A Companion to the Medieval World

WILEY-BLACKWELL COMPANIONS TO HISTORY

This series provides sophisticated and authoritative overviews of the scholarship that has shaped our current understanding of the past. Defined by theme, period and/or region, each volume comprises between twenty-five and forty concise essays written by individual scholars within their area of specialization. The aim of each contribution is to synthesize the current state of scholarship from a variety of historical perspectives and to provide a statement on where the field is heading. The essays are written in a clear, provocative, and lively manner, designed for an international audience of scholars, students, and general readers.

WILEY-BLACKWELL COMPANIONS TO BRITISH HISTORY

A Companion to Roman Britain
Edited by Malcolm Todd
A Companion to Britain in the Later Middle Ages
Edited by S. H. Rigby
A Companion to Tudor Britain
Edited by Robert Tittler and Norman Jones
A Companion to Stuart Britain
Edited by Barry Coward
A Companion to Eighteenth-Century Britain
Edited by H. T. Dickinson
A Companion to Nineteenth-Century Britain
Edited by Chris Williams
A Companion to Early Twentieth-Century Britain
Edited by Chris Wrigley
A Companion to Contemporary Britain
Edited by Paul Addison and Harriet Jones
A Companion to the Early Middle Ages: Britain and Ireland c.500–c.1100
Edited by Pauline Stafford

WILEY-BLACKWELL COMPANIONS TO EUROPEAN HISTORY

A Companion to Europe 1900–1945
Edited by Gordon Martel
A Companion to Eighteenth-Century Europe
Edited by Peter H. Wilson
A Companion to Nineteenth-Century Europe
Edited by Stefan Berger
A Companion to the Worlds of the Renaissance
Edited by Guido Ruggiero
A Companion to the Reformation World
Edited by R. Po-chia Hsia
A Companion to Europe Since 1945
Edited by Klaus Larres
A Companion to the Medieval World
Edited by Carol Lansing and Edward D. English
A Companion to the French Revolution
Edited by Peter McPhee

WILEY-BLACKWELL COMPANIONS TO WORLD HISTORY

A Companion to Western Historical Thought
Edited by Lloyd Kramer and Sarah Maza
A Companion to Gender History
Edited by Teresa A. Meade and Merry E. Wiesner-Hanks
A Companion to the History of the Middle East
Edited by Youssef M. Choueiri
A Companion to Japanese History
Edited by William M. Tsutsui
A Companion to International History 1900–2001
Edited by Gordon Martel
A Companion to Latin American History
Edited by Thomas Holloway
A Companion to Russian History
Edited by Abbott Gleason
A Companion to World War I
Edited by John Horne
A Companion to Mexican History and Culture
Edited by William H. Beezley
A Companion to World History
Edited by Douglas Northrop
A Companion to Global Environmental History
Edited by J. R. McNeill and Erin Stewart Mauldin
A Companion to World War II
Edited by Thomas W. Zeiler, with Daniel M. DuBois

For further information on these and other titles in the series please visit our website at

www.wiley.com.

A COMPANION TO THE MEDIEVAL WORLD

Edited by

Carol Lansing and Edward D. English

A John Wiley & Sons, Ltd., Publication

This paperback edition first published 2013

Edition history: Blackwell Publishing Ltd (hardback, 2007)

Blackwell Publishing was acquired by John Wiley & Sons in February 2007. Blackwell's publishing program has been merged with Wiley's global Scientific, Technical, and Medical business to form Wiley-Blackwell.

Registered Office
John Wiley & Sons Ltd, The Atrium, Southern Gate, Chichester, West Sussex, PO19 8SQ, UK

Editorial Offices
350 Main Street, Malden, MA 02148-5020, USA
9600 Garsington Road, Oxford, OX4 2DQ, UK
The Atrium, Southern Gate, Chichester, West Sussex, PO19 8SQ, UK

For details of our global editorial offices, for customer services, and for information about how to apply for permission to reuse the copyright material in this book please see our website at www.wiley.com/wiley-blackwell.

Library of Congress Cataloging-in-Publication Data

A companion to the medieval world / edited by Carol Lansing and Edward D. English.
p. cm. – (Blackwell companions to European history)
Includes bibliographical references and index.
ISBN 978-1-4051-0922-2 (cloth) – ISBN 978-1-118-42512-1 (pbk.)
1. Europe – History – 476-1492. 2. Middle Ages. 3. Civilization, Medieval. I. Lansing, Carol, 1951- II. English, Edward D.
D117.C657 2009
940.1 – dc22

2008051691

A catalogue record for this book is available from the British Library.

Cover image: 14th-century king administers justice to his subjects. Photo: The Art Archive / Real biblioteca de lo Escorial / Alfredo Dagli Orti.
Cover design by Richard Boxall Design Associates

Set in 10/12 pt Galliard by Toppan Best-set Premedia Limited
Printed in Malaysia by Ho Printing (M) Sdn Bhd

1 2013

Contents

Notes on Contributors

John Arnold is Professor in the School of History, Classics, and Archaeology, Birkbeck, University of London. He is the author of *Belief and Unbelief in Medieval Europe* (London: Edward Arnold, 2005); co-edited with K. J. Lewis, *A Companion to the Book of Margery Kempe* (Woodbridge, Suffolk: Boydell, 2004); *Inquisition and Power: Catharism and the Confessing Subject in Medieval Languedoc* (Philadelphia: University of Pennsylvania Press, 2001); *History: A Very Short Introduction* (Oxford: Oxford University Press, 2000); co-edited with S. Ditchfield and K. Davies, *History and Heritage: Consuming the Past in Contemporary Culture* (Lower Coombe, Dorset: Donhead, 1998); and most recently *What is Medieval History?* (Cambridge: Polity, 2008).

Richard E. Barton is Associate Professor at the University of North Carolina, Greensboro. He is the author of "Making a Clamor to the Lord: Noise, Justice and Power in Eleventh- and Twelfth-Century France," in *Feud, Violence and Practice: Essays in Medieval Studies in Honor of Stephen D. White*, ed. B. Tuten and T. Billado (Aldershot: Ashgate, forthcoming); "Gendering Anger: *Ira, Furor* and Discourses of Power and Masculinity in the 11th and 12th Centuries," in *In the Garden of Evil: the Vices in the Middle Ages*, ed. Richard Newhauser (Toronto: University of Toronto Press, 2005), 371–392; and *Lordship in the County of Maine, c. 890–1160* (Woodbridge, Suffolk: Boydell Press, 2004).

Constance H. Berman is Professor of History at the University of Iowa. She is the editor and a contributor to *Medieval Religion: New Approaches* (London: Routledge, 2005); *The Cistercian Evolution: The Invention of a Religious Order in Twelfth-Century Europe* (University of Pennsylvania Press, 2000); a co-editor of *Medieval Agriculture, the Southern-French Countryside, and the Early Cistercians. A Study of Forty-three Monasteries* (Philadelphia: American Philosophical Society, 1986); co-editor of *The Worlds of Medieval Women: Creativity, Influence, Imagination* (Morgantown: West Virginia University Press, 1985); the editor and translator of *Women and Monasticism in Medieval Europe: Sisters and Patrons of the Cistercian Order*, (Kalamazoo, MI: Medieval Institute Publications, 2002) and has two works in progress: *The White Nuns: Cistercian Abbeys for Women and Their Property* and *After the Millennium: Women's Work and European Economic Growth, 1050–1250.*

Richard Britnell is emeritus professor of economic history at the University of Durham, fellow of the British Academy and co-editor of the Surtees Society. He is the author of many articles, editions, and *Growth and Decline in Colchester, 1300–1525* (Cambridge: Cambridge University Press, 1986, reprint 2008); *The Commercialisation of English Society, 1000–1500* (Cambridge: Cambridge University Press, 1993; 2nd edn, 1996); co-edited with B. M. S. Campbell, *A Commercialising Economy: England 1086 to c. 1300* (Manchester: Manchester University Press, 1995); co-edited with A. J. Pollard, *The McFarlane Legacy: Studies in Late Medieval Politics and Society* (Stroud: Alan Sutton, 1995); *The Closing of the Middle Ages? England, 1471–1529* (Oxford: Blackwell, 1997); edited *Pragmatic Literacy, East and West, 1200–1330* (Woodbridge: Boydell and Brewer, 1997); and *Britain and Ireland 1050–1530: Economy and Society* (Oxford: Oxford University Press, 2004).

James W. Brodman is a Professor of History at the University of Central Arkansas, a past President of the American Academy of Research Historians of Medieval Spain, and founder and director of LIBRO: The Library of Iberian Resources Online. He has published *Ransoming Captives in Crusader Spain: The Order of Merced on the Christian-Islamic Frontier* (Philadelphia: University of Pennsylvania Press, 1986); *L'Ordre de la Merce: El rescat de captius a l'Espanya de les croades* (Barcelona: Edicions dels Quaderns Crema, 1990); *Charity and Welfare: Hospitals and the Poor in Medieval Catalonia. The Middle Ages Series* (Philadelphia: University of Pennsylvania Press, 1998); and *Charity and Religion in Medieval Europe.* Washington, DC: The Catholic University of America Press, 2009.

Olivia Remie Constable is Professor of History at the University of Notre Dame. She has published *Trade and Traders in Muslim Spain: The Commercial Realignment of the Iberian Peninsula 900–1500* (Cambridge: Cambridge University Press, 1994); *Medieval Iberia: Readings from Christian, Muslim, and Jewish Sources* (Philadelphia: University of Pennsylvania Press, 1997); *Housing the Stranger in the Mediterranean World: Lodging, Trade, and Travel in Late Antiquity and the Middle Ages* (Cambridge: Cambridge University Press, 2003); and a new book project entitled *Muslims in Medieval Europe.*

Robert W. Dyson was Lecturer in the School of Government and International Affairs and a member of the Centre for Medieval and Renaissance Studies and the Centre for the History of Political Thought at the University of Durham. Among his numerous publications are *St. Augustine of Hippo and the Christian Transformation of Political Philosophy* (London: Continuum Press, 2005); *Giles of Rome's "On Ecclesiastical Power": A Medieval Theory of World Government* (New York: Columbia University Press, 2005); *St Thomas Aquinas: The Political Writings* (Cambridge: Cambridge University Press, 2002); *St Augustine of Hippo: The City of God Against the Pagans* (Cambridge: Cambridge University Press, 1998); *James of Viterbo On Christian Government* (Woodbridge, Suffolk: Boydell Press, 1995); and *Giles of Rome on Ecclesiastical Power* (Woodbridge, Suffolk: Boydell Press, 1986).

Edward D. English is Executive Director of Medieval Studies and Adjunct Associate Professor of History at the University of California, Santa Barbara. He is finishing the first of two volumes on the society and politics of Siena in the fourteenth century. His other publications include *Enterprise and Liability in Sienese Banking, 1230–1350* (Cambridge: Medieval Academy of America, 1988) and *The Encyclopedia of the Medieval World,* 2 volumes (New York: Facts-on-File, 2005).

Stephen Gersh is Professor of Medieval Studies in the Medieval Institute at the University of Notre Dame. His publications include: *Kinesis Akinetos. A Study of Spiritual Motion in the Philosophy of Proclus* (Leiden: Brill 1973); *From Iamblichus to Eriugena. An Investigation of the Prehistory and Evolution of the Pseudo-Dionysian Tradition* (Leiden: Brill 1978); *Middle Platonism and Neoplatonism. The Latin Tradition,* 2 volumes (Notre Dame: University of Notre Dame Press, 1986); *Concord in Discourse. Harmonics and Semiotics in Late Classical and Early*

Medieval Platonism (Berlin: Mouton-De Gruyter 1996); and with Maarten J. F. M. Hoenen, *Plato in the Middle Ages. A Doxographical Approach* (Berlin: De Gruyter 2002).

Yitzhak Hen is Associate Professor at Ben-Gurion University of the Negev. He has published *Culture and Religion in Merovingian Gaul, A.D. 481–751* (Leiden: Brill, 1995); *The Sacramentary of Echternach*, Henry Bradshaw Society, 110 (London: Boydell and Brewer, 1997); co-edited with Matthew Innes, *The Uses of the Past in the Early Middle Ages* (Cambridge: Cambridge University Press, 2000); *De Sion Exibit Lex et Verbum Domini de Hierusalem. Studies on Medieval Law, Liturgy and Literature in Honour of Amnon Linder*, Cultural Encounters in Late Antiquity and the Middle Ages, 1 (Turnhout: Brepols, 2001); *The Royal Patronage of Liturgy in Frankish Gaul to the Death of Charles the Bald (877)*, Henry Bradshaw Society Subsidia series, 3 (London: Boydell and Brewer, 2001); co-edited with Rob Meens, *The Bobbio Missal: Liturgy and Religious Culture in Merovingian Gaul*, (Cambridge: Cambridge University Press, 2004); *Roman Barbarians: The Royal Court and Culture in the Early Medieval West* (London: Palgrave, 2007); and is General Editor of the Series "Cultural Encounters in Late Antiquity and the Middle Ages" for Brepols.

Martha C. Howell is Miriam Champion Professor of History in Columbia University. She has published *From Reliable Sources* with Walter Prevenier (Ithaca: Cornell University Press, 2001); *The Marriage Exchange: Property, Social Place and Gender in Cities of the Low Countries, 1300–1550* (Chicago: University of Chicago Press, 1998); and *Women, Production, and Patriarchy in Late Medieval Cities* (Chicago: University of Chicago Press, 1986); with Marc Boone, *In But Not of the Market: Movable Goods in the Late Medieval and Early Modern Economy* (2007), and *Commerce before Capitalism in Europe, 1300–1600.* (Cambridge: Cambridge University Press, 2010).

Hans Hummer is an Associate Professor in History at Wayne State University. He has published *Politics and Power in Early Medieval Europe: Alsace and the Frankish Realm, 600–1000* (Cambridge: Cambridge University Press, 2005); "The Identity of *Ludovicus Piissimus Augustus* in the *Praefatio in Librum Antiquum Lingua Saxonica Conscriptum*," *Francia* 31/1 (2004), pp. 1–14; "Die merowingische Herkunft der Vita Sadalbergae," *Deutsches Archiv für Erforschung des Mittelalters* 59, 2 (2003), pp. 459–93.

Matthew Innes is Professor of History in the School of History, Classics and Archaeology at Birkbeck in the University of London and has been an editor of the journal *Early Medieval Europe*. He has published *State and Society in the Early Middle Ages: the Middle Rhine Valley, 400–1000* (Cambridge: Cambridge University Press, 2000); co-edited, with Yitzhak Hen, *The Uses of the Past in the Early Middle Ages* (Cambridge: Cambridge University Press, 2000); *The Sword, the Book and the Plough: An Introduction to Early Medieval Western Europe, 300–900* (London: Routledge, 2006); co-authored with Marios Costambeys and Simon Maclean, *The Carolingian World* (Cambridge: CUP, 2007); and is co-editing with Warren Brown, Marios Costambeys, and Adam Kosto, *Laypeople and Documents in the Early Middle Ages* (currently in preparation for publication).

Thomas Kuehn is professor of History at Clemson University. He is the author of numerous articles and *Emancipation in Late Medieval Florence* (New Brunswick, NJ: Rutgers University Press 1982); *Law, Family, and Women: Toward a Legal Anthropology of Renaissance Italy* (Chicago: University of Chicago Press, 1991); *Illegitimacy in Renaissance Florence* (Ann Arbor: University of Michigan Press, 2002), *Heirs, Kin, and Creditors in Renaissance Florence* (Cambridge: Cambridge University Press, 2008); and has edited two collections of essays: with Anne Jacobson Schutte and Silvana Seidel Menchi, *Time, Space, and Women's Lives in Early Modern Europe* (Kirksville, MO: Truman State University Press 2001); and with John A. Marino, *A Renaissance of Conflicts: Visions and Revisions of Law and*

Society in Italy and Spain (Toronto: Centre for Reformation and Renaissance Studies, 2004).

Carol Lansing is Professor of History at the University of California, Santa Barbara. Her research focuses on medieval Italian politics, society, and culture. Her previous publications include *The Florentine Magnates: Lineage and Faction in a Medieval Commune* (Princeton: Princeton University Press, 1991); *Power and Purity: Cathar Heresy in Medieval Italy* (Oxford: Oxford University Press, 1998); *Passion and Order: Restraint of Grief in the Medieval Italian Communes* (Ithaca, NY: Cornell University Press, 2008).

James Paul Masschaele is an Associate Professor in History, at Rutgers University. He has published "The Public Space of the Marketplace in Medieval England," *Speculum*, 77 (2002), pp. 383–421; "Trade, Domestic: Markets and Fairs," in David Loades, ed., *Reader's Guide to British History* (London: Fitzroy Dearborn Publishers, 2003); and *Peasants, Merchants, and Markets: Inland Trade in Medieval England, c. 1150–c. 1350* (New York: St. Martin's Press, 1997).

Andreas Meyer is Professor at Philipps University, Marburg in Germany. He has published extensively on the hospitals, the papal curia, late Medieval piety and Italian notaries, especially those in Lucca. His books include *Zürich und Rom: ordentliche Kollatur und päpstliche Provisionen am Frau- und Grossmünster 1316–1523* (Tübingen: Niemeyer, 1986); *"Felix et inclitus notarius": Studien zum italienischen Notariat vom 7. bis zum 13. Jahrhundert* (Tübingen: Niemeyer, 2000).

Maureen C. Miller is Professor in the Department of History at the University of California, Berkeley. She has published *Power and the Holy in the Age of the Investiture Conflict: A Brief Documentary History* (New York: Bedford/St. Martin's, 2005); *The Bishop's Palace: Architecture and Authority in Medieval Italy* (Ithaca, NY: Cornell University Press, 2000); *The Formation of a Medieval Church: Ecclesiastical Change in Verona, 950–1150* (Ithaca, NY: Cornell University Press, 1993) translated as *Chiesa e società in Verona medievale (950–1150)*, ed. Paolo Golinelli (Verona: CIERRE, 1999).

Robert I. Moore is Professor Emeritus in the School of Historical Studies in the University of Newcastle. He has published *The Birth of Popular Heresy* (New York: St. Martin's Press, 1976); The Origins of European Dissent (New York: B. Blackwell, 1985); *The Formation of a Persecuting Society: Authority and Deviance in Western Europe, 950–1250*, 2nd edn (Malden, MA: Blackwell Publishing, 2007); *The First European Revolution, c. 970–1215* (Oxford: Blackwell, 2000); and *Atlas of World History* (Chicago: Rand McNally, 1992).

Steven Murray is Professor of Art History in the Department of Art History and Archaeology and Director of the Media Center in Columbia University. His publications include *Building Troyes Cathedral: The Late Gothic Campaigns* (Bloomington: Indiana University Press, 1987); *Beauvais Cathedral: Architecture of Transcendence* (Princeton: Princeton University Press, 1989); *Notre-Dame, Cathedral of Amiens: The Power of Change in Gothic* (Cambridge: Cambridge University Press, 1996); *A Gothic Sermon: Making a Contract with the Mother of God, Saint Mary of Amiens* (Berkeley: University of California Press, 2004); and *The Amiens Trilogy*, a video recording on the building and design of Amiens Cathedral.

Clifford J. Rogers is Professor of History at the United States Military Academy at West Point. He has published *War Cruel and Sharp: English Strategy under Edward III, 1327–1360* (Woodbridge, Suffolk: Boydell Press, 2000); edited, *The Wars of Edward III: Sources and Interpretations* (Woodbridge, Suffolk: Boydell Press, 1999); edited with Mark Grimsley, *Civilians in the Path of War* (Lincoln, NE: University of Nebraska Press, 2002); and is co-editor of *The Journal of Medieval Military History.*

Philipp W. Rosemann is Professor in the Philosophy Department at the University of Dallas. He has edited *Tabula* for *Opera Roberti Grosseteste Lincolniensis*, vol. 1, Corpus Christianorum, Continuatio

Mediaevalis, 130 (Turnhout: Brepols, 1995) and published *Omne ens est aliquid. Introduction à la lecture du "système" philosophique de saint Thomas d'Aquin.* (Louvain/Paris: Peeters, 1996); *Omne agens agit sibi simile: A "Repetition" of Scholastic Metaphysics* (Louvain: Leuven University Press, 1996); *Understanding Scholastic Thought with Foucault* (New York: St. Martin's Press, 1999); *Peter Lombard* (New York: Oxford University Press, 2004); edited with Thomas A. F. Kelly, *Amor amicitiae – On the Love that is Friendship: Essays in Medieval Thought and Beyond in Honor of the Rev. Professor James McEvoy*, (Louvain/Paris/Dudley, MA: Peeters, 2004); and edited *John Scottus Eriugena*, Special Issue of the *American Catholic Philosophical Quarterly* 79:4 (Fall, 2005), pp. 521–671; *The Story of a Great Medieval Book: Peter Lombard's "Sentences"* (Toronto: University of Toronto Press, 2007); and is the Associate Editor of the *American Catholic Philosophical Quarterly* and the editor of Dallas Medieval Texts and Translations.

Teofilo F. Ruiz is Professor of History at the University of California, Los Angeles. He has published *Sociedad y poder real en Castilla* (Barcelona: Ariel, 1981); *The City and the Realm: Burgos and Castile in the Late Middle Ages* (London: Variorum, 1992); *Crisis and Continuity: Land and Town in Late Medieval Castile* (Philadelphia: University of Pennsylvania Press: Philadelphia, 1994); *Spanish Society, 1400–1600* (London: Longman, 2001); *From Heaven to Earth: The Reordering of Castilian Society, 1150–1350* (Princeton: Princeton University Press, 2004); with Robin Winks *Medieval Europe and the World* (Oxford, 2005); and *Centuries of Crises* (Oxford: Blackwell Press, 2007).

Phillipp R. Schofield is Professor of History in the Department of History and Welsh History at the University of Wales, Aberystwyth. He has published numerous articles on agrarian history, manorial courts, peasant debt, diet, the social economy of the medieval village, co-edited with N. J. Mayhew, *Credit and Debt in Medieval England, c. 1180–c. 1320* (Oxford: Oxbow, 2002 and *Peasant and Community in Medieval England* (New York: Palgrave, 2003).

Kenneth R. Stow is Professor of Jewish History at the University of Haifa, the editor of *Jewish History: A Journal of Jewish Historical Studies*, and the author of numerous articles and monographs such as *Catholic Thought and Papal Jewry Policy*, 1555–1593 (New York: Jewish Theological Seminary of America, 1977); *Taxation, Community and State: The Jews and the Fiscal Foundations of the Early Modern Papal State* (Stuttgart: A. Hiersemann, 1982); *The 1007 Anonymous and Papal Sovereignty: Jewish Perceptions of the Papacy and Papal Policy in the Middle Ages.* (Cincinnati: Hebrew Union College, 1984); *The Jews in Rome*, 2 vols. Leiden: Brill, 1995–97); *Alienated Minority: The Jews of Medieval Latin Europe* (Cambridge, MA: Harvard University Press, 1992); *Theater of Acculturation: The Roman Ghetto in the Sixteenth Century* (Seattle, WA: University of Washington Press, 2000); *Jewish Dogs: An Image and Its Interpreters: Continuity in the Catholic-Jewish Encounter* (Stanford, CA: Stanford University Press, 2006).

Christopher Tyerman is Supernumerary Fellow and Tutor in History, Lecturer in Medieval History, Hertford College and New College, in Oxford. He is the author of *England and the Crusades, 1095–1588* (Chicago: University of Chicago Press, 1988); *The Invention of the Crusades* (Basingstoke, Hampshire: Macmillan Press, 1998); *Fighting for Christendom: Holy war and the Crusades* (Oxford: Oxford University Press, 2004); *The Crusades: A Very Short Introduction* (Oxford: Oxford University Press, 2005); and *God's War: A New History of the Crusades* (Cambridge, MA: The Belknap Press of Harvard University Press, 2006).

Part I

The Middle Ages

CHAPTER ONE

The Idea of a Middle Ages

EDWARD D. ENGLISH AND CAROL LANSING

Understandings of the European Middle Ages have long been shaped by the old master narrative, in contradictory ways. The name itself was, of course, coined first by Renaissance humanists to characterize what they saw as a long stagnant, barbaric period between the cultural flowering of Antiquity and its rebirth in fourteenth-century Italy.[1] The idea was taken up by Enlightenment *philosophes*, who saw the period as one of superstitious ignorance. The term medieval is still commonly used to evoke savage barbarity; medieval scholars were amused when in Quentin Tarantino's 1994 film *Pulp Fiction* Ving Rhames turned on his former torturers and threatened to "get medieval" on them.[2]

"Medieval" continues to be associated with backwardness, darkness, indiscriminate violence. Bruce Holsinger has recently analyzed the ways in which politicians and pundits in a bizarre twist of Orientalism use the term to characterize Islamic opponents like al-Qaeda and the Taliban. In 2006, Donald Rumsfeld, then US Secretary of Defense, said of Abu Musab al-Zarqawi: "He personified the dark, sadistic and medieval vision of the future – of beheadings, suicide bombings, and indiscriminate killings."[3] Some professional medievalists have echoed this approach, faintly, when they argue that the Middle Ages are best understood in terms of The Other or the grotesque.[4]

Other views of the medieval were also driven by ideology. Crucially, many of the great source collections were created in the eighteenth century by professional religious who sought to demonstrate the rationality of medieval religion while protecting the property and reputation of their contemporary Church.[5] The emphases in those collections have profoundly shaped the field of medieval history: orderly edited sources attract the most study. Popular culture has had a variety of influences as well. With the opening of travel to a wider number of people from the mid-nineteenth century, Anglophone travelers and expatriates created a huge literature describing, for example, medieval and early Renaissance Italy, especially the city states, often with an emphasis on the oppressive hands of a retrogressive Catholicism.[6] The same period – even in the United States, founded as separate from the evils of the old European regimes – saw a romantic fascination with medieval culture and architecture.[7]

The Middle Ages were popular with pre-Civil War southern aristocrats worried about honor and chivalry.[8] Movies throughout the twentieth century brought a variety of ideas about what was medieval to popular culture. This was done complete with knights riding by the occasional telephone pole and enriched by the use of a faux dialect called "speaking medieval."[9]

Political regimes in the twentieth century recognized the value of the medieval past as a tool to legitimate themselves and also to encourage tourism. Mussolini in Italy did not just promote the cult of imperial Rome but also co-opted the Italian Middle Ages and Renaissance in spectacles and schemes to "restore" buildings and piazzas.[10] In contemporary Italy, one political party claims legitimation from the medieval past by holding rallies attended by men dressed as "Lombard Knights."[11] The Middle Ages turned up again as part of the "Culture Wars" of the 1990s when the attack of the newly elected congress led by Newt Gingrich on the funding of the National Endowment for the Humanities (NEH) included ridicule of medieval projects. An NEH-funded program on teaching ways in which medieval people understood sex and gender directed by Edward English, one of this volume's editors, came under attack. Besides a plain old-fashioned anti-intellectualism, these Republican members of Congress were uncomfortable with ideas that such concepts as sexuality and gender might have history that should be discussed in colleges and universities.[12]

The discipline of medieval history was shaped in part by responses to these caricatures. Twentieth-century professional medievalists in part responded with an emphasis on the ways in which the modern world originated in the Middle Ages. Colin Morris argued for a twelfth-century "discovery of the individual."[13] Joseph Strayer's 1970 *On the Medieval Origins of the Modern State* is an influential example. Strayer promoted parliamentary systems and constitutional democracy, in response to the world wars and totalitarianism. It is, of course, correct that many aspects of the modern world ultimately derive from the European Middle Ages, including institutions such as universities and the Catholic Church. However, one effect of this approach has been to privilege the historical winners, aspects of medieval Europe that became important in later centuries, above all the nation state. To give a favorite example, arguably the liveliest cultural innovation in the thirteenth century was Mediterranean, centered on Frederick II's polyglot court and administration in Palermo. Frederick's response to papal pressure to go on Crusade was to travel to Jerusalem and hammer out a diplomatic solution, an effort that won him a papal excommunication. Sicily and the Italian south in later centuries suffered a long slide into overtaxed poverty and marginality. Textbook narratives therefore focus not on medieval Palermo, with its Muslim and Jewish bureaucrats and Arabic-speaking monarch, but on the historical winners, Paris and London.

What would the European Middle Ages look like without this contradictory intellectual baggage? The project is, of course, an impossibility: the questions of scholars are always informed by their experience. Our past is in the present. Still, some dramatic scholarship has recovered aspects of medieval culture that have simply been left out. To give an example that is not reflected in this volume, the field of medieval English literature has recently been shaken up by Jocelyn Wogan-Browne, who is mapping "the French of England": late medieval English elites kept writing in French, producing a large volume of literature that has been little studied because specialists focus on the winner, Middle English. More generally, much recent medieval scholarship has been devoted to the effort to identify and then strip away received intellectual categories and seek a fresh understanding of medieval culture and society. That approach is reflected in most of the chapters in this volume, on topics such as reform, the Crusades, the family, Romanesque and Gothic architecture. R. I. Moore even sketches an approach to a genuinely comparative world history that would set aside European exceptionalism. Ironically, medieval nevertheless often still appears as both other and origins of modern.

Notes

1 Two excellent recent studies of ideas about the Middle Ages are Arnold, *What is Medieval History?* and Bull, *Thinking Medieval.*

2 Dinshaw, *Getting Medieval*, esp. "Getting Medieval: Pulp Fiction, Foucault, and the Use of the Past," pp. 183–206; for ideas about contemporary critical theory, especially French, and medievalism, see Holsinger, *The Premodern Condition.*

3 Quoted by Holsinger, *Neomedievalism, Neoconservatism, and the War on Terror*, p. 1.

4 Freedman and Spiegel, "Medievalism Old and New."

5 Damico and Zavadil, eds, *Medieval Scholarship*; see the biographies of Bolland, Mabillon, Muratori, Waitz, and Delisle; Knowles, "Jean Mabillon"; Knowles, "The Bollandists" and "The Maurists" in *Great Historical Enterprises*; much of this came together in Edward Gibbon's work; see Pocock, *Barbarism and Religion.*

6 See the essays in Law and Østermark-Johnson, eds, *Victorian and Edwardian Responses to the Italian Renaissance.* Much of this had to do with a romantic nostalgia for a lost past that was much better, a kind of medieval dreamland inherited from Dante Gabriel Rossetti, Walter Scott, John Ruskin, and François-René de Chateaubriand.

7 See, e.g., Fleming, "Picturesque History and the Medieval."

8 Wyatt-Brown, *Southern Honor.*

9 Among a number of books on the Middle Ages in the movies, see Aberth, *A Knight at the Movies*; the "Middle Ages" also lives on in computer games.

10 Lazzaro and Crum, eds, *Donatello among the Blackshirts*, and essays in Lasansky, *The Renaissance Perfected*, esp. ch. 3, "Urban Politics: The Fascist Rediscovery of Medieval Arezzo," pp. 107–43.

11 For the contemporary party called the Lombard League in Italy, see Coleman, "The Lombard League: Myth and History."

12 For a view into the culture wars of the 1990s see a summary of the discussion in the US House of Representatives attacking the National Endowment for the Humanities sponsorship of the Summer Institute on teaching about Sex and Gender in the Middle Ages in Dinshaw, *Getting Medieval*, pp. 173–82.

13 Morris, *The Discovery of the Individual.*

Bibliography

Aberth, John, *A Knight at the Movies: Medieval History on Film* (London: Routledge, 2003).

Arnold, John, *What is Medieval History?* (Cambridge: Polity, 2008).

Bull, Marcus, *Thinking Medieval: An Introduction to the Study of the Middle Ages* (New York: Palgrave Macmillan, 2005).

Coleman, Edward, "The Lombard League: Myth and History," in Howard. B. Clarke and Judith Devlin (eds), *European Encounters: Essays in Memory of Albert Lovett* (Dublin: University College Dublin Press, 2003), or online at www.threemonkeysonline.com/als/Umberto%20Bossi%20and%20the%20Lega%20Nord.html.

Damico, Helen, and Zavadil, Joseph B., eds, *Medieval Scholarship: Biographical Studies on the Formation of a Discipline*, vol. 1: *History* (New York: Garland Publishing, 1995).

Dinshaw, Carolyn, *Getting Medieval: Sexualities and Communities, Pre- and Postmodern* (Durham, NC: Duke University Press, 1999).

Fleming, Robin, "Picturesque History and the Medieval in Nineteenth-Century America," *American Historical Review*, 100 (1995), pp. 1061–94.

Freedman, Paul, and Spiegel, Gabrielle M., "Medievalism Old and New: The Rediscovery of Alterity in North American Medieval Studies," *American Historical Review*, 103/3 (June 1998), pp. 677–704.

Holsinger, Bruce, *The Premodern Condition: Medievalism and the Making of Theory* (Chicago: University of Chicago Press, 2005).

Holsinger, Bruce *Neomedievalism, Neoconservatism, and the War on Terror* (Chicago: Prickly Paradigm Press, 2007).

Knowles, David, "Jean Mabillon," in David Knowles, *The Historian and Character and Other Essays* (Cambridge: Cambridge University Press, 1963), pp. 213–39; repr. from *Journal of Ecclesiastical History*, 10 (1959), pp. 153–73.

Knowles, David, "The Bollandists" and "The Maurists," in David Knowles, *Great Historical Enterprises: Problems in Monastic History* (London: Thomas Nelson and Sons, 1963), pp. 2–32, 34–62; repr. from *Transactions of the Royal Historical Society.*

Lasansky, D. Medina, *The Renaissance Perfected: Architecture, Spectacle, and Tourism in Fascist Italy* (University Park, PA: Pennsylvania State University Press, 2004).

Law, John E., and Østermark-Johnson, Lene, eds, *Victorian and Edwardian Responses to the Italian Renaissance* (Aldershot: Ashgate, 2005).

Lazzaro, Claudia, and Crum, Roger J., eds, *Donatello among the Blackshirts: History and Modernity in the Visual Culture of Fascist Italy* (Ithaca, NY: Cornell University Press, 2005).

Morris, Colin, *The Discovery of the Individual, 1050–1200* (New York: Harper & Row, 1972).

Pocock, J. G. A., *Barbarism and Religion*, 5 vols (Cambridge: Cambridge University Press, 1999–2011).

Wyatt-Brown, Bertram, *Southern Honor: Ethics and Behavior in the Old South* (Oxford: Oxford University Press, 1982).

Part II

Early Medieval Foundations

Chapter Two

Economies and Societies in Early Medieval Western Europe

Matthew Innes

Living through the Crisis of the Roman Empire

In 459, an 83-year-old man living in Bordeaux composed a long poem reflecting on his life. Paulinus had lived through turbulent times, and in those times had experienced both fame and fortune, disaster and disgrace. In looking back, he sought consolation of a distinctly Christian type: "I, who indeed felt that I owed my whole life to God, should show that my whole life's doings also have been subject to his direction; and, by telling over the seasons granted me by his same grace, I should form a little work, a Thanksgiving to him, in the guise of a narrative memoir."[1]

Paulinus was born into the highest echelon of imperial society, the aristocracy of huge landowners whose status was reinforced by the legal and political privileges associated with membership of the Senate of Rome. Paulinus' paternal grandfather, Ausonius, had been the real architect of his family's rise to the very top of the hierarchy. Ausonius' father was a well-to-do landowner from southeastern Gaul, and his mother the daughter of a famous Greek physician. Ausonius himself achieved fame as a teacher and poet at Bordeaux; as tutor and then chief adviser to the Emperor Gratian (reigned 367–83), and spent fifteen years at the western imperial court, serving in the highest political office of Praetorian Prefect. Paulinus was born in Pella, the site of Alexander the Great's ancient capital, whilst his father was cutting his political teeth as governor of Macedonia. Promotion to the largely honorific position of subconsul of Africa saw the family move to Carthage, and then, once the eighteen-month term had ended, to Rome, before finally settling at Ausonius' residence in Bordeaux. Paulinus there followed the typical pattern of privileged youth, with a period of wild misdeeds following his education, before his marriage saw a portion of the family property settled on him.

In his 30s, though, dual misfortunes hit Paulinus. His personal crisis was caused by the death of his father, and his brother's subsequent attempts to overturn the will, particularly the provisions making bequests to Paulinus' mother. But these familial conflicts coincided with public crisis, as the frontiers of the Roman state in the west were shattered, and, after prolonged political turmoil, barbarian war leaders settled as military protectors in much of Gaul. For a figure of Paulinus' standing, the personal and the political inevitably intersected. The chain of events here is complex, elided by Paulinus' hindsight and his presentation of these misfortunes as God's judgment on his earlier life of otiose luxury. But Paulinus attempted to ride the barbarian tiger, cashing in the luster of the family name and serving as count of the private largesse in the regime of the would-be Emperor Priscus Attalus – who in turn depended on the might of the Gothic army of Athaulf. Attalus' regime, however, proved short lived, and Athaulf's Goths were eventually, in 418, settled in southern Gaul as "guests" of the "official" regime of the Emperor Honorius. Paulinus thus found himself driven from his ancestral home, which was plundered by barbarians and menaced by displaced slaves and youths, his property lost 'partly through the ravages of barbarians acting by the laws of war, and partly through the iniquity of Romans proceeding wantonly and in defiance of all laws to my hurt at various times."[2]

Looking back, Paulinus took solace in contemplating Christ's poverty, and considered taking a monastic vow. The next forty years, however, saw a continuing seesaw of fortunes and misfortunes. Paulinus considered abandoning Gaul for the Greek estates inherited from his mother, but his wife and her kin argued against; by the time their deaths made this a possibility, the annual income sent from the east had ended, the estates presumed lost. Further conflict within his family interacted with dramatic shifts in the political scene. Paulinus' sons abandoned him for the court of the Gothic king: "both alike were fired with liberty, which they could find in greater measure at Bordeaux, albeit as partners of Gothic farmers."[3] They were able to recover some share in their ancestral possessions, whose fruits Paulinus had hoped they would share; but, when the Gothic king's earlier friendship turned to anger, the possessions were confiscated.

The death of both sons left Paulinus cut off from these twice-lost estates. Hence he settled in an urban residence at Marseilles, the major valve between Gaul and the Mediterranean economy, and sought to make his living by trading the fruits of his vineyards and orchards, even renting extra plots to be cultivated by his unfree dependants: hardly the kind of activity that would have been seen as fitting of a figure of Paulinus' rank just a few decades earlier. Eventually, however, Paulinus ran short of funds and slaves, and so had to quit Marseilles and return to Bordeaux, where he managed just about to keep up the appearance of respectability: he maintained "a household of a kind." Any hope of recovering his grandfather's estates gone, he lost the freehold on his Marseilles residence, and was left to give thanks to an unnamed Goth who, having acquired a farm that had once been owned by Paulinus, sent him a payment that, whilst not a fair price, was a godsend, and demonstrated God's goodness.

Paulinus is a vivid witness to the series of events that have overshadowed our understanding of West European history in the succeeding half millennium: the ending of Roman rule in the west. For a commentator of Paulinus' generation, the first decade of the fifth century when "foes burst into the vitals of the Roman state" were inevitably seen as a crucial turning point, and this period has been the primary focus of most modern analyses of "the fall of Rome." The testimony of Paulinus, who ended a dramatic loser in the first barbarian settlements, usefully counterpoints other examples made more familiar by modern commentators. Later figures like Sidonius Apollinaris (*c.* 430–89) were able to maintain their position and manage change more seamlessly, in part because they were politically luckier, in part because the experience of Paulinus' generation was more dramatic and more violent than that of their fifth- and sixth-century successors.

In response to misfortune, Paulinus' hopes shifted from the Roman state, which his line had long steered, to the Christian God, whom they had adopted far more recently. The refusal of Augustine of Hippo to make an unequivocal and unproblematic identification of the city of God with a Christianized empire made it possible for the likes of Paulinus to adjust their horizons.[4] They no longer identified their inherited social dominance with an obligation to uphold Roman order and so safeguard the common good through involvement in public life; instead they sought personal solace through their relationship with a God whose justice was inscrutable. It was even possible for another who suffered from the initial crisis, Paulinus' contemporary at Marseille the priest Salvian, to critique the contemporary Roman world for abandoning the true justice implicit in its laws, and therefore suffering divine displeasure.[5]

These ideological and psychological shifts need taking seriously; they did not, however, mark the wholesale collapse of the economy or society of the Roman west. As Paulinus himself makes clear, the political and military changes of the 400s and 410s, dramatic though they were, did not inaugurate a wholesale social revolution. Paulinus' misfortunes were very much personal, the loss of influence and resources wrought by his intimate involvement in intricate political maneuvers that failed. The legal, political, and social frameworks within which he and his sons attempted to make good their earlier losses were entirely familiar, with Roman structures coming under new, barbarian, management; others were able to use them to maintain their position in the way made so vivid in the letters and poems of Sidonius. Neither Paulinus nor his contemporaries believed that the Roman world order had ended.

Rome's Shadow and the Study of the Early Middle Ages

The events through which Paulinus lived have haunted Western historical thought in ways that continue to influence understandings of the post-Roman period to this day. Since at least the Renaissance, scholars have normally seen the ending of Roman rule in the West as marking a fundamental discontinuity in Western history, with the ancient and modern worlds separated by a historical gulf in the shape of the "Middle Ages" that lay between. We should not forget that no one living in the period we call the "Middle Ages" would have seen themselves as "medieval," and remember that, although "medieval" attitudes toward the ancient world were complex, and in many ways conditioned by the history of the Church, they stopped short of any sense of wholesale disjuncture. In the early modern period, the growing currency of a tripartite division of the past, however, encouraged the view that there was a fundamental break between the ancient world and the Middle Ages, and discussions of Rome's "fall" – the vocabulary echoing mankind's "fall" from grace in the Book of Genesis – could become moralizing tales seeking to imbue historical lessons, as in Edward Gibbon's multi-volume *History of the Decline and Fall of the Roman Empire* (1776–88). While isolated individuals continued to search for connections between Roman and medieval societies, the dominant view quickly became one of almost apocalyptic discontinuity, with a new order growing from the ashes of wholesale collapse and destruction. In such a scheme, the origins of European societies and nations could be sought in the various "peoples" who established themselves in the Empire's former Western provinces. Through the early modern and modern periods scholars spent much energy combing diverse sources – primarily Roman ethnography, early medieval law codes, and sagas and folklore from later medieval Scandinavia – to elucidate a common Germanic culture, distinct from and conflicting with Roman principles of social organization, from which post-Roman societies could be derived.

In the now dominant tripartite divisions of the past, scholars saw in classical antiquity – whose texts, after all, provided the basis of the literary education of the "civilized" modern man – a prism of the present, separated by an unfortunate interlude of barbarism and superstition. Although the Middle Ages played an ultimately villainous role in this historical drama, attitudes to the medieval were in important ways more ambivalent and complex. After all, the identities and institutions of *ancien régime* Europe had resolutely medieval origins, and historical argument played a prominent role in political debate. While this medievalism of precedent was increasingly marginalized in the course of the nineteenth century, the advent of state-sponsored mass education established a heroic Middle Ages at the beginning of popular narratives of nationhood, while newly professionalized historical scholarship in the universities focused on medieval origins of modern institutions. Meanwhile, the trauma of industrialization encouraged an escapist and often romantic medievalism of difference, idealizing an agrarian past of organic communities. It is no accident that this revalorization of the Middle Ages coincided with an increasingly self-confident Eurocentric world order, which enabled non-European societies to be understood as primitive and implicitly equated with Europe's medieval past.

As the contents of a book like this make clear, the research agenda of professional historians in the second half of the twentieth century has increasingly qualified and questioned these assumptions, and, where growing subspecialization allows it, the very category of the medieval is now a matter for self-conscious reflection, soul-searching even. Whilse academic medievalism is ultimately informed by the tension between the medieval as the "other" and the Middle Ages as a place of origins, it is also increasingly defined by an interrogative stance toward popular views of medieval barbarism and superstition, which are frequently tied to the worries of Western elites about the contested and fragile nature of their ideological hegemony. For students of medieval Europe after 1100, understanding the Middle Ages now involves recreating a complex but different world that cannot be reduced to the facile value-judgments of popular culture, but whose dynamism points forward to Western modernity.

Interpretations of Europe from the fourth to the eleventh centuries, however, have been slower to change, and it was only in the closing decades of the twentieth century that specialists systematically began to question entrenched narratives of Roman collapse and a subsequent new start based on the ancestral cultures of barbarian incomers. In part, this is because of the sheer length of the shadows cast by inherited narratives: the notion of barbarian tribes as our direct ancestors, sweeping aside Roman institutions, has after all been central to modern national identities. Intimately linked to the longevity of these stereotypes has been the notion that these were indeed "dark ages" in the sense that insufficient evidence survives to allow us to shed light on their history. There can be little doubt that there are indeed times and places in early Middle Ages Europe where source material is scanty, but this should not obscure the fact that these centuries are far better documented than classical antiquity, nor that there are also many early medieval societies that have left a dense enough footprint for us to recreate complex cultural debates and economic systems, political conflicts, and social dynamics. The fact that the archives and institutions of later medieval Europe are far richer than those for the period before 1100 for long acted as a disincentive for serious research on the early medieval period, but it does not mean that such research is impossible. In fact, early medievalists have arguably suffered from the very success of their colleagues working on the period after 1100, for, as the complexity and dynamism of high and late medieval culture and society have become apparent, so it has been tempting to cast the early Middle Ages as an ill-documented backwater, archaic and primitive. While blanket understandings of the Middle Ages as a whole as backward and static have been questioned, such prejudices about the early medieval period have been harder to shift.

Nonetheless, in the second half of the twentieth century specialist scholarship on Europe's early medieval centuries flourished, to the extent that the period has now become a recognizable subdiscipline of its own, with its separate conferences and journals, debates and networks. This subspecialization has further fractured any sense of the Middle Ages as a single entity, and the findings of the new early medieval scholarship have not yet been properly synthesized with more established work on the period after 1100, a fact indeed reflected in the structure of this book. But it has allowed us to move beyond old stereotypes pitting barbarian against Roman in a clash of two fundamentally antithetical civilizations, and presenting early medieval societies as a new beginning emerging in the smoldering ashes of a crucible of collapse. Whilst there has been serious debate about some of the hyper-continuity theories that characterized the early stages of rethinking, it is now commonplace to see early medieval economies and societies as the result of transformation not collapse – the result of multifaceted interactions, some violent, some not, unfolding over centuries.

Although one of the pathbreaking works in the process of reassessment – Henri Pirenne's *Mohammed and Charlemagne*[6] – put economic systems at its heart, through the second half of the twentieth century it was cultural and political history that led the way, as historians found new ways to understand conversion and Christianization, and to assess the achievements of early medieval kings. Social and economic history, which if it is to be done successfully necessitates analysis of whole systems, not sympathetic reassessment of the writings of known individuals, has lagged, largely because it poses different methodological and interpretative problems from those faced by historians dealing with religious texts or narrative histories. Nonetheless, the last decades have seen dramatic advances in our knowledge and understanding of the archaeological record, and the development of new ways of using the documentary record, which fills out dramatically from the eighth century onward. One result of these advances has been an increasing awareness of the differences between the regions that made up early medieval Europe, and the most recent attempts to synthesize have rested on a desire to catalogue and compare the diverse societies that made up the early medieval West. Nonetheless, if the chronology and context of economic and social change differed from region to region, shared structural characteristics can be identified across much of Western Europe. To understand the driving dynamics of social and economic change, though, what follows focuses on the former Roman provinces of the West; the reader should not forget that Scandinavia (never Roman), Britain and Ireland (some never Roman, the parts that were unique in the extent of post-Roman collapse), and central and southern Spain (Islamic after 711) had their own stories that interacted in complex ways with those of modern France, the Low Countries, western Germany, and Italy.

Urbanism and the Economy: The Rhythms of Change

Paulinus' reminiscences vividly evoke the reshaping of an ancient society, structured by senatorial dominance and Roman order. But, for all its turmoil, Paulinus' life continued to revolve around the polarity between the public life of the city, and the cultivated leisure of aristocratic rural retreat – a polarity that had defined the activities of the Roman ruling class throughout the empire's history. The city – Latin *civitas* – was the defining footprint of Roman rule, the arena through which landowners articulated and constructed their dominance of public life and through which they exercised cultural, economic, and political dominance. Paulinus' early life, for example, was defined by his father's path from Pella to Carthage to Rome as he climbed the ladder of office leading to formal membership of the Senate. Thereafter, the family focused its activities on the city of Bordeaux, where Paulinus' grandfather Ausonius has first risen to prominence, and on its smaller neighbor, nearby Beziers, from which they were driven out by barbarians in a vivid crux in the middle of Paulinus' poem. Even after Paulinus' fall from grace, Bordeaux, arguably a more important political center as court of the Gothic kings than it had been previously, and Marseilles, attested by archaeology and historical sources as the major valve between Gaul and the Mediterranean economy, were the central public stages for the remainder of his career.

In Western Europe north of the Alps, in contrast to the Mediterranean and the Near East, there was no indigenous tradition of urban life prior to Roman conquest. Beyond the Mediterranean shores of southern Gaul in particular, cities were, in origin, Roman implants. With their standardized layouts of public buildings and public spaces, they articulated the ideology of civilized Roman order. Cities were first administrative, political, and military centers. Within provincial societies north of the Alps, they displaced pre-Roman centers such as hill forts as the focal points of social action, and defined the identity of their territories, often taking on pre-Roman tribal names. Around the shores of the Mediterranean, and in Italy in particular, cities had generally grown more organically, but the structures of Roman rule likewise created a template within which they could flourish. Nonetheless, these differences of origin led to important contrasts between western Mediterranean societies, and those of Rome's more outlying provinces. In particular, Italy and southern Gaul had very dense urban grids, with many relatively small cities – like Paulinus' Beziers – serving as purely local foci and few places much more than a day's travel from a city of some size, but a smaller number of major provincial centres – Bordeaux, for example, in Paulinus' Aquitaine – dominating. Further north, on the other hand, cities were fewer and further apart, provincial capitals ruling a wide swathe of countryside dotted by the occasional military emplacement or secondary center.

The spread of the classical city was a central aspect of the growth of the Roman Empire, and it produced a wealth of material remains in terms of buildings, statues, and inscriptions. Hence it is easy for archaeologists and historians to adopt it as a static ideal, and therefore to interpret changes in the topography and function of cities in terms of "decline." In fact, as the social and political system was restructured through the third to fifth centuries, cities inevitably changed. It is more useful for us to understand how and why these late antique transformations took place than to pass judgment on them against some timeless criteria for "true" urbanism. First and foremost, these changes were topographical. City walls became universal, initially in the third century a response to military and political need but soon an index of a city's status. Widespread church building following the empire's conversion to Christianity redefined the public spaces and the public life of cities. The Christian Church, after all, adopted the administrative structure of the empire, with a bishop in each city as the leader of Christian life in each city's territory. Within the city, the formal classical public buildings, and the statues and inscriptions that commemorated civic benefactors and past events, mutated into new patterns of ecclesiastical patronage. Moreover, Christianization created new supernatural protectors for cities, as bishops developed the cults of long-dead Christian martyrs, whose relics were often discovered in cemeteries – in classical times places of pollution located outside the city's bounds, but now integrated into a Christian urban topography.

Changes to city life, of course, were not solely topographical and cultural. Throughout the late Roman period, cities remained the primary interface between the ever-more ambitious agencies of the government, and local landed society. Above all, it was through city councils that land and people were registered and so tax assessed and collected. One recurrent concern of the government was, therefore, to ensure that local notables took on membership of the "Senate" of their home city and so responsibility for these crucial municipal duties and obligations. The resulting torrent of legislation trying to clamp down on evasion of council ("curial") office by those qualified to take it on can easily seem to imply a crisis of public confidence in city life. In fact, it is worth remembering that the expanded imperial bureaucracy and the Church, along with the army, offered alternative career paths for ambitious locals who would previously have spent a part of their lives in municipal office, but now claimed exemptions.

It is thus no surprise that, in the course of the fifth and sixth centuries, the structures of municipal government changed, even in the East, where the empire survived: city governors, often military men directly appointed by emperors, emerged, and bishops gained an increasing stake in many aspects of city life. In the West, parallel changes took place in the context of the collapse of the imperial tiers of the governmental system and the emergence of new barbarian kingdoms in the former provinces. In some areas – classically southern Gaul – men like Paulinus and his class, shorn off from the imperial court and its patronage, increasingly took on episcopal office in the course of the fifth centuries, and served as patrons for their cities: Sidonius Apollinaris is the classic example of this process, and the example of his distant descendant Gregory of Tours (539–94), thanks to whose writings we are uniquely well informed about late-sixth-century Gaul, shows how some senatorial families were able to create new forms of cultural and social dominance through the Church. But alongside the emergence of bishops we also find another process paralleled in the East, the appearance of military governors, normally entitled *comes* "count" or *dux* "duke", their position based on the administration of a city or group of cities. We find such figures alongside bishops right across Gaul, but in Italy following the Lombard invasion it was very much city-based "dukes" rather than bishops who became the crucial figures. This points to an alternative path of social and political adaptation, with some leading Roman landowners militarizing and merging with the entourages of new barbarian kings.

These changes may be the most easily detected in the written record, but there can be little doubt that they were part of a wider process of demographic and economic transformation. Classical cities may have been first and foremost administrative and political centers, but these functions, and the resultant clustering of landowning activities, had important economic consequences, and led to significant levels of population being engaged in non-agricultural activity. From the third century onward, however, at different rates in different regions, there is a cumulative weight of archaeological hints of declining urban demography and a falling-off of urban economic activity. Urban populations are notoriously difficult to estimate from such evidence, but to take the example of Rome – the biggest and best-studied city in the West throughout our period – a population of well over a million in the Empire's heyday had declined by a factor of around 100 by the beginning of the eighth century, the nadir of the city's demographic fortunes. Rome's very size and its role as a political and ecclesiastical center make its trajectory unique: in the fourth, fifth, and sixth centuries in particular its decline was matched by the rise of the newly founded Constantinople. Nonetheless, Roman cities right across Western Europe, where they survived, show clear evidence of a similar falling-away of population, with dense early Iimperial habitation becoming more sparse, as a diminishing population clustered in small pockets around major churches or the residences of secular leaders. By 700 at the latest, even the very biggest cities – political centers like Paris or Pavia – probably had permanent populations that barely reached into the thousands, and evidence for specialized economic activity is hard to find.

The Church's adoption of the administrative geography of the Roman Empire meant that most Roman cities continued as the seats of bishops, and so eventually became the nuclei of medieval towns. Indeed, remarkably few former Roman cities simply vanished in the post-Roman period. Those that did were predominantly situated in frontier provinces, where in some cases organized Christianity itself disappeared, as in Britain, where urban discontinuity is greatest. But the presence of bishop and Church within a former Roman city did not mean the continuation of city life, and archaeological evidence for city-dwellers or urban activity is hard to come by on many sites, particularly north of the Alps. Even in Italy, where some level of continued urban occupation cannot be denied, there has been heated controversy between those who would see the post-Roman period in cataclysmic terms of collapse, and those who would see a more complex process of transformation.

To a very large extent, such debates turn on differing understandings of city life, for the case for cataclysm rests on the absence of the characteristic archaeological traces left by classical urbanism from post-classical contexts. Those arguing for urban transformation, on the other hand, have paid more sympathetic attention to the early medieval evidence, all too easily dismissed by earlier generations of archaeologists searching for classical structures in stone and the mass-produced pottery whose shards typically record classical occupation. Advances in archaeological technique and a greater awareness on the part of excavators of the possibilities of recovering early medieval evidence have helped correct this neglect. Hence, in Italy at least, it is now possible to discern the outlines of early medieval "cityscapes," and to trace the physical reshaping of the framework of the Roman city to serve new functions in a new society. Within the city walls, pockets of occupation were characteristically separated by areas where there was little habitation at all, which in some cases were given over to "market-gardening" style activity. Changes in domestic architecture similarly departed from the structures characteristic of Roman city life, with widespread construction in wood, and Roman town houses, where they continued to be occupied, partitioned up, and divided between more than one household. This style of urbanism was not merely that of "squatters" eking out a living amidst the ruins of the Roman city, as recent excavations of impressive two-storeyed aristocratic complexes in the Crypt of Balbus and the Forum of Nerva in Rome have shown. The evidence of written documents and narratives confirms that in Italy, even in the seventh and eighth centuries, cities like Lucca or Verona were the primary stages for the public activities of landowners who continued to reside in them. Where there is genuine discontinuity it may be at the level of smaller cities, which even in Roman times had little more than local significance, and are in general little excavated and more or less invisible in the written record.

North of the Alps, the evidence is trickier, with the Church far more dominant in both archaeology and written record. Nonetheless, it does clearly suggest that cities were distinct from the surrounding countryside, fulfilling special functions as cultural, social, and political centers. Thus, while the archaeology of early medieval Tours or Mainz suggests a thinner population in small clusters around the cathedral and other urban churches and the residences of major secular figures, narrative and documentary records point to their being places where the great and good of the locality met periodically, attending the major festivities of the Church's calendar and seeing to public business while in the city. Aristocrats here, in contrast to Italy, may not have habitually resided in cities, but cities still had an important role in their societies.

Even in the immediately post-Roman centuries, then, the inherited urban grid continued to exercise a profound influence in all but the most outlying former Roman provinces. But it did so in a far poorer society where there was less economic specialization and lower population generally. By the eighth, ninth, and tenth centuries, however, region by region an upturn in urban economic activity and in urban population starts to become apparent within the walls of former Roman cities. In this same period, moreover, we see both new urban sites within the former Roman provinces, and urbanism exported for the first time beyond Rome's former frontiers.

The reasons for this new urban growth were resolutely economic. In particular, in the second half of the seventh century around the North Sea, and from the second half of the eighth century in the Mediterranean, new networks of long-distance transcultural trade in luxury goods began to emerge, served by specialist ports of trade. In spite of ninth-century disruptions, as Viking and Muslim warlords made rich pickings exploiting these new connections, long-distance trade networks were eventually to prove a crucial stimulus. By the tenth century at the latest, there are clear signs of developing regional and local markets, which may have been more mundane in their nature, but were also able to exercise a far more profound influence on society. In doing so, they created a new economic pattern, distinct from that inherited from the Roman world.

In fact, patterns of urban transformation ultimately make most sense if linked to the rhythms of economic change in the post-Roman west. Although agriculture was the dominant force in the Roman economy, occupying over 90 percent of the population, long-distance exchange played an important role: fourth-century Rome was fed by African grain, just as Constantinople's growth in the fifth and sixth centuries was possible only because of annual shipments from Egypt, while large-scale movements of foodstuffs and supplies maintained the armies that were stationed in the western provinces in the fourth century. Such exchanges were not primarily commercial in their logic, for it was the Roman state that organized them, and the tax system that structured them. Late Roman traders were characteristically holders of shipping franchises, who might sail to Carthage or Alexandria to pick up a shipment of state-procured goods for Rome or Constantinople, and what private long-distance trade there was rode "piggy-back" on these routes, and would not have been possible without the fiscal incentives given to those who undertook state shipments of official supplies. The patterns of long-distance trade thus closely mirrored political change: the systems supplying Roman armies in the West ended dramatically with the collapse of the Rhine frontier in the decades around 400, while the relative decline of Rome and the rise of Constantinople in the fifth and sixth centuries led to the increasing dominance of eastern traders and eastern ships in the Mediterranean as a whole, with trade in the western Mediterranean thinning out until it connected only a handful of major centers, Marseilles, Carthage, and Rome foremost among them. The arrival, in the middle decades of the sixth century, of plague epidemics carried via trade routes connecting the Mediterranean, via the Red Sea, to China and east Africa had severe consequences – just how severe is a matter of continuing debate – for the system, but it is telling that the western Mediterranean was already so disconnected that there is very little evidence for epidemics having a significant impact there. The final jolt came with the political crisis of the Byzantine Roman Empire in the East in the seventh century. Constantinople, like Rome a century or more before, was forced to adjust, as state shipments from distant provinces ended, and became the hub of a smaller, regional, economic system by 700, as the new Islamic rulers of the empire's eastern and African provinces harvested the tax yields of their new subjects.

This ancient economy, fundamentally structured by the Roman state, was replaced by new systems of transcultural trade. While early medieval trade networks catered for the demands of ruling elites and relied on royal protection, they were not so closely tied to the structures of the state as their predecessors. The chronology of their emergence differed, region by region. Around the North Sea, specialized emporia begin to develop in the later part of the seventh century and into the eighth. While some of these related to Roman sites – at London, for example, an "emporium of many nations"[7] stood just outside the gate of the former Roman city on the Strand – more were new foundations on low-lying and easily navigable sites, such as Dorestad in the Rhine delta and Hamwic near modern Southampton on the south English coast, and, by 800, Hedeby in Denmark and Birka in Sweden. There are some grounds for seeing the development of these sites as attempts to institutionalize more fluid systems based on beach markets and itinerary merchants supplying luxury goods direct to royal courts: certainly exchanges of high-status goods (amber, ivory) from Scandinavia for wine and metalwork from Anglo-Saxon England and Frankish Gaul and Germany had a prehistory. But by 700 at the latest these were not only ports of trade, but also sizable centers of craft production, with raw materials imported and worked for re-export, and a sizable permanent population reaching several thousand.

Whether we should classify these emporia as "urban centres" or "(proto)-towns" should be doubted: the vocabulary used to refer to such sites, and the archaeological record, indicates that there were conceptually and structurally distinct from the former Roman cities that remained ecclesiastical and political centers. And by the middle decades of the ninth century they were experiencing problems, some directly and indirectly caused by Viking activities (whose relationship to the rising tide of trade between Scandinavia and Europe remains a complex and obscure issue). But even in their heyday, in the decades around 800, emporia like Dorestad or Hamwic had created regional supply networks in their hinterlands, and the ninth and tenth centuries saw these regional networks intensifying, and supporting economic specialization. It is on the back of these processes that we find evidence for increasing population and craft production right across the cities of the West in the ninth and tenth centuries, and find new towns developing around aristocratic and monastic centers of demand, whose extensive landholdings meant that they were also centers of production. In the Low Countries, for example, Dorestad disappeared in the ninth century, but the emergence of Bruges and Ghent as urban centers occurs little more than a generation later.

In the western Mediterranean, the long and lingering afterlife of the Roman economy into the seventh century meant that the emergence of new trade networks had a different chronology, and the surviving urban pattern meant that these networks grew in a different context. Nonetheless, it is clear that by the last quarter of the eighth century regular connections between the Islamic provinces of North Africa and Spain, and the northern coastline of the western Mediterranean, were taking place, at first indirectly via Naples, and Sicily and the various other islands, but soon directly. Networks connecting the Adriatic with the wider Mediterranean grew in a similar pattern, primed by the dramatic growth of Venice, a classic emporium with no Roman past, in the late eighth and ninth centuries. These networks brought high-status luxury goods – spices, incense, and silk – from the Islamic world into Western Europe, in return for a variety of West European staples – slaves definitely, particularly via Venice, but also metalwork and other Western products. The struggles between Byzantine, Frankish, and Islamic rulers to control the islands and sea lanes of the western Mediterranean in the ninth century in some ways provide a parallel to Viking activity in the North, albeit in a very different political and religious context. As in the north, while there is some evidence for dislocation, particularly in the later ninth century, the basic dynamic of growth remained. By 900 the major trading centers and networks were clearly established, and the foundations for continued growth in transcultural exchange through the tenth century and beyond well laid, while within Italy traders, and market activity, became increasingly apparent.

Although it is long-distance trade in luxury goods, in both Italy and the north, that catches the eye, the crucial factor in economic developments was the emergence of local and regional markets feeding off more intensive agricultural production.

These were the basis of new economic patterns, and they were possible only because of changes in the countryside.

A World of Villages: The Transformation of the Countryside

Cities and their fate have long been a major focus of attention. In part, this is because cities were such a fundamental feature of ancient Mediterranean civilization; in part, because to successive generations of modern Europeans the centrality of urban centers to public life was a crucial feature that made the Romans somehow "like us" and hence the post-Roman period an unfortunate and barbaric Other. Yet, in fact, the transformation of the rural landscape in the post-Roman period was perhaps more dramatic and sudden than changes in cityscapes. Arguably, it was the second half of the first millennium that saw the emergence of the underlying grid of village settlement – agglomerations of farming households, increasingly focused on parish churches with attached cemeteries – that was to determine the basic shape of the pre-industrial West European countryside. Indeed, one focus for recurrent interest in the early medieval centuries has been a search for the origins of villages and parishes, usually underpinned by a strong sense of a timeless local identity and organic agrarian order out of which subsequent social complexity grew. In many areas of Europe in the nineteenth and early twentieth centuries, scholars thus searched for a new social order that started from scratch as "new peoples" carved out a place in the post-Roman countryside, but more recent attempts to understand the archaeology in particular have pointed to more complex and drawn-out processes of change.

Thanks to several generations of sophisticated field surveys and careful excavation, the settlement patterns of the Roman countryside are well understood. This topography was dominated and ultimately defined by the luxurious rural residences of Paulinus and his class, labeled villas in archaeological and historical shorthand, although Roman authors use a more varied terminology. Villas themselves, of course, could vary in their scale and scope: not every one was like the rural palace, complete with bathhouse and landscaped vistas, lauded in Sidonius Apollinaris' poetic description of his villa at Avitacum.[8] The construction and maintenance of such residences marked a considerable investment on the part of their owners, an investment that had major economic implications, although writers like Sidonius characteristically failed to mention their role in directing and organizing agrarian production. In the West, rural economy and society were organized around villa centers. Neither the archaeology nor the written sources give any sense of the presence of strong alternative models for rural settlement with a clear definition or structure in the West, just isolated farms or scattered hamlets, mostly of simple wooden construction. These patterns stand in marked contrast to the empire's eastern provinces, where we do find genuine villages as well as, and sometimes including, elite residences. This stands as eloquent testimony to the total dominance of the landowning elite within late Roman provincial society in the West.

This does not mean that the late Roman countryside in the West was cultivated solely by gangs of laborers who were housed and fed by their masters. In fact, a slave-based system of this kind had never been widespread outside central Italy, and was in decline everywhere after the third century. Of course, the legal distinction between free and unfree people remained a central categorization for Roman and early medieval society. But slavery – the subjection of humans as legal possessions owned by a master – remained a central social institution and cultural concern because of the omnipresence of slaves as servants within elite households, not because slavery was a central component of the economic system. In fact, the legal sources reveal a complex array of different classes of peasant household in the Roman countryside, with varying degrees of subjection to villa-owners, who might also enjoy title over their lands or even their persons, or whose domination might rest on other forms of patronage. Landlord dominance was intimately tied up with the workings of the tax system, which made landowners middlemen responsible for the registration and collection of tax liabilities and public dues incurred by their dependants and tenants and so encouraging a blurring between rent and tax and formalized systems of rural patronage. The importance of villas in these systems of dominance and dependence reinforced their role as centers of aristocratic conspicuous consumption, and so major economic hubs: the demands and needs of their owners structured patterns of rural production in their hinterlands.

Against this backdrop, the more or less total disappearance of villas from the West by the seventh century is the most dramatic index of the scale of post-Roman change, and one easily obscured by a focus on cities and long-distance trade. The chronologies and patterns of villa abandonment inevitably differ from region to region: in some frontier areas, villa life showed its first signs of frailty in the empire's third-century "crisis" and never really recovered, whilst in the core provinces around the shores of the western Mediterranean villa maintenance and construction continue through the fourth and fifth centuries in spite of political change.

In some regions, again notably those provinces closer to Roman frontiers in northern Gaul and Britain, the archaeological record seems to indicate a fairly dramatic process of abandonment, with new types of settlement emerging in the fourth and fifth centuries with little apparent relationship to their predecessors. Here, villa sites, where they did become the basis of later medieval settlements, may have been the objects of conscious and ideologically loaded reuse, as is the case with a series of seventh- and eighth-century rural monasteries founded by powerful Frankish aristocratic families.

In the western Mediterranean, on the other hand, we can clearly see in the works of aristocratic authors like Sidonius the continuation of villas through the fifth century and into the sixth. Here, we seem to be dealing with more gradual processes of transformation. In some areas, notably in central Italy but also perhaps at some sites in Spain and southern Gaul, there is a suggestion that former villa sites might have remained as centers of agrarian management, but on a far more modest scale and with far less influence over their hinterlands, as large farms. Probably the classic site of this kind is Mola di Monte Gelato just north of Rome, where a former villa seems to have continued as some form of estate center throughout the post-Roman period prior to its rebuilding as a major papal estates center or *domusculta* in the eighth century; it is not impossible that some of the former villa centers that re-emerge in new forms in the north at a similar date may have had similar histories. Elsewhere in the south, we see new forms of settlement hierarchy emerging – for example, fortified hilltop centers emerging in parts of southern Gaul and Italy in the sixth century; in other areas, in the sixth and seventh centuries in particular, we see relatively unstructured patterns of scattered and often short-lived small-scale rural habitation.

The disappearance of villas is a strong indication of the collapse of a particular system of elite dominance, rooted in the close relationship between Roman landlords and the Roman state; and the disappearance of the cultural values and patterns of conspicuous consumption that the Roman senators like Paulinus used to articulate and justify their dominance. The regional patterns evident particularly in the archaeology might therefore be seen as indications of different processes and varying paces whereby the Roman ruling class mutated into the aristocracies of the early medieval west. The archaeology also makes immediately clear a further set of regional contrasts, in the speed with which alternative social models emerged.

In the north, villa collapse appears clear-cut because by the end of the fifth century at the latest a new model of settlement is already apparent. This takes the form of an agglomeration of up to half a dozen household units, each based on a single post-built wooden "hall" between 15 and 30 meters long, with a series of associated smaller wooden hut-like structures based on a rectangular sunken foundation ("sunken featured buildings", *fonds de caban* or *Grübenhauser*). These wooden building traditions have precedents within the Roman provinces of northern Gaul and Britain as well as beyond the Roman frontier, and should be seen as the products of acculturation, as new social models evolved in the post-Roman West: it is striking, for example, that beyond the frontier animals had characteristically been housed alongside humans in often much bigger "longhouses," but in the post-Roman provinces smaller "halls" were dwelt in only by people. The other feature of this new model of settlement was the presence of agglomerations of households of roughly equivalent size and status alongside one another. These "villages" may have been relatively fluid and ill-defined, particularly in the fifth to seventh centuries, when there is good evidence for a significant degree of dispersal of households across each settlement area, and for some settlement mobility, with households periodically abandoned and rebuilt at a neighboring site; it is in the eighth, ninth, and tenth centuries that more nucleated settlements, with a fixed site, emerge, characteristically as households cluster around a newly founded church and associated cemetery. Nonetheless, already in written sources from sixth century such as the writings Gregory of Tours, the Latin *villa* is used to refer to a settlement unit recognizably akin to what we would style a village, composed of a group of households tied together not by any formal tenurial hierarchy or strict economic or social dependency, but by the patterns of cooperation and conflict implicit in living in a community. In law codes and legal documents, too, individual farms, fields, and households were located in a particular *villa*, which was primarily a unit of settlement and implicitly defined in terms of community, not ownership or management.

Most research on southern Gaul, Spain, and Italy has attempted to identify a similar passage "from villa to village" for these regions. What this should not obscure is the fact that the new model of settlement that becomes apparent so clearly and quickly in the north is far more elusive and slower to emerge in the south. New building in stone disappeared here, as in the north, with the end of the villa system, but in the sixth and seventh centuries we characteristically either find new, shallower, hierarchies emerging, for example, around fortified hilltops in southern Gaul or estate centers in central Italy; or, as in Tuscany, scattered, small-scale and short-lived habitation with little obvious structure. Certainly, as in the north, settlement structure stabilized and became more nucleated in the course of the eighth, ninth, and tenth centuries. In some areas, classically Tuscany, this led to the emergence of villages, here located on hilltops and often walled, part of a wider process of *incastellamento*, the creation of defensible nucleated settlement units, which is paralleled right across the western Mediterranean in the tenth and eleventh centuries.

Changing Aristocracies: Wealth and Social Status

It is notable that, in both north and south, village structures began to crystallize, albeit in regionally different forms, in the eighth, ninth, and tenth centuries. It is also no accident that new forms of elite residences, distinct from those that populated the new villages, emerge in a roughly similar chronology. In the sixth to eighth centuries, we have little evidence either archaeological or written for any special residential structure being particularly associated with aristocratic status. Rather, aristocrats resided in wooden halls like those of their neighbors, perhaps physically bigger (as at Laucheim in Bavaria), or perhaps sited so as to articulate local dominance (for example, distanced from the major foci of settlement, as at Kircheim in Bavaria, or marked by a high palisade-like fence or a specially metalled track leading to the door, as at Wulflingen in Swabia). Fences, tracks, and doors are presented as important status-markers in law codes and narratives. Movable wealth – chests of treasure and status-affirming heirlooms, garments and wall-hangings, tableware, and high-status feast food – rather than physical structures were the crucial status-markers.

By the seventh and eighth centuries, however, particularly in the Frankish heartlands, major landowning families might also found "family monasteries" on their rural estates. These institutions, which commemorated ancestors and often housed and were run by matrons and daughters, doubled as "family trusts" holding landed resources, and as impressive residences. Those who lacked the resources for a full-scale monastic foundation might invest in the type of "hall plus church" complex evident in both the archaeology and the documentary evidence. And, in the course of the ninth and tenth centuries, new forms of secular aristocratic residence emerged, out of which developed the castles that were the defining feature of the medieval countryside and the defining mark of medieval aristocratic families. Archaeologically, the prehistory of the castle is difficult to trace precisely, because on most sites the earliest layers are overlaid by generation after generation of later development. However, the archaeology does support documents and narratives that indicate aristocratic residences being increasingly distinct and detached from the run of rural settlement by the end of the ninth century. Royal estate centers – which were, after all, managed by resident stewards who were normally recruited from the ranks of the local aristocracy – may have provided a model for the first stages of this process, for already in the reign of Charlemagne they typically featured wooden palisades and two-storey halls. Certainly in the course of the tenth century these features became the defining characteristics of the aristocratic stronghold. External defenses, for example, came to encompass earthen ramparts and eventually man-made mounds or mottes, protecting buildings of two or more storeys, perhaps initially of wood construction but increasingly upgraded to stone. By the eleventh century, such centers were simultaneously anchor points for family identity, marks of social status, and mechanisms for creating cohesive lordship over the surrounding countryside. The knightly class that resided in them was the first ruling class since Paulinus' time to be able to invest its dominance in a particular type of residence-cum-political center.

These changes in the landscape clearly indicate radical shifts in the creation, circulation, and distribution of wealth. The villas of the late Roman world and castles of the eleventh century rested on sharp inequalities of wealth and articulated the dominance of clearly defined landowning elites. But the fact that in the centuries between dominant families could not set themselves apart so dramatically is telling. In part, as the archaeology above all makes clear, there was in all probability simply less wealth to go around in these intervening centuries. Early medieval sites both urban and rural are marked by a relative paucity of material remains, implying an impoverished material culture compared to Roman and later medieval times. As a result, early medieval population levels are hard to estimate, even in relative terms, simply because habitation produced far less of the kind of remains evident from surveys and field walking. This does not necessarily mean that lives were harder for the mass of the peasantry: within a world where there were fewer surpluses, the distribution of wealth was more equitable, and landlords' pressure less, than in Roman or later medieval times. Certainly archaeological and written evidence from the earliest medieval centuries, prior to the reign of Charlemagne, indicate rural populations adopting a mixed economic strategy, designed to minimize risk and aimed primarily at self-sufficiency. The size of livestock, for example, declined as stock-breeding for the market or the table of the landlord was abandoned, and cattle were expected to have a working life in the fields prior to being slaughtered; pastoral resources likewise played an important role in domestic economies.

Early medieval rural landscapes, like early medieval cities, were undoubtedly more sparsely populated than their Roman predecessors. The shifts that had occurred since Roman times in both the structures of settlement and the overall level and distribution of wealth make the extent of population decline difficult to assess, although it was certainly less dramatic in the countryside than in urban contexts. Probably the most significant demographic fact is that from the seventh century onward there are tell-tale signs of population growth – for example, in the clearing of new land and the foundation of new settlements, and in denser population in existing settlements and cemeteries – reversing a trend of decline going back to at least the third century. This in itself may well indicate that behind the poorer material culture of the early medieval countryside lies a peasantry more confident in its control of its destiny than had previously been the case.

Nonetheless, the written evidence even from these centuries clearly indicates the existence of landowning elites. Most research has focused on the question of aristocratic origins, asking whether the barbarian peoples had a defined aristocratic class prior to their arrival in the former Roman provinces of the West, or whether aristocracies were created by kings in the process of settlement. The question itself is misleading, as it presupposes a social structure that can be characterized in terms of "Germanic" or "Roman" principles of organization, rather than one arising out of a complex set of interactions. The senatorial aristocracy of Roman times was a truly international ruling class, with interests right across the empire (think of Paulinus' holdings in Greece), and particularly connecting the core provinces of the western empire: Italy, and the Mediterranean coastlines of Gaul, Spain, and North Africa. As is apparent from Paulinus' political career, political collapse in the fifth century fractured these connections, and the aristocratic elites of southern Gaul and north-eastern Spain – who had risen to prominence thanks to the influence of men like Ausonius with the Theodosian dynasty – found themselves forced to adjust to new political, regional, circumscriptions. Even in Italy, where senatorial families attempted to keep up contacts with Constantinople and the wider imperial world through the first half of the sixth century, the Senate of Rome itself had disbanded by the first decade of the seventh century, and more regional elites of diverse origin – military officers and barbarian war leaders as well as impoverished senators and provincial landowners – emerged in place of the senatorial class. Elsewhere, patterns of transformation are harder to trace, with some evidence for a powerful military aristocracy emerging alongside the Merovingian dynasty in northern Gaul in the fifth and sixth centuries, the result of long-term interactions between the barbarian warlords from beyond the Rhine and increasingly militarized ruling elites of Roman frontier provinces. By the seventh century, a series of regional aristocracies was crystallizing around the courts of the barbarian kings and dukes of the West. Characteristically, these aristocracies were highly militarized, and had adopted distinct ethnic identities to articulate their interests, which were resolutely regional. The political success of the Carolingian dynasty in the eighth century rested on the creation of an extensive and inclusive coalition among these aristocracies, and creating a genuine "imperial aristocracy" with interests right across Western Europe, which interacted in complex ways with kin and clients whose horizons remained more regional. In spite of the political problems of the Carolingian empire in the ninth century and its fracturing into an array of successor kingdoms, the Carolingian period was fundamental in creating the conditions in which the "imperial aristocracy" and its successors could create firmer systems of local dominance, and a more clearly articulated divide between aristocrats and others, than had been the case since Paulinus' time.

The Roman senatorial elite from which Paulinus sprang has been called the richest ruling class of pre-modern times, with real justice. For Paulinus and his contemporaries, social status was straightforward: members of the Roman Senate enjoyed defined legal and political privileges, which were immediately apparent in terms of deportment, and expressed in terms of specified honorific titles given to different ranks. On a local level, "curial" status and membership of a city council brought comparable privileges. Status was thus tied up with public life and brought with it formal privileges entrenched in administrative and legal practice and underwritten by the state. In the course of the fifth and sixth centuries, these formal status-markers disappeared. Whether this led to increased social mobility is not clear. A less sharp social hierarchy without formal status barriers ought, logically, to have been more open than its predecessor, and there are good examples of upwards mobility in, for example, the career of the slave turned conman Andarchius recounted by Gregory of Tours.[9] What is clear is that elite status itself was far more subjective and inclusive than had previously been the case: it rested on perceptions about group membership, and was not defined by any objective dividing line. The rich Carolingian sources, for example, repeatedly talk of the political community of aristocratic landowners with whom kings had to deal as "the powerful," "the leading," "the best," "the noble," but in legal documents this terminology might equally easily be applied to the leading landowners of a locality or neighborhood. These were ultimately collective labels, too, which were far more rarely applied to individuals, and then usually to indicate moral approval, the sense of behaving honorably, "like a noble" rather than "like a slave".

There were economic limits to this elasticity of identity: the claims of Gregory's Andarchius, for example, were ultimately exposed as empty. The thickening-out of the documentary record from the eighth and ninth centuries – itself a product of aristocratic endowment of monastic foundations as a means of stabilizing their position – has allowed historians to understand the patterns and practices of aristocratic landholding. In general, landholdings were small and scattered: agglomerations of land parcels, some a few fields, some a whole farm, very occasionally a whole village, over a 20–50 kilometer radius, although the very highest echelons of the 'imperial aristocracy' might own several such regional clusters. These patterns did not encourage intensive exploitation: typically, larger holdings came complete with dependent peasants, whose legal status (free or unfree) and customary position varied from region to region, but who characteristically lived in family-based household units on the land they farmed and from which they fed themselves. Social status thus rested primarily on the acquisition of more units of a familiar type, for even well-to-do free peasants might own a handful of such land parcels in two or three neighboring villages, and aristocratic rank thus depended primarily on the possession of sufficient resources to allow full participation in the public political life of the region and kingdom.

From the eighth century onwards, however, we find new, more intensive forms of agricultural exploitation emerging alongside these patterns of fragmented smallholding. Crucial here was the emergence of the manorial system, in which dependent peasants, whether free or unfree, were expected to cultivate a demesne or reserve set aside solely for the profit of the landowner, in addition to paying rent on their own holdings. This system seems to have first emerged in the seventh century as a means of organizing the estates of the Merovingian kings in their heartlands around Paris, but it was soon also adopted by major Frankish churches, and it spread across Europe with Frankish rule in the course of the eighth century. The complexities of manorial structures have spawned a huge specialist bibliography, and it is possible to overestimate the importance of the manor in Carolingian and post-Carolingian Europe: they are relatively scarce, for example, in southern Gaul, while in Italy demesnes were frequently small or fragmented, and in many areas labor service was primarily important as a sign of subordination, often seen by free peasants on whom it was imposed as an encroachment on their ancestral liberty. Nonetheless, the run of estate surveys or polyptychs beginning with Charlemagne's attempts to record the resources of royal estates and quickly taken up by the great churches of the Carolingian and post-Carolingian world constitute impressive testimony as to the scale of economic resources available to those at the top of the Carolingian system. Aristocrats too began to form manors on their own estates, without their ever replacing scattered land parcels as the dominant form of aristocratic landholding (and even royal and ecclesiastical landholdings were not solely organized in manorial form); perhaps more importantly, as stewards of royal estates or recipients of life grants of royal or ecclesiastical lands, aristocrats were well placed to benefit from the new system. These changes in agricultural organization were a crucial aspect of the wider social and economic changes of the Carolingian and post-Carolingian periods: the stabilization of settlement patterns and the intensification of arable production and stock-breeding attested archaeologically, the emergence of local markets often at major manorial centers evident in the documents, and the deepening of social stratification wherever we look were possible precisely because of the more intensive exploitation in the countryside.

Aristocratic status and resources rested on family connections and inheritance. Kinship patterns within the landowning classes have been a major concern of research, in part because traditional scholarship sought to find distinctive "Germanic" kinship practices transmitted through the early medieval evidence. Certainly, early medieval aristocratic families defined themselves in different terms from those familiar to Paulinus. The complex Roman naming system, honoring ancestors and articulating an objective family identity transmitted over time, had disappeared more or less everywhere in the West by the seventh century. Instead, we find ourselves in the sometimes bewildering position of studying families that had no surnames. This does not mean that they had no family consciousness. Name elements seem to have been manipulated to articulate a family pedigree, and written sources can refer to the kin of a named individual acting collectively as a group, but the clan names used to structure many historical accounts by labeling family groupings are essentially modern creations with a limited basis in the original sources. Detailed work on the documentary record has allowed the norms of the law codes to be related to social practice, and the stress in the laws on wide clanlike groupings – often seen as a "Germanic" inheritance – has been qualified. There were occasions – times of major political conflict or family trauma – when a far-reaching array of kin, uncles, and cousins might act together. But such action was not the norm, nor was it automatic: the basic units of inheritance and ownership, which shaped the everyday obligations of practical kinship, were more restricted, and rooted in the household, focusing on a conjugal couple, their parents, and their offspring. More distant kinship bonds mattered, in part because their very fluidity made them open to manipulation and thus so useful: a powerful relation in a position to deliver patronage or protection might usefully be reminded of common ancestry, whether it came through maternal or paternal lines. In other words, rather than thinking of a fixed kinship system that assigned particular values to particular relationships, we should think of households structured by affective sociability tied together by a web of potential claims that could be activated as and when appropriate in a system whose virtue lay in its flexibility. Patterns of landholding that turned on the relatively frequent circulation of relatively small units of ownership were central to such a system. The implications of these structures for gender relations and the life cycle are among the most exciting areas of current research.

How did aristocracies whose internal structures were themselves flexible sustain and legitimate their position in a society far poorer, and far less stratified, than the later Roman world? The most obvious and recognizable change was in their militarization. The cultural and social values of Paulinus' class were those of *civilitas*, an ideology of Roman order that rested on a rigid separation between civilian society and the military, who alone were permitted to bear weapons; Roman legislation from the years around 400, indeed, voices moral panics about military attire as inherently barbarizing, not appropriate for high-status Romans or within the city of Rome. These distinctions were quickly eroded, although some barbarian regimes – most famously that of Theodoric the Ostrogoth in Italy between 489 and 526 – attempted to prop them up, with a view to creating a social partnership between tax-paying Roman civilians and the weapon-bearing barbarians who now offered them protection. By 600, even in those areas of Italy under Byzantine rule, a new militarized idiom of aristocratic status had arisen, and in everywhere bar Byzantine Italy it was closely linked to the ethnicities that had emerged as the crucial identities in the new societies of the post-Roman West. Militarization was in all probability not cheap. It rested on the recruitment of extensive entourages, with aristocrats supplying and feeding sizable military households themselves, as well as offering appropriate gifts and patronage to a larger and wider group of kin and clients. The cost of militarization indeed helps explain why fifth- and sixth-century aristocracies were unable to maintain the levels of investment in residential buildings that had characterized their Roman forebears; even where violence allowed plunder and tribute, these spoils had immediately to be recycled as gifts to ensure the continued support of followers. Certainly, the imperatives of a military aristocracy explain why it was war gear – swords, sword belts, horses – that were the archetypical status symbols in the early medieval West. Around such objects – and the feasts and other ceremonies where they were circulated and displayed – stories encoding mores and identities were woven, transmitted to us by writers such as Gregory of Tours and the eighth-century historian of the Lombards, Paul the Deacon. Aristocratic honor was thus a highly gendered cultural code, resting on sometimes painful feats of machismo, and military training separated boys from girls at an early stage in youth.

Obviously, in a new world of more diffuse political power lacking the fiscal and legal apparatus of the Roman state, military might was an important aspect of aristocratic domination. But, crucially, throughout the early medieval period aristocracies were nowhere able to maintain a monopoly on the legitimate use of force or the bearing of weapons, either in theory or in practice. Carrying weapons was the fundamental badge of freedom, and a crucial aspect of ethnic identities that were not restricted to elites but were open to all the free. Lombard and Carolingian kings in their legislation drew on this ideological link in demanding military service from all free men. Carolingian peasants were capable of mounting armed resistance to Vikings or other marauders even when their social "betters" fled, and were just as ready as their aristocratic peers to turn to the sword in the prosecution of disputes with kin or neighbors. Of course, aristocrats were immediately identifiable on account of the quality and lineage of their war gear, and their ability to distribute it to their followers. And, if and when necessary, aristocrats possessed the necessary force to subject the lesser free whether armed or not, as was discovered by the sworn groups of *Stellinga* recruited in Saxony in the Carolingian civil wars, or the fellowship of Loire valley peasants formed to resist the Vikings but slaughtered as subversive by Frankish aristocrats in 859.[10] These episodes do show aristocrats not only using violence to impose their dominance, but contesting the legitimacy of some forms of peasant armed action. But it was only extreme forms of peasant self-help that could be presented as potentially subversive: the right of free men to bear weapons was unquestioned. It was not until the end of our period, with the emergence of a new ideology of knighthood creating an identity rooted in ecclesiastically sanctioned violence for a broad-based elite in the tenth and eleventh centuries, that the automatic identification of free status with weapon bearing was broken. Even then practice lagged well behind theory. Moreover, the ideological monopoly on legitimate knightly force thus achieved came at a high price: the involvement of the Church in the sanctification of knightly violence meant that it could also rule some of its forms, notably those that might threaten Church property, out of order.

No social elite can exist purely on the basis of coercion, and the inability of early medieval aristocracies even to claim a monopoly on force means that we should look for other strategies of power. In fact, it was the very fluidity of early medieval aristocratic groupings that was crucial in enabling them to exercise power without the formal structures of rank and rule that had underpinned the position of Paulinus and his class. In a world where even governmental institutions were relatively diffuse and unspecialized, and where wealth was overwhelmingly based on control over land and its fruits, aristocrats ultimately had to cajole and persuade communities of local landowners to accept their leadership. Their economic muscle, especially as it allowed them to recruit military followings, was, of course, one means of persuasion, but coercion could not work everywhere, all the time. Public office – above all, the catch-all position of count – mattered because it gave precedence at the public meetings at which disputes between locals were resolved and through which localities interacted with royal courts. This was office of a very different type to that of Paulinus' world, where aristocrats took on roles for a fixed time period as they progressed up the *cursus honorum*. These were jobs for life, but they also necessitated the use of kinship, patronage, and landholding locally to cultivate goodwill: even powerful kings tended to appoint well-connected insiders as the most efficient means of governing. Such roles both legitimated aristocratic power – even when kings were unable to intervene, offices remained in theory legitimate public positions delegated from God via the king – and provided levers of patronage for its holders, notably in the dispensation of justice and the meting-out of punishment to wrongdoers.

The End of the Early Middle Ages?

The tenth and eleventh centuries saw the emergence of a more clearly defined aristocratic class, its dominance now explicitly articulated in the ideology of knighthood and the reality of castles. This process of transformation was one of the major topics of debate in medieval history through the second half of the twentieth century, and the controversy shows little sign of abating. Since the pioneering work of the French historians Marc Bloch on the cultural and social world of the post-Carolingian aristocracy, and Georges Duby, whose study of the area around Maçon began a wave of region-by-region analysis, these changes have been in the eyes of many a genuine revolutionary transformation in the organization of society worthy of comparison with the Industrial Revolution of the nineteenth century.[11] Characteristically, for Bloch – whose work remains hugely influential – the basis for this process was social meltdown, with the collapse of the Carolingian empire and the raids of Vikings, Magyars, and Saracens creating a world in which the protection of the powerful became the dominant organizing principle of society. Bloch, drawing on then current thinking, saw the creation of formal systems of lordship whereby men pledged themselves as the armed retainers or "vassals" of a lord in return for his protection, and the grant of a life interest in land in the form of a "benefice" or "fief" as characteristic of this new order, although, unlike most of his contemporaries, he did not see a particular tenurial form as the defining characteristic of this "feudal society."

Following Bloch, Duby and his successors traced the changing mechanisms of aristocratic power, and their detailed research into legal documentation developed a less cataclysmic picture of gradual transformation, albeit one in which the coercive violence of the aristocracy was a crucial factor. Aristocratic families, even though they frequently had their origins in the Carolingian ruling classes, developed new structures, as lineages stressing father-to-son inheritance emerged, with maternal kin and extensive bilateral links to uncles and cousins less important than in early medieval times, and the status of daughters and even younger sons diminished so as to maintain the family line down through time. In the eleventh century, surnames – characteristically evoking the new seat of family power, the castle around whose inheritance a lineage was formed – emerged, alongside the ideology of knighthood, which intersected but was never quite identical with notions of nobility. For Duby and his successors, the hallmark of this new order of aristocratic power lay not so much in the obligations between lords and their men, which emerged as increasingly complex and diverse, and certainly unable to be reduced to a single or simple model. Instead, it was a wider system of social dominance as lords were able to establish formal rights of jurisdiction over all sectors of society. Lordly jurisdiction enveloped not only their followers – Duby's earliest work had attempted to show the decline of the old Carolingian public courts and the rise of an alternative system of lords dispensing justice to their men from their new castle seats – but also, by the eleventh century, the peasantry as a whole. The emergence of a homogenized class of serfs – a major concern of Bloch's entire scholarly career – was possible as the new lords, dominating the countryside from their castles and via their bands of knights, were able to impose a host of petty dues on the peasantry, whether free or unfree – dues that rested on the claims of lords to exercise jurisdiction over an area but that were often imposed by force, and are referred to by modern scholars as the *seigneurie*.

The model of "feudal revolution" developed in the second half of the twentieth century articulated a clear sense of a disjuncture in historical development, short and sharp in its working-out but epoch making in its implications. In many ways, it also mirrored the changing constitution of medieval history as a discipline, and the increasing separation of early medievalists as a distinct subdiscipline, because it identified the "birth" of medieval society with a discrete set of tenth- and eleventh-century developments and thus cut loose the early medieval centuries. It is precisely because it straddles this historiographical divide, and conditions how the research of those either side of that divide relates to one another, that the very notion of a "feudal revolution" has been such a major focus of controversy and debate in the past few decades. Virtually every aspect of the classic model has been challenged, most often on the basis of a fuller understanding of the early medieval background, and the Carolingian period in particular, than was available to earlier generations.

The French historian Dominique Barthélemy has even gone so far as to suggest that earlier historians had in reality simply picked up a "documentary revolution", and misunderstood changes in the idioms of the records from which they worked – and in particular a tendency to write in more and more anecdotal detail about the background to property disputes – for changes in actual social organization. Move beyond the documents, so it could be claimed, and there are precedents for virtually all the forms of domination evident in the eleventh century in Carolingian evidence. Move beyond a dated and misleading picture of the Carolingian empire as a highly centralized and bureaucratic state, and acknowledge its reality as a powerful aristocratic coalition, and tenth- and eleventh-century change, whilst it cannot be denied, cannot be epoch making.

Certainly older views of internal political crisis and external marauders leading to wholesale social meltdown in late Carolingian times and after have been firmly discredited by new political histories of the period. So too the stress of much earlier work on aristocratic violence as a newly potent force for change raises more questions than it answers. After all, physical force was an integral part of early medieval society and aristocracies had been militarized since the ending of Roman rule in the West, so it is difficult to see how aristocratic coercion suddenly functioned as a force for sweeping change: it is a mistake, albeit an easy one to make, to take the polemics of anxious churchmen eager to keep knights off their estates at face value as evidence for an epidemic of violence. Aristocratic power was nothing new – it had underwritten all early medieval political systems – and patronage based on the obligations of a client to his lord and protector had strong Roman precedents and were ever present in the early medieval centuries. The granting of land for military service was nothing like so widespread or systematic as was previously believed even in the tenth and eleventh centuries, nor did it rest on explicit norms or a consistent legal vocabulary. On close examination even pictures of a dramatic shift in the functioning of justice dissolve, for the public meetings of early medieval times had been dominated by aristocratic interests and interacted with the use of patronage and force to broker settlements.

Such debates are far from having run their course, in part because finding precedents for any single aspect of aristocratic behavior is one thing but analyzing the dynamics of a social system another entirely. But looked at from the long perspective of the early medieval centuries, the most striking feature of the tenth and eleventh centuries is that, cumulatively, the undoubted changes in the mechanisms of aristocratic power show a ruling class able to create formal systems that explicitly articulated its social dominance – something that had not really existed in the West since Paulinus' time. The emergence of serfdom marked a clear divide between peasants and their landlords where previously stratification had been a matter of gradual, quantitative, shifts rather than a qualitative difference; the ideology of knighthood mapped legitimate access to force onto class divisions, and the formalization of jurisdictions and obligations in the *seigneurie* rooted them in law; the development of castles physically inscribed the new structures of dominance into the landscape, while the fluid systems of patronage and kinship that had sustained early medieval aristocracies seamlessly and gradually evolved into firmer and more fixed norms about lineage and lordship to sustain the new structures. Many, indeed most, aspects of tenth- and eleventh-century aristocratic power had plentiful precedents in early medieval precedents, but in their very formalization into the documentary record and the law they became something more than an isolated practice. Documentary change here was a direct byproduct of social transformation and the articulation of new expectations and norms about social relationships.

Again, if we think about the tenth and eleventh centuries from the long perspective of the early medieval centuries, is it any accident that these social changes cumulatively formalizing aristocratic dominance came at precisely that moment when economic growth – more wealth and more exchange of wealth – was evident right across the West European countryside? Of course, there are difficult questions of cause and effect involved in any attempt to relate social and economic change. Aristocrats with newly formalized rights over the peasantry were doubtless more able to extract surplus wealth from those who worked the land, and indeed the strong correlation between the growth of aristocratic domination in the countryside, and extraction of greater surplus from the peasantry, and economic growth can be traced back at least to Carolingian times. Nonetheless, only in a world of more wealth, and so with the potential for a steeper social hierarchy with a wider gulf between aristocrats and others, was a more formal and stable system of aristocratic domination than that of early medieval times even a possibility.

Notes

1 Paulinus, *Eucharisticon*, Preface, in Moussy (ed.), *Paulin de Pella*. I have used the English translation of Evelyn-White, in *Ausonius: Works*, appendix: Paulinus of Pella, pp. 295–351. In forthcoming work I hope to locate Paulinus' misfortunes in their legal and political context.
2 Quote from *Eucharisticon*, lines 422–5.
3 Quote from *Eucharisticon*, lines 498–502.
4 On Augustine's ecclesiology, Markus, *Saeculum*, is fundamental.
5 Salvian of Marseille, *On the Governance of God*.
6 Pirenne, *Mohammed and Charlemagne* (1939, but first published (posthumously) in French in 1937).
7 Bede, *Ecclesiastical History*, II.3, ed. and trans. Colgrave and Mynors, pp. 142–3.
8 Sidonius Apollinaris, *Letters*, 2.2, ed. and trans. Anderson, and see also his description of the villas of his friends Apollinaris and Ferreolous, 2.9.
9 Gregory of Tours, *Histories*, X:4, ed. Krusch and Levison; English translation by Thorpe.
10 Nithard, *Histoire des fils de Louis le Pieux*, IV.2, ed. Lauer; translation by Scholz, *Carolingian Chronicles*, and Nelson, *The Annals of St Bertin*, s.a. 859.
11 The pioneering works were Bloch, *Feudal Society* (the French original dates from 1939–40), and Duby, *La Société aux XIe et XIIe siècles*; see also Bisson, "La Terre et les hommes.

Bibliography

Ambrosiani, Bjorn, and Clarke, Helen, *Towns in the Viking Age*, 2nd edn (Leicester: Leicester University Press, 1995).

Ausonius, *Ausonius: Works*, trans. A. G. Evelyn-White (Cambridge, MA: G. P. Putnam & Sons, 1921.

Bede, *Ecclesiastical History*, ed. and trans. B. Colgrave and R. Mynors (Oxford: Oxford University Press, 1969).

Bisson, Thomas N., "The 'Feudal Revolution'", *Past and Present*, 142 (1994), pp. 6–42; with comments by Dominique Barthelemy, Timothy Reuter, Stephen D. White, and Chris Wickham in *Past and Present*, 152 (1996) and 155 (1997).

Bisson, Thomas N., "La Terre et les hommes: A Programme Fulfilled?," *French History*, 14 (2000).

Bloch, Marc, *Feudal Society*, 2 vols. (London: Routledge & Kegan Paul, 1961).

Bonnassie, Pierre, *From Slavery to Feudalism in South Western Europe* (Cambridge: Cambridge University Press, 1991).

Brown, Warren, and Gorecki, Piotr, eds, *Conflict in Medieval Europe* (Aldershot: Ashgate, 2003).

Bush, M. L., ed., *Serfdom and Slavery: Studies in Legal Bondage* (London: Longman, 1996).

Christie, Neil, ed., *Landscapes of Change: Rural Evolutions in Late Antiquity and the Early Middle Ages* (Aldershot: Ashgate, 2004).

Costambeys, Marios, Innes, Matthew, and Maclean, Simon, *The Carolingian World 700–900* (Cambridge: Cambridge University Press, 2009).

Davies, Wendy, *Small Worlds: The Village Community in Early Medieval Brittany* (London: Duckworth, 1988).

Davies, Wendy, and Fouracre, Paul, eds, *The Settlement of Disputes in Early Medieval Europe* (Cambridge: Cambridge University Press, 1986).

Duby, Georges, *The Chivalrous Society* (Berkeley and Los Angeles: University of California Press, 1978).

Duby, Georges, *La Société aux XIe et XIIe siècles dans la régione mâconnaise* (Paris: L'École des hautes etudes en sciences sociales, 1982).

Gregory of Tours, *Histories*, ed. B. Krusch and W. Levison, Monumenta Germaniae Historica Scriptores rerum Merowingicarum, 1.1 (Hanover: Impensis Bibliopolii Hahniani, 1951); English translation, L. Thorpe (Baltimore: Penguin, 1974).

Hamerow, Helena, *Early Medieval Settlements: The Archaeology of Rural Communities in Northwest Europe, 400–900* (Oxford: Oxford University Press, 2002).

Hansen, Inge Lynn, and Wickham, Chris, eds, *The Long Eighth Century* (Leiden: Brill, 2001).

Hodges, Richard, *Dark Age Economics: The Origins of Towns and Trade, 700–1100* (London: Duckworth, 1982).

Hodges, Richard, *Towns and Trade in the Age of Charlemagne* (London: Duckworth, 2001).

Hodges, Richard, and Bowden, William, eds, *The Sixth Century* (Leiden: Brill, 1998).

Innes, Matthew, *An Introduction to Early Medieval Western Europe, 300–900: The Sword, the Plough and the Book* (London: Routledge, 2007).

Liebeschutz, Wolfgang, *The Decline and Fall of the Roman City* (Oxford: Oxford University Press, 2001).

Little, Lester, and Rosenwein, Barbara, eds, *Debating the Middle Ages: Issues and Readings* (London: Blackwell, 1998).

McCormick, Michael, *Origins of the European Economy: Communications and Commerce, 300–900* (Cambridge: Cambridge University Press, 2001).

Markus, R. A. *Saeculum: History and Society in the Theology of St Augustine* (Cambridge: Cambridge University Press, 1970).

Moussy, C. (ed.), *Paulin de Pella, Poème d'action et des grâces de Père* (Sources chrétiennes, 209; Paris: Éditions du Cerf , 1974).

Pirenne, Henri, *Mohammed and Charlemagne* (London: G. Allen & Unwin, Ltd., 1939).

Nelson, Janet L. (trans.), *The Annals of St Bertin* (Manchester: Manchester University Press, 1990).

Nithard, *Histoire des fils de Louis le Pieux*, ed. P. Lauer (Paris: Société d'édition "Les belles Lettres", 1964).

Poly, Jean-Pierre, and Bournazel, Eric, *The Feudal Transformation 900–1200* (New York: Holmes & Meier, 1991).

Reuter, Timothy, ed., *The Medieval Nobility: Studies on the Ruling Classes of France and Germany from the Sixth to the Twelfth Century* (Amsterdam: North-Holland, 1978).

Salvian of Marseille, *On the Governance of God*, trans. E. M. Sanford (New York: Columbia University Press, 1930) or J. F. O'Sullivan (Washington: Catholic University of America Press, 1947).

Scholz, B. W., *Carolingian Chronicles* (Ann Arbor, MI: University of Michigan Press, 1970).

Sidonius Apollinaris, *Letters*, ed. and trans. W. B. Anderson (London: W. Heinemann, 1969).

Smith, Julia, *Europe after Rome: A New Cultural History* (Oxford: Oxford Universality Press, 2005).

Verhulst, Adrian, *The Rise of Cities in Northwest Europe* (Cambridge: Cambridge University Press, 1999).

Verhulst, Adrian, *The Carolingian Economy* (Cambridge: Cambridge University Press, 2002).

Wickham, Chris, *Framing the Early Middle Ages: Europe and the Mediterranean 300–800* (Oxford: Oxford University Press, 2005).

Further Reading

The shape of early medieval history in general, and early medieval social and economic history in particular, has changed beyond all recognition since the late 1990s, and students and teachers should no longer be content to focus on "old chestnuts" such as continuity versus change, or the validity of the "Pirenne thesis," when specialist research has moved so far beyond. The best example of the new research – although difficult, and voluminously large, it is the place to start for a full understanding of the economy and society of the period – is Chris Wickham, *Framing the Early Middle Ages: Europe and the Mediterranean 300–800* (Oxford: Oxford University Press, 2005). Two shorter, and more accessible, surveys, covering economy and society alongside politics and religion, are Matthew Innes, *An Introduction to Early Medieval Western Europe, 300–900: The Sword, the Plough and the Book* (London: Routledge, 2007), and Julia Smith, *Europe after Rome* (Oxford: Oxford University Press, 2005), while Marios Costambeys, Matthew Innes, and Simon Maclean, *The Carolingian World 700–900* (Cambridge: Cambridge University Press, 2009), covers a shorter period in more detail. All these general works provide a real focus on aristocratic elites, which have been the major focus of historical research for several decades now, primarily in regional case studies. Advances in scholarship mean that many classic older works such as Georges Duby, *The Early Growth of the European Economy* (London: Weidenfeld and Nicolson, 1974), are no longer accurate reflections of the state of research.

There are a number of volumes collecting the kind of archaeological and historical research that underpin rethinking on specific themes. On the economy, Richard Hodges and William Bowden, eds, *The Sixth Century* (Leiden: Brill, 1998), and Inge Lynn Hansen and Chris Wickham, eds, *The Long Eighth Century* (Leiden: Brill, 2001), are excellent starting points, as is Adrian Verhulst, *The Carolingian Economy* (Cambridge: Cambridge University Press, 2002). The classic studies of trade – if provocatively extreme in their conclusions – are Richard Hodges, *Dark Age Economics: The Origins of Towns and Trade, 700–1100* (London: Duckworth, 1982), on the North Sea, and Michael McCormick, *Origins of the European Economy: Communications and Commerce, 300–900* (Cambridge: Cambridge University Press, 2001), on the Mediterranean. On towns, there are many important conference volumes, but useful overviews are provided by Wolfgang Liebeschutz, *The Decline and Fall of the Roman City* (Oxford: Oxford University Press, 2001), Bjorn Ambrosiani and Helen Clarke, *Towns in the Viking Age*, 2nd edn (Leicester: Leicester University Press, 1995), Adrian Verhulst, *The Rise of Cities in Northwest Europe* (Cambridge: Cambridge University Press, 1999), and Richard Hodges, *Towns and Trade in the Age of Charlemagne* (London: Duckworth, 2001).

The literature on the countryside is in general less accessible, but for the archaeology Neil Christie, ed., *Landscapes of Change: Rural Evolutions in Late Antiquity and the Early Middle Ages* (Aldershot: Ashgate, 2004), is a good starting point, while Helena Hamerow, *Early Medieval Settlements: The Archaeology of Rural Communities in Northwest Europe, 400–900* (Oxford: Oxford University Press, 2002), is a thought-provoking overview. And for a penetrating and pioneering case study based on the documentary evidence, see Wendy Davies, *Small Worlds: The Village Community in Early Medieval Brittany* (London: Duckworth, 1988); on issues of free and unfree status, the starting points are Hans-Werner Goetz, "Serfdom and the Origins of a 'Seigneurial System' in the Carolingian Period," *Early Medieval Europe*, 2 (1993), pp. 29–51 and Wendy Davies, "On Servile Status in the Early Middle Ages," in M. L. Bush, ed., *Slavery and Serfdom* (London: Longman, 1996).

On the "feudal revolution" and changes in the mechanisms of aristocratic power, the classic studies of Georges Duby are translated in *The Chivalrous Society* (Berkeley and Los Angeles: University of California Press, 1978), and a good selection of French and German work to the 1970s is available translated in Timothy Reuter, ed., *The Mediaeval Nobility* (Amsterdam: North-Holland, 1978). The classic synthesis on the "feudal revolution" thesis is also available in English translation: Jean-Pierre Poly and Eric Bournazel, *The Feudal Transformation 900–1200* (New York: Holmes & Meier, 1991). The work of Pierre Bonnassie on Catalonia is collected in *From Slavery to Feudalism in South Western Europe* (Cambridge: Cambridge University Press, 1991). The best way into recent debate, focusing on violence, comes from Thomas N. Bisson's article "The 'Feudal Revolution'," *Past and Present*, 142 (1994), pp. 6–42; with comments by Dominique Barthélemy, Timothy Reuter, Stephen D. White, and Chris Wickham in *Past and Present*, 152 (1996) and 155 (1997). A taste of Barthélemy's work, which has been the major statement of continuity, is available in translation in Lester Little and Barbara Rosenwein, eds, *Debating the Middle Ages* (London: Blackwell, 1998), pt II. Wendy Davies and Paul Fouracre, eds, *The Settlement of Disputes in Early Medieval Europe* (Cambridge: Cambridge University Press, 1986), opened up new ways of thinking about the mechanisms of aristocratic power prior to the tenth century, and see more recently Warren Brown and Piotr Gorecki, eds, *Conflict in Medieval Europe* (Aldershot: Ashgate, 2003).

Chapter Three

Politics and Power

Hans Hummer

Dinner chez Charlemagne was a festive, and revealing, affair. The bedazzled guests were treated to a spectacular four-course meal, wheels of rindy cheeses, earthen bowls laden with fruits, drinking horns brimming with wine and mead, and finally the crowning entrée, in honor of the famously carnivorous emperor himself, roasted meats, ostentatiously carried in on spits by the royal hunters (including perhaps a boar or buck or two brought down by Charlemagne's own keen spear). Sinking their teeth into this bacchanalia of meats was an assemblage of Charlemagne's vast family, swollen by his many legitimate and illegitimate children, and the kin groups linked to the Carolingian brood by marriage, concubinage, and patronage; and his well-armed "friends," the powerful counts, courtiers, bishops, abbots, and other assorted magnates of the realm. As the vittles settled and the lamps burned low, the gregarious emperor would call for some reading, the deeds of ancient heroes, or perhaps a selection from his favorite book, Augustine's *City of God*.[1]

This power feasting, and the source from which much of it can be inferred, Einhard's vivid *Life of Charlemagne*, reveal a great deal about the salient features of politics and power in early medieval Europe. Political power flowed through seemingly informal and ad-hoc networks of kin groups, power-brokers, and royal apparatchiks brought together for a common purpose, often to hunt, to feast, or to fight, and thereby cement their solidarity through a combination of conviviality and bellicosity.[2] This was an empire hammered out by conquest and held together by a bewildering web of personal loyalties and mutual oaths.[3] By all appearances, it lacked the stereotypical accoutrements of government. At this feast we would be hard pressed to identify any heads of discrete departments of state, ministers, treasurers, or generals. It would be difficult too, on the basis of their actual behavior, to delineate any hard-and-fast divisions between civil, military, or ecclesiastical obligations of many of the attendees: the powerful clerics might be leading armed retinues, the counts tripling as commanders, judges, and lay abbots of influential monasteries, and the emperor, in his capacity as the defender of the faith, demanding reform of warfare, laws, and churches alike.

At a second glance, beneath the back-slapping negotiation of power, early medieval politics exhibited impressively formalized components. Most of the feasting figures would have been entitled aristocrats – abbots, bishops, counts, or *missi* – whose positions required obligations of them.[4] The counts were required to promulgate the king's will, work justice in their localities, and muster troops for the many Frankish wars. The ecclesiastical officials in particular were bounded by a written code of responsibilities, the monastic rules for abbots, who governed tightly organized institutions (monasteries), and for bishops a revered tradition of canon law, which defined episcopal duties, chief among them the responsibility to ordain priests and administer the clergy within the diocese.[5] Similar to the counts, the abbots and bishops were expected to publicize and enforce the royal will, including the raising of troops. These (non-Euclidean) parallel lines of lay and ecclesiastical authority intersected in the person of the ruler. With the titles of king and emperor came a cluster of general responsibilities: the ruler was expected to do justice, to orchestrate warfare, to defend the faith, and to protect the church and the people, especially the weak.[6] At the palace in Aachen, and among his entourage, were also royal chaplains, clerics who formed a chancery for the issuing of royal edicts and who educated the aristocratic children sent to the court for grooming. The emperor even had a system of accountancy to ensure compliance, his *missi*, usually sent out in twos, one a layman and one a cleric. In short, all of these title-holders, whether lay or ecclesiastical, were charged with responsibilities that were public in nature, meaning that they were vested with wider obligations beyond narrowly personal, familial, or institutional self-interest. Indeed, the failure to live up to these wider duties often structured the complaints against officials derided for dereliction, malfeasance (greed), and abuse of authority.[7]

Reconciling the informal and formal aspects of Frankish rule, or at least coming to some understanding of their precise relationship, has presented a major challenge for early medievalists. Among the many problems, foremost perhaps are fundamental heuristic issues. How exactly are we to talk about political entities in the early Middle Ages? What kind of terminology are we to use to describe them? The usual language of "government" is problematic because early medieval realms really do not look like states as traditionally conceived.[8] We are hard pressed to find a centrally directed bureaucracy, an elaborated system of delegated authority, clearly defined "offices," or an explicit theory of government. Even if we boil the definition of a state down to its essence, the right to raise taxes to fund its activities and pay its representatives, the early medieval realms do not qualify, at least not in the way that one typically understands tax raising. It is not that these kingdoms bear no resemblance to "states." They did have a central focus in the king or emperor and his court, a layer of local and regional officials ultimately answerable to the ruler, and if the entitled did not raise taxes, they could generate revenues from their own estates and levy dues from tenants or from the exercise of justice.[9] The problem is that the terminology of government can be a linguistic Trojan horse, sneaking in a set of contestable assumptions that can subtly transmute early medieval organization into something more familiar to bureaucratically organized societies (such as contemporary ones). One could cite many instances, but representative has been the tendency, now in decline, to separate medieval society into public and private spheres. As a neutral analytical device, this can have its uses, but in an early medieval context it quickly runs afoul of anachronism, introducing an artificial standard for distinguishing the legitimate and illegitimate exercise of power. In short, it does not work well as a way to describe or explain the actual exercise of power as it appears to us in the sources.

So why not just make use of the political terminology of the period? Medieval sources do speak of emperors, kings, dukes, counts, *missi*, bishops and abbots, of *regna* (kingdoms), the *imperium* (empire), *ducatus* (dukedoms), *comitatus* (countships), *ecclesiae* (churches), a *missatica*, and so on, but these can be frustratingly opaque (to us). They might or might not have the territorial dimension that we, or even people in the high medieval period, associate with political groupings or jurisdictions.[10] For example, a duke or king was usually set over a people, thus the "king of the Franks," not the "king of Frankland"; the "duke of the Alemanni," not the "duke of Alemannia." Counts usually appear without an accompanying territorial title or a well-demarcated territorial jurisdiction. Consequently, early medievalists are more comfortable speaking of dukedoms and countships, which convey the sense of a zone of authority springing from the activities of a person, rather than duchies or counties, which connote a stable and inhabitable territorial jurisdiction. Yet, the sources do sometimes exhibit the language of territoriality – for example, the *ducatus Alisatiae*, the dukedom of Alsace, or *Francia*, Frankland. The issue is complicated by the persistence, or revival, of late Roman terminology, which in a Roman context referred to spatial administrative units, but in the early Middle Ages only elusively so. The sources might also, especially in the ninth century when the Carolingian cultural revival was in full swing, summon the reified language of Roman government and speak of the Carolingian realm as a *res publica*, a republic. Although the native terminology is worth pondering, it offers no master key for unlocking the riddles of early medieval politics.

We might simply examine the behavior of political actors and infer from actual practice the so-called informal modes of political order. This can illuminate the rich world of customs, rituals, symbols, dispute resolution, and sociological forms that structured and mediated the operation of power.[11] This kind of work has enjoyed great popularity since the 1980s, fanned by the enthusiasm among many historians for anthropological models or insights. The idea is that the opacity of early medieval society can perhaps be overcome by donning the hat of an anthropologist and attempting to decode its language and behavior, as an ethnographer might an alien culture. This does offer a way to explain and conceptualize many aspects of political power with which formal political and institutional history, colored as they have been by modern constructs, cannot cope. On the other hand, this can introduce its own anachronisms. If more conventional political history can be said to have trusted too much in institutional forms as a way to understand the operation of power, many social historians have shown too little inclination to take them seriously enough. The general response has been either to ignore them or to dismiss them as epiphenomenal and focus instead on what "really" happened, on "practice." It is perhaps no coincidence that, until recently, much of this innovative work focused on the seventh and the tenth centuries, especially the latter, on the periods on either side of the Carolingian empire when institutional variables could, presumably, be ignored in the pursuit of a purer sociological analysis. If this fruitful work has yielded many finely grained studies of the contingencies of power, the emphasis on "strategies" and on the primacy of sociological forms has made it difficult to reconcile the formal and informal aspects of Frankish rule. In other words, it has had less success summing up the parts, relating them to macro-historical processes and constructs, and thus accounting for entities such as the Frankish empire.

In addition to heuristic problems, the task of reconciling the apparently confusing formal and informal aspects of politics and power in early medieval Europe has been hampered by another long-running impulse deeply embedded in a Western historiographical tradition powerfully stamped by the Renaissance and the Enlightment: the tendency to emphasize the Roman, Christian, Germanic, or feudal constituents of early medieval political culture and trace out these putatively elemental strands as if they were neutral standards for measuring developments.[12] Studies undertaken in this vein tend to deny the period its particularity, subordinating it to processes that chart either the end of classical civilization or the origins of the high medieval feudal order. Intentionally or not, they conjure up a bastard civilization of incomplete or partially fulfilled components or, worse, the image of a miserable Dark Age. The task, rather, is to map out the distinctiveness of early medieval political culture and to tell a story that would be meaningful to the historical experience of its actors.[13]

Behind all of these heuristic, methodological, and heuristic problems looms the cultural politics of Europe and the West over the last two centuries. The state-building and hyper-centralization of the nineteenth and twentieth centuries have had an obvious influence on the statist perceptions of many scholars. This has existed alongside a countervailing impulse of the Romantic era, which saw in the early Middle Ages a Shangri-la of intimate communities bound by shared oral traditions, a tradition that lives on in complicated ways in the social historical preoccupation with localism.[14] The Enlightenment, secularism, and the disestablishment of the Church throughout Europe also exerted a powerful pull on views of the past. The division of the past into autonomous and antagonistic lay and ecclesiastical histories, and the quest for the secular bases of political authority, have been predictable consequences. This bifurcation of ecclesiastical and lay history has perhaps sown more confusion into the treatment of early medieval politics than any other construct, and only recently have scholars been ready to confront this deeply embedded anachronism.[15]

The Second World War and its aftermath have had an enormous impact on the direction of contemporary scholarship.[16] Researchers have systematically de-emphasized any alleged Germanic contributions to early medieval society, preferring to emphasize the continuity of Roman forms, especially in the immediate post-Roman period.[17] Although not always stated, the former is associated with a now radioactive illiberal fascism, while the latter has been identified with the safer (and victorious) liberal tradition. It should be pointed out that the Franks were always difficult to appropriate for national causes because of the geographic scope of their activities: if the Frankish kings did not look particularly French, they did not appear to act in a very German way either. Ironically, despite the prevailing desire to view the past "on its own terms," the formation of a united Europe has stimulated a veritable flood of what one might call European Union scholarship on the Franks, the implicit goal of which has been to emphasize the common roots of Europe, a task seemingly consistent with the achievement of the greatest of the Frankish rulers, Charlemagne, propitiously dubbed by one of his court poets as the "father of Europe."

The point is not that these approaches are fundamentally defective, although the feudal, and especially the Germanic, traditions of scholarship now enjoy less favor and fewer practitioners. These have been displaced by historians concerned less with origins and roots than with understanding how society operates and describing it in native terms. Thus, since the mid-twentieth century, it has been common to hear scholars declaim that they are going to examine the evidence "without preconceptions," or, where it applies to the Frankish realms, to interpret the evidence in Frankish terms. This is an impossible ideal, since as outsiders we can hardly hope to do either with any sureness. Such sentiments, in fact, sound suspiciously similar to modern Western anxieties about respecting difference – a worthy concern perhaps, but a contemporary one all the same. Nonetheless, as an analytical disposition, the caveat does have its uses. It can sensitize investigators to the applicability of constructs, the limits of understanding, and protect against the most egregious scholarly hubris. The point, rather, is that there is no all-encompassing conceptual framework that will banish all of the riddles of politics and power in early medieval Europe and magically resolve its manifold puzzles. We can, however, isolate many of the fundamental features of early medieval political organization that have been painstakingly elucidated over the last century of scholarship and attempt to fit them together into a coherent story, a picture that is necessarily contingent and one that not all scholars would agree upon.[18]

In the interest of coherence, this chapter will focus on politics and power in the Frankish empire, the most successful and powerful political unit of the early Middle Ages and under whose aegis were consolidated the foundations of Europe.[19] At its height under Charlemagne, the Frankish realm encompassed the kingdom of the Franks, the kingdom of the Lombards, central Italy, Corsica, the marches in Brittany and northeastern Spain, and the Slavic marches to the east and southeast. Within the cultural ambit of the empire revolved the Celtic and Anglo-Saxon kingdoms of the British Isles, and the dukedoms of southern Italy. Thus, the Frankish rulers held sway over an enormous empire that included most of modern western, central, southern, and southeastern Europe.

The political order of the Frankish realms is itself a vast subject, but we can perhaps best get a handle on its complexity, and at the same time begin to reconcile its formal and informal aspects, if we spotlight the aristocracy, whose thirst for honors and glory shaped everything from the practice of kingship and lordship, to the organization of ecclesiastical foundations, to the exploitation of peasant labor. The immense and subtle work on the aristocracy, pioneered mostly by German researchers, has been taken up and supplemented by scholars elsewhere who have attempted to merge its constitutional preoccupations with social historical insights.[20] Both the accumulation of studies and the redirection of scholarly priorities after the Second World War have shifted the focus from royal agency to the aristocratic bases of political power.[21] Great scholarly energy has gone into the elucidation of the factions, social networks, and family groups that made up the aristocracy. The challenges here have been quite formidable. By contrast with the high and later medieval families, early medieval kindreds were not divided into self-defined "houses," or lineages, making it impossible to identify discrete units and trace them over more than a generation or two.[22]

Crucial for sifting, sorting and analyzing the thousands of names that populate the early medieval records (especially monastic charters) has been the prosopographical approach, the so-called *besitzt-geschictliche-genealogische Methode*. This method, first developed by historians of antiquity to explore connections among the Roman aristocracy, has been deployed to flesh out an individual's probable identity and social milieu.[23] The challenges for early medievalists have been greater because, whereas Roman aristocrats bore a tripartite name, early medieval Europeans usually carried only one, which might have been borne by numerous individuals. Close analysis of a combination of overlapping and repetitive genealogical, proprietary, onomastic, and associative information has allowed investigators to differentiate individuals and situate them within various levels of group activity.

Taken as a whole, this research has established that, if the boundaries of families remain elusive and aristocratic factions ephemeral, the aristocracy itself seems to have achieved remarkable continuity. This finely nuanced work has also revealed the nobility to have been extraordinarily broad and stratified: it included the lower and middling aristocracy, visible in charters as small property-owners and probably comprising the groups who filled out the regional aristocracies, as well as the so-called imperial aristocracy, the upper crust of kindreds that formed the pool from which the kings raised up the most distinguished entitled aristocrats. Although the term "aristocracy" has stood in many treatments as proxy for lay actors, the concept actually encompasses both lay and ecclesiastical spheres: the kindreds responsible for this society's counts, dukes, and warriors also produced its bishops, abbots, monks, and priests.

The king was the quintessence of the aristocracy, the personage who provided its leadership and focused its interests. Managing the competing factions and the many obstreperous individuals posed an unstinting challenge.[24] The ruler might empower or isolate particular factions, extend favor to – or withdraw it from – ambitious individuals, or open up new vistas for glory with a well-timed military campaign. The skill, or clumsiness, with which he handled these dilemmas and the inevitable crises of lordship set the parameters for possible achievements. In the heyday of the Frankish empire, the emperors granted widely dispersed honors to imperial aristocrats, whose pan-European interests might act as a centripetal force for unity alongside that of the emperorship.[25] As time passed, the regional divisions among the mass of the Frankish aristocracy became more pronounced, and, because these regional aristocracies required – or at least desired – that a king represent them, maintain their integrity, and enforce the political order, the Frankish realm fractured into several independent kingdoms during the later Carolingian period. The aristocratic groupings and the new dynasties that came into being in the tenth and eleventh centuries, and rose to prominence in the high medieval period, developed out of the factions and families of the old Carolingian aristocracy.[26]

If the aristocracy, as it came to be during the Carolingian period, served as the wellspring for the transformed aristocracy of the high Middle Ages, less clear have been the processes responsible for its formation.[27] The seventh century appears to be decisive, although the sparseness of the documentation makes it difficult to elucidate the developments with precision. Nonetheless, it would appear that by the seventh century the Frankish military aristocracy, which had descended in part from elements in the Roman army and in part from barbarian warrior groups, and the provincial Roman aristocracies of late antiquity, merged to form a common aristocracy that considered itself in terms of its political identity to be "Frankish," at least in the traditional Frankish heartlands between the Paris basin to the mid-Rhine, the area that today coincidentally (or perhaps not!) forms the heart of Europe.[28] Prior to that, the provincial aristocracy had been made up of the erstwhile Roman senatorial families, who dominated the episcopal and comital offices of the influential cities, as well as the earlier monastic establishments, which overwhelming were a suburban phenomenon.[29] These patterns in office holding were a natural outgrowth of the senatorial aristocracy's long control of the municipal government to which the administration of the bishops and counts was closely bound. To the Frankish aristocracy generally were reserved the titles associated with military power, the kingship obviously, as well as the dukeships, which possessed the power to summon and command an army; and some of the countships, since the responsibilities of counts included the oversight of royal prerogatives and possessions in localities, many of which descended from the former Roman imperial fisc.[30]

The authority of the earlier Merovingian kings, the first Frankish dynasty (481–751), over this aristocracy was much more autocratic than that of the later Carolingians.[31] This was enabled in part by the presence of the still-functioning provincial and fiscal administrations that could prosecute the king's will, if necessary, at the expense of other interests. The king's power was also enhanced by the Frankish aristocracy's military pedigree, as well as the earliest Merovingian kings' ruthless elimination of rivals. That the early Merovingian kings might raise up nobles of service and wed women of servile origin stand as potent symbols of the kings' freedom vis-à-vis the aristocracy.

The final disintegration of late-antique administrative structures during the seventh century, and thus a relative decline in the influence of urban centers, especially in the north, meant that power, wealth, and status were concentrated ever more in the countryside, where senatorial and Frankish aristocrats alike held sway over enormous estates. The leveling of status between the aristocracies, in combination with the passing of the institutional frameworks that sustained the distinctive consciousness of the senatorial families, helped facilitate the fused "Frankish" aristocracy of the early medieval period.[32] These developments also had ramifications for the bases of royal power, which came to rely ever more upon aristocratic support and consensus. A poignant symbol of this reconfiguration was the mayorship of the palace, which beginning in the early seventh century focused the interests of the dominant aristocratic faction at court and in time served as the platform for Carolingian aggrandizement.[33]

The story of the withering of the Roman order and the arrival of the so-called Dark Ages has traditionally been told in regretful tones. This seductive tale, still a stubborn fixture within the public imagination (and in the minds of some scholars), has been substantially recast by the sheer weight of scholarly research. The narrative now is one of transformation, of the formation of a new and dynamic Frankish civilization that laid the political, social, and economic groundwork of Europe.[34] As the great Belgian historian Henri Pirenne observed long ago, the seventh century staged another story, the profound shift in the center of political gravity from the Mediterranean to northern Europe, a process propelled by the Franks, under whose aegis Europe was for the first time constituted as a separate and coherent political entity.[35] Pirenne famously pinned these developments on the eruption of Islam, which he blamed for disrupting the alleged unity of Mediterranean civilization. Pirenne's thesis has been widely criticized, but he did correctly redirect historians' attention away from political collapse of the western Roman Empire, to the discontinuities of the seventh century, where developments internal to the Frankish realm, in particular the formation and activities of the fused Frankish aristocracy, are now seen to be decisive.

Two seminal and interrelated developments transformed the contours and consciousness of the Frankish aristocracy: the burst of rural monasticism and the organization of manorial estates. The former was tied to the activities of Irish monks in the Frankish heartlands who attracted the enthusiastic patronage of Frankish aristocrats.[36] Presumably, the rural monastic culture familiar to the holy men from Ireland was compatible with the needs and aspirations of the continental aristocracy. In addition, the impressive rigorous and ascetic brand of Irish monasticism appealed to Frankish aristocrats desirous of a connection to the holy unmediated by direct (and partisan) episcopal supervision. Frankish patrons expressed their enthusiasm most conspicuously with the endowment of new monasteries in the countryside, or, in the case of humbler families, with smaller donations of property.[37] Both sent sons and daughters to populate these new foundations as monks and nuns; in the case of the founding families, daughters especially might be installed as abbesses and celebrated posthumously as saints.[38]

This phenomenon had a number of profound ramifications for the peculiar shape of early medieval lordship. The sacral prestige harvested from these foundations and from association with the holy effectively abolished any lingering qualitative differences in status that separated the Frankish from the provincial senatorial aristocracies. Frankish aristocrats, once at the mercy of the whims of royal favor, could now directly tap into a powerful source of legitimacy and aspire to greater self-control. This energetic monasticism captured the imagination of many senatorial aristocrats too, whose traditional sources of legitimacy and power were undergoing profound change with the fast withering late-antique order. The abundant and vivid hagiographical literature of the seventh century attests to the formation of a reconstituted Frankish aristocracy made up of older elements reconciled to one another by this new sanctity.[39] Bobolenus, who reflected on the origins of Germanus of Grandval in his *Life* of the eponymous saint composed around 680, offers a particularly poignant witness to the process. He proudly tells us that his hero "arose from a senatorial family" (*ex genere senatorum prosapiae genitus*), and goes on to reveal a career bound up with the history of Luxeuil, founded by the greatest of the continental Irish saints, Columbanus, and its nexus of associated Frankish families. Germanus attracted the support of powerful Frankish patrons, Gundoin, the duke in Alsace, Arnulf, the bishop of Metz, and Waldelen, the abbot of Luxeuil. Bobolenus proudly recalled the noble origins of figures of senatorial, Frankish and Burgundian descent, but in his view holiness transcended them all: Germanus, he points out, was even "nobler by his sanctity" (*nobilior sanctitate*).[40]

These Irish-led foundations, and those set up by Frankish disciples, played a pivotal role in the formation of manorial estates. The precise origins of this distinctively early medieval form of agricultural exploitation is hidden, but its first appearance in monastic charters of the late seventh century in the Frankish heartlands suggests a reciprocal connection between the spread of rural monasticism, the organization of the countryside, the consolidation of a reconstituted Frankish aristocracy, and the aristocracy's subsequent dominance and long continuity.[41] It is hardly a coincidence that many of the prestigious monasteries and families of the Carolingian period, including the future Carolingian family itself, arose in this area. Try as we might, with the obvious exception of the Merovingian family, we simply cannot trace any of the kin groups dominant in the eighth century earlier than the seventh century, an indication that sweeping changes had stimulated a new aristocratic consciousness closely bound to monasticism.

These seminal developments can help illuminate the relationship of the so-called formal and informal processes of politics and power in the early Middle Ages. In effect, ecclesiastical institutions served as repositories of family property and identity.[42] The reason is that properties given to monasteries were not intended to be alienated, if one means by that that donors meant to consign the property to the unfettered control of the institution. Nor did the receiving institution assume that property granted to them could simply be done with as they pleased. Clerics have been accused of scheming to divest families of their property, and disputes over property have often been misconstrued as protests in principle to ecclesiastical control, but such interpretations are anachronistic, colored by the more heavily documented later Middle Ages, when the reformed papacy did seek to seal off church property, and reinforced by a healthy dose of modern anticlericalism.[43] Meanwhile, in the gift-giving culture of early medieval Europe, donations and counter gifts marked the beginning, or continuation, of an ongoing relationship with the holy, one of the major attractions, as has been pointed out, of Irish monasticism. Consequently, the donation charters often request that monks return the favor with prayers, or entry into the monastery's *Book of Life*, and express hopes for salvation.

Although some properties were given outright as gifts to support the monks, the donors also expected that other properties – especially those more central to the family's lordship – be returned to them by precarial contract.[44] These grants expired upon the death of the holder, but they were often taken up by their heirs. Moreover, families in especially good standing might also receive additional awards of monastic property. By these means, individuals could consolidate and pass on indivisible blocs of property, which in the normal course of events would have been divided up among heirs according to the custom of partible inheritance. It is not that, lacking these means, families would have, by infinite regression, dispersed their holdings into ever tinier parcels. Early deaths and disputes among family members often saw to the emergence of alpha males who might reconsolidate family holdings, but this was a messy and riskier process. The fact that the monastery was a divine institution, governed by an explicit set of rules, was crucial. The process of donation abstracted property from the rest of the family's complex, and ensured its stability by attaching it to the permanence of the divine order. Kin groups thus allied themselves to an eternal family whose internal organization of fathers (abbots) and brothers (monks) was naturally compatible with the wider ethos of kinship that transcended mere biological ties and structured so many of the relationships of the time. This alliance was made manifest by formal written contract, the hollowed, material – one might say scriptural – witness to the bargain. The sheer formality of the exchange reinforced the solemnity, inviolability, and impartiality of the agreement in the eyes of both donors and recipients.

This symbiotic relationship between monastic foundation and family influence effectively institutionalized the power of the aristocracy, accounting for the dominance of the great monasteries of the Carolingian era and the long continuity of the kindreds who patronized them. Perceiving the ubiquity of kinship in the sources, scholars have tried in vain to work out the genealogies of families. Hoping to elucidate the great houses responsible for the lordship of the Frankish empire, they have been tantalized, and frustrated, by clusters of gapped networks. The central difficulty is that sources of the earlier period do not reveal autonomous kin groups, self-consciously incorporated as they were in the later medieval period with a lineal name, heraldry, and castles. A response has been to dub early medieval kindreds "elusive," either because the ecclesiastical sources have eclipsed our view of them, or because the cognaticism and bilaterality of families continually produced ad-hoc arrangements that subverted the formation of stable lineages. This line of pursuit assumes that social processes, such as kinship, can, or rather should be able to, explain the puzzling phenomenon.

The peculiar shape of early medieval kin groups, however, cannot be considered in isolation from the institutional frameworks that structured families over time. Monasteries were too integral to the organization and flow of political power to be sifted out in the pursuit, ultimately chimerical, of separate lay bases of authority. Families are elusive only in sociological terms; when understood within the wider context of landholding, monastic endowment, and reform, the shifting patterns are quite explicable. Although the proprietary bases of lordship might remain stable, the succession within kindreds was not. This material component could be taken up and integrated into the lordships of powerful individuals whose dominance within the kindred was determined by the hashing-out of interfamilial politics. Royal action might inject another element of dynamism, as favor – typically the granting of an honor, such as a countship – was bestowed upon the exponents of influential groups. The ecclesiastical institution itself was not inert; its abbots, frequently derived from powerful families and owing their appointments either to kings or to factions within the monastery, might assert control over property in defiance of the interests of other patron groups. Thus, the informal aspects of power – the aggrandizement of individuals, the recurring dominance of particular families and abrupt shifts in leadership within kindreds – were bound up with the operation of formal institutions.

For the greater families, the endowment of new monasteries was a boon to their lordships. The burgeoning propertied wealth of the monastery, which could be granted out as gifts, the swelling number of minor and middling families attached to the institution by gifts and oblates, and the overarching control of the founding kindreds, often exercised through the abbacy of a family member, consolidated and augmented the scope of their influence. Not surprisingly, the family that came to dominate continental Europe in the early Middle Ages arose from the Ardennes region, in the center of the Frankish heartlands, where this potent combination of manorialization, patronage, and aggressive monastic piety first took shape.

The Carolingian ascent to power has undergone significant revision over the last several decades.[45] The triumphal narratives of Carolingian victory composed in the eighth and ninth centuries, which long exerted a powerful influence over historiographical perceptions of the period, are now approached with greater caution. The Merovingian dynasty is now seen to have been somewhat more vigorous in its latter phase, and the Carolingian ascent less inevitable, than Carolingian historians made them out to be. Nonetheless, current scholarship may be drifting too far in the other direction, underplaying signs of trouble for Merovingian kings, overplaying the crises that buffeted the early Carolingians, and paying too little attention to the changed parameters of power that would have seen to the reordering of political power, with or without a change in ruling houses.

It is important to keep in mind that Carolingian power unfolded within a solidly aristocratic context. The early Carolingian family, known to scholars in its original incarnation as the Pippinids, appeared first in the early seventh century, in the western regions of the eastern Merovingian kingdom of Austrasia where Irish monks were most active.[46] Much of what we know of the Pippinids involves their activities as mayors of the Austrasian palace and founders of a cluster of monasteries in the Ardennes region. To put it another way, the family fixed its power with monastic foundations, and as mayors harnessed the power of the Austrasian aristocracy to their own ambitions. Because they were anchored to the area through landholding institutions, they were able to weather crises and in the late seventh century extended their power when they captured the mayorship in Neustria. Their position in Neustria was consolidated by what has been labeled a "monastic policy," wherewith ecclesiastical institutions were systematically won over and subordinated to Pippinid control.

So much of what transpired in the way of politico-religious reform in the subsequent Carolingian period presumed the centrality of ecclesiastical institutions and the aid – and control – of patron saints.[47] The Carolingian extension and consolidation of power proceeded apace with the devolution of authority to bishoprics, and especially monasteries. This can be seen in the granting of donations, rights, privileges, and immunities that required reciprocal obligations of the recipient institutions, thus binding them to the legitimizing authority of the kingship: they were required to support the itinerate royal retinue, requisition troops and supplies for campaigns, and most crucially promulgate the great Carolingian reforms of education and pastoral care for both clergy and laity alike.[48] In material terms, these institutions were also expected to put some of their swelling reservoir of property at the disposal of the king in the form of *precariae verbo Regis* – that is, ecclesiastical property granted out to royal supporters at the word of the king.[49] Although rules defining the terms of these grants were issued to alleviate ecclesiastical worries about the confusion of claims and proper compensation, in time these arrangements set off many property disputes between abbots and the kings' counts.

Already, in the seventh century, Merovingian kings had endowed ecclesiastical institutions with substantial grants of royal properties, a practice that began to transform the responsibilities of counts, who were charged with the oversight of fiscal resources. A good deal of scholarly energy has been devoted to determining the relative formality or informality of comital authority – whether a count's authority was more or less personal rather than official, and whether his reach was coterminous with the *pagi*, the rural districts into which much of early medieval Europe was divided, and thus territorial.[50] In the later Merovingian and in the Carolingian periods, comital authority – to the extent that we can witness its operation, most of which is visible to us only in documents that concern ecclesiastical institutions – was closely connected to monastic establishments. In reality, the *pagi* are known to us not from any independent comital records, but overwhelming through monastic charters, which often locate donations by means of these districts. Rather than a refracted image of comital administration in need of the corrective lenses of scholarship, this "system" of *pagi* more obviously testifies to the organization of monastic property, and, where the counts are concerned, their responsibilities relative to the fiscal properties rolled into monastic endowments.

When viewed from this perspective, the Carolingians' rise to power, and in particular the methods they employed, become explicable. The co-opting of ecclesiastical institutions and the use of ecclesiastical property were not merely instrumental, a strategic manipulation of the Church to secular ends. Far from "secularizing" ecclesiastical property, as they have been accused of, the Carolingians devised a rulership that was an instinctive extension of the family's practice of lordship.[51] The process was facilitated by similar methods honed by families in other regions, and the Carolingians' own sense of entitlement and self-righteousness derived from their association with the holy. Scholars have marveled at the Carolingians' control of the historical record, when compared with the gabby and graphic depictions of the seamy side of political life in Merovingian accounts, and some have all but conjured up images of Carolingian minders supervising the composition of flattering "propaganda" and suppressing failures. The Carolingians hardly needed censors; the self-censorship of Carolingian historians and chroniclers, most of them ecclesiastical, convinced of the ruling house's serenity and aura, and dependent upon the royals for their privileged positions, virtually guaranteed that the most dissonant news would be downplayed.

The Carolingian kings, after all, had been divinely ordained to rule. The Merovingian kings, to be sure, were assumed to rule according to the divine will, but this was implicit, because of the general working-out of God's plan in the world. By contrast, God had raised up the Carolingians and instituted them by sacramental anointing through his vicar, St Peter.[52] The anointment of the first Carolingian king, Pepin, has provided the grist for generations of scholarly research, controversy, and speculation, but, whatever the precise sequence of events and rituals employed, Pepin received – through the pope – the blessing of Peter, who sat atop the hierarchy of saints. For the Frankish aristocracy, many of whose families had produced a host of late-Merovingian saints and were trained by their status consciousness to be impressed by rank, the Petrine favor bestowed upon Pepin and his successors was a powerful sign of superior dignity.[53] Peter's sanction of the Carolingian line, and the framing of Frankish authority within the context of saintly power, is graphically illustrated by a Roman mosaic of the late 790s that shows Peter granting the banner of "victory" to Charlemagne and the priestly stole of "life" to Leo III, the pope who presided over Charlemagne's coronation as emperor on Christmas Day, 800. It is hardly surprising that Einhard believed the *City of God* was the emperor's favorite book: by striking contrast with Augustine's own pessimism about the world, to contemporaries the Carolingian empire seemed an embodiment of the heavenly city on earth.

Not surprisingly, the consolidation and expansion of the Frankish empire under the Carolingians proceeded apace with the aid of saintly power and the streamlining of ecclesiastical institutions. The Frankish church was reorganized over the century between Charles Martel and Louis the Pious along thoroughly Roman lines, meaning that the Carolingian rulers encouraged episcopal control and conciliar action as a means of facilitating order.[54] Under Pepin, the yearly muster was moved to May from March in deference to Lent (and better campaign conditions); and, under both Pepin and Charlemagne, lay and ecclesiastical magnates were convened jointly at royal assemblies.[55] The fervor and idealism of Carolingian rulership were underwritten by the aggressive monastic piety of the Frankish aristocracy and disciplined along the lines of (Roman) Benedictine monasticism. The relics of Roman saints, especially the defiant martyrs of antiquity, were imported from Rome to northern monasteries, where they were placed alongside the local saints. By these means, the Carolingians, building upon the successes of their predecessors, finished what the Merovingians began and accomplished what the vaunted Roman Empire never managed: the conquest and consolidation of the regions east of the Rhine.[56] Frankish successes here have been attributed to looser supervision, the devolution of power to regional aristocracies and their toleration of local custom. In part, that is true. However, when it came to beliefs, the Franks tolerated little in the way of local traditions, and the zeal to impose Romano-Frankish Christianity took few prisoners, whether they were pagans, "corrupt" Christians, or rival Byzantine missionaries. The task of Christianization entailed a fundamental reorganization as newly won territories were integrated into the Frankish ecclesiastical network.[57] Carolingian conquests, especially those in the east, were reinforced with the implantation of monasteries, which introduced with the translation of relics a new Christian sacrality, and brought the countryside and its obstreperous inhabitants under manorial supervision.

It is important to recognize that this institutional dimension to Carolingian power, if it provided a conduit for royal action and the means for devising a political arrangement fundamentally distinct from that of the preceding Roman period, also saw to the consolidation and perpetuation of the local and regional interests that formed the pillars of the underlying Carolingian order. The founding families and patron groups continued to assert themselves because they had transformed their property into monastic capital that virtually guaranteed that it would remain safe from rivals or royal confiscation. In Bavaria, for example, although the Agilolfing ducal family lost its position when Charlemagne conquered the area in 788, the power of the Huosi family, which had long been closely associated with the church of Freising as its bishops, continued unbroken.[58] In newly won territories, such as Saxony, monastic foundations might be organized to stimulate the implantation of Frankish power and to create and integrate a new regional aristocracy.[59] Beneath Einhard's contention that the Frankish and Saxon peoples had become "one people" lay the creation of an infrastructure that rearticulated Saxon power and aligned it to Frankish authority.[60]

The resilience and regional patterns of this basic fabric of power shed light on the integrity and fragmentation of the Carolingian empire. From Pepin I to Louis the Pious, with the exception of brief moments, royal power remained undivided. This was due less to conscious policy than to the fortunate deaths or retirements of rival brothers.[61] More intentional was the effort of early Carolingian kings to monopolize military authority by their suppression of the dukes and the replacement of them with counts, who were supposed to be more beholden to the royal will.[62] These demographic accidents, ad-hoc policies, and the unusually long and victorious reign of Charlemagne helped to engender an imperial unity that inspired contemporaries and subsequent generations alike. Of long-lasting consequence too were the successes of the so-called Carolingian renaissance, the reforms launched by Charlemagne, and continued by his successors, which were undertaken to cultivate administrative discipline, an overarching cultural and linguistic cohesion, and a lofty sense of Frankish purpose.[63]

This program naturally devolved upon monasteries and churches, whose hierarchical structure, robust social networks, pastoral mission, and educational institutions, which served clerics and laity alike, made them ideal targets, and efficient promulgators, of reforms. Although united to a remarkable degree by doctrinal conformity, loyalty to the ruler, and reverence for the bishop of Rome, this "Frankish church" possessed no routine administration above the level of bishop. To the extent that it possessed central direction, it found its focus in the ruler who summoned councils and appointed many of the most important prelates. Still, it exhibited the local and regional impulses of the aristocracy that made up its leadership and patron groups; consequently, even in the heady days of imperial unity, councils frequently were assembled along regional lines and tailored to meet provincial concerns.[64] In other words, if ecclesiastical institutions could be a force for Frankish unity, they also reflected regional variations that could be used for factional ends.

Louis the Pious went furthest in the effort to make the churches and monasteries the basis for imperial unity. By contrast with his father, who retained his titles as king of the Franks and of the Lombards even after he had become emperor, an astute recognition of the multiple pillars of his power, Louis presented the more elegant scheme of an explicitly Christian empire governed by an emperor, set above subordinate kings.[65] The basic miscalculation here was not so much Louis's substitution of a familiar "Frankishness" for a newfangled "Christianity" as the glue of the empire, since neither was mutually exclusive. The bigger problem was an overestimation of the integrity of the Frankish empire and its church, and their presumed ability to remain undivided in the face of the ambitions of Louis's successors to establish independent kingdoms for themselves. Another was the unresolved tension in the relationship of the emperorship to the tradition of kingship, and their relative authorities.[66] If a king was by definition the highest authority in his realm, then what exactly was the role of the emperor? If the emperor could trump the power of a king, was that not an affront to a king's dignity? As the alpha member of the family, and the father figure, Louis the Pious, albeit after his sons' rebellions in the early 830s, which temporarily removed him from power, managed to hold the system together. The troubles resumed for good after his death, when the advantages of seniority and paternal authority were much reduced between the sons. Consequently, the eldest, Lothar, was unable to make his power as emperor dominant over his kingly brothers, Charles the Bald and Louis the German.

In recent years, scholars have wanted to downplay the traumas of political fragmentation, either by consigning emotional accounts to the realm of rhetorical artifice or mere political self-interest, or by limiting the toll to a few elites, or by emphasizing the contingent nature of the settlements and the persistence of transregional links. These have been put forth as correctives to earlier nationalist interpretations that wanted to see the future divisions (and antagonisms) of Europe prefigured in the

Carolingian partitions. In the interest of fairness, it should be acknowledged that contemporary developments, namely the drive toward European unity, have perhaps supplied a new set of political pressures. We can, however, respect the voices of the past without jumping to conclusions about their current relevance. When projected against the backdrop of the far-flung honors of the imperial aristocracy, the transregional ecclesiastical network, and the wide social networks attached to ecclesiastical institutions, the strains of fragmentation, which left many great aristocrats bereft of lordships and many ecclesiastical institutions nervously straddling the boundaries of kingdoms, were surely as distressing as Carolingian writers described. With our advantages of hindsight, we can also appreciate the long-term ramifications of the Carolingians partitions, whatever the principle actors might have intended. In other words, if the Carolingian empire established the foundations of a common European culture, its fragmentation and the emergence of the post-Carolingian realms reflected and sharpened its deep internal divisions.[67]

The burdens of Carolingian unity were such that Louis the Pious's heirs schemed to outmaneuver one another for the entire empire, but in the end settled on separate realms, most notably at Verdun in 843 and again at Meersen in 870. The unusually long reigns of Charles the Bald (829/833–77) in west Francia and Louis the German (826/833–76) in east Francia, meant that, even while the two kings lusted to unite the Carolingian realms under themselves, they spent most of their reigns consolidating their authority and effectively cementing separating kingdoms.[68] Long dependent upon the capacity of kings to confirm or grant privileges and rights, ecclesiastical institutions in the end remained dependent upon the protection of the presiding king. For their parts, Louis the Pious's sons and grandsons convened councils of bishops and transformed them into regional churches coextensive with their kingdoms.[69] So successfully was this done by Charles the Bald in the west and Louis the German in the east that, despite the continued fragmentation of royal power after their deaths, especially in the west, the west and east Frankish churches remained irreducible pillars of unity in the later kingdoms of Capetian France and Ottonian Germany.

This regionalization of power undermined the imperial aristocracy and stimulated innovations in lordship. At a more local level, lordships appear more tightly focused, often featuring the direct control of monasteries by powerful families; and aristocratic blocs became subordinated to the leadership of the emergent regional dukes.[70] Consequently, the kings were less able to interact directly with localities (with the exception of the places where they were personally dominant), ruling instead in concert with the great magnates.[71] The elaboration of this particular pattern of consensual rule was more striking in the east Frankish realm, where the so-called stem dukes lorded over distinct territorial zones, than in west Francia, where the weakness of royal authority beyond the Paris basin, the establishment of the powerful Viking dukedom of Normandy, and the erosion of ducal and comital power in Burgundy effected a more uneven distribution of power centers.

The process of Carolingian decline and the social and political transformation of Europe in the tenth and eleventh centuries have arguably presented the major historiographical question in medieval history over the last century and a half. Initially, kings and their alleged limitations in dealing with Viking, Magyar, and Saracen marauders were held responsible for the perceived chaos, a view encouraged by contemporary accounts, steeped in a Christian historiography that tended to obsess about moral decline and blame the leadership. Their views found an eager reception in nineteenth-century Europe, itself undergoing radical centralization and finding in the past champions or, in the case of the late and immediate post-Carolingian periods, abundant cautionary tales of incompetence that served as thinly veiled examples for the edification of national statesmen. A spate of recent biographies and studies have done their part to set individual rulers within their immediate context, to treat laudatory or hostile accounts with greater caution, and to elucidate both the shortcomings and the notable creativity of particular reigns.[72] Other studies have criticized the notion of post-Carolingian chaos and emphasized instead, when understood according to the norms of the time, the remarkable stability of political order at many levels in tenth-century society.[73]

Influential have been the local social histories produced or inspired by French historians. The overriding theme here has been the so-called feudal revolution, transformation, or mutation, terms that have been mobilized to unite the accumulation of studies that have sought to illuminate what have long been seen as the sweeping social, political, and cultural changes in medieval Europe between the ninth and the twelfth centuries.[74] In a German context, the focus has been on the evolving exercise of kingship and its relationship to the aristocracy and ecclesiastical reform.[75] Briefly, these changes included the emergence of non-Carolingian dynasties, the development of a patrilineal consciousness among kindreds, the creation of an autonomous church, and the consolidation of serfdom. Let it suffice to say that there has been great disagreement about the scope, nature, or reality of the proposed changes.[76] Processual historians in particular have lodged subtle epistemological critiques of the conceptual and teleological categories applied to the paradigm of transformation, and shifted attention to the "strategies" of power and the unspoken norms that can be inferred from actual behavior.

Be that as it may, much of this work, whether it be the structural approaches of traditional social history, or the more recent poststructural emphases on cultures of power, shares a preoccupation with the informal aspects of power, an analytical disposition encouraged either by the dissipation of Carolingian power and the perceived concomitant weakening of institutional order, or by a nominalist skepticism of conceptual categories.[77] The period has offered a sort of sociological or anthropological laboratory, blessedly free of the formal political and institutional nuisances that might get in the way of a more pristine social analysis. In the absence of dominant controlling authorities, social structures can be elucidated and class interests granted a primacy in driving historical change; or, rituals of power and gift-giving, norms worked out from close observation of behavior, and compromise justice can reveal the sinews of power that united or divided a particular community or society.

Although this rich work has illuminated many aspects of the political and social order of medieval Europe on the cusp of the millennium, it has tended to make tactical, rather than systematic, use of the Carolingian context. The structural analyses have emphasized the breakdown of the Carolingian system to dramatize the collapse of political order that is seen to have helped trigger the formation of a new society.[78] Here we see change, but a change predicated on a delegated system of governance at odds with the much more qualified view presented by Carolingianists. The forms of social and political order elucidated in poststructural analyses have emphasized the general stability of the period and continuities with the preceding and succeeding periods. However, the methods deployed – the elucidation of genealogies of ritualized behavior and the micro-historical explication of events, powerful methods for the exploration of the sinews of power at any particular time – have identified forms so general that it becomes difficult to gauge historical change. Lacking in many studies associated with the paradigm of transformation – or continuity – around the year 1000 is a more thoroughgoing treatment of the preceding Carolingian context and closer attention to the institutional nexuses that regulated power over time.

One must not lose sight of the institutions that mediated every scrap of documentary information used to elucidate the informal aspects of power. If we shift the focus to the institutional networks that sustained and structured aristocratic wealth and power throughout the foregoing period, we can perhaps gain a clearer sense of the processes that contributed to the transformation of power around the millennium.[79] The ecclesiastical institutions with which the consciousness of the aristocracy was intimately bound underwent a profound transformation between 950 and 1050, with fateful implications for the subsequent development of powerful kin groups. Although the church reforms of the tenth and eleventh centuries have been a standard feature of the hegemonic narrative, scholarly disjunction has consigned them mostly to a separately constituted ecclesiastical history. However, when pitched against the Carolingian context, the demands of reformers, a group that included both clerics and their lay benefactors, who now agitated for ecclesiastical self-control – the free election of abbots, an emphasis on celibacy to seal off the boundaries between the world and sacred society, subjection to the pope, and the firm relegation of lay benefactors to roles as protectors – had radical implications. Scholarly research has long taken note of the energetic castle building, the heightened patrilineal consciousness of kindreds, and the formation of focused patrimonial lordships beginning in the early eleventh century.[80] The incorporation of autonomous families around castles and patrimonial estates, in short the formation of the consciousness that came to define the outlook and organization of the high medieval aristocracy, was a consequence of the transformed institutional consciousness and behavior of monasteries and churches that struck at the foundations of the early medieval political arrangement.

Notes

1 Einhard, *Vita Karoli*, cc. 23–4, pp. 27–9.

2 On banqueting, see Althoff, "Der frieden-, bündnis-und gemeinschaftstiftende Charakter des Mahles"; on warfare, see Halsall, *Warfare and Society*, and Reuter, "Plunder and Tribute"; though, for a more conventional approach, see Bachrach, *Early Carolingian Warfare*; and, on hunting, see Jarnut, "Die frühmittelalterliche Jagd."

3 Althoff, *Family, Friends and Followers*; Becher, *Eid und Herrschaft.*

4 The literature on Frankish officials is extensive, but see in particular Borgolte, *Geschichte der Grafschaften*; Ganshof, *Frankish Institutions*; Archibald Lewis, "Dukes"; Murray, "From Roman Gaul to Frankish Gaul"; Schulze, *Grafschaftsverfassung*; Sprandel, "Dux und comes"; and Karl F. Werner, "Missus-marchio-comes."

5 On ecclesiastical officials, see Benson, *The Bishop-Elect*; Felten, *Äbte und Laienäbte*; and Heinzelmann, *Bischofsherrschaft*.

6 On rulership, see Erkens, ed., *Das frühmittelalterliche Königtum*; Kern, *Kingship and Law*; Mayer, ed., *Das Königtum*; the pertinent articles by Nelson in *Politics and Ritual* and *The Frankish World*; and Sawyer and Wood, eds., *Early Medieval Kingship*.

7 Fouracre, "Carolingian Justice"; Noble, "From Brigandage to Justice."

8 Innes, *State and Society*; for a contrasting maximalist view of state power, see Durliat, *Les Finances publiques*.

9 Airlie, Pohl, and Reimitz, eds, *Staat im frühen Mittelalter*; Davies and Fouracre, eds, *Property and Power*, pp. 1–16, 245–71; Nelson, "Kingship and Royal Government"; Wickham, *Framing the Early Middle Ages*.

10 Reynolds, *Kingdoms and Communities*.

11 Brown, *Unjust Seizure*; Davies and Fouracre, eds, *Settlement of Disputes*; Geary, "Vivre en conflit" and "L'Humiliation des saints"; Koziol, *Begging Pardon and Favor*; Rosenwein, *To Be the Neighbor of St Peter*; White, *Custom, Kinship, and Gifts to Saints*.

12 The list is inexhaustible, but notable among them are Ganshof, *Feudalism*; Fossier, *Enfance de l'Europe*; Lot, *End of the Ancient World*; and Riché, *Education and Culture*; and the tradition of German legal history represented most notably by Heinrich Brunner, *Deutsche Rechtsgeschichte*.

13 On Frankish historical and cultural identities, see Innes and Hen, eds, *Uses of the Past*; and McKitterick, *History and Memory*. With respect to the anachronisms associated with "feudalism," see Reynolds, *Fiefs and Vassals*.

14 See Otto Brunner, *Land and Lordship*, in particular the translators' introduction.

15 De Jong, "Introduction: Rethinking Early Medieval Christianity."

16 Bullough, "*Europae Pater*"; Freed, "Reflections" and "Medieval German Social History"; Sullivan, "Carolingian Age."

17 Influential has been the work spearheaded by Austrian historians and sponsored by the European Science Foundation: Goetz, Jarnut, and Pohl, eds, *Regna and Gentes*; Pohl, ed., *Kingdoms of the Empire*. Walter Goffart's weighty contributions have been brought together in his *Barbarian Tides*. See most recently, Noble, ed., *From Roman Provinces to Medieval Kingdoms*.

18 For other brief overviews of early medieval politics, see McKitterick, "Politics"; and the articles in McKitterick, ed., *New Cambridge Medieval History*, vol. 2: Fouracre, "Frankish Gaul to 814"; Nelson, "Kingship and Royal Government"; and Fried, "The Frankish Kingdoms".

19 Atsma, ed., *La Neustrie*; Geary, *Before France and Germany*; James, *Origins of France*; McKitterick, *Frankish Kingdoms*; Wood, *Merovingian Kingdoms*.

20 The literature is enormous, but see Airlie, "The Aristocracy"; Hechberger, *Adel im fränkisch-deutschen Mittelalter*; Störmer, *Früher Adel*; and the seminal work of the Freiburg circle of Gerd Tellenbach and Karl Schmid: Tellenbach, *Zur Bedeutung der Personenforschung*; Schmid, "'Freiburger Arbeitskreis'" and "Programmatisches zur Erforschung"; Keller, "Das Werk Gerd Tellenbachs," esp. pp. 389–92; and Oexle, "Gruppen in der Gesellschaft." For connections between the Frankish and Italian aristocracies, see Hlawitschka, *Franken, Alemannen, Bayern und Burgunder in Oberitalien*.

21 Freed, "Reflections"; Reuter, ed., *The Medieval Nobility*. The shifted priorities are especially clear when one compares Reuter's collection of translated articles by German historians, with those translated a generation earlier by Barraclough, *Mediaeval Germany*.

22 Schmid, *Geblüt, Herrschaft, Geschlechterbewüsstsein* and "Zur Problematik."

23 Gelzer, *Nobilitat*; Münzer, *Römische Adelsparteien*.

24 Karl Brunner, *Oppositionelle Gruppen*.

25 Fleckenstein, *Hofkapelle*; Schulze, "Reichsaristokratie."

26 Bouchard, *"Those of My Blood"*; Hlawitschka, *Vom Frankenreich*; Andrew Lewis, *Royal Succession*; Karl F. Werner, *Vom Frankenreich.*

27 Le Jan, *Famille et pouvoir*; Karl F. Werner, "Important Noble Families."

28 See Ewig's fundamental studies in *Spätantikes und fränkishes Gallien*, especially "Die fränkischen Teilreiche" and "Volkstum und Volksbewusstsein."

29 Peter Brown, *Cult of the Saints*; Heinzelmann, *Bischofsherrschaft*; Stroheker, *Der senatorische Adel*; Prinz, *Frühes Mönchtum*, pp. 19–117, 449–85; Van Dam, *Saints and their Miracles.*

30 Amory, "Meaning and Purpose of Ethnic Terminology" and "Names, Ethnic Identity, and Community"; Ebling, *Prosopographie*; Murray, "Position of the Grafio."

31 On Merovingian kingship and aristocracy, see Grahn-Hoek, *Fränkische Oberschicht*; Hannig, *Consensus fidelium*; Irsigler, *Untersuchungen*; and Wallace-Hadrille, *Long-Haired Kings.*

32 Cf. Ewig, "Volkstum und Volksbewusstsein".

33 Haar, *Studien*; Heidrich, "Les Maires".

34 Peter Brown, *Rise of Western Christendom*; McCormick, *Origins*; Wickham, *Framing the Early Middle Ages.*

35 Pirenne, *Mohammed and Charlemagne*; Havighurst, ed., *Pirenne Thesis*; and, more recently, McCormick, *Origins.*

36 Prinz, *Frühes Mönchtum*, pp. 121–445, 485–540; Ian Wood, "Vita Columbani."

37 Dierkens, *Abbayes.*

38 In addition to Prinz, *Frühes Mönc*htum, see Wemple, *Women in Frankish Society.*

39 Bosl, "'Adelsheilige'"; Prinz, *Frühes Mönchtum*, pp. 489–501; on Merovingian hagiography more widely, see Fouracre and Gerberding, *Late Merovingian France*; and Heinzelmann, ed., *L'Hagiographie.*

40 Bobolenus, *Vita Germani*, cc. 1–9, pp. 33–7.

41 Goffart, "From Roman Taxation"; Wickham, "The Other Transition"; Verhulst, ed., *Le Grand Domaine*; Rösener, ed., *Strukturen der Grundherrschaft.*

42 Hartung, "Adel, Erbrecht, Schenkung"; Hummer, *Politics and Power*; Jahn, "Tradere ad Sanctum." Susan Wood, *Proprietary Church*, now offers a superb wide-angled perspective.

43 For the conspiratorial view, see Goody, *Development of the Family.*

44 On *precariae*, see Morelle, "Les 'Actes de précaire'"; Rosenwein, "Property Transfers"; and Ian Wood, "Teutsind."

45 Fouracre, *Age of Charles Martel* and "Observations"; Gerberding, *Rise of the Carolingians*; Jarnut, Nonn, and Richter, eds, *Karl Martell.*

46 Matthias Werner, *Adelsfamilien* and *Lüttlicher Raum.*

47 Fouracre, "Origins."

48 On the reforms, see McKitterick, *Frankish Church*; and Wallace-Hadrille, *Frankish Church.*

49 Bondroit, "Les 'Precaire verbo regis'"; Constable, "Nona et Decima"; Hummer, *Politics and Power*, pp. 76–109.

50 For contrasting views on the relationship of counts to pagi, see Borgolte, *Geschichte der Grafschaften*; Innes, *State and Society*; Nonn, *Pagus und Comitatus*; and Schulze, *Grafschaftsverfassung.*

51 On alleged secularization, see Nonn, "Bild Karl Martells."

52 Semmler, *Dynastiewechsel*; Folz, *Coronation of Charlemagne.*

53 On Franco-papal relations, see Becher, "Kaiserkrönung"; Caspar, *Papsttum*; Noble, *Republic of St Peter* and "Papacy."

54 See above n. 48, as well as de Clercq, *La Legislation religieuse franque*; and Hartmann, *Synoden der Karolingerzeit.*

55 Assemblies have received surprisingly little focused attention, but see Barnwell and Mostert eds, *Political Assemblies.*
56 Peter Brown, *Rise of Western Christendom*; Wolfram, *Geburt Mitteleuropas* and *Conversio Bagoariorum*; Ian Wood, *Missionary Life.*
57 See in particular the case of Saxony, Ehlers, *Integration Sachsens*; and Lammers, ed., *Eingliederung.*
58 On the Huosi, see Störmer, *Adelsgruppen*; on Bavaria more generally, see Jahn, *Ducatus Baiuvariorum.*
59 See Ehlers, *Integration Sachsens*, and Lammers, ed., *Eingliederung.*
60 Einhard, *Vita Karoli*, c. 7, p. 10.
61 Kasten, *Königssöhne und Königsherrschaft.*
62 Karl Ferdinand Werner, "Les Principautés périphériques."
63 The implications of the Carolingian renaissance are dealt with in Rosamond McKitterick's corpus of work; see in particular *Carolingians and the Written Word* and *History and Memory.*
64 Cf. Hellgardt, "Zur Mehrsprachigkeit."
65 On Louis the Pious, see Godman and Collins, eds, *Charlemagne's Heir.*
66 Nelson, "Kingship and Empire"; Ullmann, *Carolingian Renaissance.*
67 On the post-Carolingian kingdoms, see Dunbabin, *France in the Making*; Fasoli, *I re d'Italia*; Hlawitschka, *Lotharingien und das Reich*; and Reuter, *Germany in the Early Middle Ages.*
68 Goldberg, *Struggle for Empire*; Hartmann, *Ludwig der Deutsche und seine Zeit*; Nelson, *Charles the Bald*; Screen, "Importance of the Emperor."
69 Bigott, *Ludwig der Deutsche und die Reichskirche*; Schröder, *Westfränkischen Synoden.*
70 On the emergent dukedoms, see Dhondt, *Études*; and Stingl, *Entstehung der deutschen Stammesherzogtümer.*
71 Althoff, *Amicitiae und Pacta*; Althoff and Keller, *Heinrich I. und Otto der Grosse*; Schneidmüller, *Karolingische Tradition.*
72 See in addition to the studies of particular reigns cited above, n. 68, MacLean, *Kingship and Politics.*
73 Fichtenau, *Living in the Tenth Century*; see also Koziol, *Begging Pardon and Favor*, and Rosenwein, *To Be the Neighbor of St Peter.*
74 The literature is enormous, but it has been brought together deftly in Moore, *First European Revolution*, and Poly and Bournazel, *Feudal Transformation.*
75 Tellenbach, *Church, State and Christian Society* and *Church in Western Europe*; Schmid, "Adel und Reform."
76 See Bisson, "Feudal Revolution"; and the ensuing debate between Bisson, Dominique Barthélemy, Timothy Reuter, Chris Wickham, and Steven White in *Past and Present*, 152 (1996), pp. 196–223; 155 (1997), pp. 177–225.
77 Cf. Brown and Górecki, "What Conflict Means."
78 White, "Tenth-Century Courts."
79 Hummer, "Reform and Lordship."
80 Duby, *La Société* and *Chivalrous Society*; Schmid, "Zur Problematik."

Bibliography

Primary Sources

Bobolenus, *Vita Germani Abbatis Grandivallensis*, ed. Bruno Krusch, MGH SRM, 5 (Hanover: Hahnsche Buchhandlung, 1910), pp. 25–40; esp. cc. 1–9, pp. 33–7.

Einhard, *Vita Karoli Magni*, ed. O. Holder-Egger, MGH SRG, vol. 25 (Hanover: Hahnsche Buchhandlung, 1911).

Secondary Sources

Airlie, Stuart, "The Aristocracy," in Rosamond McKitterick, ed., *The New Cambridge Medieval History* (Cambridge: Cambridge University Press, 1995), vol. 2, pp. 431–50.

Airlie, Stuart, Pohl, Walter, and Reimitz, Helmut, eds, *Staat im frühen Mittelalter* (Vienna: Österreichischen Akademie der Wissenschaften, 2006).

Althoff, Gerd, "Der frieden-, bündnis-und gemeinschaftstiftende Charakter des Mahles im früheren Mittelalter," in Irmgard Bitsch, Trude Ehlert, and Xenja von Ertzdorff, eds, *Essen und Trinken in Mittelalter und Neuzeit: Vorträge eines interdisziplinären Symposions vom 10.–13. Juni 1987 an der Justus-Liebig-Universität Gießen* (Sigmaringen: Thorbecke, 1987), pp. 13–25.

Althoff, Gerd, *Amicitiae und Pacta: Bündnis, Einung, Politik und Gebetsgedenken im beginnenden 10. Jahrhundert*, MGH, Schriften 37 (Hanover: Hahn, 1992).

Althoff, Gerd, *Family, Friends and Followers: Political and Social Bonds in Medieval Europe*, trans. Christopher Carroll (Cambridge: Cambridge University Press, 2004).

Althoff, Gerd, and Keller, Hagen, *Heinrich I. und Otto der Grosse: Neubeginn und karolingisches Erbe*, 2 vols (Göttingen: Muster-Schmidt, 1985).

Amory, Patrick, "The Meaning and Purpose of Ethnic Terminology in the Burgundian Laws," *Early Medieval Europe*, 2/1 (1993), pp. 1–28.

Amory, Patrick, "Names, Ethnic Identity, and Community in Fifth- and Sixth-Century Burgundy," *Viator*, 25 (1994), pp. 1–30.

Atsma, Hartmut, ed., *Spätantikes und fränkishes Gallien: Gesammelte Schriften*, 2 vols, Beihefte der Francia, 3/1–2 (Zurich: Artemis, 1976–9).

Atsma, Hartmut, ed., *La Neustrie: Les Pays au nord de la Loire de 650 à 850*, Beihefte der Francia 16, 2 vols (Sigmaringen: Thorbecke, 1989).

Bachrach, Bernard, *Early Carolingian Warfare: Prelude to Empire* (Philadelphia: University of Pennsylvania Press, 2001).

Barnwell, P. S., and Mostert, Marco, eds, *Political Assemblies in the Earlier Middle Ages* (Turnhout: Brepols, 2003).

Barraclough, Geoffrey, *Mediaeval Germany, 911–1250: Essays by German Historians* (Oxford: Blackwell, 1938).

Becher, Matthias, *Eid und Herrschaft: Untersuchungen zum Herrscherethos Karls des Großen*, Vorträge und Forschungen, Sonderband 39 (Sigmaringen: Thorbecke, 1993).

Becher, Matthias, "Die Kaiserkrönung im Jahr 800: Eine Streitfrage zwischen Karl dem Großen und Papst Leo III," *Rheinische Vierteljahrsblätter*, 66 (2002), pp. 1–38.

Benson, Robert L., *The Bishop-Elect: A Study in Medieval Ecclesiastical Office* (Princeton: Princeton University Press, 1968).

Bigott, Boris, *Ludwig der Deutsche und die Reichskirche im Ostfränkischen Reich (826–876)*, Historische Studien, 470 (Husum: Matthiesen, 2002).

Bisson, Thomas, "The Feudal Revolution," *Past & Present*, 142 (1994), pp. 6–42.

Bondroit, Alain, "Les 'Precaire verbo regis' avant le concile de Leptinnes (a. 743)," *Revue d'histoire ecclésiastique* 1 (1900), pp. 41, 60, 249–66, 430–47.

Borgolte, Michael, *Geschichte der Grafschaften Alemanniens in fränkischer Zeit*, Vorträge und Forschungen, Sonderband 31 (Sigmaringen: Thorbecke, 1984).

Bosl, Karl, "Der 'Adelsheilige': Idealtypus und Wirklichkeit, Gesellschaft und Kultur im merowingerzeitlichen Bayern des 7. und 8. Jahrhunderts: Gesellschaftliche Beiträge zu den Viten der bayerischen Stammesheiligen Emmeram, Rupert, Corbinian," in

Clemens Bauer, Laetitia Boehm, and Max Müller, eds, *Speculum Historiale: Geschichte im Spiegel von Geschichtsschreibung und Geschichtsdeutung* (Freiburg: Alber, 1965), pp. 167–87.

Bouchard, Constance, *"Those of My Blood": Constructing Noble Families in Medieval Francia* (Philadelphia: University of Pennsylvania Press, 2001).

Brown, Peter, *The Cult of the Saints: Its Rise and Function in Latin Christianity* (Chicago: University of Chicago Press, 1981).

Brown, Peter, *The Rise of Western Christendom: Triumph and Diversity, AD 200–1000*, 2nd edn (Oxford: Blackwell, 2003).

Brown, Warren, *Unjust Seizure: Conflict, Interest, and Authority in an Early Medieval Society* (Ithaca, NY: Cornell University Press, 2001).

Brown, Warren, and Górecki, Piotr, "What Conflict Means: The Making of Medieval Conflict Studies in the United States," in Warren Brown and Piotr Górecki, eds, *Conflict in Medieval Europe: Changing Perspectives on Society and Culture* (Burlington, VT: Ashgate, 2003), pp. 1–35.

Brown, Warren, and Górecki, Piotr, eds, *Conflict in Medieval Europe: Changing Perspectives on Society and Culture* (Burlington, VT: Ashgate, 2003).

Brunner, Heinrich, *Deutsche Rechtsgeschichte*, 2 vols (Leipzig: Duncker and Humblot, 1887–92).

Brunner, Karl, *Oppositionelle Gruppen im Karolingerreich* (Vienna: Böhlau, 1979).

Brunner, Otto, *Land and Lordship: Structures of Governance in Medieval Austria*, trans. Howard Kaminsky and James Van Horn Melton (Philadelphia: University of Pennsylvania Press, 1992).

Bullough, Donald, "*Europae Pater*: Charlemagne and his Achievement in the Light of Recent Scholarship," *English Historical Review*, 75 (1970), pp. 59–105.

Caspar, Erich, *Das Papsttum unter fränkischer Herrschaft* (Darmstadt: Herman Genthrin, 1956).

Constable, Giles, "*Nona et Decima*: An Aspect of Carolingian Economy," *Speculum* 35 (1960), pp. 224–50.

Davies, Wendy, and Fouracre, Paul, eds, *The Settlement of Disputes in Early Medieval Europe* (Cambridge: Cambridge University Press, 1986).

Davies, Wendy, and Fouracre, Paul, eds, *Property and Power in the Early Middle Ages* (Cambridge: Cambridge University Press, 1995).

De Clercq, Charles, *La Legislation religieuse franque de Clovis à Charlemagne: Étude sur les actes de conciles et les capitulaires, les statuts diocésains et les règles monastiques 507–814*, 2 vols (Louvain: Bureau du Recueil, Bibliothèque de l'Université, 1936–58).

De Jong, Mayke, "Introduction: Rethinking Early Medieval Christianity: A View from the Netherlands," *Early Medieval Europe*, 7/3 (1998), pp. 261–75.

Dierkens, Alain, *Abbayes et chapitres entre Sambre et Meuse (VIIe–XIe siècles): Contribution à l'histoire religieuse des campagnes du Haut Moyen Age*, Beihefte der Francia, 14 (Sigmaringen: Thorbecke, 1985).

Dhondt, J., *Études sur la naissance des principautés territoriales en France IXe–Xe siècles* (Bruges: De Tempel, 1948).

Duby, Georges, *The Chivalrous Society*, trans. Cynthia Postan (Berkeley and Los Angeles: University of California Press, 1977).

Duby, Georges, *La Société aux XIe et XIIe siècles dans la région mâconnaise*, 2nd edn (Paris: Éditions de l'École des hautes études en sciences sociales, 1982).

Dunbabin, Jean, *France in the Making, 843–1180*, 2nd edn (Oxford: Oxford University Press, 2000).

Durliat, Jean, *Les Finances publiques de Dioclétian aux Carolingiens (284–888)*, Beihefte der Francia, 21 (Sigmaringen: Thorbecke, 1990).

Ebling, Horst, *Prosopographie der Amtsträger des Merowingerreiches von Chlothar II. (613) bis Karl Martell (741)*, Beihefte der Francia, 2 (Munich: Fink, 1974).

Ehlers, Caspar, *Die Integration Sachsens in das fränkische Reich (751–1024)* (Göttingen: Vandenhoeck and Ruprecht, 2007).

Erkens, Franz-Reiner, ed., *Das frühmittelalterliche Königtum: Ideelle und religiöse Grundlagen*, Ergänzungsbände zum Reallexikon der germanischen Altertumskunde, 49 (Berlin: De Gruyter, 2005).

Ewig, Eugen, "Die fränkischen Teilreiche im 7. Jahrhundert (613–714)," in Hartmut Atsma ed., *Spätantikes und fränkishes Gallien: Gesammelte Schriften*, 2 vols, Beihefte der Francia, 3/1–2 (Zurich: Artemis, 1976–9), vol. 1, pp. 172–230.

Ewig, Eugen, "Volkstum und Volksbewusstsein im Frankenreich des 7. Jahrhunderts," in Hartmut Atsma ed., *Spätantikes und fränkishes Gallien: Gesammelte Schriften*, 2 vols, Beihefte der Francia, 3/1–2 (Zurich: Artemis, 1976–9), vol. 1, pp. 231–73.

Fasoli, Gina, *I Re d'Italia, 888–962* (Florence: Sansoni, 1949).

Felten, Franz, *Äbte und Laienäbte im Frankenreich: Studien zum Verhältnis von Staat und Kirche im frühen Mittelalter* (Stuttgart: Hiersemann, 1980).

Fichtenau, Heinrich, *Living in the Tenth Century: Mentalities and Social Orders*, trans. Patrick J. Geary (Chicago: University of Chicago Press, 1991).

Fleckenstein, Josef, *Die Hofkapelle der deutschen Könige*, MGH Schriften 16, 1–2 (Stuttgart: Hiersemann, 1959).

Folz, Robert, *The Coronation of Charlemagne*, trans. J. E. Anderson (London: Routledge, 1974).

Fossier, Robert, *Enfance de l'Europe: X^{e}–XIIe siècles: Aspects économiques et sociaux* (Paris: Presses universitaires de France, 1982)

Fouracre, Paul, "Observations on the Outgrowth of Pippinid Influence in the 'Regnum Francorum' after the Battle of Tertry (687–715)," *Medieval Prosopography*, 5 (1984), pp. 1–31.

Fouracre, Paul, "Carolingian Justice: The Rhetoric of Improvement and Contexts of Abuse," *La Giustizia nell'alto medioevo (secoli V-VIII)*, Settimane di studio del Centro italiano di studi sull'alto medievo, 42 (Spoleto: Centro italiano di Studi sull'alto medioevo, 1995), pp. 771-803.

Fouracre, Paul, "Frankish Gaul to 814," in Rosamond McKitterick, ed., *The New Cambridge Medieval History* (Cambridge: Cambridge University Press, 1995), vol. 2, pp. 85–109.

Fouracre, Paul, "The Origins of the Carolingian Attempt to Regulate the Cult of Saints," in P. A. Hayward and J. Howard-Johnston, eds, *The Cult of Saints in Late Antiquity and the Middle Ages: Essays on the Contribution of Peter Brown* (Oxford: Oxford University Press, 1999), pp. 143–65.

Fouracre, Paul, *The Age of Charles Martel* (New York: Longman, 2000).

Fouracre, Paul, and Gerberding, Richard, *Late Merovingian France: History and Hagiography 640–720* (Manchester: Manchester University Press, 1996).

Freed, John B., "Reflections on the Medieval German Nobility," *American Historical Review*, 91/3 (1986), pp. 553–75.

Freed, John B., "Medieval German Social History: Generalizations and Particularism," *Central European History*, 25/1 (1992), pp. 1–26.

Fried, Johannes, "The Frankish Kingdoms 817–911: The East and Middle Kingdoms," in Rosamond McKitterick, ed., *The New Cambridge Medieval History* (Cambridge: Cambridge University Press, 1995), vol. 2, pp. 142–68.

Ganshof, F. L., *Feudalism*, 3rd edn, trans. Philip Grierson (New York: Harper, 1964).

Ganshof, F. L., *Frankish Institutions under Charlemagne*, trans. Bryce and Mary Lyon (Providence, RI: Brown University Press, 1968).

Geary, Patrick J., "L'Humiliation des saints," *Annales: Économies, sociétés, civilisations*, 34 (1978), pp. 27–42.

Geary, Patrick J., "Vivre en conflit dans une France sans état: Typologie des mécanismes de règlement des conflits (1050–1200)," *Annales: Économies, sociétés, civilisations*, 42 (1986), pp. 1107–33.

Geary, Patrick J., *Before France and Germany: The Creation and Transformation of the Merovingian World* (Oxford: Oxford University Press, 1988).

Gelzer, Matthias, *Die Nobilitat der Römischen Republik* (Leipzig: Teubner, 1912).

Gerberding, Richard, *The Rise of the Carolingians and* the Liber Historiae Francorum (Oxford: Clarendon Press, 1987).

Godman, Peter, and Collins, Roger, eds, *Charlemagne's Heir: New Perspectives on the Reign of Louis the Pious (814–840)* (Oxford: Clarendon Press, 1990).

Goetz, Hans-Werner, Jarnut, Jörg, and Pohl, Walter, eds, *Regna and Gentes: The Relationship between Late Antique and Early Medieval Peoples and Kingdoms in the Transformation of the Roman World* (Leiden: Brill, 2003).

Goffart, Walter, "From Roman Taxation to Medieval Seigneurie: Three Notes," *Speculum*, 47 (1972), pp. 165–87, 373–94.

Goffart, Walter, *Barbarian Tides: The Migration Age and the Later Roman Empire* (Philadelphia: University of Pennsylvania Press, 2006).

Goldberg, Eric, *Struggle for Empire: Kingship and Conflict under Louis the German, 814–876* (Ithaca, NY: Cornell University Press, 2006).

Goody, Jack, *The Development of the Family and Marriage in Europe* (Cambridge: Cambridge University Press, 1983).

Grahn-Hoek, Heike, *Die fränkische Oberschicht im 6. Jahrhundert: Studien zu ihrer rechtlichen und politischen Stellung* (Sigmaringen: Thorbecke, 1976).

Haar, Karl-Heinz, *Studien zur Entstehungs- und Entwicklungsgeschichte des Fränkischen Maior Domus-Amts: Zur kontinuität einer spatrömischen Institution und ihrer Stellung bei den Franken vornehmlich bis zum Ausgang des 6. Jahrhunderts* (Augsburg: Blasaditsch, 1968).

Halsall, Guy, *Warfare and Society in the Barbarian West, 450–900* (New York: Routledge, 2003).

Hannig, Jürgen, *Consensus fidelium: Frühfeudale Interpretationen des Verhältnisses von Königtum und Adel am Beispiel des Frankenreiches* (Stuttgart: Hiersemann, 1982).

Hartmann, Wilfried, *Die Synoden der Karolingerzeit im Frankenreich und in Italien* (Paderborn: Schöningh, 1989).

Hartmann, Wilfried, *Ludwig der Deutsche und seine Zeit* (Darmstadt: Wissenschaftliche Buchgesellschaft, 2002).

Hartung, Wolfgang, "Adel, Erbrecht, Schenkung: Die strukturellen Ursachen der frühmittelalterlichen Besitzübertragungen an die Kirche," in Ferdinand Seibt, ed., *Gesellschaftsgeschichte: Festschrift für Karl Bosl zum 80. Geburtstag*, 2 vols (Munich: Oldenbourg, 1988). vol. 1, pp. 417–38.

Havighurst, Alfred, ed., *The Pirenne Thesis: Analysis, Criticism, and Revision*, 3rd edn (Lexington, MA: Heath, 1976).

Hechberger, Werner, *Adel im fränkisch-deutschen Mittelalter: Zur Anatomie eines Forschungsproblems* (Ostfildern: Thorbecke, 2005).

Heidrich, Ingrid, "Les Maires du palais neustriens du milieu du VIIe au milieu du VIIIe siècle," in Hartmut Atsma, ed., *La Neustrie: Les Pays au nord de la Loire de 650 à 850*, Beihefte der Francia 16, 2 vols (Sigmaringen: Thorbecke, 1989), pp. 217–29.

Heinzelmann, Martin, *Bischofsherrschaft in Gallien: Zur Kontinuität römischer Führungsschichten vom 4. bis zum 7. Jahrhundert: Soziale, prosopographische und bildungsgeschichtliche Aspekte* (Zurich: Artemis, 1976).

Heinzelmann, Martin, ed., *L'Hagiographie du haut moyen âge en Gaule du Nord: Manuscrits, textes et centres de production*, Beihefte der Francia, 52 (Stuttgart: Thorbecke, 2001).

Hellgarth, Ernst, "Zur Mehrsprachigkeit im Karolingerreich: Bemerkungen aus Anlaß von Rosamond McKittericks Buch *The Carolingians and the Written Word*," *Beiträge zur Geschichte der deutschen Sprache und Literatur*, 118 (1996), pp. 1–48.

Hlawitschka, Eduard, *Franken, Alemannen, Bayern und Burgunder in Oberitalien (774–962): Zum Verständnis der fränkischen Königsherrschaft in Italien* (Freiburg: Albert, 1960).

Hlawitschka, Eduard, *Lotharingien und das Reich an der Schwelle der deutschen Geschichte* (Stuttgart: Hiersemann, 1968).

Hlawitschka, Eduard, *Vom Frankenreich zur Formierung der europäischen Staaten- und Völkergemeinschaft, 840–1046: Ein Studienbuch zur Zeit der späten Karolinger, der Ottonen und der frühen Salier in der Geschichte Mitteleuropas* (Darmstadt: Wissenschaftliche Buchgesellschaft, 1986).

Hummer, Hans J., "Reform and Lordship in Alsace at the Turn of the Millennium," in Warren Brown and Piotr Górecki, eds, *Conflict in Medieval Europe: Changing Perspectives on Society and Culture* (Burlington, VT: Ashgate, 2003), pp. 69–84.

Hummer, Hans J., *Politics and Power in Early Medieval Europe: Alsace and the Frankish Realm, 600–1000* (Cambridge: Cambridge University Press, 2005).

Innes, Matthew, *State and Society in the Early Middle Ages: The Middle Rhine Valley, 400–1000* (Cambridge: Cambridge University Press, 2000).

Innes, Matthew, and Hen, Yitzak, ed., *The Uses of the Past in the Early Middle Ages* (Cambridge: Cambridge University Press, 2000).

Irsigler, Franz, *Untersuchungen zur Geschichte des frühfränkischen Adels* (Bonn: Röhrscheid, 1969).

Jahn, Joachim, "Tradere ad Sanctum, Politische und gesellschaftliche Aspekte der Traditionspraxis im agilolfingischen Bayern," in Ferdinand Seibt, ed., *Gesellschaftsgeschichte: Festschrift für Karl Bosl zum 80. Geburtstag*, 2 vols (Munich: Oldenbourg, 1988), vol. 1, pp. 400–16.

Jahn, Joachim, *Ducatus Baiuvariorum: Die Bairische Herzogtum der Agilolfinger* (Stuttgart: Hiersemann, 1991).

James, Edward, *The Origins of France: from Clovis to the Capetians, 500–1000* (New York: St Martin's, 1982).

Jarnut, Jörg, "Die frühmittelalterliche Jagd unter rechts- und sozialgeschichtlichen Aspekten," in *L'uomo di fronte al mondo animale nell'alto medioevo*, Settimane di studio del Centro italiano di studi sull'alto medioevo, 31 (Spoleto: Presso la sede del Centro, 1985), pp. 765–808.

Jarnut, Jörg, Nonn, Ulrich, and Richter, Michael eds, *Karl Martell in seiner Zeit*, Beihefte der *Francia*, 37 (Sigmaringen: Thorbecke, 1994).

Kasten, Brigitte, *Königssöhne und Königsherrschaft: Untersuchungen zur Teilhabe am Reich in der Merowinger- und Karolingerzeit*, MGH, Schriften 44 (Hanover: Hahnsche Buchhandlung, 1997).

Keller, Hagen, "Das Werk Gerd Tellenbachs in der Geschichtswissenschaft unseres Jahrhunderts," *Frühmittelalterliche Studien*, 28 (1994), pp. 374–97.

Kern, Fritz, *Kingship and Law in the Middle Ages*, trans. S. B. Chrimes (Oxford: Blackwell, 1939).

Koziol, Geoffrey, *Begging Pardon and Favor: Ritual and Political Order in Early Medieval France* (Ithaca, NY: Cornell University Press, 1992).

Lammers, Walther, ed., *Die Eingliederung der Sachsen in das Frankenreich* (Darmstadt: Wissenschaftliche Buchgesellschaft, 1970).

Le Jan, Régine, *Famille et pouvoir dans le monde franc (VIIe–Xe siècle): Essai d'anthropologie sociale* (Paris: Sorbonne, 1995).
Lewis, Andrew, *Royal Succession in Capetian France: Studies on Familial Order and the State*, Harvard Historical Studies, 100 (Cambridge, MA: Harvard University Press, 1981).
Lewis, Archibald R., "The Dukes in the *Regnum Francorum,* AD 550–751," *Speculum*, 51/3 (1976), pp. 381–410.
Lot, Ferdinand, *The End of the Ancient World and the Beginnings of the Middle Ages*, trans. Philip Leon and Mariette Leon (New York: Barnes and Noble, 1953).
McCormick, Michael, *Origins of the European Economy: Communications and Commerce AD 300–900* (Cambridge: Cambridge University Press, 2001).
McKitterick, Rosamond, *The Frankish Church and the Carolingian Reforms, 789–895* (London: Royal Historical Society, 1977).
McKitterick, Rosamond, *The Frankish Kingdoms under the Carolingians, 751–981* (London: Longman, 1983).
McKitterick, Rosamond, *The Carolingians and the Written Word* (Cambridge: Cambridge University Press, 1989).
McKitterick, Rosamond, ed., *The New Cambridge Medieval History*, vol. 2 (Cambridge: Cambridge University Press, 1995).
McKitterick, Rosamond, "Politics," in Rosamond McKitterick, ed., *The Early Middle Ages: Europe 400–1000*, The Short Oxford History of Europe (Oxford: Oxford University Press, 2001), pp. 21–56.
McKitterick, Rosamond, *History and Memory in the Carolingian World* (Cambridge: Cambridge University Press, 2004).
MacLean, Simon, *Kingship and Politics in the Late Ninth Century: Charles the Fat and the End of the Carolingian Empire* (Cambridge: Cambridge University Press, 2003).
Mayer, Theodor, ed., *Das Königtum: Seine geistigen rechtlichen Grundlagen*, Vorträge und Forschungen, 3 (Constance: Thorbecke, 1956).
Moore, Robert I., *The First European Revolution*, c. *970–1215* (Oxford: Blackwell, 2000).
Morelle, Laurent, "Les 'Actes de précaire', instruments de transferts patrimoniaux (France du Nord et de l'Est, VIIIe–XIe siècle)," *Mélanges de l'École française de Rome: Moyen âge*, 3/2 (1999), pp. 607–47.
Münzer, Friedrich, *Römische Adelsparteien und Adelsfamilien* (Stuttgart: Metzler, 1920).
Murray, Alexander Callander, "The Position of the Grafio in the Constitutional History of Merovingian Gaul," *Speculum*, 61/4 (1986), 787–805.
Murray, Alexander Callander, "From Roman Gaul to Frankish Gaul: 'Centenarii' and 'Centenae' in the Administration of the Merovingian Kingdom," *Traditio*, 44 (1988), pp. 59–100.
Nelson, Janet, *Politics and Ritual in Early Medieval Europe* (London: Hambledon, 1986).
Nelson, Janet, *Charles the Bald* (London: Longman, 1992).
Nelson, Janet, "Kingship and Empire in the Carolingian World," in Rosamond McKitterick, ed., *Carolingian Culture: Emulation and Innovation* (Cambridge and New York: Cambridge University Press, 1994), pp. 52–87.
Nelson, Janet, "The Frankish Kingdoms 814–898," in Rosamond McKitterick, ed., *The New Cambridge Medieval History* (Cambridge: Cambridge University Press, 1995), vol. 2, pp. 110–41.
Nelson, Janet, "Kingship and Royal Government," in Rosamond McKitterick, ed., *The New Cambridge Medieval History* (Cambridge: Cambridge University Press, 1995), vol. 2, pp. 383–430.
Nelson, Janet, *The Frankish World, 750–900* (London: Hambledon, 1996).

Noble, Thomas F. X., *The Republic of St Peter: The Birth of the Papal State, 680–825* (Philadelphia: University of Pennsylvania Press, 1984).

Noble, Thomas F. X., "From Brigandage to Justice: Charlemagne, 785–794," in Celia Chazelle, ed., *Literacy, Politics and Artistic Innovation in the Early Medieval West* (Lanham, MD: University Press of America, 1992), pp. 49–75.

Noble, Thomas F. X., "The Papacy in the Eighth and Ninth Centuries," in Rosamond McKitterick, ed., *The New Cambridge Medieval History* (Cambridge: Cambridge University Press, 1995), vol. 2, pp. 563–86.

Noble, Thomas F. X., ed., *From Roman Provinces to Medieval Kingdoms* (New York: Routledge, 2006).

Nonn, Ulrich, "Das Bild Karl Martells in den lateinischen Quellen vornehmlich des 8. und 9. Jahrhunderts," *Frühmittelalterliche Studien*, 4 (1970), pp. 70–137.

Nonn, Ulrich, *Pagus und Comitatus in Niederlothringen: Untersuchungen zur politischen. Raumgliederung im früheren Mittelalter* (Bonn: Röhrscheid, 1983).

Oexle, Otto Gerhard, "Gruppen in der Gesellschaft: Das wissenschaftliche Œuvre von Karl Schmid," *Frühmittelalterliche Studien*, 28 (1994), pp. 410–35.

Pirenne, Henri, *Mohammed and Charlemagne*, trans. Bernard Miall (New York: Norton, 1939).

Pohl, Walter, ed., *Kingdoms of the Empire: The Integraton of Barbarians in Late Antiquity* (Leiden: Brill, 1997).

Poly, Jean-Pierre, and Bournazel, Eric, *The Feudal Transformation, 900–1200*, trans. Caroline Higgitt (London: Holmes and Meier, 1991).

Prinz, Friedrich, *Frühes Mönchtum im Frankenreich: Kultur und Gesellschaft in Gallien, den Rheinlanden und Bayern am Beispiel der monastischen Entwicklung (4. bis 8. Jahrhundert)* (Munich: Oldenbourg, 1988).

Reuter, Timothy, ed. and trans., *The Medieval Nobility: Studies on the Ruling Classes of France and Germany from the Sixth to the Twelfth Century* (Amsterdam: North-Holland, 1978).

Reuter, Timothy, "Plunder and Tribute in the Carolingian Empire," *Transactions of the Royal Historical Society*, 35 (1985), pp. 391–405.

Reuter, Timothy, *Germany in the Early Middle Ages*, c. *800–1056* (London: Longman, 1991).

Reynolds, Susan, *Fiefs and Vassals: The Medieval Evidence Reconsidered* (Oxford: Clarendon, 1994).

Reynolds, Susan, *Kingdoms and Communities in Western Europe, 900–1300*, 2nd edn (Oxford: Clarendon Press, 1997).

Riché, Pierre, *Education and Culture in the Barbarian West, Sixth through Eighth Centuries*, trans. J. J. Contreni (Columbia, SC: South Carolina University Press, 1976).

Rösener, Werner, ed., *Strukturen der Grundherrschaft im frühen Mittelalter*, Veröffentlichungen des Max-Planck-Instituts für Geschichte, 92 (Göttingen: Vandenhoeck and Ruprecht, 1989).

Rosenwein, Barbara H., *To Be the Neighbor of St Peter: The Social Meaning of Cluny's Property, 909–1049* (Ithaca, NY: Cornell University Press, 1989).

Rosenwein, Barbara H., "Property Transfers and the Church, Eighth to Eleventh Centuries: An Overview," *Mélanges de l'École française de Rome: Moyen âge*, 3/2 (1999), pp. 563–75.

Sawyer, P. H., and Wood, I. N., eds, *Early Medieval Kingship* (Leeds: University of Leeds, 1977).

Schmid, Karl, "Zur Problematik von Familie, Sippe und Geschlecht, Haus und Dynastie beim mittelalterlichen Adel," *Zeitschrift für die Geschichte des Oberrheins*, 105 (1957), pp. 1–62.

Schmid, Karl, "Adel und Reform in Schwaben," in Josef Fleckenstein, ed., *Investiturstreit und Reichsverfassung*, Vorträge und Forschungen, 17 (Sigmaringen: Thorbecke, 1973), 295–319.

Schmid, Karl, "Der 'Freiburger Arbeitskreis': Gerd Tellenbach zum 70 Geburtstag," *Zeitschrift für die Geschichte des Oberrheins*, 122 (1974), pp. 331–47.

Schmid, Karl, "Programmatisches zur Erforschung der mittelalterlichen Personen und Personengruppen," *Frühmittelalterliche Studien*, 8 (1974), pp. 116–30.

Schmid, Karl, *Geblüt, Herrschaft, Geschlechterbewüsstsein: Grundfragen zum Verständnis des Adels im Mittelalter*, ed. Dieter Mertens and Thomas Zotz, Vorträge und Forschungen, vol. 44 (Sigmaringen: Thorbecke, 1998).

Schneidmüller, Bernd, *Karolingische Tradition und frühes französisches Königtum: Untersuchungen zur Herrschaftslegitimation der westfränkischen-französichen Monarchie im 10. Jh.* (Wiesbaden: Steiner, 1979).

Schröder, Isolde, *Die westfränkischen Synoden von 888 bis 987 und ihre Überlieferung* (Munich: Monumenta Germaniae Historica, 1980).

Schulze, Hans K., *Die Grafschaftsverfassung der Karolingerzeit in den Gebieten östlich des Rheins*, Schriften zur Verfassungsgeschichte, 19 (Berlin: Duncker and Humblot, 1973).

Schulze, Hans K., "Reichsaristokratie, Stammesadel und fränkische Freiheit," *Historische Zeitschrift*, 227 (1978), pp. 353–73.

Screen, Elina, "The Importance of the Emperor: Lothar I and the Frankish Civil War, 840–843," *Early Medieval Europe*, 12/1 (2003), pp. 25–51.

Seibt, Ferdinand, ed., *Gesellschaftsgeschichte: Festschrift für Karl Bosl zum 80. Geburtstag*, 2 vols (Munich: Oldenbourg, 1988).

Semmler, Josef, *Der Dynastiewechsel von 751 und die fränkische Königssalbung* (Brühl: Droste, 2003).

Sprandel, Rolf, "Dux und comes in der Merowingerzeit," *Zeitschrift der Savigny-Stiftung für Rechtsgeschichte, Germanistische Abteilung*, 74 (1957), pp. 41–84.

Stingl, Herfried, *Die Entstehung der deutschen Stammesherzogtümer am Anfang des 10. Jahrhunderts* (Aalen: Scientia Verlag, 1974).

Störmer, Wilhelm, *Adelsgruppen im früh- und hochmittelalterlichen Bayern* (München: Kommission für Bayerische Landesgeschichte, 1972).

Störmer, Wilhelm, *Früher Adel: Studien zur politischen Führungsschicht im fränkisch deutschen Reich vom 8. bis 11. Jahrhundert*, 2 vols, Mongraphien zur Geschichte des Mittelalters 6, 1–2 (Stuttgart: Hiersemann, 1973).

Stroheker, Karl Friedrich, *Der senatorische Adel im spätantiken Gallien* (Darmstadt: Wissenschaftliche Buchgesellschaft, 1970).

Sullivan, Richard, "The Carolingian Age: Reflections on its Place in the History of the Middle Ages," *Speculum*, 64 (1989), pp. 267–306.

Tellenbach, Gerd, *Church, State and Christian Society at the Time of the Investiture Contest*, trans. R. F. Bennett (Oxford: Blackwell, 1940).

Tellenbach, Gerd, *Zur Bedeutung der Personenforschung für die Erkenntnis des früheren Mittelalters*, Freiburger Universitätsreden, neue Folge, v. 25 (Freiburg: Schulz, 1957).

Tellenbach, Gerd, *The Church in Western Europe from the Tenth to the Early Twelfth Century*, trans. Timothy Reuter (Cambridge: Cambridge University Press, 1993).

Ullmann, Walter, *The Carolingian Renaissance and the Idea of Kingship* (London: Methuen, 1969).

Van Dam, Raymond, *Saints and their Miracles in Late Antique Gaul* (Princeton: Princeton University Press, 1993).

Verhulst, Adriaan, ed., *Le Grand Domaine aux époques mérovingienne et carolingienne: Die Grundherrschaft im frühen Mittelalter* (Gent: Belgisch Centrum voor Landelijke Geschiedenis, 1985).

Wallace-Hadrill, J. M., *The Long-Haired Kings, and Other Studies in Frankish History* (New York: Barnes and Noble, 1962).

Wallace-Hadrille, J. M., *The Frankish Church* (Oxford: Clarendon Press, 1983).

Wemple, Suzanne, *Women in Frankish Society: Marriage and the Cloister, 500 to 900* (Philadelphia: University of Pennsylvania Press, 1981).

Werner, Karl Ferdinand, "Important Noble Families in the Kingdom of Charlemagne," in Timothy Reuter, ed. and trans., *The Medieval Nobility: Studies on the Ruling Classes of France and Germany from the Sixth to the Twelfth Century* (Amsterdam: North-Holland, 1978), pp. 137–202.

Werner, Karl Ferdinand, "Les Principautés périphériques dans le monde Franc du VIIIe siècle," in *I Problemi dell' Occicente nel secolo VIII*, 2 vols, Settimane di Studio dell Centro Italiano di studi sull' alto medioevo, 20 (Spoleto: Presso la sede del Centro, 1973), pp. 483–514.

Werner, Karl Ferdinand, *Vom Frankenreich zur Entfaltung Deutschlands und Frankreichs: Ursprünge, Strukturen, Beziehungen Ausgewählte Beiträge: Festgabe zu seinem sechzigsten Geburtstag* (Sigmaringen: Thorbecke, 1984).

Werner, Karl Ferdinand, "Missus-marchio-comes: Entre l'administration centrale et l'administration locale de l'empire carolingien," in Walter Paravicini and Karl Ferdinand Werner, eds, *Histoire comparée de l'administration (IVe–XVIIIe siècle)*, Beihefte der Francia, 9 (Munich: Artemis, 1980), pp. 191–239.

Werner, Matthias, *Der Lüttlicher Raum in frühkarolingischer Zeit: Untersuchungen zur Geschichte einer karolingischen Stammlandschaft*, Veröffentlichungen des Max Planck Instituts für Geschichte 62 (Göttingen: Vandenhoeck and Reprecht, 1980).

Werner, Matthias, *Adelsfamilien im Umkreis der frühen Karolinger*, Vorträge und Forschungen, Sonderband 28 (Sigmaringen: Thorbecke, 1982).

White, Stephen D., *Custom, Kinship, and Gifts to Saints: The* Laudatio Parentum *in Western France, 1050–1150* (Chapel Hill, NC: North Carolina University Press, 1988).

White, Stephen D., "Tenth-Century Courts and the Perils of Structuralist History," in Warren Brown and Piotr Górecki, eds, *Conflict in Medieval Europe: Changing Perspectives on Society and Culture* (Burlington, VT: Ashgate, 2003), pp. 37–68.

Wickham, Chris, "The Other Transition: From the Ancient World to Feudalism," *Past and Present*, 103 (1984), pp. 3–36.

Wickham, Chris, *Framing the Early Middle Ages: Europe and the Mediterranean, 400–800* (Oxford: Oxford University Press, 2005).

Wolfram, Herwig, *Conversio Bagoariorum et Carantanorum: Das Weißbuch der Salzburger Kirche über die erfolgreiche Mission in Karantanien und Pannonien* (Vienna: Böhlau, 1979).

Wolfram, Herwig, *Die Geburt Mitteleuropas: Geschichte Österreichs vor seiner Entstehung, 378–907* (Berlin: Siedler, 1987).

Wood, Ian, "The *Vita Columbani* and Merovingian Hagiography," *Peritia: Journal of the Medieval Academy of Ireland*, 1 (1982), pp. 63–80.

Wood, Ian, *The Merovingian Kingdoms 450–751* (London: Longman, 1994).

Wood, Ian, "Teutsind, Witlaic and the History of Merovingian *precaria*," in Wendy Davies and Paul Fouracre, eds, *Property and Power in the Early Middle Ages* (Cambridge: Cambridge University Press, 1995), pp. 31–52.

Wood, Ian, *The Missionary Life: Saints and the Evangelisation of Europe, 400–1050* (New York: Longman, 2001).

Wood, Susan, *The Proprietary Church in the Medieval West* (Oxford: Oxford University Press, 2006).

Further Reading

Much of the relevant scholarship on early medieval politics and power, and subsidiary issues, has been summarized within the Oldenbourg series of bibliographical monographs by Reinhold Kaiser, *Das römische Erbe und das Merowingerreich*, rev. edn, Ezyklopädie deutscher Geschichte, 26 (Munich: Oldenbourg 2004); Reinhard Schneider, *Das Frankenreich*, rev. edn, Oldenbourg Grundriss der Geschichte, 5 (Munich: Oldenbourg, 2001); and Johannes Fried, *Die Formierung Europas, 840–1046*, rev. edn, Oldenbourg Grundriss der Geschichte, 6 (Munich: Oldenbourg, 2008). Roger Collins, *Early Medieval Europe*, 2nd edn (New York: Palgrave, 1999), offers a comprehensive, if idiosyncratic, survey of the period, with a focus on the political narrative. Concise surveys of early medieval politics and government in English are provided in Rosamond McKitterick, "Politics", in Rosamond McKitterick, ed., *The Early Middle Ages: Europe 400–1000*, The Short Oxford History of Europe (Oxford: Oxford University Press, 2001), pp. 21–56; and in the relevant contributions by Paul Fouracre in Paul Fouracre, ed., *The New Cambridge Medieval History*, vol. 1: c. *500–*c. *700* (Cambridge: Cambridge University Press, 2006); Paul Fouracre, Janet Nelson, and Johannes Fried, in Rosamond McKitterick, ed., *The New Cambridge Medieval History*, vol. 2: c. *700–*c. *900* (Cambridge: Cambridge University Press, 1995); and Janet Nelson in Timothy Reuter, ed., *The New Cambridge Medieval History*, vol. 3: c. *900–*c. *1024* (Cambridge: Cambridge University Press, 2000). The relationship of the formation of the early medieval political order to the collapse of the Roman Empire in the West has been substantially recast over the last several decades. Much of this work has been brought into elegant new syntheses by Chris Wickham, *Framing the Early Middle Ages: Europe and the Mediterranean 400–800* (Oxford and New York: Oxford University Press, 2005), and Matthew Innes, *Introduction to Early Medieval Western Europe, 300–900: The Sword, the Plough and the Book* (London: Routledge, 2007). For treatments of particular periods and regions within the early medieval period, see Roger Collins, *Early Medieval Spain: Unity in Diversity 400–1000*, 2nd edn (New York: Macmillan, 1995); Frank M. Stenton, *Anglo-Saxon England*, 3rd edn (Oxford: Oxford University Press, 1989); and Chris Wickham, *Early Medieval Italy: Central Power and Local Society 400–1000* (London: Macmillan, 1981); on the Frankish realms, Ian Wood, *The Merovingian Kingdoms 450–751* (New York: Longman, 1994); Patrick Geary, *Before France and Germany: The Creation and Transformation of the Merovingian World* (Oxford: Oxford University Press, 1988); and Rosamond McKitterick, *The Carolingian Kingdoms under the Carolingians, 751–987* (London: Longman, 1983); and on the post-Carolingian kingdoms, Timothy Reuter, *Germany in the Early Middle Ages,* c. *800–1056* (London: Longman, 1991); and Jean Dunbabin, *France in the Making, 843–1180*, 2nd edn (Oxford: Oxford University Press, 2000). The aristocracy is central to understanding the formation and operation of the early medieval political order. The scholarship on the aristocracy, much of it German, has been masterfully brought together in Régine Le Jan, *Famille et pouvoir dans le monde franc (VIIe–Xe siècle): Essai d'anthropologie sociale* (Paris: Sorbonne, 1995), and Werner Hechberger, *Adel im fränkisch-deutschen Mittelalter: Zur Anatomie eines Forschungsproblems* (Ostfildern: Thorbecke, 2005). F. L. Ganshof, *Feudalism*, trans. Philip Grierson, 3rd edn (New York: Harper, 1964), and *Frankish Institutions under Charlemagne*, trans. Bryce and Mary Lyon (Providence, RI: Brown University Press, 1968), are still useful on political terminology, though Ganshof's views of delegated authority should be balanced with Matthew Innes, *State and Society in the Early Middle Ages: The Middle Rhine Valley, 400–1000* (Cambridge: Cambridge University Press, 2000), which embeds office holding within the dynamics of lordship. On the symbiosis of ecclesiastical foundations, landed property, and aristocratic power, see Friedrich Prinz's classic *Frühes Mönchtum im Frankenreich: Kultur und Gesellschaft in Gallien, den Rheinlanden und Bayern am Beispiel der monastischen*

Entwicklung (4. bis 8. Jahrhundert) (Munich: Oldenbourg, 1965), and Susan Wood, *The Proprietary Church in the Medieval West* (Oxford: Oxford University Press, 2006). No adequate monographic survey of the post-Carolingian period exists, though Heinrich Fichtenau's *Living in the Tenth Century: Mentalities and Social Orders*, trans. Patrick J. Geary (Chicago: University of Chicago Press, 1991), offers a thoughtful reflection on the political culture of tenth-century Europe; and Robert I. Moore, *The First European Revolution, c. 970–1215* (Oxford: Blackwell, 2000), presents an elegant and concise treatment of the profound political and social transformations of the eleventh century.

Chapter Four

Religious Culture and the Power of Tradition in the Early Medieval West

Yitzhak Hen

No subject in the history of the early Middle Ages has more significance and more pitfalls than that of the interaction between culture and religion. Not only is the subject matter extremely vast and highly complicated; the evidence itself poses major problems – in many cases it is extremely slight, in others it is exceptionally ambiguous, and more often than not it is marred with a profound Christian bias. Nevertheless, the subject has some very real attractions, which had led in the past to the building of vast but fragile historical theories, attempting to bring the distinctive culture of the era into a schematic relationship with historical events, such as the spread of Christianity or the rise of the Carolingians to power. These attempts, however, forced modern predilections and preoccupations on the early medieval evidence, and therefore should be approached with extreme caution. Moreover, one must constantly bear in mind that examining our sources (whether literary, artistic, or archaeological), with or without the help of modern anthropological and sociological theories, will yield only a partial picture. There is always the chance that certain cultural aspects may have existed in a form that left no written records or datable artifacts, and that some meanings that were clear and obvious to those who lived at the time will remain hidden from us forever.

Yet, it would be unfair, and rather simplistic, to put all the blame on the nature of our sources or lack thereof. One has to acknowledge that our own experience in the modern world poses a major stumbling block in any attempt to understand various religious and cultural phenomena. The study of early medieval culture in general, and religious culture in particular, requires a preliminary mental readjustment. We must temporarily abandon familiar cultural territory and radically question received intellectual categories. Early medieval society was fundamentally different from our own, and the concepts that we employ to describe contemporary religious phenomena are inevitably ill adapted to the analysis of what early medieval people regarded as the divine sphere. Besides, the function of religious culture and rituals cannot be the same in a society where religion, or more precisely Christianity, was thoroughly intertwined with all areas of public and social interactions, and in one, such as ours, in which public life is largely secularized.

Bearing in mind the intricacy of the topic we are dealing with, one has to make many choices of issues, sources, and interpretations. Hence, this chapter is not a comprehensive "authoritative" survey of every aspect related to the religious culture of the early medieval West; rather it focuses on several significant issues that will highlight the problems inherent in the topic, and will provide a sufficient basis for further discussion.

Some Preliminary Historiographical Observations

In his attempt to define and characterize psychoanalysis *Weltanschauung*, Sigmund Freud provided us with both an acute and a bold appraisal of religion as a cultural system:

> Of the three powers [i.e. art, philosophy, and religion], which may dispute the basic position of science, religion alone is to be taken seriously as an enemy. Art is almost always harmless and beneficent; it does not seek to be anything but an illusion. Except for a few people who are spoken of as being "possessed" by art, it makes no attempt at invading the realm of reality. Philosophy is not opposed to science, it behaves like science and works in part by the same methods; it departs from it, however, by clinging to the illusion of being able to present a picture of the universe which is without gaps and is coherent, though one which is bound to collapse with every fresh advance in our knowledge. . . . But philosophy has no direct influence on the great mass of mankind; it is of interest to only a small number even of the top layer of intellectuals and is scarcely intelligible to anyone else. On the other hand, religion is an immense power, which has the strongest emotions of human beings at its service. It is well known that at an earlier date it comprises everything that played an intellectual part in men's lives, that it took the place of science when there was scarcely yet such a thing as science, and that it constructed a *Weltanschauung*, consistent and self-contained to an unparalleled degree, which, although it has been profoundly shaken, persists to this day.[1]

Notwithstanding the fact that Freud's views on religion were admittedly sketchy and hostile, it would be useless to impugn his observations, especially since, despite the passage of time and his own bias, they remain fundamentally sound.

The words cited above were written by Freud at a time when religion was gradually being integrated into the mainstream of medieval history. One of the first medievalists to do so was the German historian Herbert Grundmann, whose book on the religious movement in the Middle Ages was a turning point in the way historians treated religious issues in their research.[2] Religion was understood by Herbert Grundmann as an essential component in the formation of culture and society, without which no comprehensive understanding of the medieval world is possible. Consequently, religion emerged as a legitimate field of historical inquiry, and medievalists throughout the world have paid more attention to religious factors. At first, scholars concentrated on orthodox Christian phenomena, examining issues of theology, papal history, and doctrinal development. The inevitable result was a romanticized image of medieval Christianity, in which Christian unity, philosophical theology, and papal dominance were the leitmotivs. However, this romanticized image of medieval Christianity was rightly questioned by many scholars in the second half of the twentieth century. Under the influence of modern anthropology and sociology, historians realized that other forms of religious observance and convictions, which departed from the official-intellectual interpretation of Christianity, were not less important for the understanding of medieval culture and society. Thus, topics such as heresies, popular religions, and folkloric traditions were also investigated.[3]

This new trend in medieval history, initiated mainly by French scholars from the *Annales* school, enriched the narrow perspective of medieval Christianity and, as could only be expected, was harshly criticized by some conservative historians. For example, John Van Engen, who bluntly and without any qualm declares that "in medieval Christendom, religious culture rested ultimately on the 'faith' or 'belief,' meaning professed assent to certain propositions as well as inner conviction," laments the fact that "doctrinal disputes and papal policies have given way to relics, the cult of the saints, pilgrimages, miracles, purgatory and the like" – a historiographical tendency that he regards as a "dramatic shift downward."[4]

John Van Engen is right in criticizing the dichotomous view, which attempts to distinguish clearly between "elite" and "popular" religions as parts of separate cultural systems. Yet his own understanding of "medieval Christendom" as an ordered and harmonious culture, which conforms to the articulated belief system of an ecclesiastical elite, seems to me extremely naïve and anachronistic.[5] Modern research had made it clear that any attempt to define medieval Christianity in terms of dichotomy, or in terms of articulated beliefs, is a drastic simplification of a much more complicated situation. In order to understand, or at least to begin to understand, medieval Christianity one has to take into account both the official-clerical representation of Christianity, and its more "popular," sometime even unorthodox, manifestations. Only then does a richer and more nuanced picture begin to emerge. Scholars in the past decades have realized that much can be gained from a subtle and sympathetic investigation of said phenomena, and much research has been done in an attempt to understand and delineate the various intertwined components that make medieval religious culture.

Since the 1980s, it has become standard for scholars who study the interaction between culture and religion in the medieval West to look at both the "official" and the more "popular" manifestations of religio-cultural phenomena, which sometimes overlap and sometimes work in two parallel spheres. However, two conceptual problems have emerged over the years, and both should be mentioned briefly here. First, many scholars, especially in the German-speaking world, have favored the view that characterizes certain aspects of early medieval religion as being "archaic" and gradually moving toward spirituality and secularization.[6] This view was clearly formulated as an antithesis to the "Germanic" interpretation, which speaks of the "Germanization" of early medieval Christianity. It goes without saying that the issue of the "Germanization of Christianity," favored especially by German scholars before 1945, was closely linked with National Socialism, and has now been almost completely abandoned by modern scholars.[7] Nevertheless, the alternative "archaic" interpretation is not completely convincing either. "Archaism" is a long-term, *religionsgeschichtlich* way to evaluate or categorize. But those who used it in the study of culture and religion inadvertently transferred a term that is useful in some way for a long-term developmental scheme into a shorter-term scheme. Thus, they are using a developmental term typologically, and this is quite problematic. I personally prefer the notion of "enforced adaptation" so masterfully discussed by Peter Brown in his book on the rise of Christendom in Late Antiquity and the early Middle Ages.[8]

The second point is the phenomenological approach pursued by some historians of religious culture. It is a well-known fact that, from the moment Gerardus van der Leeuw introduced phenomenology to religious studies,[9] a clear dichotomy has characterized the study of religions. On the one hand stands the "systematic–phenomenological" approach to religion, which tends to focus on the synchronic elements of religion, describing and categorizing religious phenomena, while neglecting the diachronic, formative aspects – that is, the particular historical, cultural, and social contexts of these phenomena.[10] On the other hand stands the "idiographic-historical" approach. Needless to say this dichotomy satisfied no one, but, once formulated, it set the tone for the entire discipline of *Religionswissenschaft*.[11] Many studies of culture and religion in the early medieval West opted for classical phenomenology, and therefore some historians may find them too phenomenological. More attention to the contextual (both historical and cultural) aspects would make any study in the field more comprehensive and convincing. Having said that, let us plunge into the murky waters of early medieval religious culture.

Paganism, Christianity, and the Conversion of Europe

Early medieval society has traditionally been described as Christian by name, but pagan by practice, in which non-Christian rituals and superstitions were rife. This derogatory view was partly conditioned by the traditional definition of conversion, but it also derives from our sources, which mention numerous "non-Christian" practices and classify them as "pagan." But are we to understand these descriptions at face value? Could it be that the sources' campaign against pagan practices and superstitions tells us more about the authors' worries and anxieties than about the actual survival of pagan religions among the newly converted inhabitants of Western Europe?

Although most scholars agree nowadays that by the end of the sixth century the vast majority of the inhabitants of Western Europe were, in fact, baptized Christians, there is little consensus regarding the degree to which Christianity had been adopted by them. On the one hand, some historians have argued that conversion to Christianity includes very little apart from two obvious things – baptism and the renunciation of all pagan gods and worship rituals. According to these criteria, Western Europe of the early Middle Ages was indeed a Christian society. On the other hand, it has been argued that true conversion entails a change in every aspect of the individual's life, thought, and belief. Arthur Darby Nock, for example, has written in his 1933 vanguard study of conversion: "By conversion we mean the reorientation of the soul of an individual, his deliberate turning from indifference or from an earlier form of piety to another, a turning which implies a consciousness that a great change is involved, that the old was wrong and the new is right."[12] Subsequently, Ramsey MacMullen believed that "so disturbing and difficult must be conversion, or so incomplete."[13] According to Nock, MacMullen, and many others, early medieval Europe was, perhaps, Christian by name, but still pagan by practice and spirit.

However, to understand conversion as "the reorientation of the soul of the individual" and "the adhesion of the will to a theology" is to impose modern perceptions on the past. It further assumes deep knowledge and understanding of Christianity's theology and doctrine on the side of the people. Yet very few Christians have ever attained deep and thorough theological understanding like Saint Augustine (d. 430), and to judge the conversion of a society according to an Augustinian yardstick is, to my mind, misleading. The Christianity of the "ordinary" men and women, which manifested itself mainly in ritual acts and participation in ceremonies, was not the Christianity of theologians, and it is unreasonable to expect a total reorientation of the soul, and a complete adhesion to a theology.

In order to demonstrate how complex and multilayered the question of conversion is, and how vaguely it is represented in our sources, let us take the practice of divination by casting lots (*sortes*), which was unequivocally condemned as a pagan superstition by various Christian authors and policymakers.[14] For example, in the first council of Orléans, which was convened in 10 July 511 at the initiative of King Clovis (d. 511),[15] the Merovingian bishops resolved (among other things) that:

> If any cleric, monk or laymen shall think he should observe divination or auguries or casting the lots (*sortes*), which they say are "of the saints" (*sanctorum*) to whomever they should believe they should make them known, they are to be expelled from the Church's communion with those who believe in them.[16]

This resolution was subsequently repeated by several regional and "national" Church councils, such as the diocesan council of Auxerre (561–605),[17] which declared:

> It is forbidden to turn to soothsayers or to augurs, or to those who pretend to know the future, or to look at what they call "the lots of the saints" (*sortes sanctorum*), or those they make of wood or bread. But whatever a man wishes to do, let him do it in the Name of God.[18]

Moreover, it was further recycled by many penitentials, such as the one appended to the *Bobbio Missal* and dated to around 700:[19]

> If anyone consult what is called without reason "lots of the saints" (*sortes sanctorum*) or any other lots (*sortes*), she/he shall do penance for three years, one [of which] on bread and water.[20]

These canons are simple and straightforward. They rule against any form of divination or fortune telling, and they clearly associate the use of the *sortes* with unorthodox superstitious behavior, a reminiscent survival of the pagan past. Modern historians followed suit, and, taking these condemnations at face value, argued for the persistence of pagan religious practices among the newly converted Christians. By doing this, they failed to take into account "the sheer vitality of non-religious, secular institutions and traditions and their power to resist change.'[21] True, divinations had some pagan religious meanings in both the Roman and the Germanic past. But, when performed in sixth-century Francia, the various divination practices mentioned above were part of a social behavior, completely detached from its original pagan connotations. This notion gets an impressive support from numerous contemporary sources.

In his *Ten Books of History*, Gregory of Tours (d. 594) relates how Merovech, King Chilperic's son, consulted the *sortes* to check whether he would inherit his father's kingdom, as was predicted by a certain female soothsayer:

> Merovech had no faith in Guntram's soothsayer. He placed three books on the Saint's [i.e. St Martin's] tomb, the Psalter, the Book of Kings, and the Gospels: then he spent the whole night in prayer, beseeching the holy confessor to show him what was going to happen and to indicate clearly whether or not he would be allowed to inherit the kingship. He spent three days and nights in fasting, vigil and supplication: then he went up to the tomb and open the first volume, which was the Book of Kings. This was the first verse on the page which he opened: "Because thou hast forsaken the Lord thy God and hast taken hold upon other gods and hast not walked uprightly before him, the Lord thy God will deliver thee into the hands of thy enemies" [1 Kings 9: 9]. He found the following verse in the Psalms: "Surely thou didst set them slippery places, thou castedst them down into destruction. How are they brought into desolation, as in a moment! They are utterly consumed because of their iniquities" (Psalms 73: 18–19]. This was what he found in the Gospels: "Ye know that after two days in the feast of the Passover, and the son of man is betrayed to be crucified" [Matthew 26: 2]. Merovech was dismayed by these answers and for a long time he wept at the tomb of the Holy bishop.[22]

This is by no means the only example for the use of the *sortes* in a utterly Christian disguise found in the our sources. In the middle of the struggle between King Lothar I (d. 561) and his rebellious son Chramn (d. 560), to give just one more example, the *sortes* were consulted again, this time in an attempt to reach a political decision:

> [The] priests placed three books on the altar, the Prophets, the epistles and the Gospels. They prayed to the Lord that in His divine power He would reveal to them what would happen to Chramn, whether he would ever prosper and whether or not he would come to the throne. At the same time they agreed among themselves that each should read at Mass whatever he found when he first opened the book. The Book of the Prophets was opened first. There they found: "I will take away the hedge thereof, and it shall be eaten up. When I looked that it should bring forth grapes, it brought forth wild grapes" [Isaiah 4: 4–5]. Then the Book of the Apostle was opened and they found this: "For yourselves know perfectly that the day of the Lord so cometh as a thief in the night. For when they shall say, peace and safety; then sudden destruction cometh upon them, as travail upon a woman with child; and they shall not escape" [1 Thessalonians 5: 2–3]. Finally the Lord spoke through the Gospel: "And every one that heareth these sayings of mine, and doeth them not, shall be likened unto a foolish man, which built his house upon the sand. And the rain descended, and the floods came, and the winds blew, and beat upon that house, and it fell, and great was the fall of it" [Matthew 7: 26–7]. Chramn was welcomed in his churches by the Bishop whom I have named and he was allowed to take communion.[23]

If the former incident could be dismissed as a deviant aberration, brought about by Merovech's own distress and insecurity, the latter is much more compelling. It was the priests of Dijon cathedral who consulted the *sortes*, and Gregory found nothing wrong in it. Moreover, he did not even mention the fact that both Meroverch and the clergy of Dijon ignored the unambiguous conciliar decrees mentioned above, which clearly condemn the use of what may be defined as "a Christianized form of the pagan *sortes*." Could it be that Gregory, the famous bishop of Tours, understood the use of the *sortes* as a harmless and non-threatening superstitious practice that has nothing to do with religious beliefs or pagan cults?

The two incidents reported by Gregory and cited above raise a whole series of problems concerning the artificiality, in a sense, of written models and traditions. Bearing in mind the various practices and beliefs that were condemned by our Christian sources as "pagan" or "superstitious," one may ask what relationship the resurfacing of such practices bears to changing realities. Are we to understand the preoccupation of our early medieval sources with pagan practices and superstitions and their repetitive condemnations as a reflection of the reality the authors seem to describe?

Whenever this question and its implications are discussed, two names are constantly mentioned – Dieter Harmening and Jean-Claude Schmitt. Harmening argues that the repetitions and copying of certain texts are a clear sign of submission to literary conventions (*topoi*), and thus abolish any documentary value of the texts in question.[24] Schmitt, on the other hand, argues that such repetitions proved the continued existence of certain practices or beliefs, and therefore present an accurate reflection of reality.[25] Although one has to acknowledge that both Harmening and Schmitt have some strong points in support of their arguments, neither position is completely convincing. A combination of the two is needed in order to understand the texts with which we are dealing. No doubt the repetition of various unauthorized observances, such as the use of the *sortes biblicae* or the *sortes sanctorum* and their classification as "pagan" or "superstitious," is, in a sense, the result of some well-rooted literary conventions. Yet, at the same time, the preoccupation with pagan practices and superstitions in our sources reflects a certain reality. This reality was a mental reality rather than a practical one, and therefore these texts and condemnations should be regarded as evidence for what the people who wrote them thought ought to be prohibited. They should be regarded as evidence for norms, not documentary facts.

From the fourth century onwards, various practices, which the Christian authorities could not abolish, transform, or control, were defined by Christian authors as "pagan." Hence, a certain image of what is "pagan" emerged in the writings of Christians, such as Ambrose of Milan, Jerome, and Augustine, and this image was later used and recycled by preachers, theologians, missionaries, and legislators. Needless to say, the image that emerges from these writings was far from being an accurate description of an actual reality. But it helped Christianity to set up clear-cut boundaries by defining what is permitted from a Christian point of view and what is not. More often than not, the past practices that survive the conversion of the West had no religious meaning any more. And yet, they were a crucial part of Christianity's view of paganism, and consequently of itself. To paraphrase Robert Markus, the condemnation of pre-Christian patterns of behavior helped to define the identity of the Christian community, united with its bishop under a shared loyalty and value system.[26] Hence, we should be extremely cautious when attributing the label "pagan" to social customs practiced by people converted to Christianity. Not everything that survives from the pagan past or described in our sources as superstitious retained its pagan religious meaning, and in fact many of the practices condemned in the early Middle Ages as "pagan" did not necessarily bear the heavy charge of religious significance one might attribute to them in a different context.

The Threefold Liturgical Cycle

Early medieval Europe was, by and large, an agrarian society that lived according to the seasonal cycle even after the introduction of Christianity. Nevertheless, the Christian liturgical cycle became an important factor in everyday life, and local churches throughout Europe strove to create an essentially Christian rhythm that was to replace the pagan sequence of festivals. The agrarian cycle, one should stress, was never abolished. It continued to punctuate the life of the people along the Christian cycle, with some points of connection, such as Easter, which often coincided with the spring harvest. But, from the moment that a Christian rhythm was established, the pace of life even in those agrarian societies was clearly measured against a Christian scale. Let us, then, look at the threefold cycle of the Christian liturgy in an attempt to appreciate its crucial role in the formation of early medieval culture and religion.

In a series of sermons delivered to the Christian community of fifth-century Rome, Pope Leo the Great (d. 461) made a noteworthy attempt to shape the lives of Rome's inhabitants by public liturgical worship. As pointed out by Robert Markus: "What Leo's preaching to his Roman congregations reveals is an overriding concern to draw them into the rhythm of the Church's public worship. Time and again he is trying to awaken in his audience a sense of the moment in the sacred time-scheme whose deep rhythms he wishes to reverberate in the hearts and the minds of his hearers."[27] Hence, the Christianization of time became an integral part of Rome's evangelization strategy, and Leo's initiatives set the tone for many a generation of popes and clergymen.

One of Leo's most influential followers was Pope Gregory the Great (d. 604), who set up a papal scheme to Christianize time. After encouraging a ruthless confrontational process in the conversion of pagans, Gregory suddenly realized that a lenient flexible approach might be much more effective. "Because they [i.e. the Anglo-Saxons] are in the habit of slaughtering much cattle as sacrifices to devils," he wrote in his famous letter to Abbot Mellitus (d. 624), "some solemnity ought to be given them in exchange for this. So on the day of the dedication or the festivals of the holy martyrs, whose relics are deposited there, let them make themselves huts from the branches of trees around the churches which have been converted out of shrines, and let them celebrate the solemnity with religious feasts."[28] Hence, according to Gregory's new approach, the Christianization of time was perceived as a crucial prerequisite for the success of any mission, and consequently both missionaries and clergymen made a constant effort to formulate a Christian calendar for their communities. This was done by the introduction of the so-called Christian temporal cycle and more so by the introduction of sanctoral cycles, which were more local in nature and changed through time.

The temporal cycle of liturgy commemorates the events in Christ's life. It consists of two sequences of celebrations: one focuses on Christ's birth and is fixed in the Roman calendar, (that is, Advent, Christmas Day on 25 December, the *Circumcisio Domini* on 1 January, and the Epiphany on 6 January); the other focuses on Christ's death and resurrection, whose dates must be computed each year according to the lunar calendar (that is, Lent, Holy Week and Easter Day, as well as Ascension Day and Pentecost). The core of these celebrations was the mass, which was at the time the most important rite offered by the Church, and the only one our early medieval sources mention as obligatory on Christmas, Easter, and Pentecost.[29]

The congregation, which normally stood, filling up the church, had an important role in the celebration of the mass. Their role was not passive, as some may think, but a very active one. They had to respond to the celebrant and the clergy several times, they had to sing several hymns and antiphons, and at the end of the celebration they had to proceed to the altar in order to receive the sacrament. The mass also had a didactic aspect, embodied in the sermon given by the celebrant, as well as a certain cathartic effect that offered the believers some psychological relief. And yet the mass was, first and foremost, an important social event. People gathered in church not only to pray, but also to meet each other, to chatter, to discuss business, and to settle disputes. All these elements transformed the mass on major feast days into one of the most important components in the religious culture of the early medieval West.

If the temporal cycle of liturgy was fixed, with minimal place for changes and local variations, the sanctoral cycle offered each and every Christian community an opportunity to shape its own liturgical pace. Originating from the commemoration of the victims of the Roman persecutions, the cult of the saints grew in scope and importance far beyond a mere commemoration of the dead. Each year more names were added to the list of saints, and from the beginning of the fourth century onwards this list was enriched by the names of hermits, monks and nuns, bishops and abbots, who, as Isidore of Seville (d. 636) put it, "if a period of persecution had occurred, could have been martyrs."[30] The cult of the saints spread from the East into the West at a fairly early stage, and it did not take long before it gained a central position in the popular devotion and the religious culture of early medieval Europe. This process, one should stress, did not happen instantly or uniformly throughout Western Europe. Each region had its own pace and intensity, each church had its own peculiar saints, and no uniformity ever existed.

Let us take, for example, the sanctoral cycle of Arles in southern Gaul. Very few saints were venerated in Arles in the late fifth century, and only one of them can be identified as a local saint (Honoratus (d. 429)). This situation changed dramatically under Bishop Caesarius (d. 542) and his successor, Aurelianus (d. 551), who built churches, collected relics, instituted new saints' feasts, and constantly preached the Christian faith to the inhabitants of city and its environs. During their episcopacy, the number of saints venerated in Arles continuously multiplied, and by the mid-sixth century the sanctoral cycle of Arles was composed of feasts in honor of more than twenty-five saints, several of which were bishops, clerics, abbots, and monks in the region.[31] There is no way to gauge how many of these saints were solemnly venerated. But even if not all the saints' days that are mentioned in our sources were celebrated in Arles with a pompous feast, it seems only fair to conclude that the annual cycle of Arles was punctuated with various local liturgical feasts.

The sanctoral cycle of Arles is extremely revealing in another aspect as well. The exact date of the saints' death was not always known. However, the day of the relics' translation and deposition in the church, which eventually became the day on which the saint was venerated, could be planned carefully, and the sanctoral cycle of Arles shows some signs toward this direction. Three feasts in honor of local saints were assigned in Arles to the end of August, maybe in an attempt to create a cluster of local liturgical celebrations. This tendency was not unique to Arles, and it intensified throughout the latter part of the sixth century, as can be deduced from other examples. An excellent case in point is the sanctoral cycle of Auxerre in Burgundy. By the beginning of the seventh century twelve feasts in honor of local saints were celebrated in Auxerre during the month of May,[32] and this attempt to turn the month of May into a prolonged period of liturgical celebrations in the city suggests that the Christian authorities in Auxerre used and manipulated the various saints' feasts in order to Christianize time. This is exactly what Gregory the Great had in mind when he advised Mellitus that "on the day of the dedication or the festivals of the holy martyrs . . . let them make themselves huts from the branches of trees around the churches which have been converted out of shrines, and let them celebrate the solemnity with religious feasts."[33] It is, then, not at all surprising that missionaries were equipped with long lists of potential saints' feasts. The so-called Calendar of Saint Willibrord, to give just one example, lists more than a hundred saints' feasts.[34] At any given moment a Christian feast could be found in order to replace a pagan celebration, or a celebration thought to be pagan by the Church and its representatives.

The third liturgical cycle – that is, the personal cycle – is perhaps the most significant one. It gives us a rare glimpse of the religious culture and habits of the ordinary people, and it clearly reveals how deeply Christianity had infiltrated into every aspect of everyday life. The individual life cycle in the early Middle Ages was punctuated by various events that mark significant social, religious, and personal changes in life. It could only be expected that Christianity, which had only recently got a stronghold in society, would strive to gain control over these crucial junctions in the personal life cycle, and to provide them with a Christian religious context, if not a proper Christian meaning. A careful examination of the various liturgical sources reveals that, throughout the period with which we are concerned (roughly from the fourth till the ninth century), the individual life experience witnessed a dramatic Christian makeover. Slowly but surely Christianity became a crucial component in shaping the people's social practices and attitudes. A nice example is provided by the concept of marriage.

The best evidence for the Christianization of marriage in the early Middle Ages comes from a series of sacramentaries that were composed in Italy, Frankish Gaul, and Visigothic Spain. The following prayer, for instance, was incorporated into the Verona collection of *libelli missarum* (dated to the second half of the sixth century), and was subsequently copied into the so-called Old Gelasian Sacramentary (dated to the mid-eighth century):

> We ask you, O Lord, to look with favour on this offering of your maidservant. We humbly beseech your majesty on her behalf that just as you have granted her to reach the proper age for marriage, once she has been joined in the marital union through your gift, you may enable her to rejoice in the offspring she desires and may graciously bring to her and to her husband the length of years that they desire. Through . . .[35]

This and similar prayers from the various sacramentaries clearly indicate that a valiant effort was made to adapt the rite of marriage to a Christian context, and it may well be that the ceremony was moved altogether to the church and that an entire mass was sung in honor of the occasion.

Although the decree *Tametsi* of the council of Trent (1563) was the first to recognize the rite of marriage as a sacrament, this was the result of a long process that started with the Christianization of everyday life in late antiquity and the early Middle Ages. The works of Christian scholars, such as Tertullian (d. *c.* 230) and especially Augustine (d. 430), paved the way for such a change, and already by the ninth century marriage was perceived as a sacrament by Hincmar of Rheims (d. 882). This conceptual change had a dramatic effect on the ceremony that was celebrated, as the various matrimonial prayers and masses in early medieval sacramentaries clearly suggest. Although we cannot be sure that a Christian ceremony was performed every time a couple was married in the early Middle Ages, the fact that a Christian rite had already existed is extremely significant in itself.

Other prayers in various sacramentaries tell a very similar story. The Old Gelasian Sacramentary, for example, contains numerous prayers for domestic affairs, such as a mass to encourage rain, an oration to be said after a storm, or benedictions to ensure good crop. Some prayers were dedicated to medical problems, such as women's sterility, and a few were meant to ensure the health of all family members. Prayers to be said on the occasion of visiting a new house, as well as masses to secure the well-being and safe return of travellers, were also included in early medieval prayer books. Indeed Christianity had infiltrated every corner of the human life.

Religion and Political Ideology

The last issue I wish to discuss here is the interaction between religion and political ideology. The early medieval rulers of the post-Roman world inherited the Roman-imperial tradition of political thought, and subsequently rulers were described in traditional imperial nomenclature and addressed in the reverential language that has customarily been employed to address the emperor. At the same time, Roman-imperial ideals were gradually infiltrated into the various statements on the virtues that a good king should display. Yet, in the later Roman period, and more so in the sixth and the seventh centuries, Roman was inherently Christian. Hence, when Christian authors, such as Cassiodorus (d. 585), addressed their Barbarian rulers (whether Arian or Catholic) in traditional Roman-imperial language, they automatically defined their status – or rather their political ideology – in Christian terms. Thus, already by the sixth century Christian ideas and notions were an integral part of the so-called early medieval perception of kingship, and this trend was intensified during the seventh and early eighth centuries.[36]

One significant effect of this process was the frequent recourse to biblical examples and citations, which denote the Christian complexion of the newly formed political thought. It was not to Byzantium that early medieval authors looked for a royal model, but to the Bible, and more particularly to the historical books of the Old Testament. Another manifestation of the Christianization of early medieval rulership, at least in Francia, was the emergence of the royal patronage of liturgy. Large amounts of landed property, precious objects, and various immunities were bestowed by Frankish kings and queens upon monasteries and religious communities in order to secure their spiritual support. It is, then, no mere coincidence that many of the liturgical books from early medieval Europe contain prayers for the well-being of the king and his kingdom. For example, the Old Gelasian Sacramentary contains the following mass for the king:

> O God, protector of all the kingdoms and of the greatest Roman empire, let your servants N., our kings, adorn the triumph of your virtue skilfully, so that they, who are *principes* by your command, may always be powerful in their duty.
>
> O God, in whose hand lay the hearts of the kingdoms, lend the ears of your compassion to our humble prayers and give the guidance of your wisdom to our *principes*, your servants, so that drinking from your fountain for their assemblies they may please you and may rise above all the kingdoms.
>
> SECRET: Accept, O Lord, the supplicant prayers and sacrifice of your Church for the safety of N., your servant, and work the old miracles of your arm for the protection of the faith of the people, so that after the enemies of peace are surpassed, the secure Roman freedom may serve you.
>
> DURING THE ACT: Thus, O Lord, accept this oblation of your servant N., which we offer you by the ministry of the sacerdotal office, just as you regarded it worthy to bestow upon him the power of ruling, gracious and generous [as you are] receive [him under your protection]; and implored grant our entreaty, so that confident in the protection of your majesty, he may be blessed with age and kingdom.
>
> AFTER COMMUNION: O God, who prepared the eternal Roman empire by evangelical predicting, present the celestial arms to your servants N., our *princeps*, so that the peace of the churches may not be troubled by the storm of wars.[37]

These prayers, which are, to my mind, the most eloquent witness to the Christianization of the concept of rulership, beseech God to protect the kingdom's peace, to secure its stability, and to grant victory to the ruler. Not only were these prayers an emotional appeal for God's protection; they also disseminate what appears to be an utterly Christian political ideology. Although the formula *rex Dei gratia* was not yet used by our early medieval kings and their advisers, its notion was already embedded in the various masses for the kings adduced above.

When in 751 Pippin III (d. 768) assumed power over the Frankish kingdom, he simply continued the religious policy of his early medieval predecessors and propagated the very same Christian ideology of rulership. But as they did in so many matters, the Carolingians operated on a much more grandiose scale. It is enough to mention the immense effort taken by Pippin III, Charlemagne, and their successors to organize stupendous rituals and liturgical ceremonies to realize that from a fairly early stage Carolingian politics was accompanied by a massive downpour of rhetoric that highlighted, among other things, a Christian theocratic concept of rulership. Biblical examples, once again, offered an attractive general model, and as early as 775 Charlemagne (d. 814) was addressed as both David and Solomon.[38] Subsequently, this rhetoric gave rise to one of the standard tropes of Frankish political ideology under the Carolingians – that is, the equation of the Franks with the chosen people of the Old Testament – the New Israel.[39]

To sum up, as I have noted at the very beginning of this chapter, the interaction between religion and culture is one of the most significant and more elusive topics in the history of the early medieval West. There is no straightforward definition of what religious culture consists, nor do scholars agree about the degree to which religion, and more precisely Christianity, infiltrated and influenced the transformation of the post-Roman world. The two extreme views of conversion adduced above leave much to be desired. Neither is sufficient on its own to describe the complicated and most colorful situation of early medieval Europe. Although not altering completely the lives of the people, the new religion had an undeniable significant impact on the individual's life, and on society as a whole. True, this was not always a total "reorientation of the soul" accompanied by deep and thorough theological understanding, as envisaged by Nock, but certainly it entailed much more than just baptism and official renunciation of past beliefs.

Notes

1 Freud, "The Question of *Weltanschauung*," pp. 195–6. This collection of lectures was first published in Vienna in 1933. Such issues are discussed in Hen, "Arnold Angenendt's History of Medieval Religiosity."

2 Grundmann, *Religiöse Bewegungen im Mittelalter.*

3 For a penetrating short summary on the developments in historiography, see Little and Rosenwein, eds, *Debating the Middle Ages*, pp. 301–9. See also Vauchez, "Les Orientations récentes de la recherche française."

4 Van Engen, "The Christian Middle Ages," pp. 545 and 535. Van Engen refers to Jacques Le Goff and Jean-Claude Schmitt (both from the Paris École des Hautes Études en Sciences Sociales) as the main representatives of this new historiographical trend.

5 See the apposite response to Van Engen's criticism by Schmitt, *Religione, folklore e socità nell'Occidente medievale*, pp. 1–27.

6 See, e.g., Haubrichs, *Die Anfänge* and "Christentum in der Bekehrungszeit (Frömmigke itsgeschichte)"; Hattenhauer, *Europäische Rechtsgeschichte*; Angenendt, *Geschichte der Religiosität im Mittelalter.*

7 For some criticism on the concept of the "Germanisation of Christianity," see Rathofer, *Der Heliand*, pp. 51–3; Schäferdiek, "Germanisierung des Christentums." The "Germanisation of Christianity" was proposed again more recently by Russell, *The Germanisation of Early Medieval Christianity*; and see the pertinent reviews of this book by Arnold Angenendt in *Journal of Ecclesiastical History*, 49 (1998), pp. 156–7 and by Thomas F. X. Noble in *American Historical Review*, 100 (1995), pp. 888–9.

8 See Brown, *The Rise of Western Christendom.*

9 See Leeuw, *Einführung in die Phänomenologie der Religion.*

10 For a short introduction on the "phenomenological" approach to religion, see Douglas Allen, "Phenomenology of Religion."

11 See the discussion by Alles and Kitagawa, "The Dialectic of the Parts and the Whole." See also Bianchi, "History of Religions."

12 Nock, *Conversion*, pp. 7, 14.

13 MacMullen, *Christianizing the Roman Empire*, p. 74.

14 For a short introduction on the *sortes sanctorum*, see Flint, *The Rise of Magic in Early Medieval Europe*, pp. 273–86.

15 On the first Church Council of Orléans, see Pontal, *Histoire des conciles mérovingiens*, pp. 47–58.

16 *Concilium Aurelianenses I (511)*, c. 30, in Gaudemet and Basdevant, eds, *Les Canons*, vol. I, p. 88. I cite the English translation from Hillgarth, *Christianity and Paganism*, p. 103.

17 On the council of Auxerre, see Pontal, *Histoire des conciles mérovingiens*, pp. 192–3.
18 *Synodus diocesana Autissiodorensis (561–605)*, c. 4, in Gaudemet and Basdevant, eds, *Les Canons*, vol. II, p. 488; trans. Hillgath, *Christianity and Paganism*, p. 103.
19 On this penitential, see Meens, "Reforming the Clergy," and see there for further bibliography.
20 *Poenitentiale Bobbioense*, c. 26, in Lowe, ed., *The Bobbio Missal*, p. 175.
21 Markus, *The End of Ancient Christianity*, p. 9.
22 Gregory of Tours, *Libri histroiarum X*, 5.14, ed. Krusch and Levison, p. 212. I cite the English translation by Thorpe, *Gregory of Tours*, pp. 271–2.
23 Gregory of Tours, *Libri historiarum X*, 4.16, ed. Krusch and Levison, pp. 149–50; trans. Thorpe, *Gregory of Tours*, pp. 212–13.
24 Harmening, *Superstitio*, especially pp. 49–73.
25 Schmitt, "Les Superstitions" and ""Religion populaire" et culture folklorique." See also the highly controversial paper by Künzel, "Paganism, syncrétisme, et culture religieuse populaire."
26 Markus, *The End of Ancient Christianity*, p. 207.
27 Ibid., pp. 125–35; the citation is from p. 127.
28 Bede, *Historia ecclesiastica*, I. 30, ed. and trans. Colgrave and Mynors, *Bede's Ecclesiastical History*, p. 106. I cite the English translation by McClure and Collins, eds, *The Ecclesiastical History of the English People*, p. 57.
29 On the temporal cycle and the celebration of the mass, see Hen, *Culture and Religion*, pp. 61–81, and see there for further bibliography.
30 Isidore of Seville, *Etymologiae*, VII.xi.4, ed. Lindsay. I cite the translation of Barney et al., *The Etymologies of Isidore of Seville*, p. 170.
31 On the sanctoral cycle of Arles, see Hen, *Culture and Religion*, pp. 89–92.
32 On the liturgical cycle of Auxerre, see Picard, "Espace urbain et sépultures épiscopales à Auxerre" (repr. in Riché, ed., *La Christianisation*, pp. 205–2, with an updated bibliography on pp. 264–5).
33 Bede, *Historia ecclesiastica*, I.30, ed. and trans. Colgrave and Mynors, *Bede's Ecclesiastical History*, p. 106; trans. McClure and Collins, eds, *The Ecclesiastical History of the English People*, p. 57.
34 Paris, Bibliothèque nationale de France, lat. 10837, fos 34^{v}–40^{r}. *The Calendar of St Willibrord*, ed. Wilson.
35 *Sacramentarium Veronense*, XXXI.1107, ed. Mohlberg and Siffrin, p. 139; *Liber sacramentorum Romanae aecclesiae ordinis anni circuli (Sacramentarium Gelasianum)*, III. lii.1147, ed. Mohlber, Eizenhöfer, and Siffrin, p. 209. I cite the English translation from Hunter, *Marriage in the Early Church*, p. 150. Verona collection of *libelli missarum*: Verona, Biblioteca Capitolare, LXXXV (80); the Old Gelasian Sacramentary: Vatican City, Biblioteca Apostolica Vaticana, Reg. lat. 316.
36 Wallace-Hadrill, *Early Germanic Kingship.*
37 *Liber sacramentorum Romanae aecclesiae ordinis anni circuli (Sacramentarium Gelasianum)*, III.62.1505–9, ed. Mohlberg et al., pp. 217–18.
38 Cathwulf, *Epistola*, ed. Dümmler, pp. 503–5.
39 Garrison, "The Franks as the New Israel?"

Bibliography

Allen, Douglas, "Phenomenology of Religion," in Mircea Eliade, ed., *The Encyclopaedia of Religion*, vol. 11 (New York and London: Macmillan, 1987), pp. 272–85.
Alles, Gregory D., and Kitagawa, Joseph M., "The Dialectic of the Parts and the Whole: Reflections on the Past, Present and Future of the History of Religions," in Joseph M.

Kitagawa, ed., *The History of Religions: Retrospect and Prospect* (New York and London: Macmillan, 1985), pp. 145–81.

Angenendt, Arnold, *Geschichte der Religiosität im Mittelalter* (Darmstadt: Primus Verlag, 1997).

Barney, Stephane A., Lewis, W. J., Beach, J. A., and Berghof, Oliver, *The Etymologies of Isidore of Seville* (Cambridge: Cambridge Univeristy Press, 2006).

Bianchi, Ugo, "History of Religions," in Mircea Eliade, ed., *The Encyclopaedia of Religion* (New York and London: Macmillan, 1987), vol. 6, pp. 399–408.

Brown, Peter *The Rise of Western Christendom: Triumph and Diversity, AD 200–1000*, 2nd edn (Oxford: Blackwell, 2003).

The Calendar of St Willibrord, ed. H. A. Wilson, Henry Bradshaw Society, 55 (London: Harrison and Sons, 1918).

Cathwulf, *Epistola*, ed. Ernst Dümmler, MGH, Epistolae 4 (Berlin: Apvd Weidmannos, 1974).

Flint, Valerie I. J., *The Rise of Magic in Early Medieval Europe* (Princeton: Princeton University Press, 1991).

Freud, Sigmund, "The Question of *Weltanschauung*," in Sigmund Freud, *New Introductory Lectures to Psychoanalysis*, trans. James Strachey, The Pelican Freud Library, 2 (Harmondsworth: Penguin, 1973), pp. 193–219.

Garrison, Mary, "The Franks as the New Israel? Education for an Identity from Pippin to Charlemagne," in Yitzhak Hen and Matthew Innes, eds, *The Uses of the Past in the Early Middle Ages* (Cambridge: Cambridge University Press, 2000), pp. 114–61.

Gaudemet, Jean, and Basdevant, Brigitte, eds, *Les Canons des conciles mérovingiens (VIe–VIIe siècles)*, 2 vols, Sources Chrétiennes, 353–354 (Paris: Cerf, 1989).

Gregory of Tours, *Libri histroiarum X*, V.14, ed. Bruno Krusch and Wilhelm Levison, MGH SRM I.1 (Hanover: Impensis Bibliopolii Hahniani, 1951).

Grundmann, Herbert, *Religiöse Bewegungen im Mittelalter. Untersuchungen über die geschichtlichen Zusammenhänge zwischen der Kezerei, den Bettelorden und der religiösen Frauenbewegung im 12. und 13. Jahrhundert und über die geschichtlichen Grundlagen der deutschen Mystik* (Berlin: E. Ebering, 1935); English translation: *Religious Movements in the Middle Ages: The Historical Links between Heresy, the Mendicant Orders, and the Women's Religious Movement in the Twelfth and Thirteenth Century, with the Historical Foundations of German Mysticism*, trans. Steven Rowan (Notre Dame, IN: University of Notre Dame Press, 1995).

Harmening, Dieter, *Superstitio. Überlieferungs- und theoriegeschichtliche Untersuchingen zur kritisch-theologischen Aberglaubensliteratur des Mittelalters* (Berlin: E. Schmidt, 1979).

Hattenhauer, Hans, *Europäische Rechtsgeschichte* (Heidelberg: C. F. Müller Juristischer Verlag, 1992).

Haubrichs, Wolfgang, *Die Anfänge: Versuche volkssprachlicher Schriftlichkeit im frühen Mittelalter (ca. 700–1050/60)*, Geschichte der deutschen Literatur, I:1 (Frankfurt: Athenäum, 1988).

Haubrichs, Wolfgang, "Christentum in der Bekehrungszeit (Frömmigkeitsgeschichte)," in *Reallexikon der germanistischen Altertumskunde*, vol. 4 (Berlin and New York: De Gruyter, 1981), pp. 510–57.

Hen, Yitzhak, *Culture and Religion in Merovingian Gaul, AD 481–751* (Leiden, New York, and Cologne: E. J. Brill, 1995).

Hen, Yitzhak "Arnold Angenendt's History of Medieval Religiosity," *Revue belge de philologie et d'histoire*, 77 (1999), pp. 473–9.

Hillgarth, J. N., *Christianity and Paganism, 350–750: The Conversion of Western Europe*, rev. edn (Philadelphia: University of Pennsylvania Press, 1986).

Isidore of Seville, *Etymologiae*, VII.xi.4, ed. Wallace M. Lindsay (Oxford: Oxford University Press, 1911).

Künzel, Rudi, "Paganism, syncrétisme, et culture religieuse populaire au haut Moyen Ages: Réflexions et méthodes," *Annales ESC*, 47 (1992), pp. 1055–69.

Liber sacramentorum Romanae Aeclesiae ordinis anni circuli: Cod. Vat. Reg. lat. 316, Paris Bibl. Nat. 7193, 41/56 (Sacramentarium Gelasianum), ed. Leo Eizenhöfer, Petrus Siffrin and Leo Cunibert Mohlberg (Rome: Herder, 1981).

Little, Lester K., and Rosenwein, Barbara H., eds, *Debating the Middle Ages: Issues and Readings* (Oxford: Blackwell, 1998).

Lowe, E. A., ed., *The Bobbio Missal: A Gallican Mass-Book*, Henry Bradshaw Society, 58 (London: Henry Bradshaw Society Publications, 1920).

McClure, Judith, and Collins, Roger, eds and intro., *The Ecclesiastical History of the English People; The Greater Chronicle; Bede's letter to Egbert* (Oxford: Oxford University Press, 1994).

MacMullen, Ramsay, *Christianizing the Roman Empire, AD 100–400* (New Haven and London: Yale University Press, 1984).

Markus, Robert A., *The End of Ancient Christianity* (Cambridge: Cambridge University Press, 1990).

Meens, R., "Reforming the Clergy: A Context for the Use of the Bobbio Penitential," in Yitzhak Hen and Rob Meens, eds, *The Bobbio Missal: Liturgy and Religious Culture in Merovingian Gaul* (Cambridge: Cambridge University Press, 2004), pp. 154–67.

Nock, Arthur Darby, *Conversion: The Old and the New in Religion from Alexander the Great to Augustine of Hippo* (Oxford: Oxford University Press, 1933).

Picard, Jean-Charles, "Espace urbain et sépultures épiscopales à Auxerre," *Revue d'histoire de l'Église de France*, 168 (1976), pp. 205–2 (repr. in Pierre Riché, ed., *La Christianisation des pays entre Loire et Rhin (IVe–VIIe siècle)* (Paris: Cerf, 1993), pp. 205–2, with an updated bibliography on pp. 264–5).

Pontal, Odette, *Histoire des conciles mérovingiens* (Paris: Éditions du Cerf; Institut de la Recherche et de histoire des textes (CNRS), 1989).

Rathofer, Johannes, Der Heliand: *Theologischer Sinn als tektonische Form. Vorbereitung und Grundlegung der Interpretation* (Cologne: Böhlau, 1962).

Riché, Pierre, ed., *La Christianisation des pays entre Loire et Rhin (IVe–VIIe siècle)* (Paris: Cerf, 1993).

Russell, James C., *The Germanization of Early Medieval Christianity: A Sociohistorical Approach to Religious Transformation* (New York and Oxford: Oxford University Press, 1994).

Sacramentarium Veronense, ed. Leo C. Mohlberg and Peter Siffrin, Rerum ecclesiasticarum documenta, series maior 1 (Rome: Herder, 1956), p. 139.

Schäferdiek, Knut, "Germanisierung des Christentums," in Gerhard Krause und Gerhard Müller, eds, *Theologische Realenzyklopädie*, vol. 12 (Berlin and New York: de Gruyter, 1984), pp. 451–524.

Schmitt, Jean-Claude, ""Religion populaire" et culture folklorique," *Annales ESC*, 31 (1976), pp. 941–53.

Schmitt, Jean-Clause, *Religione, folklore e socità nell'Occidente medievale* (Bari, 1988); English translation: "Religion, Folklore and Society in the Medieval West," in Lester K. Little and Barbara H. Rosenwein, eds, *Debating the Middle Ages: Issues and Readings* (Oxford: Blackwell, 1998), pp. 376–87.

Schmitt, Jean-Claude, "Les Superstitions," in Jacques Le Goff, ed., *Histoire de la France religieuse*, vol. 1 (Paris: Éditions du Seuil, 1988), pp. 425–53.

Thorpe, Lewis, *Gregory of Tours: History of the Franks* (Harmondsworth: Penguin, 1974).

Vauchez, André, "Les Orientations récentes de la recherche française sur l'histoire de la vie religieuse au moyen âge," *Ricerche di storia sociale e religiosa*, 40 (1991), pp. 25–44.

Van Engen, John, "The Christian Middle Ages as an Historiographical Problem," *American Historical Review*, 91 (1986), pp. 519–52.

Wallace-Hadrill, J. M., *Early Germanic Kingship in England and on the Continent* (Oxford: Oxford University Press, 1970).

Ward-Perkins, Bryan, *The Fall of Rome and the End of Civilization* (Oxford: Oxford University Press, 2005).

Wickham, Chris, *Early Medieval Italy: Central Power and Local Society 400–1000* (Ann Arbor: University of Michigan Press, 1989).

Further Reading

Robert Markus, *The End of Ancient Christianity* (Cambridge: Cambridge University Press, 1990) and Peter Brown, *The Rise of Western Christendom: Triumph and Diversity A.D. 200–1000*, 2nd ed. (Oxford: Blackwell, 2003), are exemplary in the way they portray the evolution of Christian thought and the Christianization of Western Europe in Late Antiquity and the early Middle Ages. Similarly, Walter A. Goffart, *The Narrators of Barbarian History (A.D. 418–800): Jordanes, Gregory of Tours, Bede, and Paul the Deacon* (Princeton: Princeton University Press, 1988), is a thought provoking book on the ways in which historical narratives from the early Middle Ages ought to be used and interpreted. As far as religious-cultural phenomena are concerned, Peter Brown, *The Cult of the Saint: Its Rise and Function in Latin Christianity* (Chicago: University of Chicago Press, 1981) is the most obvious starting point, not only because it is the first major study to define the cult of the saints as a religious-cultural phenomenon, but also because it is one of the first and most influential studies that brought hagiography into the frontline of historical research. Michael McCormick, *Eternal Victory: Triumphal Rulership in Late Antiquity, Byzantium, and the Early Medieval West* (Cambridge: Cambridge University Press, 1986), which looks at the interactions between ideology and ritual, demonstrates quite neatly the continuities as well as the changes that characterized the passage from Late Antiquity to the Middle Ages. Rosamond McKitterick, *The Carolingians and the Written Word* (Cambridge: Cambridge University Press, 1989) opened up a new field of studies in early medieval history, by focusing on the use of the written word in the Carolingian period. Finally, Patrick Geary, *Phantoms of Remembrance: Memory and the Oblivion at the End of the First Millennium* (Princeton: Princeton University Press, 1994) stresses the significant role of memory in the creation of historical, cultural and religious identities in the medieval West. These books may not be the last word on the topics they study, but they are all exemplary in their discussions and use of primary sources, and they all contributed immensely to our understanding of the period in question.

The amount of literature on the various topics discussed in this chapter is enormous and cannot be listed here. For some important introductory discussions, see the various chapters in the first two volumes of *The New Cambridge Medieval History, I – c. 500–c. 700*, edited by Paul Fouracre (Cambridge: Cambridge University Press, 2005) and *II – c. 700–c. 900*, edited by Rosamond McKitterick (Cambridge: Cambridge University Press, 1995). See also *The Early Middle Ages*, ed. Rosamond McKitterick (Oxford: Oxford University Press, 2001), especially the chapters by Mayke de Jong and Ian Wood. Several of the issues adduced above were discussed more fully in my *Culture and Religion in Merovingian Gaul, AD 481–751* (Leiden, New York and Cologne: E. J. Brill, 1995). Some aspects of early medieval cultural history were also surveyed in Julia M. H. Smith, *Europe after Rome: A New Cultural History, 500–1000* (Oxford: Oxford University Press, 2005). The role of kings and their courts in the cultural transformation of the early Middle Ages is discussed in my *Roman Barbarians: The Royal Court and Culture in the Early Medieval West* (London and New York: Palgrave Macmillan, 2007).

A superb introduction to the Christianization of Europe is Peter Brown's *The Rise of Western Christendom. Triumph and Diversity, A.D. 200–1000*, 2nd edn (Oxford: Blackwell, 2003). Richard Fletcher, *The Conversion of Europe: From Paganism to Christianity 371–1386 AD* (New York: HarperCollins, 1997) offers a nice overview of the process of conversion, while Ramsey MacMullen in *Christianity and Paganism in the Fourth to Eighth Centuries* (New Haven and London: Yale University Press, 1997) looks more closely at the conflict between Christianity and Paganism in the period with which we are concerned. Two collections of essays, *Christianizing Peoples and Converting Individuals*, ed. Guyda Armstrong and Ian N. Wood (Turnhout: Brepols, 2000) and *Conversion in Late Antiquity and the Early Middle Ages: Seeing and Believing*, ed. Kenneth Mills and Anthony Grafton (Rochester, NY: University of Rochester Press, 2003), contain a wide selection of more focused studies. Superstitions and pagan survivals are at the core of Valerie I. J. Flint's book *The Rise of Magic in Early Medieval Europe* (Oxford: Oxford University Press, 1991), and of Bernadette Filotas' more recent study, *Pagan Survivals, Superstitions and Popular Culture in Early Medieval Pastoral Literature* (Turnhout: Brepols, 2005). Note, however, that Flint's very inclusive definition of magic and her main thesis about the "rescue" and incorporation of previously condemned magical practices into Christianity's own world of beliefs, practices and attitudes, is highly controversial, and to my mind is utterly wrong.

Cyrille Vogel's *Medieval Liturgy: An Introduction to the Sources*, trans. and rev. William Storay and Niels Rasmussen (Washington DC: Pastoral Press, 1986) is still the best introduction to the liturgy of the early medieval West, to which one can add Eric Palazzo's lucid supplement *A History of Liturgical Books from the Beginning to the Thirteenth Century*, trans. Madeleine Beaumont (Collegeville, MN: Liturgical Press, 1993). His short book *Liturgie et société au Moyen Âge* (Paris: Aubier, 2000), offers a nice summary on the interaction between liturgy and society.

The starting point for any discussion on the cults of saints is Peter Brown's *The Cult of the Saints: Its Rise and Function in Latin Christianity* (Chicago: University of Chicago Press, 1981). Brown's theories have many followers as well as critics. For a reappraisal of his work, see the papers in a special issue of *The Journal of Early Christian Studies*, 6:3 (1998) as well as in *The Cult of Saints in Late Antiquity and the Early Middle Ages*, ed. James Howard-Johnston and Paul A. Hayward (Oxford: Oxford University Press, 1999). On the cults of saints in early medieval Gaul, see Raymond Van Dam, *Saints and their Miracles in Late Antique Gaul* (Princeton: Princeton University Press, 1993), and more recently Brigitte Beaujard, *Le culte des saints en Gaule* (Paris: Les Éditions du Cerf, 2000).

The many aspects of the personal cycle of liturgy are discussed in numerous books and papers. I should particularly like to mention here the fundamental study by Arnold Angenendt, "*Missa specialis*: Zugleich ein Beitrag zur Entstehung der

Privatmessen," *Frühmittelalterliche Studien* 17 (1983), pp. 153–221. On marriage, see Philip L. Reynolds, *Marriage in the Western Church: The Christianisation of Marriage during the Patristic and Early Medieval Period* (Leiden, New York and Cologne: E. J. Brill, 1994). On death-bed rituals, see Frederick S. Paxton, *Christianizing Death: The Creation of a Ritual Process in Early Medieval Europe* (Ithaca and London: Cornell University Press, 1990), and Megan McLaughlin, *Consorting with Saints: Prayer for the Dead in Early Medieval France* (Ithaca and London: Cornell University Press, 1994).

On the perception of kingship in Late Antiquity and the early Middle Ages, see again Michael McCormick, *Eternal Victory: Triumphal Rulership in Late Antiquity, Byzantium and the Early Medieval West* (Cambridge: Cambridge University Press, 1986). Hans H. Anton's *Fürstenspiegel und Herrscherethos in der Karolingerzeit*, Bonner Historische Forschungen, 32 (Bonn: L. Rohrscheid, 1968) is still the most comprehensive study of Carolingian political ideology. A more recent and succinct discussion of the issue is Janet L. Nelson, "Kingship and Empire in the Carolingian World," in *Carolingian Culture: Emulation and Innovation*, ed. Rosamond McKitterick (Cambridge: Cambridge University Press, 1994), pp. 52–87 (an earlier version was published as "Kingship and Empire," in *The Cambridge History of Medieval Political Thought, c. 350–c. 1450*, ed. J. H. Burns (Cambridge: Cambridge University Press, 1988), pp. 211–51). On kings and liturgy, see my *The Royal Patronage of Liturgy in Frankish Gaul to the Death of Charles the Bald (877)*, Henry Bradshaw Society, Subsidia 3 (London: The Boydell Press, 2001). On the Christianisation of kingship, see Régine Le Jan, "La sacralité de la royauté mérovingienne," *Annales: Histoire, Sciences Sociales* 6 (2003) pp. 1217–41, and compare it with my "The Christianisation of Kingship," in *Der Dynastiewechsel von 751: Vorgeschichte, Legitimationsstrategien und Erinnerung*, ed. Matthias Becher and Jörg Jarnut (Münster: Scriptorium, 2004), pp. 163–177.

Part III

Populations and the Economy

Chapter Five

Economic Takeoff and the Rise of Markets

James Paul Masschaele

Historians of Western Europe have long viewed the period from the year 1000 to the early fourteenth century as an era of profound growth and cultural vibrancy. During those centuries, Europeans constructed the great Gothic cathedrals that still grace the centers of numerous towns, and their creative genius gave birth to many institutions, such as the university and the Common Law system, that continue to influence world affairs in the twenty-first century. Most historians also believe that the flowering of medieval civilization was underwritten by rising levels of prosperity fueled by growing trade and agricultural development. Recent research has tended to confirm the economic side of this equation, with an ongoing consensus that Europe in 1300 was considerably wealthier, more densely populated, more urbanized, and more economically sophisticated than it was at the turn of the millennium.

In spite of general agreement about an overall increase in wealth and sophistication, however, there has been extensive disagreement about both the causes and the consequences of growth. Two schools of thought have dominated research during the twentieth century. The first emphasizes commercial development as the key determinant of the period's economic fortunes. Nearly a century ago, Henri Pirenne argued for the primacy of cities and long-distance mercantile trade as the engines of expansion throughout the period.[1] Pirenne's exuberant vision of economic and commercial change found support in many quarters through the interwar years and ultimately inspired Roberto Lopez's influential model of "Commercial Revolution" that placed the period's dramatic economic change alongside the better-known Industrial Revolution as a transforming event in world history.[2] Lopez drew attention to numerous advances in how trade was conducted: new methods for organizing businesses; new institutions for pooling and investing capital (including banks); new legal and contractual ways to enforce obligations (including the use of notaries); and new ways to settle debts and transmit payments across foreign borders. Collectively these changes transformed Europe from a backward and relatively impoverished continent into one of the world's most dynamic and entrepreneurial regions.

The second leading school of thought emphasizes demographic growth as the primary force influencing the economy. Michael Postan was the main advocate of this position. Postan challenged the view that economic progress was uniform and continuous throughout the period.[3] He agreed that early growth was impressive, but he saw it as unsustainable. Ultimately the benefits conferred by commercial development were swamped by a rising population. According to Postan, population grew more quickly than the economy as a whole, leading inexorably to deprivation and suffering. By the end of the thirteenth century, Postan believed, Europe had entered a period of real economic misery: More and more people had to be supported from a relatively fixed resource base, and this could be done only with lots of belt-tightening and reduced per-capita incomes. Medieval economic "growth" was thus illusory; the overall economy was certainly larger but people were not better off in 1300 than they had been in 1000.

Postan's neo-Malthusian model held great sway through much of the second half of the twentieth century, particularly among historians working on areas north of the Alps.[4] Since the 1980s, however, its influence has waned, and historians have been increasingly inclined to move commercial development back to center stage. The scholarship produced in the era of Pirenne and Lopez is still seen as relevant in this movement, but recent work has added newer theoretical models to the mix. Greater attention is now given to the institutional framework of the economy, an approach inspired by Douglass North, whose seminal works on "transaction costs" in the 1970s and 1980s gave rise to the "new institutional economics."[5] The term "transaction costs" refers to the costs associated with making sales and conducting business, including, among other things, search costs, contract enforcement costs, transport costs, insurance costs, and the cost of taxes and tariffs. Earlier scholars were aware that these costs had to be factored into their accounts of the takeoff and growth of the medieval economy, but North's model brought new clarity and energized new thinking about the intersection between politics and economics.[6] The period from *c.* 1000 to *c.* 1300, for example, saw extensive political consolidation and long periods of relative peace. Nascent states became increasingly adept at enforcing laws and maintaining order, giving traders greater security and enhancing the predictability of transaction costs. In this environment, confidence increased and people's willingness to invest and take risks went up, leading to a virtuous cycle of wealth creation and further political consolidation.

While even the followers of Postan now accept a greater role for commerce in the economy than they did a generation ago, there are still many unanswered questions about how to reconcile the renewed emphasis on commercial development with models emphasizing demographic movements. Indeed, it is still far from clear if the two models are compatible at all or how they might be reconciled with each other. Growing commercial acumen and falling transaction costs do not automatically lead to economic transformation. Even at the end of the Commercial Revolution, Europe remained predominantly a peasant society, as indeed it would continue to be for several more centuries. It is conceivable that commerce became more efficient and more sophisticated in the high Middle Ages without changing the core structure of the economy, which was rural and agrarian.[7] While conceivable, though, such a view seems unlikely. Several recent studies have demonstrated that residents of the countryside were actively involved in commerce, and the notion of a commercially-inactive rural world can no longer be taken as self-evident.[8] Medieval peasants were not isolated from markets, nor were their aspirations limited to simple subsistence.

What is still needed, however, is a thorough reassessment of the relationship between commercial development and population growth.[9] Clearly, both were prominent aspects of economic change in the period. But the specific mechanics of the relationship have never been carefully studied. Did population growth and commercial development operate independently or were they mutually dependent? If they were co-dependent, how exactly did they relate to each other? Some elements of the relationship are obvious and have come in for scrutiny in earlier literature. The growth in urban population, for example, is generally understood as a process involving substantial immigration from the countryside, and historians have generally presupposed that rural population growth pushed people from the countryside into the towns. Similarly, the fact that peasants were often paying a portion of their rent in money already in the tenth century – in addition to payments in kind and in labor – suggests that money was circulating in the countryside early on and therefore that peasants had some degree of commercial involvement even at the very beginning of the great cycle of growth that transformed medieval society in the high Middle Ages.

But the issue is not really whether there was some kind of modest trickle-down effect linking commerce and population; the central issue is whether the two were related in a more systematic way, one that was powerful enough to end the prolonged slump that characterized the economy of the early Middle Ages and ultimately to generate the surge of the twelfth and thirteenth centuries. While it is true that the earlier period is now often seen in a more positive light, it is still nonetheless true that by comparison with what went before and what came after, the period from *c.* 500 to *c.* 900 was characterized by low population density, restricted commercial activity, and generally low levels of wealth production and economic activity. Indeed, Bryan Ward-Perkins has recently argued that Europe recovered the level of technical and economic sophistication apparent in the later Roman Empire only at the end of the commercial boom of the high Middle Ages.[10] Adam Lucas's survey of milling technology in the ancient and medieval worlds points to a similar conclusion: the technological sophistication found in excavated Roman mills completely disappeared in the early Middle Ages and was not replicated in Europe before the twelfth and thirteenth centuries.[11] Even if arguments for a cataclysmic economic collapse in the early Middle Ages are not accepted, there is little reason to doubt that the growth cycle that characterized the high Middle Ages departed from a fairly low base, or that there was a significant contrast between the two periods, one era defined by long-term decline and stagnation and the other by long-term growth.[12]

The point at which the cycle of decline gave way to the cycle of growth is difficult to isolate. Some historians see economic growth as a byproduct of the stabilizing of European society in the Carolingian period, others see the breakup of the Carolingian order in the later ninth and early tenth centuries as the backdrop to later growth; still others have suggested that growth did not begin before the middle of the tenth century, after Europe had weathered the worst of the Viking, Magyar, and Muslim attacks.[13] Evidence from this period is so meager and so difficult to interpret that a consensus on chronology is unlikely ever to develop. By the second half of the tenth century, the dense mist obscuring the contours of economic life begins finally to dissipate, allowing glimpses of an economy that had begun to develop along the lines that would characterize its fortunes throughout the high medieval growth cycle.[14]

On the agrarian side, land was being cleared and drained, new villages were appearing, and population appears to have been moving upward.[15] On the urban and commercial side, new towns and markets were being founded in places like Douai and St Omer, old Roman towns like London, Paris, and Milan were expanding, and the money supply was on an upward trajectory, thanks to the opening of new silver mines in Saxony in the 960s.[16]

In the early phases of the expansion, however, agrarian change and commercial change moved on parallel tracks but were not necessarily mutually dependent. The towns of the tenth and eleventh centuries were small: a handful may have had populations above 10,000 at the turn of the millennium, but towns with only a few thousand inhabitants were more typical.[17] Many of these early towns were glorified villages situated beside a castle or an abbey, with inhabitants who knew the smell of manure from first-hand experience. The largest of these early towns undoubtedly drew on surpluses from neighboring villages to supply their tables and workshops, but total urban demand in the tenth and eleventh centuries was simply too low to lead to any major restructuring of agricultural techniques or practices. Most towns probably supplied the lion's share of what they needed from the countryside by combining crops grown directly by residents – most towns had fields attached to their urban nucleus –with produce imported from the personal estates of lords resident in the towns. Much of the commerce in this early period involved luxury goods traded over long distances; it was not based on the production of a wide array of consumer goods sold to a broad cross-section of society. Trade in expensive luxury commodities was often lucrative for the small groups of merchants who undertook it, and it undoubtedly generated a trickle-down effect that created niches for craftsmen and smaller retailers, who could also look to the households of lords and clerics for customers. As towns grew, they naturally extended their supply lines further into the countryside, but in most of Europe before the twelfth century they needed little more than the incidental surpluses marketed by peasants living within a few kilometers of each town. Only in the twelfth century, and then only in certain parts of Europe, did urban growth proceed at a pace that was capable of transforming what went on in the countryside.

In the case of the countryside, the impetus behind population growth and rising productivity has long perplexed historians. Standard textbook accounts generally still rely on Lynn White's arguments about changing technology, including improvements in horse harnessing, plough design, and especially systems of crop rotation.[18] There is probably some truth to the model, but its central feature – the transition from two-crop rotation to three-crop rotation – is notoriously difficult to date, and accounts of the system's geographical spread and chronological development are still widely divergent.[19] Georges Duby thought that an improving climate played a role in raising yields and population levels, suggesting that a phase of warmer and drier weather began at some point in the eighth century and persisted into the twelfth or thirteenth century.[20] The notion of a "Medieval Warm Period" has gained wide currency among climatologists in the past two decades, but its onset is now generally placed in the later tenth or eleventh centuries, raising questions about its role as the spark of the demographic upswing.[21] A third possibility is that the emergence of a more structured political environment in the second half of the tenth century, associated with the Peace of God movement and/or the "feudal revolution," may have had a role to play.[22] Again, however, the argument works better for explaining the upward trend of the eleventh century than for the origins of the trend in the tenth century.

Over the longer term, these changes undoubtedly played a major role in raising agrarian productivity and facilitating demographic growth. All historians agree that Europe was much more densely populated in 1300 than it was in 900. Indeed, at the high water mark in the first half of the fourteenth century some countries reached a population level that would not be attained again until the eighteenth century. Signs of population pressure on resources are readily found at the end of the period: lands poorly suited to cultivation had been brought under the plough; many peasants had to make ends meet on farms with only a handful of acres; and one of the worst famines in recorded history afflicted a wide swathe of northern Europe in the 1310s.[23] Even historians who do not see these developments as constituting a Malthusian crisis agree that they are symptoms of a population that had grown substantially in preceding centuries.

The chronology of population growth is a question of vital importance for understanding the dynamics of the economy in the period. Most historians have seen population growth as more or less continuous throughout the entire period. Local setbacks caused by war, environmental degradation, or economic shifts undoubtedly occurred, but there were no large-scale epidemics or other setbacks between the tenth and fourteenth centuries that reversed, or even halted, the general upward trend. The degree of freedom from viral and bacterial killers is every bit as striking a feature of the period as the benign climate. By emphasizing rising agrarian productivity as the root cause of population growth, most historians have assumed that stimulated fertility accounts for the upward trend, but a relatively propitious mortality regime was probably every bit as important. Certainly by comparison to what came after, mortality factors were remarkably restrained during the high medieval growth cycle.[24]

A continuous trend is, however, not the same as a constant trend. To understand the relationship between population growth and commercial development between the tenth and fourteenth centuries, the constancy of the trend matters almost as much as its general direction. Numerous different types of rising trend are imaginable. Population might have shot up like a rocket in the tenth and eleventh centuries, for example, when there was so much fertile virgin land to exploit, and then slowed down later in the period, as the options for extending acreage became less viable.[25] Or the whole period might have been characterized by short bursts of expansion followed by longer periods of adjustment, all trending upward but not at the same pace.[26] Or the trend might have been feeble at first, as people warily adjusted to the more favorable environmental circumstances and new agrarian practices, before giving way to a phase of fast growth during which earlier changes coalesced to act in a particularly powerful way.

Of the three options just outlined, the third scenario best fits the available evidence. Arguments for a fairly rapid ascent of population in the thirteenth and early fourteenth centuries are a staple of the neo-Malthusian literature of the postwar period. Wilhelm Abel, for example, estimated that the combined population of Germany, France, and England increased from approximately twenty-two million in 1200 to approximately forty million in 1340.[27] In a local study of the English manor of Taunton, J. Z. Titow found that the number of peasants who made customary payments to their lord increased from 506 in 1209 to 1,115 in 1268.[28] Robert Fossier similarly argued that the population of Picardy entered a phase of rapid growth toward the end of the twelfth century. [29] He calculated a growth rate of 0.72 percent per annum for the last quarter of the century, a rate that would have easily doubled Picardy's population between 1200 and 1300. More recent studies concur in finding relatively rapid rates of growth in the thirteenth and early fourteenth centuries. David Nicholas has argued the case for Flanders, and studies of single English manors by Zvi Razi and Bruce Campbell have reached the same conclusion.[30] In his recent account of Genoa's economic miracle in the twelfth and thirteenth centuries, Avner Greif notes that, while the city's population increased by 100 percent between 1050 and 1200, it increased by some 230 percent between 1200 and 1300.[31] The towns and cities of Tuscany experienced comparable growth in the thirteenth century: a recent survey by Paolo Malanima suggests that urban populations in Tuscany doubled or trebled over the course of the century.[32]

It is unlikely that growth on this scale took place across Europe as a whole, or that development occurred everywhere at the same time. The phase of rapid growth probably began earlier in Italy than in Europe north of the Alps and probably began earlier in Western Europe than in Eastern Europe. Surviving records are too fragmentary to allow for detailed regional comparisons or precise calculations of the trend's starting and ending points. But they do generally concur on the main point – that growth in the thirteenth century was both fast and widespread. Relatively fast growth probably stretched back into the twelfth century and continued in some places right up to the Black Death, although growth may have began to slow by the end of the thirteenth century and was probably not as widespread in the first half of the fourteenth century.

While the arguments in favor of fast population growth in a "long" thirteenth century are old hat for economic historians, their implications for longer-term population movements have seldom been fully appreciated. Historians are accustomed to use the model of heady thirteenth-century growth to draw a contrast with the problematic conditions of the fourteenth century, when famine, war, and especially plague combined to sap Europe of much of its vitality.[33] But the rapid growth of the thirteenth century also has significant repercussions for understanding how Europe developed in the centuries *before* the great surge. Population growth on a pace comparable to that of the thirteenth century simply cannot have taken place in the tenth and eleventh centuries. A cycle of such rapid growth extending over four centuries would have given Europe a population history without parallel anywhere on the globe before the advent of the Industrial Revolution.

The problem is not just the lack of comparable experience elsewhere. An even bigger difficulty is that the numbers simply do not add up. To make sense from a mathematical perspective, a relatively rapid demographic growth that extended over a span of four or more centuries would require either a remarkably low starting point or a remarkably high end point. This can be illustrated by using some population estimates recently offered by demographic historians. Italy provides a good case in point. According to the team of economic historians led by L. Del Panta, Italy had a population of approximately 5.2 million in *c.* 1000 and 12.5 million in 1300.[34] These estimates imply a growth rate of about 0.3 percent per annum, a credible figure but one that would need to be understood as encompassing moderate growth, not the kind of surge that is commonly attributed to Italy in the high Middle Ages. To double a population in a century, as apparently happened in many Italian towns in the thirteenth century, requires a compound annual growth rate of approximately 0.7 percent per annum. But such growth could not have occurred for the population as a whole over four centuries. If it had, and if the end point was 12.5 million, then the population base of Italy at the start of the cycle in *c*. 900 would have to be placed somewhere around 750,000 people. Of course, it is likely that the population of the towns grew faster than the population of the countryside, but if the towns are extracted from the total population because of their unusually rapid growth, the figure for rural population growth over the period would have to be lowered correspondingly. Thus, even the modest rate of 0.3 percent per annum would have to be seen as too high. Stunning urban growth in the midst of lackluster rural growth is certainly possible, but seems unlikely. The basic problem, for Italy as for elsewhere, is that the two common portrayals of the period's demographic history cannot be easily reconciled: if growth occurred over a very long time then it must have been slow; if growth was vigorous, then it could not have occurred over a very long time.

Similar calculations can be made for England, whose population trend has been extensively studied in the past two generations.[35] The most widely accepted model of England's demographic history is that proposed by Edward Miller and John Hatcher, which proposes a population of approximately two million in 1086, derived from the detailed data in Domesday Book, and a population of approximately 5.5 million in 1300.[36] These figures suggest a growth rate of 0.47 percent per annum – significantly higher, it should be noted, than the rate just calculated for Italy. But even these estimates run into trouble if they are plotted on a line with a starting point in the early tenth century. If the Domesday population of two million is seen as the terminus for a growth phase that began *c*. 900 and if earlier growth was constant with that of the twelfth and thirteenth centuries, then the population of England at the start of the cycle must have been 840,000. Once again, this does not seem credible, and once again the problem stems from an uneasy juxtaposition of long growth and fast growth.

One way out of the interpretative trap is to modify the assumption that growth took place at a constant rate throughout the entire period. Indeed, the best resolution of the problem is to assume that growth began tentatively at some point in the tenth century, continued on a gentle course through the eleventh century, and then took off at some point in the twelfth century. In this scenario, relatively rapid growth can be accounted for without the need to make problematic assertions about the conditions prevailing at the outset of the growth phase. If the transition to a phase of rapid demographic growth is placed somewhere in the twelfth century, then the duration of the phase of rapid growth can be limited to a period of about two centuries, perhaps even less. Of course, the opposite view – that growth was rapid early on and then eased over time – would also solve the problem. But, while both are intrinsically possible, the weight of evidence greatly favors the position that later growth was faster. Of all of the possible scenarios for the population history of the period, by far the best documented and best supported by scholarly opinion is that growth was sustained and substantial in the thirteenth century. If a two-stage model of growth has any validity as an interpretation of the demographic history of the period, it is only in conjunction with a model that sees slow growth as the earlier phase of the cycle and fast growth as the later.

Redefining the contours of Europe's demographic growth between 900 and 1300 is important in its own right, but it is especially significant in the context of Europe's overall economic development in the period. The transition from an era of slow growth to one of much faster growth raises an obvious question: why did a demographic trend that had endured for two or more centuries shift gears and start moving at a faster speed? Many of the factors that were noted earlier as explaining the origins of the cycle in the tenth century were still operating in the twelfth. Their ability to inaugurate the process of population growth cannot, however, account for the transition to a brisker pace of growth. There were no dramatic changes in the climate associated specifically with the twelfth century, for example, nor were there qualitative changes in the provision of peace and good government.

There were, however, some dramatic changes in Europe's commercial life that began in the twelfth century and continued on into the fourteenth century, and collectively they may well have been powerful enough to trigger a demographic surge. For one thing, the money supply expanded rapidly. An exceptionally rich deposit of silver was discovered near Freiburg in the 1160s, and smaller deposits were also brought into production in Italy and Scotland at roughly the same time.[37] By the end of the twelfth century, another significant mining center had emerged in Freisach, Austria, and in the first half of the thirteenth century new mines were opened up in Bohemia and Sardinia. Later in the century another major find was made at Kutná Hora near Prague. As a result of these finds, Europe enjoyed a dramatic increase in its bullion supply, one that was unparalleled before the advent of new world silver. The impact of this new precious metal on the money supply is best documented in the case of England, where the total volume of money in circulation was in the vicinity of £50,000 in the 1150s, but probably exceeded £2,000,000 in the early fourteenth century.[38]

Another major development was an increase in the number of commercial venues operating in Europe, including fairs, markets, ports, and new towns. Europe already had a significant number of commercial centers before the twelfth century, but the twelfth and thirteenth centuries saw a veritable explosion in their number. Fairs seem to have been particularly important in the early phase of this expansion.[39] Most of the major Flemish fairs, for example, were established in the 1120s, and by the middle of the century were generating considerable business.[40] Some of the fairs of Champagne can be traced back to the 1110s, but their precocious growth began *c.* 1140 and then carried through into the thirteenth century.[41] In England, a great flurry of fair activity began *c.* 1180 and most of the country's major fairs were in existence by 1220.[42] The number of rural market centers also skyrocketed in the twelfth and thirteenth centuries, particularly between *c.* 1160 and *c.* 1280. In England alone, for example, more than 350 rural markets were operating by 1200, and several hundred more were set up in the first half of the thirteenth century.[43]

As impressive as the sheer number of new venues, however, was the growing complexity of the regional and inter-regional networks facilitated by the fairs and markets. Growing links between various venues were facilitated by increasingly effective scheduling, which permitted individual commercial sites to operate within larger temporal cycles. In the case of fairs, the cycles were annual, with each fair convening for only a few days or a few weeks of the year.[44] When one fair closed, another opened up, and the process of sequential opening and closing would then continue throughout an entire season. In the case of markets the cycles were weekly, with each market convening on a particular day of the week.[45] When a new market was set up, its creator sought to fit it into the existing cycle of markets by taking account of when other nearby markets convened. If a nearby town had a Saturday market, for example, and other established markets met on Tuesdays, Wednesdays, and Thursdays, it made sense to schedule the new market for a Monday or a Friday. Eventually, of course, all of the daily slots would be spoken for and founders then had to make judgments about how they might best compete with an existing market. In this way a competitive "market for markets" came into existence, a process that can already be observed by the later twelfth century. Success depended on a variety of factors, including the intrinsic character of the site itself and its accessibility by land and water, but often the most important determinant of a new market's success was its ability to develop a close articulation with other nearby markets.

The rationalizing of the temporal sequences of both fairs and markets was an important development for the conduct of trade over larger geographical areas. If the holder of a market or fair aspired to facilitate nothing more than local trade among peasants or between peasants and local artisans, scheduling would not have been a major concern. It was useful, of course, for locals to have a fixed time to conduct their transactions, and in the case of fairs it also made sense to convene at an opportune time in the annual agricultural cycle. But these basic considerations required little attention to the scheduling of other fairs and markets in the region. For traders who were not based in or near the market site, however, and who were interested in trading more than a few chickens or the odd bushel of grain, the temporal sequence mattered a great deal. Temporal articulation of fairs and markets allowed merchants to follow a circuit of commercial gatherings across a wider region, enabling them to tap a concentrated supply of goods and customers at one site before moving on to tap a similar concentration at another site. Merchants were thus able to reduce their search and travel costs by following a more orderly and efficient circuit of commercial gatherings. They may also have profited from the opportunity to arbitrage between different venues, but more importantly they acquired the role of commercial intermediary between different regions and production zones. Profits could now be made in such things as wine and wool, even barley and bacon; trade was no longer restricted to luxury goods traded over long distances and sold to an elite group of consumers. By modern standards this system of periodic purchasing seems an awkward way to bring buyers and sellers together, but in the context of an economy that was still dominated by peasants with limited productive capacity and feeble individual purchasing power, it marked a major step forward in the process of commercialization.

Along with the transformation of its networks of trade and distribution, Europe made major advances in manufacturing during the twelfth and thirteenth centuries. Textile production was particularly important in this regard; woolen textiles were to the medieval economy what automobiles were to the twentieth century or what computers (or perhaps biotechnology) promise to be to the twenty-first century. Prior to the twelfth century, Europeans had manufactured an assortment of textiles, and some products had even circulated over long distances. But the industry was transformed in the twelfth and thirteenth centuries in ways that had significant repercussions for the economy as a whole. While there are few statistics available, it is clear that the production of cloth rose dramatically over the period. Textile production became the major source of employment in many of the burgeoning towns, and the trade in textiles and raw materials needed for textile production became one of the dominant branches of international trade. The development of a major textile industry touched all layers of medieval society, from the peasants who grew the wool through the artisans whose steadfast toil transformed the wool into cloth to the merchants who often sought customers hundreds, sometimes thousands, of miles away from the point of production.

Advances in textile production were related to a host of other changes taking place in the twelfth and thirteenth centuries, including the growing circulation of money and the development of more sophisticated commercial networks. But it was also a function of technological change, allied with an entrepreneurial spirit that exploited the possibilities offered by new technology. The most significant technological change involved the introduction of the horizontal pedal loom, which is first documented at the outset of the twelfth century.[46] Horizontal looms transformed the weaving process from a handicraft to an industrial pursuit. They were a vast improvement on the older vertical looms, allowing weavers to create a more uniform and standardized product with a more consistent weave. By mechanizing key parts of the weaving process and using regularized mechanical force to achieve a tighter fit between warp and weft fibers, weavers were able to produce cloth that was both more durable and more aesthetically pleasing. Like most great technological innovations in world history, the horizontal loom increased the efficiency of the manufacturing process while simultaneously creating a better and more desirable product.

The expansion of textile production was heavily dependent on the commercial transformation taking place at the same time. The industry's growth was concentrated in a few select areas, or "hot zones," which included northern Italy, northeastern France, eastern England, and especially Flanders. The earliest manufacturers in these hot zones probably relied mainly on raw materials and resources that were available locally or regionally, but, as production volumes increased, producers inevitably had to draw on inputs from more distant places. The Flemish industry provides a good example. It began by using mainly local wools and developing a close symbiosis between the towns and the surrounding countryside, but by the end of the twelfth century Flemish producers had developed close trade relations with wool-growers in England and woad-growers in neighboring Picardy.[47] As the towns grew in size and wealth, foodstuffs, too, had to be imported from further afield, shipped along the coast from the fields of northern France or across the North Sea from England and eventually from northern Germany as well.[48] The conduct of this trade in agrarian staples is not well documented in the twelfth and thirteenth centuries, but it must have involved bulking operations by local merchants in contact with peasant producers as a prelude to transshipment from port to port.

Textile producers were also dependent on commercial networks to disseminate their finished product. Cloth is frequently mentioned in surviving local toll lists from the twelfth and thirteenth centuries, and by the 1240s English kings were spending hundreds of pounds every year to acquire cloth produced in Flanders and northern France.[49] Consumption at lower social levels is rarely documented before the fourteenth century but must have accounted for a substantial part of the entire market. Trade over longer distances is also apparent in the twelfth century. Genoese notarial records from the later twelfth century include contracts relating to a variety of northern textiles, and reveal distribution from the north Italian city into other parts of the Mediterranean.[50] Thus cloth produced in the towns of Flanders, northern France, and southeastern England found its way into chests and wardrobes in Constantinople, Damascus, and Alexandria. By the thirteenth century, the textile trade between northern and southern Europe included a wide array of fabrics, including many that were relatively cheap (such as rays, says, and stanforts).[51] It is difficult to assess the volume of this trade, but fragmentary evidence suggests that it was regular and substantial. It is revealing, for example, that Italian merchants discriminated carefully between the wares produced in several dozen northern towns and had, by the end of the twelfth century, developed a nuanced vocabulary to describe a wide array of different types of cloth produced in the north, often by referring to specific places of production.

The trade in textiles between north and south provides a good example of the symbiosis between manufacturing and commercial change that was reshaping the European economy in the twelfth and thirteenth centuries. Most if not all of the northern textile-producing towns were oriented in the first instance towards regional and inter-regional markets. Even in the heyday of international trade in the later thirteenth and early fourteenth centuries, northern cloth was more likely to be sold and tailored within a few hundred miles of its production site than at the other end of Europe or in the Islamic world. At the same time, however, the explosive growth that characterized the hot zones of northern Europe at the time would not have occurred without the aggregate demand of more distant places. Similarly, while the Italian merchants who facilitated the international exchange of northern textiles developed many lucrative commercial networks that were not directly related to the trade in textiles, that trade nonetheless mattered a good deal to their overall fortunes and opened up possibilities for other types of trade that would never have reached a critical mass had it not been for the impetus provided by the textile trade. In essence, the mingling of northern producers and southern entrepreneurs created a positive feedback loop that served everyone well, one that was instrumental in effecting the transformation of the European economy.

In the twelfth century, when the links between northern and southern merchants were being forged, trade occurred principally in fairs, especially the great international fairs held in Champagne. The fairs were frequented by Flemish and Italian merchants by the 1140s, perhaps even slightly earlier, and they grew by leaps and bounds in the second half of the twelfth century.[52] By the end of the century they had acquired their mature form as a cycle of six successive fairs in four different towns (Provins, Troyes, Lagny, and Bar-sur-Aube) open for business for ten months of the year. Merchants from all across Europe gathered in Champagne to trade a wide range of goods, including leather goods, spices, and above all textiles. Money-changers were active in the fairs from at least the 1140s, and the clearing of international debts constituted a central part of the fairs' business, even in the twelfth century, when the last days of every fair were set aside for credit reconciliation.[53] The fairs continued to hold a prominent place in Europe's commercial infrastructure into the fourteenth century, but by then they were no longer pivotal in bringing northerners and southerners together. To a great extent, they became a victim of their own success. Business became so brisk in the thirteenth century that Italian companies began to maintain agents year-round in the major commercial centers of northern Europe, and the periodic trade of the fairs slowly gave way to the more continuous trade of towns.[54] But by bringing two of Europe's hottest zones into contact in the middle of the twelfth century, the fairs of Champagne were a major force in the period's economic transformation.

While textiles were the driving force behind Europe's industrial and commercial transformation in the twelfth and thirteenth centuries, they were by no means the only industry to take off in the period. Agriculture also became more specialized and intensive, as can be seen, for example, in the case of wine production in Gascony and wool production in England.[55] Other extractive industries, such as fishing, mining, and fur trapping, probably also grew significantly, although there is little direct evidence with which to measure their growth.[56] In the case of manufactured goods other than textiles, great advances can be seen in the degree of specialization and commitment to market production. This reorientation of production and engagement with wider markets is exemplified by an unusual document composed in England in the middle of the thirteenth century, listing 108 English places, mostly towns, and giving a short description of what each place was known for at the time.[57] It is not clear if the anonymous author had any useful purpose for the list; probably, as its most recent editor notes, it was "the product of an idle hour." The attributes that caught the author's eye were sometimes based on architectural or cultural attributes, such as "the castle of Dover" or "the school of Oxford." But the most striking feature of the list is the frequency with which places were associated with the production of specialized commodities. Examples include the scarlet of Lincoln, the knives of Thaxted, the ale of Ely, the soap of Coventry, the iron of Gloucester, and the rope of Bridport. In many instances, the presence of a specialized industry corresponding with the author's observations can be corroborated in other sources, albeit generally of later date.

This product specialization (or "branding," as we might say today), occurred all across Europe in the twelfth and thirteenth centuries and can be attributed both to the improving commercial climate and to a new emphasis on improving product quality. The changing environment is best exemplified in the case of pottery, the only good to survive in sufficient quantity over a long enough period of time to allow for meaningful chronological comparison. The quality and variety of pottery produced in the ancient world needs little comment, but the high standards of the ancient world were not maintained following the collapse of the western Roman Empire.[58] According to Bryan Ward-Perkins, the use of potting wheels fell into abeyance in the early Middle Ages and commercially produced pottery disappeared from common household use throughout most of Europe. Alan Vince's recent summary of pottery evidence from northern Europe argues a similar position. Vince found that pottery datable to a period before the middle of the twelfth century was typically produced in the vicinity of the excavation site and lacked technical sophistication.[59] The situation changed dramatically, however, in the middle of the twelfth century. Vince found that potters began to produce a greater variety of types, styles, and sizes, and glazed ware became much more common. Local pots were essentially shunted aside in favor of wares produced in distant places that specialized in production. Pots produced in London and its environs begin to appear regularly in Scottish and Irish sites, for example, while Scandinavian and Baltic areas showed a predilection for Flemish wares.

From the middle of the twelfth century, then, Europe's economy entered a phase of relatively fast growth, one that would endure into the fourteenth century. Growth was defined by rising commodity production and product specialization, both in manufacturing and in agriculture. It was also defined by improvements in commercial infrastructure, including a substantial increase in the number of markets and fairs, and advances in urbanization. Clearly the growth in productive capacity and the growth in commercial infrastructure were intertwined phenomenon, with developments in one area feeding off developments in the other. But were these developments substantial enough to transform Europe's demographic tendencies? Medieval historians have, on the whole, answered this question negatively, treating population trends and commercial development as independent variables. Even at the end of the medieval commercial revolution, most of the population continued to reside in the countryside, and demographers have naturally focused their attention on such issues as the availability of land, the dynamics of inheritance, and the performance of agriculture. As noted above, it is now generally accepted that peasants were more active market participants than was once thought and that village land markets, credit structures, and labor relations were deeply influenced by the broader economic currents of the high Middle Ages. [60] For present purposes, however, the real question that needs to be addressed is not whether peasants were commercially active but whether their activities were substantial and sustained enough to change fundamental processes of family formation and reproduction.

Direct evidence on this issue is hard to come by, but there is more than a little indirect evidence to suggest a close relationship between Europe's commercial transformation and its demographic history. A good example is provided by geography: the hot zones of commercial transformation in the twelfth and thirteenth centuries were also areas of exceptional population growth. The most densely populated areas of Europe in the early fourteenth century were Flanders and northern France, southeastern England, and northern Italy, or, in other words, precisely the same areas that experienced the most dynamic commercial development in the period. It is self-evident in the modern world that areas that succeed in generating new jobs and wealth also experience fast population growth, and it seems reasonable to infer that similar economic logic would have operated in the twelfth and thirteenth centuries. In the case of England, whose commercial and demographic history has been relatively well studied, such a model makes sense at a regional as well as a national level.[61] England was a major player in the commercial transformation of northern Europe in the period, but the extent of commercial development within the country was very uneven. Areas like East Anglia and the east Midlands were highly commercialized and actively involved in international trade early on, while many parts of the North developed their commercial infrastructure relatively slowly and were less urbanized and less economically dynamic throughout the period.[62] Their demographic history mirrors their commercial history: East Anglia and the Midlands were densely settled regions in which, by the later thirteenth century, peasants were typically living on landed holdings of just a few acres, whereas northern England was relatively sparsely settled and peasant holdings were typically much larger.[63]

The links between commercial development and population growth were complex and wide-ranging, but one feature that stands out in the period is peasant responsiveness to new market conditions. Indeed, one of the most impressive aspects of the agrarian history of the high Middle Ages is the emergence of specialized agricultural regions created by international demand for certain products. Examples include viticulture in Gascony and other parts of France and Germany, sheep rearing in England, and woad production in Picardy. In these specialized regions, increases in production were due in the first instance to simple expansion of the area devoted to particular crops or activities, but also typically involved an intensification of land use. In the conditions of the time, this meant above all else the application of greater labor inputs per acre. Viticulture provides a particularly good example.[64] Land dedicated to vines had to be thoroughly worked before planting and then carefully hoed and fertilized while the young plants were growing. Pruning and training the shoots likewise placed a heavy demand on local labor supplies, as did harvesting and vinting. The need for high labor inputs meant that most producers operated on a small scale, working plots that were more akin to gardens than fields. Sales and transfers of vineyards in charters and notarial documents typically involve small parcels of a few acres or less, reflecting the small scale on which most peasants operated. The surge in wine consumption and wine trade that characterized the period was, in short, associated with a surge in employment in wine-producing regions. The work was hard and not particularly remunerative, but it allowed a vast multitude of small landholders and casual laborers, as well as a growing number of coopers and other more specialized artisans, to establish economic footholds and become householders.

A similar dynamic can be associated with industrial production in the period, particularly in the textile industry. Cloth manufacturing was a labor intensive form of production, and increases in output were inevitably accompanied by increased levels of employment. Even significant technological innovation did not change this fundamental relationship, because improvements and expansion in one stage of the manufacturing process had to coincide with the expansion of other less mechanized parts of the process. The revolution in weaving discussed above is a case in point, as is the growing use of mechanical fulling mills in the thirteenth century.[65] Modern experience suggests that technological innovation is driven by a desire to reduce labor costs and typically leads to the substitution of mechanical force for human labor, causing a reduction in employment. Whether or not this is really what happens in the modern economy it is a far cry from the medieval experience of technological change. In the Middle Ages technological innovation typically led to an expansion of employment. Thus, when weaving was transformed by the dissemination of horizontal pedal looms, the production of cloth began a steady ascent that created niches for a body of weavers that expanded with every passing generation. But the spin-off employment effects were even more substantial, as the armies of artisans who prepared the yarn for weaving and then processed the woven cloth also grew in proportion to the rising output of the looms. The consequences of this rising tide can be seen most readily in the growing population of towns, but many of the preliminary stages of wool preparation, such as washing, carding, and spinning, were carried out in the countryside, so that employment opportunities for peasants also rose as the industry advanced.

In both town and country, then, the commercial expansion of the twelfth and thirteenth centuries was accompanied by an expansion in the number of jobs. Increasing employment in turn fostered opportunities for household formation and created an environment in which the slow and gentle demographic growth of the tenth and eleventh centuries could give way to the relatively rapid growth of the high Middle Ages. The precise mechanics of household formation are scarcely documented in the period, but it seems reasonable to assume that individuals and families would have responded to the opportunities presented by wage earning in ways that would have had demographic consequences. Ultimately, of course, such a model rests on the assumption that human fertility was stimulated by changing economic conditions. It would, of course, be reassuring to have direct evidence of the link between economic change and reproductive decision making, but such evidence simply does not exist for the period. *Faute de mieux*, arguments about demographic tendencies in the period must rely on indirect evidence. What is reasonably clear from looking at the assembled evidence is that Europe's population levels surged in the thirteenth century and that the surge can in some instances be traced back into the twelfth century. There are many possible explanations for this surge—an improving climate, growing political stability, and decreased epidemic activity, to name just a few. But if it is asked which aspect of social and economic life changed most significantly around the time the demographic surge began, then the answer must surely lie in the expansion of the commercial economy. Without this expansion, Europe may have stayed on the path of slow growth it had followed from at least the tenth century, but it is hard to imagine it would have gone through the remarkable transformations that are synonymous with the continent in the high Middle Ages.

Notes

1 Most famously in Pirenne, *Medieval Cities.*

2 Lopez, "The Trade of Medieval Europe" and *Commercial Revolution*; Lopez and Raymond, *Medieval Trade in the Mediterranean.*

3 Most succinctly in Postan, "The Economic Foundations of Medieval Society," an article that was based on a conference paper first delivered in Paris in 1950.

4 A good account of the influence of Postan's work can be found in Hatcher and Bailey, *Modelling the Middle Ages*, ch. 2.

5 North and Thomas, *The Rise of the Western World*; North, *Structure and Change in Economic History.*

6 Examples include Kowaleski, *Local Markets and Regional Trade*, ch. 5; Munro, "The 'New Institutional Economics'"; Greif, *Institutions and the Path to the Modern Economy.*

7 A thoughtful consideration of this question can be found in Britnell, "Commercialisation and Economic Development."

8 Desplat, ed., *Foires et marchés dans les campagnes*; Cavaciocchi, ed., *Fiere e mercati nella integrazione delle economie*; Moore, *Fairs of Medieval England*; Britnell, *Commercialisation of English Society*; Masschaele, *Peasants, Merchants, and Markets*; Petrowiste, *A la foire d'empoigne.*

9 Langdon and Masschaele, "Commercial Activity."

10 Ward-Perkins, *The Fall of Rome*, esp. ch. 5.

11 Lucas, *Wind, Water, Work.*

12 The one notable exception being Bridbury, "Domesday Valuation."
13 Verhulst, *Rise of Cities*; Hodges, *Towns and Trade*; Verhulst, *Carolingian Economy*; Dyer, *Making a Living*.
14 Duby, *Early Growth*; Johanek, "Merchants, Markets, and Towns."
15 Lewis, Mitchell-Fox, and Dyer, *Village, Hamlet and Field*; Fossier, "Rural Economy and Demographic Growth."
16 Keene, "London from the Post-Roman Period to 1300"; Hinton, "Large Towns 600–1300," pp. 230–1; Wickham, *Early Medieval Italy*, p. 91; Spufford, *Money and its Use*, p. 74.
17 Bairoch, Batou, and Chèvre, *The Population of European Cities*. Estimates given in this publication tend to err on the high side.
18 White, *Medieval Technology*.
19 Baker and Butlin, eds, *Studies of Field Systems*; Fox, "Alleged Transformation"; Bakels, "Crops Produced."
20 Duby, *Early Growth*, pp. 6–11.
21 Crowley and Lowery, "How Warm?"
22 Moore, *First European Revolution*.
23 Postan, "Medieval Agriculture in its Prime: England"; Schofield, "Dearth, Debt, and the Local Land Market"; Jordan, *Great Famine*.
24 The role of mortality in the demographic history of late medieval and early modern England has been forcefully restated in Hatcher, "Understanding the Population History."
25 Herlihy, *Medieval and Renaissance Pistoia*, pp. 56–7.
26 Slicher van Bath, *Agrarian History*, pp. 77–80.
27 Abel, *Wüstungen*, p. 62.
28 Titow, "Some Evidence"; a figure of the Taunton hundredpenny payments prepared by Christopher Thornton is in Britnell, *Britain and Ireland*, p. 78.
29 Fossier, *La Terre et les hommes en Picardie*, pp. 274–99.
30 Nicholas, "Of Poverty and Primacy"; Razi, *Life, Marriage and Death*, pp. 27–32; Campbell, "Population Pressure, Inheritance and the Land Market," p. 96.
31 Greif, "Political Foundations."
32 Malanima, "Urbanisation and Italian Economy," p. 101.
33 Representative is Aberth, *From the Brink of the Apocalypse*.
34 Del Panta et al., *Popolazione italiana*.
35 Recently surveyed in Langdon and Masschaele, "Commercial Activity," pp. 54–68.
36 Miller and Hatcher, *Medieval England: Rural Society and Economic Change*, p. 29. The figure for 1300 offered here represents the midpoint of their estimated range.
37 Spufford, *Money and its Use*, pp. 109–31. On the growth of the money supply see also Mayhew, *Sterling*; Blanchard, *Mining, Metallurgy and Minting*.
38 Allen, "Volume of English Currency," p. 608.
39 Irsigler, "Fonction des foires."
40 Yamada, "Mouvement des foires."
41 Irsigler, "Fonction des foires," p. 54.
42 Moore, *Fairs of Medieval England*, pp. 22–3.
43 Letters et al., *Gazetteer*.
44 Bur, *Formation du comté de Champagne*, pp. 292–304; Moore, *Fairs of Medieval England*, pp. 9–23.
45 Masschaele, *Peasants, Merchants, and Markets*.
46 Munro, "Medieval Woollens."
47 Fossier, *La Terre et les hommes en Picardie*; Harvey, "English Trade in Wool and Cloth"; Thoen, "Count, the Countryside and the Economic Development"; Nicholas, "Of

Poverty and Primacy"; Langdon and Masschaele, "Commercial Activity," pp. 48–50; Bell, Brooks, and Dryburgh, *English Wool Market.*

48 Gras, *Evolution of English Corn Market*; Derville, "Grenier des Pays-Bas"; Hybel, "Grain Trade in Northern Europe."

49 Bienvenu, "Recherches sur les péages," esp. pp. 445–6; Despy, "Recherches sur les tariffs," esp. p. 120; Moore, *Fairs of Medieval England*, pp. 24–47; Masschaele, "Tolls and Trade."

50 Reynolds, "Market for Northern Textiles"; Krueger, "Genoese Exportation."

51 Chorley, "Cloth Exports of Flanders"; Munro, "'Industrial Crisis,'" pp. 105–15.

52 Bur, *Formation du comté de Champagne*, p. 303; Irsigler, "Fonction des foires," p. 54.

53 Bautier, *Economic Development*, p. 111.

54 Spufford, *Power and Profit*, pp. 19–22, 238–9.

55 Duby, *Rural Economy and Country Life*, pp. 138–9; Langdon and Masschaele, "Commercial Activity," pp. 48–50.

56 On the expansion of commercial fishing, see Hoffman, "Brief History of Aquatic Resource Use"; on mining, see Gimpel, *Medieval Machine*, pp. 59–74.

57 *English Historical Documents*, ed. Rothwell, pp. 881–4.

58 Ward-Perkins, *The Fall of Rome*, pp. 105–8.

59 Vince, "Use of Pottery."

60 For a recent treatment of economic interactions between peasants and the world outside the village, see Schofield, *Peasant and Community.*

61 Miller and Hatcher, *Medieval England: Towns, Commerce, and Crafts*; Britnell, *Commercialisation of English Society* and *Britain and Ireland.*

62 Campbell, "Agricultural Progress" and "Arable Productivity"; Britnell, "Borough Markets and Trade."

63 Hallam, ed., *Agrarian History of England and Wales*, vol. 2.

64 Dion, *Histoire de la vigne*; Unwin, *Wine and the Vine.*

65 Carus-Wilson, "Industrial Revolution"; Langdon, *Mills in the Medieval Economy*, pp. 40–47.

Bibliography

Abel, Wilhelm, *Die Wüstungen des ausgehenden Mittelalters*, 2nd edn (Stuttgart: G. Fischer, 1955).

Aberth, John, *From the Brink of the Apocalypse: Confronting Famine, War, Plague, and Death in the Later Middle Ages* (New York and London: Routledge, 2001).

Allen, Martin, "The Volume of the English Currency, 1158–1470," *Economic History Review*, 2nd ser., 54 (2001), pp. 595–611.

Bairoch, Paul, Batou, Jean, and Chèvre, Pierre, *The Population of European Cities: Data Bank and Short Summary of Results* (Geneva: Droz, 1988).

Bakels, Corrie C., "Crops Produced in the Southern Netherlands and Northern France during the Early Medieval Period: A Comparison," *Vegetation History and Archeology*, 14 (2005), pp. 394–9.

Baker, A. R. H., and Butlin, R. A., *Studies of Field Systems in the British Isles* (Cambridge: Cambridge University Press, 1973).

Bautier, Robert-Henri, *The Economic Development of Medieval Europe* (London: Thames and Hudson, 1971).

Bell, Adrian R., Brooks, Christopher, and Dryburgh, Paul R., *The English Wool Market, c. 1230–1327* (Cambridge: Cambridge University Press, 2007).

Bienvenu, J. M., "Recherches sur les péages angevins aux XIe et XIIe siècles," *Le Moyen Age*, 63, 4th ser., 12 (1957), 209–40, 437–67.

Blanchard, Ian, *Mining, Metallurgy and Minting in the Middle Ages* (Stuttgart: F. Steiner, 2001).

Bridbury, A. R., "The Domesday Valuation of Manorial Income," in A. R. Bridbury, *The English Economy from Bede to the Reformation* (Woodbridge: Boydell, 1992), pp. 111–32.

Britnell, Richard H., "Commercialisation and Economic Development in England, 1000–1300," in Richard H. Britnell and Bruce M. S. Campbell, eds, *A Commercialising Economy: England 1086 to* c. *1300* (Manchester: Manchester University Press, 1995), pp. 7–26.

Britnell, R. H., *The Commercialisation of English Society, 1000–1500*, 2nd edn (Manchester: Manchester University Press, 1996).

Britnell, Richard, "Borough Markets and Trade in Northern England, 1000–1216," in Richard Britnell and John Hatcher, eds. *Progress and Problems in Medieval England* (Cambridge: Cambridge University Press, 1996), pp. 46–67.

Britnell, Richard, *Britain and Ireland 1050–1530* (Oxford: Oxford University Press, 2004).

Bur, Michel, *La Formation du comté de Champagne, v. 950–v. 1150* (Nancy: Université de Nancy II, 1977).

Campbell, Bruce M. S., "Agricultural Progress in Medieval England: Some Evidence from Eastern Norfolk," *Economic History Review*, 2nd ser., 36 (1983), pp. 26–46.

Campbell, Bruce M. S., "Arable Productivity in Medieval England: Some Evidence from Norfolk," *Journal of Economic History*, 43 (1983), pp. 379–404.

Campbell, Bruce M. S., "Population Pressure, Inheritance and the Land Market in a Fourteenth-Century Peasant Community," in Richard M. Smith, ed., *Land, Kinship and Life-Cycle* (Cambridge: Cambridge University Press, 1984), pp. 87–134.

Carus-Wilson, E. M., "An Industrial Revolution of the Thirteenth Century," *Economic History Review*, 11 (1941), pp. 39–60.

Cavaciocchi, Simonetta, ed., *Fiere e mercati nella integrazione delle economie europee secc. XIII–XVIII* (Florence: Le Monnier, 2001).

Chorley, Patrick, "The Cloth Exports of Flanders and Northern France during the Thirteenth Century: A Luxury Trade?" *Economic History Review*, 2nd ser., 40 (1987), pp. 349–79.

Crowley, Thomas J., and Lowery, Thomas S., "How Warm was the Medieval Warm Period," *Ambio*, 29 (2000), pp. 51–7.

Del Panta, L., Livi Bacci, M., Pinto, G., and Sonnino, E., *La popolazione italiana dal Medioevo a oggi* (Rome: Laterza, 1996).

Derville, Alain, "Le Grenier des Pays-Bas médiévaux," *Revue du Nord*, 69 (1987), pp. 267–80.

Desplat, Christian, ed., *Foires et marchés dans les campagnes de l'Europe médiévale et moderne* (Toulouse: Presses Universitaires du Mirail, 1996).

Despy, Georges, "Recherches sur les tariffs de tonlieux dans le duché de Brabant au XIIIe siècle," *Publications de la section historique de l'Institut Grand-Ducal de Luxembourg*, 104 (1988), pp. 103–30.

Dion, Roger, *Histoire de la vigne et du vin en France des origines aux XIXe siècle* (Paris: L'Auteur, 1959).

Duby, Georges, *Rural Economy and Country Life in the Medieval West*, trans. Cynthia Postan (Columbia, SC: University of South Carolina Press, 1968).

Duby, Georges, *The Early Growth of the European Economy: Warriors and Peasants from the Seventh to the Twelfth Century*, trans. Howard B. Clarke (Ithaca, NY: Cornell University Press, 1974).

Dyer, Christopher, *Making a Living in the Middle Ages* (New Haven and London: Yale University Press, 2002).

English Historical Documents, vol. 3: *1189–1327*, ed. H. Rothwell (Oxford: Oxford University Press, 1975).

Fossier, Robert, *La Terre et les hommes en Picardie, jusqu'à la fin du XIIIe siècle* (Paris and Louvain: B. Nauwelaerts, 1968).

Fossier, Robert, "The Rural Economy and Demographic Growth," in David Luscombe and Jonathan Riley-Smith, eds, *The New Cambridge Medieval History*, vol. 4 (Cambridge: Cambridge University Press, 2004), pp. 11–46.

Fox, H. S. A., "The Alleged Transformation from Two-Field to Three-Field Systems in Medieval England," *Economic History Review*, 2nd ser., 39 (1986), pp. 526–48.

Gimpel, Jean, *The Medieval Machine: The Industrial Revolution of the Middle Ages* (New York: Penguin, 1976).

Gras, Norman Scott Brien, *The Evolution of the English Corn Market from the Twelfth to the Eighteenth Century* (Cambridge, MA: Harvard University Press, 1915).

Greif, Avner, "On the Political Foundations of the Late Medieval Commercial Revolution: Genoa during the Twelfth and Thirteenth Centuries," *Journal of Economic History*, 54 (1994), pp. 271–87.

Greif, Avner, *Institutions and the Path to the Modern Economy: Lessons from Medieval Trade* (Cambridge: Cambridge University Press, 2006).

Hallam, H. E., ed., *The Agrarian History of England and Wales*, vol. 2: *1042–1350* (Cambridge: Cambridge University Press, 1988).

Harvey, P. D. A., "The English Trade in Wool and Cloth, 1150–1250: Some Problems and Suggestions," in Marco Spallanzani, ed., *Produzione commercio e consume dei panni di lana (nei secoli XII–XVIII)*, Istituto Internazionale di Storia Economica "F. Datini", Pubblicazioni – Serie II, Atti delle "Settimane di Studio" e Altri Convegni (Florence: Leo S. Olschki, 1976), pp. 369–75.

Hatcher, John, "Understanding the Population History of England, 1450–1750', *Past and Present*, 180 (2003), pp. 83–130.

Hatcher, John, and Bailey, Mark, *Modelling the Middle Ages: The History and Theory of England's Economic Development* (Oxford: Oxford University Press, 2001).

Herlihy, David, *Medieval and Renaissance Pistoia: The Social History of an Italian Town, 1200–1430* (New Haven and London: Yale University Press, 1967).

Hinton, David A., "The Large Towns 600–1300" in D. M. Palliser, ed., *The Cambridge Urban History of Britain*, vol. 1 (Cambridge: Cambridge University Press, 2000), pp. 217–44.

Hodges, Richard, *Towns and Trade in the Age of Charlemagne* (London: Gerald Duckworth, 2000).

Hoffman, Richard C., "A Brief History of Aquatic Resource Use in Medieval Europe," *Helgoland Marine Research*, 59 (2005), pp. 22–30.

Hybel, Nils, "The Grain Trade in Northern Europe before 1350," *Economic History Review*, 2nd ser., 55 (2002), pp. 219–47.

Irsigler, Franz, "La Fonction des foires dans l'intégration des economies européenes au Moyen Age," in Simonetta Cavaciocchi, ed., *Fiere e mercati nella integrazione delle economie Europee secc. XIII–XVIII* (Florence: Le Monnier, 2001), pp. 49–70.

Johanek, Peter, "Merchants, Markets, and Towns," in Timothy Reuter, ed., *The New Cambridge Medieval History*, vol. 3 (Cambridge: Cambridge University Press, 1999), pp. 64–94.

Jordan, William Chester, *The Great Famine: Northern Europe in the Early Fourteenth Century* (Princeton: Princeton University Press, 1996).

Keene, Derek, "London from the Post-Roman Period to 1300," in D. M. Palliser, ed., *The Cambridge Urban History of Britain*, vol. 1 (Cambridge: Cambridge University Press, 2000), pp. 187–216.

Kowaleski, Maryanne, *Local Markets and Regional Trade in Medieval Exeter* (Cambridge: Cambridge University Press, 1995).

Krueger, H., "The Genoese Exportation of Northern Cloths to Mediterranean Ports, Twelfth Century," *Revue belge de philologie et d'histoire*, 65 (1987), pp. 722–50.

Langdon, John, *Mills in the Medieval Economy: England 1300–1540* (Oxford: Oxford University Press, 2004).

Langdon, John, and Masschaele, James, "Commercial Activity and Population Growth in Medieval England," *Past & Present*, 190 (2006), pp. 35–82.

Letters, Samantha, Fernandes, Mario, Keene, Derek, and Myhill, Olwen, *Gazetteer of Markets and Fairs in England and Wales to 1516*, List and Index Society, Special Series 32 and 33 (Kew: List and Index Society, 2003).

Lewis, Carenza, Mitchell-Fox, Patrick, and Dyer, Christopher, *Village, Hamlet and Field: Changing Medieval Settlements in Central England* (Manchester: Manchester University Press, 1997).

Lopez, Robert S., "The Trade of Medieval Europe: The South," in M. Postan and E. Rich, eds, *Cambridge Economic History*, vol. 2 (Cambridge: Cambridge University Press, 1952), pp. 257–354.

Lopez, Robert S., *The Commercial Revolution of the Middle Ages, 950–1350* (Cambridge: Cambridge University Press, 1976).

Lopez, Robert S., and Raymond, Irving W., *Medieval Trade in the Mediterranean World* (New York: Columbia University Press, 1955).

Lucas, Adam, *Wind, Water, Work: Ancient and Medieval Milling Technology* (Leiden: Brill, 2006).

Malanima, Paolo, "Urbanisation and the Italian Economy during the Last Millennium," *European Review of Economic History*, 9 (2005), pp. 97–122.

Masschaele, James, *Peasants, Merchants, and Markets: Inland Trade in Medieval England, 1150–1350* (New York: St Martin's Press, 1997).

Masschaele, James, "Tolls and Trade in Medieval England," in Lawrin Armstrong and Ivana Elbl, eds, *Money, Markets and Trade in Late Medieval Europe: Essays in Honour of John H. A. Munro* (Leiden: Brill, 2007), pp. 146–83.

Mayhew, Nicholas, *Sterling: A History of a Currency* (New York: Wiley, 2000).

Miller, Edward, and Hatcher, John, *Medieval England: Rural Society and Economic Change, 1086–1348* (London and New York: Longman, 1978).

Miller, Edward, and Hatcher, John, *Medieval England: Towns, Commerce, and Crafts 1086–1348* (London and New York: Longman, 1995).

Moore, Ellen Wedemeyer, *The Fairs of Medieval England: An Introductory Study* (Toronto: Pontifical Institute of Medieval Studies Press, 1985).

Moore, R. I., *The First European Revolution,* c. *970–1215* (Oxford: Blackwell, 2000).

Munro, John H., "The 'Industrial Crisis' of the English Textile Towns, *c.* 1290–*c.* 1330," in M. Prestwich, R. H. Britnell, and R. Frame, eds, *Thirteenth Century England*, vol. VII (Woodbridg: Boydell, 1999), pp. 105–15.

Munro, John, "The 'New Institutional Economics' and the Changing Fortunes of Fairs in Medieval and Early Modern Europe: The Textile Trades, Warfare, and Transaction Costs," *Vierteljahrschrift für Sozial- und Wirtschaftsgeschichte*, 88 (2001), pp. 1–47.

Munro, John H., "Medieval Woollens: Textiles, Textile Technology and Industrial Organization, *c.* 800–1500," in David Jenkins, ed., *The Cambridge History of Western Textiles*, vol. 1 (Cambridge: Cambridge University Press, 2003), pp. 181–227.

Nicholas, David, "Of Poverty and Primacy: Demand, Liquidity, and the Flemish Economic Miracle, 1050–1200," *American Historical Review*, 96 (1991), pp. 17–41.

North, Douglass C., and Thomas, Robert P., *The Rise of the Western World: A New Economic History* (Cambridge: Cambridge University Press, 1973).

North, Douglass C., *Structure and Change in Economic History* (New York: Norton, 1981).

Petrowiste, Judicaël, *A la foire d'empoigne: Foires et marchés en Aunis et Saintonge au moyen âge, vers 1000–vers 1550* (Toulouse: CNRS – Université de Toulouse-Le Mirail 2004).

Pirenne, Henri, *Medieval Cities: Their Origins and the Revival of Trade* (Princeton: Princeton University Press, 1925).

Postan, M. M., "Medieval Agriculture in its Prime: England," in M. M. Postan, ed., *The Cambridge Economic History of Europe*, vol. 1: *The Agrarian Life of the Middle Ages*, 2nd edn (Cambridge: Cambridge University Press, 1966), pp. 548–70.

Postan, M. M., "The Economic Foundations of Medieval Society," in M. M. Postan, *Essays on Medieval Agriculture and General Problems of the Medieval Economy* (Cambridge: Cambridge University Press, 1973), pp. 3–27.

Razi, Zvi, *Life, Marriage and Death in a Medieval Parish: Economy, Society and Demography in Halesowen 1270–1400* (Cambridge: Cambridge University Press, 1980).

Reynolds, R. L., "The Market for Northern Textiles in Genoa, 1179–1200," *Revue belge de philologie et d'histoire*, 8 (1929), pp. 831–50.

Schofield, Phillipp. "Dearth, Debt, and the Local Land Market in a Late Thirteenth Century Village Community," *Agricultural History Review*, 45 (1997), pp. 1–17.

Schofield, Phillipp R., *Peasant and Community in Medieval England 1200–1500* (Houndmills and New York: Palgrave Macmillan, 2003).

Slicher van Bath, B. H., *Agrarian History of Western Europe, AD 500–1850*, trans. Olive Ordish (London: Edward Arnold, 1963).

Spufford, Peter, *Money and its Use in Medieval Europe* (Cambridge: Cambridge University Press, 1988).

Spufford, Peter, *Power and Profit: The Merchant in Medieval Europe* (New York: Thames and Hudson, 2002).

Thoen, Erik, "The Count, the Countryside and the Economic Development of the Towns in Flanders from the Eleventh Century to the Thirteenth Century: Some Provisional Remarks and Hypotheses," in Erik Aerts, Brigitte Henau, Paul Janssens, and Raymond Van Uytven, eds, *Studia Historica Oeconomica. Liber Amicorum Herman Van der Wee* (Louvain: Universitaire Pers Leuven, 1993), pp. 259–78.

Titow, J. Z., "Some Evidence of the Thirteenth Century Population Increase", *Economic History Review*, 2nd ser., 14 (1961), pp. 218–24.

Unwin, P. T. H., *Wine and the Vine: An Historical Geography of Viticulture and the Wine Trade* (London and New York: Routledge, 1991).

Verhulst, Adriaan, *The Carolingian Economy* (Cambridge: Cambridge University Press, 2002).

Verhulst, Adriaan, *The Rise of Cities in Northwest Europe* (Cambridge: Cambridge University Press, 1999).

Vince, Alan, "The Use of Pottery to Chart Trade Routes in the North Sea and Baltic Areas," in Lars Berggren, Niles Hybel and Annette Landen, eds, *Cogs, Cargoes, and Commerce: Maritime Bulk Trade in Northern Europe 1150–1400* (Toronto: Pontifical Institute of Mediaeval Studies, 2002), pp. 128–42.

Ward-Perkins, Bryan, *The Fall of Rome and the End of Civilization* (Oxford: Oxford University Press, 2005).

White, Lynn T., *Medieval Technology and Social Change* (Oxford: Oxford University Press, 1962).

Wickham, Chris, *Early Medieval Italy: Central Power and Local Society 400–1000* (Ann Arbor: University of Michigan Press, 1989).

Yamada, M., "Le Mouvement des foires en Flandre avant 1200," in J. M. Duvosquel and A. Dierkens, eds, *Villes et campagnes au Moyen Âge: Mélanges Georges Despy* (Liège: Éditions du Perron, 1991), pp. 773–89.

Further Reading

A good starting point for further reading on medieval economic history is provided by the works of M. M. Postan and Roberto Lopez, both of whom exercised profound influence on the field. An overview of Postan's main views can be found in his *Essays on Medieval Agriculture and General Problems of the Medieval Economy* (Cambridge: Cambridge University Press, 1973). Postan's influence has been well summarized in John Hatcher and Mark Bailey, *Modelling the Middle Ages: The History and Theory of England's Economic Development* (Oxford: Oxford University Press, 2001). Like Postan, Lopez published many of his most influential ideas in article form; his general views are most readily accessible in *The Commercial Revolution of the Middle Ages, 950–1350* (Cambridge: Cambridge University Press, 1976).

Recent work in the field includes a number of valuable surveys. For England, see Richard Britnell, *Britain and Ireland 1050–1530* (Oxford: Oxford University Press, 2004), and Christopher Dyer, *Making a Living in the Middle Ages* (New Haven and London: Yale University Press, 2002). For France, see Philippe Contamine, Marc Bomparie, and Jean Luc Sarrazin, *L'Économie médiévale*, 3rd edn (Paris: A. Colin, 2003). For Italy, see Roberto Greci, Giuliano Pinto, and Guiliano Todeschini, *Economie urbane ed etica economica nell'Italia medievale* (Rome: Laterza, 2005). Peter Spufford, *Power and Profit: The Merchant in Medieval Europe* (New York: Thames and Hudson, 2002), is thematically narrower, but noteworthy for its broad geographical sweep.

Important works dealing with key elements of the medieval economy have also appeared in recent years. On textiles and textile production, see the first volume of *The Cambridge History of Western Textiles*, edited by David Jenkins (Cambridge: Cambridge University Press, 2003). On mills and milling, see John Langdon, *Mills in the Medieval Economy. England 1300–1540* (Oxford: Oxford University Press, 2004), and Adam Lucas, *Wind, Water, Work: Ancient and Medieval Milling Technology* (Leiden: Brill, 2006). Kathryn Reyerson, *The Art of the Deal: Intermediaries of Trade in Medieval Montpellier* (Leiden: Brill, 2002), explores how merchants acquired and processed market information. A useful synthesis of English agrarian history can be found in Phillipp R. Schofield, *Peasant and Community in Medieval England 1200–1500* (Houndmills and New York: Palgrave Macmillan, 2003). The early history of urban development is the focus of Adriaan Verhulst, *The Rise of Cities in Northwest Europe* (Cambridge: Cambridge University Press, 1999). New perspectives on demography and technology can be found in John Langdon and James Masschaele, "Commercial Activity and Population Growth in Medieval England," *Past & Present*, 190 (2006), pp. 35–82. Numerous specialized fields have been brought together in the recent festschrift for John H. A. Munro edited by Lawrin Armstrong, Ivana Elbl, and Martin Elbl: *Money, Markets and Trade in Late Medieval Europe: Essays in Honour of John H. A. Munro* (Leiden: Brill, 2007).

Chapter Six

Rural Families in Medieval Europe

Phillipp R. Schofield

An assessment of the rural family across a period extending from the early Middle Ages to the late Middle Ages inevitably presents not just a series of challenges but also a range of likely approaches. In order to examine the rural family across three quarters of a millennium, it seems appropriate, if not necessarily sensible, to divide the analysis between a number of facets of the medieval family, namely as domestic unit, as economic unit, and as a cultural unit. By so doing we will be able to move widely over shared agendas within a variety of studies across medieval Europe, engaging with historiographical traditions and grappling with analytical approaches to the family.

It is, broadly speaking, in discussion of family structure and demography, of economy and of culture, that the historiographical framing of the medieval family has been constructed. In that respect also, the history of the family has tended to follow the familiar lines of the general development of the discipline. Much of the work on the family in past time, and not just the medieval rural family, has been a product of broader discipline-wide developments, including the emergence of women's history and gender history, and the close historical engagement with the agendas of the social sciences.[1] Thus, sociological investigation of the family, consistent with the growth of a new social history in the 1960s and 1970s, encouraged an outpouring of work on family and household structures, much of it informed by work on other periods and by non-medievalists.[2] While this avenue of research has never since been entirely closed off, in more recent years the history of the medieval family has also admitted a cultural turn that has witnessed the publication of work on, *inter alia*, the nature of domestic space, the representation of the family, and its symbolic reference.[3] A good deal of this work is also heavily informed by research into the domestic economy, where discussion of, for instance, the role of women and children, treatment of the elderly, and the nature of charity all encourage a dialogue between subdisciplinary areas of research. Much of the research on the economy of the medieval family has in addition been the product of the investigation of issues ancillary to the family *per se*. Thus, for instance, discussion of land and its transfer in this period, a major theme of the economic history of the Middle Ages, has spawned a fair amount of reflection on the ways in which families in this period responded to changes in land supply, availability of capital, and the shifts within their own domestic structure. In turn, such work has encouraged further reflection upon the domestic economy, its function, and its foundation.

The major theoretical foundations for the study of the family in earlier periods have also been established by the work of those whose own research has been located in other disciplines. Thus, writing on the economy of the family has drawn upon the work of economic anthropologists such as Boserup and Sahlins. It would, however, be inappropriate to suggest that such theoretical underpinnings enjoy a universal degree of relevance; "contemporary" economic modelling, such as that undertaken on early twentieth-century Russia by Chayanov, clearly has greater significance within some historical traditions than it has in others and it may be at the second stage, of exchange between historians working within historical traditions, that such approaches are shared.[4]

Within the body of historical work focused upon the family, we can identify two main traditions, the two quite often intersecting and significantly informed by the work of the other. One of these strands is closely associated with an *Annaliste* approach, which has encouraged an investigation of the history of the family and its related topics, including the history of childhood, of age, of memory, and so on.[5] The other main strand we might best identify as emerging from work on family and household, in terms of structures and their demographic consequences, notably work linked to the Cambridge Group for the History of Population and Social Structure. Unlike the more disparate themes of an *Annaliste* tradition of *histoire totale*, the Cambridge Group project set a challenge for historians of the family working on different temporal and spatial contexts to test the extent of the nuclearization of the family. In this sense also the purpose was to place the history of the family upon a solid empirical footing and to reject some of the cosier, loosely ethnographic assumptions regarding the historical family that had persisted since at least the nineteenth century.[6] Both strands have precipitated research on the history of the family in Europe and beyond; it is clear also, as we will have cause to discuss in what follows, that this work has given impetus to medieval historians, including those working on aspects of rural and agrarian history in the period.

The Rural Family

It is now a standard of the literature on family structure that the majority of domestic units were simple, often nuclear units, typically comprising no more than two generations of family members. Crucial, then, in the distinction between differing family forms, as discussed across periods and between regions, is the proportion of more or less complex family and household types. In no small part as a result of the research encouraged by Laslett et al. in the 1960s and 1970s, we can now explore instances of "typical" family forms, before also proceeding to consider their typicality. For the family, that is the co-habiting kin group, we can describe its principal features. Inevitably, in generalizing, we lose the particular and we will need, from time to time, to consider a variety of instances. If we begin with the nuclear family, we find its type perpetuated throughout medieval Europe. Wickham notes that, for the early Middle Ages, it is the nuclear family that is most typically represented in our documents, with relatively much less direct reference to more distant kin.[7] In Catalonia, between the ninth and eleventh centuries, the predominant type of family grouping, judging from donations to ecclesiastical foundations, was nuclear, with recorded activity of single men, men and offspring, single women, single women and offspring, and parents, either acting alone or with their children, accounting for 88.6 per cent of all such recorded activity. Slightly more complex groupings were responsible for the remainder of this activity. While meaningful data on family structure are in relatively short supply for the early Middle Ages, ninth-century polyptychs offer us some reasonable sense of the average size of households, as on the estates of the abbey of Saint-Germain des Prés, where the mean size was 5.79 persons and the structure was typically simple. Listings of family units, as evidence for rentals and surveys, from the high Middle Ages offer us a fuller sense of this nuclear typicality. Thus, for example, in early fourteenth-century Greece, fiscal records, *praktika*, detail family membership and, though potentially difficult to interpret, do clearly suggest that the majority of families, between 50 percent and 75 percent, were nuclear in structure. Perhaps most obviously, the cadastral surveys of fifteenth-century Italy also suggest the preponderance of simple family and household structures, with 80.4 percent of households in the countryside around Florence and Arezzo composed of a single nucleus. Of families in the countryside, 51.2 percent were "entirely conjugal," composed of parents and, potentially, their offspring. Smith has also questioned the extent to which thirteenth-century serf lists from England (Lincolnshire) reveal any great complexity of household structure, as it was once suggested they might.[8]

This is not to say, of course, that more complex family units did not exist in medieval Europe, for inevitably they did. Laterally extended and vertically extended families occur in most identifiable cohorts of family structure. In medieval England, at Kibworth Harcourt (Leicestershire), a surviving male overlap of three generations was rare, though it was relatively more common to find family units that included females of three generations. Homans, in an analysis that predates the systematic investigation of family forms in past society, offers work that is as rich in its detail as it is potentially problematic in its emphasis on extended familial structures. He suggests that both stem-families, where one heir is advantaged over his siblings, the latter choosing either to remain as unmarried members of the main family or to seek their fortunes elsewhere, and joint-families, where there is a distribution of resources amongst siblings, or male siblings, were to be found in thirteenth-century English villages.[9] The proportion of extended family types varied across periods and across the region. There is some suggestion that, even within subregions, the proportions of extended family groups could differ quite significantly, as in early fourteenth-century Macedonia, where the proportion of, for instance, laterally extended family groups varied quite markedly between administrative districts or *themes*. Hammel notes similar distinctions for other Balkan households, his analysis of fourteenth-century listings of household structures from the estates of the Mount Athos monastery of Chilander suggesting a significant predominance of nuclear households, a feature that stands in contrast to later evidence for the joint family organization associated with the *zadruga*.[10]

If the family group, namely that of blood relations, varied significantly in its size and complexity, a further additional element of variety is evident in the household – that is, those living under the same roof.[11] In most instances, the household and the family unit must have been coterminous, with identical membership, but difference did exist where servants, slaves, and retainers lived with the family. While servants in late medieval Tuscany were a small element of the population, they did have an impact upon the structure of a small number of households.[12] Hardly suprisingly, the size and complexity of the household corresponded to relative wealth, though not to the extent that we should exclude the relatively humble from our considerations here. Amongst those that we might identify as elites living in the countryside, especially, of course, lay and religious households, there was, frequently, an evident complexity in their organization and considerable range in their size. While some of these, such as the *società della torre* and the *alberghi*, might best be identified as urban phenomena, gangs of dwellers resident within the households of the rich and powerful were not unknown to the countryside, as the domestic accounts of the great households indicate.[13] At lower levels of society, a peasant elite might also have housed servants and the passing stranger, thereby extending their household for periods of time. The housing of servants in peasant households, as *famuli*, *ancillae*, or *manipasti*, is familiar from a number of sources across Europe. The relatively intermittent accommodation of strangers, *extranei*, is also familiar, and is sometimes associated with the extension of the household at significant moments in the agrarian calendar, especially at harvest time.

While we might inevitably focus our attention upon the immediate family and household, it is also important to recognize the significance of the wider familial group, which we might think of as a functionally extended family, kin, and wider lineage.[14] Again, there are significant differences to identify here, not the least of which were determined by distinctions of wealth, mobility, and regional and local economies. We might also suspect that a strong cultural tie to kinship and blood relation either served to perpetuate such associations or was a reflection of their material significance. We will return to this in the final third of this chapter. For the moment we should note that, in certain rural contexts, individuals enjoyed the benefit of a wider kin group, often living within fairly close proximity though not within the same household. In other contexts, kin relationships might extend over significant geographical distance and might not easily be separated from other forms of collective identity, akin to clan, tribe, or economic grouping, as the knightly armorial clans in late medieval Poland illustrate. In fact, within economies where distance from the family hearth was a necessary feature of daily life, the emotional bonds of family were fiercely maintained but the actual familial identities blurred. Amongst the Cathar shepherds of the Pyrenees, for example, bonds of brotherhood did not only exist between blood brothers.[15] In other contexts, rural and village confraternities might well serve a similar function, offering an essentially non-familial grouping but one that was capable of replicating similar forms of familial support, including succor and education.[16]

The disparities described above can, in part, be explained by the variety of likely causative conditions that pertained across the period and the region. Age at marriage, for instance, inevitably helped to determine family size and structure, and was also a product of the same. While, as will be discussed further, it is impossible, in a homeostatic marriage system, to separate relativities of wealth from age at marriage, with a tendency for earlier marriage to be associated with wealthier families, historians have tended to distinguish between two dominant marriage patterns in Europe, and that especially based upon research on early modern and modern Europe. Most famously, J. Hajnal drew a distinction between northwest and southern European marriage patterns, sometimes referred to as, respectively, "European" and "non-European" marriage patterns.[17] The distinctive features of these two regimes were, for a "European" regime, late marriage, as well a significant proportion of the population who never married, a high proportion of servants, and a significant proportion of households composed of a sole occupant. By contrast, a "non-European" regime was characterized by earlier marriage, no solitaries and servants, and an almost universal proportion of those who eventually married.

Without meaningful data on age at marriage it is all but impossible to identify the predominance of one or other regime in earlier centuries and across all parts of Europe.[18] However, sufficient detailed information exists from parts of northern and southern Europe by the late Middle Ages to allow some meaningful distinction to be drawn. We might therefore identify a distinction between parts of late medieval England and northern Italy (Tuscany), with, apparently, a higher concentration of life-cycle service and later marriage evident in the former rather than in the latter. In southern Italy, there was even less evidence of life-cycle service than in Tuscany, and the likelihood that women would migrate from countryside to town in search of service work was comparatively remote.[19] Elsewhere such movement of women into urban households was less a choice and more the result of force. In the late medieval Balkans, for instance, the rural populations of Bosnia and Herzegovina were plundered for slaves, and especially female slaves, to support households within the towns of the Adriatic. Thrown into slavery, these men and women lost the support of their own families and had to develop opportunity within their new and imposed domestic setting.[20] By contrast, in late medieval England, there is especially strong evidence for the movement of young men and, above all, women from countryside to town in search of employment within urban households as servants, as studies of taxation records for York have shown.[21]

As Razi has attempted to show, different marriage patterns pertained, even within regional and local contexts, and were determined as much by relativities of wealth as they were by custom and perceived norms of behavior.[22] While these are topics to which we will need to return later in this chapter, it is evident that a crucial determinant of familial structure was wealth. Relativity of wealth helps explain some of the distinctions across time, as Howell reminds us when she notes that the age structure of the family was determined, in no small part, by the age at which offspring left the family home, a departure in itself determined by alternative opportunities, including the labor market, relative to "domestic" opportunities, including inheritance and marriage.[23] In medieval England, at Halesowen (Warwickshire), there was a direct and positive correlation between wealth and family size, the wealthiest "virgaters" tending to hold more land but also to live in a larger family groups.[24] In early fifteenth-century Italy, wealth has also been identified as a close associate of family size, suggesting that "families in the ruling class had their own demographic characteristic."[25] And, it is, of course, clear that political and religious elites, with especially advantaged access to resources, were most likely to occupy large and complex households. Klapisch also clarifies this association by suggesting that wealth alone did not determine family size and structure, but that landed wealth was the crucial component.[26]

The Economy of the Rural Family

The family and household were also, inevitably, economic units. To some extent, and we identify this as a traditional view of the rural family and its economy, the family and the economy of the family might be considered coterminous. A Chayanovian view of the peasant family, for instance, places great store upon the capacity of the family to respond to its own needs in ways largely but not wholly consistent with a subsistence or self-sustaining economy.[27] There is, as we might expect, good evidence for this close dependency of the rural family upon its own labor relative to a fairly fixed plot of land. In medieval England the concept of the *terra unius familie*, the land of and for a single villein family, was the bedrock of one form of seigneurial expectation of tenant land. Units of landholding, of 30 or 40 acres, were held by unfree tenants on the expectation of their capacity both to maintain the tenant family and to provide the lord with rent, in money, kind, and/or labor. This consonance of economic unit and family is also identified elsewhere.[28]

Within the family, we can find good evidence for a distribution of tasks partially determined by age and by gender. In medieval England, coroners' rolls illustrate the dangers of domestic occupations but may also inform us, through frequency of death and injury relative to place of incident and identity of the victim, of the normal distinctions of such activity. Thus, for instance, accidents involving females were more likely to occur close to the family hearth than were the deaths of males. Unsurprisingly also the range of tasks was determined by age and capacity. While, for instance, children, especially girls, might be employed by their parents as nurses of their younger siblings, responsibility for other significant facets of the domestic economy tended to reside with the adult members of the family. While children tended to be offered tasks consistent with their physical capacity, it is also the case that their training developed through their childhood in a manner intended to deliver them, as young adults, into the world of work. In fourteenth-century France, shepherd boys developed their range of skills as they matured, so that, by the age of about 14, they were largely equipped to meet the responsibilities of a shepherd's life. In similar manner, the male offspring of rural artisans also developed their skills in apprenticeship as the carpenters, tilers, and smiths of the medieval village. It is also evident that, in addition to capacity and expertise, roles within the domestic economy were divided according to custom and the like. Changes in custom and developments in trading opportunities would also see opportunities for employment increase or decrease accordingly. Thus, brewing of ale by females, as part of a household economy, declined in the late Middle Ages as it gave way to commercial brewing dominated by men.[29]

It would, though, be incorrect to associate the family unit in the medieval countryside with any absolute self-sufficiency. It is unlikely that many, if any, rural families in the Middle Ages came close to a dependency that was based exclusively upon themselves. While it is reasonable to suppose that the domestic unit and its landholding was the vital mainstay of most rural families in this period, it is also evident that rural families were, to varying degrees, drawn into economic dealing beyond their immediate domestic sphere. Obligations to lords and to the state, labor beyond the family, the sale of surplus produce through the market or through less formal exchange all had consequences, both advantageous and disadvantageous, for the domestic budget. We might, for instance, think of a merchant class, which moved between town and countryside, and while recognizably resident, at least in part, in the countryside was dependent upon commercial exchange and the market for the proper functioning of its economy. In fifteenth-century England, certain rural dwellers were also as much "urban" in that their main economic activity drew them into town and city. Aspiring merchants also aped their social superiors, not only by seeking marriages that placed them within their society, but also by purchasing residences in the countryside and channeling their profits into land and their rustic existence.[30]

This involvement in an economy that extended beyond the immediate domestic or familial unit is also evident in the employment of servants or the use of slaves, thereby extending the capacity of the simple biological unit of the family. It has already been noted, for instance, that households might be extended in their size and complexity at certain key moments of the agricultural year, as illustrated by complaints against the "illegal" housing of strangers who might then be employed, in competition with neighbors, as gleaners.[31] An important distinction here is to be made between households where a significant part of the domestic economy involved paid labor, including live-in servants, and those households where this was not the case. In earlier periods and in certain parts of Europe in the later Middle Ages, we should also recognize the significance of slaves within and beyond the domestic rural economy. In most parts of Western Europe, between the tenth and twelfth centuries, slavery was subsumed within structures of feudal lordship that imposed various degrees of obligation and of freedom and unfreedom upon those who came increasingly to be seen as tenants rather than slaves. In such instances, slaves occupied land and households separate from their lords and masters, their impact on the lord's domestic economy typically a product of their obligation and that, increasingly, in forms of rent.[32]

There were, of course, consequences arising from the economic relationship of household and work. The marriage patterns discussed earlier in this chapter had implications for the nature and functioning of domestic economies, as well as having a wider impact upon society and economy across the period. We tend to think of rural families as operating within a neo-local household formation system, sometimes referred to as a "peasant" or "niche" system, where opportunity for marriage is generally dependent upon the availability of land. In such systems relatives of wealth and landholding determine differences of age at marriage within particular social groups. Thus, in Halesowen (England) in the fourteenth century age at marriage appears to have been earlier for the relatively prosperous villagers, who also enjoyed extensive familial and wider kin networks, but was later for the poorer tenants. These poorer tenants were conceivably more likely to find themselves operating within a "proletarian" or "real-wages" household formation system, a system of relative displacement that stands in contrast to any view of the domestic economy focused upon the family. In such a system, those individuals who could not expect to gain significantly through familial association and above all through inheritance, could, for example, seek labor opportunities as a means of gathering the necessary resources prior to marriage. Instead, we come closer to an economy centered on the individual and his or her earning capacity relative to the labor market. Such difference in marriage and household formation systems had consequences for the family and/or households in other respects, notably in the employment of life-cycle servants, with delayed marriage as a by-product of their employment, while individuals might also use their employment to support their own family members.[33]

Establishing the relative significance of these household formation systems is far from straightforward, not least because individuals living within the same family and household might be participants in either system. This might especially be the case where a strict monogeniture advantaged one sibling while forcing the other siblings to seek their advantage elsewhere, precipitating both centrifugal and centripetal effects within the same domestic unit. The same would also be the case if the household was also home to life-cycle servants. In such an instance the life-cycle servant was a participant in one form of household formation system, essentially a "proletarian" or "real-wages" system, while other members of the household might be more appropriately seen as operating within a "peasant" or "niche" system. That said, historians have tended to explain the prevalence of one of the two systems relative to the other in terms of wealth, with wealthier rural families basing their marriage choices upon their landed resources and upon their capacity to accumulate land, chiefly through inheritance. In other contexts, families might exploit opportunities provided by institutions, including religious houses, in order to absorb non-inheriting family members.[34]

While the rural family might be other than self-sustaining in terms of labor, it also needed to engage, in economic terms, with individuals and institutions for a range of other reasons. Not the least of these was in its obligations. Lords, the Church, and the State were, to varying degrees, able to make demands upon the domestic unit in this period. This was especially the case where the family or household was directly associated with a block of landholding. Towards the close of the period the burgeoning nation state in Europe could direct its apparatus toward the individual, as systems of taxation on movable goods or head taxes illustrate, but in earlier periods landholding was typically the basis of obligation. In this respect, heads of households, as tenants, owed some element of their resource to others. Among rural elites this might include military service, while for peasants service would more likely be performed as labor. Rents in cash and kind, payments such as mortuary to the Church or death duties to the lord, had a similar impact upon the budget of the rural household.

Against such outgoings there existed opportunities to sell produce and particular skills. It was once assumed that few households in the period, be they religious houses, noble, or peasant, were involved in anything other than an economy founded on consumption – that is, the maintenance of anticipated needs rather than an enterprise more geared to profit. It is now argued that at all levels of society it is possible to detect those who looked to secure more than their consumption needs and, instead, employed their resources in ways capable of seeking profit. The domestic economy of the household, insofar as it generated any kind of surplus, also presented the opportunity for family and household to exploit that surplus, through either reinvestment or display. The purchase of household goods, the employment of labor, charitable donation, gestures of self-aggrandisement are all evident from this period, as families sought opportunities to employ whatever benefits their toils had brought them. One other surplus that families might enjoy was time; where free time independent of labor could be found, then a domestic culture might also be fostered.

The Culture of the Rural Family

The culture of the rural family also, of course, exhibited enormous variety in this period. Impossible as it is to trace every facet of household and family culture, in any period, we can at least identify a number of features redolent of the cultural investigation of the domestic space. We might begin by exploring the culture of the family group and the extent to which issues of family, kin, and relationships of blood were of central relevance to family members. Thus, for instance, as more than one historian has described, the familial regard for property is evidence both for the nature of the family economy and also for a sense of collective obligation and action. In ninth-century Brittany, for example, familial rights over land outstripped the ability of the individual to alienate family land without the consent of his or her kin. The same was also the case in fourteenth-century Greece, where the alienation of even small plots of land was subject to the agreement of the immediate family – that is, all those with actual claims upon the property.[35] While we could find many similar instances throughout medieval Europe, it would be incorrect to suggest that men and women in the medieval countryside were universally and entirely subsumed within a familial identity, and that they did not act as individuals. Discussion of, for instance, the familial attachment to land, the so-called family–land bond, has generated a good deal of reflection on the nature of the rural economy in this period.[36] By extension it may also have something to tell us regarding the contemporary perception of the vitality and significance of the family itself. No doubt the extent to which familial rights over property either superseded or were secondary to the rights of individuals was conditioned by, amongst other things, institutions, local custom, and the nature of the economy. But the culture of the family is and was an inevitable construct of such factors and, in turn, helps determine their force.

There is also little doubt that, where it was of significance, families found opportunity to represent power relations within the family.[37] Distinctions of age and of gender were rehearsed in a number of ways. In late medieval Italy it is possible that an implicit indication of power is evident in listings of family members in the *catasto*, including the organization of subgroups listed according to the age of the male head of the household.[38] Welsh hall houses of the later Middle Ages, including the houses of well-to-do peasants and yeomen, exhibit features consistent with a familial organization that placed the male head of the household on a dais at the end of the hall furthest from the entrance, in a manner entirely consistent with that to be found in higher-status households.[39] Herlihy also notes that women, not infrequently closer in age to their offspring than were their husbands, acted as intercessors between child and father. We see this in the German poem *Helmbrecht*, where, while the father rejects his mutilated robber-son, it is the mother who offers him a crust "as if to a child." In so doing mothers were seen as replicating, within the domestic setting, the role of the Virgin and of other female saints.[40] The culture of space and its use within the household can also be identified in other contexts, not least in its evolution. In some parts of Europe we can chart a development of the domestic space in the countryside, a response to changes in fashion, political circumstance, and the wider economy. While we could as appropriately discuss such developments under the heading of "economy" or "family and household structure," shifts in the organization of the physical household had inevitable cultural import. Thus, for example, we witness, in certain parts of Europe, the creation of "new" space in the medieval house, in response to changing economic circumstance and the opportunity to employ non-kin as domestic servants within the household. The movement within late medieval house construction to incorporate private rooms and solars, also evident amongst the relatively wealthy in parts of Europe in the high and late Middle Ages is testimony both to a changing regard for privacy and personal space and for the opportunity to occasion such a shift in design. The domestic ritual of the household, more evident to us in higher-status households than in their relatively lowlier equivalents, was also an opportunity to confirm positions within the domestic unit, either by explicit reference or by more subtle, and implicit, suggestion. Goldberg has described, admittedly in an urban context, how fifteenth-century books of hours furnished the female members of households with spiritual material that allowed them to adapt their religious expression to their domestic setting, while, also in fifteenth-century England, nonconformity found its expression in reading groups and gatherings, at the core of which was the family.[41]

That family and household occupied a centrality of sorts is also evident from their roles as a focus for key events of the life cycle. Thus, the vital events of birth, marriage, and death were, of necessity, familial, at least in certain respects, and these tended to be cultural. Celebration or recognition of vital events resided with the family, though often mediated through some external institution such as lordship, of which more below. In similar terms, violence between families might, for instance, have its rituals and cultures of expression, as those who have studied feud in the countryside have described. Blood feud in late medieval Denmark, for instance, was not solely the prerogative of the nobility but might also involve all "good men," including peasants.[42] In such circumstances the roles of victim and of aggressor were determined by blood relationship, with kinship a determining factor in the formal process of remedy. Even where opportunity was presented to calm the insistent demands of the feuding parties, principally through the intervention of law and the "state," it was the representation of the family and wider kin, an explicit acknowledgment of blood rights, that tended to hold sway even with some diminution of familial authority toward the end of the period.[43]

Families were also a signal source of their own collective memories, a potentially crucial component in asserting rights over property and ordering succession. While the wider community and neighbors also had an important role to play in gathering and storing information, as, for instance, witnesses to proof-of-age inquests suggest, the immediate family and the wider kin group had a recognized responsibility to preserve information on, *inter alia*, lineage, ties of blood, and the property of the family. Thus, throughout much of Europe and across the period, certain features of the family, such as degrees of consanguinity and affinity, were determined by the individual and collective capacity of families to remember who was related to whom, and by what degree. Again we might expect the medieval family's capacity to effect such a role to be influenced by a wider context, not the least of which would be the degree to which society preserved an orality relative to accessible sources of public and private written record, such as notaries. It has also been suggested that the development of durable surnames in the high Middle Ages reflects, among a variety of social groups, anxiety over the transfer of property and a clear desire to preserve identities in ways that ensured an appropriate transmission within the family.[44]

We should also note, in this discussion of memory and the family, that female members of the family may have had a particular role to play. In most pre-industrial contexts the capacity for any society to generate a large proportion of families comprising more than two generations is remote.[45] Issues of survivability, of age at marriage, and of treatment of the elderly, while significant in demographic terms, also have considerable cultural relevance.[46] Where, for instance, we find an early age at marriage for females relative to that of males, then we might expect a distinct approach to memorializing the family, in ways determined by gender, with stronger bonds existing between surviving female members across more than one or two generations.[47] High-status women in Carolingian Europe were, as van Houts has described, custodians of a family memory and enjoined their male relatives to reflect upon their wider familial responsibilities.[48] That said, we should also recognize that the terminology of familial relationships is often not so extensive in this period as to encourage a sense that family members carried with them a detailed knowledge of their own lineage, and administrative records seldom identify blood relations at more than two or three removes from the individual.[49]

Beyond the immediate family and household, interaction with other family and kin groups might generate its own range of broadly cultural responses, with established modes of dealing. The coming-together of families, at point of marriage, promoted events and rituals at least in part intended to make public, to cement, and to celebrate such unions. The thirteenth-century German poem that describes a public exchange of vows and the ritual treading by the groom on the foot of the bride is mirrored in other public exchanges elsewhere in Europe.[50] The exchange of goods by dowry made explicit this coming-together of families, as did the institution of godparenthood, which provided a means of celebrating the virtues of the family while at the same time extending its associations and networks. In the late-thirteenth-century Pyrénées, for example, the acceptance of the role of godparent and attendance of baptism brought opportunities for influence as it also brought obligation for support and the development of the offspring of the family.[51] It is also important to note that the family, inheritance, and, in particular, marriage were routes to success and social advancement. It is has been noted by more than one commentator that high-status males across medieval Europe might advance their position through marriage; in such circumstances also a cultural shift might be effected within the family through association by the female line with a new household.[52]

In a number of respects also the culture of the family, as also in the case of the economy and the structure of the family, was conditioned by factors external to it. Not the least of these external factors, especially for a servile peasantry, were lordship and the Church. The direct consequences of lordship for unfree peasant families, of serfs and villeins, in different parts of Europe and at different points in the Middle Ages, were, broadly speaking, to inhibit freedom of choice and action. Vital events – birth, death, and marriage – were each of consequence for lords keen to protect their tenantry as an economic investment and to regulate any transfer of property, particularly in the instances of marriage and death. We might reasonably expect such events to be imbued with ritual and cultural significance, which indeed they were, as we have already discussed in the case of marriage, but they were also events informed by the lord's own expectations. In particular, marriage and death both frequently attracted some financial penalty or license, an expectation that the Church also placed upon the same events while at the same time contriving to draw them within its aegis. It has, for instance, been suggested that the limited incidence of joint-family organization (*zadruge*) in parts of Macedonia in the late Middle Ages may be a consequence of lordly insistence that households were divided according to conjugal units.[53] Lords might also choose to effect changes in strategies of inheritance, to insist upon retirement of the infirm, to control the remarriage of widows, and so on. Such direct involvement could not but influence the nature of familial identities and the integrity of family and household bonds. In similar ways, attitudes to family, both within the countryside and in the towns, were influenced by external views of the family and of relations within and beyond it. Attitudes to marriage and to degrees of consanguinity, to illegitimacy, affinity and the treatment of children, including infanticide, were each mediated by the Church's teaching in this period. The Church's claim on property and the competing claims of family are also highly relevant, not least in a period when such competition appears to have heightened. In such circumstances the durability of family and the force of its claim upon the individual relative to the claims of other bodies, such as the Church, the lord, the State, the local community, were contested.

Conclusion

To a large degree our focus upon the central facets of the rural family across the Middle Ages is determined by the preoccupations of earlier historians. In terms of the body of secondary work on the medieval rural family, a significant proportion of that work was generated by local or regional studies that included, as one element of their analysis, a demographic and social structural account of the area of study. In many respects, study of the domestic economy has emerged in a similar way, though, in recent years, and especially within an Anglophone historiography, there has also been a program of research on markets and commerce, part of which has included study of the family economy and its place within wider commercial networks. Inevitably also our view is conditioned by the sources that survive, as well as the preparedness of historians to engage with them. In that sense a progress through constitutional and juridical sources of the family, including the statements of canon lawyers, through listings of family groups and heads of households, through qualitative sources and the material and archaeological remains of the medieval family and household also reflects the changes in historical approach and fashion outlined above. Indirectly, the combination of these approaches has brought historians to a fuller view of the medieval rural family, so that we now, through a series of case and thematic studies, have arrived at a broad consensus on, *inter alia*, the typicality of familial structure, the relative significance of factors external to the immediate family, and the strength of familial ties. In certain degree the prevalence of certain historical "projects," such as the quest to identify the extent of nuclearization, risks a reduction of diversity, and the failure to concentrate upon the particular and the local, or indeed to generate new questions around the medieval family, whether rural or urban. That said, the extent to which family and kinship mattered in this period relative to the individual and to other forms of association capable of providing support and nurture remains an issue of some historical relevance and investigation. It may though be the case that, in a European historiography that is increasingly Anglophone and, at the same time, open to the research of those working on Central and Eastern Europe, the next generation of major research questions will be generated from outside Western Europe.

Notes

1 Lambert and Schofield, *Making History.*
2 See, e.g., Laslett with Wall, *Household and Family.* One study of the post-medieval family in Europe, but with clear reference for those interested in the medieval family and household, is Flandrin, *Families in Former Times*, while Scott, ed., *The Peasantries of Europe*, also has a good deal on rural families in the later Middle Ages and earlier.
3 See, e.g., on space and the household, Gilchrist, *Gender and Material Culture.*
4 Wickham, *Framing the Early Middle Ages*, pp. 536ff; for Chayanov, see, *inter alia*, M. Bourin, "Preface", in Feller and Wickham, eds, *Le Marché de la terre*, pp. viii–ix, and the observation that Chayanov does not have the same relevance in a French historiographical tradition.
5 See, e.g., Duby and le Goff, *Famille et parenté dans l'occident médiéval.* In addition, particular aspects of life cycle, little explored in this chapter, have generated some significant areas of research. There is, for instance, a growing literature on childhood, most famously prompted by the thesis of Ariès, *L'Enfant et la vie familiale.* Among studies of childhood that include reference to families and their children in the countryside, two broad statements are Orme, *Medieval Childhood*, and Shahar, *Childhood in the Middle Ages.* Themes with potential relevance for the study of the medieval rural family are infanticide and illegitimacy, and both have received attention in recent decades. The study of infanticide in the Middle Ages, in part a product of a psycho-historical approach, was especially prominent in the 1970s, and attracted more attention from historians of childhood than it did from medievalists, as the debate between Kellum and Helmholz illustrates: Kellum, "Infanticide in England"; Helmholz, "Infanticide in the Province of Canterbury." Studies of the treatment of children, as well as attitudes to illegitimacy and the illegitimate, have also been considered by historians interested in demography and social structure, as, for instance, Smith, "Marriage Processes in the English Past."
6 Laslett, "Introduction: The History of the Family," pp. 1–89.
7 Wickham, *Framing the Early Middle Ages*, p. 551.
8 Catalonia: To Figueras, *Familia i hereu a la Catalunya Nord-Oriental*, pp. 76–7; early medieval France: Herlihy, *Medieval Households*, pp. 56, 69–70; Greece: Laiou-Thomadakis, *Peasant Society*, p. 81. Similar observations have also been made for northwestern Russia in the late Middle Ages and early modern period: Moon, *Russian Peasantry*, p. 158. Italy: Klapisch, "Household and Family in Tuscany," pp. 279–80. England: Smith, "Hypothèses sur la nuptialité," pp. 120–4.
9 Howell, *Land, Family and Inheritance in Transition*, pp. 232–5; Homans, *English Villagers of the Thirteenth Century*, pp. 119–20.
10 Laiou-Thomadakis, *Peasant Society*, pp. 79–81; Hammell, "Household Structure in Fourteenth-Century Macedonia," pp. 259–62. On the problems associated with a simple association between household structure and the concept of *zadruga*, as well as a generally useful discussion of *zadruga*, see Todorova, *Balkan Family Structure and the European Pattern*, pp. 127–33.
11 Laslett, "Introduction: The History of the Family," pp. 23ff.
12 Klapisch, "Household and Family in Tuscany," pp. 277–8.
13 Woolgar, *Great Household*, cc. 2–3; Klapisch, "Household and Family in Tuscany," pp. 280–1.

14 Razi, "Myth of the Immutable English Family."
15 Bieniak, "Clans de chevalrie," pp. 321–8; Le Roy Ladurie, *Montaillou*, pp. 126–7.
16 Lynch, *Individuals, Families, and Communities*, pp. 89–91, while here describing rural confraternities, has argued that the inclination for such organization is best seen as an essentially urban phenomenon.
17 Hajnal, "European Marriage Patterns in Perspective," and "Two Kinds of Pre-Industrial Household Formation System," pp. 65–104.
18 But note Herlihy, *Medieval Households*, pp. 76–7, 104–11.
19 Smith, "Hypothèses sur la nuptialité," pp. 109–10; Lynch, *Individuals, Families, and Communities*, pp. 49–51.
20 Stuard, "To Town to Serve: Urban Domestic Slavery," pp. 39–55.
21 Goldberg, *Women, Work and Life-Cycle*, pp. 280ff.
22 Razi, *Life, Marriage and Death*, pp. 50–64; Razi, "Myth of the Immutable English Family," pp. 3–44.
23 Howell, *Land, Family and Inheritance in Transition*, pp. 235–6.
24 Razi, *Life, Marriage and Death*, p. 86, and references therein.
25 Klapisch, "Household and Family in Tuscany," p. 274.
26 Klapisch and Demonet, "'A une pane et uno vino'," p. 53.
27 Chayanov, *The Theory of Peasant Economy*, pp. 107–13.
28 See, e.g., Epstein, "Peasantries of Italy," p. 91.
29 Hanawalt, *The Ties that Bound*, pp. 156ff, 177–8; Shahar, *Childhood in the Middle Ages*, pp. 243–5; Whittle, "Housewives and Servants in Rural England," p. 71.
30 e.g. Kermode, *Medieval Merchants*, pp. 110–12.
31 Schofield, "Social Economy of the Medieval Village."
32 Pelteret, *Slavery in Early Mediaeval England*, pp. 256–9.
33 See, for a useful summary of the theory in this respect, Poos, *A Rural Society after the Black Death*, pp. 141–8.
34 See, e.g., Leyser, *Rule and Conflict*.
35 Davies, *Small Worlds*, p. 71; Kravari, "Les Actes privés des Monastères de l'Athos," pp. 85–6.
36 Feller and Wickham, eds, *Le Marché de la terre*.
37 Rösener, *Peasants in the Middle Ages*, p. 172.
38 Klapisch and Demonet, "'A une pane et uno vino.'"
39 Suggett, *Houses and History in the March of Wales*, p. 85.
40 Herlihy, *Medieval Households*, pp. 121–2; for *Helmbrecht*, see Shahar, *Childhood in the Middle Ages*, p. 252.
41 Goldberg, "What was a Servant?" pp. 8–9.
42 Netterstrøm, "Feud, Protection and Serfdom," pp. 373–4.
43 Flandrin, *Families in Former Times*, pp. 15–16. On the reduced claim of kin *vis-à-vis* the state, see, e.g., Pollock and Maitland, *The History of English Law*, vol. ii, pp. 473–4.
44 See, e.g., Bourin and Durand, *Vivre au village au Moyen Âge*, pp. 37–8. See also Duby, "Family Structures," pp. 108–9.
45 See, e.g., Herlihy, *Medieval Households*, p. 71.
46 See, e.g., Laiou-Thomadakis, *Peasant Society*, p. 82. Also van Houts, *Memory and Gender*.
47 See, above, for instance at Kibworth Harcourt, where three-generational female associations were more common than were similar male associations. Also, Klapisch, "Household and Family in Tuscany," p. 272.
48 Van Houts, *Memory and Gender*, c. 4, esp. pp. 66–73. Note also Goody, *The Development of the Family and Marriage*, p. 235, and the particular significance of matrilineal lines of succession.

49 See, e.g., Davies, *Small Worlds*, p. 68.
50 Rösener, *Peasants in the Middle Ages*, pp. 178–9.
51 Le Roy Ladurie, *Montaillou*, p. 127. On godparenthood, see also Lynch, *Individuals, Families, and Communities*, pp. 70–3 and references therein.
52 See, e.g., Goody, *The Development of the Family and Marriage*, p. 229 and references.
53 Hammell, "Household Structure in Fourteenth-Century Macedonia," p. 270. But see also n. 10 above, and references there to *zadruga*.

Bibliography

Ariès, P., *L'Enfant et la vie familiale sous l'Ancien Régime* (Paris: Plon, 1960).

Bieniak, J., "Clans de chevalerie en Pologne du xiiie au xve siècle," in G. Duby and J. le Goff, eds, *Famille et parenté dans l'occident médiéval* (Rome: École Française de Rome, 1977), pp. 321–33.

Bourin, M., and Durand, R., *Vivre au village au Moyen Âge: Les Solidarités paysannes du xie au xiiie siècle* (Rennes: Universitaire de Rennes, 2000).

Chayanov, A. V., *The Theory of Peasant Economy* (Homewood, IL: published for the American Economic Association, by R. D. Irwin, 1966).

Davies, W., *Small Worlds: The Village Community in Early Medieval Brittany* (Berkeley and Los Angeles: University of California, 1988).

Duby, G., "Family Structures in the West during the Middle Ages," in G. Duby, *Love and Marriage in the Middle Ages* (Cambridge: Polity Press, 1994), pp. 105–12.

Duby, G., and le Goff, J., eds, *Famille et parenté dans l'occident médiéval* (Rome: École Française de Rome, 1977).

Epstein, S. R., "The Peasantries of Italy, 1350–1750," in T. Scott, ed., *The Peasantries of Europe from the Fourteenth to the Eighteenth Centuries* (London: Longman, 1998), pp. 74–108.

Feller, L., and Wickham, C., eds, *Le Marché de la terre au moyen âge* (Rome: École Française de Rome, 2005).

Flandrin, J. L., *Families in Former Times: Kinship, Household and Sexuality* (Cambridge: Cambridge University Press, 1979).

Gilchrist, R., *Gender and Material Culture: The Archaeology of Religious Women* (London: Routledge, 1997).

Goldberg, P. J. P., *Women, Work, and Life-Cycle in a Medieval Economy: Women in York and Yorkshire, c.1300–1520* (Oxford: Oxford University Press, 1992).

Goldberg, P. J. P., "What was a Servant?" in A. Curry and E. Matthew, eds, *Concepts and Patterns of Service in the Later Middle Ages* (Woodbridge: Boydell, 2000), pp. 1–20.

Goody, J., *The Development of the Family and Marriage in Europe* (Cambridge: Cambridge University Press, 1983).

Hajnal, J., "European Marriage Patterns in Perspective," in D. V. Glass and D. E. C. Evesley, eds, *Population in History: Essays in Historical Demography* (London: Edward Arnold, 1965), pp. 101–43.

Hajnal, J., "Two Kinds of Pre-Industrial Household Formation System," in R. Wall, ed., *Family Forms in Historic Europe* (Cambridge: Cambridge University Press, 1983), pp. 65–104.

Hammell, E. A., "Household Structure in Fourteenth-Century Macedonia," *Journal of Family History*, 5 (1980), pp. 242–73.

Hanawalt, B. A., *The Ties that Bound: Peasant Families in Medieval England* (Oxford: Oxford University Press, 1986).

Helmholz, R. H., "Infanticide in the Province of Canterbury during the Fifteenth Century," *History of Childhood Quarterly*, 2 (1975), pp. 282–340.

Herlihy, D., *Medieval Households* (Cambridge, MA: Harvard University Press, 1985).

Homans, G. C., *English Villagers of the Thirteenth Century* (Cambridge, MA: Harvard University Press, 1941; repr. 1970).

Howell, C., *Land, Family and Inheritance in Transition: Kibworth Harcourt, 1280–1700* (Cambridge: Cambridge University Press, 1983).

Kellum, B. A., "Infanticide in England in the Later Middle Ages," *History of Childhood Quarterly*, 1 (1974), pp. 367–88.

Kermode, J., *Medieval Merchants: York, Beverley and Hull in the Later Middle Ages* (Cambridge: Cambridge University Press, 1998).

Klapisch, C., "Household and Family in Tuscany in 1427," in P. Laslett with R. Wall, *Household and Family in Past Time* (Cambridge: Cambridge University Press, 1972), pp. 267–81.

Klapisch, C., and Demonet, M., ""A une pane et uno vino": The Rural Tuscan Family at the Beginning of the Fifteenth Century," in Robert Forster and Orest Ranum, eds, *Family and Society: Selections from the Annales: économies, sociétés, civilizations*, trans. Elborg Forster and Patricia M. Ranum (Baltimore: Johns Hopkins University Press, 1976), pp. 41–74.

Kravari, V., "Les Actes privés des Monastères de l'Athos et l'unité du patrimoine familial," in D. Simon, ed., *Eherecht und Familiengut in Antike und Mittelalter* (Munich: Oldenbourg Wissenschaftverlag, 1992), pp. 77–88.

Laiou-Thomadakis, A. E., *Peasant Society in the Late Byzantine Empire: A Social and Demographic Study* (Princeton: Princeton University Press, 1977).

Lambert, P. and Schofield, P., *Making History: The Theory and Practices of a Discipline* (London: Routledge, 2004).

Laslett, P., "Introduction: The History of the Family," in P. Laslett with R. Wall, *Household and Family in Past Time* (Cambridge: Cambridge University Press, 1972), pp. 1–89.

Laslett, P., with Wall, R., *Household and Family in Past Time* (Cambridge: Cambridge University Press, 1972).

Le Roy Ladurie, E., *Montaillou: Cathars and Catholics in a French Village, 1294–1324* (Harmondsworth: Penguin, 1980).

Leyser, K., *Rule and Conflict in an Early Medieval Society: Ottonian Saxony* (London: Edward Arnold, 1979).

Lynch, K. A., *Individuals, Families, and Communities in Europe, 1200–1800: The Urban Foundations of Western Society* (Cambridge: Cambridge University Press, 2003).

Moon, D., *The Russian Peasantry, 1600–1900* (London: Longman, 1999).

Netterstrøm, J. B., "Feud, Protection and Serfdom in Late Medieval and Early Modern Denmark (*c.*1400–1600)," in P. Freedman and M. Bourin, eds, *Forms of Servitude in Northern and Central Europe: Decline, Resistance, and Expansion* (Turnhout: Brepols, 2005), pp. 369–84.

Orme, N., *Medieval Childhood* (New Haven: Yale University Press, 2003).

Pelteret, D. A. E., *Slavery in Early Mediaeval England: From the Reign of Alfred to the Twelfth Century* (Woodbridge: Boydell, 1995).

Pollock, Sir F., and Maitland, F. W., *The History of English Law*, 2 vols. (Cambridge: Cambridge University Press, 1968).

Poos, L. R., *A Rural Society after the Black Death: Essex 1350–1525* (Cambridge: Cambridge University Press, 1991).

Razi, Z., *Life, Marriage and Death in a Medieval Parish: Economy, Society and Demography in Halesowen, 1270–1400* (Cambridge: Cambridge University Press, 1980).

Razi, Z., "The Myth of the Immutable English Family," *Past & Present*, 140 (1993), pp. 3–44.

Rösener, W., *Peasants in the Middle Ages* (Cambridge: Polity Press, 1992).
Schofield, P. R., "The Social Economy of the Medieval Village," *Economic History Review* (2007; "on-line early" at http://www.blackwell-.synergy.com/doi/full/10.1111/j.1468-0289.2007.00406.x).
Scott, T., *The Peasantries of Europe from the Fourteenth to the Eighteenth Centuries* (London: Longman, 1998).
Shahar, S., *Childhood in the Middle Ages* (London: Routledge, 1990).
Smith, R. M., "Hypothèses sur la nuptialité en Angleterre aux xiiie–xive siècles," *Annales: économies, sociétes, civilisations*, 38 (1983), pp. 107–36.
Smith, R. M., "Marriage Processes in the English Past: Some Continuities," in L. Bonfield, R. Smith, and K. Wrightson, eds, *The World we have Gained: Histories of Population and Social Structure* (Oxford: Oxford University Press, 1986), pp. 43–99.
Stuard, S.M., "To Town to Serve: Urban Domestic Slavery," in B. A. Hanawalt, ed., *Women and Work in Pre-Industrial Europe* (Bloomington: Indiana University Press, 1986), pp. 39–55.
Suggett, R., *Houses and History in the March of Wales: Radnorshire, 1400–1800* (Aberystwyth: Royal Commission on the Ancient and Historical Monuments of Wales, 2005).
To Figueras, L., *Familia i hereu a la Catalunya nord-oriental (segles x–xii)* (Barcelona: L'Abadia de Montserrat, 1997).
Todorova, M. N., *Balkan Family Structure and the European Pattern* (Budapest: CEU Press, 2006).
van Houts, E., *Memory and Gender in Medieval Europe* (Basingstoke: Palgrave, 1999).
Whittle, J., "Housewives and Servants in Rural England, 1440–1650: Evidence of Women's Work from Probate Documents," *Transactions of the Royal Historical Society*, 6th ser. 15 (2005), pp. 51–74.
Wickham, C., *Framing the Early Middle Ages: Europe and the Mediterranean, 400–800* (Oxford: Oxford University Press, 2005).
Woolgar, C. M, *The Great Household in Late Medieval England* (New Haven: Yale University Press, 1999).

Further Reading

There are relatively few general statements on the medieval rural family. An accessible and highly relevant work is D. Herlihy, *Medieval Households* (Cambridge, MA: Harvard University Press, 1985). The history of the family, including the medieval rural family, is also considered in A. Burguiere et al., eds, *A History of the Family*, vol. I: *Distant Worlds, Ancient Worlds* (Cambridge, MA: Harvard University Press, 1996). More generally, P. Laslett, with R. Wall, *Household and Family in Past Time* (Cambridge: Cambridge University Press, 1972), remains a major contribution to the study of family and household form in past societies.

There are also a number of national and regional studies that include detailed statements on family and household in this period. These include M. Bourin and R. Durand, *Vivre au village au Moyen Âge: Les Solidarités paysannes du xie au xiiie siècle* (Rennes: Universitaire de Rennes, 2000); B. A. Hanawalt, *The Ties that Bound: Peasant Families in Medieval England* (Oxford: Oxford University Press, 1986); P. R. Schofield, *Peasant and Community in Medieval England* (Basingstoke: Palgrave, 2003). P. Fleming, *Family and Household in Medieval England* (Basingstoke: Palgrave, 2001), provides an overview of discussion of central facets of the medieval family in England, while C. Woolgar, *The Great Household in Medieval England* (New Haven: Yale University Press, 1999), describes higher-status households in the period. Perhaps the single most important case study of family structure and household form is D. Herlihy and C. Klapisch-Zuber, *Tuscans and their Families: A Study of the Florentine Catasto* *of 1427* (New Haven: Yale University Press, 1985); A. E. Laiou-Thomadakis, *Peasant Society in the Late Byzantine Empire: A Social and Demographic Study* (Princeton: Princeton University Press, 1977), has also promoted a good deal of work on the Byzantine peasant family, as examined through nominal listings. Much of the more particular research on the family in past society is also published in edited collections, such as G. Duby and J. le Goff, eds, *Famille et parenté dans l'occident médiéval* (Rome: École Française de Rome, 1977), and in dedicated journals such as the *Journal of Family History* (Sage Journals) and *Continuity and Change* (Cambridge: Cambridge University Press).

An important statement on age at marriage and its implications for our understanding of the medieval family, especially in the medieval English countryside, is provided by R. M. Smith, "Hypothèses sur la nuptialité en Angleterre aux xiiie–xive siécles," *Annales: économies, sociétes, civilisations*, 38 (1983), pp. 107–36. Smith has written extensively on household formation systems and marriage in this period; among his key works the following is highly relevant to the study of the medieval rural family: R. M. Smith, "Some Issues Concerning Families and their Property in Rural England 1250–1800," in R. M. Smith, ed., *Land, Kinship and Life-Cycle* (Cambridge: Cambridge University Press, 1984), pp. 1–86. Historians of medieval England, following the lead of early modernists, have paid close attention to the life cycle of family members, especially in the late Middle Ages. Regional and local studies that have explored this aspect are P. J. P. Goldberg, *Women, Work, and Life-Cycle in a Medieval Economy: Women in York and Yorkshire, c.1300–1520* (Oxford: Oxford University Press, 1992), and L. R. Poos, *A Rural Society after the Black Death: Essex 1350–1525* (Cambridge: Cambridge University Press, 1991). While life-cycle service may, following Hajnal, have been of less significance elsewhere in medieval Europe, historians of the family and household in other European countries have been eager to define structure and the degree of effective familial support.

The economy of the medieval family can be approached from a number of directions. One major aspect of our consideration must be the extent to which the majority of rural families in this period – that is, peasant families (whether serfs, slaves, or free tenants) – owed part of their produce or labor as obligation to their social superiors, the Church, the lord and the State. Two recent works that combine overall assessment with collections of case studies are P. Freedman and M. Bourin, eds, *Forms of Servitude in Northern and Central Europe: Decline, Resistance, and Expansion* (Turnhout: Brepols, 2005), and M. Bourin and P. Martínez-Sopena, *Pour une anthropologie du prélèvement seigneurial dans les campagnes médiévales (xie–xive siècles): Réalités et représentations paysannes* (Paris: Publications de la Sorbonne, 2004). There are relatively few opportunities to itemize a peasant family budget in this period, but, for one important attempt at such an assessment, see C. Dyer, *Standards of Living in the Middle Ages* (Cambridge: Cambridge University Press, 1989). Higher-status secular households and religious households, which, in certain instances, we might also consider to be rural households, provide fuller information on their domestic economies; see, for instance, C. M. Woolgar, *The Great Household in Late Medieval England* (New Haven: Yale University Press, 1999). Also of relevance here is the relationship of family with the Church; the development of the institution of marriage is considered in J. Goody, *The Development of the Family and Marriage in Europe* (Cambridge: Cambridge University Press, 1983), and in M. M. Sheehan, *Marriage, Family and Law in Medieval Europe: Collected Studies* (Toronto: Pontifical Institute, 1996).

Classic works on the culture of the household and of the family in the medieval countryside include, most obviously, E. Le Roy Ladurie, *Montaillou: Cathars and Catholics in a French Village, 1294–1324* (Harmondsworth: Penguin, 1980, and various editions). Much discussion of familial culture resides in studies directed at particular aspects of culture and society in this period, including works on religiosity and aspects of faith, of education, and so on. Thus, for instance, there is considerable evidence for elements of domestic culture in work on medieval literacy and "textual communities," as described in B. Stock, *The Implications of Literacy Written Language and Models of Interpretation in the Eleventh and Twelfth Centuries* (Princeton: Princeton University Press, 1983), and also P. Biller and A. Hudson, eds, *Heresy and Literacy, 1000–1530* (Cambridge: Cambridge University Press, 1994). The family as a source of memory is discussed in E. van Houts, *Memory and Gender in Medieval Europe* (Basingstoke: Palgrave, 1999), while B. A. Hanawalt, *The Ties that Bound: Peasant Families in Medieval England* (Oxford: Oxford University Press, 1986), offers some insight into the family and household as centers of education and nurture, issues also considered in, *inter alia*, S. Shahar, *Childhood in the Middle Ages* (London: Routledge, 1990). Investment in the rural house and a description of its variety is discussed in J. Chapelot and R. Fossier, *The Village and House in the Middle Ages* (London: Batsford, 1985), and also, in one of a number of regional and local case studies, in A. Bazzana and E. Hubert, eds, *Maisons et espaces domestiques dans le monde Méditerranéen au Moyen Âge* (Rome and Madrid: École Française de Rome-Casa de Veláquez, 2000).

Chapter Seven

Marriage in Medieval Latin Christendom

Martha Howell

Marriage in medieval Europe began as a secular bond constituted according to more or less formal rules that differed from class to class and varied from place to place. In fact, although people in the early Middle Ages surely made distinctions among heterosexual unions, for example, by recognizing only certain pairings as having granted inheritance rights to children, even those unions would probably not have been regarded as "marriages" by people in later centuries.[1] In the early part of the Middle Ages, even the nobility had no single normative form of marriage. Some unions, for example, did not involve a formal property transfer (what scholars have labeled *Friedelehe*), while other unions, which have been called *Muntehe*, required the property exchange and are thought to have signified the transfer of guardianship (*Munt*) over the woman from the father to the husband.[2] During the centuries to follow, marriage acquired a clearer definition as a secular bond and was, at the same time, given profound religious and spiritual significance. These developments, however, did less to stabilize the meaning of marriage than to create tensions, because the secular and religious meanings were often in conflict and were themselves internally inconsistent.

Although the existing scholarship makes this complexity visible, individual scholars have tended to work from within disciplinary subfields in approaching this history and thus have concentrated on only part of the story. Social historians, for example, have typically focused on the sociopolitical bonds created by marriage, legal scholars on the property relations constituted by marriage or on the legal status of the marital bond itself, and religious or cultural historians on the spiritual and cultural significance of marriage. Many of them have taken the relationship between the present and the past as their organizing structure, seeking to expose the way marital practices in those centuries anticipated the modern Western marital ideal. Implicitly if not always explicitly, they have treated medieval marriages either as embryo of that model – in which people marry by free choice, live in stable nuclear families, and consider their marriage a lifetime commitment to romance, friendship, and partnership – or as its primitive opposite.

This chapter attempts to tell the story somewhat differently, neither foregrounding one aspect of marriage's history in these centuries nor interpreting marital practices then through the lens of the modern ideal. Instead, I have sought to emphasize the multiple and unstable meanings and purposes of marriage, the tensions surrounding those definitions, and the sociocultural logics that informed people's understandings and practices of marriage in those long centuries. Marriage in 700 or 1300 – no less than in 2000 – did crucial work. Marriage could link people in semi-permanent sociopolitical bonds, granting rights to claim – and imposing obligations to provide – property, assistance of many kinds, and even affection. It could stabilize class status through time by channeling capital through generations. It could inscribe the terms of gender hierarchy by regulating the sexual division of labor, distinguishing legitimate from illegitimate sex, and assigning patriarchal authority to heads of families. Because these potentialities were not always realized, however, because they were often mutually incompatible, and because they were differently prioritized by different people, marriage itself was an unstable institution, and it was subject then, as now, to intense political and cultural scrutiny.

Secular Imperatives

Throughout the Middle Ages, parents, "friends," and employers had a huge influence on the marriage decision, because marriage was, above all, a means of creating social, political, and economic alliances. Hence, people usually married in what seem to have been direct reflections of these practical matters. For the nobility, this often meant that parents actually selected their children's spouses, and it always meant that the interests of family property, power, and position governed when and to whom a child was married. Boys and girls of this class were regularly betrothed as infants and formally married as adolescents. By the later Middle Ages, merchant families sometimes adopted similar practices in an effort to secure and deepen their own social networks. For ordinary people of non-servile condition, however, such matters were usually less rigorously controlled, and the evidence we have indicates that both men and women of these classes usually married later in life, generally between 18 and 28. Nevertheless, children of free peasants, artisans, or merchants were expected to – and almost always did – marry someone whose property, skills, or connections could strengthen the natal family's position and secure the fortunes of the new household. Unfree people who married were subject to the same logic, but, since they were usually expected to acquire their lord's permission before marrying, their superiors played a major role in the decision, often, for example, forbidding marriages outside the manorial village or arranging matches between villages.

Because marriage was essentially a sociopolitical institution, only those with access to sufficient economic resources were able to marry. Elites usually married at relatively high rates, for they had property and complex alliances to secure, but even among those groups there were many who did not marry. In regions where primogeniture was the rule, for example, the younger sons of landed nobility were sometimes excluded from the marriage market, for they could neither continue the household's line nor found one of their own.[3] Studies of Italian urban elites have similarly demonstrated that "excess" daughters of merchant families were sent to monasteries, so that family money could be invested in the marriages of others.[4] On average, some scholars have estimated, as many as one quarter of medieval people never married, perhaps more if we were to include the truly poor in the count.[5] Those who did not marry were by and large left to find alternative means of securing a social place, whether as religious, as servants in another household, or as dependants in a relative's household. It is hard to say whether these people lived celibate lives. We know, mostly from late medieval evidence, that all social classes produced illegitimate children, but we have no records suggesting that the rates of bastardy and single motherhood were as high in the Middle Ages as they would be in later centuries.[6] Property, no one then doubted, was the bedrock of marriage, and the property exchange set the terms of marriage. The economic and sociopolitical rights that attached to property structured the relations between husband, wife, and their children, as well as the relations with kin, thus giving specific meaning to marriage and expressing people's ideas about its meaning. Accordingly, the assets that each spouse brought into marriage or acquired thereafter were carefully controlled during the marriage by informal and formal rules about who could use it and for what purposes, who inherited it at the end of the marriage, and what rights the surviving spouse had to it during his or her remaining life. The range of possibilities was enormous, and a detailed map of the variations by class, region, or period would be almost unreadable. It is, moreover, no easy task to get information about these matters because until the later Middle Ages we have distressingly few sources. There are, to be sure, a few marriage contracts setting forth the terms of property exchange from the earlier centuries, some wills and other records of inheritance and bequest, a scattering of court cases where such matters were adjudicated, the rare summary of practice, and a few narrative sources that describe the rituals of property exchange in marriage. But, even in their totality, they do not provide the density necessary for confident generalizations; worse still, all but a very few of these sources treat royalty or high nobility. For ordinary people everywhere – and, in fact, for most of the elite as well – we have almost nothing from these centuries.[7]

This situation is considerably worse for northern Europe than it is for the areas bordering the Mediterranean. The south was direct heir to legal institutions of the Roman Empire, and after the tenth century, southern Europeans revived many of those practices. Among them were secular notaries (lawyers of a kind), who drafted and preserved property agreements. People in the south who had property to exchange in marriage or to pass on at death (even in small amounts) customarily hired a notary to record their wishes, and beginning about 1200, we thus have good evidence of how people across much of the social spectrum in that region organized property relations in marriage and how they passed property at death.[8]

In contrast, northerners typically left few such records during the Middle Ages, and the scattered documents we do have from this region usually involved people at the very top of the social order.[9] The paucity of documents from this region, like the relative abundance of documentation from the south, reflects the region's legal history. Following older Germanic traditions, northerners allowed relations between private individuals – what legal scholars refer to as "private law" – to be governed by custom or, to put it another way, by common practice. In this region, it was even casually said that "people make law," a phrase invoking the conviction that private law arose from the practices of the people, not from a lawyer's office, not from the sovereign's chancery, and not from the courtroom. Because everyone knew the local practice, there was in principle no need for written law or written records. As a result, custom remained local; it varied considerably from region to region, and, unsurprisingly, it changed as circumstances changed.

It was not until the later Middle Ages, and especially after about 1500, that northern customs were gradually recorded, in the process being rendered considerably more stable and uniform. Judicial practice accomplished the first steps because, as individuals brought their disputes about application or interpretation of local custom to the civil courts that had developed in the course of the Middle Ages, they left records revealing something about the norms and how they evolved over time. We also have a limited number of statutes issued by territorial sovereigns that sought to regularize, change, or clarify custom.[10] There are also some written customals, or summaries of local practice. These were rare before about 1300, but by the mid-sixteenth century almost all regions and many localities had published such compilations, in response in part to pressures from territorial sovereigns who wished to regularize and publicize law in order to simplify governance. In addition, people in this region occasionally turned to the marriage contract to make adjustments to customary rules, or they used wills or last testaments to manage inheritance rather than just for the charitable gifts that the Church considered a spiritual duty. Most often, it was the rich or the well connected who were in a position to overwrite local custom or, in some cases, were able to invoke customs particular to their class.[11] There were some occasions in the later Middle Ages, however, when ordinary people also used written documents to modify custom, and in a few exceptional cases they did so in great enough numbers to create an archive able to reveal the pattern of choices.[12]

A combination of such "records of practice" and customals, along with contemporary chronicles and commentaries, has permitted historians to sketch the patterns of customary marital property law in northern Europe during the later Middle Ages, trace its variations over time and space, and compare it to practices in the southern regions of Roman law. Throughout much of the north, some form of what historians call "community property law" prevailed. In the classic communal regime, all the assets of both husband and wife were merged into one undifferentiated marital property fund over which the husband had full managerial control.[13] Community property regimes usually recognized children as exclusive and inalterable heirs of their parents' property, granting them what in law are called devolutionary rights and allowing parents no latitude in the choice of heirs. "God chooses heirs" went the adage of the day. Such regimes also granted the widow succession rights to communal property, either some or all of it, in recognition of her position as replacement for her deceased husband. The common fund (or community account) was thus an unspecified mass of property in which family members shared collective rights.

In structure, these customary communal arrangements stood in stark contrast to the Roman system typical of southern Europe. There marital property was divided into two separate accounts, one reflecting the wife's contribution to the marriage, and the other reflecting the husband's. Legal historians have labeled these "Roman" systems "dotal," because the wife's property was called her dowry or *dos* in Latin (*dot* in French). The terms of these marital property agreements were typically set by marriage contracts that listed the bride's dowry (often its monetary value was also expressed); the dowry was separately managed during the marriage, and she was promised return of that amount upon her widowhood, typically along with an increase that was figured as a percentage of the dowry itself.[14] The property contributed by the husband was not sequestered in the same way as his wife's, however, since all property in the marital household except that specifically marked for her or her beneficiaries belonged to him. Children were the normal heirs of these marriages, but in most regions parents had the right to distribute their estate unequally among their children, and even to will patrimonial property to others.

Formally, this system was very different from the communal systems of the north. The southern regime positioned the husband and wife as independent representatives of their respective natal families, and has for that reason been labeled "separatist." In contrast, communal regimes created a radically unitary partnership, apparently breaking all property ties with natal kin and forming new ones between the spouses and the children they would have together. In practice, however, very few systems were purely separatist or communal, and, in any case, the practices in any region or among any social class could change over time. For example, in northern France, where it was customary for people to form common property funds at marriage, the nobility typically allowed only a portion of movable goods to fall into that account. Either by means of special agreements or by way of special provisions of local customary law, land and other valuables that had been brought to marriage were placed in separate accounts reserved for the husband and wife respectively. Thus was created a hybrid system, neither communal nor separatist, but some of each.

Hybridity was also achieved by the French customary *douaire* that developed in the central Middle Ages. This was the widow's right to property (or income) from her husband's estate, which represented a way of expressing the husband's obligation to care for his wife after his death, as in life.[15] This was a centerpiece of northern French customary law until the French Revolution, but *douaire*-like arrangements also made an appearance elsewhere, including in English Common Law (the dower) and those manorial customs providing widow's "free bench" (the widow's right to occupy the marital home during her life). The French *douaire* did not, however, replace the community account, but existed alongside it, in sometimes baroque ways. In the Parisian region, for example, the community account was restricted to most movable wealth brought to the marriage and to property acquired after the marriage. Immovable wealth brought to the marriage by either spouse, however, sometimes along with specially named movables that had been contributed to the marriage, was held apart from the common fund, serving as the lineal property of the respective spouses. The property reserved by the husband funded his widow's *douaire*, but she also had a claim to part of the community fund (as well as rights to her own lineal property).[16]

Most of the evidence we have about marital property law in the medieval centuries gives us a snapshot of a place and time, even of a single marriage, and some legal histories have been written as though that snapshot can stand for a regional system with a long life. In fact, however, marital property law was unstable everywhere during the Middle Ages, fluctuating over time, according to the social place of the people involved, and with respect to geography. To be sure, this does not mean that people had free choice in deciding the terms of their own marriages. Instead, they were bound by local custom or simply by the mores of the community or kin network, and it was rare for any couple to exceed these boundaries by wide margins.[17] That some did helps explain why changes occurred over time and why there was so much variation even within regions, but the changes happened slowly enough for them to be usually imperceptible within one person's lifetime, and a couple marrying in, say, 900 or 1200 surely considered themselves to have little latitude.

Although in practice each form of marital property law typically contained elements reminiscent of the other, it is also true that certain classes tended to prefer one to the other. The customs of the nobility in the early Middle Ages (about whom we have the most information during this period) were decidedly communal in spirit, while in the central and late Middle Ages the landed classes opted for more separatist arrangements.[18] As the Middle Ages drew to a close, Europe's merchant class also came to prefer more separatist arrangements, while artisans and peasants tended to stay with communal systems. Thus, there can be little doubt that the instability and hybridity of marital property law was in part a measure of people's efforts to adjust the law to their individual circumstances and structure their property arrangements to reflect social needs. Separatist regimes privileged the natal line, assuring that a wife's property (which had come from her family) was not diminished during the marriage and was returned to her, to her children, or to her natal kin when her husband died. When people chose these regimes or built such features into their existing customs, they were seeking to preserve capital in family lines, thus expressing a deep commitment to lineage itself and announcing that their assets would hold value over time. It is no wonder, then, that the landholding classes along with the capitalist class emerging at the very end of the Middle Ages tended to choose such strategies, for they could live from income produced by assets that held value from generation to generation. Communal regimes, in contrast, preferred the conjugal household and gave its head (the husband or his widow) wide latitude in managing property. Such practices seem to express less reliance on (and perhaps loyalty toward) the lineage and more confidence that the conjugal unit was a manager of wealth rather then simply the transmitter of fixed assets from generation to generation.[19]

Enter the Church

During the earliest centuries of its history the Christian Church had been ambivalent about marriage and especially about sexual pleasure in marriage, but that ambivalence had all but disappeared by the central Middle Ages. Indeed, from about the twelfth century forward, churchmen consistently praised marriage as a legitimate, if second-order, alternative to celibacy, even if they typically offered only cautious endorsement of marital sex. Preachers celebrated the union as a potential vehicle of grace, and confessors offered detailed counsel on proper comportment for husband and wife alike. By the thirteenth century, marriage was widely considered a sacrament.[20]

As the church gave spiritual meaning to the martial bond, its lawyers also set the legal terms of marriage. First, canonists determined that mutual consent alone constituted a valid marriage. A binding union was immediately contracted if words of "present consent" were used (*per verba de praesenti*, as in "I marry you"). A promise to marry, in contrast, was expressed by words of future consent (*per verba de futuro*, as in "I will marry you"); if followed by consummation, this union was also binding. Although there had to be witnesses to the exchange of vows if the marriage was to stand up in ecclesiastical court, no particular form of publicity, no formal solemnization, and no parental consent were required. As early as the Fourth Lateran Council of 1215, however, canonists had declared that marriages were to be announced publicly by means of a reading of the banns, in order to allow members of the community to protest the union should there be impediments (prior marriage, consanguinity, and the like). At least from that period on, the Church sought to assure that banns were read at specified times and places, that witnesses were present, and that a priest officiated.[21] Marriages performed without the proper publicity and rituals were considered "clandestine" unless followed by appropriate solemnization, and they were condemned by canonists and preachers alike.[22] Nevertheless, clandestine marriages – those by "consent alone" or without the rituals laid out by the Church – were reluctantly deemed "valid" if not "legitimate" until the Council of Trent reversed itself in 1563. As an early sixteenth-century theologian wrote in explaining the medieval Church's position regarding the validity of clandestine marriages, "it is not of the essence of marriage to contract it in the presence of the church and according to the custom of the country, but a matter of propriety. The fitness of the parties [and the consent between them] is of the essence of marriage."[23]

Second and third, the canonists rendered marriage monogamous and indissoluble. Without exception, extramarital sex was uniformly condemned as adultery, and it was sporadically prosecuted. The insistence on the indissolubility of marriage was even more vigorously sustained, so that until the sixteenth century, when Protestants allowed divorce in certain cases, Western Europeans possessed few effective means for ending a bad marriage and entering a new one, all of them expensive or inordinately clumsy.[24]

The rules promulgated by medieval canonists were not, however, easily absorbed into European culture. Because marriage had traditionally been organized to serve the interests of parents, kin, and the network of alliances important to them, noble men had regularly shed wives who had not produced an heir, who were no longer of use in securing political alliances, or who stood in the way of a better match. Ordinary people were often equally casual about the status of their unions: a husband who had been absent for years was taken for dead and his wife was considered a widow; men who changed addresses often changed wives as well, in effect winding up as bigamists. Thus, when the Church deemed marriage indissoluble and as courts began to prosecute what they called bigamy, people from all social ranks had reasons to object, and they would only slowly come to accept these rules as the norm.

The prohibition of what the Church referred to as incest (marriages defined as endogamous) would also sharply conflict with lay practices. Although marriages in early medieval Europe were in principle exogamous in that women typically married out of their natal lines, taking property with them in the form of dowry or simply as marriage portions, many people nevertheless married closely related kin, thus managing to keep property in the family line, broadly defined.[25] Among the nobility, for example, cousins married first cousins and uncles took nieces as wives. We have little good evidence about the patterns among ordinary people in these early centuries, but it is reasonable to assume that in peasant communities people did the same, for the pool of marriageable people was too small to permit very strict rules about exogamy.[26] By the central Middle Ages, however, the Church had radically expanded the category of prohibited kinship, forbidding marriages between kin related by blood to the seventh degree. According to the Fourth Lateran Council, which reduced the boundary to the fourth degree, all descendants of a common great-great-grandparent were ineligible spouses, and no one could marry a godparent or the child of a godparent. Although royalty and similarly high-placed people were sometimes able to circumvent those rules, even they had trouble obtaining the necessary exemptions. There is some debate among scholars about the reasons for the Church's insistence on such strict rules of exogamy. Jack Goody has famously argued that the Church fashioned the rules for its own material benefit, reasoning that widows who had married far out of their line would be inclined to leave their property to the Church rather than return it to the families who had sent them out.[27]

The principle allowing a couple to form a valid marriage by mutual consent alone provoked especially vigorous opposition, for parents and public officials alike considered the Church's position an infringement of their rights to control the marriage decision.[28] Although families anticipated that the bride and groom would find one another "acceptable," the couple's wishes took second place or, perhaps better said, were expected to accord with the larger interests of kin and community. Thus, elites with significant property at stake, and ordinary householders as well, frequently went to court to block marriages contracted without their approval, typically using their control over property to discourage such unions and to punish those who disobeyed. In England and Flanders, to mention just two examples, fathers and mothers denied customary inheritance rights to children who married without consent, a powerful disincentive in an age when marriages were financed and life chances determined, directly or indirectly, by inheritances.[29] Despite intense pressure from families, however, the canonists never made parental approval a formal condition of a valid marriage. It was only in 1563 with the decree of *Tametsi* issued by the Council of Trent that the Catholic Church effectively brought families back into the picture.[30] Protestants, although discarding most of the medieval Church's doctrine on marriage, embedded the couple's consent in a complex of events that also guaranteed familial and community supervision.[31] By the end of the sixteenth century, virtually every European country, either by adopting *Tametsi* or by promulgating rules of its own, had formally banned clandestine marriages. England was the only significant exception, and it was not until Lord Hardwicke's Act of 1753 that the medieval canon law was repealed in that nation.[32]

The Bonds of Kinship and Conjugality in the Later Middle Ages

Historians agree that marriage changed during the second half of the millennium. George Duby has given us perhaps the most influential argument about the beginnings of the transformation.[33] According to Duby, around the turn of the millennium aristocrats who had long used marriage to solidify the *lignage* ("lineage," the collaterally extended kin group) began to deploy marriage to form the *ménage*. This conjugal unit, which was under the control of its male head and connected to a patriarchally defined line extending vertically through generations, displaced the laterally extensive and considerably less coherent *lignage*. No longer would the female line (if not females themselves) bear the same importance as the male, no longer would the hierarchies of generational and gender authority be as multiple and mobile, and no longer could the alliances formed by marriage change so quickly. In Duby's interpretation, the Church's insistence on monogamy and on the indissolubility of marriage powerfully fueled this development, but it also had roots in secular imperatives. The new marriage system served the class interests of these elites, who were becoming ever more dependent on land, because the indissoluble and closed *ménage* allowed them to accumulate and hoard land as no looser kin confederation could. Men could then pass it on, intact, to their directly descendent heirs. To do so, however, they had to rigidify the definition of legitimacy, and that required a new commitment to monogamy; it was thus, Duby argued, that the Church's teachings about marriage were eventually accepted by this class. Because this system tended to privilege senior males (in a system that could take the strict form of primogeniture), it had an additional sociocultural effect as well: junior males, denied full inheritance rights, were set adrift and made available for adventures of various kinds, including the warfare and *amour* so celebrated in the romance literature of the day.[34]

The *ménage* Duby described has been called "modern" to distinguish it from the less cohesive aristocratic household of earlier centuries. But his *ménage* was hardly the nuclear household of modernity. It was a large, extended household closely bound to (patrilineal) kin by both residence and political connections. The marriages that formed these households were, like aristocratic marriages of the past, explicitly based on property and political interests, and those interests made the marriage decision very much a "family" affair and marriage an alliance of groups. Historians agree, however, that during the closing centuries of the Middle Ages, principally in northwestern Europe and almost exclusively among townspeople, independent peasants, and a rising class of yeomen, the *ménage* did become synonymous with the nuclear family. As historians have understood the term, this household was formed by a couple who had married as adults, who were close in age, and who had exercised a significant degree of choice in the selection of their spouse and the site of their residence. The couple governed their households, had full possession of the property that financed their marriage, and directly participated, through the household's head, in community affairs. The households thus formed were relatively free of control by kin, and they were populated only by the couple, their minor children, a few servants, and the occasional dependent relative.[35]

In contrast, households typical of the European past (not to mention the rest of the then contemporary world), both those of aristocracy and of the peasantry, were extended in one way or another. Husbands and wives in aristocratic households lived with a crowd of relatives and retainers, and typically they shared little private space or private time. The households of ordinary people were smaller, but few were nuclear. In some villages, several generations resided together under the governance of a senior male, the literal patriarch.[36] In others, brothers formed joint households with their spouses and unmarried siblings. In still others, the peasant household, although composed only of the couple and their children, did not qualify as nuclear in the sense historians have usually intended, because it was not independent. Rather, it was embedded in a manorial economy where the household's labor was controlled, the social and geographic mobility of its members limited, and any political capacity denied them.

Many historians have argued that the independent nuclear family achieved a degree of intimacy unlike that imagined or experienced in any extended or dependent households. In this interpretation, the classic nuclear family was the birthplace of what has come to be called the "companionate marriage." This is a scholar's term, used as shorthand for a disparate, rather unstable, and somewhat contradictory collection of features that are understood to have been woven together to form a unique and powerful cultural narrative over the course of the centuries between about 1300 and 1700. A companionate marriage is understood to be the union of an adult woman and man who had freely chosen to wed, principally in pursuit of both romance and friendship, and who imagined their union to be a partnership fueled by mutual interests, shared activities, and sustained desire.[37] Even if property was essential to the definition in these early centuries, property was considered an expression of the emotional bonds that united the couple, not an impediment to them.[38] These ideals found their most secure home in the classic nuclear family, because, it is argued, in such "closed" households conjugal intimacy could be cultivated, kin and community shut out, and resources – both socioeconomic and cultural – accumulated for the benefit of the couple and their offspring. Conjugal pairs forming such closed, nuclear residential units easily, it has been reasoned, achieved the private and absorbing relationship evoked by the term companionate marriage.[39]

Some historians have added marital property law to demography, for, in exactly the same northern regions of Europe where the nuclear family took clearest shape, husbands and wives traditionally shared property. In such community property arrangements, as we have seen, much of the property brought to the marriage or acquired during its course was deposited in a common account, and either surviving spouse, widow or widower, succeeded to some or all of it. In the words of at least one scholar, such property arrangements were "egalitarian" in form and produced more egalitarian conjugal relations.[40] This form of marital property law contrasts strongly with strictly dotal systems modeled on Roman law, which, as we have also seen, were "separatist" in spirit, thus seeming an unlikely nurturer of the friendship and mutual cooperation that help define the companionate marriage. Demography and law thus combined, in the minds of many historians, to locate the companionate marriage most firmly among early modern Europe's middling sorts, especially in northern Europe, in what is now England, northern France, the old Low Countries, and parts of Germany.[41] In this historiography, the term becomes both class and place specific, linking the ideology of the companionate marriage to the practicalities of household management and to the demographic history of northwestern Europe.

Whatever the importance of demography and property law, however, the principle of consent so vigorously upheld by the medieval Church is thought to have been the chief fuel of the companionate marriage. By making choice – individual choice – the essence of marriage, it gave women and men liberty to marry whom they wished, free of the demands of parents who put the material interests of the family ahead of their wishes and free of the pressures implicit in community norms. Romance could now prevail, the reasoning goes, while class, political status, family connections, or any of the other attributes that might have made a potential spouse suitable in the eyes of parents, kin, or neighbors could be ignored.[42]

This language of romantic love, although borrowing heavily from the rhetoric of Christian spirituality, came most directly to later medieval Europe via the troubadours and the courtly love literature of the central Middle Ages. These poems and stories provided a narrative in which human love was elevating, sexual passion but an earthly version of the divine, and fidelity to the beloved an ennobling virtue. Although begun in aristocratic circles, in the centuries to come romance and sexual passion would be combined with stories about marriage by choice to form a narrative that would circulate well outside the genres of the romance or lyric poetry.[43]

Comic literature of the later Middle Ages took up these themes with special gusto, regularly equating choice with romance and sometimes linking both to marriage. These stories also frequently positioned the couple's desire against the family's material and political concerns, making parents, particularly fathers, seem the enemy of love, even the destroyer of marriage. In the *fabliau* known as *Vilain mire*, for example, an impoverished young noblewoman is forced by her father to marry a brutal but prosperous peasant; in *Les Trois bossus*, another woman is given to a stingy and jealous hunchback. In *Auburée*, a poor girl of good family is courted by the son of a merchant who refuses to allow his son to follow his heart, instead forcing him to marry into a moneyed family; meanwhile, the abandoned girl is given over to an old, but rich, man. In all three stories, however, the "bad" marriages fail: the young noblewoman who had been denied her true love takes a lover, cuckolding the old man; the miserable wife of the hunchback refuses to obey her husband; and the first woman gives the brutal peasant a sound beating.[44]

Romance and marriage often show up in the legal record as well. One court case, for example, describes women who were prosecuted for witchcraft because they had concocted a potion that was supposed to "make a husband fall madly in love and live as a good spouse."[45] Similar tropes appear in French pardon tales from the fifteenth century, the texts that supported the official *rémissions* issued to delinquents who had managed to convince the court that they deserved to be let off.[46] Like the *fabliaux*, these tales frequently feature the tensions between property, represented by the family, and free choice, sometimes explicitly described as true love.[47] One defense, for example, describes the elopement of a young noble and his beloved, who chose this route to marriage because one or the other of their families was blocking their union. Another case gives us the story of Odet de Ven, who was "determined to marry Katherine, daughter of Odet Daulin, lord of Cassagne." Having no other means of courting her, so carefully was she apparently sequestered, he snuck into her room at night and carried her away against her will. Soon he won her over, however, and she agreed to have him. The couple then presented themselves to her family, who accepted the match, and they were subsequently wed with appropriate rites. Another less happy but nevertheless satisfyingly resolved tale concerns a young woman who was forced to marry "against her will," and then compelled to live with her spouse's parents, although it had been promised that the couple would reside with her family, not his; in justifiable retribution, she burned down her in-laws' house.

Marital Woes

Such records leave no doubt that the language of individual choice, desire, romance, and love circulated around marriage in late medieval Europe. We can also be certain that this language fueled the narrative of the companionate marriage that was to acquire hegemony in the early modern centuries. But it is not at all clear that the doctrine of consent "freed" medieval people to marry for love alone, that desire itself was considered an appropriate basis for marriage, or that the intimacy of nuclear households implied "companionate," much less egalitarian, relations between wife and husband. The route from the nuclear household of the late Middle Ages to the ideal of companionate marriage was considerably less direct than we have assumed and the ideal itself was just that – an ideal that may have been imagined by many but was lived by few.

First, it can be argued that the doctrine of consent did more to disturb contemporary ideas about marriage than it did to unleash people to marry for the love they had previously been denied. When canonists made consent the sole legal basis of marriage, they wrenched the notion out of a social context where it had long rested and where the multiple interests that make up marriage had been clearly expressed. These included, above all, the property exchange, which was usually agreed to at a formal betrothal. Traditionally considered at least as important as the couples' consent, it directly signaled the parents' approval, and, because it was typically witnessed by members of the community, it signaled theirs as well. The priest's blessing, which was added to the mix in later centuries of the Middle Ages, performed similar work, for it incorporated the couple in a spiritual as well as a secular community. By unraveling that rich nexus, canonists created an artificial binary that did more to cause trouble than to open the way to the modern European ideal of marriage. The consenting spouses were now positioned as opponents of the family and the community, not as members of these groups with interests that were similar to theirs – and that would in fact very soon be theirs, as they established their own households, managed shops, or set to farming, and bore children. Even more paradoxically, canonists also positioned the couple as adversaries of the Church, for the principle of consent alone allowed the couple to ignore ecclesiastical rules about bigamy and consanguinity or to bypass the formal religious rituals.

In practice, most of the unions that the Church labeled clandestine marriages were direct expressions of this paradox. The vast majority of these "valid but illegitimate" marriages were formed to hide a previous liaison or a prohibited degree of kinship and to avoid the bother and expense of ecclesiastical rituals rather than to marry against the wishes of parents.[48] In fact, to judge from some recently published evidence, the huge minority of people outside northern France and Italy (where officials then had enough power to prevent most such marriages) who were considered to have married clandestinely had intended no deception or revolt at all. Instead, these people were simply following longstanding practices in which people married when they could form a self-supporting household, and they did so openly, according to local custom.[49] Both the bride and groom were fully adult, and first-time spouses were typically about the same age; they had each consented to the marriage and probably initiated the courtship on their own, but both their families (who were helping to set up the new household) and the community accepted their union. Their marriages were clandestine only because they had not conformed to the increasingly rigid rituals required by the Church. Marriages of "choice" these surely were, but choice was neither the antithesis of family or community interests nor the sign of romantic love *tout court*.

A recent study by Tine De Moor and Jan Luiten van Zanden similarly suggests that the motives of wage workers who married in northwestern Europe during the fourteenth and fifteenth centuries cannot be reduced to romance. The couples they studied had, to be sure, chosen to marry independently of kin and Church, and a sexual liaison had typically begun their relationship. But these unions were sometimes short-lived, hardly normative marriages at all, and people entered and left them in response to job opportunities and other practical considerations as often as in search of romance.[50]

Widows in the same region were particularly hardheaded. Although the records we have give us little insight into the emotional content of their second, third, or fourth marriages, there is no doubt that these women chose spouses for their ability to help maintain a household and a business.[51] How much romance played a role is not clear, and certainly not directly recorded. Widowers seem to have been as practical, for indirect evidence suggests that they often married widows who were about the same age. Like the widows themselves, these men seem to have been more interested in the security of a settled household, along with its workshop or business, than in the attractions of youth.[52] Even when old men married women barely out of girlhood – and some did – it is hard to know how much romance and sexual desire motivated their choices. Although the comic literature delights in telling that story, texts like the fourteenth-century *Ménagier de Paris* foreground the day-to-day practicalities of these December–May marriages, not romance.[53] And, even if the husbands in these marriages had in fact sought romance, we can be sure that few of the young women they married would have thought themselves smitten. If they "freely consented" to the match, which all but a small minority surely did, they did so principally for material and social reasons.[54]

Second, if choice cannot be automatically associated with sexual desire and romance in the late medieval centuries, neither then can desire and romance be securely linked to marriage. In fact, the poems, songs, and stories of the troubadours and courtiers that gave Europeans a rich narrative about romance were rarely about conjugal love.[55] Andreas Capellanus's *Art of Courtly Love*, for example, argues that love and marriage are incompatible. Courtly love was typically extramarital, and it entailed secrecy and deceit, not sharing and partnership. The chivalric romances themselves delighted in the plight of illicit lovers, with only a few exceptions like von Eschenbach's version of *Parzival* making an argument for conjugal love.[56] The later *Roman de la Rose* features the foolish lover familiar from the *fabliaux*, and only Marie de France and then Christine de Pizan offered serious challenges to the dominant narrative: marriage was a vexed institution and romance was often its enemy.

The comic tales that have come to us from the period also regularly make romance a problem in marriage. Most of these texts do not in fact tell how love seals marriage; instead, they tell of love gone wrong, of sexual desire run amok, of adultery, and of tension – sometimes bloody battles – in marriage. Scholars have even labeled much of the comic literature of the age "anti-marriage" because their stories about conjugal relations are so vexed.[57] Chaucer's *Canterbury Tales*, for example, are so heavily infused with the complexities of marital relations that scholars long ago identified a "marriage group" consisting of the Wife of Bath's prologue, the Clerk's Tale, the Merchant's Tale, and the Franklin's Tale, all of which take the difficulties of marriage as their theme. As the introduction to a recent collection of marriage tales from the period comments, "we might add [to that list] The Knight's Tale of two marriages, the Miller's fabliau of the foibles of courtly love, the Reeve's fabliau of domestic life, The Shipman's Tale of cuckoldry and exchange, Melibee's tale of household governance, The Nun's Priest's Tale of a literally henpecked husband."[58] The fifteenth-century *Quinze joies de mariage* (*Fifteen Joys of Marriage*) repeats the themes.

The husbands in these tales are tormented by flirtatious and vain wives who are more interested in jewels, fashion, and other men than in housekeeping or the serious issues of the day. No happy marriages here. The author of the *Fifteen Joys* is also thought to have put to pen the hundred stories in the famous *Les Cent Nouvelles Nouvelles* composed at the Burgundian court, in part after Boccaccio and previous fabliaux but in part after stories supplied by various members of the court, including the future Louis XI of France. The same themes, the same tropes, pervade these tales: trickery in marriage, cuckoldry, love gone wrong, the social order upended. The first tale recounts a tale of adultery; the fourth of cuckoldry; the seventh of a strange (and very funny) *ménage à trois*; the eighth of an out-of-wedlock pregnancy . . . and so on – plenty of sex and romance, little of marital bliss.[59]

Such stories surely did not describe the typical marriage; rather they expressed this culture's worries about the meaning of marriage and served as kinds of cautionary tales about the dangers of unbridled sexual desire, of uncontrolled women, and of reckless youth. Read as cautionary tales, they seem to insist that a good marriage is passionless, that a good wife is submissive, and that a good household is a soberly managed business. Many scholars have concluded that contemporaries themselves agreed. Heide Wunder has, for example, argued that romance was considered a dangerous ground for marriage among the early modern German burghers she studies – just as the comic literature of the period suggests it was. What they meant by "love," she insists, was commitment, affection and regulated desire, not passion.[60] Significantly, it was exactly in this period that Protestants sought to domesticate passion, putting it to work in making marriage a moral project with an intensity unknown to the medieval Church. Luther, Calvin, and their followers taught that marriage was a gift to humankind, given by God for the benefit of human souls, an indispensable site of spiritual growth for men, women, and children.[61] It was thus incumbent on husbands and wives to honor the institution not only by honoring one another, but, somewhat surprisingly and entirely oxymoronically, by accepting what one scholar has termed "the *duty* to desire" one's spouse.[62] Sex in marriage was praised, but only because it secured the marriage and thus fulfilled spiritual obligations, not because it brought pleasure. By the seventeenth century, Catholics had taken up much of this rhetoric, with the result that all Christians in the West were being similarly instructed not only about the moral status of marriage but also about the importance of harnessing sexual desire to marriage. Anthropologists studying the way the ideal of the companionate marriage has found its way around today's world similarly emphasize that romantic love is not the motive for the modern companionate marriage. As the editors of a recent collection of articles commented, "While romantic love may be something that companionately married couples strive to maintain during married life . . . privileging romantic attraction and individual choice when selecting a spouse is, in fact, quite different from being able (and wanting) to prioritize the ongoing affective primacy of the conjugal unit."[63]

Third, if marriage in the late medieval centuries was not necessarily a "free" choice based on romance and sexual longing, neither was the nuclear household necessarily an irenic oasis of companionship and egalitarian partnership. To be sure, as countless historians have emphasized (myself included), a couple heading a nuclear household was responsible for what has been called a "family enterprise" on which their well-being, and the well-being of their offspring, depended.[64] This reality forced cooperation between spouses; the work they did to support that household and the earnings they shared could foster mutual respect, deep affection, and comfortable companionship. There is no doubt that the rhetoric of the companionate marriage – choice, desire, friendship, and so on – provided a narrative that expressed the ideal of such marriages.

But this household was not a stable or impermeable body, and the couple was not a single body. To understand what marriage meant to couples in such households, we must take account of these tensions even as we acknowledge that shared responsibilities could in fact build sturdy emotional bonds. "Partnership," I want to emphasize, did not imply equality, and, because it did not, marriages in family economies were not necessarily peaceful, and sexual desire was not necessarily their fuel. Talk of romance, sexual desire, companionship, and friendship did important cultural work, but its work was less to describe marriages as they actually existed than to provide themes that could resolve its contradictions.

Let us begin by examining the notion that nuclear households were "closed" or stable. In fact, they were embedded in and considerably more open to community, Church, and kin than we imagine the modern Western household to be. Kinship, demography, and the market economy itself could easily erode its foundations, and even invade its space. A woman's father, her uncles or brothers, even her mother or aunt, could intervene between wife and husband, lending their power – whether economic or political – to her. A man married to a women born of a leading merchant family in medieval Paris or London or Ghent, for example, was directly dependent on the sociopolitical relations established by his marriage, and he would have carefully cultivated them, allowing fathers, brothers, uncles, mothers, and aunts a say in his household and his business. Neighbors and Church officials exercised other kinds of control, mostly through surveillance but also through law itself. A man who could not govern his household lost respect in the community, and, with it, he sometimes lost public office. Guilds required that prospective members prove legitimate birth. The Church granted legal separations to women who could prove excessive cruelty, lack of support, or even adultery.[65]

Demography also rendered the nuclear household unstable and permeable. In those days, only a minority of marriages actually survived into a couple's old age; in fact, scholars have estimated that death then brought an early end to marriages just as frequently as divorce does today.[66] In the north of Europe, widows with property regularly remarried, even within months of their husbands' deaths. About 30 percent of the marriages in samples of marriage contracts from fifteenth-century Douai (a city in the medieval county of Flanders), were, for example, of widows.[67] Alongside these combined households, there were a significant number of female-headed households in this region, for not all widows chose to remarry and some could not find an appropriate mate. In the south, there were many more unmarried widows, probably because marital property systems there made the widow's financial support dependent on her remaining unmarried. In late medieval Florence, for example, prosperous widows tended not to remarry because they would then lose rights to property left to them.[68] Everywhere, however, men seem to have regularly remarried when widowed, even taking three, four, or five different wives during a long life and having children with each of them. It is thus wrong to imagine that cities of this day, or even villages, were populated by stable nuclear families.

The demographically "combined family" of medieval Europe was sometimes as emotionally unstable as such families are today. Although we have evidence suggesting that combined families co-habitated comfortably and even willingly shared economic resources, we are also confronted with court cases that display children squabbling with their half-siblings or stepparents about inheritances. In addition, we have countless folk tales that feature cruel stepmothers, absent mothers, and lost fathers, all of which suggest the tension produced by combining families. Thus, even though the French called stepmothers *belles-mères*, they also coined the word *marâtre* to describe stepmothers as evil twins.

If nuclear households were permeable and unstable, they were also hierarchical. By the terms of law and culture, wives in these settings were enclosed in a space ruled by men; their labor, whether for subsistence or for the market, was at the service of his household; their bodies were to be available to him, at will. As husbands, men represented the family in the community. They had explicit authority to "govern" family members, which included the right to beat both wives and children for "disobedience." Gender hierarchy was thus constructed by and constructive of the nuclear household.[69]

Even community property law, which in structure seems to position men and women as equals, formally inscribed male dominance. These regimes were not egalitarian except in the narrow sense that in their strictest form they gave widows the same succession rights that widowers enjoyed. During the marriage, however, they were anything but egalitarian, for the classic communal property regime made the husband the sole and absolute manager of the conjugal fund, including all property that his wife might have brought to the marriage or acquired in its course.[70] Such an arrangement, it is easy to imagine, would hardly have produced the harmonious partnership imagined by the term "companionate" marriage.

The structural inequality between husband and wife in nuclear households was thus in tension with the fact that wives and husbands had to work together and that a wife's performance as co-manager of the household was essential to its material success. The gender system came under even greater pressure, as the commercial economy expanded in the late Middle Ages, because commerce loosed women's labor and their property from the control of husbands and fathers. Women who worked for wages now answered to employers, who organized ever more complex and rationalized putting-out systems. Their work schedules, their wages, even the spaces of their work now became matters of (unequal) negotiation between the women and their employers; husbands and fathers were effectively marginalized. Gender hierarchy could also be shaken when women managed their own enterprises. Because the husband was, in law, the head of household, he was solely responsible for all debts incurred by family members, including his wife's, even those generated by her own business. A businesswoman, thus positioned to act in her husband's name, could ruin him if she failed.[71] If she was successful, she posed another kind of threat, for her earnings gave her a voice or a claim to a voice that social, cultural, and legal norms denied.[72] Even when a woman worked under her husband's authority, perhaps managing the sales from his shop or assisting in the manufacturing process itself, there could be trouble. Anxiety over market conditions, disputes about business decisions taken, a wife's inadequacies as a salesperson of her husband's wares, a husband's ineptness in the workshop – such issues easily disturbed marital harmony, giving women reason to complain or men reason to doubt their own competence, and a husband's authority was implicitly eroded.

In areas of community property law, tensions could be worse, for a widow there could assume the male position as head of household, thereby acquiring many of the powers of her deceased husband and literally inverting the gender hierarchy. In most of the regimes, widows were given control of a significant portion of marital property (sometimes all of it), and the archives of the day confirm that they often went on to manage their late husbands' enterprises, sometimes retaining managerial control even when sons had come of age. A widow could also serve as a guardian of minor children, with no more supervision by her late husband's kin than he would have had to endure as a widower.[73] In some places widows who headed households even represented them in community affairs. When a widow remarried – and many did – she lost these powers, but if the second husband was the widow's junior (perhaps her deceased husband's apprentice) or if she had written a marriage contract to preserve her control of the property she brought to the marriage, his effective powers were limited. It is no wonder then that the widow was a stock figure of comic tales of the period, her unloosed sexuality signaling not just her ability to transfer property from one man to another but also her capacity to displace a man as head of household. Indeed, it is no wonder that Phyllis riding Aristotle was a favorite image in popular literature of the day.[74]

****

Much of the history of medieval marriage is lost to us, for we have very few sources from the early centuries of the millennium, and those we have tell us little about most people's experiences of marriage. It is clear, however, that even then the interests of family, of the bride and groom themselves, and of the larger community differed by class, and that they changed over time, making marriage unstable in form and meaning. During the central Middle Ages, as the Church acquired control of the legal definition of marriage and as a cultural narrative of romance and passion was grafted onto the ecclesiastical rule of consent, marriage acquired even greater complexity.

The comparatively rich historical record of the later Middle Ages fully exposes the resulting tensions. Secular lawmakers, moralists, religious authorities, cultural commentators, and ordinary people alike, all agreeing that marriage was the fundament of social, gender, and moral order, were engaged in a vigorous debate about marriage's meaning and its proper form. The tasks they assigned to it were, however, so diverse and the interests they expected it to serve were so various that no single cultural narrative could resolve its contradictions and no set of laws fully stabilize it. Marriage was irredeemably many things, and it would necessarily change as material circumstances changed. What it was and what it should be were, then as now, never finally settled.

Notes

1 As Ruth Mazo Karras recently put it: "In contemporary society marriage requires an act or performative utterance by someone authorized by the relevant jurisdiction to perform it. If that act has taken place (and if the parties have met certain qualifications, such as age or gender, again depending on the jurisdiction), the marriage is valid; if it has not,

it is not. In the early Middle Ages the line between who was married and who was not is not quite so clear, to us or perhaps even to them" (Karras, "The History of Marriage and the Myth of Friedelehe," p. 119). For marriages in these centuries more generally, see Guichard and Cuvillier, "Barbarian Europe."

2 Traditionally, historians have argued that only the *Muntehe* automatically granted inheritance rights to children and thus that it alone was a "real" marriage. For a summary of this scholarship, see Duby, *The Knight, the Lady and the Priest*. More recent scholarship has, however, challenged conventional understandings of the difference between the two, arguing that contemporaries typically made no such rigid distinctions. Both kinds of marriage were, in their eyes, fully legitimate and in fact were scarcely distinguishable. See Karras, "The History of Marriage and the Myth of Friedelehe," p. 119.

3 For a discussion of this pattern, see Duby, *Medieval Marriage*. Later restatements and elaborations include his *The Knight, the Lady, and the Priest* and *Love and Marriage*.

4 See, in particular, Sperling, *Convents and the Body*.

5 For women's rates of celibacy, see Bennett and Froide, eds, *Singlewomen in the European Past*.

6 See, for an overview, Laslett, Oosterveen and Smith, eds, *Bastardy and its Comparative History*.

7 The scholarly literature on the subject of medieval and early modern marital property law is vast. Some of the best overviews are Brissaud, *A History of French Private Law*; Erickson, *Women and Property*; Bonfield, ed., *Marriage, Property, and Succession*; Planitz, *Deutsche Rechtsgeschichte*; Yver, *Egalité entre héritiers et exclusion des enfants dotés* and "Les Deux Groupes de coutumes"; Ourliac and Malafosse, *Histoire du droit privé*; Ourliac and Gazzaniga, *Histoire du droit privé francais*; Godding, *Le Droit privé*; Jacob, "La Charte d'Hesdin," *Les Époux, le seigneur et la cité*, and "Les Structures patrimoniales"; Gilissen, "Le Statut de la femme"; Lepointe, *La Famille dans l'ancien droit*; Olivier-Martin, *Histoire de la coutume*; Le Jan, "Femmes, pouvoir et société"; Chevrier, "Sur quelques caractères"; Hughes, "From Brideprice to Dowry"; Petot and Vandenbossche, "Le Statut de la femme"; Schmidt, *Overleven na de dood*; Caeneghem, *A Historical Introduction to Private Law*.

8 On the late medieval south in particular, see Hilaire, *Le Régime des biens entre époux*; Mayali, *Droit savant et coutumes*; Lafon, *Les Epoux bordelais*; Favarger, *Le Régime matrimonial*; Poudret, *La Situation du conjoint survivant*.

9 Thus, what we know about northern people's conceptions of marriage itself in this age has until recently come more from Church courts, where people argued about their marital status, arranged legal separations, or brought suits for violation of marital vows, than from any information we might tease out of marital property records.

10 It is not until almost the end of the Middle Ages, however, that these became frequent and not until later that issuers acquired the authority necessary for reliable enforcement.

11 On customs peculiar to the nobility in the *Nord* of France, see Jacob, "Les Structures patrimoniales."

12 For a study of one such case, see Jacob, *Les Époux, le seigneur et la cite*, and Howell, *The Marriage Exchange*.

13 In most places, however, the classic regime did not prevail. Instead, only a portion of the couple's wealth was contributed to this fund, or the rights of the husband or of his widow to manage it were circumscribed in some way. Nevertheless, the principle remained: husband and wife, along with the successor to marriage and the children born of it, shared rights to a significant portion of marital property.

14 By the late Middle Ages, the rules about control of the dowry during both marriage and widowhood varied from place to place; in some, widows could themselves control the dowry, although that right was usually limited and often challenged. See Chabot,

"La Loi du lignage." On Italian marital property law more generally, see Kuehn, *Law, Family and Women.*

15 See Le Jan, "Femmes, pouvoir et société," for a fuller discussion of this history; also see Godding, *Le Droit privé.*

16 In some other areas, such as most of Dutch-speaking Flanders, where no *douaire* was provided for widows, immovable property brought into the marriage was nevertheless not deposited in the communal account; instead, each spouse held that property separately during marriage, and it returned to his or her respective lineal families at death. Thus, here too custom constructed a dual system, in which part of the property of each spouse (typically inherited immovables) was held "separate" for the familial line and the remainder (typically movables and immovables that had been acquired during marriage) was held jointly.

In a few areas, however, all property was considered communal. In what became the classic or so-called universal community property regime, a widow received no dower and no lineal properties were held apart; instead, all property was communal, under the husband's control during marriage. The wife, however, was firmly positioned as successor to her husband with respect to her share of communal property (typically 50%), able to block his ability to borrow against it or alienate it during his life, and automatically positioned as first "creditor" of his estate at his death. For these details, see Godding, *Le Droit privé*, and Jacob, *Les Époux, le seigneur et la sité* and "Les Structures patrimoniales".

17 Bourdieu, "Normes et déviances," argues that we should not, however, take "custom" as fixed, since individuals can manipulate local inheritance practices to reflect particular circumstances, such as the number of children or the number of male children, the size of the property to be passed on, etc.

18 For a discussion of this pattern in southern Europe, see Hughes, "From Brideprice to Dowry."

19 See Wunder, *He is the Sun, She is the Moon*, which, although concentrating on the 1400–1700 period, provides an especially lucid discussion of this social logic. In these households, she notes, "the bride and groom combined their resources to provide the basis for an independent life as a married couple. This life had to be secured by the work of the spouses, usually throughout their lives: through housekeeping in the narrower sense, but at times and in case of need through every conceivable kind of work" (Wunder, *He is the Sun, She is the Moon*, p. 68). See also Howell, *The Marriage Exchange*, for a development of this argument.

20 Brundage, *Law, Sex, and Christian Society*; Brooke, *The Medieval Idea of Marriage*; Reynolds and Witte, Jr, eds., *To Have and to Hold.* See also Witte, Jr., *From Sacrament to Contract.* As Witte explained it, "marriage was conceived at once (1) as a created, natural association, subject to the laws of nature; (2) as a consensual contract, subject to the general laws of contract; and (3) as a sacrament of faith, subject to the spiritual laws of the church . . . It was the sacramental quality of marriage, however, that provided the theological and legal integration of these three perspectives into a systematic model of marriage" (Witte, Jr, *From Sacrament to Contract*, p. 93).

21 Canon 51 of the Fourth Lateran Council read, in part: "we absolutely forbid clandestine marriages; and we forbid also that a priest presume to witness such. Wherefore, extending to other localities generally the particular custom that prevails in some, we decree that when marriages are to be contracted they must be announced publicly in the churches by the priests during a suitable and fixed time, so that if legitimate impediments exist, they may be made known . . . if anyone should presume to contract a clandestine or forbidden marriage of this kind within a prohibited degree, even through ignorance, the children from such a union shall be considered illegitimate, nor shall the ignorance of the parents be pleaded as an extenuating circumstance in their behalf, since they by

contracting such marriages appear not as wanting in knowledge but rather as affecting ignorance . . . The parochial priest who deliberately neglects to forbid such unions, or any regular priest who presumes to witness them, let them be suspended from office for a period of three years and, if the nature of their offense demands it, let them be punished more severely . . . (Halsall, ed., *Internet Medieval Sourcebook*).

22 In late medieval England, the usual practice was an exchange of vows in the presence of witnesses (a vow in the present tense was a valid – if clandestine – marriage; a vow in the future tense was a betrothal), followed by the calling of banns and a church solemnization: McSheffrey, "Place, Space, and Situation." Roughly the same practices prevailed in fifteenth-century France. Marriage normally took place in two stages – a betrothal (promise of the future) followed by solemnization. The marriage was not consummated until the latter step had been completed. There too, however, marriages could be formed simply by vows in the present, with or without subsequent solemnization. See the examples provided by Charbonnier, "Les Noces de sang."

23 Hay, *William Hay's Lectures on Marriage*, p. 31; cited in Witte, Jr, "The Reformation of Marriage Law," p. 302.

24 On the history of medieval ecclesiastical marriage law in England, see Helmholz, *Marriage Litigation*, Sheehan, *Marriage, Family, and Law*, and Pedersen, *Marriage Disputes.* For France and Europe more generally, see Turlan, "Recherches sur le mariage"; Brundage, *Law, Sex, and Christian Society*; Donahue, "Clandestine Marriage," p. 315, and "The Canon Law on the Formation of Marriage and Social Practice"; Esmein, *Le Mariage en droit canonique*; Gottlieb, "Getting Married in Pre-Reformation Europe"; Brooke, *The Medieval Idea of Marriage.* Noonan, "Marriage in the Middle Ages 1," p. 454, provides an account of the theoretical basis of the doctrine of consent and analysis of its practical and doctrinal importance. Although he acknowledges that the standard "scarcely maximized free choice . . . [it] acknowledged rights of the individual not dependent on family." The basis of the consent doctrine, he concluded, was "the liberty of love," quoting a fifteenth-century commentator, "marriage signifies the conjunction of Christ and the Church, which is made through the liberty of love." On the early modern period, see in particular Bels, "La Formation du lien de mariage," Hanley, "Engendering the State," and Witte, *From Sacrament to Contract.*

25 See Goody, *Production and Reproduction*, for an explanation of this "Eurasian" system.

26 For a recent study of the way the tensions between lay interests in endogamous marriages and the Church's insistence on exogamy in the late Middle Ages and early modern period, see Sperling, "Marriage at the Time of the Council of Trent."

27 Goody, *Development of the Family and Marriage.* While most scholars have acknowledged that the rules had this effect, many have vigorously resisted the implication that the Church devised them for this purpose. In addition, some have quite reasonably pointed out that the churchmen in question were members of the same aristocratic families whose interests they presumably shared and thus would not have consciously worked against their kin.

28 See Baldwin, "Consent and the Marital Debt," for some arguments on the issue.

29 For a study of this strategy in pre-Reformation England, see Carlson, *Marriage and the English Reformation.* Also see Outhwaite, *Clandestine Marriage.* For Flanders, see Greilsammer, *L'Envers du tableau.* In 1438, the city of Ghent issued an ordinance forbidding clandestine marriages and disinheriting women seduced into such unions (in F. De Potter, *Petit cartulaire du Gand*, pp. 66–9; my thanks to Walter Prevenier for bringing this document to my attention).

30 Henceforth marriages that did not take place in the presence of the parish priest and before appropriate witnesses would be deemed invalid; these rules gave families power over choice. *Tametsi* did not become the law everywhere in Catholic Europe, however,

for the French refused to promulgate the decree. Instead, they made the rules about marriage a matter of state and formally linked them to inheritance law, thus also rejecting the venerable doctrine of "consent alone." Hanley, "The Jurisprudence of the Arrêts," provides a review of the steps in, and the institutional context of, this program during the sixteenth century, as well as an argument about "the family–state compact" that resulted. Turlan, "Recherches sur le mariage," argues that medieval French civil courts regularly resisted Church law on the basis of customary law, ruling that marriages made without parental consent were invalid and that marriages that had not met the Church's standard of publicity were valid (although Turlan also notes that those standards were vague until the end of the period).

31 As John Witte has recently summarized it, the Protestants charged that the medieval Church "discouraged and prevented mature persons from marrying by its celebration of celibacy, its proscriptions against the breach of vows to celibacy, its permission to breach oaths of betrothal, and its numerous impediments. Yet it encouraged marriages between the immature by declaring valid secure unions consummated without parental permission as well as oaths of betrothal followed by sexual intercourse. It highlighted the sanctity and solemnity of marriage by deeming it a sacrament. Yet it permitted a couple to enter this holy union without clerical or parental witness, instruction, or participation. Celibate and impeded persons were thus driven by their sinful passion to incontinence and all manner of sexual deviance. Married couples, not taught the Scriptural norms for marriage, adopted numerous immoral practices" (Witte, "The Reformation of Marriage Law," pp. 294–5).

32 See Outhwaite, *Clandestine Marriage*, for this history.

33 Duby, *Medieval Marriage*, *The Knight, the Lady and the Priest*, and *Love and Marriage*.

34 More recent scholarship has complicated Duby's portrait in several ways. A new volume of essays by specialists working in various time periods, social settings, and geographical locations, for example, disturbs the idea that collateral kinship relations throughout Europe declined after 1000 at the rate and in the way Duby described. Further, although they provide additional support to his claim that lineal kinship became more important at the end of the Middle Ages, the essays do useful damage to the notion that primogeniture was becoming the norm (even among the aristocracy) and they offer some interesting case studies about the logic of alternative practices of defining kinship and cementing these ties through marriage, even among Europe's medieval aristocracy. For these arguments, see Sabean, Teuscher, and Mathieu, eds, *Kinship in Europe*. See also the older Goody, Thirsk, and Thompson, eds, *Family and Inheritance*.

35 See, in particular, Hajnal, "European Marriage Patterns in Perspective," Laslett and Wall, eds, *Household and Family in Past Time*, and Smith, "Some Reflections."

36 See Mulder-Bakker and Browne, eds., *Household, Women, and Christianities*, for a fuller discussion of this pattern.

37 Lawrence Stone, *The Family, Sex and Marriage*, provides perhaps the fullest account. See also Shorter, *The Making of Modern Marriage*; Leites, "The Duty to Desire"; MacFarlane, *Marriage and Love in England*; Hanawalt, *The Ties that Bound*; Traer, *Marriage and the Family*; Watt, *The Making of Modern Marriage*. Recent surveys include Hartman, *The Household and the Making of History*; Houlbrooke, *The English Family*, largely superseded by Fleming, *Family and Household*. The "partnership" aspects of such marriages are particularly emphasized in Mitterauer and Sieder, *The European Family*. For a discussion of the companionate marriage in its modern settings, see Hirsch and Wardlow, eds, *Modern Loves*, and Collier, *From Duty to Desire*.

38 On this point, see Howell, "From Land to Love."

39 To be sure, scholars have not argued that the typical marriage in the earlier centuries of European history, or for that matter elsewhere in the world, was "affect-less," to employ a

term famously coined by Lawrence Stone. To judge from the few indications about such matters that we have from the earlier years of European history, it is clear that husband and wife in, say, 900 or 1100 could be attentive to one another's needs and were by no means indifferent to their spouse's person. Occasionally they even spoke of conjugal love, although by that term they seem to have meant something closer to affection and appreciation than passion. *Dilectio* was typically used to refer to conjugal love; for this vocabulary and an argument that the medieval discourse on marriage, as opposed to the discourse on women, was not misogynist, see Schnell, "The Discourse of Marriage."

40 Gilissen, "Le Statut de la femme." Also, for a development of the argument linking consent, nuclear households, and communal property law, see De Moor and van Zanden, "Girl Power." My thanks to the authors for allowing me to cite this draft. Wunder, *He is the Sun, She is the Moon*, suggests a similar interpretation: the independence of the nuclear household forced husbands and wives into an economic partnership on which the future of the household depended. "Emancipation from the older bonds of dependency was achieved not by individuals but only by the working married couple" (Wunder, *He is the Sun, She is the Moon*, p. 69). See also Hirsch and Wardlow, *Modern Loves*, who consider the privileging of the conjugal unit over other family ties to be a defining feature of the companionate marriage (see, in particular, p. 4).

41 For examples of this reasoning, see Houlbrooke, *The English Family*; Fleming, *Family and Household*, Schmidt, "Touching Inheritance" and *Overleven na de dood*, and Otis-Cour, *Lust und Liebe*.

42 In general, on the importance of consent in validating choice and mutual desire as the principles of marriage, see Brooke, *The Medieval Idea of Marriage*; Brundage, *Law, Sex and Christian Society*; Kelly, "Clandestine Marriage and Chaucer's 'Troilus'"; Herlihy, *Medieval Households* and "Family"; Murray, "Individualism and Consensual Marriage"; Outhwaite, ed., *Marriage and Society*. See also Noonan, "Marriage in the Middle Ages," for the doctrinal basis of the link between love and consent.

43 Scholars have in recent decades produced a sophisticated body of work investigating the way marriage and conjugal love were represented in a wide range of medieval texts. Old debates about the meaning of courtly love have been replaced by subtle readings of theological, legal, and imaginative texts that struggled to understand and assess love, marriage, and their relationship. Representative studies include Cartlidge, *Medieval Marriage*; Hagstrum, *Esteem Enlivened by Desire*; Ertzdorff and Wynn, eds, *Liebe, Ehe, Ehebruch in der Literatur des Mittelalters*; Edwards and Spector, eds, *The Olde Daunce*; Dallapiazza, *Minne, Husere und das Ehlich Leben*; Schulz, *Liebe, Ehe und Sexualität im Vorreformatorischen Meistersang*; Kelly, *Love and Marriage in the Age of Chaucer*; Otis-Cour, *Lust und Liebe*.

44 Lorcin, "Le Sot, la fille et le prêtre," provides a fuller analysis of these and other tales from the period. For the *fabliaux* themselves, see Montaigion and Raynaud, eds, *Recueil general et complet*.

45 Gonthier, "Les Rapports du couple," p. 163.

46 Charbonnier, "Les Noces de sang."

47 Although fictions of a kind themselves, these texts are a considerably better index of cultural assumptions than the *fabliaux*, because the defense would not have been accepted (not even for the money that usually accompanied the pleas for leniency) if it had not closely tracked cultural norms. A murder had to be justified, for example, on the grounds that the death was the unavoidable and unintended outcome of a legitimate fight. The excuse for too severely beating a wife had to turn on her insubordination, slovenliness, or some other infraction of wifely duties. The stories of love and resistance to familial pressures were similarly framed to justify the clandestine marriage. On pardon tales as sources for social history, see, in particular, Davis, *Fiction in the Archives*.

48 As a recent scholar put it, the canonical rules actually produced clandestine marriages because they were both "too simple and too complex. Too simple, because the arranged marriage of noble houses left no essential role for churchmen to play in *effecting* a marriage; too complex because they suggested that several customary features had to be present at once . . . – the already agreed-upon marriage pact, an exchange of property, and the sexual act itself . . ." (Resnick, "Marriage in Medieval Culture," p. 352 (emphasis in original)).

49 Sperling's data are from 1564. In that year, some 44% of petitioners from all over Catholic Europe who applied to Rome for a dispensation from kinship prohibitions considered themselves to have been married clandestinely. Although some of these marriages may have been undertaken secretly, most were clandestine only in the technical sense that the ceremony had violated the rules about the banns, even in a minor way, or had been performed without the proper rituals: Sperling, "Marriage at the time of the Council of Trent." The same patterns prevailed in late medieval and early modern England: see Outhwaite, *Clandestine Marriage*, Sokol and Sokol, *Shakespeare, Law, and Marriage*, and McSheffrey, *Marriage, Sex, and Civic Culture.* For Italy, see Perol, "Le Marriage et les lois somptuaires," and Bellavitis, *Identité, mariage, mobilité sociale.*

50 De Moor and van Zanden, "Girl Power."

51 On this issue, see Howell, *The Marriage Exchange*, esp. ch. 4.

52 Eight of the twelve widows who wrote marriage contracts in a sample of forty-one contracts taken from the early 1420s in Douai (in the medieval county of Flanders), for example, had minor children, which suggests that the women were no longer fresh-faced girls: Douai, Archives Municipales de Douai (AMD), FF 609, and AMD, FF 616. Most of them were marrying widowers.

53 Brereton and Ferrier, eds, *Le Ménagier de Paris.*

54 For evidence of remarriage by women and men alike in this region, see Howell, *The Marriage Exchange*, Danneel, *Weduwen*, Schmidt, *Overleven na de dood*, and the sources they cite.

55 Hoecke and Welkenhuysen, *Love and Marriage*; Donaldson, "The Myth of Courtly Love"; Newman, *The Meaning of Courtly Love.* Jane Burns has recently argued, however, that "the amorous paradigms governing courtly love in the European Middle Ages display significant variations from one national literature to the next." Dominant in French literary texts is the image of the "self-absorbed Narcissus," on the one hand, and the "fetishist Pygmalion," on the other. In fact, she continues, the entire body of such literature is more varied: in some we find women "who move through the courtly world while deploying varied forms of resistance to its misogynistic, hierarchical and normative paradigms of gendered interaction" (Burns, "Courtly Love"). See also her extensive bibliography.

56 For this argument, see Brooke, *The Medieval Idea of Marriage.*

57 As Camille noted in *The Medieval Art of Love*, in the medieval literary tradition, marriage was positioned as incompatible with romantic love, even as its antithesis.

58 Salisbury, ed., "Introduction." Others have objected, however, that Chaucer regularly made explicit connections between love and marriage; see Brewer, "Love and Marriage in Chaucer's Poetry"; also Kelly, "Clandestine Marriage and Chaucer's 'Troilus.'"

59 Vigneulles, *Les Cent Nouvelles Nouvelles.*

60 Wunder, *He is the Sun, She is the Moon.*

61 See, for a discussion of these teachings, Peters, "Gender, Sacrament and Ritual"; Harrington, *Reordering Marriage and Society*; Witte, *From Sacrament to Contract*; Davies, "Continuity and Change in Literary Advice on Marriage" and "The Sacred Condition of Equality"; Todd, *Christian Humanism and the Puritan Social Order.*

62 Leites, "Duty to Desire" (emphasis added); see also Morgan, *The Puritan Family.*

63 Hirsch and Wardlow, eds, *Modern Loves*, p. 3.

64 The literature on the "family economy," along with its relationship to the nuclear household and the sexual division of labor in the late medieval and early modern centuries, is vast, thanks to about a generation of work by feminist social historians. For guides to the literature, see Howell, *Women, Production and Patriarchy* and *The Marriage Exchange*.

65 For good evidence about these patterns in late medieval London, see McSheffrey, *Marriage, Sex, and Civic Culture*.

66 For a study of that nicely exposes the instability and permeability of the nuclear household, see Chaytor, "Household and Kinship."

67 AMD FF 609; AMD FF 616.

68 For studies of Florence that expose these patterns, see Klapisch-Zuber and Herlihy, *Les Toscans et leurs familles*, Klapisch-Zuber, *Women, Family and Ritual*, and Chabot, "La Loi du lignage."

69 Mitterauer and Sieder, *The European Family*, and Stone, *The Family, Sex and Marriage*, are among studies that emphasize the patriarchal character of the late medieval and early modern nuclear household. Both also argue, however, that more egalitarian gender relations developed over time, as the small household's functions were reduced when economic and political tasks were transferred to a public world dominated by men. The ever-more "intimate" nuclear household could thus become the site of more purely "affective" and egalitarian relations.

70 For evidence of these norms, see Howell, *The Marriage Exchange*.

71 Hence the logic of the "femme sole," "kopvrouw," "coopwiif" and *femme marchande publique* (and various) in French, *Kauffrau* (and various) in German, which allowed a husband to separate himself legally from his wife and her creditors. The same logic informed the German convention of *Schlüsselrecht*, which, by granting the wife a certain credit line with local retailers and service providers, limited the obligations she could incur in the course of provisioning the household.

72 See Medick, "Zur strukturellen Funktion von Haushalt und Familie" and "The Proto-Industrial Family," for a study of this tension in villages where wage work was available to women.

73 For a study of these practices in late medieval Ghent, see Danneel, *Weduwen*.

74 The "woman on top" trope was famously described by Davis, "Women on Top."

Bibliography

Anderson, Michael and Harris, C. C., eds, *The Sociology of the Family: New Directions for Britain* (Keele: University of Keele, 1979).

Baldwin, John W., "Consent and the Marital Debt: Five Discourses in Northern France around 1200," in Angeliki E. Laiou, ed., *Consent and Coercion to Sex and Marriage in Ancient and Medieval Societies* (Washington: Dumbarton Oaks Research Library and Collection, 1993), pp. 257–70.

Bellavitis, Anna, *Identité, mariage, mobilité sociale: Citoyennes et citoyens à Venise au XVI siècle* (Rome: École française de Rome, 2001).

Bels, P., "La Formation du lien de mariage dans l'église protestante francaise (XVIe et XVIIe siècle)," in *La Femme: Recueils de la Société de Jean Bodin pour l'histoire comparative des institutions*, 12 (Brussels: Éditions de la Librairie encyclopédique, 1962).

Bennett, Judith, and Froide, Amy M., eds, *Singlewomen in the European Past, 1250–1800* (Philadelphia: University of Pennsylvania Press, 1999).

Bonfield, Lloyd, ed., *Marriage, Property, and Succession* (Berlin: Duncker & Humbolt, 1992).

Bourdieu, Pierre, "Normes et déviances: Les Stratégies matrimoniales dans le système de reproduction," *Annales ESC*, 27 (1972), pp. 1105–25.
Brereton, Georgine E., and Ferrier, Janet Mackay, eds, *Le Ménagier de Paris: A Critical Edition* (Oxford: Oxford University Press, 1981).
Brewer, D. S., "Love and Marriage in Chaucer's Poetry," *Modern Language Review*, 49 (1954), pp. 461–4.
Brissaud, Jean, *A History of French Private Law* (trans. of 2nd French edn) (Boston: Little Brown, 1912).
Brooke, Christopher N. L., *The Medieval Idea of Marriage* (Oxford: Oxford University Press, 2002).
Brundage, James A., *Law, Sex, and Christian Society in Medieval Europe* (Chicago: University of Chicago Press, 1987).
Burns, E. Jane, "Courtly Love: Who Needs it? Recent Feminist Work in the Medieval French Tradition," *Signs*, 27/1 (2001), pp. 23–57.
Burguière, André, ed., *A History of the Family* vol. 2 (Cambridge: Polity Press, 1996).
Caenegem, Raoul Charles van, *A Historical Introduction to Private Law* (Cambridge: Cambridge University Press, 1992).
Camille, Michael, *The Medieval Art of Love: Objects and Subjects of Desire* (New York: Abrams, 1998).
Carlson, Eric J., *Marriage and the English Reformation* (Cambridge, MA: Blackwell Publishing, 1994).
Cartlidge, Neil, *Medieval Marriage: Literary Approaches, 1100–1300* (Cambridge: D. S. Brewer, 1997).
Chabot, Isabelle, "La Loi du lignage: Notes sur le système successoral florentin (XIVe–XVe–XVIIe siècles)," *Femmes, dots et patrimonies: Clio, histoire, femmes et sociétés*, 7 (1998), pp. 51–72.
Charbonnier, Pierre "Les Noces de sang: Le Mariage dans les lettres de rémission du XVe siècle," in Josiane Teyssot, ed., *Le Mariage au Moyen Âge: XIe–XVe siècles: Actes du Colloque de Montferrand du 2 mai 1997* (Montferrand: Association "Il était une fois Montferrand," 1997), pp. 133–55.
Chaytor, Miranda, "Household and Kinship: Ryton in the Late 16th and Early 17th Centuries," *History Workshop Journal*, 10 (1980), pp. 25–60.
Chevrier, G., "Sur quelques caractères de l'histoire du régime matrimonial dans la Bourgogne ducale aux diverses phases de son développement," in *Les Droits des gens mariés: Mémoires de la Société pour l'Histoire du Droit et des Institutions des anciens pays bourguignons, comtois et romands*, 27 (Dijon: Faculté de Droit et de Sciénce Politique, 1966), pp. 257–85.
Collier, Jane F., *From Duty to Desire: Remaking Families in a Spanish Village* (Princeton: Princeton University Press, 1997).
Conze, Werner, *Sozialgeschichte der Familie in der Neuzeit Europas* (Stuttgart: Klett, 1976).
Dallapiazza, Michael, *Minne, Husere und das ehlich Leben: Zur Konstitution bürgerlicher Lebenmuster in spätmittelalterlichen und frühhumanistischen Didaktiken*, Europäische Hochschulschriften I, Deutsche Literatur und Germanistik, 455 (Frankfurt am Main: Lang, 1981).
Danneel, Marianne, *Weduwen en wezen in het laat-middeleeuwse Gent* (Leuven: Garant, 1995).
Davies, Kathleen M., "Continuity and Change in Literary Advice on Marriage," in R. B. Outhwaite, ed., *Marriage and Society: Studies in the Social History of Marriage* (New York: Europa Publications, 1981), pp. 58–80.
Davies, Kathleen M., "The Sacred Condition of Equality: How Original Were Puritan Doctrines of Marriage," *Social History*, 5 (1977), pp. 563–80.

Davis, Natalie Z., *Fiction in the Archives: Pardon Tales and their Tellers in Sixteenth-Century France* (Stanford CA: Stanford University Press, 1987).

Davis, Natalie Z., "Women on Top: Symbolic Sexual Inversion and Political Disorder in Early Modern Europe," repr. in Barbara A. Babcock, ed., *The Reversible World: Symbolic Inversion in Art and Society* (Ithaca, NY, Cornell University Press, 1978), pp. 147–90.

De Moor, Tine, and van Zanden, Jan Luiten, "Girl Power: The European Marriage Pattern (EMP) and Labour Markets in the North Sea Region in the Late Medieval and Early Modern Period," paper read in the workshop "The Rise, Organization, and Institutional Framework of Factor Markets, 23–25 June 2005."

Donahue, Charles, "Clandestine Marriage in the Later Middle Ages: A Reply," *Law and History Review*, 10 (1992), pp. 315–22.

Donahue, Charles, "The Canon Law on the Formation of Marriage and Social Practice in the Later Middle Ages," *Journal of Family History*, 8 (1983), pp. 144–58.

Donaldson, E. Talbot, "The Myth of Courtly Love," *Ventures*, 5 (1965), pp. 16–23.

Duby, Georges, *The Knight, the Lady, and the Priest: The Making of Modern Marriage in Medieval France* (New York: Pantheon Books, 1983); trans. from the French: *Le Chevalier, la femme et le prêtre: Le Mariage dans la France féodale* (Paris: Hachette littérature générale, 1981).

Duby, Georges, *Love and Marriage in the Middle Ages* (Chicago: University of Chicago Press, 1994).

Duby, Georges, *Medieval Marriage: Two Models from Twelfth-Century France* (Baltimore, MD: Johns Hopkins University Press, 1978).

Edwards, Robert R., and Spector, Stephen, eds, *The Olde Daunce: Love, Friendship, Sex, and Marriage in the Medieval World*, SUNY Series in Medieval Studies (Albany, NY: State University of New York Press, 1991).

Erickson, Amy Louise, *Women and Property in Early Modern England* (London: Routledge, 1993).

Ertzdorff, Xenja von, and Wynn, Marianne, eds, *Liebe, Ehe, Ehebruch in der Literatur des Mittelalters: Vorträge des Symposiums von 13. bis 16. Juni 1983 am Institut für Deutsche Sprache und Mittelalterliche Literatur der Justus Liebig-Universität Giessen*, Beiträge zur deutschen Philologie, 58 (Giessen: W. Schmitz, 1984).

Esmein, Adhémar, *Le Mariage en droit canonique*, ed. R. Genestal, 2 vols (Paris: Librairie du Recueil Sirey, 1928).

Favarger, Dominique, *Le Régime matrimonial dans le comté de Neuchâtel du XV*[e] *au XIX*[e] *siècle* (Neuchâtel: Éditions Ides et Calendes, 1970).

Fleming, Peter, *Family and Household in Medieval England* (New York: Palgrave 2001).

Gilissen, Jean, "Le Statut de la femme dans l'ancien droit belge," in *La Femme. Recueils de la Société de Jean Bodin pour l'histoire comparative des institutions*, 11–13 (Brussels: Éditions de la Librairie Encyclopédique, 1959–62).

Glass, D. V., and Eversley, David Edward, eds, *Population in History: Essays in Historical Demography* (London: E. Arnold, 1965).

Godding, Philippe, *Le Droit privé dans les Pays-Bas méridionaux du 12*[e] *au 18*[e] *siècle*, Mémoires de la Classe des Lettres, Collection in 4o, 2nd sér., pt 1 (Brussels: Academie Royale de Belgique, 1987).

Gonthier, N., "Les Rapports du couple d'après les sources judiciaries à la fin du Moyen Âge," in Josiane Teyssot, ed., *Le Mariage au moyen âge: Xi*[e]*–Xv*[e] siècles: *Actes du Colloque de Montferrand du 2 mai 1997* (Montferrand: Association "Il était une fois Montferrand," 1997), pp. 155–65.

Goody, Jack, *The Development of the Family and Marriage in Europe* (Cambridge and New York: Cambridge University Press, 1983).

Goody, Jack, *Production and Reproduction: A Comparative Study of the Domestic Domain* (Cambridge: Cambridge University Press, 1976).

Goody, Jack, Thirsk, Joan, and Thompson, E. P., eds, *Family and Inheritance: Rural Society in Western Europe 1200–1800* (Cambridge: Cambridge University Press, 1976).

Gottlieb, Beatrice, "Getting Married in Pre-Reformation Europe: The Doctrine of Clandestine Marriage and Court Cases in Fifteenth-Century Champagne," Ph.D. dissertation (Columbia University, 1974).

Greilsammer, Myriam, *L'Envers du tableau: Mariage et maternité en Flandre médiévale* (Paris: Armand Colin, 1990).

Guichard, Pierre, and Cuvillier, Jean Paul, "Barbarian Europe," in André Burguière, ed., *A History of the Family* (Cambridge, MA: Harvard University Press, 1996), pp. 318–78.

Hagstrum, Jean H., *Esteem Enlivened by Desire: The Couple from Homer to Shakespeare* (Chicago: University of Chicago Press, 1992).

Hajnal, J., "European Marriage Patterns in Perspective," in D. V. Glass and D. E. C. Eversley, eds, *Population in History: Essays in Historical Demography* (London: E. Arnold, 1965), pp. 101–43.

Halsall, Paul, ed., *Internet Medieval Sourcebook* (New York: P. Halsall, 1996).

Hanawalt, Barbara A., *The Ties that Bound: Peasant Families in Medieval England* (Oxford: Oxford University Press, 1986).

Hanley, Sarah, "Engendering the State: Family Formation and State Building in Early Modern France," *French Historical Studies*, 16/1 (1989), pp. 4–27.

Hanley, Sarah, "The Jurisprudence of the Arrêts: Marital Union, Civil Society, and State Formation in France, 1550–1650," *Law and History Review*, 21/1 (2003), pp. 1–41.

Harrington, Joel F., *Reordering Marriage and Society in Reformation Germany* (Cambridge: Cambridge University Press, 1995).

Hartman, Mary S., *The Household and the Making of History: A Subversive View of the Western Past* (Cambridge and New York: Cambridge University Press, 2004).

Hay, William, *William Hay's Lectures on Marriage*, trans. John C. Barry (Edinburgh: Stair Society, 1967).

Helmholz, Richard H., *Marriage Litigation in Medieval England* (Cambridge: Cambridge University Press, 1974).

Herlihy, David, *Medieval Households* (Cambridge, MA: Harvard University Press, 1985).

Herlihy, David, "Family," *American Historical Review*, 76/1 (1991), pp. 1–16.

Hilaire, Jean, *Le Régime des biens entre époux dans la région de Montpellier du début du XIIIe siècle à la fin du XVIe siècle: Contribution aux études d'histoire du droit écrit* (Montpellier: Causse, Graille & Castelnau, 1957).

Hirsch, Jennifer S., and Wardlow, Holly, eds, *Modern Loves: The Anthropology of Romantic Courtship and Companionate Marriage* (Ann Arbor, MI: University of Michigan Press, 2006).

Hoecke, Willy van, and Welkenhuysen, Andries, *Love and Marriage in the Twelfth Century* (Leuven: Leuven University Press, 1981).

Houlbrooke, Ralph A., *The English Family 1450–1700* (London: Longman, 1984).

Howell, Martha C., *Women, Production and Patriarchy in Late Medieval Cities* (Chicago: University of Chicago Press, 1986).

Howell, Martha C., *The Marriage Exchange: Property, Social Place, and Gender in Late Medieval Cities* (Chicago: University of Chicago Press, 1998).

Howell, Martha C., "From Land to Love: Commerce and Marriage in Northern Europe during the Late Middle Ages," *Jaarboek voor middeleeuwse Geschiedenis*, 10 (2007), pp. 216–53.

Hughes, Diane Owen, "From Brideprice to Dowry in Mediterranean Europe," *Journal of Family History*, 3 (1978), pp. 262–96.

Jacob, Robert, "La Charte d'Hesdin (1243) et la vocation successorale du conjoint survivant dans les pays Picard et Wallon," *Tijdschrift voor Rechtsgeschiedenis*, 50 (1982), pp. 351–70.

Jacob, Robert, *Les Époux, le seigneur et la cité: Coutume et pratiques matrimoniales des bourgeois et paysans de France du Nord au moyen âge* (Brussels: Facultés Universitaires Saint-Louis, 1990).

Jacob, Robert, "Les Structures patrimoniales de la conjugalité au moyen-âge dans la France du Nord: Essai d'histoire comparée des époux nobles et routiers dans les pays du groupe de coutumes 'Picard-Wallon,'" Thèse de doctorat (Université de Paris 2, 1984).

Karras, Ruth M., "The History of Marriage and the Myth of *Friedelehe*," *Early Medieval Europe*, 14/2 (2006), pp. 119–51.

Kelly, Henry A., "Clandestine Marriage and Chaucer's 'Troilus'," *Viator*, 4 (1973), pp. 435–59.

Kelly, Henry A., *Love and Marriage in the Age of Chaucer* (Ithaca, NY: Cornell University Press, 1975).

Klapisch-Zuber, Christiane, *Women, Family and Ritual in Renaissance Italy*, trans. Lydia Cochran (Chicago: University of Chicago Press, 1985).

Klapisch-Zuber, Christiane, and Herlihy, David, *Les Toscans et leurs familles: Une étude du Castado Florentin de 1427* (Paris: École des hautes études en sciences sociales, 1978).

Kuehn, Thomas, *Law, Family and Women: Toward a Legal Anthropology of Renaissance Italy* (Chicago: University of Chicago Press, 1991).

Lafon, Jacques, *Les Epoux bordelais 1450–1550: Régimes matrimoniaux et mutations sociales* (Paris: SEVPEN, 1972).

Laiou, Angeliki E., ed., *Consent and Coercion to Sex and Marriage in Ancient and Medieval Societies* (Washington: Dumbarton Oaks Research Library and Collection, 1993).

Laslett, Peter, Oosterveen, Karla, and Smith, Richard M., eds, *Bastardy and its Comparative History: Studies in the History of Illegitimacy and Marital Nonconformism in Britain, France, Germany, Sweden, North America, Jamaica, and Japan* (Cambridge, MA: Harvard University Press, 1980).

Laslett, Peter, and Wall, Richard, eds, *Household and Family in Past Time: Comparative Studies in the Size and Structure of the Domestic Group over the Last Three Centuries in England, France, Serbia, Japan and Colonial North America, with Further Materials from Western Europe* (Cambridge: Cambridge University Press, 1972).

Leites, Edmund, "The Duty to Desire: Love, Friendship, and Sexuality in Puritan Theories of Marriage," *Journal of Social History*, 15/3 (1982), pp. 383–408.

Le Jan, Régine, "Femmes, pouvoir et société dans le haut moyen âge," in Régine Le Jan, ed., *Les Médiévistes français*, 1 (Paris: Picard, 2001).

Lepointe, Gabriel, *La Famille dans l'ancien droit*, 2nd edn (Paris: Domat-Montchrestien, 1947).

Lorcin, Marie-Thérèse, "Le Sot, la fille et le prêtre: Le Mariage dans les contes à rire," in Josiane Teyssot, ed., *Le Mariage au moyen âge: XIe–XVe siècles* (Montferrand: Association "Il était une fois Montferrand," 1997), pp. 125–33.

MacFarlane, Alan, *Marriage and Love in England: Modes of Reproduction, 1380–1840* (Oxford: B. Blackwell, 1986).

McSheffrey, Shannon, "Place, Space, and Situation: Public and Private in the Making of Marriage in Late Medieval London," *Speculum* 79 (2004), pp. 960–90.

McSheffrey, Shannon, *Marriage, Sex, and Civic Culture in Late Medieval London* (Philadelphia: University of Pennsylvania Press, 2006).

Mayali, Laurent, *Droit savant et coutumes: L'Exclusion des filles dotées*, Xiième–Xvième *siècles* (Frankfurt am Main: Klostermann, 1987).

Medick, Hans, "Zur strukturellen Funktion von Haushalt und Familie im Übergang von der traditionellen Agrargesellschaft zum industriellen Kapitalismus: die proto-industrielle Familienwirtschaft," in W. Conze, ed., *Sozialgeschichte der Familie in der Neuzeit Europas*, Neue Forschungen, Industrielle Welt, 21 (Stuttgart: Klett, 1976), pp. 254–82.

Medick, Hans, "The Proto-Industrial Family: The Structural Function of Household and Family during the Transition from Peasant Society to Industrial Capitalism," *Social History*, 3 (1976), pp. 291–316.

Mitterauer, Michael, and Sieder, Reinhard, *The European Family: Patriarchy to Partnership from the Middle Ages to the Present* (Oxford: Basil Blackwell, 1982).

Montaigion, Anatole de, and Raynaud, Gaston, eds, *Recueil général et complet des fabliaux des XIIIe et XIVe siècles* (Paris: Librairie des Bibliophiles, 1872–90).

Morgan, Edmund S., *The Puritan Family: Religion and Domestic Relations in Seventeenth-Century New England* (New York: Harper & Row, 1966).

Mulder-Bakker, Anneke B., and Browne, Jocelyn Wogan, eds, *Household, Women, and Christianities in Late Antiquity and the Middle Ages*, Medieval Women, Texts and Contexts, 14 (Turnhout: Brepols, 2005).

Murray, Jacqueline, "Individualism and Consensual Marriage: Some Evidence from Medieval England," in Constance M. Rousseau and Joel T. Rosenthal, eds, *Women, Marriage and Family in Medieval Christendom: Essays in Memory of Michael M. Sheehan CSB* (Kalamazoo, MI: Medieval Institute Publications, 1998), pp. 121–51.

Newman, Francis X., *The Meaning of Courtly Love* (Albany, NY: State University of New York Press, 1968).

Noonan, John, "Marriage in the Middle Ages: Power to Choose," *Viator*, 4 (1973), pp. 419–34.

Olivier-Martin, Francois, *Histoire de la coutume de la prevoté et vicomté de Paris*, 2 vols (Paris: Éditions Cujas, 1995).

Otis-Cour, Leah, *Lust und Liebe: Geschichte der Paarbeziehungen im Mittelalter* (Frankfurt am Main: S. Fischer Verlag, 2000).

Ourliac, Paul, and Gazzaniga, Jean-Louis, *Histoire du droit privé francais de l'an mil au Code Civil* (Paris: A. Michel, 1985).

Ourliac, Paul, and Malafosse, Jehan de, *Histoire du droit privé*, vol. 3 in *Le droit familial* (Paris: Presses Universitaires de France, 1971).

Outhwaite, R. B., ed., *Marriage and Society: Studies in the Social History of Marriage* (New York: St Martin's Press, 1981).

Outhwaite, R. B., *Clandestine Marriage in England, 1500–1800* (Rio Grande, OH: Hambledon Press, 1995).

Pedersen, Frederick, *Marriage Disputes in Medieval England* (London: Hambledon, 2000).

Perol, Céline, "Le Marriage et les lois somptuaires en Toscane au XIVe siècle," in Josiane Teyssot, ed., *Le Mariage au moyen âge: XIe-XVe siècles* (Montferrand: Association "Il était une fois Montferrand," 1997), pp. 87–95.

Peters, Christine, "Gender, Sacrament and Ritual: The Making and Meaning of Marriage in Late Medieval and Early Modern England," *Past & Present*, 169 (2000), pp. 63–96.

Petot, P., and Vandenbossche, A., "Le Statut de la femme dans les pays coutumier francais du XIIIe au XVIIe siècle," in *La Femme. Recueils de la Société de Jean Bodin pour l'histoire comparative des institutions*, 12 (Brussels: Éditions de la Librairie Encyclopédique, 1962).

Planitz, Hans, *Deutsche Rechtsgeschichte* (Graz-Köln: Böhlau, 1971).

Potter, Frans de, *Petit cartulaire du Gand* (Ghent: S. Leliaert, A. Siffer & Cie, 1885).

Poudret, Jean. F., "La Situation du conjoint survivant en pays de Vaud XIIIe–XVIe siècle," in *Les Droits des gens mariés. Mémoires de la Société pour l'histoire du droit et des institutions des anciens pays bourguignons, comtois et romands*, 27 (Dijon: Faculté de Droit des Science Économiques de Dijon, 1966).

Resnick, Irven M., "Marriage in Medieval Culture: Consent Theory and the Case of Joseph and Mary," *Church History*, 69/2 (June 2000), pp. 350–71.

Reynolds, Philip L., and Witte, John, Jr, eds, *To Have and to Hold: Marrying and its Documentation in Western Christendom, 400–1600* (Cambridge: Cambridge University Press, 2007).

Rousseau, Constance M., and Rosenthal, Joel T., eds, *Women, Marriage, and Family in Medieval Christendom: Essays in Memory of Michael M. Sheehan, CSB* (Kalamazoo, MI: Medieval Institute Publications, 1998).

Sabean, David Warren, Teuscher, Simon, and Mathieu, Jon, eds, *Kinship in Europe: Approaches to the Long-Term Development (1300–1900)* (Oxford and New York: Berghahn Books, 2007).

Salisbury, Eve, "Introduction," in Eve Salisbury, ed., *The Trials and Joys of Marriage* (Kalamazoo, MI: Published for TEAMS in association with the University of Rochester by Medieval Institute Publications, Western Michigan University, 2002).

Schmidt, Adriadne, *Overleven na de dood: Weduwen in Leiden in de gouden eeuw* (Amsterdam: Bert Bakker, 2001).

Schmidt, Adriadne, "Touching Inheritance: Mannen, vrouwen en de overdracht van bezit in Holland in de 17e eeuw," *Historisch Tijdschrijf Holland*, 33/4 (2001), pp. 175–89.

Schnell, Rudiger, "The Discourse of Marriage in the Middle Ages," trans. Andrew Shields, *Speculum*, 73/3 (1998), pp. 771–86.

Schulz, Ulrike-Marianne, *Liebe, Ehe und Sexualität im Vorreformatorischen Meistersang: Texte und Untersuchungen*, Goppinger Arbeiten zur Germanistik, 624 (Goppingen: Kümmerle, 1995).

Sheehan, Michael M., *Marriage, Family, and Law in Medieval Europe: Collected Studies*, ed. James K. Farge (Toronto: University of Toronto Press, 1996).

Shorter, Edward, *The Making of Modern Marriage* (New York: Basic Books, 1975).

Smith, Richard, "Some Reflections on the Evidence for the Origins of the 'European Marriage Pattern,' in England," in C. C. Harris and Michael Anderson, eds, *The Sociology of the Family: New Directions for Britain*, Sociological Review Monograph, 28 (Keele: University of Keele, 1979), pp. 74–112

Sokol, B. J., and Sokol, Mary, *Shakespeare, Law, and Marriage* (Cambridge: Cambridge University Press, 2003).

Sperling, Jutta, *Convents and the Body Politic in Late Renaissance Venice* (Chicago: University of Chicago Press, 1999).

Sperling, Jutta, "Marriage at the Time of the Council of Trent (1560–70): Clandestine Marriages, Kinship Prohibitions, and Dowry Exchange in European Comparison," *Journal of Early Modern European History*, 8/1–2 (2004), pp. 67–108.

Stone, Lawrence, *The Family, Sex and Marriage in England 1500–1800* (1977; abridged edn, New York: Harper & Row, 1985).

Teyssot, Josiane, *Le Mariage au moyen âge: XI*e*–XV*e *siècles: Actes du Colloque de Montferrand du 3 mai 1997* (Montferrand: Association "Il était une fois Montferrand," 1997).

Todd, Margo, *Christian Humanism and the Puritan Social Order* (Cambridge: Cambridge University Press, 1987).

Traer, James F., *Marriage and the Family in Eighteenth Century France* (Ithaca, NY: Cornell University Press, 1980).

Turlan, Julliette M., "Recherches sur le mariage dans la pratique coutumière, XIIe-XVIe siècles," *Revue historique de droit français et étranger*, 4th sér., 35 année (1957), pp. 477–528.

Vigneulles, Philippe de, *Les Cent Nouvelles Nouvelles*, ed. Charles H. Livingston et al., Travaux d'humanisme et Renaissance, 120 (Geneva: Droz, 1972).

Watt, Richard, *The Making of Modern Marriage: Matrimonial Control and the Rise of Sentiment in Neuchâtel, 1550–1800* (Ithaca, NY: Cornell University Press, 1992).

Witte, John, Jr., "The Reformation of Marriage Law in Martin Luther's Germany: Its Significance Then and Now," *Journal of Law and Religion*, 4/2 (1986), pp. 293–351.

Witte, John, Jr., *From Sacrament to Contract: Marriage, Religion, and Law in the Western Tradition* (Louisville, KY: Westminster John Knox Press, 1997).

Wunder, Heidi, *He is the Sun, She is the Moon: Women in Early Modern Germany* (Cambridge, MA: Harvard University Press, 1998).

Yver, Jean, *Egalité entre héritiers et exclusion des enfants dotés: Essai de géographie coutumière* (Paris: Sirey, 1966).

Yver, Jean, "Les Deux Groupes de coutumes," *Revue du Nord*, 35 (1953), pp. 197–220.

Further Reading

Brooke, Christopher N. L., *The Medieval Idea of Marriage* (Oxford: Oxford University Press, 2002).

Brundage, James A., *Law, Sex, and Christian Society in Medieval Europe* (Chicago: University of Chicago Press, 1987).

Duby, Georges, *The Knight, the Lady, and the Priest: the Making of Modern Marriage in Medieval France* (New York: Pantheon Books, 1983); trans. from the French: *Le Chevalier, la femme et le prêtre: Le Mariage dans la France féodale* (Paris: Hachette littérature générale, 1981).

Erickson, Amy Louise, *Women and Property in Early Modern England* (London: Routledge, 1993).

Goody, Jack, *The Development of the Family and Marriage in Europe* (Cambridge and New York: Cambridge University Press, 1983).

Hajnal, J., "European Marriage Patterns in Perspective," in D. V. Glass and D. E. C. Eversley, eds, *Population in History: Essays in Historical Demography* (London: E. Arnold, 1965), pp. 101–43.

Herlihy, David, "Family," *American Historical Review*, 76/1 (1991), pp. 1–16.

Hughes, Diane Owen, "From Brideprice to Dowry in Mediterranean Europe," *Journal of Family History*, 3 (1978), 262–96.

Klapisch-Zuber, Christiane, *Women, Family and Ritual in Renaissance Italy*, trans. Lydia Cochran (Chicago: University of Chicago Press, 1985).

Leites, Edmund, "The Duty to Desire: Love, Friendship, and Sexuality in Puritan Theories of Marriage," *Journal of Social History*, 15/3 (1982), pp. 383–408.

Noonan, John, "Marriage in the Middle Ages 1: Power to Choose," *Viator*, 4 (1973), pp. 419–34.

Reynolds, Philip L., and Witte, John, Jr, eds, *To Have and to Hold: Marrying and its Documentation in Western Christendom, 400–1600* (Cambridge: Cambridge University Press, 2007).

Sheehan, Michael M., *Marriage, Family, and Law in Medieval Europe: Collected Studies*, ed. James K. Farge (Toronto: University of Toronto Press, 1996).

Stone, Lawrence, *The Family, Sex and Marriage in England 1500–1800* (1977; abridged edn, New York: Harper & Row, 1985).

Wunder, Heidi, *He is the Sun, She is the Moon: Women in Early Modern Germany* (Cambridge, MA: Harvard University Press, 1998).

Chapter Eight

Gender and Sexuality

John Arnold

A civic fountain was a major landmark in a thirteenth-century Italian commune: an essential source of water, an expression of civic identity, and a semi-formal meeting place. In 1265 the Tuscan town of Massa Marittima completed its fountain, situated just off the main piazza, comprising a loggia framed by three tall arches. At some point thereafter – perhaps a decade later – the wall behind the water troughs was decorated with murals. Those for the right and centre arches are now lost, though the latter might have incorporated a depiction of the Virgin Mary. But in the left arch one mural still survives, some 6 × 5 meters in size. The image the medieval commune chose to place there is of a penis tree.

Penis trees are rare, though not unknown, in medieval art. The one at Massa Marittima is probably the earliest depiction, and is certainly the largest and most public. In the bottom right, a group of four women stand sedately, talking with each other, whilst a black bird flies in from the right of the frame. Bottom left, four women (maybe the same four women) fight and squabble: two tussle over a sack whilst pulling each others' hair, as black birds fly overhead, and another is being poked from behind – perhaps sodomized – by a disembodied phallus. The fourth woman reaches up to the verdant tree that dominates the frame. In its branches are the penises: twenty-five or more, erect and carrying scrotal sacs, but detached from their presumed owners. How one interprets this is open to debate, but George Ferzoco – who has done more than any other scholar to introduce and explain the mural to a wider audience – has persuasively argued that it is an allegory of the bad effects of Ghibelline government. The black bird undoubtedly signifies imperial power. The left-hand side of the frame clearly depicts "disorder"; sodomy, in particular, has a long history of association with civic misgovernment. The figures might be interpreted as "witches," as a much later written text – the German inquisitors' manual, the *Malleus maleficarum* (*c.* 1475) – tells of women who magic away men's penises and hide them in trees. It is, at any rate, a very public picture, telling the good people of Massa Marittima something important about themselves and their political environment.[1]

For a variety of reasons, the Massa Marittima mural presents an interesting place to begin a chapter on the very broad theme of gender. It may challenge some popular perceptions of the period: for one, the mistaken notion that medieval people, as part of a religious culture, were utterly repressed about sexual and bodily matters; for another, the more informed perception that medieval "bawdiness" or "ribaldry" was a low-class, unthinking, somewhat meaningless cultural reflex. What was crude, sexual, and bodily *could* be linked to "low" things – it played a role in the language of insult, and elite depictions of peasants sometimes took pleasure in gratuitously depicting those who worked in such a fashion.[2] But here we have penises, sodomy, and disorder lavishly depicted, at no little expense, in the service of civic identity. And that presents a matter of further importance. It is clear that the Massa Marittima mural is a political image. It is also clear that its visual language draws upon imagery that is not simply "gendered" as a by-product of other factors, but that speaks directly through the depiction of masculine virility and impotence, the right and wrong ordering of sexuality and power, and fears of female disorder. Gender, politics, power, and public communication here go hand in hand. The mural can serve, therefore, as a manifesto for current and future study of medieval gender: this is a field not limited to the study of women, not restricted to matters of family and domesticity, and not something marginal to medieval people's own view of the world around them. Gender is here center stage; and its study will clearly provide insight to a variety of issues.

This is not for a moment to suggest that the study of women, families, or society is, or should be, a "marginal" field. The current study of gender is completely indebted to historiography in these areas, and the work undertaken within the paradigms of women's history and the history of the family continues to have profound importance for our understanding of the past. Indeed, as I will suggest toward the end of this chapter, women's history continues to present gender history with important methodological and political lessons. But it is nonetheless true that "gender," particularly since the 1980s, has come to incorporate more than these areas, and has adopted approaches and insights different from the methodologies and politics of the 1960s and 1970s. In this chapter I shall begin by sketching some of the main historiographical currents affecting the study of medieval gender, and turn then to the nature of medieval patriarchy, and the representation of femininity, masculinity, and manhood. We will look further at medieval sexualities in particular, and I will conclude with some thoughts on the tension between representation and reality, ideas and practice.

Historiography and Gender

Medieval historians have long paid attention to the role and position of *some* women in the period. The relative frequency of female regents meant that certain figures – Boudicca, Eleanor of Aquitaine, Blanche of Castile – attracted attention from the earliest days of modern medievalism. The importance of "the lady" to discourses of courtly love, and the vibrancy of particular characters such as Chaucer's Wife of Bath, prompted some early discussion of the cultural position of women. The first sustained interest in "women" *en masse* – and conceived collectively as something like a "fourth estate" (as the title of Shulamith Shahar's general textbook puts it) – came, however, from nineteenth-century demographers. In the 1880s the German scholar Karl Bucher posed the *Frauenfräge* (the "Woman Question"): noting an apparent "surplus" of unmarried women in late medieval sources, he suggested that, whilst most women desired marriage, in the post-plague era not all were able to find a husband, and that this "problem" had an effect upon society. Further pioneering work in the early twentieth century continued to focus upon economic issues, notably Eileen Power's discussion of medieval nunneries as marginalized and impoverished foundations, and Marion K. Dale's study of women in guilds.

The growth of a self-conscious "Women's History" in the 1970s and 1980s (for medievalists, more particularly in the mid-1980s to the early 1990s) drew upon these roots, adapting the methods and paradigms of social history to the study of women, and asking questions prompted particularly by economic and demographic issues.[3] But some new elements were also present. Pre-eminent was the degree to which feminist politics informed and inspired this work. For several of the key writers whose first works appeared in the mid-1980s, the project of their histories was to demonstrate the mechanisms and effects of patriarchy in past societies, and their analyses emphasized the degree to which women's lives were restricted and marginalized. At the same time, in demonstrating that which had previously been "hidden from history," there was a concern to give back a voice to these women, and to argue that their lives were an important, albeit much occluded, part of the historical process. Thus one would point to the economic importance of "women's work" (brewing, gleaning, huckstering, and other tasks) to the household – and also to how this work was undervalued and marginalized by the culture of its time.

"Gender history," as something distinguished from "women's history," arose in the late 1980s. Still inspired by feminism, it sought to question the nature of the apparently universal category "woman," and, in the terms set out by Joan Wallach Scott's highly influential article of 1986, aimed to think about "gender" as an analytical category that could be applied to issues of language and representation beyond the social realm – in politics, for example. For Scott and others – notably her friend and discussant, the influential theorist Judith Butler – the categories upon which the projects of social history and women's history tend to depend ("women," "working class," "race") are not self-evident, stable, pre-given, or unchanging, but produced in and through language and culture. For Butler, even our very flesh is experienced and apprehended only via cultural constructions, never as a pure and unmediated foundation. Any attempt to analyze "women" as an undifferentiated group with a core of stable identity is thus, for these and other writers, a project doomed to failure. According to Scott, the historian faces a further challenge in that she cannot access the foundational "experience" of those she seeks to discuss, first because the sources we use are texts (and hence bound up with issues of genre, rhetoric, and representation); and, secondly and more essentially, because the very "experience" of any past subject was, itself, subject to the cultural mediation and construction of its own time. In this conceptualization, there is no pure and unfettered "experience" to then be "distorted" or interpreted by culture; all that happens to us is, in the very terms in which we experience it, always already mediated by culture. Writing a history of "women" thus no longer seems possible, in a priori terms. The project instead is transformed into the writing of histories that examine how "women" (and "men," and other interlocking categories of race, class, age, and sexuality) are constructed and deployed within particular discourses at different historical and cultural junctures.[4]

These perspectives fall within what is sometimes (rather unhelpfully) labeled "postmodernism," or (more precisely) poststructuralism – analyses that emphasize the importance of language in the construction of social reality, and the degree to which that language is shifting and unstable rather than tethered to any fixed external referent. A key thinker here was the French historian and philosopher Michel Foucault, whose work on the history of sexuality has provided a further set of intellectual tools for the study of gender (despite the fact that he himself did not really consider the topic). Foucault was concerned to shift debate away from a straightforward narrative of sexual "liberation" from earlier "repression," and to suggest instead that modern "sexualities" are constructed largely through those same discourses of medicine, science, and psychology that appear liberatory or repressive. Past sexualities – or, rather, past experiences of desire and pleasure, which may or may not cohere into something as specific as a "sexuality" – form different shapes to that of modern experience. Thus Foucault would argue that "the homosexual" is an identity made through late-nineteenth-century medical discourse; earlier senses of male–male sexual desire saw it as activity rather than identity, and did not make a primary divide of the sexual world into "homo-" and "heterosexual."[5] For those who work on periods well before the development of the discourses of science and medicine, Foucault's ideas have opened up the possibility of viewing medieval sexual ideas and identities in ways different from modern gay/straight dichotomies, and have prompted an examination of those medieval discourses that laid claim to sexual matters – particularly sin and confession, and aspects of secular law, though also elements of literature and conduct manuals.

None of the influential theorists discussed above focused on the Middle Ages, and some, such as Foucault, tend to assume a convenient and spurious simplicity to medieval society and culture, against which later complexity can be set. Nonetheless, they have had a profound influence on the study of medieval gender. The recent prioritization of what might broadly be termed "cultural" elements is notable – histories of gender and literacy, art, religion, and so forth. The shift away from "woman" as a universalized category has been accompanied by "third-wave" feminisms that tend to emphasize female agency, even within repressive regimes, and look to the specifics of individual negotiations of gender rather than overarching patterns and tendencies. Most importantly, however, medievalists mostly now consider that, rather than simply "recovering" the experience of earlier women (and men), they are analyzing the idealizations and constructions of our sources, the interdependency of those sources' gendered images, and the element of power involved in the explicit and implicit narration of what it meant to be a medieval woman (lady, wife, widow, maiden, whore, singlewoman, concubine) or man (knight, squire, husband, artisan, *litteratus*, peasant, knave). As we will see, however, the issue of the lived experience of gender has not gone away; and, whilst "gender history" has become particularly influential since the 1980s, the project of "women's history" has not died out.

Patriarchies, Misogynies, Femininities

A tale is told in medieval Italy (the north Italy of the Massa Marittima penis tree), most famously in Boccaccio's *Decameron*. A man, Nastagio degli Onesti, walking in the woods one day, came across a knight hunting down a naked girl who had rejected his advances. The knight's dogs held her down whilst the knight cut her open, ripped out her heart, and fed it to his animals. She then arose and the hunt resumed, the scene re-enacted in an endless cycle. Having witnessed this violence, Nastagio brought to the woods the woman he loved, and her kinsfolk, and showed them the repeated tableau of chase and evisceration; this as encouragement that she in turn should yield to Nastagio. This story, and other narratives of rape, violence, and female passivity, were recounted in various ways in late medieval Italy, including being represented visually on bridal chests and panels painted for wedding celebrations.[6]

The historiography since the 1980s has frequently sought to emphasize feminine agency rather than oppression. But it must always do so against a backdrop of endemic and structural misogyny. Medieval society was patriarchal, and medieval culture was misogynistic; it is ludicrous to argue otherwise. In medieval literature of various types the besetting female fault of inconstancy is punished graphically and repeatedly, and engrained female lust satisfied regardless of consent or female agency. The song remained much the same, from hovel to castle. In Caxton's version of the much older *Book of Chess*, the section concerning "the Queen" ends with a narrative about a queen who allowed the king of Hungary to take her husband's castle, on the promise that he would wed her. The Hungarian monarch slept with her for the night, then had her raped by all his troops; on the third day she was executed, a wooden staff driven through her from genitalia to throat. The fate was deserved, the text tells us, for her sexual and military betrayal. In various French *fabliaux*, countless wives are sexually assaulted by randy priests and others, "bumped and battered with such force" that they cannot help but submit; and, in any case, the priest only does "what women everywhere want done."[7] The examples multiply in cackling chorus across various genres, and find sophisticated echo in the high literary productions of Boccaccio, Chaucer, and others. Intellectual thought, with roots in antique philosophy, the Bible, and patristic writings, emphasized the innate weakness of women and superiority of men. Humoral theory posited woman as a kind of insufficiently finished creature, not "baked" long enough in the womb to become hot and dry, as rational man was made. Instead, her cold and wet physiology doomed her to an unstable nature, having to emit a monthly surplus of fluid (a highly dangerous discharge, which could kill herbs, stop trees fruiting, and cause rabies in dogs) and prone to emotional confusion and uncontrolled passions. Women were in some senses "outside" the differentiated male roles of *oratores*, *bellatores*, and *laboratores*. They more readily divided into maiden, wife, and widow – identities predicated on the presence or absence of a male authority, and endowed with restrictive social expectations in various works of moral guidance.[8]

These ideas had direct results in some of the structures that controlled women's lives. There was an expectation that women would be governed by men, whether father, husband, or priest. Women could not hold secular or religious office; they were the ones who brewed ale, but were never the official ale-tasters who governed the trade; they belonged to various craft guilds, but never acted as treasurer or became masters; they contributed perhaps disproportionately to charity via religious confraternities, but never sat at the head of the annual feast. In law, their roles were much restricted. As an early fourteenth-century English legal note explains, a woman could bring an appeal against a man only if he killed her husband who then died in her arms, if she was raped, or if her goods were stolen and the thief *immediately* taken with the property still in his possession (and the case brought immediately to trial). Other appeals – including more drawn-out cases of theft – could not be brought by a woman because "women are changeable in nature."[9] Nor could a woman act as a witness in law, and, in various cases where she was either the accused or the wronged party, her husband or father was expected to act on her behalf. In the case of rape – as today, a crime hardly ever resulting in successful prosecution – in England, after 1382, the wrong done was understood primarily as an assault against the honor and property of the family, rather than of the victim herself.[10]

One could continue thus onward, multiplying the specific ways in which women encountered limitations to their actions and opportunities, were subject to the will of others (often backed up by violence and intimidation), and were mocked, ridiculed, despised, and fantasized by both popular and elite culture. But, although it is true that medieval society was patriarchal and medieval culture misogynistic, there are also more complex truths beyond the surface of anti-women invective. Whilst misogyny in general worked to sustain the social disadvantages of women, specific enunciations of misogyny could have particular purposes, not always connected simply to female oppression. Take, for example, the fairly well-known description of women by Odo of Cluny (994–1049): "If men could see beneath the skin, the sight of women would make them nauseous . . . Since we are loath to touch spittle or dung even with our fingertips, how can we desire to embrace such a sack of dung?"[11] The strong association of women with the low and the bodily is common across medieval culture; but it is worth noting that Odo's primary purpose was not to denigrate women but to help monks protect their fragile chastity. The attractiveness of women, even the very *thought* of women, within a monastic setting, held the potential for sin. Odo's misogyny had a function, and that function was specifically directed toward the thoughts, feelings, and fallibilities of a small group of men, rather than womankind. One might see an element of this, in reversed fashion, in the encounters between women and clerics in various *fabliaux* and other bawdy tales. The satirical target of such stories was most usually the cuckolding priest or friar, and the weak and deceived husband; the stereotyped notion of feminine insatiability was more backdrop than main feature. Nor was Odo's strand of monastic misogyny the same as the association, growing in strength in the late Middle Ages, between women and "sins of the tongue" – gossip and scolding, in particular.[12] And this, in turn, was not the same as the subtle misogyny of the troubadour "courtly love" tradition, which presented women as either trapped in the position of *domna* ("lady"), who is unattainable, stuck on a pedestal, and paradoxically masculine in terms of her authority (acting as the lover's "lord and master"); or else consigned to the low-status ranks of women-in-general, who are unreasonable, take lovers indiscriminately, and are to be despised.[13]

This is not to argue that these attitudes were utterly unconnected, or lacking in collective force. But it is nonetheless useful to view medieval culture as drawing upon a number of different misogynies, rather than simply voicing one unified (male) viewpoint. This points up, at the very least, the varying discursive contexts within which ideas of femininity were expressed, and the ends to which they were put; with a particular caveat concerning monastic views, which talked about women whilst thinking primarily about men. It also reminds us that the force and effect of misogyny was contextually dependent. Various medieval queens were accused of adultery, and this is undoubtedly an indication that, despite their legitimate access to power via lineage and/or marriage, it was, as Pauline Stafford puts it, "as 'woman' that they were often judged."[14] The fact of gender could be used to trump the differentials of status. At the same time, however, whilst accusing a queen of adultery draws upon common stereotypes of female sexual incontinence, it is also a notably *specific* use of the trope, usually implicated in struggles between political factions. That is, the misogyny that attempts to bring down a queen is operating in a different realm and in a different manner from an otherwise identical accusation leveled between neighbors in a Church court.

One can also find challenges to medieval misogynies, whether directly, implicitly, or through resistant reinterpretation of the traditions. The most famous example of the direct challenge is that of the fifteenth-century French writer Christine de Pizan. In her books *The Book of the City of Ladies* and *The Treasure of the City of Ladies* Christine tackled head-on the literary misogyny espoused in the poem *The Romance of the Rose*:. "why on earth was it," Christine asks, "that so many men, both clerics and others, have said and continue to say and write such awful, damning things about women and their ways." To challenge these unfair assumptions, she "builds" through writing a "city of Ladies" who give good example of their sex, and tackles directly some abiding issues, such as why women were not allowed equal access to law.[15] The late medieval English mystic Margery Kempe of Bishop's Lynn was at various points challenged as to the legitimacy of her potentially scandalous actions and speech, in large part on the grounds of her sex, and she drew upon discourses of Christian fraternity and affective piety in rebuttal. In religion, in particular, more positive images of femininity were also available, most obviously the literally inimitable Virgin Mary, but also the various Virgin Martyrs of early Christianity, and later saints such as Zita of Lucca (a pious maidservant) and Agnes of Bohemia (daughter of the king of Bohemia). Female saints, in both life and death, were still restricted by their sex, and Caroline Walker Bynum has argued that, whereas the narratives of male saints' lives often depict dramatic conversions marked by liminal (symbolically marginalized) experiences, female saints were always already liminal, and their piety was usually presented as an unbroken amplification of their existent roles. Nonetheless, female saints proffered positive images of womanhood, and displayed the possibility of female agency – admittedly most often in the protection of their own chastity, but also (as in Agnes of Bohemia's case) in the setting-up of religious foundations, or (in the case of Katherine of Alexandria, a virgin martyr, who debated with the court philosophers of a pagan emperor) in notable female learning and authority.[16] Motherhood had strongly positive connotations, and was on occasion used to describe the caring role a male abbot had toward his monastic community. Even some negative stereotypes could be re-cited in useful ways by some women: the expectation that widows, being "without a man," were weak and in need of protection seems to have been deployed as a narrative tactic in certain legal cases, for example.[17]

That medieval misogyny was not univocal does not mean that it was without power. Indeed, in some respects the multifaceted demands upon women, sometimes contradictory, could make their lives more complicated. As Dyan Elliott has argued, a respectable bourgeois woman, as representative not only of her own honor but of that of her husband and household, had to tread a very specific line in her outward comportment. Dress too showily, and she transgressed notions of humility and piety.

But dress down too much and she both damaged her husband's honor, and potentially failed to present him with a sufficiently enticing sexual object; if he were to stray elsewhere, the fault would lie with her.[18] However, that differing expectations were contradictory may at some points have opened up a space of potential resistance. One might see this at work in the case of any holy woman who used discourses of extreme piety and mysticism to counteract some of the social expectations of her position. The most obvious example is again Margery Kempe, whose self-canonizing activities allowed her, in part, to relinquish the role of wife and bourgeois businesswoman she had previously performed.

Masculinities

A key insight of feminist gender theory has been that women are the primary bearers of "gender." That is, in most times and places, it is women who are discussed, analyzed, described, idealized, and demonized, and it is "femininity" that is abstracted into a presumed category of universal applicability; in contrast, masculinity and male roles emerge tacitly, as implications, the presumed and unstated opposites of feminine weakness. This has applicability to the Middle Ages, most pervasively in the creation story of Adam and Eve: Adam is created from clay, in and of himself; Eve is made from Adam, as his helpmeet, but beset by the frailties of curiosity and desire, which lead to their expulsion from Eden. Woman, thereafter, is the problem: the imperfected nature of woman a matter for discussion by jurists, medical theorists, theologians; the tendency for woman to bring down man a concern for monastic writers in particular.

At the same time, however, the Middle Ages to some extent refute the universal applicability of the tenet. For men are understood to come in several different varieties: most obviously the "three orders" of those who fight, those who pray, and those who labor, but also those who trade, those who make, those who dig, and those who read (and sometimes write) texts. "Masculinity" had no univocality, but was always multiple. And, in various areas, male roles and behavior were not tacitly assumed, but explicitly discussed. The most immediately accessible of these medieval masculinities is that of the chivalric knight; accessible because, from the twelfth century onward, it was much depicted and debated, in chivalric romances and prose histories, in tapestries and illuminations, in songs and poetry, and in manuals explicitly concerned to teach young men how to become knights. The earliest extant manual is the anonymous, early thirteenth-century poem *Ordene de chevalerie* (*Order of Chivalry*), which sets some patterns adopted in other, later works such as Raymond Llull's *Libre que és de l'Orde de cavalleria* (*The Book of the Order of Chivalry*) and Geoffroi de Charny's *Le Livre de chevalerie* (*The Book of Chivalry*). Chivalry is most often presented via an explanation of its codes and meanings by an experienced knight to an interlocutor – Saladin, in the *Ordene*; a young squire in Lull's *Book*. It has a strong Christian inflection, as the knight labors in God's service, and his protection of the weak against the strong is an act of charity. The process of becoming a knight is ritualized – in the *Ordene*, the knight must bathe to purify himself, and be reclothed in new garb – and the accoutrements of knighthood are given symbolic, spiritual meanings: the sword's two edges indicating justice and loyalty, for example.[19]

Chivalry is an ideology built around a set of productive tensions: inner/outer, nature/breeding, individual/collective, glory/humility, heterosexual desire/homosocial fellowship. The external accoutrements of chivalry matter – the bucklers, stirrups, shield, helmet, sword, the very important fact that one is on horseback – but so, too, do the "innate" qualities of strength and bravery. Chivalry primarily associates itself with, and glorifies, nobility and aristocracy, but at points suggests that any man might potentially be chivalric, and thus elevated through such natural disposition. The individual knight, fighting alone and for "his name" (as does Lancelot in the influential thirteenth-century Lancelot–Grail cycle), is a recurrent trope of individual self-sufficiency; but so, too, is the importance of horizontal bonds of comradeship (most famously the Arthurian round table) and of vertical bonds of fealty to "valiant lords". Almost every work on chivalry makes it plain that one's honor and renown are worthy prizes – but also that *real* merit comes from service to God, which may go unrewarded in this life. The desire to win the love of a fair lady (usually a highly idealized and somewhat abstract lady) is familiar in poems, treatises, and tales; but the knight most often feels *male* eyes upon him and his deeds, and in chivalric romances the strongest affective relationships are often with other men rather than with women. Perhaps most importantly, and in a fashion not dissimilar to medieval views of femininity, chivalry is a code to which one aspires but cannot easily (or ever) fully attain. As Geoffroi de Charny explains, in regard to those most suited to the pursuit of chivalry:

> the more these men see and themselves perform brave deeds, the more it seems to them, because of the high standards their natural nobility demands of them, that they have done nothing and that they are still only at the beginning. And as a result of this, they are still not satisfied, for they have heard talk as to how one should fight on the battlefield . . .[20]

As a model for gendered behavior, suitable to one particular stratum of the social order, this is far from being a static or tacit identity. It has considerable power and motive force through its express demands, and, as with femininity, the abilities and actions of a real individual are given meaning *relative* to a set of impossible ideals.

Another masculinity with more or less well-defined codes was that of the clergy. The clearest examples are monastic, since monks, of course, lived under a Rule that set out not only practical aspects of their daily lives, but modes of comportment, self-development, and identity. The control and disciplining of individual will are of high importance, as the monk attempts to move closer to God and to transcend his bodily predilections. Monks have a necessarily collective identity, men together, under the care and rule of an abbot (figured in various texts as "father," and sometimes also as "mother"). To be successfully male in this guise is to fit in, to control oneself, and to subordinate oneself to the rule of others. These elements are paramount even in the otherwise extraordinary identities of figures such as St Bernard of Clairvaux or exemplary early Christian martyrs. The mastery of the flesh, and the submission of thought and aspiration, are the ideal. For the secular clergy, the inflection is perhaps rather different. Until the twelfth century (and in practice, in some places, long thereafter) the parish clergy had married, and their sense of identity was probably much closer to that of their lay neighbors than other clerics. But following the "monasticization of the clergy" (as it has been described), they too were to valorize the control of bodily desire, and to find alternative forms of manhood beyond those provided by family and household. The education of clergy, and the close association of *clerici* with *litterati* ("literate" in the sense of mastering Latin), brought a different kind of authority.[21]

The masculine identity perhaps least discussed was that pertaining to most: the manhood of non-noble, non-clerical males. It is not easy to access, as we lack sources that specifically glorify or codify it. It must surely have varied to some degree by class and location – how to be a good man (*prud'homme* or *bon homme* are ill-defined but suggestive terms found in a variety of sources, most notably in civic contexts) would involve some different activities when one was a successful cloth merchant from those of a tenant farmer. What one can glean suggests a balance, not dissimilar to one of chivalry's binary tensions, between the pursuit of individual worldly fortune (a portion of which should be bestowed in alms and other charity) and collective neighborliness. A late medieval English text, *How the Wise Man Taught his Son*, emphasizes the importance of fitting in: do not seek office, do not boast of success, pay your debts, the Wise Man advises: "And son, if you be well at ease, and sit warm among your neighbors, do not get new-fangled ideas, or be hasty to change, or to flit."[22] Although, here as elsewhere, the ultimate importance of fulfilling the precepts of Christian charity is emphasized, male identity is again primarily achieved in the eyes of others. But here one does not seek to stand out or aspire. One should work hard, be in control of oneself and one's household (most notably one's wife, but also the servants), and play a suitable role within the community.[23] The "Other" of this kind of masculinity is not simply femininity, though that is still there: it is more predominantly an "Other" of disparaged male identities, particularly that of "youth" (shiftless, irresponsible, prone to yield to passing desires and whims) and "old age" (physically incapable, dependent).[24] The clarion call of honest labor and collective endeavor underpins some of the calls to rebellion made by the "rebel letters" of the 1381 English rising: "Jack Miller asks help to turn his mill aright," "Jack Carter prays you all to make a good end of that you have begun" and so forth.[25] To be used in such a context implies that they could be effective, emotional spurs to action. At the same time, elements of the chivalric identity notionally restricted to the nobility had, by the late fourteenth century, a clear attraction to other laymen, particularly among the upper civic bourgeoisie. The Trinity Guild in Bishop's Lynn, a guild that comprised the civic oligarchy in the fourteenth and early fifteenth centuries, commissioned a fine goblet (now on display in King's Lynn museum) decorated with Arthurian scenes. Christine de Pizan herself wrote a chivalric manual, and William Caxton "Englished" Raymond Llull's *Libre* – both of which were, among other things, commercial propositions for an assumed civic audience.

To return to the opening point of this section, one would not claim that medieval masculinities were utterly separated by the tripartite ordering of society. That men of all roles and classes were potentially in thrall to certain ideological elements – strength, self-control, the opinion of other men – seems highly likely. One can see some very specific "citations" of one code of masculinity within an apparently contrasting context, such as when Peter Abelard (born into the minor nobility, it should be remembered) describes his intellectual encounters with others in terms of combat, victory, and knightly prowess.[26] Thirteenth-century Arthurian romances tended to spiritualize the quests of their protagonists, perhaps as a clerical effort to "reform" knighthood, perhaps also as a way for clerics to read themselves into the story of masculine valiance. If we are right to see some yearning here – perhaps particularly on the part of a clergy that was disbarred from achieving the lay markers of mature manhood such as fathering children – one can also note that, whilst ideals of masculinity asserted strength, virility, masterhood and so forth, this did not mean that all men effortlessly cloaked themselves in such ideological armor. The codes of manhood could be cited against specific individuals. This happened at a parish level, for example, as priests were upbraided for failing to keep their vows of celibacy, and were associated (in written fiction, and perhaps also in popular views and actual fact) with sexual incontinence and violence.[27] It also occurred in the realm of high politics, as with Richard II of England, whose deposition from the throne was justified in part in regard to his continuing "youth" and unmanly behavior.[28] Modern gender theory has increasingly emphasized the instability of masculinity, in both the unresolved tensions of its idealized demands, and the problems of performing masculinity successfully in lived reality. One can make some points similarly for the Middle Ages – not, it should be noted, in an effort to make one feel sorry for men having to be men, but as a political act and an historiographical insight. It may be worth demonstrating the shakiness of the foundations upon which some gendered assumptions rest, as a means of critique for present claims and attitudes. It is certainly useful to demonstrate how the apparent order of past things may have contained within it tensions and contradictions, the attempted salve or resolution of which could provide the motive force for historical change in society and culture.

Sexualities

> Love is an inborn suffering that results from the sight of, and uncontrolled thinking about, the beauty of the other sex. This feeling makes a man desire before all else the embraces of the other sex, and to achieve the utter fulfillment of the commands of love in the other's embrace by their common desire.
>
> (Andreas Capellanus, *De amore*, I, i)[29]

Medieval people knew about sex. That is, not only did medieval people *have* sex (obviously they did, or else we would not now be here), but they discussed it, imagined it, explained it, worried about it, desired it. Andreas Capellanus, a cleric writing in the late twelfth century, discusses "love" (which "can exist only between persons of a different sex"), which leads him to lengthy discussion about emotions, social status, and the suitability or otherwise of various love matches. But it is clear throughout his text that this love includes, is indeed grounded in, bodily desire. "When a man sees a girl ripe for love," Andreas expounds, he starts to think of her, of the different parts of her body, desiring her more and more; "he begins to picture the role he can play and to pry into her body's hidden features. He longs to exercise the functions of each part."[30] The language – influenced by classical rhetoric – is slightly abstract; but that which it describes is quite clearly not.

Studies of human sexuality tend to seek out possible universal features to sexual habits, dispositions, and prohibitions – or else ask if all is historically and culturally varied. Certainly elements of what Andreas describes appear more or less "universal," not only in the basic grunt of desire, but also in the male perspective, which desires to possess, to "know," to uncover, and to pry and reveal. This continues as a strand in modern, Western sexuality. But other elements in *De amore*, and in Western medieval culture more broadly, differ somewhat from modern perspectives. A large amount of Andreas's discussion is given over to social status, as a major hurdle to the possibility of not only consummation but of desire itself. With regards to sex, the most immediate thing that comes to his mind once he has established the hegemony of heterosexuality is thus class. This would find echoes in vernacular poetry of the period, such as early Troubadour verse (some of which is bluntly sexual and rampant with chivalric masculinity). Elsewhere, medieval culture placed sex in a different frame. That most studied by scholars is religious: sex in canon law, sex in theological treatises, sex in confessional discourse. The French historian Pierre Payer, in an argument both inspired by and revising the work of Michel Foucault, has suggested that there was a "comprehensive" view of sex in late medieval theology. By this he means that theological discussion constituted an internally coherent "discourse" on sexuality, which explained, managed, and delineated human sexual experience in a fashion comparable to later scientific discourses. The essential viewpoint of this medieval theology was that sex was natural and inevitable – ordained by God for the procreation of the species – but desire (lust) was something against which all had to fight. Lust diminishes reason, and threatens to reduce men (most particularly men) to the state of animals; for this reason, it must be controlled.[31]

The Church certainly laid claim to the governance of human sexual experience. From the twelfth century, marriage was sacramentalized by the Church, bringing with it prohibitions against consanguinous union (to the fourth degree, following the tenets of the Fourth Lateran Council of 1215) and placing issues of adultery, unmarried sex, and abandonment within the purview of the Church courts. Confessors' manuals, a genre massively expanding in number and scope in the thirteenth century, discuss sexual acts and sexual desire within the framework of sin. Here, for example, is an anonymous (probably mendicant) manual from the early thirteenth century:

> [L]ust . . . has many types, namely simple fornication, which is illicit love between an unmarried man and an unmarried woman; adultery, which is any violation of wedlock, as when a married woman comes to another man or vice versa; incest, which is illicit sex between blood relatives or kinsfolk; debauchery, which is the illicit deflowering of a virgin. The following four types [of lust] are better known through acts than words, namely abuse, softness, shamefulness, sodomitical vice [*abusus, mollites, flagitium, sodomiticum vitium*]. Priests should take care when questioning about such matters, as it can happen that [such things] proceed from confession.[32]

Here, again, the framework within which sex is understood differs somewhat from modern conceptions; incest, for example, includes sex between godparents and godchildren, and the last four sins are neither entirely clear in their meaning, nor map onto modern conceptions of normal/"perverted," or (less judgmentally) straight/queer.

All of this might suggest that sex was strongly "controlled" during the medieval period. For certain groups this was the case: monks and nuns had always been subject to admonishment, monitoring, and cloistering, and an essential part of their religious identity was their pursuit of chastity. Indeed, one might argue that a particularly medieval category of sexuality was "virginity": a highly desired state, achieved only with great spiritual resource, promised a mighty reward in heaven. "One is not born a virgin, but rather becomes one," as Sarah Salih has insightfully remarked: virginity was a positive, relatively well-defined "sexual" identity in the Middle Ages, discussed and lauded within religious discourse more than any other.[33] And it was only finally achieved and guaranteed upon death, for lust could strike down even the elderly – and the "true" virgin could be seen as one who had never been soiled even by the *thought* of sex. The virginal image was not confined to antique martyrs and medieval nuns: holy men were often virgins, and the power of virginity was emphasized in some Arthurian romances, embodied in Galahad, the only knight sufficiently pure and perfected to gain the Holy Grail. But the last example reminds us that discourses such as these were always situated and not universal: there is plenty of other literature for and about medieval knights that places unfettered heterosexual activity at the core of their identities, and it is clear that for some men of privilege (or those aspiring to privilege) rape was on a par with hunting – both activities, indeed, sometimes conducted by young men acting in groups.[34]

The Church certainly laid the most universal *claim* to the control and meaning of sexuality, but that is not quite the same thing as saying that it achieved it. Confession occurred but once a year, and, whilst preaching on sin may well have presented a framework for the interpretation of sexual activity, it was neither the only way in which sex was discussed and understood, nor did it exercise hegemony over human activities. Indeed, it never expected to do so: lust was a sin, and sin was part of the human condition. The confessional discourse on sex did not expect to eradicate misbehavior; it provided, rather, a differentiated field within which sexual activities were given moral meaning, and a means by which all but the most "serious" transgressions could be ameliorated in the eyes of God.[35] Whilst the Church fairly consistently preached that desire was something to be controlled – that the only really *good* sex was that involving minimal pleasure, between man and wife, for the purposes of procreation – it is clear that other parts of medieval culture were more than capable of fantasizing sexual pleasure, taking pleasure (both satirical and voyeuristic) in forbidden sexual liaisons, and thinking of sex in ways ungoverned by religious strictures. "Ribald" does not really do justice, for example, to some of the vernacular *fabliaux* of the thirteenth and fourteenth centuries; they could more truly be called joyously filthy. Medieval medical discussions of sexual relations provide a third contrast. These discourses were informed by classical learning as much as by medieval theology, and located various elements of sexual habits and identities in bodily functions and natural arrangements. The humoral theory of health implicated sexual activity in non-moral fashion; one can find doctors (following Galen) advising lords and kings who were separated from their wives that they seek sexual relief elsewhere, in order to maintain their bodily balance and health.[36]

So, whilst there are elements to medieval sex that are completely recognizable across the centuries, other aspects more clearly indicate cultural specificity. Which part of the balance is emphasized by modern historians depends, in part, upon what they seek. An area of considerable importance to the development of studies of medieval sex has been gay history, prompted particularly by a desire to reveal that has been "hidden from history" in past ages; but also (and somewhat in tension with this first project), following Foucault and others, to question whether "homosexuality" is a category that can be applied to a past age. There does seem to be a sense in some medieval texts that certain men prefer sex with other men. A medical writer, Peter of Albano, argued that the internal plumbing of some men was differently arranged, making sexual pleasure from receiving anal penetration "natural" to them. He further notes that other men *choose* to have sex with men; this is "on account of depraved and filthy habit" and much to be condemned. [37] John Boswell, in a foundational book, argued that there was a gay "sub-culture," associated with medieval cities and places of learning, that used the term "Ganymede" for those who loved other men. He further argued – much more controversially – that the medieval Church had tacitly accepted same-sex love between men, until the high Middle Ages and the development of a more repressive society. [38]

On the other side of the argument, however, it has been pointed out that there was no (apparently) clear-cut category akin to that of "homosexual"; and that, in a distinction important to Foucault's theories, medieval texts overwhelmingly discuss acts rather than identities.[39] That is, in the Middle Ages there was discussion of "sodomy," and this was a type of activity through which many were *potentially* liable to transgress. In fact, what exactly was meant by sodomy was not clear cut for much of the period, as the quotation from the confessor's manual above indicates. For some writers, it included any sexual activity not likely to result in procreation, which could include sex between a man and woman where the woman was on top rather than underneath.[40] Later usages – in civic statutes, for example – would seem to associate "sodomy" most particularly with sex between men; but further, confusing and destabilizing, distinctions are sometimes drawn, most often between those acting "like a woman" (presumably those being penetrated) and those doing the penetrating, but also between those initiating, and those acquiescing to sexual relations. In any case, it may be argued that sodomy was an activity – and that even the term "sodomite" indicated not a stable, innate, and perduring identity (in the way in which "homosexual" has been used since the late nineteenth century) but at most a tendency to fall repeatedly into the same sin, much as one might say "usurer" or "blasphemer." One could (in this theoretical conception) stop being a sodomite – although it was such a serious crime that those convicted were likely to be executed, finding any possibility of "redemption" only after death.

Another strand of literary scholarship (motivated by a different political perspective, drawn from Queer Theory) has relinquished the chase for clear-cut "gay people" in the past, in favour of "queering" areas that have hitherto been overlooked. Thus the emotionally laden language of *amicitia* ("friendship"), which informs letters between twelfth-century intellectuals, has been read for its sexual subtexts, and the homosocial activities of literary knights have been emphasized. Queer readings are provocations, and to try to ask how much is lost against how much is gained in such interpretative strategies is perhaps to miss their very point. Nonetheless, one can perhaps draw a useful distinction between provocative readings that are happy simply to have disturbed categorizations, and those that seek to pursue further, more extended revisions in dialogue with other perspectives. Two recent examples of the latter come from Judith Bennett (on lesbianism) and Richard E. Zeikowitz (on homosexuality). Bennett, noting that the number of "real" lesbians one can find in medieval archives are paltry, has argued that a project of searching for past connection should not fixate solely upon acts of genital sexual activity. Modern lesbian cultures include many other aspects, notably the production of different forms of family, and women-friendly spaces. In these aspects, Bennett argues, one might search for medieval forebears who are "lesbian-like" Zeikowitz, meanwhile, has argued that the nature of the erotic should not be limited to the physical act of sex. In his reading, of literary and historical texts, an erotic potential was present in a variety of activities and conjunctions between medieval knights, and this helps to explain those occasions (such as prosecution of the Knights Templar) when "sodomy" suddenly becomes such a fraught issue. Sodomy's main meaning, in his interpretation, is to police the boundaries of *legitimate* male–male emotion and erotic potential.[41]

In various ways, the potential destabilizations associated with the category of "sodomy" can be read back into all areas of discussion. As already noted, medieval people knew about and discussed sex. But the contexts within which they discussed it, and the meanings it accrued, do not necessarily map on to modern conceptions of "sexuality," even when points of contact can be established. It has been argued that modern Western culture has made sexuality a field unto itself, a primary locus for identity and meaning. Whether this was the case for medieval people is uncertain. Elements of sexuality were framed by ecclesiastical discussions of sin – but in that framing they were but a subset of a wider set of issues, about moral and social conduct, Christian identity, and individual salvation. All sexual activity outside marriage (and some inside marriage) was sinful; and even those refraining from all sexual activity had to struggle with the specter of inner desire and the images that flickered on the walls of one's imagination. But at the same time they struggled with other desires – for wealth, status, recognition, health, and so forth. Within this religious discourse, one's salvational state was the primary aspect of identity, not the precise nature of one's appetites or sinful actions. In a parallel fashion, *elements* of sexual activity were framed by medical discourse, and other elements by secular law (particularly in civic statutes). In some areas, something like a category of identity is produced; but the contexts of knowledge and policing always extend well beyond that which is purely sexual.

One can chase this argument round and around, not least by asking whether assertions about modern sexual identity are as stable as they first seem, or whether the medieval can helpfully interrogate, and destabilize, the modern. What is ultimately at issue is the individual, subjective experience of sexuality; something not easily accessible, if at all, to the historian of the Middle Ages. But the struggle seems worth the prize, not only for sexuality but for gender identities in general. For that reason, let us turn lastly to gender as a lived experience, and see what the older projects of social history and women's history may still have to offer to more recent cultural approaches.

Gender as Lived Experience

The depiction of women within medieval religious discourse, as we have seen, was fairly negative if not unremittingly hostile. Most women were denied formal positions of authority in the Church (as in every other part of life), could not preach or perform the sacraments, were barred from church for a period after childbirth, and were associated most often with the sin of lust. One might surmise that this sketch, albeit somewhat brief and crude, provides a reasonable analysis of "gender" in relation to medieval religion. But to stop here would be a mistake, for we would miss the opportunity to explore perhaps the most interesting and important aspects of gender: how real people, in their everyday existence, experienced and negotiated the often contradictory codes by which culture laid claim to their lives. Much work has been done on a few, extraordinary women in regard to religious discourse, and Caroline Walker Bynum has argued that the emphasis that female saints and mystics placed upon food and the body is the product of individual agency to some extent "rewriting" the given script, finding a way of making female "limitations" into sites of potential power.[42] More recently there has been a focus on the great mass of ordinary women and their activities in everyday religion. As Katherine French and others have demonstrated, women joined confraternities (sometimes single sex, sometimes with men), pooled resources to act as "patrons" and to bestow alms, owned and read religious texts, went on pilgrimage and made individually tailoured wills, and acted as key participants in the life of the parish, helping, amongst other things, to provide essential material support to the local church.[43] It may have been the case that, when attending that church, such women had to endure a tedious monologue of misogynist invective, emphasizing female subjection to male authority and so forth; but recent work on some late medieval sermons concerning marriage has found a much more textured and complex clerical "voice" that encouraged negotiation and some degree of mutual respect within marriage.[44] In other words, the "playing-out" of gender within actual lives could be considerably more complex than some general depictions (including those given above) might make it appear.

There are some underlying issues here, methodological, epistemological, and political. Part of what scholars such as French and Bynum represent is a feminism that seeks (in a nuanced fashion) to emphasize the agency of women rather than their oppression – a "third-wave" feminism, as I have sketched it briefly above. Other voices insist, however, on recognizing some major limits to that agency: Judith Bennett points out, for example, that women wage-earners in late medieval England earned only around 70 percent of what their male counterparts took home – a proportion that is only very slightly higher in late-twentieth-century England.[45] Neither group of scholars claims that its viewpoint provides a satisfactory "overall meaning" to the history of gender. Gender is not, ultimately, the set of abstractions one can extract and collate from learned treatises, wall-paintings and illuminations, sermons and poems. It is, rather, the *experience* of being a gendered person inhabiting a (changing, aging) body, surrounded by other people (family, neighborhood, co-workers) and their expectations, in a society organized along various hierarchical and unequal lines (manorial serfdom, tripartite *ordos*, trade guilds, clerical offices, civic oligarchies) but equipped with certain palliative mechanisms to which one might, at certain times, have access (secular and ecclesiastical law, markets, kinship, custom). That was not, I realize, a very punchy sentence. But the conditional phrases and subclauses attempt to summon up the complexity of the situation, and the shifting perspectives intrinsic to it. In all this, one might imagine historiographically a slight return to women's history – social history, more broadly – in useful complement to the textual, and sometimes abstract, emphases of cultural history.

To return to the issue of religion: historiographically, an important shift came about in the latter part of the twentieth century, away from religion as a set of generalized abstractions and formal processes, handed down from on high to society, to what the French called *la religion vécue* – lived religion, religion of the people, as something embodied and produced and performed and experienced. More or less parallel moves can be found in other areas of social history, focused most recently, for example, on the experience of ordinary people in national politics. Gender history could be seen as undergoing a similar move. For some practitioners, the basic project of making visible the lives of women continues to be of importance, as a job not yet nearly fulfilled. Those working on aspects of masculinity are involved in a similar task, though more one of "shedding new light" than of revealing the utterly unknown. In addition, one can see a returning interest in trying to gain a sense of the experience of gender – albeit one that, at its best and following Joan Scott, relinquishes any naive belief in the transparency of past culture, or the ability to gain direct access to past thoughts and feelings. The shift might be sketched as a change of question: not simply "how did it feel to be a woman in this time and place?" but "through what means, and with what possibility of agency, did one feel oneself to be what kind of woman (or man) in this time and place?" There has been recent work done on the "singlewoman" in late medieval English history, some from the perspective of bringing to light the histories of those who were never married. This is in itself an important job, not least for the recognition that such people could constitute a surprising proportion of the population. But, as Cordelia Beattie demonstrates, there is another approach available: to understand the discourses that constructed a notion of "singleness" in various medieval discourses, and the varied contexts in which they were likely to come into effect in a particular person's life.[46] The notion of "singlewoman" is not a category into which we can safely place a person and thus "explain" her; it is, rather, a potential conception, capable of differing inflections dependent upon who is speaking, which may be claimed by or forced upon a particular woman in certain circumstances.

This approach invites further reflection (familiar from many other strands of gender theory) on the ways in which *other* forms of social categorization can intersect with, and inflect, those of gender. The most obvious field is that of class; or, more broadly for our period, "status." Work on masculinity, as already discussed, demonstrates the important potential differences between different "orders" of manhood. Studies on women demonstrate similar, but less obvious, distinctions. Whilst the stereotypical conception of women as having unruly sexuality *could* be applied across all social levels – as an accusation leveled at a queen, as we have seen – it was in fact *most* often a concern when applied to the lowest levels of society. In various ways, the hindrances of femininity struck hardest when one was poor.[47] But being of "higher" status did not necessarily bring with it the greatest freedoms: most obviously, marriage was something placed clearly under family control for upper-class women (and in societies where daughters could potentially receive part of the family's lands). This is not to romanticize plebeian marriage as completely free and equal – but it does mean that when ordinary people married, particularly in northern Europe, they more often had a choice of partner, and were more often expected to negotiate married life in some form of partnership. The general concepts of gender mattered; but how exactly they played out in real people's lives depended upon circumstance – and that, of course, changed as life went on.

As social historians have pointed out for some time, life cycle could have a tremendous effect on ordinary women's lives. There were, first, differing cultural expectations of maidens, wives, and widows; these, in fact, probably further differed dependent upon where one lived. For example, marriage in northwestern Europe tended to be between men and women of roughly similar age, forming a new household unit, whereas in the south and elsewhere the bride was often notably younger than her husband, the couple might live with more extended family, and even when married they could be understood to continue to "represent" their distinct natal backgrounds.[48] The expectations incumbent upon a "wife" could therefore differ; and the focus upon a young woman's "maidenhood" might carry greater cultural importance in a society where her potential for marriage was part of the wider family's repertoire of tools for the maintenance of status and socioeconomic advantage. The practices of life differed with life cycle.[49] Young women in late medieval England, for example, might experience a period of relative economic independence in paid service, though with the expectation that this would change upon marriage. When married, if in a town, the wife could play a different role as partner to her husband; there is evidence, for example, of wives clearly acting as business partners to their spouses, and sometimes acting essentially independently, though the practices of record keeping present the husband as the more "visible" entity. Widowhood could spell financial disaster, depending upon the attitude of one's children and the terms of a will; but it might alternatively bring relative economic freedom (though also more restricted social expectations). In each of these "stages" of life, and in combination with other factors (social status, geographical location, external economic, and political factors), the ways in which individual women's lives were marked by gender would vary; and the degree to which they could challenge, subvert – or perhaps more often attempt gently to negotiate – the demands of a patriarchal society would vary too.

And in various areas there was always a potential gap between ideals and practice. Work on the social history of sexuality has tended to stress a gap – sometimes quite considerable – between ecclesiastical conceptions of sexual morality and the lived experience of sex. Guido Ruggiero, studying the prosecution of sex crime in late medieval Venice, has noted, for example, that, whilst the records of the secular courts use much of the rhetoric of sin – citing various offences as insults to God – the actual punishments they imposed could tell a very different story. The rape of unmarried women, for example, was depicted in censorious fashion; but those who committed such crimes were punished very lightly. Only in regard to the crime of sodomy were civic authorities as harsh as, or possibly harsher than, clerical rhetoric; and, even then, one might argue that (as in the Massa Marittima mural) the horror of sodomy had slightly different meanings: an offence "against nature and against God" in theology, a threat to the possibility of civic order from a secular viewpoint. In less fraught circumstances, Judith Bennett has demonstrated that the imposition of *leyrwite* – a manorial fine for unmarried sex – indicates a good deal of communal tolerance for carnal pleasure that was condemned by the Church; *except* when it was combined with poverty and famine, presumably because the village was less than happy at having a fatherless mouth in need of food.[50] One is also unsurprised to note that real clerics were themselves not always able to live up to the codes of celibacy and alleged "emasculinity" ascribed to them; as Jennifer Thibodeaux argues, one could in fact see clerical sexual misdemeanors as springing in part from the unresolved tension that surrounded the nature of their male role.[51] Only very occasionally do we get to glimpse something of the ways in which individual people dealt with the emotional, social, legal, and spiritual demands of gender. Where we can see something – as is occasionally the case with the very rich records of certain inquisitorial trials – one is immediately aware of the complex and above all else *shifting* nature of these experiences. A *châtelaine* called Beatrice de Lagleize confesses to her past affairs, with an aspiring Cathar "good man" and two parish priests: her experience of these loves involved negotiations of public honor and shame, the relative freedoms of social status, and a fear that a woman who sleeps with a priest will never "see the face of God." A gay man, Arnaud de Verniolles, attempts to persuade the inquisitor that his sexual experiences were not at the blackest end of the medieval moral spectrum, and desperately tries out various potential legitimations: that his health demanded that he have sex frequently, and, if no women were available, it was sensible to go with men; that his nature inclined him innately toward men; that he had once slept with a prostitute and caught a disease, and thereafter thought it more prudent to go with men . . . Arnaud twists and turns, caught up in the gaze of inquisitorial power, finding himself unexpectedly in the very worst trouble (sentenced ultimately to life imprisonment).[52] He provides a very sharp and harsh example of what was surely a much wider phenomenon, and not simply for a medieval gay man: that one might find areas of life, in periods of one's life, that provided greater or lesser freedom of action and expression; but that gendered ideals could snap shut over you with a brutal finality in certain particular circumstances.

"Gender" is thus never one thing, and never a constant, in the Middle Ages. It is sometimes convenient to talk about a gender "ideology" for an era, but even this begs further questions. What constitutes an ideology? Do some statements in the Bible, in Aristotle, and in Galen provide "*an* ideology," or do they rather stake sometimes competing claims over *certain* aspects of life? They tend, in any case, to be evoked in differing circumstances; and, whilst the tiny educated elite in Europe might, at any given moment after (say) the eleventh century, be immersed in texts that repeat some or all of these ideas, the extent to which this provides "an ideology" for the much wider realm of social interactions and governance is less than clear. Preaching, as the most widespread tool of dissemination in medieval Europe, is of considerable importance here; and it provides interestingly conflicting evidence. Analysis of preaching *exempla* suggest some familiar strains of gender expectation: the association of women with sexual temptation, for example. But, as already noted, the texts of sermons themselves, where they survive, can present rather more nuanced and socially rooted accounts of what it means to be a man and a woman. Even if one decides that the multifarous statements and ideas about gender do constitute a medieval ideology, there is a question still to be answered as to its strength and resources. Some elements of gender are probably most policed within the household and within the local community, simply but powerfully enforced by the pull and sway of social expectation. But the unwritten and communal nature of such expectations can provide a space for relative freedom, a small degree of play, in comparison to the specific (but much more limited) codifications of law. Where there is interplay between the two – where the community invokes the law, and delivers those who displease it to the power of the state – one sees gender at its strongest. But such interactions are not found every day, nor do they provide a complete index to all experiences of gender. One might helpfully think sideways, in our future explorations of these topics. As social historians have demonstrated, the abstract ideas and laws concerning serfdom and unfreedom can look much more clear cut and much more decisive than its lived reality. Being "unfree" imposed definite social, legal, and economic limits, and in some circumstances could be very much resented; but it was also a kind of never-ending obstacle course to be negotiated, within which one exercised labor, commerce, and social engagement as best one could, with varying individual outcomes. It dictated much about a person and his or her life, but not necessarily everything; and its lived experience changed depending upon local and historical circumstance. Perhaps, in a similar fashion, one could see gender as a set of potential exclusions and definitions, at points invoked very sharply by authorities with more or less power to control an individual; but similarly a realm within which other elements of life were conducted, feelings experienced, changes interpreted, and stories narrated.

Notes

1 Ferzoco, *Il murale di Massa Marittima.* Ferzoco convincingly suggests that the right-hand arch contained a mirroring mural, depicting the effects of Guelf "good government." There are currently various reproductions of the image on-line; for example http://stregheria.com/penistree_wideweb__430x325.jpg, accessed Feb. 25, 2008. My thanks to George for his work, these ideas, and much else. Thanks also to Cordelia Beattie, Sean Brady and Victoria Howell for comments on a draft of this chapter.
2 Freedman, *Images*, pp. 133–73.
3 For example, see the introductory discussions of past historiography in Howells, *Women, Production and Patriarchy*; Bennett, *Women in the Medieval Countryside*; Goldberg, *Women, Work and Lifecycle.*
4 Scott, "Gender"; Butler, *Bodies that Matter*; Scott, "Evidence of Experience."
5 Foucault, *History of Sexuality.*
6 Hughes, "Representing the Family," pp. 12–15.
7 Caxton, *Game of Chess*, second traytye, pars 11; "The Priest Who Peeked," in DuVal, ed., *Fabliaux*, p. 28.
8 Casagrande, "Protected Woman."
9 Extract from *Year Books of Edward II, 1313–14*, trans. in Goldberg, ed. and trans., *Women in England*, p. 239.
10 Dean, *Crime in Medieval Europe*, pp. 82–6.
11 Odo of Cluny, *Collationem Libri Tres*, II, ix, *Patrologie Latine* 133 col. 556.
12 Bardsley, *Venomous Tongues.*
13 Kay, *Subjectivity in Troubadour Poetry*, pp. 84–110.
14 Stafford, "Powerful Women," p. 413.
15 Pizan, *Book of the City of Ladies*, pp. 5–6, 29–30.
16 Lewis, *Cult of St Katherine.*
17 Beattie, *Medieval Single Women*, p. 30.
18 Elliott, "Dress as Mediator."
19 *Ordene de chevalerie*, in Busby, ed. and trans., *Raoul de Hodenc*, p. 172.
20 Charny, *Knight's Own Book of Chivalry*, pp. 57–8.
21 For a provocative reading of some of these developments, see McNamara, "*Herrenfrage*," pp. 3–29.

22 "How the Wise Man Taught his Son," in Rickerts, ed., *Babees Book*, pp. 43–7.
23 Goldberg, "Masters and Men," in Hadley, ed., *Masculinity in Medieval Europe*, pp. 56–70.
24 On this, and in regard to chivalric and learned masculinities also, see further Karras, *From Boys to Men*.
25 Dobson, ed., *Peasants' Revolt*, p. 382.
26 Peter Abelard, *Historia calamitatum*, in Radice, ed. and trans., *Letters of Abelard and Heloise*, pp. 58, 61.
27 An English chancery court petition (TNA: PRO C49/27/14) claims that "many priests, secular as well as religious, have been greviously vexed and wrongfully troubled by diverse indictments of felony," calling for the king to "aquit all and every priest . . . of all manner of felony of rape" (my modernization). My thanks to Cordelia Beattie for this reference.
28 Fletcher, "Manhood, Youth and Politics."
29 Capellanus, *On Love*, p. 33.
30 Ibid., p. 35.
31 Payer, *Bridling of Desire*.
32 Goering and Payer, "*Summa Penitentie Fratrum Predicatorum*," p. 31.
33 Salih, *Versions of Virginity*.
34 Ruggiero, *Boundaries of Eros*.
35 See further Arnold, *Belief and Unbelief*, pp. 156–63.
36 Jacquart and Thomasset, *Sexuality and Medicine*.
37 Cadden, *Meanings of Sex Difference*, pp. 214–16.
38 Boswell, *Christianity, Social Tolerance, and Homosexuality*.
39 See particularly Foucault, *History of Sexuality*, p. 43.
40 Kuster and Cormier, "Old Views and New Trends."
41 Bennett, "'Lesbian-Like'"; Zeikowitz, *Homoeroticism and Chivalry*.
42 Bynum, *Holy Feast and Holy Fast*.
43 French, *Good Women of the Parish*.
44 Schnell, "Discourse on Marriage."
45 Bennett, *History Matters*.
46 Beattie, *Medieval Single Women*.
47 Farmer, *Surviving Poverty in Medieval Paris*.
48 See Martha Howells, Chapter 7, this volume.
49 See Goldberg, *Women, Work and Lifecycle*; Phillips, *Medieval Maidens*; Barron and Sutton, eds, *Medieval London Widows*.
50 Ruggiero, *Boundaries of Eros*; Bennett, "Writing Fornication."
51 Thibodeaux, "Man of the Church?"
52 Arnold, *Inquisition and Power*, pp. 197–225.

Bibliography

Arnold, John, *Inquisition and Power: Catharism and the Confessing Subject in Medieval Languedoc* (Philadelphia: University of Pennsylvania Press, 2001).

Arnold, John, *Belief and Unbelief in Medieval Europe* (London: Hodder Arnold, 2005).

Bardsley, Sandy, *Venomous Tongues: Speech and Gender in Late Medieval England* (Philadelphia: University of Pennsylvania Press, 2006).

Barron, Caroline, and Sutton, Anne F., eds, *Medieval London Widows, 1300–1500* (London: Hambledon, 1994).

Beattie, Cordelia, *Medieval Single Women: The Politics of Classification in Late Medieval England* (Oxford: Oxford University Press, 2007).

Bennett, Judith M., *Women in the Medieval Countryside: Gender and Household in Brigstock before the Plague* (Oxford: Oxford University Press, 1987).
Bennett, Judith, "'Lesbian-Like' and the Social History of Lesbianism," *Journal of the History of Sexuality*, 9 (2000), pp. 1–24.
Bennett, Judith M., "Writing Fornication: Medieval Leyrwite and its Historians," *Transactions of the Royal Historical Society*, 6th ser., 13 (2003), pp. 131–62.
Bennett, Judith M., *History Matters: Patriarchy and the Challenge of Feminism* (Philadelphia: University of Pennsylvania Press, 2006).
Boswell, John, *Christianity, Social Tolerance, and Homosexuality: Gay People in Western Europe from the Beginning of the Christian Era to the Fourteenth Century* (Chicago: University of Chicago Press, 1980).
Busby, Keith, ed. and trans., *Raoul de Hodenc*: Le Roman des Eles; *The Anonymous* Ordene de chevalerie (Philadelphia: University of Pennsylvania Press, 1983).
Butler, Judith, *Bodies that Matter: On the Discursive Limits of "Sex"* (London: Routledge, 1993).
Bynum, Caroline Walker, *Holy Feast and Holy Fast: The Religious Significance of Food to Medieval Women* (Berkeley and Los Angeles: University of California Press, 1987).
Cadden, Joan M., *Meanings of Sex Difference in the Middle Ages: Medicine, Science, and Culture* (Cambridge: Cambridge University Press, 1993).
Capellanus, Andreas, *On Love*, ed. and trans. P. G. Walsh (London: Duckworth, 1982).
Casagrande, Carla, "The Protected Woman," in Christine Klapisch-Zuber, ed., *A History of Women in the West II: Silences of the Middle Ages* (Cambridge, MA: Harvard University Press, 1992), pp. 70–104.
Caxton, William, *The Game of Chess* (London: n.p., 1870) (facs. BL King's Library C.10. b.23).
Charny, Geoffroi de, *A Knight's Own Book of Chivalry*, trans. Elspeth Kennedy (Philadelphia: University of Pennsylvania Press, 2005).
Dean, Trevor, *Crime in Medieval Europe* (Harlow: Longman, 2001).
Dobson, Richard Barrie, ed., *The Peasants' Revolt of 1381*, 2nd edn (London: Macmillan, 1983).
DuVal, John, ed. and trans., *Fabliaux Fair and Foul* (Binghamton, NY: Medieval and Renaissance Texts and Studies, 1992).
Elliott, Dyan, "Dress as Mediator between Inner and Outer Self: The Pious Matron of the High and Later Middle Ages," *Mediaeval Studies*, 53 (1991), pp. 279–308.
Farmer, Sharon, *Surviving Poverty in Medieval Paris: Gender, Ideology, and the Daily Lives of the Poor* (Ithaca, NY: Cornell University Press, 2002).
Ferzoco, George, *Il murale di Massa Marittima/The Massa Marittima Mural*, 2nd edn (Florence: Consiglio Regionale della Toscana, 2005).
Fletcher, Chris D., "Manhood, Youth and Politics in the Reign of Richard II," *Past and Present*, 189 (2005), pp. 3–39.
Foucault, Michel, *The History of Sexuality, Volume I*, trans. R. Hurley (London: Penguin, 1979).
Freedman, Paul, *Images of the Medieval Peasant* (Stanford, CA: Stanford University Press, 1999).
French, Katherine L., *The Good Women of the Parish: Gender and Religion after the Black Death* (Philadelphia: University of Pennsylvania Press, 2007).
Goering, Joseph, and Payer, Pierre J., eds, "The *Summa Penitentie Fratrum Predicatorum*: A Thirteenth-Century Confessional Formulary," *Mediaeval Studies*, 55 (1993), pp. 1–50.
Goldberg, P. J. P., *Women, Work and Lifecycle in a Medieval Economy* (Oxford: Oxford University Press, 1992).
Goldberg, P. J. P., ed. and trans., *Women in England, 1275–1525: Documentary Sources* (Manchester: Manchester University Press, 1995).

Hadley, Dawn, ed., *Masculinity in Medieval Europe* (London: Pearson, 1999).
Howells, Martha C., *Women, Production and Patriarchy in Late Medieval Cities* (Chicago: University of Chicago Press, 1986).
Hughes, Diane O., "Representing the Family: Portraits and Purposes in Early Modern Italy," *Journal of Interdisciplinary History*, 17 (1986), pp. 7–38.
Jacquart, Danielle, and Thomasset, Claude, *Sexuality and Medicine in the Middle Ages*, trans. M. Adamson (Princeton: Princeton University Press, 1988).
Karras, Ruth Mazo, *From Boys to Men: Formations of Masculinity in Late Medieval Europe* (Philadelphia: University of Pennsylvania Press, 2002).
Kay, Sarah, *Subjectivity in Troubadour Poetry* (Cambridge: Cambridge University Press, 1990).
Kuster, Harry J., and Cormier, Raymond J., "Old Views and New Trends: Observations on the Problem of Homosexuality in the Middle Ages," *Studi medievali*, 25 (1984), pp. 587–610.
Lewis, Katherine J., *The Cult of St Katherine of Alexandria in Late Medieval England* (Woodbridge: Boydell, 2000).
McNamara, Jo Ann, "The *Herrenfrage*: The Restructuring of the Gender System, 1050–1150," in Clare A. Lees, ed., *Medieval Masculinities: Regarding Men in the Middle Ages* (Minneapolis: University of Minnesota Press, 1994), pp. 3–29.
Payer, Pierre J., *The Bridling of Desire: Views of Sex in the Later Middle Ages* (Toronto: University of Toronto Press, 1993).
Phillips, Kim M., *Medieval Maidens: Young Women and Gender in England 1270–1540* (Manchester: Manchester University Press, 2003).
Pizan, Christine de, *The Book of the City of Ladies*, trans. R. Brown-Grant (London: Penguin, 1999).
Radice, Betty, ed. and trans., *The Letters of Abelard and Heloise* (London: Penguin, 1974).
Rickerts, Edith, ed., *The Babees Book* (London: Chatto and Windus, 1908).
Ruggiero, Guido. *The Boundaries of Eros: Sex Crime and Sexuality in Renaissance Venice* (New York: Oxford University Press, 1985).
Salih, Sarah, *Versions of Virginity in Late Medieval England* (Cambridge: D. S. Brewer, 2001).
Schnell, Rüdiger, "The Discourse on Marriage in the Middle Ages," *Speculum*, 73 (1998), pp. 771–86.
Scott, Joan Wallach, "Gender: A Useful Category of Historical Analysis," *American Historical Review*, 91 (1986), pp. 1053–75.
Scott, Joan Wallach, "The Evidence of Experience," *Critical Inquiry*, 17 (1991), pp. 773–97.
Stafford, Pauline, "Powerful Women in the Early Middle Ages: Queens and Abbesses," in Peter Linehan and Janet L. Nelson, eds, *The Medieval World* (London: Routledge, 2001), pp. 398–415.
Thibodeaux, Jennifer, "Man of the Church, or Man of the Village? Gender and the Parish Clergy in Medieval Normandy," *Gender and History*, 18 (2006), pp. 380–99.
Zeikowitz, Richard E., *Homoeroticism and Chivalry: Discourses of Male Same-Sex Desire in the Fourteenth Century* (New York: Palgrave, 2003).

Further Reading

Blamires, Alcuin, ed., *Women Defended and Women Defamed: An Anthology of Medieval Texts* (Oxford: Oxford University Press, 1998). A collection of translated medieval texts discussing "women," from a variety of perspectives.

Baldwin, John W., *The Language of Sex: Five Voices from Northern France around 1200* (Chicago: University of Chicago Press, 1996). An important study of intellectual views, mostly connected with the University of Paris, at a key point in time.

Bardsley, Sandy, "Women"s Work Reconsidered: Gender and Wage Differentiation in Late Medieval England," *Past & Present*, 165 (1999), pp. 3–29. Both overview and critique of recent perspectives on female labor.

Erler, Mary, and Kowaleski, Maryanne, eds, *Gendering the Master Narrative: Women and Power in the Middle Ages* (Ithaca, NY: Cornell University Press, 2003). A collection of essays by a number of important scholars, indicating the state of recent debate.

Goldberg, P. J. P., ed. and trans., *Women in England, 1275–1525: Documentary Sources* (Manchester: Manchester University Press, 1995). Wonderful collection of translated medieval sources from England, largely from a social history perspective.

Goodich, Michael, *The Unmentionable Vice: Homosexuality in the Later Medieval Period* (New York: Dorset Press, 1979). The first book written on the topic, and still an important overview.

Hadley, Dawn, ed., *Masculinity in Medieval Europe* (London: Pearson, 1999). A collection of essays; with the collection edited by Murray (below). It was of foundational importance.

Jordan, Mark D., *The Invention of Sodomy in Christian Theology* (Chicago: University of Chicago Press, 1997). A key work on the theological and intellectual concepts.

Karras, Ruth Mazo, *From Boys to Men: Formations of Masculinity in Late Medieval Europe* (Philadelphia: University of Pennsylvania Press, 2002). The first single-author study that covers males in terms of chivalry, intellectuals, and artisans.

Karras, Ruth Mazo, *Sexuality in Medieval Europe: Doing unto Others* (London: Routledge, 2005). A very useful and insightful overview of recent debate.

Klapisch-Zuber, Christine, ed., *A History of Women in the West II: Silences of the Middle Ages* (Cambridge, MA: Harvard University Press, 1992). Older in viewpoint, but an important summary of certain medieval attitudes and practices.

McCarthy, Conor, ed., *Love, Sex and Marriage in the Middle Ages: A Sourcebook* (London: Routledge, 2003). Interesting collection of translated medieval texts, arranged by genre and demonstrating variety of viewpoint and practice.

Murray, Jacqueline, ed., *Conflicted Identities and Multiple Masculinities: Men in the Medieval West* (London: Routledge, 1999). A key set of essays, setting the agenda for much subsequent work.

Partner, Nancy, ed., *Studying Medieval Women: Sex, Gender, Feminism* (Cambridge, MA: Medieval Academy of America, 1993). A collection of articles first published in the journal *Speculum*, all with great insight and all provoking key methodological and political debates.

Scott, Joan Wallach, "History-Writing as Critique," in Keith Jenkins, Sue Morgan, and Alun Munslow, eds, *Manifestos for History* (London: Routledge, 2007), pp. 19–38. A recent, self-consciously polemical, address to the current state of gender history by its most key figure.

Shahar, Shulamith, *The Fourth Estate: A History of Women in the Middle Ages* (London: Routledge, 1983). A classic textbook; superseded on detail by subsequent work, but still an important and readable overview.

Chapter Nine

Society, Elite Families, and Politics in Late Medieval Italian Cities

Edward D. English

Late medieval social history has been among the most fruitful areas of research since the Second World War. This has been especially true for Italian towns and cities between 1200 and 1500. Their histories have provided models for study for much of the urban landscape of the rest of Europe. Given the scope and aims of this collection of essays and the vast bibliography produced for the topic of this essay, it is appropriate to limit this essay to Italian towns and cities during that period in comparative terms. Urban elites across Europe are comparable in the ways that they used mercantile interests and rural bases of power to maintain dominance. The historiography of Italian urban society, especially that of elites, reflects the major scholarly trends since the mid-twentieth century and can indicate where future research might head, not only for Italy but also for urban elites more generally.[1]

Town life on the Italian peninsula took off after 1200. While there had been some continuation of urban concentrations from the fifth century, cities really grew in terms of population and cultural significance in the thirteenth century. By then they were more or less freed of imperial capacity and were well into developing the economic activities and capacities that gave them the wealth that placed them at the center of the European economy. Pierre Racine quotes the work of four major scholars on the booming cities throughout the peninsula. The success of these towns was based on revolutions in politics, the production and preservation of documents along with the requisite literacy, the conduct of commerce and banking, and the appearance of the new mendicant orders that aimed to provide the pastoral care of those in the city, promote papal authority, and ensure religious conformity.[2] Of primary significance for this chapter was the emergence of urban regimes in which the evolution of political institutions created a documentary bonanza. Further wealth became concentrated in the hands of the elite families that formed the oligarchic cores of the communes.[3]

Sources

During the course of the thirteenth century, merchant families grew very rich from a "commercial revolution" in institutional innovations, and the elaboration of credit instruments and accounting practices. Although it is still not clear how they initially accumulated capital, many of these families either drew upon the resources of their rural estates and moved to the city or developed their urban proprieties, and then invested in banking (especially lucrative papal banking), and moved representatives and capital round Europe to take advantage of developing markets.[4] Other members of the elite were not so venturesome but still managed to thrive in the new urban environments. Suffice it to say that the Italian peninsula during the thirteenth century became the economic dynamo of the European economy and among the most wealthy and sophisticated economies before the industrial revolutions after 1800.

Economic success and political sophistication were based on the keeping of careful records and enough literacy to take advantage of them. This sea of archival and manuscript survivals is of fundamental importance. As Trevor Dean asserts, the quality and quantity of this written material are far beyond those of the rest of Europe. Quoting John Larner, Dean goes on to say: "More source materials survive than a hundred scholars could adequately master."[5] After Italian unification in 1870, scholars who were then able to exploit the opening of state archives produced a veritable ocean of publications on the cities of Italy. This also fostered a growth in interest in local history. From the time of Jacob Burckhardt in the last half of the nineteenth century, foreign researchers and writers further enriched our understandings of these innovation communes and lordships, going far beyond trying to discover the elusive origins of the "Renaissance."[6]

Written sources for society, families, and politics include notarial documents in the tens of thousands, the proceedings of communal councils, collections of statutes, fiscal evaluations and records, diplomatic correspondence, familial letters, contemporary chronicles and histories, and theoretical studies of political ideas, judicial records, and account books and merchant correspondence. These sources are further enriched by the writings of clerics involved in pastoral care, sermonizing, and promoting devotion to new urban saints. From the twelfth century the survival of secular material was promoted by the revival and modernization of the procedures and ideas of Roman Law. The recording of the notariate was further fostered by the recognition of the value of written records by both public institutions and private individuals. This was helped by the recognition of the memorial value of records of actual transactions with their details as offering legal proof. Notarial practice offered possibilities for noting how things had been done in the past and for devising innovative contracts for using the law and institutions for specific and new needs and ends.[7]

From the thirteenth century, writers in a more secular vein such as Brunetto Latini, Dante, Boccaccio, Petrarch, Leonardo Bruni, Leon Battista Alberti, and many others produced literary masterpieces that can also be used to understand the culture and society of Italy between 1250 and 1450. Lauro Martines has pointed out how less famous writers such as Gentile Sermini and Piero Veneziano can be read intelligently to illustrate traits, social concepts, and issues in order to enlighten the reader on community and familial ideas about demography, gender, age, sexuality, and daily life.[8]

Another kind of source that is of fundamental importance for our understanding of these societies, families, and politics is called *ricordanze* or family memoires/diaries. They are almost unique to Florence, and little exists resembling them for the rest of Europe.[9]

Historians of art and architecture have also turned their attention to subjects of social and political interest in studies of the portrayal of children, women, marriage, and the Blessed Virgin among numerous other subjects. The "Good Government" frescos in the town hall of Siena have spawned a large literature on how they represent a good and well-governed society.[10] Historians of architecture have studied palaces and other kinds of domestic and private space. Archeological studies of urban remains for this late period are relatively rare because of the problem that the sites, essentially peoples' basements or cellars, are presently occupied. Archaelogy has been more productive for rural sites and strongholds occupied by these elites. Further publication of these findings would be beneficial.

The richness of these sources has facilitated some of the best historical studies on society, the family, and politics anywhere in Europe between 1200 and 1500, including in-depth studies of a wide variety of urban topics. They can provide a comparative perspective for similar studies for the rest of Europe.

Families

Writings about families in the Middle Ages and Early Renaissance period, from family chronicles themselves to histories of Italian republics and towns under the lordship of a particular family, have been around for a long time.[11] Early modern antiquarians compiled detailed studies, often commissioned, of families, especially royal ones, well into the twentieth century. Their work has often proved very useful because of their collective biographical approach. In the early 1960s Phillipe Ariès laid the foundation for more contemporary work on the family, or at least the treatment of children within it, with the publication of *L'Enfant et la vie familiale sous l'ancien régime*, soon translated as *Centuries of Childhood: A Social History of Family Life*. This was followed by studies of later periods.[12] Ariès did show that familial institutions, ideas, and practices have a history. He also encouraged interest in familial mentalities and emotions in the past.

In a recent article in the *American Historical Review* Nara Milanich has called for a new paradigm for the study of the family in the past.[13] She also points out how the history of the family has been used for modern political and mythical agendas, and not just in Latin America. Milanich rightly asserts that the family is the basis for much of everything regarding the state, sexuality, domestic arrangements, and childrearing. However, its study has fallen into a "quiet senescence." She goes on to point out the value of discriminating between the family life and dominant cultures of the elite and those of other classes. This includes difference in family size, whether nuclear or extended, and the extent to which they were affective or patriarchic. Her point about cultures of inequality should not be underestimated for the Middle Ages. Her work and that of others such as Jack Goody could be brought into more comparative use by historians of the Middle Ages.[14] Goody's other publications comparing European social practices with those of the East are intended to offer an additional comparative view of the family, kinship, and capitalism outside Europe.[15] There can be little doubt that we need a new paradigm for the study of the pre-modern family, and its comparison with cultures that are more modern could lead to a better understanding of the functioning of kinship and the foundations of capitalistic ideas and practices. Katherine Lynch has recently encouraged this comparative approach in her book on families and their other relationships with urban institutions. The family might be called the foundation of human society, and it functions in a wider and extra-familial community.[16]

Among the richest sources of material about the family at nearly all levels of society for late medieval Italy is the great *catasto* or tax evaluation for the city of Florence and its Tuscan subjects or region. Cadastral surveys were common enough in the fourteenth century, but the one carried out in 1427 for the Florentine state is one of the most detailed and exhaustive survey or fiscal census of population ever done in the pre-industrial age. It found some 60,000 households and counted more than 260,000 people. David Herlihy and Christiane Klapisch-Zuber used this great monument of medieval counting to produce one of the most important, thorough, and pioneering studies on any place in the later Middle Ages.[17] They found that there were two types of domestic systems functioning at this low point in population level, patrician and artisanal or peasant.. Their findings on patrician households are fundamental.[18] They demonstrate a context for the distribution of wealth in the city state of Florence. They show kinds of wealth, marital statuses, relationships within a household with respect to its head, age distributions within a synchronic population, and wealth in the city and outside of it. By this time Florence had become the economic capital of it city state. They go on to describe marriage patterns involving usually considerably older men and younger women. They integrate these practices with the fates of children, the implications of life cycles, patterns of birth and death, gender distributions, and the effects of wealth on determining household size and structure.

Their major findings for elites included a dramatic account of the distribution of wealth. In 1427 Florence included 14 percent of the lay population of its part of Tuscany (essentially all but the region controlled by Siena), but held two-thirds of the wealth. According to Herlihy and Klapisch-Zuber: "Florence was thus a blazing sun of affluence, surrounded by dim planets of wealth in the smaller Tuscan cities – all of them set in a dark, nearly desolate rural space."[19]

Within Florence the top 100 families or 1 percent of urban households held a quarter of the city's wealth, roughly a sixth of the wealth of the entire Florentine State. Herlihy and Klapisch-Zuber also found that the Tuscan marriage model differed from the European one described by Hajnal. Contrary to the pattern suggested by him, the principal characteristics of Tuscan marriages in 1427, as described by them, were "a young age at first marriage for women (16), with almost no permanent spinsters in the community, outside the convents; an advanced age at first marriage for men, with a significant number of permanent bachelors."[20] The consequence of this was a large gap in age between husband and wife. This was most extreme among Florentine elites: the wealthiest men married first at an average age of 31. This helped produce a large pool of unmarried young men. Other results were dowry inflation, as families of young girls competed for desirable and appropriate husbands. There was also a large proportion of widows, as younger wives outlived their husbands.

The authors did not hesitate to extend some of their findings into observations about the wider culture and economy of this Tuscan state, including the proletarization of populations and their debt servitude to urban elites. The book also graphically demonstrated the long-term baleful effects of the numerous visitations of the plague over the second half of the fourteenth century. Though now thirty years old, this work is still the starting point for late medieval social and demographic history. It also laid the groundwork for later work on the social world of elites in Florence and a comparison with other cities.

The rest of this chapter will concentrate first on the social world of the oligarchs and nobles who ran these cities. From among the wealth of scholarly works on these themes, we can employ work on specific families, marriage markets dominated by dowry inflation, the effects of plagues and demographic trends, and succession practices. The chapter will then conclude with a section on the social and political dynamics of the cities in which these families lived, their exercise of power, and the negotiated reciprocal possibilities of factionalism as a stable profitable way of politics.

In addition to the *catasto* records, the archives and libraries of the city of Florence contain many other records of family and political life. These include thousands of notarial documents, private materials from prominent lineages, and the records of the dowry investment fund from over the course of the fifteenth century. Two examples of studies based on the accounts books and correspondence of elite families are the books by Richard A. Goldthwaite and F. William Kent.[21] Though they complement one another in many ways, they reach quite different conclusions on whether these lineages were losing wider family solidarity and falling more and more into nuclear units. Goldthwaite followed Ariès's ideas about the progressive nuclearization or fragmentation of these families. To him economic forces encouraged less cohesiveness in terms of fewer joint business projects, and more individual private residential properties instead of shared ownerships. He based much of his findings on account books, which do indicate such a fall in mutual activities and interests. Kent worked on a different set of families with different sources. Reading diaries and private papers, he found a continued survival of extended households and a stress on kinship ties, especially in political and social matters. His families and lineages jointly hold few corporate properties other than the old family palaces or towers within Florence, chapels, and patronage rights. Kent also demonstrated the importance of neighborhood ties and vertical patronage links through society. Both scholars indicated how the individual members of these families had ties to other institutions within the city, such as confraternities, guilds, and political factions built around other families.

There are now many studies of individual elite families from Florence, other Italian towns and regions, and elsewhere.[22] Scholars have studied a wide variety of particular aspects of families and oligarchs; an example is the collection edited by Ciappelli and Rubin on memory, kinship, art, and neighborhood.[23] There is clearly a rich and enticing future for such studies in Florence and elsewhere. There is need for more work outside of the dominant Florentine, and, to a lesser extent, Venetian paradigms. For example, there needs to be more research on the families who became tyrants themselves and their allied oligarchic lineages in places such as Milan or Padua.

One inhibiting obstacle has been the sources. There are few if any *ricordanze* outside Florence, and even basic familial account books are rare.[24] To study the histories of elite families in another republic such as Siena, one has to reconstruct information about familial activity and interests from notarial chartularies. These can be supplemented by the vast collections of individual parchments written by notaries before 1400. From the mid-fourteenth century, these parchments gradually become rarer, as their participants grew more and more reliant on the records kept by the notary in his own chartulary. When deprived of the contextual information provided by *ricordanze* or diaries, historians have to reconstruct objectives and interests out of more reticent documents than those available to Professors Goldthwaite and Kent. Large numbers of letters between the commune and its leading citizens do survive in Siena, for example, but they are rarely very personal or enlightening about matters internal to the lineages involved. Some towns, such as Bologna and Lucca, do have rich judicial sources, but they have not been mined for elite activities. Though not blessed with many judicial records, the archives of Siena do contain a wealth of material on the economic activities, political machinations, marriage strategies, religious interests, and patronage connections of its leading families. This is likely to be the case elsewhere in the period between 1300 and 1500.

Another area of study on elite families has been patterns of marriage alliances and strategies, accompanied by research on dowry inflation and ideas about relationships. Anthony Molho published a major study on how propertied families, mostly of considerable substance, maintained their power and affluence within the context of economic and regime changes and the terrible revisits of the plague after 1350 and into the fifteenth century. Molho integrated the surviving letters, memoir books, and abundant fiscal records to enrich Julius Kirshner's and his systematic analysis of the *Monte delle doti* (Dowry Fund). This work contains bits of information on about 19,000 marriages, beginning in 1425. These record the investments by fathers in a fund that would pay them interest and would eventually allow them to withdraw the deposits increased by interest when their daughters married. Molho argued that individuals subordinated their personal desires to a deeper concern for their families. The fund encouraged patterns of endogamy among the Florentine aristocracy. According to Molho's analysis of the *catasto* or tax evaluation from 1480, the Florentine elite comprised about 500 rich individuals. This group belonged in his view to 417 lineages, at the core of which was an inner elite of 110 people. He also defines an additional three status groups. With such definitions, he suggests patterns of endogamy and lateral alliances of marriages within the circle of his elite. Molho's book contains a wealth of information on a large list of families, but rarely goes beyond repeating the detailed studies by others on certain lineages, such as that of the Alberti. The individuals and their choices get lost in the details of financial transactions. Research on the marriage patterns of particular lineages within elites could nuance his perceived patterns of individual choice sacrificed to the influence of lineage objectives and interests.

The legal aspects of these systems of marriage, dowries, exile, emancipation by fathers, illegitimacy, and succession have been illuminated by Julius Kirshner and Thomas Kuehn in many studies in the decades since 1980.[25] They have paid special attention to both legal theory and judicial practice to show how the legal system limited peoples' intentions but also created opportunities to craft innovative and desired solutions to problematic legal objectives. Anyone studying families in Italy or the legal systems of the north needs to take into consideration what options were open to people and how they manipulated these options often toward more satisfying and creative ends. It must also be remembered that the ethical aspects of marriage and succession were shaped by and within canon law and ecclesiastical courts.[26] Legal sources such as *consilia*, opinions written by scholars on particular juridical problems, do offer much promise in our understanding of these systems of law.

However, the great majority is either unpublished or exists in sometimes questionable editions produced in the sixteenth century. They are not readily accessible but can be found throughout the local libraries of Italy. It must also be remembered that, although *consilia* seem to discuss real people in real legal difficulties, this may not be the case. They often treat theoretical problems that might be useful and instructive for the real world. Still the content of their arguments and the discussion of solutions can be useful when studying the options and possibilities of individuals, families, and lineages in the legal system.

Other scholars have studied dowry systems in the later Middle Ages and early Renaissance. Venice provided another rich opportunity to study marriage as an evocative social act with political objectives and consequences. Stanley Chojnacki's numerous studies of the patrician class in Venice do provide a contrast with upper-class families in Florence, especially with regard to the roles and opportunities of women. Christiane Klapisch-Zuber portrayed the women of Florence as rather hapless victims and pawns, like the literary images of "Griseldas" with little choice in such matters and few rights over marital property by the fourteenth century.[27] Chojnacki, on the other hand, found a much better situation, at least for elite women, in fourteenth- and fifteenth-century Venice. Women there could seemingly manipulate the system to their advantage. Dowry inflation was supposed to be controlled, with the intention to level the playing field for the city's oligarchs and the legally defined noble class. According to Chojnacki, women exercised more power in Venice because of the value of their dowries to their husbands, their greater freedom in testamentary bequests, the political rewards to their husbands if they worked with the families tied to them through their wives and other female connections, and just plain affection that could occur between husbands and wives.[28]

Work on patrician families elsewhere in Italy and the rest of Europe might confirm either of these views on the status of elite women within oligarchic and patriarchic lineages. We need research reconstructing the actual transmission of wealth between the parties contracting the marriages at the moment of agreements and clarifying when the contents of dowries were physically passed between them in fulfillment of contracts. This is needed to understand fully how these systems worked for individuals and lineages. This requires the tracking of particular properties and bits of wealth over time within the context of the life cycles of male and female lineage members. This would also entail the systematic study of wills and last testaments. In order to understand a will, one should know as much as possible about the person writing it and the familial and legal options open to him or her.

Demography

The early fourteenth century brought the beginning of many crises that affected the populations of Italy and Northern Europe. Both areas suffered extensive famines between 1317 and 1329.[29] The chronicles and records of the Italian cities describe these in considerable detail. The upper classes there and in the north were accused of hoarding and manipulating the food supply. In the ensuing bread riots, the houses and storage places of the elites were among the first spaces to be attacked by the starving rioters. The governments of the town responded by trying to regulate the supply of food, banishing useless mouths, and to prevent forestalling the market by various mechanisms. They had only limited success. While we are unsure of the mortality rates, they were undoubtedly considerable. There might also have been some effect on the longer-term physical health of many in the surviving population, though this remains unclear in medical thought or in the historical record. There can be little doubt that the elites in Italian cities did try to benefit from the reoccurring crises. With their extensive agricultural holdings in the countryside and influence on the road systems surrounding the urban areas, they were in a perfect position to carry out just such manipulations of supply.

Populations seem to have peaked in the first decade of the fourteenth century, generally reaching numbers not attained again until the eighteenth or nineteenth centuries. It was into this evolving Malthusian crisis that the Black Death arrived in 1347. There is presently a dispute on whether these fourteenth-century plagues were really the same disease as the modern bubonic plague first described in the 1890s by Alexander Yersin, who studied occurrences in China and India and later in North America. Scholars such as Samuel Cohn and Graham Twigg have raised real doubts about this diagnosis of the fourteenth-century disease and suggested other diseases such as earlier versions of the flu virus or anthrax.[30] There can be little doubt, however, that it killed 30–40 percent of the population in its first visitation between 1347 and 1349. It must be remembered that it recurred regularly and with great severity for the next 150 years and beyond. The upper-class members of the towns in Italy and elsewhere did not escape a considerable mortality, though there is a need for study on its effects on the numbers of family members, clients, and henchmen making up the big rich lineages. Did they really flee to their rural estates, like the group at the core of Boccaccio's *Decameron*? Did local politics change because of demographic changes? Did certain grand lineages suffer more than others, thus changing whatever balances of power that might have existed? Did the balance of economic and political resources change?

Elite Political Dynamics

Recent scholarship on the politics of Italian cities between 1200 and 1500 has focused with various degrees of intensity on several aspects of elite culture. These include the changing roles of those lineages labeled magnates, factional conflict, social and political clientage, architectural and artistic patronage, the relationship of lords with the other major families in their subject cities, the use of space in urban environments and neighborhoods, lordship in rural areas around cities, concepts of nobility, women's roles in linking together lineages, mercantile and landed wealth, and domestic life. This chapter will end with a discussion of the question of magnates, the powers involved in rural lordships, and the use of urban space and image for political and social prestige.

In the early to mid-thirteenth century, the inhabitants of many towns of northern Italy came to be governed by communal forms of government. Their leading citizens swore oaths to protect their towns, though most people had little say in the matter. They were run by small oligarchies made up of members from a commercial and feudal elite.[31] Even at the core of these governing groups there was an inner circle that came to exercise real power. Often with overlapping sources of wealth and power, some groups were merchants and some had rural and urban landed interests.[32]

Some had various levels of interest and ability in military affairs or violence.[33] Some were essentially new in terms of their wealth and prestige; and some were related to the old rural feudal nobility.[34] Lack of sources and surnames hampers a deeper understanding of who these men were. They did consider the new commune to be theirs and barely distinguishable from their personal holdings.

This was to be a continuing aspect of all elite relationships to government down to the present day. Under the influence of the twentieth-century sociologists Vilfredo Pareto, Achile Loria, and Gaetano Mosca, the scholars who studied them were frequently part of the elite themselves or were playing to gain its favor. Under the influence of a more materialist historical view, others from the nineteenth century and on were much opposed to upper-class dominance and posited a struggle between classes. In the late thirteenth century, some members of the city of Florence sought to limit the power of some of their overbearing fellows. In the 1280s and 1290s, following precedents from Bologna and Siena, they passed laws restricting a group they called magnates, making them ineligible for some communal offices and subject to harsh penalties for any recourse to violence on their social inferiors. Well into the fourteenth century, families were added to the list of magnates, while others managed to get themselves removed from such restrictions. Those labeled magnates were a slice of the oligarchy in most of these cities. Florence has provided the paradigm for the study of these members of elite and oligarchic ruling classes. This is in part due to its exaggerated general influence on historical studies of late medieval Italy but also because of it rich sources and the persuasive qualities of the historians who have studied the city on the Arno, such as Gaetano Salvemini and the anti-Marxist Nicola Ottokar.[35] Magnate tyranny and violence over other classes probably did extend to the countryside. At the same time, the commune also exploited the rural population in a variety of fiscal ways. Though the magnates were excluded from the highest offices in a commune such as Siena, their friends, clients, and business partners did have their hands on the levers of power. On the other hand, the magnates who did not have seats in the towns or many links with their more mercantile brethren probably did suffer more serious problems because they became marginal to the real power elite. At the same time, there were magnates with different capacities. Their history varies from place to place, demonstrating that, while Florentine history can provide a starting point for analysis for other urban concentrations in Italy or elsewhere, it is better not to assume that there is always a similar pattern everywhere. In Florence certain magnate families did what they could do lose their magnate label, while at the same time economic and demographic factors worked to break down their ties to a lineage.[36] Some were allowed to change their names legally. By the late fourteenth century in Florence they were marginalized or absorbed in factions jockeying for positions of power in the city. In Siena in the same era, certain great magnate houses rose up in rebellion to seize control of the city, as so many of their contemporaries had already done in other cities of northern Italy. Their rival lineages would band together even with deadly enemy families and factions to oppose the control of one of the great families such as the Salimbeni or Tolomei. In the end absorption was not peaceful, as it seems to have been in Florence. One probable difference was that the Sienese families had maintained rural strongholds and wealth that were further strengthened by private armies and gangs of henchmen ready to do their bidding. Much more work needs to be done on the reality of their rural lordships, sources of manpower, the terms of their relationships with that of manpower, patterns of rural strongholds and wealth, and geography of their systems of clientage within the cities themselves. Philip Jones's idea about the interconnection between rural and feudal elites and the commercial ones in the towns can be found in these magnates.[37]

These lineages were at the core of the various factions contending for control of a town, a struggle for offices, and thus power of policies and fiscal matters. Dale Kent has studied Florence in the era of initial dominance by the Medici family. According to Kent, the Medici succeeded because of their roles as personal patrons and party leaders. They outshone rival lineages and factions in these matters and came to control the committees of government.[38] Though few places have the documents that Kent uses to show how the Medici did it, patronage and clientage were at the core of the politics of all medieval towns. Many existed in a sort of unstable equilibrium, as a few ambitious families jockeyed for dominance. Venice did have laws and traditions that helped keep the city serene. In Siena, particular families tried their hands on several occasions in the late fourteenth century. They failed because the commune was able to muster support of the other great lineages afraid of another clan's dominance. Eventually the contending old lineages were defeated in battle or wounded so badly in the factional battles that they gave up. The systems of patronage underlying these conflicts need more study, both in the city and outside it, to get all links that sometimes look like a sort of "bastard feudalism" involving private armies of professionals or press-ganged peasants.

Part of the influence of elites was their control over space in towns and the impressive buildings they erected for their lineages from the mid-thirteenth century.[39] Their compounds came to be almost villages within the city walls. In Siena, for example, elite families often had their own somewhat fortified piazza (a *castellare*) in which they built a fortress with a tower, apartments, a church, and rows of shops or storerooms. The main palace was divided into shares passed on for generations. Maintenance was joint. Patronage of their church was controlled. They even rotated the use of the most elaborate residence within the lineage. Succession to the most strategic rural and urban strongholds was carefully passed to male members of the family. Over the course of the fourteenth century, these common properties came to be divided into shares too small to be significant or were bought up by the more successful lines within the lineage. Property-holding patterns by elites need more detailed research, if we are going to have a better understanding of the history of these families and lineages. Control of streets and neighborhoods, prominent participation in rituals, and the construction of prestige familial monuments in churches were also part of this game, theater, and display of power.[40] Again the scholarship has been fullest on Florence and Venice, but much can be done elsewhere.

Notes

1 See the Bibliography for useful articles that offer suggestive comparative perspectives, such as: Britnell, "England and Northern Italy" and "The Towns of England and Northern Italy"; Jones et al., "The Later Medieval English Urban Household"; Kowaleski, "The History of Urban Families in Medieval England"; also Howell, *Women, Production, and Patriarchy* and *The Marriage Exchange*. Robert Putnam (*Making Democracy Work*) has

described Italian civil society in the Middle Ages without taking fully into consideration the role of elites in manipulating society and social capital for their own best interests.

2 Racine, *Les Villes d'Italie*, p. 1, quoting Élisabeth Crouzet-Pavan, Jean-Claude Maire Vigueur, Robert S. Lopez, and Giulia Barone. Racine goes on to organize his textbook according to these themes.

3 The so-called mendicant revolution certainly did affect changes in the practices of religion in these cities and among their elites. This was especially true in terms of ideas about usury and gaining salvation; for wills, see Cohn, *Death and Property in Siena* and *The Cult of Remembrance and the Black Death*. Those topics would require at the very least another essay.

4 The classic discussion of the "commercial revolution" remains that of Lopez, *The Commercial Revolution of the Middle Ages*, and Jones, *Italian City-State*, pp. 152–332; see also Masschaele, Chapter 5, this volume.

5 Dean, *Towns of Italy*, p. 1; he refers to Larner, *Italy in the Age of Dante*, p. 11, and further points to thoughts of Jones, *Italian City-State*, on pp. 156–7, 202–3.

6 The literature on the "Renaissance" and the urban cultures of the Italian cities is vast, but one interesting place to begin is Witt, *In the Footsteps of the Ancients*. Educational ideas and practices in terms of socialization for moral purposes for society have been a topic of controversy among scholars; see Grendler, *Schooling in Renaissance Italy*, and Black, *Humanism and Education*.

7 For recording keeping, notaries, and literacy in Italy, see the basic works of Cammarosano, *Italia medievale*; Langeli, *Notai*; Albini, *Le scritture del commune*; Petrucci, *Writers and Readers in Medieval Italy*; see also the fundamental article by Diane Owen Hughes on notarial documents as historical sources: "Toward Historical Ethnography"; for the "documentary revolution," see Maire Vigueur, "Révolution documentaire et révolution scripturaire." There is now an excellent manual for studying material in the vernacular in Italy: Redon et al., *Les Langues de l'Italie médiévale*; see also Britnell, Chapter 20, this volume.

8 Martines, *Strong Words*, and Martines and Baca, eds, *An Italian Renaissance Sextet*.

9 Jones, "Florentine Families and Florentine Diaries," and Grubb, *Family Memoirs from Verona and Vicenza*.

10 Rubinstein, "Political Ideas in Sienese Art," Skinner, "Ambrogio Lorenzetti's *Buon Governo* Frescoes," and Frugoni, *A Distant City*, among numerous others.

11 See, as an example for an English noble family, Given-Wilson, "Chronicles of the Mortimer Family."

12 Stone, *Family, Sex and Marriage*, and Shorter, *The Making of the Modern Family*; they displayed little understanding of the family or childhood in the Middle Ages. The initial efforts at psychohistory showed even more misunderstanding of medieval attitudes especially in terms of parental attachment: deMause, "The Evolution of Childhood." These studies did follow the traditional idea of the Middle Ages as a brutal time. This is not to say that there was not plenty of child abuse and neglect in the period, but only to point out that it is exaggerated by these authors, who were concerned primarily in finding the origins of the modern family, especially the nuclear one. Margaret L. King and Albrecht Classen have produced fine bibliographical references and useful recent studies of the state of the question for historical study of childhood: King "Concepts of Childhood," and Classen, "Phillip Ariés and the Consequences," in Classen, *Childhood in the Middle Ages and the Renaissance*, pp. 1–65. See also the classic study Boswell, *The Kindness of Strangers*, and Hanawalt, "Medievalists and the Study of Childhood," and, for a comparison to the experience of children in Italy, see her *Growing up in Medieval London*.

13 Milanich, "Whither Family History?"

14 The family and it structures have long been of interest to anthropologists; for an introduction to anthropological approaches to the family history, see Françoise Zonabend, "An Anthropological Perspective on Kinship and the Family," in Burguière et al., eds, *A History of the Family*, vol. 1, pp. 8–68, 655–8, with a useful glossary of anthropological terminology on pp. 648–54. Jack Goody has written an important but controversial book about the regulation of the family by the Church: *The Development of the Family and Marriage in Europe*; see the critical essays by Mitterauer, Saller, Sheehan, and Bonfield in *Continuity and Change*, 6/3 (Dec. 1991). Committed Catholic scholars, such as David Herlihy and Michael M. Sheehan, have strongly disagreed with Goody's image of a church regulating family life to its own material benefit in terms of succession. This is an argument that needs more study.

15 Goody, *The Oriental, the Ancient and the Primitive* and *The East in the West.* The most interesting aspect of the recent study by Linda Mitchell (*Family Life in the Middle Ages*) is her inclusion of chapters on the family in Islam and Judaism.

16 Lynch, *Individuals, Families, and Communities in Europe*; she also points out the connections between urban and rural society, the different practices of plebeians and patricians, and the consistent importance of clientage and neighborhood.

17 Herlihy and Klapisch-Zuber, *Tuscans and their Families*, is an English translation and a much abridged version of *Les Toscans et leur familles* from 1978. Their research was computer assisted but in the "punch-card age," when coding, gathering data, and the ensuing analysis were much more awkward and laborious than is the case now. That possible pieces of information on such matters as occupation, that are contained in this remarkable set of documents, were not gathered hardly detracts from its value and remarkable insights into a particular population. A searchable online version has lived on at www.stg.brown.edu/projects/catasto/ along with a database of office-holders in Florence between 1282 and 1532 at www.stg.brown.edu/projects/tratte/. One can also find information there on the code-books employed and Herlihy's own work on naming practices.

18 Though much praised, the version in English of Herlihy and Klapisch's work did not go without criticism: see Smith (then a prominent member of the Cambridge Population Group), "The People of Tuscany and their Families"; see also the comments by scholars in "Family in Medieval Tuscany: Critiques and a Reply," *Journal of Interdisciplinary History*, 11/3 (1981), 477–506; other reviews raising questions are J. N. Stephens in the *English Historical Review*, 103 (1988), pp. 110–12, and F. W. Kent in *Speculum*, 55 (1980), 129–31; for rural families and information on the Cambridge Population Group, see Schofield, Chapter 6, this volume.

19 Herlihy and Klapisch-Zuber, *Tuscans and their Families*, p. 97.

20 Ibid., p. 215; Hajnal, "European Marriage Patterns in Perspective."

21 Goldthwaite, *Private Wealth in Renaissance Florence*, and Kent, *Household and Lineage in Renaissance Florence.*

22 For Florence and its region, see Fabbri, Lansing, and Pirillo; for elsewhere in Italy, see Allegrezza, Carocci, Grubb, and Queller. For outside Italy, see the works by Nicholas, Rheubottom, McKee, Mertes, Jones, Kowaleski, and Thrupp in the Bibliography.

23 One example of the breadth of such work is collected in Ciapelli and Rubin, eds, *Art, Memory, and Family*, which is about the many connections among family, society, kin, neighborhood, art, and memory.

24 For there existence in other places, see Grubb, *Family Memoirs from Verona and Vicenza.*

25 Kirshner, *Pursuing Honor while Avoiding Sin*, and Kuehn, *Heirs, Kin, and Creditors*, to name only two of their numerous publications involving the civil law and social institutions. For a comparative and Mediterranean perspective, see Sperling and Wray, eds, *Across the Religious Divide.*

26 See the work of Michael M. Sheehan in Farge, ed., *Marriage, Family, and Law*, and the recent monumental study Donahue, *Law, Marriage, and Society*. Such ecclesiastical court records have been assumed to have been pretty much nonexistent in Italy and outside England. However, this is proving not to be the case as scholars work in more ecclesiastical archives; see Brucker, *Giovanni and Lusanna*, for insight into ideas about marriage and class; Dean and Lowe, eds, *Marriage in Italy*; for a general study of marriage in the Middle Ages, see Howell, Chapter 7, this volume.

27 See, in particular: Klapisch-Zuber, "The *Cruel Mother*: Maternity, Widowhood, and Dowry in Florence in the Fourteenth and Fifteenth Centuries" and "The Griselda Complex: Dowry and Marriage Gifts in the *Quattrocento*" in *Women, Family, and Ritual in Renaissance Italy*; for similar ideas about the status of women in Florence see Cohn, *Women in the Streets*; see also the articles by Isabelle Chabot; for a general study of gender in the Middle Ages, see Arnold, Chapter 8, this volume.

28 Most of Chojnacki's essays are collected in *Women and Men in Renaissance Venice*; see also Guzzetti, "Dowries in Fourteenth-Century Venice." Queller and Madden raise interesting questions about dowries in Venice in "Father of the Bride"; for the relationship between elite women, fashion, and consumerism, see Stuard, *Gilding the Market*.

29 Jordan, *The Great Famine*.

30 Cohn, *The Black Death Transformed*, and Twigg, *The Black Death*.

31 Bertelli, *Il potere oligarchico nell stato-cittá médiévale*.

32 Bordone, Castelnuovo, and Varanini, *Le aristocrazie dai signori rurali al patriziato*.

33 Gasparri, *I milites cittadini*; Grillo, *Cavalieri e popoli in armi*; and Maire Vigueur, *Cavalieri e cittadini*.

34 Heers, *Le Clan familial au Moyen Age* and *Parties and Political Life in the Medieval West*.

35 Salvemini, *Magnati e popolani in Firenze dal 1280 al 1295* (originally published in 1899), and Ottokar, *Il comune di Firenze all fine del Dugento* (originally published in 1926); see also the work of Lansing, *The Florentine Magnates*, Raveggi et al, *Ghibellini, Guelfi e Popolo Grasso*, and numerous others.

36 Klapisch-Zuber, *Retour à la cite*; see also her numerous articles leading up to this important book; Caduff, "Magnati e popolani nel contado fiorentino"; for magnates on a more general level, see Centro italiano di studi di storia e d'arte, Pistoia, *Magnati e popolani nell'Italia comunale*; Société des historiens médiévistes de l'enseignement supérieur public, *Les Élites urbaines au Moyen Age*; Clauzel, "Les Élites urbaines et le pouvoir municipal"; for elites and urban revolts, see Cohn's two recent books: *Popular Protest in Late Medieval Europe* and *Lust for Liberty*.

37 Jones, *Economia e società nell'Italia médiévale*.

38 Kent, *The Rise of the Medici*.

39 For Italy among many recent studies, see Friedman, "Places and the Street in Late-Medieval and Renaissance Italy," and, for Florence, see Goldthwaite, *The Building of Renaissance Florence*; for a comparative perspectives on space in towns in the north, see Arnade, Howell, and Simons, "Fertile Spaces," and Boone, "Urban Space and Political Conflict in Late Medieval Flanders.

40 Crum and Paoletti, *Renaissance Florence*.

Bibliography

General Studies

Ariès, Philippe, *Centuries of Childhood: A Social History of Family Life*, trans. Robert Baldick (New York: Vintage Books, 1962).

Beattie, Cordelia, Maslakovic, Anna, and Jones, Sarah Rees, eds, *The Medieval Household in Christian Europe*, c. *850–c. 1550: Managing Power, Wealth, and the Body* (Turnhout: Brepols, 2003).

Bonfield, Lloyd, "Canon Law and Family Law in Medieval Western Christendom," *Continuity and Change*, 6/3 (1991), pp. 361–74.

Boswell, John, *The Kindness of Strangers: The Abandonment of Children in Western Europe from Late Antiquity to the Renaissance* (New York: Pantheon Books, 1988).

Brundage, James A., *Law, Sex, and Christian Society in Medieval Europe* (Chicago: University of Chicago Press, 1987).

Burguière, André, Klapisch-Zuber, Christiane, Segalen, Martine, and Zonabend, Françoise, eds, *A History of the Family*, vol. 1: *Distant Worlds, Ancient Worlds* (Cambridge MA: Belknap Press of Harvard University Press, 1996).

Casey, James, *The History of the Family* (Oxford: Basil Blackwell, 1989).

Classen, Albrecht, ed., *Childhood in the Middle Ages and the Renaissance: The Results of a Paradigm Shift in the History of Mentality* (Berlin: Walter de Gruyter, 2005).

Crawford, Katherine, *European Sexualities, 1400–1800* (Cambridge: Cambridge University Press, 2007).

Davis, Isabel, Müller, Miriam, and Rees Jones, Sarah, *Love, Marriage, and Family Ties in the Later Middle Ages* (Turnhout: Brepols, 2003).

deMause, Lloyd, "The Evolution of Childhood," in Lloyd deMause, ed., *The History of Childhood* (New York: Psychohistory Press, 1974), pp. 1–73.

Epstein, Steven A., "The Medieval Family: A Place of Refuge and Sorrow," in Samuel K. Cohn, Jr, and Steven A. Epstein, eds, *Portraits of Medieval and Renaissance Living: Essays in Memory of David Herlihy* (Ann Arbor, MI: The University of Michigan Press, 1996), pp. 149–71.

Given-Wilson, Chris, "Chronicles of the Mortimer Family, *c.* 1250–1450," in Richard Eales and Shaun Tyas, eds, *Family and Dynasty in Late Medieval England*, Harlaxton Medieval Studies, 9 (Donington: Shaun Tyas, 2003), pp. 67–86.

Goody, Jack, *The Development of the Family and Marriage in Europe* (Cambridge: Cambridge University Press, 1983).

Goody, Jack, *The Oriental, the Ancient and the Primitive: Systems of Marriage and Family in the Pre-Industrial Societies of Eurasia* (Cambridge: Cambridge University Press, 1990).

Goody, Jack, *The East in the West* (Cambridge: Cambridge University Press, 1996).

Hajnal, J., "European Marriage Patterns in Perspective," in D. V. Glass and D. E. C. Eversley, eds, *Population in History: Essays in Historical Demography* (London: E. Arnold, 1965), pp. 101–43.

Herlihy, David, *Medieval Households* (Cambridge, MA: Harvard University Press, 1985).

Herlihy, David, "Family," *American Historical Review*, 96/1 (Jan. 1991), pp. 1–16.

Kertzer, David I., and Barbagli, Marzio, eds, *The History of the European Family*, vol. 1 *Family Life in Early Modern Times, 1500–1789* (New Haven: Yale University Press, 2001).

King, Margaret L., "Concepts of Childhood: What We Know and Where We Might Go," *Renaissance Quarterly*, 60/2 (Summer 2007), pp. 371–407.

Lett, Didier, *Famille et parenté dans l'Occident medieval V*[e]*–XV*[e] *siècle* (Paris: Hachette, 2000).

Lynch, Katherine A., *Individuals, Families, and Communities in Europe, 1200–1800: The Urban Foundations of Western Society* (Cambridge: Cambridge University Press, 2003).

Milanich, Nora, "Whither Family History? A Road Map from Latin America," *American Historical Review*, 112/2 (Apr. 2007), pp. 439–58.

Mitchell, Linda E., *Family Life in the Middle Ages* (Westport, CT: Greenwood Press, 2007).

Mitterauer, Michael, "Christianity and Endogamy," *Continuity and Change*, 6/3 (1991), pp. 295–333.

Neel, Carol, ed., *Medieval Families: Perspectives on Marriage, Household, and Children* (Toronto: University of Toronto Press, 2004).

Sabean, David Warren, Teuscher, Simon, and Mathieu, Jon, eds, *Kinship in Europe: Approaches to Long-Term Development (1300–1900)* (New York: Berghahn Books, 2007).

Saller, Richard, "European Family History and Roman Law," *Continuity and Change*, 6/3 (1991), pp. 335–46.

Saller, Richard P., and Kertzer, David I., "Historical and Anthropological Perspectives on Italian Family Life," in David I. Kertzer and Richard P. Saller, eds, *The Family in Italy from Antiquity to the Present* (New Haven: Yale University Press, 1991), pp. 1–19.

Segalen, Martine, *Historical Anthropology of the Family* (Cambridge: Cambridge University Press, 1986).

Sheehan, Michael M. , "The European Family and Canon Law," *Continuity and Change*, 6/3 (1991), pp. 347–60.

Shorter, Edward. *The Making of the Modern Family* (New York: Basic Books, 1977).

Sperling, Jutta, and Wray, Shona Kelly, eds, *Across the Religious Divide: Women's Properties in the Wider Mediterranean (1300–1800)* (New York: Routledge, 2010).

Verdery, Katherine, "A Comment on Goody's Development of the Family and Marriage in Europe," *Journal of Family History*, 13/2 (1988), pp. 265–70.

Viazzo, Pier Paolo, "What's So Special about the Mediterranean? Thirty Years of Research on Household and Family in Italy," *Continuity and Change*, 18/1 (2003), pp. 111–37.

Witt, Ronald G., *In the Footsteps of the Ancients: The Origins of Humanism from Lovato to Bruni* (Leiden: Brill, 2000).

Comparative Europe

Arnade, Peter, Howell, Martha C., and Simons, Walter, "Fertile Spaces: The Productivity of Urban Space in Northern Europe," *Journal of Interdisciplinary History*, 33/2 (Spring 2002), pp. 515–48.

Bassett, Steven, ed., *Death in Towns: Urban Responses to the Dying and the Dead, 100–1600* (Leicester: Leicester University Press, 1992).

Boone, Marc, "Urban Space and Political Conflict in Late Medieval Flanders," *Journal of Interdisciplinary History*, 33/4 (Spring 2002), pp. 621–40.

Britnell, Richard H., "England and Northern Italy in the Early Fourteenth Century: The Economic Contrasts," *Transactions of the Royal Historical Society*, 5th ser., 39 (1989), pp. 167–83.

Britnell, Richard H., "The Towns of England and Northern Italy in the Early Fourteenth Century," *Economic History Review*, 44/1 (Feb. 1991), pp. 21–35.

Clauzel, Denis, "Les Élites urbaines et le pouvoir municipal: Le `Cas' de la bonne ville de Lille aux XIVe et XVe siècles," *Revue du Nord*, 78 (Apr.–June 1996), pp. 241–67.

De Clerq, Wim, Dumolyn, Jan, and Haemers, Jelle, "*Vivre noblement*: Material Culture and Elite Identity in Late Medieval Flanders," *Journal of Interdisciplinary Studies*, 38/1 (Summer 2007), pp. 1–31.

Donahue, Charles, Jr, *Law, Marriage, and Society in the Later Middle Ages: Arguments about Marriage in Five Courts* (Cambridge: Cambridge University Press, 2007).

Farge, James K., ed., *Marriage, Family, and Law in Medieval Europe: Collected Studies* (Toronto: University of Toronto Press, 1996).

Dyer, Christopher, *Standards of Living in the Later Middle Ages: Social Change in England c. 1200–1520* (Cambridge: Cambridge University Press, 1989).

Fleming, Peter, *Family and Household in Medieval England* (New York: Palgrave, 2001).

Hanawalt, Barbara A., *Growing Up in Medieval London: The Experience of Childhood in History* (Oxford: Oxford University Press, 1993).

Hanawalt, Barbara A., "Medievalists and the Study of Childhood," *Speculum*, 77/2 (Apr. 2002), pp. 440–60.

Hatcher, John, and Bailey, Mark, *Modelling the Middle Ages: The History and Theory of England's Economic Development.* (Oxford: Oxford University Press, 2001).

Howell, Martha C.,*Women, Production, and Patriarchy in Late Medieval Cities* (Chicago: University of Chicago Press, 1986).

Howell, Martha C., *The Marriage Exchange: Property, Social Place, and Gender in Cities of the Low Countries, 1300–1550* (Chicago: University of Chicago Press, 1998).

Jones, Sarah Rees, et al., "The Later Medieval English Urban Household," *History Compass*, 5/1 (2007), pp. 112–58.

Jordan, William Chester, *The Great Famine: Northern Europe in the Early Fourteenth Century* (Princeton: Princeton University Press, 1996).

Kowaleski, Maryanne, "The History of Urban Families in Medieval England," *Journal of Medieval History*, 14/1 (Mar. 1988), pp. 47–63.

Lopez, Robert S., *The Commercial Revolution of the Middle Ages, 950–1350* (Englewood Cliffs, NJ: Prentice-Hall, 1971).

Macfarlane, Alan, *The Origins of English Individualism: The Family, Property and Social Transition* (Oxford: Basil Blackwell, 1978).

Macfarlane, Alan, *Marriage and Love in England: Modes of Reproduction, 1300–1840* (Oxford: Basil Blackwell, 1986).

McFarlane, K. B., *The Nobility of Later Medieval England* (Oxford: Clarendon Press, 1973).

Mertes, Kate, *The English Noble Household, 1250–1600: Good Governance and Political Rule* (Oxford: Basil Blackwell, 1988).

Nicholas, David M., *The Domestic Life of a Medieval City: Women, Children, and the Family in Fourteenth-Century Ghent* (Lincoln, NE: University of Nebraska Press, 1985).

Nicholas, David M., *The Metamorphosis of a Medieval City: Ghent in the Age of the Arteveldes, 1302–1390* (Lincoln, NE: University of Nebraska Press, 1987).

Nicholas, David M.,. *The Van Arteveldes of Ghent: The Varieties of Vendetta and the Hero in History* (Ithaca, NY: Cornell University Press, 1988).

Rheubottom, David, *Age, Marriage, and Politics in Fifteenth-Century Ragusa* (Oxford: Oxford University Press, 2000).

Société des historiens médiévistes de l'enseignement supérieur public, *Les Élites urbaines au Moyen Âge (XXVIIe Congrès de la SHMS, Rome, mai 1996)* (Paris: Publications de la Sorbonne, 1997).

Stone, Lawrence, *The Family, Sex and Marriage in England 1500–1800* (New York: Harper & Row, 1977).

Thrupp, Sylvia L., *The Merchant Class of Medieval London* (1948; Ann Arbor, MI: University of Michigan Press, 1962).

Italy

General Studies on Italy

Abulafia, David, ed., *Italy in the Central Middle Ages* (Oxford: Oxford University Press, 2004); note especially the articles by Edward Coleman and Stephen Epstein.

Albini, Giuliana, *Le scritture del commune: Amministrazione e memoria nelle città dei secoli XII e XIII* (Turin: Scriptorium, 1998).

Ascheri, Mario, *Le città-stato* (Bologna: Il Mulino, 2006).

Barone, Giulia, *Da frate Elia agli spiritual* (Milan: Biblioteca francescana, 1999).

Boucheron, Patrick, *Les Villes d'Italie (vers 1150–vers 1340)* (Paris: Belin, 2004).

Cammarosano, Paolo, *Italia medievale: Strutture e geografia delle fonti scritte* (Rome: La nuova Italia scientifica, 1991).

Collodo, Silvana, and Pinto, Giuliano, eds, *La società médiévale* (Bologna: Monduzzi Editore, 1999).

Crouzet-Pavan, Élisabeth, *Enfers et paradis: L'Italie de Dante et de Giotto* (Paris: Albin Michel, 2001).

Dean, Trevor, ed., *The Towns of Italy in the Later Middle Ages* (Manchester: Manchester University Press, 2000).

Gaulin, Jean-Louis, Jamme, Armand, and Rouchon Mouilleron, Véronique, eds, *Villes d'Italie: Texts et documents des XIIe, XIIIe, XIVe siècles* (Lyons: Presses Universitaires de Lyon, 2005).

Gilli, Patrick, *Villes et sociétés urbaines en Italie, milieu XIIe–milieu XIVe siècle* ([Paris]: Sedes, 2005).

Heullant-Donat, Isabelle, and Perol, Céline, *Les Villes d'Italie du milieu du XIIe au milieu du XIVe siècle: Économies, sociétés, cultures, pouvoirs (approaches de la question)* (Paris: Hachette, 2004).

Hughes, Diane Owen, "Toward Historical Ethnography: Notarial Records and Family History in the Middle Ages," *Historical Methods Newsletter*, 7/2 (Mar. 1974), pp. 61–71.

Jehel, George, *Les Villes d'Italie di XIIe au milieu du XIVe siècle: Sociétés, pouvoirs, économies, cultures* (Nantes: Éditions du temps, 2004).

Langeli, Attilio Bartoli, *Notai: serivere documenti nell'Italia medievale* (Rome: Viella, 2006).

Larner, John, *Italy in the Age of Dante and Petrarch, 1216–1380* (London: Longman, 1980).

Maire Vigueur, Jean-Claude, "Révolution documentaire et révolution scripturaire: Le Cas de l'Italie médiévale," *Bibliothéque de l'École des chartes*, 153/1 (Jan. June 1995), pp. 177–85.

Menant, François, *Les Villes italiennes, XIIe–XIVe siècle: Enjeux historiographiques, méthodolgie, bibliographie commentée* (Paris: Armand Colin, 2004).

Milani, Giuliano, *I comuni italiani* (Bari: Editori Laterza, 2005).

Najemy, John M., ed., *Italy in the Age of the Renaissance* (Oxford: Oxford University Press, 2004); note especially the articles by Julius Kirshner, Diane Owen Hughes, Andrea Zorzi, Dale Kent, and John M. Najemy.

Petrucci, Armando, *Writers and Readers in Medieval Italy: Studies in the History of Written Culture* (New Haven: Yale University Press, 1995).

Putnam, Robert D., *Making Democracy Work: Civic Traditions in Modern Italy* (Princeton: Princeton University Press, 1993).

Racine, Pierre, *Les Villes d'Italie du milieu du XIIe siècle au milieu du XIVe siècle* (Paris: Armand Colin Éditeur, 2004).

Redon, Odile, Ricci, Lucia Battaglia, Beltrami, Pietro G., Brunet, Jacqueline, and Grieco, Allen J., *Les Langues de l'Italie médiévale*, L'atelier du médiéviste, 8 (Turnhout: Brepols Publishers, 2002).

Smith, R. M., "The People of Tuscany and their Families in the Fifteenth Century: Medieval or Mediterranean?" *Journal of Family History*, 6 (1981), pp. 101–28.

Particular Studies on Italy

Allegrezza, Franca, *Organizzazione del potere e dinamiche familiari: Gli Orsini dal Duecento agli inizi del Quattrocento*, Nuovi studi storici, 44 (Rome: Istituto storico italiano per il Medio Evo, 1998).

Bertelli, Sergio, *Il potere oligarchico nell stato-cittá medievale* (Florence: La Nuova Italia Editrice, 1978).

Bettotti, Marco, "Famiglia e lignaggio: L'aristocrazia in Italia," can be found on *Reti medievali* at www.rm.unina.it/repertorio/famiglia1.html.

Black, Robert, *Humanism and Education in Medieval and Renaissance Italy* (Cambridge: Cambridge University Press, 2001).

Bordone, Renato, Castelnuovo, Guido, and Varanini, Gian Maria, *Le aristocrazie dai signori rurali al patriziato*, ed. Renato Bordone (Bari: Editori Laterza, 2004).

Brown, Judith C., and Davis, Robert C., eds, *Gender and Society in Renaissance Italy* (New York: Longman, 1998).

Brucker, Gene A., ed., *Two Memoirs of Renaissance Florence: The Diaries of Buonaccorso Pitti and Gregorio Dati* (New York: Harper & Row, 1967).

Brucker, Gene A., *Giovanni and Lusanna: Love and Marriage in Renaissance Florence* (Berkeley and Los Angeles: University of California Press, 1986).

Carocci, Sandro, *Baroni di Roma: Dominazioni signorili e lignaggi aristocratici nel Duecento e nel primo Trecento*, Nuovi studi storici, 23 (Rome: Istituto sorico italiano per il Medio Evo, 1993).

Carocci, Sandro, ed., *La nobiltà romana nel Medioevo*, Collection, 359 (Rome: École française de Rome, 2006).

Cavalca, Desiderio, "Il ceto magnatizio a Firenze dopo gli ordinamenti di giustizia," *Rivista di storia el diritto italiano*, 40–1 (1967–8), pp. 85–132.

Centro italiano di studi di storia e d'arte, Pistoia, *Magnati e popolani nell'Italia comunale (Pistoia, 15–18 maggio 1995)* (Pistoia: Centro italiano di studi di storia e d'arte, 1997).

Chabot, Isabelle, "Widowhood and Poverty in Late Medieval Florence," *Continuity and Change*, 3/2 (Aug. 1988), pp. 291–311.

Chabot, Isabelle, "*La sposa in nero*: La ritualizzazione del lutto delle vedove fiorentine (secoli XIV–XV)," *Quaderni storici*, 29/2 (Aug. 1994), pp. 421–62.

Chabot, Isabelle, "Lineage Strategies and the Control of Widows in Renaissance Florence," in Sandra Cavallo and Lyndan Warner, eds, *Widowhood in Medieval and Early Modern Europe* (New York: Longman, 1999), pp. 127–44.

Chabot, Isabelle, "Reconstruction d'une famille: Les Ciurianni et leurs *Ricordanze* (1326–1429)," in Les Médiévistes de l'Université de Provence, eds, *La Toscane et les Toscanes: Cadres de vie société, croyances (Mélanges offerts à Charles-M. de la Roncière)* (Aix/Marseilles: Université de Provence, 1999), pp. 137–60.

Chojnacki, Stanley, *Women and Men in Renaissance Venice: Twelve Essays on Patrician Society* (Baltimore: Johns Hopkins University Press, 2000).

Cicchetti, Angelo, and Mordenti, Raul, *I libri di famiglia in Italia*, I: *Filologia e storiografia letteraria* (Rome: Edizioni di storia e letteratura, 1985).

Ciappelli, Giovanni, *Una famiglia e le sue ricordanze: I Castellani di Firenze nel Tre-Quattrocento* (Florence; Leo S. Olschki, 1995).

Ciappelli, Giovanni, and Rubin, Patricia Lee, eds, *Art, Memory, and Family in Renaissance Florence* (Cambridge: Cambridge University Press, 2000).

Cohn, Samuel K., Jr, *Death and Property in Siena, 1205–1800: Strategies for the Afterlife* (Baltimore: Johns Hopkins University Press, 1988).

Cohn, Samuel K., Jr, *The Cult of Remembrance and the Black Death: Six Renaissance Cities in Central Italy* (Baltimore: Johns Hopkins University Press, 1992).

Cohn, Samuel K., Jr, *Women in the Streets: Essays on Sex and Power in Renaissance Italy* (Baltimore: Johns Hopkins University Press, 1996).

Cohn, Samuel K., Jr, *Creating the Florentine State: Peasants and Rebellion, 1348–1434* (Cambridge: Cambridge University Press, 1999).

Cohn, Samuel K., Jr, ed., *Popular Protest in Late Medieval Europe* (Manchester: Manchester University Press, 2004).

Cohn, Samuel K., Jr, *Lust for Liberty: The Politics of Social Revolt in Medieval Europe, 1200–1425* (Cambridge, MA: Harvard University Press, 2006).

Cortese, Maria Elena, *Signori, castelli, città: L'aristocrazia del territorio fiorentino tra X e XII secolo* (Florence: Leo S. Olschki, 2007).

Crum, Roger J., and Paoletti, John T., eds, *Renaissance Florence: A Social History* (Cambridge: Cambridge University Press, 2006).

Dean, Trevor, and Lowe, K. J. P., eds, *Marriage in Italy, 1300–1650* (Cambridge: Cambridge University Press, 1998).

Epstein, Steven A., *Wills and Wealth in Medieval Genoa, 1150–1250* (Cambridge, MA: Harvard University Press, 1984).

Fabbri, Lorenzo, *Alleanza matrimoniale e patrizio nella Firenze del '400: Studio sulla famiglia Strozzi* (Florence: Leo S. Olschki, 2007).

Friedman, David, "Places and the Street in Late-Medieval and Renaissance Italy," in J. W. R. Whitehand and P. J. Larkham, eds, *Urban Landscapes: International Perspectives* (New York: Routledge, 1993), pp. 69–113.

Frugoni, Chiara, *A Distant City: Images of Urban Experience in the Medieval World*, trans. William McCuaig (1983; Princeton: Princeton University Press, 1991).

Gasparri, Stefano, *I milites cittadini: Studi sulla cavalleria in Italia*, Nuovi studi storici, 19 (Rome: Istituto storico italiano per il Medio Evo, 1992).

Goldthwaite, Richard A., *Private Wealth in Renaissance Florence: A Study of Four Families* (Princeton: Princeton University Press, 1968).

Goldthwaite, Richard A., *The Building of Renaissance Florence: An Economic and Social History* (Baltimore: Johns Hopkins University Press, 1980).

Grendler, Paul F., *Schooling in Renaissance Italy: Literacy and Learning, 1300–1600* (Baltimore: Johns Hopkins University Press, 1989).

Grillo, Paolo, *Cavalieri e popoli in armi: Le istituzioni militari nell'Italia médiévale* (Bari: Editori Laterza, 2008).

Grubb, James S., *Provincial Families of the Renaissance: Private and Public Life in the Veneto* (Baltimore: Johns Hopkins University Press, 1996).

Grubb, James S., *Family Memoirs from Verona and Vicenza, 15th–16th Centuries* (Rome: Viella, 2002).

Guzzetti, Linda, "Dowries in Fourteenth-Century Venice," *Renaissance Studies*, 16 (2002), pp. 430–73.

Heers, Jacques, *Le Clan familial au Moyen Age: Étude sur les structures politiques et sociales des milieux urbains* (Paris: Presses Universitaires de France, 1974).

Heers, Jacques, *Parties and Political Life in the Medieval West*, trans. David Nicholas; Europe in the Middle Ages, 7 (Amsterdam: North-Holland, 1977).

Herlihy, David, "Family Solidarity in Medieval Italian History," in David Herlihy, Robert S. Lopez and Vsevolod Slessarev, eds, *Economy, Society and Government in Medieval Italy: Essays in Memory of Robert L. Reynolds* (Kent, OH: Kent State University Press, 1969), pp. 173–84.

Herlihy, David, "Mapping Households in Medieval Italy," *Catholic Historical Review*, 58/1 (Apr. 1972), pp. 1–24.

Herlihy, David, *The Family in Renaissance Italy*, Forums in History, 125 (St Charles, MO: Forum Press, 1974).

Herlihy, David, "The Medieval Marriage Market," in Dale B. J. Randall, ed., *Medieval and Renaissance Studies (Proceedings of the Southeastern Institute of Medieval and Renaissance Studies, Summer 1974)*, no. 6 (Durham, NC: Duke University Press, 1976), pp. 3–27.

Herlihy, David, *Women, Family and Society in Medieval Europe: Historical Essays*, ed. Anthony Molho (Providence, RI: Berghahn Books, 1995).

Herlihy, David, and Klapisch-Zuber, Christiane, *Tuscans and their Families: A Study of the Florentine Catasto of 1427* (New Haven: Yale University Press, 1985); this is a partial English translation of *Les Toscans et leur familles: Une étude du catasto de 1427* (Paris: L'École des hautes études en social sciences, 1978).

Hughes, Diane Owen, "Urban Growth and Family Structure in Medieval Genoa," *Past and Present*, 66 (Feb. 1975), pp. 3–28.

Hughes, Diane Owen, "Domestic Ideals and Social Behavior: Evidence from Medieval Genoa," in Charles Rosenberg, ed., *The Family in History* (Philadelphia: University of Pennsylvania Press, 1975), pp. 115–43.

Hughes, Diane Owen, "Kinsmen and Neighbors in Medieval Genoa," in Harry A. Miskimin, David Herlihy, and A. L. Udovitch, eds, *The Medieval City* (New Haven: Yale University Press, 1977), pp. 95–111.

Hughes, Diane Owen, "From Brideprice to Dowry in Mediterranean Europe," *Journal of Family History*, 3/3 (Fall, 1978), 262–96.

Hughes, Diane Owen, "Sumptuary Law and Social Relations in Renaissance Italy," in John Bossy, ed., *Disputes and Settlements: Law and Human Relations in the West* (Cambridge: Cambridge University Press, 1983), pp. 69–99.

Hughes, Diane Owen, "Representing the Family: Portraits and Purposes in Early Modern Italy," *Journal of Interdisciplinary History*, 17/1 (Summer, 1986), pp. 7–38.

Hughes, Diane Owen, "Invisible Madonnas? The Italian Historiographical Tradition and the Women of Medieval Italy," in Susan Mosher Stuard, ed., *Women in Medieval History and Historiography* (Philadelphia: University of Pennsylvania Press, 1987), pp. 25–57.

Jones, Philip J., "Florentine Families and Florentine Diaries in the Fourteenth Century," *Papers of the British School at Rome*, 24 (1956), 183–205.

Jones, Philip J., *Economia e società nell'Italia medievale* (Turin: Giulio Einaudi, 1980).

Jones, Philip J., *The Italian City-State: From Commune to Signoria* (Oxford: Clarendon Press, 1997).

Kent, Dale, *The Rise of the Medici: Faction in Florence, 1426–1434* (Oxford: Oxford University Press, 1978).

Kent, Francis William, *Household and Lineage in Renaissance Florence: The Family Life of the Capponi, Ginori, and Rucellai* (Princeton: Princeton University Press, 1977).

King, Margaret L., *Venetian Humanism in an Age of Patrician Dominance* (Princeton: Princeton University Press, 1986).

King, Margaret L., *The Death of the Child Valerio Marcello* (Chicago: University of Chicago Press, 1994).

Kirshner, Julius, *Pursuing Honor while Avoiding Sin: The Monte delle Doti of Florence*, Quaderni di *Studi senesi*, 41 (Milan: A. Giuffrè, 1978).

Kirshner, Julius, "Wives' Claims against Insolvent Husbands in Late Medieval Italy," in Julius Kirshner and Suzanne F. Wemple, eds, *Women of the Medieval World: Essays in Honor of John H. Mundy* (Oxford: Basil Blackwell, 1985), pp. 256–303.

Kirshner, Julius, "Materials for a Gilded Cage: Non-Dotal Assets in Florence 1300–1500," in David I. Kertzer and Richard P. Saller, eds, *The Family in Italy from Antiquity to the Present* (New Haven: Yale University Press, 1991), pp. 184–207.

Kirshner, Julius, "*Maritus lucretur totem uxoris sue premortue* in Late Medieval Florence," *Zeitschrift der Savigny-Stiftung für Rechtsgeschichte (Kanonistische Abteilung)*, 121 (1991), pp. 111–55.

Kirshner, Julius, and Molho, Anthony, "The Dowry Fund and the Marriage Market in Early Quattrocento Florence," *Journal of Modern History*, 50/3 (Sept. 1978), 403–38.

Klapisch-Zuber, Christiane, *Women, Family, and Ritual in Renaissance Italy* (Chicago: University of Chicago Press, 1985).

Klapisch-Zuber, Christiane, "Ruptures de parenté et changements d'identité chez les magnats florentins du XIVe siécle," *Annales: Économies, sociétés, civilisations*, 43/5 (Sept.–Oct. 1988), pp. 1205–40.

Klapisch-Zuber, Christiane, "Women and the Family," in Jacques Le Goff, ed., *Medieval Callings* (Chicago: University of Chicago Press, 1990), pp. 285–311.

Klapisch-Zuber, Christiane, "Kinship and Politics in Fourteenth-Century Florence," in David I. Kertzer and Richard P. Saller, eds, *The Family in Italy from Antiquity to the Present* (New Haven: Yale University Press, 1991), pp. 208–28.

Klapisch-Zuber, Christiane, "Honneur de noble, renommée de puissant: La Définition des magnats italiens (1280–1400)," *Médiévales*, 24 (Spring 1993), pp. 81–100.

Klapisch-Zuber, Christiane, "La Construction de l'identité sociale: Les Magnats dans la Florence de la fin du Moyen Âge," in Bernard Lepetit, ed., *Les Formes de l'expérience: Une autre histoire sociale* (Paris: Éditions Albin Michel SA, 1995), pp. 151–64, 326.

Klapisch-Zuber, Christiane, "Family Trees and the Construction of Kinship in Renaissance Italy," in Mary Jo Maynes, Ann Waltner, Brigitte Soland, and Ulrike Strasser, eds, *Gender, Kinship, Power: A Comparative and Interdisciplinary History* (New York: Routledge, 1996), pp. 101–14.

Klapisch-Zuber, Christiane, *L'Ombre des ancêtres: Essai sur l'imaginaire médiéval de la parenté* (Paris: Fayard, 2000).

Klapisch-Zuber, Christiane, *L'Arbe des familles* (Paris: Éditions de La Martinière, 2003).

Klapisch-Zuber, Christiane, *Retour à la cite: Les Magnats de Florence, 1340–1440* (Paris: Éditions de l'École des hautes etudes en sciences sociales, 2006).

Klapisch-Zuber, Christiane, "Quel Moyen Age pour le nom?" in Monique Bourin, Jean-Marie Martin, and François Menant, eds, *L'Anthroponymie: Document de l'histoire sociale des mondes méditerranéens médiévaux* (Rome: École française de Rome, 1996), pp. 473–80.

Klapisch-Zuber, Christiane, "Identité de sexe, identité de classe: Femmes nobles et populaires en Italie (XIVe–XVe siècles)," in André Burguière, Joseph Goy and Marie-Jeanne Tits-Dieuaide, eds, *L'Histoire grande ouverte: Hommages à Emmanuel Le Roy Ladurie* (Paris: Fayard, 1997), pp. 394–404.

Klapisch-Zuber, Christiane, "Vrais et faux magnats: L'Application des ordonnances de justice au XIVe siècle," in *Magnati e popolani nell'Italia comunale (Pistoia, 15–18 maggio 1995)*, Quindicesimo convegno di studi (Pistoia: Centro italiano di studi di storia e d'arte, 1997), pp. 273–91.

Klapisch-Zuber, Christiane, "Un noble florentin à ses crayons: Lapo da Castiglionchio et sa généalogie," in *La Toscane et les Toscanes: Cadres de vie société, croyances (Mélanges offerts à Charles-M. de la Roncière)* (Aix/Marseilles: Université de Provence, 1999), pp. 113–35.

Klapisch-Zuber, Christiane, "Les Acteurs politiques de la Florence communale (1350–1430)," in Jean Boutier, Sandro Landi, and Olivier Rouchon, eds, *Florence et la Toscane, XIVe–XIXe siècles: Les Dynamiques d'un état italien* (Rennes: Presses Universitaires de Rennes, 2004), pp. 217–39.

Kuehn, Thomas, *Emancipation in Late Medieval Florence* (New Brunswick: Rutgers University Press, 1982).

Kuehn, Thomas, *Law, Family, and Women: Toward a Legal Anthropology of Renaissance Italy* (Chicago: University of Chicago Press, 1991).

Kuehn, Thomas, "Law, Death, and Heirs in the Renaissance: Repudiation of Inheritance in Florence," *Renaissance Quarterly*, 45/3 (Autumn 1992), pp. 484–516.

Kuehn, Thomas, *Illegitimacy in Renaissance Florence* (Ann Arbor: University of Michigan Press, 2005).

Kuehn, Thomas, *Heirs, Kin, and Creditors in Renaissance Florence* (Cambridge: Cambridge University Press, 2008).

Lansing, Carol, *The Florentine Magnates: Lineage and Faction in a Medieval Commune* (Princeton: Princeton University Press, 1991).

Lansing, Carol, *Passion and Order: Restraint of Grief in the Medieval Communes* (Ithaca, NY: Cornell University Press, 2008).

La Roncière, Charles Marie de, "Tuscan Notables on the Eve of the Renaissance," in Philip Ariès and Georges Duby, eds, *A History of Private Life, II: Revelations of the Medieval World* (Cambridge, MA: Harvard University Press, 1988), pp. 157–309.

La Roncière, Charles Marie de, *Firenze e le sue campagne nel Trecento: Mercanti, produzione, traffici*; Biblioteca storica toscana, 48 (Florence: Leo S. Olschki, 2005).

Leverotti, Franca, *Famiglia e istituzioni nel medioevo italiano dal tardo antico al rinascimento* (Rome: Carocci, 2005).

McKee, Sally, "Greek Women in Latin Households of Fourteenth-Century Venetian Crete," *Journal of Medieval History*, 19/3 (1993), pp. 229–49.

Maire Vigueur, Jean-Claude, ed., *D'une ville à l'autre: Structures matérielles et organisation de l'espace dans les villes européenes (XIIIe–XVIe siècle)* (Bologna: 2004); (Rome: École française de Rome, 1989).

Maire Vigueur, Jean-Claude, *Cavalieri e cittadini: Guerra, conflitti e società nell'Italia comunale* (Bologna: Il Mulino, 2004); this is an Italian translation of *Cavaliers et citoyens: guerre, conflits et société dans l'Italie communale, XIIe-XIIIe siècles* (Paris: Éditions de l'École des hautes etudes en sciences socials, 2003).

Martines, Lauro, *Strong Words: Writing and Social Strain in the Italian Renaissance* (Baltimore: Johns Hopkins University Press, 2001).

Martines, Lauro, and Baca, Murtha, eds, *An Italian Renaissance Sextet: Six Tales in Historical Context* (New York: Marsilio, 1994).

Menzinger, Sara, *Giuristi e politic nei comuni di popolo: Siena, Perugia e Bologna, tre governi a confronto* (Rome: Viella, 2006).

Milani, Giuliano, *L'esclusione dal commune: Conflitti e bandi politici a Bologna e in altere città italiane tra XII e XIV secolo*; Nuovi studi storici, 63 (Rome: Istituto storico italiano per il Medio Evo, 2003).

Molho, Anthony, "Visions of the Florentine Family in the Renaissance," *Journal of Modern History*, 50/2 (June, 1978), pp. 304–11.

Molho, Anthony, "Deception and Marriage Strategy in Renaissance Florence: The Case of Women's Ages," *Renaissance Quarterly*, 41/2 (Summer 1987), pp. 193–217.

Molho, Anthony, *Marriage Alliance in Late Medieval Florence* (Cambridge, MA: Harvard University Press, 1994).

Mordenti, Raul, *I libri di famiglia in Italia, II: geografia e storia*. La memoria familiare, 4 (Rome: Edizioni di storia e letteratura, 2001).

Ottokar, Nicola, *Il comune di Firenze all fine del Dugento* (1926; repr. 2nd edn, Turin: Giulio Einaudi, 1974).

Queller, Donald E., *The Venetian Patriciate: Reality versus Myth* (Urbana, IL: University of Illinois Press, 1986).

Queller, Donald E., and Madden, Thomas F., "Father of the Bride: Fathers, Daughters, and Dowries in Late Medieval and Early Renaissance Venice," *Renaissance Quarterly*, 46/4 (Winter 1993), pp. 685–711.

Pirillo, Paolo, *Famiglia e mobilità sociale nella Toscana medievale: I Franzesi della Foresta da Figline Valdarno (secoli XII–XV)* (Figline: Comune di Figline Valdarno, 1992).

Raveggi, Sergio, Tarassi, Massimo, Medici, Daniela, and Parenti, Patrizia, *Ghibellini, Guelfi e Popolo Grasso: I detentori del potere politico a Firenze nella seconda metà del Dugento* (Florence: La nuova Italia, 1978).

Rossetti, Gabriella, "Les *Élites* mercantili nell'Europa dei secoli XII–XVI: Loro cultura e radicamento," in Alberto Grohmann, ed., *Spazio urbano e organizzazione médiévale (Atti della session C23, Eleventh International Economic History Congress, Milano, 12–16 settembre 1994)* (Naples: Edizioni scientifiche italiane, 1994), pp. 39–59.

Rubinstein, Nicolai, "La lotta contro i magnati a Firenze: La prima legge sul *sodamento* e la pace del Card. Latino," *Archivio storico italiano*, 93/2 (1935), pp. 161–72.

Rubinstein, Nicolai, *La lotta contro i magnati a Firenze: II, le origini della legge sul sodamento* (Florence: Leo S. Olschki, 1939).

Rubinstein, Nicolai, "Political Ideas in Sienese Art: The Frescoes by Ambrogio Lorenzetti and Taddeo di Bartolo in the *Palazzo Pubblico*," *Journal of the Warburg and Courtauld Institutes*, 22 (1958), pp. 179–207.

Salvemini, Gaetano, *Magnati e popolani in Firenze dal 1280 al 1295*, ed. Ernesto Sestan. *Opere di Gaetano Salvemini*, 1. 2nd edn (Milan: Giangiacomo Feltrinelli, 1974; for the twelve appendices see the first edition (Florence: G. Carnesecchi e figli, 1899), pp. 305–432).

Salvemini, Gaetano, *La dignità cavalleresca nel Comune di Firenze a altri scritti*, ed. Ernesto Sestan. *Opere di Gaetano Salvemini*, 2 (Milan: Giangiacomo Feltrinelli, 1972).

Skinner, Quentin, "Ambrogio Lorenzetti's *Buon Governo* Frescoes: Two Old Questions, Two New Answers," *Journal of the Warburg and Courtauld Institutes*, 62 (1999), pp. 1–28.

Strocchia, Sharon T., *Death and Ritual in Renaissance Florence* (Baltimore: Johns Hopkins University Press, 1992).

Stuard, Susan Mosher, *Gilding the Market: Luxury and Fashion in Fourteenth-Century Italy* (Philadelphia: University of Pennsylvania Press, 2006).

Vallerani, Massimo, "La città e le sue istituzioni: Ceti dirigenti, oligarchia e politica nella medievistica italiana del Novecento," *Annali dell'Istituto storico italo-germanico in Trento*, 20 (1994), pp. 165–220.

Black Death and its Consequences

Aberth, John, *From the Brink of the Apocalypse: Confronting Famine, War, Plague, and Death in the Later Middle Ages* (New York: Routledge, 2001).

Benedictow, Ole J., *The Black Death, 1346–1353: The Complete History* (Woodbridge: Boydell Press, 2004).

Bowsky, William M., ed., *The Black Death: A Turning Point in History?* (New York: Holt, Rinehart and Winston, 1971).

Carmichael, Ann G., *Plague and the Poor in Renaissance Florence* (Cambridge: Cambridge University Press, 1986).

Cohn, Samuel K., Jr, *The Black Death Transformed: Disease and Culture in Early Renaissance Europe* (London: Arnold, 2002).

Herlihy, David, *The Black Death and the Transformation of the West*, ed. with an introduction by Samuel K. Cohn, Jr (Cambridge, MA: Harvard University Press, 1997).

Horrox, Rosemary, ed., *The Black Death* (Manchester: Manchester University Press, 1994).

Twigg, Graham, *The Black Death: A Biological Reappraisal* (London: Batsford, 1984).

Further Reading

The study of urban élites and families in late medieval cities has produced a large bibliography, especially for Italy. The extensive bibliography below is indicative of that. Casey, *History of the Family*, remains a good introduction to the study of the European family. Carol Neel in *Medieval Families* has collected the foundational articles. David Herlihy in *Medieval Households* takes a wider approach with a clearly structured analysis of the family. The volumes by Jack Goody listed in the bibliography are important for his questions about the family in Europe and give a beginning to a comparative perspective to the wider world. Lynch, *Individuals, Families, and Communities in Europe*, Mitchell, *Family Life in the Middle Ages*, and Crawford, *European Sexualities*, bring the literature more up-to-date.

For Italy, among the best works in English that reflect the state of the scholarship are in the collections edited by David Abulafia, *Italy in the Central Middle Ages*, and John Najemy,

Italy in the Age of the Renaissance. Several French and Italian scholars, such as Ascheri, Boucheron, Gilli, Menant, Milani, and Racine have produced excellent introductions to the history of these cities.

Two collections contain important articles on élites and dominating classes: Société des historiens médiévistes de l'enseignement supérieur public, *Les Élites urbaines au Moyen Age*, and Centro italiano di studi di storia e d'arte, Pistoia, *Magnati e popolani nell'Italia comunale.* For particular Italian élite families see Goldthwaite, *Private Wealth in Renaissance Florence*, and Kent, *Household and Lineage in Renaissance Florence.* For wider perspectives on the politics, society and economy of Florence, whose history still dominates much of the scholarship, see the recent books by John M. Najemy, *A History of Florence 1200–1575* (New York: Blackwell, 2006) and Richard Goldthwaite, *The Economy of Renaissance Florence* (Baltimore: The Johns Hopkins University Press, 2009). The classic studies of magnates in Florence are Salvemini, *Magnati e popolani in Firenze dal 1280 al 1295* and Ottokar, *Il comune di Firenze all fine del Dugento.* They must be read in conjunction with Raveggi, et al., *Ghibellini, Guelfi e Popolo Grasso*, Lansing, *The Florentine Magnates*, and George W. Dameron, "Revisiting the Italian Magnates: Church Property, Social Conflict, and Political Legitimization in the Thirteenth Century Commune," *Viator*, 23 (1992), 167–87. Klapisch-Zuber carries the study of magnate families into the fourteenth century in her recent *Retour à la cité: les magnats de Florence.* For some comparisons of families and local cultures and politics within Italy see the works listed in the bibliography by Allegrezza, Carocci, Chojnacki, King, Queller, and Vallerani.

One can approach the marriage strategies, legal options, and social institutions for Italians living within the context of the *ius commune* and Roman Law through the numerous publications by Chabot, Herlihy, Hughes, Kirshner, Klapisch-Zuber, Kuehn, and Molho. The controversies over the Black Death and its consequences are discussed in Sam Cohn's *The Black Death.* Lastly, the collection edited by Roger Crum and John Paoletti, *Renaissance Florence*, contains important essays on urban space, art, and society in Florence.

Part IV

Religious Culture

Chapter Ten

New Religious Movements and Reform

Maureen C. Miller

Reform is a recurrent motif in the history of Christianity and it has given rise to dramatic historical narratives in which valiant churchmen combat rampant abuses. Since the 1970s, however, historians have become much more skeptical that clerical complaints describe real crises, but also more convinced that those calling for reform had significant political and ideological goals. Reformers sought to achieve particular visions of Christian society and its leadership. This shift from the empirical study of the condition of the church to the politics of reforming agendas and their consequences has affected interpretation of both the Carolingian reform and the eleventh-century or "Gregorian" reform. It has also revealed more connections between these two eras of ecclesiastical refashioning. The rise of the papacy remains a central narrative of medieval reform, but scholars now increasingly recognize the role that lay people played in shaping a new ecclesiology and founding new kinds of institutions. A key result of eleventh-century reform is that it gave rise to a profusion of new experiments in religious life that opened the pursuit of Christian perfection to all men and women, particularly through the cultivation of the *vita apostolica*.

The Early Middle Ages

In the mid-twentieth century, the standard narrative of the religious history of early medieval Europe emphasized a long, messy, but ultimately effective period of missionary work among the "barbarians" followed by a rapid and energetic systematization of ecclesiastical structures in the late eighth and ninth centuries by Carolingian monarchs and the leading clerics gathered at their court. In this version of early medieval religious history, the conversion of the Merovingian king Clovis (481–511) led to the acceptance of Christianity by the Franks, who in turn evangelized the peoples they conquered. Through missionaries like the Anglo-Saxon Boniface (d. 754), the Franks were brought into more regular relations with Rome, which eventually yielded an alliance between the Carolingians and the papacy. Boniface and his co-laborers in the missionary field made these new rulers of the Franks painfully aware of the failings of the clergy, the evils of lay control of bishoprics and monasteries, and the resurgence of pagan superstitions among the people. An oft-repeated vignette is Boniface's alarm at a Bavarian priest baptizing people "in the name of the fatherland and the daughter" (*in nomine patria et filia*). Such reports prompted the early Carolingian kings – Pippin III (751–68), then Charlemagne (768–814) – to reform the Frankish church by calling numerous councils, most famously a series held in 813, and issuing capitularies, such as the *Admonitio Generalis* of 789. The latter required bishops to establish schools; the education of the clergy was a central concern of Carolingian reform. The movement also clarified Church organization, establishing metropolitans over ecclesiastical provinces and subjecting suffragan bishops within those regions to the disciplining authority of their archbishop. Bishops, in turn, were to discipline their clergy and ensure that pastoral care was offered in their dioceses. The liturgy was progressively Romanized through the dissemination of newly acquired texts and contact with the papal curia. Order was brought to the empire's numerous monasteries through the propagation of the Benedictine Rule, and Chrodegang of Metz's rule for canons reformed cathedral chapters. As a result of monarchical leadership of reform, the Church was integrated into Carolingian structures of power.[1]

Over the past several decades, historians have been slowly modifying this picture without abandoning its basic framework. A major impetus for revision has been the work of Peter Brown and the emergence of the field of "late antiquity." Roughly encompassing the third to the mid-eighth centuries, this post-classical era is characterized by Brown and others in highly positive terms as one of creative synthesis. This contrasts sharply with the assumptions about the early Middle Ages undergirding the account of Carolingian reform summarized above. That early Middle Ages began with the collapse of the western Roman Empire and was characterized by barbarian invasions and the destruction or mere embattled survival of Roman cultural institutions. It ended with the Carolingians restoring order and a new imperial unity. If the pre-Carolingian era was, instead, a period in which many Roman institutions and ideas survived to be creatively combined with Germanic concepts and practices, what was the Carolingian accomplishment? Was there really a "crisis" in the eighth-century Church that necessitated "reform"?

Generally, Carolingianists have come to admit many more continuities across the seventh to ninth centuries, but they have also used the model of cultural creativity deployed by Brown to renew claims for a distinctive and highly significant Carolingian contribution. On the topic of liturgical reform, for example, instead of portraying the Frankish Church as all but cut off from Roman influence from the late sixth century, historians acknowledge continuing contact through pilgrims, bishops, and kings. What was once viewed as a "Romanization" of the liturgy under the Carolingians is now considered a creative adaptation of Roman rites to Frankish circumstances by bishops, such as Chrodegang of Metz.[2] The gradualist vision of late antiquity has also modified understandings of evangelization and reform. Rather than seeing the missionary endeavors of the seventh and eighth centuries as generally successful but followed by backsliding and a resurgence of pagan superstitions demanding "reform," historians of religion are now deeply skeptical of claims of conversion. Instead they posit a gradual process of Christianization and an accommodation of the faith to the beliefs, values, and practices of Germanic societies.[3] Carolingian reform, in this narrative, is still a systematization of ecclesiastical life and institutions, but one that ordered a distinctively Frankish Church. Peter Brown himself, discussing the accomplishment of Charlemagne in his *Rise of Western Christendom*, abandons altogether the term "reform" with its connotation of return to an earlier pristine state. He frames the ruler's interventions in ecclesiastical life as *correctio*, a contemporary description that leaves open the standard used in correcting or shaping up Christian society.[4]

In part related to the rise of the concept of Christianization, scholars have broadened their descriptions of what constituted reform in the Carolingian era. Ecclesiastical organization and clerical education are still central, but they are now joined by an appreciation of Carolingian interest in preaching, pastoral care, vernacular instruction of the laity, and liturgy as a means of Christianization. The goal of reform was not so much the correction of specific abuses, but the creation of a Christian society.[5] This richer picture of Carolingian reform has reinforced emphasis on the Carolingian symbiosis of Church and State.

> In the preface of the *Admonitio Generalis*, or General Exhortation, of 789 [Pierre Riché noted], Charlemagne compared himself to Josiah, the biblical king who sought "to restore to God's service, by inspecting, correcting, and exhorting, the kingdom that God had committed to him." . . . Like a new Moses, he was a religious lawgiver; like a new David triumphing over the foes of Israel, the Frankish king led a new chosen people to its salvation.[6]

This vision of Christian kingship empowered the monarch to intervene in ecclesiastical life, selecting bishops and legislating reforms. But it also led bishops to elaborate the idea of kingship as a ministry, making royal power conditional upon the righteous exercise of the office.

While adopting the notion of a gradual transformation and Christianization of Europe, the significance of the Carolingian reform has been reconceived. Rather than rectifying a crisis in ecclesiastical order, it created a new vision of order: that of a Christian society led by monarchs and bishops working together for the salvation of God's chosen people. In this new formulation, the extent or reality of abuses and the effectiveness of reform efforts are less important than the ideological work accomplished by Carolingian monarchs and bishops. By issuing capitularies and calling reform councils, the Carolingians articulated claims to authority not only over the Church, but over all Christian society. Kings were not the only ones, however, to use reform to bolster their power. As Makye de Jong has pointed out, "more and more the church transformed its religious authority into political authority based on the superiority of episcopal *auctoritas* over royal *potestas*."[7]

Indeed, greater attention to developments beyond the reign of Charlemagne has made historians aware of a shift in the dynamic of reform from monarch to bishops. By 844, Rosamond McKitterick has observed, "the bishops not only assumed the initiative and defined their own role in their society, they now took it upon themselves to define the role of the king, rather than have the king by his own legislative action defining his role in the community."[8] This shift is highly significant, as it foreshadows the independent action and prerogatives of ecclesiastical leaders that were championed in the eleventh-century, or "Gregorian," reforms. Recent work on Carolingian reform has found other connections to these later reforms. Makye de Jong, for example, has underscored a new emphasis on clerical chastity and priestly purity in the ninth century, while McKitterick has documented an increasing preoccupation with the exaltation of the priestly and episcopal office.[9] Continuities have also been suggested between the Carolingian monastic reforms of Benedict of Aniane and the tenth-century wave of monastic reform usually seen as presaging the "Gregorian" era.[10]

"Gregorian Reform"

The classic work that established the traditional narrative of eleventh-century religious change is Augustin Fliche's *La Réforme grégorienne*. In three learned and richly annotated volumes published from 1924 to 1937, Fliche crafted a narrative so compelling that it still informs accounts today. His story begins in the late ninth and tenth centuries, when political disorder allowed lay people to invade Church lands, take over ecclesiastical institutions, and found their own "proprietary" churches. The "church in the power of the laity" was plagued by abuses: incompetent and immoral priests, monasteries of lax discipline where true religious could not pursue their vocations in peace, and corrupt bishops who were often the relatives of rich and powerful local lords. The first heroic efforts at reform came in monasteries, particularly Cluny, which was founded in 909. This Burgundian house was dedicated to reviving a strict interpretation of the Benedictine Rule; its foundation charter explicitly exempted it from the control of local lords, its lands placed under the direct protection of St Peter. Cluny became a beacon of reform, its abbots and monks helping to rekindle discipline at other monasteries, until it was the center of an expansive network of reformed institutions extending throughout France and into Iberia, the German empire, and northern Italy. By the late tenth century calls for more general reform of the Church begin to be heard. In northern Italy, bishops such as Atto of Vercelli (r. 924–61) and Ratherius of Verona (c. 887–974) decried the number of clerics who were ignorant or poorly educated, and who had wives and concubines. In Lotharingia the precocious study of canon law produced a new awareness of the trampled rights of the Church and calls for an end to lay meddling in ecclesiastical affairs. Simony, the "heresy" of paying for spiritual things (administration of sacraments, appointment to church offices) and "nicolaitism" or clerical unchastity emerged as critical abuses demanding reform.

Fliche's story was above all, however, one of popes. For this French Catholic scholar, it was the reform and revival of the papacy in the mid-eleventh century that led to real change. Although he gives credit to Emperor Henry III for settling a messy three-way papal schism at the Synod of Sutri in 1046 and bringing reform-minded leaders to Rome, it was Pope Leo IX (r. 1049–54) who established a cadre of reformers, many from his native Lotharingia, and set the papacy on a new course. In this entourage was Hildebrand, who would become Pope Gregory VII (r. 1073–85). Fliche dedicated an entire volume to Gregory and credited this pope with reforming the Church. Central to his narrative was Gregory's dramatic clash with the German king Henry IV (r. 1056–106) over royal appointment of bishops, or "lay investiture." The investiture conflict continued after Gregory's stormy pontificate, but Fliche credits this uncompromising figure with turning the tide. His courageous championing of the liberty for the Church carried out reform and revived

Christianity. This would reach new heights in the twelfth and thirteenth centuries, Europe's great "age of faith."[11]

Fliche's Catholic polemic was apparent and, predictably, provoked a response. In 1936 a young German scholar, Gerd Tellenbach, published a slim volume that has had an enduring impact: *Libertas: Kirche und Weltordnung in Zeitalter des Investiturstreites.* Translated into English in 1940 under the title *Church, State and Christian Society at the Time of the Investiture Contest*, this work has remained in print and had a formative influence on the field. Tellenbach recast the story, shifting emphasis from reform to the investiture conflict and from abuses to ideas about authority: "The Investiture Controversy," the author begins, "was a struggle for right order in the world." Three notions of hierarchy coexisted in eleventh-century Europe, according to Tellenbach. One was an ascetic, monastic hierarchy in which the only truly meritorious status was achieved in the next world by effectively renouncing this world while in it. This Christian conceptualization of world order coexisted with another that Tellenbach labeled "sacramental" or "priestly." This schema ranked individuals through their sacramental functions, their ability to save souls by administering grace, and – in contrast to the ascetic hierarchy – was aimed at conquering and converting the world rather than fleeing it. Finally, the "royal theocracy" world view allotted a special superior place to kings as God's appointed representatives on earth with the "duty of leading the people towards God." Before the mid-eleventh century, the ascetic world view had predominated within the Church and, thus, conflict had not arisen with the royal theocratic perspective. From the late 1050s, however, debates among reformers, reflected in the third book of Humbert of Silva Candida's *Libri adversus simoniacos*, launched a frontal assault on the position of the laymen, particularly kings, within the Church. The clash between Gregory VII and Henry IV over investiture was the result of the sacramental-priestly world view challenging the royal-theocratic. "The superiority of the Church over the State derives," Tellenbach concluded, "from Catholic belief in the Church and its vocation . . . Hence Protestant Christianity immediately reoriented its attitude towards the state."[12] Tellenbach's was a German Lutheran response to Fliche's French Catholic interpretation.

Scholarship over the rest of the twentieth century has been content to explore details of these two, broad paradigms. The Catholic periodical *Studi Gregoriani*, for example, published from 1947 on in Rome, dedicated itself to "the history of 'Libertas ecclesiae,' the freedom of the Church." The polemical literature that the investiture conflict sparked, so central to Tellenbach's narrative of the clash of ideas, was extensively studied, and Fliche's insight that canon law was a central tool and inspiration in reform generated abundant and productive research.[13] But, by the 1960s, scholars were still awaiting Tellenbach's revision and expansion of his initial, stunning foray into the field, while criticism of Fliche's papal-centric interpretation was accumulating, both within Catholicism and without. The slender, idea-packed volume of *Libertas* offered less fodder to critics than the three tomes of *La Réforme grégorienne.* Fliche's emphasis on Gregory VII was easily questioned, and generally historians have moved away from the using the term "Gregorian reform." Scholarly appreciation of the reforming achievements of other popes in the second half of the eleventh century, and other non-papal actors, increased. Indeed, criticism of the role Fliche accorded Lotharingian reformers and his emphasis on Cluny helped produce a much richer picture of reform efforts.[14] Tellenbach's reliance on Humbert of Silva Candida and the inherent teleology of his account have been criticized, but generally German and Anglophone scholarship has been sympathetic to his interpretation. Norman F. Cantor and Brian Tierney, in particular, have done much to enshrine Tellenbach's interpretation in American curricula.[15]

The great majority of medieval historians, however, turned to social and economic history in the 1970s and 1980s, leaving the entire topic of reform and the investiture conflict relatively moribund. The actors, it is true, were all elites: popes, kings, cardinals, princes, bishops, and monks. The sources, for sure, were the very essence of the old history: legal collections, letters, diplomas, theological and political treatises. The few, derivative studies appearing prompted Karl Morrison in 1987 to lament an "immobilization of interpretative discourse" on this "central theme in European history."[16] To a large degree, he is correct. Pursuant to mobilizing discourse, let us summarize where current interpretation stands on the broad issues and consider promising new directions.

The Origins of the Eleventh-Century Reform Movements

While Carolingianists are now less inclined to ventriloquize uncritically the lamentations of ecclesiastical leaders like Boniface in order to explain royal efforts at reform, most historians are more confident that a real crisis in the tenth century provoked the next great effort at Church reform. This was, after all, the era of viking, Arab, and Magyar invasions. Opinions have changed, however, on the proximate causes of the perceived crisis in ecclesiastical life. In the early twentieth century, Catholic authors such as Fliche blamed lay people: it was the laity's domination of the Church that befouled it with abuses. It was not hard, of course, to find tenth-century examples of lay elites sequestering Church lands and appointing unfit priests to parishes and derelict abbots to monasteries. A new explanation emerged with Tellenbach's *Libertas*. Influenced by German idealism, but in some ways paralleling the early *Annales* interest in *mentalité*, Tellenbach found the origins of reform and the investiture crisis in people's heads: it was two conflicting world views that led to calls for change and to conflict. One world view was essentially Carolingian: that anointed kings ordered and directed all Christian society, including the Church. The other placed priests at the top of the hierarchy, since they were responsible for souls, even those of kings. These two incompatible notions of right order in the world resulted in a movement for reform led by the papacy that came to a clamorous crescendo in Pope Gregory VII's struggle with Emperor Henry IV.

Tellenbach himself considered the ultimate causes of the conflict beyond discernment,[17] but his interpretation constituted the first step toward contemporary "no-fault" explanations. Disorder was the fundamental cause of ecclesiastical disarray, and in the tenth century, well, disorder happens. Instead of trying to assess who behaved most badly in the midst of disorder, historians now take the more positive tack of assigning credit for actively working toward or accomplishing reform. In doing so they turned Fliche's interpretation upside down. Instead of the papacy rescuing the Church from the domination of the laity, scholars now champion lay people as the makers of reform. In a now classic article in the *American Historical Review*, John Howe brought together overwhelming evidence of the lay nobility's role in founding reformed monasteries and supporting episcopal, monastic, and papal reform efforts.[18] Other scholars emphasized the impact common lay people had through their participation in peace councils and in movements against married and simoniacal priests such as the Milanese *pataria*.[19]

Although the exact relationship of monastic reform to the late-eleventh-century papal reforms has been debated, there is broad consensus that tenth-century monastic reforms prepared the way for more general calls for reform of the entire Church in the eleventh. Fliche highlighted the role of Cluny in reforming other monasteries and building a powerful network of affiliated houses dedicated to a strict observance of the Benedictine Rule. His linkage of Cluny to the "Gregorian" reform of the late eleventh century was firmly rejected by Tellenbach, who saw monastic and papal reform as two separate movements with different ends.[20] H. E. J. Cowdrey and others, however, have countered by abandoning emphasis on causation and instead demonstrating the close collaboration of Cluny with papal reform efforts and the common ideas and beliefs that animated both movements.[21] The prominence of Cluny within narratives of monastic reform was challenged by Kassius Hallinger, however, in his monumental two-volume study of the Lotharingian monastery of Gorze and its affiliated houses. Hallinger successfully demonstrated that monastic reform was a broader phenomenon in the tenth century than Cluny-centered narratives suggested and that the reform of Gorze and other German monasteries occurred independently.[22] But the importance of Cluny has been reasserted by Joachim Wollasch. He argued that other movements in monastic reform were more dependent for their impetus upon local lords, both lay and ecclesiastical, with the result that reform waned when the support of patrons diminished. Gorze itself, Wollasch points out, had to be reformed again in the early eleventh century. Cluny, on the other hand, with its unique freedom from all secular and ecclesiastical lordship, became a more independent and enduring source of reform.[23]

Characterizations and Evaluations of Eleventh-Century Reform

The reigning interpretations of eleventh-century reform are currently those of Gerd Tellenbach and I. S. Robinson. Fifty years after the publication of *Libertas*, Tellenbach completed a lengthier study of the same historical events that largely restates, with some modifications, his earlier thesis. It has achieved wide diffusion both in Germany, where it was published as a "handbook" of Church history, and in Anglophone scholarship through its inclusion in the Cambridge Medieval Textbooks series. Whereas *Libertas* focused on the investiture conflict, Tellenbach's mature consideration is framed differently: its focus, as the title clearly indicates, is *The Church in Western Europe from the Tenth to the Early Twelfth Century*. This shift is important and reflects a broader trend away from the investiture conflict as the narrative frame of accounts of ecclesiastical change in late eleventh-century Europe. Chiefly, it is a response to the work of Rudolf Schieffer, whose 1981 monograph *Die Entstehung des päpstlichen Investiturverbots für den deutschen König* sundered historical confidence that the issue of lay investiture was at the root of the war between emperor and pope. In a meticulous examination of the evidence, Schieffer demonstrated that there was no mention of investiture in the correspondence leading up to Gregory's excommunication of Henry in 1076 and no definite prohibition of lay investiture until 1078. With this direct link between reform initiatives and the open breach between papacy and empire eliminated, historians had to reconsider their master narrative. Most now see the investiture conflict as the result of Gregory's war with Henry, not its cause.[24]

Tellenbach still devotes a third of his book to a narrative of the conflict between Gregory VII and Henry IV and is clearly reluctant to let go of investiture: he declares Schieffer's arguments "convincing" but contends that gradual "change in the conception of the laity's role in the church" led to growing concern about the practice. But the major change he charts in the book is the rise of papal monarchy and a new ecclesiology. The "revolution" is in the Church: the papacy's new ability to challenge lay power and promote its view of "right order in the world" – one in which the authority of priests is superior to the power of princes – was the central development of the era.[25] Tellenbach is skeptical of the extent of abuses such as clerical concubinage and simony; he sees opposition to lay influence in the Church as the key preoccupation of reformers. Reform in the eleventh century was about driving lay people out of the positions of power they held over Church offices and lands. He also argues that their "radical principles" were never realized and that Gregory's pontificate was a "tragedy." Tellenbach's sympathies are clearly with the emperors, whose "traditional" notions of right order endured: rulers in Western Europe continued to care for the Church and to foster Christianity within their kingdoms. But in the end Tellenbach admits that, if Gregory's radical principles "were hardly ever realized . . . even the compromises which were achieved transformed the Christian world." The transformation, in Tellenbach's view, was largely negative: the "idea of a church of the clergy" replaced the older notion of *ecclesia* as a unity of all Christians, and "the church took on conceptually the new form of a closed spiritual hierarchy."[26]

Some scholars, most notably Dominque Iogna-Pratt, have echoed Tellenbach's negative judgment, linking this more restrictive ecclesiology with a persecuting sociology. At the same time that the Church was being defined as a hierarchy of clerics, society was conceived as Christian so as to exclude, and ultimately persecute, Jews and heretics.[27] R. I. Moore has also posited connections between the Gregorian reform and the emergence of a "persecuting society" in the central Middle Ages. Papal reform's "struggle to impose Roman authority over local tradition" played a part in turning dissent into heresy.[28]

More positive characterizations and evaluations of reform have been articulated, but they tend to shift emphases rather than to confront Tellenbach head-on. The quandary here is how to launch a positive interpretation of eleventh-century reform without returning to Catholic apologetics. The least restrained by this qualm is H. E. J. Cowdrey, whose massive biography of Pope Gregory VII unabashedly proclaims him "one of the very greatest of popes" and is principally dedicated to proving that he was driven by "an inner spirituality that has been insufficiently appreciated." This scholarly work is a corrective to a tendency to evaluate Gregory and the reform movements as chiefly political – about power and property rather than religious beliefs. But Cowdrey's refusal to "present Gregory comprehensively against the background of his times or to establish his place in the longer development of the medieval church or of Latin Christendom"[29] leaves Tellenbach's interpretation unchallenged.

I. S. Robinson achieves a more objective tone and even-handed erudition in addressing both reform and the investiture struggle. After writing both a history of the eleventh- and twelfth-century papacy and a biography of Emperor Henry IV, he was invited to write the chapter of the *New Cambridge Medieval History* on "Reform and the Church, 1073–1122." Robinson differs from Tellenbach on several points. First, without trying to adjudicate the empirical problem of gauging the severity of abuses, Robinson urges us to take seriously the fact that both pro-imperial and pro-papal observers unanimously condemned simony and clerical unchastity. All agreed on the need for reform; they differed as to the definition of abuses and the best means to rectify them. Secondly, Robinson underscores different idealized notions of the past as central to eleventh-century views of reform. The "golden age" papal supporters wanted to revive was the fourth to sixth centuries, the era of Constantine and Gregory the Great, when emperors obeyed popes. Imperial supporters idealized a more recent past, the Ottonian era, when kings and bishops worked together to bring peace and reform to Church and society.[30]

Robinson would agree with Tellenbach that notions of hierarchy and the role of the laity were central themes of eleventh-century reform. He also shares Tellenbach's emphasis on questions of property as fundamental to both the perception of abuses and plans for reform. Most importantly, Robinson too sees the emergence of papal monarchy and a new ecclesiology as the most significant results of eleventh-century reform and the investiture struggle. He concludes:

> In Gregory VII's calls for obedience from bishops and in his opponents' accusations of "tyranny" we can identify a clash between two rival ecclesiologies: the centralising, monarchical ecclesiology of the reform papacy and the ecclesiology which the eleventh-century episcopate had inherited from the Carolingian and Ottonian ages.
>
> Theirs was a Christendom composed of autonomous "territorial churches" (*Landeskirchen*), governed by bishops meeting frequently in provincial or national synods, collaborating closely with kings in the regulation of ecclesiastical affairs. The ecclesiology which inspired the reforming activities of Gregory VII envisaged the universal church as a single unified institution directed by Rome. The central fact of the church's life, according to this vision, was the papal primacy, "which embraced the whole church like a single diocese, gathering to itself the fullness of power of the whole hierarchy, for the power of binding and loosing to the pastoral duty of preaching."[31]

What was most shocking and divisive to contemporaries were the violent *means* Gregory used to pursue his reform agenda: his use of military force to compel obedience, his appeals to social inferiors to rise up against their lords, and his sanction of direct lay action against unchaste priests. Tellenbach also depicted papal "style" and methods as new, but Robinson would define Gregory VII's improvised "emergency measures" as distinguishing reform in his era and warranting use of the term "Gregorian reform."[32] In the end, Robinson's evaluation of the emergence of a monarchical papacy and its attendant ecclesiology is more even-handed. He acknowledges both the institutional creativity of eleventh-century papal reformers as well as the legitimate criticisms of their excesses.

It merits underscoring at this point that, although the field has moved far from Fliche's confessional perspective, his emphasis on the papacy has certainly carried the day: whether for it or against it, historians agree that the most significant result of the eleventh-century reform movements and the investiture conflict was the emergence of papal monarchy. Real interpretative differences occur mainly in judging how or why this is significant. Tellenbach and his followers see it negatively, as hindering the development of the state and the establishing of a more "modern" restriction of religion to the private sphere. Those who disagree with this teleology toward the "modern" and the nation state emphasize the institutional creativity of the papacy, pointing out how the Church's institutional practices fostered the development of bureaucratic techniques and the rule of law.

Robinson deserves credit for rising above the confessional and nationalistic polemics of the French Catholic interpretation of Augustin Fliche and the German Lutheran stance of Gerd Tellenbach. He has achieved this relative equanimity to a certain extent by abandoning hope of empirical resolution of central questions and concentrating instead on listening attentively and critically to the rhetoric of the sources. The highly polemical character of those sources to a certain degree warrants such an approach. Robinson began his career studying the propagandistic tracts of the investiture conflict and in his biography of Henry IV grappled extensively with the problem of distilling empirical "truth" from rabidly partisan accounts. The concentration on discourse, however, ignores the possibilities offered by decades of local studies in sources extensively mined for social and economic history. It also misses the opportunity to engage with newer narratives of medieval history emerging from *Annales*-inspired "total history." Steps have been taken on both these fronts.

The salutary convergence of the turn to social and economic history and the tendency toward systematic regional coverage in European scholarship has yielded a great deal of data on ecclesiastical institutions and life in the eleventh and twelfth centuries. In Italy, for example, over the 1960s, 1970s, and 1980s, the "Settimane di studio" held at Mendola organized and presented research in documentary sources from regions throughout the peninsula on basic institutions of medieval Christianity (dioceses, parishes, monasteries, hermitages, canons).[33] French scholars, following the lead and model of Georges Duby's *thèse* on the Maconnaise, have reconstructed regional societies on the basis of charters throughout France and in Italy, and conferences on specific themes have gathered regional evidence on key reform topics, such as the secular clergy.[34] Specific studies of reform in local communities have also been accomplished and reveal that reform initiatives are evident from the late tenth and early eleventh centuries, that they occur in regions that remained staunchly pro-imperial, and that papal reforming initiatives often had a very limited impact.[35] The role of lay people as the makers of reform, in founding and supporting reform institutions (discussed above), was revealed in local documentary sources, such as charters. In sum, research in different sources, particularly local socioeconomic documents, calls into question the importance to reform of the papal–imperial struggle that still dominates accounts. More concerted systematic analysis of the empirical work done on local communities is necessary: this is a harvest awaiting the gathering.

The most productive recent work on eleventh-century reform has been engaging with newer narratives of the transformation of Europe over the central Middle Ages. These narratives still focus on explaining how more powerful monarchies and a more unified European culture emerged in the thirteenth century, but their explanations emphasize demographic, social, and economic developments (for example, the expansion of settlement, the rise of banal lordship). Did religious reform figure in these processes? R. I. Moore has suggested that the establishment of new communities and the social tensions engendered by rapid change made more important the priest's role as mediator, not just in a sacramental sense between parishioners and God, but in the terrestrial realm as peacemaker. Communities also increasingly wanted their priestly mediators to be impartial, not beholden to the local lord. Moore thus links opposition to simony and to clerical marriage to the terrestrial ties their priestly mediators had with local families and rulers. The concerns of the reform movement, in sum, grew out of new social conditions.[36] Other scholars have connected support for reform with the rise of new elite lineages and with the rapid multiplication of ecclesiastical institutions as Europe's population surged.[37] Kathleen G. Cushing has also argued that the reform movement had a decisive social impact: it helped define some of the new values that transformed the rough *milites* of the eleventh century into a more stable and educated aristocracy.[38]

A significant factor in the consolidation of that aristocracy was the disinheritance of women. Georges Duby pointed out that the enforcement of clerical celibacy and the Church's more restrictive definition of marriage contributed significantly to both lay and ecclesiastical efforts to protect property. Moore too has drawn attention to a confluence of interests among secular and ecclesiastical lords in this regard.[39] The significance of this attention to gender and property has been underscored by Conrad Leyser, who noted:

> it inverts conventional assumptions about the meaning of Reform. The famous and violent conflict between popes and kings, and between Pope Gregory VII and King Henry IV in particular, leads us instinctively to cast Reform as a battle between Church and State, clergy and laity. In Duby's perspective, however, the clash between Pope and King which dominates the media in fact conceals a fundamental collusion between clerical and lay interests, or at least a negotiated settlement, over the distribution of property.

Leyser and others have called attention to the rhetoric of gender: the ways in which reformers attack other men as being unduly influenced by women or contaminated by contact with them. He argues, rightly I think, that assessing the historically specific aims of such gendered discourses is more useful than interpreting them psychologically as male neurosis and misogyny motivating demands for priestly celibacy.[40] Indeed, Leyser's insight that the deployment of these gendered accusations reveals competition between monks and bishops suggests new ways to understand reform: were reform efforts in the tenth and eleventh centuries aimed at overturning the dominance that bishops had achieved in the Carolingian era and restructuring the Church to give greater weight to monastic institutions and values? Whether through the study of gender or local sources, the challenge before historians is to get beyond the dramatic story of Gregory VII's conflict with Henry IV and understand better the chronological and geographical contours of reform on a European-wide scale.

New Religious Movements

In 1935 Herbert Grundmann used the term *Religiöse Bewegungen* or "religious movements" to characterize a new interest in the "apostolic life" and in Christian poverty that emerged in the twelfth century and ultimately flowered in the thirteenth with the mendicants. A key insight Grundmann had was that medieval Christians trying to cultivate the *vita apostolica* could end up as either heretics or saints: the "religious movement" encompassed both the Humiliati, whose way of life was ultimately sanctioned by Pope Innocent III, and the Waldensians, who were condemned as heterodox and persecuted. Grundmann also posited a connection between reform and the twelfth-century religious movement that he described: the early seekers of the apostolic life had their religious desires "awakened" by the Gregorian reform. Reform and this twelfth-century religious movement, however, were distinct. This was chiefly because Grundmann defined ecclesiastical reform in the era of Gregory VII narrowly as completing "the structure or *ordo* of the hierarchical Church, which rested on the idea of apostolic succession, reserving the execution of Christian salvation to those who had been ordained to it either directly or indirectly by the successors of Peter and the apostles."[41] Historians today have a more capacious understanding of reform as including and generating varied religious movements. The eleventh and twelfth centuries were marked by a plethora of religious experiments, only some of which developed into enduring institutions or "orders." But certainly one of the most significant and lasting results of eleventh-century reform was this new variety in the forms and organization of religious life. In the early Middle Ages, to lead a religious life meant to leave the world and enter a monastery. From the eleventh century, not only did interpretations of monastic life change – with the emergence of reforming congregations like Cluny and eremitical orders like the Carthusians – but new models of what it meant to live a religious life, many pursued "in the world," emerged.[42] Since other contributions to this volume are devoted to monasticism, the mendicants, popular religion, and poverty, I will limit myself to pointing out the connections between reform and these new religious movements.

A comparison of the careers of Dominic of Sora (*c.* 960–1032) and Robert of Arbrissel (*c.* 1045–116) is a good place to start. Both were ordained to the priesthood, but fled to the wilderness to become hermits. Dominic spent years as a monk before retreating to a mountaintop with his abbot's permission; Robert was archpriest in the diocese of Rennes and then studied in Angers before he embarked upon an eremitic life in the forest of Craon. Both, however, traveled a great deal over the rest of their lives, preaching, attracting followers, and founding religious communities. Dominic littered southern Umbria, Lazio, and the Abruzzi with small monasteries. Robert founded first a community of regular canons at La Roë, and then a mixed encampment of male and female followers that ultimately became the monastery of Fontrevaud and several daughter houses. Both were remembered as charismatic preachers and as ascetics; both cultivated chastity and exhorted fellow clerics to follow their example. Dominic has a stronger liturgical profile: his preaching is always depicted in the context of the mass and his priestly virtues highlighted. He drove out married priests and their wives. Poverty is a stronger theme in Robert's *vitae*, but he too worked for reform. As archpriest, Baudri of Dol recounts, "while restoring peace among those at odds, freeing the church from shameful servitude to lay people, and putting a stop to the sinful fornications of clergy and laity, he utterly abhorred simony, and manfully opposed all vices."[43] Although Grundmann included only Robert in his religious movement, these religious seekers followed similar paths and worked for reform.

If hermit-preachers were one trend in religious life related to reform, regular canons were another. From the ninth century, communal living arrangements had been urged on the secular clergy to help them live chaste and virtuous lives. The formation of clerical communities at parish churches can be documented across the tenth century; they served as training centers for the schooling and formation of priests. But many rural communities and urban parishes were fortunate to have one priest, and bishops realized the formidable financial obstacles to gathering all their clergy into communal living arrangements. Attempts to achieve the ideal, however, led not only to the founding of communities of secular clerics but also to the composition of customs or institutes to order their communal religious life, the most popular of which were those of the canons regular of St John Lateran, St Victor in Paris, St Ruf in Avignon, and St Mary in Porto (Ravenna). Called "regular" because they lived under a rule (usually that of St Augustine, supplemented by a set of customs), these clerics cultivated the apostolic life, many dedicating themselves to pastoral care. Bishops are chiefly responsible for fostering the establishment of communities of regular canons, but Hildebrand (later Gregory VII) promoted them as a means for reforming the secular clergy at the Lateran Synod of 1059, and later popes continued these efforts.[44]

Although the model of the apostolic life was initially urged on the secular clergy by reformers as a valorizing ideal, lay people were also inspired by it. Their enthusiasm begins in the eleventh century with popular reforming movements such as the *pataria*. Best documented in Milan, but also evident in other Italian cities, this grassroots pressure group had clerical leaders – such as the Ariald of Carimate and Landulf "Cotta" – but the mass of its supporters were lay men and women. Reform issues are most prominent in the *pataria*, particularly the "strike" organized against married and simoniacal priests in Milan in which lay people refused the sacraments from impure clerics. But the defining aspects of the *vita apostolica* are already evident. Popular preaching figures prominently in accounts of the *pataria* and would become the most contested aspect of lay movements: the Waldensians and Humiliati were forbidden to preach publicly without episcopal sanction and were condemned as heretical when they failed to heed such strictures. Andrea of Strumi's life of Ariald also extols how the patarene leader's "every effort and action was directed toward putting into practice what he read in Sacred Scripture," particularly in giving to the poor and to beggars.[45]

Relieving the suffering of the poor became the central mission in lay cultivation of the apostolic life, and it found more ready acceptance and support from ecclesiastical leaders than did lay enthusiasm for preaching. From the twelfth century the lay foundation of hospitals soared. Intensely local institutions, these places for the care of the poor and infirm were often established and run by lay people. In Catalonia, for example, Bishop Deodat of Barcelona built a hospital in 1024, a layman named Arnau founded one next to the cathedral at Urgell in 1024, and Arsendis, wife of Arnau Mir, in 1068 asked her spouse to establish four shelters for the infirm in local communities. Verona had so many hospitals by the early thirteenth century that the bishop attempted to consolidate them.[46]

In sum, eleventh-century reform was a key catalyst in transforming religious life in medieval Europe. Monastic reform and new monastic congregations were supported by the reformed papacy, which also fostered lay groups galvanized by reform issues such as simony and clerical unchastity. Lay activism, once awakened, supported and created new kinds of institutions and orders, from hospitals to confraternities to the Mendicants. This accomplished a radical democratization of the religious life in Western Europe.

Notes

1 A good example of this mid-twentieth century synthesis is Boussard, *Civilization*, pp. 92–117.
2 Claussen, *Reform of the Frankish Church*, pp. 265–89.
3 Wood, *Missionary Life*, especially pp. 1–20; Russell, *Germanization*, pp. 26–44.
4 Brown, *Rise of Western Christendom*, pp. 439–46.
5 McKitterick, *Frankish Church*, is the classic articulation of this new view.
6 Riché, *Carolingians*, p. 117.
7 De Jong, "*Sacrum palatium et ecclesia*," p. 1245.
8 McKitterick, *Frankish Church*, p. 15.
9 De Jong, "*Imitatio Morum*," pp. 49–64; McKitterick, *Frankish Church*, p. 63.
10 Gaillard, *D'une reforme à l'autre*.
11 Fliche, *La Réforme grégorienne*, vol. 1, pp. 23–92, 108–59; vol. 2, pp. 103–8, 420–4.
12 Tellenbach, *Church, State and Christian Society*, pp. 1 (quotation), 55–60, 97–9, 108–9, 167–8 (quotation).
13 Robinson, *Authority and Resistance*; Kuttner, "Revival of Jurisprudence"; Blumenthal, *Investiture Controversy*, pp. 70–3, 102; Gilchrist, *The Collection in Seventy-Four Titles*.
14 Capitani, "Esiste un 'età gregoriana'?"; Hicks, "The Investiture Controversy."
15 Cantor, *Church, Kingship, and Lay Investiture*; Tierney, *Crisis of Church and State*; Tierney, "Freedom and the Medieval Church."
16 Morrison, review, p. 999.
17 Tellenbach, *Church, State and Christian Society*, p. 163; Tellenbach, *The Church in Western Europe*, p. 140.
18 Howe, "Nobility's Reform," pp. 317–39.
19 Moore, "Family, Community and Cult," pp. 49–69; Moore, *First European Revolution*, pp. 14–15, 81–8; Remensnyder, "Pollution, Purity, and Peace," p. 282; Howe, *Church Reform & Social Change*, pp. 97–122, 160–2.
20 Tellenbach, *Church, State and Christian Society*, pp. 82–3, 186–92; Tellenbach, *The Church in Western Europe*, pp. 113–14, 117–20, 342; Howe, *Church Reform & Social Change*, p. xv.
21 Cowdrey, *The Cluniacs and the Gregorian Reform*; Iogna-Pratt, *Order and Exclusion*, pp. 16–25, 360–4.
22 Hallinger, *Gorze-Kluny*; Rosenwein, *Rhinoceros Bound*, pp. 16–18; Blumenthal, *Investiture Controversy*, pp. 7–19.
23 Wollasch, "Monasticism," pp. 163–85.
24 Blumenthal, *Investiture Controversy*, pp. 113–27.
25 Tellenbach, *The Church in Western Europe*, pp. 177–84; see also pp. xiv–xv, 65–74, 135, 185–222, 237, 251–52, 304–34.
26 Ibid., pp. 157–84, 187 (quotation), 249–52, 334–7, 348, 351.
27 Iogna-Pratt, *Order and Exclusion*, pp. 16–25, 359–65.
28 Moore, *Formation*, pp. 69–72; Moore, "Heresy, Repression, and Social Change."
29 Cowdrey, *Pope Gregory VII*, pp. vii, 694.
30 Robinson, "Reform and the Church," pp. 271–86.

31 Ibid., pp. 322–3.
32 Tellenbach, *The Church in Western Europe*, 204–5, 322–34; Robinson, "Reform and the Church," 332–4.
33 *La vita comune del clero*; *L'eremitismo in Occidente*; *Le istituzioni ecclesiastiche . . . Diocesi, pievi e parrocchie*; *Chiesa, diritto e ordinamento.*
34 As just a few examples, Magnou-Nortier on Narbonne, Devailly on Berry, and Toubert on Latium specifically address evidence for reform: Magnou-Nortier, *La Société laïque*, pp. 447–518; Devailly, *Le Berry*, pp. 239–85, 475–517; Toubert, *Les Structures*, pp. 789–933. See also *Le Clerc séculier au moyen age.*
35 Laudage, *Priesterbild*, pp. 94–115; Cushing, *Reform and the Papacy*, p. 107; Milo, "Dissonance"; Miller, *Formation*, pp. 50–8; Ramseyer, *Transformation of a Religious Landscape*, pp. 191–2, 195.
36 Moore, "Family, Community and Cult"; Moore, *First European Revolution*, pp. 61–2.
37 Howe, *Church Reform & Social Change*, pp. 97–116, 158–62; Miller, *Formation*, pp. 22–62, 175–7.
38 Cushing, *Reform and the Papacy*, pp. 139–59.
38 Duby, *The Knight*, pp. 116–20, 282–4; Moore, *First European Revolution*, pp. 81–111.
40 Leyser, "Custom, Truth, and Gender," pp. 77–8, 80 (quotation); Miller, "Masculinity, Reform, and Clerical Culture"; for psychological approaches see McNamara, "The *Herrenfrage*"; Elliott, *Fallen Bodies*, pp. 14–34, 81–126.
41 Grundmann, *Religious Movements*, p. 7; on Grundmann, see Van Engen, "The Christian Middle Ages," pp. 522–4.
42 Constable, *Reformation*, pp. 44–87; Bynum, *Jesus*, pp. 9–21; Van Engen, "The Christian Middle Ages," pp. 523–30.
43 Venarde, *Robert of Arbrissel*, pp. xx–xxix, 1–21 (quotation, p. 11); Howe, *Church Reform & Social Change*, pp. 24–66.
44 Miller, *The Formation*, pp. 39–62, 80–6; Bynum, *Jesus as Mother*, pp. 22–58; Blumenthal, *Investiture Controversy*, 68–9, 101–2; Cowdrey, *Pope Gregory VII*, pp. 45–6.
45 Vauchez, *The Laity*; Violante, "I laici"; Cowdrey, "The Papacy, the Patarenes"; Golinelli, *La Pataria*, pp. 35–47, 59–61, 88.
46 Brodman, *Charity and Welfare*, p. 30; de Sandre Gasparini, "L'assistenza," pp. 25–59; Miller, *Formation*, pp. 87–92.

Bibliography

Benson, Robert, ed., *Imperial Lives and Letters of the Eleventh Century*, trans. Theodor E. Mommsen and Karl F. Morrison (New York: Columbia University Press, 1962; repr., 2000).

Blumenthal, Uta-Renate, *The Investiture Controversy: Church and Monarchy from the Ninth to the Twelfth Century* (Philadelphia: University of Pennsylvania Press, 1988).

Boussard, Jacques, *The Civilization of Charlemagne* (New York: McGraw, 1968).

Brodman, James William, *Charity and Welfare: Hospitals and the Poor in Medieval Catalonia* (Philadelphia: University of Pennsylvania Press, 1998).

Brown, Peter, *The Rise of Western Christendom*, 2nd edn (Malden, MA: Blackwell, 2003).

Bynum, Caroline Walker, *Jesus as Mother: Studies in the Spirituality of the High Middle Ages* (Berkeley and Los Angeles: University of California Press, 1982).

Cantor, Norman F., *Church, Kingship, and Lay Investiture in England 1089–1135* (Princeton: Princeton University Press, 1958).

Capitani, Ovidio, "Esiste un 'età gregoriana'? Considerazioni sulle tendenze di una storiografia medievistica," *Rivista di storia e letteratura religiosa*, 1 (1965), pp. 454–81.

Chiesa, diritto e ordinamento della "societas Christiana" nei secoli XI e XII: Atti della nona Settimana internazionale di studio, Mendola, 28 agosto–2 settembre 1983 (Milan: Vita e pensiero, 1986).

Claussen, M. A., *The Reform of the Frankish Church: Chrodegang of Metz and the* Regula canonicorum *in the Eighth Century* (Cambridge: Cambridge University Press, 2004).

Constable, Giles, *The Reformation of the Twelfth Century* (Cambridge: University Press, 1996).

Cowdrey, H. E. J., *The Cluniacs and the Gregorian Reform* (Oxford: Clarendon Press, 1970).

Cowdrey, H. E. J., "The Papacy, the Patarenes and the Church of Milan," in H. E. J. Cowdrey, *Popes, Monks and Crusaders* (London: Hambledon Press, 1984), pp. 25–48.

Cowdrey, H. E. J., *Pope Gregory VII 1073–1085* (Oxford: Clarendon Press, 1998).

Cowdrey, H. E. J., *The Register of Pope Gregory VII 1073–1085: An English Translation* (Oxford: Oxford University Press, 2002).

Cushing, Kathleen G., *Reform and the Papacy in the Eleventh Century: Spirituality and Social Change* (Manchester: Manchester University Press, 2005).

De Jong, Makye, "*Imitatio morum*: The Cloister and Clerical Purity in the Carolingian World," in Michael Frassetto, ed., *Medieval Purity and Piety: Essays on Medieval Clerical Celibacy and Religious Reform* (New York: Garland, 1998), pp. 49–80.

De Jong, Makye, "*Sacrum palatium et ecclesia*: L'Autorité religieuse royale sous les Carolingiens (790–840)," *Annales: Histoire, Sciences Sociales*, 58/6 (2003), pp. 1243–69.

De Sandre Gasparini, Giuseppina, "L'assistenza ai lebbrosi nel movimento religioso dei primi decenni del duocento veronese: Uomini e fatti," in Maria Chiara Billanovich, Giorgio Cracco, and Antonio Rigon, eds, *Viridarium floridum: Studi di storia veneta offerti dagli allievi a Paolo Sambin* (Padua: Antenore, 1984), pp. 25–59.

Devailly, Guy, *Le Berry du Xe siècle au milieu du XIIIe: Étude politique, religieuse, sociale, et économique* (Paris: Mouton, 1973).

Duby, Georges, *The Knight, the Lady, and the Priest*, trans. Barbara Bray (Chicago: University of Chicago Press, 1993).

Elliott, Dyan, *Fallen Bodies: Pollution, Sexuality, & Demonology in the Middle Ages* (Philadelphia: University of Pennsylvania Press, 1999).

Fliche, Augustin, *La Réforme grégorienne*, 3 vols., Spicilegium sacrum Lovaniensis, Études et documents 6, 9, 16 (Louvain: Spicilegium sacrum Lovaniensis, and Paris: E. Champion, 1924–37).

Gaillard, Michèle, *D'une reforme à l'autre (816–934): Les Communautés réligieuses en Lorraine à l'époque carolingienne* (Paris: Publications de la Sorbonne, 2006).

Gilchrist, John T., *The Collection in Seventy-Four Titles: A Canon Law Manual of the Gregorian Reform* (Toronto: Pontifical Institute of Mediaeval Studies, 1980).

Golinelli, Paolo, ed., *La Pataria: Lotte religiose e sociali nella Milano dell'XI secolo* (Milan: Jaca Book, 1984).

Grundmann, Herbert, *Religious Movements in the Middle Ages*, trans. Steven Rowan, ed. Robert L. Lerner (Notre Dame, IN: University of Notre Dame Press, 1995).

Hallinger, Kassius, *Gorze-Kluny: Studien zu den monastischen Lebensformen und Gegensätzen im Hochmittelalter*, 2 vols (Graz: Akadem. Druck-u. Verlagsanst., 1971).

Hicks, Sandy B., "The Investiture Controversy of the Middle Ages, 1075–1122: Agreement and Disagreement among Historians," *Journal of Church and State*, 15 (1973), pp. 5–20.

Howe, John, *Church Reform & Social Change in Eleventh-Century Italy: Dominic of Sora and his Patrons* (Philadelphia: University of Pennsylvania Press, 1997).
Howe, John, "The Nobility's Reform of the Medieval Church," *American Historical Review*, 93/2 (1988), pp. 317–39.
Iogna-Prat, Dominique, *Order and Exclusion: Cluny and Christendom Face Heresy, Judaism, and Islam (1000–1150)*, trans. Graham Robert Edwards (Ithaca, NY: Cornell University Press, 2002).
Kuttner, Stephan, "The Revival of Jurisprudence," in Robert L. Benson, Giles Constable, and Carol D. Lanham, eds, *Renaissance and Renewal in the Twelfth Century* (Cambridge, MA: Harvard University Press, 1982; repr. Toronto: Medieval Academy Reprints for Teaching/ University of Toronto Press, 1991), pp. 299–323.
Laudage, Johannes, *Priesterbild und Reformpapsttum im 11. Jahrhundert* (Cologne: Böhlau, 1984).
La vita comune del clero nei secoli XI e XII: Atti della settimana di studio: Mendola, settembre 1959, 2 vols (Milan: Vita e pensiero, 1962).
Le Clerc séculier au moyen age: XXIIe Congrès de la S.H.M.E.S. (Amiens, juin 1991) (Paris: Publications de la Sorbonne, 1993).
Le istituzioni ecclesiastiche della "societas Christiana" dei secoli XI–XII: Diocesi, pievi e parrocchie: Atti della sesta settimana internazionale di studio, Milano, 1–7 settembre 1974 (Milan: Vita e pensiero, 1974).
L'eremitismo in Occidente nei secoli XI e XII: Atti della seconda settimana internazionale di studio, Mendola, 30 agosto–6 settembre 1962 (Milan: Vita e pensiero, 1965).
Leyser, Conrad, "Custom, Truth and Gender in Eleventh-Century Reform," *Studies in Church History*, 34 (1998), pp. 75–91.
McKitterick, Rosamond, *The Frankish Church and the Carolingian Reforms, 789–895* (London: Royal Historical Society, 1977).
McNamara, Jo Ann, "The *Herrenfrage*: The Restructuring of the Gender System, 1050–1150," in Clare A. Lees, ed., *Medieval Masculinities: Regarding Men in the Middle Ages* (Minneapolis: University of Minnesota Press, 1994), pp. 3–29.
Magnou-Nortier, Elisabeth, *La Société laïque et l'Église dans la province ecclésiastique de Narbonne (zone cispyrénéenne) de la fin du VIIIe à la fin du XIe siècle* (Toulouse: Association des publications de l'Université de Toulouse-Le Mirail, 1974).
Milo, Yoram, "Dissonance between Papal and Local Reform Interests in Pre-Gregorian Tuscany," *Studi medievali*, ser. 3, 20 (1979), pp. 69–86.
Miller, Maureen C., *The Formation of a Medieval Church: Ecclesiastical Change in Verona, 950–1150* (Ithaca, NY: Cornell University Press, 1993).
Miller, Maureen C., "Masculinity, Reform, and Clerical Culture: Narratives of Episcopal Holiness in the Gregorian Reform Era," *Church History*, 72/1 (2003), pp. 1–28.
Miller, Maureen C., *Power and the Holy in the Age of the Investiture Conflict* (Boston: Bedford-St Martin's, 2005).
Moore, R. I., "Family, Community and Cult on the Eve of the Gregorian Reform," *Transactions of the Royal Historical Society*, ser. 5, 30 (1980), pp. 49–69.
Moore, R. I., *The First European Revolution* c. *970–1215* (Oxford: Blackwell, 2000).
Moore, R. I., *The Formation of a Persecuting Society: Power and Deviance in Western Europe, 950–1250* (Oxford: Blackwell, 1998).
Moore, R. I., "Heresy, Repression, and Social Change in the Age of Gregorian Reform," in Scott L. Waugh and Peter D. Diehl, eds, *Christendom and its Discontents: Exclusion, Persecution, and Rebellion, 1000–1500* (Cambridge: University Press, 1996), pp. 19–46.
Morrison, Karl F., review of Brigitte Szabó-Bechstein, *Libertas ecclesiae: Ein Schlüsselbegriff des Investiturstreits und seine Vorgeschichte, 4.–11. Jahrhundert*, *Speculum*, 62 (1987), pp. 998–9.

Ramseyer, Valerie, *The Transformation of a Religious Landscape: Medieval Southern Italy, 850–1150* (Ithaca, NY: Cornell University Press, 2006).

Remensnyder, Amy G., "Pollution, Purity, and Peace: An Aspect of Social Reform between the Late Tenth Century and 1076," in Thomas Head and Richard Landes, eds, *The Peace of God: Social Violence and Religious Response in France around the year 1000* (Ithaca, NY: Cornell University Press, 1992), pp. 280–307.

Riché, Pierre, *The Carolingians: A Family Who Forged Europe*, trans. Michael Idomir Allen (Philadelphia: University of Pennsylvania Press, 1993).

Robinson, I. S., *Authority and Resistance in the Investiture Contest: The Polemical Literature of the Late Eleventh Century* (Manchester: Manchester University Press; New York: Holmes & Meier, 1978).

Robinson, I. S., *Henry IV of Germany, 1056–1106* (Cambridge: Cambridge University Press, 1999).

Robinson, I. S., *The Papacy 1073–1198: Continuity and Innovation* (Cambridge: Cambridge University Press, 1990).

Robinson, I. S., *The Papal Reform of the Eleventh Century: Lives of Pope Leo IX and Pope Gregory VII* (Manchester: Manchester University Press, 2004).

Robinson, I. S., "Pope Gregory VII (1973–1085)," *Journal of Ecclesiastical History*, 36/3 (1985), pp. 439–85.

Robinson, I. S., "Reform and the Church, 1073–1122," in David Luscombe and Jonathan Riley-Smith, eds, *The New Cambridge Medieval History IV*: c. *102–1198, Part I* (Cambridge: Cambridge University Press, 2004), pp. 268–334.

Rosenwein, Barbara H., *Rhinoceros Bound: Cluny in the Tenth Century* (Philadelphia: University of Pennsylvania Press, 1982).

Russell, James C., *The Germanization of Early Medieval Christianity: A Sociohistorical Approach to Religious Transformation* (Oxford: Oxford University Press, 1994).

Sullivan, Richard E., "The Carolingian Age: Reflections on its Place in the History of the Middle Ages," *Speculum*, 64 (1989), pp. 267–93.

Tellenbach, Gerd, *Church, State and Christian Society at the Time of the Investiture Contest*, trans. R. F. Bennett (Oxford: Basil Blackwell, 1940; repr. Cambridge, MA: Medieval Academy of America, 1991).

Tellenbach, Gerd, *The Church in Western Europe from the Tenth to the Early Twelfth Century*, trans. Timothy Reuter (Cambridge: Cambridge University Press, 1993).

Tierney, Brian, *The Crisis of Church and State 1050–1300* (Englewood Cliffs, NJ: Prentice-Hall, 1964).

Tierney, Brian, "Freedom and the Medieval Church," in R. W. Davis, ed., *The Origins of Modern Freedom in the West* (Stanford, CA: Stanford University Press, 1995), pp. 64–100.

Toubert, Pierre, *Les Structures de Latium medieval: Le Latium méridional et la Sabine du IXe siècle à la fin du XIIe siècle*, 2 vols (Rome: École française de Rome, 1973).

Van Engen, John, "The Christian Middle Ages as an Historiographical Problem," *American Historical Review*, 91 (1986), pp. 519–82.

Vauchez, André, *The Laity in the Middle Ages: Religious Beliefs and Devotional Practices*, trans. Margery J. Schneider, ed. Daniel E. Bornstein (Notre Dame, IN: University of Notre Dame Press, 1993).

Venarde, Bruce L., *Robert of Arbrissel: A Medieval Religious Life* (Washington: Catholic University of America Press, 2003).

Violante, Cinzio, "I laici nel movimento patarino," in Piero Zerbi, ed., *Studi sulla Cristianità medioevale: Società, istituzioni, spiritualità* (Milan: Vita e pensiero, 1972).

Weinfurter, Stefan, *The Salian Century: Main Currents in an Age of Transition*, trans. Barbara M. Bowlus (Philadelphia: University of Pennsylvania Press, 1999).

Wollasch, Joachim, "Monasticism: The First Wave of Reform," in Timothy Reuter, ed., *The New Cambridge Medieval History, vol. III* c. *900*–c. *1024* (Cambridge: Cambridge University Press, 1995), pp. 163–85.

Wood, Ian, *The Missionary Life: Saints and the Evangelisation of Europe 400–1050* (Harlow: Longman/Pearson, 2001).

Further Reading

The essential work on Carolingian reform is still Rosamund McKitterick, *The Frankish Church and the Carolingian Reforms, 789–895* (London: Royal Historical Society, 1977).; see Richard E. Sullivan, "The Carolingian Age: Reflections on its Place in the History of the Middle Ages," *Speculum*, 64 (1989), pp. 267–93, on the place of ecclesiastical history in the broader historiography of Carolingian Europe.

For eleventh-century reform and the investiture conflict, the best point of entry into the subject is Uta-Renate Blumenthal, *The Investiture Controversy: Church and Monarchy from the Ninth to the Twelfth Century* (Philadelphia: University of Pennsylvania Press, 1988), but the key works are still Augustin Fliche, *La Réforme grégorienne*, 3 vols., Spicilegium sacrum Lovaniensis, Études et documents 6, 9, 16 (Louvain: Spicilegium sacrum Lovaniensis, and Paris: E. Champion, 1924–37); Gerd Tellenbach, *Church, State and Christian Society at the Time of the Investiture Contest*, trans. R. F. Bennett (Oxford: Basil Blackwell, 1940; repr. Cambridge, MA: Medieval Academy of America, 1991), and *The Church in Western Europe from the Tenth to the Early Twelfth Century*, trans. Timothy Reuter (Cambridge: Cambridge University Press, 1993); and I. S. Robinson, "Reform and the Church, 1073–1122," in David Luscombe and Jonathan Riley-Smith, eds, *The New Cambridge Medieval History IV*: c. *102–*c.*1198, Part I* (Cambridge: Cambridge University Press, 2004), pp. 268–334. Useful collections of sources with introductions are Brian Tierney, *The Crisis of Church & State 1050–1300* (Englewood Cliffs, NJ: Prentice-Hall, 1964), and Maureen C. Miller, *Power and the Holy in the Age of the Investiture Conflict* (Boston: Bedford-St Martin's, 2005). On Gregory VII, I. S. Robinson, "Pope Gregory VII (1073–1085)," *Journal of Ecclesiastical History*, 36/3 (1985), pp. 439–85, is a masterful bibliographical survey of work on Gregory from 1947 to 1985; an encyclopedic biography has been provided by H. E. J. Cowdrey, *Pope Gregory VII 1073–1085* (Oxford: Clarendon Press, 1998); Cowdrey has also translated the main corpus of Gregory's letters: H. E. J. Cowdrey, *The Register of Pope Gregory VII 1073–1085: An English Translation* (Oxford: Oxford University Press, 2002). Paul of Bernreid's life of Pope Gregory VII, along with the life of Pope Leo IX and Bonizo of Sutri's *Liber ad amicum*, have been translated by I. S. Robinson in *The Papal Reform of the Eleventh Century: Lives of Pope Leo IX and Pope Gregory VII* (Manchester: Manchester University Press, 2004). On Henry IV, Robinson's *Henry IV of Germany, 1056–1106* (Cambridge: Cambridge University Press, 1999), is an excellent detailed political biography; Stefan Weinfurter, *The Salian Century: Main Currents in an Age of Transition*, trans. Barbara M. Bowlus (Philadelphia: University of Pennsylvania Press, 1999), provides a cogent analysis of the investiture conflict in the broad context of changing concepts of lordship in the eleventh-century empire. The anonymous life of Henry IV and his letters are still available in English in Robert Benson, ed., *Imperial Lives and Letters of the Eleventh Century*, trans. Theodor E. Mommsen, Karl F. Morrison (New York: Columbia University Press, 1962; repr. 2000). R. I. Moore, "Family, Community and Cult on the Eve of the Gregorian Reform," *Transactions of the Royal Historical Society*, ser. 5, 30 (1980), pp. 49–69, and Dominique Iogna-Prat, *Order and Exclusion: Cluny and Christendom Face Heresy, Judaism, and Islam (1000–1150)*, trans. Graham Robert Edwards (Ithaca, NY: Cornell University Press, 2002), are the best introductions to recent perspectives.

Giles Constable, *The Reformation of the Twelfth Century* (Cambridge: University Press, 1996), beautifully describes the new variety of religious life and its relation to reform, although the first two chapters of Herbert Grundmann, *Religious Movements in the Middle Ages*, trans. Steven Rowan, ed. Robert L. Lerner (Notre Dame, IN: University of Notre Dame Press, 1995), are still a wonderfully readable introduction to the *vita apostolica*. The historiography of medieval Christianity is still best treated in John Van Engen, "The Christian Middle Ages as an Historiographical Problem," *American Historical Review*, 91 (1986), pp. 519–82.

Chapter Eleven

Monastic and Mendicant Communities

Constance H. Berman

Christian monasticism has its biblical roots in the austerities of the forty days Jesus of Nazareth spent in the desert, but also in the community of his followers who lived together after his ascension. It is the institutional practice of a "higher" Christian life, today most often thought to encompass the vows of poverty, chastity, and obedience. Early Christian monks or nuns sought closeness to God by pursuing lives of self-denial and austerity, or asceticism. Such Christians had parallels in Jewish ascetic groups such as the Essenes or the community at Masada, as well as in Greek philosophical communities.[1] From the earliest Christian centuries there were ascetic Christian women who lived monastic lives as consecrated virgins or veiled widows in family homes, devoting their lives to prayer and chastity. Eventually communities of such women were founded, for instance, that at Bethlehem founded by St Jerome's friend and patron, Paula.[2] When the spokesmen for medieval Christian monasticism looked back to their origins, however, they pointed to the "desert fathers" as the founders of monasticism: St Anthony the hermit (d. *c.* 250), whose life was written by Athanasius, patriarch of Alexandria (*c.* 298–373), and St Pachomius (*c.* 292–346), the converted soldier, founder of a monastic community at Tabennisa in the Egyptian desert, modeled on a Roman military camp.[3] There was further identification by medieval monastics and mendicants with the *vita apostolica*, the life of the early apostles, and with the Gospel sisters Martha and Mary, who represented the active and contemplative lives respectively.[4]

To become a monk or a nun was to deny oneself marriage, family, political office, and clerical duties, to leave father and mother, sister and brother, possessions and worldly concerns, and bearing arms, to follow a higher Christian life. At first, monasticism was a flight from the life of the cities. The words "monk" and "monasticism" come from the Greek word *monos* for "alone," and the *monacus* or *monaca* was originally someone living alone in the desert. Only later was a distinction made between those *monachi* who were organized into communities living a common life (*koinos bios*, hence cenobitic communities) and those who continued to live alone in the desert or *eremus* (hence hermits or eremitical communities). There were also those monastics who wandered from place to place (the *gyrovagues*) and those who traveled to holy places as pilgrims. The monastic life might be embraced by married couples, who took vows to live chastely within marriage, or by those who lived by begging (mendicancy). In late antiquity mendicants were one type of monks, and the life of begging or mendicancy one aspect of early monasticism.[5]

In the early centuries of Christianity, monastics often saw themselves as "athletes for Christ," competing with one another in the practice of asceticism or self-mortification. They rejected clerical service in urban Christian communities in their search for a more perfect life of prayer. Monks were distinct from priests in not having been ordained, and in having no share in the ecclesiastical hierarchy, or in priestly ordination for celebration of the mass. Both monks and nuns took religious vows, and there was hence little gender distinction within early monasticism, although usually men's and women's communities were separate. On occasion such communities were "double" ones, with men and women living chastely together under a single roof, sharing a single church, but otherwise segregated. Such double communities appeared for brief periods in the West – the most famous being Whitby in seventh-century Anglo-Saxon England, early twelfth-century Fontevrault in Anjou, and the fifteenth-century Bridgittine house of Syon, which was part of an order founded by Birgitta of Sweden *c.* 1370.[6]

Early monasticism made its inroads primarily among the most devout within Christian communities. Although some monks or hermits, like the great desert saint, Simeon Stylite, who lived on a pillar in the Syrian wilderness for decades, became figures of great sanctity and authority, early monasticism was often viewed with dismay by Christian authorities. Such Christians "fleeing to the desert" abandoned familial and civic responsibilities, and in their failure to reproduce or hold civic office threatened the Roman social fabric and brought opprobrium on their religion. Monks wandering from place to place in a self-absorbed pursuit of their own salvation disrupted clerical attempts to gain legitimacy for Christianity, and they were often a burden on urban Christian communities. Hordes of monks are described as descending like locusts on the cities of the Empire, begging for food and shelter, involving themselves in ecclesiastical politics and elections, arrogant about their own celibacy and perfection, and respecting no authority but their own.[7] Their praise of chastity and condemnation of priestly marriage pushed the clerical hierarchy toward increased celibacy, fear of contamination by women, and anti-feminism if not outright misogyny, leaving the role of women within early Christianity to be undermined and forgotten.[8]

But, while monastic praise of virginity and chastity increasingly monasticized the clergy, particularly in the West, monasticism itself was being tamed. It was soon defined as a life lived in community in obedience to a leader or rule. Monks and hermits who had once gone for years without seeing another soul were enjoined to participate in weekly celebration of mass, even if they then returned to their individual cells. Excessive self-mortification was replaced by moderation and humility. Monks and nuns were enjoined by bishops and other reformers to seek perfection by regular prayer for the souls of the larger Christian community, and to share a common table, a common purse, and personal poverty. Stability was adopted as a monastic virtue and would lead eventually to idealization of monastic enclosure, particularly for women. Monastic reformers evoking the discipline of the military camp or obedience to the paterfamilias of the great Senatorial household gradually brought the extremists of asceticism under control through obedience to an abbot or abbess, whose power mimicked that of the Roman father. Indeed the term abbot comes from the Hebrew word for father, *ab* (in Syriac *abba*, in Latin *abbas*, *abbatis*), and the abbess in this sense is not a mother, but a female father.

When persecutions of Christians ended in the fourth century, churches and communities had begun to spring up outside the walls of Roman cities on the burial spots of local martyrs and saints. Monastic prayers and burial in monastic cemeteries would become valued because of the vicinity of those saints.[9] As monastic communities increasingly imitated the social organization of the late Roman family, so too did the typical monastery imitate the physical layout of the great Greek or Roman house, with its series of arcaded rooms looking inward on atrium and peristyle with its pools and colonnaded garden. The Roman *domus* was thus transformed into a monastic enclosure with the church adjoining a garden surrounded by a colonnaded cloister linking it to chapter house, refectory, scriptorium, and living quarters.[10]

Increasingly nuns and monks took religious vows of obedience to a monastic rule (*regula*); thus monks were henceforth considered "regular" clergy, in contrast to the "secular" clergy who had taken priestly orders (been ordained) but had not taken monastic vows. Rather than performing the mass (the exclusive activity of priests), monks and nuns punctuated their lives with regular prayer or praise, the Divine Office, celebrated at set times each day, the monastic hours. This Divine Office, which derived from Jewish recitation of the Hebrew Psalms, would eventually encompass the collective recital of the entire book of Psalms over the course of a week. It required no priestly intermediary and did not exclude monastic women, whose prayers were considered to be equal to those of men within the monastic life.[11] In the early Middle Ages few monks were priests. Only from the ninth or tenth century would most monks be ordained as priests; reform movements tended to resist and reverse this clericalization of monasticism.[12]

Abbesses and abbots in late antiquity were those wealthy Christians who founded monasteries, using their own wealth to support and endow those communities. Gradually rules evolved about who should rule religious communities. Abbots and abbesses should be at least 20 years old. They could not inherit their positions. After the eleventh-century Gregorian reform, they were not to be appointed by a ruler. Instead they were to be elected by the community through electors, by direct ballot, or by compromise or scrutiny, or chosen by divine inspiration, as when a white dove descended onto the head of the appropriate candidate. Once selected, the abbess or abbot was consecrated by a bishop and charged with his or her duties as head of the community. A newly consecrated abbess, for instance, was enjoined to perform the Divine Office, to oversee the community with wisdom, intelligence, good counsel, courage, goodness, and understanding, to preserve God's commandments day and night, to attend to sacred reading, spurn the worldly and ephemeral, practice good works, overcome pleasure or voluptuousness, love honorable chastity, practice virtue, use authority with modesty, and make an example of her life. Receiving the rule of her community in chastity, sobriety, goodness, moderation, and prudence, she was to rule without separating herself from the sisters in more luxurious apartments, eating separately from the sisters, or having favorites, but to correct faults with firmness and without either too much severity or too much laxity.[13] Both abbesses and abbots were the spiritual leaders of their communities, but an abbot who was also a priest had additional functions: celebrating mass, hearing confession and granting penance, consecrating new members, or offering last rites to the dying.[14]

As for administration of property, it is likely that many abbesses carried a greater share of those duties than did abbots, for abbots were more able to delegate responsibilities to officers or obedientiaries: priors who assisted the abbot or ruled dependent houses, cellerars charged with providing food to the monastic table, and others administering monastic properties.[15] Although there were great and wealthy houses of nuns, on average women's houses were smaller, supported fewer nuns, and had less endowment to manage than men's houses.[16] Abbesses had to have priests to assist them in certain duties, but might consequently undertake a larger share of property administration. Nuns could be either virgins, chaste, veiled widows, or wives if their husbands also took monastic vows, and abbesses often ruled their communities because of their wealth or connections to the outside world – gaining authority through their status as members of a prominent family, or through earlier experience in the world as married women, although sometimes proving themselves by rising through community ranks. Most historians have concluded that enclosure of medieval nuns remained flexible enough to allow abbesses to leave the monastery when necessary for monastic business. The vitae of abbots of great monastic communities often praise their skill in acquiring property, constructing buildings, and managing resources, but abbesses too were adept in managing the monastic property with great skill – despite a tendency for the medieval monks who most often authored our narrative sources to downplay such abilities among monastic women.[17] Indeed recent studies suggest that abbesses were less likely than abbots to incur debts, and more successful in juggling resources, to provide for both the poor at their gates and the needs of their communities. In times of famine, abbesses remitted rental payments owed by tenants; in good times they encouraged gifts from admirers to increase the properties they held already.[18]

If early monks and nuns took vows at all, those vows only vaguely resembled the later triad of poverty, chastity, and obedience. While the desert tradition of physical deprivation would continue to be celebrated in later monastic readings such as the Collationes of John Cassian (*c.* 360–435), the life of heroic asceticism was gradually replaced by the virtues of moderation, humility, and obedience to a rule and an abbot.[19] Such moderated practices are associated with the great rules of monastic life established in late antiquity: advice by Basil of Caesaria (c. 330–79), still used by Greek monks today; the letters of Augustine, bishop of Hippo in North Africa (354–430), from which the later Augustinian Rule derives, and in Italy both the anonymous "Rule of the Master" and the more famous Rule of Benedict of Nursia (*c.* 480–*c.* 530). The Rule of Benedict, which became the most important monastic rule in the West, was long believed to be the work of a single inspired genius, but is now known to be a collation of earlier rules. It was spread quickly from his famous monastic house at Montecassino south of Rome, with the backing of Pope Gregory the Great (540–604, pope from 590), one of the great intellectuals of the transition between late antiquity and the early Middle Ages, who included a Life of Benedict of Nursia in his widely read Dialogues.[20] As for Benedict's Rule, foremost was obedience to an abbot, who was to urge moderation and humility and manual labor to avoid boredom or listlessness, within a schedule of communal recitation of the entire book of Psalms each week. It also stressed private prayer, devout reading, and manual labor, an activity that in many Western monasteries came to be centered on copying in the scriptorium or writing room. Indeed, we owe the survival of most texts from the ancient world to the copying by such medieval monks and nuns.[21] Benedict's Rule was used by communities of women as well as men, and famous abbesses of late antiquity are associated with authors of monastic rulers: Macrina, the sister of Basil of Caesaria, and Scholastica, the sister of Benedict of Nursia, are both thought to have headed their communities of nuns.[22] Much stricter than Benedict's Rule, particularly in terms of monastic enclosure, was a rule written by Caesarius, bishop of Arles (d. 543), for use by his sister and her nuns at a community in that city.[23] In general, however, the Rule of Benedict was successful because of its lack of excessive specificity, and communities using it could develop customs appropriate to their own needs.

In most of the West, where monasticism was established in former Roman provinces, monks and nuns were subject to the local bishop, who had replaced Roman civic authorities. That was different in Ireland, however, where Roman civilization had never penetrated and bishops lived in monasteries and were subject to abbots (and abbesses like Bridget of Kildare (*c.* 450–523); Celtic monks and nuns were famous for their manuscript copying and illumination, but followed more ascetic monastic practices than elsewhere.[24] Among them was the ascetic practice of setting out to sea on tiny crafts to wash up on whatever shore, establishing hermitages and monasteries at Skelling Michael off the southern coast of Ireland, at Iona and Lindisfarne in northern Britain – whence they converted Britain from the north.[25] They encountered the Benedictine Rule introduced by monks sent from Rome to convert Britain. Their influence traveled northward from Canterbury. In Northumbria, at the great synod of Whitby in 664 Roman practice triumphed over that of the Celtic in terms of monastic practice and calendrical calculations. Anglo-Irish monks and nuns continued missionary efforts to the Continent, establishing long-lived houses of monks at places like Luxeuil, and Bobbio, as well as assisting in the conversion of the Saxons at the time of the martyred monastic missionary Boniface and the emperor Charlemagne.[26]

Generally, the fierce Merovingian Franks were more sympathetic to nuns than their Carolingian successors, and great double monasteries ruled by abbesses at Chelles and Jouarre near Paris and the Benedictine nuns at the Holy Cross in Poitiers, founded by the Thuringian captive princess Queen Radegunda (d. 587), represent the height of the foundation of houses of nuns in Frankish lands until the tenth century. Indeed, women's monasticism at the time of the Carolingians was limited by the reforms of monastic practices authored by the monk Witiza, better known as Benedict of Aniane (*c.* 747–821).[27] During the chaos of Norman, Saracen, and Magyar raids of the ninth and tenth centuries, monastic communities of all types were threatened by non-Christian invaders, who had no respect for the religion that protected the treasure kept in monastic coffers.[28] Abbesses in Britain and elsewhere encouraged their nuns to make themselves as unattractive as possible to avoid being assaulted by invaders. In France, communities of monks moved the relics of their saints further and further from the rivers and sea. In Britain, communities of nuns, like that at Whitby, disappeared in the Viking era only to be replaced later by houses of monks.[29] The exception was in Ottonian Germany and Italy, where imperial women favored nuns' houses in Rome, Brescia, and north of the Alps at places like Gandersheim (founded 852) and Quedlinburg (founded 936).[30]

As Europe emerged from the trauma of the later invasions, monasticism's story turns to the foundation of the abbey of Cluny by the Duke of Aquitaine at a site in Burgundy bordering Empire, Francia, and the road south to Italy and Rome.[31] Cluny became the most famous monastery in eleventh-century Europe, its growth and reputation a result both of dedication to St Peter and papal protection from local interference, and of a series of long-lived and saintly early abbots. It had close ties to the Reconquest of Spain, whose Christian leaders transferred some of the spoils to Cluny's building program, and its leaders were involved in the events of the Gregorian reform. Its reputation for reform and the desire to have daughter houses of monks emulate its customs inspired lay patrons to give their monasteries to Cluny to be reformed. The invention of the feast of All Souls by Abbot Odilo (994–1049) added to Cluny's fame as a liturgical center, offering impressive anniversary masses for the dead. Many asked to be buried in Cluniac cemeteries, or to enter Cluniac houses at the very end of life.[32] Cluny gradually acquired a congregation of such once-independent monastic communities in which the abbot of Cluny was monarch and all Cluniac monks took their vows from him. Similar reform movements were found in the Empire, at Hirsau and Gorze, for instance, but it was primarily Cluny and its impressive church, its elaborate liturgical furnishings, and the constant prayers for the dead by its priest/monks that dominated eleventh-century Europe.[33]

Declining revenues and a disputed election in the early twelfth century led to claims by rivals that a crisis had developed in Cluniac monasticism, but recent studies have not confirmed this.[34] Although its revenues from the reconquest of Spain may have been lower, Cluny's ties to Spain, Italy, and other parts of Europe continued in the twelfth century.[35] Cluny's eighth abbot, Peter the Venerable (1122–156), was a powerful force in western Christendom, reorganizing the abbey's finances, welcoming the dying Peter Abelard, writing powerful letters in response to Cistercian complaints, refusing to support the Second Crusade, instead writing treatises against Jews, against heretics, and against Saracens (for the last commissioning translations of the Koran from scholars in Spain) to assist in his creation of a "Christian armory" for propagation of the faith. Peter's writings show that he saw himself and Cluny at the center of Christendom,[36] but the Cluny cartulary too shows the abbey continuing to receive new gifts in the twelfth century, acquiring churches and tithes once in lay hands, and forging new relationships between its prayers and the community.[37]

The Cluniac monarchy was primarily one of monks, but in 1055 a Cluniac house for the female relatives of Cluny's abbot, Hugh the Great (1049–109), was founded at Marcigny. It was to contain ninety-nine nuns, including a prioress, but no abbess. That it was asserted that the Virgin Mary ruled them from heaven and the abbot of Cluny on earth tells us much about Cluniac self-confidence.[38] Marcigny was the only Cluniac house for nuns, but there were a number of eleventh-century foundations for religious women following the Benedictine Rule: le Ronceray founded in 1028 in Angers, the Abbaye-aux-Dames at Saintes in 1047, and that of la Trinité in Caen founded in 1062 by Matilda of Flanders, wife of the future king of England, William the Conquerer.[39] Nonetheless, the spotlight of monastic history moves *c.* 1100 toward new groups of reformers seeking a more austere life in the "deserts" of Western Europe.[40] The history of monasticism begins to be told from this point forward as an ever-repeating tripartite drama of reform, success, and decadence and then reform again. But such a cyclical narrative has limited credibility, drawing as it does from a Cistercian narrative justifying their break from the monastery of Molesme. It implies that Cistercians replaced the Cluniacs. Instead, newer groups supplemented the old, as a diversity of monastic opportunities arose in an expanding Western Europe. This new reform movement may have appeared first in the late eleventh century, when some Gregorian reformers began a critique of the older monasticism. New communities and congregations appeared at Fonte Avellano, Vallombrosa, and Camaldoli, then at la Grand Chartreuse in the Alps. Ideas were carried north to Grandmont, Molesme, Cîteaux and Prémontré and into the forests of Normandy and Brittany, where we see foundations by Vidal of Savigny, Bernard of Tiron, Gerald of Salles, and the double houses founded by Robert of Arbrissel at Fontevrault and Stephen of Obazine. Savigniac houses in Britain were important in the reign of Stephen, but it was also a period of hermits and anchorites, and the foundation of a new double house of sisters and canons by Gilbert of Sempringham. But there were also many independent foundations, often ephemeral, often swallowed up by the more successful.[41]

These new monastic reformers were inspired by Gregorian ideas about the separation of spiritualities and temporalities, about monastic ownership of churches and tithes, and whether as contemplative monks and nuns not providing for the care of souls they should be subject to tithes.[42] They also worried about worldly wealth and power, about lordship over villages of dependent tenants that was no different from secular manorialism, and about how their vows of personal poverty squared with lives in wealthy communities, for the more poverty stricken a monastic house appeared, the more secular donors, identifying such poverty with sanctity, flocked to make gifts to those poor monks and nuns.[43] In reformers' eyes such support would lead only to wealth, ease, and monastic decadence. Taking their vows of poverty as seriously as Francis of Assisi and his followers would in the next century, these twelfth-century reformers thus attempted to divorce themselves from corporate wealth – in some cases refusing any endowment, including ownership of churches and tithes, and limiting ties to the feudal economy and growing cities.[44] They struggled, too, with just how open their communities should be to provide for pilgrims and travelers, to offer education to the children of local nobles, or to care for the sick and the hungry. Many refused to adopt the elaborate architecture used to attract pilgrims, and the liturgy associated with anniversary masses, and argued that monastic vows of poverty, humility, and obedience could be fulfilled only if monastic buildings, food, clothing, and liturgical furnishings were austere and simple, and monastic communities isolated from the world.[45]

Thus many twelfth-century reformers retreated to the new deserts or wildernesses of Western Europe not only in search of solitude, but to live by the labor of their own hands. They were constantly plagued by followers emulating their sanctity but needing behavioural guidance from formal rules, or by patrons attempting to give them land, and such monastic reformers may be distinguished from one another by how they avoided ownership of property, villages, churches, and tithes, and the responsibilities for parishes.[46] A variety of houses of monks and nuns, in addition to the Grandmontine hermits, did so by animal husbandry, which was less labor intensive than agriculture, and could rely on pasture lands belonging to others.[47] Most limited the expense of monastic life by a return to the "primitive" simplicity and "apostolic poverty" of early monastic life in architecture and decoration, food and clothing, and efforts to avoid interactions with outsiders. In their efforts to avoid property ownership, some of the founders thus anticipated the thirteenth-century mendicants.

Some may be differentiated by their attitude toward the care of souls in parishes. The followers of Norbert of Xanten, the Praemonstratensian or Norbertine canons and canonnesses, as well as other "regular" canons, organized themselves into communities of priests living coenobitic lives, taking over abandoned churches and undertaking parochial care.[48] Other reformers, including those who eventually became Cistercians, shared a common table and dormitory of coenobitic monasticism, turning their backs on the world around them in favor of the contemplative life, and denounced the elaborate liturgy of the pilgrimage churches and prayers for souls. They argued that monks should not hold tithes and should not undertake priestly duties, but should isolate themselves from the care of souls, and the associated income from altars, churches, tithes, and dependent tenants, but sought exemption from payment of tithes on the labor of their own hands.

Most other groups that were eremitical at the outset – the Arrouaise canons, the canons of Prémontré, and many of the smaller congregations that would be incorporated by the Cistercians had been eremitical at the outset but evolved into coenobitic monks and nuns sharing a common table and gathering at intervals each day for the recitation of the divine office.[49] While many of these groups devised new reform customaries, others would revert to more traditional ways.[50] Thus Gerald of la Sauve Majeure, who began as a hermit, was soon joined by canons from Bordeaux who had founded a new village and priory in the vicinity, and like other reformers accepted knights as adult converts to his community. Gradually La Sauve and its congregation reverted to practices similar to those of the earlier Cluniacs, co-founding villages with local lords, accepting child oblates, providing medical services to pilgrims and fighters to Spain, and accepting patrons for burial at the end of life.[51]

As the diversity of possibilities for the religious life increased in this period, it was accompanied by an increased specialization in charitable services that were gradually shifting from bishops, priests, and traditional monasteries to new smaller and more specialized religious foundations: hospices and hospitals for the sick or for travelers, leprosaria, and by the thirteenth century residences for students at university cities, all of which were founded in order to provide prayers for a patron family's souls.[52] Some of this increased specialization may have arisen as the duties once undertaken by the families of parish priests disappeared with the enforcement of clerical celibacy and the outlawing of clerical marriage in the first half of the twelfth century. There is evidence, too, that some of the new hermitages and independent monasteries had been founded by clerical families, those who chose to live together after taking vows of chastity, rather than being forced to live apart because of changing mores in the Church.[53] Throughout the West, such new communities were established by patrons (including women) whose political roles sometimes precluded their own entrance into religious life, but others were founded by knights, peasants, urban artisans, or holy women who had themselves converted to that life.[54]

Tithes and churches were a potent issue. While the hermits of Grandmont in central France refused to own land, living on the increase of their flocks and herds held in pasture lands belonging to great lords, they also considered themselves laymen and subject to ecclesiastical tithes; at first control of their funds was vested wholly in the converts or lay brothers rather than the choir monks.[55] The Carthusians also remained eremitical in the organization of their daily lives; unlike the Cistercians with their system of granges, the Carthusians attempted to create large walled enclaves from which all other owners had been expelled. They lived in separate apartments and ate alone, coming together only for mass in the church. These hermits originally lived at the top of a mountain in the Savoy, with lay brothers at the gatehouse at the bottom as a buffer with the outside world.[56] The congregation of Tiron, on the other hand, which attracted primarily artisans, also acquired large numbers of churches.[57] Hospitaller and Templar outposts in the West also attracted specialist knights and sergeants, but often had tithes and ecclesiastical incomes that might come up against the tithe exemptions of some of the new monks.[58]

The move toward new eremitical and monastic foundations in this period was associated with individuals of great charisma who became wandering preachers and reformers, often with notions of reviving the life of equality of early Christians. They began as clerics disenchanted with the new urban schools or converted knights and peasants or monks rejecting the social hierarchies of earlier monasticism fleeing to the "new deserts" and urging others to abandon earlier lives in a search for new monastic lives based on notions of equality of men and women, rich and poor, urban artisan and peasant.[59] Whereas in an earlier age recruits to religious houses had been oblates (the children dedicated to monastic communities by parents), the new religious communities recruited adults who entered the religious life at mid-career, or founded reform communities after experiencing a mid-life crisis and conversion. Such conversions were by secular clerics, knights, and even the merchant, Godric of Finchale, who became a hermit.[60] The knight Pons de Léras, founder of Silvanès, was typical. A "convert" to the religious life, he renounced his violence, determined to lead a religious life, converted his land into moveable assets, settled his wife and children in religious communities, and departed on a pilgrimage before founding a hermitage that eventually became a Cistercian abbey. His life encompasses the period over which the term "convert," or "conversus," came to mean a lay brother among the Cistercians, and the author of this Vita, confused by rapidly changing terminology, described Pons as having "out of humility" remained a lay brother or conversus rather than a monk.[61] Among such conversion stories the most famous is that of early thirteenth-century Francis of Assisi, but there are many others, evidence of a rediscovery of the individual in twelfth-century Europe. Such conversion stories, like all narratives, have accepted conventions, but they differed by gender; for men such conversions meant a change to a new type of life, whereas for women such stories are often about achieving a long-sought-after religious life against family objections.[62]

For the twelfth century the most famous of such conversion stories is presented by the Cistercians as the story of their foundation; it is the interlocked account of two group conversions to the new and stricter religious life at Cîteaux. In the first, Cîteaux's foundation in 1098 is described as accomplished by a group of reform monks seeking to live (or convert to) a stricter life who left the "decadent" monastery of Molesme to found the new monastery at Cîteaux. The second part describes how Cîteaux was rescued from obscurity by another group conversion, that of the secular cleric Bernard of Fontaines and his followers. Led by Bernard, who would become better known as Bernard of Clairvaux, these men left their secular lives to enter

Cîteaux in 1112, and then were sent a year later to found the daughter-house at Clairvaux, where Bernard ruled as abbot until his death in 1153.[63] Elevated to sainthood in 1174, Bernard of Clairvaux has been identified as a "Doctor of the Church" for his influential Latin sermons on such topics as the Song of Songs. Bernard's charismatic preaching and active advocacy of the monastic life as lived at Clairvaux encouraged many individuals, among them the future Pope Eugenius III (ruled 1145–53), to enter that abbey, or to affiliate their own independent monastic foundations with Clairvaux and the Cistercians.[64]

By the end of the twelfth century an order of Cistercian monks and nuns was in place, with over 500 houses of monks and an as yet uncounted smaller number of houses of nuns.[65] This was not by an overflowing of monastic foundations from Burgundy. The order's success was created by Cistercian incorporation of independently founded congregations and houses, each with its local recruits and endowment, many of them intent on living monastic lives without dependence on the manorialism that had supported earlier monasteries. Most such houses and their associated granges were located in regions of long settlement, where Cistercians and others rationalized long-fragmented landholdings into consolidated farms or granges, practiced a newly intensive pastoralism, sought papal exemption from tithes on the fruit of their own labor, and used the labor of lay brothers and sisters (often recruited along with land purchases from earlier occupants) to provide products demanded by growing cities of the twelfth century.[66]

Bernard of Clairvaux and his followers were active among twelfth-century monastic reformers in emphasizing the duties of the abbot or abbess as a loving mother as well as a stern father.[67] Their concern with monastic caritas, an attitude of love, respect, and equality owed to all members of a monastic community, would later be expanded to apply to the relationships among Cistercian monastic communities: no community should rule over another, or demand payment of taxes from another; all should contribute to the material aid of the needy.[68] In this Cistercian idealism of the early to mid-twelfth century there was a brief moment when notions of social hierarchy were rejected. Since all were adult converts to the religious life, all were to be equal as brothers or sisters. Peasants who became lay brothers or sisters were treated as equal to the educated clerics or noble ladies who ruled monastic houses. Conversi (and conversae) were placed in charge of satellite farms (granges), so that monks (and nuns) could remain within the monastic enclosure, but they were equal in status to those choir nuns and monks, although receiving larger portions of food each day because they did more manual labor. Many of them were illiterate, but not all were peasants. There is evidence not only in the vitae, but in the charters, that knights with little education converting to the Cistercian life sometimes preferred lay-brother status and its abbreviated round of daily prayer. By the 1180s, however, such notions of equality among the Cistercians were disappearing, and knights were required to become choir monks. Cistercians also began to use the words conversus and conversa to mean lay brother or lay sister.[69]

As for these lay brothers and lay sisters, the Cistercians certainly did not invent this new "second class" of monks and nuns, but they were among the first to articulate descriptions of the purpose of these lay brothers in written documents. Such rules about incorporating lay brothers may have led other independently founded reform communities of the twelfth century to adopt Cistercian practices. Out of such shared practices would come the establishment of an annual, universal, and mandatory General Chapter of abbots gathering at Cîteaux each year and the developing notion of a religious order as an administrative institution. Although once believed to date to early in the twelfth century, the innovations that we associate with a religious order as enjoined on all monks and nuns in 1215 by the Fourth Lateran Council in 1215 probably emerged a generation after the early charismatic leaders had disappeared, and most completely during the reign of Pope Alexander III (1159–81).[70] Such an order as recommended in 1215 was distinct from earlier congregations organized around charismatic individuals like Bernard of Clairvaux or the monarchical principles of Cluny. The invention of such an umbrella group of monastic communities, characterized by a collective or individual head, written customs, internal visitation, exemption from local episcopal interference, and internal dispute resolution, was invented after much trial and error, borrowing and sharing among various reform groups, and, although by 1215 the Cistercians had emerged as the model, it is likely that most new reformers had contributed to the development.

Women were active in this reform movement. Although we have no evidence that women were among those leaving Molesme to found Cîteaux in 1098, there were women in the monastic community at Molesme, and a house at Jully was founded by Molesme in 1113 to accommodate those women who had also converted to the religious life and whose relatives had entered Clairvaux.[71] Although not sharing in the deliberations of the abbots at Cîteaux, Cistercian nuns were part of the order, and, like those of monks, women's houses were subjected to the regularizing influence of the General Chapter, particularly in the period from 1180 to 1250.[72] A house of nuns was founded at le Tart in the early 1120s with the help of Stephen Harding, abbot of Cîteaux, and would have its own congregation of houses of nuns by the end of the century; Cistercian nuns at Montreuil near Laon reported *c.* 1150 by Herman of Tournai are described as "working in the fields like the brothers of Clairvaux, rather than spinning or weaving."[73] Cistercian affiliation of men's houses brought incorporation of associated houses of nuns, but there were also new foundations like that at Las Huelgas in Burgos made in the 1180s by the king of Castile, who wanted to create a congregation of all Cistercian women's houses in the parts of Spain under its authority.[74] The opening of the thirteenth century saw a great surge of women's houses founded or affiliated with the Cistercians, many supported by Blanche of Castile, queen of France (d. 1252), and her friends. By the thirteenth century's end, Cistercian women's houses outnumbered those for men.[75]

Cistercians were not alone in having women in their midst. In addition to the double communities of canons and canonesses founded by Norbert at Prémontré, Robert of Arbrissel at Fontevrault, and Gilbert of Sempringham, there were many other independently founded houses of religious women of the period, some headed by women of great intellectual strength who seriously examined what the religious life meant for them. The twelfth-century abbess of the Paraclete, Heloise (1098–162), complained to her former husband, Peter Abelard (1079–142), that the Rule of Saint Benedict was ill suited to women's lives, but rejected the rule he wrote, which subjected religious women to men, for a rule she had written herself.[76] Hildegard of Bingen (1098–179) provided texts of her visions and dressed her nuns in beautiful colors, as well as writing letters about theological subjects to the intellectuals of her day.[77] Herrad, abbess of Hohenburg (1125–95) compiled an encyclopedia, the famous *Hortus Deliciarum*, for the education of her nuns.[78] These three abbesses of new religious communities that have nonetheless been treated as traditional Benedictine houses had access to the latest educational trends. The next generations of religious women (not only nuns but beguines, anchorites, and penitents) were excluded not only from the clerical university but from much of the urban apostolate of the mendicant friars. Instead, living increasingly enclosed lives, they would be upheld as models of sanctity for their visions, their penitential lives, and their pious proof of orthodoxy against heresy.[79]

Such women seen as models of penitence are part of a shift *c.* 1200 toward an urban apostolate and the rise of the "mendicant" orders. Part of the shift was in location: from the twelfth-century abbeys in the countryside, with ties to the cities primarily through urban markets where they sold their surpluses, to a mission aimed more directly at the cities, with the remodeling, rebuilding, and restoration of urban churches and cathedrals, and new attention given to the spiritual needs of the urban population through preaching and indoctrination with the tenets of the faith.[80] This is often presented in the history of monasticism as the result of the onset of decadence within new groups like the Cistercians, but this is only partially true, for communities of Cistercian nuns experienced their greatest expansion in the early thirteenth century. On the other hand, it was clear that Cistercian abbots, periodically engaged in preaching against dualist and anticlerical heretics, Cathars or Albigensians and others, in southern France, had been ineffective. Although the first mission to the south by Bernard of Clairvaux in the 1140s may be linked to the increased distancing of Cistercian monks from nuns in that decade, and a rhetoric associating women with heretics, later Cistercian abbots were ineffective in persuasion and ended up advocating force against Cathar perfects whose austere life styles allowed them to seize the higher ground in debate with Cistercian abbots who were increasingly viewed as wealthy, land-hungry, self-satisfied northerners taking sides in local affairs.[81] It was, in fact, in the attempts to find a new self-presentation in such preaching against heresy, as well as in biblical injunctions to preach the Gospel, that new "mendicant" groups arose in the early decades of the thirteenth century. Their early history is obscure, based on lives written for sanctification. As with earlier groups like the Cistercians, moreover, there is a tendency to read later institutions back into earlier events, accompanied by conflation between the two main groups, the followers of Francis and Dominic, eventually the Order of Friars Minor, the Franciscans, and the Order of Preachers, the Dominicans. Although traditionally called mendicants because they are said to reject monastic ownership of property, what is most striking about these new religious orders is their lack of any pretense of monastic stability, except for their nuns. The men of these preaching and mendicant groups all struggled with the tension that had exercised Bernard of Clairvaux before them, between the active life of preaching as exemplified by the biblical Martha and the contemplative life of monastic prayer represented by her sister Mary, as well as the issue of the *cura monialium*, the care of nuns' souls.[82] The men as well as the women also identified with Mary Magdalene as the representative of a life of penitence and a universal hope that even such a sinner could convert and be saved.[83]

Dominic de Guzmán (c. 1170–221), probably a regular canon, passed through southern France when he accompanied his bishop Diego of Osma on a trip to Rome. Perceiving the ineffectiveness of Cistercian preaching, he proposed that debate with the Cathar heretics would be more successful if it were to be conducted by poor, wandering Christian clerics, dressed in simple garb, looking as poor and holy as the Cathar perfects.[84] He gained the attention of the former Cistercian abbot Fulk, bishop of Toulouse.[85] Together they inspired an existing house of Catholic nuns at Prouille to support their mission of preaching against those with Cathar ideas in the vicinity; Prouille would become the first Dominican community. When Fulk granted houses in Toulouse for Dominic and his fellow preachers in 1213–14, those became the core of the first Dominican community of friars. Later, *c.* 1221, a house of Dominican nuns would be founded at San Domenico e Sisto in Rome by Honorius III and placed under the care of Diane d'Andalo, who had made her profession in Dominic's hand before his death in 1221.[86] Such communities of Dominican nuns were endowed like traditional nuns and strictly enclosed from the start.[87] By the mid-fourteenth century there were probably more communities of Dominican sisters than of friars, the latter tending to be limited to one per city. Some of the German communities of nuns provide us with important group lives in the form of sister books.[88]

From the outset, then, the emphasis of Dominic's charisma was on preaching against heresy by poor wandering clergy, well educated in the theological issues at stake and the supervision of a certain number of enclosed nuns. This led naturally to the organization of an international order, the establishment of houses for preachers in the major cities, hostels as institutions of higher learning, the *studia generale* in major university centers, and an association with the proving of the faith through the medieval Inquisition. Dominicans followed the Augustinian Rule, possibly because this had been Dominic's original affiliation, but also because new orders had been prohibited by the Fourth Lateran Council. The specific customs established in the 1220s led to the creation of an order. Like that of the Franciscans, there was a single head, a procurator-general of some sort, as well as provincial chapters; this was also the form for the military–religious orders.[89] While called mendicants, the emphasis for Dominicans was on preaching and eventually on university study, rather than on the rejection of property. In many ways this Dominican way of life became the model for all other new mendicant, preaching, teaching orders – most notably the Carmelites and Austin Friars, as well as for the more orthodox "conventuals" among the Franciscans.[90]

The origins of the Franciscans are less precise, although thirteenth-century conversion stories are epitomized by that of Francis of Assisi (1181/2–226), their founder.[91] Growing up in a wealthy bourgeois family in Assisi, Francis eventually decided against chivalry and the life of the knight to convert to the religious life. This conversion was not so different from earlier such conversions, but Francis's was a much more dramatic tale. Renouncing his family and possession in the central square of his native town, stripping himself bare of even his fine clothing, Francis began teaching the Gospel, wandering from place to place, restoring churches, living without property as a beggar or day laborer, enjoining upon his followers never to save anything for the following day. His miraculous ability to discern the hidden resources saved by those followers and his growing popularity led him in 1209 to seek papal authorization from Innocent III (1198–216) for the preaching of his "little brothers." Innocent III is often described by later historians as having by his authorization of Francis and his followers wisely co-opted a potentially heretical group.[92] Encouraged to write a rule to be approved by the Pope, Francis's third attempt was approved by Honorius

III (1216–27) in 1223. Francis's followers, like those of Dominic, gradually became a religious order.

Although the story of the conversion of Francis of Assisi is well known, tracing the early history of the Franciscans is more difficult because of early fractures among Francis and his followers about the notion of "apostolic poverty."[93] These early debates led to revised Vitae and suppressed earlier texts. Francis, moreover, seems to have been anticipated in some ways by earlier groups such as the Waldensians and the Humiliati, both of which had been given papal approval at least for a limited time.[94] Many Franciscan communities had originally been communities of penitents, some of them subject to customs established for penitent women (called the Order of San Damiano) *c.* 1218 by Cardinal Hugolino, the future Pope Gregory IX (1227–41). This seems a deliberate obfuscation, given that Francis had settled his companion, Clare of Assisi (1194–253) at the church of San Damiano, where she and her nuns were strictly enclosed. Eventually a rule by Clare, the Forma Vitae was approved for her own community, which differed from both that of Francis and that of Hugolino.[95] Clare maintained that her nuns should own no property. They had to do this at the cost of being enclosed and thus living on the proceeds of the begging of the brothers rather than begging themselves. This was maintained only until her death. Most of the Franciscans gradually came to be "conventuals" involved in the foundation of conventual houses located near cities and universities with their own *studia*. A legal fiction allowed the Franciscans, like the Dominicans, to own buildings, settle in communities, and build great hall churches like that of the Jacobins in Toulouse, for their preaching.[96] As a variety of penitential groups came to be included under the Franciscan Order, some of the most radical practitioners of absolute poverty, including some (called Spirituals or *fratricelli*) inspired by Francis himself, were thrust out of the order and declared heretical.[97]

From the inception of mendicant orders grave doubts were expressed about the propriety of women's preaching or begging, and women were not only actively discouraged from such a religious life, but increasingly enclosed and separated from contact with even their priests. The establishment of nuns' choirs, grills, and screens to isolate the nuns from the celebration of mass often limited their ability to see the crucial moment of the elevation of the host.[98] Perhaps in part because of this exclusion, it was religious women of the thirteenth century who orchestrated notions of a feast of Corpus Christi and increasingly revered the Eucharistic wafer as a relic of Christ, one that must be carefully protected.[99] Concerns about enclosure, separation, and adequate income to avoid having to leave the cloister soon extended to all houses of nuns, and abbesses were somewhat hampered in their administrative tasks after Boniface VIII issued Periculoso, "On the Enclosure of Nuns," in 1298 as part of his volume of church law, the *Liber Sextus.* Begging by religious women was forbidden, and there were limits on the admission of women over what a monastic endowment could support, but the enforcement of Periculoso remained limited until its reissue in 1263 by the Council of Trent.[100]

Finally, what was it like to live in medieval monastic and mendicant communities? While the Rule of Saint Benedict at first glance seems to cover every possibility, it was its flexibility about the local details of monastic life that would make it so popular over the centuries. There is abundant work on the liturgical practices, monastic customaries, and scriptoria for houses of monks and increasingly for houses of nuns as well; Barbara Rosenwein has discussed Western monks engaged in perpetual prayer and Alison Beach the collaboration of monks and nuns in scriptoria.[101] Particularly in the enclosed atmosphere of the medieval nunnery, it must have been difficult for most nuns when one of their sisters received the gift of tears or had mystical experiences leaving her bedridden and in the care of the rest of the community, and many must have prized the quiet of a religious life without such saintly companions.[102] The sister books and accounts of late medieval nuns, on the other hand, suggest the various artistic patronage and activities of such religious women and their secular patrons, whether sponsoring chapels or initiating pious practices, such as the use of the rosary or devotion to the Body and Blood of Christ, and there is considerable evidence not only for monks, but also for nuns, as artists, composers and copyists of music, and authors of monastic chronicles, or books for their community's education.[103] Recent work has suggested that the constant worries among abbesses to ensure that priests were available to provide for the Cura Monialium were mitigated to some extent by theories among some priests and monks that such care of nuns' souls was not only an obligation, but an opportunity for salvation. Finally, in the accounts and account books for German and other nuns and in the survival of manuscripts and artifacts from their houses, we are beginning to realize that medieval nuns not only produced manuscripts and manuscript art, but important textiles, particularly for the altars of their own and other churches.[104] In such communities of monks and nuns much attention was given to devotional innovations – to the celebration of particularly favored saints or particular times of the liturgical year, in windows and chapels, in dramas and liturgical innovations, including in music, and in meditations on particular art or relics, and even in special meals funded by patrons to celebrate anniversaries or significant moments in a monastery's history.

Such monastic and mendicant communities were central institutions of the medieval Church. They served as missionaries converting the pagans, and as copyists preserving the legacy of the ancient world. Most importantly these communities provided places for men and women to pursue religious lives, whether as enclosed contemplatives or as active preachers, knights, inquisitors, and educators. Many religious communities offered specific social and religious services to members of the surrounding society – praying for the souls of the dead, caring for the sick or poor or lepers, educating the children of the laity, or preaching against heresy. While by the end of the Middle Ages the active life of the mendicant orders in the towns had become different from the prayer and contemplation of monks and nuns living in isolated communities, such distinctions between monastic and mendicant communities were a relatively late development in the history of medieval monasticism.

Notes

1 On such "pre-Christian" monasticism, see Chadwick, *The Church in Ancient Society*; on Greek philosophical asceticism, see Long, *Hellenistic Philosophy*.

2 On ascetic women within early Christianity, see Clark, *Women in the Early Church*, and McNamara, *A New Song*.

3 A detailed and nuanced account is Constable, *The Reformation of the Twelfth Century*, but see also Nelson, "Medieval Monasticism." Such modern surveys as Lawrence,

Medieval Monasticism, tend to recount that history in terms like those of medieval narratives such as Eberbach, *Le Grand Exorde de Cîteaux*.

4 See Constable, "The Interpretation of Mary and Martha."

5 *The Rule of Saint Benedict in English*, trans. Fry, where ch. 1, p. 20, describes the four types of monks; see also Dietz, *Wandering Monks, Virgins, and Pilgrims*.

6 For details on such nuns, the standard account is McNamara, *Sisters in Arms*.

7 Caner, *Wandering, Begging Monks*.

8 On Gregorian reformers in this light, see McNamara, "Canossa and the Ungendering of the Public Man."

9 Peter Brown, *The Cult of the Saints*.

10 Horn, *The Plan of St Gall*; Hales, *The Roman House*.

11 On liturgy, see, e.g., Boynton and Cochelin, eds, *From Dead of Night to End of Day*; on women's communities, see Sorrentino, "In Houses of Nuns, in Houses of Canons."

12 Constable, *The Reformation of the Twelfth Century*; on increased clerical hegemony in central and later Middle Ages, see R. I. Moore, *The Formation of a Persecuting Society*.

13 Parisse, *Les Nonnes au Moyen Age*, provides the details.

14 Increasingly there was resistance to abbesses arrogating such duties – see, e.g., the issue of the abbess of las Huelgas, in *Les Registres d'Innocent IV*, ed. Berger, no. 589, to be discussed further in Berman, *The White Nuns*, forthcoming.

15 The duties of such officers are outlined in detail in such monastic customaries as *Les "Ecclesiastica Officia" cisterciens du XIIe siècle*, ed. Choisselet and Vernet.

16 Johnson, *Equal in Monastic Profession*.

17 Abbots' lives are often the source for modern histories; on attitudes to nuns, see Berman, "The Labors of Hercules."

18 See Oliva, *The Convent and the Community*, on making ends meet; for increasing property donations and other gifts because of the poverty of the nuns, see Berman, "Abbeys for Cistercian Nuns."

19 On reading Cassian, see *The Rule of Saint Benedict*, trans. Fry; on such asceticism, see, e.g., *The Wisdom of the Desert Fathers*, trans. Ward.

20 The most accessible account of new findings on the rule is still Knowles, "The *Regula Magistri* and the *Rule* of Saint Benedict"; *The Dialogues of Gregory the Great Book Two: Saint Benedict*, trans. Uhlfelder, sect. 33, is about Scholastica's death.

21 Reynolds and Wilson, *Scribes and Scholars*, pp. 75–9.

22 On such monastic sibling pairs, see Schulenburg, *Forgetful of their Sex*, and, more recently, Griffiths, "Siblings and the Sexes."

23 *The Rule for Nuns of St Caesarius of Arles*, ed. McCarthy.

24 On Irish monasticism, see Bitel, *Isle of the Saints*.

25 See Horn, *The Forgotten Hermitage of Skellig Michael*, and Brown, *The Lindesfarne Gospels*.

26 Fuhrmann, *Irish Medieval Monasteries*.

27 Wemple, *Women in Frankish Society*.

28 Certainly this is the account of the monks writing *The Anglo-Saxon Chronicle*, ed. Garmonsway.

29 Schulenburg, *Forgetful of their Sex*, pp. 144–54; "The Wandering Relics of Saint-Philibert," in Herlihy, ed, *The History of Feudalism*, pp. 8–12.

30 Gilsdorf, *Queenship and Sanctity*; on Brescia, see Wemple, "S. Salvatore/S. Giulia"; on Rome, see Hamilton, "Monastic Revival in Tenth Century Rome."

31 This is the account of the *Exordium Magnum* (see *Les "Ecclesiastica Officia" cisterciens du XIIe siècle*), found in standard histories.

32 Hillebrandt, "Le Doyen à Cluny"; Rosenwein, *To Be the Neighbor of Saint Peter*.

33 Hallinger, *Gorze-Kluny.*
34 Van Engen, "The 'Crisis of Coenobitism' Reconsidered."
35 Duby, "Le Budget de l'abbaye de Cluny."
36 Iogna-Prat, *Order and Exclusion*, pp. 338–57.
37 *Recueil des chartes de l'abbaye de Cluny.*
38 Wischermann, *Marcigny-sur-Loire.*
39 *Cartulaire de l'abbaye royale de Notre-Dame*, ed. Grasilier; *Cartulaire de l'abbaye du Ronceray d'Angers*, ed. Marcegay; on La Trinity in Caen, see Chibnall, ed., *Charters and Custumals of the Abbey of Holy Trinity Caen*, ed. Chibnall, and *Charters and Custumals of the Abbey of Holy Trinity Caen, part 2*, ed. Walmsley.
40 Leyser, *Hermits and the New Monasticism.*
41 Milis, *Angelic Monks and Earthly Men*; Golding, *Gilbert of Sempringham*; on smaller communities being swallowed up, see Berman, *The Cistercian Evolution.*
42 Constable, *Monastic Tithes.*
43 On Cistercian ideals, see Lekai, *The Cistercians, Ideal and Reality.*
44 For instance, the early Grandmontines as described by Becquet, "La Première crise de l'Ordre de Grandmont."
45 Conrad Rudolph, "The `Principal Founders' and the Early Artistic Legislation of Cîteaux," pp. 1–45.
46 Lackner, *Eleventh-Century Background of Cîteaux.*
47 On pastoral economy's advantages for small groups, see Berman, *The Cistercian Evolution*, pp. 189–96.
48 See Miller, *The Formation of a Medieval Church*, and works by Caroline Walker Bynum, including *Docere verbo et exemplo.*
49 Lackner, *Eleventh-Century Background of Cîteaux, passim.*
50 As, for instance, *Les "Ecclesiastica Officia" cisterciens du XIIe siècle.*
51 *Le Grand Cartulaire de la Sauve Majeure*, ed. Higounet.
52 See Mundy, "Charity and Social Work in Toulouse," or Berman, "Monastic Hospices in Southern France."
53 On family conversions, see *Cartulaire de l'abbaye cistercienne d'Obazine*, ed. Barrière, for example, no. 103 (1150–9).
54 Regarding countesses of Flanders, for instance, see Jordan, *Women, Power, and Religious Patronage.*
55 Lackner, *Eleventh-Century Background of Cîteaux*; on Grandmontines, pp. 196–203; on Carthusians, pp. 203–14.
56 For enclosures, see *Cartulaire de la Chartreuse de Bonnefoy*, ed. Lemaître.
57 *Cartulaire de l'abbaye de la Sainte-Trinité de Tiron*, ed. Merlet.
58 See Carraz, *L'Ordre du Temple*; on disputes over tithes and pastures, see Berman, *Medieval Agriculture*, pp. 50–2; for nuns, see Berman, *The Cistercian Evolution*, pp. 193–5.
59 See, e.g., Venarde, ed., *Robert of Arbrissel.*
60 On Godric, see Reginald of Durham, *Libellus de vita et miraculis S. Godrici.*
61 On Pons, Kienzle, "The Tract on the Conversion of Pons of Léras," and Berman, "The Life of Pons de Léras."
62 A series of such conversions are described in *Self and Society in Medieval France*, ed. Benton; cf. *The Life of Christina of Markyate*, ed. Talbot.
63 See Elder, ed., *The New Monastery*, pp. 9–18.
64 On affiliations to Clairvaux, see Pacaut, "La Filiation clarevallienne."
65 See Bondéelle-Souchier, "Les Moniales cisterciennes et leurs livres manuscripts," and Barrière et al., eds, *Cîteaux et les femmes*; there is no gazetteer of women's houses like Janauschek, *Originum Cisterciensium*, which lists all houses of monks, but the nuns' houses tend to be included in van der Meer, ed., *Atlas de l'Ordre cistercienne.*

66 Berman, *Medieval Agriculture, passim.*
67 Bynum, *Jesus as Mother*, pp. 110–69, or its earlier journal version, "Jesus as Mother and Abbot as Mother," the latter republished in Berman, ed., *Medieval Religion*, pp. 20–48.
68 See discussion of the Charter of Charity in Martha Newman, *The Boundaries of Charity*, and Stock, *The Implications of Literacy.*
69 Berman, "Distinguishing between the Humble Peasant Lay-Brother and –Sister."
70 This is the central argument of Berman, *The Cistercian Evolution.*
71 Berman, "Were There Twelfth-Century Cistercian Nuns?"
71 See Berman, "Beyond the Rule of Saint Benedict."
73 *De miraculis sanctae Mariae Laudenensis* of Herman of Tournay, in *Patrologia Latina* (*PL*), ed. Migne, 156: 962–1018, col. 996.
74 Conner, "The Abbeys of Las Huelgas and Tart and their Filiations," but see also Barrière, "Obazine, monastère double en Limousin."
75 See n. 65 above.
76 McLaughlin, "Heloise the Abbess"; Venarde, *Women's Monasticism and Medieval Society*, pp. 121–4, for discussion of those letters; see also Griffiths, "'Men's Duty to Provide for Women's Needs,'" repr. in Berman, ed., *Medieval Religion*, pp. 290–315.
77 Newman, *Sister of Wisdom.*
78 Griffiths, *The* Garden of Delights.
79 Elliott, *Proving Woman*; *Mary of Oignies, Mother of Salvation*, ed. Mulder-Bakker.
80 Little, *Religious Poverty and the Profit Economy.*
81 Kienzle, *Cistercians, Heresy and Crusade.*
82 Knox, *Creating Clare of Assisi.*
83 Jansen, *The Making of the Magdalen.*
84 Thouzellier, *Hérésie et hérétiques.*
85 See also Schulman, *Where Troubadours were Bishops.*
86 On Diana d'Andalo and Jordan of Saxony, see *To Heaven with Diana!*, trans. Vann.
87 *Cartulaire de Notre-Dame de Prouille*, ed. Guiraud, no. 1; on Dominican women more generally, see Lehmijoki-Gardner, *Dominican Penitent Women.*
88 Lindgren, *Sensual Encounters*; on sister books, see "Die Chronik der Anna von Munzingen," ed. König; "Der Nonne von Engeltal Büchlein von der Gnaden Uberlast," ed. Schröder; "Aufzeichnungen über das mystische Leben der Nonnen von Kirchberg bei Sulz Predigerordens," ed. Roth; *Das "St Katharinentaler Schwesternbuch,"*; ed. Meyer; "Die Stiftung des Klosters Oetenbach," ed. Zeller-Werdmüller and Bächtold; "Aufzeichnungen über das mystische Leben der Nonnen," ed. Roth; *Das Leben der Schwestern zu Töss beschrieben von Elsbet Stagel*, ed. Vetter; "Les 'Vitae sororum' d'Unterlinden," ed. Ancelet-Hustache; "Mystisches Leben in dem Dominikanerinnenkloster Weiler bei Eßlingen," ed. Bihlmeyer.
89 See Riley-Smith, *Hospitallers*;, and Housley, ed., *Knighthoods of Christ.*
90 On mendicants in the university, see Courtenay, *Parisian Scholars in the Early Fourteenth Century*, and Moorman, A *History of the Franciscan Order.*
91 Brooke, *The Image of Saint Francis.*
92 See Moore, *Pope Innocent III* or Bolton, *Innocent III.*
93 Moorman, *A History of the Franciscan Order*; Brooke, *Early Franciscan Government.*
94 Brasher, *Women of the Humiliati*; Audisio, *The Waldensian Dissent*; on the Cathar threat in Ialy, see Lansing, *Power and Purity.*
95 Knox, *Creating Clare of Assisi*, 25–55, but see also Mueller, *The Privilege of Poverty.*
96 On Italian mendicant architecture and religion, see Thompson, *Cities of God*; on Dominican architecture more generally, see Sundt, "*Mediocres domos et humiles habeant fratres nostri.*"

97 Burr, *The Spiritual Franciscans.*
98 Bruzelius, "Hearing is Believing." Wealthy houses could be exceptional; for Naples see Bruzelius, *The Stones of Naples*, and Knox, *Creating Clare of Assisi*, pp. 114–21.
99 Rubin, *Corpus Christi.*
100 Makowski, *Canon Law and Cloistered Women.*
101 Rosenwein, "Perpetual Prayer at Agaune," and Beach, "Claustration and Collaboration."
102 McNamara, *The Ordeal of Community*, has suggested that living in community with sisters or brothers not chosen by oneself would often have been difficult.
103 Bynum, *Wonderful Blood*; the collection of articles in Mews, ed. *Listen, Daughter* and Winston-Allen, *Stories of the Rose.*
104 On art, see Hamburger, *Nuns as Artists*; on chronicles, Winston-Allen, *Convent Chronicles*; on textiles made by nuns, see the forthcoming work on heath monasteries by June Meacham.

Bibliography

The Anglo-Saxon Chronicle, ed. G. N. Garmonsway (London: Dent, 1982).

Audisio, Gabriel, *The Waldensian Dissent: Persecution and Survival*, c. *1170*–c. *1570* (Cambridge: Cambridge University Press, 1999).

"Aufzeichnungen über das mystische Leben der Nonnen von Kirchberg bei Sulz Predigerordens während des XIV. und XV. Jahrhunderts," ed. F. W. E. Roth, *Alemannia*, 21 (1893), pp. 123–48.

Barrière, Bernadette, "Obazine, monastère double en Limousin," *Archéologia*, 155 (June 1980), pp. 19–33.

Barrière, Bernadette, "The Cistercian Monastery of Coyroux in the Province of Limousin in Southern France, in the 12th–13th Centuries," *Gesta*, 31/1 (1992), pp. 76–82.

Barrière, Bernadette, Henneau, Marie-Élizabeth, Bonis, Armelle, Dechavanne, Sylvie, and Wabont, Monique, eds, *Cîteaux et les femmes* (Paris: Créaphis, 2001).

Beach, Alison I., "Claustration and Collaboration between the Sexes in the Twelfth-Century Scriptorium," in Sharon Farmer and Barbara H. Rosenwein, eds, *Monks and Nuns, Saints and Outcasts: Religion in Medieval Society* (Ithaca, NY: Cornell University Press, 2000), pp. 57–75.

Becquet, Jean, "La Première crise de l'Ordre de Grandmont," *Bulletin de la Société archéologique du Limousin*, 87 (1960), pp. 283–324.

Berman, Constance H., *Medieval Agriculture, the Southern-French Countryside, and the Early Cistercians: A Study of Forty-Three Monasteries* (Philadelphia: American Philosophical Society, 1986).

Berman, Constance H., "Abbeys for Cistercian Nuns in the Ecclesiastical Province of Sens: Foundation, Endowment and Economic Activities of the Earlier Foundations," *Revue Mabillon*, 73 (1997), 83–113.

Berman, Constance H., "Were There Twelfth-Century Cistercian Nuns?" *Church History*, 68 (1999), pp. 824–64, repr. in Berman, ed., *Medieval Religion*, pp. 217–48.

Berman, Constance H., *The Cistercian Evolution: The Invention of a Religious Order in Twelfth-Century Europe* (Philadelphia: University of Pennsylvania Press, 2000).

Berman, Constance H., "The Labors of Hercules, the Cartulary, Church and Abbey for Nuns of La Cour-Notre-Dame-de-Michery," *Journal of Medieval History*, 26 (2000), pp. 33–70.

Berman, Constance H., ed., *Medieval Religion: New Approaches* (London: Routledge, 2005).

Berman, Constance H., "Distinguishing between the Humble Peasant Lay-Brother and -Sister and the Converted Knight in Medieval Southern France," in Janet Burton and Emilia Jamroziak, eds, *Religious and Laity in Northern Europe* (Turnhout: Brepols, 2006), pp. 263–83.

Berman, Constance H., "Beyond the Rule of Saint Benedict: The Imposition of Cistercian Customs and Enclosure of Nuns in the Twelfth and Thirteenth Centuries," *Magistra: A Journal of Feminine Spirituality in History*, 13 (2007), pp. 3–40.

Berman, Constance H., "Monastic Hospices in Southern France: The Cistercian Urban Presence," *Revue d'Histoire ecclésiastique*, 101 (2007), pp. 747–74.

Berman, Constance H., "The Life of Pons de Léras, Knights and Conversion to the Religious Life in the Central Middle Ages," *Church History and Religious Culture*, 88 (2008), pp. 119–37.

Berman, Constance H., "Two Medieval Women's Property and Religious Benefactions in France: Eleanor of Vermandois and Blanche of Castile," *Viator*, 41 (2010), pp. 151–82.

Berman, Constance H., *The White Nuns* (forthcoming).

Bitel, Lisa, *Isle of the Saints: Monastic Settlement and Christian Community in Early Ireland* (Ithaca, NY: Cornell University Press, 1990).

Bolton, Brenda, *Innocent III: Studies on Papal Authority and Pastoral Care* (Aldershot: Variorum, 1995).

Bondéelle-Souchier, Anne, "Les Moniales cisterciennes et leurs livres manuscrits dans la France d'ancien régime," *Cîteaux*, 45 (1994), pp. 193–336.

Boynton, Susan, and Cochelin, Isabelle, eds, *From Dead of Night to End of Day: The Medieval Customs of Cluny* (Turnhout: Brepols, 2005).

Brasher, Sally Mayall, *Women of the Humiliati: A Lay Religious Order in Medieval Civic Life* (New York: Routledge, 2003).

Brooke, Rosalind B., *Early Franciscan Government: Elias to Bonaventure* (Cambridge: Cambridge University Press, 1959).

Brooke, Rosalind B., *The Image of Saint Francis: Responses to Sainthood in the Thirteenth Century* (Cambridge: Cambridge University Press, 2006).

Brown, Michelle P., *The Lindesfarne Gospels: Society, Spirituality and the Scribe* (Toronto: University of Toronto Press, 2003).

Brown, Peter, *The Cult of the Saints: Its Rise and Function in Late Christianity* (Chicago: University of Chicago Press, 1981).

Bruzelius, Caroline A., "Hearing is Believing: Clarissan Architecture, ca. 1213–1340," *Monastic Women's Architecture: Gesta*, 31 (1992), pp. 83–91.

Burr, David, *The Spiritual Franciscans: From Protest to Persecution in the Century after Saint Francis* (University Park, PA: Pennsylvania State University Press, 2001).

Burton, Janet, *Monastic and Religious Orders in Britain, 1000–1300* (Cambridge: Cambridge University Press, 1994).

Burton, Janet, and Jamroziak, Emilia, eds, *Religious and Laity in Northern Europe* (Turnhout: Brepols, 2006).

Bynum, Caroline Walker, "Jesus as Mother and Abbot as Mother: Some Themes in Twelfth-Century Cistercian Writing," *Harvard Theological Review*, 70 (1977), pp. 257–84.

Bynum, Caroline Walker, Docere verbo et exemplo: *An Aspect of Twelfth-Century Spirituality* (Missoula, MT: Scholars Press, 1979).

Bynum, Caroline Walker, *Jesus as Mother: Studies in the Spirituality of the High Middle Ages* (Berkeley and Los Angeles: University of California Press, 1982).

Bynum, Caroline Walker, *Wonderful Blood: Theology and Practice in Late Medieval Northern Germany and Beyond* (Philadelphia: University of Pennsylvania Press, 2007).

Caner, Daniel, *Wandering, Begging Monks: Spiritual Authority and the Promotion of Monasticism in Late Antiquity* (Berkeley and Los Angeles: University of California Press, 2002).

Carraz, Damien, *L'Ordre du Temple dans la basse valleé du Rhône: Orders militaries, croisades et sociétés méridionales* (Lyons: Presses Universitaires de Lyon, 2005).
Cartulaire de l'abbaye cistercienne d'Obazine (XIIe–XIIIe siècle), ed. Bernadette Barrière (Clermont-Ferrand: Université de Clermont-Ferrand II, 1989).
Cartulaire de l'abbaye du Ronceray d'Angers, (1028–1184), ed. Paul Marcegay (Paris: Picard, 1900).
Cartulaire de l'abbaye royale de Notre-Dame de Saintes de l'ordre de Saint Benoit, ed. Thomas Grasilier (Niort: Clouzot, 1871).
Cartulaire de l'abbaye de la Sainte-Trinité de Tiron, ed. Lucien Merlet (Chartres: Garnier, 1883).
Cartulaire de la Chartreuse de Bonnefoy, ed. Jean-Loup Lemaître (Paris: Éditions du Centre national de la recherche scientifique, 1990).
Cartulaire de Notre-Dame de Prouille, ed. J. Guiraud, 2 vols (Paris, 1907).
Chadwick, Henry, *The Church in Ancient Society: From Galilee to Gregory the Great* (New York: Oxford University Press, 2001).
Charters and Custumals of the Abbey of Holy Trinity Caen, ed. Marjorie Chibnall (London: British Academy, 1982).
Charters and Custumals of the Abbey of Holy Trinity Caen, part 2: The French Estates, ed. John Walmsley (Oxford: British Academy, 1994).
Clark, Elizabeth Ann, *Women in the Early Church* (Wilmington, DE: Galzier, 1983).
Conner, Elizabeth, "The Abbeys of Las Huelgas and Tart and their Filiations," in John A. Nichols and Lillian Thomas Shank, eds, *Hidden Springs: Cistercian Monastic Women*, Medieval Religious Women, 3/1 (Kalamazoo, MI: Western Michigan University, 1995), pp. 29–48.
Constable, Giles, "The Interpretation of Mary and Martha," in Giles Constable, *Three Studies in Medieval Religious and Social Thought* (Cambridge: Cambridge University Press, 1995), pp. 1–141.
Constable, Giles, *Monastic Tithes from their Origins to the Twelfth Century* (Cambridge: Cambridge University Press, 1964).
Constable, Giles, *The Reformation of the Twelfth Century* (Cambridge: Cambridge University Press, 1996).
Courtenay, William J., *Parisian Scholars in the Early Fourteenth Century: A Social Portrait* (Cambridge: Cambridge University Press, 1999).
Das Leben der Schwestern zu Töss beschrieben von Elsbet Stagel, samt der Vorrede des Johannes Meyer und dem Leben der Prinzessin Elisabet von Ungarn, ed. Ferdinand Vetter, Deutsche Texte des Mittelalters, 6 (Berlin: Weidmann, 1906).
Das "St Katharinentaler Schwesternbuch": Untersuchung, Edition, Kommentar, ed. Ruth Meyer (Tubingen: Max Niemeyer, 1995).
"Der Nonne von Engeltal Büchlein von der Gnaden Uberlast," ed. Karl Schröder, *Litterarischer Verein in Stuttgart* (1871), pp. 1–44.
The Dialogues of Gregory the Great Book Two: Saint Benedict, trans. Myra L. Uhlfelder (New York: Bobbs-Merill, 1967).
"Die Chronik der Anna von Munzingen: Nach der ältesten Abschrift mit Einleitung und Beilagen," ed. J. König, *Freiburger Diözesan Archiv*, 13 (1880), pp. 129–236.
"Die Stiftung des Klosters Oetenbach und das Leben der seligen Schwestern daselbst, aus der Nürnberger Handschrift," ed. H. Zeller-Werdmüller and Jakob Bächtold, *Zürcher Taschenbuch*, NS 12 (1889), pp. 213–76.
Dietz, Maribel, *Wandering Monks, Virgins, and Pilgrims: Ascetic Travel in the Mediterranean World, AD 300–800* (University Park, PA: Pennsylvania State University Press, 2005).

Duby, Georges, "Le Budget de l'abbaye de Cluny entre 1080 et 1155: Économie domaniale et économie monétaire," in Georges Duby, *Hommes et structures au moyen âge* (Paris: Mouton, 1973), pp. 61–82.

Eberbach, Conrad d', *Le Grand Exorde de Cîteaux ou Récit des débuts de l'Ordre cistercien*, trans. Anthelmette Piébourg, intro. Brian P. McGuire (Turnhout: Brepols, 1998).

Les "Ecclesiastica Officia" cisterciens du XIIe siècle: Texte latin selon les manuscrits édités de Trente 1711, Ljubljana 31 et Dijon 114. Version française, annexe liturgique, notes, index et tables, ed. Danièle Choisselet and Placide Vernet, Documentation cistercienne, 22 (Reiningue: Abbaye d'OElenberg, 1989).

Elder, E. Rozanne, ed., *The New Monastery: Texts and Studies on the Early Cistercians* (Kalamazoo, MI: Cistercian Studies, 1998), pp. 9–18.

Elkins, Sharon, *Holy Women of Twelfth-Century England* (Chapel Hill, NC: University of North Carolina Press, 1988).

Elliott, Dyan, *Proving Woman: Female Spirituality and Inquisitorial Culture in the Late Middle Ages* (Princeton: Princeton University Press, 2004).

Felten, Franz J., "Verbandsbildung von Frauenklöstern: Le Paraclet, Prémy, Fontevraud mit einem Ausblick auf Cluny, Sempringham, und Tart," in Hagen Keller and Franz Neiske, eds, *Vom Kloster zum Klosterverband* (Munich: Wilhelm Fink, 1997), pp. 277–341.

Fuhrmann, Joseph Paul, *Irish Medieval Monasteries on the Continent* (Washington: Catholic University, 1927).

Geary, Patrick, *Furta Sacra: Thefts of Relics in the Central Middle Ages* (Princeton: Princeton University Press, 1978).

Gilchrist, Roberta, *Gender and Material Culture: The Archaeology of Religious Women* (London: Routledge, 1994).

Gilsdorf, Sean, *Queenship and Sanctity: The Lives of Mathilda and the Epitaph of Adelheid* (Washington: Catholic University of America Press, 2004).

Golding, Brian, *Gilbert of Sempringham and the Gilbertine Order* c. *1130*–c. *1300* (Oxford: Oxford University Press, 1995).

Le Grand Cartulaire de la Sauve Majeure, ed. Charles Higounet (Bordeaux: Fédération historique du Sud-Ouest, 1996).

Griffiths, Fiona, *The* Garden of Delights: *Reform and Renaissance for Women in the Twelfth Century* (Philadelphia: University of Pennsylvania Press, 2007).

Griffiths, Fiona, "Siblings and the Sexes within the Medieval Religious Life," *Church History*, 77 (2008), pp. 26–53.

Griffiths, Fiona, "'Men's Duty to Provide for Women's Needs': Abelard, Heloise, and their Negotiation of the *Cura monialium*," *Journal of Medieval History*, 30 (2004), 1–24; repr. in Constance H. Berman, ed., *Medieval Religion: New Approaches* (London: Routledge, 2005), pp. 290–315.

Hales, Shelly, *The Roman House and Social Identity* (Cambridge: Cambridge University Press, 2003).

Hallinger, Kassius, *Gorze-Kluny: Studien zu den monastischen Lebensformen und Gegensätzen im Hochmittelalter*, 2 vols (Rome, "Orbis Catholicus," Herder, 1950–1).

Hamburger, Jeffrey F., *Nuns as Artists: The Visual Culture of a Medieval Convent* (Berkeley and Los Angeles: University of California Press, 1997).

Hamilton, Bernard, "Monastic Revival in Tenth Century Rome," *Studia Monastica*, 4 (1962), pp. 35–68.

Herlihy, David, ed., *The History of Feudalism* (New York: Harper and Rowe, 1970),

Hillebrandt, Maria, "Le Doyen à Cluny: Quelques remarques sur sa terminologie et son histoire," *Annales de Bourgogne*, 72 (2000), pp. 397–429.

Horn, Walter, *The Plan of St Gall: A Study of the Architecture and Economy of, and Life in, a Paradigmatic Carolingian Monastery* (Berkeley and Los Angeles: University of California Press, 1979).

Horn, Walter, *The Forgotten Hermitage of Skellig Michael* (Berkeley and Los Angeles: University of California Press, 1990).

Housley, Norman, ed., *Knighthoods of Christ: Essays on the History of the Crusades and the Knights Templar, Presented to Malcolm Barber* (Aldershot: Ashgate, 2007).

Iogna-Prat, Dominique, *Order and Exclusion: Christian Society Faces Heresy, Judaism and Islam, 1000–1150* (Paris, 1998; Ithaca, NY: Cornell University Press, 2002).

Janauschek, Leopold, *Originum Cisterciensium* (Vienna, 1877; Englewood Cliffs, NJ: Gregg Press Reprint, 1964).

Jansen, Katherine Ludwig, *The Making of the Magdalen: Preaching and Popular Devotion in the Later Middle Ages* (Princeton: Princeton University Press, 2001).

Johnson, Penelope, *Equal in Monastic Profession: Religious Women in Medieval France* (Chicago: University of Chicago Press, 1991).

Jordan, Erin L., "Gender Concerns: Monks, Nuns, and Patronage of the Cistercian Order in Thirteenth-Century Flanders and Hainaut," *Speculum*, 87 (2012), pp. 62–94.

Jordan, Erin L., *Women, Power, and Religious Patronage in the Middle Ages* (New York: Palgrave Macmillan, 2006).

Jordan of Saxony, *To Heaven with Diana! A Study of Jordan of Saxony and Diana d'Andaló*, trans. Gerald Vann (New York: Pantheon, 1960).

Kienzle, Beverly M., "The Tract on the Conversion of Pons of Léras and the True Account of the Beginning of the Monastery of Silvanès," *Cistercian Studies Quarterly*, 29 (1995), pp. 219–43.

Kienzle, Beverly M., *Cistercians, Heresy and Crusade in Occitania 1145–1229: Preaching in the Lord's Vineyard* (York: York Medieval Press, 2001).

Knowles, David, "The *Regula Magistri* and the *Rule* of Saint Benedict," in David Knowles, *Great Historical Enterprises: Problems in Monastic History* (London: Nelson, 1963), pp. 135–95.

Knowles, David, *From Pachomius to Ignatius: A Study in the Constitutional History of the Religious Orders* (Oxford: Clarendon Press, 1966).

Knox, Lezlie, *Creating Clare of Assisi* (Leiden: Brill, 2008).

Lackner, Bede K., *Eleventh-Century Background of Cîteaux* (Washington: Cistercian Publications, 1972).

Lansing, Carol, *Power and Purity: Cathar Heresy in Medieval Italy* (New York: Oxford University Press, 1998).

Lawrence, C. H., *Medieval Monasticism*, 3rd edn (London: Longman, 2001).

Leclercq, Jean, "Cisterciennes et filles de S. Bernard: À propos des structures variées des monastères de moniales au moyen age," *Studia monastica*, 32 (1990), pp. 139–56.

Lehmijoki-Gardner, Maiju, *Dominican Penitent Women* (Mahwah, NJ: Paulist Press, 2005).

Lekai, Louis J., *The Cistercians, Ideal and Reality* (Kent, OH: Kent State University Press, 1977).

"Les *Vitae Sororum* d'Unterlinden: Édition critique du ms 508 de la bibliothèque de Colmar," ed. Jeanne Ancelet-Hustache, *Archives d'histoire doctrinale et littéraire du moyen âge*, 5 (1930), pp. 317–519.

Leyser, Henrietta, *Hermits and the New Monasticism: A Study of Religious Communities in Western Europe, 1000–1150* (London: Macmillan, 1984).

The Life of Christina of Markyate: A Twelfth Century Recluse, ed. and trans. C. H. Talbot (Toronto: Medieval Academy Reprints, 1998).

Lindgren, Erika Lauren, *Sensual Encounters: Monastic Women and Spirituality in Medieval Germany* (New York: Columbia University Press, and Guttenberg E project, 2008).

Little, Lester K., *Religious Poverty and the Profit Economy in Medieval Europe* (Ithaca, NY: Cornell University Press, 1978).

Long, A. A., *Hellenistic Philosophy: Stoics, Epicureans, Sceptics* (Berkeley and Los Angeles: University of California Press, 1986).

McLaughlin, Mary M., "Heloise the Abbess: The Expansion of the Paraclete," in Bonnie Wheeler, ed., *Listening to Heloise: The Voice of a Twelfth-Century Woman* (New York: St Martin's Press, 2000), pp. 1–18.

McNamara, Jo Ann Kay, *A New Song: Celibate Women in the First Three Christian Centuries* (New York: Haworth Press, 1983).

McNamara, Jo Ann Kay, *The Ordeal of Community: Two Early Monastic Rules for Women* (Toronto: Peregrina, 1993).

McNamara, Jo Ann Kay, "Canossa and the Ungendering of the Public Man," in Sabrina Petra Ramet and Donald W. Treadgold, eds, *Render unto Caesar: The Religious Sphere in World Politics* (Washington: American University Press, 1995), pp. 131–50; repr. in Constance H. Berman, ed., *Medieval Religion: New Approaches* (London: Routledge, 2005), pp. 102–22.

McNamara, Jo Ann Kay, *Sisters in Arms: Catholic Nuns through Two Millennia* (Cambridge, MA: Harvard University Press, 1996).

Mahn, J.-B., *L'Ordre cistercien et son gouvernement des origines au milieu du Xiii^e^ siècle 1098–1265* (Paris: Boccard, 1945).

Makowski, Elizabeth, *Canon Law and Cloistered Women: Periculoso and its commentators, 1298–1545* (Washington: Catholic University of America Press, 1997).

Mary of Oignies, Mother of Salvation, ed. Anneke B. Mulder-Bakker, trans. Margot H. King and Hugh Feiss, and with contributions by Brenda Bolton and Suzan Folkerts (Turnhout: Brepols, 2006).

Mews, Constant, ed., *Listen, Daughter: The* Speculum virginum *and the Formation of Religious Women in the Middle Ages* (New York: Palgrave, 2001).

Milis, Ludo, "Ermites et chanoines réguliers au XIIe siècle," *Cahiers de la civilisation médiévale*, 22 (1979), pp. 39–80.

Milis, Ludo, *Angelic Monks and Earthly Men: Monasticism and its Meaning to Medieval Society* (Woodbridge: Boydell Press, 1992).

Miller, Maureen C., *The Formation of a Medieval Church: Ecclesiastical Change in Verona, 950–1150* (Ithaca, NY: Cornell University Press, 1993).

Moore, John C., *Pope Innocent III 1160/61–1216: To Root up and to Plant* (Leiden: Brill, 2003).

Moore, R. I., *The Formation of a Persecuting Society: Authority and Deviance in Western Europe, 950–1250* (Malden, MA: Blackwell, 2007).

Moorman, John, *A History of the Franciscan Order from its Origins to the Year 1517* (Oxford: Oxford University Press, 1968).

Mueller, Joan, *The Privilege of Poverty: Clare of Assisi, Agnes of Prague, and the Struggle for a Franciscan Rule for Women* (University Park, PA: Pennsylvania State University Press, 2006).

Mundy, John H., "Charity and Social Work in Toulouse," *Traditio*, 22 (1966), pp. 203–87.

"Mystisches Leben in dem Dominikanerinnenkloster Weiler bei Eßlingen im 13. und 14. Jahrhundert," ed. Karl Bihlmeyer, *Württembergische Vierteljahreshefte für Landesgeschichte*, NS 25 (1916), pp. 61–93.

Nelson, Janet L., "Medieval Monasticism," in Peter Linehan and Janet L. Nelson, eds, *The Medieval World* (London: Routledge, 2001), pp. 576–604.

Newman, Barbara J., *Sister of Wisdom: St Hildegard's Theology of the Feminine* (Berkeley and Los Angeles: University of California Press, 1987).

Newman, Martha, *The Boundaries of Charity: Cistercian Culture and Ecclesiastical Reform, 1098–1180* (Palo Alto, CA: Stanford University Press, 1996).

Oliva, Marilyn, *The Convent and the Community in Late Medieval England: Female Monasteries in the Diocese of Norwich 1350–1450* (Woodbridge: Boydell, 1998).

Pacaut, Marcel, "La Filiation clarevallienne dans la genèse et l'essor de l'Ordre cistercien," in *Histoire de Clairvaux: Actes du Colloque de Bar-sur-Aube/Clairvaux, 22–23 June, 1990* (Bar-sur-Aube: Némont, 1991), pp. 135–47.

Parisse, Michel, *Les Nonnes au Moyen Âge* (Le Puy: Bonneton, 1983).

Recueil des chartes de l'abbaye de Cluny, formé par Auguste Bernard et complété, revisé et publié par Alexandre Bruel in six volumes (Paris: Imprimerie Nationale, 1876–1903).

Reginald of Durham, *Libellus de vita et miraculis S. Godrici, heremitae de Finchale* (London: J. B. Nichols and Son, 1847).

Les Registres d'Innocent IV, ed. Elie Berger, 4 vols (Paris: Thorin, 1884–1921).

Reynolds, L. D., and Wilson, N. G., *Scribes and Scholars: A Guide to the Transmission of Greek and Latin Literature*, 3rd edn (Oxford: Clarendon Press, 1991).

Riley-Smith, Jonathan, *Hospitallers: The History of the Order of St John* (London: Hambledon Press, 1999).

Rosenwein, Barbara H., "Perpetual Prayer at Agaune," in Sharon Farmer and Barbara H. Rosenwein, eds, *Monks and Nuns, Saints and Outcasts: Religion in Medieval Society* (Ithaca, NY: Cornell University Press, 2000), pp. 37–56.

Rosenwein, Barbara H., *To Be the Neighbor of Saint Peter: The Social Meaning of Cluny's Property, 909–1049* (Ithaca, NY: Cornell University Press, 1989).

Rubin, Miri, *Corpus Christi: The Eucharist in Late Medieval Culture* (Cambridge: Cambridge University Press, 1991).

Rudolph, Conrad, "The 'Principal Founders' and the Early Artistic Legislation of Cîteaux," in Meredith Lillich, ed., *Studies in Cistercian Art and Architecture*, vol. III (Kalamazoo, MI: Cistercian Publications, 1987).

The Rule for Nuns of St Caesarius of Arles, ed. Maria Caritas McCarthy (Washington: Catholic University of America, 1960).

The Rule of Saint Benedict in English, trans. Timothy Fry (Collegeville, MN: Liturgical Press, 1982).

Schulenburg, Jane T., *Forgetful of their Sex: Female Sanctity and Society, ca. 500–1100* (Chicago: University of Chicago Press, 1998).

Schulman, Nicole M., *Where Troubadours Were Bishops: The Occitania of Folc of Marseille (1150–1231)* (New York: Routledge, 2001).

Self and Society in Medieval France; the Memoirs of Abbot Guibert of Nogent, ed. and intro. John F. Benton (Toronto: Medieval Academy Reprints, 1984).

Sorrentino, Janet, "In Houses of Nuns, in Houses of Canons: A Liturgical Dimension to Double Monasteries," *Journal of Medieval History*, 28 (2002), pp. 361–72.

Stock, Brian, *The Implications of Literacy: Written Language and Models of Interpretation in the Eleventh and Twelfth Centuries* (Princeton: Princeton University Press, 1983).

Sundt, Richard A., "*Mediocres domos et humiles habeant fratres nostri*: Dominican Legislation on Architecture and Architectural Decoration in the 13th Century," *Journal of the Society of Architectural Historians*, 48 (1987), pp. 394–407.

Thompson, Augustine, *Cities of God: The Religion of the Italian Communes 1125–1325* (University Park, PA: Pennsylvania State University Press, 2005).

Thouzellier, Christine, *Hérésie et hérétiques: Vaudois, cathares, patarins, albigeois* (Rome: Edizioni di Storia e Letteratura, 1969).

van der Meer, Frederik ed., *Atlas de l'Ordre cistercienne* (Paris: Séquoia, 1965).

Van Engen, John, "The 'Crisis of Cenobitism' Reconsidered: Benedictine Monasticism in the Years 1050–1150," *Speculum*, 61 (1986), pp. 269–304.

Venarde, Bruce L., *Women's Monasticism and Medieval Society: Nunneries in France and England, 890–1215* (Ithaca, NY: Cornell University Press, 1997).

Venarde, Bruce, ed., *Robert of Arbrissel: A Medieval Religious Life* (Washington: Catholic University of America Press, 2003).

Wemple, Suzanne, "S. Salvatore/S. Giulia: A Case Study in the Endowment and Patronage of a Major Female Monastery in Northern Italy," in Julius Kirshner and Suzanne F. Wemple, eds, *Women of the Medieval World: Essays in Honor of John H. Mundy* (Oxford and New York: B. Blackwell, 1985), pp. 85–102,

Wemple, Suzanne, *Women in Frankish Society: Marriage and the Cloister 500–900* (Philadelphia: University of Pennsylvania Press, 1981).

The Wisdom of the Desert Fathers, trans. Benedictina Ward (Oxford: SLG Press, 1981).

Winston-Allen, Anne, *Convent Chronicles: Women Writing about Women and Reform in the Late Middle Ages* (University Park, PA: Pennsylvania State University Press, 2004).

Winston-Allen, Anne, *Stories of the Rose: The Making of the Rosary in the Middle Ages* (University Park, PA: Pennsylvania State University Press, 1997).

Wischermann, Else Maria, *Marcigny-sur-Loire: Grüdungs- und Frügeschicte des ersten Cluniac enserinnenpriora*tes *1054–1150* (Munich: Fink, 1986).

Further Reading

Recommended readings range from standard histories of monasticism telling a very traditional tale based on medieval monks' own narratives, such as David Knowles, *From Pachomius to Ignatius: A Study in the Constitutional History of the Religious Orders* (Oxford: Clarendon Press, 1966), to the more innovative work of Henrietta Leyser, *Hermits and the New Monasticism: A Study of Religious Communities in Western Europe, 1000–1150* (London: Macmillan, 1984), Lester Little, *Religious Poverty and the Profit Economy in Medieval Europe* (Ithaca, NY: Cornell University Press, 1978), and the works of Caroline Bynum and Giles Constable, all listed in the Bibliography above. For those who read French, Michel Parisse's *Les Nonnes au Moyen Age* (Le Puy: Bonneton, 1983) is particularly valuable; Peter Brown, *The Cult of the Saints: Its Rise and Function in Late Christianity* (Chicago: University of Chicago Press, 1981), and Patrick Geary, *Furta Sacra: Thefts of Relics in the Central Middle Ages* (Princeton: Princeton University Press, 1990), both provide interesting insights on monastic life and relics. On the mendicants, the most interesting studies are Lezlie Knox, *Creating Clare of Assisi* (Leiden: Brill, 2008), David Burr, *The Spiritual Franciscans: From Protest to Persecution in the Century after Saint Francis* (University Park, PA: Pennsylvania State University Press, 2001), and Rosalind B. Brooke's new volume, *The Image of St Francis: Responses to Sainthood in the Thirteenth Century* (Cambridge: Cambridge University Press, 2006).

Chapter Twelve

Hospitals in the Middle Ages

James W. Brodman

Hospitals in the Middle Ages were, first of all, places of hospitality – that is, shelters for those who were temporarily or permanently without a home. The earliest, dating from the fourth century, served pilgrims and the poor of cities in the eastern Mediterranean. By the sixth century, such shelters were also found in Western Europe, where they also served travelers. Here, with the decline of urban life, the relatively few hospitals were mainly rural and frequently associated with monasteries. After 1000, however, with Western Europe's urban renaissance, hospitals became prominent here for the first time. By the end of the twelfth century, they numbered in the thousands, as virtually every community of any size acquired one or more of these institutions. The thirteenth and fourteenth centuries saw a rapid proliferation of hospitals, and by the end of the Middle Ages cities such as Paris counted upward of sixty such institutions.

Unlike modern hospitals, those of the Middle Ages were charitable institutions that served the poor and so never levied a direct charge against those who were treated. The poor themselves were not defined according to any fixed economic standard but rather were identified by their vulnerability or loss of status. Thus, the impecunious aristocrat was as eligible for assistance as the transient beggar. While wealthy individuals might personally provide direct assistance to those in need, hospitals were the earliest and most important societal or institutional response to individual suffering. In a rural environment of almost universal poverty characteristic of the early Middle Ages, hospitals principally served pilgrims and other travelers. But, as European society grew more urban, this clientele expanded not only in numbers but also in scope. In the twelfth century, hospitals also began to serve orphans and abandoned children, mothers and their newborns, the sick and the dying, the victims of plague and captivity, the injured and wounded, and the more-generalized category of the poor. Some institutions provided longer-term care to the victims of chronic diseases, such as ergotism and leprosy, to social outcasts, such as reformed prostitutes or the mentally disturbed, and to the elderly who required some form of assisted living.

The initial motivation for assisting these myriad categories of the needy was religious. Not only did the love of God also imply a care for one's neighbor, but, in the quest for personal salvation, one's solicitude toward the needy was seen as a fit atonement for sin, and so charitable giving would help tilt the scales of eternal justice in a heavenly direction. Because of this association between charity and religion, much of the initial patronage and support of hospitals was ecclesiastical – from bishops, cathedral chapters, monasteries, and even individual clerics. The secular elite, however, also founded and endowed hospitals, but in the same spirit as they patronized churches and monasteries. In the high Middle Ages, associations of less exalted lay persons also came to support hospitals. These included overtly religious groups, such as confraternities and parish organizations, but also more secular associations, such as guilds and town councils that had to cope with the epidemiological and demographic crises of the later Middle Ages.

At first, hospitals provided inmates with a place to sleep and something to eat. As they expanded in size and scope, hospitals augmented the extent of their care. While only institutions such as leprosaria provided long-term shelter for the chronically ill, many institutions came to provide palliative and medical care to those suffering from acute illness or who sought an honorable place to die. Consequently, by the fourteenth century, physicians, surgeons, barbers, and apothecaries begin to appear on the rosters of hospitaller personnel. The "nursing" staff itself was varied in composition. Many were members of religious orders or local congregations of professed religious; some were lay folk who served without pay for love or for the promise of care in old age; others were hired and like modern caregivers paid a salary.

Historians, particularly beginning around 1960, began to study not only the histories of individual hospitals but also a wide gamut of intersections between these medieval houses of charity and their surrounding society. The earliest attention to the medieval hospitaller movement, however, began some two centuries earlier during the erudite reaction to the Enlightenment's critique of medieval religion; at this time ecclesiastical scholars assembled a number of collections of primary documents to illustrate the history of several Catholic religious orders, among them those that engaged in hospitaller work.[1] The fascination with medieval sources grew even greater in the nineteenth century and, among the collections of documents to appear, are those of statutes that regulated the life of medieval hospitaller communities and their care of patients. Likewise, in the late nineteenth century coincident with the modern state's earliest embrace of social welfare responsibilities, the first histories of European hospitals and charity were published, and, as with most history of this age, the attention was focused upon the formation and development of institutions.[2]

This pattern of investigation – emphasizing the development of institutions, both religious orders as well as free-standing hospitals – continued until the 1960s, when scholars broadened their approach to consider the social context of medieval benevolence. The first works of note dealt with canon law and its implications for the development of the obligation of charity.[3] Since 1970 there has been an explosion of interest in the subject along two principal lines of investigation. One thread of inquiry has centered on the study of particular urban societies and groups. This has produced illuminating studies of hospitals and charity for Italian communes such as Venice, Genoa, and Florence, for the English communities of York and Cambridge, and for Brussels and other urban centers of the Low Countries, as well as for Barcelona and other towns in the Iberian Peninsula.

Social historians, on the other hand, have concentrated their attention upon both ends of the social spectrum. Particularly pivotal has been the work of Michel Mollat and his associates, not only in France but throughout the Continent. This has focused upon the medieval underclass and society's attitude toward poverty. From 1962 to 1974, Mollat and his associates produced some 90 seminar papers, 220 articles, and several theses on the subject of medieval poverty, including many on hospitals and poor relief.[4] Mollat himself published what must be considered to be the pivotal work in the modern study of medieval charity and poor relief: *Les Pauvres au Moyen Age* (1978). This history surveys Western Europe's attitudes from the fifth to the sixteenth centuries toward the poor and the various systems and criteria evolved to treat those on the margins of society. Chapter 8, in particular, introduces medieval hospitals to a broader audience. Subsequently, Mollat contributed to an extended survey of the history of hospitals in medieval France from the sixth to the fifteenth centuries.[5]

Most prominent of Mollat's disciples was the future Polish politician Bronisław Geremek, who has published studies of the underclass of late medieval Paris and a broad history of poverty and social welfare.[6] Elsewhere in Europe, Mollat's influence has inspired local historians to explore the medieval origins of their own hospitals and institutions of charity. Most notable is the conference convened in Lisbon in 1972 that inaugurated the modern study of hospitals within Portugal and Spain.[7] Within France, national congresses in 1972, 1985, and 1996 turned from Mollat's broad surveys to studies of particular hospitals and institutions.[8] Charity, however, was not just for the underclass. Giovanni Ricci's article on the deserving poor helped to broaden the scope of study to include assistance to members of the middle and upper classes.[9]

Mollat's pioneering work prepared the way for a large body of local studies of hospitals as well as several new regional histories. For France, in addition to the volume edited by Jean Imbert cited above, these include a collection of articles on Languedoc, edited by M.-H. Vicaire, John Hine Mundy's studies of medieval Toulouse, and a lengthy survey of the hospitals of the Rhône Valley by Daniel Le Blévec.[10] For the Low Countries, the work of P. de Spiegler and Paul Bonenfant joins a much older history by Walter Marx.[11]

For England, the principal modern survey is that of Nicholas Orme and Margaret Webster. More analytical is Sethina Watson's work on the origins of hospitals in England.[12] Local studies have been done by Patricia Cullum for York, Miri Rubin for Cambridge, and Carole Rawcliffe for Norwich.[13] Walter Godfrey's half-century-old survey of English almshouses has yet to be superseded.[14] Publication of hospital statutes and other records, begun in the nineteenth century, continues.[15] Dieter Jetter has provided a general survey of the history of hospitals in medieval Germany, and Jerzy Kłoczowski touches briefly on the subject for Poland.[16]

In Spain and Portugal, historians inspired by Michel Mollat began publishing studies in the 1970s. For Catalonia, a landmark collection of studies was produced by Manual Riu and his associates in the early 1980s.[17] One contributor, Carme Batlle, has gone on to provide histories of hospitals in two Catalan towns, Barcelona and La Seu d'Urgell.[18] Josep Baucells i Reig, director of the Cathedral Archives of Barcelona, has worked with medieval Barcelona's almshouse and Prim Bertran i Roigé with that of Lleida.[19] Josep Christian Guilleré's numerous works on Girona trace the hospitaller history of that northern Catalan community.[20] The hospitals of Lleida (Lérida) have been studied by Josep Lladonosa i Pujol and most especially by Josep Tarragó.[21] Based in part upon these works, the most comprehensive regional study of Catalonia's medieval hospitals is my own *Charity and Welfare*.[22] For the Kingdom of Valencia, incorporated into Christian Spain in the thirteenth century, the works of two historians stand out. First of all, there is Robert Ignatius Burns, who has traced the crystallization of thirteenth-century Christian institutions, including hospitals, in that realm. For non-ecclesiastical hospitals, infant care, and the later Middle Ages, there is the work of Agustín Rubio Vela.[23]

For Spain in general, and particularly Castile, Fermin Hernández Iglesias's old history has been replaced by that of Carmen López Alonso.[24] Some attention has been paid to the network of the pilgrim shelters that developed in northern Spain between the Pyrenees and the pilgrim site of Santiago de Compostela. Among those of local governance are the Hospital del Rey and the Hospital de Santa Maria la Real, subjects of histories by Luis Martínez Garcia. There have been other studies of Santo Domingo de la Calzada and the Rioja.[25] Pyrenean hospices were the particular work of charitable confraternities and small religious orders (especially the Orders of Aubrac, Roncesvalles, and Somport), which have been studied by a number of historians.[26] Appropriately the military order of St James (Santiago) also maintained hospices along the eponymous *camino*, but this activity has not been given any adequate attention. Elsewhere in Castile, however, pre-modern hospitals have attracted little notice.[27]

The bibliography for hospitals in medieval Italy far exceeds that found elsewhere in Europe, although curiously no one has essayed a general history for the entire region. Instead, scholarship mimics the geopolitical realities of the peninsula and so is generally confined to a particular city and its *contado*. There are, furthermore, few histories of hospitals *per se*. Instead the focus is upon the community and the perspective more secular than religious. Indeed, Augustine Thompson, whose recent study of the religious life of the Italian communes intends to refute historians who propose solely secularist explanations for Italian history, mentions hospitals only in passing.[28] Thus, hospitaller history in Italy is mostly social history.

The earliest work of this nature is Brian Pullan's monumental study of Renaissance Venice. In subsequent decades, John Henderson has followed in his footsteps with his work on Florence, Samuel K. Cohn for Siena, and Steven Epstein for Genoa. A congress held in 1987 has produced an important collection of articles on charity and hospitals in the important northern commune of Milan. There has been no parallel study for Rome, and so its hospitals and charitable provision remain much understudied.[29]

Everywhere in Europe, the first specialized shelters were for the care of lepers. Given the chronic character of this affliction, these institutions, unlike most other hospitals, provided long-term care. The earliest leprosaria appeared in the twelfth century and they became quite common in the thirteenth century but, with the abatement of the disease, declined in number in the fourteenth. By far the most important modern scholar of medieval leprosy is Françoise Beriac, whose 1988 work has yet to be superseded. A decade later came a much more narrow study by François-Olivier Touati, who demonstrated efforts to give leper communities a monastic character. He has also collaborated with Nicole Bériou in a study of the conflict of authorities between a desire to care for lepers and a need to segregate them from the community. R. I. Moore, on the other hand, stresses only society's alienation from the poor. For lepers in northern Europe, there is a study by Peter Richards, for Asturias in northern Spain one by José Ramon Toliver, and for Majorcan lepers one by Antonio Contreras. Some leper studies have centered around the Order of St Lazarus, a confraternity founded in Jerusalem to care for leprous members of the crusader community and whose master until 1253 had to be a leper. While this order acquired numerous houses throughout Western Europe, evidence is equivocal about the extent to which it cared for lepers who were not members of the brotherhood.[30]

There was also a group of medieval religious orders that devoted all or part of their resources to the operation of hospitals. In the twelfth century, the earliest exemplars were several military orders that followed the Rule of St Augustine instead of the Benedictine Rule.[31] Most important is the Order of St John or the Hospitallers; others who emulated St John's mix of military and hospitaller activities include the Teutonic Order, the Spanish Order of Santiago, and the small English Order of St Thomas of Acre. While most historians have focused upon the military side of their apostolates, there are now a few studies of their hospital work, most notably conference collections, edited respectively by Malcolm Barber and Helen Nicholson, which contain contributions by the principal scholars in this still small field.[32]

After the fall of Jerusalem and the calamity of the Third Crusade, ransoming orders appeared to rescue Christians taken captive through war or piracy. The Trinitarian Order was founded in 1198, just after the calamitous loss of Jerusalem and the failure of the Third Crusade. It became active throughout Western Europe and the Levant, where it established and operated hospices for captives as well as for the more traditional travelers and the poor. Its principal modern historian is Guilio Cipollone, who has authored several books and, in 1998, brought a large number of scholars to Rome to celebrate the 800th anniversary of the order. In 1986 I published a book on the second ransoming order, the Mercedarians, who originated in Catalonia *c.* 1230; unlike the Trinitarians, the work of this order in the Middle Ages was focused entirely on ransoming and aiding Christians held in captivity within the Islamic world. Mercedarian history in the late Middle Ages and early modern era is told by Bruce Taylor. Ransoming was also the work of a few military orders, particularly the Spanish Order of Santiago. Yvonne Friedman has sketched the differences that distinguished ransoming customs in the Levant from those of Western Europe; Jarbel Rodriguez discusses the social dimensions of ransoming in the later Middle Ages.[33]

The Order of St Anthony, established in southern France at the beginning of the twelfth century to treat victims of ergotism, and the Order of the Holy Spirit, begun at Montpellier at the end of the same century, are the two major charity orders to arise in the Middle Ages whose principal work was the operation of hospitals. Both came to operate hundreds of hospitals throughout Western Europe and beyond. The former has been studied recently by Adalbert Mischlewski. There is no comparable modern history for the Order of the Holy Spirit, the standard history being now more than a century old.[34] Primary sources for both orders are scanty and problematic and so we simply do not have a good picture of the extent of their hospitaller activity (beyond that it was extensive), its character, or its influence upon the development of local hospitals. Consequently, both orders provide fertile ground for additional exploration.

Recent studies of hospitals have focused upon particular clienteles and modes of treatment. Among the former are women and children. Studies of women have proceeded along three tracks: women who served in hospitals, women with special needs, such as pregnant women, and social outcasts, such as prostitutes. Even though the great majority of those who tended to the poor, sick, and crippled in medieval hospitals were women, surprisingly little has been written about the social origins, manner of life, or character of service of these medieval nurses.[35] Undoubtedly the lack of easily accessible sources has been a barrier to the exploration of women's roles in the hospital movement, because most female hospitallers served either as individuals or as members of small, independent congregations of professed sisters. Modern scholars, however, have focused upon more visible groupings, such as communities of nuns or beguines.[36] As for women who were patients in hospitals, apart from a scattering of references in larger works, there has been little study of the special needs of pregnant women and new mothers. The most popular subject for contemporary historians instead has been women on the margins, particularly prostitutes. Included in such studies have been the hospitals that sheltered prostitutes in old age or that attempted their reform and reintegration into society.[37]

Studies of the care of children in the Middle Ages began as a reaction to Philippe Ariès's controversial assertion that high mortality rates among infants and pre-adolescents caused medieval parents not to love their children as much as modern mothers and fathers. Subsequent histories of medieval childhood attempt to show some measure of society's concern for children by studying how children in need were assisted, particularly abandoned children, orphans, and girls too poor to afford dowries for marriage. The most general treatments are Shulamith Shahar's *Childhood in the Middle Ages* and John Boswell's study of child abandonment. Other works consider orphans, orphanages, apprenticeships, and dowering charities.[38]

Medieval hospitals provided extended care to the elderly, including retired clergy, favorites of the royal court, and affluent members of the community, and also an honorable place for the poor to die. As in other areas, the study of care of the elderly is in its infancy and has yet to produce any major works. Consequently, references to gerontology are only found scattered throughout larger works. Among the topics that have received treatment are corrodians and donates – that is, those who entered hospitals in return for payment and those who traded their own service to a hospital for care in old age. By the fourteenth century, there was a concern that the elderly, precisely because many were able to subsidize their own care, were displacing other categories of the needy in the patient population. At the end of the Middle Ages, insanity was also recognized as a distinctive malady, and institutions arose to care for the mentally troubled.[39]

Since clergy generally served in hospitals only as administrators and chaplains, laymen and laywomen played an essential role in the operation of medieval hospitals. Of course, lay folk made up the overwhelming majority of those served as patients, and, if we extend the term "laic" to include those who lived under religious vows but outside holy orders, lay women and men made up the vast majority of hospital personnel as well. Furthermore, both individually and corporately, lay people established and provided the material support for hospitals through a stream of donations, legacies, and endowments. This lay participation in the hospital movement has raised many questions.

The first of these questions addresses the religious character of hospitals and whether their fundamental purpose was related to the spiritual well-being of their patrons and patients or whether patient care and the alleviation of suffering were of paramount importance. An older debate framed this as a question of Catholic versus Protestant ideas of charity, with the former focused on the spiritual welfare of donors and the latter upon the physical needs of those actually served.[40] More recently, and among medievalists, this has become a question of patronage, with many arguing that the increasing instances of lay control over hospitals, dating from the mid- to late thirteenth century, and the introduction of medical services by physicians and surgeons, produced a shift from religious to secular purposes.[41] Indeed some historians doubt that lay-sponsored charity was capable of having a religious purpose.[42]

This debate, however, posits a false dichotomy. Much recent scholarship, for example, has shown that little medieval charity was unconditional and doled out indiscriminately to all comers; insteadmost assistance was focused upon the actual needs of the deserving poor.[43] Furthermore, the movement toward laic control in the later Middle Ages over hospitals is merely one of degree. While clerics established and patronized a proportionally larger number of hospitals earlier in the Middle Ages than later, both laymen and clergy founded and supported hospitals throughout this long era. And, even though the care of patients becomes progressively more sophisticated, hospitals, whatever the form of their governance, continued to provide patients with religious solace and Christian burial throughout the entire medieval period. What we see at the end of the Middle Ages are not institutions that are either religious or secular, but rather ones that combined objectives that derived from both worlds. Indeed, André Vauchez argues that the communes of Italy spawned a new idea of holiness, the saint of charity who founded and served in hospitals.[44]

A second area of interest is the character of laic patronage. Earlier in the Middle Ages, lay initiatives emanated almost exclusively from the aristocracy, while from the late twelfth century they are increasingly initiated by urban groups. Some town initiatives derived from the penitential movement that grew up in the urban centers of Italy and the Low Countries in the later twelfth century. Among these lay religious devotees are the beguines and the Humiliati, who, among their communal practices, established and served in small hospitals. Confraternities and guilds also established hospitals, not only for their own membership but for others as well. Another locus for lay initiatives was the parish, which distributed alms to the needy and which less frequently also operated neighborhood hospitals.[45]

A third question is that of the shared governance of hospitals between secular and ecclesiastical authorities. If many hospitals were established by bishops, monasteries, cathedral chapters, and religious orders, why did the Church fail to exercise effective jurisdiction over hospitals? Or, to pose the question in another way, why was it that many hospitals came to fall under the control of laic confraternities and municipal councils? While some historians, as we have seen, have found the answer in the inevitable rise of secularism, others have argued that Malthusian crises of the fourteenth century overwhelmed earlier ecclesiastical foundations and required the institutional participation of government.[46] Most recently, Augustine Thompson in his magisterial study of the Italian communes argues that modern ideas that separate Church from

State are anachronistic. Instead, he argues for a more integrated view of society in which the religious and the secular intermingled constantly on a variety of levels.[47] Did the Church ever attempt to gain a monopoly over hospitals? During the pontificate of Pope Innocent III, there were signs that some reformers contemplated systematic organization and supervision of all hospitals. Such plans, however, never went beyond the stage of theory for two reasons: the Church's unwillingness to accept responsibility for the funding of hospitals and a laic participation in the hospital movement that was too broad ever to be organized into corporations, such as religious orders, that could be effectively supervised by ecclesiastical officials.

Another broad area of current interest is the introduction of medical care into the hospital. Historians disagree exactly when and how this occurred. Andrew Crislip, in a study of fourth-century Egyptian monasteries, argues that early monastic health care served as the model for the first Christian hospitals, citing the foundation established by Bishop Basil of Caesarea just after his ordination as bishop in 370 that served orphans, the elderly, the sick, and invalids. Timothy Miller makes the case that the Byzantine hospitals of the early Middle Ages continued this marriage between hospitality and medical care, although scholars such as Michael Dols and Vivian Nutton have challenged the view that any hospital could provide meaningful medical care prior to the twelfth century.[48] For Western Europe, however, the study of hospitals and medicine dates from only the twelfth century.

Much of the discussion for the implementation of medical care in the hospitals of the West revolves around the role of the Order of St John in diffusing Eastern medical knowledge and practice to the West. Jonathan Riley Smith argues in his history that the knights learned their medicine from Muslim sources in the Levant. Timothy Miller, on the other hand, believes that the origin of this knowledge was Byzantine and that, furthermore, the knights, through their hospitals in Europe, disseminated oriental medical practice to Western Europe. Most recently, Piers Mitchell, in a study of medical practice in the Crusader East, asserts that St John's hospital in Jerusalem evolved only slowly from a pilgrim shelter into a genuine medical hospital as the crusaders absorbed medical knowledge from both Byzantine and Muslim sources. Like Miller, however, he argues that the Levant was a far more important influence in the medicalization of Western hospitals than Spain or Sicily, which were other points of transfer of knowledge from East to West. Susan Edginton, in a study of medical practice at St John's hospital in Jerusalem, dissents and avers instead that Hospitaller medicine was inspired by already existing West European models. Anthony Luttrell and Daniel Le Blévec, however, doubt that St John had any real influence in the transfer of medical practice from East to West by arguing that in Europe the order maintained at best small pilgrim hospices that contained no medical facilities, at least before the thirteenth century.[49]

Physicians, surgeons, apothecaries, barbers, and other medical personnel begin to appear in the sources for West European hospitals in the thirteenth century and become quite common in the fourteenth, particularly in Mediterranean Europe. Some of the best studies have been done for Iberia; notable are Michael McVaugh's and Lluís García Ballester's work in the Crown of Aragon that deal with medical practice by both Christian and Jewish practitioners. Various anthologies of articles have also appeared that treat the introduction of medical practice in other regions of Europe. Nancy Siraisi has written a general introduction to late medieval medicine and Danielle Jacquart and Claude Thomasset have focused on medicine and women. Monica Green introduces female practitioners. Fernando Serrano Larráyoz's work on late medieval Navarre, however, reminds us that outside major towns medical care was mostly for the elite, although even in remote areas the privileged had access to practitioners trained at Europe's best universities.[50]

A generation ago, medievalists had only a general awareness of the existence and function of hospitals in the Middle Ages. Now, as the result of a growing body of scholarship, a basic outline of their origins, evolution, and function has emerged. As a result of this study, the phenomenon has become for us immeasurably more complicated than was once thought. For example, generalizations about conditional and unconditional assistance, the identity of the poor, the nature of care, and the roles of clergy and lay people in the hospital movement have had to be cast aside or seriously modified. Instead of a neatly definable movement with clear characteristics, historians are discovering that hospitals, and more broadly speaking the social services afforded by medieval charity, were a large and complex phenomenon, yet one strangely difficult to quantify – in short, something messy.

Indeed, the inchoate character of the hospitaller phenomenon has produced a serious paradox in our understanding of medieval society. How is it that something as pervasive as medieval hospitals – certainly by the end of the Middle Ages numbering in the many thousands – has remained relatively invisible in our contemporary treatments of the Middle Ages? Part of the explanation arises from the fact that modern Western society itself has turned to the challenge of universal health care only since the Second World War. The rise of the modern study of medieval hospitals certainly coincides with the emergence of this contemporary issue. Historians, however, who have undertaken a study of the medieval origins of our modern welfare policies have found that the medieval institutions provide formidable obstacles to generalization. As we have seen, this has led some historians, such as or R. I. Moore or Kenneth Baxter Wolf, to argue that ideas of charity and care had very shallow roots in medieval society, that the medieval establishment feared the poor rather than having any empathy toward such unfortunates.[51] In light of the substantial infrastructure represented by medieval hospitals and their focus of care upon those regarded as deserving, however, such arguments do not ring true. Rather, the paradox arises from the lack of any sort of centralizing organization in the medieval hospital movement. Literally anyone, from the poor widow to kings and popes, could and did establish hospitals. The Church's religious orders encompassed only a small minority of hospitals, and the efforts of bishops to establish a measure of oversight over hospitals were never particularly consistent or effective. If the papacy became a medieval accrediting agency for the university movement, it failed to do so for the hospital movement. As a consequence, hospitals defy generalization precisely because there were so many of them – of different size, purpose, endowment, resources, governance, and so on. This is not to deny that these institutions fulfilled a significant purpose, but it does point out the difficulties in assessing just what that impact was.

It is for this reason that most current studies of hospitals remain narrow in their focus. Many deal with individual hospitals or those within a particular community. A few historians have begun to investigate individual care-giving religious orders and others, such as the Knights of St John, that had a hospitaller dimension. Lacking to date, however, have been any meaningful comparative studies that recognize these organizations as part of a distinctive subset of medieval religious culture. Social historians are focusing on questions of class and gender. As illuminating as much of their work is, their conclusions are all too often overly narrow and tend to minimize any role for religion in the medieval hospital movement. Historians of science are investigating the development of the profession of medicine, the training, licensing, and practice of medical professionals, and the diagnosis and treatment of illness and particular diseases in the Middle Ages. Archeological evidence and new studies of medical practice in the Islamic world have advanced these efforts. Yet, because hospitals served the poor rather than the rich, historians of medicine have considered hospitals only tangentially. Structurally hospitals grew in size and became more diverse in function in the last centuries of the Middle Ages, producing, for example, the first of the so-called general hospitals. While this evolution has been noted in particular communities, there has been little of the sort of comparative study that might lend greater insight into the penetration of medicine into hospital care, the social function of hospitals, the impact of war, disease, and economic turmoil on hospitals, the community's commitment to the support of hospitals, and the relative strength of civic and ecclesiastical control over these institutions.

Consequently, despite the fact that the modern bibliography has become very large, there remains much to be done to investigate the histories of individual hospitals, of groups that sponsored and operated hospitals, and of the character of care afforded medieval patients. But needed even more are comparative studies that will help us probe the broader significance of medieval benevolence. It is only then that historians will be able to assess the impact of the charity movement upon medieval Europe and gauge its role in crystallizing and shaping modern attitudes and practices toward the poor.

Notes

1 See, e.g., Linás, ed., *Bullarium coelestis ac regalis ordinis B. Mariae Virginis de Mercede Redemptionis Captivorum*; Reines, ed., *Bullarium ordinis Sanctissimae Trinitatis Redemptionis Cativorum collectum et scholiatum*; Aguado, eds., *Bullarium equestris ordinis S. Iocobi de Spatha*.

2 These early works can be cited. For England, Clay, *The Mediaeval Hospitals of England*. For Spain, Hernández Iglesias, *La beneficencia en España*, and Bofarull y Sartario, *Gremios y confradias*. For French statutes, Le Grand, ed., *Statuts d'Hôtels-Dieu et de léproseries*.

3 See, e.g., Imbert, *Les Hôpitaux en droit canonique*, and Tierney, *Medieval Poor Law*.

4 Many of these are collected in Mollat, ed., *Études sur l'histoire de la pauvreté*.

5 Imbert, ed., *Histoire des hôpitaux en France*.

6 Geremek, *Margins of Society* and *Poverty*.

7 The proceedings were subsequently published as *A pobreza e a assistência aos pobres na península ibérica*.

8 The proceedings were published as *Actes du 110ᵉ Congrès national des sociétés savantes*; *Assistance et assistés jusqu'à 1610: Actes du 97ᵉ congrès national des sociétés savantes*; and Dufour and Platelle, eds, *Fondations et œuvres charitables au Moyen âge: Actes du 121e Congrès*.

9 Ricci, "Naissance du pauvre honteux," pp. 158–77.

10 Vicaire, ed., *Assistance et charité*; Mundy, "Charity and Social Work," pp. 203–87; Le Blévec, *La Part du pauvre*.

11 Spiegeler, *Les Hôpitaux et l'assistance à Liège*; Bonenfant, "Hôpitaux et Bienfaisance publique," pp. 1–195; Marx, *The Development of Charity in Medieval Louvain*.

12 Orme and Webster, *The English Hospital*; Watson, "The Origins of the English Hospital," pp. 75–94.

13 Cullum, *Cremetts and Corrodies* and "Hospitals and Charitable Provision"; Rubin, *Charity and Community*; Rawcliffe, *The Hospitals of Medieval Norwich*.

14 Godfrey, *The English Almshouse*.

15 Harper-Bill, *Charters of the Medieval Hospitals of Bury St Edmunds*; Cheney, "The Earliest English Diocesan Statutes," pp. 1–29; "Register of the Hospital of St Mary."

16 Jetter, *Geschichte des Hospitals*; Kloczowski, *A History of Polish Christianity*.

17 Riu, ed., *La pobreza y la asistencia a los pobres en la Cataluña medieval*.

18 Batlle, *La Seu d'Urgell medieval* and *L'assistència als pobres a la Barcelona*.

19 Baucells, ed., *El maresme i la Pia Almoina*; Bertran, "El menjador de l'almoina de la catédral de Lleida," pp. 89–124.

20 Guilleré, "Assistance et charité à Gérone," pp. 191–204; *Diner, poder i societat*; *Girona al segle XIV*; and *Girona medieval*.

21 Lladonosa, *La pediatria als antics hospicis de Lérida* and "Noticia sobre els hospitals," pp. 291–308; Tarragó, *Hospitales en Lérida*.

22 Brodman, *Charity and Welfare*.

23 Burns, *Crusader Kingdom of Valencia*; Rubio, *Pobreza, enfermedad y asistencia hospitalaria en la Valencia*.

24 Hernández, *La beneficencia en España*; López, *La pobreza en la España*.

25 Martínez, *La asistencia a los pobres en Burgos* and *El Hospital del Rey*; Saenz, *El hospital de peregrinos y la cofradia de Santo Domingo de la Calzada*; Hergueta, "Noticias Históricas del Maestre Diego de Villar."

26 Jugnot, "Deux fondations," pp. 321–41; Ostolaza, ed., *Colección diplomática*, pp. 85–6, no. 2; 88–9, no. 3; Durán, *El hospital de Somport*.

27 For hospitals along the camino de Santiago, see Brodman, *Charity and Welfare*, pp. 28–30; Porras, *Orden de Santiago*; Forey, "The Military Orders and the Ransoming of Captives," pp. 259–79. One Castilian city that has been studied is Valladolid: Rucquoi, "Hospitalisation et charité à Valladolid," pp. 393–408.

28 Thompson, *Cities of God*.

29 Pullan, *Rich and Poor in Renaissance Venice*; Henderson, *Piety and Charity in Late Medieval Florence*, "Hospitals of Late Medieval and Renaissance Florence," pp. 63–92, and *The Renaissance Hospital*; Cohn, *Death and Property in Siena*; Epstein, *Genoa and the Genoese and Wills and Wealth in Medieval Genoa*; Alberzone and Grassi, eds, *La carità a Milano*.

30 Beriac, *Histoire des lépreux*; Bériou and Touati, *Voluntate dei Leprosos*; Touati, *Maladie et société*; Moore, *Formation of a Persecuting Society*; Richards, *Medieval Leper*; Tolivar, *Hospitales de leprosos en Asturias*; Dols, "Leper in Medieval Islamic Society," pp. 891–916; Contreras, *La asistencia publica a los leprosos en Mallorca*; Marcombe, *Leper Knights*; Barber, "The Order of Saint Lazarus," pp. 439–56.

31 Those who followed the Rule of St Benedict, such as the Templars, generally did not operate hospitals. On this point, see, Brodman, "Rule and Identity," pp. 383–400.

32 Barber, ed., *The Military Orders*, vol. 1: *Fighting for the Faith*; and Nicholson, ed., *The Military Orders*, vol. 2: *Welfare and Warfare*.

33 Cipollone, *Cristianità-Islam*; the acta of the Congress are published as Cipollone, ed., *La liberazione dei "captivi"*; Brodman, *Ransoming Captives*; Taylor, *Structures of Reform*;

Brodman, "Military Redemptionism," pp. 24–7; Friedman, *Encounter between Enemies*; Rodriguez, *Captives and their Saviors in the Medieval Crown of Aragon*.

34 Mischlewski, *Un ordre hospitalier*, Brune, *Histoire de l'Ordre Hospitalier du Saint-Esprit*.

35 One example is Brodman, "Religion and Discipline," pp. 123–32.

36 Forey, "Women and the Military Orders," pp. 63–92; Green, "Women's Medical Practice," pp. 434–73; Le Blévec, "Le Rôle des femmes," pp. 171–90; Johnson, *Equal in Monastic Profession*. On the beguines, see Brasher, *Women of the Humiliati*; Simons, *Cities of Ladies*.

37 Otis, *Prostitution in Medieval Society*; Karras, *Common Women*; Rossiaud, *Medieval Prostitution*.

38 Ariès, *Centuries of Childhood*; Shahar, *Childhood in the Middle Ages*; Boswell, *The Kindness of Strangers*; Gavitt, *Charity and Children*.

39 Sheehan, ed., *Aging and the Aged in Medieval Europe*; Cullum, *Cremetts and Corrodies*; Rosen, "The Mentally Ill," pp. 377–88.

40 For a discussion of this, see Tierney, *Medieval Poor Law*, pp. 47–9, and Brodman, *Charity and Welfare*, pp. 135–7, 203.

41 This argument has been made for Castile by Carmen López, for Valencia by Agustín Rubio, for England by Miri Rubin, for Italy by Philip Gavitt. See Brodman, *Charity and Welfare*, pp. 131–3, 202.

42 Wolf (*Poverty of Riches*, pp. 20–9, 44–5), for example, argues that lay society rejected the social gospel in favor of a mendicant spirituality that idealized poverty; Ruiz (*From Heaven to Earth*, pp. 42–3, 112, 115, 121) argues that lay charitable giving was nothing more than a businessman's bargain with God.

43 For example, on the association between material need and religious, see Henderson, *Piety and Charity in Late Medieval Florence*, pp. 252–4.

44 Vauchez, *Sainthood in the Late Middle Ages*, pp.199–206, 243, 275.

45 Andrews, *The Early Humiliati*; Brasher, *Women of the Humiliati*. For a general overview of scholarship on confraternities, see Vauchez, "Les Confréries au Moyen Age," pp. 467–77; Vauchez, *The Laity in the Middle Ages*. Parish history has yet to be adequately explored by modern historians. One of the few useful studies is French, *People of the Parish*.

46 For example, in medieval Genoa, where urban institutions were highly developed, charity remained fundamentally the responsibility of ecclesiastical corporations until the fifteenth century, at which time laymen and the town itself began to assume an important role – but only because the former were no longer able to shoulder the burden alone. See Epstein, *Genoa and the Genoese*, pp. 303–4.

47 Thompson, *Cities of God*, p. 3.

48 Crislip, *From Monastery to Hospital*; Miller, *The Birth of the Hospital in the Byzantine Empire*; Dols, "The Origins of the Islamic Hospital," pp. 367–90; Nutton, "Review Essay," pp. 218–21.

49 Riley-Smith, *The Knights of St John*; Miller, "The Knights of Saint John," pp. 709–33; Mitchell, *Medicine in the Crusades*; Edgington, "Medical Care," pp. 27–34; Luttrell, "The Hospitaller's Medical Tradition," pp. 64–81; Le Blévec, *La Part du pauvre*, vol. 1, pp. 94–6.

50 García Ballester, *La medicina a la Valencia*; McVaugh, *Medicine before the Plague*. Anthologies include Barry and Jones, eds, *Medicine and Charity before the Welfare State*, and Bowers, *The Medieval Hospital and Medical Practice*. On medicine and women, see Siraisi, *Medieval and Early Renaissance Medicine*; Jacquart and Thomasset, *Sexuality and Medicine in the Middle Ages*; Green, "Women's Medical Practice," pp. 434–73; Serrano, *Medicina y enfermedad*.

51 Moore, *Formation of a Persecuting Society*; Wolf, *The Poverty of Riches*, pp. 20–9.

Bibliography

A pobreza e a assistência aos pobres na península ibérica durante a idade media Actas das 1.as jornadad luso-espanholas de história medieval, Lisboa, 25–30 de Setembro de 1972, 2 vols (Lisbon: Instituto de Alta Cultura, 1973).

Actes du 110e Congrès national des sociétés savantes, 3 vols; vol. 1: *Santé, médecine et assistance au moyen âge* (Paris: Editions du CTHS, 1987).

Aguado de Cordova, Antonio Francisco, ed., *Bullarium equestris ordinis S. Iocobi de Spatha* (Madrid: Ioannis de Ariztia, 1719).

Alberzoni, Maria Pia, and Grassi, Ororato, eds, *La carità a Milano nei secoli XII–XV: Atti del Convegno di Studi Milano, 6–7 novembre 1987* (Milan: Editoriale Jaca Book, 1989).

Andrews, Frances, *The Early Humiliati* (Cambridge: Cambridge University Press, 1999).

Ariès, Philippe, *Centuries of Childhood: A Social History of Family Life*, trans. Robert Baldick (New York: Vintage Books, 1962).

Assistance et assistés jusqu'à 1610: Actes du 97e congrès national des sociétés savantes, Nantes, 1972 (Paris: Bibliothèque national, 1979).

Barber, Malcolm, ed., *The Military Orders*, vol. 1: *Fighting for the Faith and Caring for the Sick* (Aldershot: Ashgate, 1994).

Barber, Malcolm, "The Order of Saint Lazarus and the Crusades," *Catholic Historical Review*, 80 (1994), 439–56.

Barry, Jonathan, and Jones, Colin, eds, *Medicine and Charity before the Welfare State* (London: Routledge, 1991).

Batlle i Gallart, Carme, *La Seu d'Urgell medieval: La ciutat i els seus habitants* (Barcelona: Editorial Rafael Dalmau, 1985).

Batlle i Gallart, Carme, *L'assistència als pobres a la Barcelona medieval (s. XIII)* (Barcelona: Editorial Rafael Dalmau, 1987).

Baucells i Reig, Josep, ed., *El maresme i la Pia Almoina de la Seu de Barcelona: Catàleg del fons en pergamí de l'Arxiu Capitular de la Catedral de Barcelona* (Barcelona: Generalitat de Catalunya, 1987).

Beriac, Françoise, *Histoire des lépreux au moyen age, une société d'exclus* (Paris: Éditions Imago, 1988).

Bériou Nicole, and Touati, François-Olivier, *Voluntate dei Leprosos: Les Lépeux entre conversion et exclusion aux XIIème et XIIIème siècles* (Spoleto: Centro Italiano de Studi sull'alto Medioevo, 1991).

Bertran i Roigé, Prim, "El menjador de l'almoina de la catédral de Lleida: Notes sobre l'alimentació dels pobres lleidatans al 1338," *Ilerda*, 40 (1979), pp. 89–124.

Bofarull y de Sartario, Manuel de, *Gremios y confradias de la antigua Corona de Aragón.* Colección de documentos inéditos del Archivo General de la Corona de Aragón, vols. 40, 41, 2 vols (Barcelona: En la imprenta del Archivo and L. Benaiges, 1876–1910).

Bonenfant, P., "Hôpitaux et Bienfaisance publique dans les an ciens Pays-Bas des origines à la fin du xviiie siècle," *Annales de la Société Belge d'Histoire des Hôpitaux*, 3 (1965), pp. 1–195.

Boswell, John, *The Kindness of Strangers: The Abandonment of Children in Western Europe from Late Antiquity to the Renaissance* (New York: Pantheon Books, 1988).

Bowers, Barbara, ed., *The Medieval Hospital and Medical Practice* (Aldershot: Ashgate, 2006).

Brasher, Sally Mayall, *Women of the Humiliati: A Lay Religious Order in Medieval Civic Life* (New York: Routledge, 2003).

Brodman, James William, "Military Redemptionism and the Castilian Reconquest, 1180–1250," *Military Affairs*, 44 (1980), pp. 24–7.

Brodman, James W., *Ransoming Captives in Crusader Spain: The Order of Merced on the Christian–Islamic Frontier* (Philadelphia: University of Pennsylvania Press, 1986).

Brodman, James W., *Charity and Welfare: Hospitals and the Poor in Medieval Catalonia* (Philadelphia: University of Pennsylvania Press, 1998).

Brodman, James W., "Rule and Identity: The Case of the Military Orders," *Catholic Historical Review*, 87 (2001), pp. 383–400.

Brodman, James William, "Religion and Discipline in the Hospitals of Thirteenth-Century France," in Barbara Bowers, ed., *The Medieval Hospital and Medical Practice* (Aldershot: Ashgate, 2006), pp. 123–32.

Brune, Paul, *Histoire de l'Ordre Hospitalier du Saint-Esprit* (Paris: C. Martin, 1892).

Burns, Robert I., SJ, *The Crusader Kingdom of Valencia: Reconstruction on a Thirteenth-Century Frontier*, 2 vols (Cambridge, MA: Harvard University Press, 1967).

Cheney, C. R., "The Earliest English Diocesan Statutes," *English Historical Review*, 75 (1960), pp. 1–29.

Cipollone, Giulio, O.SS.T., *Cristianità-Islam: Cattività e liberazione in nome di dio: Il tempo di Innocenzo III dopo "il 1187"* (Rome: Editrice Pontificia Università Gregoriana, 1992).

Cipollone, Giulio, O.SS.T., ed., *La liberazione dei "captivi" tra cristianità e islam: Oltre la crociata e il Ǧihād: Tolleranza e servizio umanitario* (Vatican City: Archivio Segreto Vaticano, 2000).

Clay, Rotha Mary, *The Mediaeval Hospitals of England* (London: Methuen, 1909; repr. London: Cass, 1966).

Cohn, Samuel K., *Death and Property in Siena, 1205–1800* (Baltimore: Johns Hopkins University Press, 1988).

Contreras Mas, Antonio, *La asistencia publica a los leprosos en Mallorca: Siglos XIV al XIX* (Mallorca: En Tall, 1990).

Crislip, Andrew, *From Monastery to Hospital: Christian Monasticism and the Transformation of Health Care in Late Antiquity* (Ann Arbor, MI: University of Michigan Press, 2005).

Cullum, Patricia Helena, "Hospitals and Charitable Provision in Medieval Yorkshire, 936–1547," D.Phil. thesis (University of York, 1989).

Cullum, Patricia Helena, *Cremetts and Corrodies: Care of the Poor and Sick at St Leonard's Hospital, York, in the Middle Ages* (York: Borthwick Papers, No. 79, 1991).

Dols, Michael W., "The Leper in Medieval Islamic Society," *Speculum*, 58/4, (1983), 891–916.

Dols, Michael W., "The Origins of the Islamic Hospital," *Bulletin of Medical History*, 61 (1987), pp. 367–90.

Dufour, Jean, and Platelle, Henri eds, *Fondations et œuvres charitables au Moyen Âge: Actes du 121e Congrès national des sociétés historiques et scientifiques: Section d'histoire médiévale et philologie, Nice, 1996.* (Paris: Les Éditions du CTHS, 1999).

Durán Gudiol, Antonio, *El hospital de Somport entre Aragón y Bèarn (siglos XII y XIII)* (Saragossa: Guara Editorial, 1986).

Edgington, Susan, "Medical Care in the Hospital of St John in Jerusalem," in Helen Nicholson, ed., *The Military Orders*, vol. 2: *Welfare and Warfare* (Aldershot: Ashgate, 1998), pp. 27–34.

Epstein, Steven, *Genoa and the Genoese, 958–1528* (Chapel Hill, NC: University of North Carolina Press, 1996).

Epstein, Steven, *Wills and Wealth in Medieval Genoa, 1150–1250* (Cambridge, MA: Harvard University Press, 1984).

Forey, A. J., "Women and the Military Orders in the Twelfth and Thirteenth Centuries," *Studia monastica*, 29 (1987), pp. 63–92.

Forey, A. J., "The Military Orders and the Ransoming of Captives from Islam (Twelfth to Early Fourteenth Centuries)," *Studia monastica*, 33 (1991), pp. 259–79.

French, Katherine L., *People of the Parish: Community Life in a Late Medieval Parish* (Philadelphia: University of Pennsylvania Press, 2000).

Friedman, Yvonne, *Encounter between Enemies: Captivity and Ransom in the Latin Kingdom of Jerusalem* (Leiden: Brill, 2002).

García Ballester, Lluís, *La medicina a la Valencia medieval: Medicina i societat en un país medieval mediterrani* (Valencia: Institució Valenciana d'Estudis i Investigació, 1988).

Gavitt, Philip, *Charity and Children in Renaissance Florence: The Ospedale degli Innocenti, 1410–1536* (Ann Arbor, MI: University of Michigan Press, 1990).

Geremek, Bronislaw, *The Margins of Society in Late Medieval Paris*, trans. Jean Birrell (Cambridge: Cambridge University Press, 1987).

Geremek, Bronislaw, *Poverty: A History*, trans. Agnieszka Kolakowska (Oxford: Basil Blackwell, 1994).

Godfrey, Walter H., *The English Almshouse with Some Account of its Predecessor, the Medieval Hospital* (London: Faber and Faber, 1955).

Green, Monica, "Women's Medical Practice and Medical Care in Medieval Europe," *Signs*, 14/2 (1989), pp. 434–73.

Guilleré, Christian, "Assistance et charité à Gérone au début du XIVème siècle," in R. I. U., Manuel, ed., *La pobreza y la asistencia a los pobres en la cataluña medieval: Volumen misceláneo de estudios y documentos*, Anuario de Estudios Medievales, 9 (Barcelona: Consejo Superior de Investigaciones Científicas, 1980), pp. 191–204.

Guilleré, Christian, *Diner, poder i societat a la Girona del segle XIV* (Girona: Ajuntament de Girona, 1984).

Guilleré, Christian, *Girona medieval: L'etapa d'apogeu, 1285–1360* (Gerona: Diputació de Girona: Ajuntament de Girona, 1991).

Guilleré, Christian, *Girona al segle XIV*, trans. Núria Mañé, 2 vols (Girona: Publicacions de l'Abadia de Montserrat, 1993–4).

Harper-Bill, Christopher, ed., *Charters of the Medieval Hospitals of Bury St Edmunds* (Rochester, NY: Boydell Press, 1994).

Henderson, John, "Hospitals of Late Medieval and Renaissance Florence: A Preliminary Survey," in Lindsay Granshaw and Roy Porter, eds, *The Hospital in History* (London and New York: Routledge, 1989), pp. 63–92.

Henderson, John, *Piety and Charity in Late Medieval Florence* (Oxford: Clarendon Press, 1994).

Henderson, John, *The Renaissance Hospital: Healing the Body and Healing the Soul* (New Haven: Yale University Press, 2006).

Hergueta, Narciso, "Noticias Históricas del Maestre Diego de Villar, médico de los reyes Alfonso VIII, Doña Berenguela y San Francisco, de los hospitales y hospederías que hugo en la Rioja en los siglos XII y XIII, y de la Villa de Villar de Torre," *Revista de archivos, bibliotecas y museos*, 10 (1904), pp. 423–34; 11 (1904), pp. 126–32.

Hernández Iglesias, Fermin, *La beneficencia en España*, 2 vols (Madrid: Tipogràfica de Manuel Minuesa, 1876).

Imbert, Jean, ed., *Histoire des hôpitaux en France* (Toulouse: Privat, 1982).

Imbert, Jean, *Les Hôpitaux en droit canonique* (Paris: J. Vrin, 1947).

Jacquart, Danielle, and Thomasset, Claude, *Sexuality and Medicine in the Middle Ages*, trans. Matthew Adamson (Princeton: Princeton University Press, 1988).

Jetter, Dieter, *Geschichte des Hospitals*, vol. 1: *Westdeutschland von des Anfängen bis 1850* (Weisbaden: Franz Steiner Verlag, 1966).

Johnson, Penelope, *Equal in Monastic Profession: Religious Women in Medieval France* (Chicago: University of Chicago Press, 1991).

Jugnot, G., "Deux fondations augustiniennes en faveur des pèlerins: Aubrac et Roncevaux," in Marie-Humbert Vicaire, ed., *Assistance et charité*, Cahiers de Fanjeaux, 13 (Toulouse: E. Privat, 1978), pp. 321–41.

Karras, Ruth Mazo, *Common Women: Prostitution and Sexuality in Medieval Europe* (Oxford: Oxford University Press, 1996).

Kłoczowski, Jerzy, *A History of Polish Christianity* (Cambridge: Cambridge University Press, 2000).

Le Blévec, Daniel, *La Part du pauvre: L'Assistance dans les pays du Bas-Rhône du XIIe au milieu du XVe siècle*, Collection, 265, 2 vols (Rome: École française de Rome, 2000).

Le Blévec, Daniel, "Le Rôle des femmes dans l'assistance et la charité," in M.-H. Vicaire, ed., *La Femme dans la vie religieuse du Languedoc (XIIIe–XVe s.)*, Cahiers de Fanjeaux, 23 (Toulouse: Edouard Privat, 1988), pp. 171–90.

Le Grand, Léon, ed., *Statuts d'Hotels-Dieu et de léproseries: Recueil de textes du XIIe au XIVe siècle* (Paris: Alphonse Picard et Fils, 1901).

Lladonosa i Pujol, Josep, *La pediatria als antics hospicis de Lérida* (Lerida: Primer Congres de Pediatres de Llengua Catalan, 1978).

Lladonosa i Pujol, Josep, "Noticia sobre els hospitals medievals de Lleida," in *Colli Alentorn Miquel: Miscel.lània d'homentage en el seu visitante aniversari* (Barcelona: Fundacion Jaume I, 1984), pp. 291–308.

Linás y Aznor, José, ed., *Bullarium coelestis ac regalis ordinis B. Mariae Virginis de Mercede Redemptionis Captivorum* (Barcelona: Raphaëlis Figueró, 1696).

López Alonso, Carmen, *La pobreza en la España medieval* (Madrid: Ministerio de Trabajo y Seguridad, 1986).

Luttrell, Anthony, "The Hospitaller's Medical Tradition, 1291–1530," in Malcolm Barber, ed., *The Military Orders*, vol. 1: *Fighting for the Faith and Caring for the Sick* (Aldershot: Ashgate, 1994), pp. 64–81.

McVaugh, Michael R., *Medicine before the Plague: Practitioners and their Patients in the Crown of Aragon, 1285–1345* (Cambridge: Cambridge University Press, 1993).

Marcombe, David, *Leper Knights: The Order of St Lazarus of Jerusalem in England*, c. *1150–1544* (Rochester, NY: Boydell, 2003).

Martínez Garcia, Luis, *La asistencia a los pobres en Burgos en la baja edad media: El hospital de Santa Maria la Real, 1341–1500* (Burgos: Excma. Diputación Provincial de Burgos, 1981).

Martínez García, Luis, *El Hospital del Rey de Burgos: Un señorío medieval en la expansion y en la crisis (siglos XIII y XIV)* (Burgos: Ediciones J. Garrido Garrido, 1986).

Marx, Walter John, *The Development of Charity in Medieval Louvain* (Yonkers, NY: printed by the author, 1936).

Miller, Timothy S., *The Birth of the Hospital in the Byzantine Empire*, 2nd edn (Baltimore: Johns Hopkins University Press, 1997).

Miller, Timothy S., "The Knights of Saint John and the Hospitals of the Latin West," *Speculum*, 53 (1978), pp. 709–33.

Mischlewski, Adalbert, *Un ordre hospitalier au moyen âge: Les Chanoines reguliers de Saint-Antoine-en-Viennois* (Grenoble: Presses Universitaires de Grenoble, 1995).

Mitchell, Piers D., *Medicine in the Crusades: Warfare, Wounds and the Medieval Surgeon* (Cambridge: Cambridge University Press, 2004).

Mollat, Michel, ed., *Études sur l'histoire de la pauvreté (Moyen Âge–XVIe siècle)*, 2 vols (Paris: Publications de la Sorbonne, 1974).

Mollat, Michel, *Les Pauvres au Moyen Age: Étude sociale* (Paris: Hachette, 1978); English translation: *The Poor in the Middle Ages: An Essay in Social History.* trans. Arthur Goldhammer (New Haven: Yale University Press, 1986).

Moore, R. I., *The Formation of a Persecuting Society: Power and Deviance in Western Europe, 950–1250* (Oxford: Basil Blackwell, 1987).

Mundy, John H., "Charity and Social Work in Toulouse, 1100–1250," *Traditio*, 22 (1966), pp. 203–87.

Nicholson, Helen, ed., *The Military Orders*, vol. 2: *Welfare and Warfare* (Aldershot: Ashgate, 1998).

Nutton, Vivian, "Review Essay," *Medical History*, 30 (1986), pp. 218–21.

Orme, Nicholas, and Webster, Margaret, *The English Hospital, 1070–1570* (New Haven: Yale University Press, 1995).

Ostolaza, Maria Isabel, ed., *Colección diplomática de Santa Maria de Roncesvalles (1127–1300)* (Pamplona: Consejo superior de investigaciones científicas, 1978).

Otis, Leah Lydia, *Prostitution in Medieval Society: The History of an Urban Institution in Languedoc* (Chicago: University of Chicago Press, 1985).

Porras Arboledas, Pedro Andrés, *La Orden de Santiago en el siglo XV* (Madrid: Dykinson, 1997).

Pullan, Brian, *Rich and Poor in Renaissance Venice: The Social Institutions of a Catholic State to 1620* (Cambridge, MA: Harvard University Press, 1971).

Rawcliffe, Carole, *The Hospitals of Medieval Norwich* (Norwich: University of East Anglia, Centre of East Anglia Studies, 1995).

"Register of the Hospital of St Mary: A Calendar, Ordinances," in The ORB: On-line Reference Book for Medieval Studies, http://the-orb.net/encyclop/culture/towns/yarmout4.html (accessed Feb. 23, 2004).

Reines, Lorenzo, ed., *Bullarium ordinis Sanctissimae Trinitatis Redemptionis Cativorum collectum et scholiatum* (1761; MS copy, Archive of San Carlos, Rome, 1965).

Ricci, Giovanni, "Naissance du pauvre honteux: Entre l'histoire des idées et l'histoire sociale," *Annales: Économies, sociétés, civilizations*, 38(1983), pp. 158–77.

Richards, Peter, *The Medieval Leper and his Northern Heirs* (Cambridge: D. S. Brewer, 1977).

Riley-Smith, Jonathan, *The Knights of St John in Jerusalem and Cyprus*, c. *1050–1310* (London: Macmillan, 1967).

Riu, Manual, ed., *La pobreza y la asistencia a los pobres en la Cataluña medieval*, 2 vols (Barcelona: CSIC, 1980–2).

Rodriguez, Jarbel, *Captives and their Saviors in the Medieval Crown of Aragon* (Washington: Catholic University of America Press, 2007).

Rosen, George, "The Mentally Ill and the Community in Western and Central Europe during the Late Middle Ages and Renaissance," *Journal of the History of Medicine*, 19 (1986), pp. 377–88.

Rossiaud, Jacques, *Medieval Prostitution*, trans. Lydia G. Cochrane (Oxford: Basil Blackwell, 1988).

Rubin, Miri, *Charity and Community in Medieval Cambridge* (Cambridge: Cambridge University Press, 1987).

Rubio Vela, Agustín, *Pobreza, enfermedad y asistencia hospitalaria en la Valencia del siglo XIV* (Valencia: Institucion Alfonso el Magnanimo, 1984).

Rucquoi, Adeline, "Hospitalisation et charité à Valladolid," in *Les Sociétés urbaines en France médidionale et en Péninsule Ibérique au moyen âge. Actes du Colloque de Pau, 21–23 Septembre 1988* (Paris: Centre national de la recherche scientifique, 1991), pp. 393–408.

Ruiz, Teofilo F., *From Heaven to Earth: The Reordering of Castilian Society, 1150–1350* (Princeton: Princeton University Pres, 2004).

Saenz Terreros, M. V., *El hospital de peregrinos y la cofradia de Santo Domingo de la Calzada desde su fundación hasta la crisis del antiguo regimen* (Longroño: Instituto de Estudios Tiojanos, Consejo Superior de Investigaciones Científicas, 1986).

Serrano Larráyoz, Fernando, *Medicina y enfermedad en la corte de Carlos III* el Noble *de Navarra (1387–1425)*, Temas de Historia de la Medicina, No. 2 (Pamplona: Fondo de Publicaciones del Gobierno de Navarra, 2004).

Shahar, Shulamith, *Childhood in the Middle Ages* (London: Routledge, 1990).

Sheehan, Michael, ed., *Aging and the Aged in Medieval Europe: Selected Papers from the Annual Conference of the Centre for Medieval Studies, University of Toronto, held 25–26 February and 11–12 November 1983* (Toronto: Pontifical Institute for Medieval Studies, 1, 1900).

Simons, Walter, *Cities of Ladies: Beguine Communities in the Medieval Low Countries, 1200–1565* (Philadelphia: University of Pennsylvania Press, 2001).

Siraisi, Nancy G., *Medieval and Early Renaissance Medicine: An Introduction to Knowledge and Practice* (Chicago: University of Chicago Press, 1990).

Spiegeler, P. de, *Les Hôpitaux et l'assistance à Liège (Xᵉ–XVᵉ s.): Aspects institutionnels et sociaux* (Paris: Les Belles Lettres, 1987; Lettres de l'Université de Liège Fasc. 249 of Bibliothèque de la Faculté de Philosophie).

Tarragó Valentines, J. F., *Hospitales en Lérida durante los siglos XII al XVI* (Lerida: n.p., 1975).

Taylor, Bruce, *Structures of Reform: The Mercedarian Order in the Spanish Golden Age* (Leiden: Brill, 2000).

Thompson, Augustine, *Cities of God: The Religion of the Italian Commune, 1125–1325* (University Park, PA: Pennsylvania State University Press, 2005).

Tierney, Brian, *Medieval Poor Law: A Sketch of Canonical Theory and its Application in England* (Berkeley and Los Angeles: University of California Press, 1959).

Tolivar Faes, J., *Hospitales de leprosos en Asturias durante las edades media y modera* (Oviedo: Imprenta "La Cruz", Instituto de Estudios Asturianos, 1966).

Touati, François-Olivier, *Maladie et société au moyen âge: La Lépre, les lepreux et les léproseries dans la province ecclésiastique de Sens jusqu'au milieu de XIVᵉ siècle*. Bibliothèque du Moyen Age, 11 (Brussels: De Boeck Université, 1998).

Vauchez, André, "Les Confréries au moyen age: esquisse d'un bilan historiographique," *Revue historique*, 275/2 (1986), pp. 407–67.

Vauchez, André, *The Laity in the Middle Ages: Religious Beliefs and Devotional Practices*, ed. and intro. Daniel E. Bornstein, trans. Margery J. Schneider (Notre Dame, IN: Notre Dame University Press, 1993).

Vauchez, André, *Sainthood in the Late Middle Ages*, trans. Jean Birrell (Cambridge: Cambridge University Press, 1997).

Vicaire, Marie-Humbert, ed., *Assistance et charité*, Cahiers de Fanjeaux, 13 (Toulouse: E. Privat, 1978).

Watson, Sethina, "The Origins of the English Hospital," *Transactions of the Royal Historical Society*, ser. 6, 16 (2006), pp. 75–94.

Wolf, Kenneth Baxter, *The Poverty of Riches: St Francis of Assisi Reconsidered* (Oxford: Oxford University Press, 2003).

Further Reading

Barber, Malcolm, ed., *The Military Orders*, vol. 1: *Fighting for the Faith and Caring for the Sick* (Aldershot: Ashgate, 1994). This contains key studies of the hospital activities of the military orders.

Brodman, James W., *Charity and Welfare: Hospitals and the Poor in Medieval Catalonia* (Philadelphia: University of Pennsylvania Press, 1998). This is a useful survey of the various types of hospitals and the services they provided to clients.

Gavitt, Philip, *Charity and Children in Renaissance Florence: The Ospedale degli Innocenti, 1410–1536* (Ann Arbor, MI: University of Michigan Press, 1990). This is an excellent study of one particular institution that served orphans in the Late Middle Ages, highlighting the problems of infant mortality.

Geremek, Bronislaw. *Poverty: A History*, trans. Agnieszka Kolakowska (Oxford: Basil Blackwell, 1994). This is a fundamental study of the ideas of poverty and the social responses to it.

Henderson, John, *The Renaissance Hospital: Healing the Body and Healing the Soul* (New Haven: Yale University Press, 2006). This recent study highlights the dual religious and care functions of the hospital.

McVaugh, Michael R., *Medicine before the Plague: Practitioners and their Patients in the Crown of Aragon, 1285–1345* (Cambridge: Cambridge University Press, 1993). This is the best available study in English of medical practice in the High Middle Ages.

Miller, Timothy S., *The Birth of the Hospital in the Byzantine Empire*, 2nd edn (Baltimore: Johns Hopkins University Press, 1997). This is the classic, if sometimes controversial, study of hospitals and medicine in the Byzantine world.

Nicholson, Helen, ed., *The Military Orders*, vol. 2: *Welfare and Warfare* (Aldershot: Ashgate, 1998). This volume contains useful studies of the configuration and practices of medieval hospitals.

Rubin, Miri, *Charity and Community in Medieval Cambridge* (Cambridge: Cambridge University Press, 1987). This is an important local study that traces the development of hospitals and other charitable activities during the High and Late Middle Ages.

Vauchez, André, *The Laity in the Middle Ages: Religious Beliefs and Devotional Practices*, ed. and intro. Daniel E. Bornstein, trans. Margery J. Schneider (Notre Dame, IN: Notre Dame University Press, 1993).

Chapter Thirteen

Popular Belief and Heresy

Carol Lansing

In June of 1345, the commune of Florence burned to death Giovanni di Jacobo Cherucci, otherwise known as Brother John the Hermit and Friend of God.[1] His court sentence enumerates a long list of frauds, including using phoney religious claims to seduce women. Brother John is something of a puzzle for a historian of medieval popular belief and heresy, for several reasons. First, what might his case suggest about what some lay people actually believed, given his evident insincerity and his victims' gullibility? Secondly, to my knowledge he was never charged with heresy. Can he nevertheless be considered a heretic, since he was sentenced for things that got other people condemned for heresy – if nothing else, pretended sanctity and illicit preaching. Thirdly, he was also charged with things that were often used against people considered heretical, including fraud, greed, and sexual voracity. Historians tend to discount those charges as stereotypical smears, but Brother John was apparently guilty. The case is thus vivid evidence of the complexities of studying medieval religious belief. It can serve to introduce some of the themes of this chapter: popular currents of belief and doubt, the problem of hostile sources, the ways later understandings have shaped ideas about medieval belief, how medieval heresy was defined, and how contemporaries viewed that definition.

Brother John the Hermit and Friend of God was tried, not in an ecclesiastical tribunal, but in the Florentine criminal court. According to his six-page sentence, he claimed that when he was 8 the Virgin Mary told him to leave his parents and live as a hermit in the Babylonian desert. He stayed there for ten years and ate no bread or wine, only roots, herbs, and manna provided to him by the Holy Spirit. As a result, he had no stomach or viscera. A sign on his left breast was given to him as a mark of divine inspiration. Actually, his sentence reads, he had never been to Babylonia, did not have a dried-up belly, and had received the mark when someone cut him with a sword, in Sicily. He was a holy man only "in word and in mantle." Brother John made these claims and displayed his body, to get money and goods, particularly in Mantua, Ferrara, the Bolognese countryside, and Florence, even from nuns.

One specialty was love charms for women. These required that he use a piece of thread to measure the woman's vulva and vagina; then he bound it up with some of his sperm in a bit of linen, which the woman was to wear around her neck for forty days. The promised result was indissoluble love between man and woman. The sentence lists four women who bought charms, whose Christian names the court explicitly considered it better to keep secret, including a nun. They did not hesitate to mention the women's targets: one Florentine wanted a charm because she was in love with Jacopo de' Cavalcanti. In their cases Brother John succeeded in his goal, which was to penetrate them from the rear. This was simply phoney magic. However, when he tried the same strategy with a woman of the village of Villa Nova, he promised her not a love charm but to free her from the sins she had committed with the local priest. She realized what he intended and refused him. He did deceive four other women in the Florentine countryside, promising to free them from sin and then enjoying carnal knowledge. Brother John also sold bits of writing that allowed a person to travel among enemies unharmed, protected by Jesus. He was so full of grace that he was able to walk on hot coals without burning his feet, flagellating himself. And he knew who was in Purgatory and how to free them. He told a Florentine woman named Silvestra that for five soldi he would free her mother and brother from Purgatory and lead them to glory. Brother John even managed to extort money from two nuns at the Florentine convent of San Pier Gattolino, again promising with the use of candles and the paternoster to lead people from Purgatory to eternal life.

The Problem of Sources

What can we make of this text? First, it evidently repeats Brother John's confession, mentioning, for example, when he could not remember a victim's name. It is very possible that he confessed under torture. Torture was allowed in civic and ecclesiastical courts when there were strong indications of guilt that did not meet the stringent requirements for proof; a confession made during torture also had to repeated away from the place of torture to be considered valid.[2] Civic records of the sentences of people who were tortured – often thieves – generally include all the points of their confessions, even those that were not relevant to the charge. His sentence does that: for example, he also admitted to bigamy, detailing how he had married three women in three different cities.

Can we give his coerced sentence any credence? The problematic status of this text is all too typical of the evidence for popular belief, heretical or not. In general, the study of medieval popular belief and heresy repeatedly underscores the ways in which the nature of the evidence shapes our information about the past. Most of the evidence is normative, efforts by clerics to teach right belief or identify wrong. These include sermons and exempla, designed to foster right belief, sometimes through tales of the correction of error or doubt. Penitentials and confessor's manuals, by contrast, do list sins, including errors of belief as well as of practice, in order to teach priests how best to respond to them. All of this evidence is indirect. For heresy in particular, most of the evidence is also hostile, accounts written by clerics who were quick to impose stereotypes and had strong incentives to picture these religious groups as organized alternatives to the Catholic Church. For the eleventh and twelfth centuries, most accounts are from chronicles, letters, and treatises. They have been heavily scrutinized by a number of superb historians.[3] For the eleventh century, there are references to scattered small groups, notably an aristocratic circle of canons at Orléans who probably believed in a variant of Gnosticism, and a circle of radical ascetics at Monforte, in the Piedmont. Another group was the Patarenes of Milan, who assailed what they along with the Gregorian reformers perceived as clerical corruption, including simony and marriage. In the early twelfth century, the same kinds of sources describe charismatic wandering preachers like Tanchelm in the Low Countries, who attacked what he considered clerical immorality and, according to very hostile sources, parodied the sacraments, most famously by marrying an image of the Virgin and then demanding wedding gifts. The best documented is Henry of Lausanne, a popular evangelical preacher who urged penance and criticized clerical wealth and abuses, inspiring in Le Mans popular rage against the clergy. Henry challenged papal teachings over the sacraments and ceremonies, marriage, baptism, confession, and prayers for the dead. The late twelfth century saw the appearance of movements that became widespread, notably the group that became the Waldensians, who stressed poverty and preaching and were initially condemned over disobedience to Church authority. The Cathars also appeared in this period, a faith based in part on Scripture that broke radically with Catholicism. Cathars believed in varieties of dualism and teaching poverty and physical purification as a means of escaping the corruption of matter. Their origins have been much debated.[4]

With the creation of the papal inquisitions in the 1230s, the evidence multiplies and changes form. The inquisitors pursued not only Cathars and Waldensians, but radical Franciscans, mystics, converted Jews. At the end of the fourteenth century, Church courts in England pursued the Lollards, followers of the Oxford theologian John Wyclif, who developed his emphasis on the primacy of the authority of Scripture. For these groups, most of the influential sources are the descriptions in thirteenth- and fourteenth-century manuals designed to aid inquisitors in catching heretics. One core problem is whether these hostile texts can be read against the grain. They are certainly revealing of the justification and mechanisms of persecution. Their authors had a considerable investment in representing heresy as an organized, serious threat to the Church. We also have the depositions of witnesses and accused heretics that were recorded by inquisitions, as well as their sentences. These range from the very terse statements of thousands of people questioned in big inquests like the one held in the Languedoc in 1245–6, to extraordinarily detailed depositions. Significantly, the texts we have are not verbatim transcripts, but rather later redactions. Scribes translated depositions into Latin, omitted the questions and often condensed the answers into a third-person narrative. Ironically, because these texts record people's statements about their beliefs and practices, they are a main source not only for heresy but for popular belief more generally. Individual statements of belief were rarely recorded by secular institutions, which is one reason Brother John's sentence is an oddity.

Is it possible to learn anything of people's beliefs and experience from sources that are hostile, depositions given under duress and shaped by the inquisitorial process? John Arnold in 2001 asked a harder question: is it even ethical for a historian to make the attempt, since it means profiting from the work of the inquisitors, using information people provided only because they were under terrible threats? If you strip away the inquisitor's influence but use the confession to answer your own questions, do you not step into his role?[5] Most historians, Arnold included, do see value in attempting to reconstruct the beliefs and experience of accused people who would otherwise be lost to history. Arnold took a Foucauldian approach, examining them in terms of the construction of discourse. Adriano Prosperi recently wrote of using these sources in terms of the remembrance of victims: we as historians are able to seek to recover the names and identities of people who suffered because of thoughts, words, spoken or written, or deeds, that broke with the obligatory "remembering them, in opposition to the logic of the inquisition which sought to cancel their names and memories."[6] This is a moving justification. However, as I will suggest, it can also encourage a sentimental view. The fact that people were the victims of persecution does not mean they were all admirable. Brother John with his sleazy scams became a victim as well!

To use these hostile texts requires a precise understanding of the legal, political, and social factors that produced the documents to try to work out what ideas or accounts might actually have come from the person questioned rather than from the coercive methods and formulaic questions of the tribunal. The study of popular belief and heresy has thus fostered the meticulous attention to textual criticism that is the hallmark of the best medieval scholarship; the most devastating reviews point out textual sloppiness. One classic example is Leonard Boyle's discussion of Emmanuel Le Roy Ladurie's 1975 *Montaillou.*[7] Ladurie drew on the extraordinarily detailed depositions collected by the inquisitor Jacques Fournier to create a brilliant, highly successful ethnography of a fourteenth-century village in the Pyrenees, including beliefs about time, magic, death, the afterlife. Boyle demonstrated at length that Ladurie's emphasis on collective mentalities and apparent research method – collecting references to specific beliefs and practices without careful regard to context or to the original manuscript – led him into some serious errors.[8]

Only a scattering of texts survive in which lay groups and individuals stated their beliefs directly. This is particularly true for those deemed heretical. Most famously, Marguerite Porete's brilliant mystical treatise *The Mirror of Simple Souls*, burned as heretical in Valenciennes in 1306, survived in anonymous copies in monastic libraries. Romana Guarnieri in 1946 was able to identify an old French version because it contained specific passages condemned by Parisian theologians in 1309, a condemnation that led to its unrepentant author's execution. Latin and Middle English copies have since been found as well.[9] A few Cathar texts also survive because they were preserved in inquisitorial archives.[10] Anne Hudson has discovered and made available a range of Lollard sources, most of them clerical in origin.[11]

Belief and Skepticism

What then of Brother John's sentence? In his case, the questions could not have been formulaic. It may be that the fascination with sex reflects the preoccupations of his questioner. Like Bishop Fournier, the judge asked for details that had little to do with the evidence needed for proof. Or perhaps these were details that he volunteered and the possibly amused notary chose to record.[12] It is not easy to find a context to assess the credibility of the text: we know religious frauds existed, but our details often come from contemporary comic stories, like those of Boccacio, in which religious tricksters used phoney relics and recipes to get sex and money. Perhaps some people found him not a holy man but a buffoon. Like Riperando, a man executed for religious fraud in Bologna fifty years earlier, the tale of Brother John would be amusing – setting aside the sexual predation – if he had not been burned alive.[13] It is also the case that Brother John's scams played cleverly on some of the central themes in late medieval religious culture. One was extreme bodily austerity as proof of divine favor, a pattern particularly associated with women. Holiness could be discerned by visible signs.[14] A second was the idea of Purgatory as an "accountable afterlife" in which pious actions and donations could affect the souls of the dead.[15] Brother John's promise to remit sin and free souls from Purgatory was an extreme version of a highly popular set of practices.

As Brother John's case suggests, medieval people who were not Jews or Muslims operated within a Christian world view.[16] As his scams also imply, this does not mean that everyone was deeply pious. What, after all, could he himself have believed? The question of the extent to which this was an age of faith has long been ideological: historians who argue for widespread orthodox piety often rely on normative evidence and also bring a set of religious convictions to the material.[17] There is certainly no lack of evidence for religious skepticism, once you look for it.[18] People certainly doubted things like the power of the saints or the power of relics. When the corpse of Saint Vincent was carried through a French town and a woman was told to set her work down as a gesture of respect, "She jeeringly said that it was more likely to be the body of some heathen Moor or Spaniard than a martyr."[19] People also questioned the Church's teachings on central points, often the Eucharist. One comment often found in depositions to inquisitors is that, even if the body of Christ was as big as a mountain, the priests would have eaten it up long ago.[20] People could be quite scornful. The Lollard Margery Baxter was recorded as saying: "If that sacrament were God, the true body of Christ, there would be infinite gods, because a thousand priests and more every day make a thousand gods, and afterwards eat those gods, and once they are eaten discharge them through their hinder parts into the stinking latrine, where you can find plenty of such gods . . ."[21] Clerics responded in a number of ways. Alexander of Ashby in a model sermon on the Eucharist urged: "Do not believe that this does not take place, do not doubt whether it takes place, do not inquire how it takes place."[22] Theologians came to distinguish between simple doubt, which could be corrected, and the distorted arguments of the intellectually arrogant.[23] Many well-known Eucharistic miracles explicitly answered doubt, like the Miracle of Bolsena, which led to the institution of the Corpus Christi feast.

People also challenged the Church's social teachings. There are rich studies of twelfth-century preachers like Henry of Lausanne who questioned clerical control of the sacraments – rites of passage such as baptism and marriage – and found enthusiastic followers.[24] It is sometimes possible to find critics of teachings on sexuality. For example, the Church had long condemned all non-procreative sex as sodomy, and from the eleventh century theologians like Peter Damian blasted same-sex relations between men.[25] In the thirteenth century, the condemnation of sodomy was also written into secular law in many places. A rare and poignant case also from the mid-fourteenth-century Florentine court reveals dissent and a willingness to point out hypocrisy. A man named Agostino confessed that he had been an active sodomite for the past twelve years. "And like a man totally inflamed with this grave crime, he stated that he did not consider it a crime but rather *congrue*, fitting." In effect, he gave no credence to the Church's condemnation of sex between men, which to him seemed appropriate. He also said that a lot of other people deserved death if he was to be executed for this reason. Like Brother John, he was burned, on 15 May 1348.[26]

These were criticisms of points of doctrine. Although scholars have argued the contrary, atheism was also imaginable. A prior of Holy Trinity, Aldgate, complained around 1200 that "there are many people who do not believe that God exists. They consider that the universe has always been as it is now and is ruled by chance . . . nor do they think that the human soul lives on after the death of the body."[27] Fra Giordano da Pisa preached in Florence in 1304–5 that many people did not belief in the invisible goods of Paradise. "Today they feel safe from the threats and pains of hell and simply do not believe in them," doubting God's existence because, Giordano thought, they could not reconcile it with the terrible evil in the world.[28] Witnesses in the posthumous trial of Pope Boniface VIII reported not only sodomy and demon worship but comments like "Christ was not the Son of God; he was a crafty and hypocritical man." When Boniface lay dying after the attack at Anagni, as a priest celebrated mass a cardinal said: "Holy Father, behold the Body of Christ." Boniface was furiously angry and shoved him in the face, saying: "The thing you say I should behold is no more the Body of Christ than I am; it is bread." Urged to commend himself to the Virgin, he replied: "That good donkey never existed, nor did her son."[29] The event was a political show trial and it is not clear that Boniface actually said these things, though they have a certain authentic ring. The point is that these were thinkable ideas.

Heresy

Brother John was evidently a fraud and perhaps a skeptic. Was he a heretic? He certainly confessed to things that got other people condemned for heresy, if nothing else the pretense of sanctity and the claim that he could remit sin. Why was he not treated as a heretic? Heresy, after all, was often proven on the basis of practice rather than belief, what people actually did rather than what they said they believed. Again, it was common to charge heretics with being frauds and tricksters, so that sincere belief was not a necessary criterion.[30] What did distinguish variant belief from heresy? Historians have long argued that heresy was not an objective category but a construct, a label used by authorities to condemn people, beliefs, and practices on the grounds that they deviated from the Church's teachings. Heresy, like beauty, lies in the eye of the beholder. No one considered him or herself a heretic. Further, charges of heresy were made by people who claimed legitimate authority within the Christian tradition. Assertions of authority were legitimated by texts, so that heresy charges could become a struggle that hinged on the status of documents. When Bernard of Clairvaux sought Peter Abelard's condemnation at the Council of Sens in 1141, he had first to get the assembled prelates to vote to condemn a specific list of theological points drawn from Abelard's writings. Bernard needed a document accepted by the authority of a Church council to legitimate the claim that these specific views were heretical. Abelard's student famously said that the clerics voted them at dinner, and that it was unclear whether they were saying *condemnamus*, we condemn, or just *namus*, we are drowning, presumably in drink.[31] In the case of Brother John, the issue was not whether he believed in his preposterous scams, but the role of Church authorities. He was not a heretic because he was charged with fraud in a civic court. The sentence even mentions canon law, but in reference to the bigamy, not his religious claims.

How did this understanding come about? The idea that sectarian difference is heresy is hardly exclusive to Christianity, nor is the obligation to correct and punish. The execution of heretics could certainly serve to bolster political authority in Islam as well.[32] In the Christian tradition, the understanding of sectarian division as heresy has existed since the second century, when the attempt to build a unitary canon of belief sparked efforts to classify and attack variants as heresy. It is important to recognize that the construction of variant belief as heresy is rooted in the idea of an original pure Christian doctrine. This was clearly formulated in the fifth-century Canon of St Vincent of Lérins: "in the Catholic Church itself we take the greatest care to hold *that which has been believed everywhere, always and by all.*" The doctrine of the Church is eternal, and those who claim membership but choose not to hold to that doctrine are heretics. However, the idea of an original pure doctrine has long been subject to historical critique. Walter Bauer, in his pioneering *Orthodoxy and Heresy in Earliest Christianity* (published originally in 1934), challenged the notion that Christianity initially spread in a doctrinally pure form and then some groups deviated into heresy. Bauer analysed the century after the apostolic age to argue that variant forms of belief existed and that orthodoxy was essentially the majority view in Rome. It was Rome's monarchical bishop who built a tight knit organization and in the second century campaigned to extend Rome's sphere of influence in the Western Church, in part by imposing orthodoxy. In effect, claims about what became papal primacy and claims about correct doctrine went together. Heresy charges are an exercise of power. The medieval definition of heresy was most clearly formulated in the thirteenth century by Robert Grosseteste: heresy is an opinion chosen by human perception, contrary to Holy Scripture, publicly avowed and obstinately defended.

It was largely Augustine who set the course for the Church's treatment of people considered heretics, providing both for fraternal correction and also for compulsion. The first execution was Priscillian, bishop of Avila, decapitated for heresy in 385. The crucial clarification of the legal status of heretics eight centuries later was again linked to bolstered papal authority, now understood in terms of sovereignty. Pope Innocent III in the 1199 decretal *Vergentes in senium* defined heresy as *lèse-majesté*, high treason in Roman law, an offense against the divine majesty of Christ and by extension the sovereign status and unique judicial authority of his representative, the pope. The definition of heresy as treason against papal sovereignty opened the way for papal inquisitions and provided for the severe penalties for treason in Roman law to be imposed on convicted heretics. In Western Europe, although there was important secular legislation on heresy, notably imperial, the redefinition of heresy reinforced papal monarchy.

While the narrative of medieval heresy was written largely by the winners, it is important to recognize that many contemporaries did not accept the papal and inquisitorial view. Violent resistance was fairly common, ranging from attacks on papal legates and inquisitors to riots.[33] The best documented is a famous episode from Bologna that offers a rare look at what some medieval townsfolk thought about the question. In 1299 the Dominican inquisitors in Bologna condemned two living men and an exhumed corpse as relapsed heretics, and handed them over to the civic authorities to be burned. Probably, the two men were tortured. One of them, a popular local named Bompietro, asked for the sacrament at the last and was denied. Hundreds of townspeople reacted to the sentence and executions with outrage and even urged violence against the inquisitors and the Dominican convent. When the inquisitor, Fra Guido da Vicenza, threatened them with sanctions, they believed him: 320 people confessed their actions and comments to the tribunal. The record of their confessions survives and is an unparalleled look at popular ideas about a papal inquisition's pursuit of heresy. Angry Bolognese townsfolk challenged the inquisitor's morality and authority, saying things like it is the inquisitors who should be burned and not Bompietro, who was a good man and a good Christian. Fra Guido was really just after his money, or, some said, wanted his sister. Some Bolognese went further and questioned the validity of the inquisitorial project itself. A woman named Ysotta di Pietro confessed she had said that heresy must come from the friars.[34] Paolo Trintinelli, a local noble, protested against the sentences when they were read in his parish church, eloquently denying the authority of the inquisitor and his documents. What was done to the two men was an evil deed, Paolo said, and the inquisitor can have whatever he wants written. He himself would not give one bean for those sentences.[35] Seven hundred years later, scholars arrived at much the same view as Ysotta di Pietro and Paolo Trintinelli: heresy did come from the friars, in the sense that it was a construct rather than an objective category.

In part because of the relative nature of the subject, the history of the study of medieval heresy has taken fascinating turns. If heresy had no objective existence, then what is it exactly that a historian of heresy studies? Is it sectarian difference? Or, is it the process by which some authorities came to condemn other Christians as heretical? Currently, a strong body of research analyzes that process within the broader frame of the history of persecution. Yet another approach – important to an older generation of scholars but currently less fashionable – is to treat popular heretical movements as dissent, asking why some beliefs and sectarian groups enjoyed widespread popularity despite their condemnation as heresy by Church authorities.

For all of these reasons, the narrative of medieval heresy has been and remains fascinatingly unstable. Occasionally, scholars score wonderful coups, like Guarnieri's recovery of *The Mirror of Simple Souls.* Another instance concerns the first major dissident group for whom we have evidence: the circle of clerics and layfolk at Orléans in 1022, including the queen's confessor. They were questioned in the presence of the French monarchs, ultimately confessed, and as many as fourteen were burned, the first known executions for heresy since Priscillian in the fourth century. There are seven sources, notably a detailed account by Paul of Saint-Père du Chartres that is thought to have been directly based on the memories of an eyewitness and perhaps an account of the trial.[36] Historians long debated whether the episode should be read as evidence of Bogomil influence, imported from outside. R. I. Moore and others argue that the groups' emphasis on secret knowledge suggests instead home-grown gnosticism.[37] R. H. Bautier placed the group in a dramatically different light: he analyzed the episode in the context of a power struggle over the Orléans bishopric between Robert the Pious and Eudes II Count of Blois, in which the Blois faction succeeded in seriously embarrassing the crown.[38] Bautier thus demonstrated that this was a heterodox religious sect manipulated as a weapon in a political intrigue.

Another is the so-called heretical sect of the Free Spirit. Scholars basing their views on evidence from inquisitorial manuals considered them to be a late medieval antinomian movement, mystics who believed that their experience of illumination made them exempt from the obligations of ordinary morality, as Norman Cohn luridly termed them in *The Pursuit of the Millennium*, an "elite of amoral supermen."[39] Robert Lerner in 1972 demonstrated that the apparent antinomian amorality of the Free Spirit was "rooted in the problem of the sources . . . none was charged with theft or murder and "most charges of fornication were unofficial, imaginative or vague." "The mystics were instead highly ascetic in their pursuit of perfection." Lerner found them rather like contemporary hippies. Did they even exist as a movement? The Free Spirit were "so closely related" to orthodox mystics "that it is somewhat artificial to draw a line between them: works that are called Free-Spirit today may well be called orthodox tomorrow and vice versa."[40] Most scholars now consider them inquisitorial fantasy: mystics, of course, existed and not all were orthodox, but the heretical sect was the product of inquisitorial methods of questioning. Since the 1990s scholars on these kinds of textual grounds have challenged the existence of groups thought to have been the major popular movements, notably the Cathars and the Waldensians.

All of this has made the study of medieval heresy a particularly challenging and useful valuable laboratory for historical method. It has also unfortunately made the field rather isolated, seen perhaps as arcane. This is particularly true of intellectual heresy, which scholars tend to separate from popular groups. Textbook accounts like Malcolm Lambert's magisterial *Medieval Heresy*, now in its third edition, explicitly trace popular movements. Intellectual heresy raises complex questions, not the least because theologians like Berengar of Tours or Peter Abelard were persecuted for positions that later came to be accepted. And yet, popular and intellectual currents were often interwoven, not only in the cases in which theologians like Peter Olivi or John Wycliffe sparked popular movements. The popular preacher Arnold of Brescia after all was a student of Abelard!

Women and Gender

One way in which scholars have integrated the history of heresy into the broader narrative has been study of the roles of women. Historians interested in recovering something of the experience of women have long debated whether they were attracted to heresies, and if so why. Gottfried Koch in his 1962 *Frauenfrage und Ketzertum im Mittelalter* argued for a general movement of women into the religious life, both regular and outside established orders.[41] Some scholars argued that heretical groups – notably the Cathars – had a particularly strong appeal because they offered opportunities denied women in the orthodox Church. Cathars in theory allowed women to preach and perform the ritual purification that was roughly equivalent to a Catholic sacrament. That idea has been much debated, debunked by historians showing that the active roles of Cathar women were easily overrated, then revived by others.[42] Shannon McSheffrey and others have explored the roles of women among the Lollards. Susan Snyder, studying heresy in Bologna, found that many of the women associated with the followers of the apocalyptic radical Fra Dolcino were not married but concubines, and argued that their marginal status made them more apt to be drawn to teachings that challenged the Church on issues of sexuality.[43] Some groups were distinctly female, most famously the Guglielmites, a group of elite women in Milan who venerated a woman named Guglielma as the Holy Spirit and founded a new church with a female pope. Recent work has also shifted from a focus on the roles of women to gender expectations, as, for example, in John Arnold's analysis of the case from the Fournier register of Arnaud de Verniolles, a subdeacon accused of repeated sodomy.[44]

Persecution

The field is now at a fascinating juncture. Two emphases dominate: persecution and deconstruction. R. I. Moore has done much to move the study of heresy into the main narrative. His *Formation of a Persecuting Society* was something of a bombshell in 1987. Moore changed the terms of the discussion by pointing out that the rise in the twelfth and thirteenth centuries of organized persecution of groups deemed heretical simply cannot be explained in terms of the medieval justification, the threat they posed to Christian society. Instead, he argued, this was part of a broader pattern, a turn to persecution of constructed threats that included Jews, lepers, and sexual minorities as well as heretics. Similar stereotypes were imposed on all of them. For Moore, persecution was decidedly not the result of popular antipathy. It was an effort by a growing educated administrative elite to consolidate their power. This was a decisive turn; Europe became, as he put it, a society that relied upon persecution. Moore's sweeping argument has sparked considerable debate. Some specialist historians challenged his account as overgeneralized, notably his account of the persecution of European Jews. Moore's book also tended to turn scholarly attention toward persecution and away from social and political analysis of heretical groups as organized protests. Scholars ask not whether some individuals did seek to challenge the Catholic Church, but why they were persecuted.

Studies of persecution include Dominique Iogna-Prat's *Ordonner et exclure* (1998), a book that meticulously sets out the logic of persecution in twelfth-century terms.[45] What justified action against non-Christians? Iogna-Prat demonstrated that Cluniac monks equated their own monastic order with the universal Church. The great abbot Peter the Venerable defended the Church by preaching against its enemies. Persecution was justified by an all or nothing logic: humankind shares a common destiny, and society is made up of forms of solidarity that are as obligatory for Muslims and Jews as for Christians.

Other scholars have turned to the mechanisms of the inquisition. James Given in 1997 treated the Languedocian inquisitions of 1275–325 not in terms of the history of religion but rather as the cutting edge of medieval state formation. He analyzed inquisitorial practice in terms of their techniques of domination: systems of record keeping, interrogation, and punishment. Then, he turned to how Languedocians responded: individual and collective resistance, and efforts to manipulate the tribunals. For Given, then, the inquisitions provide a case study of growth of bureacratic systems of governance, one that is particularly revealing because their detailed records do offer glimpses of resistance.[46] More recent work on inquisitions includes a massive volume derived from a Vatican conference of 1998.

Dyan Elliott in a 2004 study looked at inquisitions into heresy as an aspect of what she sees as the criminalization of late medieval female spirituality. Elliott argues that the mechanisms developed after the Fourth Lateran Council of 1215 to discern sanctity and to uncover heresy tended in practice to draw the categories of saint and heretic together.[47] Both kinds of tribunals sought to test or prove a person's spiritual state. Further, "representations of female sanctity were in many ways sculpted to confound the heretic. Central features of women's spirituality that first emerged in this period – its physicality, eucharistic devotion, confessional practice – all answer to this need, providing vivid proof of orthodox contentions."[48] Ironically, the use of techniques like inquisitions to test sanctity fostered a growing skepticism, and the emphasis on bodily piety led to physical tests. Confessors investigated the veracity of a mystical rapture by testing to be sure that the woman's body was truly insensate. Douceline of Digne's ecstatic rapture was tested by hot lead being poured on her feet.[49] With growing skepticism and the elaboration of techniques for the discernment of spirits, the categories of saint and heretic joined, as in the case of Joan of Arc.

Deconstruction

Another significant tendency in recent scholarship has been somewhat inaccurately termed deconstruction. This is a sharpening of the emphasis on source criticism that has always been crucial to research on heresy. Again, much of our information about medieval heresies was shaped by the views of clerical authorities with a considerable investment in portraying them as a serious threat to the institutional Church, and colored by later assumptions, notably later inquisitorial manuals. The project then has been to strip away assumptions and to seek to work out what perhaps did take place. Much of this research has been meticulous and invaluable. One important instance is *Inventer l'hérésie?*, a 1996 collection of articles derived from a seminar at Nice led by Monique Zerner that was devoted to the close analysis of the logic of the production and conservation of the sources for popular heresy before the Albigensian Crusade and the creation of the papal inquisitions.[50] In what political circumstances did people who came to be accused of heresy function? One example is an essay by Michel Rubellin on Valdès, who initiated the Waldensians. Rubellin argues that historians have been too quick to locate Valdès in broader narratives, understanding him in terms of the actions of his later followers and missing what can be reconstructed of his actual role in Lyons in 1170–183.[51] Rubellin makes a compelling case that Valdès was probably a lay functionary of the church of Lyons who became a partisan supporter of the reform program of Archbishop Guichard against the cathedral canons. The next bishop, Jean Bellesmains, backed the canons, deplored lay involvement in reform, and expelled Valdès.

Some of this work has been extreme, like the research it critiques only selectively attentive to the sources. Scholars in recent years have sought to right the balance. The most important debates concern whether what have been considered widespread popular religious movements actually existed, notably the Waldensians and the Cathars. Michel Roquebert in the recent volume honoring Jean Duvernoy critiqued this tendency, which he reads as deconstructing the Cathars.[52] Mark Pegg is one proponent: he has argued repeatedly that it is misleading to use the conventional term Cathar. It is a term they never used, calling themselves the good Christians, good men or women, and it implies connections among groups of believers in southern France and northern Italy.[53] Scholars generally continue to use it nonetheless. First, it is less value-laden than the alternatives. To speak of the good Christians versus the Catholics sounds like a sixteenth-century Protestant reformer, and of course much of the intellectual baggage we carry to this material derives from that era. Further, there is good evidence for connections, as a number of historians have pointed out.

Some recent work might be termed post-revisionist. Claire Taylor in a fine regional study of Aquitaine argues in opposition to this scholarship that the heretics there *c.* 1000 were dualists probably influenced by missionaries from the Balkans, who spoke to concerns of an oppressed and disillusioned population. Cathar dualists appeared in one region, the Agenais, from the 1150s to the 1170s.[54] Peter Biller in a 2006 article argued a strong case against the deconstruction of Waldensianism.[55] While the "baggage of post-medieval confessional historiography and its myths needs to be cleared out of the way," there is solid archival evidence for Valdès, some inquisitors took pains to write accurate accounts, and considerable evidence does describe an organized entity. What then of the problem of terminology? David Burr took an approach that is a model of reasonableness in his magisterial history of the Spiritual Franciscans. He noted that the term "spirituals' was a party label applied to Franciscan rigorists only from 1310–11, so that the use of the term for the earlier period is an anachronism that suggests a unified movement, when in fact – as Burr was at pains to demonstrate – several groups existed. Why then his use of the term? The groups had much in common and by the 1270s were on their way to becoming a movement, though never a unitary one.[56] Another strong tendency has been work that crosses the often artificial boundaries between orthodoxy and heresy, or between heretical groups, like Francis Andrews's study of the Humiliati or recent dissertations on late medieval Italian religion by Susan Snyder and Janine Peterson.

I would like to return finally to the tendency to sentimentalize heretics.[57] Historians tend to imagine them as clean-living sincere believers persecuted by the institutional Church. This harkens back to Reformation-era Protestants who considered some medieval heretics to be their forerunners.[58] The emphasis on sincerity reflects Protestant attitudes as well.[59] The view is also is a legacy of some Enlightenment authors, who saw heretics as heroes struggling against persecution. John Stuart Mill in *On Liberty* (1859) portrayed heretics as social benefactors. Ideas and doctrines remain vital only when they are tested and defended. Mill acknowledged that people like heretics who energetically assert an unpopular religious view may themselves be one-sided. However, they bring into discussion suppressed and neglected truths, and wiser minds can then provide balance. His list of heroic benefactors whose religious truth was put down by persecution is a telling one: Arnold of Brescia, Fra Dolcino, Savonarola, the Cathars, the Waldensians, the Lollards, the Hussites.[60]

Scholarship – including my own work – can sometimes sentimentalize them as well. Moore has written of the local or little community, dominated and oppressed by universal monopolizing papacy and clerical elite. Pegg pictures the simple faith of peasants. Louisa Burnham in her eloquent study of the beguines sees them as martyrs. As Steven Justice has pointed out, we side with heretics even though we often have little sympathy for the religious views that motivated them. We tend to think of them as bravely going to the stake for their faith, and of course some did. It is worth noting that the early Dominicans – often unpopular foreigners living in modest convents inserted into the towns – who took on heavily armed Cathar nobles embedded in the local power structure – were brave on behalf of their faith as well. And, as I have suggested, some of the people condemned for heresy may well have been snake-oil salesmen, and not sincere believers. Brother John the Hermit and Friend of God is instructive here: probably there were plenty of people like him who used religious claims to extort money. These were victims of persecution, but hardly brave martyrs.

Notes

1 Archivio di Stato di Firenze (ASF), Podestà 127, 181[r]–183[v].
2 Peters, *Torture*, pp. 54–8.
3 See, e.g., Russell, Moore, and Lambert, all in Zerner, ed., *Inventer l'hérésie?*
4 Bernard Hamilton has posited a strong argument for Bogomil influence in "Bogomil Influences."
5 Arnold, *Inquisition and Power*, "Introduction," discusses the debates over these issues.
6 Prosperi, "I Caratteri originali," pp. 762–3.
7 Le Roy Ladurie, *Montaillou.*
8 Boyle, "*Montaillou* Revisited."
9 Porete, *Speculum simplicium animarum.*
10 Published in *Heresies of the High Middle Ages*, ed. and trans. Wakefield and Evans.
11 Hudson, *The Premature Reformation.*
12 Justice, "Inquisition, Speech and Writing."
13 Lansing, "Idolatry and Fraud."
14 See Elliott, *Proving Woman*, for bibliography.
15 Chiffoleau, *La Comptabilité*; LeGoff, *Birth of Purgatory.*
16 See Hen, Chapter 4, this volume.
17 See, e.g., Thompson, *Cities of God*, and Van Engen, "The Christian Middle Ages."
18 Murray, "Piety and Impiety."
19 Quoted by Arnold, *Belief and Unbelief*, p. 222.
20 Ibid., p. 223.
21 Quoted by Justice, "Inquisition, Speech and Writing," p. 24.
22 Quoted by Bartlett, *England under the Norman and Angevin Kings*, p. 479.
23 Rubin, *Corpus Christi*, p. 333, quoting Humbert of Romans.
24 Nelson, "Society, Theodicy and the Origins of Heresy," is an early synthetic analysis of this tendency.
25 See Arnold, Chapter 8, this volume.
26 Archivio di Stato di Firenze (ASF) Podestà 276, 321[r]–322[v]. See Rocke, *Forbidden Friendships.*
27 Arnold, Chapter 8 this volume, cites Bartlett, *England under the Norman and Angevin Kings*, p. 478.
28 Murray, "Piety and Impiety," pp. 101–2.
29 *Boniface VIII en procès.*
30 Keane, "Sincerity, 'Modernity,' and the Protestants."
31 Clanchy, *Abelard.*
32 Eddé, "Hérésie et pouvoir politique en Syrie."
33 See Lambert, *Medieval Heresy*, pp. 135, 144.
34 *Acta Sancti Officii Bononie*, no. 259, p. 199.

35 Ibid., nos. 21, 22, pp. 47–9.
36 See Lambert, *Medieval Heresy*, pp. 343–7, for a detailed account of the sources.
37 Moore, *Origins*, pp. 24–30.
38 Bautier, "L'Hérésie d'Orléans."
39 Cohn, *The Pursuit of the Millennium*, chs. 8 and 9.
40 Lerner, *The Heresy of the Free Spirit*, p. 227.
41 Koch, *Frauenfrage und Ketzertum im Mittelalter.*
42 See Abels and Harrison, "The Participation of Women," Biller, "Cathars and Material Women," and Brenon, *Les Femmes cathares.*
43 Snyder, "Woman as Heretic."
44 Arnold, *Inquisition and Power*, ch. 5.
45 Iogna-Prat, *Order and Exclusion.*
46 Given, *Inquisition and Medieval Society.*
47 Elliott, *Proving Woman.*
48 Ibid., p. 2
49 Bornstein, "Violenza al corpo di una santa."
50 Zerner, ed., *Inventer l'hérésie?*
51 Rubellin, "Au temps où Valdès n'était pas hérétique."
52 Roquebert, "Le Déconstructionisme et les études cathares"
53 See Pegg, *The Corruption of Angels.*
54 Taylor, *Heresy in Medieval France.*
55 Biller, "Goodbye to Waldensianism?"
56 Burr, *The Spiritual Franciscans*, pp. viii–ix.
57 Peters, "Moore's Eleventh and Twelfth Centuries," mentions "Moore's sentimental affection" for what he terms the Little Community.
58 Friesen, "Medieval Heretics or Forerunners of the Reformation?"
59 See Keane, "Sincerity, 'Modernity,' and the Protestants."
60 Mill, *On Liberty*, p. 53. See the essays in Laursen and Nederman, eds, *Beyond the Persecuting Society.*

Bibliography

Abels, Richard, and Harrison, Ellen, "The Participation of Women in Languedocian Catharism," *Mediaeval Studies*, 41 (1979), 215–51.

Acta Sancti Officii Bononie, ed. Lorenzo Paolini and Raniero Orioli (Rome: Istituto storico italiano per il Medio Evo, 1982).

Andrews, Francis, *The Early Humiliati* (Cambridge: Cambridge University Press, 1999).

Arnold, John, *Inquisition and Power: Catharism and the Confessing Subject in Medieval Languedoc* (Philadelphia: University of Pennsylvania Press, 2001).

Arnold, John, *Belief and Unbelief in Medieval Europe* (London: Hodder Arnold, 2005).

Bartlett, Robert, *England under the Norman and Angevin Kings 1075–1225* (Oxford: Oxford University Press, 2000).

Bauer, Walter, *Orthodoxy and Heresy in Earliest Christianity*, ed. Robert Kraft and Gerhard Krodel (Philadelphia: Fortress Press, 1971).

Bautier, R. H., "L'Hérésie d'Orléans et le mouvement intellectuelle au début du xie siècle," in *Actes du 95e Congrès National des Sociétés savantes (Rheims, 1970): Section philologique et historique* (Paris: Bibliothèque Nationale, 1975), vol. I, pp. 63–88.

Biller, Peter, "Cathars and Material Women," in Peter Biller and A. J. Minnis, eds, *Medieval Theology and the Natural Body* (York: York Medieval Press, 1997), pp. 61–107.

Biller, Peter, "Goodbye to Waldensianism?" *Past & Present*, 192 (2006), pp. 3–33.

Bornstein, Daniel, "Violenza al corpo di una santa: Fra agiografia e pornografia. A proposito di Douceline di Digne," *Quaderni medievali*, 39 (1995), pp. 31–46.

Boyle, Leonard, "*Montaillou* Revisited: Mentalité and Methodology," in J. A. Raftis, ed., *Pathways to Medieval Peasants* (Toronto: Pontifical Institute of Medieval Studies, 1981), pp. 119–40.

Brenon, Anne, *Les Femmes cathares* (Paris: Perrin, 1992).

Burnham, Louisa, *So Great a Light, So Great a Smoke: The Beguin Heretics of Languedoc* (Ithaca, NY: Cornell University Press, 2008).

Burr, David, *The Spiritual Franciscans: From Protest to Persecution in the Century after Saint Francis* (University Park, PA: Pennsylvania State University Press, 2001).

Chiffoleau, Jacques, *La Comptabilité de l'au-delà* (Rome: École française de Rome, 1980).

Clanchy, Michael, *Abelard: A Medieval Life* (Oxford: Blackwell, 1997).

Cohn, Norman, *The Pursuit of the Millennium: Revolutionary Millennarians and Mystical Anarchists of the Middle Ages* (New York: Oxford University Press, 1957; rev. edn, 1970).

Coste, Jean, ed., *Boniface VIII en procès: Articles d'accusation et dépositions des témoins (1303–11)* (Rome: L'Erma di Bretschneider, 1995).

Eddé, Anne-Marie, "Hérésie et pouvoir politique en Syrie au XIIe siècle: L'Exécution d'al'Suhrawardî en 1191," in Andrez Vauchez, ed., *La Religion civique à l'époque médiévale et moderne (Chrétienté et Islam)*, Collection, 213 (Rome: École française de Rome, 1995), pp. 235–44.

Elliott, Dyan, *Proving Woman: Female Spirituality and Inquisitorial Culture in the Later Middle Ages* (Princeton: Princeton University Press, 2004).

Frassetto, Michael, ed., *Heresy and the Persecuting Society in the Middle Ages: Essays on the Work of R. I. Moore* (Leiden: Brill, 2006).

Friesen, Abraham, "Medieval Heretics or Forerunners of the Reformation? The Protestant Rewriting of the History of Medieval Heresy," in Alberto Ferreiro, ed., *The Devil, Heresy and Witchcraft in the Middle Ages* (Leiden: Brill, 1998), pp. 165–90.

Given, James B., *Inquisition and Medieval Society: Power, Discipline and Resistance in Languedoc* (Ithaca, NY: Cornell University Press, 1997).

Hamilton, Bernard, "Bogomil Influences on Western Heresy," in Michael Frassetto, ed., *Heresy and the Persecuting Society in the Middle Ages: Essays on the Work of R. I. Moore* (Leiden: Brill, 2006), pp. 93–114.

Henderson, John B., *The Construction of Orthodoxy and Heresy: Neo-Confucian, Islamic, Jewish and Early Christian Patterns* (Albany, NY: State University of New York Press, 1998).

Heresies of the High Middle Ages, trans. and ed. Walter Wakefield and Austin P. Evans (New York: Columbia University Press, 1969).

Hudson, Anne, *The Premature Reformation: Wycliffite Texts and Lollard History* (Oxford: Oxford University Press, 1988)

Iogna-Prat, Dominique, *Ordonner et exclure* (1998); *Order and Exclusion: Cluny and Christendom Face Heresy, Judaism and Islam (1000–1150)*, trans. Graham Robert Edwards (Ithaca, NY: Cornell, 2002).

Justice, Steven, "Inquisition, Speech and Writing: A Case from Late-Medieval Norwich," *Representations*, 48 (Autumn 1994), pp. 1–29.

Keane, Webb, "Sincerity, 'Modernity,' and the Protestants," *Cultural Anthropology*, 17 (2002), pp. 65–93.

Koch, Gottfried, *Frauenfrage und Ketzertum im Mittelalter: Die Frauenbewegung im Rahmen des Katharismus und des Waldensertums und ihre sozialen Wurzeln* (12.–14. Jahrhundert), 2nd edn (Berlin: Akademie-Verlag, 1962).

Lambert, Malcolm, *Medieval Heresy: Popular Movements from the Gregorian Reform to the Reformation*, 3rd edn (Oxford: Blackwell, 2002).

Lansing, Carol, "Idolatry and Fraud: The Case of Riperando and the Holy Managlia," in Michael Frassetto, ed., *Heresy and the Persecuting Society: Essays on the work of R. I. Moore* (Leiden: Brill, 2006), pp. 253–69.
Lansing, Carol, *Power and Purity: Cathar Heresy in Medieval Italy* (Oxford and New York: Oxford University Press, 1998).
Laursen, John Christian, and Nederman, Cary, eds, *Beyond the Persecuting Society: Religious Toleration before the Enlightenment* (Philadelphia: University of Pennsylvania Press, 1998).
LeGoff, Jacques, *The Birth of Purgatory*, trans. Arthur Goldhammer (Chicago: University of Chicago Press, 1986).
Lerner, Robert, *The Heresy of the Free Spirit in the Later Middle Ages* (Berkeley and Los Angeles: University of California Press, 1972).
Le Roy Ladurie, Emmanuel, *Montaillou, village occitan de 1294 à 1324* (Paris: Gallimard, 1975); English translation: *Montaillou: The Promised Land of Error*, trans. Barbara Bray (New York: George Braziller, 1978).
Merlo, Grado, *Eretici e inquisitori nella società piemontese del Trecento* (Turin: Claudiana, 1977).
Mill, John Stuart, *On Liberty* (London: Parker and Son, 1859).
Moore, Robert I., *The Formation of a Persecuting Society* (1987; 2nd edn, Oxford: Blackwell, 2007).
Moore, Robert I., *The Origins of European Dissent* (London: Penguin, 1977).
Murray, Alexander, "Piety and Impiety in Thirteenth-Century Italy," in S. J. Cuming and Derek Baker, eds, *Popular Belief and Practice*, Studies in Church History, 8 (Cambridge: Cambridge University Press, 1972), pp. 83–106.
Nelson, Janet L., "Society, Theodicy and the Origins of Heresy: A Reasessment," in S. J. Cuming and Derek Baker, eds, *Popular Belief and Practice*, Studies in Church History, 8 (Cambridge: Cambridge University Press, 1972), pp. 65–77.
Pegg, Mark, *The Corruption of Angels: The Great Inquisition of 1245–46* (Princeton: Princeton University Press, 2001).
Peters, Edward, "Moore's Eleventh and Twelfth Centuries: Travels in the Agro-Literate Polity," in Michael Frassetto, ed., *Heresy and the Persecuting Society in the Middle Ages: Essays on the Work of R. I. Moore* (Leiden: Brill, 2006), pp. 11–29.
Peters, Edward, *Torture*, 2nd edn (Philadelphia: University of Pennsylvania Press, 1996).
Peterson, Janine, "Contested Sanctity: Disputed Saints, Inquisitors and Local Communities in Northern Italy, 1250–1400," Ph.D. dissertation, Indiana University, 2006.
Porete, Marguerite, *Margaretae Porete Speculum simplicium animarum*, ed. Paul Verdeyen, Corpus Christianorum Continuatio Mediaevalis, 69 (Turnhout: Brepols, 1986).
Prosperi, Adriano, "I Caratteri originali di una controversia secolare," in *L'Inquisizione, Atti del Simposio internazionale, Città del Vaticano, 29–31 ottobre 1998* (Vatican City: Biblioteca Apostolica Vaticana, 2003), pp. 731–64.
Rocke, Michael, *Forbidden Friendships: Homosexuality and Male Culture in Renaissance Florence* (Oxford and New York: Oxford University Press, 1996).
Roquebert, Michel, "Le Déconstructionisme et les études cathares," in Anne Brenon and Christine Dieulafait, eds, *Les Cathares devant l'histoire: Mélanges offerts à Jean Duvernoy* (Cahors: L'Hydre Éditions, 2005), pp. 105–33.
Rubellin, Michel, "Au temps où Valdès n'était pas hérétique: Hypothèses sur le rôle de Valdès à Lyon," in Monique Zerner, ed., *Inventer l'hérésie? Discours polémiques et pouvoirs avant l'Inquisition*, Collection du Centre d'Études Médiévales de Nice, vol. 2 (Nice: Centre d'études médiévales, Faculté des lettres, arts et sciences humaines, Université de Nice Sophia-Antipolis, 1998), pp. 192–217.
Rubin, Miri, *Corpus Christi: The Eucharist in Late Medieval Culture* (Cambridge: Cambridge University Press, 1991).

Russell, Jeffrey B., *Dissent and Reform in the Early Middle Ages* (Berkeley: University of California Press, 1965).

Snyder, Susan, "Woman as Heretic: Gender and Lay Religion in Medieval Bologna," Ph.D. dissertation (University of California, Santa Barbara, 2002).

Taylor, Claire, *Heresy in Medieval France: Dualism in Aquitaine and the Agenais, 1000–1249* (Rochester, NY: Boydell Press, 2005).

Thompson, Augustine, *Cities of God: The Religion of the Italian Communes, 1125–1325* (University Park, PA: Pennsylvania State University Press, 2005.)

Van Engen, John, "The Christian Middle Ages as an Historiographical Problem," *American Historical Review*, 91 (1986), pp. 519–52.

Zerner, Monique, ed., *Inventer l'hérésie? Discours polémiques et pouvoirs avant l'Inquisition*, Collection du Centre d'Études Médiévales de Nice, 2 (Nice: Centre d'études médiévales, Faculté des lettres, arts et sciences humaines, Université de Nice Sophia-Antipolis, 1998).

Further Reading

The bibliography on popular belief and heresy is vast and this chapter can only suggest a few directions. For further bibliography, see John Arnold, *Belief and Unbelief in Medieval Europe* (London: Hodder Arnold, 2005), an invaluable account of medieval belief, including heresy, that synthesizes much recent scholarship. Malcolm Lambert, *Medieval Heresy: Popular Movements from the Gregorian Reform to the Reformation*, 3rd edn (Oxford: Blackwell, 2002), remains the best general introduction to the history of heresy, with extensive bibliography. For work published before 1980, see the invaluable Carl Berkhout and Jeffrey Burton Russell, *Medieval Heresies: A Bibliography, 1960–79* (Toronto: Pontifical Institute of Mediaeval Studies, 1981). For the Cathars, see Malcolm Barber, *The Cathars: Dualist Heretics in Languedoc in the High Middle Ages* (New York: Longman, 2000), and the Cahiers de Fanjeaux series published by the Centre d'Études Historiques de Fanjeaux. For England, see Ian Forrest, *The Detection of Heresy in Late Medieval England* (Oxford: Oxford University Press, 2005). On literacy, see Peter Biller and Anne Hudson, eds, *Heresy and Literacy, 1000–1530* (Cambridge: Cambridge University Press, 1994). For the Waldensians, see Euan Cameron, *Waldenses: Rejections of Holy Church in Medieval Europe* (Oxford: Blackwell, 2000). Translated source collections include the invaluable *Heresies of the High Middle Ages*, trans. and ed. Walter Wakefield and Austin P. Evans (New York: Columbia University Press, 1969), and *The Birth of Popular Heresy*, trans. R. I. Moore (London: Edward Arnold, 1975).

Chapter Fourteen

Jews in the Middle Ages

Kenneth R. Stow

Writing about 1560, the Jewish historian Joseph ha-Kohen named his survey of Jewish history the *'Emeq ha-bakha*, the *Valley of Tears*. The notion that medieval Jewish life was an unending series of tribulations has not only animated subsequent historians, but left its mark on modern Jewish memory. Medieval Jewish history is too often identified with the "history of anti-Semitism," a term that, used in isolation, has sometimes served as a shorthand for avoiding confrontation with real historical issues; for instance, why did Christians find Jews so formidable, although Jews as a social, political, and certainly a religious force were exceedingly weak.

Even Joseph ha-Kohen understood that the motives underlying approaches to the Jews from the outside were not always commensurate with simple patterns and patterning. Subtly describing the accusation, made at Trent in northern Italy in 1475, that Jews had killed the child Simonino, ha-Kohen told how the pope, a Franciscan, and his envoy, a Dominican bishop, defended the Jews.[1] This was far from what might have been expected from members of these two religious orders. All was not black and white. There were intricacies to Jewish medieval existence. There were also positive aspects. Had there been no massacres in the Rhineland during the First Crusade of 1096, and other tragedies like them later on, or the mass of restrictive canonical and civil legislation that caused Jews great unease (we do not really know how much), the modern historian of medieval Jewry would still have much to say.

To begin with, Jews pursued intense learning, produced important literary works, sustained families, and reared children in a demonstrably Jewish way. Jews functioned politically through quasi-autonomous communal entities, and they carried on complex economic endeavors. These last were dependent from about the year 1200 on Christian attitudes toward the Jewish lending and, to a lesser extent, Jews selling Christians wine, although in Mediterranean regions, especially Sicily and Spain, Jews long continued to be artisans. In the earlier Middle Ages, Jews played what some have called a significant role in international commerce, but by the twelfth century this was no longer true. Speaking of Jews in terms of agriculture makes little sense throughout the Middle Ages. The great majority of Jews were always town-dwellers, even when towns and cities were few. Jews thus contributed to the development of urbanism, especially in Northern Europe. At the same time, and the above caveat notwithstanding, whatever Jews did in medieval Europe, it was always under the heading of a people living in a thoroughly Christian environment. This was a basic fact that could never be ignored, nor can it be even today.

This fact stands out most clearly when noting the so-called ritual stonings that took place annually in Italy and Spain in the later Middle Ages. In the former, at least, the event was demonstrably staged; it was never a spontaneous outburst. The setting was Easter week, when Christians putatively were concentrated on the death of their Lord and those held responsible – namely, the Jews. Vengeance was the theme of the day. But rulers abhorred uncontrolled violence, and even the participants themselves may often have sensed the ritual's artificiality. Most of the time, relations between Christians and Jews were tranquil, sometimes friendly, sometimes exceedingly so and – according to some – excessively so, at the table or even in bed, against which priests, but especially Dominicans and Franciscans from the thirteenth century onward, railed. The proper order of society had to be re-established. What better way to accomplish this than through regulated violence. It was through negotiation, therefore, that the rules of ritual stoning were fixed: how long the stoning would go on, and who might participate, but mostly what object could be stoned, which was usually the walls of Jewish homes, not the windows or doors that a stone might penetrate. When the stones ceased to fly, "business as usual" was resumed.

However, reality did not always follow the plan. Once, an angered Italian Jew tampered with the ritual's script by throwing a stone back. In Spain, the script was always in difficulty. From no later than the fourteenth century, for the most part, there was no longer a Jewish–Christian equilibrium to re-achieve. In people's minds, the remaining (that is, unconverted) Jews of Spain posed enormous dangers. Converts were viewed suspiciously and assumed to be intrinsically unfaithful, and it was feared that the ever-growing number of converts would be seduced back to Judaism.[2]

Instability, accompanied by vaguely observed rules, was thus the constant Jewish lot, as well as the Jews' worst enemy. Despite long interludes of calm, Jews themselves must have felt perennially insecure. But non-Jews, too, felt threatened. And this was the great "rub." Something intangible about the Jews was felt to challenge Christian society at its roots. This, as we will see, was anxiety about the *Corpus Christi* and its purity (a multi-valent term that applies to the Eucharist itself, as well as the civic body politic, and more). The result was distrust and often a desire to have Jews expelled, even on a kingdom-wide basis. Worse, there arose desires for revenge, whether by unrestrained violence or punishments decreed by overwrought rulers, including on charges of killing Christian children, the accusation we know as ritual murder – which, too, it should be added, was perceived as an assault on the *Corpus Christi*. Let us now see how what we have just described, whether the positive, the negative, or the intangible, worked itself out in real life.

Jews and their Rulers

In a justly famous essay, the great Jewish historian Salo Baron suggested that, in the area of self-rule, medieval Jewish life was stable. He perceived medieval Jews as enjoying charters that gave them true, autonomous, and defined corporate rights, and these, in turn, enabled them to govern their communities from within. By contrast, he argued that Jewish stability was upended and the Jews themselves discomforted when modern society denied them these very rights, especially in the nineteenth century, by way of their legal Emancipation. Emancipation granted full civic rights, at least in law, but Jews could not know whether the loss of autonomy, the counterpart of the rights granted, was advantageous. Would the bestowal of the latter compensate for the disappearance of the former?[3] Baron's perspective, however, was too elegant. He pictured a sudden revolutionary turn, belying what was actually a centuries-long process. The change from what has been called Jewish corporate status to that of individuality within the framework of the modern state was, rather, a gradual one. Besides, the Jews' medieval legal situation had grown increasingly unstable as time passed.

The source of Baron's perception was his understanding of the medieval Jewish community as an autonomous corporation headed by rabbis, who, in truth, were often placed directly under communal officials, especially after the thirteenth century, for instance, as it was decreed at Worms in 1312. With respect to Jewish autonomy itself, its nature was anything but corporate. Whatever self-rule Jews exercised, it would be more accurate to regard it in the light of traditions that began in late Roman law (about the mid-fourth century CE) and then continued into the Middle Ages. These traditions accorded Jews the right to live by their own laws when those laws *did not contradict* the law of the realm and the canons of the Church, which left a large margin for self-rule. Self-rule was reinforced when Jews were likened to the *genera*, the tribal or ethnic bodies (to use a wholly modern term) that dominated social and political organization in the successor states to the Roman Empire – for a *genus* automatically enjoyed a great deal of autonomy.[4]

In the Mediterranean regions – Spain, Italy, and parts of France (and eventually the lands under Carolingian rule) – Jews were also considered "Roman citizens" (albeit the idea of Roman citizenship was growing ever more vague and archaic). Originally, this status was advantageous. Not only did Jews enjoy the privileges accorded to the other *genera*, but they were to be governed from above by legal traditions that guaranteed their rights, beginning with the privilege of permanent, unchallenged residence in Christian lands; and this was wholly apart from Christian theological teachings on the subject, which, in the event, were themselves highly influenced with respect to the Jews by Roman Law.

However, in the long run, this plus became a minus. As the centuries progressed and the other *genera* disappeared or amalgamated into the predecessors of what we now call national states, the Jews uniquely retained their original status, which made them stand out. They derived their rights from what was becoming, Italy excepted, an outmoded legal and political structure. Moreover, as European society became ever more a *societas fidei*, a society of the – Christian – faith, or faithful, Jews found themselves increasingly on the outside from every possible angle. How indeed could they amalgamate into a political–social body that (ever more) saw itself as the embodiment of the *Corpus Christi*? In practice, and as Roman law fell into general disuse, Jews came to live by, and depend on, special charters. And, despite Baron's favorable opinion, these charters made the Jews dependent on the perennially fickle grace of the king, to whom they were firmly subordinated. In simple terms, the Jews' civil status came to be one that was theirs alone; and, eventually, it was this clearly unpleasant, as well as unpredictable, status that decided their fate. When pressures (of many kinds: civil, as well as theological) became unmanageable, it was easier to expel the Jews than to defend them.

Nonetheless, as long as the situation persisted, it did allow the Jews considerable control over internal affairs; and here Baron was correct. Jews preferred it this way, and they were wary about giving up their privileges, including in exchange for rights like those Emancipation eventually promised. Until early modern times, these privileges left Jews in full, or nearly full, control of private and family life, especially matrimony and inheritance. Jews were authorized as well to deal with internal disputes, although they lacked "primary jurisdiction," the undisputed obligation to try cases among Jews before a strictly Jewish tribunal. A discontented Jew could easily circumvent communal authority, as communal protests indicate. Communities also protested against unauthorized persons representing them before lay rulers, another indication of the absence of authoritative powers.

Jewish communal rule, therefore, lacked legal, as well as civil, precision. This is to say, it lacked the definition that is the backbone of long-range political stability. Hence, it seems counterintuitive that the medieval Jewish community has so regularly been called a corporation, indeed, "a corporation among the corporations." For what corporate status most especially offers to both governmental, but especially non-governmental, bodies is the very definition Jews were missing. Most likely, the term corporation began to be used to describe the Jewish community by historians who applied the same Marxist historical perspective to Jews that was commonly used to describe the *pre*-French Revolutionary world. The Marxist notion of "the feudal corporation" is the rough equivalent of the better-known concept of "class"; its simplistic charm has kept it alive even in a post-Marxian world.

In the medieval world, the idea of the corporation emerged only during the thirteenth century. Jewish communities themselves were first organized in places like the Rhineland hundreds of years earlier. In addition, today, when speaking of corporations, we think of the corporate body of the state or of great business conglomerates. With respect to the Middle Ages, this perception is anachronistic. In the Middle Ages and the early modern period, a corporation was a *societas* (the term still used in Europe for corporations), meaning a gild or worker's body with rights and rules. It applied neither to governments nor to autonomous self-governing social groups. Moreover, the Jewish community could not even be correctly deemed a *societas* (albeit authorities, especially in Italy, occasionally used the term, alternating with *universitas*, when referring to Jewish communal bodies). For even gilds, the true *societates*, had guaranteed rights, and these the Jews never effectively possessed as an organized body. Indeed, late ancient Roman law had explicitly denied Jewish communities corporate rights and jurisdiction, and the spirit – and often the application – of this law lived on; the point was also one that medieval jurists were fond of repeating. They understood that the denial of true corporate status placed limits on internal Jewish self-rule. Normally, we do not interfere in Jewish marital affairs, said Bartolus, the greatest of medieval jurists, except, he noted, where the matter infringes on our own legal rules. The right to interfere in Jewish affairs was always there, and it would be more and more invoked over time.[5]

The Jews' unique legal situation thus created an oxymoron: self-rule, which, for the most part, went unchallenged, as Baron perceived it, and which was to internal

Jewish advantage, but a self-rule that was accompanied by an intrinsic instability and weakness, which Baron *mis*understood and which ultimately proved fatal to Jewish continuity. For what most generated instability was the Jews' growing dependence on their rulers and on what has already been called their rulers' fickleness and their arbitrary whims. Yet what else should be expected when one's existence was tied to ephemeral charters of privilege rather than to a fundamental – what today we would call constitutional – set of rules. It is paradoxical that these charters originated as grants of special – for instance, commercial – rights given to permanent residents of a region. This was the case when the first "defense" (*tuitio*, *protectio*) charters, as they are technically known, were granted by Carolingian rulers (in what is today France) in the ninth century. Over time, however, and as said, only the Jews came to be dependent on charters. The legal instrument that had granted special privilege now became the Jews' sole and, patently, unreliable guarantor of continued residence.

More worryingly, nobody could truly explain why – that is, nobody could find the legal justification for why – Jews lived under a special rule of law, a *ius speciale*. To account for this, it was said, about 1157, that Jews were "attached" to the Royal Chamber (the treasury and the permanent part of the realm), and, then, from 1234, that they were "Chamber Serfs," not true slaves or serfs, but people utterly dependent on the king. Variations said Jews were "like slaves (legally)," or "the king's slaves," or "like (royal) property."[6]

Hence, the Jews' legal status was an artificial one, and, when it no longer worked, kings could freely expel them, which, as said, they did. Nor were these kings responding to a request from the Church. In England (1290), leading nobles and even the commons feared kings would manipulate Jews to force them into bankruptcy. In France (1306), kings were set on stopping lending, converting the Jews, and "preventing ritual murder," which they thought really took place. Failing to achieve these goals, kings rid themselves of Jews. The case in Spain, in 1492, was roughly similar: the decree of expulsion said that Jews "seducing" converts back to Judaism were damaging "the republic." Germany, with its local rule, witnessed a patchwork of small expulsions alternating with attacks, although some places did retain their Jews. We are accustomed to think of Jews as having always lived in Eastern Europe. Yet, in Poland, where Jews first settled no later than the thirteenth century, real growth began only in the sixteenth. One should not judge Jewish life there by medieval or West European standards.

The story ends, though, paradoxically. The process that climaxed with Jewish Emancipation was actually one that began when the old status Jews had once enjoyed under Roman law began to be reinstated from about the mid-sixteenth century. More and more, Jews were placed under what was called "common law," *ius commune*, which in continental Europe means a modernized Roman law. We can trace the process especially well in Italy and, of all places, in the Papal State. The problem was that, the more these rights were reinstated, the more the Jews were forced to give up directing their own affairs, including, for instance, in the matters of marriage and inheritance. From this perspective, of a slowly expanding regime of *ius commune*, what above I called Emancipation can be seen as the gradual culmination of a long series of changes in Jewish life rather than a revolution. The process was ineluctable, and, in many ways and in many places, it granted Jews unprecedented and maximum stability. Where, however, the process was "successfully" challenged, as in modern Germany, when Emancipation was reversed by Hitler's "Nuremberg Laws" of 1935, the result was disaster.[7]

How, then, did Jews chose to run their own affairs under these conditions? Lacking formal empowerment by outside authority, but also, as we shall see, sufficient political theory and understanding of their own, they chose to view the community as a Court of Law. This approach vested power in those called judges (*dayyanim*), scholars, and rabbis, alongside communal heads known as *parnasim* – however, as individuals. These people were not perceived, as we perceive our elected officials today, as agents of ongoing representative bodies. A famous rabbinic dictum says that we know there is authority for a court in these precincts, since a great scholar once dwelled here; by distinction, Christians would say that we know a court exists here, because the (Platonic) "form" of the court, or of a deliberative body, is "eternal." Thus the Christian body politic, or the source of authority, was continuous. Among Jews, authority was dependent on personality and personal leadership, and it was temporary by definition.

About the year 1000, Rabbi Gershom, The Light of the Exile, as he was known (d. 1028), sought to eliminate this predicament. He said that a community could enter into an agreement to regulate public behavior by having *all* its members swear an oath. These agreements, called *haramot* (pl. of *herem*), created "dedicated" communal space, exclusive, if not "sanctified," realms of communal action. One was prohibited, when a *herem* existed (the word does not mean *niddui*, or excommunication), from turning to a court as though no binding rules and decrees existed. In effect, the *haramot* (translated into terms we understand today) established a public sphere, governed by an assembly vouchsafed with the law-making powers. They turned the whole of the community into a representative assembly, which, as medieval Christian theorists put it, possessed the "fullness of power" (*plenitudo potestatis*) to ensure that its decrees be enforced and which also exercised "full power" (*plena potestas*) to bind the community through its votes. The validity of its decisions was continuous, remaining in force even when those who made the decisions were no longer alive.

What granted validity to this assembly's pronouncements was that, in the words of Rabbi Jacob Tam (d. 1171), they were made *be-da'at kulam* (through universal consultation). Rabbenu Tam, as he is called, understood the principles of representation well. What he meant by this expression was that all were to be consulted and asked their opinion about impending decisions. His inspiration, however, was external, specifically the dictum of Roman Law, then in vogue, which said that, to ordain statutes, the opinion of all communal members (or their representatives) must be sought: *quod omnes tanget ab omnibus approbetur*. Once rules, fundamental laws, had been made, decisions about specific applications might be made by the majority. This had also been Rabbi Gershom's intention. Neither he nor Rabbenu Tam understood "universal consultation" to mean "unanimity," as has been said. Nor were these two alone in sharing this view. One complex *responsum* asks whether a law was still valid even if a member of the community who was not consulted *before* its adoption did not object *afterward*. The questioner is echoing the principle of *quod omnes tanget* in its most explicit sense – universal consultation *before* the fact, *be-da'at kulam*.[8]

Still, most medieval Jews failed to understand R. Tam and R. Gershom – or they preferred feigning ignorance. Fighting for rabbinic pre-eminence toward the end of the thirteenth century, a time when lay *parnassim* were successfully challenging rabbinic communal authority, Rabbenu Meir of Rothenberg said that, where an assembly was not constituted or its leader chosen *be-da'at kulam*, then a great scholar should lead. Everything still hinged on individual, scholarly prestige. This and other statements of R. Meir may be responsible for some historians mistaking the crux of debate as one of whether simple majorities or unanimity should decide communal questions. The real crux was whether, and how, to apply theories of representation.

Yet the historians who speak of majorities and unanimity may be partially right. By using these terms, they are reflecting the reality that Jews failed to develop ongoing governmental – communal institutions, and that they remained mired in the concept of rule by informal majorities or by transient courts, whose authority rested on the scholarly – and often arguable – renown of a specific rabbinic judge.

Jews and Culture

In part, this situation was an effect of the Jews' political instability. Institutions grow strong in the kind of secure physical surroundings that Jews lacked. At the same time, political instability, accompanied, as we shall see, by a strong measure of cultural alienation, should not be confused with cultural isolation. Medieval Jews were not cut off – nor did they cut themselves off – from external cultural influence. Rabbenu Tam's concept of representational rule came to him, we said, from the outside. Indeed, scholars today are increasingly appreciating how open medieval Jews were to outside influence, including in daily Jewish life. For that matter, until at least the time of the First Crusade, some Jews apparently had Christian business partners. This is revealed by the word *makar*, as it appears in the Hebrew Crusade chronicles and which translates the Latin *sodalis*, or "business partner." Jews, the texts say, had Christian *makarim*; the word meant neither "friend" nor "acquaintance," as it would mean today. One thing sold in these partnerships may have been cosmetics or medicines. The 1084 Charter of Rudiger of Speyer tells explicitly that Jews were renowned for preparing and dealing in these items.

Medieval Jews knew Latin in depth. More sophisticated Jews cited papal theory, and some were conversant with medieval law. Jews were no less conversant with medieval vernacular literature. One text, describing a supposed massacre and forced conversion in early eleventh-century Normandy, employs for its own ends the image of a sword with a golden hilt. The swords slips and pierces the hand of its wrongful wielder, an image that comes directly from the grail legends of late-twelfth-century writers like Chrétien de Troyes, carrying the message that one does not, as some grail legends suggest, pursue the grail by pursuing Jews. In this same vein, one scholar has contrasted the hesitation of Rabbi Amnon of the prayer *Unetanah toqef* when faced with the prospect of conversion to that of Lancelot in Chrétien's tale "The Knight of the Cart."[9]

Acculturation also penetrated the realm of rabbinic learning. The Tosafist commentators on the Talmud were not, as is often said, people who preferred concrete to theoretical, philosophical thought (the kind prevalent in Andalusia, along with mystical, eventually kabbalistic, trends). Rather, they were typical medieval legists, debating law just as it was studied in the Christian law schools of Europe. One easily espies an endless series of methodological parallels in Jewish and Christian legal study.

For one, it was no accident that the printed Talmudic page is arranged precisely as were Roman Law texts when both were first printed about 1500.

Acculturation further took place in what historians call the realm of "private life" – in particular, that of the family. In Italy, especially Rome, albeit toward the very end of the Middle Ages, the order of the process leading to marriage followed precisely that used by Roman Christians. The *kiddushin* (= *matrimonium*) followed the *erusin* (= *impalmamento*) by no more than a few weeks; the *huppah* (= *nozze*) itself was postponed for up to a full year after. In Ashkenaz, *kiddushin* and *huppah* were performed virtually, as today, one right after the other. Nonetheless, some adaptations like these ended in true originality. Elements that were adopted were also adapted, "Judaized," we might say, to the point that the internalized came to look like it sprouted naturally from the original core. Rabbenu Tam's insistence on *da'at kulam* had framed a foreign legal concept, *quod omnes tanget*, in a fully rabbinic setting. Much later on, at Rome, the idea of an irrevocable gift, *donationes inter vivos*, was neatly grafted onto the rabbinic concept of a *mattanah gemurah*, a total gift. Yet, whereas Christians used the Latin term to indicate a permanent bond with somebody they were *de facto* adopting – legal adoption of persons as we know it today is a development of a much later century – Jews were using the Hebrew term to create real adoption, as we now understand it: it was the child him or herself who became the irrevocable gift. With Christians, the irrevocable gift was only the donation to the "adoptee."[10]

It goes without saying that there was Jewish initiative, too, Jewish originality in both learning and culture. Jewish medieval culture could be highly original. The stories created by the writers known as Yossipon or Ahimaaz ben Paltiel in southern Italy rest firmly on a base of pre-existent Jewish midrash. Ahimaaz bespeaks a Jewish ideal type who is at once learned, pious, charitable, a man of means and commercial acumen, as well as the head of a biological family. This was far distant from the then emerging Christian ideal (in the eleventh century when Ahimaaz was writing) of the celibate priest. Yossipon combined Roman historical lore with the work of Josephus Flavius to create an ingenious history of the Jews, but also of the Romans, in order to prove that Esau's true descendants were Christians, not the Jews, as Christians were then claiming; nor, consequently, were Christians the True Israel, as the latter also said (Israel being Jacob's second biblical name).[11]

Nobody needs reminding about the achievements of Jewish philosophy. Thomas of Aquinas, for one, constantly cites Maimonides' original philosophical interpretations. Jewish philosophy did far more than transmit the ideas of Arabic philosophy to the West, as was once thought. Christians readily learned the Bible, too, from Jewish teachers, anxious as the former were to learn the burgeoning method of *peshat* – roughly, the literal meaning of the text. Jews produced poetry in many forms. In Spain, the basis was an extraordinarily rich biblical Hebrew vocabulary. The themes – women, wine, even young boys – were notably secular. Poetry did not need to be religious, although often it was.[12]

Certain cultural modes were unique to Jews. Collections of midrashim, inventive, often charming and clever, biblical interpretation, sometimes with a moral bent, are an example; Christians dabbled in midrash, influenced by Jews, but the art never reached Jewish heights. True ingenuity resides in Talmudic interpretations. A 200-year process succeeded in translating a text, the Talmud – written, first, in the

Near East, in an agrarian environment, and later perfected to suit the cosmopolitan atmosphere of Abassid Baghdad and its thriving Muslim culture – into terms applicable to an incipiently urban eleventh-century Europe. The effort was enormous. There was a need for a dictionary, which was achieved in Rome about 1101, and then for a word-by-word parsing, achieved by Solomon Yitzhaki, better known by the acronym Rashi, about the same time. Rashi's grandsons then elaborated a detailed commentary, preparing the raw text for use in resolving concrete daily and long-range problems; what these scholars, known as the Tosafists, would have unhesitatingly called pure theoretical, school exercises had, in fact, great resonance with reality – so much so that, later on, these commentaries became the basis of practical codes of law that came to be shared in one way or another by Jews living in Germany, France, Spain, England, and Italy. The codes united Jews in their practices, wherever they were, with only minor exceptions, such as the kinds of foods prohibited on the Jewish Passover and small variations in marital processes.

This so brief survey of Jewish cultural invention would not be complete without noting that which was truly new – the Kabbalah. This mystical form of biblical interpretation arose in Spain and southern France in the later twelfth and thirteenth centuries. It might be philosophical, truly mystical, or even magical, and it appears largely in a book called the *Zohar*, the *Book of Splendor*, every one of whose disarmingly simple statements harbors an entire series of codes and ideas. A parallel kind of mystical, but perhaps even more a pietistic code arose at about the same time in the Rhineland, centered in the coterie known as the Pious of Ashkenaz. Their major text, *The Book of the Pious*, is a conglomerate of moral *exempla*. Such *exempla* existed among Christians, too. However, those in *Sefer Hasidim* invariably pose a moral conundrum, a problem for which there is no true answer, the point being to press the devotee to seek a higher road to the knowledge of God and the observance of what was called the "Divine Will." To attain this goal was an ideal, whose limits one probed and tested, but was never quite able wholly to attain, or even intellectually to grasp in full. In seeking to pursue their quest, pietists suggested possible endeavors, trials of observance, which portended activities that would put the devotee above (and perhaps in conflict with) the law, the *halachah*. But whether any of the pietists ever embarked on these endeavors, which we know only from tales of dreams, is, and will, remain unknown.[13]

Sexuality and Family

One element that stands out in *The Book of the Pious* is sexuality, which is fully recognized and legitimated. Pietists controlled their libidos; they did not suppress them. What, it is asked, does one do should sexual thoughts arise during prayer. The answer is not to pray that they go away. It is to press one's thumbs into the pew in front of one. Restraint was balanced by recognizing the naturalness of physical drives. This was very Jewish, and very unChristian, certainly with respect to currently emerging Christian clerical ideals. Christian clergy were warned to stay away from women completely. The Hassidim included women in their numbers, and praised them, such as Dolcia, the wife of Eleazar haRokeah, one of the leading members of the Pietist coterie.

Jewish family life in general seems to have stood out from that of Christians. Comparisons of Jewish and Christian families, especially in Ashkenaz, begin with the small Jewish family, averaging two (surviving) children. The deciding factor was probably medical technology, and one suspects that Jewish and Christian city-dwellers had families of similar size. In common, too, with some Christian women, especially those living in a proto-bourgeois middle-class urban setting, Jewish women engaged in business. Many Jewish women, it has been said, lent Christian women small sums, even for food, and often in the presence of their children, who may have felt humiliated seeing their mothers so reduced, a humiliation that, in turn, may have strengthened anxieties about Jewish intentions. A notable example of Jewish women who lent money was Dolcia, mentioned just above, although perhaps she was lending larger sums, since she seems to have supported her husband and family through this practice. But almost certainly unlike Christian compeers, Dolcia, as her husband relates – subsequent to her murder by errant Christians – was capable of holding her own in learned rabbinic debate. Her older daughter knew how to read; indeed, a famous Christian comment is that Jews send even their daughters to school.[14]

Jewish women, later on, enjoyed privileges that may have been theirs alone. In Italy, Jewish daughters had the *right* to refuse a match. Brothers took an oath unconditionally to accept *halizah*, which means to opt out of performing levirate marriage, marriage with the childless widow of a deceased brother. For their part, sons in sixteenth-century Italy were told they might follow their hearts rather than parental will in choosing a partner; this decision was achieved only after a 300-year debate.[15]

Sentiment, feeling, were integral to marriage. Rashi himself made it clear that, at a certain time of life, a man left his mother to cleave to a wife, who must also be respected, especially during sexual intercourse. That Jewish parents cherished children is expressed not only in dirges, like that penned by the Rokeah, when his wife and two young daughters were murdered. The idea is present, too, in the much earlier *Scroll of Ahimaaz*, about 1054; the great hero Shefatyah is said to have "cherished" his daughter Cassia greatly. He was also angered, because his wife had done everything in her power to hold back Cassia's betrothal, eventually to her first cousin, although endogamous matches like this were far from a foregone conclusion. Cassia's mother did not want the match – or so we are told; Ahimaaz was writing entertainment, as much as he was telling about his ancestors in the small town of Oria near the heel of the Italian boot, a town that still names one of its neighborhoods the *Rione Giudea*, the Jewish zone.[16] A real-life mother may have hesitated for many reasons before letting her daughter marry, one of which would have been exposing her to childbirth at a relatively young age (which, given the late onset of menarche in pre-industrial societies, was not likely to have been before 16). Relatedly, rabbinic texts discuss whether various methods of birth control were licit, in particular, a type of cervical sponge called in Hebrew a *mokh* (a spongy natural growth).[17]

The moving – and dividing – issue between Jewish and Christian perceptions of the family was the centrality Jews accorded marriage and the family in anchoring society and setting standards. The Church, specifically the Catholic Church, made peace with the biological family only during the Renaissance, when it decided it would achieve more by controlling family life than by continuing to relegate it to a distant second place with respect to the idea of celibacy, as it had done from early on. Jews, by contrast, retained the notion of the family as a pillar of society that was the norm in the ancient world. Jews also saw marriage as creating sanctity through spousal interaction, in particular sexuality; one Jewish work, the *Iggeret ha-Qodesh*, says that properly channeled sexuality leads to precisely this end. In Judaism, sexuality has never been a sin, condoned, as it was by the Church, to avoid greater trespass. Later Jewish polemicists reflecting on the Church's denigration of sexuality – for instance, the author of the early fourteenth-century *Nizzahon Yashan* – wondered whether monks and nuns "burned up" in their unconsummated sexual passion; perhaps he was thinking of the Jewish adage that a man, *'ish*, without a woman, *'ishah*, is *'esh*, fire.

An even greater challenge to Christian ideals was the ability of Jews to divorce. For the Church, marriage was an unbreakable sacrament, plausible only as it signified the inviolable union of Christ and the Church. Jewish marriage as a legal institution is the product of a civil contract, meaning that it is capable of being annulled. Even more threatening, Jewish marriage may be reconstituted. Jews in all periods divorced and remarried, of which there are many records throughout the Middle Ages and afterward.

The *Corpus Christi* and its Absence

This enormous difference over so fundamental a social institution as the family illustrates neatly that opposition between Jews and Christians was not limited to questions of belief, or, to be more precise, to belief detached from a social and cultural context. For Christians, that context may be encapsulated by the word "body." Christian marital union reflected the unified body, the *corpus*, of the Church, but that body was also, and explicitly, identified as the body of Christ. The Church called itself the mystical *body* of Christ, the *corpus mysticum*.[18] Indeed, all Christian society pictured itself in corporeal terms. Medieval towns, we have said, described themselves as the *Corpus Christi*, the collective earthly embodiment of Christ's body. Jews, of course, resided outside this body, and there, Christian thinkers intoned, Jews ought to be kept – lest they contaminate it.

Jews never appreciated this conceptualization of society, nor did they openly reflect on it; the precise lines of their assailants' thinking mattered little during an attack and afterward; what remained was essentially the memory of murder committed in the name of Christ. More importantly, Jews lacked the primeval image of Christ, or of any other corporeal model, on which to model their society. To this iconographical deficiency may be partly ascribed the Jewish failure to go beyond the vision of the community as a time-bound court and its venue. Jews had no tools to understand the "body politic" as the corporate structure that it is.

This image of the body and its centrality is essential to understand the conundrum of Jews facing Christians during the Middle Ages. In the past, historians discussing this subject traditionally began elsewhere. Hayyim Hillel Ben Sasson's classic *History of the Jewish People*, for instance, teaches that it was "hatred" that motivated the (Catholic) Church to act, which, in turn, motivated the common people to attack and governments to expel.[19] Another favorite picture is that of a more tolerant Christianity toward the beginning of the Middle Ages (through about the time of the Crusades) succeeded by a more violent one later on. Named as the source of moderation was the so called Augustinian theory of witness, whose influence is said gradually to have waned.

Yet was there ever a period of "moderation," and was there truly an "Augustinian theory" to undergird it? Libels, accusations, and persecutions multiplied in later medieval times. And so did massacres, expulsions, and, possibly, forced conversion (whether all, or most, conversions were forced is a difficult riddle). But the early Middle Ages, too, experienced forced conversions, and anxiety about alleged Jewish machinations was common. Most of the laws restricting Jews were also enacted no later than the year 1000, some much earlier, despite the frequent, yet incorrect, perception that these laws were late. As for the traditional recourse to "hatred" to explain what went on, this term describes emotion, not historical process. The real historical roots of disdain for Jews lie in repeatedly stated concerns about what Jews *might* do to harm the Christian body – now, and in the future; constant apprehension was a far greater menace than a supposed rage about what Jews purportedly *had* done in the past – namely, the killing of Jesus.

As for an Augustinian theory of witness, it may have existed in Augustine's own writings, although this is arguable, but in practice it was never evoked. Nor was Augustine's complex theorizing based exclusively, if at all, as it is sometimes said, on Psalm 59: 8, "do not slay them, lest my people forget (or be forgotten)." Augustine cited this verse as a proof text, not as an explanation for his motives, but, in the event, he alone cited it. The first pope – and only the second Christian thinker in 800 years – to mention the verse, regardless of context, was Pope Innocent III, in the thirteenth century, who was justifying his unprecedented directive of 1215 (on which more below) ordering Jews to wear distinguishing clothing. And he had reason to be concerned about possible consequences; in 1216 Innocent felt compelled to write that the purpose behind his directive was not to expose Jews to danger.

Augustine himself accepted Jews in Christian society, because he was a follower of Paul, for whom a Jewish social presence was fundamental. He was not motivated by an exegetical rationale of his own creation. Jews, Paul had said, would eventually recognize Christ and join the Christian body, at which time the End of Days would arrive. Like Paul, Augustine, in his *The City of God*, assigned the Jews the distinct role of harbingers of mankind's final redemption. Likewise, in the final chapter (10) of his tract *Against the Jews*, Augustine wrote that Christians must love Jews and persuade them to embrace Christianity "through the sweetness of lips." Yet Augustine said this to counterbalance the first nine chapters of the tract, which excoriate Jews as being carnal in their essence, the opposite of the "spiritual" Christian. Here, too, Augustine was echoing Paul, especially Paul's ambivalence: his love for his Jewish fellows, alongside his criticism of their failure to recognize the value of faith in Jesus. Throughout Augustine's tract, Jews symbolize evil, Christians good. Thus Augustine wrote in another work, the *Contra Faustum*, that Jews bear the sign of Cain. This did not mean that Jews were marked as murderers or deicides. For Augustine, the sign of Cain imprinted on the Jewish forehead was Judaism itself, "this blatant and appropriate sign of their observance" (12. 12–13), which he believed was lethal for the soul. Did not the Jews' sorry state prove the point?

For the time being, Augustine said, again following Paul, the Jewish presence must be that of the "elder (of Genesis 25: 23, cited in Romans 9: 12) serving the younger," alluding to the elder Esau and the younger Jacob, an inversion of identities we have noted above. Through their servitude, Jews bore testimony to Christian truth. The Jews, Augustine said in every case when he mentioned this testimony, were *capsarii*, the older slaves who carry the schoolbooks of their younger master – and herein lies the key to his thought. The Jews, now taking the place of Esau, symbolize evil and carnality, Christians, spirituality and good. Understood in these terms, which subsequent Christian exegesis universally accepted, the concept of "Jewish witness" portended no promise of moderate treatment. Through the manner of their existence, Jews bore witness to the denigrated real-life status that was evil's fruit. Like the *capsarius*, the Jews bore the books, the Hebrew Bible, but their closed mindedness to its true (Christological) portent had left them spiritually – as well as civilly, in terms of their restricted legal and social existence – enslaved.[20]

As "slaves" resisting Christ, moreover, Jews were deemed rebellious. They had also placed themselves dangerously outside the *Corpus Christi*. The idea of the Christian body originates in 1 Corinthians 10: 16–18. All those who accept the cup and bread, the meal of the Lord (eventually named the Eucharist), says Paul, become one with his body. As explained by the early sixteenth-century English Catholic theologian John Colet, this meant that "all men, nourished by the One [God himself], may *be* one in that by which they are nourished."[21] Colet was expanding on the twelfth-century Odo of Cambrai, who said: "He feeds us with his blood and body so that . . . *we are him* and he is one with us?" As taught by Paul and through centuries of Christian exegesis, the Eucharist, Christian society, and the Christian individual are corporeally one and interchangeable.

This body's purity must also be maintained. Paul makes this point in 1 Corinthians 10: 19, where he refers obliquely to Ezekiel 44: 7. The prophet admonishes the priests soon to rebuild the Jerusalem temple so that only *true* Jews may offer "the sacrifice: my *bread*, which is the fat and the blood." This description is virtually identical to Paul's imaging of the Eucharist, which, itself, is a "sacrifice"; should the impure, those not truly Jews, approach the altar, Ezekiel implies, they (ritually) pollute it. It seems clear that Paul intentionally transposed Ezekiel's admonition, and definition, onto the Eucharist and its celebrants. Yet, for Christians who imbibe the blood of the (Eucharistic) sacrifice, Ezekiel's demand for purity became even more acute. At stake were not only ritual purity, but the well-being and perfection of that unity which was at once both Christian society and *each* of its individual members. And, as both were defined by Paul in 1 Corinthians 10: 19, Jews had no place in the structure.

Christians, especially Christian thinkers, were principally exercised, however, not by the question of Jewish membership in the body. Their anxieties centered on the consequences of Christians associating with Jews and threatening the body's integrity. Most feared of all were common dining and sexuality. Expressed by churchmen like the ninth-century Agobard of Lyons – in terms of Paul's exegetical inversion of the roles of Jacob (the Christian) and Esau (the Jew) – there was concern that the proximity of real Jews might introduce impurities into "Jacob's" spiritual wholeness. The remedy, one remedy, was expulsion. In Galatians 4: 30, Paul says that those who follow Jewish practice should be expelled, as was the son of Hagar (the roles of Isaac and Ishmael were also inverted). Paul himself no doubt intended believers in Christ who demonstrated imperfect faith by circumcising themselves like Jews. Later Christian exegetes transferred Paul's admonition to Jews. The fourteenth-century legal scholar Oldradus da Ponte directly cited Galatians 4: 30 to explain why Jews who had violated the rules regulating their behavior might *legally* be expelled. Legists in the fifteenth century recalled Oldradus' words on a number of occasions.[22]

Christian exegetes did not stop here. Jews were not simply carnal, as first Paul, then Augustine, had phrased it; nor were they merely "servants." Commenting on Matthew 15: 26, where Jesus says he has brought "the bread" (later interpreted to mean the Eucharist) for "the children, not . . . the dogs," Augustine's rough contemporary John Chrysostom of Antioch said "the dogs" are the Jews; the Christians were now "the children" (Matthew himself probably intended believers in Jesus by this term). Subsequent Christian exegetes took up Chrysostom's charge. Equating Jews and dogs became common. It also suited the ideal of maintaining purity. From early ancient times, dogs were forbidden to enter temples lest they pollute them. The impurity was passed on through contact or touch.

The tone on dangers created by physical contact with Jews was set by Agobard of Lyons, for whom any intimacy with Jews was polluting, but especially that derived from sharing a common table. Should a priest dine with Jews, his acquired impurity passes on to all who receive the Eucharist from his hands, nullifying the sacrament's salvific powers.[23] Agobard was no doubt influenced by the third-century Cyprian, whom he cited. Cyprian lambasted priests who had participated in pagan rites to avoid pollution; and, as the law *Christianorum ad aras* taught, Jewish and pagan rites were identical.[24]

Dangerous contact with Jews was not always direct. Impurity was said to be transferred should Jews even see the Eucharist in procession; and once it was said that Jews should not hear the mass being sung. Complementarily, Jewish prayers were called *ululates*, "the barking of dogs"; even sound diffused pollution. The fear of pollution through contact may also explain the decision of Innocent III to force Jews to wear special clothing. The Jews with whom Innocent was acquainted were Romans, as was Innocent himself. They looked, spoke, dressed, and ate much as he did himself. To dine with them must have seemed natural, as it was on occasion to have sexual contact. Yet both actions made Christians unfit to receive the Eucharist – and it was precisely Pope Innocent who obliged every Christian to receive the Eucharist annually at Easter time. To avoid conflict, he ordered Jews visibly to be singled out.

Yet Innocent did not carry the notion of pollution through contact to its limit. There were those who accused Jews of polluting the Body of Christ through deadly touch – namely, through murder, whether by attacking the Eucharist directly, the so-called Host Libel, or by attacking the Eucharist's principal earthly incarnation, Christian children. Such murders – as one writer claimed about 1400, speaking of the child known as the Good Werner of Obserwessel – were committed with the intent simultaneously to destroy the *corpus verum* (the Eucharist), the *corpus mysticum* (the Church), and also the "real body" of Christ embodied by the physical body of the murdered child. These supposed murders also served another purpose. They "proved" not simply the truth of the Eucharist itself; for that, there were hundreds of tales of Eucharistic miracles not involving Jews. Rather, tales of ritual murder, alongside those of host desecration, "demonstrated" Christianity's ability to survive any threat, as well as its "supersession" of Judaism as God's choice.

The potential victim of Jews machinations was every single Christian. This is attested to by stories in which the victim, instead of being a real person, is an infinitely malleable waxen image, the wax signifying the individual and the whole at the same time; ritual murder was perceived as being much more than a re-enactment of the Crucifixion. However, ritual murder's ultimate implication may have been verbalized only at the turn of the twentieth century. Speaking of the fifteenth-century Lorenzino di Marostica, a suspected victim of Jewish wrath, Bishop Antonio de Pol said that, in murdering Lorenzino, the Jews sought to kill "not an individual Christian, but Christianity itself."[25]

The murderous Jew, need it be said, was also pictured as a dog. In recounting the story of the supposed martyrdom of Simon of Trent in 1475, one Dr Tiberino – a humanist, at that – said that the Jews "barked" (*ululare*) when they brought the kidnapped Simon into the room "to perpetrate their perverse desires." One of these perversions, greater than murder, was, as illustrations suggest, to circumcise Simon. Symbolically, at least, Simon's assailants were bent on voiding his baptism, the fate Paul had described for all Christians who became circumcised. As Antonio de Pol would put it in the later nineteenth century, also speaking of ritual murder, such crimes were attempts to "kill Christianity itself," or at least to pollute it, as Pope Pius IX would intimate in 1871, the year after Rome's Jews were freed from the ghetto where they had lived for 300 years. These Jews, the pope said, were barking up and down the city streets (*latrare per le vie*), polluting them and, for that matter, all Christian spatial sanctity; the ghetto itself he had seen as a kennel.[26] Continuing this papal line, the Jesuit Giovanni Oreglia warned (in 1882) that Jews and Christians occupying the same school bench were generating a "dangerous familiarity" (*una pericolosa famigliarità*). Ideas born in the Middle Ages had endured into modern times, and, what is more, they had penetrated lay society. As though in direct response to Oreglia's admonition, the Italian racial laws of 1938, which spoke openly of pollution within the Italian fascist "body," ordered Jewish children to be expelled from Italian schools.

Yet it must be cautioned that the story has a second side. One tradition within the Church perceived the Jews in wholly negative and destructive terms, another in those of law and obligation. This stretched the formal, papally headed Church between two poles. Though Innocent III was set on preventing what he believed was pollution, he also recognized Jewish rights and made it clear they were to be observed. We have said that he even specified that the distinguishing clothing he had ordered Jews to wear was no pretext to cause them physical harm. Innocent IV firmly denounced the idea that Jews used Christian blood in their rituals, hence, the blood libel itself. The popes were not so clear about the Talmud. When the challenge arose in the thirteenth century whether the Talmud was not a new and distorted Jewish law, Gregory IX and at first Innocent IV ordered the Talmud burned. Yet, when Innocent IV later became convinced that the Talmud was essential to Judaism, he put a halt to the bonfires, limiting himself to denouncing purported blasphemies in the Talmudic text. [27] Innocent IV also suggested that papal courts (meaning papal inquisitorial tribunals, which are not to be confused with the later Spanish national Inquisition at the end of the fifteenth century) might punish Jews erring in their own faith, when Jewish authorities did not. In response to a Jewish petition, however, the late-fourteenth-century papal inquisitor Nicholas Eymerich explained that a Jew could be prosecuted by the inquisition only for denying God. In the same vein, a papal letter of 1278 says that the pope would like to force Jews to attend conversionary sermons, but canonical restrictions did not allow punishment should Jews refuse to attend. The Church actually permitted Jews to lend at interest, which was prohibited to Christians entirely. Jews were allowed to accept "not immoderate interest," a backhanded way of saying yes when the letter of the law said clearly no.

As time progressed, restrictions were more insistently enforced. However, even the most draconian of popes, who tried desperately to convert Jews and restrict all their activities – namely, Popes Benedict XIII, Paul V, and Pius V, in the fifteenth and sixteenth centuries – paid at least lip service to laws calling for the Jews' safety and preservation. Just like Augustine, a thousand years before them, these popes felt bound by the writings of Paul, for whom Jews were both "enemies," dwelling outside the Body of Christ, yet, "for the sake of their fathers" (Romans 11: 28) "friends, who would eventually unite with that body, heralding the 'End of Days.'" No wonder that the Church taught that Jews should be heavily restricted, but still enjoy basic rights (which is what the Latin *tolerare*, "to give privileges," means in papal texts; the word does not mean "to tolerate," in the sense of just allowing Jews to exist).

Much of this Jews understood. They knew about privileges and protection, but they also knew Christians called them dogs. One polemic text, the *Nizzahon Yashon*, retorted that "they [the Christians] bark," and it further likened the Eucharist to human sacrifices to the ancient pagan god Molokh.[28] Hence, Christians were the polluters; they had not superseded the Jews as God's people. On the other hand, Jewish writers knew that the real danger they faced was from the laity, like the lesser nobles who decimated them in the cities of the Rhineland at the start of the First Crusade in 1096.[29] Trouble with rulers began shortly after, in 1171, when Count Theobald of Blois put to death by fire more than thirty Jews charged with ritual murder. About ten years later, King Philip Augustus of France is reported, it appears correctly, to have believed Jews annually sacrificed and consumed the heart of a Christian child. The result was expropriation and expulsion from the Île de France, which Philip ruled directly. More and more, Jews would experience pressures to convert, burnings of the Talmud, alongside its expurgation, and, eventually, country-wide expulsion at the hands of arbitrary lay rulers; reports of earlier tragedies at lay hands, about the year 1000, are all literary.

Jews responded as best they could, which means in writing; defensive *acts* were out of the question. In a letter surely never sent, Meir b. Shimshon asked the Archbishop of Narbonne in southern France to take the pope as his guide about lending. The bishop should not take as his model the current French king, Louis IX, who forbade Jews entirely to lend and may have been the prime mover in burning the Talmud about 1240. Other "never mailed" letters appended to the (sole extant) manuscript recounting the Blois massacre satirically praise the king. But their message is, in fact, sharp criticism, strongly implying that kings are easily moved by accusations like that of ritual murder. Most notably, a Hebrew narrative of a (fictitious) massacre in the year 1007 condemns the king as Haman reincarnate, while the pope, the author says, obeys the law, as seen in his bull of protection (later made law) *Sicut iudaeis non*. The Jews, the anonymous author goes on, are under rightful papal authority (*memshelet reshutkhah*). Yet this also exposes them to papal claims of direct jurisdiction should, for instance, Jewish books contain blasphemies. Papal protection, therefore, depended on Jews bowing to heavy legal restriction and – to return to where we began – the ceding of autonomous privilege.[30]

Jewish life and the permanence of Jewish settlement in Western Europe was becoming ever more precarious, soon to culminate not only in royally ordered expulsions, but also in repeated massacres, especially in Germany, principally on charges that Jews had desecrated the Eucharistic host.

These charges did not cease with the Middle Ages. In some sectors, the anxiety generated by the thought that Jews are "dogs" who wish to desecrate the host, the *corpus verum*, the "true body," still runs deep. We saw it among high churchmen in later nineteenth-century Rome, including Pope Pius IX. Yet even today there are those who see the Jews as those who yearn to steal the children's "bread." One need go no further than the children's game played in contemporary Chile "Who," the children chant, standing in a circle around a lone child at the center, "stole the bread [the Eucharist, to be sure] from the oven?" "The Jewish dog," goes the answer, the Jewish dog; and then the child in the middle is struck.[31] The original accusation of John Chrysostom lives on. Some myths persevere, so much so, in fact, that, when we think of Jewish life in the Middle Ages, our minds reach out to them first and to their too often dire effects. The memory of cultural achievement and of well-wrought acculturation is relegated all too often to second place.

Notes

1 Joseph ha-Kohen, *Emeq habakha*, pp. 94–5, 131; Hsia, *Trent 1475, passim.*
2 Toaff, *Il vino*, pp. 224–5, 67; Nirenberg, *Communities of Violence*, pp. 200–30.
3 Baron, "Ghetto and Emancipation," p. 524.
4 Colorni, *Legge*, pp. 25–30, 34–43.
5 Stow, "Holy Body," pp. 151–71.
6 Langmuir, "Tanquam servi," pp. 27–33.
7 Stow, "Jewish Pre-Emancipation," *passim.*
8 Stow, *Alienated Minority*, pp. 187–91.
9 Einbinder, "Signs of Romance," p. 224; Stow, *Jewish Dogs*, p. 259; Lampert, *Gender*, pp. 101–39.
10 Stow, *Theater of Acculturation*, pp. 68–9.
11 Gerson Cohen, "Esau as Symbol," pp. 40–4.
12 Shirman, *Studies in the History of Hebrew Poetry*, e.g. pp. 90–7.
13 Marcus, "Hierarchies, Religious Boundaries," pp. 7–26.
14 Stow, "The Jewish Family," pp. 1085–10.
15 Stow, *Theater of Acculturation*, pp. 82–4.
16 Klar, *Scroll of Ahimaaz*, pp. 25–6.
17 Feldman, *Marital Relations*, pp. 161–2.
18 Rubin, *Corpus Christi*, pp. 259–67; Stacey, "From Ritual Crucifixion," *passim.*
19 Ben Sasson, *History of the Jewish People*, pp. 414–20, 477, 484.
20 Stow, *Jewish Dogs*, pp. 33–5, 169.
21 Abulafia, *Christians and Jews*, p. 130.
22 Zacour, *Jews and Saracens*, pp. 52, 54, 57.
23 Gilboa, *Agobardi, passim*
24 Linder, *Jews in Legal Sources*, pp. 224, 234, 235, 247.
25 Caliò, "Antisemitismo e culto," *passim.*

26 Miccoli, "Santa Sede," vol. 2, pp. 1371–574.
27 Grayzel, *Church and Jews*, vol. 1, pp. 29–33, 238–45, 250–3, 274–8.
28 Stow, *Jewish Dogs*, pp. 137–44; Berger, *Jewish Christian Debate, passim.*
29 Stow, "Conversion Apostasy," pp. 911–33; Cohen, *Sanctifying the Name, passim*; Yuval, *Two Nations, passim*; Haberman, *Sefer gezerot*, pp. 24–60, 72–82.
30 Stow, The "1007 Anonymous", *passim.*
31 Agosin and Sepúlveda, *Amigas*, p. 13; Nirenberg, *Communities of Violence*, p. 220; Stow, *Jewish Dogs*, pp. 33–5, 169.

Bibliography

Abulafia, Anna Sapir, *Christians and Jews in the Twelfth-Century Renaissance* (London: Routledge, 1995).

Agosin, Marjorie, and Sepúlveda, Emma, *Amigas, Letters of Friendship and Exile* (Austin, TX: University of Texas Press, 2001).

Baron, Salo W., "Ghetto and Emancipation," *Menorah Journal*, 14 (1928), pp. 515–26.

Ben Sasson, Haim Hillel, *A History of the Jewish People* (Cambridge, MA: Harvard University Press, 1976).

Berger, David, *The Jewish Christian Debate in the High Middle Ages: A Critical Edition of the Nizzahon vetus* (Philadelphia: Jewish Publication Society, 1979).

Caliò, Thomasso, "Antisemitismo e culto dei santi in età contemporanea: Il caso del beato Lorenzino de Marostica," in Paolo Golinelli, ed., *Il pubblico dei santi: Forme e livelli di ricezione dei messaggi agiographfici* (Rome: Viella, 2000).

Cohen, Gerson D., "Esau as Symbol," in Alexander Altmann, ed., *Jewish Medieval and Renaissance Studies* (Cambridge, MA: Harvard University Press, 1967).

Cohen, Jeremy, *Sanctifying the Name of God: Jewish Martyrs and Jewish Memories of the First Crusade* (Philadelphia: University of Pennsylvania Press, 2006).

Colorni, Vittore, *Legge ebraica e leggi locali* (Milan: Giuffrè 1945).

Einbinder, Susan, "Signs of Romance: Hebrew Prose and the Twelfth Century Renaissance," in Michael A. Signer and John Van Engen, eds, *Jews and Christians in Twelfth-Century Europe* (Notre Dame, IN: University of Notre Dame Press, 2000).

Einbinder, Susan, *Beautiful Death: Jewish Poetry and Martyrdom in Medieval France* (Princeton: Princeton University Press, 2002).

Feldman, David M., *Marital Relations, Birth Control, and Abortion in Jewish Law* (New York: Schocken Books, 1974).

Gilboa, Akiva, ed. and trans., *Agobardi Lugdunensis Archiepiscopi Epistolae Contra Iudaeos* (Latin text with Hebrew translation) (Jerusalem: Akadmlon, 1964), from E. Duemmler, ed., *Agobardi Lugdunensis Archiepiscopi Epistolae*, Monumenta Germaniae Historica, Epistolae Karolini Aevi, 3 (Berlin: Apud Weidmannos, 1899).

Grayzel, Solomon, *The Church and the Jews in the Thirteenth Century*, vol. 1 (1933; rev. edn, New York: Hermon, 1966).

Haberman, Abraham, *Sefer gezerot ashkenaz ve-zarfat* (Jerusalem: Mossad Bialik, 1945).

Ha-Kohen, Joseph, *Emeq habakha*, ed. Meir Letteris (Cracow: n.p., 1895).

Hsia, Ronnie Po-Chia, *Trent 1475* (New Haven: Yale University Press, 1992).

Klar, Benjamin, *The Scroll of Ahimaaz* (in Hebrew) (repr. Jerusalem: Mossad Bialik, 1974).

Lampert, Lisa, *Gender and Jewish Difference from Paul to Shakespeare* (Philadelphia: University of Pennsylvania Press, 2004).

Langmuir, Gavin I., "*Tanquam servi*: The Change in Jewish Status in French Law about 1200," in Gavin I. Langmuir, *Toward a Definition of Antisemitism* (Berkeley and Los Angeles: University of California Press, 1990), pp. 167–94.

Linder, Amnon, *The Jews in Legal Sources of the Early Middle Ages* (Detroit: Wayne State University Press, 1997).

Lipton, Sara, Images of Intolerance: The Representation of Jews and Judaism in the Bible (Berkeley and Los Angeles: University of California Press, 1999).

Marcus, Ivan G., "Hierarchies, Religious Boundaries and Jewish Spirituality in Medieval Germany," *Jewish History*, 1/2 (1986), pp. 7–26.

Miccoli, Giovanni, "Santa Sede: Questione ebraica e antisemitismo fra Otto e Novecento," in C. Vivanti, *Gli ebrei di Italia* (Turin: Einaudi, 1996), vol. 2, pp. 1371–574.

Nirenberg, David, *Communities of Violence: Persecution of Minorities in the Middle Ages* (Princeton: Princeton University Press, 1996).

Rubin, Miri, *Corpus Christi: The Eucharist in Late Medieval Culture* (Cambridge: Cambridge University Press, 1992).

Shirman, Haim, *Studies in the History of Hebrew Poetry and Drama* (Jerusalem: Mossad Bialik, 1979).

Stacey, Robert, "From Ritual Crucifixion to Host Desecration: Jews and the Body of Christ," *Jewish History*, 12/1 (1998), pp. 11–28.

Stow, Kenneth, *Alienated Minority: The Jews of Medieval Latin Europe* (Cambridge, MA: Harvard University Press, 1992; repr. 1994).

Stow, Kenneth, *Theater of Acculturation: The Roman Ghetto in the 16th Century* (Seattle: University of Washington Press, 2001).

Stow, Kenneth, *Jewish Dogs: An Image and its Interpreters* (Stanford, CA: Stanford University Press, 2006).

Stow, Kenneth, "The Jewish Family in the Rhineland," "Conversion Apostasy and Apprehensiveness: Emicho of Flonheim," "The '1007 Anonymous' and Papal Sovereignty," and "Holy Body, Holy Society," all reprinted in Kenneth Stow, *Popes, Church, and Jews in the Middle Ages* (Aldershot: Ashgate Variorum, 2007), VIII, IV, X.

Stow, Kenneth, "Jewish Pre-Emancipation: *Ius commune,* the Roman Comunità and Marriage," in Kenneth Stow, *Jewish Life in Early Modern Rome: Challenge, Conversion, and Private Life* (Aldershot: Ashgate Variorum, 2007), XVIII.

Toaff, A., *Il vino e la carne* (Bologna: Il Mulino, 1989).

Yuval, Israel Jacob, *Two Nations in your Womb* (Berkeley and Los Angeles: University of California Press, 2006).

Zacour, Norman, *Jews and Saracens in the Consilia of Oldradus de Ponte* (Toronto: University of Toronto Press, 1990).

Further Reading

Cohen, Gerson D., "Esau as Symbol," in Alexander Altmann, ed., *Jewish Medieval and Renaissance Studies* (Cambridge, MA: Harvard University Press, 1967). Fundamental on iconography of supersession.

Cohen, Jeremy, *Sanctifying the Name of God: Jewish Martyrs and Jewish Memories of the First Crusade* (Philadelphia: University of Pennsylvania Press, 2006). Excellent study of medieval Jewish martyrdom.

Colorni, Vittore, *Legge ebraica e leggi locali* (Milan: Giuffrè 1945). Colorni is the only true scholar of medieval law to have written on this crucial subject regarding Jews.

Einbinder, Susan, *Beautiful Death: Jewish Poetry and Martyrdom in Medieval France* (Princeton: Princeton University Press, 2002). Excellent literary and historical study of Ashkenazi poetry.

Grayzel, Solomon, *The Church and the Jews in the Thirteenth Century*, vol. 1 (1933; rev. edn, New York: Hermon, 1966). The earliest edited collection of papal letters on the Jews.

Hsia, Ronnie Po-Chia, *Trent 1475* (New Haven: Yale University Press, 1992). Thorough investigation of the most clamorous of all blood libels.

Lampert, Lisa, *Gender and Jewish Difference from Paul to Shakespeare* (Philadelphia: University of Pennsylvania Press, 2004). Innovative comparison of medieval Jewish and women's images.

Linder, Amnon, *The Jews in Legal Sources of the Early Middle Ages* (Detroit: Wayne State University Press, 1997). The *sine qua non* for revision of old platitudes about Augustinian theory and for understanding the status of Jews in early medieval law.

Lipton, Sara, *Images of Intolerance: The Representation of Jews and Judaism in the Bible* (Berkeley and Los Angeles: University of California Press, 1999). Unparalleled iconographic study of Jewish images in manuscript illumination.

Miccoli, Giovanni, "Santa Sede: Questione ebraica e antisemitismo fra Otto e Novecento," in C. Vivanti, *Gli ebrei di Italia* (Turin: Einaudi, 1996), vol. 2, pp. 1371–574. Deep analysis of Catholic institutional anti-Semitism in the nineteenth and early twentieth centuries with relation to a feared modernity.

Nirenberg, David, *Communities of Violence: Persecution of Minorities in the Middle Ages* (Princeton: Princeton University Press, 1996). Jews and social violence in medieval Spain.

Shirman, Haim, *Studies in the History of Hebrew Poetry and Drama* (Jerusalem: Mossad Bialik, 1979). Still best comprehensive study (in Hebrew) of the subject.

Stow, Kenneth, "The '1007 Anonymous' and Papal Sovereignty," in Kenneth Stow, *Popes, Church, and Jews in the Middle Ages* (Aldershot: Ashgate Variorum, 2007), IV. Revisionary approach to reading medieval Hebrew chronicles as expressing ideals, not chronography.

Stow, Kenneth, "The Jewish Family in the Rhineland," in Kenneth Stow, *Popes, Church, and Jews in the Middle Ages* (Aldershot: Ashgate Variorum, 2007), VIII. Attempt to analyze Jewish family demographically and structurally.

Stow, Kenneth, *Alienated Minority: The Jews of Medieval Latin Europe* (Cambridge, MA: Harvard University Press, 1992; repr. 1994). Book-length essay on the Jews of Medieval Latin Europe.

Stow, Kenneth, "Conversion Apostasy and Apprehensiveness," in Kenneth Stow, *Popes, Church, and Jews in the Middle Ages* (Aldershot: Ashgate Variorum, 2007), VII. Emicho of Flonheim as a creator of apostates, despised equally by ecclesiastics and Jews.

Stow, Kenneth, *Theater of Acculturation: The Roman Ghetto in the 16th Century* (Seattle: University of Washington Press, 2001). Social and anthropologically oriented evaluation of Jewish life in Rome based on testimonies and other documentation set down in Hebrew by Jewish (rabbinic) notaries.

Stow, Kenneth, *Jewish Dogs: An Image and its Interpreters* (Stanford, CA: Stanford University Press, 2006). Study of how Jews and Christians confronted each other principally over issues of purity and contamination.

Stow, Kenneth, "Jewish Pre-Emancipation: *Ius commune*, the Roman Comunità and Marriage," in Kenneth Stow, *Jewish Life in Early Modern Rome: Challenge, Conversion, and Private Life* (Aldershot: Ashgate Variorum, 2007), XVII. Argues that increasing Jewish inclusion in the legal system of *ius commune* prepared the way for a gradual, rather than sudden, emancipation.

Yuval, Israel Jacob, *Two Nations in your Womb* (Berkeley and Los Angeles: University of California Press, 2006). Provocative discussion of Jewish role in prompting Christians to formulate attitudes toward the former.

Chapter Fifteen

Muslims in Medieval Europe

Olivia Remie Constable

Although Islam arose in seventh-century Arabia, the religion and its followers would have a profound impact on medieval Europe. With the arrival of Islamic rule in the Iberian Peninsula after 711, and later in Sicily, regions that are now considered to be part of Europe became Muslim. Much of Spain, known as al-Andalus in Arabic, remained under Muslim control for nearly eight centuries – almost the entire medieval period – until the fall of Islamic Granada in 1492. Arab administration in Sicily was briefer, stretching from the ninth to the eleventh centuries, yet we find an enduring legacy of Muslim culture in both regions. This is evident in local languages, literature and music, architectural heritage, and even in the shape of the land itself, which for centuries was planted, terraced, and irrigated with crops and techniques imported from the East.

Over time, the presence of Muslim neighbors became a concern for medieval Christians throughout Europe. While some parts of Mediterranean Europe were under Muslim rule or subject to Muslim raids, in other regions free or enslaved Muslims later lived under Christian rule. Even in areas that had no direct contact with Muslims, such as England, Christians became increasingly aware of the existence of Islam. Even before the launching of the First Crusade to Jerusalem, in 1095, West European rulers and their subjects were engaged in diplomatic, military, and economic contacts with Muslims, both within Europe and overseas.

During the era of the crusades, stretching from the eleventh century into the fifteenth century, Christian and Muslim armies met in battle, whether in the Near East or southern Europe. Although it has been debated whether the effort to expand Christian territories in Spain (often called the *reconquista*) was truly a crusade, it was undoubtedly part of the larger phenomenon of Christian military endeavors in Muslim lands. At the same time, Christian churchmen became increasingly preoccupied with the problem (as they saw it) of Islam, and the complementary goals of conquest and conversion. Muslims even became part of the European imagination, finding a place in Latin and vernacular literature and pageants, whether as the bellicose enemy in the *Song of Roland*, in more romantic roles in other *chansons de geste*, or as fantastical characters in mummers plays and royal entries.

This chapter will examine these two parallel aspects of Muslims in medieval Europe, looking mainly at the history of actual Muslim states in Sicily and Spain, and their enduring legacy for European culture, but also giving attention to the perceptions of Muslims and Islam in European thought. It will also discuss medieval Muslim attitudes toward Europe and Western Christians. Modern scholars are divided in their opinions on these issues. Although there is general agreement that relations between medieval Muslims and Christians, and their attitudes toward each other, varied according to time and place, scholars differ in their overall interpretation of this interfaith encounter. Some, pointing to the ongoing military confrontations, conversion efforts, resettlements, and the ultimate expulsion of Muslim communities from medieval Europe, see relations as fundamentally hostile and intolerant. Others, while acknowledging these hostilities, put more emphasis on the long periods of peaceful interaction and tolerance between the two communities, stressing the translation of scientific and philosophical texts, the transfer of medical knowledge and agrarian technology, and the many shared traditions of commerce, daily life, and popular culture. Both visions have merit and can be supported by medieval evidence, yet neither is self-sufficient. Instead, the two must go together, since the time frame is too long, the regions too varied, and the peoples and politics too complex for a single interpretation. In order to cover such diversity, this chapter will proceed chronologically, looking at changing conditions for Muslims in medieval Europe from the eighth to the sixteenth centuries.

It has been famously argued by the historian Henri Pirenne that the early medieval Muslim incursions into the Mediterranean world changed the course of European history. From being a "Roman Lake," where economic, religious, and intellectual life had continued in much the same way in the fifth and sixth centuries as they had under earlier Roman rule, Pirenne proposed that the arrival of Islam annexed the Mediterranean, forcing Western Christians to focus their political and economic energies in northern Europe. Thus, claimed Pirenne, Charlemagne developed his northern empire as a result of Muhammad and the spread of Islam. Subsequent historians have spent considerable time critiquing Pirenne's thesis, and many of its details have been discredited. Nevertheless, Pirenne's central insight – that the rise of Islam had profound consequences for the course of European history, and for definitions of Europe and Western Christianity – remains sound. Whereas prior historians had envisioned the rise of medieval Europe as a struggle between Roman and Germanic elements, Pirenne saw that Islam, far from being merely a distant culture on the other side of the Mediterranean, was also an important factor in the development of medieval Europe.

Within the first few decades of the revelation of Islam, Muslim armies forged their way westward across North Africa, reaching the Straits of Gibraltar by the early eighth century. The forces that crossed over to southern Spain in 711 included both Arabs from the Near East and Berbers who had joined the Muslim army as it made its way westward. Many of the troops were recent converts to Islam, and represented a mixture of ethnic, linguistic, and cultural traditions. This variety persisted in al-Andalus during later centuries, especially with the acculturation of local Visigothic and Hispano-Roman peoples. Over time, most of the Andalusi population converted to Islam, and Arabic became the dominant language of religion, administration, and culture, but many people probably also spoke romance dialects. The population remained ethnically and culturally mixed, with some regions being predominantly Arab, while other areas were mainly settled by Berbers. This diversity was less apparent during periods of strong Arab rule in the capital city of Cordoba, from the middle of the eighth century until the end of the tenth century, but it manifested itself in the subsequent small decentralized states of the Taifa period (eleventh century). In the later eleventh and twelfth centuries, al-Andalus would be ruled by two Berber dynasties from North Africa, the Almoravids (*al-Murabitun* in Arabic) and the Almohads (*al-Muwahhidun*).

The Muslim armies arriving in Spain in 711 were directed by an Arab general and led by a Berber commander, and the expedition was overseen, at a distance, by the Umayyad caliph in Damascus. The Umayyad dynasty had ruled since 661, but in 750 a rival dynasty, the Abbasids, claimed the caliphal title and moved their seat of power to their newly founded capital of Baghdad. This recentering of the Islamic world with the shift from Syria to Iraq had consequences for the later history of Muslim Spain and North Africa, which were now on the periphery of an empire that looked east as much as west.

In 711, however, the caliph in Damascus was very interested in events in Iberia, and people in Spain were likewise aware of Eastern affairs. Two eighth-century Latin chronicles record the Muslim conquest of 711, and also mention events in Byzantium and Syria. These are our earliest sources, since no Arabic accounts of the conquest survive from before the ninth century. Although these Christian authors recount the horrors of a military conquest, they do not question the legitimacy of Muslim rule, nor are they particularly hostile toward Islam. They indicate a process of conquest that combined military force with negotiation, with some Spanish towns making treaties with Muslim leaders. This is confirmed by the survival of one such treaty, dated 713, that records the surrender of Murcia. In return for submission and payment of tribute, the Christian inhabitants of the town would be left in peace.[1]

The Muslim conquest of Visigothic Spain was not the final phase of Islamic military expansion, since further raiding expeditions crossed the Pyrenees into France. The most famous of these ended in a battle near Poitiers, where a Muslim army was defeated by the Franks, led by Charles Martel, in 732. The Battle of Poitiers has been seen as a critical turning point in medieval history, and it is sometimes said that, had it not been for Martel's victory, France would have become a Muslim country. It seems more likely, however, that the incursions across the Pyrenees were only raids, seeking booty not conquest, and there is no indication of any Muslim settlement north of Narbonne.

During the first four decades of Muslim rule, al-Andalus was ruled by a series of Arab governors appointed by the Umayyad caliph and sent out from Syria. All this changed in the middle of the eighth century, however, with the Abbasid revolution and the demise of the Umayyad caliphate in Damascus. Most of the members of the Umayyad family were killed, but one prince, Abd al-Rahman, fled westward across North Africa. According to historical tradition, his mother was a Berber, and he found refuge with her tribe. When Abd al-Rahman arrived in al-Andalus, he claimed the throne, and was accepted as ruler in 756. Notably, he did not seek to be caliph, since this unique title was currently claimed by the Abbasid ruler in Baghdad. Instead, for the next two centuries, the Spanish Umayyads called themselves *emirs*, a lesser title without the universal religious significance of caliph. Nevertheless, neither did the

Cordoban Umayyads recognize the Abbasid caliphate. While all other regions of the Muslim world proclaimed the name of the Abbasid caliph during Friday prayers (the *khutba*), and imprinted his name on coins and other official items, this was never done in Umayyad Spain. Thus, al-Andalus was both part of a larger Muslim world, and yet politically separate from it. This distinction would affect subsequent relations between al-Andalus and Christian Europe.

Charlemagne entered into separate diplomatic relations with Abbasid Baghdad and Umayyad Cordoba. According to Frankish sources, Charlemagne exchanged embassies with the Abbasid caliph Harun al-Rashid, with the friendly result – according to the chronicler Einhard – that "Harun sent Charlemagne the only elephant he possessed, simply because the Frankish king asked for it."[2] There is no record of this exchange in Arabic sources. Contemporary relations with Cordoba were less cordial. In 778 the Muslim governor of Zaragoza sought to assert his independence from the Umayyads, and sent an emissary to Charlemagne asking for his support. In response, Carolingian forces marched south, but, when they arrived at Zaragoza, the governor refused to surrender the city. Charlemagne therefore returned home over the Pyrenees, where his army's rear guard, including his nephew Roland, was ambushed and killed by Basques.[3] This event would later inspire one of the most famous medieval French epics, the *Song of Roland*, composed at least three centuries after the event, which turned Roland's attackers into Muslims. In its twelfth-century version, this narrative is striking for the stereotypical and hostile portrayal of Muslims that was characteristic of its period (see further discussion below). The contemporary sources, in contrast, are much more prosaic in their attitude toward Muslim Spain. Despite the tragic events in 778, the Carolingians continued to make forays into north-eastern Spain, and Barcelona surrendered to Frankish control in 801, resulting in the semi-official creation of the Spanish March (roughly the area of modern Catalonia). This region would remain within a French sphere of influence for many centuries.

Although Umayyad emirs in Cordoba had some difficulty asserting their authority over outlying provinces, for the most part Umayyad rule in the eighth and ninth centuries saw increasing consolidation and centralization. Umayyad armies regularly mustered to defend the northern borders of al-Andalus against the emerging Christian Spanish kingdom of Asturias-Leon. This mountainous region of the northern peninsula was the only area that had never come under Muslim rule, and by the eighth century small Christian kingdoms were emerging. The economy of al-Andalus also developed rapidly, laying the groundwork for a local and international commerce that would expand in the tenth century. Cordoba flourished, and the growing Muslim population of the city was reflected in repeated expansions of the main mosque. Despite the ongoing refusal to acknowledge the Abbasid caliphs, Muslim Spain remained closely tied to other regions of the Islamic world. Eastern books and scholars made their way to Cordoba, and Andalusi Muslims traveled eastward for trade, pilgrimage, and education. It is clear that people in the Islamic west viewed the Near East as the cultural, religious, and intellectual center of the Muslim world. In 822, for example, a musician from Baghdad arrived at the Cordoban court, entrancing everyone with news of the latest Eastern fashions and tastes in music and literature.

While al-Andalus was under independent Umayyad rule, North African provinces remained loyal to the Abbasid caliphs in Baghdad. In 800 the region of Ifriqiyya (roughly modern Tunisia) was granted by caliph Harun al-Rashid to an Arab governor, Ibrahim ibn Aghlab. Subsequently, the Aghlabid dynasty governed almost autonomously until 909, although they always acknowledged the supremacy of the Abbasids. Because of their location in the central Mediterranean, the Aghlabids were well placed to initiate naval expeditions to Mediterranean islands and mainland Italy. During the 820s, the Aghlabids began their conquest of Sicily, but progress was slowed by regional resistance and the difficulties of directing an overseas campaign, as well as the fact that there was dissension between Arab and Berber factions in the Aghlabid armies. By 902 Sicily was more or less under Aghlabid control. As in Spain, Muslim Sicily had a very mixed population. Arabs comprised the ruling elite on the island, but there was also a significant Berber population, and Greek and Latin Christians long continued to constitute the majority of the population.

Muslim ships (usually described as pirates in Christian sources) also began to harass cities in mainland Italy. Bari was attacked by Muslims, probably from Tunisia, and became the base of an independent Arab emirate from 847 until 871. In 846 a raid was launched on Rome; the *Liber Pontificalis* described how Muslim forces "made a surprise attack on St Peter the prince of the apostle's church with unspeakable iniquities."[4] This assault prompted the Carolingian emperor Lothar to send an army and money to fund walls to protect the papal city against further incursions. But more raids followed, with attacks on Salerno in 871, and on Monte Cassino and San Vincenzo al Volturno in the early 880s. From 882 until 915 a Muslim base was established at the mouth of the Garigliano river, south of Rome, and in 891 renegade Andalusis founded a colony at Fraxinetum, near modern Saint-Tropez. From here, they raided along the French coast, and even into the western Alps, attacking travelers. In the early 970s they captured Mayeul, Abbot of Cluny, and held him for ransom, an affront that spurred the Christian destruction of Fraxinetum in 973.

Not all aggression in the ninth century can be categorized along religious lines, however, since some south Italian cities hired Arab mercenaries to aid them against Christian neighbors, and several made pacts of non-aggression with the Aghlabids. Some ports, notably Amalfi, engaged in commerce with al-Andalus, North Africa, and Egypt. These are important points to keep in mind, since they indicate that contemporaries may have been more concerned with security and commerce than religion. Indeed, it is doubtful whether most Europeans, even in areas close to Islamic regions, fully understood Islam as a religion. Christian chronicles of this period refer to Muslims as often as *saraceni*, *arabi*, or *mauri* (the latter particularly for North Africans), as by religious designations such as *musulmani* or *hagareni*.

Nevertheless, Christian intellectuals recognized the need to learn more about Islam. In many cases, European Christian ideas about Islam were influenced by Eastern Christian writers, such as the eighth-century John of Damascus, who viewed Islam as a Christian heresy. This idea appears in Christian Spanish texts by the ninth century, including an inflammatory Latin biography of Muhammad (*Istoria de Mahomet*), probably written *c.* 850, that describes the prophet as a "heresiarch." However, despite the hostile elements in this text, it is striking in that it also repeats details from the canonical Muslim version of the life of the Prophet.[5] This suggests that data from both Muslim and Christian sources went into creating Western Christian understandings of Islam. Because of their proximity to Muslim Spain,

Iberian Christians were more likely to have access to Arab sources than coreligionists elsewhere in Europe.

Christians in al-Andalus (*mozarabs*) were a protected community, as in other areas of the Muslim world. Along with Jews, they were designated "people of the book," because the Bible was considered a divinely revealed text, even if superseded by the later revelation of the Qur'ān. In return for the payment of taxes, acquiescence to legal, religious, and social restrictions, and subservience to Muslim political rule, Christians and Jews were allowed to follow their own religious, legal, and cultural traditions. In general this situation worked smoothly, and it promoted an atmosphere of peaceful coexistence that allowed minority communities to prosper both economically and intellectually. In rare instances, however, religious hostilities and social tensions led to violence. In the middle of the ninth century, a number of Christians in Cordoba were inspired by the kind of enmity expressed in the *Istoria de Mahomet*, and by a radical preacher named Eulogius, to speak out against Islam. These actions brought about their execution, and the "Martyrs of Cordoba" have become a famous and unusual example of violence toward Christians living under Muslim rule. This kind of isolated internal violence was very different from the ongoing external hostilities in Muslim–Christian border regions, expressed as military, naval, or piratical actions.

The persecution of Andalusi Christians was rare, but these incidents attracted the attention of Christians elsewhere in Europe. The story of the death of a boy called Pelagius, in 925, reached the German court of Otto I, probably as a result of diplomatic contact in the 950s, and was memorialized in verse by Hrotsvit of Gandersheim (d. *c.* 975). Her passion poem, which begins by describing Cordoba as "an ornament bright, a city famous in lore," has often been cited as an example of northern Christian admiration for the Umayyads and their capital city. It was quite the reverse, however, since she was referring to Cordoba before "the faithless tribe of unrestrained Saracens fell upon the stout people of this town."[6] Although there is no evidence that she understood much about Islam, other than what she may have gathered from talking to Andalusi envoys at Otto's court, Hrotsvit was one of the first northern European authors to write about Muslims and their religion.

Hrotsvit's words are symptomatic of increasing contact, diplomacy, commerce, and hostility between Christians and Muslims in tenth-century Europe. Changing relations were in part due to political consolidation both in Christian Europe and in Muslim regions. In Spain, the Christian kingdoms of Leon, Navarre, and Aragon, and the County of Barcelona, all gained firmer footing during the tenth century. At the same time, we see major changes in al-Andalus, with the declaration of a new Umayyad caliphate in 929, by the ruler Abd al-Rahman III (912–61). Along with his assertion of caliphal power, Abd al-Rahman began to mint gold coins in Spain, something that had long been considered a caliphal prerogative. The minting of gold not only signaled a change in Umayyad political status, but it also indicated Cordoba's access to African gold routes.

Abd al-Rahman III's assumption of the caliphal title probably had more to do with outdoing a new rival power in North Africa, the Fatimids, than it had to do with snubbing the Abbasids. The Fatimids had begun as a Shiite religious movement, following a charismatic leader who overthrew the Aghlabid dynasty and proclaimed himself caliph in 909. This, more than the declaration by Abd al-Rahman ten years later, was a watershed event. The Fatimids challenged the unitary caliphate in Baghdad, while asserting a Shi'ite claim to political power in the face of the Sunni rule by both the Umayyads and the Abbasids. Subsequently, the Fatimids would push their control westward toward Morocco, where they came into conflict with Umayyad claims to territorial influence. At the same time, the Fatimids also looked toward the Mediterranean, founding one of the first important Muslim Mediterranean ports, al-Mahdiyya, and establishing a Fatimid fleet. Abd al-Rahman responded by pouring resources into a new naval base at the Andalusi port of Almeria. This initiated a new era of Muslim naval strength in the western Mediterranean, which would last into the eleventh century.

Meanwhile, the Fatimids also claimed rulership over Sicily, where they appointed the Kalbid family as governors on the island. Over time, the Kalbids came to rule the island virtually independently, especially after the Fatimids had transferred their seat of power to Egypt in 972, but they always maintained their loyalty to the Shiite caliphs. This was in contrast to the governors appointed in Tunisia, the Zirids, who declared independence from the Fatimids.

Since Muslim control of Sicily was achieved only by the end of the Aghlabid period, most Islamization and Arabization of the island occurred in the tenth century. However, because of the troubled administration, remote location, mixed population, and relatively short time span, Muslim acculturation never penetrated as deeply in Sicily as it had in North Africa and al-Andalus. When the Muslim traveler Ibn Hawqal visited Sicily in 973, he admired the fertility of the island, and the many mosques and markets in Palermo, but he had little good to say about Sicilians, whom he perceived as idle, irreligious, and uncultured. He proposed that this was because Sicilians ate too many onions.[7] Ibn Hawqal's opinions may not reflect accurately on the majority of Sicilians (who were, in any case, mostly still Christian at this point), but it is notable that Muslim Sicily never produced as many artifacts of high Islamic culture – scholarly books, literature, or architectural monuments – as we find in al-Andalus. Nevertheless, we know of a certain number of Sicilian intellectuals, including theologians, jurists, scientists, and poets. Arabic Sicilian poetry is particularly noteworthy, and it is linked stylistically with poetic forms that were evolving in Muslim Spain. At the same time, Sicily was also thriving economically, both in the agrarian and the commercial sectors, with merchants and other travelers solidifying connections between the island and other regions of the Mediterranean World.

The declaration of two new Muslim caliphates in North Africa and Spain, and the increasingly broad territorial interests of the Umayyads and the Fatimids, both on land and sea, began to shift the mood of international relations in the Mediterranean. The Muslim raids of the ninth century gave way to more organized naval and diplomatic activities. Because Fraxinetum was reputed to have connections with Umayyad Spain, in 953 Otto I sent an ambassador to Cordoba to complain about attacks on travelers in the Alps. In response, Abd al-Rahman III dispatched the *mozarab* bishop Recemund (called Ibn Zayd, in Arabic sources) as an envoy to Otto. It seems likely that Recemund, or one of his companions, was the source for the information on Pelagius that Hrotsvit later put into verse. In contrast to the unilateral accounts of Carolingian diplomacy, these exchanges between Otto and Abd al-Rahman are recorded in both Muslim and Christian texts. Ibn Hayyan, the most important Arabic chronicler for the Umayyad period, mentions the embassy sent from Europe to discuss the problem of Fraxinetum, and he also notes Muslim diplomatic contacts with other Christian states, such as Barcelona.[8]

In these diplomatic exchanges, the caliph sent Christian or Jewish envoys, not Muslims, to conduct negotiations. This choice may reflect practical considerations, since Andalusi Christians and Jews were more likely to speak Latin or European vernacular languages, but it also reflects the curious phenomenon that medieval Muslims almost never traveled by choice to Christian lands. Thus, almost all Arabic information about Europe was based on the accounts of others. The same, of course, was true for the writings of most medieval Europeans regarding Islam. But we do have a number of first-hand Christian accounts of Muslims and Muslim lands. Whereas European merchants, pilgrims, scholars, and diplomats traveled southward in increasing numbers into Muslim territories, for economic, spiritual, intellectual, or political reasons, there were no corresponding lures northward for Muslim travelers. Only Muslim soldiers regularly crossed frontiers into foreign domains, since even raiding expeditions stopped after the early eleventh century. In general, by the central Middle Ages, the Muslim understanding of *jihad* (any struggle on behalf of Islam) was one of defensive maintenance, while Christian military endeavors (what we commonly refer to as crusades) were aimed at both defending Christian lands and regaining areas perceived as lost to Islam.

Why this apparent Muslim disinterest in northern Europe? This question remains a mystery, although there are several probable explanations. First, Arab maps show Europe off on the edge of the world, far from the civilized Islamic center, and Muslims perceived northern regions as cold, wet, and barbaric. In the tenth century, the geographer al-Mas'udi wrote that in Europe

> the power of the sun is weak . . . cold and damp prevail in their regions, and snow and ice follow one another in endless succession. The warm humor is lacking from [Europeans]; their bodies are large, their natures gross, their manners harsh, their understanding dull, and their tongues heavy. Their color is so excessively white that it passes from white to blue . . . their hair is lank and reddish because of the prevalence of damp mists.[9]

Secondly, even if a brave soul were drawn to such an unpleasant place, there were no facilities in Europe to accommodate the needs of a Muslim traveler – no mosques, baths, *halal* butchers, or Muslim communities to welcome them. In contrast, Christians in Muslim lands could easily find churches and other Christians. Thirdly, because there had always been Christians in Muslim lands, there was a well-understood concept of safe-conduct (*aman*) for non-Muslims traveling in Islamic lands; there was no parallel institution for Muslims arriving in Europe. Finally, any of the European exports that might tempt a Muslim merchant (furs, amber, silver, tin, slaves) were already brought to Muslim markets by European traders, so there was no need to make a trip to acquire them.

In one rare instance of a Muslim observer in early medieval Europe, a Muslim prisoner of war, Harun b. Yahya, was taken to Rome *c.* 886, and he eventually returned home with a detailed description of the city's walls, churches, and inhabitants.[10] There is also another account, from the 960s, by an Andalusi Jewish merchant, Ibrahim b. Yaqub, who traveled from Spain to Germany, Bohemia, and Eastern

Europe. Although he was not a Muslim, his observations were shaped by his Andalusi perspective. He was sometimes positively impressed, for instance, writing that

> the city of Prague is built of stone and chalk and is the richest in trade in all these lands. The Russians and the Slavs bring goods there from Cracow; Muslims, Jews, and Turks from the land of the Turks also bring goods and market weights; and they carry away slaves, tin, and various kinds of fur. Their country is the best of all those of the Northern peoples, and the richest in provender . . . it is remarkable that the people of Bohemia are dark and black-haired; blonds are rare among them . . .[11]

This account provides one of the earliest references to Muslims traveling into Europe from the east. Although there is material evidence of contact between northern Europe and the Near East, including hoards of eastern Muslim coins discovered in Scandinavia, most of these items were probably brought back by northern peoples who had traveled eastward – such as the Rus traders coming down the Volga, described by the tenth-century Arab author Ibn Fadlan – rather than by Muslims traveling west.[12]

At the time of the exchange of embassies between Abd al-Rahman III and Otto I, Umayyad rule in al-Andalus was at its apex. Cordoba ranked as one of the largest cities in the world, with an estimated population of 100,000, and it had become a major religious and intellectual center, attracting scholars from all over the Islamic Mediterranean. Muslims in al-Andalus no longer looked eastward for cultural inspiration, since they were now trend-setters for literature, music, and fashion. Al-Andalus had become wealthy, through agriculture and trade, and through access to gold routes coming across North Africa. All kinds of valuable new crops began to be cultivated in the peninsula – including sugar, rice, hard wheat, citrus fruits, and cotton – most of which originated in India and the Far East, and could be grown in Spain only with innovative techniques of cultivation and irrigation. This medieval "green revolution" was promoted on the highest levels, with rulers sponsoring research gardens and acting as patrons to botanists and other scientists.

The art of the garden reached new heights in al-Andalus. The complex interplay of architecture, plants, and water can be seen in the extensive gardens that have been excavated in the ruins of Umayyad palaces, especially at the site of Medina al-Zahra, a royal retreat constructed outside Cordoba by Abd al-Rahman III. According to legend, the gardens were designed in order that his consort, who was homesick for her native Granada, could look over the terraces of blossoming trees and be reminded of the snows of the Sierra Nevada. Andalusi music, art, and literature all testify to the centrality of the garden as a site for pleasure, love, and courtly life. The Umayyad princess, Wallada, was a patron of poets, and also a poet in her own right. The verses written between her and her lover, the poet Ibn Zaydun, often reflect these themes, as when he refers to the "garden wherein long ago our glances plucked roses which youthful passion displayed in their freshness, as well as sweetbriar."[13] Another celebrated poetic form, the *muwashshahat*, evolved in al-Andalus and was characterized by classical Arabic verses that ended with lines in romance (the *kharja*). These poems generally celebrate amorous dalliance and drinking, often in garden settings. The *muwashshahat* form has become famous for its probable influence on troubadour poetry in Christian Spain and Provence.

The Umayyad state under Abd al-Rahman III achieved the greatest degree of centralization that it had yet know. Early in his reign, Abd al-Rahman had been faced with regional revolts, but these were put down and the subsequent declaration of a new caliphate aided his consolidation effort. The Andalusi northern border remained problematic, however, since northern Christian kingdoms were expanding and taking political shape at this period. Military forays into the border regions along the Tagus river were routine events for both sides, as were diplomatic exchanges between Cordoba and northern rulers. Merchants and other travelers also seem to have moved freely between al-Andalus and the north, suggesting that, despite border skirmishes, the general atmosphere was relatively secure.

But by the end of the tenth century, during the reign of Abd al-Rahman's grandson, Hisham II, the balance began to shift. Because Hisham was a minor when he came to the throne, he ruled under the joint regency of his mother, Subh, and Muhammad ibn Abi Amir, who held the title of *hajib* (chancellor). This man was also known as al-Mansur ("the Victorious"), because of his military successes, and he retained control over Andalusi affairs even after Hisham had come of age. Al-Mansur seems to have been especially effective at controlling the different factions – Arabs, Berbers, and the Saqaliba (originally Slavs imported to serve in Andalusi armies) – within the military. He became famous for his aggressive border campaigns (Arab sources mention over fifty raiding expeditions), especially his attacks on Barcelona in 985 and Santiago de Compostela in 997. The latter was both a symbolic and a military victory, since al-Mansur carried off the cathedral doors and bells, hanging the latter in the mosque of Cordoba.

The "sack" of Compostela was a blow to Christian morale at a moment when the recently rediscovered tomb of St James was becoming a focus for Iberian Christian veneration, identity, and solidarity. Christians elsewhere in Europe were also beginning to notice the shrine. By the eleventh century, pilgrims flocked to Compostela, helping to integrate Iberian Christians within the broader European religious community. The importance of the shrine was also recognized in al-Andalus, as is clear, not only from al-Mansur's actions, but also in the writing of Ibn Hayyan, who reported that "Santiago is a city in the most remote part of Galicia, and one of the sanctuaries most frequented, not only by the Christians of al-Andalus, but by the inhabitants of the neighboring continent, who regard its church with veneration equal to that which the Muslims entertain for the Kaba at Mecca."[14]

After al-Mansur died in 1002, al-Andalus soon dissolved into civil war. Between 1008 and 1031, there were numerous claimants to the Umayyad throne, including Hisham II, each backed by a different military or regional faction. By the 1030s, after the death of the last Umayyad contender, al-Andalus had fractured into many small city states (called *taifas*) ruled by local military commanders or notable families. Some taifa states, such as Seville and Toledo, were in Arab hands, while others (for example, Granada) were in Berber control or were ruled by Saqaliba dynasties (Valencia). Each taifa state envisioned itself as the heir to Umayyad grandeur. Some taifa rulers tried to preserve the glamorous court life of an earlier era, acting as patrons to court poets, musicians, architects, and gardeners. But no taifa ruler had the resources, either from agriculture or from commerce, to support this kind of lifestyle, especially when it was also necessary to maintain an army to battle neighboring taifas and Christian kingdoms.

Constant border issues necessitated a variety of responses besides military confrontation, and they invalidate any idea that eleventh-century politics were simply drawn along religious lines. Taifa states allied with each other, but taifa rulers also allied with Christian kings against other Muslim or Christian states. After the death of the Christian king Ferdinand I in 1065, his realm was divided between his three sons into the separate kingdoms of Galicia, Castile, and Leon. The brothers immediately went to war against each other, during which the younger two, Alfonso and Garcia, at times sought refuge at the taifa courts of Toledo and Seville. Alfonso (who became Alfonso VI) would later marry the daughter of the emir of Seville.[15] Muslim and Christian mercenaries also served in armies on both sides. For example, the Castilian nobleman Rodrigo Diaz (also known as El Cid) fought for the emir of Zaragoza against the Count of Barcelona, and he later had Muslims among his own troops when he captured Islamic Valencia. In many cases, peace was maintained through the payment of tribute. This strategy had been deployed in earlier centuries, when Christian rulers often paid sums to Cordoba, but the situation was reversed in the eleventh century when taifa kingdoms regularly handed over protection money (called *parias*) to Christian kingdoms. These hefty sums were both a drain on taifa finances, and a boon to northern Christian economies. As the pilgrimage to Santiago was becoming a burgeoning industry, and as Gregorian reformers were introducing new religious vigor into northern Spain, *paria* payments helped to finance ambitious new Christian construction projects, including monasteries and cathedrals in Leon and Castile.

The increasing political and economic disarray in the taifa states was matched by administrative unification and growing military strength in the north. By 1072 Alfonso VI had recombined the kingdoms of Leon, Castile, and Galicia, and he began to turn his attention to territorial gain. He conquered the city of Toledo (where he had once taken refuge from his older brother) in 1085. This was a significant symbolic victory: Toledo was not only an important Muslim city, in a strategically central location, but it had been the Visigothic capital before 711. The capture of Toledo is often seen as shifting the balance between Christian and Muslim power in medieval Iberia. Nevertheless, it was also part of a larger movement, often called *reconquista* – the effort to reconquer Spanish lands lost to Islam. Although some medieval chroniclers portrayed the dream of retaking former Visigothic territories as stretching back to the eighth century, in fact the idea of reconquest began to take on a coherent ideology and force only during the tenth and eleventh centuries. Much of the *reconquista* effort was internal to Spain, but there was also external support. Already in 1064, a combined French, Catalan, and Aragonese army had laid siege to the Muslim fortress of Barbastro, near Zaragoza, and Pope Alexander II supported the endeavor by granting soldiers on this campaign the first known indulgence for fighting against Muslims. Later, the granting of a papal indulgence would become a critical element in the legitimation of a crusade.

Alfonso VI's conquest of Toledo raised new and difficult questions about how to incorporate this Muslim city into the Christian kingdom of Castile–Leon. These issues would continue to be important as the *reconquista* effort pushed deeper into Andalusi territory during the twelfth and thirteenth centuries, and many of Alfonso's solutions would set a model for later conquests. First, there were the linked problems of how to Christianize an Islamic city, and what to do with the Muslim population.

Both the physical and institutional infrastructure of the Muslim city (mosques, bathhouses, religious schools, legal and tax structures, and so on) and its human inhabitants needed attention. Alfonso promised that all Muslims who wished to remain in Toledo would be protected; they could continue to practice Islam and keep their property in return for paying a poll tax (this levy has been compared to the tax on Christians and Jews living under Muslim rule). Those Muslims who preferred to leave Toledo and relocate in Islamic regions further south were granted safe passage. At the same time, Alfonso also guaranteed that the main mosque of the city would retain its identity – but this promise was soon violated when the building was converted into a cathedral. Supposedly this happened when Alfonso was absent from the city, providing an opportunity for his French wife, Constance, and the newly appointed archbishop of the city, a French Cluniac, to seize control of the building. On Alfonso's return, sources report that he was furious and threatened punishment, but the Muslims of the city persuaded him not to act, lest it prompt retaliation against their community. The event is sometimes interpreted as an example of northern European hostility to Islam and misunderstanding of the tolerant *convivencia* that Alfonso sought to promote. While there may be some truth in this characterization, it seems unlikely that the queen and archbishop acted without any knowledge of the king, and it is telling that the building remained a cathedral (indeed, within three years, Pope Urban II declared its primacy among all sees in Spain – an ambition that had surely already been mooted in 1085). It seems likely, therefore, that this was a face-saving ploy to deal with an untenable situation. Certainly, as Christian armies captured more Muslim cities, it became routine to convert the main mosque into a church as a primary step in the process of Christian consolidation. The Muslim population was usually allowed to retain one or more smaller mosques in an area of the city designated for their residence (often called the *moreria*).

But Muslims were not the only inhabitants of newly conquered Toledo. There was a second issue presented by the significant population of Jews and *mozarabs*. Neither was as problematic as the Muslim community, since both were familiar with Christian rule in other areas of Castile–Leon. However, the *mozarabs* felt that they had a moral claim to Toledo, since they saw themselves as true heirs to the Visigoths. Although they were highly Arabized after centuries of living under Muslim rule (for example, *mozarab* documents from Toledo continued to be written in Arabic into the thirteenth century), they preserved Christian traditions from the eighth century. This presented something of a conundrum in an era emerging from the turmoil of Gregorian Reform. It is, therefore, significant, and emblematic of the reverence for their Visigothic heritage, that the Christian community in Toledo was allowed to continue to use its older form of the liturgy.[16] Alfonso also appointed a *mozarab* as governor of Toledo.

Thirdly, there was the issue of settling new Christian inhabitants. Both in Toledo and in later Christian campaigns, the promise of land and houses in formerly Muslim territories was an incentive for those serving in Christian armies. Christian kings also wanted to attract other immigrants, especially women and families, to populate their new lands. To this end, it became normal to divide up conquered cities, and to give out land to all comers, a process meticulously described in documents (called *repartimientos*) listing all the royal grants. Although no *repartimiento* text survives for Toledo, we have them for a number of other newly Christian cities.

The capture of Toledo did not go unnoticed in the Muslim world, and it sparked other taifa states to band together and call upon aid from North Africa. In response, the Almoravid dynasty sent forces from Morocco to Spain and routed Alfonso's army in 1086, at the Battle of Zallaqa. This effectively secured the northern Andalusi frontier, and pushed Alfonso's forces back north almost as far as Toledo. At first it appeared that this was enough, and the Almoravids returned to North Africa, but shortly afterward they came back to al-Andalus, this time as conquerors. Some taifa states held out against them, notably Zaragoza (which later fell to the king of Aragon in 1118), but the Almoravids were soon in control of most of al-Andalus. Their presence, and the subsequent rule of another North African dynasty, the Almohads (1147–228), stalled the progress of the *reconquista* for most of the twelfth century.

The eleventh century was also a turning point in Sicily and southern Italy, where Norman mercenaries led by two brothers, Robert and Roger Guiscard, began to take territory for themselves in the middle of the century. Robert, the older brother, focused on campaigns in Calabria and Apulia, while Roger concentrated on Muslim Sicily, taking Messina in 1061 and then moving westward across the island. The political situation in Sicily was fractured at the time of the Norman arrival, and Roger worked in alliance with one Muslim faction against another. As a result, he met more resistance in some areas than others. In Palermo, the city was supported by naval assistance from North Africa, but it fell to the Normans in 1072.

By 1091 the entire island was under Norman control, and Roger found himself ruling a mixed population of Greek and Latin Christians, Muslims, and Jews. Norman rulers were faced with the task of incorporating these various groups within their new regime. Although the Muslim population was promised protection, and allowed to maintain their religion and law, most mosques were converted into churches. In many rural areas Muslims lost their freedom, as Sicilian domains were parceled out among the Norman elite. Lists of *villeins* on Norman estates include the names of many Muslim tenants now tied to the land. Military accounts also show Muslims serving in Norman armies, and the Norman court employed Muslim bureaucrats, officials, and other professionals. Although the Normans are credited with reincorporating Sicily firmly within the West European Christian sphere, they also assimilated aspects of Muslim culture into their administration. During the twelfth century, elements of Norman Sicilian court ceremonial were modeled on Islamic forms, and some royal business was conducted in Arabic. Several Norman kings took Arabic titles, which then appeared on coins and in Arabic documents and inscriptions.

By the end of the eleventh century, therefore, on the eve of the First Crusade to Jerusalem, the military expansion of Christian rule into Muslim territories was already well underway in both Spain and Sicily. For the next century, these western borderlands would remain areas of contention, as Almoravid and Almohad armies defended the Andalusi frontiers in Iberia and the Normans made forays into North Africa, but there was little change in the overall control of land. Borders in Spain remained relatively unchanged until the early thirteenth century. In the Mediterranean, Christian naval and merchant ships gradually gained control of critical maritime routes for trade and communications.

The twelfth century witnessed changing attitudes as Christians and Muslims came into more frequent contact, both on the battlefield and elsewhere. In European thought, Islam and Muslims came to occupy a more prominent position in many spheres. There was greater interest in Islam in Christian theological writing (often with a view to conversion), growing enthusiasm for the scientific and intellectual resources available in Arabic texts, and a romanticization of Muslims in vernacular literature, while at the same time there was an increasingly hostile attitude toward Muslims in general. Within Muslim writings, this growing hostility is likewise clear, especially in the articulation of the doctrine of Islamic holy war (*jihad*). It is probable that the solidification of ideas about *jihad* in this period came in response to Christian military incursions.

By the twelfth century, European intellectuals were well aware that Arabic translations of ancient Greek texts by Aristotle, Galen, and other writers were available in both Spain and Sicily, as well as important medieval Arabic treatises on science, medicine, and similarly useful subjects. Thus, despite a general aversion to Islam, northern scholars traveled south to Palermo, Toledo, and other cities to seek texts and translators. Some of these men, including Gerard of Cremona and Michael Scot, maintained connections with intellectual activity in both southern Italy and Spain. It has often been said that there were "schools of translation" in Spain and Sicily, particularly in Toledo, but this wording is misleading. The process was not nearly as organized as the word "school" implies. Instead, we should envision small groups of scholars with different language competencies, often combinations of Christians, Muslims, and Jews, working together to translate texts in a two-stage process. A Christian who knew Latin and vernacular might work with a Jew who knew Arabic and vernacular; the Jewish partner would translate the Arabic orally into vernacular, and the Christian would then write his words down in Latin. Some European scholars may also have learned Arabic themselves. Through this process of travel, translation, and the transmission of texts, new scientific, philosophical, and medical ideas began to circulate throughout Europe.

Christian courts in Spain and Sicily became a locus for intellectual activity, and Christian kings became patrons to scholars and translators, both Muslims and Christians. In Palermo, the Muslim geographer al-Idrisi worked at the court of Roger II (1130–54), and his Arabic treatise on world geography became known as the "Book of Roger." Although written at a Christian court, Idrisi's work became more influential in the Muslim world than in Europe. Later, the emperor Frederick II (1215–50) supported the teaching of medicine in Salerno, and hosted scholars working on translations of Arabic works on zoology, optometry, mathematics, anatomy, astrology, and other fields. In Castile, King Alfonso X (1252–84) was also known as a patron of scholars, gaining the title "the Wise" (*el Sabio*) for his interest in intellectual matters. A wide variety of scientific and other texts were produced under his oversight, many of them translations from Arabic, including astronomical tables, a lapidary treatise, and a book on chess.

Christian intellectuals also took a deep interest in Arabic religious and philosophical texts. The writings of Aristotle, together with those of his great Muslim commentator Ibn Rushd (known as Averroes in Latin), would have a profound impact on Western Christian theology. Peter Abelard, Thomas Aquinas, and others would long wrestle with Aristotelian thought, especially its implications for the interplay of faith and reason. Other theologians took an interest in the Qur'ān itself. Peter the Venerable, Abbot of Cluny, traveled to Spain in 1142 and commissioned a Latin translation of this text with an eye to refuting its content in order to convert Muslims to Christianity. Peter wrote, famously, that he wished to bring Muslims to conversion through love rather than compulsion, and he realized that he could not dispute the claims of Islam without a better understanding of its primary text. Nevertheless, Peter was adamant in his opposition to Islam, which he regarded as a heresy, and his writings on the subject vilify both the Qur'ān and Muhammad. His Latin treatise was surely aimed at Christian readers, concerned about Islam and seeking polemical ammunition, rather than intended to convert a Muslim audience. Other Christian theologians, including the thirteenth-century Catalan Ramon Llull and a number of Dominican writers, also longed to convert Muslims through disputation and reason. To this end, they proposed the establishment of language schools to teach Arabic to preachers, but it is doubtful whether these schools were ever fully established or whether they promoted conversions. Indeed, it has been proposed that a knowledge of Arabic may actually have been more practical for ministering to Muslims who had already converted to Christianity, or to Arabic-speaking Christians, than for winning over new converts.

Even while some European churchmen recognized Islam as a monotheistic religion, although they considered it heretical, popular Christian opinion frequently regarded Muslims as pagans, who were said to worship Muhammad and the Greek pantheon. The twelfth-century *Song of Roland* is often cited for this kind of thinking, with its description of a Muslim king who "hates God's name, Mahound (Muhammad) he serves, and to Apollyon (Apollo) he prays."[17] At the same time, Muslims also became the object of Christian literary imagination, not always as the enemy, in *chansons des geste* and other stories. For example, the young Christian nobleman Beton was brought up at a Muslim court, and Huon, duke of Bordeaux, in the tale of the same name, was invited by a Muslim emir to play chess with his daughter.[18] This Muslim princess is just one among a number of "Saracen" women who play romantic and exotic roles in medieval Christian literature. Not all were princesses, however; the heroine in the Old French romance of *Aucassin et Nicolette* was born a Muslim slave.

At the same time that imaginary Muslim slaves were appearing in Christian literature, real Muslim slaves were working in elite households in Mediterranean Europe. Slavery provided another avenue for Christian–Muslim encounters. In Spain and Sicily, and in the burgeoning port cities of southern France and northern Italy, Muslim slaves were bought and sold in the wake of military conquests. Although Christian rulers generally promised protection to Muslims in newly conquered regions, some unlucky people were captured, then either ransomed or enslaved. The same was often true when Christians were captured by Muslims. In Genoa, local records show the sale of Muslim slaves from Valencia shortly after that city's conquest by James I in 1238. Notarial records also indicate that many of these Muslims later converted to Christianity. We cannot know if they converted for reasons of faith or practicality, but there was no Muslim community to support their continued practice of Islam, while conversion might eventually lead to freedom. Literature and reality may sometimes have reflected each other. One is reminded of the tale of Nicolette in one Genoese document, which recorded the marriage of a Christian man to a converted and manumitted Muslim slave woman.

During the thirteenth century, as Christian-held territories expanded, increasing numbers of Christians in southern Europe became familiar with Muslims and former

Muslims, free and unfree, as part of their daily lives. In Spain, the number of Muslims living under Christian rule (*mudejars*) expanded dramatically in the first half of the thirteenth century, with a wave of conquests following the watershed Christian victory against the Almohads at Las Navas de Tolosa in 1212. Cordoba fell to the Crown of Castile in 1236, followed by Seville in 1248, and Murcia in 1266. In the Crown of Aragon, King James I captured the Balearic Islands in 1229, and Valencia in 1238. By the end of the century, only the mountainous southern region of Granada remained in Muslim hands, under the rule of the Nasrid dynasty, which paid tribute to Castile to maintain its independence.

Surrender arrangements were different in each captured city, but in general the Muslim population was allowed to remain if they wished, under the protection of the king, and to keep their religion and laws so long as they paid taxes and did not resist Christian authority. In most cities, the Muslim community was relocated to the *moreria*, where they had their own houses, markets, and mosques. Christian legislation, such as the *Siete Partidas* of Alfonso X, ruled that, "although the Moors do not acknowledge a good religion, so long as they live among Christians with their assurance of security; their property shall not be stolen from them or taken by force." At the same time, Muslims were subject to severe penalties for certain crimes, especially sexual relations with a Christian woman or conversion of a Christian to Islam.[19]

Many Muslims chose to leave conquered regions rather than to live under Christian rule, and it became a heated debate among Islamic jurists as to whether it was even possible to follow a proper Muslim life in a Christian land. Most legal scholars ruled that it was impossible, and urged Muslims to emigrate to Granada or North Africa. The Andalusi jurist Ibn Rushd (d. 1126), the grandfather of Averroes, ruled that "the obligation to emigrate from the lands of unbelief will continue right up until Judgment Day," while a later opinion warned that a Muslim living in Christian lands "must beware of the pervasive effect of their [Christian] way of life, their language, their dress, their objectionable habits, and influence on people living with them over a long period of time."[20] As a result, most *mudejars* who were able to emigrate, especially members of the educated and wealthy elite, including theologians, jurists, and other professionals, did so. This meant that the remaining *mudejar* community in Spain was very different from the other religious minority under Christian rule, the Jews. Because the Jews had nowhere to flee (and were never suspected of being a fifth column), and because they already had a long tradition of living under Christian rule, the Iberian Jewish community retained its elite families and professional classes, and some rose to positions of trust and power in Christian administrations. *Mudejars*, in contrast, often found themselves at the bottom of the Iberian economic and social hierarchy.

In Sicily, the situation was somewhat different, since all Muslims there had lived under Christian rule since the late eleventh century. When the Muslim traveler Ibn Jubayr visited Palermo in 1183, he observed a mixed situation. He found that

> the Muslims of this city preserve the remaining evidence of their faith. They keep in repair the greater number of their mosques, and come to prayers at the call of the muezzin. In their own suburbs they live apart from the Christians. They do not congregate for the Friday service, since the *khutba* is forbidden. On feast days (only may) they recite it with intercessions for the Abbasid caliphs. They have a *qadi* (Muslim judge)

> to whom they refer their law suits, and a cathedral mosque where, in this holy month, they assemble under its lamps. The ordinary mosques are countless, and most of them are used as schools for Quran readers. But in general, these Muslims . . . enjoy no security for their goods, their women, or their children

despite the official Norman policy of tolerance.[21] Ibn Jubayr's concerns proved well grounded; the later twelfth century saw revolts and increasing repression of the Muslim population, and the situation further deteriorated under Swabian rule after 1194. Early in his reign, the emperor Frederick II took military action against Muslim rebels, and in the 1220s he ordered the deportation of most Sicilian Muslims to Lucera, on the Italian mainland. Lucera survived as a Muslim town until 1300. Although a few Muslims still remained on the island, the mass exodus to Lucera effectively marked the end of Muslim life on Sicily.

By the central medieval period, there were also Muslims living under Christian rule in Eastern Europe. These Muslims had not been conquered, and they may have settled in the region as merchants or mercenaries. Ibrahim ibn Yaqub noted Muslims in Prague in the tenth century, and Arabic sources mention Muslim villages in Hungary during the twelfth century. In the thirteenth century, Latin documents from Hungary indicate that Muslims paid special taxes to the crown in return for royal protection, but there was also a growing Christian insistence on conversion. By the fourteenth century, as in Italy, the Muslim population in Hungary had disappeared.

Muslim communities would continue to exist in Iberia until the reign of Ferdinand and Isabel in the late fifteenth century. The joint title of this royal couple, as "the Catholic Monarchs," emphasized their determination to pursue the final conquest of Muslim Granada in 1492, and to expel both the Jews (in 1492) and the Muslims (from the Crown of Castile in 1502, and from the Crown of Aragon in 1525). Thereafter, only converted Jews (*conversos*) and Muslims (*moriscos*) remained in Spain, although some Christians came to doubt the validity of their conversion. These suspicions added fuel to the activities of the Inquisition. Modern scholars also disagree about the degree to which *mudejars*, and later *moriscos* (despite their conversion), were able to preserve Muslim belief. Without an educated religious class, versed in Arabic and Islamic law and doctrine, it must have been difficult to maintain faith. The question is made particularly impenetrable by the fact that almost no documentation survives to record the Muslim point of view, and thus virtually all our evidence is from Christian sources. Some of these Christian texts depict a passive and subjugated population, while others betray fears that *mudejars* or *moriscos* would rebel against their Christian rulers. It seems reasonable to assume that, while some *mudejars* and *moriscos* submitted to Christian rule, either willingly or pragmatically, others more actively resisted Christian authority. Over time, while the formerly Muslim population gradually assimilated with Christian neighbors, in terms of language, religion, food ways, and in other respects, they also inserted aspects of their own culture into mainstream Spanish life. This continued a process of acculturation that had been in motion since the eighth century.

By the early sixteenth century there were no longer any Muslim communities resident in Western Europe. However, the Ottoman conquest of Constantinople, in 1453, opened the way for an entirely new scenario for Christian–Muslim relations in

Eastern Europe. The early modern period also witnessed the colonial expansion of West European trade and political influence into Islamic lands, both in the Mediterranean world and beyond, and brought new developments in diplomacy, commerce, and technology. There were likewise important theological shifts in both religious traditions in the post-medieval period. These changes profoundly altered the encounter between Christian and Muslim regions, shifting relationships away from an earlier medieval Mediterranean framework onto a new early modern world stage. Although the medieval heritage of Muslims in Europe remains important today, in many ways the contemporary encounter between Christians and Muslims in the twentieth and twenty-first centuries owes more to precedents established in the post-medieval period.

Notes

1 *Chronicle of 754*, in Wolf, ed. and trans., *Conquerors and Chroniclers*, pp. 111–58; *Treaty of Tudmir*, in Constable, ed., *Medieval Iberia*, pp. 37–8.
2 Einhard, *Life of Charlemagne*, p. 70. These embassies, and the elephant, are also mentioned in the *Royal Frankish Annals*, pp. 82, 87, 92.
3 Einhard, *Life of Charlemagne*, p. 64.
4 *Lives of the Ninth-Century Popes*, p. 96.
5 *Istoria de Mahomet*, in Wolf, "Earliest Latin Lives," pp. 97–9.
6 Wilson, *Hrotsvit of Gandersheim*, p. 29.
7 Ibn Hawqal, "Sicily," in Lewis, ed. and trans., *Islam*, vol. II, pp. 87–101.
8 Ibn Hayyan, "On the Campaigns and Diplomacy of Abd al-Rahman," in Constable, ed., *Medieval Iberia*, pp. 67–72.
9 Al-Mas'udi, "Neighbors to the North," in Lewis, ed. and trans., *Islam*, vol. II, p. 122.
10 Ibn Rusteh, *Atours précieux*, pp. 146–8.
11 Ibrahim b. Yaqub, in Lewis, *Muslim Discovery*, p. 145.
12 Ibn Fadlan, "Description of the Russian Vikings (921–922)," in Davis, ed., *Eagle, Crescent, and Cross*, pp. 154–8.
13 Ibn Zaydun, in Monroe, ed. and trans., *Hispano-Arabic Poetry*, p. 182.
14 Ibn Hayyan, quoted in al-Maqqari, *History*, vol. II, p. 193.
15 Zaida, the mother of Alfonso's only son, was first a concubine, and then his wife. She took the name Elizabeth after her conversion to Christianity.
16 The Mozarabic Rite, one of only two surviving Latin non-Roman liturgical forms (the other being the Ambrosian Rite in Milan), is still celebrated regularly in the cathedral of Toledo.
17 *Song of Roland*, p. 51.
18 *Boke of Duke Huon of Burdeux*, pp. 177–81.
19 *Siete Partidas*, vol. V, pp. 1438–42.
20 Harvey, *Islamic Spain*, pp. 56–8.
21 Ibn Jubayr, *Travels of Ibn Jubayr*, pp. 348–9.

Bibliography

Aucassin and Nicolete, trans. Andrew Lang (New York: Holiday House, 1936).
Boke of Duke Huon of Burdeux (London: Early English Text Society, nos. 40–1, 1882–3).
Constable, Olivia R., ed., *Medieval Iberia: Readings from Christian, Muslim, and Jewish Sources* (Philadelphia: University of Pennsylvania Press, 1997).

Daurel and Beton: A Twelfth-Century Adventure Story, trans. Janet Shirley (Felinfach: Llanerch, 1997).

Davis, Charles, ed., *The Eagle, the Crescent, and the Cross* (New York: Appleton-Century-Crofts, 1967).

Einhard, *The Life of Charlemagne*, trans. Lewis Thorpe (Harmondsworth: Penguin Books, 1969).

Harvey, L. P., *Islamic Spain 1250–1500* (Chicago: University of Chicago Press, 1990).

Ibn Jubayr, *The Travels of Ibn Jubayr*, trans. R. J. C. Broadhurst (London: Jonathan Cape, 1952).

Ibn Rusteh, *Les Atours précieux*, French trans. Gaston Weit (Cairo: Publications de la Société de Géographie d'Égypte, 1955).

Lewis, Bernard, ed. and trans., *Islam from the Prophet Muhammad to the Capture of Constantinople* (New York: Walker and Company, 1974).

Lewis, Bernard, *The Muslim Discovery of Europe* (New York: Norton, 1982).

The Lives of the Ninth-Century Popes (Liber Pontificalis), trans. Raymond Davis (Liverpool: Liverpool University Press, 1995).

al-Maqqari, *History of the Mohammedan Dynasties of Spain*, trans. Pascual de Gayangos (London: Oriental Translation Fund, 1843).

Monroe, James T., ed. and trans., *Hispano-Arabic Poetry* (Berkeley and Los Angeles: University of California Press, 1974).

Pirenne, Henri, *Mohammed and Charlemagne* (London: George Allen and Unwin, 1954).

"Royal Frankish Annals," in *Carolingran Chronicles* trans. Bernhard Scholz (Ann Arbor: University of Michigan Press, 1970).

The Siete Partidas, 5 vols. trans. S. P. Scott, new edition by Robert Burns (Philadelphia, University of Pennsylvania Press, 2001).

The Song of Roland, trans. Dorothy Sayers (Harmondsworth: Penguin, 1957).

Wilson, Katharina M., ed., *Hrotsvit of Gandersheim: A Florilegium of her Works* (Rochester, NY: D. S. Brewer, 1998).

Wolf, Kenneth, ed. and trans., *Conquerors and Chroniclers of Early Medieval Spain* (Liverpool: Liverpool University Press, 1990).

Wolf, Kenneth. "The Earliest Latin Lives of Muhammad," in Michael Gervers and Ramzi Jibran Bikhazi, eds, *Conversion and Continuity: Indigenous Christian Communities in Islamic Lands, Eighth to Eighteenth Centuries* (Toronto: Pontifical Institute of Mediaeval Studies, 1990) pp. 89–101.

Further Reading

A number of recent books concern the history of Muslim Spain and the relationship between Muslims and Christians in the Iberian Peninsula during the Middle Ages. Among these, Hugh Kennedy, *Muslim Spain and Portugal: A Political History of al-Andalus* (New York: Longman, 1996), surveys the outlines of Andalusi history and politics from the earliest period until the fall of Granada. Other volumes treat a narrower chronological scope. Both Thomas Glick (*Islamic and Christian Spain in the Early Middle Ages* (Princeton: Princeton University Press, 1979)) and Ann Christys (*Christians in Al-Andalus, 711–1000* (Richmond: Curzon, 2002)) write about Christian–Muslim relations in early medieval Spain, whereas Brian Catlos (*The Victors and the Vanquished: Christians and Muslims of Catalonia and Aragon, 1050–1300* (Cambridge: Cambridge University Press, 2004)) and Robert Burns (*Islam under the Crusaders: Colonial Survival in the Thirteenth-Century Kingdom of Valencia* (Princeton: Princeton University Press, 1973)) discuss the situation of Muslims living under Christian rule in the twelfth and thirteenth centuries. Robert Burns has also authored many other important and useful books on Muslims and Christians in the Crown of Aragon in the thirteenth century. On the situation of Muslims in Spain during the fourteenth and fifteenth centuries, see L. P. Harvey, *Islamic Spain, 1250–1500* (Chicago: University of Chicago Press, 1990), which examines both Muslims in Granada and *mudejars* in Christian kingdoms, and Kathryn Miller, *Guardians of Islam: Religious Authority and Muslim Communities of Late Medieval Spain* (New York: Columbia University Press, 2008), which investigates *mudejar* communities and the preservation of Muslim religious traditions in late medieval Spain.

Somewhat less has been written on Muslims in Sicily, though a good basic survey remains Ahmad Aziz, *History of Islamic Sicily* (Edinburgh: Edinburgh University Press, 1975). More recently, the situation of Sicilian Muslims and their influence during the Norman period (eleventh and twelfth centuries) has been discussed by Alex Metcalfe, in *Muslims and Christians in Norman Sicily: Arabic Speakers and the End of Islam* (London: Routledge, 2003), and Jeremy Johns, in *Arabic Administration in Norman Sicily* (Cambridge: Cambridge University Press, 2002). On the reign of Frederick II and his creation of the Muslim colony at Lucera in the early thirteenth century, see Julie Taylor, *Muslims in Medieval Italy: The Colony at Lucera* (Lanham, MD: Lexington Books, 2003).

A more general treatment of medieval Muslims living in the Christian regions of Spain, Sicily, and the Crusader States can be found in the collection of essays *Muslims under Latin Rule, 1100–1300*, edited by James Powell (Princeton: Princeton University Press, 1990). On Muslims in medieval Eastern Europe, see Nora Berend, *At the Gate of Christendom: Jews, Muslims, and Pagans in Medieval Hungary* (Cambridge: Cambridge University Press, 2001). Regarding Muslim–Christian intellectual contacts and influences, see John Tolan, *Saracens: Islam in the Medieval European Imagination* (New York: Columbia University Press, 2002). On the ways in which Islam was perceived in medieval Europe, see Maria Menocal, *The Arabic Role in Medieval Literary History* (Philadelphia: University of Pennsylvania Press, 1987), which examines the influence of Arabic literary forms on troubadour poetry.

Part V

Politics and Power

Chapter Sixteen

Conflict Resolution and Legal Systems

Thomas Kuehn

In the metahistorical account of the path to modernity, law and judiciary occupied a distinct place. The modern world was marked by states with unitary law codes and centralized court systems. Justice was a state monopoly. Law was rational and systematic. Penal offenses were investigated and prosecuted by state agents, and even private conflicts had to be taken to courts.

The medieval situation was antithetical to the modern. Then law was plural, overlapping, and predominantly local. Courts were weak or nonexistent; laws customary; justice in the hands of venal lords or prelates, or even in the hands of private individuals altogether (feud and revenge). Law was anything but rational, being instead highly ritualized and formal, with modes of proof including torture or ordeal. Historical research celebrated those developments (for example, founding of the law school of Bologna, ecclesiastical abolition of ordeals at the Fourth Lateran Council, Magna Carta) and those individuals (for example, Henry II of England, Emperor Frederick II, Louis IX of France, Gratian, Accursius) that contributed to the rationalizing, centralizing, and professionalizing of law, courts, and the state.[1]

This contrast between medieval and modern lives on. It is at the heart of the professional identity formation of lawyers and judges to this day. The role of much of legal history has been to legitimize current law and the legal profession. But truly critical legal historical studies, in league with allied disciplines of legal anthropology and sociology, look to social and political facts and to the uses of the law and have raised challenges to this legitimizing progressive narrative.[2]

The influence of legal anthropology, which studies forms of conflict resolution in "stateless" societies, has been felt especially in revisions of historical understanding of disputing, use of law, and courts in the Middle Ages. The relative statelessness of the Middle Ages made the anthropological perspective especially inviting and useful. Unitary law codes and state apparatus of enforcement diminish in importance as it becomes clear that societies without such things are not plunged into anarchy or lacking in ways to settle disputes peacefully and effectively. In study of the Middle Ages, then, one finds that feud and vendetta lasted throughout the period as "normative" forms of dispute processing, flanked by other customary and extra-judicial forms. But it is also clear that the Middle Ages were not just a negative backdrop or a stage to transcend in order to arrive at modern states and laws. There were moments of centralization of political power and courts, as with the Carolingian and Anglo-Saxon monarchs, that left a legacy of importance for later developments. There was also the legacy of the sophisticated and written Roman law.[3] Legal developments of the Middle Ages were complex, but among the most important of the period. It was then that canon law arose, law schools blossomed, legislative bodies formed, judicial procedures became regularized, and modern states had their origins.

Disputes and Settlements in the Early Middle Ages

The advent of Germanic peoples and their customs into the Roman empire governed by a complex and sophisticated law and courts has long been taken as a retrograde step in the evolution of law. In fact, it is increasingly clear that the Germanic peoples, especially for those, like the Burgundians, who began their migration from areas close to the borders with Rome, had already been heavily influenced by Roman legal forms. Indeed, it is also clear that Romans were influenced in directions that brought them close to Germanic patterns, or had not everywhere adapted the centralized system of the imperial law, as in what has been termed West Roman vulgar law. The fact that so-called barbarian codes were written, in Latin, is indicative of some cultural and legal rapprochement.

Further, it is very likely that historians have exaggerated the consistent, systematic, and centralized character of the Roman law in late antiquity. The functioning of the law on the peripheries belied the rhetoric of emperors intent on imposing rule and authority. Imperial law was more often negotiated than imposed, formulated (in the form of imperial rescripts) more often than decreed, in reaction to judicial rulings and interpretations in the provinces, and invoked or not by litigants as it suited their self-interests. Less formal extra-judicial forms of dispute settlement were always available and officially honored.[4]

One feature common to Germanic laws was the *wergeld* (in fact, the value of a free man that could be fractionally distributed across various offenses). It ostensibly substituted for a private act of revenge some form of material compensation put in terms of a monetary sum. An example is the Burgundian Code's establishment of a fee of 15 *solidi* for knocking out teeth of a Burgundian or Roman noble, 10 *solidi* for teeth of free-born Burgundians or Romans, 5 *solidi* for teeth of lower-class persons.[5] These sums were not judicially imposed fines. They were customary forms of compensation, re-establishing the proper social balance between parties where one had been damaged by the other's actions or inactions, intentional or not. As direct revenge or banishment from the group was considered to be the only sanctions available to primitive peoples, substitution of material compensation for revenge is usually seen as a positive evolutionary step.

In fact, anthropology has discovered that forms of group pressure are almost immediate when a dispute between some members of the group becomes apparent. Formal rituals of peace – foreswearing one's claim to an act of revenge – were the result aimed for. When individuals and their kin were unable on their own to find an accommodation, there might be recourse to a third party as arbitrator. It would be up to him (presumably impartial, chosen by agreement of the parties) to determine and impose an equitable solution.

On its face, arbitration of this sort was less formal but not all that different from procedures available in the Roman Empire. In Roman formulary procedure, parties expressed their claims to a magistrate, who determined if there was an issue of law and wrote a formula to cover it (this is where the *praetor* came to have great influence in expanding and correcting the older *ius civile*). The formula was passed to a lay *iudex*, who followed its terms in finding for plaintiff or defendant, depending on what matters of fact he found proved, while he had great latitude in conducting the trial. His determination, thanks to the formula, was thus supposedly in keeping with the law. The arbitrator was not to be concerned with law in any specific terms, as opposed to some general sense of right, equity, and justice; he was out to find a point of agreement between disputing parties.

By the end of the empire, formulary procedure had been replaced by *cognitio*, in which a *iudex* as government official heard the whole case, being responsible for framing the legal issues and for making the final judgment, as well as weighing the evidence and testimony of witnesses. In such a more professionalized procedure, issues of law could be allowed to emerge in the course of the process, instead of being framed at the outset. Technical terms lost or changed meaning, and the distinction between law and fact became blurred, as a result. For some scholars this resulted in the formation of an unsystematic, degenerate, "vulgar" law; for others this is the organic growth and vitality of the law.[6] It was certainly a more professional form, and thus more distinct from arbitration. But the judges' latitude, while open to the sorts of influence and corruption that generated many complaints and concerns in the late empire, allowed for effective resolution of disputes to the satisfaction of both parties. Even bishops, who were accorded judicial powers, were praised more for being mediators and peacemakers than for being instruments of judgment.[7]

Arbitration remained a viable feature of law throughout the Middle Ages (as, indeed, it remains today, with powerful advocates for it as an alternative to expensive formal litigation). Though arbitration would always seem an informal alternative to law, it was in fact later a vibrant part of it. The learned jurists of the schools that arose after the twelfth century elaborated a distinction they found in Roman legal texts between the *arbiter* (like the *iudex*, bound to law) and the *arbitrator* (the "friendly" composer of differences, operating on good faith and without legal formalities).[8] In fact, in legislation and in practice (as in the texts of late medieval notaries) the two were often combined, leading to a powerfully useful procedural institution that some communities mandated for certain types of disputes (as those between close kin).[9] Not only was arbitration not a Germanic import, it was decidedly not a procedure to be discarded as an evolutionary stage surpassed by later developments.

Ordeals and Proof

The key legal–judicial problem was what to do when arbitration did not work – when the parties could not or would not agree and pursued their vendettas or when an end otherwise could not be found. Certainly there is plenty of evidence of deep moral reluctance to take money for blood previously shed. In such serious cases both social peace and political order were in jeopardy. The Christian Germanic kings sought to impose their authority and prerogatives, to judge and punish malefactors for putative failure to keep faith with the monarch, for breaking the royal peace. Royal ideologies centered on the king's maintaining peace, especially for those (widows, orphans, clergy) unable to maintain it for themselves.[10] In fact, studies of the administration of justice between the sixth and tenth centuries highlight the constant difficulty for any territorial power to compel parties to appear before them and the need for severe penalties for contumacy. Monarchs like the Anglo-Saxon Aethelstan launched down a path of defining a category of crimes and a class of outlaws.[11]

By the seventh century a form of dispute processing had developed in Merovingian Gaul, known to historians from charters called *placita*. The very name shows the limits of judicial power, however, in the etymology offered in some of these documents: it is called a *placitum* because it pleases both parties ("placitum vero dictum est eo quod ambabus partibus placet"). Most *placita* that survive do so because they establish property ownership. There is a pattern to these, as they draw on stock formulae, and detail accusation and response before a tribunal, interchanges of evidence, and a summation of the result, with attestation that proper procedure was followed. The prominence of clergy in these surviving disputes can be explained by the fact that alienations of property to an ecclesiastical institution could well put it at odds with the donor's kin, and the regularizing of procedure to defend property rights would be a prime interest for such institutions. In any case, once one went to court, rules of law began to matter, as did the political power behind it.

The modes of proof in these cases have drawn much attention. Written evidence might well be presented, but it was also the case that, where written evidence lay to hand, the case was much less likely to come to court. Witness testimony was also highly important, and at times reliable witnesses trumped impressive documents. Written records and witness testimony were the most prominent forms of proof. In some areas, such as Catalonia, these forms of proof were wielded by a fairly professionalized judiciary operating with a sophisticated legal procedure and written (in this case, Visigothic) law.[12]

In the absence of documentary evidence, witness testimony, or consensus as to facts, laws like those of the Burgundians from the early sixth century envisioned two options – oath taking and ordeal. Oath taking (clearing oneself from an accusation by an oath along with others, often called oath-helpers) may have derived from vulgar Roman law; it was not part of the written imperial law. The presence of oath-helpers meant the accused had social support and standing in the community. Increased reliance on oaths may have arisen with the Christianization of the empire, as the oaths on Scriptures or relics called upon God. Ordeal (*iudicium Dei*) may have had a Germanic origin, but it is little mentioned before the earliest written Germanic laws of the sixth century; again, it may also have been the Church that encouraged the practice. The presence of clergy and the proper invocation to God to render judgment through water, fire, or combat was a vital part of the ordeal.[13] But the ordeal remained within a judicial procedure.

Oath and ordeal both brought the divine into proceedings. So too did books of penitence and the ultimate ecclesiastical sanction, excommunication. Inquest, on the other hand, was a procedure that brought the king or his agent into proceedings. Charlemagne dispatched his *missi* (generally a layman and an ecclesiastic together) into the corners of France and Italy to take sworn testimony about evident and hidden offenses. Extending a royal prerogative to investigate fiscal rights, these inquiries turned up cases that were placed in royal courts. Thus the counts and their traditional courts, where feud, oath, and ordeal might be corrupted and justice denied, could be circumvented. The oath administered to those *boni homines* who would testify about matters of fact and general knowledge in the area (thus jurors, from *iurare*) were central; and acts establishing inquests invoked obligations of service and loyalty to the king and anathema on those who failed to appear. Interests of ecclesiastical institutions in property gave them privileges of access to such inquests; reporting these activities from a distance to the royal court injected a measure of record keeping and made the judge an observer of proper procedure. Again, most of the records that survive deal with property, benefices, and immunities, records of which might obviate future disputes; matters of murder, assault, and so on probably remained in private hands and not in need of a jurisdictional settlement.[14]

Meaning of Ordeal

The inquest procedure continued to influence legal and administrative developments, notably in England, where the Normans used it in the Domesday survey of 1086 and again in the twelfth century in more properly legal matters with Henry II. The eclipse of Carolingian power weakened this more proactive and investigative procedure. Instead, from the ninth century one encounters much more frequent notice of forms of ordeal. A suspect might be made to pluck a ring from the bottom of a cauldron of boiling water, with the state of his injuries after three days determining guilt or innocence. Preservation, or not, from walking over a number of glowing ploughshares (six, nine, or twelve) was another variant. The most lasting form would prove to be the duel – trial by combat.

The reliance on chance or strength, rather than on reason and evidence, was long taken as proof of the fundamental irrationality of medieval law. The abolition of ordeals and their replacement by rational modes of proof in judicial circumstances were taken as positive steps. Anthropologists, however, pointed to the ready logic and situational rationality of all sorts of procedure in different societies, including those invoking the divine. Peter Brown applied their insights to the ordeal and argued for the functional social logic of the system, which hinged on members of the community coming to consensus on conducting an ordeal and determining whether the elements had pointed toward acquittal or conviction.[15] In this guise, said Brown, ordeal was reassuring and peace generating in the small, face-to-face society of the medieval village. Ordeal was employed only when all other forms of proof (written evidence, witness testimony, and oaths) were lacking or had yielded no conclusive result. The later legal procedural development is then to be explained by transformations in the community (that is, population growth, capitalism, a merchant class), such that it no longer found the ordeal satisfying, useful, or probative.

Robert Bartlett challenged Brown, following a line of criticism mounted in anthropology against the functionalist approach, which marked Brown's work. To Bartlett ordeal was not a device of small communities but a device of "hard, intrusive, rule-making lordship." He argued that ordeals could result in division as much as consensus, and the decisions lay with judges and priests, not the community (a more complex process than that witnessed by modern anthropologists). Nor did the ordeal "wither" from prior social change by 1200; instead it was spreading into frontier areas (Scandinavia, Poland, Wales, and Ireland) and remained vigorous where it began, despite a line of doubt and criticism of it. Ordeals came into disrepute because there was a "crisis in clerical confidence" in the use of ordeals, a growing wariness that arose even as ordeals spread and increased, about inconsistencies in the practice and the inaccessibility of divine judgments, the sin of tempting God. From this basis arose the decree of the Fourth Lateran Council forbidding clergy to participate in ordeals and the subsequent clerical derision of ordeal as irrational.[16] The result was a further disentanglement of the priestly from the secular that had been fundamentally pursued in the Gregorian reforms beginning in the mid-eleventh century.

"Revolution" in Law

Harold J. Berman has argued most forcefully for seeing the Gregorian Reform movement as a sudden transformative moment for the Western legal tradition.[17] That is when "law became disembedded' from religion, central authorities (secular and ecclesiastical) emerged, as did "a class of professional jurists." Ultimately the development of distinct feudal, manorial, mercantile, and urban laws showed, Berman claims, that rising "modern' legal systems were not only the result of policies of elites but responses to social and economic changes.

The essence of the revolution Berman described is the application of rational analysis by the likes of Gratian, Abelard, and Bracton (effectively marrying Greek philosophy to Roman jurisprudence) to the laws. His is thus a conceptual account of law far removed from effective procedures and the operation of courts on the ground. Berman exaggerated the degree of discontinuity in the developments he traced, but he also stood in a tradition that stressed a discontinuity around the same time. Others, operating with a narrower view of law, have seen a revolution in law in the recovery/rediscovery of the texts of Roman law, specifically to the *Digest*.[18]

The *Digest* was part of an assemblage of compilations made between 529 and 534 by the order of the last Roman emperor with great impact on law, Justinian (ruled 527–65). Alongside the *Institutes*, a textbook for use in imperial law schools, and the *Codex*, a systematic arrangement of legislation and imperial decrees (soon supplemented by the *Novels*, a volume of Justinian's legislation), the *Digest* presented topically arranged snippets, in fifty books, of the writings of the great Roman jurisprudents. These texts, then, were those of legal experts – technical, abstract, dense.

Justinian's compilation (the whole known as the *Corpus iuris civilis*) made it to Italy, but it was extraneous to the legal life of the Lombard kingdom there, and even largely to the remnant Byzantine footholds in the south and northeast of the peninsula. Roman law persisted, as it had before Justinian, largely in anthologies and epitomes. These might be consulted to help a judge determine a rule, but there was no systematic science of interpretation in the hands of a class of jurists. That is what the legal renaissance is taken to encompass – the formation of a systematic and autonomous legal science, found in schools, such as the one that arose in Bologna, associated with the shadowy figure of Irnerius (d. *c.* 1130). It was in the late eleventh and twelfth centuries that Roman legal thought and institutions regained influence. Then "an aptitude and a capacity for looking at everyday events and defining them juridically became part of the new cultural heritage and encouraged specialization, lent substance to the new professions of the practice and the theory of the law." Then the Church and empire and the growing market towns (in Italy and to some extent in southern France and northern Spain) found that the "abstract and reiterated legal concepts made Roman law . . . a mine of precious materials that jurists, as specialists arrogating to themselves a monopoly on the theorization of social relations, could recuperate and reutilize."[19]

Alongside the revived Roman-based legal science there also arose an increasingly abstract and professional canonical legal science of the Church. The figure of the monk Gratian (d. *c.* 1150) is as shadowy as that of Irnerius, but his compilation of texts of various provenances around legal topics and problems, which came to be known as the *Decretum*, became the textual basis to canon law studies, just as the *Digest* and *Codex* were for civil law. The Church, of course, was a vibrant institution whose legislation and adjudicative roles were in high gear from the eleventh century. Papal decretal letters, giving judgments on a wide variety of matters, were assembled in various compilations, official and not, beginning around 1200. It was Gregory IX (1227–41) who finally gave them official form in 1234 in five books known as the *Liber extra*. Boniface VIII (1295–303) would add the *Liber sextus* in 1298, and some final additions to the so-called *Corpus iuris canonici* came in the early fourteenth century. The story of these and related developments (the spread of universities, the elaboration of interpretative approaches of decretists, decretalists, glossators, post-glossators, and commentators) are all well known.

Many accounts of these developments have assumed that the more rational approach to law was inevitably influential and eagerly accepted in jurisdictions and courts. While legislators might have reason to hold onto customs and rules that underwrote their power in society, the force of reason on procedures was not to be denied. In fact, effects of these developments on courts and procedures, on means of conflict resolution, in other words, are less certain in more recent studies of litigation and dispute resolution.

Ius commune and *Ius proprium*

Taken together canon law and civil law (and some other minor pieces) became a *ius commune*, a common law (not to be confused with the royal "common law" of England). There is much ideological baggage, then and now, attached to the term, especially as contemporary Europe moves hesitatingly toward a union. In the Middle Ages the fundamental sense was that these rules, institutions, and ideas were a living force available everywhere (in jurisdictional terms, everywhere subject nominally to the empire, but in a larger sense, as *ratio scripta*, a standard of justice truly universally applicable). But, as such, they also stood in contrast, in any one place, to local customs and legislation, the *ius proprium*. Thus, while there was one universal common standard, there were many *iura propria*. The patterns and rules contained especially in Roman law gave impetus to feudal monarchs and lords and to city fathers to assemble and draft local customs. In Italy, for example, the Roman law rules of inheritance that had daughters sharing equally with sons ran up against prevailing patterns derived from Lombard customs favoring sons over daughters. Adaptation of Roman dowry then carried a rule excluding dowered daughters from family patrimony in favor of sons or other close agnatic males. This became a norm broadly enacted into law throughout Italy and southern France.[20] Pisa was one of the first cities to enact a statute compilation that showed the influence of Roman law, both in adaptations of language and institutions and in conscious modification or avoidance. Venice posed as more systematically rejecting the Justinianic legacy.[21] Eventually even relatively modest villages would sport written collections of their *iura propria*.[22] These dealt with areas of private law, but also mainly defined rules for local institutions, officials, and locations, including markets. These statutes did not just copy out existing customs; in some instances they greatly modified or were even opposed to normative traditions.

Courts and Procedures

These lords and communities established and staffed courts of law, as did bishops. These courts had their peculiarities in regard to procedure and standards of proof, and their powers were fairly weak and were to crystallize only slowly across the twelfth and thirteenth centuries. Recourse to outsiders as *podestà* in many Italian communities by and around 1200 added a vital veneer of impartiality to draw people away from their weapons or the mediating services of friends or others and into court. As these officials came increasingly to be drawn from the ranks of university-trained experts, the procedures in these courts came to move ever so subtly into more complicated forms.

Procedural developments occurred on two fronts – the scholastic (though this was too highly influenced by the activities and needs of the higher ecclesiastical courts) and the practical-judicial. As Roman jurists had not tended to separate procedure from substantive law (leaving the former embedded as so many *actiones* scattered throughout the law), while canonists were in need of procedures for ever-busier ecclesiastical courts, the procedures arrived at have come to be called romano-canonical procedure. The culmination of the process was the *Speculum iudiciale* of Guglielmus Durandus of 1271, expanded in 1289–91. In general, the result of these developments has been characterized in terms of the formation of two procedural models – the accusatory and the inquisitory – with the usual evolutionistic presumption being that the latter was more conducive to centralizing state power and came to replace or edge aside the former as time passed. While that characterization retains some broad utility, it is also overly simplistic and ahistorical.

As the name implies, the accusatory procedure was driven by a plaintiff lodging claims against a defendant. The influence of jurisprudence and practice was to result in a typical sequence of precise procedural phases, increasingly taking written form. The accuser began with a *libellus* of claims or charges and the legal action being invoked; the defendant then responded, including by citing *exceptiones* in his favor; a judicial formula of *contestatio litis*, fixing the commitment of the parties to go to trial before the judge on the alleged *actiones* and *exceptiones* was then drawn up; next came presentation of evidence and witnesses to the judge, leading to his sentence. The judge both investigated and ruled, though he approached witnesses with the *articuli* (allegations on which they were to be examined) provided by the parties. The effective abolition of ordeals arose from and precipitated rules of evidence and proof, including the admissability of witnesses and the credibility of evidence.[23]

Inquisitory procedure, adapting the late Roman *cognitio* and the Carolingian inquest, driven by ecclesiastical needs actively to remove notorious sinners from areas of responsibility and to search out heretics, gave latitude to the judge to initiate and pursue cases. He could operate more quickly and secretively, without formal complaint or lodging of claims, and the pace and order of proceedings were entirely in his hands. Possibilities of defense were drastically limited and, under appropriate legal circumstances, torture could be applied to witnesses and defendants to compel testimony they were otherwise reluctant to give. The focus here was not on parties and their dispute (indeed a real accuser might well be absent) but on the facts and the justice they deserved. One of the hallmarks of inquisitory procedure became an elaborate system of proofs. Full proofs, such as corroborating testimony of two credible eyewitnesses, allowed the judge to determine the facts; *probationes semiplenae* were numerous but none of them was decisive alone. The judge had to proceed by rules, including those setting *indicia* for the application of torture, and determine if half proofs concordantly amounted to full proof.

One of the foremost scholars of legal procedure in the Middle Ages, Massimo Vallerani, has vigorously denied the applicability of any evolutionistic scheme to these procedural forms. The accusatory and inquisitory procedures grew side by side during the decades around 1200, aimed at different sorts of cases, persons, and circumstances. They were, in fact, two different ways of sorting out the relationship between "law" and "facts." To put it in his terms:

> In sum, the two systems not only examine different facts (recounted by the offended party in the accusation; in the inquisition by an external report, as the denunciation of police or anonymous notices), but they also have opposite conceptions of the ways to reconstruct a fact (by a dialectical confrontation of the parties' testimony in the first, by a guided investigation on the body of the defendant in the second) or the final goal of judgment (to judge about a pretense of a disputant; to punish the guilty). At the level of logic the greatest difference is with regard to the notion of fact. In the accusation the fact is given life independent from reality and internal to the procedural discourse: the fact is a dialectical construction that must be defined by the parties in debate and put to proof by the judge. There are two distinct moments, that correspond to the theory of argumentation and to the theory of proof. In the inquisition fact is instead given an existence independent from law, as one postulates an objective reality that needs to be known and not merely discussed, because the procedure serves exactly to establish a *veritas* that coincides with reality. This presupposes a single judgment, concentrated in the hands of authority, without significant input from the parties and above all from the defendant.[24]

In the accusatory procedure the political independence of the judge is vital, as he must not favor one party over the other; in the inquisitory the judge is political from the start, defender of a particular order and endowed with the capacity to inquire into facts.

What Vallerani finds in studying judicial records of communities such as Bologna and Perugia is that inquisitional procedure did not operate quite so differently from accusatory, was not so free of the parties and their concerns, as one would think. Effectively there was a hybrid third procedure on the ground, as political and social forces reacted to legal procedure, veering from programs of general law enforcement to ad-hoc accommodations and amnesties, thus limiting the power of foreign judges and the range of *arbitrium* they could exercise in cases.[25] In other words, beyond the procedure used and the judgment arrived at in court, there was always the matter of enforcement, acceptance of judicial rulings, and public peace.

Whatever procedure was used, it inevitably changed the form of confrontation for the parties. Their disputes had to be distilled into legal terms recognizable to courts as actionable claims, and that required the services of notaries and attorneys. It took time for people to become accustomed to legal forms and to expect some amount of vengeance, retribution, and balancing of accounts from courts. Those less able to pursue their grievances by more direct means were more likely to find the courts a viable possibility. Daniel Lord Smail has examined the motives and actions of litigants in Marseilles who found utility in taking their enmities and debt claims to Angevin courts.[26] Whatever the forms of evidence and proof, those matters were, in the final analysis, incidental in large part to what the users of courts hoped to gain by going to them.

The presence of two forms of procedure, or the influence of one on the other, provided a needed flexibility as conditions changed. Negotiating and changing penalties was an important political factor that could not be left to foreign judges and learned law alone. Subsequently, with an important boost from early fourteenth-century papal legislation, there arose a less formal, more streamlined version of accusatory procedure, known as summary procedure, that was geared to keeping the courts attractive venues for disputing. A flexible array of procedures, including informal arbitration (though properly notarized for publication and record, if not strictly for enforcement), was what these communities needed, rather than some single rigid form.[27]

Both inquisitory and summary procedures tended to enlarge the sphere of activity and discretion left to the judge. A variety of consequences followed. One was that jurisprudence came to stress the need for procedure and the evidence it generated to ensure that judicial decisions were based on something more than a judge's conscience.[28] Another was the limitation of the effect of private (negotiated or arbitrated) peace settlements with regard to publicly levied fines and penalties for crimes. Governments and inquisitory courts continued to assert the public nature of crimes and their penalties; but it was also the case that revocation of penalties such as exile or outlawry required a prior arrangement of peace between the parties, lest there simply be a return to violence. The process is apparent in a city such as Bergamo, where thirteenth-century statutes gave wide play to private settlement of disputes, but where the statutes of 1331 reduced the effect of private peace accords for avoiding capital penalties and even monetary fines to minor crimes, and finally statutes of 1391 allowed private peace pacts the effect of limiting fines by only one quarter.[29] The signorial rule of the Visconti over Bergamo and other communities of Lombardy fostered inquisitorial courts and an inflated sense of the public nature of offenses, which was not removed by private settlements.

Another procedural innovation seemingly went the other way – away from politics and toward privileging professional expertise and terminology. In an accusatory proceeding, either the parties, eager to arrive at a conclusion, agreed to seek *consilium* from an expert, or the judge sought guidance and got the parties to agree to an outside expert. This was known as *consilium sapientis*, and it was generally incumbent on the judge to align his decision with that of the expert. Statutes specified the procedure of approaching the *sapiens* and put restraints on him or them to assure fairness.[30] The parties might also seek *consilium* to bolster their own case. This was the *consilium pro parte*, which, paradoxically, had more resonance in jurisprudence because the *consultor* was best advised to rehearse all the pros and cons of an issue, thus making the text a useful professional reference. The consulting jurists tended to uphold procedural formalities and terminological distinctions and continually had to confront the differences between *ius commune* and local laws and customs, in which case they disposed of regular professional interpretative devices.[31] As the scholastic law became more attuned to the legal problems of actual societies (thus moving away from primary attention to textual exegesis), especially in the aftermath of the conceptually challenging and synthetic works of great fourteenth-century jurists such as Bartolus of Sassoferrato (1313–57) and Baldus de Ubaldis (1323–400), *consilia* became an important feature of professional practice for *doctores legum*. In the "heyday of *consilia*" their efforts made the *ius commune* a truly integrative force in communities. Toward the end of the fifteenth century states increasingly erected more central courts, including those serving as points of appeal from other courts, and the judges of those courts became more powerful in accommodating learned law to legislation and shifting political and economic realities. Learned jurisprudence began to cede way to judges and case law, though a doctrine of precedent remained foreign to the civil-law tradition.

English Common Law

Peculiarities of the insular English situation under the Anglo-Saxon monarchs had already put in place some key elements of later law before the Norman Conquest of 1066. Most accounts of the development of English law, beginning with Maitland, have posited the central transformation in the work of Henry II (1154–89) and his advisers. The law then became centralized and "common" to the kingdom in royal courts, staffed with itinerant professional justices. Royal courts took over land-law jurisdiction through the instrument of novel disseisin, working on the pretense that all land was held from the king after the Conquest.[32] Criminal law was greatly transformed, as actions became classified as felonies against the king's peace, punishable by death or other physical penalties. Vital to the workings of the system was the returnable writ – a royal order to the sheriff to make the defendant appear to answer the complaint contained in the writ. These had different names, depending on the action set forth, and were registered (the registry constituting the earliest basis to common law). The success of royal courts in attracting business away from local and feudal courts is often attributed to the surer, professional, impartial nature of justice obtained there. In a revealing study from the 1980s, however, Robert C. Palmer demonstrated that county courts in England (as one example of a non-royal venue) were not unprofessional arenas from which litigants were eager to escape. Rather, until the fourteenth century, they were integrated with the workings of royal courts, not least because of the operation of the sheriff and his staff.[33]

S. F. C. Milsom has revised Maitland's argument by claiming that the Angevin reforms fundamentally changed landholding rights, doing much more than moving their adjudication to royal courts. Patrick Wormald has advanced a different revision.

He sees the Anglo-Saxon period as much more important (thus implicitly arguing for greater post-Conquest continuity), notably so in criminal law. There is at least greater willingness to see the immediate post-Conquest years to 1135 (which opened a relatively anarchic stretch of two decades) as formative of many of the essential later elements of the common law.[34]

It is hard to deny that the Conquest set the basis for a powerful kingship, especially once Henry II had engineered a restoration of royal authority in the mid-twelfth century. Writs, shire courts, hundred courts, royal courts, and other devices lay to hand, to be sure. But Henry aggressively turned them into instruments of dispute settlement and royal justice. The procedural device that became perhaps most characteristic of English law was the jury. The sworn inquest of local persons of good repute was a tool the Normans brought with them. It became the key means of prosecution of suspect persons – actually in a bifurcated form, the "grand" jury that decided whether to prosecute and for what wrongs, and the "petty" jury that heard the facts and returned a verdict of guilt or innocence (replacing after 1219 the ordeal, which was no longer available). The English criminal procedure thus remained an accusatory one and did not depend on a state prosecutor. Rulings of judges became formative and controlling, and that set precedent, rather than legislation, as the basis of many legal rules.

The English criminal and torts procedures did not necessarily draw all claims and accusations to the courts. Revenge and feud went on, sometimes in, but often out of, court.[35] From the royal perspective, juries and itinerant judges were designed to overcome fear or reluctance to bring accusations; but the results, even in the form of a verdict of one's neighbors, were not always geared to maintaining peace and social balance. Punishment and compensation were not the same thing. Still, as Palmer has argued in a study of a land dispute, "it is the very absoluteness of [litigants'] claims and defenses and the one-sidedness of the judgments that push them to compromise."[36] Inefficiencies and repeated opportunities for defeated litigants to reopen disputes were vital to dispute resolution and to bringing repeat business to the royal courts. The writ system over time tended to limit options to bring action. If one's grievance did not find coverage by an existing form of writ, one might have no recourse. So, even where forms of compensation remained available in tort actions, such as trespass, it was not always open when circumstances did not fit tightly described models. Later courts of equity, based on Roman law in some measure, beginning with royal courts and later centering on Chancery, were offered as recourse. They became more prominent from the end of the thirteenth century, precisely the time when another pivotal monarch, Edward I (1272–307), provided legislation allowing for trusts, land purchases, and security for debts.

While less directly or consistently influenced by the terminology and methods of the civil law, the developments in England were not unrelated to those on the Continent. Monarchs and princes sought to define crimes in terms of obligations and loyalties owed to them and to bring actions for such offenses, and their punishment, under the purview of their judicial mechanisms. While Henry II was forging innovations at the Assizes of Clarendon (1166) and Northampton (1176), contemporaries such as Frederick I Barbarossa and Philip of Alsace were engaged in parallel courses. Alfonso VIII (1158–214) in Castile and Alfonso IX (1188–217) for Leon extended the use of inquest procedure for criminal cases, even if, by the *Siete partidas* of Alfonso X (1252–84), the result was a form of inquisitory proceeding.[37]

Conclusion

By the late Middle Ages, despite the elaboration of consistent procedures, especially the romano-canonical, and thus the greatly enlarged possibility of official intervention in serious crimes, there remained an enormous variety of judicial practices, even within the same region. Feudal, civic, corporate, and ecclesiastical courts often used their own customs, and would continue to do so over succeeding centuries. A more consistent and coherent form can be attributed only to the grand tribunals (for example, Parlement of Paris, Westminster, Roman Ruota), inquisition courts, and to doctrinal accounts of procedure.

The epoch of famines, plagues, wars, and insurrections of the fourteenth and fifteenth centuries culminated in demographic growth, impoverishment, and uprooting of populations. Toleration of rootlessness declined; fear of theft and violence grew. Repressive mechanisms seemed more comforting. This was the era when *ius commune* and romano-canonical procedure were "received" in Germany and transformed the courts and the governments of princes and cities that established them. In 1495 Maximilian I (1493–519) declared a territorial peace (*Landfriede*) for the empire and decreed establishment of an imperial court (*Reichskammergericht*) to resolve disputes and thus preserve that peace. It was to be staffed at least for half its judges by persons trained in Roman law, following romano-canonical procedures, largely in written forms. This arose in part from and gave further impetus to the succession of legal reformations, routinizing and reforming civil law and procedures in a number of polities. The resulting relative homogenizing of law in the empire fit the interests of merchants and bankers and began to make secular tribunals more effective rivals of Church courts. The criminal legislation of Charles V (1519–55) in 1532 (*Constitutio criminalis Carolina*) would cap the development against the added backdrop of religious upheaval.

The common elements of continental procedure (writing, secrecy, learned theory of proofs) exalted the role of the trained technical expert, notably in the great courts. In minor courts, on the local level of community or lord, the ignorant judge, the antithesis of the educated professional, was both an embarrassing presence and a necessary evil. Between the different judicial levels an increasing reliance on writing and the consequent omnipresence of notaries, especially on the Continent, was a linking feature.[38] Even here, the power of the notary's record shifted from resting on signatures and attestations attached to it to being the *instrumentum* drafted by someone with *publica fides.*

In early modern Europe, sovereign intervention in justice assumed various forms (advocacy, letters of remission, pardon), many of them lucrative.[39] All took advantage of the fundamental ambiguity of a regime wavering between grace and law. Anyone who had access to both had a good chance of winning the judicial game. Appellate process made justice prevail on the basis of supplication and grant of grace. In the end, again, it was not abstract justice that was truly going to guarantee political order.

Notes

1 Especially Pollock and Maitland, *History of English Law*.
2 Hispanha, *Introduzione alla storia del diritto europeo*.
3 Wormald, *Making of English Law*, and Alessi, *Il processo penale*.
4 Harries, *Law and Empire in Late Antiquity*.
5 *The Burgundian Code*, p. 41.
6 Stein, *Roman Law in European History*.
7 James, "'Beati pacifici'."
8 Martone, *Arbiter-Arbitrator*.
9 Kuehn, *Law, Family, and Women*, pp. 19–74.
10 Carbasse, *Introduction historique au droit penal*, and Sorrentino, *Storia del processo penale*.
11 Padoa Schioppa, *Italia ed Europa nella storia del diritto*, pp. 53–81.
12 Bowman, *Shifting Landmarks*.
13 Wood, "Disputes in Late Fifth- and Sixth-Century Gaul," and Fouracre, "'Placita' and the Settlement of Disputes in Later Merovingian Francia."
14 Nelson, "Dispute Settlement in Carolingian West Francia," and Collins, "Visigothic Law and Regional Custom."
15 Brown, "Society and the Supernatural"; see also Hyams, "Trial by Ordeal".
16 Bartlett, *Trial by Fire and Water*.
17 Berman, *Law and Revolution*. His argument, in fact, is more sweeping – that the modern West ("not only modern legal institutions and modern legal values but also the modern state, the modern church, modern philosophy, the modern university, modern literature, and much else that is modern" (p. 4)) had its origins in the period 1050–150.
18 Stein, *Roman Law in European History*, pp. 43–5.
19 Bellomo, *The Common Legal Past of Europe*, pp. 52, 58.
20 Bellomo, *Ricerche sui rapporti patrimoniali tra coniugi*, and Mayali, *Droit savant et coutumes*.
21 Cozzi, "Authority and the Law in Renaissance Venice."
22 Useful here is Rossetti, *Legislazione e prassi internazionale a Pisa*.
23 Alessi, *Prova legale e pena*.
24 Vallerani, *La giustizia pubblica medievale*, p. 80.
25 Vallerani, Massimo, *La giustizia pubblica medievale*; Sbriccoli, "*Vidi communiter observari*."
26 Smail, *Consumption of Justice*.
27 Bellabarba, "Pace pubblica e pace private".
28 Padoa Schioppa, *Italia ed Europa nella storia del diritto*, pp. 269–80.
29 Ibid., pp. 222–38.
30 The classic study is Rossi, *Consilium sapientis iudiciale*; see also the essays in Ascheri, Baumgärtner, and Kirshner, eds, *Legal Consulting in the Civil Law Tradition*.
31 Sbriccoli, *L'interpretazione dello statuto*.
32 Palmer, "The Origins of Property in England" and "The Economic and Cultural Impact of the Origins of Property."
33 Palmer, *The County Courts of Medieval England*.
34 Milsom, *The Legal Framework of English Feudalism*; Wormald, *The Making of English Law*; Hudson, *The Formation of the English Common Law*.
35 See the interesting recent work of Hyams, *Rancor and Reconciliation in Medieval England*.
36 Palmer, *The Whilton Dispute*.
37 Alessi, *Il processo penale*, pp. 52–60.

38 Clanchy, *From Memory to Written Record.*
39 Pardon petitions are incisively analyzed by Davis, *Fiction in the Archives.*

Bibliography

Alessi, Giorgia, *Il processo penale: Profilo storico* (Bari: Laterza, 2001).

Alessi, Giorgia, *Prova legale e pena: La crisi del sistema tra evo medio e moderno* (Naples: Jovene, 1979).

Ascheri, Mario, Baumgärtner, Ingrid, and Kirshner, Julius, eds, *Legal Consulting in the Civil Law Tradition* (Berkeley and Los Angeles: Robbins Collection, 1999).

Bartlett, Robert, *Trial by Fire and Water: The Medieval Judicial Ordeal* (Oxford: Oxford University Press, 1986).

Bellabarba, Marco, "Pace pubblica e pace privata: Linguaggi e istituzioni processuali nell'Italia moderna," in Marco Bellabarba, Gerd Schwerhoff, and Andrea Zorzi, eds, *Criminalità e giustizia in Germania e in Italia/Kriminalität und Justiz im Deutschland und Italien* (Bologna: Il Mulino; Berlin: Duncker und Humblot, 2001), pp. 189–213.

Bellomo, Manlio, *The Common Legal Past of Europe, 1000–1800*, trans. Lydia G. Cochrane (Washington: Catholic University of America Press, 1995).

Bellomo, Manlio, *Ricerche sui rapporti patrimoniali tra coniugi: Contributo alla storia della famiglia medievale* (Milan: Giuffrè, 1961).

Berman, Harold J., *Law and Revolution: The Formation of the Western Legal Tradition* (Cambridge, MA: Harvard University Press, 1983).

Bowman, Jeffrey A., *Shifting Landmarks: Property, Proof, and Dispute in Catalonia around the Year 1000* (Ithaca, NY, and London: Cornell University Press, 2004).

Brown, Peter, "Society and the Supernatural: A Medieval Change," *Daedalus*, 104 (1975), pp. 133–51.

The Burgundian Code, trans. Katherine Fischer Drew (Philadelphia: University of Pennsylvania Press, 1972).

Carbasse, Jean-Marie, *Introduction historique au droit penal* (Paris: Presses Universitaires de France, 1990).

Clanchy, M. T., *From Memory to Written Record, England 1066–1307*, 2nd edn (Oxford: Blackwell, 1993).

Collins, Roger, "Visigothic Law and Regional Custom in Disputes in Early Medieval Spain," in Wendy Davies and Paul Fouracre, eds, *The Settlement of Disputes in Early Medieval Europe* (Cambridge: Cambridge University Press, 1986), pp. 85–104.

Cozzi, Gaetano, "Authority and the Law in Renaissance Venice," in J. R. Hale, ed., *Renaissance Venice* (London: Faber and Faber, 1973), pp. 293–345.

Davis, Natalie Zemon, *Fiction in the Archives: Pardon Tales and their Tellers in Sixteenth-Century France* (Stanford, CA: Stanford University Press, 1987).

Fouracre, Paul, "*Placita* and the Settlement of Disputes in Later Merovingian Francia," in Wendy Davies and Paul Fouracre, eds, *The Settlement of Disputes in Early Medieval Europe* (Cambridge: Cambridge University Press, 1986), pp. 23–43.

Harries, Jill, *Law and Empire in Late Antiquity* (Cambridge: Cambridge University Press, 1999).

Hispanha, Antonio Manuel, *Introduzione alla storia del diritto europeo* (Bologna: Il Mulino, 1999).

Hudson, John, *The Formation of the English Common Law: Law and Society in England from the Norman Conquest to Magna Carta* (London and New York: Longman, 1996).

Hyams, Paul, *Rancor and Reconciliation in Medieval England* (Ithaca, NY: Cornell University Press, 2003).

Hyams, Paul, "Trial by Ordeal: The Key to Proof in the Early Common Law," in Morris S. Arnold, T. A. Green, S. Scully, and Stephen D. White, eds, *On the Laws and Customs of England: Essays in Honor of Samuel E. Thorne* (Chapel Hill, NC: University of North Carolina Press, 1981), pp. 90–126.

James, Edward, "'*Beati pacifici*': Bishops and the Law in Sixth-Century Gaul," in John Bossy, ed., *Disputes and Settlements: Law and Human Relations in the West* (Cambridge: Cambridge University Press, 1983), pp. 25–46.

Kuehn, Thomas, *Law, Family, and Women: Toward a Legal Anthropology of Renaissance Italy* (Chicago: University of Chicago Press, 1991).

Martone, Luciano, *Arbiter-Arbitrator: Forme di giustizia privata nell'età del diritto commune* (Naples: Jovene, 1984).

Mayali, Laurent, *Droit savant et coutumes: L'Exclusion des filles dotées, xiième–xvème siècles* (Frankfurt am Main: Klostermann, 1987).

Milsom, S. F. C., *The Legal Framework of English Feudalism* (Cambridge: Cambridge University Press, 1976).

Nelson, Janet L., "Dispute Settlement in Carolingian West Francia," in Wendy Davies and Paul Fouracre, eds, *The Settlement of Disputes in Early Medieval Europe* (Cambridge: Cambridge University Press, 1986), pp. 45–64.

Padoa Schioppa, Antonio, *Italia ed Europa nella storia del diritto* (Bologna: Il Mulino, 2003).

Palmer, Robert C., *The County Courts of Medieval England, 1150–1350* (Princeton: Princeton University Press, 1982).

Palmer, Robert C., "The Economic and Cultural Impact of the Origins of Property: 1180–1220," *Law and History Review*, 3 (1985), pp. 375–96.

Palmer, Robert C., "The Origins of Property in England," *Law and History Review*, 3 (1985), pp. 1–50.

Palmer, Robert C., *The Whilton Dispute, 1264–1380: A Social–Legal Study of Dispute Settlement in Medieval England* (Princeton: Princeton University Press, 1984).

Pollock, Frederick, and Maitland, Frederic William, *The History of English Law to the Accession of Edward I*, ed. S. F. C. Milsom (Cambridge: Cambridge University Press, 1968).

Rossetti, Gabriella, *Legislazione e prassi internazionale a Pisa (secoli xi–xiii): Una tradizione normativa esemplare* (Naples: Liguori, 2001).

Rossi, Guido, *Consilium sapientis iudiciale: Studi e ricerche per la storia del processo romano-canonico* (Milan: Giuffrè, 1958).

Sbriccoli, Mario, *L'interpretazione dello statuto: Contributo allo studio della funzione dei giuristi nell'età comunale* (Milan: Giuffrè, 1969).

Sbriccoli, Mario, "Vidi communiter observari: L'emersione di un ordine penale pubblico nelle città italiane del secolo XIII," *Quaderni fiorentini per la storia del pensiero giuridico moderno*, 27 (1998), pp. 231–68.

Smail, Daniel Lord, *The Consumption of Justice: Emotions, Publicity, and Legal Culture in Marseille, 1264–1423* (Ithaca, NY, and London: Cornell University Press, 2003).

Sorrentino, Tommaso, *Storia del processo penale: Dall'ordalia all'Inquisizione* (Catanzaro: Rubettino, 1999).

Stein, Peter, *Roman Law in European History* (Cambridge: Cambridge University Press, 1999).

Vallerani, Massimo, *La giustizia pubblica medievale* (Bologna: Il Mulino, 2005).

Wood, Ian, "Disputes in Late Fifth- and Sixth-Century Gaul: Some Problems," in Wendy Davies and Paul Fouracre, eds, *The Settlement of Disputes in Early Medieval Europe* (Cambridge: Cambridge University Press, 1986), pp. 7–22.

Wormald, Patrick, *The Making of English Law: King Alfred to the Twelfth Century*, vol. 1 (Oxford: Blackwell, 1999).

Further Reading

Several good anthologies regarding medieval dispute settlements are listed in the Bibliography. Also useful, though more wide-ranging, is Warren C. Brown and Piotr Górecki, eds, *Conflict in Medieval Europe: Changing Perspectives on Society and Culture* (Aldershot: Ashgate, 2003), notably the editors' joint essays, "What Conflict Means: The Making of Medieval Conflict Studies in the United States, 1970–2000," pp. 1–35, and "Where Conflict Leads: On the Present and Future of Medieval Conflict Studies in the United States," pp. 265–85.

In addition to the outstanding example of traditional legal historical scholarship of the great Frederic William Maitland, see S. F. C. Milsom's revisions, *Historical Foundations of the Common Law*, 2nd edn (London: Butterworth, 1981). For continental law, see Franz Wieacker, *Privatrechtsgeschichte der Neuzeit unter besonderer Berüchsichtigung der deutschen Entwicklung*, 2nd edn (Göttingen: Vandenhoeck und Ruprecht, 1967), Italian trans., *Storia del diritto privato moderno*, 2 vols (Milan: Giuffrè, 1980); R. C. van Caenegem, *An Historical Introduction to Private Law* (Cambridge: Cambridge University Press, 1992); Antonio Pertile, *Storia del diritto italiano dalla caduta dell'impero romano alla codificazione*, 2nd edn, 4 vols (Turin: Unione Tipografico, 1894); Paul Koschaker, *Europa und das römishce Recht*, 4th edn (Munich: Beck, 1966); Mario Caravale, *Ordinamenti giuridici dell'Europa medievale* (Bologna: Il Mulino, 1994). Ennio Cortese, *Le grandi linee della storia giuridica medievale* (Rome: Il Cigno, 2000), an excellent survey, shows the conservative power of the modern paradigm in its substance and organization, as do many of the essays in Antonio Padoa Schioppa, ed., *Legislation and Justice* (Oxford: Clarendon Press, 1997). An important critical sociological take is that of Pierre Bourdieu, "La Force du droit: Éléments pour une sociologie du champs juridique," *Actes de la recherche en sciences socials.* 64 (Nov. 1986), pp. 3–19, or the English version, "The Force of Law: Toward a Sociology of the Juridical Field," *Hastings Law Journal*, 38 (1987), pp. 814–53.

A systematic overview by a scholar of Roman law is Peter Stein, *Legal Institutions: The Development of Dispute Settlement* (London: Butterworth, 1984). His work relies in part on important works of legal anthropology, which include Sally Falk Moore, *Law as Process: An Anthropological Approach* (London: Routledge, 1978); Simon Roberts, *Order and Dispute: An Introduction to Legal Anthropology* (New York: Penguin, 1979); John Comaroff and Simon Roberts, *Rules and Processes: The Cultural Logic of Dispute in an African Context* (Chicago: University of Chicago Press, 1981); William Ian Miller, *Bloodtaking and Peacemaking: Feud, Law, and Society in Saga Iceland* (Chicago: University of Chicago Press, 1990); Anton Blok, *Honour and Violence* (Cambridge: Polity Press, 2001); Jacob Black-Michaud, *Cohesive Force: Feud in the Mediterranean and the Middle East* (New York: St Martin's Press, 1975); Norbert Rouland, *Legal Anthropology*, trans. Philippe G. Planel (Stanford, CA: Stanford University Press, 1994). See also Thomas Kuehn, "Antropologia giuridica dello stato," in Giorgio Chittolini, Anthony Molho, and Pierangelo Schiera eds, *Origini dello Stato: Processi di formazione statale in Italia fra medioevo ed età moderna* (Bologna: Il Mulino, 1994), pp. 367–80.

Also useful on Roman law is Hans Julius Wolff, *Roman Law: An Historical Introduction* (Norman, OK: University of Oklahoma Press, 1951). A useful analysis of procedure and forms of proof in the early Middle Ages is Luca Loschiavo, *Figure di testimoni e modelli processuali tra antichità e primo medioevo* (Milan: Giuffrè, 2004), who argues forcefully that Germanic law used witness testimony and documents, not relying heavily on oath helpers, and that Christianity added a new emphasis on determining moral truth in legal procedure. In addition to Hyams's book and article cited in the bibliography, see his "Nastiness and Wrong, Rancor and Reconciliation," in Warren C. Brown and Piotr Górecki, eds, *Conflict in Medieval Europe: Changing Perspectives on Society and Culture* (Aldershot: Ashgate, 2003), pp. 195–218.

An earlier account with some similarities to Berman's is Walter Ullmann, *Law and Politics in the Middle Ages: An Introduction to the Sources of Medieval Political Ideas* (Ithaca, NY: Cornell University Press, 1975). A nice critical review of Berman is Edward Peters, "The Origins of the Western Legal Tradition," *Harvard Law Review*, 98 (1984–5), pp. 686–96. Classic on the rise of Roman law is Francesco Calasso, *Medio evo del diritto* (Milan: Giuffrè, 1954), who offered a critical stance on the textual account of the legal renaissance, centering it in wider movements of population, economic and urban renewal, and the expanding role of the Church. A more internal account of legal change, centering on the role of a professional class of judges, is Charles M. Radding, *The Origins of Medieval Jurisprudence: Pavia and Bologna, 850–1150* (New Haven and London: Yale University Press, 1988). An important account generally internal in its focus on texts, interpretative techniques, and the existence of a self-conscious class of jurists is Paolo Grossi, *L'ordine giuridico medievale* (Bari: Laterza, 1995). The great modern editions of the essential texts are *Corpus iuris canonici*, ed. Emil Friedberg, 2 vols (Leipzig: Tauchnitz, 1879); *Corpus iuris civilis*, ed. T. H. Mommsen, W. Kroll, R. Krueger, and R. Schoell, 3 vols (Berlin: Weidmann, 1928–9). Easily available portions in English translation are Justinian, *The Digest of Roman Law: Theft, Rapine, Damage and Insult*, trans. C. F. Kolbert (Harmondsworth: Penguin, 1979); Gratian, *The Treatise on Laws (Decretum DD. 1–20) with the Ordinary Gloss*, trans. Augustine Thompson and James Gordley (Washington: Catholic University of America Press, 1993). On canon law, a fine survey is James Brundage, *Medieval Canon Law* (London and New York: Longman, 1995). On institutional development of universities, see Alan B. Cobban, *The Medieval Universities: Their Development and Organization* (London: Methuen; New York: Harper and Row, 1975); Manlio Bellomo, *Saggio sull'università nell'età del diritto comune* (Catania: Giannotta, 1979), and *Società e istituzioni in Italia dal medioevo agli inizi dell'età moderna*, 3rd edn (Catania: Giannotta, 1982). For an interesting perspective on the imperial quality of *ius commune* against later works of Hermann Conring, see Constantin Fasolt, *The Limits of History* (Chicago: University of Chicago Press, 2004), pp. 155–218. Two other books published by Liguori that are useful for understanding civic legislative activity are Claudia Storti Storchi, *Intorno ai Constituti pisani della legge e dell'uso (secolo xii)* (Pisa: GISEM; Naples: Liguori, 1998) and Gabriella Rossetti, ed., *Legislazione e prassi internazionale nell'Europe medievale: Tradizioni normative, ordinamenti, circolazione mercantile (secoli xi–xv)* (Pisa: GISEM; Naples: Liguori 2001).

An excellent comparative study of legal procedure in this period is Chris Wickham, *Courts and Conflict in Twelfth-Century Tuscany* (Oxford: Oxford University Press, 2004), originally published as *Legge, pratiche e conflitti: Tribunali e risoluzione delle dispute nella Toscana del xii secolo* (Rome: Viella, 2000). On legal procedure, see Linda Fowler Magerl, *Ordo iudiciorum vel ordo iudiciarius: Begriff und Literaturgattung* (Frankfurt am Main: Klostermann, 1984); I. Rosoni, *Quae singula non prosint collecta iuvant: La teoria della prova indiziaria nell'età medievale e moderna* (Milan: Giuffrè, 1995). In addition to his book, see Massimo Vallerani's "I fatti nella logica del processo medievale: Note introduttive," *Quaderni storici*, 108 (Dec. 2001), pp. 665–93; and Mario Ascheri, "Il processo civile tra diritto comune e diritto locale: Da questioni preliminari al caso della giustizia estense," *Quaderni storici*, 101 (Aug. 1999), pp. 355–87. On judicial discretion, see Massimo Meccarelli, *Arbitrium: Un aspetto sistematico degli ordinamenti giuridici in età di diritto comune* (Milan: Giuffrè, 1998). For a further slant on Mario Sbriccoli's ideas, see his "Legislation, Justice, and Political Power in Italian Cities, 1200–1400," in Antonio Padoa Schioppa, ed., *Legislation and Justice* (Oxford: Clarendon Press, 1997), pp. 37–55. A nice overview of judicial changes in the era is Andrea Zorzi, "Negoziazione penale, legittimazione giuridica e poteri urbani nell'Italia comunale," in Marco Bellabarba, Gerd Schwerhoff, and Andrea Zorzi, eds, *Criminalità e giustizia in Germania e in Italia/Kriminalität und Justiz im Deutschland und Italien* (Bologna: Il Mulino; Berlin: Duncker and Humblot, 2001), pp. 13–34. For a social historical take on summary procedure, see Simona Cerutti, *Giustizia sommaria: Pratiche e ideali di giustizia in una società di Ancien Régime (Torino xviii secolo)* (Milan: Feltrinelli, 2003). Also valuable on *consilia* is Mario Ascheri, *Tribunali, giuristi e istituzioni dal medioevo all'età moderna* (Bologna: Il Mulino, 1989). Important on the ideas and activities of jurists are Adriano Cavanna, "Il ruolo del giusista nell'età del diritto comune," *Studia et documenta historiae et iuris*, 44 (1978), pp. 95–138, Osvaldo Cavallar, *Francesco Guicciardini giurista: I Ricordi degli onorari* (Milan: Giuffrè, 1991), David S. Chambers and Trevor Dean, *Clean Hands and Rough Justice: An Investigating Magistrate in Renaissance Italy* (Ann Arbor: University of Michigan Press, 1997), Patrick Gilli, "Les *consilia* juridiques de la fin du Moyen Âge en Italie: Sources et problèmes," in *Les Élites lettrées et le droit en Italie au Moyen Âge* (in press) and online at *Reti medievali.*

On the development of law and courts in England, in line with Maitland and an eloquent exponent of his views, and critical of Milsom, is R. C. van Caenegem, *The Birth of the English Common Law*, 2nd edn (Cambridge: Cambridge University Press, 1988). See also his comparative account of English and continental law, *Judges, Legislators and Professors: Chapters in European Legal History* (Cambridge: Cambridge University Press, 1987). Other useful accounts are Arthur R. Hogue, *Origins of the Common Law* (Bloomington, IN: Indiana University Press, 1966; repr. Indianapolis: Liberty Press, 1985); Paul A. Brand, *The Making of the Common Law* (London: Hambledon Press, 1992). On legal developments around the time of the Reformation, see John Witte, Jr, *Law and Protestantism: The Legal Teachings of the Lutheran Reformation* (Cambridge: Cambridge University Press, 2002), esp. pp. 33–50; Wolfgang Kunkel, "The Reception of Roman Law in Germany," and Georg Dahm, "On the Reception of Roman and Italian Law in Germany," in Gerald Strauss, ed., *Pre-Reformation Germany* (New York: Harper & Row, 1972), pp. 263–81 and 282–315 respectively.

In addition to Clanchy on the importance of writing in judicial applications, see Armando Petrucci, *Writers and Readers in Medieval Italy: Studies in the History of Written Culture* (New Haven and London: Yale University Press, 1995), pp. 236–50; Mario Amelotti and Giorgio Costamagna, *Alle origini del notariato italiano* (Rome: Consiglio Nazionale del Notariato, 1975); Mario Montorzi, Fides in rem publicam: *Ambiguità e tecniche del diritto comune* (Naples: Jovene, 1984). Pardon petitions are incisively analyzed by Natalie Zemon Davis, *Fiction in the Archives: Pardon Tales and their Tellers in Sixteenth-Century France* (Stanford, CA: Stanford University Press, 1987).

CHAPTER SEVENTEEN

Medieval Rulers and Political Ideology

ROBERT W. DYSON

The political thought of the Middle Ages is above all a Christian and ecclesiastical thought. Its ramifications are, of course, too extensive to describe fully in a single chapter. We shall here concentrate on one complex and important issue: the question of the respective roles of *regnum* or *imperium* and *sacerdotium* – royal or imperial and priestly authority. We select this question at the cost of omitting much that is important; but we do so because, in terms of the controversial literature that it produced, it is the main driving force of ideological debate from the fifth to the fourteenth centuries.

The Two Powers Problem

Down to the fourth century, Christianity was regarded with an official hostility that expressed itself most notably in recurrent persecutions of the Church by the Roman authorities. But in 312, in circumstances somewhat obscured by hagiography, the emperor Constantine himself became a Christian, and in 313 published an edict – the Edict of Milan – granting toleration to the Christian faith.[1] Thus began the process of assimilation by which, under Theodosius I (378–95), Christianity was transformed into the established religion of the Roman Empire.[2] But this process produced a difficulty that was to persist for a millennium. The Byzantine emperors still perceived themselves as sovereigns of the civilized world, with nothing lying outside their scope. The emperor, as supreme, is head of both Church and State: this doctrine is known as "caesaropapism." But the Church is the channel through which the grace of Christ flows into the world; upon it depends the salvation of mankind. How can the Church confess itself to be subject to the command of merely temporal rulers? Since the coming of Christ, the world has contained two powers, each with a compelling claim to supremacy. In the terminology introduced in the twelfth century by St Bernard of Clairvaux, there are now two "swords," a material and a spiritual. How are their fields of activity to be defined? What is to happen where they intersect, or if they come into conflict?

Caesaropapism was an issue for the Church, especially the Western Church, from the first. Though they relinquished the title *pontifex maximus*, the Christian emperors, in exercising authority over the Church, were not content always to abstain from theology. Constantine presided in person over the Council of Nicaea (325), and himself proposed the word *homoousios* ("consubstantial") as a solution to the Arian controversy. For their part, Christians were ready enough to call upon the secular magistrates for support when they felt it necessary to do so. When the Donatist schism arose in Africa in 312, both sides appealed to the authorities for adjudication, thereby apparently confirming the subordination of ecclesiastical matters to civil jurisdiction.[3] But the Church wished nonetheless to retain complete autonomy in spiritual matters. As it grew in material wealth, it also wished to exclude the secular authorities from interference with its property.

Christian authors thus found it necessary at an early stage to define in exact ideological terms the distinction between spiritual and secular power. St Augustine (354–430), though not the first Patristic author to address this question, was the figure to whom later generations ascribed the greatest authority.[4] In principle, he thinks, Church and State are separate orders, distinguishable in terms of easily specifiable functions. There is no "problem" of Church and State because there is no reason why the two orders should come into conflict. The State is divinely appointed to deal with temporal things, the Church with spiritual ones. Proper recognition should be given by each to each, and neither should intrude into the province of the other. Commenting on chapter 13 of St Paul's Epistle to the Romans, Augustine says:

> We are composed of body and soul. For as long as we are in this temporal life, we use temporal things for the support of this life. As to that part of us that pertains to this life, it is fitting that we be subject to the powers: that is, to the men who administer human affairs . . . But as to that part of us by which we believe in God and are called to His kingdom, it is not fitting for us to be subject to any man who seeks to subvert in us that very gift which God has deigned to give us for the attainment of eternal life. If, therefore, anyone supposes that, because he is a Christian, he does not have . . . to pay taxes or tribute, or that he does not have to render due honor to the powers that deal with such things, he falls into great error. But if anyone supposes that he should be subject to a man who is raised up to some high position in the administration of temporal affairs in such a way that that man is deemed to have power even over his faith, he falls into even greater error.[5]

In about 412, Augustine writes in a similar sense to Apringius, proconsul of Africa:

> I do not doubt that when you exercise that power which God has given to you as a man over men, you keep in mind the Divine tribunal before which even judges will have to stand and render an account of their judgments . . . It is of you that the Apostle said . . . that you bear not the sword in vain and that you are "a minister of God, a revenger to execute wrath upon him that doeth evil."[6] But it is one thing to rule a province and another to rule the Church. The former must be administered by engendering fear; the latter must gently commend herself through mildness.[7]

These passages effectively mark the beginning of an ideology of dualism – it may be called the "Augustinian/Gelasian principle" – that was to persist throughout the

Middle Ages. Secular and spiritual powers are ordained to preside over the two parts of man, and each part requires different techniques of rule. The governance of exterior life requires coercion; that of the soul, gentleness. In view of the similarities between the two documents, we may assume that Pope Gelasius I had Augustine's letter to Apringius in mind when in 494 he wrote his famous letter to the emperor Anastasius II:

> There are two orders, O August Emperor, by which this world is principally ruled: the consecrated authority of the pontiffs, and royal power [*auctoritas sacrata pontificum, et regalis potestas*]. But the burden laid upon the priests . . . is the heavier, for it is they who are to render an account at the Divine judgment even for the kings of men.[8]

Like so many Christian authors who discuss it, Augustine attributes the separateness of secular and spiritual jurisdictions to Christ's words at Matthew 22: 21: "Render to Caesar the things that are Caesar's, and to God the things that are God's."

Dualism from Gelasius I to Charlemagne

Augustine himself nowhere suggests that secular rulers are formally subject to ecclesiastical jurisdiction in temporal things. He does, however, insist – he could hardly do otherwise – that spiritual considerations far outweigh material ones, and have a prior claim on our allegiance. He insists also that Christian rulers, like all Christians, must serve God according to their station in life, and so must "make their power the handmaid of His majesty."[9] Inevitably, ecclesiastical authors began to insist with increasing force that the relation between the two powers cannot be a partnership of equals. Augustine admonished Apringius to remember the divine tribunal at which he would have to account for his judgments. Gelasius echoes Augustine, but with a clear shift in meaning. Now, it is the *priests* who will have to answer for kings, and the priests who therefore carry the heavier burden. He continues:

> Know, O most clement Son, that though you take precedence over the human race in dignity, nonetheless you bend your neck in devout submission to those who preside over things Divine, and look to them for the means of your salvation. In partaking of the heavenly sacraments . . . you acknowledge that you ought to be subject to the order of religion rather than ruling it [*subti te debere cognoscis religionis ordine potius quam praeesse*] . . . For if the ministers of religion, acknowledging that your rule . . . has been given to you by Divine disposition, obey your laws lest they seem to obstruct the proper course of worldly affairs, with what good will, pray, ought you to obey those who have been charged with the dispensation of the holy mysteries?

It is significant that Gelasius should have invoked the classical Roman distinction between *potestas* and *auctoritas*, "power" and "authority." Kings have power, but it is the pontiffs who have authority.[10] Augustine's largely metaphysical dualism has started to crystallize into the clearer and much more contentious doctrine that rulers are juridically subordinate to the Church. The implication of *potius quam praeesse* is clear. It is not possible for emperors to regard themselves as subject to the Church spiritually, yet sovereign over it temporally. In his fourth Tractate (*c.* 496), Gelasius says in remarkably peremptory terms that the civil authorities should "fear" to intervene in matters of religion; they are "permitted" to have power; they cannot "presume" to judge things divine. The pontiffs have final responsibility for directing even temporal things. In doing so they should "make use of the resources of the imperial government" (*quatenus spiritualis actio a carnalibus distaret incursibus*): "so that spiritual activity may be removed from carnal distractions."[11] There is much judicious imprecision in Gelasius's words, but their purport is clear. The task of emperors and kings is to protect the Church *a carnalibus incursibus*. Secular government exists to do those things that are beneath the Church's dignity.

In the second half of the eighth century, the papacy embarked on a course of diplomacy intended to create in the West a countervailing force to the caesaropapism of the Byzantine emperors. The foundations of this diplomacy were established in the late sixth century by Gregory I (590–604),[12] who, wishing to strengthen papal authority in regions where imperial influence was weakest, had cultivated cordial relations with the Franks in Gaul. Its first substantial phase occurred between 751 and 754.[13] Pepin "the Short," Mayor of the Palace of the Merovingian king Childeric III, wished to dispose of the feeble Merovingians and establish his own family as a royal dynasty in name as well as in fact. In 751 he sought the opinion of Pope Zachary: should the name of king belong to him who actually wields power or to a nominal king who is really a nonentity? The pope gave the desired reply, accompanied by a command that Pepin should become king forthwith, and in November 751 Childeric was banished to the monastery of Saint-Bertin. In 754 Pope Stephen II traveled to the Frankish kingdom to request Pepin's support against the Lombards in Italy and, while there, crowned and anointed him king. In doing so, Stephen stressed that God was entrusting to Pepin the special office of guardian of the Roman Church, in which capacity he was to bear the title *Patricius Romanorum*. In subsequent correspondence, Stephen emphasized that, through his papal coronation, Pepin had become St Peter's strong right arm, charged with securing justice for Christ's Church. For the first time, a pope was claiming to have consecrated a king as his secular lieutenant – a role that Pepin was apparently content to accept. Pepin's actions against the Lombards marked the end of papal dependence on Byzantine military power. The ceremony of anointing, inspired by the Old Testament[14] but performed for the first time in the West in 754, was to figure centrally in subsequent medieval coronations, functioning as something like the sacramental conferment of royal power.[15]

Papal relations with the Frankish monarchy culminated a generation later. On 25 April 799, Pope Leo III, suspected of simony, adultery, and perjury, was attacked and beaten by his enemies in the streets of Rome. He appealed to Pepin's son and successor Karl – Charlemagne – to judge between him and his accusers. In November 800 Charlemagne came to Rome to preside over the trial. This enforced answerability to a temporal ruler was not something that the pope accepted willingly. His action on Christmas Day 800 may reasonably be attributed to a desire to retrieve his position. On 23 December, Leo swore his innocence in St Peter's Basilica, before an assembly of Roman and Frankish clergy. Two days later, at the end of the Christmas Mass – to Charlemagne's surprise, apparently – he crowned Charlemagne, not as king of the Franks, but as "Emperor of the Romans." The pope had purported to bestow upon Charlemagne nothing less than temporal authority over the civilized world: in effect, to remove the imperial crown from Byzantium and transfer it to a candidate appointed by himself.

But what could entitle the pope to dispose of Constantine's successor in the East in favour of a Frankish newcomer? In this connection, we encounter the potent ideological document known as the *Donatio Constantini*, the "Donation of Constantine."[16] The *Donatio* is a clumsy eighth-century forgery, possibly confected in the Monastery of Saint-Denis, where Stephen II had stayed during his Frankish expedition of 754. Stephen may well have used it in negotiating with Pepin. Its basis is an earlier document, the *Legenda Sancti Silvestri*, which had circulated in Rome at the end of the fifth century. The gist of the *Donatio* is as follows. Cured of leprosy by Pope Sylvester I (314–35), a grateful Constantine bestowed upon Sylvester and his successors "imperial power, the dignity of glory, strength, and honour." He decreed that the pope "should have dominion over the four principal dioceses of Antioch, Alexandria, Constantinople, and Jerusalem, and all the Churches of God in the world." He handed to him moreover the Lateran palace, "the crown of our head; a mitre . . . all the advantages of our high imperial rank, and the glory of our power." The *Donatio* observes that Sylvester "by no means wished to use the golden crown above the clerical crown that he wore for the glory of St Peter": the pope had regarded temporal power as inferior from the first, which is why there are still emperors. But the implication is plain. Constantine's successors had worn the crown by the pope's permission. In crowning Charlemagne, Leo III had transferred his own property from one trustee to another. Nothing is known about the crown used in 800; but, when Charlemagne's son Louis I, "the Pious', was crowned in 816 by Stephen IV, the crown was said to be the very one given to Sylvester by Constantine. It is easy to imagine the symbolic power of this object, genuine or not.

Such was the basis both of Charlemagne's claim to be "Emperor of the Romans" and to the pope's claim to jurisdictional supremacy over him. Charlemagne's coronation – the *translatio imperii*, as it came to be called – signals the final division of Christendom into "Latin" or European and "Greek" or Eastern contingents, demarcated by territorial as well as ecclesiastical and doctrinal frontiers. The question of who was the real emperor of the Romans was not settled until the capture of Constantinople during the Fourth Crusade (1204); but it had by then become largely an academic one. Charlemagne's empire did not long survive him, and the complicated events that occurred between Charlemagne's death and the papal coronation of Otto I in 962 are matters on which we cannot dwell. It is enough to observe that, by the end of the eighth century, the papacy had contrived to establish its own independent spiritual sovereignty in the West (though at the cost of having to deal recurrently with the caesaropapist ambitions of the Western emperors). It had begun, moreover, to assemble, in the form of the principle of dualism and the *Donatio Constantini*, an intellectual arsenal in defense of the proposition that, while the world contains two powers, one is decidedly subordinate to the other. Though its authenticity was from time to time doubted, the *Donatio Constantini* was not finally discredited as a forgery until 1440, when it succumbed to the careful textual analysis of the Italian humanist Lorenzo Valla.[17]

Dualism in the High Middle Ages: Papal Monarchy

From the eleventh century, though they do not always refer to him directly, the Church's ideological champions rely greatly on themes associated with St Augustine.

They emphasize the division of mankind into two "cities": the *civitas Dei*, the eternal fellowship of those predestined to salvation; and the *civitas terrena*, the collectivity of those excluded from Divine grace. They tend to identify the Roman Church with the *civitas Dei* on earth, and secular political arrangements with the visible part of the *civitas terrena*. Some authors also lay stress upon Augustine's doctrine that earthly government originated in and expresses selfish and sordid impulses. The standard example occurs in the letter written by Pope Gregory VII to Bishop Hermann of Metz in March 1081, during the pope's great controversy with the emperor Henry IV over lay investiture.[18]

> Is not a sovereignty devised by men of this world who knew not God subject to that which the providence of Almighty God established for His own glory and graciously bestowed upon the world? . . . Who does not know that kings and princes derive their origin from men ignorant of God who raised themselves up above their fellows by pride, plunder, treachery, murder . . . at the instigation of the devil, the prince of this world: men blind with greed and intolerable in their audacity?

Gregory does not mention Augustine, but his words illustrate an unmistakably Augustinian tendency. The Church's sovereignty reflects the glory and grace of God; this world's kingdoms exemplify audacity and greed. In a pamphlet called *Ad Gebehardum* (*c.* 1085), Manegold of Lautenbach, a partisan of Gregory VII, in effect compares the responsibility of kings to those of a swineherd. He is answering the assertion of the imperialist Wenrich of Trier that a subject's oath of fealty is binding unconditionally. Why, Manegold asks, should a king who breaks faith with his subjects be less liable to dismissal than a swineherd who neglects his master's pigs? A homely analogy, perhaps, but one with an implication that is clear.

During the high Middle Ages, the themes of dualism, the two "Cities," and the connection between politics and sin were fashioned into an elaborate theory of ecclesiastical, and especially papal, supremacy. The visible Church is the City of God on earth, and hence the repository of divine justice. Political activity is ignoble at best, and at worst actuated by greed and rapacity. Only the guidance of a purer hand can redeem kingdoms from squalor. This disjunction can form the basis of any or all of the following claims: that royal authority flows from the Church or depends upon its validation; that princes are entirely subject to the Church's supervision and command; and even that the Church can depose unworthy rulers. The most ambitious papalist authors – Giles of Rome (*c.* 1247–1316) is the outstanding instance – canvassed what has been called a "hierocratic" papal ideology. The pope is the ruler *de iure* of the entire world, with *plenitudo potestatis* in spiritual and temporal things alike. As *vicarius Christi*, "vicar" of Christ – a title coined by the great thirteenth-century pontiff Innocent III (1198–1216) – he stands at the head of the hierarchy of earthly powers. He can judge any case without exception. He can appoint, direct, and punish kings and emperors and dismiss them by absolving subjects from their oath of allegiance. He can preside over all disputes, domestic or international. He can confiscate the property of sinners and transfer it to the righteous, even if that property is a kingdom. From him there is no appeal, because in this world there is no higher authority to whom appeal might be made. Under these conditions, the ancient theory of natural law became transformed into the doctrine that all human law, if it is to be valid, must reflect the divine law as mediated to the world through the Church.[19]

These conclusions emerged from a series of bitter conflicts between the Church and secular rulers, during which popes and papal publicists drew upon the authorities of Scripture, theology, philosophy, and canon law to establish the Church's independence of secular control and its supremacy over all temporal powers.[20] Major landmarks are the pontificates of Gelasius I (492–96), Gregory VII (1073–85), Innocent III (1198–1216), and Boniface VIII (1294–1303). Papalism finds its quintessential expression at the climax of the epochal contest of 1296–1303 between Boniface VIII and Philip IV of France, in the celebrated Bull *Unam sanctam* (1301): "We declare, state, define and pronounce that it is absolutely necessary for salvation that every human creature be subject to the Roman Pontiff."[21]

Exponents of papalism relied invariably upon the authority of Christ's words at Matthew 16: 18–19:

> And I say also unto thee, That thou art Peter, and upon this Rock I will build my Church; and the gates of hell shall not prevail against her. And I will give unto thee the keys of the kingdom of heaven; and whatsoever thou shalt bind on earth shall be bound in heaven, and whatsoever thou shalt release on earth shall be released in heaven.

According to the universal belief of Western Christendom, Christ had by these words created the office of the papacy and bestowed upon Peter and his successors the *potestas clavium*, the "power of the keys." The pope is endowed with divine authority to open and close heaven. It was in the fifth century, by Leo I (440–61), that this "Petrine doctrine" was made the basis of the papal claim to jurisdictional supremacy over the *respublica Christiana*.[22] What it can mean, once accepted, is limited only by the ingenuity of those who rely on it. Between the fifth and the thirteenth centuries, it was interpreted, with growing confidence and explicitness, as authorizing the pope to exercise monarchical government over every aspect of earthly life.

Such claims were made in the apparently genuine conviction that it is his moral and spiritual status that justifies the pope's intervention in secular affairs. The pontiffs who made the grandest assertions of *plenitudo potestatis* were inevitably accused of personal ambition; but none ever claimed that the *potestas clavium* establishes the pope as a secular monarch *simpliciter*. To do so would be to contradict the principle of dualism implicitly accepted on all sides from the fifth century. But no one who shared the religious values of Catholic Europe could doubt that the *potestas clavium* confers a supreme jurisdiction in matters of sin. What, then, are its limits? Is there any department of life from which sin is absent? Ours is a fallen world. Augustine, elaborating St Paul, had set the concepts of sin and grace at the center of Western religious sensibility. Sin, purgatory, damnation, absolution, extreme unction: these belong to the fabric of every believer's life. We are pilgrim members of the City of God, journeying toward a supernatural destination. All Christians, great and small, depend upon divine grace for their salvation, and hence upon the Church as the means of its sacramental transmission. All Christians, from emperor to peasant, can therefore become subject to papal jurisdiction *ratione peccati*: "by reason of sin."

The expression *ratione peccati* was devised by the decretalists of the thirteenth century. The principle that it expresses received its definitive, though not its first, statement in Innocent III's decretal *Novit* (1204), written to justify Innocent's intervention between King John of England and Philip Augustus of France, when Philip invaded John's great fief of Normandy. Philip Augustus enlisted the French clergy's support against the pope. Why, the bishops of France wanted to know, should the pope interfere in a temporal dispute capable of being settled in the king's feudal courts? Innocent III replied at length:

> Let no one suppose that we wish to diminish or disturb the jurisdiction and power of the king . . . For we do not intend to judge concerning the fief, judgment of which belongs to him . . . but to decide concerning a sin, the judgment of which belongs to us beyond doubt, and we can and should exercise it against anyone . . . No right-minded man does not know that it belongs to our office to rebuke any Christian for any mortal sin and to coerce him with ecclesiastical penalties if he rejects our correction . . . That we can and should rebuke is evident from the pages of both the Old and New Testaments . . . when the Lord gave the keys of the kingdom of heaven to the blessed Peter he said: "Whatsoever thou shalt bind on earth shall be bound in heaven, and whatsoever thou shalt release on earth shall be released in heaven." . . . Though we are empowered to proceed in this fashion against any criminal sin in order to recall the sinner from error to truth and from vice to virtue, this is especially true when the sin is against peace, which is the bond of love . . . Finally, when a treaty of peace was made between the kings and confirmed on both sides by oaths which, however, were not kept for the agreed period, can we not take cognizance of such a sworn oath, which certainly belongs to the judgment of the Church, to repair a broken treaty of peace?[23]

The logic invoked here is at once simple and powerful. The pope has authority to coerce sinners; if kings sin, he may coerce kings. Without doing any mischief to the Augustinian/Gelasian principle, the degree of temporal intervention that the *ratione peccati* principle can be used to justify is theoretically limitless.

Opposition to the Church's Claims

The Church's universalist claims did not, of course, go unopposed. From the time of Charlemagne, we encounter a royalist and imperialist literature that argues for an ideology of independent theocratic or sacral kingship – an ideology largely influenced by Germanic conceptions of government developed especially during the ninth-century Carolingian "renaissance.[24] This ideology does not depart from the Augustinian/Gelasian principle; indeed, it depends heavily upon it. There are two powers indeed; but the one is not subordinate to the other, nor is secular power directly in the Church's gift. Does not St Paul tell us that the powers that be are ordained of God and must be obeyed?[25] Nowhere do the Scriptures say that kings are appointed by the Church; frequently they do say that kings are to be honoured as the servants of God. The function of Christian emperors is to unite and defend the *populus Dei* and govern its exterior life under the Church's guidance, but not in juridical subordination to it. Kings are chosen by God; at their coronation they are blessed by the Church, not authorized by it. They are anointed to rule temporal things, and answerable to the Church only spiritually. The principle of dualism cuts both ways: the Church has no more right to intervene in temporals than kings or emperors have to intervene in spirituals. This is a summary of a wide and repetitious literature. We cannot survey it in detail, but early instances are Notker the Stammerer's biography of Charlemagne and the letters of Charlemagne's English counsellor Alcuin.[26] Weightier examples are furnished by tracts produced during the Investiture Controversy: Wenrich of Trier's *Epistula ad Hildebrandum* (*c.* 1081); the anonymous *De unitate ecclesiae conservanda* (*c.* 1090); Hugh of Fleury's *Tractatus de regia potestate et sacerdotali dignitate* (*c.* 1108); the "York Tractates" (*c.* 1100); Gregory of Catino's *Orthodoxa defensio imperialis* (*c.* 1111). A confident synopsis of royalist arguments is given in a later pamphlet (*c.* 1301), possibly by John of Paris, called *Quaestio de potestate papae* or *Rex pacificus*.

Down to the thirteenth century, the ecclesiastical argument is in general more impressive than the royalist or imperialist one. Both sides rely upon the same unquestioned scriptural and philosophical authorities, but those authorities lend themselves to different interpretations. The Church's representatives had on the whole a more assured, literate, and educated grasp of the issues. Also, the contention that princes are subject to the pope only in spirituals tended to founder upon the seemingly unanswerable *ratione peccati* principle: that there is nothing that is not, or cannot become, a spiritual matter. But a more developed royalist literature begins to make its appearance at the turn of the fourteenth century, especially in France. Philip IV's conflict with Boniface VIII produced two able pamphlets in particular: *Disputatio inter clericum et militem* and *Quaestio in utramque partem*. Outstanding among more substantial works of the early fourteenth century are John of Paris's *Tractatus de potestate regia et papali* (*c.* 1302), Marsilius of Padua's *Defensor pacis* (1324), and the diffuse writings of the English Franciscan William of Ockham (1280–349).

We mention Marsilius's *Defensor* especially, as being probably the most influential political treatise of the later Middle Ages.[27] Marsilius does not rest content with the assertion that spiritual and temporal power are separate but equal. Priests indeed have exclusive authority in matters of sin; but the punishment of sin and the reward of virtue pertain to the world to come. Priestly authority is great, but it does not in any way extend to the things of *this* world. Priests may teach and persuade, but they may neither coerce nor require kings to coerce on their behalf. In everything belonging to this world, priests and popes are subject to temporal government, and the best form of temporal government is a republican commonwealth whose laws are made by the "weightier part" of the people and enforced by secular coercive authority. Law depends not upon the approval or validation of the Church, but upon the will of the people, the *legislator humanus*. The *universitas civium*, the whole citizen body, will be better able than monarchs to create laws conducive to the common good. By the same reasoning, the Church should be organized not as a monarchy, but along republican lines. It should be governed by councils consisting of both clergy and laymen, and this government should extend even to the definition of doctrine. The *universitas fidelium* is more likely than an individual to discover the will of God. The Church's supreme legislative and judicial organ, therefore, should be not the pope but a General Council of the whole Church. This doctrine – versions of which are found also in John of Paris, the younger William Durandus, and William of Ockham – is called "conciliarism." It has ancient roots, in the seven Ecumenical Councils and in the work of Archbishop Hincmar of Rheims in the ninth century; but the "conciliar movement" of the fifteenth century was a movement of reform arising in specific circumstances that we must now briefly consider.

Political Change, the " Western Schism," and the Conciliar Movement

From the beginning of the fourteenth century, we notice a decline, amounting to a collapse, of the Church's efforts to assert its temporal authority. A couple of late flowers – Augustinus Triumphus's *Summa de potestate ecclesiastica* and Alvarus Pelagius's *De planctu ecclesiae* – appeared during the pontificate of John XXII (1316–34), but these treatises add nothing to the arguments exhausted by Giles of Rome in his *De ecclesiastica potatestate* (*c.* 1301). Broadly speaking, we may account for the demise of papalism as an ideology in terms of two factors: one intellectual, the other political.

The intellectual factor is the thirteenth-century "recovery" of Aristotle presided over so largely by St Thomas Aquinas (*c.* 1225–74).[28] By identifying earthly ends as valuable, albeit proximate, ends that can be sought without sin, Christian Aristotelianism tended to undermine the "Augustinian" principle that the papalists so much favoured: that politics has no positive good to contribute to our lives, and that the only truly important things are spiritual ones. By the same token, it re-endued government and citizenship with the ethical character assigned to them by classical political thought. In St Thomas's unfinished *De regimine principum* and in the *Summa theologiae*, the distinction between tyranny and good government becomes intelligible again. Government is an activity worthwhile in its own right, ordered to goods that are genuine goods, and not dependent for its moral quality upon the supervision of a higher authority. It is the Aristotelian idea of a *communitas perfecta*, a self-sufficient political community, that enables Marsilius to develop an argument by which the Church is excluded from a material role in public life and laymen are admitted to an active part in the governance of civic religion. Also, St Thomas's formulation of the ancient idea of natural law helped to restore reason to its role as a moral faculty independent of theology. More than anyone else, St Thomas rehabilitated the classical modes of thought about human nature and association, and hence about the relation between the temporal and spiritual powers, which subsequent authors were to use in formulating secular, republican, and "modern" accounts of politics.

As to more immediately political considerations: ineluctable forces of change had been operating in Europe since the pontificate of Gregory VII. Between 1150 and 1250, the question of *imperium* and *sacerdotium* had been the occasion of distracting controversies between the imperial Hohenstaufen dynasty and successive popes. The contests between Frederick Barbarossa and Popes Hadrian IV (1154–9) and Alexander III (1159–81), and between Frederick II and Innocent III, had enabled kings to consolidate their kingdoms unhindered by either pope or emperor.[29] The renewal of Roman law studies at Bologna and Pavia in the later eleventh century[30] lent growing efficiency and prestige to the civil courts, reduced the need of monarchs to rely upon ecclesiastics as bureaucrats, counselors, and lawyers, and eroded the belief that princes exist to perform tasks too lowly for the Church's consideration. The period following the death of Frederick II in 1250 saw a fragmentation of the empire and the growth of recognizably modern nation states, especially the kingdoms of France and England. Their aspirations were inimical to the papacy's universalist claims. Also, they were expensive to govern and defend. They were administered by complex bureaucracies and judicial systems. Wishing, in the interests of centralization, to free themselves from reliance upon feudal magnates, their kings began to employ mercenary armies instead of the old feudal levies. They looked increasingly to the Church's wealth as a source of revenue and, as a concomitant, encouraged their subjects to regard the Church as wealthy, slothful, and exploitative. They called into being national representative assemblies to mobilize support for new taxes on Church property. Philip IV's confrontation with Boniface VIII furnishes the clearest illustration of these tendencies: it was Philip who, in 1302, summoned the Estates General of France to sustain him in his struggle with Rome. French politics and diplomacy in the late thirteenth century were shaped by the determination that the king should be answerable to no one for the governance of his own realm. It was this that led France into war with Edward I of England over the territories that, as Duke of Guienne, the latter held in France; and the same determination brought Philip IV into conflict with Boniface VIII. Encouraged by energetic ministers – Pierre de Flotte, Guillaume de Nogaret, Enguerrand de Marigny – Philip was resolved to strengthen his kingdom by all available means and to tolerate no obstacle.[31] For a number of interconnected reasons, the ideology of papal imperialism was, by the end of the thirteenth century, well on the way to obsolescence.

The humiliating public defeat of Boniface VIII by Philip IV inflicted immense damage on the Church's vigour and independence. The curia migrated from Rome to Avignon in 1305. Avignon was not in France but in Provence, which belonged to the Angevin house of Naples; but the Avignon papacy necessarily became an instrument of French political interests. The Church's reputation suffered enormously during the first half of the fourteenth century. It remained in Avignon until 1377, and the conduct of its princes there became a matter of international scandal. The people of Europe, dying in uncounted numbers of the Black Death, felt themselves abandoned. Pious voices, including those of St Catherine of Siena and St Bridget of Sweden, were raised in protest, and a powerful current of opinion wished to disengage the Church from undue French influence. The emperor Charles IV sponsored Urban V's unsuccessful attempt in 1367 to re-establish the curia in Rome. At the initiative of Pope Gregory XI, the Church finally returned to Rome on January 17, 1377.[32]

The hope occasioned by this return withered almost immediately. When Gregory XI died in March 1378, the ensuing conclave was accompanied by violent disorder. The Italians, and Charles IV, did not want a French pope; the French did not want an Italian. A rabble beseiged the conclave hall, demanding an Italian. On April 9, Bartolomeo Prignano, archbishop of Bari, was elected as Urban VI. But the new pope's unsuspected and ungovernable temper alienated everyone. He berated bishops and cardinals for their absenteeism, luxury, and simony; he cursed and threatened; he is said to have had five uncooperative cardinals tortured. He ignored the French cardinals' pleas for a return to Avignon and announced his intention of packing the Sacred College with Italians. In September 1378 sixteen French cardinals declared Urban VI's election invalid, as having been swayed by intimidation. The suggestion was also cultivated that the new pope was insane. In another conclave they chose Robert of Geneva as Clement VII. Clement VII returned to Avignon; but now there were two popes. Most of Italy, the Empire, England, Poland, and Hungary declared for Urban VI; France, Scotland, Naples, and the Spanish kingdoms supported Clement VII. Urban VI died in October,1389.

His successors were Boniface IX, Innocent VII (1404), and Gregory XII (1406). At Avignon, Clement VII was succeeded in 1394 by Benedict XIII.

The Western Schism[33] brought the conciliar theories of Marsilius and William of Ockham measurably close to realization. In 1393, at the suggestion of weighty authorities – Henry of Langenstein; Conrad of Gelnhausen; Jean Gerson; Pierre d'Ailly – Charles VI of France asked the University of Paris for a solution.[34] The university recommended a General Council of the Church to end the deadlock: a proposal supported by cardinals on each side of the Schism and by the universities of Oxford and Cologne. But the Council of Pisa (1409) managed only to make a difficult situation farcical. Gregory XII and Benedict XIII declined to cooperate; they convoked councils of their own, at Aquileia and Perpignan. The Council of Pisa deposed Gregory XII and Benedict XIII and elected Peter Philargi, archbishop of Milan, as Alexander V. But neither Gregory XII nor Benedict XIII would acknowledge himself deposed; so now there were three popes.

When Alexander V died in 1410, his successor, John XXIII (anti-pope, d. 1419), was prevailed upon by the emperor Sigismund to summon the Council of Constance, which met from November 5, 1414 to April 22, 1418. Largely through judicious manipulation of the voting process, the Council secured the abdications of John XXIII and Gregory XII, who received the Sees of Tusculum and Porto by way of compensation. It declared Urban VI, Boniface IX, Innocent VII, and Gregory XII to have been true popes, and made a fresh start by electing Odo Colonna as Pope Martin V. Benedict XIII remained as antipope in Aragon until his death in 1423. His remaining cardinals elected another antipope, Clement VIII, but Clement VIII submitted to Martin V in 1429.[35]

The Council of Constance made a brave, and almost successful, attempt to transform the ideological nature of the Church: "to turn into a tepid constitutionalism the Divine authority of a thousand years."[36] Its decree *Haec sancta* declared that the body of the Church Militant is superior to its head. It asserted that a general council of the Church has its authority directly from the Holy Spirit; that in everything pertaining to faith, the extinction of schism and the reform of the Church, every Christian is bound to obey it; and that all refusing to do so, "even . . . the papal dignity itself," should be subject to ecclesiastical and civil penalties. In its decree *Frequens* the council made arrangements for the holding of regular councils to manage the Church's business. In convening them, the pope was to act merely as a kind of chief executive. They were to be held "in such places as the pope shall be required to designate and assign, with the consent and approbation of the council . . . or as, in his absence, the council itself shall designate." In effect, the Council of Constance asserted, against the trend of centuries, that the Church is a constitutional monarchy. On the face of it, this "Gallican doctrine," as it came to be called, was an impressive vindication of the doctrines of Marsilius and Ockham.

Haec sancta has been called "the most revolutionary official document in the history of the world."[37] This may be so as to its intent; it is hardly true as to to its effectiveness. The conciliar initiative failed almost entirely to take a grip on ecclesiastical government. The next council, at Siena, was summoned in 1423 but prorogued in less than a year. The Council of Basle, fitfully in session from 1431 to 1449, managed to accomplish only a demonstration of its own futility. Directionless, sparsely attended, and assembling erratically, the Council proved unable to resist the monarchical influence of Pope Eugenius IV (1431–47). The dissensions to which it gave rise nearly produced another schism. In 1437 the Council purported to depose Eugenius IV and elected Duke Amadeus VIII of Savoy as Felix V. Felix was largely unacknowledged outside Savoy and Switzerland, but the renewed threat of schism brought the conciliar movement to an end. Felix V's submission to the "real" Pope Nicholas V in 1449 restored the pope to his position as supreme head of the Church.[38]

The conciliar "movement" did not really move very far, but it may be described as an effective distraction of papal attention from the secular sphere. So far as the papacy's directly political aspirations are concerned, events in Europe had by the end of the fifteenth century gone beyond the possibility of effective interference. The question of *regnum* or *imperium* and *sacerdotium* was no longer one of significant ideological concern. The political countenance of Europe had changed irrevocably, and a wholly secularized type of political theory was emerging – a theory captured most readily in the writings of its most famous exponent, Niccolò Machiavelli.

Notes

1 See Bettenson, *Documents of the Christian Church*, p. 15. Also Alföldi, *Conversion of Constantine*; Barnes, *Constantine and Eusebius*; Jones, *Constantine and the Conversion of Europe*.
2 See Cochrane, *Christianity and Classical Culture*, ch. 9; Greenslade, *Church and State from Constantine to Theodosius*; King, *Emperor Theodosius and the Establishment of Christianity*; Lippold, *Theodosius der Grosse und Seine Zeit*.
3 See especially Frend, *The Donatist Church*.
4 See Deane, *Political and Social Ideas of St Augustine*; Dyson, *The Pilgrim City*; *St Augustine of Hippo*.
5 *Expositio quarumdam propositionum ex epistula ad Romanos* 72; cf. *Epistulae* 134: 1–3. All translations from the Latin in this chapter are mine.
6 Romans 13: 4.
7 *Epistulae* 134: 1–3.
8 *Epistulae* 12: 2, quoted in Carlyle and Carlyle, *History of Medieval Political Theory*, vol. 1, p. 191.
9 *De civitate Dei*, 5: 24.
10 See Dyson, *Normative Theories*, pp. 88–90; also Ullmann, *Growth of Papal Government*, pp. 14–26. For different views, see Caspar, *Geschichte des Papsttums*, vol. II, pp. 65, 753; Zeigler, "Pope Gelasius and his Teaching on the Relation of Church and State."
11 *Tractatus* 4: 11, quoted in Carlyle and Carlyle, *History of Medieval Political Theory*, vol. 1, pp. 190–1.
12 See Richards, *Consul of God*; Markus, *Gregory the Great and his World*.
13 See Geary, *Before France and Germany*; Wood, *The Merovingian Kingdoms*. Also Duchesne, *Beginnings of the Temporal Sovereignty of the Popes*; Halphen, *Charlemagne and the Carolingian Empire*.
14 Cf. 1 Samuel 10: 1.
15 Bouman, *Sacring and Crowning*.
16 For the text of the *Donatio*, see Bettenson, *Documents of the Christian Church*, pp. 98–101. See also Coleman, *Constantine the Great and Christianity*; Ullmann, *Growth of Papal Government*, pp. 74ff; Fuhrmann, "Konstantinische Schenkung und Sylvesterlegende

in neuer Sicht," p. 523; "Konstantinische Schenkung und abendländisches Kaisertum," p. 63.

17 See Valla, *Discourse on the Forgery of the Alleged Donation of Constantine.*

18 For a translation of this letter and of the so-called *Dictatus papae*, see Dyson, *Normative Theories*, app. II; see also MacDonald, *Hildebrand*; Tellenbach, *Church, State and Christian Society.*

19 See Dyson, *Natural Law and Political Realism*, vol. 1.

20 For a broad treatment of these controversies, see Dyson, *Normative Theories*, *passim*; *Natural Law and Political Realism*, vol. 1, ch. 6; Miethke and Bühler, *Kaiser und Papst im Konflikt*; Pennington, *Pope and Bishops*; Prodi, *Papal Prince*; Tierney, *Crisis of Church and State*; Ullmann, *Growth of Papal Government*; Wilks, *Problem of Sovereignty.*

21 For a translation of *Unam sanctam*, see Dyson, *Normative Theories*, app. III.

22 See especially Klinkenberg, "Papsttum und Reichskirche," p. 37; Ullmann, "Leo I and the Theme of Papal Primacy," pp. 25, 295; *Growth of Papal Government*, ch. 1.

23 Innocent III, *Novit* (*Extra.* 2: 1: 13: *Corpus iuris canonici* 2: 242ff); and see especially Ullmann, *Medieval Papalism*; Watt, *Theory of Papal Monarchy*; Sayers, *Innocent III.*

24 See especially Ullmann, *Carolingian Renaissance and the Idea of Kingship.*

25 Romans 13: 1.

26 See Collins, *Charlemagne*; Halphen, *Charlemagne and the Carolingian Empire*; King, ed., *Charlemagne*; Ullmann, *Growth of Papal Government*, ch. 3 and ch. 7, sect. 7.

27 See Gewirth, *Marsilius of Padua and Medieval Political Philosophy*; Nederman, *Community and Consent.*

28 See Dyson, *Natural Law and Political Realism*, vol. 1, ch. 7; Dunbabin, "The Reception and Interpretation of Aristotle's *Politics*"; Finnis, *Aquinas*; Flüeler, *Rezeption und Interpretation des Aristotelischen "Politica" im späten Mittelalter*; Gilby, *Principality and Polity*; Grabmann, "Forschungen über die lateinischen Aristoteles übersetzungen"; Jaffa, *Thomism and Aristotelianism*; Kempshall, *Common Good in Late Medieval Political Thought*; Nederman, *Medieval Aristotelianism and its Limits*; Steenberghen, *Aristotle in the West*; *Thomas Aquinas and Radical Aristotelianism.*

29 For a general account, see Previté-Orton, ed., *The Shorter Cambridge Medieval History*, vol. 2. See also Tierney, *Crisis of Church and State*, pt III.

30 Müller, "The Recovery of Justinian's Digest in the Middle Ages," p. 1; cf. Radding, *The Origins of Medieval Jurisprudence.*

31 See Bisson, "The General Assemblies of Philip the Fair," p. 537; Brown, *Politics and Institutions in Capetian France*; Fawtier, *The Capetian Kings of France*; Hallam, *Capetian France*; Prestwich, *Edward I*; Strayer, *Reign of Philip the Fair.*

32 See Jarrett, *Emperor Charles IV*, p. 209; Jorgensen, *Saint Catherine of Siena*, p. 237; Renouard, *The Avignon Papacy*, p. 66; Pirenne, *A History of Europe*, vol. 2, p. 23; Flick, *Decline of the Medieval Church*, vol. 1, p. 213.

33 See especially Delaruelle, Labande, and Ourliac, *L'Église au temps du grand schisme et de la crise conciliaire*; Valois, *La France et le grand schisme.* See also Smith, *Great Schism*; Ullmann, *Origins of the Great Schism*; Previté-Orton and Brooke, eds, *Cambridge Medieval History*, vol. 8: *The Close of the Middle Ages.*

34 See Black, *Council and Commune*; Figgis, *Studies of Political Thought from Gerson to Grotius*; Jacob, *Essays in the Conciliar Epoch*; Tierney, *Foundations of the Conciliar Theory.*

35 See Mundy and Woody, *The Council of Constance*; Stump, *The Reforms of the Council of Constance (1414–1418)*; Vooght, "Le Conciliarisme à Constance et à Basle."

36 Figgis, *Studies of Political Thought from Gerson to Grotius*, p. 31.
37 Ibid.
38 See especially Black, *Monarchy and Community*.

Bibliography

Alföldi, A., *The Conversion of Constantine and Pagan Rome* (Oxford: Clarendon Press, 1969).

Barber, M., *The Two Cities: Medieval Europe 1050–1320* (London: Routledge, 1992).

Barnes, T. D., *Constantine and Eusebius* (Cambridge, MA.: Harvard University Press, 1984).

Bettenson, H., *Documents of the Christian Church* (Oxford: Oxford University Press, 1947; repr. 1975).

Bisson, T. N., "The General Assemblies of Philip the Fair: Their Character Reconsidered," *Studia Gratiana*, 15 (1972), pp. 537–64.

Black, A. J., *Monarchy and Community: Political Ideas in the Later Conciliar Controversy, 1430–1450* (Cambridge: Cambridge University Press, 1970).

Black, A. J., *Council and Commune: The Conciliar Movement* (London: Burns & Oates, 1979).

Black, A. J., *Political Thought in Europe, 1250–1450* (Cambridge: Cambridge University Press, 1992).

Bouman, C. A., *Sacring and Crowning: The Development of the Latin Ritual for the Anointing of Kings and the Coronation of an Emperor before the Eleventh Century* (Groningen: J. B. Wolters, 1957).

Brown, E. A. R., *Politics and Institutions in Capetian France* (Aldershot: Variorum, 1991).

Burns, J. H., ed., *The Cambridge History of Medieval Political Thought,* c. *350–*c. *1450* (Cambridge: Cambridge University Press, 1988).

Canning, J., *A History of Medieval Political Thought* (Cambridge: Cambridge University Press, 1987).

Carlyle, R. W., and Carlyle, A. J., *A History of Medieval Political Theory in the West*, 6 vols (Edinburgh and London: W. Blackwood, 1928–36; repr., 1970).

Caspar, E., *Geschichte des Papsttums*, vol. II (Tübingen: J. C. B. Mohr, 1933).

Cochrane, C. N., *Christianity and Classical Culture* (Oxford: Oxford University Press, 1943).

Coleman, C. B., *Constantine the Great and Christianity* (New York: Columbia University Press, 1914).

Coleman, J., *A History of Political Thought from the Middle Ages to the Renaissance* (Oxford: Blackwell, 2000).

Collins, R., *Charlemagne* (Basingstoke: Macmillan Press, 1998).

Deane, H. A., *The Political and Social Ideas of St Augustine* (New York: Columbia University Press, 1966).

Delaruelle, E., Labande, E.-R., and Ourliac, P., *L'Église au temps du grand schisme et de la crise conciliaire (1378–1449)* (Paris: Bloud & Gay, 1962–4), vol. 14 of A. Fliche and V. Martin, eds, *Histoire de l'église depuis les origines jusqu'à nos jours.*

Duchesne, L., *The Beginnings of the Temporal Sovereignty of the Popes,* AD *754–1073*, trans. A. H. Matthew (London: Kegan Paul, Trench, Trübner, 1908).

Dunbabin, A. J., "The Reception and Interpretation of Aristotle's *Politics*," in N. Kretzmann, A. Kenny, and J. Pinborg, eds, *The Cambridge History of Later Medieval Philosophy* (Cambridge: Cambridge University Press, 1982), pp. 723–37.

Dyson, R. W., *The Pilgrim City: Social and Political Ideas in the Writings of St Augustine of Hippo* (Woodbridge: Boydell Press, 2001).

Dyson, R. W., *Normative Theories of Society and Government in Five Medieval Thinkers* (Lewiston, ME, Queenston, Ontario, and Lampeter: Edwin Mellen Press, 2003).

Dyson, R. W., *Natural Law and Political Realism in the History of Political Thought*, vol. 1 (Berlin, New York and Oxford: P. Lang, 2005).

Dyson, R. W., *St Augustine of Hippo: The Christian Transformation of Political Philosophy* (London: Peter Lang, 2006).

Fawtier, R., *The Capetian Kings of France: Monarchy and Nation (987–1328)*, trans. L. Butler and R. J. Adams (London: Macmillan, 1960).

Figgis, J. N., *Studies of Political Thought from Gerson to Grotius* (Cambridge: Cambridge University Press, 1923).

Finnis, J., *Aquinas: Moral, Political and Legal Theory* (Oxford: Oxford University Press, 1998).

Flick, A. C., *The Decline of the Medieval Church*, vol. 1 (New York: Alfred A. Knopf, 1930).

Flüeler, C., *Rezeption und Interpretation des Aristotelischen "Politica" im späten Mittelalter* (Amsterdam and Philadelphia: John Benjamins, 1992).

Frend, W. H. C., *The Donatist Church* (Oxford: Oxford University Press, 1952).

Fuhrmann, H., "Konstantinische Schenkung und Sylvesterlegende in neuer Sicht," *Deutsches Archiv*, 15 (1959), pp. 523–40.

Fuhrmann, H., "Konstantinische Schenkung und abendländisches Kaisertum," *Deutsches Archiv*, 22 (1966), pp. 63–78.

Geary, P. J., *Before France and Germany: The Creation and Transformation of the Merovingian World* (Oxford: Oxford University Press, 1988).

Gewirth, A., *Marsilius of Padua and Medieval Political Philosophy*, vol. 1 (New York: Columbia University Press, 1951).

Gilby, T., *Principality and Polity: Aquinas and the Rise of State Theory in the West* (London: Longmans, Green, 1958).

Grabmann, M., "Forschungen über die lateinischen Aristoteles übersetzungen," *Beiträge zur Geschichte der Philosophie und Theologie des Mittelalters*, 17 (1918).

Greenslade, S. L., *Church and State from Constantine to Theodosius* (London: SCM Press, 1954).

Hallam, E., *Capetian France 987–1328* (London and New York: Longman, 1980).

Halphen, L., *Charlemagne and the Carolingian Empire* (Amsterdam and New York: North-Holland, 1977).

Jacob, E. F., *Essays in the Conciliar Epoch* (Manchester: Manchester University Press, 1953).

Jaffa, H., *Thomism and Aristotelianism* (Chicago: University of Chicago Press, 1952).

Jarrett, B., *The Emperor Charles IV* (London: Eyre and Spottiswoode, 1935).

Jones, A. H. M., *Constantine and the Conversion of Europe*, rev. edn (New York: Collier Books, 1962).

Jorgensen, J., *Saint Catherine of Siena*, trans. I. Lund (London: Longmans, Green, 1938).

Kempshall, M. S., *The Common Good in Late Medieval Political Thought* (Oxford: Oxford University Press, 1999).

King, N. Q., *The Emperor Theodosius and the Establishment of Christianity* (London: SCM Press, 1961).

King, P. D., ed., *Charlemagne: Translated Sources* (London: Methuen, 1986).

Klinkenberg, H. M., "Papsttum und Reichskirche," *Zeitschrift der Savigny Stiftung für Rechtsgeschichte Kanonistische Abteilung*, 38 (1952), pp. 37–112.

Lewis, E., *Medieval Political Thought*, 2 vols (New York: Knopf, 1954).

Lippold, A., *Theodosius der Grosse und Seine Zeit* (Munich: W. Kohlhammer, 1968).
MacDonald, A. J. M., *Hildebrand: A Life of Gregory VII* (London: Methuen, 1932).
Markus, R. A., *Gregory the Great and his World* (Cambridge: Cambridge University Press, 1997).
Miethke, J., and Bühler, A., *Kaiser und Papst im Konflikt* (Düsseldorf: Schwann, 1988).
Müller, W. P., "The Recovery of Justinian's Digest in the Middle Ages," *Bulletin of Medieval Canon Law*, 20 (1990), pp. 1–29.
Mundy, J. H., and Woody, K. M., eds, *The Council of Constance*, trans. L. R. Loomis (New York: Columbia University Press, 1961).
Nederman, C. J., *Community and Consent: The Secular Political Theory of Marsiglio of Padua's Defensor Pacis* (London: Rowman & Littlefield, 1995).
Nederman, C. J., *Medieval Aristotelianism and its Limits: Classical Traditions in Moral and Political Philosophy* (Aldershot: Variorum, 1997).
Pennington, K., *Pope and Bishops: The Papal Monarchy in the Twelfth and Thirteenth Centuries* (Philadelphia: University of Pennsylvania Press, 1984).
Pirenne, H., *A History of Europe*, vol. 2 (New York: G. Allen & Unwin, 1952).
Prestwich, M., *Edward I* (New Haven: Yale University Press, 1997).
Previté-Orton, C. W., ed., *The Shorter Cambridge Medieval History*, 2 vols (Cambridge: Cambridge University Press, 1952; repr. 1971).
Previté-Orton, C. W., and Brooke, Z. N., eds, *Cambridge Medieval History*, vol. 8: *The Close of the Middle Ages* (Cambridge: Cambridge University Press, 1936).
Prodi, P., *The Papal Prince: One Body and Two Souls*, trans. S. Haskins (Cambridge: Cambridge University Press, 1987).
Radding, C., *The Origins of Medieval Jurisprudence: Pavia and Bologna, 850–1150* (New Haven: Yale University Press, 1988).
Renouard, Y., *The Avignon Papacy: 1305–1403* (Hamden, CT: Archon Books, 1970).
Richards, J., *Consul of God: The Life and Times of Gregory the Great* (London and Boston: Routledge & Kegan Paul, 1980).
Sayers, J. E., *Innocent III, Leader of Europe 1198–1216* (London: Longman, 1994).
Smith, J. H., *The Great Schism* (London: Hamilton, 1970).
Steenberghen, F. van, *Aristotle in the West: The Origins of Latin Aristotelianism* (New York: Humanities Press, 1970).
Steenberghen, F. van, *Thomas Aquinas and Radical Aristotelianism* (Washington: Catholic University of America Press, 1980).
Strayer, J., *The Reign of Philip the Fair* (Princeton: Princeton University Press, 1980).
Stump, P. H., *The Reforms of the Council of Constance (1414–1418)* (Leiden: E. J. Brill, 1994).
Tellenbach, G., *Church, State and Christian Society at the Time of the Investiture Contest* (Oxford: Blackwell, 1970).
Tierney, B., *Foundations of the Conciliar Theory: The Contribution of the Medieval Canonists from Gratian to the Great Schism* (Cambridge: Cambridge University Press, 1955).
Tierney, B., *The Crisis of Church and State, 1050–1300* (Englewood Cliffs, NJ: Prentice Hall, 1980).
Ullmann, W., *Medieval Papalism: The Political Theories of the Medieval Canonists* (London: Methuen, 1949).
Ullmann, W., "Leo I and the Theme of Papal Primacy," *Journal of Theological Studies* 2nd Ser. 11/1, pp. 25–51 (1960).
Ullmann, W., *The Growth of Papal Government in the Middle Ages* (London: Methuen, 1962), pp. 25–61.
Ullmann, W., *The Carolingian Renaissance and the Idea of Kingship* (London: Methuen, 1969).

Ullmann, W., *The Origins of the Great Schism* (London: Burns, Oates & Washbourne, 1948; repr. Archon Books, 1972).
Valla, Lorenzo, *Discourse on the Forgery of the Alleged Donation of Constantine*, ed. and trans. C. B. Coleman (New Haven: Yale University Press, 1922).
Valois, N., *La France et le grand schisme*, 4 vols (Paris: A. Picard et fils, 1896–1902).
Vooght, P. de, "Le Conciliarisme à Constance et à Basle," in B. Botte, ed., *Le Concile et les Conciles* (Paris: Éditions de Chevetogne, 1960), pp. 143–81.
Watt, J. A., *The Theory of Papal Monarchy in the Thirteenth Century* (New York: Fordham University Press, 1965).
Wilks, M., *The Problem of Sovereignty in the Later Middle Ages* (Cambridge: Cambridge University Press, 1983).
Wood, I., *The Merovingian Kingdoms* (London: Longman, 1994).
Zeigler, A. K., "Pope Gelasius and his Teaching on the Relation of Church and State," *Catholic Historical Review*, 27 (1942), pp. 412–37.

Further Reading

For scholarly surveys of the field in general, see A. J. Black, *Political Thought in Europe, 1250–1450* (Cambridge: Cambridge University Press, 1992); J. H. Burns, ed., *The Cambridge History of Medieval Political Thought*, c. *350–*c. *1450* (Cambridge: Cambridge University Press, 1988); J. Canning, *A History of Medieval Political Thought* (Cambridge: Cambridge University Press, 1987); J. Coleman, *A History of Political Thought from the Middle Ages to the Renaissance* (Oxford: Blackwell, 2000). See also M. Barber, *The Two Cities: Medieval Europe 1050–1320* (London: Routledge, 1992); W. Ullmann, *Principles of Government and Politics in the Middle Ages* (New York: Barnes & Noble, 1961), and *A History of Political Thought: The Middle Ages* (Harmondsworth: Penguin, 1970). Dated but still of value, especially for its many (untranslated) quotations from primary sources, is R. W. Carlyle and A. J. Carlyle, *A History of Medieval Political Theory in the West*, 6 vols (Edinburgh and London: W. Blackwood, 1928–36; repr., 1970). There is a detailed analysis of the work of some key contributors to medieval political thought in R. W. Dyson, *Normative Theories of Society and Government in Five Medieval Thinkers* (Lewiston, ME, Queenston, Ontario, and Lampeter: Edwin Mellen Press, 2003). Volume 1 of the same author's *Natural Law and Political Realism* in the *History of Political Thought* (Lewiston, ME, Queenston, Ontario, and Lampeter: Edwin Mellen Press, 2003) may be consulted for the classical antecedents of medieval political theory. For the political thought of St Augustine and its influence on the development of medieval ideology, see especially R. W. Dyson, *St Augustine of Hippo: The Christian Transformation of Political Philosophy* (London: Peter Lang, 2006), and H. A. Deane, *The Social and Political Thought of Saint Augustine of Hippo* (New York: Columbia University Press, 1966). For conciliarism, see A. J. Black, *Council and Commune: The Conciliar Movement* (London Burns & Oates, 1979), and B. Tierney, *Foundations of the Conciliar Theory: The Contribution of the Medieval Canonists from Gratian to the Great Schism* (Cambridge: Cambridge University Press, 1955). There are useful collections of documents in translation in H. Bettensen, *Documents of the Christian Church* (Oxford: Oxford University Press, 1947; repr. 1975), B. Tierney, *The Crisis of Church and State, 1050–1300* (Englewood Cliffs, NJ: Prentice Hall, 1980), and E. Lewis, *Medieval Political Thought*, 2 vols (New York: Knopf, 1954).

Chapter Eighteen

Papal Monarchy

Andreas Meyer

The Foundations

From the middle of the third century at the latest, the Bishops of Rome based their concept of themselves on the words of Jesus: "Thou art Peter, and upon this rock I will build my church . . . Whatsoever thou shalt bind on earth shall be bound in heaven: and whatsoever thou shalt loose on earth shall be loosed in heaven."[1] As we know very little about the real Peter, there is no historical evidence for the dogmatic fiction of his pre-eminent position in the early years of the Christian Church. Indeed, it is difficult to discern any structures in the early history of the Church in general. If, none the less, we try here to indicate what they were, it is in the full awareness that contemporaries perceived such structures even less distinctly than we do, so that our main purpose is to provide a firm framework for this narrative. In addition, many texts became particularly influential only very much later.

Peter was regarded as one of the oldest of the disciples of Jesus, and one of the first witnesses of his resurrection. After the Pentecostal experience, he and James the Greater probably presided over the controlling body of the Christian community in Jerusalem, which was formed in imitation of the twelve tribes of the Old Testament. The Twelve led the community as a whole, while missionary work was the responsibility of seven "deacons" chosen by the community. When the Jerusalem community first suffered persecution in the year AD 42, Peter only just managed to escape, and James was executed. We do not know where Peter took refuge at this time. The community, which remained the centre of Christianity until the destruction of Jerusalem by Titus in AD 70, was now led by Mary, James the Lesser, and members of their families.

The first mention of the work of the Apostles Peter and Paul in Rome is in a letter written by the Roman community around AD 96 to the community in Corinth. Only after the middle of the second century, when the Christian communities were well established and the graves of the Apostles, by analogy with the cult of heroes, were venerated outside Rome, were further memorials to them set up in Rome itself: for Peter at the foot of the Vatican Mount and for Paul on the road to Ostia. Veneration of the two saints is still linked with those places to this day. The tradition was also acknowledged outside Rome, for neither Corinth nor Antioch, where Peter is known to have lived and worked, ever claimed his tomb as their own.

After the second half of the second century, we begin to hear of holders of office in the eastern communities of the empire (κληρος = a group chosen by God), who were distinguished from the other members of the community and divided into a hierarchy of their own. They were headed by the "episcope," who had overall authority, conducted divine service, received new members into the community through baptism, and was in charge of discipline and doctrine in his community. He would meet other "episcopes" of the same region to discuss doctrinal and disciplinary questions. The institution of synods and councils, still so important in the Church as a body today, developed out of these gatherings.

In large communities like that of Rome, elders (presbyters) joined the episcopes to take divine service on important days, to celebrate the Eucharist in subdivisions of communities, and to prepare catechumens for baptism. In the third century, further hierarchically arranged holders of office were recognized: subdeacons, acolytes, exorcists, lectors, and doorkeepers (*ostiarii*). These positions are encountered later as the hierarchy of degrees in holy orders.

Around 220 the Bishop of Rome, Calixtus I, recognized marriage between partners who were not legally of the same rank, deviating in this respect from Roman law. He also reduced the number of deadly sins penalized by excommunication, and reserved absolution of such sins to himself, basing his measures on reference to the authority of the Roman Church and the saying of Jesus that God would separate the chaff from the wheat.[2] But in making these pragmatic decisions Calixtus was dissociating himself from older Christian traditions, and the result was tension within his community. Ultimately, however, it was the question of how to treat backsliders from the faith during the persecutions under Emperor Decius (249–51) that first led to what can be clearly discerned as a split in Rome: a schism.

The splendor of Rome as the capital of the empire, its international and cultural importance, must also have shed luster on the Christian community of the city and its bishops at an early date. The importance of Rome is evident, for instance, in visits to the city from the second century onwards by prominent Christians as well as by the supporters of controversial doctrines. But when, in the late second century, Bishop Victor I made his authoritarian pronouncement on the question of a single date for Easter, his claim to primacy was disputed.

As a consequence of the doctrine of the apostolic succession, which was gradually taking shape, two terms that characterize the doctrine of the papacy to this day developed: *cathedra* and *sedes apostolica*. They express the concept that the occupant of the See of Rome is in the doctrinal tradition of the apostles, in this case Peter and Paul.

The year 235 is the first certain date we have for the Roman community. At that time, ceremonies of liturgical commemoration were also becoming strongly associated with outstanding figures of the community (for instance, a day to commemorate Peter and Paul on July 29, and one to commemorate Lawrence on August 10), and the unvarying part of the mass (the canon) formed.

We do not know where the Bishop of Rome lived before the Constantinian watershed. All that can be proved is that after the sixth century his residence was near the Lateran Basilica, close to the city wall and outside the urban dwelling area, a factor that proved particularly useful at later dates when he was at odds with parts of the local population.

When Constantine moved the center of imperial rule to the east in the year 324, the Bishop of Rome acquired increasing political importance, first in Rome itself, then in the rest of the western empire. By 318 Constantine had made episcopal courts part of Roman civil procedure. If a state court referred a civil action to the episcopal court, the bishop judged it by virtue of imperial authority. If both parties to the action agreed, proceedings could be conducted by the bishop from the first.

When the Greek-speaking part of the population of Rome moved east in the course of the fourth century, Latin became the ecclesiastical language of the city. The bishops of the fourth and fifth centuries initially established themselves as presiding over doctrine in Rome by integrating sections of communities under their own bishops, or by excluding other sections as heretics. Both are signs that structures were forming on the model of the state in classical antiquity. At this time the Roman upper class became Christian, as we can see from the senatorial garb worn by Peter and Paul in the mosaic in the apse of Santa Pudenziana.

It was also the responsibility of the Bishop of Rome to protect the population at times of crisis and to provide the people with food. With these duties, which had devolved upon him after the collapse of the civil administration under the city prefects, the income of the Church increased and its administrative arm became more effective. The bishop had the support of seven deacons, who formed a college under the leadership of an archdeacon. This arrangement gave the bishop further authority over the presbyters active throughout the city. Under Gelasius I (492–6) the division of Church property into four was introduced, and later became canon law: one quarter each went to the bishop, the clergy, charity to the poor, and ecclesiastical buildings. Pope Gelasius also had the first catalogue of all Church property drawn up in the form of a polyptych.

As, in accordance with Roman law, all legal business had to be recorded in writing, and as the Church therefore had members skilled in that art (*notarii*), written documentation was characteristic of very many areas of ecclesiastical life at an early date. Ecclesiastical notaries took written records of the Roman synods, were commissioned by the bishop to edit the Acts of the Martyrs, to ensure that the cult of the saints was standardized, and to record the episcopal writings. All documents seem to have been kept in a *scrinium* (shrine, archive) after the time of Julius I (337–52). The retention of the documents in archives made it possible to support papal claims even outside Rome on a continuous basis. Jurisprudence, a legacy of late antiquity, thus began to shape the life of the Church very early.

Soon a certain rivalry developed between the Bishop in Rome and the patriarchs in Constantinople. The Bishop of Rome's claim to primacy was first openly made in the second half of the fourth century, and it appeared fully formed under Leo I a hundred years later. An important part was played by the *Pseudo-Clementines*, documents written in the East in the third century and translated into Latin around the end of the fourth century, for in one of these fictitious letters Clement purports to describe how Peter transferred to him, as his successor, the power of binding and loosing. This letter, which was thought to be genuine, proved to the Bishops of Rome that they, like Clement, held all the powers of Peter. Leo reinforced this doctrine with the help of Roman law, presenting the Bishop of Rome as the legitimate heir to the functions handed on by Christ to Peter. Thereafter, every Bishop of Rome thought of himself as the representative (*vicarius*) of Peter, not just the successor to his own immediate predecessor. Leo thus not only depersonalized the office of pope; he also brought it into line with the contemporary monarchy of the Roman emperor by applying the imperial Roman idea of the *principatus* – the highest power in the jurisdiction – to the papal concept of the primacy. In short: "The Emperor's domain was the Pope's Church."[3] Although Emperor Valentinian III, in an edict of 445, recognized the primacy of the pope in ecclesiastical jurisdiction and incorporated it into the constitution, it was still the emperor who, for some time into the future, called the great councils, presided over them, and then furthered the acceptance of the doctrinal beliefs on which decisions had been made.

Damasus I (366–84) had a basilica as fine as San Pietro built over the tomb of the Apostle Paul, thus making the ritual parallels between the two saints clear. Ever since then, the two apostles have been depicted together as the predecessors of the Bishop of Rome, who had inherited the highest pastoral power from one and the highest doctrinal authority from the other. In line with this thinking, Leo I eulogized the two apostles, in a sermon for their day on June 29, as the true patrons of Rome, replacing Romulus and Remus, and had the Bishops of Rome painted in medallions in San Paolo, beginning with Peter. Leo was also the first Bishop of Rome to have himself buried in San Pietro.

The Early Stages

Theodoric (493–526), the Gothic king of Rome, who was an Aryan, declined the traditional imperial role of patron of the Church, thus leaving the Catholic Church free to develop as it pleased. It is, therefore, not surprising that, in his theological dispute with Emperor Anastasios, Pope Gelasius I (492–6) formulated the influential doctrine of the proper relationship between the sacred and secular powers that rule the world in a reciprocal relationship (the doctrine of the Two Powers), giving greater weight to priests because they must also account for secular rulers before the judgment seat of God. However, Gelasius also stressed the principle of mutual non-interference. In addition, he claimed supreme authority in the Church for the Bishop of Rome. This doctrine was to re-emerge in Rome in the second half of the eighth century, and it was influential in the move toward greater ecclesiastical autonomy under the Carolingians in the ninth century. It gained very wide distribution because it was taken up in the *Pseudo-Isidorian Decretals*. Finally, Gregory VII (1073–85) made it a useful weapon in the struggle for the hierocratic precedence of the priestly office, and Gratian uses it in his *Decretum* as an argument against secular claims to rule the Church.

The work known as the *Symmachian Forgeries* was written against the background of the Laurentian Schism in Rome (498–506), when the majority favored the deacon Symmachus, originally from Sardinia, as pope over the Roman arch-presbyter Laurentius. According to these documents, Constantine the Great and Sylvester I had decreed, citing 1 Corinthians 2: 15, that the pope was subject to the judgment of neither the emperor nor the Council, but was responsible solely to God for his actions (*nemo iudicabit primam sedem*). These texts exerted their greatest influence when Charlemagne was not granted the right to judge the complaint against the pope in December 800.

The legend of St Sylvester, first appearing at the end of the fourth century and elaborated in the *Constitutum Constantini* in the eighth century, also reinforced the view that spiritual and papal authority took precedence over its secular and royal counterpart. None the less, throughout the entire first millennium the Ecumenical Council, in which the Bishop of Rome did not as a rule participate personally, remained the supreme authority in all ecclesiastical affairs. It passed sentence on patriarchs, and in 680/1 even on Pope Honorius I (625–38). But the fact that the man condemned had been pope was remembered only in the east of the empire, while it soon faded from memory in the West.

After the fall of the western Roman Empire in 476, the Bishops of Rome showed that they considered themselves the equal of the emperor by wearing the pallium, and they also began bestowing it on the bishops of Ostia associated with them, although the pallium was really an imperial privilege. In processions, they had candles and incense carried ahead of them as if they too were emperors. But the reality did not by any means correspond to their ideas in every particular, as evinced in particular by the facts that the Catholic baptism in 498 of Clovis, king of the Franks, was not registered in Rome; that the early Gallic and Spanish synods met without reference to Rome; and that the Frankish and Visigoth churches were subject to the king and not to the pope.

At the time, the authority of the Bishop of Rome reached beyond his immediate vicinity only in that his letters were collected and handed down to posterity in Gaul and Spain as well as in Rome. They could thus be cited later in certain situations as historically ratified ecclesiastical law. It was presumably at the time of Symmachus (498–514) that the monk Dionysius Exiguus, who was originally from the Balkans, put together a collection of early papal letters on systematic principles, and it proved its worth in practice. After Pope Adrian I (772–95) had extended it and dedicated it to Charlemagne in 774, the so-called *Dionysio-Hadriana* played a major part as an authoritative collection of old decretal law. The letters were known as decretals because the popes usually decided on a single case (*decernimus, iussimus*) in them, but nonetheless established a generally acknowledged guideline, by analogy with the imperial rescripts.

When Emperor Justinian (527–65) restored the Imperium Romanum after the death of Theodoric in 526, he treated the Bishops of Rome as imperial Western patriarchs whose election he ratified before they were consecrated. Unmoved by the Gelasian dictum, Justinian emphasized, in his Sixth Amendment, the responsibility of priests for the salvation of souls and of emperors for civil welfare. At the same time he secured for himself ultimate authority for maintaining the true faith and ecclesiastical discipline, and he also considered himself responsible for the elimination of heretics (Amendment 132). In addition, Justinian established the principle that the bishops exercised functions in the civil life of cities by order of the ruler, and could participate in the appointment of local state officials. If subsequent popes played an ever greater part in Roman administration, it was thus very much in line with Justinian's intentions. Finally, in Amendment 131, Justinian decreed that the four Ecumenical Councils were on a par with the Gospels, and stated that the Bishop of old Rome was the highest of all priests, but the Bishop of new Rome – that is,

Constantinople – came directly after him in order of rank. However, the Lombard invasion of Italy in 568 brought Byzantine ecclesiastical rule to an abrupt end.

Gregory I (590–604), who also gave himself, in a sermon to the Roman people and with reference to Mark 10: 44, the modest-sounding papal title, still in use today, of *servus servorum Dei* (servant of the servants of God), encouraged Christian missions to the Anglo-Saxons, thus laying the foundations for the Roman orientation of the Church there. England became the first place outside Italy to take Roman ecclesiastical law and the Roman liturgy as its model. From that time on, English monks and bishops went to Rome for edification and to learn Church law. The link between the Celtic Christian traditions of Ireland and Scotland and the Roman traditions in turn influenced the missionaries who went to continental Europe after the end of the seventh century. Particularly important in spreading Rome-centered ecclesiastical law and the Roman liturgy was Winfrid/Boniface, who encouraged the high regard in which Rome was held in the kingdom of the Franks and on the right bank of the Rhine. In the course of the early Middle Ages all the Germanic nations, some of the Slavic peoples, and Hungary joined the Roman Catholic Church. The Germanic peoples in particular revered St Peter as "prince of the apostles" and the "gatekeeper of heaven," a view that also increased their respect for his successors.

When the Lombards conquered northern and central Italy, and the adherents of Muhammad subjugated Syria, Palestine, and North Africa, Byzantine influence in Italy decreased yet further. Rome was now on the outermost periphery of the empire, and was linked with Ravenna, the seat of the imperial exarch, only by a single road, the Via Flaminia. It had also lost the greater part of its population during the Gothic Wars (535–52). From then on its few remaining inhabitants lived in the low-lying areas of the Subura and of the Field of Mars. Constans II (d. 663) was the last emperor of antiquity to visit the city on the Tiber; Constantine I (708–15) was the last Bishop of Rome to travel to Byzantium.

The warlike confrontations of the sixth and seventh centuries meant that the landed property of the Bishop of Rome, once spread over the entire empire, was now increasingly confined to central and southern Italy and Sicily. Sicily above all was a centre of supplies for Rome and its bishop, having survived the Gothic Wars intact. As a rule, the leaders of the patrimonies there were Roman clerics. After the late sixth century the members of the papal court, who were directly dependent on the pope, became further and further divided from the traditional groups of the higher clergy and the notaries. In the seventh century, the papal court became even more like the imperial administration in its organization.

Although even in the East no one disputed the fact that the Bishop of Rome occupied the foremost see of Christendom, from this point on the universal validity of the papacy in doctrinal matters gained increasing acceptance only in the Latin Church of the fallen western Roman Empire, or those parts of it that had not been conquered by Islam, and in the countries of the Latin mission among the Germanic peoples, the western and southern Slavs, and Hungary. From the seventh century onward, the iconic dispute in particular heightened the latent alienation of Byzantium and Rome, until at last Christian unity collapsed in the schism of 1054, an event hardly even noticed by contemporaries. During the Crusades this split, which was particularly obvious after the conquest of Constantinople in 1204, was expressed in the rise of a Catholic ecclesiastical organization in the East. Politically motivated attempts to restore union in 1274 and 1439 were ultimately ineffectual because the popes laid too much emphasis on their own primacy. In Italy, on the other hand, the theological confrontations with Byzantium already mentioned reinforced the efforts to achieve autonomy made from 666 onwards by the archbishops of Ravenna and the emergent Venetian church. As a result, the ecclesiastical power of the papacy was confined at this time to central and southern Italy and to Sicily.

The early eighth century, for which we have few sources, was a factor in creating many of the problems characteristic of the Church in succeeding centuries: its relationship with Frankish and German rulers; the construction and consolidation of the ecclesiastical state; and its dependence on the Roman nobility. Because of that lack of sources, however, our knowledge of this crucial period is on the whole rather vague. Although disputes with Byzantium over taxation and forms of worship became increasingly fierce, Greek elements in the law, the liturgy, the art, and the administration of the Roman Church continued to exist for a long time. When Emperor Leo III withdrew jurisdiction over Saloniki, Sicily, and southern Italy from Pope Gregory II (715–31) because of his dislike of the pope's prohibition of the worship of icons, and confiscated the papal possessions in Sicily, the papacy not only lost most of its landed property but found its ecclesiastical sovereignty increasingly confined to central and northern Italy.

Although the emperor was nominally still the sovereign, from now on the pope ran the actual government of Rome and the duchy belonging to it. That is evident, for instance, in Gregory II's negotiations with Lombard rulers for the return of conquered towns, and the work of Gregory III (731–41) in fortifying the city walls of Rome. When King Aistulf not only took the exarchate of Ravenna in 751 but also threatened Rome, Pope Stephen II (in 754) became the first pope to travel to France, where he concluded an alliance with King Pépin in which Pépin promised parts of Italy to St Peter and his vicar. Aistulf threatened Rome yet again in 756, whereupon the Franks took up arms against the Lombard king and forced him to give up part of the exarchate of Ravenna to Peter's representative on earth. This bitter experience kept King Desiderius, who with papal support had succeeded Aistulf in the year 757, from repeating his predecessor's mistake until 771. When he did repeat it, Charlemagne conquered the Lombard kingdom and further expanded Pépin's promise in Rome in 774.

The Donation of Pépin comprised the duchy of Rome and parts of Byzantine Italy that had been conquered by the Lombards in the eighth century: Ravenna and the Pentapolis, a narrow strip of territory along the Via Flaminia. Presumably the popes of the time intended to rule as secular lords over all the bishoprics that were still under their ecclesiastical authority, since the reduction in their numbers by Emperor Leo III. Political circumstances prevented this plan from being fully realized, but none the less, the increase in the secular power of the papacy led to the election of the popes becoming the subject of subsequent power struggles. These were particularly fierce when Rome was largely left to itself, as in the late eighth and the tenth centuries. In such circumstances, a pope could reign successfully only if he came from one of the important Roman families, outmaneuvered his predecessor's supporters once he had been elected, and instead promoted the interests of his family and its friends. In this way nepotism became one of the most important methods of personal papal policy.

Under Stephen IV (768–72), not only did seven bishops of the duchy of Rome have particularly close ties with the papal court because, as cardinals, they conducted weekday services in the Lateran Church, but the *Constitutum Constantini* also dates from this time. In this text Constantine describes his conversion to Christianity by the Princes of the Apostles and Pope Sylvester. Its main historical importance was in purporting to give the reason for moving the seat of government to Constantinople: earthly emperors were not supposed to reside in the place where the representative of the Emperor of Heaven had his own see. In addition, this text mentions privileges and donations – sovereignty over certain imprecisely designated Western countries and islands – in favor of the Roman Church. It states that the pope, as head of the Catholic Church, has imperial rank, and consequently the emperor himself symbolically held his stirrup and had bestowed on him the tiara and other signs of honor, while the papal clergy are placed on a par with the imperial senate. The *Constitutum Constantini* is the first text to describe the residence of the Bishop of Rome, the Lateran, as a former imperial palace (*palatium*). This document, the fictional character of which was recognized by Nikolaus von Kues in 1433 and by Lorenzo Valla around 1440, shows how heavily fixated on Byzantium the Church still was in the eighth century. "Its principal tendency seems to have been to legitimate or at least give a reason for the papal claim to Italy and the removal, necessary for that purpose, of the country from the imperial Byzantine group of territories."[4] So the alliance of the popes with Pépin the Frank had not yet changed the Roman mentality. Rome still looked eastward rather than westward.

After the late seventh century, Anglo-Saxon missionaries spread the fame of Rome as the highest ecclesiastical authority on the Continent of Europe. Boniface, who had been acting for the Pope as "Archbishop of Germania" since 733, thereupon paved the way for the alliance of the papacy with the Franks and the momentous association of the papacy and the empire. In 751 Pope Zachary (741–52) authorized Pépin, Mayor of the Palace, to overthrow the Merovingians and take over the kingship of the Franks. However, it was not Rome that upheld Zachary's opinion that the holder of power should also bear the title of king. In 754 Pope Stephen II (752–7) fled from the Lombards to France, where he anointed Pépin in Saint-Denis and made him *Patricius Romanorum*, Patron of Italy. Pépin stated his devotion to St Peter and promised to protect the saint's successors. Thereafter the King of the Franks needed not just election by the great men of the realm but also anointing by the Church, which reinforced the influence of the Church on the kingship. Since the treaties then concluded have not come down to us, however, it is not clear exactly what happened at the time. Later, their contents were differently interpreted by both the Roman and the Frankish sides.

Charlemagne (768–814), Pépin's son and successor, introduced the Roman liturgy and Roman law into the entire empire. But, despite his veneration for Peter and his successors, he left no one in any doubt that he – like the Emperor of Byzantium in the East – was both secular and spiritual lord of his domains. That is particularly evident from the letter that he wrote in 796 to Leo III (795–816): "It is our duty, with God's help, to defend the holy Church of Christ in all outside places against attack by the heathens and destruction by unbelievers, and to consolidate it within by recognition of the Catholic faith. Your own task, Holy Father, is to raise your hands to God, together with Moses, and thus support our battle, so that at your request and under the leadership of God the Christian people will gain the victory everywhere over the enemies of his holy name."[5]

Nothing changed when Leo III, on Christmas Day of 800, crowned the King of the Franks and the Lombards emperor in St Peter's. His own position had been weakened since the year 799, when an attack on him had failed and he had to take refuge with Charlemagne in Paderborn. Although Charlemagne, citing the *Symmachian Forgeries*, declined to start any legal investigation of accusations made against the pope, he could judge the conspirators only when he had been crowned emperor, or he would have been breaking the law passed by Leo III and Constantine V in 740, to the effect that only the emperor could pass sentence on those guilty of high treason. In the West the Empress Irene, then ruling in Byzantium, was regarded as a usurper because she had had her son, the rightful *Basileus*, blinded.

Louis I showed who the Franks thought was responsible for the coronation of the emperor when, in 817 and following the Byzantine example, he crowned his eldest son Lothair co-emperor to rule with him. Only when Carolingian power in Italy disintegrated, after the death of Louis II, was Pope John VIII (872–82) able to demonstrate that it was the pope who bestowed the dignity of emperor when, in 875 and 881, he favored Charles the Bald and Charles III respectively over all other candidates. The disputes of Nicholas I (858–67) over the patriarchate of Constantinople, over Bulgaria, and over the marriage of King Lothair II are not just the expression of papal power, although the inclusion of Bulgaria in the jurisdiction of the Roman Church failed, but also show that the secular ruler was regarded as a sinful Christian in the association of the churches and was thus subject to the judgment of the pope.

When Charlemagne divided the Frankish church into provinces under archbishops, and allowed the pope the right to determine the extent of these ecclesiastical provinces and the archiepiscopal sees, the old ecclesiastical principle of the collegiality of all bishops was abandoned in favor of a hierarchical system headed by the pope. With this the Bishop of Rome won decisive influence over the Frankish church, both formally and in practice. An even clearer pointer to the future, however, was the fact that Gregory IV (827–44), when he was expected to settle the quarrel between Emperor Louis the Pious and his sons in 830, issued a decretal formulating the principle that the pope alone had fullness of power (*plenitudo potestatis*), while Christ had given bishops only partial responsibility (*pars sollicitudinis*). The conflict, which remained unresolved at the time, led to textual changes in the law of the late Church of antiquity in the so-called *Pseudo-Isidorian Decretals* of between 835 and 838, in which the utterances of theologians were presented as decretals of the Bishops of Rome, and later Roman claims as laws made by earlier popes. The author of this collection has recently been identified as Paschasius Ratbertus, a monk and later abbot of Corbie. For reasons valid at the time, it was in the interests of Paschasius to secure, with the aid of these fictional papal decretals, the independence of the bishops from secular power (in this case that of Louis the Pious) and also from the metropolitans (in this case Hinkmar of Reims) and the provincial synods (here the synod of Diedenhofen). Only the pope could judge them and other *causae maiores*. Consequently, it was in this collection of documents relating to ecclesiastical law that the papal decretals first outweighed all other kinds of decisions. This forgery too was to acquire its real explosive force only some way into the future. "During the move toward reform in the eleventh century, when a conviction arose that the Church must be more strongly orientated toward Rome, and the ancient Church must be brought back to life, when the need for exemplary organizational structures was felt, the hour of Pseudo-Isidore had come." Gratian adopted the texts from Pseudo-Isidore into his *Decretum*, especially those relating to procedural law, and they acquired enormous effectiveness. The fact that this legal collection was a forgery, although suspected earlier, was not proved until 1628.[6]

In the ninth and tenth centuries the direct sovereign power of the pope was still confined to Rome, the duchy of Rome, and the patrimonies that remained to it. At the same time, the popes were exposed to the rivalry of the Roman nobility. Their weakness showed particularly clearly when the leading political orders of the West disintegrated before the onslaught of the Saracens, Normans, and Hungarians. Now they were victims of individual despots in central Italy and groups of Roman nobles. Only the intervention of the German King Otto I (936–73) brought temporary relief. John XII crowned him emperor on February 2 962 in St Peter's. Thereupon, and until 1530, the anointing and coronation of the emperor (with the exception of Louis the Bavarian in 1328) was reserved for the pope. However, he himself remained dependent for a very long time on a strong imperial power.

At the time analogies with the royal German administration first became evident. Instead of papyrus, parchment was used increasingly as the material on which documents were written; the *cancellarius* was in charge of correspondence instead of the *bibliothecarius*; chaplains surrounded the pope. German bishops had brought to Rome, for the imperial coronation of Otto I, a collection of liturgical texts that under the Carolingians had been brought into the kingdom of the Franks and had later been altered there: this was known as the *Pontificale Romano-Germanicum*. At the same time the buildings of the Lateran became the center of episcopal administration. Popes now also had themselves buried in San Giovanni. It was emphasized that the palace (*palatium*) was the centre of papal sovereignty, and the clergy and judges bore its name, as the titles of *diaconi sacri palatii* and *iudices sacri palatii* show. Rome was once again divided into twelve regions (Italian: *rioni*) on the Augustan model, which regulated military matters. Once again, great stress was laid on ancient institutions. Otto III was the first Western emperor who even made Rome his seat of government, in order to usher in the *renovatio imperii Romanorum*. He was also the first Western emperor to venture to appoint popes well known to him from outside Italy, in the persons of Gregory V in 996 and Sylvester II in 999. But after his death in 1002, and Pope Sylvester's in 1003, the papacy and sovereignty in Rome reverted to the dominant families of the Crescentii and the counts of Tusculum.

Expansion

The advice of the Bishop of Rome, or his decision, had long been sought in difficult matters. The pope had also heard appeals when one side in a dispute felt that it had been unjustly condemned. But before the middle of the eleventh century he had few legal competences in the Latin Church. He was involved in setting up new bishoprics and Church provinces, he gave privileges to churches and monasteries, and he began bestowing the pallium on archbishops. The pallium, a circular woolen stole with strips of fabric adorned with crosses hanging down in front of and behind the wearer, has been known as part of the papal insignia since the sixth century, and probably derives from the sash worn by Roman officials. It was originally a mark of honor, which had to be requested by the archbishop himself. After the ninth century it became a sign of office, and the archbishop's rightful exercise of power depended on its bestowal. The pallium was laid on the tomb of St Peter before it was given to an archbishop; it denoted his participation in the papal power of government, and helped Rome to give symbolical expression to its position of pre-eminence within the Church. After the late eleventh century, archbishops had to go to Rome in person to receive it. In analogy to this gift, the pope subsequently gave foreign prelates the miter as a sign of special favour.

Movements for ecclesiastical reform, first felt in monastic life in Lorraine and Burgundy in the tenth century, increased with the coming of the new millennium. They were strongly influenced by the thinking of hermits. The new desire for a more deeply Christian way of life, abjuring the transitory world and turning the attention of humanity to the aim of achieving Heaven, soon affected all groups in Christianity. One expression of this movement was the rapidly rising number of monasteries seeking to rid themselves of the influence of their local bishops through papal privileges. Papal exemption, like canonization, a process that gradually developed after the first papal canonization (of St Ulrich of Augsburg in 993), was a successful instrument for making the primacy of the pope felt.

In the course of the eleventh century the idea of reform perceptibly affected all areas of western Christianity. It was also behind the papal reform of the time and continued into the early twelfth century. Papal reform picked up the idea, began following it through on its own initiative, and in so doing acquired its new character, building itself a new position in western Christendom on those foundations. This was the time when the papacy, under great stress and amidst violent upheavals, detached itself from the authority of secular rulers.

With the reforming synod of Pavia, led by Pope Benedict VIII and Emperor Henry II in 1022, the new ideas reached the center of the Church. The synod laid strong emphasis on the celibacy of the clergy, from subdeacons upwards, and disqualified the children of clerics from any claim to Church property. In 1046 Henry III intervened in the confusion surrounding the chair of St Peter at the ecclesiastical assemblies of Sutri and Rome, although they were still held in traditional synodal form, when, forcefully and in full awareness of his responsibility, he ended the crisis in the Church over three popes who had not been clearly legitimized. Henry's intervention was not only approved but praised in Rome and the empire. When the Romans gave the emperor the hereditary dignity of a *Patricius Romanorum*, Henry also had the right to designate the next pope, and as a result the next four popes were Germans. They brought in a new style of papacy, backed by the general movement for reform in the Church. Leo IX in particular (1049–54) brought the universal importance of the papacy throughout the West to the fore. Through his able and even radical colleagues, whom he brought to Rome from Lorraine and Burgundy, the college of cardinals quickly developed from what had previously been mainly a source of liturgical assistance into a body standing beside the popes in the government of the Church as a whole. Hand in hand with this development went the expansion of the Roman Curia into the central authority of Church management. Leo IX, who before his election had been a member of the imperial court chapel, of the German king's chancellery, and Bishop of Toul, brought to his new position experience that was reflected, for instance, in the papal privileges that were now outwardly similar to imperial documents. Under Leo IX, the papacy became a significant quantity even outside Rome. Still under the same Pope, it became clear that the see of the Bishop of Rome could no longer be treated as the emperor's own church. Church reform gave rise to the wish for complete freedom and independence of the papacy, which did not want to be part of any imperial ecclesiastical system, but to stand above all empires. The early death of Henry III in 1056 greatly smoothed the way for these endeavors. The settlement agreed with the Normans, the new power in southern Italy, brought Rome further freedom of action.

Under Nicholas II, the Lateran synod of 1059 passed the law that regulated the election of the Bishop of Rome. In future a preliminary vote by the cardinal bishops was to be followed by the vote of all the cardinals. Only then were the rest of the Roman clergy and the laymen to assent to the decision.

Opposition to the widespread practices of the marriage of priests and of simony, taken as meaning any participation by a layman in the awarding of church offices, soon became the most effective instrument toward achieving the freedom that the Church now demanded. By the freedom of the Church (*libertas ecclesiae*) the reformers understood not only freedom from secular interference but also a close link between Rome and the other churches. The reformers forcefully imposed their views. In opposing married clergy and bishops who practiced simony, they did not shrink from appealing to laymen, who were open to the argument that sacraments not administered by celibate priests were invalid, and might entail the loss of the soul's eternal salvation. They thus made laymen more obedient only to the pope, not to the bishops.

Pope Gregory VII championed the ideas of the purity and freedom of the Church with uncompromising radicalism. He was also convinced of the unlimited supremacy of the pope both inside and outside the Church. His letters show him as the first pope to correspond with the entire world of the time. Even kings and emperors had to bow to his will. In the *Dictatus papae* (1075), he not only powerfully and clearly formulated the papal claim, which contradicted Church tradition in many points; he also put his principles into practice when he excommunicated the impulsive and poorly advised Henry IV of Germany (1056–105, d. 1106), and absolved his subjects of their oath of loyalty. The scene at Canossa in January 1077 is the ultimate expression of the change in the relationship between the two supreme powers. "The son of Henry III, who had liberated the chair of St Peter from deep indignity and indeed had made it the supreme see again, stood outside one of the castles of his realm, a penitent."[7] The desanctification of the Roman–German kingship went hand in hand with the centralization of the Church in law and liturgy. Even the defeat and exile of Gregory VII in 1084 did not change that. The interplay between papal legates and the *pataria* brought an end to the independence of the Milanese church. Ravenna too, where a powerful imperial anti-pope had been installed between 1080 and 1100 in the person of Wibert, who took the name of Clement III, soon lost its ecclesiastical autonomy.

Urban II (1088–99) drew support in his opposition to the emperor and the anti-pope mainly from the Normans of southern Italy and the nobility of France and Lorraine. He encouraged reforming Benedictines and canons. His greatest success, however, was the crusade he initiated, ending in 1099 with the conquest of Jerusalem and the setting-up of a patriarchate dependent on Rome. When Philip I of France separated from his wife Berta in 1092, he felt the force of Urban's moral authority. A little later, marriage was raised to the rank of a sacrament, which was ultimately in the pope's area of competence.

After Paschal II (1099–18) had found a solution to the procedural question of investiture in England and France, by distinguishing between a Church office and Church property and between sacred and secular rights (regalia), Calixtus II and Emperor Henry V found a similar solution in the Concordat of Worms of 1122. The First Lateran Council of 1123 confirmed this agreement.

The Papal Curia now developed into the real centre of administration, and came to resemble the courts of Western rulers not only in its name but also in its structure. As head of the scribal office, the chancellor now definitively took over from the *bibliothecarius*. Under John of Gaeta, who was notable in forming the style of papal documents and was chancellor to Urban II and later Pope Gelasius II (1118–19), Carolingian minuscule replaced the ancient curial script used for papal records. At the time it was usual for a cardinal to be head of the chancellery. The authority of the archdeacon was absorbed into the new office of treasurer, who was responsible for the finances and perhaps also for the archives and the library. There were papal chaplains after Paschal II at the latest. The parallel with secular courts was also expressed in ceremonial. After his election, the pope was robed in a purple cloak, and his throne in San Giovanni was made of porphyry, both purple and porphyry having previously been reserved for the *Basileus*. Porphyry slabs subsequently became popular as flooring in Roman churches.

The idea of a structurally unified Catholic Church headed by the pope gained acceptance, because synods, held by the pope himself or a legate as his *alter ego* and now taking place more frequently, sometimes outside Rome, made it easier to adopt the papal directives. The synods had thus lost their character as assemblies of equals. The strong position of the papacy was evident, for instance, in the fact that legates, who ranked above archbishops, appointed or dismissed bishops and abbots, and could alter ecclesiastical structures by dividing or merging dioceses.

In the development of Church reform, and the conflict between the two hegemonic powers (*duae potestates*) arising from it, two legal systems had in fact clashed, the new papal and the old imperial systems. Although the conflict ended without any real victor, the papal legal system still emerged from these disputes as the supreme spiritual power in the West. For, unlike the empire, the papacy succeeded in developing a firmly established law that claimed universal validity, and continued to develop in line with the idea of the unlimited power of the pope (*plenitudo potestatis*), who was answerable only to God.

This law first makes itself felt in the then newly made collections of Church law (the collection of seventy-four titles, the collections of Anselm of Lucca, Deusdedit, and Ivo of Chartres). They were usually based on *Pseudo-Isidore*, which purported to provide them with an "ancient Church" suiting their own ideals. They differ from older collections because they regularly also contained the decisions of contemporary popes, thus emphasizing the role of the papacy in the development of the law. These texts could be decisions made at papal synods, or the decretals of individual popes in concrete cases. It is noticeable that the second group comprised not only directives and prohibitions, but above all dispensations – that is, decisions on whether and how far departures from the norm could be allowed. In Ivo's collections, for instance, the number of dispensations exceeds that of normative texts: as Ivo saw it, a dispensation was not so much a short-term emergency measure as the alleviation of a norm obviously regarded as too stern in practice. From now on, papal dispensations in law making and in practice were a major factor in ecclesiastical government. Not only was the pope the supreme legislator of the Church; it was also he who decided on deviations from the norm.

All laws, dispensations, and privileges, as well as the activity of synods and legates, would have been ineffective if those affected had not in general agreed with them. Hermits, monks, and canons regular were against simony and married priests because of their own ideals, and were thus automatically allies of the papacy. The bishops, on the other hand, had more reservations in their attitude to these papal initiatives, for, apart from the metropolitan, who rose to be primate in his own country, they were the real losers in the formation of the ecclesiastical hierarchy. Laymen were made receptive to the ideals of Church reformers by a genuine concern for their own souls. If religious lay movements threatened the Church as it developed its hierarchy, from the twelfth century onward they were disqualified as being heretical, and after the meeting of Lucius III with Emperor Frederick I in 1184 they were opposed with the aid of the secular arm. After Clement III (1187–91), criticism of the papacy was regarded as a major crime.

The attempt of the jurist Gratian, who taught in Bologna around the middle of the twelfth century, to reconcile previous and often contradictory ecclesiastical norms with each other, using the new scholastic methods, showed the new way ahead. Gratian called his work *Concordia dicordantium canonum*, but it was known to his contemporaries as the *Decretum Gratiani.*[8] Although assembled without any official commission, it quickly became the standard collection of ecclesiastical law. Commentaries on it were written, and it was in circulation in the law schools. Since it was left incomplete, it soon received additions (*paleae*) and later appendices. Finally, collections of texts were made, handed down independently of the *Decretum* and known as *Extravagantes.* In these collections, assembled in France, Italy, Spain, and England, papal decretals predominated, in particular those of Alexander III (1159–81). They express not only the far-reaching validity of the papal dispositions of the time but also their overwhelming weight within the new Church law. Because of the conflicts of the time between pope and emperor, Germany did not play an important part in this development. When Bernardus Balbi systematically gathered all the important *extravagantes* together in five books in Pavia around 1190, he was explicitly creating a work intended to be useful to judges and teachers of law. His collection gained general recognition, and served as the model for all further collections.

Papal law thus became accepted not through instructions from on high, but because collectors and commentators assembled a unified and useful legal code out of the disparate texts. Those who suffered by this development were primarily the holders of partial powers within the Church. In the long run, archbishops, bishops, synods, and councils lost their old status and were subject to the new and ever-expanded papal law. The last conflicts of this kind took place at the Council of Constance (1414–18) – as is particularly obvious in the decretals *Haec sancta* and *Frequens*, which stated the supremacy of the council over the pope and called for the regular holding of further councils – and the Council of Basel (1431–47), at which

Felix V was elected as the last anti-pope in history. On the basis of this experience, the Popes subsequently sought to avoid or prevent general councils.

The cardinals, who came together in a college in the twelfth century, won greater importance. In the process, a not insignificant role was played by the schisms of 1130–8 and 1159–78, ending with the Second and Third Lateran Councils, for the question of who was rightful pope was no longer decided by who ruled in Rome but who had more supporters in the West. Here the cardinals, recruited with increasing frequency from outside Rome, played a considerable part. From now on they and the pope made decisions in the Consistory, not only on the *causae maiores*, which were reserved for the Pope, and in which new material was always being put forward, but also in appeals and cases where one party, bypassing the local authorities, had turned directly to the pope. Obviously many of these parties hoped for a more impartial judgment from the papal court than from their own bishop, who could be perceived as liable to influence by powerful local groups. When the number of legal cases became a heavy burden, Alexander III (1159–81) began delegating them to papal judges working locally. The cardinals were also involved in the award of new privileges and the confirmation of old ones, as their records of solemn privileges show. After 1179 the papal election was also reserved for them. The election should be made with a two-thirds majority, and it was amended by the Conclave in 1274 on the model of Italian communes. On behalf of the pope, the cardinals traveled to all the countries of the Western world as legates *a latere*. Purple has been their color since the middle of the thirteenth century.

At this time the institutions of the Curia were also extended. Its many residences outside Rome led to the installation of papal clerks (*scriptores*), instead of the traditional Roman scribes (*scriniarii*), to write down the charters. Under Alexander III books of formulae arose, and the *Cursus* (stylistic turns of phrase), was fixed. The high importance of papal documents had led to increasing instances of forgery. The chancellery was still headed by the chancellor, while the treasurer not only managed the income and expenditure of the papal court but also administered all the curials. Lists of rents and properties made it easier to keep track of the papal possessions; among them, the *Liber censuum* of Cencius (1192) was pre-eminent. But the financial situation of the Curia was still weak. A few of the earlier chancellors and treasurers became popes themselves, a fact that reflects the importance of those functions.

While the writing of papal history died out again after Cardinal Boso (d. after 1178), papal ceremonial was still widely displayed. The tiara gained increasing significance as the most important symbol of secular power. Popes had themselves buried in imperial sarcophagi. In the Lateran palace, Pope Innocent II had Emperor Lothair III depicted in painting as the papal vassal for the Matilda Estates, and Clement III had the Donation of Constantine painted in the outer hall of San Giovanni. The relics that the Lateran claimed to hold (including the Tablets of the Law given to Moses) symbolized the fact that, as the Popes understood it, Rome had replaced Jerusalem as the holiest place in Christendom. As a result the papal chapel was referred to thereafter as *Sancta sanctorum*.

Reaching out to the World

Although Bernard of Clairvaux, in his treatise on the papacy *De consideratione papae*, intended for Eugene III (1145–53), emphasized the pope's position as the successor to St Peter and not to Emperor Constantine, only Celestine V (1294) briefly embodied the widespread longing for a truly spiritual pope who would renew the Church and usher in the age of the Holy Spirit in the manner desired by Joachim of Fiore. But Celestine found his office too much for him, and resigned it after a few months.

Since the popes only expanded and consolidated matters arising after the Investiture Controversy, but proposed no new theories, there was ultimately no very successful development in the relationship of the new papal power to the traditional political forces. Claims to the pre-eminence of spiritual and papal power over secular power were indeed constantly being made – most clearly in the maxim *papa est vero imperator* (the pope is the true emperor), current from 1170 onwards – but the political powers were not going to bow unconditionally to the pope's superior authority. As a result, vehement disagreement kept breaking out again: Alexander III against Emperor Frederick I and King Henry II of England; Innocent III against Philip II of France and King John of England (John Lackland); Gregory IX and Innocent IV against Emperor Frederick II. But finally, despite the papal bull *Unam sanctam*,[9] Boniface VIII suffered a humiliating defeat in conflict with Philip IV of France. John XXII (1316–34), Benedict XII (1334–42), and Clement VI (1342–52) were unable to carry through their claim to appoint the king of Germany and future emperor against the opposition of Louis of Bavaria, although Innocent III, in the decretal *Venerabilem*, had already stated firmly that the office of emperor, unlike that of kings, was primarily in the gift of the Church.[10] The "Golden Bull of 1355–6 responded only with silence to their demand, which was based on the curial translation theory.

The political commitment of the popes was also evident in their promotion of the crusades. However, they had no lasting success in this area, and not only after the fall of Acre to the Muslims in 1291. From the fourteenth century onwards the necessity of defense against the increasingly urgent threat posed by the Turks superseded ideas of the liberation of Jerusalem. The only pope who ever set off for the east in person was Pius II (1458–64), and he died on his way, in Ancona harbour.

The more the popes saw themselves as heads of the universal Church, the more of their old support in the city of Rome they lost. Safeguarding or recovering their property in central Italy, and after 1130 their feudal overlordship of the kingdom of Sicily, was a strenuous business. In Tuscany and northern Italy, both of them part of the kingdom of Italy, which was allied to the German crown, the Matilda Estates were another source of conflict from 1102–15 onward. Expansion of the secular property of the pope into a genuine Church state, however, clashed not just with the imperial rights of sovereignty but also, and regularly, with the Roman commune and its leaders, including Arnold of Brescia (d. 1154), Brancaleone degli Andalò (d. 1258), Cola di Rienzo (d. 1354), or Stefano Porcaro (d. 1453). The result, from the twelfth to the fourteenth centuries, was a series of bitter conflicts often leading to schisms, and the absence for decades of the Bishop of Rome from his proper sphere of influence. The popes had papal residences first in Anagni, Rieti, Viterbo, and Orvieto, later in Avignon. And there was criticism of the political methods employed by many popes to impose their rule on central Italy or to expand it. Nepotism in particular, deliberate favor shown to close relations, cast a shadow over the spiritual authority of the papacy from the time of Innocent III onward, and led to violent upheavals when new popes took office. The conflicts between Rome and the other papal residences meant that, after the thirteenth century, many papal functionaries bound to Rome lost their rights; services held in Rome were no longer community occasions involving the bishop, the clergy, and the people; and constitutional ceremonies such as the pope's enthronement in San Pietro, or his taking possession of the Lateran, lost their former significance, while coronation with the tiara became more important.

The papacy's claim to feudal sovereignty over kingdoms (Aragon, England, Portugal, Sicily, Hungary), its eastern policy after the taking of Constantinople in 1204, conflict with the Cathars of the south of France, ruthless opposition to the Hohenstaufens and their supporters in the empire and in Italy, as well as the unsuccessful union with the Orthodox Church (1274) all created widespread discontent and ended in failure. The house of Anjou, established in southern Italy in 1265, proved even more conscious of their own power than the Hohenstaufens, and the downfall of the international political standing of the papacy followed hard on the heels of the fall of the empire. Boniface VIII's determined attempt to impose full papal powers on France were foiled by Philip IV, and ended in the capture of the Pope in Anagni in 1303. It is true that after the death of Emperor Henry VII (1305–13), Pope Clement V (1305–14) issued the constitution *Pastoralis cura*, which strictly limited imperial powers of jurisdiction to the area of the empire, rejected the idea of the imperial office as a supranational institution, and denied all imperial claims to universal sovereignty. The price paid for that was the papacy's subjection, for over a hundred years, to the hegemonic power of France. But after 1340, when Spain and Portugal began quarreling over newly discovered islands and previously unknown parts of the world, the papacy successfully joined the game again, as an authority able to confer legitimacy by calling on the Donation of Constantine.

The split in the college of cardinals caused a long vacancy in the see after the death of Benedict XI (1303–4), ending only in 1305 with the election of the Archbishop of Bordeaux, who took the name of Clement V. When he had been consecrated pope in Lyons, he went first to his native place before, in 1309, going to Avignon, which was then subject to the kings of Naples, a subsidiary line of the French Capetian dynasty as counts of Provence. The Holy See had already acquired the neighboring Comtat Venaissin in 1274, left vacant by the count of Toulouse. John XXII (1316–34) added to the papal possessions in 1320 with Valréas, which he exchanged with the Knights of St John for estates seized from the disbanded Knights Templar. Clement VI then bought the city of Avignon in 1348. While John XXII resided in the bishop's palace there, Benedict XII, Clement VI, and Urban V built a magnificent papal palace to replace it, with a Chapel of St John and St Peter, providing space for the Roman ceremonials as well as the papal courts (*Audientia sacri palatii, Audientia litterarum contradictarum*). The papal treasury was also accommodated in the palace.

The insecure situation of the Church state in central Italy, where papal rule was constantly questioned and neighboring powers (Milan, Florence, Naples, and Sicily) had little interest in the pope's presence, did not tempt the popes of southern French origin to leave Avignon. The return of the papacy to Rome was also delayed because, under Clement V, the Italians in the college of cardinals had already lost their old numerical superiority: 111 of the 134 cardinals created in Avignon were Frenchmen.

Among them, the most influential group came from the Limousin, including three of the six Avignon popes. Only the danger represented by the Grandes Compagnies after the defeat of the King of France by Edward III at Poitiers in 1356, and the moral pressure exerted on Urban V (1362–70) and Gregory XI (1370–78) by Birgitta of Sweden and Catherine of Siena, two women with a high reputation for sanctity even in their lifetimes, brought the Curia back to Rome in 1377. An earlier attempt in 1367 had failed after a few months.

The reasons for the schism that broke out in the autumn of 1378 and split Christendom until 1417 were the wish of the Romans to see an Italian on the *Cathedra Petri*, the fact that the college of cardinals consisted predominantly of Frenchmen, and the ardent desire of Urban VI for reform. Unlike earlier schisms, this split was caused by the cardinals themselves, and they maintained it for decades. Ultimately the secular powers profited most from this dead-end situation, by extending their own dominance over the Church.

All kinds of ways of restoring Church unity were discussed: military victory of one pope over the other (*via facti*), the simultaneous resignation of both popes (*via cessionis*), negotiation (*via conventionis*) or withdrawal of support by the secular power (*via subtractionis*). Because there was no satisfactory answer to the question of whether the pope in Rome or the pope in Avignon had canonical legitimacy, and also because the Roman Curia was dominated by a clique of Neapolitan families, in this obvious state of emergency support increased for the idea, deriving from early Christianity, that the Council, as representing the Church as a whole, held the highest power and authority, and if necessary could judge a pope. Finally, then, the *via concilii* was taken, involving the colleges of cardinals on both sides. In 1409 the Church Fathers, assembled in council in Pisa, removed from office both the Pope in Rome, Gregory XII (1407–15, d. 1417), and his adversary in Avignon, Benedict XIII (1394–417, d. 1423), and elected a new pope, Alexander V (1409–10). However, the two deposed popes did not accept the judgment, so that now there were three rival popes with three obediences. Only the Council of Constance (1414–18), called by Alexander V's successor, John XXIII (1410–15, d. 1419), together with King Sigismund, brought an end to this stalemate with the deposition of John XXIII on May 291415, the resignation of Gregory XII on July 4 1415, and the deposition of Benedict XIII on July 26 1417.

The council could now have ended the *causa unionis* swiftly by electing a new head of the Church. However, many of the Fathers taking part in the council were afraid that the *causa reformationis* would be lost after the choice of a pope, for the schism appeared to its contemporaries to be the result of deep-seated shortcomings in the Church. Nor was it clear who was to elect the new pope. In view of the responsibility borne by the council in this period without a pope, and its achievement in ending the schism, it was agreed that, in a departure from canon law, the council should participate in the election of the pope. After long and bitter disputes on the question of whether, as before, Italians and Frenchmen should predominate in the college of cardinals and at the papal court, on November 11 1417 twenty-three cardinals and six deputies from each of the five nations to have taken part in the council, making fifty-three electors in all, chose as pope the Roman Oddo Colonna, who had been made a cardinal in 1405 by Innocent VII. He took the name of the saint whose day it was, becoming Martin V. He was the first in a series of Italian popes that – interrupted only by the pontificates of the Borgias and Adrian VI (1522–3) – lasted until the election of John Paul II in 1978.

Martin V returned to Rome in 1420 and began setting up papal rule in the Church state again. From now on the secular power of the popes was concentrated mainly in central Italy and Rome, although Eugene IV resided outside Rome again between 1434 and 1443 because of unrest in the city. A legate held office in Avignon until 1791.

As a result of Eugene IV's clumsy handling of affairs, the Church assembly split at the Council of Basel in 1437. While what remained of it in Basel took radicalism even further, and set up an anti-pope in the form of Felix V (1439–49), the council in Florence decided on union with the Greek Church. But this new attempt to unify the Christian churches failed because it laid emphasis on the primacy of the pope.

Nicholas V (1447–55) began a programme of rebuilding in Rome. He had the fortress of San Pietro, first built in the late thirteenth century, extended into a palace, and also planned the rebuilding of the Basilica. The two Popes Sixtus IV (1471–84) and Julius II (1503–13), who were related to each other, were particularly outstanding for their work on the buildings. We owe to them the Ponte Sisto (1475), the Sistine Chapel, the new building of the Ospedale di Santo Spirito not far from the Vatican, the Via del Governo Vecchio between the Piazza Navona and the Ponte Sant'Angelo, and the Via Giulia as a road linking the two upper bridges over the Tiber. As in Avignon, magnificent cardinals' palaces were built (the Palazzo Capranica, the Palazzo Venetio, the palazzo later named the Cancellaria) and "national churches" for the many curials, craftsmen, and pilgrims who came from abroad.

On the model of the palace at Avignon, the Vatican increasingly became the center of papal rites. Traditional processions now passed only through the papal palace, so that the Station churches entirely lost their significance. Only the procession to the Lateran after the coronation of the pope still recalled the tradition of the early and high Middle Ages. Sixtus IV also changed the constitution of the commune of Rome and made the city's magistrature subject to the papal chamber. The papal domination of Rome is shown most clearly in Michelangelo's new designs for the Capitol.

After the papal Curia had finally been established in Rome in 1443, the number of non-Italians in the college of cardinals swiftly and steadily fell. They last held the qualified majority (67 percent) in 1455. A generation later, in 1484, they first lost the blocking minority, and in 1559 they lost it for four centuries.

The Pope as Monarch in the Church

The papacy reached the summit of its spiritual and secular authority in the towering figure of Innocent III (1198–216). Innocent exercised his office in the full awareness of his divine vocation as *vicarius Christi*. Under him that term, which had arisen in the form of *vicarius Petri* in the eleventh century, became an established part of the papal titles. As the pope understood himself, he stood between God and man as the representative of Christ the priest-king, judging all, including nations and realms, and himself judged only by God. This enormous and also dangerous claim could be fully realized only within the Church, and in the secular sphere only when the political powers were willing to accept it. However, Innocent proved flexible in this respect.

The most important instrument of spiritual dominion was the cleverly handled law. Like Gregory VII, Innocent was imbued by ideas of spiritual responsibility, but he was better than his predecessor at sensing the right amount of moderation. In addition, he was able to seize the opportunities offered by the time, when imperial and royal power in Sicily and the empire was crippled over a long period by the death of Henry VI in 1197 and the ensuing double election. The Fourth Lateran Council, which he called in 1215, became the most brilliant ecclesiastical assembly of the medieval West.

In legal and administrative matters experienced popes such as Gregory IX, Innocent IV, and Boniface VIII built on the foundations already laid to extend the pre-eminence and responsibility of the pope. However, this progress proved ambivalent, for it stood in the way of an understanding with the eastern Church, and also led to the way in which the Church as a whole continued to be disastrously affected, as so often in the past, by schisms and confusion in the Church in Rome.

Innocent III was the first pope to put together the decrees he had issued and publish them, in 1210, as an official collection of decretals, in order to establish papal law in the universities and law courts now developing. Honorius III followed his example in 1226. Both collections were superseded when Gregory IX published the *Liber-Extra (vagantium)* in 1234, the official collection of law developed after Gratian and influenced by the papacy.[11] Finally Boniface VIII in 1298, with the *Liber Sextus*, and John XXII in 1317, with the *Clementines*, published the law that had come into force since then in two further collections, which all remained valid until 1917.[12] Although the stocks of medieval manuscripts have suffered severe losses, the 700 extant manuscripts of the *Liber extra*, and 500 manuscripts of the *Liber sextus*, still provide evidence of the effectiveness of papal law, which also had commentaries written on it, was systematically expounded in *Summae*, was prepared for practical use in further texts, and was taken over by synods. It also served as the model for collections of secular law.

From 1215 onwards, the cathedral chapter acted as a college of electors to choose bishops. But the majority principle was accepted here only after it had become usual, because of many contentious episcopal elections, for a bishop chosen freely and fairly to be confirmed in his office by the pope. With this ruling, the papacy had won decisive political influence on the tenure of bishoprics. The pope and the cardinals, sitting together in the Consistory, decided on the confirmation of these appointments. New bishops subsequently had to a pay a fee (*servitium commune*) corresponding to one-third of their first year's income, and after the time of Boniface VIII it was divided between the pope and the cardinals. As a result, the Roman Church was soon living largely at the expense of the transalpine churches, which were wealthier than the Italian bishoprics.

Clement IV (1265–68), in the *Licet ecclesiarum*, decreed that the pope not only had the right to give all ecclesiastical benefices and also to bestow candidacies for them; he also reserved for himself the gift of ecclesiastical livings whose holders had died in the Curia.[13] As the norms that arose in the thirteenth century by the promulgation of the *Liber sextus* (1298) became recognized as inalienable law, the influence of the papacy within the Church rose immeasurably. However, the contemporaries of the popes of the time accepted it, for not only did the clergy continue visiting the Curia in their thousands to improve their position in the struggle for benefices; they also went to receive absolutions and dispensations. More and more lay people were seeking the latter, as can be seen from countless petitions in the registers of the papal penitentiary, beginning in the fifteenth century, for dispensations to marry a close relation or for the free choice of a confessor.

The successful establishment of papal authority after the thirteenth century can be understood only if we take account of the role of the new orders of the Franciscans and Dominicans and especially of the university of Paris, which had its organization and its rights validated by the pope at an early date, serving as the model for many other universities. All three institutions encouraged the idea of the primacy of the pope in their own ways. Because of their monastic structure, the older reforming orders were unsuitable for the concerns of the time in respect of missionary work, the care of souls, and opposition to heresy. The mendicant orders, on the other hand, saw themselves not only as saviors of the Church but as directly subject to the pope. The Dominicans served him as inquisitors, while the Franciscans spread the Roman liturgy throughout the world. Thanks to the *Pax mongolica*, Clement V and John XXII created new Church provinces between Persia and China in the fourteenth century, and bishoprics that they entrusted to the mendicant orders. Benedict XII, a member of the Cistercian order, energetically tackled the task of reforming it, and enacted reformed constitutions in 1335 for the Cistercians, in 1336 for the Benedictines and Franciscans, and in 1339 for the Canons Regular. He thereby extended the influence of the papacy to wider circles.

None the less, the Cathars in southern France and the heretical Beguines and Waldensians were constantly questioning the spiritual authority of the pope. The radical criticism that had provoked John XXII's conflict with King Louis the Bavarian no longer stopped short at the existing structure of the Church. John Wyclif in England, Jan Hus in Bohemia, and later Martin Luther emphasized the sole authority of Holy Scripture, thus questioning wide areas of medieval ecclesiastical law.

Innocent III tightened the organization of the papal chancellery, which had been headed by vice-chancellors since the time of Honorius III. Its task was to produce the papal writings. As a rule these were answers (rescripts) to petitions that had been made (supplications). The unbroken series of registers of letters begins under Innocent III, while the register of supplications does not begin until 1342. In all, the late medieval papal registers contain well over two million documents, although the writings were never all recorded, and there have been major losses since. However, what we have shows clearly the universal importance of the papacy for ecclesiastical and religious life.

When the duty of annual confessions was introduced in 1215, the Apostolic Penitentiary arose as the supreme ecclesiastical office of confession, "a kind of control centre for the administration of the Christian conscience."[14] It gave absolution from offenses against Church law, or dispensations from undeserved disadvantages, for instance, when rising clerics had been born out of wedlock.

The Apostolic Chamber also grew at this time, for its responsibility throughout the West was now to collect taxes for the crusades imposed on all benefices, dues paid on their enthronement by bishops, as well as money from the sale of pardons, and after the early fourteenth century annates, income drawn from the benefices left vacant in the Curia. To this end, the chamber created an almost universal network of collection areas where these monies and taxes were gathered. After the middle of the thirteenth century Italian merchants transferred these sums to Rome or Avignon. Those who were slow to pay were excommunicated, with weighty consequences in the longer term. Under Boniface VIII the series of papal accounts began (*Introitus et exitus*) so that we have very precise ideas of the financial power of the late medieval papacy. But the more strongly the Curia paraded its financial interests, the more the papacy lost in religious substance, spiritual reputation, and political weight, as compared to the nation states, now growing stronger, whose rulers successfully expanded their national churches.

Under Innocent III, the *Audientia sacri palatii* (also known as the *Rota* from the time when the Curia had been based in Avignon) also became the supreme ecclesiastical court. But not all cases went to it. The pope reserved certain important cases for his own judgment, or entrusted the decision to cardinals. As early as the late twelfth century, he was also handing on many cases to delegated judges outside. The auditors of the Rota had been bound to consult together since 1331. Documentary records of the Rota in Rome began in 1464.

The rapidly growing administrative apparatus of the Curia lived at first on taxes and bribes, for, in spite of strict regulations concerning fees, it was vulnerable to corruption throughout this period. Soon the keep of the curials was mainly provided by Church benefices, which was the reason why Clement IV, as mentioned above, reserved the gift of benefices to himself. In the time that followed, the popes interpreted this rather imprecisely formulated constitution in their own favor, and to the disadvantage of those groups that had previously given ecclesiastical benefices. After King Edward III of England, in the *Statute of Provisors* (1351) and the *Statute of Praemunire* (1353), had set limits to the papal competences for England, and forbidden the sending of papal fees to the Curia, the reforming decretals made in 1418 in Constance and the concordats concluded there with the nations taking part in the council, the Pragmatic Sanction of Bourges (1438) and the Vienna Concordat of 1448, were applied to the papal power to dispose of Church benefices in other countries too. These reforms, in their turn, favored the development of national churches. However, they also decreased the papal income, and consequently after the middle of the fifteenth century the profits from the newly discovered alum mines of Tolfa, and above all the Curia's trade in offices, were supposed to compensate for this loss.

When Pope Urban II called for a crusade at the Council of Clermont in 1095, the indulgence quickly became a means whereby the pope reached every single believer. After 1300, it was also possible to acquire complete indulgence by visiting the main churches of Rome in Holy Years. Finally, Clement VI opened the floodgates when, in 1350, he allowed a Jubilee indulgence in return for payment. Criticism of indulgences and of the further intensification of curial fiscalism became ever louder in the following period. Looking back, we may say that the contemporaries of the popes at this time had only a faint idea of the real volume of papal finances. As a result, speculation flourished, especially in Germany. The sensed value of German monetary payments to Rome around 1500 was certainly considerably higher than it was in fact, especially by comparison with Spain and France, which the Germans unjustly thought were better situated. But "sensed suffering was to have enormous explosive power as an argument against Rome in the Reformation.

The popes of the late fifteenth century were less concerned with positioning themselves as a moral authority than with adding to the new reputation of the papacy and the Church as a leading cultural force. Often men with a humanist education, they greatly encouraged the arts and sciences. Sixtus IV, for instance, refounded the papal library. The activity of many artists made Rome a center of the Italian Renaissance toward the turn of the century. In their manner of life, however, there was little difference between the *vicarii Christi* and secular princes of the Italian Renaissance. Even the author of the *Liber pontificalis* was noticeably interested in scandal around 1435, and added the story of Pope Joan to the old history book. The Italianization of the Curia on all levels gave new impetus to nepotism, which was not, however, frowned upon so much by contemporaries as it would be today. The Renaissance popes obviously took little interest in the root-and-branch Church reform ardently desired by so many. In view of the strongly divergent interests of the Curia and of the higher and lower clergy, but also because of the rise of national churches, putting such reform into practice would have been utopian anyway. Over time, the claims and the reality of the papal *plenitudo potestatis* had moved too far from each other to allow it; their institutions and structures of communication were not well enough developed. The Church's hierarchy of command remained precarious throughout this period, and the papacy was constantly forced to depend on acceptance of its authority. To that extent, the monarchical constitution of the Catholic Church had moved far beyond its highest point, and in the sixteenth century it would have to make way for painfully new ecclesiastical organizations.

Notes

1 Matthew 16: 18–19.
2 Matthew 13: 24–30
3 Postel, *Die Ursprünge Europas*, p. 42.
4 Schimmelpfennig, *The Papacy*, p. 96.
5 Quoted ibid., p. 101.
6 Cf. the contributions of Klaus Zechiel-Eckes, Martina Hartmann, and Horst Fuhrmann (from whom the quotation above comes) in Hartmann and Schmitz, eds, *Fortschritt durch Fälschungen?*
7 Schwaiger, "Papst, Papsttum", in *Lexikon des Mittelalters*, vol. 6, cols. 1667–85, quoted here, col. 1674.
8 *Corpus iuris canonici*, vol. 1.
9 Ibid., vol. 2, cols 1245–6, *Extravag.* com. 1.8.1.
10 Ibid., vol. 1 (X 1.6.24).
11 Ibid, vol. 2, cols. 1–928 (quoted X).
12 Ibid., vol. 2, cols 929–1124, (quoted VI), esp. cols 1125–1200 (quoted Clem.).
13 Ibid., vol. 2, col. 1021 (VI 3.4.2).
14 Schmugge, *Kirche, Kinder, Karrieren*, p. 12.

Bibliography

Barber, Malcolm, *The Cathars: Dualist Heretics in Languedoc in the High Middle Ages* (New York: Pearson Education, 2000).
Barraclough, Geoffrey, *The Medieval Papacy* (London: Thames and Hudson, 1968).
Brundage, James A., *Medieval Canon Law* (London: Longman, 1995).

Corpus iuris canonici, ed. Emil Friedberg (Leipzig: Ex officina Bernhardi Tauchnitz, 1879).

Cushing, Kathleen, *Reform and the Papacy in the Eleventh Century* (Manchester: Manchester University Press, 2005).

Fink, Karl August, *Papsttum und Kirche im abendländischen Mittelalter* (Munich: C. H. Beck, 1981).

Frenz, Thomas, *Papsturkunden des Mittelalters und der Neuzeit*, 2nd edn (Stuttgart: Franz Steiner Verlag, 2000).

Hartmann, Wilfried, and Schmitz, Gerhard, eds, *Fortschritt durch Fälschungen? Ursprung, Gestalt und Wirkungen der pseudoisidorischen Fälschungen. Beiträge zum gleichnamigen Symposium an der Universität Tübingen vom 27. und 28. Juli 2001*, Monumenta Germaniae Historica, Studien und Texte 31 (Hanover: Hahn, 2002).

Histoire du christianisme: Des origines à nos jours, vols 1–7 (Paris: Desclée, Fayard, 1990–2000).

Miethke, Jürgen, "Geschichtsprozess und zeitgenössisches Bewusstsein: Die Theorie des monarchischen Papats im hohen und späten Mittelalter, " *Historische Zeitschrift*, 226 (1978), pp. 564–99.

Miethke, Jürgen, "Kirchenreform auf den Konzilien des 15. Jahrhunderts. Motive – Methoden – Wirkungen, " in Johannes Helmrath and Heribert Müller, eds, *Studien zum 15. Jahrhundert: Festschrift für Erich Meuthen*, 2 vols (Munich: R. Oldenbourg, 1994), S. 13–42.

Morris, Colin, *The Papal Monarchy: The Western Church from 1050 to 1250* (Oxford: Clarendon Press, 1989).

The New Cambridge Medieval History, 8 vols (Cambridge: Cambridge University Press, 1995–2005).

Paravicini-Bagliani, Agostino, *The Pope's Body*, trans. David S. Peterson (Chicago: University of Chicago Press, 2000).

Pennington, Kenneth, *Pope and Bishops: The Papal Monarchy in the Twelfth and Thirteenth Centuries* (Philadelphia: University of Pennsylvania Press, 1984).

Pennington, Kenneth, *Popes, Canonists and Texts, 1150–1550* (Aldershot: Variorum, 1993).

Postel, Verena, *Die Ursprünge Europas: Migration und Integration im frühen Mittelalter* (Stuttgart: Kohlhammer, 2004).

Robinson, Ian Stuart, *The Papacy 1073–1198: Continuity and Innovation* (Cambridge: Cambridge University Press, 1990).

Salonen, Kirsi, *The Penitentiary as a Well of Grace in the Late Middle Ages: The Example of the Province of Uppsala, 1448–1527* (Helsinki: Academia Scientarum Fennica, 2001).

Schimmelpfennig, Bernhard, *The Papacy*, trans. James Sievert (New York: Columbia University Press, 1992).

Schmugge, Ludwig, *Kirche, Kinder, Karrieren: Päpstliche Dispense von der unehelichen Geburt im Spätmittelalter* (Zurich: Artemis, 1995).

Schwaiger, Georg, "Papst, Papsttum", in *Lexikon des Mittelalters* (Munich: Artemis-Verlag 1993) vol. 6, cols. 1667–85.

Somerville, Robert, *Papacy, Councils and Canon Law in the 11th–12th Centuries* (London: Variorum, 1990).

Smith, Julia M. H., ed., *Early Medieval Rome and the Christian West: Essays in the Honour of Donald A. Bullough* (Leiden: Brill, 2000).

Tellenbach, Gerd, *The Church in Western Europe from the Tenth to the Early Twelfth Century*, trans. Timothy Reuter (Cambridge: Cambridge University Press, 1993).

Tewes, Götz-Rüdiger, *Die römische Kurie und die europäischen Länder am Vorabend der Reformation*, Bibliothek des Deutschen Historischen Instituts in Rom, 95 (Tübingen: Niemeyer, 2001).

Ullmann, Walter, *The Papacy and Political Ideas in the Middle Ages* (London: Variorum, 1976).

Zimmermann, Harald, *Das Papsttum im Mittelalter: Eine Papstgeschichte im Spiegel der Historiographie* (Stuttgart: Ulmer, 1981).

Zutshi, Patrick, "Innocent III and the Reform of the Papal Chancery," in Andrea Sommerlechner, ed., *Innocenzo III Urbs et Orbis (Atti del congresso internazionale, Roma, 9–15 settembre 1998*), 2 vols (Rome: Società romana di storia patria, Istituto storico italiano per il Medio Evo, 2003), vol. 1, pp. 84–101.

Further Reading

The books of the English Protestant writer Barraclough and the critical Catholic German historian Schimmelpfennig may be recommended to readers who want a brief but comprehensive and succinctly written survey of the papacy in the Middle Ages. Barraclough's book, unlike Schimmelpfennig's, is lavishly illustrated but is a generation older, which detracts from its value to those in search of bibliographical information.

The crucial phase in the developmental history of the medieval papacy was certainly during the eleventh and twelfth centuries. At this time the foundations were laid for what the papacy would become in later centuries. Among the many titles dealing with this period, those of Tellenbach, Morris, and Cushing are outstanding. Tellenbach's book is very densely written and has a wealth of bibliographical references, but is nonetheless published in handy format, while Morris offers a very extensive account of events, and Cushing has written a good textbook on the subject.

The papal monarchy in full flower is the subject of works by Pennington and Paravicini-Bagliani, and the two books complement each other very well. While Pennington considers constitutional aspects of the papal monarchy and those concerned with ecclesiastical law, thus also providing an impressive insight into canon law, Paravicini-Bagliana emphasizes the ceremonial and cultural sides of the phenomenon.

The Roman empire of antiquity to some extent lives on in the papacy, as the fact that the further development of the law in the Middle Ages took place in the bosom of the Church makes particularly clear. Credit is due to Brundage for writing a profound but still very readable introduction to medieval ecclesiastical law. Anyone wishing to go farther into this field can turn to three volumes of the *History of Medieval Canon Law*: vol. 1: Lotte Kéry, *Canonical Collections of the early Middle Ages: (ca. 400–1140). A Biographical Guide to the Manuscripts and Literature* (Washington: Catholic University of America Press, 1999); vol. 2: Detlev Jasper and Horst Fuhrmann, *Papal Letters in the Early Middle Ages* (Washington: Catholic University of America Press, 2001); vol. 3: Wilfried Hartmann and Kenneth Pennington, *The History of Medieval Canon Law in the Classical Period, 1140–1234: From Gratian to the Decretals of Pope Gregory IX* (Washington: Catholic University of America Press, 2008).

Papal documents in a very comprehensive sense (papal records, papal registers, petitions to the pope) are the subject of a book by Frenz, which not only offers an illustrated outline of the diplomatic aspects of the papal records, but is also a first-class bibliographical aid for all seeking access to the rich tradition of papal documentation. Zutschi's contribution to the subject shows how jurisprudence and administration went hand in hand around the year 1200, laying the foundations for a modern bureaucracy. Salonen, taking as his example the register of the papal penitentiaries, shows how the curial records can be useful in formulating questions concerning modern social and religious history.

CHAPTER NINETEEN

Urban Historical Geography and the Writing of Late Medieval Urban History

TEOFILO F. RUIZ

Medieval towns and their motley inhabitants have long attracted scholarly attention. Not unlike other areas of medieval history, the study of cities and urban societies can be traced back to a handful of pioneering and towering canonical works. Jacob Burckhardt's incomparable *The Civilization of the Renaissance in Italy*, though admittedly about Renaissance culture, is a book deeply grounded in a select number of Italian cities as sites for the emergence of novel aesthetic notions, new ways of thinking about the state, civic festivals, and the like. Maitland's enduring *Domesday Book and Beyond*, while grounded in institutional history, pays significant and path-breaking attention to urban centers or emerging English towns (boroughs and the like). And, of course, Henri Pirenne's paradigmatic work *Medieval Towns* helped shape the way in which we have studied urban medieval history over the last century and a half. To these, should be added the influential synthesis by Rörig and the less-known work of Edith Ennen. In the case of Rörig, he brought to light the importance of urban developments in the Baltic region and the role of the Hansa in urban life. As to Ennen, she provides a most useful typology of the different zones or regions for urban development: from the Roman survivals in the Mediterranean, through a transitional zone north of the Roman habitats, to areas in northern Europe that developed independent of Roman influence, In doing so, Ennen put to rest the long sway of Rome as the original and sole fountain of urban development in Europe.[1]

These foundational works rested upon a long tradition, extending into antiquity, of histories of cities and towns or travelers' descriptions of urban life. Urban history had also a fecund life in the urban accounts and chronicles of the late Middle Ages and burst into glorious manifestations during the Renaissance. Machiavelli's interest in Florentine history, Guicciardini's impressive *History of Florence*, Alberti's utopian musings about urban layouts and its connections to the "good" life, or Campanella's delightful *The City of the Sun* are only the high points of long historical concerns with describing and imagining the city.[2] Although each town or city was, and is, *sui generis*, our collective desire to provide comprehensive accounts of urban life in the Middle Ages or in other historical periods remains a powerful force. On very different keys, the works of Marino Berengo and David Nicholas – the first a more traditional, yet formidable, social history with no interest in questions of historical geography; the second, a formidable synthesis, incorporating all the new approaches to medieval urban history (including a very healthy serving of urban historical geography) – show that our interest in these topics has not declined at all and that the study of the medieval town remains an appealing subject even in this age of methodological uncertainty.[3]

Medieval Urban History

In the following pages I would like to provide a brief summary of urban history and to review the diverse historiographical trends that have propelled the account of urban societies in the medieval West to the present. How do we write the history of the medieval town at the beginning of the twenty-first century? How do methodological trends or historiographical concerns today differ from traditional approaches to urban medieval history? In superficially surveying works on the history of towns – and specifically studies of urban historical geography since the late 1970s – we need to locate the discussion within long-existing historical trends and analysis of city life and institutions. Essentially, we would like to know where we have been in our understanding of medieval cities; where we are at present; and where we may be, or should be, going to in the future in our attempts to explicate the genesis, evolution, and structures of urban societies in the medieval West. In doing so, this chapter focuses, though not exclusively, on the contributions and growing interest among some scholars in urban geography and in the relations between urban social structures and place. The social and cultural significance of urban space may stand as one of the promising areas of research, although, as I discuss below, not as much of a breakthrough as we should be contemplating at the dawn of a new century.

Cities and Towns

Although we often use the terms cities and towns interchangeably, as I often do in this chapter, it should be made very clear at the onset that, in principle, they were not one and the same. Susan Reynolds's definition of towns as "centers of non-agricultural activities, characterized by a diversity of occupations, especially those involved in trade and industry, located in a permanent settlement of large size and high density," leaves, as shall be seen below, some questions unanswered.[4] The distinction between city and town, or even the definition as a town, often did not depend on size, social structure, economic activity, or even relations with outside powers. It was, more often than not, a juridical distinction and, in some cases, tied to papal or royal grants of the right to be called a *civitas*. To give examples from the region in late medieval Europe I know best, Burgos, an urban settlement fulfilling all the conditions spelled out by Reynolds, in the kingdom of Castile, was a city, while Segovia, similar in size, social structures, and the like, under the same royal jurisdiction and, like Burgos, an episcopal see, was a community of *villa* (a town and never a city) and *tierra* (land) – that is, a juridical arrangement in which Segovia's hinterland (its *alfoz* or contado) joined the urban setting in a complex overlapping of jurisdictions, rights, obligations, and formal representation at the meetings of the Cortes or representative assemblies.[5] In England, the long debate on urbanization has gone back and forth in defining what was a town and what was not, and that includes wild variation in the estimate of urban populations. Moreover, as we all know, most towns in medieval Europe were essentially agro-towns – that is, substantial towns with a population of over 1,000 inhabitants or more, but with little commercial or artisan activity, with its inhabitants depending mostly on agricultural production for their livelihood. That was certainly the case for Santa Coloma de Queralt, a small town in the Tarragona countryside and for numerous other places in the West.[6]

Madrid, which is a far more significant example and which throughout the late Middle Ages barely met many of Reynolds's requirements as a town (it had little or no manufacturing; it was small; there was little commerce), was, and remained, a *villa* (a town) even after its spectacular growth in the mid-sixteenth century as the designated official capital of the Spanish monarchy. It is confusing, but we must keep the distinction in mind, even if, for practical purposes, both terms are used as synonyms. What follows from this aside is that towns or cities were often very different from each other. While some common features may be discerned and patterns of development identified that appear, on the surface, to follow along the same lines, to know about one town or city is not to know all cities. The local context always undermines the natural desire to see medieval urban history as a whole.

Urban History Reconsidered

Medieval towns were places of wonder. Many late medieval urban centers, above all those in Mediterranean Europe and the transitional areas once held by Rome, traced their foundations to Roman times.[7] And urban elites spent a great deal of time and effort in establishing links to the classical past even if these claims were totally fictitious. In spite of that need to historicize our own urban past, medieval towns were radically different from their ancient counterparts in terms of social structure, planning, or lack of it, and the production of culture. In truth, urban environments in the Middle Ages, above all in the late medieval world when towns and cities blossomed through Europe, held promises for a different kind of life, unlike those of an earlier age.

From the eleventh century onward, many towns and cities in the West generated a novel and dynamic social group: the bourgeoisie. Bourgeois culture and political ambitions served as the locomotive for dramatic social and economic changes that would transform European society. As sites for cultural production and institutions – the university, cathedral schools, and the like – medieval urban centers attracted a diversity of people and were also – in that limited sense in which we mean these terms when talking and writing about the Middle Ages – sites of freedom. No serfdom endured in the towns (though the number of slaves was on the rise in fifteenth century Mediterranean urban centers).

Towns' elites played unique roles in the politics of the age. More often than not, cities supported royal attempts to thwart the power of the nobility and to impose kingly rule over the jumble of fragmented institutional jurisdictions. In some places, such as most of Italy and the Low Countries, urban governments became fairly autonomous from royal control and functioned, once again in the limited sense in which we use these words, as "sovereign" powers. In large numbers, the children of the urban elites, often university trained, flocked into the growing royal bureaucracies, or, by the thirteenth century, into the Church. Not being fully a part of the traditional tripartite division of society – as imagined by ecclesiastic and scholars in the late thirteenth century[8] – the bourgeoisie injected into the social and economic structures of the medieval world novel ideas and ambitions. Finally, changes in systems of values, new notions of property, salvation, charity, and other such examples of the bourgeoisie's radical departure from the traditional medieval *mentalities* ushered in new cultural forms.[9] These cultural artifacts emerged, to a large extent, as both the work of, and to be consumed by, the middling sorts. That urban culture, although often borrowing from courtly models, reflected the dynamism and innovative character of urban life, and if I mention this here – in what seems a digression – it is gently to remind the reader that the history of towns and their inhabitants in the late Middle Ages was as much about culture and social transformations as it was about geography and space.

These social, political, and cultural outcomes were not equally distributed throughout the medieval West. Italian and Flemish towns – which either maintained a fairly unbroken link to their classical past, as was the case with Rome, Florence, Naples, and other cities and smaller towns in Italy, or were precocious in their commercial and industrial development, as was the case with Flemish manufacturing towns – were at the vanguard of the urban revolution. Places such as Barcelona, Seville, Lisbon, Valencia, and Burgos served as loci for the development of truly urban societies in the Iberian Peninsula. Paris outstripped by far any other city in the French realm. As such, Paris drew and drained, as it continues to do to this day, the kingdom's resources and became unequivocally identified with the entire realm. London played a similar role for England, though not as decisively as Paris did for France. Hanseatic cities in Germany and throughout the Baltic region represented a diverse constellation of urban societies.

Not every town in Italy was like Florence or Venice. Barcelona, Seville, and Valencia were the exception rather than the rule. By the early fourteenth century, London and Paris had really no rivals in their respective realms. Thus, in writing about urban centers, it may be wise to emphasize the differences as much as we tend to emphasize the similarities. Each town, as noted earlier, was *sui generis*, and their individual economic structure often dictated the nature of social relations and the power, or lack of it, of their respective ruling elites. Italian, Flemish, and German towns, for example, did not have to contend (or at least not as much) with the growing power of kings and their centralizing programs. This allowed for the kind of autonomy and political latitude denied to places such as Paris, where the king, with the exceptions of sporadic rebellions, had matters firmly in hand.

Town and Country: Rethinking the City

To complicate matters further in what is becoming a far too long introduction, towns held diverse and complicated relationships with their respective hinterlands. There is no way around this problem. The old dichotomy between town and country is no longer tenable in the light of recent scholarship. Instead of positing the contrasts between urban and rural societies, we must, in the light of scholarly contributions since the late 1980s, see urban societies as in permanent symbiosis with their surrounding countryside.[10] Not only was there a significant and constant seasonal influx of people from the countryside into the city – seeking work during the slow periods in the agricultural cycle – but members of the urban elites had permanent establishments in the surrounding countryside, as they began to gobble up (from the late twelfth century onward) nearby villages and turned them into entailed estates. This was certainly the case in Burgos, Avila, and other Castilian towns in the late Middle Ages.[11]

As to the movement of people from countryside to city, we know that London was a magnet for rural population and that, at one time or another, people from London's sprawling hinterland and even from very distant regions in the realm traveled to and inhabited the city at some point in their lives. Seville, which was a very large city by Iberian standards, had an extensive segment of its population engaged in agricultural labor in the nearby rich Aljarafe. In the outlying neighborhoods of the city, such as San Gil, San Julián, and even in Triana, as many as 50 percent of the neighbors were employed in cultivating the land or in tending livestock.[12] Siena, which suffered serious decline right after the Black Death, was able to replenish its population within a few months by attracting immigrants, as Bowsky has shown, from the nearby Sienese contado.[13] Towns served as sites for judicial procedures, civil and ecclesiastical appeals, litigation, spiritual solace, and festive display. All these functions attracted throngs of nearby villagers. In a reverse order, urban dwellers marched out from the confines of their towns' walls for royal entries – the most paradigmatic example of the bond between urban and rural spaces – and festivities, as I have shown elsewhere for fifteenth-century Jaén and Valladolid.[14] The reality is that the boundaries between city and countryside, which seem so clearly delineated by encircling walls and gates, rather than separating distinct populations – that is, rural and urban – were porous boundaries that permitted a continuous toing and froing between the two worlds.

Few historians would believe that we cannot study cities in the Middle Ages without acknowledging the contributions of, and links to, the surrounding countryside. So, in examining the recent contributions of urban historical geography, a certain level of skepticism must be maintained about an approach that, while decidedly insisting on the relation between countryside and town, focuses most of its attention on the archeology, topography, and geography – social and physical – of urban space. In the same manner in which urban historical geography has left out cultural history as an important analytical tool, so it has left out the countryside. This is particularly a shortcoming when, in exploring the social geography of towns – that is, how different groups were distributed in the space within city walls– there is little attention to the seasonal ebb and flow of rural people in and out of the city. We ignore only at our peril the social, economic, cultural, and political structures that joined, rather than separated, bourgeois culture, trade, and manufacturing to that of villagers, agricultural cycles, and country life.

Urban Historical Geography: What is it?

In the late 1980s and early 1990s, a series of conferences held in Britain and Germany successfully generated publications that sought to define further – though not always satisfactorily – a field of inquiry described as urban historical geography. In this respect, these conferences took place in the context of a long and productive stream of scholarship on historical geography sponsored by the Cambridge Studies in Historical Geography. The series, published by Cambridge University Press, includes many volumes on different aspects of historical geography, cutting across wide swathes of chronological and geographical periods.[15] Thus, urban historical geography represents a subfield of the vast enterprise that engages the historicity of place, whether urban, rural, or regional.

As to that subset of studies, linking older concerns with urban morphology and geography and propelled by growing concerns with the preservation and conservation of the medieval core of modern towns, practitioners of urban historical geography borrowed freely from, and worked in unison with, scholars in geography, archeology, and other ancillary fields that focus on the development of urban societies. Although, as is freely admitted, many of these concerns with the spatial organization of towns harkened back to Marc Bloch and even to an earlier historiographical tradition, the principal aim of urban historical geographers is, beyond their concerns with "spatial structures," "to show the interaction between structure, human agency, and individual experiences."[16] Thus, urban historical geographers pay close attention to urban planning, such as planning that existed in the Middle Ages, to the architecture of civic monuments, and "to the impact of human activity on urban change and development."[17]

Tilting between geography and history, it is not always clear, in reading some of the practitioners of this methodological approach, whether urban historical geography represents a bold new departure in the field of medieval urban history or the reshuffling and reinventing of older historiographical traditions. Most of the articles published in 1988 and emerging from a joint Anglo-German conference on the subject, although interesting and worthy contributions to our understanding of urban history, do not necessarily raise entirely new questions or contribute bold methodological breakthroughs. Although the German scholars tend, on the whole, to be closer to geographical and sociological explanatory schemes than are their English counterparts, the reality is that none of them engages in new lines of inquiry. While emphasis on social geography, that is, an attempt to locate specific social groups in certain quarters of medieval towns, a focus on urban development, topography, and such allied topics are always welcome additions to traditional historiographical interest on social relations and political developments, there is nothing here that urban historians have not noted in their work or addressed since the mid-1970s.

For example, we have known of the patterns of inhabitation of artisans in Paris thanks to *Le Livre de la taille de Paris, l'an 1296* published in 1958. William Courteney, in his study of university students and masters, provides us with a clear understanding of where they lived in Paris, as Richard and Mary Rouse do for bookmakers and illuminators in the late thirteenth century. In Burgos, the cathedral's *Libros de contabilidad* allows for a partial reconstruction of the city's social geography, as does the cathedral of Avila's *Libro de cuentas.*[18] Though most of these books are of recent vintage, the preoccupation with social geography was not inspired by recent work in urban historical geography. Recently, David Nicholas's excellent synthetic work on the late medieval city pays particular attention to the manner in which the influx of artisans shaped the "social geography of medieval urban centers." Nicholas also illustrates the relationship between urban development and the emergence of notions of public space and buildings from the thirteenth century onward.[19]

Other recent works, such as Keith D. Lilley, *Urban Life in the Middle Ages, 1000–1450*, though emphasizing the legal aspects of urban development and life, are sensitive to the relations between space, or what Lilley describes as "geographies of urban law," landscape, property, and social order.[20] This approach represents a new front in what has been essentially a very long trend in urban history, predating urban historical geography. If I may engage in yet another immodest act of self-reference, my early work on Burgos in the mid-1970s was already strongly concerned with urban space and what today may be called urban social geography.[21] In this, of course, I was not a pioneer at all, but followed longstanding methodological approaches present in Castilian local history, *Annales*, and *Past & Present* historiography.

If we look carefully at some of the articles dealing with medieval urban historical geography collected in the *Urban Historical Geography* volume (with emphasis on the articles dealing with England, which have a more historical bent than those on Germany, which, as noted above, are mostly either geographical or sociological studies), Christopher Dyer's very fine piece "Recent Developments in Early Medieval Urban History and Archeology in England," although engaging an earlier period than the one that is the focus for this chapter, reflects a greater interest in revisiting older questions than in exploring novel approaches to the history of urban societies. Dyer examines such issues as: what is the relation between town and country? What were the nature and role of royal and princely interventions in the development of urban societies? Dyer is, as most scholars of medieval Europe know, a most accomplished scholar, and the author of impressive works on rural and urban history.[22] His prominence in the field makes what he has to say in his essay worth noticing. And, even if the questions have been asked and somewhat answered before, this does not deter from Dyer's valuable intervention, which aims mostly at providing new historiographical leads while revisiting some of the central issues in the study of urban developments.[23] The contributions he makes in this piece are indeed important, but they do not rise to the level of methodological breakthroughs. In the same vein, Brian Graham's "The Town in the Norman Colonisation of the British Isles" also engages old questions by placing the rise of urban societies in England within the framework of a discussion on whether there was or was not feudalism in the pre-Conquest period and the intimate relation between rural developments and the rise of towns.[24] It is Terry Slater, however, who, in his "English Medieval Town Planning," surveys some old (but very interesting) scholarship that, drawing from archeological, geographical, and topographical studies, provides us with the possibilities of a new understanding of medieval urban developments. The painstaking reconstruction of towns, revealing "no single act of planning," draws upon "considerations of plot dimensions." Borrowing from Conzen's imaginative work, Slater discusses the use of burgage analysis, based upon the measurement of modern plot frontages in the light of surviving cartographic sources and basic medieval documentation. Even more to the point, the micro-historical analysis of what Slater describes as the "total plot history" – that is, the "reconstruction of the individual histories of particular plots in terms of area, building fabric, land use, ownership and occupation [as gathered] from deeds, directories, rentals, surviving building fabric, and, sometimes, archeology" – is indeed a very promising avenue of research.[25]

Although Conzen's work is not included in the aforementioned volume on urban historical geography, his topographical approach to reconstructing urban medieval life is most deserving of notice and amply cited by Slater and others. From his influential work carried out in the 1960s and beyond to a series of his articles (collected and published in 1981 and 1990 respectively), Conzen's emphasis on town planning as a way to study urban history has had a significant impact in historical–geographical approaches to our understanding of urban developments.[26] Please note, however, that many of these pioneer works on town planning, including Slater's own work on burgage, date from the 1960s and 1970s. The point here is that historians have been deploying these tools for a long time, and that, as hinted above, these questions are not new.

Thus, in looking at the history of towns, urban historical geography may offer, on the one hand, some significant contributions and enduring ways of understanding the relationship between social and spatial, between individual buildings and the social geography of specific urban localities. On the other hand, medieval archeology, appropriate borrowing from geography, mapping cities, and exploring the social distribution of urban inhabitants have been part of our scholarly arsenal long before urban historical geography emerged as a well-defined historiographical tool. Think of Braudel's *The Mediterranean and the Mediterranean World in the Age of Philip II* as a most worthy example of the signal role of geography – even if not directly tied to urban developments – in historical processes, or the even older and pioneer laying-out of the geographical context by Euclides da Cunha in his *Os Sertöes*.[27] Rather than a critique of urban historical geography, what I wish to emphasize here is that these approaches are welcome and necessary in moving our understanding of medieval urban societies forward, but they do not represent a truly paradigmatic shift in how we do urban history, or a "total," if one can invoke a Braudelian methodological approach, history.

My essay has referenced work on England and seems to neglect other parts of medieval Europe (with the exception of Castile, from where I draw examples as well). In part, this choice has been prompted by two considerations. First, historians of medieval urban and rural England have long pioneered the use of archeology and town planning in their research. The ongoing debate on how urban or not England may have been in the Middle Ages and concomitant studies of population density in urban settlements have long animated English historiography. Secondly, on the Continent, while historians have long used some of these same tools, paid attention to spatial considerations, and addressed many of the questions similarly raised by historians of England, they have not thought of their inquiry as falling into some special category designated as urban historical geography. Rather, great works on the history of towns, on the relationship between city and countryside, and on urban social distribution have been part of broad examinations of urban life that did not necessitate the creation of new heuristic categories.

New Approaches

Perhaps we should think of other recent works that make truly novel contributions as to how to read and understand urban life and the social and spatial structure of towns. Daniel L. Smail's impressive book *Imaginary Cartographies* provides us with an example of other innovative ways of looking at the life of cities and on how to plot urban spatial realities. As Smail shows convincingly, notaries and others in late medieval Marseilles engaged in a systematic mapping of the city. Boundaries, rights of way, streets, and other spatial references in property transactions, wills, and other such instruments created, in Smail's felicitous formulation, an "imaginary [and textual] cartography" of the city. Although we have had access to such imaginary maps for a long time – that is, to the raw sources for urban history – and have used these sources in attempts to reconstruct the development of medieval towns before the appearance of maps, what Smail has provided us with is a conceptual and methodological framework in which to link the written word, legal systems, space, and power into a new and provocative rendering of late medieval urban societies.[28] Along the same lines, the relationship between text (mostly literary in this case) and place can provide new fruitful avenues for our understanding of urban life.[29]

Missing also from the archeological and geographically inflected methodology of urban historical geography is the deployment of art and other cultural artifacts (as noted earlier) to enhance our knowledge of urban life and structures. Although these sources have been used in the past – think of Burckhardt – and continue to be used in the present, there is not, in the work of either urban historical geographers or others, a consistent effort to mine works of art and literature for what they show us about urban architecture, development, and daily life. One single example will suffice here. Chiara Frugoni's *A Day in a Medieval City* illustrates the pulse of urban daily life through a profusion and stunning display of visual images (paintings, manuscript illuminations, and other such materials) and literary texts (mostly Boccaccio). Frugoni does not only provide illustrations, a technique that we have long used in the past in scholarly works and in the classroom; she also offers a parallel non-textual account in which we can see and further imagine the city and its inhabitants.[30]

We also need resources to teach the city and to transmit our new understandings of urban society to undergraduate students. While almost every source reader in medieval history today includes some excerpt that illustrates urban social history, there are few collections of sources available for teaching. One exception to that is the recent publication of Maryanne Kowaleski's *Medieval Towns: A Reader*, which provides a wealth of material on different aspects of urban life.[31] Considering new web-based technologies, we now have the ability to come closer to the realities of what late medieval cities may have truly looked like through electronically published books, as, for example, those sponsored by the American Historical Association through its Gutenberg-e project. In the Gutenberg-e project, music, art, texts, and computer recreations provide a multidisciplinary approach to specific topics. In this bold new world, the contributions of urban historical geography become even more relevant. Plot histories, street histories, and computer models of urban layout and buildings can borrow from the spadework done by researchers in archives and in archeological digs. What can be achieved in this regard is impressive indeed.

I am thinking specifically of the virtual-reality portals created at UCLA, including the reconstruction of the cathedral of St James of Compostela as it may have existed in *c.* 1300, or the recreation of the monastery of St Gall, as it was meant to be built according to its famous map. These large projects, directed by John Dagenais and Patrick Geary respectively and involving undergraduates and graduate students as well, can, in the future and with better technologies yet, be extended to the recreation of virtual medieval towns in which art, literary sources, archeology, topography, metrological, and plot patterns and measures are put to the service of fully understanding medieval towns and their inhabitants. Our work on these topics has just begun.

Notes

1 See Burckhardt, *The Civilization of the Renaissance in Italy*. There are many different editions. Maitland, *Domesday Book and Beyond*; Pirenne, *Medieval Cities*, and also *Les Villes et les institutions urbaines*. The comparative model for the study of urban societies is an approach already suggested by Bloch in "Toward a Comparative History of European Societies"; Rörig, *Die Europäische Stadt und die Kultur des Bürgertums im Mittelalter*, was published posthumously and translated into English as *The Medieval Town* in 1967. See also Ennen, "The Variety of Urban Development," pp. 11–18, as well as *Die Europäische Stadt des Mittelalters*.

2 In many respects, many of the great historical works of classical antiquity were deeply bound to descriptions of urban centers. Worthy examples of writers whose work revolved around either the history of the great polis or descriptions of them are Thucydides, Livy, Pausanias, and others. In the Renaissance, the great histories of cities from Machiavelli's *Istorie fiorentine* or *Florentine Histories* to Guicciardini's *Storie fiorentine* or *The History of Florence*, and the utopian urban planning works of Alberti in his *La Città ideale nel Rinascimento* and Campanella, *Civitas Solis* or *The City of the Sun*, already show an understanding of the relationship between urban history and space. For urban utopias of antiquity and the Renaissance, see Manuel and Manuel, *Utopian Thought in the Western World*.

3 See Berengo's extensive (over 1,000 pages) *L'Europa della città*, which is a magisterial synthesis of social and institutional history, and Nicholas's superb and multiperspectival synthesis, *The Later Medieval City*, which I have used throughout as context for these discussions. See also Nicholas, *The Growth of the Medieval City*.

4 In Reynolds, *An Introduction to the History of English Medieval Towns*, pp. ix–x, as cited in Dyer, "Recent Developments in Early Medieval Urban History and Archeology in England," p. 69 n. 3.

5 See Asenjo, *Segovia*, pp. 88–128; Estepa Diez et al, *Burgos en la edad media*.

6 For Santa Coloma, see Milton's unpublished UCLA Ph.D. dissertation, "Commerce and Community in a Medieval Town."

7 On the three categories of urban centers – based upon whether they had been part of the Roman Empire, in transitional areas, or in non-Roman regions – see Ennen, "The Variety of Urban Development."

8 See Le Goff, "A Note on Tripartite Society, Monarchical Ideology, and Economic Renewal," pp. 53–7. In addition, see Le Goff's magisterial essay on urban changing values, "Merchant's Time and Church's Time in the Middle Ages," pp. 29–42.

9 For changes in mentality see Ruiz, *From Heaven to Earth*, pp. 12–36 and *passim*. See the bibliography therein.

10 See, e.g., Berengo, *L'Europa della città*, pp. 111–70. In Spanish historiography, see also the debate on *ciudad y campo* (city and countryside) and the influential article by MacKay, "Ciudad y campo en la Europa medieval," pp. 27–53. Also in the same volume of *Studia historica*, see Estepa Diez, "El alfoz y las relaciones campo-ciudad en Castilla y León," pp. 7–26.

11 See Ruiz, *Crisis and Continuity*, pp. 140–74, 235–61; Casado Alonso, *Señores, mercaderes y campesinos*, pp. 451–510.

12 Collantes de Terán, *Sevilla en la baja Edad Media*, pp. 353–7.
13 Bowsky, "The Impact of the Black Death upon Sienese Government and Society," pp. 19–34.
14 Ruiz, *Crisis and Continuity*, pp. 235–61. For festivals that brought the urban population to the countryside, see Ruiz, "Festivités, couleurs et symboles du pouvoir en Castille au XVe siècle," pp. 521–46; "Elite and Popular Culture in Late Fifteenth-Century Castilian Festivals," pp. 296–318; also *Spanish Society*, chs 5–6.
15 Among the volumes published in the Cambridge Studies in Historical Geography that may be of interest to medievalists, I should note Kain and Prince, *The Tithe Surveys of England and Wales*, and Cosgrove and Daniels, eds, *The Iconography of Landscape*. The entire series contains numerous volumes, though not many titles deal with urban spaces.
16 Denecke and Shaw, eds, *Urban Historical Geography*, p. 18
17 Ibid., pp. 20–6.
18 See *Le Livre de la taille de Paris, l'an 1296*, ed. Michaëlsson; Courtenay, *Parisian Scholars in the Early Fourteenth Century*; Rouse and Rouse, *Manuscripts and their Makers*; see also the important information about urban topography and neighborhood inhabitation in the Archivo catedral de Burgos, Libros de contabilidad; Ruiz, *Crisis and Continuity*, chs 8 and 9.
19 Nicholas, *The Later Medieval City*, pp. 74–87, 275–6, 322–9, and *passim*. See also Nicholas's other works on Flemish urban history and on the relation between town and countryside: *The Metamorphosis of a Medieval City* and *Town and Countryside*.
20 Lilley, *Urban Life in the Middle Ages*, pp. 75–105, 138–211.
21 See a collection of these early articles, specifically Ruiz, "The Economic Structure of the Area of Burgos" and "Two Patrician Families in Late Medieval Burgos." See also Estepa Diez, *Burgos en la edad media*, pp. 107–11.
22 See also Dyer, *Bromsgrove*; *Lords and Peasants in a Changing Society*; and *Everyday Life in Medieval England*, as well as many others of his books and articles.
23 Denecke and Shaw, eds, *Urban Historical Geography*, pp. 69–80.
24 Ibid., pp. 37–52.
25 Slater, "English Medieval Town Planning," pp. 95–6. See also Slater, "The Analysis of Burgages Patterns in Medieval Towns," "The Analysis of Burgage in Medieval Towns," and numerous other references found in "English Medieval Town Planning."
26 See Conzen, *The Urban Landscape*; *Geographie und Landesplanung im England*; and *Alnwick, Northumberland*. See also Slater, ed., *The Built Form of Western Cities*.
27 Da Cunha's book, originally published in 1902, has been translated into English as *Rebellion in the Backlands*.
28 Smail, *Imaginary Cartographies*.
29 An example of this methodological approach can be found in Tomasch and Gilles, eds, *Text and Territory*.
30 See Frugoni, *A Day in the Medieval City*, and, far more importantly, *A Distant City*.
31 Kowaleski, *Medieval Towns*.

Bibliography

Alberti, Leon Batista, *La Città ideale nel Rinascimento* (Torino: UTET, 1975).

Asenjo, María, *Segovia: La ciudad y su tierra a fines del medievo* (Segovia: Imp. Taravilla, 1986).

Berengo, Marino, *L'Europa della città: Il Volto della società urbana europea tra Medievo ed Età moderna* (Turin: G. Einaudi, 1999).

Bloch, Marc, "Toward a Comparative History of European Societies," in F. C. Lane and J. C. Riemersman, eds, *Enterprise and Secular Change* (Homewood, IL: R. D. Irwin, 1953).

Bowsky, William, M, "The Impact of the Black Death upon Sienese Government and Society," *Speculum*, 39 (1964), pp. 19–34.

Braudel, Fernand, *The Mediterranean and the Mediterranean World in the Age of Philip II*, trans. Siân Reynolds, 2 vols (London: Collins, 1972–3).

Burckhardt, Jacob, *The Civilization of the Renaissance in Italy* (New York: Modern Libray, 2002).

Campanella, Tommaso, *Civitas Solis*, or *The City of the Sun*, trans. A. M. Elliott and R. Millner (London: Journeyman Press, 1981).

Casado Alonso, Hilario, *Señores, mercaderes y campesinos: La comarca de Burgos a fines de la edad media* (Valladolid: Junta de Castilla y León, 1987).

Collantes de Terán, Antonio, *Sevilla en la baja edad media: La ciudad y sus hombres* (Seville: Ayuntamiento de Sevilla, 1977).

Conzen, M. R. G., *The Urban Landscape: Historical Development and Management*, ed. J. W. R. Whitehand (London and New York: Academic Press, 1981).

Conzen, M. R. G., *Alnwick, Northumberland: A Study in Town-Plan Analysis* (London: George Phillip, 1960).

Conzen, M. R. G., *Geographie und Landesplanung im England* (Bonn: F. Dümmlers Verlag, 1952).

Cosgrove, Denis, and Daniels, Stephen, eds, *The Iconography of Landscape: Essays on the Symbolic Representation, Design, and Use of Past Environments* (Cambridge: Cambridge University Press, 1988).

Courtenay, William J., *Parisian Scholars in the Early Fourteenth Century: A Social Portrait* (Cambridge: Cambridge University Press, 1999).

Da Cunha, Euclides, *Rebellion in the Backlands*, trans. Samuel Putnam (Chicago: University of Chicago Press, 1944).

Denecke, Dietrich, and Shaw, Gareth, eds, *Urban Historical Geography: Recent Progress in Britain and Germany* (Cambridge: Cambridge University Press, 1988).

Dyer, Christopher, *Bromsgrove: A Small Town in Worcestershire in the Middle Ages* (Worcester: Worcestershire Historical Society, 2000).

Dyer, Christopher, *Everyday Life in Medieval England* (London: Hambledon Press, 1994).

Dyer, Christopher, "Recent Developments in Early Medieval Urban History and Archeology in England," in Dietrich Denecke and Gareth Shaw, eds, *Urban Historical Geography: Recent Progress in Britain and Germany* (Cambridge: Cambridge University Press, 1988), pp. 69–80.

Dyer, Christopher, *Lords and Peasants in a Changing Society: The Estates of the Bishopric of Worcester, 680–1540* (Cambridge: Cambridge University Press, 1980).

Ennen, Edith, "The Variety of Urban Development," in John F. Benton, ed., *Town Origins: The Evidence from Medieval England* (Boston: Heath, 1968), pp. 11–18.

Ennen, Edith, *Die Europäische Stadt des Mittelalters* (Göttingen: Vandenhoech & Ruprecht, 1972).

Estepa Diez, Carlos, et al., *Burgos en la edad media* (Valladolid: Junta de Castilla y León, 1984).

Estepa Diez, Carlos, "El alfoz y las relaciones campo-ciudad en Castilla y León durante los siglos XII y XIII," *Studia historica*, 2 (1984), pp. 7–26.

Frugoni, Chiara, *A Distant City: Images of Urban Experience in the Medieval World*, trans. William McCuaig (Princeton: Princeton University Press, 1991).

Frugoni, Chiara, *A Day in the Medieval City*, trans. William McCuaig (Chicago: University of Chicago Press, 2005).

Graham, Brian J., "The Town in the Norman Colonisations of the British Isles," in Dietrich Denecke and Gareth Shaw, eds, *Urban Historical Geography: Recent Progress in Britain and Germany*, Cambridge Studies in Historical Geography, 10 (Cambridge: Cambridge University Press, 1988), pp. 37–52.

Guicciardini, Francesco, *Storie fiorentine dal 1378 al 1509*, or *The History of Florence*, trans. Mario Domandi (New York: Harper & Row, 1970).

Kain, Roger J. P., and Prince, Hugh C., *The Tithe Surveys of England and Wales* (Cambridge: Cambridge University Press, 1985).

Kowaleski, Maryanne, *Medieval Towns: A Reader* (Peterborough: Broadview Press, 2006).

Le Goff, Jacques, "A Note on Tripartite Society, Monarchical Ideology, and Economic Renewal in Ninth to Twelfth-Century Christendom," in Jacques Le Goff, *Time, Work & Culture in the Middle Ages*, trans. Arthur Goldhammer (Chicago: University of Chicago Press, 1980), pp. 53–7.

Le Goff, Jacques, "Merchant's Time and Church's Time in the Middle Ages," in Jacques Le Goff, *Time, Work & Culture in the Middle Ages*, trans. Arthur Goldhammer (Chicago: University of Chicago Press, 1980), pp. 29–42.

Le Livre de la taille de Paris, l'an 1296, ed. Karl Michaëlsson (Göteborg: Almqvist & Wilksell, 1958).

Lilley, Keith, D., *Urban Life in the Middle Ages, 1000–1450* (New York: Palgrave, 2002).

Machiavelli, Niccolò, *Istorie fiorentine*, or *Florentine Histories*, trans. Laura F. Banfield and Harvey C. Mansfield, Jr (Princeton: Princeton University Press, 1988).

MacKay, Angus, "Ciudad y campo en la Europa medieval," *Studia historica*, 2 (1984), pp. 27–53.

Maitland, Frederic, W., *Domesday Book and Beyond: Three Essays in the Early History of England* (Cambridge: Cambridge University Press, 1897).

Manuel, Frank E., and Manuel, Fritzie P., *Utopian Thought in the Western World* (Cambridge, MA: Belknap Press, 1979).

Milton, Gregory, B., "Commerce and Community in a Medieval Town: Santa Coloma de Queralt, 1293–1313," unpublished Ph.D. dissertation (Los Angeles: UCLA, 2004).

Nicholas, David, *The Later Medieval City, 1300–1500* (London: Longman, 1997).

Nicholas, David, *The Growth of the Medieval City: From Late Antiquity to the Early Fourteenth Century* (London: Longman, 1997).

Nicholas, David, *The Metamorphosis of a Medieval City: Ghent in the Age of the Arteveldes, 1302–1390* (Lincoln, NE: University of Nebraska Press, 1987).

Nicholas, David, *Town and Countryside: Social, Economic and Political Tensions in Fourteenth-Century Flanders* (Bruges: De Tempel, 1971).

Pirenne, Henri, *Medieval Cities: Their Origins and the Revival of Trade*, trans. Frank D. Halsey (Princeton: Princeton University Press, 1948 (originally published in 1927)).

Pirenne, Henri, *Les Villes et les institutions urbaines*, 2 vols (Paris: Librairie Felix Alean, 1939).

Reynolds, Susan, *An Introduction to the History of English Medieval Towns* (Oxford: Clarendon Press, 1977).

Rouse, Mary A., and Rouse, Richard H., *Manuscripts and their Makers: Commercial Book Producers in Medieval Paris, 1200–1500* (Turnhout: Harvey Miller, 2000).

Rörig, Fritz, *Die Europäische Stadt und die Kultur des Bürgertums im Mittelalter* (Göttingen: Vandenhoech & Ruprecht, 1955). English translation as *The Medieval Town* (Berkeley and Los Angeles: University of California Press, 1967).

Ruiz, Teofilo F., "Festivités, couleurs et symboles du pouvoir en Castille au XVe siècle: Les Célébrations de mai 1428," *Annales ESC*, 3 (1991), pp. 521–46.

Ruiz, Teofilo F., "The Economic Structure of the Area of Burgos, 1200–1350" and "Two Patrician Families in Late Medieval Burgos: The Sarracín and the Bonifaz," in T. F. Ruiz, *The City and the Realm: Burgos and Castile, 1080–1492* (Aldershot: Variorum, 1992), II, VI.

Ruiz, Teofilo F, "Elite and Popular Culture in Late Fifteenth-Century Castilian Festivals: The Case of Jaén," in B. A. Hanawalt and K. I. Reyerson, eds, *City and Spectacle in Medieval Europe* (Minneapolis, MN: University of Minnesota Press, 1994), pp. 296–318.

Ruiz, Teofilo F., *Crisis and Continuity: Land and Town in Late Medieval Castile* (Philadelphia: University of Pennsylvania Press, 1994).

Ruiz, Teofilo F., *Spanish Society, 1400–1600* (London: Longman, 2001).

Ruiz, Teofilo F. *From Heaven to Earth: The Reordering of Castilian Society, 1150–1350* (Princeton: Princeton University Press, 2004).

Slater, Terry, "The Analysis of Burgages Patterns in Medieval Towns," *Area*, 13 (1981), pp. 211–16.

Slater, Terry, "The Analysis of Burgage in Medieval Towns: Three Case Studies from the West Midlands," *West Midlands Archeology*, 23 (1981), pp. 53–66.

Slater, Terry, "English Medieval Town Planning," in Dietrich Denecke and Gareth Shaw, eds, *Urban Historical Geography: Recent Progress in Britain and Germany* (Cambridge: Cambridge University Press, 1988), pp. 93–105.

Slater, T. R., ed., *The Built Form of Western Cities: Essays for M. R. G. Conzen on the Occasion of his 80th Birthday*, ed. T. R. Slater (Leicester: Leicester University Press, 1990).

Smail, Daniel, L, *Imaginary Cartographies: Possession and Identity in Late Medieval Marseille* (Ithaca, NY: Cornell University Press, 2000).

Tomasch, Sylvia, and Gilles, Sealy, eds, *Text and Territory: Geographical Imagination in the European Middle Ages* (Philadelphia: University of Pennsylvania Press, 1998).

Further Reading

Beyond the books listed in the Notes and Bibliography, the following may prove to be useful. Although there are numerous books on diverse aspects of medieval West European urban history, I have limited the titles to recent works, most of them in English, to areas in which the concerns with the relation between space and social geography have been explicitly made.

Bairoch, Paul, et al., *La Population des villes européennes, 800–1850: Banque de données et analyse sommaire des résultats* (*The Population of European cities, 800–1850: Data Bank and Short Summary of Results)* (Geneva: Droz, 1988). A courageous attempt to provide a wide range of sources that allow us to trace European urban population and its change over time from the early Middle Ages to the mid-nineteenth century.

Buisseret, David, ed. *Envisioning the City: Six Studies in Urban Cartography* (Chicago: University of Chicago Press, 1998). Buisseret's edited volume includes articles on Chinese mapping practices, European late Renaissance and early modern cartography, and the role of mapping in the design of urban spaces. Its comparative perspective opens new vistas on the theme.

Campbell, Bruce M. S., et al., *A Medieval Capital and its Grain Supply: Agrarian Production and Distribution in the London Region*, c. *1300* (London: Institute of British Geographers, Historical Geography Research Group, 1993). This study examines one of the most important issues in urban history – that is, how were growing urban centers supplied with sufficient food to allow for population growth and expansion.

Carter, Harold, *An Introduction to Urban Historical Geography* (London: E. Arnold, 1983). Now almost a quarter of century since its original publication, Carter's book provides a brief introduction to the signal issues in the field.

Clark, Peter, ed., *Country Towns in Pre-Industrial England* (New York: St Martin's Press, 1981). Following from his earlier book on urban change, Clark's collection provides comparative analysis of English urban life on the eve of industrialization.

Clark, Peter, and Slack, Paul, *English Towns in Transition 1500–1700* (New York: Oxford University Press, 1976). One of the pioneer books on the social changes and history of early modern English towns.

Cosgrove, Denis E., *Social Formation and Symbolic Landscape* (Totowa, NJ: Barnes & Noble Books, 1985). This is an important theoretical statement about the symbolism of place and its social meaning.

Duncan, James, and Ley, David, eds, *Place/Culture/Representation* (London and New York: Routledge, 1993). This very interesting volume has an important contribution by Denis Cosgrove and Mona Domash on the methodological implications of writing a new cultural or historical geography or history of urban spaces, as well as significant contributions from Brian Stock, John Agnew, and others. Although many of its essays address either modern or non-European urban landscapes, their theoretical underpinnings make this a valuable contribution to the formulation of the relationship of culture and space in urban settings.

Ennen, Edith, *The Medieval Town*, trans. Natalie Fryde (Amsterdam: North-Holland, 1979). This is an English translation of Ennen's original German text, which remains an innovative and path-breaking study.

Epstein, S. R., ed., *Town and Country in Europe, 1300–1800* (Cambridge: Cambridge University Press, 2001). A superb collection, this book contains a truly West European-wide comparative perspective on the relationship between urban centers and their hinterland in the Middle Ages and the early modern period.

Everson, Paul, and Williamson, Tom, eds, *The Archaeology of Landscape: Studies Presented to Christopher Taylor* (Manchester and New York: Manchester University Press, 1998). Although more focused on landscape than on urban settings, the essays in this book provide a useful guide to recent work on historical archeology, one of the most important tools we have for our understanding of urban historical geography.

Girouard, Mark, *The English Town: A History of Urban Life* (New Haven: Yale University Press, 1990). Written by a renowned art and architectural historian, this delightful book is a wonderful introduction, as are his other books on country houses, Victorian architecture, and other topics, to the richness of English town life before the onset of modernity.

Hindle, Brian Paul, *Medieval Town Plans* (Princes Risborough: Shire, 1990). A most useful study of town planning, or what passed for urban planning, in medieval Europe. It offers an entry into how medieval civic leaders sought to transform their respective towns.

Howe, John, and Wolfe, Michael, eds, *Inventing Medieval Landscapes: Senses of Place in Western Europe* (Gainesville, FL: University Press of Florida, 2002). Although, once again, emphasizing rural landscapes rather than urban ones, this selection of articles offer a strong comparative perspective, ranging from Ireland to Islamic Spain, on questions of space, place, and, implicitly, the relation of the countryside to the town.

Menjot, Denis, ed., *Les Villes frontière, moyen âge–époque moderne* (Paris: L'Harmattan, 1996). A collection of essays exploring specific aspects of urban life on the frontier. It provides comparative perspectives on the role of location in the development of peculiar urban institutions.

Vanneste, Dominique, *Space and Place: Mirrors of Social and Cultural Identities? Studies in Historical Geography* (Leuven: Geografisch Instituut, Katholieke Universiteit, 1996). A series of essays on the links of space, social filiation, and cultural production.

Waller, Philip, ed., *The English Urban Landscape* (Oxford: Oxford University Press, 2000). Focusing on urban landscapes, this collection of articles traces the changes in urban geography from the first Roman urban foundations through the Middle Ages and the early modern period into the contemporary world. Attention is also given to the literary representations of urban spaces.

Some of these journals contain useful articles for our understanding of urban historical geography: *Historical Geography*. Published by the Department of Geography, California State University, Northridge, *c.* 1978 to the present and *Journal of Historical Geography*. 1975 to the present.

Chapter Twenty

Bureaucracy and Literacy

Richard Britnell

Given the scale of government operations under the later Roman emperors, medieval rulers had potentially no shortage of precedents from which to develop advanced administrative practices. An official handbook, the *Notitia Dignitatum*, composed soon after the division of the empire between its eastern and western halves in 395, supplied information about the principal officers of state and their duties, their staff, and the administrative structure in which they operated. This text survived the collapse of the western empire, and was preserved in a Carolingian manuscript, bearing witness to the vast amount of record keeping that the administration of the empire had required. In addition to this literary testimony, there long remained a living reminder of ancient ways. The eastern empire preserved the basic features of the late Roman administrative structure into the seventh century, by which time they had long been abandoned in the West. The territories under the Greek emperors were divided into prefectures, which were in turn subdivided into provinces headed by civil governors. Their central financial administration was divided between the two principal offices of the *res privata* responsible for administering the imperial estates) and the *sacrae largitiones* (responsible for other sources of income). In Western Europe, the Church preserved a tradition of Latin literacy, and also long maintained an archival tradition both at the Lateran in Rome and in bishoprics elsewhere. Yet, though this ensured that Roman law and literature had a major impact on the culture of Latin Christendom, the same cannot be said for Roman administrative models. The universal disappearance of Roman bureaucratic methods indicates the severity of the discontinuities that interrupted so many developments in ancient civilization during the fifth and sixth centuries.

The Early Middle Ages (400–750)

The breakup of the unity of the empire undoubtedly contributed to the collapse of its administrative traditions, which had in some respects developed as measures of centralization. The communications network initiated by Augustus, and developed under his successors as the *cursus publicus*, had required an expensive and far-flung structure of posting stations that lost its point with the disintegration of the empire. The management of the Roman corn supply from overseas depended upon an administrative structure of clerks and administrators issuing receipts, paying carriers and shippers, and keeping accounts, and this was undermined by the contraction of Rome and the declining demand for grain there, especially following the Vandal conquest of North Africa and the capture of Carthage in 439. The central finances of the Western emperors were undermined by recurrent invasions, the weakening and forfeited control of the provinces, and the concurrent loss of income from imperial estates and taxation.[1] A similar fate overtook the administration of large senatorial estates, with interests extending across the Roman and Hellenistic world. These events could not fail to shake administrative systems. And yet in many respects the Roman provinces had operated as subunits whose administrations were able to function independently of imperial control. The late Roman imperial system, it is said, stifled local initiative; its weakening, then, might be expected to encourage it. The administration of justice, the management of government property, the minting of currency, and the levying of taxes could surely have continued to evolve from Roman precedent all over the Roman world, even given the fragmentation of imperial authority amongst local kings, counts, and bishops. And indeed, for a while it did. Germanic leaders preferred to see themselves as the inheritors of Roman ways, and it was in their interests to preserve many features of Roman statecraft. The Visigoths in Spain and the Franks in Gaul long maintained what survived of the Roman system of taxation, and so probably did the Lombards in Italy until the late sixth century. Procedures of assessment were locally modified, until eventually what had once been taxes became indistinguishable from customary rents and other seigniorial dues, but in parts of Gaul elements of the former structure were perceptible into the seventh and eighth centuries.[2] Nor is it enough to invoke disorder as a general explanation for the collapse of Roman administrative traditions, since temporary and localized crises do not explain the failure to reinstate past normalcy in periods of more secure rule. Only the collapse of the ancient economy, and the sheer inability of rulers to govern as the Romans had done even at a local level, can explain the discontinuities in systems of trade, minting, estate management, and taxation that our documentation and archaeological evidence attest. Administrative practices were given up as they became impossible to continue, and the abandonment of ancient archival systems inevitably followed the decay of the administrative practices they had been designed to record.

Archival survivals from the early Middle Ages are so few that the description of administrations of any kind is problematic, but there is undoubtedly a story worth the search. Pride of place for administrative sophistication long remained with the eastern empire with its capital in Constantinople, though the organization there departed widely from Roman precedent during the seventh century. This was at least partly a result of the large sections of the empire to Islam, which accelerated a long-term tendency for imperial administration to become more palace centred. The large old ministries, with their complex system of subordination, were broken up so that more officers were directly answerable to the emperor. In place of the earlier separation between *res privata* and *sacrae largitiones*, a series of three major departments was created, each headed by an administrator (*logothetes*) under the general supervision of a single principal minister called the *sakellarios*. There were other officers with special responsibility for the mint and the arsenal, charitable institutions, state factories, and the imperial estates. Another set of officers was responsible for the central administration of justice. In the provinces, civil and military organizations were integrated into a single structure of administrative districts, the "themes," each headed by a military commander. The continuing dependence of this administration on literacy and record keeping is implied by the appointment of a court archivist, the *protoasekratis*.

Away from Constantinople the most formal European administrations were probably ecclesiastical. That of the papal palace in Rome imitated some structures from the imperial court in the East. At the heart of the administration an office called the *scrinium*, created in the fifth century, administered the pope's possessions and other sources of income. The responsibilities of the pope for administering justice, almsgiving, and other charitable work were handled by papal notaries and "defenders" of the Church. The papacy probably maintained the most active writing office of any West European government, since it was expected to answer questions sent for resolution by bishops throughout the Church, and from at least the time of Pope Leo I (440–61) the texts of papal letters were recorded in registers modeled on those of the imperial administration. The papal chancery maintained a formula book to assist the drafting of letters by the time of Gregory the Great (590–604), if not earlier. There was a papal archive, which was located in the Lateran by the mid-seventh century. Bede was able to reconstruct details of Augustine's mission to the English in the years between 596 and 604 from the texts of letters preserved either in the registers or elsewhere in the papal *scrinium*; these were supplied to him, with the permission of Pope Gregory II, by Nothelm, a London priest, later archbishop of Canterbury.[3] The papacy also maintained some measure of bureaucratic formality in the management of its properties; each of the patrimonies into which the papal estates were divided had its own office staffed by clerks and officials.[4] Given the higher level of literacy amongst men in holy order, the wider Church might be expected to protect bureaucratic traditions better than elsewhere, and that is probably the case. At least some bishops employed clerks, chiefly for the writing of letters, leases, and other legal documents, and they were also likely to maintain depositaries for such records. Fifty-five papyri from the period between 445 and 700 survive from the archives of the archbishop of Ravenna.[5] The oldest parchment letter to have survived in Western Europe is one written by the bishop of London to the archbishop of Canterbury in about 704.[6] Such activities hardly warranted the maintenance of much bureaucratic organization, and the archives in question are likely to have been small, even in Italy. Apart from this limited use of administrative literacy, it is impossible to be sure that churchmen maintained traditions of financial and legal recording through the early Middle Ages. It seems unlikely that they did, to judge from the originality of new and unprecedented series of archives from many parts of Europe in the twelfth century and later. Even the updating of estate surveys cannot be shown to have shared any continuity with Roman practice, though common experience suggested the occasional need for such records in different contexts. There is a surviving fragment of an estate survey from the archbishopric of Ravenna, and Gregory the Great (590–604) is said to have recorded the returns due from the papal estates in a *polyptychum*. The abbey of St Martin at Tours compiled some sort of land register around the year 700. These examples show that the estate surveys of the ninth century and later, of which the famous polyptych of Saint-Germain-des-Prés (*c.* 825–8) is the most impressive, were not without earlier medieval precedent, but they are too rare and too dissimilar to attest the existence of any common tradition.[7]

Apart from the pope, few European rulers maintained formally bureaucratic administrations, though their households were doubtless large enough to require some managerial expertise. The problems of supply were to some extent resolvable by two characteristic expedients: renders from dependants were made fixed, customary, and consequently more memorable, and households moved around from one estate center to another to consume what was available.[8] However, the larger kingdoms had courts that required complex provisioning, and probably needed some written record of their entitlements. The Visigothic king Leovigild (568–86) and his successors are likely to have maintained an elaborate palace organization in Toledo, though the provinces were ruled by dukes and counts.[9] The Lombards had a similar palace, probably less complex, in Pavia. Moreover, palaces needed to communicate in some way with noblemen, bishops, and other royal agents in the provinces. The Formulary of Marculf (*c.* 660) demonstrates that Merovingian kings sent a variety of written instruments to their agents authorizing donations, granting protection, answering petitions, and making appointments; evidently there were clerks on hand. Even English kings in this period had access to clerical assistance if they required it. In addition to the small number of surviving charters, there are written laws from Kentish kings of the seventh century. The text known as the tribal hidage may originally have been drafted for a Mercian king of the seventh century. It is inevitably uncertain how formally different governments organized their need for writing skills. The Merovingian court had a writing office of some sort, headed by a *referendarius*, a term adopted from papal practice, and royal charters show some continuity of wording and form.[10]

To judge from the number and character of surviving documents, and references to documents, most governments required clerks to draw up legislative and administrative codes, or to respond to ad-hoc needs, rather than to maintain a daily routine. It is unlikely that writing was extensively used in day-to-day internal palace administration, even if leading royal officers were sometimes literate enough to write their own names. It is still less likely that those administrations were rigorously departmentalized. Even the principal officers of kings were likely to be described by reference to their status in the household rather than any particular function within it. The power of the Carolingian dynasty before 751 was sanctioned only by their status as "mayors of the palace" for the Merovingian kings. The word *comes* ("count"), commonly used of kings' principal officers, implies a companion or supporter of the king rather than any specific duty, and a count's responsibilities were often military. Though literacy created opportunities for some specialization within courts, it is unlikely that most roles within royal households were strongly differentiated except in terms of rank.[11]

The need for written records in lay society through this period was patchy, and was probably achieved without much in the way of independent bureaucratic organization. It is attested, if only exceedingly spasmodically, both by rare surviving legal documents and by formularies that supplied models for letter writers.[12] In England no known charters were issued by laymen before the late seventh century.[13] The evidence encourages the supposition that such uses of literacy were very occasional. The households of even minor secular and ecclesiastical rulers required administrative systems for the collection of dues, for the management of day-to-day routines, and perhaps for the fulfillment of tasks outside the household. Many minor magnates required literacy for the occasional writing of letters and petitions, or formal recording of land grants, and for these purposes there were clerks to be found, but most of the administrative work of private estates in Europe passed unrecorded during the seventh and eighth centuries, and for long afterwards.

It is tempting to suppose that the scarcity of records from this early period is the result simply of the passage of time, and to some extent that must be true. Parchment replaced papyrus for the writing of legal instruments only between about 650 and 800, and up to that point original deeds were particularly vulnerable. Nevertheless, our knowledge of early medieval documents is not wholly dependent upon the survival of originals to the present day; most medieval deeds, even from later periods, are known from registered copies, later confirmations, and references in chronicles. If few original texts are known from the sixth, seventh, and eighth centuries, this means that few were known in the twelfth and thirteenth centuries, when religious houses, in particular, registered their title deeds in cartularies, when many a learned monk wrote the history of his abbey, and when early authentications of property rights were highly valued.

The High Middle Ages (750–1100)

The Carolingian empire, with its reconstruction of a large palace-centred administration, raised government administration in Western Europe to a new level of formality. "There was a huge explosion in the volume of written documentation."[14] Charles Martel had established his own writing office as mayor of the palace in about 740. After Pippin III's consecration in 751, which inaugurated Carolingian kingship over the Franks, the staff in the royal writing office grew, and the office of chancellor (*cancellarius*) first appears. Charlemagne's court employed up to three or four notaries at a time, all of whom were churchmen. Louis the Pious (814–40) raised the status of this office by appointing chancellors of higher status at court. Besides supervising the notaries' production of documents, they had custody of the royal archive. The royal writing office was chiefly concerned, as in the past, with a widening variety of mandates and legal instruments – donations of property or privilege, assignments to religious benefices, and confirmations of previous documents. An early ninth-century formulary from the royal court contains fifty-five different formulae, implying that at least that number of different forms of official documentation was envisaged. About 1,200 royal charters survive from the period between 751 and 877, many of the originals, and their details attest the existence of office traditions, some going back to the Merovingian period. An increase in business can be partly explained by reference to the expansion of the Carolingian empire, a growing number of religious and lay petitioners, and an increasing need to communicate with royal agents at a distance from the court.[15] Other uses of literacy in government also increased under the Carolingians. The recording of legislative and organizational decisions in written capitularies was vastly extended over Merovingian practice, and so apparently was the recording of legal judgments. Judges were expected to act in accordance with written law. Charlemagne probably had the royal estates described, and tenant obligations recorded, in written surveys, though these have not survived. A surviving polyptych of royal demesne at Chur (Coire) in Switzerland, dating from the tenth century, may derive from an earlier Carolingian survey.[16] Royal practice in this respect probably triggered the production of more widespread making of estate surveys. Even more impressively, Charlemagne's estate instructions known as the *Capitulare de villis* (807) required that the bailiffs of royal estates should submit various kinds of annual accounts and reports, implying an ongoing administrative routine to be supervised by royal officials.

Just as the decline of Roman administrative practices cannot be ascribed wholly to the political decay of the empire, neither can the growing production of records in the Carolingian empire during the eighth and ninth centuries be explained solely by territorial expansion. There were parallel increases in smaller political units, such as the English kingdoms of Mercia and Wessex. Offa of Mercia (757–96) is the first English king thought to have maintained clerks in his employment for writing documents. Æthelwulf of Wessex (839–58) employed a Frankish chief notary.[17] King Alfred of Wessex (871–99) expected his principal servants to be able to read English, both because the law was written into books and because they occasionally needed to respond to written instructions; his administration is known to have issued sealed letters. The earliest surviving English administrative writs date from the late tenth century. By the tenth and eleventh centuries the kings of England probably had a permanent secretariat attached to the royal household and accompanying it as it moved around. Edward the Confessor had a chancellor, Regenbald.[18] In some parts of Europe an increase in the need for literacy is suggested by an increasing number of surviving documents or references to documents. Only 15 royal charters survive from the kingdom of the Asturias in the eighth century, but there are 112 from the later ninth century.[19] It is also noteworthy that, though the Carolingian empire fragmented in 888, and some of its administrative practices were abandoned, this was not accompanied by any steep contraction in pragmatic literacy; the separate Carolingian and post-Carolingian kings and dukes issued charters and in some cases maintained their own chanceries. West Francia maintained a chancery manned by notaries, as before, though its standards of efficiency and knowledge declined in the tenth century. Berengar of Friuli maintained another chancery at Pavia, headed successively by the bishops of Piacenza, Asti, and Modena as arch-chancellors.[20] In the course of time, increasing demand for written records encouraged the employment of clerks in an increasing number of magnate households within the former empire. Writing offices were being formed in the households of the dukes of Normandy and Brittany in the early eleventh century.[21]

Both within the territory of the Carolingian empire and elsewhere the volume of extant records increased significantly from the mid-eighth century into the ninth, and sometimes into the tenth, for reasons that have little to do with the scale of government operations and have more to do with the development of legal procedures and the widespread growth of clerical literacy. The documentary evidence of charters and wills was becoming increasingly important for winning legal disputes.[22] From this period date some of the more impressive early medieval monastic charter collections, whose contents show how the issuing and acquisition of records was increasing in a wider variety of institutions outside royal courts. The remarkable cartulary of Redon Abbey in Brittany, compiled in the later eleventh century, contains 283 deeds from the period 797–924.[23] The distribution of records by time and place was governed by local events, especially by the endowment and subsequent fortunes of religious houses. The founding of Cluny Abbey in 910 gave rise to a truly impressive and exceptional monastic archive, which allows a rare insight into the development of local society in its vicinity.[24]

The volume of extant records from many regions of Western Europe dips in the tenth and eleventh centuries because of the widespread local political instability associated with the renewed invasions and political instability. However, record keeping in the Ottonian Empire increased, and the tenth century was also less disturbed in Mediterranean Europe than in the West. In these regions archives are often richer than in earlier centuries.[25] One of the larger episcopal collections is from Lucca in Tuscany, where the number of extant documents rises from 281 in the eighth century to 765 in the ninth and 1,710 in the tenth.[26] The papal bureaucracy became less conspicuous for its activity in this period, though the Lateran Palace in Rome continued to produce letters and charters, through the tenth and eleventh centuries. A number of tenth-century papal notaries are known from a series of documents many years apart, implying considerable continuity of personnel, though there is some reason to suppose that work was being farmed out to city notaries before the reform of the papal chancery in the mid-eleventh century. Some of the new ideas implemented then drew on procedures in the chancery of the Western emperors.[27]

All this while, however, it remains important not to envisage even the greatest chanceries or writing offices as evidence of bureaucratic government. The offices themselves may not have been very busy: the names of seven notaries are recorded from the thirteen-year reign of Radulf of West Francia (923–36), but only forty-nine royal *acta* are known, less than four a year.[28] From the contemporary twelve-year reign of Athelstan in England (927–39) there are seventy-three texts purporting to be royal *acta*, of which fewer than half have any chance of being authentic as they stand.[29] Evidence of this sort gives no warrant for regarding clerical activity at court as a repetitive daily routine. Large areas of day-to-day administration and jurisdiction depended on oral communication and did not require any permanent record. The potential was already available in the later eleventh century for greater archival activity. England's Domesday Book, compiled in 1086–7, is an impressive instance of what could be achieved. Yet the nearest approaches to bureaucratic administration in Europe were outside Latin Christendom altogether. The Greek empire combined a lavish court with a complex military and naval system, requiring systematic taxation. It has been claimed that "the administration of the East Roman Empire in the tenth century was, whether for good or for evil, more effective than that of any other state, anywhere to the west of China, in that age."[30] Another major European administration of the tenth century was the Muslim Caliphate of Cordova under 'Abd-al-Ruhman III and his successors. Its central secretariat was under the supervision of the viziers of the *diwan*. The need to communicate with provincial civilian and military administrations was such that the government maintained a postal service.[31]

The Later Middle Ages (1100–1500)

By the later eleventh century the habitual resort to writing in different areas of government had laid a firm foundation, through much of Western Europe, for what the following centuries were to bring – a surge in the number and range of administrative records to levels unprecedented since the days of the Roman Empire.[32] Up to this point the driving forces had been state building and the development of judicial practices; governments had characteristically used the written word for recording laws, for communicating instructions, and for recording grants of property and franchises. From now on these considerations weighed even more. A growing volume of business reduced the capacity of administrations to rely on memory and encouraged the systematic registration of information in rolls or ledgers. In addition, in the twelfth century, and more spectacularly in the thirteenth, economic development began to add weighty additional pressure against old ways of doing things, and so contributed independently to the reason why governments as well as their subjects needed to write things down. Economic change undermined the facility with which regular administrative procedures could be guided by static texts – whether books of law or statements of custom – and contributed to the pressure to create systematically updated information. The desirability of keeping regular financial accounts further encouraged the development of a new range of clerical practices, and moved governments nearer to dependence on regular bureaucratic procedures.

Many of the impressive features of archival practice in the later Middle Ages represent a large quantitative increase from earlier practices rather than any fundamental change of documentary practice. In this category the greatest change is in the surviving number of letters, warrants, charters, and other legal instruments, which is all the more impressive because of the increasing practice of registering documents received in cartularies. Where none had existed before, the establishment of royal chanceries became general throughout Europe in the twelfth and early thirteenth centuries.[33] In some instances, as in Norway and Sweden, the appointment of chancellors preceded by some decades the formalization of central administration with a definite permanent office. In Hungary a chancellor is known from the reign of Béla III (1148–96), but the office became permanent only in the thirteenth century.[34] Some institutions also registered outgoing documents, following a precedent first set by the papacy.[35] The extant series of papal registers, almost complete from 1198 onwards, contains on average over 1,000 letters a year through the thirteenth and fourteenth centuries.[36] The registration of outgoing charters and royal letters in England was begun during the chancellorship of Hubert Walter (1199–205). The English chancery became so committed to recording outgoing documentation that by the early fourteenth century there were ten major series of enrolments; by the mid-fourteenth century chancery clerks issued 30,000–40,000 letters each year.[37] The kings of Aragon registered outgoing documents from 1257. The French monarchy also experimented with registering royal deeds about the same time, though its activity in this respect was desultory by English or Aragonese standards before 1307.[38] Even in the fourteenth century the total output of the French chancery is impossible to assess, because only documents deemed to be of lasting significance were enrolled.[39] The great increase in government clerical activities in the writing and recording of letters and charters is indicated by the growing size of royal chanceries. By 1343, after a period of rapid growth, that of the French kings employed ninety-eight notaries, and produced thousands of royal *acta* each year. Although essentially in continuity with earlier medieval practice, the surge of clerical activity in the twelfth and thirteenth centuries did not imply a static routine, since it was accompanied by a considerable multiplication of different types of instrument. This is well illustrated by the growing range of legal writs by which the chancery of the English kings allowed plaintiffs to initiate actions in the royal courts of law.[40] Royal chanceries, and the chanceries of magnates with regalian rights, were inevitably exceptionally large because of the wide range of administrative procedures for which they were responsible. To a lesser extent, however, many smaller magnates, as well as bishops and abbots, were involved in the increasing production of documents of these kinds.

Both governmental and lesser administrations also had increasing responsibility for safeguarding, and sometimes registering, incoming documents. The commonest form of this activity, undertaken at quite humble levels of property ownership in the thirteenth century, was archiving records on shelves, in cupboards, or in chests, and perhaps simply listing them.[41] A further step, frequently taken for records thought to be of permanent significance such as title deeds and related documents, was their transcription into registers, either in full or in abbreviated versions. Large numbers of surviving cartularies do record the charters of monasteries, colleges, and lay families.[42] The registration of more ephemeral incoming records was less usual, though an exception might be made for petitions requiring more than routine processing. One of the most important archives of this kind is the series of registers of petitions to the Roman curia, which begins in 1342.[43]

Public provision for the registration of legal instruments was an innovation of the twelfth and thirteenth centuries that took many forms. In southern Europe, especially, the key figure was the notary, whose notebook was a publicly recognized validation of the contracts he had drawn up for his clients. The earliest Genoese notarial records date from the mid-twelfth century. Thousands of such registers were being maintained by the late thirteenth century; Milan alone is said to have had more than 1,500 notaries, "many of whom are excellent at drawing up contracts." The earliest surviving French notarial register contains 1,031 deeds drawn up in the space of nine months in 1248.[44] In northern Europe notaries were less frequently employed for ordinary secular transactions. Instead, kings, princes, free cities, and other governing bodies developed their own ways of establishing authenticity. England had several systems, some of which were delegated to the recognizance rolls of urban courts after 1283. One of the most certain ways of registering a title to freehold property in England involved a complex process through the king's courts that ended in the drawing-up of a formal agreement (a "final concord" or "fine"), of which a copy was retained in the royal archive.[45] In France lay authorities undertook the authentication of private deeds under their seals from the late twelfth century, but especially after 1220. Usually they did so without registering the deeds they had so authenticated, but there are examples of registration from Normandy and elsewhere from the later fourteenth century.[46] Systems devised by city governments inevitably varied from place to place. Lübeck and Hamburg registered legal instruments in a series of registers preserved in the city archive; at Cologne records were similarly recorded in registers, but these were maintained by parochial officers and stored in parochial coffers.[47]

The production of estate surveys was another administrative task with a long tradition behind it, even though it is doubtful how continuous that tradition was either within different regions of Europe or across different linguistic and cultural boundaries. The survival of Carolingian surveys implies the existence of models for this activity in France, Germany, Italy, and northern Spain. The tenth century is less well supplied with such records than the ninth, but the increasingly numerous *censiers* of the eleventh century onward, which were more than merely lists of rents, served essentially the same purpose. Documents of this kind, and the *terriers* that became common from the thirteenth century onward, were texts that needed periodic updating to accommodate changes of tenant and rent. These compilations, needed for reference by rulers and their administrators, were laborious to compile, and so could be updated only occasionally. Characteristically they were compiled by means of an inquest (*inquisitio*) that involved calling local jurors together to provide information and to swear to its truth. The early tradition of estate surveys in England has left few traces, though there are examples from before the Norman Conquest that demonstrate its existence. The royal initiative displayed in the Domesday survey is the most notable example of this type of record in royal administration. This is all the more remarkable for including surveys of the estates of the king's subjects as well as his own.[48] Inquests into royal and princely estates and other legal rights take many different forms from the twelfth century onward.

They may detail military tenures and obligations, like the Sicilian *Catalogus baronum* of 1149–50, later renewed, the series of *Feoda campagnie* from twelfth- and thirteenth-century Champagne, or the thirteenth-century English exchequer transcripts of the *cartae baronum* of 1166.[49] Other surveys detailed the estates and rents of kings and princes, like the *Debita Regi Navarre* of 1313, drawn up for the count of Bigorre, son of the king of France, or the *Capcio seisine Ducatus Cornubie*, made in 1337 for the king of England's eldest son as duke of Cornwall.[50] Edward I of England (1271–307) undertook one of the most ambitious royal surveys of land tenure and royal rights in 1279–80, perhaps intending to replace Domesday Book as a document of record.[51] In France, inquests into royal rights were a key feature of the extensive administrative reforms of Philip V (1316–22) and Philip VI (1328–50).[52] Surveys of various sorts had analogies throughout the major and minor aristocracy, both religious and secular, by the thirteenth century, and were no longer associated with major estate administrations. Henry de Bray, a minor English landowner, wrote his estate book with his own hand in 1322 as a guide to his heirs.[53]

Besides this increased activity in forms of literate administration that may be regarded as traditional, to some extent, governments of the twelfth and thirteenth centuries added important types of documentation for which there was little medieval precedent, and for which any Roman models had long been lost. Sometimes new administrative departments were created to handle these developments, many of which required the systematic recording of detail, in formalized ways as a continuous annual routine. One such set of innovations derived from the increasing size and complexity of government finance, and the need to supervise receipts and expenditure. No European governments achieved any system as comprehensive as a modern annual budget, drawn up in a single government office, but it nevertheless became usual for all sources of income, and all reasons for expenditure, to be recorded somewhere within the administrative system. These activities are well represented by the functioning of the exchequer of England, which was established in about 1109 for the purpose of auditing the king's income from the shires. The annual accounts or "pipe rolls" that were drawn up in the English exchequer in the course of this procedure were accompanied in the course of time by several supplementary record series, and themselves gave rise to the need for preliminary accounts by sheriffs, keepers of estates, collectors of taxes, and other royal agents in the shires. Sources of royal income that were not collected through the Exchequer were initially accounted for elsewhere, in the king's household, for example.[54] In France the number of surviving royal accounts is much smaller than that from England, but it is enough to demonstrate that by the age of St Louis (1226–70) the *Chambre de comptes* handled multiple accounts from local officers. An inventory of 1328 shows that at that time the *Chambre* had at least 7,000–8,000 accounting documents archived within its collections and considered to be of current significance. There were presumably others of lesser importance. The papal curia had three major series of accounts by the late thirteenth century, the *Introitus et exitus*, the *Collectoriae camerae*, and the *Obligationes et solutiones*.[55] The administrations of some principal noblemen were also early; the county of Flanders has fragmentary accounts from the twelfth century, demonstrating that an annual system of auditing and accounting was in existence by 1187.[56] Accounts of taxation, customs duties, loans, and other receipts and expenditure become critically important for the writing of urban financial, economic, social, and demographic history in this period, particularly for the cities of Italy, Flanders, and Germany.[57] Early surviving examples are from Ypres (1267), Mons (1279), Osnabrück (1285), and Breslau (1299).[58] As with other branches of documentation, the practice of keeping accounts rapidly disseminated into the administration of small towns and private estates, even where the bureaucratic provision was minimal. The institutional households of abbeys, colleges, and hospitals often kept accounts by 1300, and so did private households.[59] The recording of estate incomes in some shape or form, which became widespread, in England took the distinctive form of a standard principle for the detailed recording of income from manors year by year. The bishops of Winchester required detailed annual accounts of their estate income following the election of Bishop Peter des Roches in 1206; the earliest extant roll is from 1208–9.[60]

Another new departure was the recording of litigation in royal, seigniorial, and urban courts. Unlike surveys based on inquests, these were composed in the course of transacting business and were sometimes written or annotated in the course of ongoing litigation. They had the limited purpose of allowing the clerks of the court to keep track of individual cases and to assist the collection of payments due to the court, though in the course of time, where they were preserved, they sometimes came to be used as evidence of royal or seigniorial rights. Because of their ephemeral usefulness, such records have survived only very patchily, but where they are extant they constitute an invaluable source for historians of medieval society. The form of court records depended heavily on the judicial system, the status of the court in question, the composition of its business, and clerical tradition; styles of jurisdiction and styles of recording were two different things, and it pays to examine them separately. But, for all these differences, there was a general need to record procedure and decisions, as the amount of business handled by the busier royal courts increased to the point that memories could no longer cope. Such material is abundant in England, where royal justice was exceptionally extensive; there are vast quantities of documentation from the king's courts from the 1190s onwards.[61] Legal recording was well established in the kingdom of Scotland during the thirteenth century.[62] In France decisions made in *parlement* were recorded at least from the mid-thirteenth century.[63]

There was a similar development of record keeping in ecclesiastical courts at all levels from the papal courts in Rome down to local episcopal and archdeaconry courts.[64] And, as with the development of accounting, these recording practices moved from royal and princely courts down the social scale to local jurisdictions, both urban and rural. England is particularly well provided with records from seigniorial and urban courts.[65]

The categorization of archival forms in this way is no more than an illustration of the ways in which literacy became an essential feature of administrative systems in the twelfth and thirteenth centuries. A complete classification system would have not only to make numerous subdivisions between different types of legal and financial record, but also to include all sorts of other forms in which laws and administrative ordinances, minutes of meetings, reports, correspondence, and memoranda were preserved on parchment and paper sheets in rolls and registers.

As administrations adopted the habit of ongoing administrative record keeping, the practice mushroomed to accommodate different gaps in the system, particularly during the thirteenth century. A centralized system of audited accounts placed heavy pressures on local collectors of rents and taxes to keep presentable records of their activity. Literacy in the legal system similarly extended to the procedures whereby cases were brought before the courts, and to the way in which litigants presented their arguments.[66] Béla IV of Hungary (1235–72) required even top-ranking nobles to initiate business by petitioning his chancellors rather than by word of mouth.[67] The internal needs of government administration also generated copying and recopying. The absence of modern copying systems meant that each document sent out had to be written at least twice if a copy was to be retained. A series of records recording sums of money due annually could imply another series recording sums that remained outstanding. Once information was collected, it was advantageous for it to be made available to different officials in different forms, and this implied the employment of yet more clerks to perform different tasks. Even lengthy administrative records were transcribed more than once to supply copies to the various officials or departments. In the chancery of Frederick II as king of Sicily, all royal orders were written out three times, and financial transactions four times. The issue and receipt rolls of the English Exchequer were kept in triplicate.[68] Some records were not merely copied but re-edited to meet particular needs; the English *originalia* rolls, which originated in the late twelfth century, comprised extracts from chancery records, copied out and passed as information to the exchequer about debts due to the crown.[69] It may be added that the increasing tendency of governments to keep detailed records of its judicial and financial activities created a great incentive for their subjects to do likewise; that was simple self-defence.

Where studies of government bureaucracies exist, they usually show both specialized administrative departments and specialized roles within them, as well as a hierarchy of responsibility. Within the same administration there were different office traditions concerning the form and presentation of documents. There was commonly a tripartite division between a chancery that issued letters, mandates, charters, and other official writings, a finance department for keeping and auditing accounts, and a judicial system administering criminal and civil jurisdiction, though the separations of function were often not rigid; the English Exchequer, besides being the principal auditing department, also acted as a court of law for cases involving the interests of the crown. The divisions, universally apparent in the greater kingdoms, were often replicated in smaller administrations. In thirteenth-century Siena, for example, there was a chancery, headed by a chancellor, with two notaries (in 1262) for writing and sealing letters, registering copies or summaries, and maintaining the commune's archive. There was a finance office, the *Biccherna*, headed by a chamberlain, with subordinate officers and a notary who kept the city accounts in duplicate. There was also a judicial system, headed by the *podestà* and subordinate judges, with its own notarial staff; five volumes of material survive from the year 1298 alone.[70] This said, the rigidity with which office routines were maintained can never be taken for granted, and neither can the formal separation of administrative roles. Alternation between war and peace, for example, was sure to generate a switch in administrative priorities and a reallocation of responsibilities amongst royal servants. Especially in the upper reaches of administrations, roles were often merged or separated quite freely in accordance with different individual abilities, changing political advantages, and the immediate demands of the moment. Nor did government bureaucracy extend far beyond palaces, and the communal headquarters of city populations, into the workings of local administration. The obligations of government were so few that there was little to administer away from the center except government property. The government activity that impinged upon the majority of the population – the administration of justice, the collection of taxes – was either a matter for occasional, ad-hoc intervention or mediated through local lords. For all the interest of its birth and early nurture, bureaucracy as we understand it, even by 1500, had barely left the cradle.

It becomes more difficult to discuss developments in administrative practice after 1350, though the changing fortunes of European states in the fourteenth and fifteenth centuries, and the emergence of new territorial entities like the Italian territorially extended city states, implies considerable change in detail. The difficulties arise partly because, despite an abundance of material, later administrations have attracted less interest from historians. It is also because the main outlines of development were so well established by the early fourteenth century, and so widespread across Europe, that change mostly consisted of local variations in detail, which are laborious to identify, complicated to describe, and difficult to classify, rather than the sort of development that can be outlined simply and systematically as a European phenomenon. The use of the vernacular tended to increase, and paper increasingly supplemented or replaced parchment in the making of records, but these are fairly superficial aspects of ongoing administrative practice. Perhaps the biggest transformation, difficult to pin down but nonetheless pervasive, and of relevance to the history of bureaucracy, was a tendency to increasing formalism in legal instruments, legal recording, and accounting, which often reduced the amount of ad-hoc information that records contain. This could be explained partly by supposing that, once the age of institutional innovation was over, office work became increasingly subject to "routinization." Another explanation may be that, in the late Middle Ages, clerks, like most other sorts of employee, became more expensive, and more difficult to obtain and retain, so that it was more necessary than before to economize on their labor.

The availability of clerks to staff the growing administrative tasks of medieval Europe, as well as to meet occasional needs of ordinary people, depended on an educational system that changed over time. With the collapse of Roman institutions, literacy became largely confined to churchmen educated in bishopric or monastic schools. Kings depended upon ecclesiastical scriptoria for their early experiments in pragmatic literacy, and the earliest royal chancellors were often bishops. The multiplication of schools long depended upon the conversion of Europe, and the founding of bishoprics and monasteries, augmented from the twelfth century by the early growth of universities. Elite institutions of clerical education remained of the greatest importance for the higher branches of administration throughout the Middle Ages. Senior administrators were commonly drawn from the ranks of the upper clergy until well into the early modern period. Cathedral and monastic schools remained important throughout the period; St Paul's School was the most progressive London school of the early sixteenth century. In the course of the twelfth and thirteenth centuries these older educational institutions were not replaced but rather augmented by a wide range of alternatives. As landed families increasingly acquired their own clerical staff, they had the possibility of private education; even a single usefully literate chaplain could tutor members of the household in basic literacy. Opportunities for literacy were also increased by the spread of schools unattached to monasteries and principal churches, even if still in clerical hands, that both provided basic levels of literacy and acted as feeders to more advanced schooling. Towns, in particular, were important in this respect, because of the high value placed on literacy for mercantile, legal, and administrative employment. Eight schools in Milan taught Latin to laymen in 1288, and there were many more schools of other kinds.[71] Even market towns and larger villages acquired schools from the twelfth century onward. In Poland the creation of such schools, though they concentrated on literacy in Polish rather than Latin, accompanied the formation of parishes in the later thirteenth century. In the fifteenth century there were schools in at least one in ten parishes in the diocese of Châlons-sur-Marne.[72] The multiplication of schools permitted a rapid diffusion of literacy into lay society whose extent and quality are impossible to assess with any accuracy, though it was undoubtedly important for social change. It was not all dependent on the teaching of Latin, especially in countries like Italy and France, where the vernacular language had made great strides as the language of administration, commerce, and law by the thirteenth century.[73] But grammar schools that taught Latin remained important for any young man with aspirations, since it was needed for higher education of any sort, or for entry to an ecclesiastical career. In most of Europe, too, Latin texts and documents remained sufficiently numerous to constitute a serious handicap to a clerk whose literacy was restricted to the vernacular. Where Latin remained the normal language of administration, as in England or parts of Eastern Europe, it was more useful than the vernacular. By the fourteenth century a competent English administrator needed French as well.[74] The multiplication of opportunities for acquiring literacy meant that clerks could be reared up from quite humble origins, through higher institutions of education, to positions in government administration. Once there they would have to learn office routines, terminology, phraseology, and scripts, by in-house training.

The expansion of administrative systems with the accompanying increase in record keeping can be seen as an aggressive policy pursued by rulers and landlords in their desire to increase their control over men and resources, and it certainly was that to some extent; indeed, this perception justifies seeing record keeping elsewhere in society as partly a defensive measure. William I of England's decision to commission Domesday Book seems to be such an assertion of control. Yet the pursuit of power cannot be an adequate explanation for bureaucratic development, because it fails to account for the chronology of change across the medieval period; the desire for power and control was not weak in the seventh and eighth centuries, nor in the Gaelic-speaking parts of Ireland and Scotland in the thirteenth, but administrations there operated largely without formal administrative offices or written records.[75] The growth in the territorial size and population of states, and the growth of royal control, will account for the exceptional volume of record keeping in England and France, though that argument too would need qualifying to account for the precocious development of pragmatic literacy in the Italian and Flemish cities, or the parallel development of accounting and jurisdictional material generated by lordships of all sizes; problems of scale will not explain the differences between the management of eleventh-century estates and those of the thirteenth century, since there was no relevant difference in their size. A purely cultural explanation of increasing bureaucracy as a status symbol, though no doubt justifiable in some details of procedure, such as the wording of charters, forms of script, and the design of the seals used to ratify them, fails to do justice to the evident utility of the new developments; thirteenth-century governments could not have operated without them.

In addition to any atavistic desires of administrators for power and status, a rounded explanation for the growth of administration and administrative literacy must take account of their responsiveness to new and far-reaching social and economic changes. The movement "from memory to written record" was a response not only to the ambitions of state-builders for power and status but also to the environment in which they operated. The growth of towns and of local and long-distance trade, the multiplication of monetary transactions, the growing significance of sales and prices for the management of property, the growth of credit and indebtedness, the development of a property market, the widespread replacement of customary social relation in the countryside by contractual tenures, and the growth of litigation concerning commercial, tenurial and property relationships, all worked toward societies in which memory was no longer adequate from one year to the next in determining how the rights should be exercised and how business should be managed. The growth of monetary transactions, largely independent of government control, encouraged the keeping of accounts of all sorts for purely practical reasons. The general growth of civil litigation, which owed more to the growing demands of litigants than to government policies, encouraged the recording of judicial processes. Just as the decline of pragmatic literacy in the early Middle Ages was not simply a response to the waning power of Rome and Constantinople, so its vigorous recovery in the later Middle Ages was more than an adaptation to merely political change.

Notes

1 Jones, *Later Roman Empire*, vol. I, p. 204.

2 Wickham, *Framing the Early Middle Ages*, pp. 86–7, 96–8, 105–17.

3 Bede, *Historia ecclesiastica gentis Anglorum*, ed. Plummer, 2 vols, 2.6; Cheney, *Study of the Medieval Papal Chancery*, pp. 23, 26, 28–9; Noble, "Literacy and Papal Government in Late Antiquity and the Early Middle Ages," pp. 84–94; Scheibelreiter, "Church Structure and Organisation," in *NCMH*, vol. I, pp. 678–9.

4 Tabacco, *Struggle for Power in Medieval Italy*, pp. 84–5.
5 Posner, *Archives in the Ancient World*, p. 217.
6 Chaplais, "The Letter," pp. 3–23.
7 Percival, "The Precursors of Domesday," pp. 5–27.
8 Wormald, "Kings and Kingship," pp. 600–1.
9 Wickham, *Framing the Early Middle Ages*, p. 98.
10 Attenborough, ed., *Laws of the Earliest English Kings*; Sawyer, *From Roman Britain to Norman England*, p. 111.
11 Giry, *Manuel de diplomatique*, pp. 706–13; Nelson, "Rulers and Government," p. 122; Wood, "Administration, Law and Custom," pp. 65–6.
12 Wood, "Administration, Law and Custom," pp. 64–5.
13 Sawyer, *Anglo-Saxon Charters*, pp. 343–46.
14 McKitterick, "Conclusion," p. 323.
15 Giry, *Manuel de diplomatique*, p. 724; McKitterick, *The Frankish Kingdoms under the Carolingians*, pp. 80–5; Nelson, "Kingship and Royal Government," p. 409.
16 Van Caenegem, *Manuel des études médiévales*, p. 134; Nelson, "Literacy in Carolingian Government," pp. 261–2, 264.
17 Nelson, "Kingship and Royal Government," p. 410; Stenton, *Latin Charters of the Anglo-Saxon Period*, p. 37.
18 Harmer, *Anglo-Saxon Writs*; Keynes, "Royal Government and the Written Word in Late Anglo-Saxon England," pp. 231, 244, 247, 257.
19 Nelson, "Kingship and Royal Government," p. 410n.
20 Sergi, "The Kingdom of Italy," pp. 350, 355–6.
21 Bates, "West Francia," p. 416.
22 Keynes, "Royal Government and the Written Word in Late Anglo-Saxon England," pp. 248–55.
23 Guillotel, *Cartulaire de l'abbaye Saint-Sauveur de Redon*, pp. 72–6.
24 Duby, *La Société aux XIe et XIIe siècles dans la région mâconnaise.*
25 Guyotjeannin, Pycke, and Tock, *Diplomatique médiévale*, p. 106; Pasquali, *Agricoltura e società rurale in Romagna nel Medioevo*, p. 165.
26 Osheim, *Italian Lordship*, p. 13.
27 McKitterick, "The Church," pp. 137–8; Blumenthal, "The Papacy," pp. 17–20.
28 Guyotjeannin, Pycke, and Tock, *Diplomatique médiévale*, p. 223.
29 Sawyer, *Anglo-Saxon Charters*, nos 386–458, pp. 165–81.
30 Toynbee, *Constantine Porphyrogenitus and his World*, p. 195.
31 Hitti, *History of the Arabs*, pp. 527, 529.
32 Clanchy, *From Memory to Written Record*, pp. 44–80.
33 Britnell, "Pragmatic Literacy in Latin Christendom," p. 8.
34 Helle, "The Norwegian Kingdom," pp. 381–2; Lindkvist, "King and Provinces in Sweden," pp. 227–8; Schück, "Chancery," p. 72; Várdy, *Historical Dictionary of Hungary*, p. 187.
35 For the papal chancery, see Cheney, *Study of the Medieval Papal Chancery*; Herde, *Beiträge zum päpstlichen Kanzlei- und Urkundenwesen im 13 Jahrhundert.*
36 Cheney, *Study of the Medieval Papal Chancery*, p. 15.
37 Clanchy, *From Memory to Written Record*, pp. 68–71; Prestwich, "English Government Records," pp. 98–9.
38 Burns, *Society and Documentation in Crusader Valencia*, p. 159; Guyotjeannin, "French Manuscript Sources," p. 63.
39 Guyotjeannin, Pycke, and Tock, *Diplomatique médiévale*, p. 223.
40 Haas and Hall, eds, *Early Registers of Writs*, no. 87, pp. xi–xxii.

41 e.g. Clanchy, *From Memory to Written Record*, pp. 145–72; Aston, "Muniment Rooms and their Fittings in Medieval and Early Modern England," pp. 235–47.
42 Clanchy, *From Memory to Written Record*, pp. 101–2; Davis, *Medieval Cartularies of Great Britain*, pp. xi–xvi; Guyotjeannin, Pycke, and Tock, *Diplomatique médiévale*, pp. 277–86.
43 Cheney, *Study of the Medieval Papal Chancery*, p. 18.
44 Abulafia, *The Two Italies*, pp. 12–13; Bonvesin de la Riva, *De magnalibus Mediolani*, pp. 64–5; Guyotjeannin, "French Manuscript Sources," p. 52.
45 Clanchy, *From Memory to Written Record*, pp. 68–9; Simpson, *History of the Land Law*, pp. 122–5.
46 Guyotjeannin, "French Manuscript Sources," pp. 52–3.
47 Groten, "Civic Record Keeping in Cologne," p. 83, and North, "Records of Lübeck and Hamburg," pp. 89–93.
48 Douglas and Greenaway, eds, *English Historical Documents*, vol. II: *1042–1189*, pp. 875–84; Fossier, *Polyptiques et censiers*, pp. 33–43.
49 Van Caeneghem, *Manuel des études médiévales*, pp. 145–7; Davis, "Domesday Book," p. 24; Guyotjeannin, "French Manuscript Sources," p. 54.
50 Hull, ed., *The Caption of Seisin of the Duchy of Cornwall.*
51 Raban, *Second Domesday?*
52 Jones, "The Last Capetians and Early Valois Kings," pp. 410–11.
53 Willis, *The Estate Book of Henry de Bray*, p. 3.
54 Chrimes, *Introduction to the Administrative History of Medieval England*, pp. 50–66, 135–38; Galbraith, *Introduction to the Use of the Public Records*, pp. 41–5.
55 Van Caenegem, *Manuel des études médiévales*, p. 152.
56 Ibid., p. 154.
57 e.g. Blanshei, *Perugia*; Bowsky, *The Finance of the Commune of Siena*; Fiumi, *Demografia urbanistica in Prato.*
58 Marez and Sagher, eds, *Comptes de la ville d'Ypres*; Van Caenegem, *Manuel des études médiévales*, p. 157; Piérard, ed., *Les Plus Anciens Comptes de la ville de Mons.*
59 e.g. Highfield, ed., *Early Rolls of Merton College, Oxford*; Woolgar, ed., *Household Accounts from Medieval England.*
60 Harvey, *Manorial Records*, pp. 25–40; Vincent, "The Origins of the Winchester Pipe Rolls," pp. 25–42.
61 Galbraith, *Introduction to the Use of the Public Records*, pp. 45–51; Public Record Office, *Guide to the Contents of the Public Record Office*, vol. I, pp. 114–38.
62 Barrow, "The Pattern of Non-Literary Manuscript Production," p. 139.
63 Guyotjeannin, "French Manuscript Sources," p. 65.
64 Swanson, "*Universis Christi fidelibus*," p. 150; Poos, ed., *Lower Ecclesiastical Jurisdiction in Late-Medieval England.*
65 Harvey, *Manorial Records*, pp. 41–53; Martin, "English Town Records," pp. 123–25; Razi and Smith, eds, *Medieval Society and the Manor Court.*
66 e.g. Arlinghaus, "From 'Improvised Theatre' to Scripted Roles," pp. 215–37.
67 Cheney, *Study of the Medieval Papal Chancery*, p. 32.
68 Dunbabin, *Charles I of Anjou*, p. 23; Prestwich, "English Government Records," p. 100.
69 Chrimes, *Introduction to the Administrative History of Medieval England*, p. 75.
70 Waley, *Siena and the Sienese in the Thirteenth Century*, pp. 59–64.
71 Bonvesin de la Riva, *De magnalibus Mediolani*, pp. 66–7.
72 Verger, "Schools and Universities."
73 Britnell, "Pragmatic Literacy in Latin Christendom," pp. 18–23.

74 Clanchy, *From Memory to Written Record*, pp. 197–200, 207–11.
75 Britnell, *Britain and Ireland*, pp. 276–77, 484.

Bibliography

Primary Sources

Attenborough, F. L., ed., *The Laws of the Earliest English Kings* (Cambridge: Cambridge University Press, 1922).

Bede, *Historia ecclesiastica gentis Anglorum*, ed. Charles Plummer, 2 vols (Oxford: Clarendon Press, 1896).

Bonvesin de la Riva, *De magnalibus Mediolani*, ed. Maria Corti (Milan: Bompiani, 1974).

Douglas, David C., and Greenaway, George W., eds, *English Historical Documents*, vol. II: *1042–1189*, 2nd edn (London: Eyre and Spottiswood, 1981).

Guillotel, Hubert, et al., eds, *Cartulaire de l'abbaye Saint-Sauveur de Redon* (Rennes: Asssociation des Amis des Archives historiques du diocèse de Rennes, Dol et Saint-Malo, 1998).

Haas, Elsa de, and Hall, G. D. G., eds, *Early Registers of Writs* (London: Selden Society, 1970).

Highfield, J. R. L., ed., *The Early Rolls of Merton College, Oxford* (Oxford: Oxford Historical Society, 1964).

Hull, P. L., ed., *The Caption of Seisin of the Duchy of Cornwall (1337)* (Torquay: Devon and Cornwall Record Society, 1971).

Mares, G. des, and Sagher, E. de, eds, *Comptes de la ville d'Ypres de 1267 à 1329*, 2 vols (Brussels: Kiessling et cie, P. Imbreghts, successeur, 1909–13).

Piérard, Christiane, ed., *Les plus anciens comptes de la ville de Mons, 1279–1356*, 2 vols (Brussels: Palais des Académies, 1971–3).

Poos, L. R., ed., *Lower Ecclesiastical Jurisdiction in Late-Medieval England* (Oxford: British Academy, 2001).

Willis, Dorothy, ed., *The Estate Book of Henry de Bray*, ed. D. Willis (London: Camden Society, 3rd ser., 1916).

Woolgar, C. M. ed., *Household Accounts from Medieval England*, 2 vols (Oxford: British Academy, 1992).

Secondary Sources

Abulafia, David, *The Two Italies* (Cambridge: Cambridge University Press, 1977).

Arlinghaus, Franz-Josef, "From 'Improvised Theatre' to Scripted Roles: Literacy and Changes in Communication in North Italian Law Courts (Twelfth–Thirteenth Centuries)," in Karl Heidecker, ed., *Charters and the Use of the Written Word in Medieval Society* (Turnhout: Brepols, 2000), pp. 215–37.

Aston, Trevor, "Muniment Rooms and Their Fittings in Medieval and Early Modern England," in R. Evans, ed., *Lordship and Learning: Studies in Memory of Ralph Evans* (Woodbridge: Boydell Press, 2004), pp. 235–47.

Barrow, Geoffrey W. S., "The Pattern of Non-Literary Manuscript Production and Survival in Scotland, 1200–1330," in Richard H. Britnell, ed., *Pragmatic Literacy, East and West, 1200–1330* (Woodbridge: Boydell Press, 1997), pp. 131–45.

Bates, David, "West Francia: The Northern Principalities," in *New Cambridge Medieval History (NCMH)*, vol. III, pp. 398–419.

Blanshei, Sarah R., *Perugia, 1260–1340: Conflict and Change in a Medieval Urban Society* (Philadelphia: American Philosophical Society, 1976).
Blumenthal, Uta-Renate, "'The Papacy', 1024–1132," in *NCHM*, vol. IV (ii), pp. 8–37.
Bowsky, William M., *The Finance of the Commune of Siena* (Oxford: Clarendon Press, 1970).
Britnell, Richard H., ed., *Pragmatic Literacy, East and West, 1200–1330* (Woodbridge: Boydell Press, 1997).
Britnell, Richard H., "Pragmatic Literacy in Latin Christendom," in Richard H. Britnell, ed., *Pragmatic Literacy, East and West, 1200–1330* (Woodbridge: Boydell Press, 1997), pp. 3–24.
Britnell, Richard H., *Britain and Ireland, 1050–1530: Economy and Society* (Oxford: Oxford University Press, 2004).
Burns, Robert I., *Society and Documentation in Crusader Valencia* (Princeton: Princeton University Press, 1985).
Chaplais, Pierre, "The Letter from Bishop Wealdhere of London to Archbishop Brihtwold of Canterbury: The Earliest Original 'Letter Close' Extant in the West," in M. B. Parkes and Andrew G. Watson, eds, *Medieval Scribes, Manuscripts and Libraries: Essays Presented to N. R. Ker* (London: Scolar Press, 1978), pp. 3–23.
Cheney, C. R., *The Study of the Medieval Papal Chancery* (Glasgow: Jackson, 1966).
Chrimes, S. B., *An Introduction to the Administrative History of Medieval England* (Oxford: Blackwell, 1959).
Clanchy, M. T., *From Memory to Written Record: England 1066–1307*, 2nd edn (Oxford: Blackwell, 1993).
Davis, G. R. C., *Medieval Cartularies of Great Britain: A Short Catalogue* (London: Longmans, Green and Co., 1958).
Davis, R. H. C., "Domesday Book: Continental Parallels," in J. C. Holt, ed., *Domesday Studies* (Woodbridge: Boydell Press, 1987), pp. 15–39.
Duby, Georges, *La Société aux XIe et XIIe siècles dans la région mâconnaise* (Paris: Armand Colin, 1953).
Dunbabin, Jean, *Charles I of Anjou: Power, Kingship and State-Making in Thirteenth-Century Europe* (London: Longman, 1998).
Fiumi, Enrico, *Demografia urbanistica in Prato* (Florence: Leo S. Olschki, 1968).
Fossier, Robert, *Polyptiques et censiers* (Turnhout: Brepols, 1978).
Galbraith, V. H., *An Introduction to the Use of the Public Records* (London: Oxford University Press, 1934), pp. 45–51.
Giry, A., *Manuel de diplomatique* (Paris: Hachette, 1894).
Groten, Manfred, "Civic Record Keeping in Cologne, 1250–1330", in Richard H. Britnell, ed., *Pragmatic Literacy, East and West, 1200–1330* (Woodbridge: Boydell Press, 1997), pp. 81–8.
Guyotjeannin, Olivier, "French Manuscript Sources", in Richard H. Britnell, ed., *Pragmatic Literacy, East and West, 1200–1330* (Woodbridge: Boydell Press, 1997), pp. 51–71.
Guyotjeannin, Olivier, Pycke, Jacques, and Tock, Benoît-Michel, *Diplomatique médiévale* (Turnhout: Brepols, 1993).
Harmer, F. E., *Anglo-Saxon Writs* (Manchester: Manchester University Press, 1952; repr. Stamford: Paul Watkins, 1989).
Harvey, P. D. A., *Manorial Records*, rev. edn (London: British Records Association, 1999).
Helle, Knut, ed., *The Cambridge History of Scandinavia*, vol. I: *Prehistory to 1520* (Cambridge: Cambridge University Press, 2003).
Helle, Knut. "The Norwegian Kingdom: Succession Disputes and Consolidation," in Knut Helle, ed., *The Cambridge History of Scandinavia*, vol. I: *Prehistory to 1520* (Cambridge: Cambridge University Press, 2003), pp. 369–91.

Herde, Peter, *Beiträge zum päpstlichen Kanzlei- und Urkundenwesen im 13 Jahrhundert* (Munich: Kallmunz, 1961).

Hitti, Philip K., *History of the Arabs*, 10th edn (London: Macmillan, 1970).

Jones, A. H. M., *The Later Roman Empire, 284–602*, 4 vols (Oxford: Blackwell, 1964).

Jones, Michael, "The Last Capetians and Early Valois Kings, 1314–1364," in *NCMH*, vol. VI, pp. 388–421.

Keynes, Simon, "Royal Government and the Written Word in Late Anglo-Saxon England," in Rosamund McKitterick, ed., *The Uses of Literacy in Early Medieval Europe* (Cambridge: Cambridge University Press, 1990), pp. 226–57.

Kittell, Ellen, *From* Ad hoc *to Routine: A Case Study in Medieval Bureaucracy* (Philadelphia: University of Pennsylvania Press, 1991).

Lindkvist, Thomas, "King and Provinces in Sweden," in Knut Helle, ed., *The Cambridge History of Scandinavia*, vol. I: *Prehistory to 1520* (Cambridge: Cambridge University Press, 2003), pp. 221–34.

McKitterick, Rosamond, *The Frankish Kingdoms under the Carolingians* (London: Longman, 1983).

McKitterick, Rosamond, "Conclusion," in Rosamund McKitterick, ed., *The Uses of Literacy in Early Medieval Europe* (Cambridge: Cambridge University Press, 1990), pp. 319–33.

McKitterick, Rosamond, ed., *The Uses of Literacy in Early Medieval Europe* (Cambridge: Cambridge University Press, 1990).

McKitterick, Rosamond, "The Church," in *NCMH*, vol. III, pp. 137–8.

Martin, Geoffrey, "English Town Records, 1200–1350," in Richard H. Britnell, ed., *Pragmatic Literacy, East and West, 1200–1330* (Woodbridge: Boydell Press, 1997), pp. 119–30.

Nelson, Janet L. "Literacy in Carolingian Government," in Rosamund McKitterick, ed., *The Uses of Literacy in Early Medieval Europe* (Cambridge: Cambridge University Press, 1990), pp. 258–96.

Nelson, Janet L. "Kingship and Royal Government," in *NCMH*, vol. II, pp. 383–430.

Nelson, Janet L. "Rulers and Government," in *NCMH*, vol. III, pp. 95–129.

New Cambridge Medieval History (*NCMH*), ed. P. Fouracre et al., 7 vols in 8 parts (Cambridge: Cambridge University Press, 1995–2005).

Noble, Thomas F. X., "Literacy and the Papal Government in Late Antiquity and the Early Middle Ages," in Rosamond McKitterick, ed., *The Uses of Literacy in Early Mediaeval Europe* (Cambridge: Cambridge University Press, 1990), pp. 82–133.

North, Michael, "Records of Lübeck and Hamburg, *c.* 1250–1330," in Richard H. Britnell, ed., *Pragmatic Literacy, East and West, 1200–1330* (Woodbridge: Boydell Press, 1997), pp. 89–93.

Osheim, Duane J., *An Italian Lordship: The Bishopric of Lucca in the Late Middle Ages* (Berkeley and Los Angeles: University of California Press, 1977).

Pasquali, Gianfranco, *Agricoltura e società rurale in Romagna nel Medioeve* (Bologna: Pàtron, 1984).

Percival, John, "The Precursors of Domesday: Roman and Carolingian Land Registers," in Peter H. Sawyer, ed., *Domesday Book: A Reassessment* (London: Edward Arnold, 1985), pp. 5–27.

Posner, Ernst, *Archives in the Ancient World* (Cambridge, MA: Harvard University Press, 1972).

Prestwich, Michael, "English Government Records," in Richard H. Britnell, ed., *Pragmatic Literacy, East and West, 1200–1330* (Woodbridge: Boydell Press, 1997), pp. 95–106.

Public Record Office. *Guide to the Contents of the Public Record Office*, 2 vols (London: Her Majesty's Stationery Office, 1963).

Pulsiano, Phillip, ed., *Medieval Scandinavia: An Encyclopedia* (New York: Garland, 1993).

Raban, Sandra, *A Second Domesday? The Hundred Rolls of 1279–80* (Oxford: Oxford University Press, 2004).

Razi, Zvi, and Smith, Richard, eds, *Medieval Society and the Manor Court* (Oxford: Clarendon Press, 1996).

Sawyer, Peter H., *Anglo-Saxon Charters: An Annotated Bibliography* (London: Royal Historical Society, 1968).

Sawyer, Peter H., ed., *Domesday Book: A Reassessment* (London: Edward Arnold, 1985).

Sawyer, Peter H., *From Roman Britain to Norman England*, 2nd edn (London: Routledge, 1998).

Scheibelreiter, Georg, "Church Structure and Organisation," *NCMH*, vol. I, pp. 678–9.

Schück, Herman, "Chancery," in Phillip Pulsiano, ed., *Medieval Scandinavia: An Encyclopedia* (New York: Garland, 1993), pp. 71–2.

Sergi, Giuseppe, "The Kingdom of Italy," in *NCMH*, vol. III, pp. 346–71.

Simpson, A. W. B., *A History of the Land Law*, 2nd edn (Oxford: Clarendon Press, 1986).

Stenton, F. M., *The Latin Charters of the Anglo-Saxon Period* (Oxford: Clarendon Press, 1955).

Swanson, Robert, "*Universis Christi fidelibus*: The Church and its Record," in Richard H. Britnell, ed., *Pragmatic Literacy, East and West, 1200–1330* (Woodbridge: Boydell Press, 1997), pp. 147–64.

Tabacco, Giovanni, *The Struggle for Power in Medieval Italy: Structures of Political Rule*, trans. R. B. Jensen (Cambridge: Cambridge University Press, 1989).

Toynbee, Arnold, *Constantine Porphyrogenitus and his World* (London: Oxford University, 1973).

Van Caenegem, Raoul C., *Manuel des études médiévales: Typologie des sources*, new edn (Turnhout: Brepols, 1997).

Várdy, Steven B., *Historical Dictionary of Hungary* (Lanham, MD: Scarecrow Press, 1997).

Verger, Jacques, "Schools and Universities," in *NCMH*, vol. VII, p. 226.

Vincent, Nicholas, "The Origins of the Winchester Pipe Rolls," *Archives*, 21 (1994), pp. 25–42.

Vincent, Nicholas, "Why 1199? Bureaucracy and Enrolment under John and His Contemporaries," in Adrian Jobson, ed., *English Government in the Thirteenth Century* (Woodbridge: Boydell Press, 2004), pp. 17–48

Waley, Daniel, *Siena and the Sienese in the Thirteenth Century* (Cambridge: Cambridge University, 1991).

Wickham, Chris, *Framing the Early Middle Ages: Europe and the Mediterranean, 400–800* (Oxford: Oxford University Press, 2005).

Wood, Ian, "Administration, Law and Custom in Merovingian Gaul," in Rosamund McKitterick, ed., *The Uses of Literacy in Early Medieval Europe* (Cambridge: Cambridge University Press, 1990), pp. 63–81.

Wormald, Patrick, "Kings and Kingship," in *NCMH*, vol. I, pp. 571–604.

Further Readings

Historians of government and politics vary greatly in the amount of attention they pay to administration. Contributors to the *New Cambridge Medieval History*, ed. P. Fouracre et al., 7 vols in 8 parts (Cambridge: Cambridge University Press, 1995–2005), are sometimes helpful, and usually supply useful bibliographies. For the early Middle Ages there is up-to-date information in Chris Wickham, *Framing the Early Middle Age: Europe and the Mediterranean, 400–800* (Oxford: Oxford University Press, 2005). The Carolingian period is well served by Rosamond McKitterick, ed., *The Uses of Literacy in Early Medieval Europe* (Cambridge:

Cambridge University Press, 1990), and the period around 1300 by Richard H. Britnell, ed., *Pragmatic Literacy, East and West, 1200–1330* (Woodbridge: Boydell Press, 1997). A detailed case study of later medieval development, covering the period 1262–1372, is Ellen Kittell, *From* "Ad Hoc" *to Routine: A Case Study in Medieval Bureaucracy* (Philadelphia: University of Pennsylvania Press, 1991). For specialized studies of the long-term development of bureaucracy and literacy in England, see S. B. Chrimes, *An Introduction to the Administrative History of Medieval England* (Oxford: Blackwell, 1959), and M. T. Clanchy, *From Memory to Written Record: England 1066–1307*, 2nd edn (Oxford: Blackwell, 1993).

Chapter Twenty-one

The Practice of War

Clifford J. Rogers

Hell, we are told in *Revelation*, enters the world preceded by four outriders. The first is war, specifically war of conquest. The second is also war – internal war. The third is famine, but famine of a particular sort that leaves supplies of wine and oil unharmed. This may allude to Deuteronomy 20: 19, in which the Israelites are commanded not to harm the fruit trees when they besiege a city, and to Micah 6: 14–15, in which the people go hungry and oil and wine are given up to the sword. The third horseman, in other words, is the famine that oppresses the poor in the wake of war. The fourth rider is death.

Medieval warriors sometimes paid lip-service to the joys of peace, but still often looked forward with enthusiasm to the prospect of going on campaign.[1] War could bring rich prizes of gold, slaves, or captives, even new towns and lands to rule. War was also colorful and exciting, the very fount of honor and glory, the prime test of manhood and virtue.[2] Yet we must be careful as we study the subject not to forget that war in the Middle Ages was conducted first and foremost simply by inflicting harm, suffering, and misery upon the enemy's population. The fourteenth-century English soldier Walter Strael was sufficiently useful to the crown to be able to obtain a pardon for having committed

> many murders, larcenies, robberies, and sacrileges, having assaulted towns and fortresses, killed men, women, and children, set fires, raped women and violated maids, burned and destroyed churches, chapels, and monasteries, held men for ransom, ransomed towns and countryside, and done all other evils, crimes, wrongdoings and delicts which he could.[3]

There we have an unvarnished picture of the nature of war in the Middle Ages. For many, and for many of those caught up in its wake, medieval warfare was hell on earth.

Overview

There are inherent problems with trying to tackle a subject like the medieval conduct of war in a short essay. Military structures, practices, and technologies were not static across the era.[4] Change came particularly rapidly in the late Middle Ages. Beowulf's mail shirt, his "war-net woven by the skill of the smith," would still have been familiar to any soldier on a fifteenth-century battlefield, but on the other hand a tenth-century *thegn* would have found a good suit of fifteenth-century Gothic plate armor as wondrous and terrifying as Grendel himself. Similarly, while a charger magically pulled out of the Bayeux Tapestry (*c.* 1080) might have passed muster as a suitable horse for a poor esquire serving in Italy under the infamous mercenary Gattamelata ("the Honeyed Cat") in the fourteenth century, a top-quality destrier of the latter era would have been a jaw-dropping anomaly among the horses of Robert Guiscard or William the Conqueror three centuries earlier. Some historians see the rise of infantry in the fourteenth century and the development of effective gunpowder siege artillery in the mid-fifteenth as "revolutionary" (though others strongly disagree).[5] In addition to changes over time – whether evolutionary or revolutionary – there were also substantial variations in military structures and practices by region: the Irish way of war was quite different from that of the English, the fearsome *almugavars* of Catalonia had no real equivalents among French infantrymen, and so on.[6]

Still, considering the long chronological sweep under consideration, the commonalities are more striking than the differences. Warfare in sixth-century Italy had much in common with warfare in ninth-century France, eleventh-century Spain, or thirteenth-century Prussia. Other than needing to learn how to take full advantage of stirrups, a late Roman auxiliary cavalryman would not have required much adjustment in his skills, equipment, or attitudes to serve as a member of a Carolingian *scara* fighting in eighth-century Saxony, as a Norman knight at Civitate in 1053, as a mounted sergeant of the Kingdom of Jerusalem fighting at Hattin in 1187, or even in the Castilian host that gathered to oppose the Black Prince's army at Nájera in 1367.

In a single short chapter there is, of course, no way to discuss how warfare changed from place to place or century to century; that could hardly be attempted even in a thick book. Bearing in mind the level of generalization employed here, however, it will be possible to give the reader a broad sense of how war was normally conducted in this era.

The first steps in beginning a war were to summon an army, and to develop a plan for how to use it in order to accomplish the political goals that inspired the war. It must be understood, here, that "political" goals are those for which the community is willing to fight together (a definitionally necessary element of "war"): when belligerents are driven by the desire to avenge an insult to a ruling family's honor, or in order to enforce Catholic orthodoxy within a region where heretical beliefs have become widespread, these goals are no less "political" than the intention to seize control over a disputed and strategically located port, or the desire to force foreign raiders to cease their forays. Once a ruler and his principal nobles decided on what sort of war should be waged, against whom, and why, these political leaders normally themselves took in hand the task of raising forces to carry on the military operations decided upon. They then participated themselves in the campaigning, both as fighters and as leaders. Very consistently across the sweep of the Middle Ages, they conducted war using a mix of the same basic tools: ravaging and devastation of the countryside and of ill-fortified towns and manors; formal sieges of stronger places; open field battles; and various forms of "little war," including raids, ambushes, and *coups de main*.[7]

Gathering a Force

Medieval rulers and magnates normally exercised authority over three different but heavily overlapping groups in three different ways. First, they had at their immediate command the men of their households, who were paid, equipped, and fed directly from the lord's treasury. Secondly, they had a group of lesser lords with estates of their own who had done homage and fealty to them, formally recognizing a personal relationship of lordship and dependency. Especially in the high Middle Ages, many of the men of this second group were vassals holding fiefs in return for which they owed military service, and many of those in the first group were their landless sons and brothers. The extent to which such feudal arrangements structured medieval military institutions before the twelfth century is debatable, especially since the publication of Susan Reynolds's impressive *Fiefs and Vassals*. Thirdly, they had their subjects: those who were juridically subject to the territorial authority the lord wielded, either as a sovereign or as the representative of a sovereign. In order to raise an army, kings and princes made use of all these skeins of power.

When a ruler raised an army, his own household troops (reinforced for war) typically formed the core of his mounted forces. Around this core would coalesce a larger body of men-at-arms (armored cavalrymen) made up of contingents led by his vassals, friends, allies, kinsmen, and other supporters, and often supplemented by mercenaries, both horsemen and footmen. Magnates' followings were built up in much the same way as the army as a whole, though on a smaller scale: permanent household troops; freelances hired for the occasion; dependent lords with their retinues; relatives or neighbors who owed no service but welcomed an opportunity to fight, to earn glory, distinction, gratitude, and plunder.

Particularly if the army was being assembled for defensive purposes, it might also include other soldiers who were summoned for service based on their obligations as subjects of a sovereign authority, rather than by the more personal bonds of lordship or other contractual agreement. These forces would typically be led by men holding offices as regional administrators – counts (before that became simply a term for high-level nobles), sheriffs, seneschals, town mayors, and so on. It was widely accepted that every free man had the obligation to serve his king when the homeland was invaded, and by making use of this principle rulers could raise quite large armies.

Of course, "quite large" is a rather vague description. By the thirteenth century we can say with some precision how large at least some armies were, thanks to richer chronicle sources that can sometimes be checked against pay records or other documentary evidence. Before then, the sources are generally less rich, and historians' interpretations of them have varied widely. Some scholars have posited that Charlemagne (*c.* 745–814) may have been able to raise forces as large as 100,000 men; another, John France, concludes that figure is too large by a factor of five, and that a normal "large" Carolingian army would have been "of the order of between a few hundred and 3–5,000."[8] One reason for this wide range of opinion is a related dispute over whether the main power of Frankish armies consisted of armored cavalrymen or common footmen, which in turn is a part of two larger and still fiercely contested debates: first, was there ever truly a period of medieval warfare "dominated" by cavalry, and, secondly, to what extent did late Roman military institutions persist through the period of the Germanic Migrations?[9]

Even for the Norman invasion of England in 1066, which is doubtless the best documented of all medieval campaigns to that point, we cannot say with any certainty even roughly how many men were in the opposing armies, or what proportion of the Conqueror's men were knights. The only contemporary specification of the size of either army is William of Poitiers's claim that Duke William commanded 60,000 men at the battle, but until very recently modern historians have quite consistently estimated both the Conqueror's force and King Harold's at only around 7,000–8,000 combatants. The latest study of the subject, however, now argues that both the English and the Normans may perhaps have numbered in the "tens of thousands."[10] By the time we get into the twelfth century, we are on firmer ground regarding numbers. The organizers of the Fourth Crusade in 1201 planned on leaving Venice with a force of 4,500 knights, 9,000 squires, and 20,000 footmen, but in the end sailed with only around one-third of that strength. Edward III of England led a force of similar size (around 2,700 men-at-arms and 11,000–13,000 other troops) on the field of Crécy in 1346. His adversary, Philip VI of France, pushed the limits of medieval possibility in 1340, when he had an astounding 22,500 men-at-arms (fully armored aristocratic cavalrymen), as well as 2,700 infantrymen, under royal pay in a single field army, in addition to garrisons and field forces in other theaters.[11] Lesser rulers deployed smaller armies, and wars were often carried on by forces numbering in the hundreds or low thousands: the Lithuanians attacked Estonia in 1205 with 2,000 men; the army Hainault sent to aid Namur in 1172 included 680 horsemen and 1,500 foot; Simon de Montfort won the battle of Muret (1213) with under 1,000 cavalry and a few footmen.[12] Even Louis VI of France, in his first campaigns, fought at the head of just 300–500 knights.[13]

One reason for the relatively small size of these forces was that soldiers were normally expected to provide their own gear, including weapons, armor, tents or canopies, and horses. Bows, spears, and shields were cheap, but swords were costly, armor and riding horses more so; proper warhorses represented a level of expenditure far higher still. In the thirteenth century, for example, a knight's horses, arms, and armor could easily cost him the equivalent of six months' pay – which would be something like five *years'* pay for a foot soldier![14] The time required for intensive military training was also very expensive, especially the time investment needed to learn to fight effectively on horseback, in formation, and borne down by the weight of armor. The greater the expense, the fewer men who could bear it. Yet, despite the efforts of some modern historians to downplay their significance, armored cavalrymen were of crucial importance, especially for long-range offensive campaigning. Thus, the elites (interpreted broadly) were called on to participate in warfare much more often than the mass of society. Less wealthy men, especially in the early Middle Ages, were often organized into small groups who together owned as much land as a minor aristocrat, so that one of them could go to the army fully equipped with the help of his neighbors' resources.[15] Later the same end was increasingly accomplished through more centralized and monetized forms of taxation and the hiring of paid troops.

Developing a Strategy

The process of collecting a field army took weeks, allowing plenty of time for its leaders to decide how it should be used once it was fully gathered. Strategic decisions were normally preceded by long discussion and debate; the ruler's chief nobles expected to be consulted and listened to, on military matters just as in other political affairs.

The principal object of strategy was to make submission more attractive than fighting – to persuade your enemy to do your will, whatever that might be. The overall political strategy often involved plenty of carrots, but war was the main stick wielded by diplomacy. Making war was, in the first instance, simply about harming your enemy. Whatever damage you did to him weakened him (making him less of a threat to you) and gave him an incentive to surrender by showing what he could expect if he continued to resist. Hence, for example, when Robert the Wily first began his conquest of Calabria, he ordered his men "to burn, pillage and ravage all those lands which he had invaded, and to do all they could to instill terror in the inhabitants."[16] The amount of pain one belligerent needed to inflict on the other in order to gain his ends depended on a variety of considerations, including the scale of the concessions he was demanding.

It is important to understand that for much of the Middle Ages – until the fourteenth century, perhaps – rulers and their followers could often make war pay for itself, and more than pay for itself, even without factoring in the benefits gained by a favorable peace settlement. The greatest lords, by definition, had many well-armed men who owed them military service. Often, the magnates had "purchased" the service owed at a fixed cost, by the grant of lands or set revenues. Thus the *marginal cost* of going to war was low, from the overlord's perspective; it might even be negative, since lords were often entitled to a share of the plunder and ransoms collected by their men. In any season where the service owed was not "collected," it was simply lost. This made it worthwhile to wage war in pursuit of relatively minor aims, such as the acquisition of a single border castle or even an arrangement that left a disputed town in the hands of its original owner, but converted it from a freehold to a fief.

The other side of that equation is that, from the perspective of an unpaid soldier fulfilling a military obligation, the gross marginal cost of serving remained high. If there was no campaign in a given year, he could retain the money that would otherwise go to purchasing provisions at inflated prices, refurbishing equipment, replacing horses killed or lamed on campaign, and so on. In order to minimize the tension generated by these differences, rulers generally aimed to conduct war in such a way as to make campaigning profitable both for themselves and, especially, for their men. All three of the principal modes of medieval warfare could bring vast rewards to the victors. The attacker had basically three choices of target to go after: the other side's army, or its fortifications, or its countryside. Thus, a campaign might focus on battle, siege, or ravaging. The biggest immediate profits generally came from victorious battles, which meant prisoners to ransom or sell, valuable horses, armor and weapons to seize, and a rich camp to plunder. Looting towns could be comparably rewarding, though few towns could match the wealth concentrated in a major army, which drew together more rich men than could be found in any but the largest cities. General engagements and major sieges, however, also entailed great risks. Moreover, especially between the encastellation of the eleventh century and the artillery revolution of the fifteenth century, the weaker side often had the motive and the ability to avoid battle without giving up hope for victory in the war. If the defender chose to focus on holding his strongholds rather than fighting a general engagement, the attacker would be faced with the prospect of conducting extended sieges. Each such operation meant the certainty of large fixed costs in money and time, and usually also involved significant hardship and suffering, from hunger and exposure to the elements. Thus, an invader might decide to leave the fortified sites alone and go after the farms and villages of the countryside, which could not secure themselves from harm either by flight or, practically, by fortification. Indeed, this would almost always be done in the initial stages of a campaign, even if the strategic plan aimed ultimately at a big battle or siege.

Devastation and Shadowing

Medieval armies moving through enemy territory generally moved on a broad front, frequently as much as twenty or even thirty miles across.[17] The main column or columns would typically move down roads, to accommodate the wagons. These were necessary to carry the tents, cauldrons, and other heavy gear of the men-at-arms, and to sustain a rolling reserve of wine and flour, which served to ensure the troops a steady supply of victuals, rather than leaving their stomachs vulnerable to the fluctuations of pillaging, which might bring in a surfeit one day and nothing the next. Many of the foot soldiers of the army and some of the horsemen would march along with the baggage train and the noncombatants, with small groups of soldiers frequently splitting off to pillage farmsteads or hamlets visible from the road. Well out in front, perhaps a day's march in advance of the main body, would be the "outriders," horsemen who served as scouts and stood off the enemy cavalry, while also participating in the work of destruction. In between these men and the main body would be a cloud of small contingents of cavalry and mounted infantry descending on the villages and farmsteads to forage for supplies and plunder valuables. The troops would then destroy what they had not chosen to remove. Fire was the main tool for this task: it allowed for a great deal of damage to be done with a minimum of time and effort.

If the lord of the area under attack had not been taken completely by surprise, he would probably have his own cavalry in the field, shadowing the invading force. These soldiers would use ambushes and sudden small-scale attacks to impose caution on the enemy outriders and foragers, and could warn the country folk of the danger descending upon them. If they did their work well, the invaders' outriders might encounter only evacuated dwellings, emptied of their inhabitants and of the most valuable and most portable of the goods that normally filled them. A thorough defensive stripping and harassment operation could sometimes starve and ruin an army on the offense. The more rapidly the attackers moved and the less their strike had been anticipated, the more they would find left for them to pillage, and to eat.

Medieval armies therefore often made night marches in order to surprise their enemies. At sunrise, peasants or townsmen heading out to tend their fields or gardens would be seized by the soldiers, bound at the wrists and perhaps the neck, and pulled along behind the riders – if they were not killed outright, which was common (especially for men) in some places and times. Depending on prevailing mores, the captives might be enslaved, or might be ransomed back to those of their friends and kinsmen who had not fallen victim to the raiders. Those who claimed to be unable to produce a suitable ransom might be tortured, raped, mutilated, starved, or beaten. Sometimes they would be allowed to pay their ransom in services, including sexual or military servitude.[18] In order to avoid such abuse, the people of the countryside who were able to do so would, of course, flee to shelter in the nearest fortified place, or, with their livestock, to hiding places in nearby woods or swamps. They might even try seeking safety in a church, but warriors engaged in devastation did not typically respect the right of sanctuary.[19]

Skirmishes and Ambushes

Soldiers could not carry out the work of havoc entirely without risk. Devastation served multiple purposes simultaneously. Plunder both enriched the troops engaged in pillaging and supplied them with victuals. By the same token it impoverished and weakened the enemy. Burning homes, mills, granges, and threshing floors, smashing wine presses, staving in casks, barking fruit trees, and trampling crops also encouraged the victims to submit or negotiate for peace, and, if they did not, deprived them of resources and revenues that otherwise could support their resistance. Ravaging could also be used to push enemies into a particular action, such as giving battle, abandoning an offensive, or lifting a siege. The effectiveness of all these was roughly proportional to the extent of the land laid waste, so effective ravaging required wide dispersal. A small band of ten or twenty men-at-arms and a dozen or two light-armed pillagers was vulnerable to ambushes or sudden strikes launched by the garrisons of individual castles, or by detachments from a field force assigned to shadow and harass an invading army that was too strong to be challenged more directly.

By definition, the skirmishes that arose from such encounters were usually of little significance individually (though there were exceptions, as when an important leader chanced to be killed). Collectively, however, they were of great importance – and deserve much more attention from historians than they have so far been given. The balance of success in these combats could push the flood of devastation in toward the core of the invading army, and even confine it to a narrow channel, or conversely it could let the destruction flow out for dozens of miles. That, in turn, could make the difference between a bedraggled and demoralized column of hungry warriors and bony horses stumbling home without having accomplished anything, and a proud cavalcade of victorious troops, loaded down with plunder and eager to strike again the next campaigning season if the defenders still refused to submit. Even in times and places when footmen were the most important soldiers when it came to open battle, cavalrymen were the key to success in cloud of small combats that determined the overall effectiveness of ravaging operations.

Assaults

Modern parlance generally considers any sort of attack on a fortification to fall under the category of "siege warfare," but a proper siege, as the etymology indicates, involves a "sitting-down" in front of the stronghold to be captured, and can usefully be distinguished from an attempt to seize a place by a simple direct attack. A proper siege typically brought an end to a mobile campaign, but even in the midst of fast-moving ravaging operations fortified positions ranging from stockaded manor houses to walled cities often came under attack. Our modern sense of what a medieval fortress was has been distorted by the passage of time. The castles and town defenses we can still see and touch are the ones built to last for centuries; the many built of timber, earthwork, or adobe brick are now mostly gone.[20] A determined garrison, even if quite small, could hold a first-class fortification against an entire army for a long time. Most defenses did not aspire to such an ambitious role; they aimed only to protect against local threats or small ravaging parties. Such second-class strongholds, often made of timber and earth, would normally be evacuated or surrendered when approached by a full-scale invasion force. Hard fighting was most likely to occur when the outcome of an assault was not obvious in advance: when relatively weak positions were threatened by small detachments.

A man striking down from a rampart against an assailant balanced precariously on a siege ladder had a huge advantage, but still a brisk assault had a reasonable chance of success if the defenders were not hardened warriors, or if the attackers' bowmen could sweep them off the walls. Even if the defenders managed to repulse the first effort to surmount (or burn or undermine) their ramparts, the experience might lead them to negotiate a surrender, rather than face the risks of a second attempt. It is this that explains the apparent paradox of campaigns that see towns and castles falling and being sacked on a daily basis, but culminate in grand sieges lasting months, ultimately without success.

If, however, a minor stronghold managed to hold out for just a day or two, its defenders and all the country folk who had fled to the safety of its walls were likely to escape without harm, other than the damage to their property outside. It would not be worth the time of the main force to mount a regular siege, and detachments could not safely remain behind to do so when the invading army moved on. That point is one of the main explanations for why minor nobles and small towns found it worth the substantial expenses required to construct even second-class enceintes.

Siege Warfare

To acquire control over a region by force – or to compel an enemy to grant a political concession so onerous that only a serious threat of outright conquest would make submission preferable – could sometimes be accomplished principally through repeated campaigns of devastation, which over time could leave the victims with no other choice but starvation. But, so long as a lord kept the strongest fortifications of the region under his control, he could ensure that any would-be conqueror would gain little profit from the occupation of the countryside. To gain lasting and worthwhile control over an area normally, therefore, required the capture of these strong points.[21] During the early Middle Ages, these were principally walled towns, but starting around the turn of the millennium castles strong enough to serve as reservoirs of lordship even against large-scale invasion forces began to proliferate.

In order to take possession of a stronghold, the besieger had to go over, under, or through the walls. The basic difficulty of going over the walls – the difficulty of fighting from a ladder – has already been alluded to, but even to have that perilous opportunity normally required an attacker to pass through a rain of projectiles launched by the defenders: everything from millstones, beehives, solid-iron javelins, pots of blinding quicklime, and burning oil, to arrows, crossbow bolts, and trebuchet stones, to cheap but not-to-be-despised thrown rocks. Launched from above, these missiles benefited from a favorable trajectory and struck with increased force. Before scaling ladders could be planted it was often also necessary to fill a ditch or moat, and perhaps to break through the defenders of an outer palisade. And then, in addition to the missiles launched by the men at the top of the wall, the troops attempting to scale the ramparts would usually be vulnerable to highly effective enfilading fire directed at them from projecting towers. Hence, against a well-constructed and well-manned defense, a simple attempt at escalade usually failed, at least early in a siege. Given sufficient time, the attackers could improve their odds by using stone-throwing engines to weaken the walls by knocking off the elements of superstructure that were designed to protect the defenders atop the ramparts, such as wooden hoardings or stone merlons and machicolations. With a great deal of effort (and substantial risk to their crews) besiegers could also build and move up to the walls giant wooden siege towers. One purpose of these constructions was to provide covered ladders and drawbridges for assault troops, but their main function was to provide firing positions higher than the level of the wall-walk, from which bowmen could use their missiles to keep the defenders from effectively resisting an escalade attempt.

Besiegers occasionally used the same techniques employed in ore mining to bypass defenses from below. Far more commonly, however, mining was used to go not under, but rather through walls. The sappers would tunnel under the base of the walls, but then, rather than pushing the passage to the interior of the stronghold, they would extend their galleries laterally under the fortifications, holding up the masonry with stout wooden beams. The empty space could then be filled with combustibles; once the supports had been burned away, a broad stretch of wall would tumble down. Men with pickaxes could also be sent to undermine a wall directly at its base, rather than under the earth. Of course, the defenders would not simply allow these men to chop away at their walls unmolested. To have any real chance of success, the miners had to be shielded by some sort of mobile shelter made of timber and rawhide, and protected by suppressive fire, preferably – again – from bowmen in a tall siege tower. It was also possible to breach a wall by use of battering rams, though this failed far more often than it succeeded, and rams needed the same sort of protection and support as pickaxe men.

The last major means of demolishing walls was by long-range battery. The main stone-throwing engine of the early and high Middle Ages was the traction trebuchet. The largest of these engines, powered by a crew of dozens or even hundreds pulling simultaneously on a set of ropes attached to the base of the throwing arm, could throw stones weighing as much as a hundred kilograms or more. Smaller versions of the machine were more common. These could fire as many as seventy head-sized stones in an hour, and could effectively batter down wooden palisades or destroy mud-brick walls. It was not until the development of large cannon in the mid-fifteenth century, however, that artillery could rapidly bring down strong walls of heavy masonry.

Until then, it normally took months of labor to prepare the way for an assault with much chance of success. Moreover, the defenders did not have to stand by and watch passively as siege towers were built, batteries set up, and mines dug. They could use sally parties or trebuchets of their own to smash and burn the besiegers' engines; they could reinforce or repair walls from the rear as they were hammered from the front, or build new ramparts a short distance behind a section of wall threatened with breaching; they could dig countermines, break into the besiegers' shafts, and massacre the diggers at their work. And, even if the walls could be breached, or surmounted with the aid of siege towers, the final assault was likely to be costly in men injured and killed. Moreover, if the target of the siege was a walled town, taking it by storm rather than by surrender would usually mean the death of many citizens who otherwise might have become revenue-producing taxpayers, and the destruction of much of their productive capital goods.

The best way to take a town, thus, was to be let in through the gates, whether by surrender, treachery, or some combination of the two. Otto of Freising called the experience of being besieged "the most pitiful fate of all," and every misery of the defenders was a motive for them to end the siege through a negotiated surrender. Right at the start of a siege, the defenders would face the painful experience of having to stand by and watch while their lands outside the walls were burned and destroyed. Once the siege began in earnest, the besiegers, who were normally far more numerous than the defenders, could stage frequent assaults using relays of troops, forcing those inside the stronghold to stand watch after watch, until they grew exhausted. During extended sieges, scarcity of supplies drove food prices up to astronomical levels, which meant sharp hunger and sometimes outright starvation, especially for the poor. Trebuchet stones lobbed over the ramparts day and night might not do much killing, but they added one more constant worry to the lives of those on the receiving end. A greater worry still was the fear that one or another of the assaults on the walls might finally succeed, despite the disadvantages of the attackers. When a fortification was taken by storm, those inside faced a very high risk of death or rape and the near certainty of destitution, even if they survived. Competent besiegers made these threats explicit and repeated them frequently to the defenders, along with promises of good treatment in return for rapid surrender. All war is a continuation of political intercourse; in medieval siege warfare, this fact was often very much to the fore. The large majority of successful sieges, indeed, ended through a political process of negotiation, rather than through an assault. The negotiations, however, were heavily influenced by the military action that accompanied them, and a primary purpose of the attacks on the town was to press the defenders towards surrender.

It is impossible to say with any sort of precision what proportion of all sieges did end in success for the besiegers, but it is certainly the case that a great many did not. In general, when a commander began a formal siege, he invested a significant amount of his prestige in its success, so normally sieges were not abandoned lightly. Still, the leaders often had no choice but to break off their efforts, when money ran out, when the troops fulfilled their service obligations and could not be persuaded to stay on, when epidemic disease broke out in the siege camps, when food supplies became insufficient, or when a crisis at home (such as a rebellion or a counter-invasion) demanded their attention and their presence elsewhere. Sometimes the defenders could take advantage of surprise, and of the dispersed perimeter that the conduct of a proper siege normally required, to sally out and inflict such damage on the besiegers as to make the continuation of the operation impractical. Finally, many sieges failed because a relief army approached, and either defeated the besiegers in battle, or drove them off with the threat of a battle they thought they would not win.

Battle

The role and importance of battle in medieval warfare have been much debated among specialists. Campaigns of devastation (without battle) and sieges played a much larger role in medieval warfare than in modern times; that leaves a smaller slice of the importance pie for battle. In that sense, battle was of relatively low importance in medieval warfare.[22] But "relatively" is a key word there, for battle was still of very great importance indeed. Just as the practice of devastation was of great importance even in campaigns focused on siege or battle, so the *possibility* of battle was one of the most important considerations that shaped how any siege or ravaging-oriented operation would be conducted. For example, when David I of Scotland, who had been laying waste the north of England in 1138, got word of an English army approaching from the south, he pulled in his troops and his army retreated to his own kingdom. Once the English army had withdrawn from the area, the Scots launched a new campaign of devastation, advancing nearly to Durham. But then, at a new report of an approaching enemy force, the raiders again fell back nearly to the Scottish border, and began a siege of Norham.[23] It was the threat of battle – and especially his awareness that the English had a decisive advantage in armored heavy cavalry – that drove his actions.

Medieval armies typically comprised three principal classes of combatant: bowmen, heavy infantry, and cavalry. Commanders arraying their forces for battle took into account the terrain and the enemy, but a fairly typical deployment was to position the heavy infantry in the center of the main battle line, with the cavalry on the flanks and the bowmen in front. Another fairly common arrangement was for the horse to be stationed behind the foot. In this deployment, the infantry basically served as a shield from behind which the horsemen could charge like the strike of a flashing sword. When circumstances or terrain led commanders to choose to array their divisions in one line (rather than in three or more successive lines), they kept a small reserve, which would normally be positioned in the rear.

For cavalry and infantry alike, the principal key to tactical success was to maintain a well-ordered formation.[24] In the case of heavy infantry, this gave a major advantage to the side that stood on the defense, especially if it was stationed on rising ground. Keeping ranks and files even and properly spaced while advancing was difficult, but not impossible. Each of the small units that composed a battle line formed up with reference to the banner of its commander, and each soldier was enjoined to take careful note of where he was supposed to be with respect to it. Marching slowly and frequently looking to his banner to check his position, a soldier could manage the trick. If not, if some soldiers got out of line with the others, then, when the disordered force struck the well-ordered stationary one, there would be a number of places along the line where the individual men found themselves having to fight two enemies at once, a very dangerous proposition. This could also happen if one side simply formed less densely than another, so that on a given frontage it had fewer men. To prevent this from happening, medieval infantry normally formed up in very close array, with shield rims touching or overlapping. This, however, posed another danger – a less common but more deadly form of loss of order. Under certain circumstances, tightly arrayed footmen could find their formations compressed to the point where the press of bodies prevented soldiers from fighting effectively. Once that happened (as, for example, at Agincourt in 1415) further attacks from the other side were likely to cause even further compression, and very large numbers might die, trampled, smothered, suffocated, crushed.[25]

That horrendous situation normally emerged only when the destroyed formation was pressed from the rear as well as from the front, either by a "reinforcing" body or by an enveloping cavalry force. Mounted attacks were, of course, especially effective when directed against an enemy's flank or rear. Horsemen could and sometimes did also charge directly at the front of an infantry wall; despite what many historians have written, a well-trained war stallion *could* be ridden right into a line of men – such an impact is clearly described, for example, in more than one account of the battle of Bannockburn (1314).[26] Often, when footmen saw the cavalry close enough and moving fast enough that it would not be able to stop or turn before impact, they would get out of its way, breaking their own formation and bringing success to the horsemen. If the infantrymen stood their ground, and were armed with suitable pole-arms, the horse would probably impale itself, which might or might not allow the footmen to survive its impact.

More often, cavalry was used at the start of a combat to fight other cavalry, while infantry fought infantry. When horsemen charged each other, they could do so either in closed order (stirrup to stirrup) or in open order (with a horse-width gap between each rider and the next). The latter method was probably somewhat more common. When two lines in open order charged each other, the formations would pass through each other, the passage being composed of as many individual jousts as there were combatants on each side. Some would be struck down; the others would slow, circle, rally to their banners, and charge back in the opposite direction, then repeat the process either until one side broke or until the two groups lost their impetus and halted in a mass to exchange blows from standing horses (as often depicted in medieval manuscript illuminations). When lines in closed order charged each other, unless one side panicked well before contact, the formations would almost inevitably slow to a walk before they reached each other, then fight it out blade to blade and horse to horse.

Since horsemen generally fought in thinner formations, and moved to contact much more rapidly, it was common for the cavalry battle on the flanks to be decided while the infantry fight in the center was still far from resolution. That then allowed the victorious mounted men to turn in at the flanks and rear of the enemy footmen, though they sometimes pursued the fugitive riders or pushed on to plunder the enemy camp instead of doing so. If they resisted those temptations, however, they would almost always bring their side victory in the battle, since few infantry formations could withstand cavalry attacks in the rear while simultaneously fighting in the front. Thus, winning the mounted fight was typically the key to winning a battle, at least until the very end of the thirteenth century. In the following decades, a series of remarkable victories won by armies fighting entirely on foot – from Stirling Bridge (1296), Courtrai (1302), and Morgarten (1315) to Laupen (1339) and Crécy (1346) – demonstrated that, when properly handled and fighting on suitable terrain, good infantry could not only withstand a cavalry charge, but even defeat and (under the right circumstances) destroy a mounted force.[27]

Still, a force superior in horsemen could usually minimize the severity of a defeat, even if circumstances or bad leadership prevented it from winning a victory. Normally a large proportion of the losses suffered by the defeated side were suffered during the pursuit, rather than during the face-to-face fighting. The nature of medieval combat, especially between well-armored combatants, meant that, so long as the struggle continued, far more men were wounded than were killed outright. Most of the wounded on the winning side would have their wounds washed with wine (an effective antimicrobial) and bandaged, and would recover. On the losing side, by contrast, a large portion of the wounded were likely to be captured or killed after the battle had been decided if the victors launched a vigorous pursuit, even over a short distance. For this reason, the final casualty totals in medieval battles were often very lopsided.[28]

Little War and Private War

The medieval practice of war comprised much more than full-scale campaigns in which substantial armies took the field, ravaged enemy lands, conducted major sieges, and sometimes fought general engagements. Much warfare took place on a smaller scale, in the form of raids, ambushes, and *coups de main* undertaken by single garrisons, the retinues of individual lords, or small forces collected from several neighboring strongholds. Such operations could be part of a larger war, or could constitute small wars themselves, for it was not until the late Middle Ages (and not fully even then) that war making was reserved to sovereign authorities. A minor baron could declare war on a neighboring lord, on a town, even on a monastery. Depending on time and place, the prosecution of such a conflict might closely resemble a national war, though on a smaller scale, or it might be restricted to a more limited style of fighting, excluding the burning of property or attacks on noncombatants.[29]

The most common forms of small war action were raids and rescues. Frontier troops in wartime had, in effect, a permanent license and constant opportunity to rob and kidnap. Not only were they allowed to engage in these profitable but normally illicit activities, they were expected to, and successful raids brought captains praise both from their men and from their lords. Even more than in larger-scale campaigns of devastation, surprise and rapid movement were key to effective raids. It was important to raise and concentrate the force, and to move into enemy territory as far as possible, without the enemy learning of the operation. Thus, the first stages – the rendezvous and the initial drive over the frontier – were very often done at night. At the break of dawn, the raiders could scatter, collect booty, inflict damage on their enemies, and regroup before the local defenders could rally sufficient strength to oppose them. Getting their plunder home again without fighting was more problematic: the cattle, prisoners, and booty wagons could not move nearly as fast as horsemen rushing to recover the captured people and property, nor even as fast as hard-marching infantry. Hard fighting was likely to ensue if the rescue force caught up with the reivers. There were at least three such fights recorded, for example, in the *Annals of Connacht* for just the year 1416. In two of them, the leaders of the raiding parties were killed. In the third, the rescue force pressed the retreating raiders hard until the latter met the footmen they had left waiting for them; then together they turned on their pursuers and defeated them, killing fifty men.[30]

As with full-scale campaigns of devastation, raids served the dual purpose of, on the one hand, enriching the raiders, and, on the other hand, weakening the lords of the victims, and putting pressure on them to grant the political concessions sought by war. Even when they were nominally part of a larger war effort, however, raiding attacks were often made less for their own sake than as instruments of local extortion. A major preoccupation of garrison soldiers was typically the extraction of protection money or "peace money" from the inhabitants of nearby towns and villages, and payments for safe conducts from merchants and other travelers passing through their area. Those who refused or hesitated to pay were punished by destructive strikes, ambushes, and kidnappings until they came to an agreement with the soldiers. It was more efficient to get the peasants and townsmen to plunder themselves than to do it directly, and was less likely to kill the golden goose.

When it could be done, garrison soldiers also found it very profitable to seize castles and fortified towns from the enemy. Single garrisons, even groups of garrisons, rarely had enough strength to mount regular sieges, so such attempts usually rested on opportunities created by surprise, deception, treason, or some combination of the three. Robert the Wily, for example, captured his first real stronghold by disguising his soldiers as members of a funeral procession. The Black Douglas retook his ancestral castle from an English garrison by attacking the unsuspecting men while they were in church, outside the walls, for Palm Sunday.[31] Any number of places were captured even more simply, by ladders laid against the wall in the dead of night. Such attacks were very effective if a proper watch was not maintained, and to maintain a proper density of sentinels required a great investment of manpower.

Another way to capture a fortress without a formal siege, or simply to be rid of a troublesome garrison, was to lure the defenders out from behind their walls and into a trap. A typical gambit was to set a cavalry force in ambush, then have a small body of troops herd captured peasants and plundered livestock down a road within sight of the targeted garrison's watchtowers. If a pursuit force tried to recover the booty, the strike force would let them pass, then break from cover and charge into them from the rear. Opportunistic ambushes, set up without specific targets in mind, were also very common. Again, as with raids, all these various forms of small-war action served to sustain and enrich the soldiers who undertook them while reducing the enemy's strength and will to continue the struggle. Minor actions insufficient to do significant harm to an enemy king directly might nonetheless do substantial harm to him indirectly, by persuading regionally important nobles to switch sides if their sovereign failed to protect them. Local warfare both served and was shaped by local politics, as well as by larger strategic considerations.

Truce and Peace

In the Middle Ages even more than in the Ancient and Modern worlds, the locus of real power was interpersonal rather than legal or structural. The threat of violent force always had to be taken into account, and so, as Hincmar of Rheims wrote in the ninth century, everyone (by which he meant every lord) studiously strove to be surrounded by as many youths and vassals as he could support and sustain without recourse to robbery and rapine.[32] Yet that last-mentioned limitation could be a dangerous one, for, as William the Conqueror observed, "there is no doubt that whoever is bold enough to dispose of his enemy's possessions as though they were his own will overcome his enemy."[33] Many successful rulers found war making profitable, honorable, and even pleasant, and needed only a modicum of political motivation (or a fig leaf of legal justification) to begin a war. As conflicts continued, however, they grew less attractive. In short wars, wage bills were low (especially if soldiers owed stints of unpaid service, as was often the case); in long wars, costs mounted rapidly, while the easy pickings of plunder and forage were used up and disappeared. For the defender, long wars often meant the gradual loss of strongholds, vassals, and lands, alongside the drain of wealth. It became harder and harder for both sides to keep their men in service, requiring steadily increasing expenditures of political capital and goodwill to maintain the struggle. Thus, there was strong incentive for the two sides to seek some sort of agreement after a relatively short interval of fighting, even if – as was usually the case – the weaker side had enjoyed substantial success in resisting the attacks of the stronger side. The thick nets of kin, friends and vassals that stretched between almost any two neighboring rulers ensured that there would normally be influential men and women on both sides who were eager to work for a reasonable peace. Thus most wars ended as they began and as they were conducted: in a process that was inherently political, though belonging to a particularly bloody and destructive branch of politic life.

Notes

1 Peace extolled: Gray, *Scalacronica*, pp. 191–3; cf. the tale of Hawkwood and the friars ("I live from war and peace would destroy me"), quoted in Caferro, *John Hawkwood*, p. 1, and Born, *Poems*, pp. 372, 398, 436, and *passim*.

2 Although historians of chivalry and of gender have made a start at addressing the issue, there is still a great deal of room for study of the linkages between warfare and masculinity in the medieval period. As starting points, see Bennett, "Military Masculinity," and Karras, *Boys to Men*, ch. 2.

3 Rogers, "By Fire and Sword," p. 36. Historians of medieval warfare have for decades now emphasized the huge importance of devastation in medieval warfare. Among others, see Gillingham, "War and Chivalry" and "William the Bastard"; Reuter, "Plunder and Tribute"; Strickland, *War and Chivalry*; Rogers, "By Fire and Sword."

4 Those wishing to survey how war changed over time can start with Keen (ed.), *Medieval Warfare*, and Contamine, *War in the Middle Ages*. Hall, *Weapons and Warfare*, offers a particularly sophisticated approach to the interactions between technological and military change during the late Middle Ages.

5 I have argued for an "infantry revolution" in the early fourteenth century and an "artillery revolution" in the mid-fifteenth, as part of a process of punctuated equilibrium evolution. See Rogers, "Military Revolutions." I stand by those arguments, despite the critiques of Stone, "Technology, Society, and the Infantry Revolution," and DeVries, "Catapults."

6 Medieval warfare has been most thoroughly analyzed for Britain, France, the Low Countries, Carolingian Francia, and the Crusades, followed by Iberia and then Italy. The military history of medieval Central Europe (especially for the high Middle Ages) is in need of much more study.

7 These categories of war making are discussed from a soldier's-eye perspective in Rogers, *Soldiers' Lives*. Many of the points made in this chapter are developed more fully there.

8 France, "Composition and Raising of the Armies of Charlemagne," p. 69. Another proponent of the low-end figures, Timothy Reuter, concludes Carolingian and Ottonian armies "did not normally exceed two thousand fighting men" ("Carolingian and Ottonian Warfare," p. 28).

9 On cavalry, contrast Verbruggen, "Role of Cavalry," with Bachrach, "Verbruggen's 'Cavalry'." On the issue of late antique–early medieval change versus continuity, contrast Halsall, *Warfare and Society*, and Reuter, "Carolingian and Ottonian Warfare," with the expansive *opus* of Bernard S. Bachrach, particularly the summative "'A Lying Legacy' Revisited," which is a response to Abels and Morillo, "A Lying Legacy?"

10 Lawson, *Battle of Hastings*, pp. 161, 184–6, 192.

11 Crusade: Queller and Madden, *Fourth Crusade*, pp. 11, 47. Crécy: Rogers, *War Cruel and Sharp*, pp. 423–6, and Ayton, "The English Army at Crécy," p. 189, are roughly in agreement on the size of the English force. Jonathan Sumption, however, suggests (rather unconvincingly), based on shipping records, a much smaller figure of 7,000–10,000 for the English (*Hundred Years War*, p. 497). 1340: Contamine, *Guerre, état, et société*, p. 70.

12 Respectively: *The Chronicle of Henry of Livonia*, p. 47; Gilbert of Mons, *Chronicle*, p. 64; Peter of Vaux-de-Cernay, *History*, p. 209.

13 Suger, *Œuvres*, 11.

14 Contamine, *War in the Middle Ages*, pp. 94–6.

15 See, e.g., Halsall, *Warfare and Society*, pp. 93–5.

16 William of Apulia, *Deeds*, bk 2, p. 22.

17 Rogers, "By Fire and Sword," pp. 36–7. Rogers, *Soldiers' Lives*, pp. 72–97, covers movement through enemy territory.

18 See, e.g., Wright, "Ransoms of Non-Combatants," pp. 328–9.

19 This is discussed well, in a particular context, in Strickland, *War and Chivalry*, pp. 78–91.

20 Higham and Barker, *Timber Castles*, pp. 17–18.

21 Jim Bradbury's *The Medieval Siege* does an excellent job of surveying a large number of medieval sieges, based on the primary sources. So too, within its more limited purview, does Randall Rogers, *Latin Siege Warfare*.

22 There has been a strong tendency in recent years to describe siege warfare as the main or predominant form of warfare in the Middle Ages; see, e.g., Bachrach, "Medieval Siege Warfare." This perspective emerged largely in response to the medieval military histories of the early twentieth century (e.g. Oman, Delbrück), which were far too battle focused, but in my opinion the current orthodoxy has swung somewhat too far in the opposite direction.

23 Richard of Hexham, *History*, pp. 44–5.

24 Verbruggen, *Art of Warfare*, pp. 74–7, 97–102, 183–8, and *passim*; Rogers, "Offensive/Defensive," p. 169 n. 15; and *Soldiers' Lives*, pp. 162–6, 192–4.

25 Rogers, "Offensive/Defensive," p. 160, and "Agincourt."

26 Rogers, *Soldiers' Lives*, pp. 183–6, 188–97, for this and the following two paragraphs.

27 The implications of this fourteenth-century "infantry revolution" are discussed in Rogers, "Military Revolutions."

28 Rogers, *Soldiers' Lives*, pp. 214–16 (casualty rates). Ibid., pp. 224–8, briefly summarizes medieval military medicine; Mitchell, *Medicine*, and Patterson, "Military Surgery," offer more detail.

29 For the following several paragraphs, see my *Soldiers' Lives*, ch. 7.

30 *Annala Connacht*, 1416.2, 1416.10, 1416.12.

31 William of Apulia, *Deeds*, bk 2, pp. 22–3; Barbour, *Bruce*, pp. 204–10.

32 Hincmar of Reims, *De ordine palatii*, p. 82.

33 William of Poitiers, *Gesta Guillelmi*, p. 27.

Bibliography

Abels, Richard, and Morillo, Stephen, "A Lying Legacy? A Preliminary Discussion of Images of Antiquity and Altered Reality in Medieval Military History," *Journal of Medieval Military History*, 3 (2004), 1–13.

Annala Connacht: The Annals of Connacht (AD 1224–1544), ed. and trans. A. Martin Freeman (Dublin: Dublin Institute for Advanced Studies, 1944; electronic edn compiled by Pádraig Bambury (Cork: Corpus of Electronic Texts, 2001), via http://celt.ucc.ie/publishd.html).

Ayton, Andrew, "The English Army at Crécy," in Andrew Ayton, Philip Preston, et al., *The Battle of Crécy, 1346* (Woodbridge, Boydell, 2005), pp. 159–251.

Bachrach, Bernard S., "Medieval Siege Warfare: A Reconnaissance," *Journal of Military History*, 58 (1994), pp. 119–33.

Bachrach, Bernard S., "Verbruggen's 'Cavalry' and the Lyon-Thesis," *Journal of Medieval Military History*, 4 (2006), pp. 137–63

Bachrach, Bernard S., "'A Lying Legacy' Revisited: The Abels–Morillo Defense of Discontinuity," *Journal of Medieval Military History*, 5 (2007).

Barbour, John, *The Bruce*, ed. and trans. A. A. M. Duncan (Edinburgh: Cannongate Classics, 1997).

Bennett, Matthew, "Military Masculinity in England and Northern France *c.* 1050–*c.* 1225," in D. M. Hadley, ed., *Masculinity* in *Medieval* Europe (London: Longman, 1999), pp. 71–88.

Born, Bertran de, *The Poems of the Troubadour Bertran de Born*, ed. and trans. W. D. Paden et al. (Berkeley and Los Angeles: University of California Press, 1986).

Bradbury, Jim, *The Medieval Siege*, 2nd edn (Woodbridge: Boydell Press, 2002).

Caferro, William, *John Hawkwood: An English Mercenary in Fourteenth-Century Italy* (Baltimore: Johns Hopkins University Press, 2006).

The Chronicle of Henry of Livonia, trans. James A. Brundage (New York: Columbia University Press, 2004).

Contamine, Philippe, *Guerre, état et société à la fin du moyen âge: Etudes sur les armées des rois de France, 1337–1494* (Paris: Mouton, 1972).

Contamine, Philippe, *War in the Middle Ages*, trans. Michael C. Jones (Oxford: Basil Blackwell, 1987).

DeVries, Kelly, "Catapults are not Atomic Bombs: Towards a Redefinition of 'Effectiveness' in Premodern Military Technology," *War in History*, 4 (1997), pp. 454–70.

France, John, "The Composition and Raising of the Armies of Charlemagne," *Journal of Medieval Military History*, 1 (2002), 61–82.

Gilbert of Mons, *Chronicle of Hainault*, trans. Laura Napran (Woodbridge: Boydell, 2005).

Gillingham, John, "Richard I and the Science of War in the Middle Ages," "William the Bastard at War," and "War and Chivalry in the *History of William the Marshal*," in Matthew Strickland, ed., *Anglo-Norman Warfare* (Woodbridge: Boydell, 2000), pp. 194–207, 143–60, 251–64.

Gray, Thomas, *Scalacronica, 1272–1363*, ed. and trans. Andy King (Woodbridge: Surtees Society/Boydell, 2005).

Hall, Bert S., *Weapons and Warfare in Renaissance Europe* (Baltimore: Johns Hopkins University Press, 1997).

Halsall, Guy, *Warfare and Society in the Barbarian West, 450–900* (London: Routledge, 2003).

Higham, Robert, and Barker, Philip, *Timber Castles*, 2nd edn (Exeter: University of Exeter Press, 2004).

Hincmar, Archbishop of Reims. *De ordine palatii/Hinkmar von Reims*, ed. Thomas Gross und Rudolf Schieffer (Hanover: Hahn, 1980).

Karras, Ruth Mazo, *From Boys to Men: Formations of Masculinity in Late Medieval Europe* (Philadelphia: University of Pennsylvania Press, 2003).

Keen, Maurice, ed., *Medieval Warfare: A History* (Oxford: Oxford University Press, 1999).

Lawson, M. K., *The Battle of Hastings 1066* (Stroud: Tempus, 2003).

Mitchell, Piers D., *Medicine in the Crusades: Warfare, Wounds, and the Medieval Surgeon* (Cambridge: Cambridge University Press, 2004).

Patterson, Linda M., "Military Surgery: Knights, Sergeants, and Raimon of Avignon's Version of the *Chirurgia* of Roger of Salerno (1180–1209)," in Christopher Harper-Bill and Ruth Harvey, eds, *The Ideals and Practice of Medieval Knighthood, II* (Woodbridge: Boydell, 1988), pp. 117–46.

Peter of Vaux-de-Cernay, *History of the Albigensian Crusade*, trans. W. A. Sibly and M. D. Sibly (Woodbridge: Boydell Press, 1998).

Queller, Donald E., and Madden, Thomas F., *The Fourth Crusade: The Conquest of Constantinople* (Philadelphia: University of Pennsylvania Press, 1999).

Reuter, Timothy, "Plunder and Tribute in the Carolingian Empire." *Transactions of the Royal Historical Society*, 5th ser., 35 (1985), pp. 75–94.

Reuter, Timothy, "Carolingian and Ottonian Warfare," in Maurice Keen, ed., *Medieval Warfare* (Oxford: Oxford University Press, 1999), pp.13–35.

Reynolds, Susan, *Fiefs and Vassals: The Medieval Evidence Reinterpreted* (Oxford: Oxford University Press, 1994).

Richard of Hexham, *History of the Acts of King Stephen*, in *Church Historians of England*, trans. Joseph Stevenson, vol. 4, pt 1 (London: Seely's, 1856).

Rogers, Clifford J., "The Military Revolutions of the Hundred Years' War," in Clifford J. Rogers, ed., *The Military Revolution Debate* (Boulder, CO: Westview, 1995), pp. 55–93.

Rogers, Clifford J., "The Offensive/Defensive in Medieval Strategy," in *From Crecy to Mohacs: Warfare in the Late Middle Ages (1346–1526). Acta of the XXII*nd *Colloquium of the International Commission of Military History (Vienna, 1996)* (Vienna: Heeresgeschichtliches Museum/Militärhistorisches Institut, 1997), pp. 158–71.

Rogers, Clifford J., *War Cruel and Sharp: English Strategy under Edward III, 1327–1360* (Woodbridge: Boydell, 2000).

Rogers, Clifford J., "By Fire and Sword: *Bellum hostile* and 'Civilians' in the Hundred Years War," in *Civilians in the Path of War* (Lincoln, NE: University of Nebraska Press, 2002), pp. 33–78.

Rogers, Clifford J., *Soldiers' Lives through History: The Middle Ages* (Westport, CT: Greenwood, 2007).

Rogers, Clifford J., "The Battle of Agincourt," in L. J. Andrew Villalon and Donald J. Kagay, eds, *The Hundred Years War, vol. 2: Different Vistas* (Leiden: Brill, 2008).

Rogers, Randall, *Latin Siege Warfare in the Twelfth Century* (Oxford: Clarendon Press, 1991).

Stone, John, "Technology, Society, and the Infantry Revolution of the Fourteenth Century," *Journal of Military History*, 68 (2004), pp. 361–80.

Strickland, Matthew, *War and Chivalry* (Cambridge: Cambridge University Press, 1996).

Suger, *Œuvres complètes*, ed. A. Lecoy de La Marche (Paris: Société de l'Histoire de France, 1867).

Sumption, Jonathan, *The Hundred Years War*, vol. 1: *Trial by Battle* (London: Faber and Faber, 1990).

Verbruggen, J. F., *The Art of Warfare in Western Europe during the Middle Ages: From the Eighth Century to 1340*, trans. S. Willard and R. W. Southern, 2nd English edn (Woodbridge: Boydell Press, 1997).

Verbruggen, J. F., "The Role of Cavalry in Medieval Warfare," *Journal of Medieval Military History*, 3 (2005), pp. 46–71.

Villehardouin, Geffroi de, and Joinville, Jean de, *Memoirs of the Crusades: Villehardouin and Joinville*, trans. Frank T. Marzials (New York: Dutton Everyman Paperback, 1958).

William of Apulia, *The Deeds of Robert Guiscard*, trans. G. A. Loud (Leeds Medieval History Texts in Translation, at http://www.leeds.ac.uk/history/weblearning/MedievalHistoryTextCentre/medievalTexts.htm).

William of Poitiers, *The Gesta Gvillelmi of William of Poitiers*, ed. and trans. R. H. C. Davis and Marjorie Chibnall (Oxford: Oxford University Press, 1998).

Wright, N. A. R., "Ransoms of Non-Combatants during the Hundred Years War," *Journal of Medieval History*, 17 (1991), pp. 323–32.

Further Reading

Primary Sources

The majority of medieval chronicles include descriptions of warfare, and many have military conflict as their principal theme or topic. The following works are among the most valuable for students aiming to understand the conduct of medieval war.

Ambroise, *The History of the Holy War*, trans. Marianne Ailes (Woodbridge: Boydell Press, 2003).

Barber, Richard, ed. and trans., *Life and Campaigns of the Black Prince*, 2nd edn (Woodbridge: Boydell, 2002).

Barbour, John, *The Bruce*, ed. and trans. A. A. M. Duncan (Edinburgh: Cannongate Classics, 1997).

Díaz de Gamez, Gutierre, *The Unconquered Knight: A Chronicle of the Deeds of Don Pero Niño, Count of Buelna*, ed. and trans. Joan Evans (online edn Cambridge, Ontario: In Parentheses Publications, 2000, at http://www.yorku.ca/inpar/gamez_evans.pdf).

Froissart, Jean, *Chronicles*, trans. Thomas Johnes, 2 vols (London: William Smith, 1848; available online via http://books.google.com).

Gray, Thomas, *Scalacronica, 1272–1363*, ed. and trans. Andy King (Woodbridge: Surtees Society/Boydell, 2005).

James I of Aragon, *The Book of Deeds of James I of Aragon: A Translation of the Medieval Catalan*, Llibre dels Fets, trans. Damian Smith and Helena Buffery (Aldershot: Ashgate, 2003). (The Forster translation, available online via www.libro.uca.edu, is also serviceable.)

Muntaner, Ramón, *The Chronicle of Muntaner*, trans. Lady Henrietta Margaret Goodenough (online edn: Cambridge, Ontario: In Parentheses Publications, 2000, at http://www.yorku.ca/inpar/muntaner_goodenough.pdf).

Peter of Vaux-de-Cernay, *History of the Albigensian Crusade*, trans. W. A. Sibly and M. D. Sibly (Woodbridge: Boydell Press, 1998).

Villehardouin, Geffroi de, and Joinville, Jean de, *Memoirs of the Crusades: Villehardouin and Joinville*, trans. Frank T. Marzials (New York: Dutton Everyman Paperback, 1958).

Secondary Works

The literature on the conduct of war in the Middle Ages is extensive. In addition to J. F. Verbruggen, *The Art of Warfare in Western Europe during the Middle Ages: From the Eighth Century to 1340*, trans. Summer Willard and R. W. Southern, 2nd English edn (Woodbridge:

Boydell Press, 1997), and Maurice Keen, ed., *Medieval Warfare: A History* (Oxford: Oxford University Press, 1999), Helen J. Nicholson, *Medieval Warfare: Theory and Practice of War in Europe, 300–1500* (New York: Palgrave Macmillan, 2004), is an excellent and very concise introduction to the subject. *De re militari: The Society for the Study of Medieval Military History* offers a huge amount of source material and modern literature on its superb website (www.deremilitari.org) and also publishes the *Journal of Medieval Military History.* Other especially valuable books include:

France, John, *Victory in the East: A Military History of the First Crusade* (Cambridge: Cambridge University Press, 1994).

France, John, *Western Warfare in the Age of the Crusades* (Ithaca, NY: Cornell University Press, 1999).

Mallett, Michael, *Mercenaries and their Masters* (Totowa, NJ: Towman and Littlefield, 1974).

Powers, James F., *A Society Organized for War: The Iberian Municipal Militias in the Central Middle Ages, 1000–1284* (Berkeley and Los Angeles: University of California Press, 1988; online reprint: The Library of Iberian Resources at http://libro.uca.edu/socwar/index.htm).

Prestwich, Michael, *Armies and Warfare in the Middle Ages: The English Experience* (New Haven: Yale University Press, 1996).

Smail, R. C., *Crusading Warfare 1097–1193* (Cambridge: Cambridge University Press, 1956; 2nd edn, 1995).

Strickland, Matthew, and Hardy, Robert, *The Great Warbow: A History of the Military Archer* (Stroud: Sutton, 2005).

Chapter Twenty-two

Expansion and the Crusades

Christopher Tyerman

The idea of a "medieval world" is a peculiarly West European construct, even if it has been embraced by other historical traditions, such as the Japanese. The idea of medieval China, medieval India, let alone medieval America, medieval sub-Saharan Africa, or medieval Australia makes no sense. In a global context, the term "medieval" is vague, if not suspect, with no necessary agreed or unambiguous material or intellectual substance. If a "medieval world" lacks conceptual precision or definition, any notion of its expansion is consequently fraught with obscurities, ambiguities, and doubt.

This may seem excessively pedantic. At least in Western Europe, "medieval" may mean something concrete. It refers to a period of European history defined by the great nineteenth-century German textual editing project of the *Monumenta Germaniae Historica* as lasting roughly from *c.* 500 to *c.* 1500, from the political fall of the western Roman Empire to its spurious cultural rebirth a thousand years later. If there existed unifying themes transcending geography, demography, or ethnicity, two distinct elements stood out. The period was characterized, culturally, by the survival and development of late Roman ideas of law, power, and religion (that is, Christianity). Socially and politically, ruling elites depended, except in a very few urban commercial centers, on exploitation of settled agriculture through the inherited, coerced, or consented control of a peasant work force. The interplay of these two circumstances created distinctive identities, institutions, and mentalities that have come to be seen as recognizably "medieval." Lordship was based on military power sanctioned by public religion. Ecclesiastical and secular aristocracies shared wealth and attitudes. In the absence of effective or extensive coercive policing or administrative power, communal consensual traditions shaped decision making, from village and town to royal court or army. Although the continent was rich in local vernaculars, primarily but not exclusively Germanic, Romance, and Celtic, Latin provided an enduring vehicle of cultural memory, religious uniformity, academic inquiry, international conversation, social control, and status definition. Technological conservatism and stagnation rested on the poverty of investment and the abundance of cheap or pressed labor. Warfare remained central to social control and political activity, its reliance on private warriors even when paid for by public funds producing a distinctive aristocratic culture. This developed from a ubiquity of arms-bearers into a practical code of manners and status known as chivalry. In the absence of strong central institutions of secular government and law, the Church, with universal claims to truth and authority, in many areas and for much of the time constituted the most significant and robust public institution. It exerted profound influence through its monopolist provision of education, public rituals, and understanding and contact with the divine or transcendent, in particular through the cults of saints. The almost exclusively agrarian economy was only partially, if increasingly, commercialized, and only very locally and primitively industrialized, but nonetheless sustained ever more elaborate and extensive coinage currencies. The reach of government was confined by inadequate endowment, limited fiscal traditions, a cultural dislike of innovation, and rudimentary, if growing, techniques and habits of bureaucracy. All these were typical – although not exclusive – of medieval Europe.

Defining the "medieval world" as specific to a period of European history does not solve the conceptual problem, but merely focuses it. What might have expanded in this period: "Europe," "Christendom," "Christian Europe," "Latin Europe," "Latin Christendom," or other permutations? Whichever term or concept is chosen conditions whether such expansion is to be regarded as territorial, political, cultural, demographic, linguistic, economic, religious, or imaginative. Some historians rest their definition on allegiance to the papacy, the use of Latin in law, learning, and government, and a system of lordship and subservient peasantry to delineate what John France has recently described as a "Catholic core," excluding the Celtic, Slavic, and Scandinavian marches as the "Catholic fringe" in that they lacked some or all of the three defining features, or possessed them only incompletely. Robert Bartlett follows a not dissimilar typology, his core based like France's on the lands once included in Charlemagne's empire – France, Germany west of the Elbe, north Italy – plus southern Britain.[1]

Bartlett attempts to cut through the conceptual and historical morass: "whatever else may have been expanding in the High Middle Ages, there is no doubt about the widening bounds of Latin Christendom, the area of Christendom that recognised papal authority and celebrated the Latin liturgy."[2] However, this certainty is somewhat undermined by his later admission that Christendom meaning Christian territory not just Christian believers was as much a consequence of "expansion" as a basis for it.[3] For France and Bartlett, a unified identity came from acceptance of the initially spiritual but later more theocratic primacy of the oldest institution in Western Europe, the Roman papacy, allied to the Church's perpetuating of an attenuated Latin culture derived from the late Roman Empire and its eighth- and ninth-century Carolingian revival. While initially attractive, this is fraught with historical problems. What of those regions in Scandinavia or central Europe that, by 1050 at least, accepted papal primacy, celebrated Catholic saints, established dioceses and canon law in the Catholic style, used Latin as the language of educated elites, and followed traditions of royal authority and Church–State relations similar or identical to those found in the former Carolingian empire? What of Catholic Wales and Ireland? France gets round this difficulty by inventing the idea of a "Catholic fringe" surrounding his "Catholic core," while Bartlett seems eclectically to lump some parts of this fringe, but not others, into the areas whose penetration by the culture and powers of the core led to their being "Europeanized,", thus "Making Europe." Expansion, for Bartlett, can be covered by what he describes as the "aristocratic diaspora" from the central regions of Latin Christianity: wherever Roman Catholics conquered, there was expansion.

Yet this organization of past space, culture, and societies may mislead. Nora Berend has argued from the example of Hungary that distinctions between "west," "east," or "east-central" Europe distort clear understanding of the communities between the Atlantic and the Eurasian steppes.[4] Hungary may, in some respects, have experienced a different history from other regions, but it was no less part of Latin Christendom for that and in many other respects conformed entirely to patterns exhibited elsewhere – for example, of ecclesiastical and royal power and the tensions between them. Similarly it is worth noting that the initial impetus for the Christianization of pagan Prussia in the thirteenth century came not from any "core" land, but from Poland, another region, like Hungary or Bohemia, that, from the tenth century, can hardly be excluded from Latin Christendom. Only by following rather uncritically the typology of propagandists, partial polemicists, chroniclers, or the conquerors themselves can the image of a coherent expansion of Europe or Christendom be sustained in such terms.

The identity of a Latin Christian "core" was a literary and political invention as much as a social reality involving the concoction of a neat supremacism based, in part, on contrasting a praiseworthy "us" with an alien "them." Successive Roman popes and clergy from the eleventh century narrowly defined territorial Christendom and the rights of the "Christian people" to serve their wholly self-interested and self-conscious political program. In that context, the crusades were less a universal force or general expression of the expansion of Christendom or "Europe" than a highly selective means of justifying specific and rather contrasting acts and processes of invasion, conquest, and subjugation. The crusade was originally invented in the 1090s by Pope Urban II as a war that operated as a penitential act because undertaken on the direct command of God through his agent, the pope, to restore the Holy Land consecrated by Christ Himself. Subsequently there were crusades against pagan Slavs and Balts, Iberian, Syrian and Egyptian Muslims, Russian and Greek Orthodox Christians, but there was none against Sicilian Muslims, British Celtic Christians, or pagan Cumans in Hungary. Even within the pale of active crusading objectives there is no consistency. In extending the territorial, ecclesiastical, commercial, legal, and economic frontiers of lay and religious powers based in the area once ruled by the Carolingians, crusading was neither coherent nor crucial. In 1095 Urban II called for, in his own words, the liberation of the Eastern Church and the restoration of Christian rule of the Holy Places, not the annihilation of Islam nor the colonization of the Near East.[5] By contrast, Bernard of Clairvaux in 1147 encouraged German crusaders to "convert or wipe out" their pagan Slav former allies.[6] Most papal crusade bulls, like the rest of papal foreign and most other policy, were reactive to local demands: in Iberia to support political competition and conquest; in the Baltic to justify land grabs by friendly Christian nations and ecclesiastical and commercial empire-builders or to legitimize the creation of the tyrannical order-states of the Teutonic Knights in Prussia and Livonia. Only in the Holy Land could it be said that the presence of Latin rulers and settlers, with the possible exception of Italian mercantile interests, conformed to no natural or native pattern of frontier, border, or marcher exchange and interaction. Here, at least, the ideals and practice of crusading determined political events not vice versa. And it was here that both conquest and crusade failed most dismally and completely.[7]

It is undeniable that, between 950 and 1300, large areas around the periphery of what is today called Europe came under the political control of rulers whose religious allegiance was to the Roman pope. In the wake of conquest came new settlers, laws, public institutions, and identities. Slavs became Germans; descendants of the pagan Wendish prince Nicklot of the Abotrites (d. 1160), enemy to the crusaders in 1147, fought as German crusaders in Prussia in 1218. This acculturation process was not limited to religious frontiers, consistent, or one way, as demonstrated by English responses to French conquest and Anglo-French/Norman penetration of the Celtic regions of the British Isles.[8] Franks in Syria adopted native habits, in clothes, housing, and food, for example, and, increasingly, language, but were not assimilated into native society; their ultimately failed settlement was too large to be absorbed, too small to transform. The post-conquest experiences of Castile and Valencia were comparable only in terms of the ideological construct of *reconquista* and not in the nature of the demographic or religious settlement, which in Valencia retained a prominent position for the mudejar community (that is, the Muslims under Christian rule). Just as the Baltic, Outremer, and Spain differed from each other, so Sicily in the twelfth century displayed a Mediterranean eclectic heterogeneity in politics, culture, and administration, with models from Fatimid Egypt and Byzantium exerting as much influence over the conduct of public business as any from northern Italy or France.[9] Although this changed in the thirteenth century, with the marginalization of, in particular, the indigenous Muslim population and the imposition of more obviously West European systems of government first under Frederick II and later the Angevins, the new circumstances cannot be said to have been an immediate consequence of conquest. Across the Adriatic and Ionian Sea, while the Latin emperors of Constantinople presided over the husk of an ephemeral failed state between 1204 and 1261, neither imposing their own authority nor forging stable alliances with indigenous Greeks or neighboring Bulgars, some Frankish rulers of the Peloponnesus successfully managed a system of cultural and social cooperation, a Greek *convivencia*, with the local Orthodox population that allowed their statelets an attenuated existence until the mid-fifteenth century.[10]

Faced with this diversity of "many expansions",[11] it may be thought no general thesis can be sustained, especially as expansion by conquest was paralleled – for example, in the Baltic, central Europe, or the Celtic British Isles – by commercial partnership and peaceful "emulation," the attractiveness of cultural, social, economic, and political structures associated with Catholic Europe. Yet it has been argued that the fragmented experience of the changing complexions of the marches of Latin Christendom was lent cohesion by the papacy and its chosen weapon of ideological expression and political action, the crusade. While the former proposition may be sound, it does not follow that the latter is. Crusading reflected rather than determined local circumstances even before it became, *c.* 1300, the preserve of order states, in Livonia, Prussia, and Rhodes; of frontier rulers on the make, such as Peter I of Cyprus, Sigismund of Hungary, John Hunyadi or Ferdinand and Isabella of Spain; or of popes desperate to assert control over central Italy in the fourteenth century or of those in the fifteenth, such as Calixtus III or Pius II, who saw crusading against the Turk as a way of restoring confidence in the post-Schism papacy.[12] Before 1300, frontier crusades displayed hardly any unity of origin or purpose even if sustained by a consistent rhetoric. Those directed at the eastern Mediterranean operated within different practical or imaginative perimeters except that any crusading succeeded only when facing politically, economically, or technologically disadvantaged enemies. German crusaders conquered Prussia and Livonia, but not Lithuania. The First Crusade succeeded almost by accident against an insouciantly divided Near East; far better equipped, organized, and funded later expeditions dashed themselves to pieces against the more organized Ayyubids and Mamluks of Egypt.

However, some contemporaries did imagine these holy wars as part of a wider cosmic conflict between right and wrong, good and evil, Christians and infidels. Urban II in the 1090s drew equivalence between recovering lost Christian lands in Palestine and in Iberia. His policy shot through with images of the Early Church and the Apocalypse, Urban seems to have been conscious of an opportunity to reverse the tide of temporal history that, since the seventh century, had run decisively against Christianity. His penitential war of liberation for the Holy Places therefore operated on two levels, terrestrial political conquest signifying the transcendent immanence of God. Urban's early career as a Cluniac monk may have made him particularly aware of the Christian frontiers in Iberia and the Near East. His apprenticeship with Gregory VII in the 1080s perhaps introduced him to the concept of penitential warfare. Whether or not his scheme of the 1090s to liberate Jerusalem was a conscious imitation of Gregory's 1074 plan to lead an army to restore a claimant to the Byzantine throne and press on to the Holy Sepulchre, Urban's early twelfth-century biographer clearly regarded the First Crusade as a continuation of Gregory's work.[13]

Placing the campaign inaugurated in 1095 in the context of Christian conquests in Iberia (Toledo fell to Alfonso VI of Leon-Castile in 1085) and Sicily (conquered by Roger of Hauteville, 1060–92) was not unique to Urban and his circle. His imperialist opponents were also developing a grand strategy of eastern conquest, although possibly more in the realms of eschatological propaganda than political or military planning. Elsewhere, as John Cowdrey has noted, there are signs of how campaigning against non-Latins across various frontiers had penetrated contemporary rhetoric, at least in Italy, which occupied an ambiguous position as both the historic centre and a literal frontline of Latin Christianity. In the mid-1070s, Prince Gisulf of Salerno was being encouraged by Archbishop Alanus to take the fight beyond his local Norman rivals to Byzantium and against the Turks.[14] Popes had been encouraging campaigns against Muslim forces in the western Mediterranean for generations before the grant of a papal banner to the Norman invaders of Muslim Sicily in 1060. It is perfectly possible, although the manuscript evidence is highly contentious, that Pope Sergius IV offered remissions of sins to encourage the assembly of a relief expedition in the wake of Caliph al-Hakim of Egypt's destruction of the Holy Sepulchre in 1009.[15] His successor Benedict VIII certainly approved of the Pisan–Genoese attack on Muslim pirates in Sardinia in 1015–16. Early eleventh-century writers like the Burgundian Ralph Glaber or Adhemar of Chabannes from Limoges displayed sharp awareness of the struggle on Christendom's frontiers.[16] Many involved in such campaigns, such as Alfonso VI of Castile or the Norman invaders of Sicily, however secular their primary motives and methods, were happy to accept a religious gloss to the their conquests. Alfonso VI placed his capture of Toledo in 1085 explicitly in the context of a recovery for Christians of a city "for 376 years in the hands of the Moors . . . where my ancestors once reigned in power and wealth."[17] The Benedictine monk Amatus of Montecassino, who died in 1085, so avoiding having his interpretations infected by the tropes of the First Crusade, ascribed similarly elevated motives to the Norman leader in Italy Robert Guiscard (that is, "the Weasel"), who allegedly declared his desire to free Christians from Muslim rule and so "avenge the injury done to God."[18] By formulating frontier battles in this way, both Amatus and Alfonso VI showed a recognition of history as the frame for current conflicts and a perspective that embraced the idea of a Christian people – that is, a form of Christendom that they saw as being expanded in their time, attitudes fuelled by vernacular epics, such as the contemporary *Song of Roland*. With success in Iberia and Sicily, and expansionist raids such as the Genoese attack on Mahdia in 1087, which was described in the setting of a pilgrimage to Rome, events appeared to back the image: Christendom on the march.

There is some evidence that this perception was shared at the other end of the Mediterranean. Seeking a pattern to affairs after the unexpected invasion of Syria and Palestine by the First Crusade, the Damascene scholar al-Sulami arrived at a conclusion not entirely dissimilar to Urban II's, linking the invasion to parallel attacks on Muslim Spain and Sicily. Al-Sulami went further. Writing in 1105 during the early Frankish conquest of the Palestinian coast, he acutely observed how the invaders' objectives changed. Initially "Jerusalem was the summit of their wishes." However, once they had seen the internal divisions and political rivalries among the local Muslim rulers, the Franks' "ambitions grew in strength and extended to what they beheld," fighting "until they made themselves rulers of lands beyond their utmost hopes . . . so they are convinced that all the lands will become theirs, and all the people prisoners in their hands."[19] While allowing for his revivalist polemical intent and deliberate exaggeration of the threat the Franks posed, al-Sulami captured the opportunistic, unplanned quality of the establishment of the initial Frankish enclaves in Syria and Palestine.

Although Guibert of Nogent breathlessly hailed the conquests in the Holy Land as Christendom's "new colony,"[20] colonization had played no obvious part in Urban II's original scheme. The need to occupy conquests, from Antioch and Edessa in 1098 onwards, was a result of the circumstances of the expedition rather than its purpose. Not only had conquests to be secured for the security and supplying of the Western invasion army; the absence of an indigenous Christian ruling class in Palestine forced the crusaders to plan for political rule, especially once the alliance with the Greeks, who may have featured in Urban II's mind as putative rulers of a restored Jerusalem, had been temporarily abandoned in 1098–9. That so few wished to remain argues for no widespread or central colonizing motive. The Latin garrison that stayed in the Holy Land after 1099 stimulated extensive Western settlement, but retained the unique self-conscious character of its foundation and purpose. The kings declared themselves ruler of the Latins, their social, cultural, religious, legal, and fiscal relations with other local communities determined by material necessity not a program of transformation. William of Tyre summed up the peculiarity of the twelfth-century kingdom of Jerusalem by depicting it as a providential frontier state dedicated to the protection of the greatest relics in Christendom, the Holy Places.[21] The space occupied by the Western invaders of the Near East was as much of imagination and the spirit as of territory. Although it is demonstrable that the First Crusade was a consequence of closer contact between Western Europeans and the central and eastern Mediterranean rather than its cause, without the Holy Sepulchre, while Western merchants might have sought markets and trading posts in the coastal ports, there would have been no Frankish knights maneuvering or farmers settling in the hills of Judea, Samaria, and the Golan, the plains of Sharon, or the deserts of the Negev and Transjordan.

Despite al-Sulmai's assertion, the ambition of those who settled in what became known in the west as Outremer did not encompass a strategy of Near Eastern conquest. According to Albert of Aachen, usually well informed of north Italian affairs, the Lombards on the crusade of 1101–2 did toy with the idea of invading Iraq and attacking Baghdad, but such overheated optimism soon evaporated as they and the other armies of 1101 were each defeated by the Turks of Anatolia.[22] Thereafter, Frankish plans for regional domination were limited and reactive. Damascus, with which the Franks had intimate commercial and usually amicable political relations, was besieged in 1126, 1129, and 1148 to try to pull southern Syria into the Frankish rather than the Iraqi or Aleppan sphere of influence. Egypt was invaded four times in the 1160s not so much to inaugurate an annexation of the Fertile Crescent as to prevent it from falling into hostile Syrian hands, there being little overtly spiritual purpose even in retrospective Frankish propaganda. In war and politics, the Franks of Outremer operated less as agents of cultural and religious transformation than as Near Eastern *atabegs*, military leaders, based on cities and castles, holding down a subservient and alien peasantry with regiments of professional troops. As long as they paid their taxes, the destiny of their subjects' souls appeared to be of almost total indifference to the Franks. They were there to rule not to convert. The social impact of settlement relied on the numinous quality of the lands occupied rather more than any special economic attraction. This made twelfth-century Outremer very different from other frontiers where the cross was brandished above Latin conquest and settlement.

One explanation for this contrast has been ascribed to the Franks of Outremer, unlike Germans in the Baltic, encountering other "core" cultures, Greek and, especially, Muslim.[23] Where al-Andalus and its Berber allies and masters, "fringe" Muslim communities, failed to repel Christian attacks, the core "ummah" of the Near East did. However, whether facing "fringe" Muslims or not, the Christian Spanish conquerors had their own territories immediately at their backs and further off over the Pyrenees a large potential pool of sympathetic rulers, recruits, and taxpayers. The histories and objectives of Spanish kings and the Franks of Outremer were also very different. In Outremer, ironically, only when hold over territory became much more circumscribed in the thirteenth century did alternative strategies of evangelization take some hold, but even then they were largely aimed at securing the traditional goal of Jerusalem but by other means. This may be explained by two external influences: the attitudes toward conversion associated with the friars and a greater awareness of the wider Asiatic context of events in Syria and Palestine linked to the irruption of the Mongols in the Near East as well as eastern and central Europe. Even so, the mission of the Franks in Outremer was not the religious or demographic transformation of the area, except when it was seen that only conversion would give them peace, security, and control of the Holy Land, a realization that was a direct product of failure and retreat, an experience less conclusive elsewhere on the periphery of Latin Christendom.[24]

If distance distinguished and restricted Outremer as a theater of expansion, conversely religious justifications and incentives associated with the Jerusalem journey infected frontier adventures and penetration across marcher regions elsewhere, even when, as in both Iberia and northern Europe, there were sufficient and longstanding local religious antagonisms and conflicts. In 1100 Peter I of Aragon took the cross to go to Jerusalem, ignoring Urban II's view of a few years earlier that it was as meritorious to fight Muslims in Spain as in Palestine. However, a year later Peter was still contesting with the infidel in Spain, being described as a *crucifer* at the siege of Zaragoza, where he apparently displayed banners of the cross and built a siege machine nicknamed "Juslibol," God Wills It, the slogan of the First Crusade.[25] Within a generation, campaigns against Muslim rulers across the peninsular and in the Balearic Islands regularly attracted papal bulls granting Jerusalem style remission of sins, an equivalence officially recognized by the First Lateran Council of 1123. The rhetoric of war became unashamedly imitative. The archbishop of Compostella floated a scheme for North African conquest that would end up in the Holy Land to be undertaken by "soldiers of Christ" supported by "remission of sins." Chroniclers in Leon and Castile sharpened the spiritual dimension of their martial accounts, not least in response to the defensive not expansionist reality of wars against the Almoravid invaders from the Maghrib. St James the Apostle was transmuted into a "knight of Christ." Although many campaigns were still described without crusading overtones and civil even amicable relations with Muslims of al-Andalus, as opposed to those from North Africa, were still recognized as possible and prudent, the institutions that emerged in the wake of the First Crusade found eager Iberian adherents. In his will of 1131 Alfonso I of Aragon-Navarre (d. 1134) left his kingdom jointly to the newly founded Outremer orders of the Templars and Hospitallers and to the canons of the Holy Sepulchre. Alfonso also tried to found a *militia Christi* to fight Muslims and, significantly, to cut a new path to Jerusalem.[26] Alfonso did not equate Iberia with the Holy Land. From the 1170s, home-grown Iberian military orders were established to underpin and manage territorial gains made at the expense of the lords of al-Andalus.

A less robust borrowing and refashioning of images occurred in northern Europe, a process very different from that in Spain. In Iberia, the enemy was Muslim, the same as in the Holy Land, and the prospect of aiding the Jerusalem garrison was frequently, if implausibly, rehearsed. In the north the sanctification of German attacks on their Slav neighbors was only briefly linked directly with the fate of Jerusalem in Bernard of Clairvaux's delicate and uneasy rhetoric of justification for the first Baltic crusade in 1147. Bernard talked explicitly about "the complete wiping out or, at any rate, the conversion" of the pagans across the Elbe, an uncanonical missionary viciousness repeated by Innocent III in 1209 when he encouraged Waldemar II of Denmark to drag "the barbarian nations into the net of the orthodox faith . . . to root out the error of paganism and spread the bounds of the Christian faith."[27] To cover the ideological awkwardness of associating the Jerusalem holy war with local Baltic territorial conquest, the wars along the southern shore of the Baltic, in Livonia, and in Prussia were lent a somewhat spurious spiritual cachet by redesignating the areas attacked and subjugated by German and Danish conquerors as saintly patrimonies, the Virgin Mary's in Livonia, St Peter's in Prussia. A further patina of legitimacy was afforded by the regular refrain of the conquerors' apologists that the lands they were annexing had once been Christian, their enemies therefore apostates who threatened the integrity of the Church, the wars recast as a northern *reconquista*. In a region of shifting cultural and political frontiers, where missionaries followed merchants and no group could claim obvious, secure, or lasting technological or economic supremacy, such inventions and interpretations of the past were not difficult to erect.[28]

Yet the debt to the Jerusalem war persisted. Although the pagan Baltic reached its settled form only in the thirteenth century, its refashioning as holy Christian ground boasted a lengthy pedigree. In 1108 a Flemish cleric working in Magdeburg composed a propagandist *excitatoria* that likened the battleground across the Elbe as "our Jerusalem."[29] The branding of the summer raids into Wendish territory in 1147 as wars of the Cross was eased by the ubiquitous images of the first Jerusalem campaign. The Christian rulers in the area had, like their French co-religionists, embraced the new description for martial and spiritual self-advancement. Eric I of Denmark went on crusade in 1103. The emperor Henry IV floated a scheme for a Jerusalem pilgrimage and perhaps a crusade in 1103–4. Twenty years later, the future German king, Conrad III of Hohenstaufen, won his spurs on a military excursion in the Holy Land. The language of the First Crusade began to infuse literature as much as politics, familiar heroes such as Roland donning the unmistakable mantle of a *miles Christi*.[30] With the escalation of conflict along the German/Danish–Slav borderlands in the western Baltic, religion inevitably became a touchstone of identity and allegiance, even if a far from immutable one, as Wendish princes calculated their religious allegiance according to changing political circumstances and advantage. This was not how some observers wished to portray events. The missionary priest and chronicler Helmold of Bosau was very keen to equate the Wendish campaign of 1147 with the simultaneous Holy Land expedition, even though his own evidence clearly exposed the dominance of secular motives and practice.[31]

For all the literary and clerical posturing, the crusade – cross, preaching, privileges, Jerusalem, remission of sins – became an established feature of northern European wars only during the pontificates of crusade enthusiasts Celestine III and Innocent III. Before they launched the Livonian crusade in the 1190s, there had been only one crusade bull (in 1171) since 1147.[32] Celestine and Innocent were both reacting to appeals from the empire-building Hartwig II, archbishop of Bremen. As in Iberia, the crusade piggybacked on existing circumstances of war and conquest: German and Danish penetration of Pomerania, Livonia, and Estonia. The expansion of Latin Christian power in the region was driven by ecclesiastical and mercantile interests in Bremen, Lübeck, even Cologne, matched by the desire for foreign conquest and economic exploitation of the eastern Baltic by the kings of Denmark and Sweden. As the Danish chronicler Saxo Grammaticus made clear, vigorous expansionist policies of leaders such as Archbishop Absalom of Lund could be described in retrospect and probably at the time as wars backed by religion, traditional conflicts against pagans that had been a feature of West European frontier politics for centuries.[33] The accretion of crusading institutions and motifs changed this. Although preserving existing traditions of justified war against pagan neighbors, the institutions and motifs of the Jerusalem crusade permeated attitudes to what was a much older pastime.

The chronology of crusading in Iberia and northern Europe demonstrates how far it fitted existing patterns of political exchange rather than being stimulated by any new inspiration. In Spain, the crusades of the second decade attempted to reverse the defeats suffered at the hands of the Almoravids, while those of 1147–8, at Almeria, Lisbon, and Tortosa, reflected the collapsing power of the Almoravids. Crusades were a means of attracting wider recruitment and authorizing foreign help, as with the Geneose at Almeria and Tortosa. The next surge of crusading coincided with the beginning of the reversal of Almohad gains around 1200, culminating in the campaign that ended in the great Christian victory of Las Navas de Tolosa in 1212. Yet crusade bulls were aimed in 1197 against Alfonso IX of Leon, who had allied with the Almohads. The army that won in 1212 was, by the time battle was joined, largely stripped of any external crusader assistance, most of the French crusading force having abandoned the campaign as insufficiently lucrative and the weather far too hot. Although, unlike later in the Baltic, there was no permanent crusade in Iberia, in the thirteenth century and beyond crusade bulls gave rulers access to Church money through taxation and to the penitential giving of the laity. Yet it was only as the main conquest of al-Andalus was nearing completion that the local orders of Alcantara (1238) and Calatrava (1240) received permanent papal privileges granting automatic indulgences to any who fought with then against the Moors.[34] The role of the crusade in conquest became indistinct as a form of devotion, military endeavor, or fiscal ruse. Although James I of Aragon took the cross as part of his campaign to annex the region of Valencia, he and his successors did little to oppress, convert, or expel the resident Muslim majority. *Realpolitik* not religion determined the course and outcome of the so-called *reconquista*. An exception to this may be seen in the development of theories employing crusade in the extended Christendom. This gained credence from the thirteenth to the sixteenth centuries and formed a basis of justifications for bulls authorizing the occupation of the Canary Islands in the fourteenth and fifteenth centuries, the attacks by Spanish monarchs on the North African littoral at the end of the fifteenth and early sixteenth centuries, and, ultimately, the conquest of the Americas.[35] Whether the crusading impulse – that is, regarding the enterprise as a penitential duty imposed by God – inspired such developments or merely served as a means of explaining, justifying, and understanding them must remain open to doubt.

The chronology of crusading in the Baltic in part conformed to the Iberian model by providing a conceptual coherence and respectability to the achievement of secular ambitions. The alliance of the archbishop of Bremen and merchants from Bremen and Lübeck lay at the heart of the penetration of Livonia around 1200. Papal bulls legitimized economic exploitation and settlement. They also allowed the German sponsors of the Livonian enterprise to raise men and money beyond their normal areas of authority. Cloaking colonization and conquest in the guise of religious war encouraged the leaders of the German settlement in Riga to establish a standing army of a military order, the Swordbrothers, in direct imitation of the Holy Land orders. Although the Swordbrothers immediately proved awkward, violent, self-interested, and rapacious, soon competing for political power with their ostensible ecclesiastical master the bishop of Riga, they nonetheless provided defense and order, as well as channeling men and resources into the Livonian German enclave.[36] The Livonia crusade did not create the terms for expansion, but it encouraged the means and lent the enterprise a necessary respectability to ease the consciences and swell the support of the most hard-bitten or piratical German merchant or warrior.

The Danish and Swedish crusades similarly gilded existing regional political and economic impulses. A feature of Danish royal power in the twelfth century was the repeated campaigns against the pagans of the southern and eastern Baltic. They were couched at the time and especially later as religious, as with the extirpation of paganism at Rugen in 1168–9. These campaigns increased royal authority in attempting to secure control or leverage over the lucrative trade routes across the Baltic Sea, an endeavor that put the Danes in direct competition with the Lübeck mercantile colony at Riga. Similar competition marked the ecclesiastical empire building of the archbishops of Lund, Magdeburg, and Bremen. Although Pope Alexander III had recognized Danish interest in Estonia in the crusade bull of 1171, it was only in 1206, after more than a generation of Danish attacks along the Baltic coast from Prussia to Finland, that Waldemar led an army including papally authorized *crucesignati* to conquer Oesel. Similarly, despite attacks on Estonia in the 1190s, only in 1218–19 was the crusade applied to the Danish ambitions in the north-east Baltic, producing a campaign that led to the building of a Danish fort at Reval (Tallinn).[37] While Danish kings enjoyed their status as crusaders, their policy in the region was hardly conditioned by it. The Swedes, too, managed to attract papal approval for their raiding around the Gulfs of Finland and Riga, but only in the early thirteenth century. Swedish involvement in Finland dated back to the twelfth century, but received explicit crusading sanction in 1237, almost three decades after Swedish missionaries had begun work among the Suomi of south-west Finland.[38] Inevitably, Danish and Swordbrother activity in Estonia and Swedish penetration of Finland brought them up against the Orthodox Russians of Novgorod, a neat congruence of religious and territorial rivalry that so often provided the context for crusade bulls. Thus, the Swedes, alongside the Danes and Swordbrothers, normally fierce competitors, were drawn into the anti-Russian crusade of 1240–2. Thereafter, much of the crusading associated with Swedish control of Finland and Karelia was approved by the papacy in the context of its hostility to what it saw as the schismatic Russian Orthodox Church.[39]

Yet, however contingent on existing plans and interests, the institutions of the crusade in the Baltic exerted a particular and highly significant influence on the course and nature of German expansion around the Baltic basin. This did not concern the ecclesiastical reordering of the region, spearheaded by religious orders such as the Cistercians and the acquisitive new bishoprics at Riga, Reval, or Chelmno. Nor even was it directly associated with the policy of enforced conversion, a notable feature of defining the new Prussia in the thirteenth century. Beside and behind these developments stood the role of the military orders; the Swordbrothers of Livonia founded at Riga around 1200; the Knights of Dobryzn (Dobrin), established by the 1220s on the Vistula in imitation of the Swordbrothers; and the Teutonic Knights who had been invited to oversee the conquest of pagan Prussia by the Polish Duke Conrad of Mazovia in 1225. Leading attacks on the Prussians along the Vistula from 1230, in 1237 the Teutonic Knights absorbed the rump of the Swordbrothers and their rule in Livonia, two years after they had appropriated the Knights of Dobryzn.[40] If anywhere in the thirteenth century could be described as a crusader state, it was the principality the Teutonic Knights created in Prussia. Nowhere was the expansion of Latin Christendom so obviously served and dominated by the crusading ideal, its institutions, and its oppressive mentality.

The conquest, settlement, and Germanization of Prussia were very different affairs from the incursions further north in Livonia, Estonia, and Finland. For one thing, the advance came from inland toward the coast, not vice versa, this lending an immediate strategic and economic advantage to the invaders, as they could exert a stranglehold on the movement of commerce and goods. For another, whereas, in Livonia and Estonia, the Teutonic Knights after the 1230s had to compete with urban patriciates, and in Riga and Reval with the ecclesiastical hierarchy and Danish kings, by the 1240s in Prussia the Knights ruled supreme. By cleverly playing off the German emperor and the pope, the order secured privileges from both. As early as 1226, the Master of the Order, Hermann von Salza, was recognized by Emperor Frederick II as a *Reichsfurst* in his intended conquests in Kulmerland and Prussia. In 1234 Pope Gregory IX recognized Prussia as a fief of St Peter. In 1245 Innocent IV granted the Knights the right to proclaim a crusade more or less at will, inaugurating a period of permanent crusade. Failed bloody rebellions in the 1260s, 1286, and 1295 confirmed the military nature of the conquest. From the treaty of Christburg in 1249, the order pursued a policy of limiting civil rights to Germans and a privileged elite of Christianized Prussians, excluding pagans, the unfree, and the dissident. This policy could be sustained only through continuous war, the building of a network of forts and fortified towns, and the careful fostering of immigration and protected settlement of a range and depth not seen in Livonia, Estonia, or Finland, nor, indeed, in Syria and Palestine. Even so, as elsewhere in the region, order-sponsored German settlement beyond burgesses in towns and lords in the countryside was a slow and laborious process. Rural agrarian plantation only really began in the late thirteenth century, after the great rebellions had been suppressed. Even then it became a work of scores of years rather than a few decades. Yet by the fifteenth century, despite the decline in the order's fortunes after defeat by the Poles and Lithuanians at the battle of Tannenberg/Grunwald in 1410, Prussia had become and remained an integral part of Germany and the Latin world in a way Livonia and Estonia, where ethnic and cultural diversity persisted, were not.[41]

The creation of a confessional, militarist state in the thirteenth and fourteenth centuries in Prussia was unique, not for its polity being based on religious exclusivity or warfare, features shared by many if not most contemporary states, but for being ruled by a religious military order. Prussia and its dependencies were institutionally, socially, and culturally defined by religion and war in a so-called *Ordenstaat*. Elsewhere military orders played a prominent role in defense, politics, trade, and settlement, but nowhere equalled the authority enjoyed by the Teutonic Knights in Prussia. The nearest equivalent was, perhaps, the Hospitaller rule in Rhodes (1309–1522) and Malta (1530–1798), but the Hospitallers were ruling Christian populations to whom they brought a measure of protection and profit. In Prussia, the benefits of Teutonic rule were very restricted and imposed through the destruction or, some argue, redirection of indigenous culture. Yet such were the perceived advantages of an *Ordenstaat* that some commentators around 1300 took it as model for a reconquered Holy Land.[42]

Away from Prussia, Livonia, and Estonia, military orders also played a significant, if subsidiary, role in establishing Latin settlements, consolidating Latin conquests, and defending Latin gains. In twelfth-century Outremer, the military orders not only took on responsibilities for castles and for contributing to the army; by virtue of land grants they also entered the business of attracting immigrants. At the Hospitaller settlement of Bethgibelin, near Ascalon, incomers were attracted from southern France, north Italy, and Spain.[43] Similarly, in twelfth-century Spain, the Christian kings initially employed the Templars and Hospitallers in their armies and to man newly acquired frontier forts. In return, the orders received lands away from the battle zones to add to their networks of properties across Western Europe. In theory, this would provide an ideal basis for the orders to begin to organize civilian settlements in the new territories. This proved illusory, partly because of the uncertainty of the political situation consequent on the Almohad revival after the 1150s, partly because of the difficulty in finding settlers, even from their own estates elsewhere. The evidence of the orders' settlement charters (*cartas de poblacion*) suggests that the orders as landlords experienced difficulty retaining as well as attracting settlers in some areas. This was not a question of fear. Many areas for a long time far from the war zone, such as the lower Ebro, were still being settled in the later thirteenth century. The difficulty in finding settlers reflected the lack of economic benefit, a problem shared by secular landlords. Thus, as landlords of settlement, the orders played no particularly distinctive role.[44]

The Spanish kings appreciated that local military orders had advantages not possessed by the Holy Land orders. Usually founded by pious noblemen, wealthy merchants, or ecclesiastical grandees, originally often to protect a specific stronghold or small section of the frontier, between the 1150s and 1180s every kingdom except Navarre boasted its their own military orders such as Calatrava (1158) in Castile; Santiago (1170) and Alcantara (by 1176) in Leon; Evora, later Avis (by 1176), in Portugal. Some were ephemeral, but those that lasted received royal approval, patronage, and protection. Unlike the Holy Land orders, which also continued to enjoy royal patronage, especially in Aragon and Catalonia, the Spanish orders had no need to send money or men to the east. Being essentially local and national, even though attracting donations of property from across Christendom, these orders were more amenable to regional royal pressure and dependent on royal encouragement and patronage. However, as with their Holy Land exemplars, the Spanish orders acted as part of the process of expansion. As their dates of foundation suggest, they did not spearhead conquest and their experiences as colonizers conformed to wider, non-crusading regional patterns. In an analogous manner, the role of the Holy Land orders in areas of non-crusading Latin conquest, such as, arguably Celtic Wales and especially Ireland, acted as just one of many ecclesiastical and secular groups that cashed in on the rewards available to those who took part in such land grabs and subsequent occupation and rule.

The colonizing activities of the military orders point to a more general contribution to conquest and expansion exerted by crusade institutions. The military orders channeled human and material resources from all parts of Christendom to the frontiers on which they fought. In similar, if impermanent, fashion, the whole apparatus of crusading provided rulers and commanders eager to expand their or their faith's territorial rule with a massive pool of men and money. The recruitment advantages are obvious and continued well into the fifteenth century. While the Habsburg crusades against the Moorish pirates of the western Mediterranean or the Ottomans in the east may have gilded essentially national campaigns, previously and elsewhere the crusade lent international support for local conflicts as well as opening up the unexpected involvement of Western Europeans on the distant eastern Mediterranean. Except in Outremer, it is difficult to judge the difference made by such international aid. Certainly, Western crusaders materially helped the Teutonic Knights survive the thirteenth-century revolts, especially in Prussia, and to sustain their eternal struggle against pagan Lithuania in the fourteenth. Crusaders extended by far the resources at the disposal of the local Christian armies. But later, such assistance, in Hungary in 1396 or 1456, for example, came in defense not expansion of Latin territory. From at least 1300 onward, crusading must be seen as part of the defense and retreat of Latin Christendom, a subject to which modern historiography is only just beginning to afford proper attention.

Materially, crusading allowed commanders to collect money from their and their followers' subjects. As early as William Rufus's tax to pay for his mortgage for his crusading brother Robert of Normandy in 1096, the legitimacy of the cause of the cross had permitted extraordinary fiscal levies to be extracted. Even a king of limited authority, such as Louis VII of France, was able to tax the Church and perhaps the towns in his demesne. Increasingly, fiscal experiments were devised for the crusade, in 1166 and, famously, 1188, the Saladin Tithe. After Innocent III's failed scheme for an ecclesiastical tax in 1199, in 1215 the Fourth Lateran Council authorized crusade taxation of the Church that became the staple of crusade funding for the next century. At the same time the expedient of offering the crusade indulgence for cash redemption, perfected in the bull *Quia Maior* of 1213, opened up a new lucrative and socially embracive source of funding that, while controlled by the Church, was available to secular crusade commanders. During the early decades of the thirteenth century, too, regular alms, donations, and legacies were collected.[45] Each fundraising campaign had specific targets in mind, but they existed in the context of continual charitable giving, in much the same way as emergency charity appeals operate in modern first-world countries. In the later Middle Ages, crusading increasingly resembled a series of charity campaigns rather than war mobilization, providing the most regular link between the mass of the faithful and the wars planned or conducted in their name. Even Louis IX's attack on Egypt in 1249–50, in part an ambitious attempt to conquer the Nile valley, while it operated as a royal, almost national, French campaign was bankrolled by crusade fnds raised and held initially from and by the Church.[46]

Except in Outremer, the expansion of Latin Western Europe was not initiated by crusaders, the ideology and practice of holy war of the cross inconsistently supporting existing movements. The expansion of Latin Christendom into Poland, Bohemia, and Hungary owed nothing to crusading, although Hungary's strategic position and support for successive twelfth- and early thirteenth-century crusades helped cement its position in the community of Latin Christendom. However, it could be argued that the ideology of Holy War, popularized by the success of the First Crusade and refined by practice and theorists over the next century and more, lent a conceptual coherence to Latin expansionist enterprises that, in turn, played a more than marginal role in them. This ideology survived, even where private enterprise and collective leadership from different countries, nations, and regions were replaced by the patronage and resources of the state in sixteenth century, as in the American conquests.

The key to this ideology was the inescapable, umbilical relationship of crusading ideology and propaganda with the papacy.

The First Crusade had been born from two aspects of the papal reform movement. Beside the desire to liberate the Churches, west and east, from illegitimate secular or infidel control and restore, if only metaphorically or mystically, the supposed conditions of the Early Church, Urban II had justified his right to offer spiritual privileges by virtue of his authority as possessed of the power, given to St Peter by Christ, to bind and loose on earth and heaven (Matthew 16: 19).[47] This latter power was deemed universal and coterminous with Christendom and the rights of Christians acting with papal approval. By the mid-thirteenth century the canon lawyer Sinibaldo Fieschi, later Pope Innocent IV, produced a general theory under which Christians, by virtue of the pope being responsible for all human souls not just those of believers, had the right to chastise infidels and take their lands. Due cause consisted of infidels breaking "natural law' – for example, sexual perversions and idolatry – both accusations leveled frequently at Muslims and pagans by Christian polemicists. Innocent's theory still excluded forced conversion, but allowed wide latitude for Christian interference in the lands of infidels, particularly if they opposed peaceful missionizing, as happened more or less everywhere around the borders of Christendom. Innocent summed up the authority behind the theory in stating that the pope "has jurisdiction and power over infidels *de jure* but not *de facto*," a position that accepted temporal reality while offering opportunities for aggression and conquest.[48]

Allied to such theoretical and legalistic refinements were the simpler, starker rhetoric and images of Christians against infidels that appealed to Scriptural and early medieval precedent. Crusading and its attendant myths, legends, and propaganda offered those trying to dominate non-Latin Christian areas a sense of justice, identity, and superiority, from Lübeck merchants to Spanish Iberian (and later American) freebooters. Crusading also promised remission of sins and the prospect of financial subsidy and free or cheap military support. Small wonder crusading was eagerly adopted by those plying their ambitions on the marches of Christendom from the twelfth to the fourteenth centuries and those rulers facing catastrophe in central Europe and the Balkans in the fifteenth. But even here the appeal was not universal. Papal appeals for Western crusades to prop up the Latin Empire of Constantinople (1204–61) largely fell on deaf ears.[49] Western claims to parts of the Peloponnesus and central Greece ceased even to attract papal crusade bulls after the 1320s. Frankish settlers in Romania, the heirs of crusaders on the Fourth Crusade, carefully avoided the stereotypical intolerance and triumphalism that soaked crusading attitudes. At least from the mid-fourteenth century, they saw at first hand how the defeat in the Holy Land was not an isolated Christian retreat. In late fifteenth-century Hungary, as Janos Bak has argued, the nobility showed a marked lack of interest in crusading against the Turks, an indifference that contributed markedly to the blood-soaked course of the 1514 Hungarian crusade, which degenerated into a fratricidal war of social protest.[50]

Yet in the area of mentalities, images, and propaganda a final link between crusading and the expansion of Latin Europe exists. The crusades gave to conquerors a sense of mission, but also communal identity, as champions of a *societas Christiana*, a unity that lay at the heart of papal policy and rhetoric. However, papal theocracy frayed and failed in the fourteenth and fifteenth centuries, taking with it aspects of the allure of crusading and the fiction of a unified Christendom, even though such concepts retained potency beyond the opening of the Reformation. Holy war increasingly became attached to the dynastic and nationalist ambitions of rulers of individual *patria* within Christian Europe, which themselves became sacralized, from cities such as Florence, to kingdoms, especially in fourteenth- and fifteenth-century England and France and, by 1500, the new united Spanish realm. Each saw itself as a holy land with a providential destiny, which, in the case of Spain, was associated with a mission to conquer the infidel, in North Africa, the Atlantic, and the New World. Not all the formal panoply of crusading followed the new *conquistadors* of Habsburg Spain, but many did, from indulgences, bulls, and fiscal mechanisms to an attitude of religious bellicosity and cultural supremacy that harked back legally to Innocent IV and emotionally to Urban II if not beyond. While many regions of late medieval Latin Christendom witnessed contraction not expansion, it was perhaps not entirely inappropriate that the resurgence of Latin European expansionism, now around the globe, should, however unwittingly, have been inaugurated by a self-confessed messianic crusade enthusiast, Christopher Columbus.[51]

Notes

1 France, *Crusades and the Expansion of Catholic Christendom*; Bartlett, *Making of Europe*.
2 Bartlett, *Making of Europe*, p. 5.
3 Ibid., esp. pp. 251–3.
4 Berend, "How Many Europes?" pp. 77–92.
5 See Urban's letter to the Flemish of December 1095, the earliest authentic statement of his crusade plans: Hagenmeyer, *Die Kreuzzugsbriefe*, pp. 136–7.
6 Bernard of Clairvaux, *Letters of St Bernard*, trans. Scott James, p. 467.
7 On crusading, see Mayer, *Crusades*; Tyerman, *God's War*; on the Baltic, see Christiansen, *Northern Crusades*; on Spain, see now O'Callaghan, *Reconquest*.
8 Christiansen, *Northern Crusades*, pp. 53–6, 72; Bartlett, *Making of Europe*, pp. 274–7; Thomas, *English and the Normans*; Holt, *Colonial England*; Davis, *First English Empire*.
9 See Johns, *Arabic Administration in Norman Sicily*; for inter-faith relations in general, see Powell, ed., *Muslims under Latin Rule*.
10 Lock, *Franks in the Aegean 1204–1500*.
11 France, *Crusades and the Expansion of Catholic Christendom*, p. 328.
12 In general, see Housley, *Later Crusades*.
13 Urban II to Catalan counts 1096–9: Kehr, *Papsturkunden in Spanien. 1 Katalonien*, pp. 287–8; Cowdrey, "Pope Gregory VII's 'Crusading' Plans of 1074," pp. 27–40; Duchesne, ed., *Liber Pontificalis*, 2.293.
14 Cowdrey, "Gregory VII's 'Crusading' Plans," p. 31.
15 For a recent discussion, Morris, *Sepulchre of Christ and the Medieval West*, p. 137.
16 Tyerman, *God's War*, p. 55 and nn. 39 and 40 for refs.
17 Trans. O'Callaghan, *Reconquest*, p. 30.
18 *Storia de' Normanni di Amato di Montecassino*, ed. de Bartholomaeis, vol. 12, p. 234; quoted by Morris, *Papal Monarchy*, p. 142.
19 Trans. Holt, *Age of the Crusades*, p. 27.
20 Guibert of Nogent, *Gesta Dei per Francos*, 4.245.

21 On William of Tyre, see Edbury and Rowe, *William of Tyre*, esp. pt II; on Outremer, cf. Prawer, *Latin Kingdom of Jerusalem*, with Ellenblum, *Frankish Rural Settlement in the Latin Kingdom of Jerusalem*.
22 Albert of Aachen, *Historia Hierosolymitana*, 4.563.
23 This is one of the themes of France, *Crusades and the Expansion of Catholic Christendom*.
24 In general, Kedar, *Crusade and Mission*.
25 Ubieto Arteta, *Coleccion diplomatica de Pedro I de Aragon y Navarra*, p. 113 n. 6, p. 115 n. 9. In general, see O'Callaghan, *Reconquest*, esp. pp. 31–49.
26 O'Callaghan, *Reconquest*, pp. 38–41.
27 Bernard of Clairvaux, *Letters of St Bernard*, trans. Scott James, p. 467; Riley-Smith and Riley-Smith, *The Crusades*, pp. 77–8, for a translation of Innocent's letter to King Waldemar.
28 In general, Christiansen, *Northern Crusades*; Bartlett, *Making of Europe*; Urban, *Baltic Crusade*.
29 Translated in Riley-Smith, *Crusades: Idea and Reality*, pp. 75–7.
30 Tyerman, *God's War*, p. 677 and nn. 4 and 5.
31 Helmold, *The Chronicle of the Slavs*.
32 *Patrologia Latina*, 200, cols 860–1.
33 See Tyerman, *God's War*, esp. pp. 681–3.
34 O'Callaghan, *Reconquest*, pp. 50–76 and ch. 7; Forey, *Military Orders*, pp. 23–32.
35 Muldoon, *Popes, Lawyers and Infidels*, esp. pp. 88–91, 119–31; cf. Housley, *Later Crusades*, pp. 288, 308–10.
36 Christiansen, *Northern Crusades*, pp. 79–82, 99–103, 128; cf. refs in Forey, *Military Orders*.
37 Christiansen, *Northern Crusades*, pp. 109–13, 199–200.
38 Ibid., pp. 113–22.
39 Ibid., pp. 133–5.
40 Forey, *Military Orders*, pp. 32–7.
41 See notes 1, 7, and 28 above for general accounts.
42 See now Leopold, *How to Recover the Holy Land*, pp. 19, 34, 78, 178–9.
43 Delaville le Roulx, *Cartulaire générale de l'ordre des Hospitaliers*, 1.272–3, no. 399.
44 For a summary, see Forey, *Military Orders*, pp. 71–3.
45 For these measures, see Tyerman, *God's War*, pp. 76, 276–7, 298, 381, 389–91, 499–500, 617, 631–2; Tyerman, *England and the Crusades*, pp. 16–17, 45, 75–80; trans. of *Quia Maior*, Riley-Smith and Riley-Smith, *Crusades*, pp. 119–24.
46 Tyerman, *God's War*, pp. 777–9.
47 Hagenmeyer, *Die Kreuzzugsbriefe*, pp. 136–7.
48 Muldoon, *Popes, Lawyers and Infidels*, p. 10 and, generally, pp. 3–48.
49 See Barber, "Western Attitudes to Frankish Greece in the Thirteenth Century."
50 Bak, "Hungary and Crusading in the Fifteenth Century"; Housley, "Crusading as Social Revolt: The Hungarian Peasant Uprising of 1514."
51 Tyerman, *God's War*, pp. 906–15; Housley, *Religious Warfare in Europe 1400–1536*, esp. pp. 30–1 and 80–3.

Bibliography

Primary Sources

Albert of Aachen, *Historia Hierosolymitana*, in *Recueil des historiens des croisades: Documents occidentaux*, 5 vols (Paris: l'Académie des inscriptions & belles-lettres, 1844–95).

Bernard of Clairvaux, *The Letters of St Bernard of Clairvaux*, trans. Bruno Scott James (London: Burns & Oates, 1967).

The Chronicle of Henry of Livonia, trans. James A. Brundage (Madison: University of Wisconsin Press, 1961; repr. New York: Columbia University Press, 2003).

Delaville le Roulx, J., *Cartulaire generale de l'ordre des Hospitaliers*. 4 vols. (Paris: E. Leroux, 1894–1906).

Duchesne, L., ed., *Le Liber pontificalis*, 3 vols (Paris: E. de Boccard, 1955–7).

Guibert of Nogent, *Gesta Dei per Francos*, *Recueil des historiens des croisades: Documents occidentaux*, 5 vols (Paris: l'Académie des inscriptions & belles-lettres, 1844–95).

Hagenmeyer, H., ed., *Die Kreuzzugsbriefe aus den Jahren 1088–1100* (Innsbruck: Wagner'sche universitäts-buchhandlung, 1901), pp. 136–7

Helmold, *The Chronicle of the Slavs, by Helmold, priest of Bosau*, trans. with introduction and notes by Francis Joseph Tschan (New York: Columbia University Press, 1935).

Kehr, Paul Fridolin, *Papsturkunden in Spanien: Vorarbeiten zur Hispania Pontificia: I. Kalalanien* (Berlin: Weidmannsche Buchhandlung, 1926).

Ubieto Arteta, A., *Coleccion diplomatica de Pedro I de Aragon y Navarra* (Zaragoza: Consejo Superior de Investigaciones Científicas. Escuela de Estudios Medievales, 1951).

Secondary Studies

Bak, J., "Hungary and Crusading in the Fifteenth Century," in N. Housley, ed., *Crusading in the Fifteenth Century* (New York: Palgrave Macmillan, 2004), pp. 116–27.

Barber, M., "Western Attitudes to Frankish Greece in the Thirteenth Century," in B. Arbel et al., eds, *Latins and Greeks in the Eastern Mediterranean after 1204* (London: Cass, in association with The Society for the Promotion of Byzantine Studies, The Society for the Study of the Crusades and the Latin East, 1989), pp. 111–28.

Bartlett, Robert, *The Making of Europe: Conquest, Colonization and Cultural Change 950–1350* (London: Allen Lane, 1993).

Berend, N., "How Many Europes?" in P. Linehan and J. Nelson, eds, *The Medieval World* (London: Routledge, 2001), pp. 77–92.

Christiansen, Eric, *The Northern Crusades* (London: Penguin, 1997).

Cowdrey, H. E. J., "Pope Gregory VII's 'Crusading' Plans of 1074," in B. Z. Kedar, H. E. Mayer, and R. C. Smail, eds, *Outremer: Studies in the History of the Crusading Kingdom of Jerusalem Presented to Joshua Prawer* (Jerusalem: Yad Izhak Ben-Zvi Institute, 1982).

Davies, R. R., *The First English Empire: Power and Identities in the British Isles 1093–1343* (Oxford: Oxford University Press, 2000).

Edbury, P. W., and Rowe, J. G., *William of Tyre, Historian of the Latin East* (Cambridge: Cambridge University Press, 1988).

Ellenblum, Roni, *Frankish Rural Settlement in the Latin Kingdom of Jerusalem* (Cambridge: Cambridge University Press, 1998).

Forey, Alan, *The Military Orders: From the Twelfth to the Early Fourteenth Centuries* (Houndmills: Macmillan Education, 1992).

France, John, *Western Warfare in the Age of the Crusades, 1000–1300* (London: Taylor & Francis 1999).

France, John, *The Crusades and the Expansion of Catholic Christendom, 1000–1714* (London: Routledge, 2005).

Holt, James Clarke, *Colonial England, 1066–1215* (London: Hambledon Press, 1997).

Holt, P. M., *The Age of the Crusades: The Near East from the Eleventh Century to 1517* (London: Longman, 1986).

Housley, Norman, *The Later Crusades, 1274–1580: From Lyons to Alcazar* (New York: Oxford University Press, 1992).

Housley, Norman, "Crusading as Social Revolt: The Hungarian Peasant Uprising of 1514," *Journal of Ecclesiastical History*, 49 (1998), 1–28.

Housley, Norman, *Religious Warfare in Europe, 1400–1536* (Oxford: Oxford University Press, 2002).

Johns, Jeremy, *Arabic Administration in Norman Sicily: The Royal Dīwān* (Cambridge: Cambridge University Press, 2002).

Kedar, Benjamin Z., *Crusade and Mission: European Approaches toward the Muslims* (Princeton: Princeton University Press, 1984).

Leopold, Antony, *How to Recover the Holy Land: The Crusade Proposals of the Late Thirteenth and Early Fourteenth Centuries* (Aldershot: Ashgate, 2000).

Lock, Peter, *The Franks in the Aegean, 1204–1500* (London: Longman, 1995).

Mayer, Hans Eberhard, *The Crusades*, trans. John Gillingham, 2nd edn (Oxford: Oxford University Press, 1988).

Morris, Colin, *The Papal Monarchy: The Western Church from 1050 to 1250.* (Oxford: Clarendon Press, 1989).

Morris, Colin, *The Sepulchre of Christ and the Medieval West: From the Beginning to 1600* (Oxford: Oxford University Press, 2005).

Muldoon, James, *Popes, Lawyers, and Infidels: The Church and the Non-Christian World 1250–1550* (Philadelphia: University of Pennsylvania Press, 1979).

O'Callaghan, Joseph F., *Reconquest and Crusade in Medieval Spain* (Philadelphia: University of Pennsylvania Press, 2003).

Powell, James M., ed., *Muslims under Latin Rule, 1100–1300* (Princeton: Princeton University Press, 1990).

Prawer, Joshua, *The Latin Kingdom of Jerusalem: European Colonialism in the Middle Ages* (London, Weidenfeld and Nicolson, 1972).

Riley-Smith, J., and Riley-Smith, L. *The Crusades: Idea and Reality 1095–1274* (London: Arnold, 1981)

Thomas, Hugh M., *The English and the Normans: Ethnic Hostility, Assimilation, and Identity, 1066–c. 1220* (Oxford: Oxford University Press, 2003).

Tyerman, Christopher, *England and the Crusades, 1095–1588* (Chicago: University of Chicago Press, 1988).

Tyerman, Christopher, *The Invention of the Crusades.* Houndmills, Basingstoke, Hampshire: Macmillan Press, 1998.

Tyerman, Christopher, *Fighting for Christendom: Holy War and the Crusades* (Oxford: Oxford University Press, 2004).

Tyerman, Christopher, *The Crusades: A Very Short Introduction* (Oxford: Oxford University Press, 2005).

Tyerman, Christopher, *God's War: A New History of the Crusades* (Cambridge, MA: Belknap Press of Harvard University Press, 2006).

Urban, William L., *The Baltic Crusade* (Dekalb, IL: Northern Illinois University Press, 1975).

Further Reading

In English, modern understanding of the creation and nature of a distinctively Latin Christian political and religious culture in the High Middle Ages that could be described as "Christendom" and, in a later, different but closely related guise, Europe, owes much to R. W. Southern's classic *Making of the Middle Ages* (New Haven: Yale University Press, 1953) and, more specifically on the theme of expansion, to his research pupil Robert Bartlett's influential *The Making of Europe: Conquest, Colonization and Cultural Change 950–1350* (London:

Allen Lane, 1993). The role of the crusades in this process has recently been examined by John France, *The Crusades and the Expansion of Catholic Christendom, 1000–1714* (London: Routledge, 2005). The idea the interaction of one, coherent culture with a variety of neighbours has invited consideration of the theory and practice of the concept of the frontier, a geographic and conceptual space of unique exchange, conflict and synthesis. Useful and innovative collections of essays have been produced by R. Bartlett and A. Mackay, eds, *Medieval Frontier Societies* (Oxford: Clarendon Press, 1989) and by D. Abulafia and N. Behrend, eds, *Medieval Frontiers: Concepts and Practices* (Aldershot: Ashgate, 2002). This area has been acutely and succinctly analysed by Nora Behrend in "Frontiers," in H. Nicholson, ed., *Palgrave Advances in the Crusades* (Basingstoke and New York: Palgrave, 2005), that also has very helpful notes and brief bibliographies. For individual regions where crusading was claimed as part of the imposition of "Latin" culture, religion, or rule, see R. I. Burns, *The Crusader Kingdom of Valencia: Reconstruction on a Thirteenth-Century Frontier* (Cambridge, MA: Harvard University Press, 1967); E. Christiansen, *The Northern Crusades* (London: Penguin, 1997); A. Murray, ed., *Crusade and Conversion on the Baltic Frontier, 1150–1500* (Aldershot: Ashgate, 2001); R. Ellenblum, *Frankish Rural Settlement in the Latin Kingdom of Jerusalem* (Cambridge: Cambridge University Press, 1998), and C. MacEvitt, *The Crusades and the Christian World of the East: Rough Tolerance* (Philadelphia: University of Pennsylvania Press, 2008). For a flavour of what so-called expansion meant on the ground, see the often grisly, blood-soaked, tendentiously partisan but vivid and riveting contemporary account by Henry of Livonia of the conquest of what is now modern Latvia and Estonia by Germans between 1196 and 1227, *The Chronicle of Henry of Livonia*, trans. James A. Brundage (Madison: University of Wisconsin Press, 1961; repr. New York: Columbia University Press, 2003).

Part VI

Technologies and Culture

Chapter Twenty-three

Romanesque and Gothic Church Architecture

Stephen Murray

The Problem: Historiographic Overview

The terms "Romanesque" and "Gothic" have been applied to represent and classify architectural monuments in Western Europe between the late tenth and fifteenth centuries.[1] We might draw a contrast with the designations applied to the architecture of previous periods from the collapse of the Roman Empire to the tenth century – Early Christian, Byzantine, Merovingian, Carolingian, and Ottonian – each term makes unproblematic reference to the historical and geographical context. "Romanesque" and "Gothic," on the other hand, are historicizing terms referring to a more or less fictive past to frame the concept of "style" through a descriptive epithet applied to a set of easily recognizable "essential" visual forms, intended to invoke organic coherence and unity in multiple artifacts. Both epithets are value-laden: "Romanesque" is more than "Roman-like" – "esque" implies inferiority or decline, suggesting that architectural forms were dependent upon Roman architecture just as romance languages (Italian, French, and Spanish) were understood as decadent derivatives of Latin. "Gothic," a term first applied to architecture by Italian humanists of the sixteenth century, also makes reference to the past: the period of the fifth-century Germanic (Gothic: that is, Ostrogoths, Visigoths, and so on) invasions that transformed the Western provinces of the Roman Empire. Obviously either word could be applied to any historical or cultural manifestation in the aftermath of the fall of the Roman Empire: but by usage Romanesque has been restricted to the architecture of the tenth to the twelfth centuries and Gothic to that of the twelfth to the fifteenth. In the most general sense, both epithets come from the profoundly rooted cognitive need to control and to organize a mass of data through classification.[2] Despite the pejorative overtones, the nineteenth-century romantic yearning to rediscover lost cultural and national roots lent Romanesque and Gothic architecture a new life that went beyond the narrow limits of the scientific discourse of the Academy, and filled northern cities with replicas of medieval buildings.

Gothic

Although "Gothic" designates a later phase of architectural production than "Romanesque," it has deeper historical roots and should therefore be considered first. On the lips of an Italian humanist of the fifteenth century the epithet would have assumed peculiar resonance through its reference to the "barbarians" held responsible not just for the physical destruction of the Roman Empire but also for the corruption of antique cultural forms and the purity of the Latin language.[3] That association was exacerbated by continuing threats to Italian soil from Franks and Germans, and by a concerted program to enhance papal authority through a return to canonic Latin cultural forms.[4] "Gothic" in this context was synonymous with crude or rustic. The term took on additional levels of meaning when first applied to architecture since a link was found between the sinuous, diaphanous forms of a type of building with pointed arches and slender articulation and the forest, where primitive Germans had pulled together the tops of trees to make a sacred space. Thus, what had begun as a simile ("it looks like a forest") was turned into "history" – how it actually happened. The deeply rooted concept of a "low" point in cyclical cultural change as morphology – the passage from birth to maturity to decline and death – was inherited from Roman writers such as Vitruvius and Pliny the Elder.[5] It was necessary to create a myth of "Otherness" in order to launch the story of the Renaissance. It was in this way that the great tripartite chronological division was created: Antiquity, the "Middle Ages," the "Renaissance".

It should be remembered, however, that the "Gothic" monuments encountered by such humanists were not Chartres or Amiens Cathedrals, but manifestations peculiar to Italian soil. While Raphael's famous chronological classification of Roman monuments (1519), including a reference to "Germanic" forms, is generally given pride of place in the historiography of Gothic, more important was Vasari's account of "German" architecture as overcharged with confused decoration and inappropriately flimsy in appearance.[6] However, while Italians might have found the idea of primitive Germans in forests offensive, to northerners the same story brought powerful references to cultural and national roots and to artistic forms appropriately rooted in Nature.[7] In the "scientific" atmosphere of the eighteenth and nineteenth centuries, however, many hesitated to apply such a palpably anachronistic term to describe the combination of architectural forms found in cathedrals such as Chartres or Amiens, and other terms (pointed style – *style ogival*) also found considerable currency. Paradoxically, it is in our own age that the term has achieved universal currency, while at the same time being questioned by many architectural historians as a useful notion to facilitate the representation and organization of multiple buildings of a similar type.

Romanesque

"Romanesque" was coined in the early nineteenth century when the "scientific movement" brought the need to describe and classify cultural products (including languages and artifacts) just as specimens collected in expeditions of exploration were being classified and the story of creation told as "natural history."[8] As far as architecture was concerned, the desire to describe and classify was deeply rooted in the encyclopedic movement of the eighteenth century and the antiquarianism of, for example, the reformed Benedictine Maurist movement in France, or the growing popularity in England of illustrated volumes where the great buildings of the Middle Ages were represented in both words and images. And during the nineteenth century improved image technology (lithography, photography) and road and rail communications together with accelerated scholarly discourse facilitated an encyclopedic approach characteristic of the *statistique monumental* where a considerable corpus of monuments can be stored in the pages of a book. Soon after 1800 the term "Romanesque" was coined in England (William Gunn) and *roman* or *romane* in France (Charles de Gerville).[9]

It should be remembered that there was considerable fluidity both in the understanding of the chronology of individual monuments and in the meaning of the word itself: "Romanesque" and "Romantic" were still interchangeable. The currency and precision of the word gained momentum as scholarly publishing was propagated by increasing numbers of institutions – the local *Société des antiquaires* (starting in the 1820s), for example – and then in the next decade the *Société française d'archéologie* with its twin publications, *Bulletin monumental* and *Congrès archéologique*. England lost its early dominance in the historiography of Romanesque (English scholars preferred "Saxon" and "Norman") as generations of French scholars engaged in a discourse intended to reconcile the concept of a set of essential forms (round arches; heavy vaulted superstructures; articulation through the systematic application of the applied classical orders; new forms of choir and western frontispiece) with regional variations in France and beyond. For more than a century scholars of Romanesque continued to debate the question, proposing a range of different regional "schools" and "sub-schools" (Arcisse de Caumont, Viollet-le-Duc, Lasteyrie, and so on).[10] The word "Romanesque," like "Gothic," thus passed from being a rather generalized term equally applicable to language and other cultural phenomena to designate a specific "style" peculiar to the visual arts (particularly architecture) and discernible through a set of "essential" features. Applied in this very specific fashion there was certainly no pan-European "Romanesque" but rather a series of temporal and regional manifestations.

Together with the argument over regional sameness and difference in Romanesque came a general assumption of temporal "development" or improvement, seen, for example, in the transition from rubble masonry to cut stone or ashlar; in the "correctness" of classicizing forms; in the skill and precision with which buildings were laid out; in the deployment of new architectural forms, and in the increasing readiness to risk high masonry vaulting over large spans. In this way scholars have applied terms like "proto-Romanesque," "pre-Romanesque," "first Romanesque," "mature Romanesque," and "transition to Gothic." Palpable "progress" was linked with the emergence of national genius, as French, English, and Germans looked to the monuments of the Middle Ages as a sign of nascent cultural and national identity.

The questionable origins of our descriptive epithets and growing skepticism about positivistic systems of classification have led many recent art historians to limit their use of the designations as descriptive of unified "styles" and to focus instead on other attendant issues: semiotics (the "language" of architecture), patronage, institutional structures (particularly monasticism), devotional practices such as pilgrimage and the cult of saints, liturgical performance, and the socioeconomic and underpinnings of architectural production.[11] Yet the terms "Romanesque" and "Gothic" have taken on a life of their own: in publications intended for wider audiences they are currently used uncritically as neutral labels. Attempts to tell the story of medieval architecture without recourse to these terms have fallen flat.

Most recently, it has been realized that the combination of figurative description ("it looks like . . ."), anachronism, and animus have lent peculiar force to the concepts of Romanesque and Gothic. What might have been intended by Italian humanists as a negative slap might become a proud discovery of cultural roots in the north – certainly this was the case in the nineteenth-century Gothic revival and possibly already in the Middle Ages.[12] Moreover, we should acknowledge that the ability to recognize the differences that we understand as "Romanesque" and "Gothic" can certainly be found in medieval mentality and visuality, and that, while these *particular* designations did not exist at the time, the words used by medieval people would have a similar combination of temporal and spatial reference with judgment: "the new work"; "in the manner of the Romans"; "in the manner of the French."[13]

Representation and Production of Space

The Power of the Monument

Writing the history of architecture poses a peculiar problem: one's experience of any individual monument is one of intense "here-and-nowness," resulting from the presence of the sentient witness and interlocutor in an architectural space that may be overwhelming. The visitor may, moreover, be in the highly impressionable state of the pilgrim.[14] In an extended formal description of a particular building the interlocutor may want to represent the monument as one-of-a-kind. Yet buildings – particularly medieval churches – have the power to transport the user *elsewhere* in time and space – whether retroactively to the monuments associated with Christ's life and death on earth – the foundation of the Church, the lives of the saints – or forward in time to the Second Coming and the final vision of the Heavenly City.[15] Similarly, the evangelists who brought Christianity to the north were from the Mediterranean world – yet by their mission, martyrdom, and continuing presence (through the cult of relics), these outsiders provided the most critical element in the creation of the local identity commemorated in church dedications.

The Power of Architecture

Our church, then, has the power to *represent* critical aspects of the story of Christianity and to serve as a *medium*, able to transport the visitor far away in time and space. Yet it also assumes meaning through its relationship to other buildings existing in the *same* time and contiguous space – when we say that a church is "Romanesque" or "Gothic," we are appealing to a concept of Universals that creates meaning and identity through our ability to relate "token" to "type": in other words, the accidental qualities of the particular specimen before our eyes to a larger class of object, in our case involving hundreds – even thousands – of buildings, constructed over a given period of time and located in a given geographical space.[16] To represent such a complex network of connections within the linear matrix of speech or the written page poses real problems, however, as architecture is *explained* through the presentation of a procession of monuments where underlying etiological assumptions are unavoidable: *post hoc ergo propter hoc*. We can reveal the nature of the universal thing only through the rehearsal of its "essential" characteristics as found in a mature specimen. In Romanesque, these characteristics will include rounded arches – sculptural articulation systematically applied to a muscular architectural envelope often (but not always) designed with vaulting in mind. Such a combination of forms may be represented through the presentation of a "mature" specimen, such as the church of Saint-Sernin at Toulouse (high altar consecrated in 1096), Saint-Étienne at Nevers (dedicated 1097), or Cluny III (begun 1088). The recounting of the story of origins will then produce a kind of *entelechy* – a self-fulfilling prophesy, where the outcome can be nothing other than what has already been seen and described. This is doubly a problem for Gothic, where the story of origins has endlessly privileged mid-twelfth-century Saint-Denis and the procession of monuments presented in terms of continuing improvement and reaching a climax in the paradigmatic cathedrals of Chartres (1194), Amiens (nave, 1220), and Cologne (choir, 1247). Told in the art historical explanatory mode associated with Heinrich Wölfflin and his disciples like Paul Frankl, Gothic became a thing or a force "out there" and buildings represented animistically as somehow striving toward a higher level of Gothicness only then to fall off into decadence.[17]

The Problem of Context

The desire to escape from the story of style told in terms of origins and influence has led historians to seek to explain Romanesque as the expression of a set of contextual circumstances: focusing more on the *process* than the *product*. Rapid tenth-to-eleventh-century demographic recovery following the end of the period of Viking invasions may be associated with the dynamic interaction of increased political stability, agrarian productivity, and the growth of towns with their thriving industrial and commercial activities. Church reform was associated with an energized papacy and new monastic orders, notably the Cluniacs and Cistercians, whose values were potentially opposed to the materialism of the growing bourgeois population of the towns. Old-established power structures were challenged and reshaped by a new type of castle keeper and adventurer.[18] This was the age of the Norman Conquest of England; the First Crusade; the continuing *Reconquista* in Spain. Such adventures might produce wealth: the most lavish construction project in northern Europe (Cluny III) was funded by King Alphonso VI of Léon–Castille. However, the limit of our ability to *explain* the dynamics of architectural form by invoking such material circumstances is revealed by the fact that, although the mid-twelfth century was not marked by any major historical event (like the Fall of Rome or the Viking invasions, for example) nor any sudden economic or dynastic shift, buildings began to look radically different in Gothic. The different context of Gothic is one of quantitative rather than qualitative change, as urban populations played a bigger role, reformed monasticism became less important, and the mendicants began to appear in northern cities.

The Production of Space: Plotting

Rather than focusing narrowly upon the "development" of "Romanesque and Gothic style" as a means of classifying multiple artifacts, we might move the discourse to wider issues involving the representation and production of space.[19] Space should, of course, be considered in terms of multiple edifices stamped out over an extent of territory and displaying various degrees of sameness and difference. However, there are two other kinds of space that come into play. First, the creation of geopolitical space –the eleventh-to-thirteenth centuries were a time when the pattern of the political boundaries of Western Europe began to settle into their modern configuration. The outcome, achieved through intense local struggles, was by no means clear at the start. Yet buildings provided one of the most powerful means of exercising control – visual as well as logistical – of the land, projecting the *appearance* of legitimacy and manifest destiny. Such control was exercised in several ways, including the construction of cities, castles, and churches. Castle design and production were revolutionized in the late-eleventh-to-twelfth centuries through the introduction of the stone-built donjon; cities transformed in the late twelfth century through the construction of walls (often ashlar) enclosing new suburbs. One could make the case that the rapid technological change in medieval architectural production that we associate with Gothic resulted partly from the twelfth-century shift of resources and expertise from castles to church building. The multiplication of church spaces with powerful historicizing elements and references to prestigious prototypes in the Mediterranean world projected *centralized control* – whether on the part of a king, a duke, or a monastic institution.

Social space in the production of architectural form involves the realization that buildings result from the aspirations and desires entertained by multiple builders: for a church this would characteristically bring an abbot or bishop; a seigneur to provide protection and funds, and the artisans who were actually capable of building. "Change" in architectural form (the "transition" from Romanesque to Gothic) must be understood in terms of *critical response* (the assessment of existing architectural forms) and a paradigm shift in which new prototypes are identified – northern prototypes played an increasing important role in the generation of Gothic.

A useful way to conceive of the projection of architectural form in medieval buildings is through the invocation of the *desires* of the builders and the means by which they identified and communicated those desires through deliberate reference to prototypes, translating them into material form in a process that we can understand as alternating contraction and expansion. In this way, buildings *compressed* as mnemonic images were represented verbally and graphically in the interactions between patron and builder, and those images were modified and eventually laid out upon the ground and *expanded* into material edifices.[20] The sociological, logistical, and formal aspects of building were linked by the activity of "plotting," as the need to realize the as-yet-unbuilt edifice led individuals of very different backgrounds (ecclesiastical patron, seigneur, or provider of funds; master mason) to conspire together to control what might otherwise be the accidental outcome of circumstances, manipulating the building site through a combination of arithmetic and geometry expressed in the shapes formed by ropes stretched on the ground to form the building plot.[21] Enhanced knowledge of arithmetic and geometry fostered by the teaching of the liberal arts certainly helped in the generation of Gothic, as did the survival of the Roman agrarian surveying techniques practiced by the *agrimensores*.[22] Of the greatest importance was the twelfth-century shift from an oral to a literate culture: the ability to control the destiny of the unbuilt monument gained enormously from the increasing use of written contracts and accounts.

Buildings are not merely the *result* or product of material circumstances: architecture can help fix or change the outcome of history.[23] Gothic expresses a new intensity in the plotting process where patrons like Abbot Suger of Saint-Denis played a critical role in the realization of the striking new forms of the chevet of Saint-Denis to promote the ambitious agenda of the monastery. Gothic should be understood, above all, as a *paradigm shift*, where builders found their desirable prototypes, not so much in Rome, the Near East, or distant shrines associated with the tombs of the saints, but rather in the great buildings realized in the twelfth-to-thirteenth-century north, especially in and around Paris – churches like Saint-Denis and Notre-Dame of Paris.

Telling the Story of Romanesque and Gothic

We have seen that the story of Romanesque has been told through an unstable combination of temporal and spatial factors as something that "develops" over time but that is expressed as a series of distinctly regional manifestations with stylistic "influences" spreading from one region to another. Preoccupation with purely art historical issues of style and influence can get us no further: the force of Romanesque, then, is best represented on the page as a series of dialectic oppositions. Such tension is inherent in the concept of a period (tenth to twelfth centuries) characterized by dynamic growth, invention, and the production of new kinds of artifact and technology, yet one where buildings and artifacts were also deliberately formed to make references to distant prototypes and a more or less fictive past.

Here-and-Now/Elsewhere; Modernitas/Romanitas

Architecture had provided the most visible means of projecting Roman power and cultural values throughout the empire, and sizable northern cities had been plotted with a gridded street system and public buildings expressing a way of living and a set of values associated with *Romanitas*.[24] Long after the western Roman Empire had been overrun by the Germanic invaders of the fifth century, northerners looked at surviving monuments with awe. Political theory and institutional structures in the north relied heavily upon Roman precedents for the institution and projection of power as well as alliances with the Roman Catholic Church.[25] As monastic life was invented and reinvented, moreover, leaders were drawn to architectural representations of the early Church in the sites associated with the life, mission, and death of Christ in the Near East, in the establishment of the Church and the cult of saints in Rome, and in the increasing importance of pilgrimage and the cult of St James with his tomb at Santiago de Compostela in Spain. The story of Romanesque may, indeed, be told in terms of the interaction of the north and the Mediterranean World – not as the spread of a "style" through impersonal "influences" but rather as enhanced communications and prosperity allowed northerners to direct their attention to desirable prototypes; as patrons and masons traveled; as images were transmitted, and as enhanced prosperity and technology facilitated the reproduction, elaboration, and transformation of these prototypes.

In this interaction we must, of course, also recognize the power of northern architectural forms – particularly the great hall employed by Germanic peoples and the architectural language of the timber-framed structure.[26] Northern factors also come to play in the identity of the builders themselves. Patron and churchman were not able to realize their desired building alone – they needed artisans. While elite masons and carpenters as well as some materials (columns and capitals) might be brought to the building site from elsewhere, northern builders had to work with local labor, local materials, and local traditions.

Basilica/Centralized Structure

Within this dialectic framework we might recognize the existence of the two very different types of structure available to early medieval builders in monuments surviving from Antiquity. The first type was the spacious wooden-roofed basilica with smooth, unarticulated walls. Such structures were relatively inexpensive and flexible in their potential function. Able to accommodate large numbers of people, they were ideally suited to the needs of Roman public life and readily adaptable for use as churches – the prototypical early churches of Rome (St Peters, the cathedral of St John in Lateran) were of this type, which would be well known to northerners through the churches of Ravenna and Monte Cassino, and the earliest great churches built in northern cites (Saint-Denis and Saint-Étienne in Paris, for example). Simple architectural forms could be combined with sumptuous decorative programs, including elegant light-reflective marble columns, late-Antique capitals (often reused), painted or mosaic mural decoration, and gold and silver liturgical equipment and lamp mountings. In great Carolingian monasteries like Centula (dedicated 799), for example, northern builders, in response to liturgical needs, elaborated interior spatial complexity and exterior massing of the basilica through the combination of Western and Eastern transepts and multiple towers. The image of such a basilica, plotted in the famous monastic plan of Saint-Gall, was used to project Benedictine reform. The power structure of the German Ottonian empire relied heavily upon references to Byzantium and Rome as well as to its Carolingian roots: ninth- and tenth-century monastic churches (St Cyriakus at Gernrode (founded 961), for example) as well as imperial cathedrals like Speyer (*c.* 1030) would generally be dominated by such a wooden-roofed basilica, with Western and Eastern transepts and multiple towers.

The second type of structure inherited from Rome and the first centuries of Christianity was the special-use centralized building: a circle, a square, or an octagon. Such forms assumed extraordinary power through reference to the fourth-century monuments enshrining the holy sites of Christ's birth and death – the rotundas of the Holy Sepulchre and the Resurrection (*Anastasis*) in Jerusalem; the church of the Nativity in Bethlehem.[27] This type of building was considered particularly appropriate for use in baptisteries, mausolea, and seigneurial chapels. Such buildings might be vaulted. Examples in the West can be found in the mausoleum of Theoderic (*c.* 520); the church of St Vitale (526–47) at Ravenna; the palatine chapel constructed for the emperor Charlemagne at the end of the eighth century, and the oratory of Germigny-des-Prés built by Bishop Theodulf of Orléans around 800.

The generation of medieval architectural form may be understood partly in terms of the continuing interest on the part of patrons and builders in the reconciliation of the complexity and focus of the centralized structure with the generous space-enclosing envelope of the great basilica. Abbot William of Volpiano embraced such a combination in his spectacular church of Saint-Bénigne of Dijon begun in 1001.[28] The dialectic between basilica and the centralized structure was never finally "resolved" – the reconciliation of the two special forms continued to preoccupy the builders of churches throughout the Middle Ages.

Regional Interaction/Regional Identity: Supraregionalism

Abbot William of Volpiano was originally from Lombardy in northern Italy: he had come north to Cluny (Burgundy) in 987, later undertaking the reform and rebuilding of Saint-Bénigne in Dijon. The new church with its spectacular rotunda made references to monuments in the Near East as well as in Rome: the cosmopolitan nature of the enterprise may have been enhanced by the presence of Italian masons.[29] While the patron's desire to endow the yet-to-be-built church with meaning through references to prestigious prototypes provides one critical element in the conception and form of the project, an equally important factor is in the background and training of the artisans. In the eleventh century architectural production, still predominantly rural, was transformed through the increased availability of teams of skilled masons who might work alongside native-born village men: we may talk about a kind of "supraregionalism."[30] In the early Middle Ages, despite the collapse of urban life in the north, centers of fine masonry production (including the carving of classicizing capitals) continued to operate around the Mediterranean littoral, especially in northern Italy, southern Gaul, the Pyrenees, and Catalonia. In Lombardy, masons' communities achieved legal recognition at a very early date: the area saw the construction of churches with finely wrought masonry walls and the exploitation of brick construction. Exteriors are frequently articulated with vertical strips running directly into arcaded bands at cornice level – a means of creating dramatic effects of light and shadow, of lending eloquence to exterior masses, and of projecting rainwater beyond walls and foundations. Such forms can be seen in San Vincenzo in Prato (originally built 814–33), and in San Pietro in Agliate (*c.* 875?) near Milan, which has a basilical nave separated from aisles by columns, and a barrel-vaulted sanctuary raised over a groin-vaulted crypt. It is, above all, the appearance of the vertical strips linked with cornice arcading ("Lombard Bands") that lend an air of sameness to buildings from the tenth-to-twelfth centuries spread over a considerable swathe of geography: from Lombardy to Catalonia (Monserrat, 957 and later), to Burgundy (Chapaize, *c.* 1050 and later), and Switzerland that led Puig i Cadafalch, Conant, and others to talk about a "First Romanesque Style" that "spread" and "developed."[31]

Another area where we can find precocious architectural production "anticipating" the forms of Romanesque is the Asturian kingdom in northern Spain. Having been occupied first by the Visigoths, most of the Peninsula had been conquered by Islamic forces in the eighth century. The reconquest of the Peninsula was an obsession on the part of Christian emperors and kings, for whom the land of Spain became an object of desire. St James played an important role both in attracting the pilgrim to continue onward to the holy site at the end of the earth, but also in his role as *Matamoros* (Moor slayer) leading Christian armies to victory. Concomitant with the geopolitical drive was the northern fascination with intellectual and visual forms of Spanish Islamic culture, with its access to a treasure trove of Antique literary and scientific sources. To the northwest of the peninsula the Christian kingdom of the Asturias or Galicia was formed in the eighth century and under energetic kings such as Alfonso the Catholic (739–57). The sumptuous court church (*c.* 830) of S. Julién de los Prados or "Santullano" just outside Oviedo, the capital city, is a wooden-roofed basilica whose spacious transept facilitated royal access.[32] The nave is decorated with a program of images of church councils rendered by artists familiar with late-Antique monumental illusionistic ("Pompeian") painting; the choir has three short barrel-vaulted compartments. Santa Maria de Naranco (built to serve the royal palace near Oviedo under Ramiro I; consecrated 848) is a basilical structure used in transverse fashion to facilitate royal liturgical performances and audiences.[33] It is made up of lower and upper chambers – both barrel-vaulted – and loggias at each end. Continuing architectural production in northern Spain and the Pyrenees is marked by such remarkable monuments as St Michel de Cuxa (955–74) and Ripoll (*c.* 1020–32).

Romanesque "Schools" in France

For almost two centuries architectural monuments in eleventh-to-twelfth-century France have been categorized and explained in terms of "schools."[34] The early importance of Burgundy and the Auvergne in Romanesque architectural production resulted partly from the fact that the coast and rivers of western France had received the full brunt of Viking attacks in the ninth century – monks from western monasteries sometimes found refuge in central France, leading the way to economic recovery in the tenth and eleventh centuries. The role of reformed Benedictine monasticism was most important in Burgundy – the Cluniac and Cistercian movements both had their start here. Close links between Lombardy and Burgundy resulted from two levels of architectural production – monastic leaders whose interests in Church reform were focused upon a re-energized papacy in Rome, and the availability of itinerant masons. It is certainly true that some of the traits we have observed in Lombardy can also be found in Burgundian churches – particularly the systematic articulation of the exterior through the application of Lombard bands and early experiments with vaulting – both were features of, for example, the church of Chapaize (*c.* 1050 and later), and Saint-Philibert of Tournus (mid-tenth to mid-twelfth century).

The idea of a "school" is based upon the discovery of a set of unifying characteristics peculiar to the monuments of a particular region – for example, in the domed churches characteristic of western and south-western France – however, the use of domes, in fact, transcends any of the schools as traditionally designed. The characteristics of the Auvergnat "school," moreover (barrel-vaulted two-storey nave; generous transept arms stepped up to a central octagonal tower; ambulatory and radiating chapels), were, in fact, peculiar only to a handful of churches (all from around 1100) in the area (Notre-Dame du Port of Clermont-Ferrand, Orcival, Issoire, Saint-Nectaire, Saint-Saturnin). And the Romanesque churches of Normandy and Burgundy embodied a wide variety of plans and spatial configurations. The most we can do is to recognize the existence of "clumps" of buildings sharing in common elements derived from some local prototype (the cathedral of Autun and Paray-le-Monial derived from Cluny III, for example).

Modernitas

The eleventh and twelfth centuries were marked by a strong sense of "newness" – of having transcended the bounds of the old order. This is most famously expressed in Raoul Glaber's description of a world that soon after the year 1000 seemed to throw off its sense of advancing age through the assumption of a *white mantle of churches*.[35] The beautiful metaphor invoked ideas of transformation or transfiguration (the appearance of a radiant Christ between Moses and Elijah) to suggest that a world that had become old and weary had been recreated just as the white garment worn by the catechumen expresses the transformation of baptism. And the eleventh century also saw the rapid growth of towns and cities and the proliferation of castles – mostly involving a combination of earthworks and wooden palisades. In the mid-twelfth century we find the first use of the word *modernitas*. The art historical use of the word "Romanesque" privileges retrospective references to Antiquity and reuse of *spolia* – contemporaries, however, may have been equally concerned with novelty and invention. We can certainly find much evidence for such innovation in the forms of our buildings.

Arched Masonry

Medieval builders abandoned Roman masonry construction having a concrete core faced with (semi-)cut stones, favoring instead solid masonry bound together with mortar. In some areas excellent mortar allowed walls to remain relatively thin (Anglo-Saxon England, for example). Rubble (*petit appareil*) was normally combined with cut stone (ashlar) to form the voussoirs of arches, windows, and door frames and, sometimes, the corners of walls (quoins). In some cases reused Roman cut stones lent regularity to masonry surfaces; alternatively, new material might be roughly shaped and laid up in horizontal courses or rhythmic patterns created through herring-bone coursing. The use of the rounded arch is sometimes considered the essential *Leitmotif* of Romanesque, yet pointed arches were used at an early date in Italy (derived from Islamic prototypes) and Burgundy, where they were employed in Cluny III (begun in 1088) and popularized in Cistercian monastic architecture. By the late eleventh century increasing quantities of ashlar masonry were employed – made possible by the formation of masonic communities, with increasingly large numbers of artisans trained for specialized work on more sophisticated buildings. This trend was accelerated by intense competition resulting from the production of masonry castles in the late-eleventh century and from the availability of bodies of professional artisans within increasingly populous towns.

More Sophisticated Plans: Choirs with Ambulatory

Heightened aspirations on the part of the patrons and the availability of highly trained masons lie behind the invention and deployment of one of the most remarkable features of medieval ecclesiastical architecture – the choir surrounded by ambulatory and radiating chapels. Early Christian and Early Byzantine choirs remained spatially open and architecturally undeveloped, and the triple-apsed plan used widely in the

West in the early Middle Ages offered limited space; the tenth century saw the beginning of a series of remarkable developments that linked the regions of Western Europe in the quest for a choir design that provided a discrete and more generous space for the clergy with their increasingly complex liturgical demands for processional paths and altars. Of critical importance was the provision of a space for the display of relics, whether in a crypt forming the underpinnings of an elevated choir, or on the elevated platform itself. By the tenth century interest was turning toward a new kind of plan where the eastern hemicycle of the choir was not bounded by a solid wall (that is, an apse) but by an arcade opening on to flanking aisles linked by a curving passage or ambulatory encircling the hemicycle. Experiments with such forms took place over a wide swathe of geography from Rome (the transformation of the choir of St Peters in the fifth century with the addition of an annular passage) and continuing in western France (Saint-Martin of Tours, tenth century), Chartres, Auvergne (cathedral of Clermont, mid-tenth century), and Burgundy, where the choir of the church of Saint-Philibert at Tournus (late tenth century) embodies the first surviving example of a fully worked-out system of ambulatory and radiating chapels. The form became canonic after it was used in Cluny III and in the great so-called pilgrimage churches.

Exterior Forms and Massing: Transept; Towers

The breaking of the silhouette of the great church through transept arms, towers, and turrets was a feature of Carolingian, Ottonian, and Romanesque monastic church design. The exterior surfaces of the churches of Ottonian Germany were enlivened with arcades, pilasters, and corbels – the source of inspiration may surely be found in northern Italy. The point where the body of the basilica is intersected by the eastern transept (*in medio ecclesiae*), the center of liturgical operations, might be marked by a great crossing tower. Towers might also flank the choir (northern Italy) or crown the transept façades.

Western Frontispieces

One of the greatest innovations of Carolingian architecture was the western transept crowned by a central tower enshrining an upstairs space mounted over a vaulted crypt. Prime examples include Centula (dedicated 799) and Corbie (ninth century). The western chapel might serve for special liturgical celebrations, at Easter time, for example, and might carry a particular dedication, whether to Christ the Savior or to St Michael. Charlemagne's chapel at Aachen also had such a *Westwerk* principally as a means of projecting the power of the emperor. Such an arrangement is continued by the builders of the great Ottonian churches and cathedrals, including Corvey (dedicated 885) and Mainz (dedicated 1036). Great central towers with or without a western transept were still popular in the eleventh and twelfth centuries: Saint-Benoît-sur-Loire (begun 1060s), Ely Cathedral (twelfth century), Ebreuil (twelfth century). But builders began increasingly to experiment with western frontispieces composed of three segments matching the three divisions of the aisled nave (the *harmonious façade*). Early experiments can be found in a range of buildings, including Rhenish churches, but the best-known early example of the type is found at

Saint-Étienne and La Trinité of Caen (both begun mid-eleventh century) – monuments certainly known to the builders of the abbey church of Saint-Denis, where the new frontispiece with its twin towers and triple portals articulated by four great buttresses provided a paradigm for later churches.

Galleried Elevations

The great Roman prototypes (St Peter; St Paul; St John in Lateran, and so on), had two-storey elevations with marble columns and a smooth upper wall punctuated with clerestory windows. Romanesque builders, on the other hand, embraced a range of different kinds of elevation, in some cases eschewing the use of aisles altogether (Bourges and Souvigny in the eleventh century, and in a mass of smaller churches) or employing aisles of the same height as the main vessel (a one-storey elevation). The galleried elevation quickly became a favorite for prestigious churches, however, and was used in the great "pilgrimage churches" as well as in a range of churches scattered over regions from the Nivernais (Saint-Étienne of Nevers (dedicated 1097)) to the Auvergne, to Normandy (Jumièges (1037–66); Saint-Étienne of Caen (1060s)) and Anglo-Norman England and northern Italy (St Ambrogio, Milan, eleventh century; Pisa Cathedral, begun 1063). The deployment of the gallery was a sign that builders desired to make reference to prototypes in Carolingian, Ottonian, and possibly Byzantine architecture. Historians preoccupied with the "development" of the structural potential of the architectural envelope in relation to vaulting have seen galleries as providing the essential prop to buttress high barrel vaults – the galleries of "pilgrimage churches," for example, had quadrant vaults (forming a quarter of a circle) butting against the central nave and presumably providing some degree of lateral support to the central vault. However, the Jumièges nave has groin vaulted galleries with no high vault. The liturgical functions of the gallery remain unclear – but probably included the provision of a space for antiphonal choirs and for additional altars.

Interior Mural Articulation

In the early Middle Ages two-dimensional forms (applied marble, mosaics, mural painting) provided the means to render the interior sumptuous and to equip the church with cycles of images conveying the stories of Christ, the Virgin Mary, and the Saints. However, Roman builders had already combined the applied classical orders with arched masonry to convey eloquence to interiors as well as exteriors. And in the "First Romanesque" churches of Lombardy and northern Spain builders expressed their interest in three-dimensional sculptured articulation. This is first expressed in exterior articulation (Lombard bands; corbel tables), but then is applied to interior forms, particularly with the articulation of interiors with applied pilasters or engaged colonnettes linked with the roofing system or vaults to articulate the bay system. The desire on the part of Romanesque builders for taller, more massive, structures led them to deploy compound piers rather than the traditional column to support the main arcade. Such piers might be made eloquent through the application of colonnettes to surfaces and angles; the thickness of the main arcade similarly was subject to articulation with inner and outer orders, linked with the colonnettes of the pier – portal embrasures might be articulated in the same way. Particularly exciting is the application of a torus (a rounded molding) to the outer order of the arcade arch: the Normans pioneered this practice (Saint-Étienne of Caen, 1060s), initiating fruitful speculations on the relationship between features of the elevation, articulated in a linear fashion, and the language of support conveyed through applied colonnettes. The Anglo-Norman enterprise in England provided multiple opportunities for such speculation in great churches like Ely, Norwich, and Durham. The enhanced linearity and eloquence of such structures affords an immediate background to "Gothic."

Domes

Domed churches are associated particularly with western and south-western France – their use transcends any of the traditional regional "schools."[36] Whereas Byzantine domes embodied ceramic material – lighter than stone – Romanesque builders employed solid masonry – bringing considerable weight and sometimes causing structural difficulties that have led to extensive rebuilding. The dome might sit on squinches or pendentives and required a square bay and very solid support. Domed churches generally do not have aisles. Domes are ubiquitous under crossing towers, generally combined with squinches.

Vaults

Masonry vaulting has sometimes been seen as the *sine qua non* for the definition of Romanesque and the entire story of medieval architecture sometimes told in terms of the interaction of two types of structure: the thin-walled wooden-roofed basilica with columns and the muscular vaulted structure. Medieval builders inherited the basic types of vault (barrel vault; groin vault; dome) from Roman practice – however, whereas Roman vaults were of concrete or might embody lightweight ceramic material, Romanesque builders favored solid masonry: generally rubble-and-mortar with ashlar transverse arches. Romanesque barrel vaults can be quite thick, up to 2 meters at the haunch, sometimes tapering to half a meter at the crown. The popularity of vaulting is normally explained in relation to practical concerns: fear of fires resulting from lightning or the predations of the Vikings in the ninth century; acoustic benefits, and (important in the north) the insulating properties of the vault. Equally important, however, is the prestige conveyed by a difficult-to-master technique and the references to prototypes distant in time and space.

Interest in vaulting in the north certainly resulted from enhanced communications with the Mediterranean littoral especially Lombardy and northern Spain, where builders had continued to construct vaulted or partially vaulted structures. Carolingian or Ottonian churches of the ninth and tenth centuries might embody a vaulted infrastructure (crypt) in the westwork or under the choir. Although the "progressive" story of Romanesque has been eschewed here, it seems true that the confidence of eleventh-century builders increased as vaults were constructed at growing heights: over aisles, over galleries, and finally over the main vessel. The ability to look after the lateral forces generated by a masonry canopy at a height of 100 feet over the central vessel must have been considered a real challenge, particularly in edifices with clerestory windows. When and where in the north were the great breakthrough monuments constructed? Most students of medieval architecture have concluded that this must have been in the eleventh century and that Burgundy and adjacent areas played a critical role. Major monuments included the narthex of the church of Saint-Philibert at Tournus (*c.* 950–1120), the nave of the lost church of Cluny II (mid-tenth century) and dependent buildings; Cluny III (1088); the church of Chapaize (1060s), and Saint-Étienne of Nevers (dedicated 1097).

Gothic

We have represented Romanesque in a series of opposing principles (novel, as well as historicizing) applied to buildings over a wide geographical extent, and in a set of architectural features that would not have necessarily have come together in the same building. Gothic, on the other hand, is more easily represented as a unifying principle of design applied in multiple buildings, with pioneering experiments beginning in the area in the Île-de-France and areas to the north and east. Gothic architecture may be understood as a paradigm shift where a structural revolution went hand-in-hand with a new understanding of the language of architectural articulation. The structural revolution has traditionally been explained in terms of the introduction of the new lightweight rib vault – generally composed of semi-cut stones or *pendans* (not rubble); quite thin and articulated by means of an elegant crisscross diagonal rib of ashlar masonry forming the lines of intersection of the four fields of the vault.[37] The rib vault had already been employed in Romanesque (Durham Cathedral) and the enhanced linear articulation associated with its deployment may generally be linked with Anglo-Norman architecture. The search for the origins of the rib vault will take us to Islamic monuments in Spain and ultimately to Roman and Near Eastern architecture. However, it takes more than rib vaulting to make Gothic. Critically important was the rationalization of stone production to provide a copious supply of fine ashlar masonry that could be employed in a rigid structural envelope with substantial footings and deeply projecting lateral buttresses to stiffen a tall structure with (generally) high vaults. In the case of aisled basilicas, the deep lateral buttresses were projected upwards as rigid pylons (*culées*) from which flying buttresses could be launched against the superstructure to support high vaults. This structural combination allowed builders to employ a considerable expanse of glass in windows of a size unprecedented in the north. The deployment of the structural muscles of the edifice around the exterior envelope freed interior articulation from restraint, opening the potential for continuing speculation.

The starting point may be understood in terms of the opposition between the *modern* exterior elements (culées; flying buttresses – forms never seen before) and the *historicizing* articulation of the interior, based upon the applied classical orders made up of multiple colonnettes with their bases and capitals. Applied classical orders had already been used in Roman and Romanesque architecture, but Gothic builders took the liberty of extending the colonnette vertically until the capital had altogether parted company from the base, and height had lost any rational relationship with the diameter. This was a kind of deliberate counter-classicism allowing the elements of articulation to speak a language that was quite different from that of the structural frame. Panofsky suggested that this was the language of reason: however one might argue the opposite: that the increasingly linear articulation of the Gothic church created a language of illusion and fantasy with the appearance of apparently weightless vaults and sheets of shimmering glass.[38] Inspired by the new sense of freedom, Gothic builders went on speculating with the elements of articulation, pulling the building together into a coherent network of lines. This was facilitated by the exploration of various kinds of elision (linkage) that unified the multiple levels of the elevation; by moving toward an emphasis upon concavity rather than convexity; by eventually eliminating the capital, entirely changing the language of support; and finally by unleashing the essentially organic qualities of Gothic articulation in buildings that began increasingly to look like forests. We have seen that it has been recently suggested that the founding simile ("like a forest") was one that was already known to and consciously exploited by the builders of late Gothic German churches.[39]

The story of Gothic, like that of Romanesque, has been told as an unfolding "development" where the outcome is known at the start. Having found the "mature" "High Gothic" specimen in the cathedral of Chartres (1194), Soissons (1190s), or the nave of Amiens (1220s–1230s), most commentators will then undertake the search for the "first" church embodying the essential features of Gothic. For almost two centuries now this point of origin has been found in the church of Saint-Denis to the north of Paris, as rebuilt in the mid-twelfth century. The architectural features pioneered at Saint-Denis were then exploited in the great ring of churches and cathedrals that ring Paris (Saint-Germer-de-Fly, Noyon, Laon, Soissons, Chartres, Amiens, Beauvais, and so on) constituting a powerful expression of a "style" that "spread" to surrounding areas (southern France, England, Spain, Germany, Italy, and so on), where it was expressed in a range of "regional variations."

The importance of Saint-Denis, however, is not that it was the "first" Gothic building (the very notion of "first" is misconceived), but that the abundance of written sources for this monument allow us to understand more about the human context of architectural production than in any other building of its period. What we find at Saint-Denis is the harnessing of architectural form (historicizing as well as innovative) in the service of an aggressively projected ideological and soteriological program. That program, propagated most effectively by Abbot Suger, was to link the destiny of the monastery with both the rising fortunes of the Capetian monarchy and the reformed Catholic Church, retelling history as well as architectural history to make this the first bridgehead of Apostolic Christianity into Gaul; the favored house of kings; the premier monastery of all Gaul; the first "Gothic" building. This retelling of history was accompanied by shrewd economic and political actions to ensure that Saint-Denis remained the economic hub of the very profitable commercial exchanges in the vital markets to the north of the burgeoning city that was to become the capital of France.

Abbot Suger first refurbished the old nave with its cylindrical columns, thin upper wall and wooden roof: projecting a powerful image of *Romanitas*. Then the twin-towered western frontispiece with three decorated portals and newfangled rib vaults juxtaposed the northern expression of *Modernitas*. The new chevet, extending to the east of the old liturgical choir, provided an elevated platform surrounded by dazzling windows where the dark marble tomb of the Apostles was backlit, creating an overwhelming crescendo for the pilgrims who made their way there (the abbot tells us) in increasingly large numbers. Thus, at Suger's death (1151) his church was made up of three distinct components: nave, frontispiece, chevet – each speaking a very different language. Whereas the first language was anchored in references to the past, the second and third opened up potentially endless layers of modernism as the Anglo-Norman references of the west end gave way to a new kind of synthesis in the chevet where the slenderness of cylindrical columns and thin walls was combined with an envelope with the fluent use of rib vaults, the language of multiple skinny colonnettes, and an experimental buttressing system with deep external buttresses intended to support the rib-vaulted superstructure: historians have argued over whether or not flying buttresses were involved.

The opulence of the liturgical performances that accompanied the consecrations of Saint-Denis and the startling modernity of the newly constructed chevet together with the inflated historical and political claims they projected must have served as a real stimulus (and/or irritant) for the other abbots and bishops of the northern dioceses who had witnessed the events. There was no "school" of Saint-Denis, but there was certainly a quickening of the pace of reconstruction of the great churches of the area surrounding Paris, led by the building activity of the capital city itself, where Notre-Dame, begun around 1160, marked a new stage in the paradigm shift that was Gothic. If we cannot be sure about the form of the superstructure of Saint-Denis, at Notre-Dame it is quite certain that the new chevet, completed in the 1170s, was equipped with flying buttresses. The structure with its four-storied galleried elevation took an enormous leap forward in height, reaching well over 100 feet. Dominating the urban landscape, the cathedral announced the destiny of Paris as capital of France. A comparison of the metropolitan cathedral with the archiepiscopal cathedral of Sens, which had been begun a decade or so earlier, reveals how hard it is to categorize "Gothic" in terms of a unified set of architectural forms. The two buildings share some important characteristics, notably the smooth envelope unbroken by a transept, and the use of sexpartite vaults. Yet they are so very different – the four-storey elevation of Notre-Dame with its drive to great height combined with thinness and dainty articulation and columns in the main arcade; Sens with its three storeys; enormous mass, great width, and alternating double columns and piers with deeply projecting responds.

The same kind of conclusion can be drawn from a study of the ring of great cathedrals and abbey churches that went up in the area surrounding the Île-de-France in the mid-to-later twelfth century: Senlis (1150s), Noyon (1150s), Laon (toward 1160), Saint-Remi of Reims (1170s), Soissons (1170–90), and so on: at first sight they seem to have the characteristics of a kind of "family," and some of them share important features, such as the use of the galleried elevation. Yet a closer examination reveals very significant differences, and no two churches seem to have resulted directly from the design of the same master or "workshop."

The older scholarship (Bony) suggested that the essentially multifarious nature of early Gothic was pulled into a single strand as a result of the "breakthough" cathedral – namely, Gothic Chartres (1194).[40] With its enormous scale, simplified three-storey elevation, towering clerestory, and quadripartite vaults supported by a massive buttressing system, Chartres conveys an impression of startling simplicity where less is more – an appearance much appreciated by mid-twentieth-century disciples of Modernism. And then after Chartres comes the crescendo of "High Gothic" – Reims (1210), Amiens (1220), and Beauvais (1225). Students of Gothic remained, for many years, preoccupied with the etiological linkages between these monuments and the idea that they were, in a sense, the "offspring" of Chartres, and have generally been unable to create a verbal narrative able to represent the continuing *multifariousness* of Gothic. Bourges Cathedral provides an excellent case study, since it is in no sense the direct "offspring" of any single prototypical building, owing much in the overall design of its envelope to Notre-Dame of Paris, and in its articulation to monuments in the Soissons, but reaching beyond such immediate prototypes to monuments like the Romanesque Cluny III and beyond that to St Peters in Rome.

What is most important about French architectural production of the late-twelfth to mid-thirteenth centuries is that builders developed a combination of easily recognizable forms (pointed arches with their cusps and gables, crocket capitals, and so on) that created a new kind of *koine* (common language) – one associated with the successful amalgamation of a resurgent monarchy and revitalized Church, propagated by the cult of saints, and propelled in material terms a massive flow of cash from increased agrarian and industrial production and enhanced commercial exchange.

In traditional accounts of Gothic it has been hard to represent adequately the spontaneity of local architectural manifestations in regions like Burgundy, Normandy, western France, Germany (particularly the Rhineland), England, Italy, and Spain, where local masons continued to experiment with forms peculiar to their own region, while at the same time looking over their shoulders at developments elsewhere, particularly France.[41] This is especially true of England and of Germany, where patrons and masons had formed their own peculiar habits of taste and design, yet where French masons might be invited to direct the work particularly of prestigious projects like the reconstruction of Canterbury after the fire of 1174. The numerous lavish building projects in late-twelfth- and early thirteenth-century England are extraordinary given the relatively limited population of that country (much less than France) and the undeveloped state of cities. English taste tended to favor thicker and more sumptuously articulated walls and sculptural detailing and the privileging of horizontal rather than vertical expansiveness. Certain historians have juxtaposed this "Englishness" with the availability of French forms to construct a theory of the ideology of architectural form where resistance to a Francophile king, Henry III, was expressed in cathedrals such as Lincoln, Wells, and Salisbury – however, the interpenetration of the two cultural spheres was already so complete that rigid distinctions will sometimes break down.[42] But it is certainly true to say that French Gothic forms had, by the mid-thirteenth century, acquired international cachet not just because of their inherent beauty and wide applicability, but also because of their association with France and its great kings, especially Philip Augustus and Louis IX.

The abbey church of Saint-Denis, the cathedrals of Amiens and Reims, the Sainte-Chapelle – such monuments became *objects of desire* in the eyes of the kings and Church leaders of contiguous areas. King Henry III of England is said to have coveted the Sainte-Chapelle, wanting to wheel it back to London in a handcart. It is notions like this that we should apply to the construction of lookalike monuments: Westminster Abbey, the cathedrals of Léon, Burgos, and Toledo in Spain, and Cologne cathedral in Germany do not result from "influences" or the "spread of Gothic style" but rather from the increasing attention paid by the kings and bishops of surrounding areas to prototypes on French soil.

The same notion may be applied to the phenomenon of "change" in late Gothic. An important aspect of Gothic was, as we have seen, the continuing commitment to *modernitas*. What used to be dealt with in morphological terms must now be reconsidered as a social phenomenon, as builders responded to existing prototypes and decided what features to emulate and what to modify. The economic dimension is also important: France was the battlefield in the Hundred Years War, while the English enriched themselves with the spoils of war and profits from the wool trade and Flemish and German cities thrived with increased commercial interactions. Thus, it is not surprising to find the most prolific expressions of late Gothic in Germany and England. Builders generally favored simplified, architectural envelopes and stripped-down articulation with a predominance of concave or convex forms. At the same time there was intense interest in the development of elaborate tracery compositions, often focusing upon the forms of micro-architecture: baldachins, choir screens, and tombs.

Conclusion

"Romanesque" and "Gothic," whatever their original negative undertones, have both become synonymous with triumphant change and the emergence of a distinctly northern identity. Both brought features that refer to the past (historicism), yet both also bring innovation (modernity). Told in developmental terms, the story of Romanesque and Gothic conveys the illusion of inevitability – this is one of the reasons for the skepticism of current medievalists about the validity of the very concept. The last great historian of Gothic style, Jean Bony, dissatisfied at the end of his life with the determinism of his story, introduced what he called the "accidental theory," where many outcomes were possible.[43]

The reconciliation of the old, style-based art history with the exploration of architectural production as a means of projecting power and ideological structures will produce a surprising conclusion. Each great church has the force to convince the visitor that it represents the *only* possible outcome of its building campaigns. And the similarities that we can recognize across a thousand edifices spread over time and space create an overwhelming sense of something powerfully imposed by some central force or intention. This sense is only increased by the business of verbal representation and narrative. It is in this way that the modern interlocutor falls willy-nilly into the builders' plot – which was to overwhelm the visitor with the sense of accident-free inevitability, creating the illusion of manifest destiny.

Notes

1 Gombrich, *Norm and Form*; Frankl, *The Gothic*; Bizzarro, *Romanesque Architectural Criticism*.
2 Lakoff, *Woman, Fire and Dangerous Things*.
3 Frankl, *The Gothic*, pp. 237–84.
4 Rowland, *Culture of the High Renaissance*, pp. 199–241.
5 Gombrich, *Norm and Form*, pp. 81–9.
6 Frankl, *The Gothic*, pp. 272–3, 290.
7 Crossley, "Return to the Forest," pp. 71–80; Brooks, *The Gothic Revival*, pp. 23–48.

8 Foucault, *The Order of Things*, pp. 128–31; Bergdoll, *Foundations of Architecture*, p. 18.
9 Bizzarro, *Romanesque Architectural Criticism*, p. 150; Dynes, "Art, Language and Romanesque"; Seidel, *Songs of Glory*; "Rethinking Romanesque."
10 Bizzarro, *Romanesque Architectural Criticism*, p. 153.
11 Kimpel and Suckale, *Die gotische Architektur*. For a very useful overview of the current state of the field, see Davis, "Sic et non."
12 Crossley, "Return to the Forest."
13 Gervase of Canterbury, the twelfth-century chronicler, distinguished clearly between what we would call Romanesque and Gothic in the choir of Canterbury Cathedral, rebuilt after 1174; see Frisch, *Gothic Art*, pp. 14–23.
14 Gennep, *The Rites of Passage*.
15 Stookey, "The Gothic Cathedral as the Heavenly Jerusalem."
16 Armstrong, *Universals*.
17 Frankl, *Gothic Architecture*: see especially the critical introduction by Crossley, pp. 7–31.
18 Rosenwein, *Rhinoceros Bound*.
19 Lefebvre, *Production of Space*.
20 Murray, "Slippages."
21 Brooks, *Reading for the Plot*.
22 Dilke, *The Roman Land Surveyors*.
23 Binski, *Westminster Abbey and the Plantagenets*.
24 Woolf, *Becoming Roman*.
25 Geary, *Before France and Germany*.
26 Horn and Born, *Barns of the Abbey of Beaulieu*.
27 Krautheimer, "An Introduction to 'An Iconography of Medieval Architecture.'"
28 William of Volpiano, *Guillaume de Volpiano*.
29 Conant, *Carolingian and Romanesque Architecture*, p. 85.
30 Warnke, *Bau und Überbau*.
31 Puig i Cadafalch, *Le Premier Art roman*, pp. 1–10; Conant, *Carolingian and Romanesque Architecture*, pp. 17–66.
32 Conant, *Carolingian and Romanesque Architecture*, p. 43.
33 Ibid., p. 44.
34 Bizzarro, *Romanesque Architectural Criticism*, p. 153.
35 Quoted in Nichols, *Romanesque Signs*, p. 16.
36 Seidel, *Songs of Glory*.
37 Bergdoll, *Foundations* (Viollet-le-Duc, "Construction").
38 Panofsky, *Gothic Architecture and Scholasticism*, p. 20.
39 Crossley, "Return to the Forest."
40 Bony, *French Gothic Architecture*.
41 Nussbaum, *German Gothic Church Architecture*.
42 Brieger, *English Art*.
43 Bony, *French Gothic Architecture*, pp. 1–3.

Bibliography

Armstrong, David M., *Universals: An Opinionated Introduction* (Boulder, CO: Westview Press, 1989).

Bergdoll, Barry B., *Foundations of Architecture: Selections from the Dictionnaire raisonné [by Viollet-le-Duc]*, trans. Kenneth D. Whitehead (New York: G. Braziller, 1990).

Binski, Paul, *Westminster Abbey and the Plantagenets: Kingship and the Representation of Power, 1200–1400* (New Haven: Yale University Press, 1995).

Bizzarro, Tina W., *Romanesque Architectural Criticism: A Prehistory* (Cambridge and New York: Cambridge University Press, 1992).

Bony, Jean, *French Gothic Architecture of the 12th and 13th Centuries* (Berkeley and Los Angeles: University of California Press, 1983).

Brieger, Peter H., *English Art, 1216–1307*, Oxford History of English Art, 4 (Oxford: Oxford University Press, 1957).

Brooks, Chris, *The Gothic Revival* (London, Phaidon, 1999).

Brooks, Peter, *Reading for the Plot: Design and Intention in Narrative* (Cambridge, MA: Harvard University Press, 1984).

Conant, Kenneth J., *Carolingian and Romanesque Architecture*, Pelican History of Art (Harmondsworth: Penguin, 1959).

Crossley, Paul, "The Return to the Forest Natural Architecture and the German Past in the Age of Dürer," in Thomas W. Gaehtgens, ed., *Künstlerischer Austausch: Akten des XXVIII. Internationalen Kongresses für Kunstgeschichte, Berlin, 1922*, 3 vols (Berlin: Akademie Verlag, 1993), vol. II, pp. 71–80.

Davis, Michael T., "*Sic et non*: Recent Trends in the Study of Gothic Ecclesiastical Architecture," *Journal of the Society of Architectural Historians*, 58 (1999), pp. 414–23.

Dilke, Oswald A. W, *The Roman Land Surveyors: An Introduction to the Agrimensores* (New York: Barnes and Noble, 1971).

Dynes, Wayne, "Art, Language and Romanesque," *Gesta*, 28 (1989), pp. 3–10.

Foucault, Michel, *The Order of Things: An Archaeology of the Human Sciences* (New York: Vintage Books, 1970).

Frankl, Paul, *The Gothic: Literary Sources and Interpretations through Eight Centuries* (Princeton: Princeton University Press, 1959).

Frankl, Paul, *Gothic Architecture*, ed. and intro. Paul Crossley (New Haven and London: Yale University Press, 2000).

Freedberg, David, *The Power of Images: Studies in the History and Theory of Response* (Chicago: University of Chicago Press, 1989).

Frisch, Teresa G., *Gothic Art, 1140–c. 1450: Sources and Documents in the History of Art* (Englewood Cliffs, NJ: Prentice Hall, 1971).

Geary, Patrick J., *Before France and Germany: The Creation and Transformation of the Merovingian World* (New York: Oxford University Press, 1988).

Gennep, Arnold van, *The Rites of Passage* (Chicago: University of Chicago Press, 1969).

Gombrich, Ernst H., *Norm and Form* (Chicago: University of Chicago Press, 1966).

Horn, Walter W., and Born, Ernest, *The Barns of the Abbey of Beaulieu at its Granges of Great Coxwell and Beaulieu-St Leonards* (Berkeley and Los Angeles: University of California Press, 1965).

Krautheimer, Richard, "An Introduction to 'An Iconography of Medieval Architecture,'" *Journal of the Warburg and Courtauld Institutes*, 5 (1942), pp. 1–33.

Kimpel, Dieter, and Suckale, Robert, *Die gotische Architektur in Frankreich, 1130–1270* (Munich: Hirmer, 1985).

Lakoff, George, *Women, Fire and Dangerous Things: What Categories Reveal about the Mind* (Chicago: University of Chicago Press, 1990).

Lefebvre, Henri, *The Production of Space*, trans. Donald Nicholson-Smith (Oxford: Blackwell, 1991).

Murray, Stephen, "Slippages of Meaning and Form," in Mark Turner, ed., *The Artful Mind: Cognitive Science and the Riddle of Human Creativity* (Oxford: Oxford University Press, 2006), pp. 189–207.

Nichols, Stephen G., *Romanesque Signs: Early Medieval Narrative and Iconography* (New Haven: Yale University Press, 1983).

Nussbaum, Norbert, *German Gothic Church Architecture* (New Haven: Yale University Press, 2000).

Panofsky, Erwin, *Gothic Architecture and Scholasticism*, Wimmer Lecture, 1948 (Latrobe, PA: Archabbey Press, 1951).

Puig i Cadafalch, Josep, *Le Premier Art roman: L'Architecture en Catalogne et dans l'occident méditerranéen aux Xe et XIe siècles* (Paris: H. Laurens, 1928).

Rosenwein, Barbara H., *Rhinoceros Bound: Cluny in the Tenth Century* (Philadelphia: University of Pennsylvania Press, 1982).

Rowland, Ingrid D., *The Culture of the High Renaissance: Ancients and Moderns in Sixteenth-Century Rome* (Cambridge: Cambridge University Press, 1998).

Seidel, Linda, *Songs of Glory: The Romanesque Façades of Aquitaine* (Chicago: University of Chicago Press, 1981).

Seidel, Linda, "Rethinking Romanesque; Re-engaging Roman[z]," *Gesta*, 50 (2006), pp. 109–23.

Stalley, Roger A., *Early Medieval Architecture*, Oxford History of Art (Oxford: Oxford University Press, 1999).

Stookey, L. H., "The Gothic Cathedral as the Heavenly Jerusalem: Liturgical and Theological Sources," *Gesta*, 8 (1969), pp. 35–41.

Warnke, Martin, *Bau und Überbau: Soziologie der mittelalterlichen Architektur nach den Schriftquellen* (Frankfurt-am-Main, Syndikat, 1976).

William of Volpiano, *Guillaume de Volpiano et l'architecture des rotondes*, ed. Monique Jannet-Vallat and Christian Sapin (Dijon: Éditions Universitaires de Dijon, 1996).

Woolf, Greg, *Becoming Roman: The Origins of Provincial Civilization in Gaul* (Cambridge, Cambridge University Press, 1998).

Further Reading

Bergdoll, Barry B., "Introduction," in *Foundations of Architecture: Selections from the Dictionnaire raisonné [by Viollet-le-Duc]*, trans. Kenneth D. Whitehead (New York, G. Braziller, 1990), pp. 1–30. A very useful introduction to the ideas of E. E. Viollet-le-Duc, the greatest thinker and writer on medieval architecture. Includes translation of Viollet-le-Duc's articles on "Construction," etc.

Bizzarro, Tina W., *Romanesque Architectural Criticism: A Prehistory* (Cambridge and New York: Cambridge University Press, 1992). A very useful account of the history of the notion of "Romanesque."

Bony, Jean, *French Gothic Architecture of the 12th and 13th Centuries* (Berkeley and Los Angeles: University of California Press, 1983). Dependent upon both German and French intellectual traditions, this is the *summa* of the old style-based art history.

Conant, Kenneth J., *Carolingian and Romanesque Architecture*, Pelican History of Art (Harmondsworth: Penguin, 1959). Now quite old, but still, a very useful and concise account of Romanesque.

Davis, Michael T., "*Sic et non*: Recent Trends in the Study of Gothic Ecclesiastical Architecture," *Journal of the Society of Architectural Historians*, 58 (1999), pp. 414–23. This piece ranks with Crossley's introduction to the new edition of Frankl, *Gothic Architecture*, as one of the two best "state of the discipline" essays for Gothic architecture.

Frankl, Paul, *Gothic Architecture*, ed. and intro. Paul Crossley (New Haven and London: Yale University Press, 2000). Follows the dialectical style analysis system pioneered by H. Wölfflin. See especially the critical introduction by Crossley.

Frankl, Paul, *The Gothic: Literary Sources and Interpretations through Eight Centuries* (Princeton, Princeton University Press, 1959). An extraordinarily rich account, diachronically arranged, of historiographic sources for the Gothic.

Lefebvre, Henri, *The Production of Space*, trans. Donald Nicholson-Smith (Oxford: Blackwell, 1991). Provides a framework for the representation of architectural production in a context that is simultaneously sociological, mnemonic and material.

Stalley, Roger A., *Early Medieval Architecture*, Oxford History of Art (Oxford: Oxford University Press, 1999). The best attempt to tell the story of medieval architecture in a "post-style-history" mode.

CHAPTER TWENTY-FOUR

Aristocratic Culture: Kinship, Chivalry, and Court Culture

RICHARD E. BARTON

Medieval aristocrats were fundamentally social animals. I mean not merely that aristocrats lived in groups, but rather that their lives, their social and individual identities, and, in many cases, their sociopolitical fortunes were largely defined, shaped, and revised through social interactions, particularly with other aristocrats.

If such comments seem true on a basic level, it would nevertheless take far more space than is available here to explore each permutation of them. Instead, this study focuses on three contexts in which aristocratic identity, values, and sociopolitical standing were constantly being forged, broken, and reforged. Each context – kinship structures, the social world of court, and normalizing discourses of behavior that we might term chivalry – has produced a significant body of modern scholarship. Not uncoincidentally, each of these three contexts has also been shaped by distinct theoretical axes of analysis deriving at least in part from cross-disciplinary fertilization. This chapter attempts to discuss these three contexts in which aristocratic identity and culture were formed with an eye toward accomplishing three interrelated goals: first, to discuss the strengths and weaknesses of the prevailing literature; secondly, to call attention to the methodological assumptions that underlie each context; and, thirdly, to suggest some profitable future lines of research. Such an agenda is ambitious, and it hardly needs to be said that I will only be able to pick and choose key works. This chapter will not, therefore, be, and in fact cannot be, a definitive treatment of the massive historiography of chivalry and aristocratic culture.

Lineage and Kinship Structures

The concept of family lies at the heart of aristocratic conceptions of self and of others.[1] Already in the eleventh century, and undoubtedly long before this, aristocrats had taken pains to describe and enumerate their kindreds in self-conscious ways. Antiquarian historians between 1500 and 1850 were also fascinated with noble lineages, in part because those lineages were still politically and socially potent well into the nineteenth and twentieth centuries. Indeed, the local historical societies that sprang up throughout Europe in the nineteenth century featured genealogical pieces in a good percentage of their numbers. When professional historians first turned to the study of aristocrats in the second half of the nineteenth century, therefore, a good deal of their initial efforts was devoted to correcting the enthusiasms of earlier genealogists. This necessarily meant subjecting genealogy to the "scientific" and/or positivist methods and, in practice, meant renewed focus on individual aristocratic families as defined by the possession of a certain title and/or set of properties. At times this process meant overturning the received wisdom collected by several centuries of antiquarian genealogical work – for example, by significantly pruning the list of "companions of the Conqueror" or by demolishing the historicity of the western French "crusade of 1158."[2] Yet, despite the rigorous source criticism that accompanied this valuable correction of the labor of previous centuries, these early historians of aristocracy did not fundamentally question the theoretical structures that they had inherited – the study of aristocracy, if far more rigorous, remained the study of individual families and of their fortunes over time.

The problems of aristocratic genealogy and title inherited from the pre-modern era inevitably shaped the questions posed by scholars working on the aristocracy during the late nineteenth and early twentieth centuries. Chief among these questions was the problem of the antiquity of the aristocratic lineages that emerged in the eleventh and twelfth centuries. This problem was compounded by the fact that the earliest written genealogies of aristocratic lineages – produced around 1100 – tended to claim that the founder of their house was an adventurer who received lands and/or an heiress in return for service.[3] For instance, the house chronicle of the counts of Anjou claimed that the comital line derived from a forester named Tertullus; likewise, the powerful lords of Bellême, who played an active role in French politics from the tenth through the twelfth centuries, were widely thought in the 1140s to be descended from a simple crossbowman.[4] These texts prompted a generation of historians – including Marc Bloch – to argue that the aristocracy of the central Middle Ages was biologically "new."[5]

Beginning in the 1950s, however, scholars such as Karl Werner, Jacques Boussard, and others mined regional archives for genealogical evidence with which to test this hypothesis. They found that almost all the princely (and indeed some of the seigneurial) dynasties of the central Middle Ages were descended from the elites of the early Middle Ages.[6] For instance, one scholar has argued that the source of the Angevin comital dynasty was not Tertullus the anonymous forester, but rather Ingelgerius, who, although not a count or prince, was nonetheless a "noble man" (*nobilis vir*) who enriched his family through service to Carolingian princes and through favorable marriage.[7] In arguing strenuously for biological continuity, Werner and his followers made good use of a new methodology, which argued that kinship could be accurately traced through patterns of given or leading names (German: *leitnamen*). That is, scholars could associate particular names or groups of names with certain kindreds, and could thus reasonably argue that possession of a given name indicated membership in a particular kindred. To offer but one simple example, if one encountered a "Count Fulk" in a tenth-century charter stemming from the west of France, it made good sense to assume that this person was a count of Anjou, since the Angevin counts featured only two given names – Fulk and Geoffrey – between 929 and 1151. While this method is not without its critics, the point here is merely that it helped researchers establish more plausible family trees for ninth- and tenth-century aristocratic families and, in so doing, helped convince most scholars that the high medieval noble families were not completely "new," but actually shared substantial biological continuity with their Carolingian predecessors.[8]

From questions of genealogy and antiquity of lineage, scholarship turned in the 1960s and 1970s to questions concerning the structure of aristocratic kindreds. The key early figures in this scholarship were Karl Schmid and Georges Duby, whose independent arguments that a change in aristocratic family structure and consciousness occurred around the year 1000 were embraced and popularized by a generation of scholars.[9] Duby's work in particular fell in fertile soil, as his numerous studies of the French nobility published in the 1960s and 1970s reached a wide audience in France, England, and the United States.[10] The so-called Schmid thesis, especially as promoted and expanded by Duby and others, maintained that aristocrats of the early Middle Ages had conceived of their kindred very broadly, as a diffuse, horizontally organized group of kin containing both agnates and cognates (German: *Sippe*). In contrast, the thesis maintained that aristocrats began to narrow their conceptions of kindred around the year 1000 into a more tightly defined agnatic patrilineage, in which it was expected that property and aristocratic identity would descend in a linear manner from father to son (thus excluding cousins, affines, younger sons) (German: *Geschlecht*). Schmid and Duby based their theories on close analysis of patterns of onomastic evidence found in French charters and German memorial books (Latin: *Libri memoriales*).[11] Both types of sources, rich with genealogical information concerning the local aristocracies, appeared to reveal deeper societal structures that oriented individuals into larger groups. To give but one example, chosen largely at random, we know that in 1106 a certain Ademar Walter made gifts to Cluny, in the course of which he (or the monks) sought the approval of his brother (a monk at Cluny), his wife, and three sons.[12] This sort of evidence, when taken in the aggregate, would seem to allow scholars to make conclusions about the structure of families like Ademar's; in this case, it looks as if Ademar conceived of his family in a mostly agnatic, patrilinear way. Although conclusions of this sort have been subject to critiques since the 1960s, the richness of the prosopographical evidence contained in the sources – however topos-ridden they might be – has encouraged scholars to seek in them answers to questions about family structure and consciousness.

Indeed, the link between familial structure and individual aristocratic consciousness was one of the crucial insights derived from this new scholarship. It was one thing to say that Ademar defined his family as including his brother, wife, and children. It was another to argue that apparent changes in family structure between the tenth and twelfth centuries were responsible for important changes in belief structures and attitudes. Duby and his disciples did just that, arguing that changes in inheritance practice, attitudes toward violence, and marriage strategies (to name only a few) accompanied, conditioned, and/or stemmed from changes in family structure.[13] According to this influential thesis, changes in social, economic, and political conditions in the late tenth century led aristocrats to narrow their definitions of family and, thereby, to limit the marriages of their sons (and daughters) and alter the patterns by which their children inherited property. Since the family was now defined in a patrilinear way, it followed that the lineage would need to protect the economic and seigneurial resources of the lineage by preventing younger sons from marrying and by restricting inheritance to (usually) the eldest (that is, primogeniture).

All of this social practice was accompanied by changes in mental outlook, and was to be contrasted with practices and attitudes of the more fluid world of the ninth century, in which a more broadly defined kindred might well seek the benefits of marrying off younger sons and in which all worthy offspring could expect to inherit some portion of the paternal (and maternal) estates.

The scholarship surrounding this thesis draws from theories of structuralism that dominated the social sciences during the 1950s and 1960s. These theories, best known through the work of the French anthropologist Claude Lévi-Strauss but much altered and expanded, posited the existence of deep structures within society that could reveal to the trained observer, whether anthropologist or historian, fundamental truths about that society. Identification of the structure and the ways in which they interrelated could, moreover, allow one to comprehend and perhaps even predict behavior. To return to Ademar Walter, once scholars had labeled the structure of eleventh-century aristocratic French culture as agnatic and patrilinear, they could offer explanations for why Ademar felt it desirable to associate particular kinsmen in his gift of property. That is, because kinship structures emphasized linear descent of property, title, and individual honor from father to son, it was not surprising that Ademar sought only the approbation of his immediate family. Similarly, the same scholarly understanding of kinship structures allowed some historians to argue (from relatively little direct evidence) that fathers strategically limited the marriage and career choices of younger sons in order to protect the agnatic inheritance rights of the eldest.[14] Several implications seemed to follow from this argument. Duby argued that structures of kinship and resulting patrilineal attitudes explained the rowdy behavior of the youths (Latin: *juvenes*) whose troublesome behavior is apparent in some chronicle sources, while a number of scholars adduced the existence of a large pool of "landless younger sons" as an explanation for the popularity of crusading.[15] In these ways and many others, the historical profession's interest in structuralism in the 1960s and 1970s[16] offered exciting new ways of interpreting social and political dynamics, as well as individual motivations.

Since the 1970s, however, structuralism has declined in popularity and, as a result, scholars have grown less comfortable with the specific conclusions of Schmid, Duby, and their peers concerning aristocratic families and solidarities. Scholars such as Constance Bouchard, Stephen White, Régine Le Jan, Amy Livingstone, and David Crouch have called into question specific aspects of the Schmid–Duby thesis. White's close analysis of clauses in charters that remember relatives (such as Ademar's mentioned above) were highly formulaic and, more significantly, tied to very specific tenurial and legal circumstances. The image or conception of kinship contained in such formulae could not be taken as the sole, or even the most dominant, one, for individuals like Ademar.[17] In a string of articles beginning in 1979 and culminating in her 2001 book, Bouchard demonstrated the problems that had emerged from the scholarly practice of reifying family structures as either broad (*Sippe*) or narrow (*Geschlecht*); she found elements of patrilineal thinking in many Carolingian families, as well as plenty of evidence of individuals valuing broader kin groupings (including affines) after 1000.[18] Le Jan's magisterial survey of kinship and power relations among the Frankish elites definitively demonstrated that a shift from *Sippe* to lineage had already occurred by the ninth century, and could therefore not have been responsible for the changes so often attributed to it in the eleventh.[19] As Crouch points out,

Le Jan's argument is less of an assault on the Schmid–Duby master thesis than it is a criticism of its dating, for Le Jan accepts a major shift in kinship patterns and in allied conceptualizations, but merely dates them to the ninth century, and not the eleventh.[20] Close regional analyses of (mostly French) aristocracies have also begun to call into question Duby's assumptions about primogeniture and the practice of limiting marriages to eldest sons. Evergates stated very simply that "such a model is not convincing for the twelfth century."[21] Livingstone's work on the Chartrain, for instance, offers a picture of a highly contextualized and pragmatic society in which one family might practice primogeniture at one time, but another (or sometimes the same family at a later date) might favor division of the patrimony.[22] Pauline Stafford, working with mostly English evidence, has also criticized the old meta-narrative while offering a picture of fluctuation, shifting norms and values, and multiple simultaneous conceptions of kindred.[23]

In the place of the neat binary opposition of clan and lineage, with major changes taking place around 1000 and with a host of secondary effects spinning off from those changes, historians have not yet advanced a single normalizing thesis.[24] Instead, the operative conception has been complexity, fragmentation, and diversity. Indeed, rather than construct models based on intangible structures, studies are starting instead to focus upon practice – that is, on how individuals themselves experienced ("practiced") kinship.[25] In some ways this merely means that historians have been less willing to generalize on a large scale, and have become content with the sort of micro-analyses offered by White, Bouchard, Livingstone, and others.[26] These studies shift focus from society and structures to individuals, and emphasize the variety of strategies that an individual might employ in seeking to define and strengthen his or her family. As befits a post-structuralist era, the emphasis lies on plurality of options and in the simultaneous existence of multiple possible definitions and practical applications of notions of kinship. Sometimes an aristocrat might find it useful to think in a linear fashion (say in securing consent to donations), while in other situations that same aristocrat might well choose to define his family in a much broader way (say when engaging in feud or assembling a contingent to go on crusade).[27] Although there are still historians engaged in studies that either explicitly or implicitly embrace elements of the Schmid–Duby thesis,[28] it appears that a new caution had emerged concerning our ability to use "family" or kindred as the overriding axis for analyzing aristocratic behavior and mentality. This is not to deny the centrality of family to high medieval aristocrats, but it is to point out both that they did not use the term "family" as we do today[29] and that, as the studies cited above show, it is not at all clear that aristocrats always valued their kin in the same ways. Indeed, lost in historians' fixation with kindred over the past generation has been serious study of other affective relationships, in particularly with the "kith" or friends.[30] Although offering serious methodological challenges, some historians have begun to investigate the ways in which relationships of this sort may have shaped aristocratic behavior and mentality as much as did relationships with their kin.[31]

Chivalry and Courtliness

If kinship has provided one important, if problematic, lens through which to interpret aristocratic behavior and attitudes, chivalry has, for a very long time, offered an even more important one. As a framework for understanding the Middle Ages (and beyond), the term chivalry has a long history, and current scholarly efforts to define it and explain its place in medieval society are as much confounded by centuries of popular conceptions and misconceptions as they are by the sources themselves. Chivalry, as understood by most recent scholars, comprises a set of unwritten and largely self-motivated norms for aristocratic behavior, both in the realm of war and in the realm of peace.[32] It is often defined as a "code of behavior" (although one cannot point to a written code before the thirteenth century), and just as often as an "ethos."[33] While most scholars admit to the difficulties in establishing a universal definition of chivalry, precisely because it could mean different things to different individuals at different times, it is clear that for a very long time aristocrats in Europe were motivated by such a code or ethos.[34] As such, it is generally agreed that the study of noble conduct, as gleaned through the confrontation of theoretical prescriptions with actual aristocratic practice, is still of central importance to medieval history. Yet, given that agreement, there is still plenty of room for debate.

First, problems of definition have remained central. What exactly is "chivalry"? When, if ever, was the word used? All have agreed that the word chivalry (Old French: *chevalerie*) is difficult to parse. It appears in Old French literary texts beginning with *Roland* in the early twelfth century, although it is not particularly common until the end of that century.[35] But, if the term is found before 1200, it did not yet at that date signify a code of conduct, as it would by the fourteenth century, when the knight Geoffrey de Charny wrote a treatise on conduct entitled *Livre de Chevalerie*.[36] Indeed, Glyn Burgess has shown that in the twelfth century *chevalerie* should be glossed in one of the following three ways: as "a group of knights," "a military act or series of acts performed by a chevalier," or "the possession of skills required to perform such acts."[37] Since, as we shall see, most scholars believe that the ideals of chivalry developed in the twelfth century (if not before), there is a bit of a semantic problem to be overcome. Yet there were other words in Old French (*chevalier*, *prudhomme*) and in Latin (*miles*, *caballus*) whose existence in the twelfth century (and before) is well documented, and that might, therefore, suggest that the conception of "chivalry" as an ethos or code existed before the meaning of *chevalerie* expanded to include it. After all, as with the concept of "crusade,"[38] it is certainly possible for an action or a set of attitudes to exist before the creation of a general noun to describe them.

A second semantic problem involves the identity of those who may have participated in a chivalric lifestyle. Although it might seem self-evident that chivalry involved knights, scholars have recognized for many years that the concept of "knight" is a problematic one, compounded by centuries of popular stereotyping. Working backward from the later Middle Ages, when chivalry and knights may be clearly glimpsed in vernacular as well as Latin texts, early scholars assumed that the Latin word *miles* corresponded to the concept of "knight." But scholars such as Georges Duby and Marc Bloch recognized that words such as *miles* could change their meaning over time, and that just because the knights of the fourteenth century called themselves *milites* did not at all mean that the *milites* of the eleventh century should be thought of as knights. Throughout the 1960s and 1970s a great deal of scholarly energy was spent debating what individual authors of the eleventh and twelfth centuries meant by the word *miles.* Duby's thesis concerning the gradual formation of a noble class, with legal as well as social barriers preventing upward social mobility, became intimately linked to this semantic debate. In Duby's many articles and in the important work of his pupil, Jean Flori, a new orthodoxy seemed to grow up that saw the gradual elevation of *miles* from simple soldier to a term of honor and status.[39] This French school suggested that the upper aristocracy gradually co-opted the military term to emphasize its own claims to martial prowess, while simultaneously imbuing in it some of the honor or *dignitas* that had always distinguished the great from the small. Some neo-Romanizing scholars insist that it retained a purely military connotation; the *miles* was a soldier, without any connotation of social rank or special code of conduct.[40] But most scholars accept that the Roman military term *miles* had become imbued with connotations of status and rank from at least the twelfth century; as a result, most have been willing to translate *miles* as "knight" when it appears from the eleventh century onward.[41] As Jean Flori first demonstrated, norms, perhaps even a code, for noble behavior existed long before the word "chivalry" took on its present connotations;[42] as nobles started self-consciously using the word *miles* in honorific ways toward the end of the twelfth century, they were merely crystallizing notions that already had a long history. David Crouch, whose wide-ranging work since the 1990s offers the best overview of the subject, has offered an important argument that builds on Flori's thesis. Crouch notes the existence of a focused ideal of noble behavior in the *preudhomme*, who appears in vernacular writing from its earliest incarnation in the Song of Roland.[43] Despite equal problems of definition concerning the word *preuz*, Crouch ably shows that the *preudhomme* embodied a broad range of implications: he was the competent warrior, the wise counselor, and the amiable courtier all wrapped into one.[44] Thus, despite the late appearance of the word *chevalerie* used to describe a code or ethos, the concept of a self-consciously applied set of norms of noble conduct was not born around 1200, but existed from a much earlier date.

Scholars of chivalry have also debated other crucial concepts, including the content of the ethos that chivalry represented, historians' ability to use (or misuse) literary evidence, and the circumstances surrounding its first appearance. The romanticization of "the age of chivalry" and the "bold exploits of noble knights" that marked the writing of early nineteenth-century authors such as Sir Walter Scott, whose *Ivanhoe* (1819) cast a long shadow into the twentieth century through literature and film, led most serious historians to eschew chivalry as, well, un-serious.[45] Those who did study the concept, including Léon Gautier, tended to adopt a heavily moralistic or, more properly, religious understanding of chivalry as a notion fostered by the Church to improve the morality of uncouth warriors. The devout Gautier famously reduced "the ancient code of chivalry" to ten "commandments", and unselfconsciously noted their resemblance to the Decalogue. Among the ten were such gems as "Thou shalt believe all that the Church teaches and shalt obey all her commandments (#1)," "Thou shalt defend the Church (#2)," "Thou shalt respect all weaknesses and constitute thyself the defender of them (#3)," and "Thou shalt perform scrupulously thy feudal duties, if they be not contrary to the laws of God (#7)." Other commandments required honesty, generosity, love of country, and fearlessness in battle.[46] Yet, as Crouch has shown, if Gautier's interpretative framework was heavily influenced by his own Catholicism and his conclusions now seem faintly risible, he nonetheless knew his literature.

The century after Gautier's work saw several new approaches to the study of chivalry. One approach was dismissive, as English empiricists and certain continental writers, such as Johann Huizinga, noted with distaste the hollowness of Gautier's crypto-religious chivalric ideals.[47] Another rejected Gautier's religious veneer in favor of an increasingly secular understanding of codes of aristocratic conduct. Sidney Painter was one of the first to distinguish between the "courtly ideal," "feudal chivalry," and "religious chivalry."[48] In Germany, investigations into knighthood and chivalry also emphasized the fundamentally secular origins and characters of both.[49] In 1984 Maurice Keen reinvigorated scholarly examination of chivalry with his seminal book on the subject. The age of Gautier and the romantics was long gone, and Keen took pains to emphasize "the secular origins of chivalry."[50] Although, like Painter, he admitted that chivalry was formed from a fusion of "martial, aristocratic, and Christian"[51] elements, his meticulous scholarship and judicious interpretation ushered in a new era in the historiography of chivalry, one in which moral and religious values played an increasingly small role. Indeed, in France, the scholarship of Duby and Flori had linked chivalry to broad social changes around the year 1000 (just as Duby had done with family structures) and to increasing consciousness of status and class. Not surprisingly their work focused on the ways in which a chivalric ethos served to set the elite aristocracy apart from other free men. In England, John Gillingham advanced a unique view of chivalry as a "secular code" that emphasized practical and military elements. Gillingham's thesis saw chivalry as based in age-old secular notions of honor, which only cohered into a code when elites came to place a high value on the limitation of brutality in combat, and particularly in the "relatively humane" treatment of prisoners.[52] His arguments were echoed and expanded by Matthew Strickland, in an important book published in 1996.[53] Although taking a broader view that emphasized the dynamism and fluidity of noble self-conceptions and behavior, and thus espoused a wide definition of chivalry, Bouchard's excellent synthesis of 1998 also adopted a fairly secularist and hard-headed view of the realities and exigencies of noble conduct.[54]

English historian David Crouch's many works on the subject of chivalry and noble conduct represent the most recent and nuanced treatment of the subject. We have already seen that he has accepted Flori's dating of "chivalry" to the years around 1200, and that he offered the *preudhomme* as the eleventh- and twelfth-century predecessor of the *chevalier*. Crouch points to the famous *Ordene de chevalerie* of 1220 as a *terminus ante quam* for the acceptance of chivalry as a self-conscious code of noble behavior, but he produces plenty of evidence to demonstrate that similar, if less formally defined, concepts surrounding the *preudhomme* had existed since at least 1100. The key for Crouch seems to be a process of hardening of definitions whereby the *preudhomme*, or noble gentleman, came to be equated with the mounted warrior, or *chevalier*. In that process, he is not as distant from the thesis of Flori and Duby as it might appear, even though his methodologies and assumptions about class formation suggest a significant rift with the French school. At any rate, Crouch notes that it would be unthinkable to call a *chevalier* of the early twelfth century "chivalrous," with all its modern connotations; only between 1180 and 1220 did the concept of noble or gentle conduct come to be fused with that of the warrior code.[55]

Crouch's genius lies in his ability to draw from existing historiographical and methodological traditions to offer an interpretation that respects its predecessors but points in new directions. In keeping with other recent accounts of chivalry, he emphasizes loyalty, forbearance, hardiness and ferocity, and honor as the main categories of ideal noble conduct.[56] Citing the Anglo-Norman historian Henry of Huntingdon, for instance, Crouch isolates the features of a *preudhomme*: he was "*preuz*, honest, good, kind, straightforward, truthful, modest, valiant, steadfast, active and respectable."[57] But, although he rightly avoids Gautier's religious enthusiasms and excesses, Crouch allows his definition to include moral leadership and righteousness.[58] He points to copious twelfth-century literary and historical evidence to support this point, of which Bernard of Clairvaux's famous call for a "new knighthood" (which justified, in part, the Templars) is one example. Thus Crouch's approach avoids the semantic literalism of Flori and the narrower definitions of Gillingham and Strickland in favor of a broad image of the chivalrous knights as a broadly competent warrior, courtier, and moral actor.

What the recent works on chivalry and its predecessor, *preudhommie*, share is an intense focus on actual behavior. Here scholars since Keen and Flori have been concerned to abolish the old myth that chivalry was simply a form of hypocrisy in which real individuals paid lip-service to higher ideals in order to make themselves look or feel good. But the modern scholarship, by first rendering the definition of chivalry more secular and more linked to courtliness, has been able to demonstrate that some real aristocrats did seem to care about acting in ways that might be lauded in vernacular or Latin writing. To be sure, the vast bulk of the evidence for aristocratic behavior in the twelfth and thirteenth centuries still comes from literature, with all the epistemological problems that reading literature poses for historians. But the post-1980 generation has worked hard to uncover evidence from Latin chronicles, charters, and prescriptive manuals with which to test and compare the literary evidence. The best cases arrive when it is possible to construct an image of an aristocrat from multiple sources, for then, if the image is consistent, one does not have to worry as much about topoi and normative strictures of genre. That is, if only one chronicler calls an aristocrat "probus", it is possible to argue that this is a stylized convention; if authors from different locations (and particularly those writing in Latin as well as Old French) offer the same broad interpretation, then it becomes easier to argue that there is a semblance of reality in the descriptions.

Two examples may suffice. One is found in the person of Helias of La Flèche, count of Maine for most of the period 1091–110. Helias had to fight hard to claim the countship successfully from a cousin in 1091, and had an even more difficult time retaining his position in the face of Norman incursions into Maine between 1097 and 1100. His position as count was secured only when Norman dynastic politics were settled in 1106 with the victory of Henry I over his brother Robert Curthose.[59] Given his peripheral, but recurring role in Norman history, he figures in all the major Norman historical writers of the early twelfth century (both Latin and Old French), as well as in a local Manceaux episcopal *vita*. In all these sources, Helias appears as the epitome of the *preudhomme*: bold, straightforward, proud (in the good sense), brave, distinguished, handsome, and rhetorically gifted.[60] To Orderic Vitalis, he was upright and honorable, distinguished in appearance, eloquent, gentle when possible but strict when necessary, and filled with awe for God.[61] To Wace, he was "a good knight, handsome, noble and very tough."[62] To the author of the Manceau *Actus* he was noble, courageous, prudent, and generous.[63]

The classic example of an actual aristocrat who displayed chivalric virtues is, of course, William Marshal. William's story is well known, and need not be recounted in detail here. A younger son of the royal constable John Marshal, William forged a steady upward climb through the social ranks; he began *c.* 1160 as one of the squires in the household of his kinsman, the Norman chamberlain William of Tancarville, and ended up in the early thirteenth century as a great earl, a marcher lord, and the protector of England.[64] Remarkable as William's career may have been, what makes him significant for the study of chivalry is the fact that the Marshal's friend John of Earley commissioned a 19,000-line biography of the earl in Old French (the so-called *Histoire de Guillaume le Maréchal*) shortly after William's death in 1219.[65] This happy fact has allowed scholars such as Duby, Gillingham, and especially Crouch to confront the record sources (charters, letters, pipe rolls, and so forth) with a narrative written in the style of a *chanson de geste*. The *Histoire*, not surprisingly, considers William to be without peer in words or deeds; it even calls him "the best knight who ever was or ever will be."[66] Among the Marshal's many virtues were loyalty, bravery, prowess, good manners, courtliness, and worthiness.[67] And yet, as Crouch has done so ably, one can also use the historical record with the *Histoire* to trace William's difficult path through the households of successive lords. The close historical analysis, moreover, has allowed Crouch to offer a fuller picture of the Marshal than the *Histoire* might suggest; it shows a hard life eking out honor on the tournament fields, jockeying for favor among the other household knights, and hoping for general advancement or, best of all, a wealthy heiress. The financial woes and seigneurial relationships discussed in Crouch's biography suggest a rounder, more complex individual than the man of loyalty, manners, and prowess presented in the *Histoire*, without, nevertheless, compromising the *Histoire*'s general image. Although the Marshal's case is, at this point, unique in allowing this degree of historical and literary conjuncture, it presents a vision of the *preudhomme* or *chevalier* that rings true to that found in both the Latin historians and the Old French *chansons de geste*.

By the later Middle Ages, of course, when the concept of chivalry is less problematic, one is presented with a plethora of riches. Prescriptive treatises on chivalry and noble behavior abound, including the *Ordene de chevalerie* mentioned above and well-known works by Ramon Llull, Geoffrey de Charny, and Christine de Pisan.[68] Geoffrey de Charny is of special interest, for he not only wrote about chivalry, probably at the behest of King Jean II, but he was one of the most renowned knights of his age, and died carrying the Oriflamme at the Battle of Poitiers.[69] Chroniclers such as Jean Froissart assumed chivalry to be a motivating factor in every aspect of noble life.[70] Courtesy books abounded. Kings founded fraternal orders devoted to the principles of chivalry.[71] And elaborate rules for heraldry and display were established. Even if we can be certain that not all aristocrats acted chivalrously at all times, the concept had become, in Crouch's words, "a self-conscious code" that permeated late medieval culture. By this period, romance literature, prescriptive treatises, court life, and, at least some of the time, warfare, were in full concordance; the chivalrous man was good, wise, courteous, brave, and upstanding.[72]

Recent scholarship, however, has raised one further problem concerning chivalry, one that is centered on the date and origins of chivalry. Despite broad acceptance of the basic arguments and chronology sketched above, a few scholars have taken issue with the understanding of chivalry that sees it as a twelfth-century phenomenon, with or without Crouch's suggestions concerning the interim stage of *preudhommie*. In a classic article from 1988, for instance, Janet Nelson traced the origins of knighthood deep into the Carolingian period. For Nelson, "knighthood" entailed specific associations of social status, economic power, and Christian legitimization with the mounted warrior.[73] In her reading of Nithard's *Histories* and other ninth-century texts she identifies a firm conception of *nobilitas* as a quality distinguishing the best men.[74] That the term *nobilitas* could simultaneously refer to a group of men with self-consciousness of class and to the behavior and conduct that they practiced has obvious implications for the history of chivalry. And yet Nelson does not argue that "chivalry" existed in the ninth century, only that the Carolingians also possessed well-understood social hierarchies based on wealth, military training, and behavior.

In his most recent work, however, Dominique Barthélemy does not shy away from using the term "chivalry" to describe the Frankish period.[75] Indeed, he pushes back further than did Nelson, and argues that chivalry is consonant with the entire post-Roman, post-statist world of the Middle Ages. Thus, while the heroic, honor-based, but self-limiting values of the Germanic tribes (and particularly the Franks) might have been tamped down a bit by contact with Rome, those ideals re-emerged in the sixth century in forms that can be recognized as "chivalric."[76] Just as Crouch saw a *habitus* of the *preudhomme* in the eleventh century, one that prefigured the appearance of the term *chevalerie*, so then does Barthélemy argue for a chivalric *habitus* in place during the early Middle Ages.[77] This chivalry entailed "the sociability of chevaliers, the norms of interaction between them, with practices such as challenges to duels, forgiveness in the place of formal submission, and, more and more frequently, negotiated settlements between adversaries."[78] Although admitting that vengeance was a staple of Frankish society, Barthélemy argues that methods for avoiding or mitigating the need for vengeance were in widespread practice in ways that thus prefigured the noble restraint described by Gillingham for the eleventh and twelfth centuries. Other elements of so-called classic chivalry could be glimpsed in the early Middle Ages: quasi-Christianized "defense of the weak," dubbing, hostage exchange, a "clubby" sense of noble status, veneration of mounted combat, forbearance, and so forth. Despite the apparent novelty of this argument, however, Barthélemy does not deny some importance for the twelfth century. He sees the "revelation" of chivalric traits and their rapid spread through Latin and vernacular writings after 1100 as the point at which noble chivalry was internationalized into a source of "seigneurial universalism."[79] Thus he gives credence to the role of princely courts as locations where older Frankish concepts were honed, practiced, and elevated into the codes that become visible in such richness in the twelfth century, while nonetheless advocating a certain degree of continuity in noble culture. It is a provocative thesis, and one that still awaits scholarly judgment. It does offer an important corrective to the dominant role scholars have given to the twelfth century (while still respecting the "mutation" that occurred in that period) in reminding us that certain aspects of noble culture and behavior have an even more ancient pedigree than is usually granted.

As should be clear, since the early 1980s there has been an explosion of writing about chivalry and its role in shaping collective and individual beliefs and actions. Despite the plethora of excellent recent surveys (Bouchard, Crouch, Barthélemy), it is hard to predict how the field will move in the next generation. One very promising line of thinking involves using concepts of chivalry and noble conduct to explore the implications of other aspects of aristocratic behavior. Gillingham and Strickland, for instance, have done so very successfully with regard to the practice of warfare and, in Gillingham's case, imperialism. Richard Kaeuper's impressive work on chivalry and violence marks another example of the application of chivalric thought to one aspect of aristocratic practice.[80] Kaeuper masterfully blends knowledge of vernacular romance with a nuanced understanding of the historical sources to produce a rich and fulfilling image of the complex relationship between chivalric ideals and violence. His central theme is the tensions that existed between aristocratic needs to take vengeance for slights to honor and the chivalric ideal of forbearance. Kaeuper clearly shows a range of opposed discourses surrounding this tension, whether between and within the clergy or between kings and nobles. He does not resolve that tension, but allows it to exist as an interpretative axis around which individual knights could gauge the competing and simultaneous impulses toward violence and clemency. In so doing Kaeuper offers not the definitive definition or interpretation of chivalry, but rather a model for complex social analysis grounded in both literary and historical texts, one that eschews rigid structures and chronologies and instead embraces multiple voices, tensions, and possibilities.

Courts, Courtliness, and Civilizing Processes

To this point I have studiously said little about the locations in which the dynamics of kinship and noble conduct played out. And yet a sizable body of literature has emerged over the past thirty years that argues for the crucial importance of secular (and sometimes ecclesiastical) courts as sites in which aristocratic values and behavior were shaped, performed, and interpreted. The courts of great men, whether lay or ecclesiastical, were vibrant, dynamic social entities that claimed the power to shape individual behavior in the fishbowl of intense competition and peer evaluation. Courts served multiple functions: they could render judicial judgments as a legal court, they were centers of cultural and political patronage, they cemented friendships (and enmities), and they trained men in proper conduct. At court a knight might learn the qualities of the *preudhomme* or *chevalier* from the stories and reputations of other knights, and could, he might hope, return from war and other events with stories and reputations that might in turn influence his peers. Courts were, in addition, the site of intense competition for status, as the many courtiers competed for patronage, status, and reputation at the expense of each other. Indeed, Walter Map famously noted that "cupidity is the lady of the court"; her darts stung all men into selfishly striving for gain.[81] Commentaries such as Map's, despite their frequent cynicism, reveal the important social and political role that courts played in shaping noble behavior.

As with all of the concepts discussed in this chapter, it is difficult to describe "the court" precisely. Map observed that, while he existed at court, he knew not what it was, and scholars have often faced similar difficulties.[82] The etymological root of the concept is clear; the court takes its name from the Latin word *curia*, which originally referred to the units into which the Roman people were divided, but which, by the early Middle Ages, had taken on a whole host of specialist meanings. When one encounters a princely or seigneurial *curia* in the eleventh century, for instance, one has to investigate closely whether the word refers to a legal assembly, a more general social and political assembly around a particular lord, or elements of both.

Courts as centers of power and social formation existed from the earliest Middle Ages, and among the fruits of recent research has been scholarship reminding us of the "courtliness" of the centuries prior to 1000. Janet Nelson, for instance, demonstrates that Charlemagne's court boasted many of the same features as those that Elias's well-known "courtly society" of the early modern period possessed. To wit, Charlemagne's court possessed a spatial dimension, it shaped those dwelling in it into a "self-conscious elite," it served as a center for sociability and conversation, and the competition that it provoked among courtiers served to enhance royal authority.[83] Matthew Innes has also emphasized the role of Carolingian courts in shaping the social, moral, and ethical development of the men who participated it. He quotes one ninth-century writer who explicitly describes the king's court as a school (*schola*) or a course of discipline, since it "corrects men's vestments, their deportment, their speech and actions, and in general holds them to the norms of restraint appropriate to a good life."[84]

In an influential work published in 1985, C. Stephen Jaeger also argued for the prominence of pre-millennial courts in shaping the "ethical ideals" that were later called "chivalric."[85] Jaeger located the origin of those ethical ideals not in Carolingian royal courts, however, but in the work of Ottonian clergymen who in essence created a new code of conduct designed to appeal to the emperor and thereby help those clergymen secure the fruits of patronage for themselves. Jaeger's thesis was novel and invigorating, for it found the origins of courtliness and chivalry not in France, and not in romance literature, but rather in Germany and in a neo-classicizing rhetoric.[86] Because of his focus on Germany, Jaeger was also the first modern commentator to make use of the sociological theories of Norbert Elias. Elias had written his magnum opus, *The Civilizing Process*, in 1939, but it had languished in relative obscurity until it was translated into English in the 1970s. Jaeger employed Elias's idea that courts had served to "civilize" the warrior class in arguing that "courtier-bishops" cultivated virtues such as affability, moderation, and mildness. These traits allowed the bishops to navigate the competitive world of patronage at royal (and other princely courts); the success of those traits (and others) not only shaped literature, but shaped the behavior of those nobles who also wished to improve their ability to navigate the currents of the court.[87] In Jaeger's view, then, the court is the locus for profound modifications of culture and behavior.

The courts of the twelfth century and later are better known, and have traditionally figured more prominently in explanations of the development of manners and chivalric behavior. This is partly because the explosion of vernacular literature that occurred in twelfth-century Europe is widely believed to have been linked to the patronage of royal and princely courts. As a result, one important strand of writing about courts and their culture has emphasized the courts as centers of literary patronage at which the values inherent in such texts – whether romance, history, or moral treatise – were imparted to the members of the court. While Bezzola's classic study is perhaps the most famous example of this genre, there are many other exemplars.[88] Other approaches have focused more heavily on political patronage, and at the origins and status of the men who frequented courts. Judith Green has demonstrated the tight connections that bound together the members of the English King Henry I's court, and Nicholas Vincent's study of the court of Henry II offers a glimpse into both the composition of that court and the court's role in shaping behavior.[89] An important collection edited by Martin Aurell looks broadly at the multiple roles that the Plantagenet court might play, including judicial, residential, civilizing, propagandizing, and socializing.[90] If the richness of twelfth-century evidence seems to have encouraged this efflorescence in scholarship on the court, the exponentially larger corpus of material from the later Middle Ages – including financial records of the courts themselves – has produced a proportionately large body of scholarship. From older treatments that emphasize the role of an "international court culture," to more recent studies of connection between material foundations of court life and the culture that emerged from it, and to the perennial topic of the role of courts in shaping notions of romantic love, the later Middle Ages have also witnessed a rapid growth in writing about courts.[91]

Most scholarship on courts and courtliness since the 1970s has been shaped, whether explicitly or implicitly, by the methodologies and arguments of the German sociologist Norbert Elias. As mentioned above, in 1939 Elias wrote a major study of the process by which the pre-modern European aristocracy acquired manners and became civilized; this process took centuries and was centered in princely courts, where, according to Elias, kings used courtly ideals to bind a previously fractious nobility more tightly to royal interests. Later in his career Elias wrote a more general treatment of court society that emphasized the court's role as a place of discipline and control.[92] The breadth of Elias's vision and the obvious attraction of some of his arguments (his sections on the use of forks at table, and on control of bodily functions like spitting, have become well known even to a popular audience) has deeply influenced scholarship. As we have seen, Jaeger's seminal book on courts embraced Elias's basic concept, while nonetheless relocating the process to the tenth and eleventh centuries.[93] To be sure, scholars have taken issue with elements of Elias's thesis, for Elias was not trained in medieval history; for instance, Jaeger sees courtesy as one of the causal forces in a process of civilizing, rather than merely the product of that process (as Elias argued). Nonetheless, despite criticism of details of his argument, Elias's meta-narrative has come to exert an impressive influence. Some scholars interested in the history of emotions, for instance, have adopted Elias's broad thesis to explain changes in emotional regimes over time. Thus, in an important study of the emotions that King Henry III of England may have experienced in his bedchamber, Hyams argues that the wall-paintings depicting *debonerete* and other courtly virtues were probably intended to encourage Henry to moderate his more angry impulses and act in a more refined manner.[94]

Elias's focus on manners has also led scholars to direct their attention to books of courtesy written in Latin and the vernacular from the twelfth century onward. While these works – such as Étienne de Fougère's *Livre des Manières* or Daniel of Beccles's *Urbanus* – may offer an empirical interest for historians of daily life, Elias's teleological framework brought them a special significance in the broader history of high and later Middle Ages.[95] Thus Robert Bartlett has devoted a long section of his important survey of twelfth-century England to such manuals, while Crouch has used Étienne de Fougère's work in the context of the codification of *preudhommie* into *chevalerie*.[96] In several major articles, moreover, Gillingham has shifted the "invention" of civility in England several centuries earlier than Elias and others had maintained and has demonstrated how medieval concepts of civility and civilization were developed (partly) through a dialectical comparison between English manners and Irish and other Celtic "savagery."[97] And Frédérique Lachaud has subjected Daniel of Beccles's *Urbanus* to a close reading in order to show how it developed out of and subsequently influenced twelfth-century English court culture.[98] It is worth noting that a good deal of this work on manners has centered on English history (although there is also much valuable work by German historians); French scholars do not yet seem to have subjected manners and the Elias thesis to the same scrutiny as their Anglophone colleagues.

For all of the strengths and influence of Elias and his thesis, it is appropriate to sound some notes of caution. Elias was neither a medievalist nor a historian, and, while his thesis has a certain prima-facie logic to it (the increasing use of forks at table, for instance), too much credence in his teleological leanings may well prove misplaced. After all, the purpose of his study was, like all teleology, to explain the present; in his hands, developments of the past inevitably demonstrate heuristic value only insomuch as they fit into that teleology. This is not to say that medieval authors were unaware of changes, or that they could not compare societies and judge some "better," "more advanced," and/or "more civilized."[99] It is to caution, however, against attributing too much meaning to prescriptive texts whose authors might well have articulated views that did not accord with all, or even most, of the aristocrats who attended court. In the case of the emotion of anger, for instance, it is not at all clear that we should trace a path from the violent *ira regis* of the period before 1150 to a model of debonair royal patience in the thirteenth century. By reading didactic texts such as the *Architrenius* in a vacuum, however, it would be easy to conclude precisely this point.[100] But at no point in the Middle Ages did kings (and other aristocrats) surrender fully to such emotional control; instead, anger remained a constant, if seldom-used, tool in the arsenal of aristocratic power relations. Anger, when properly displayed or performed, could remind those who witnessed it of the angry man's personal vision of his social status and could, therefore, hope either to restore damaged relationships or to reforge new ones.[101] And precisely because the manner books are full of prescriptions against growing angry at court, we can be certain that anger, whether conscious and managed or "hydraulic" and unthinking, was also a common element of court life well into the later Middle Ages.[102] We are again faced with the classic dichotomy between models and practice, between what might have been good to do in most circumstances and between what might have been necessary on particular occasions, between an ideal "code" of behavior and a rounder, more human range of social responses.

Despite these notes of caution, it is clear both that the court represents a highly promising arena for research and that Elias's theses will continue to provide inspiration to future generations of scholars. Indeed, the court is a natural locus within which the two other strands of this chapter may be glimpsed and reinterpreted. After all, as many scholars have noted, courts of the Middle Ages had at their nucleus the household (Latin: *familia*) of a great person,[103] and there would thus seem to be much profit in comparing the bonds of kith, kin, and lordship through the prism of the court. And, as we have seen, the ideals and values of chivalry that developed by the twelfth century were also products of the courts, where knights gathered for other purposes might well hear stories of prowess and of manners both good and bad.[104] Even Walter Map, for all his contempt for the hypocrisies of court life, admitted that precisely those qualities that were emphasized in books of manners and practiced, at least sometimes, at court – namely, affability, courtesy, and generosity – were what distinguished noble behavior and wisdom from ignobility and ignorance. Prowess without that veneer of courtesy and chivalry was simply not noble, and thus knights were well advised to learn how to blend their prowess with courtesy in order to prove their nobility.[105]

The theme that links all three elements of this chapter – kinship, chivalry, and court life – is thus social interaction. Aristocrats were quintessentially social creatures, who craved approval from their kin, friends, and peers, and who sought and demonstrated that approval through deeds both martial and courtly. By at least the twelfth century, moreover, the court, where aristocrats gathered for dozens of reasons, had come to be the location *par excellence* in which such approval was sought, demonstrated, and interpreted. Given this common denominator, we can identify some new and promising approaches to the history of aristocratic dynamics that are suggested by the conjuncture of these themes. For one, recent methodologies that emphasize practice over models such as structuralism offer a new way to explore the dynamics of relationships between real individuals. If an emphasis on practice necessarily leads to complexity, fluidity, mutability, and the lack of a master narrative, it seems that this is a pill that some historians are more than happy to swallow. Recent interest in defining the relationship of chivalric values to princely and individual aristocratic goals and behaviors, as well as studies of the complex discourses about manners and courtesy that engaged courts from the twelfth century onward, also suggest new lines of research into the relationships between power and behavior. Elias, of course, saw the civilizing process as intimately connected to the growth of princely power, but, as Elias's model is altered and, perhaps, pushed aside in favor of alternate chronologies, it is to be hoped that the disciplinary power of courts, of chivalric conduct, and of the kindred comes to be read in new light. And, finally, the study of manners, from both prescriptive and descriptive texts, has pointed the way to a whole host of new research topics concerning emotion, gesture, bodily motion and comportment, speech and silence, and group dynamics. The possibilities are boundless and, indeed, exciting.

Notes

1 Crouch, *Birth of Nobility*, pp. 99–123.
2 Douglas, "Companions"; Angot, *Les Croisés.*
3 Poly and Bournazel, *Feudal Transformation*, pp. 92–3.
4 *Gesta consulum andegavorum*, pp. 26–9; Orderic Vitalis, *Historia Ecclesiastica*, vol. 2, pp. 306–7.
5 Bloch, *Feudal Society*, pp. 284–5.
6 Bouchard, *"Those of my Blood"*, pp. 13–16.
7 Settipani, "Les Comtes d'Anjou," pp. 212–18; Bouchard, *"Those of my Blood"*, pp. 32–3.
8 Bouchard, *"Those of my Blood"*, pp. 7–10; Martindale, "The French Aristocracy," pp. 8–10.

9 Schmid, "The Structure of the Nobility"; Duby, *La Société*, pp. 215–27. For a recent commentary, see Bouchard, *"Those of my Blood"*, pp. 59–73.
10 e.g., Duby, "The Nobility in Medieval France," pp. 100–3; "Lineage, Nobility and Knighthood," pp. 67–75.
11 Duby, *La Société*, pp. 215–27; Schmid, "Zur Problematik."
12 Bernard and Bruel, *Recueil des chartes de l'abbaye de Cluny*, vol. 5, no. 3849.
13 In the very broadest framework, this aggregate of changes has come to be known as the "Feudal Revolution." See White, "Feuding and Peace-Making," "Inheritances and Legal Arguments," and *Custom, Kinship and Gifts to Saints.*
14 Duby, "Lineage, Nobility and Knighthood," p. 74.
15 Duby, "Youth in Aristocratic Society," pp. 117–18; Riley-Smith, *First Crusade and the Idea of Crusading*, p. 43.
16 Burke, *French Historical Revolution*, p. XX
17 White, *Custom*, pp. 86–129.
18 e.g., Bouchard, *"Those of my Blood"*, p. 38.
19 Le Jan, *Famille et pouvoir*, pp. 387–413.
20 Crouch, *Birth of Nobility*, pp. 115–16.
21 Evergates, "Nobles and Knights," p. 18.
22 Livingstone, "Diversity and Continuity," pp. 415–21.
23 Stafford, "La Mutation familiale," pp. 103–25.
24 Crouch, *Birth of Nobility*, p. 121.
25 Not surprisingly, Pierre Bourdieu's theories of praxis have been influential to some of these writers (e.g. Stephen White); see Bourdieu, *Outline.*
26 Bouchard, "The Structure"; White, "Inheritances"; Livingstone, "Diversity and Continuity."
27 White, *Custom*, pp. 86–129; White, "Feuding and Peace-Making," *passim*; Riley-Smith, *First Crusaders*, pp. 81–105.
28 Some scholars engaged in study of the ninth and tenth centuries still rely heavily on *namengruppen* analyses, most often to construct genealogies, but occasionally (and with risk) to offer causal explanations for political events. Cf. Keats-Rohan, "Two Studies," pp. 8–9, and Jackman, "Rorgonid Right," p. 138.
29 For a classic deconstruction of the medieval word *familia*, see Guerreau-Jalabert, "La Désignation," pp. 90–1.
30 Pitt-Rivers, "The Kith and the Kin," pp. 89–105.
31 Althoff, *Family, Friends and Followers*; Meddings, "Friendship," pp. 187–204.
32 Keen, *Chivalry*, pp. 1–17; Crouch, *Birth of Nobility*, p. 21.
33 "Code": Gillingham, "1066," p. 32. "Ethos": Keen, *Chivalry*, p. 17.
34 Keen, *Chivalry*, p. 1; Crouch, *Birth of Nobility*, pp. 7–8.
35 Burgess, "The Term 'Chevalerie,'" pp. 343–58.
36 Charny, *A Knight's own Book of Chivalry.*
37 Burgess, "The Term 'Chevalerie,'" pp. 357–8.
38 Tyerman, "Were There Any Crusades."
39 Duby, *The Chivalrous Society*; Flori, *L'Idéologie*; *L'Essor.*
40 Bachrach, "Medieval Military Historiography," pp. 209–11.
41 Flori, *L'Essor*, pp. 223–30; Morillo, "*Milites*, Knights and Samurai," pp. 175–7.
42 Flori, *L'Essor*, pp. 339–42.
43 Crouch, *Birth of Nobility*, pp. 29–86.
44 *Preuz* stems from the Latin *probus* (honest, upstanding). See Crouch, *Birth of Nobility*, p. 30.
45 For this and much of what follows, see Crouch, *Birth of Nobility*, pp. 7–14.
46 Gautier, *Chivalry*, pp. 9–27.

47 Crouch, *Birth of Nobility*, pp. 14–15.
48 Painter, *French Chivalry*. Cf. Crouch, *Birth of Nobility*, pp. 15–16.
49 Bumke, *The Concept of Knighthood*, pp. 1–8, 22.
50 Keen, *Chivalry*, pp. 18–43.
51 Ibid., p. 16.
52 Gillingham, "1066," p. 32; "Conquering the Barbarians," pp. 76–84.
53 Strickland, *War and Chivalry*.
54 Bouchard, *Strong of Body*.
55 Crouch, *Birth of Nobility*, pp. 29–86; *Tournament*, p. 150.
56 Crouch, *Birth of Nobility*, pp. 56–80.
57 Ibid., p. 50. See also Crouch, *William Marshal*, pp. 183–92; *Tournament*, pp. 149–53.
58 Crouch calls this the "Davidic Ethic": *Birth of the Nobility*, pp. 71–9. Cf. Keen, *Chivalry*, 44–63; Kaeuper, *Chivalry*, pp. 63–88.
59 On Helias, see Barton, "Henry I."
60 Orderic Vitalis, *Historia Ecclesiastica*, vol. 5, p. 232; Wace, *The Roman de Rou*, ll. 9977–10030; *Actus Pontificum Cenomannis*, pp. 385, 400–6.
61 Orderic Vitalis, *Historia Ecclesiastica*, vol. 5, p. 232: "probus, honorabilis, corpore praecellebat fortis et magnus, eloquio . . . suavis et facundus, lenis quietis et asper rebellibus, and in timore Dei ad opus bonum fervidus."
62 Wace, *The Roman de Rou*, ll. 9986–7: "Helies fu boen chevaliers, bels fu e genz e bien pleniers."
63 *Actus Pontifictum Cenomannis*, p. 385 (*nobilis*, *viriliter*), p. 404 (*liberalitas*), p. 406 (*liberalis comes*). His actions at ibid., p. 402, speak to military prudence. For several more examples of *preudhommes*, see Crouch, *Birth of the Nobility*, pp. 42–6.
64 The portrait of the Marshal offered by Crouch, *William Marshal*, is far richer and far more credible than the impressionistic sketch offered in Duby, *William Marshal*.
65 *History of William Marshal*; Crouch, *William Marshal*, pp. 1–5.
66 *History of William Marshal*, ll. 2079–83, 3155.
67 Ibid., ll. 2428, 3081–4, 3085 ("proz est e corteis e leials").
68 Llull, *Book of the Ordre*; Charny, *Knight's own Book*; Pizan, *Book of Deeds of Arms*.
69 Keen, *Chivalry*, p. 12.
70 e.g., Froissart, *Chronicles*.
71 Keen, *Chivalry*, pp. 179–99.
72 Ibid., pp. 12–17.
73 Nelson, "Ninth-Century Knighthood," p. 255.
74 Ibid., pp. 261–2.
75 Barthélemy, *La Chevalerie*.
76 e.g., ibid., p. 64. King Sigibert was "un bon exemple d'une courtoisie et d'une clémence presque chevaleresques."
77 *Habitus* is Pierre Bourdieu's term for an implicitly recognized set of beliefs and social practices that structure other beliefs and social practices (Bourdieu, *Outline*, pp. 78–87). Crouch uses it to define the pre-codified "chivalry" of the *preudhomme* (Crouch, *Birth of the Nobility*, pp. 52–3), and Barthélemy uses it in a similar way to describe Frankish quasi-chivalric practices (Barthélemy, *La Chevalerie*, pp. 477–81).
78 Barthélemy, *La Chevalerie*, p. 478.
79 Ibid., p. 480.
80 Kaeuper, *Chivalry and Violence*;, "The Societal Role."
81 Map, *De nugis*, p. 4.
82 Ibid., p. 2; Vale, *Princely Court*, pp. 16–17.

83 Nelson, "Was Charlemagne's Court a Courtly Society?" pp. 40–2, 46–7, 53. Cf. Elias, *The Court Society.*
84 Innes, "'A Place of Discipline,'" p. 59.
85 Jaeger, *Origins of Courtliness*, p. 4.
86 Ibid., pp. 9–16 and *passim.*
87 Jaeger, *Origins of Courtliness*, pp. 211–35.
88 Bezzola, *Les Origines et la formation*; Short, "Literary Culture."
89 Green, "Networks and Solidarities"; Vincent, "The Court of Henry II."
90 Aurell, ed., *La Cour Plantagenêt*, pp. 9–46 and *passim.*
91 Mathew, *The Court of Richard II*; Vale, *Princely Court*; Jaeger, "Mark and Tristan."
92 Elias, *The Civilizing Process*; *The Court Society.*
93 Jaeger, *Origins of Courtliness*, pp. 5–9.
94 Hyams, "What did Henry III . . . Think?"
95 Fougères, *Livre des manières*; Daniel of Beccles, *Urbanus magnus.*
96 Bartlett, *England under the Norman and Angevin Kings*, pp. 582–6; Crouch, *Birth of Nobility*, pp. 83–6.
97 Gillingham, "Civilizing the English?";, "From *Civilitas* to Civility."
98 Lachaud, "L'Enseignement."
99 Cf. Gillingham, "Civilizing the English?" pp. 20–2.
100 Johannes de Hauvilla, *Architrenius*, bk 6, ll. 28–77.
101 Barton, "'Zealous Anger'," argues this point for western France between 1050 and 1150, but it could easily be extended to later periods. Cf. Map, *De nugis*, pp. 30–4.
102 For a classic twelfth-century example of this tension between performative anger and impulses towards moderation, see Peter of Blois, *Dialogus*, ll. 1–280.
103 Vale, *Princely Court*, pp. 15–33.
104 Crouch, *Birth of the Nobility*, pp. 21–5, 37–46. Walter Map notes how court officials liked to lighten the weight of serious talk with pleasantries: *De nugis*, 210.
105 Map, *De nugis*, p. 416. The classic example of seeking such a balance between prowess and courtesy is Chrétien de Troyes's *Erec and Enide.*

Bibliography

Actus Pontificum Cenomannis in Urbe Degentium, ed. G. Busson and A. Ledru (Le Mans: Archives historiques du Maine, 1902).

Althoff, Gerd, *Family, Friends and Followers: Political and Social Bonds in Early Medieval Europe*, trans. Christopher Carroll (Cambridge: Cambridge University Press, 2004).

Angot, Alphonse, *Les Croisés de Mayenne en 1158: Étude critique* (Laval: Goupil, 1896).

Aurell, Martin, ed., *La Cour Plantagenêt (1154–1204)* (Poitiers: CESCM, 2000).

Bachrach, Bernard S., "Medieval Military Historiography," in Michael Bentley, ed., *Companion to Historiography* (London: Routledge, 1997), pp. 203–20.

Barthélemy, Dominique, *La Chevalerie: De la Germanie antique à la France du XII*[e] *siècle* (Paris: Fayard, 2007).

Bartlett, Robert, *England under the Norman and Angevin Kings, 1075–1225* (Oxford: Oxford University Press, 2000).

Barton, Richard E., "'Zealous Anger' and the Renegotiation of Aristocratic Relationships in Eleventh- and Twelfth-Century France," in Barbara H. Rosenwein, ed., *Anger's Past: The Social Uses of an Emotion in the Middle Ages* (Ithaca, NY: Cornell University Press, 1998), pp. 153–70.

Barton, Richard E., "Henry I, Helias of Maine and the Battle of Tinchebray," in Donald Fleming and Janet Pope, eds, *Henry I and the Anglo-Norman World* (Woodbridge: Boydell, 2007), pp. 63–90.

Bernard, Auguste, and Bruel, Alexandre, eds, *Recueil des chartes de l'abbaye de Cluny*, 6 vols (Paris: Imprimerie Nationale, 1876–1903).

Bezzola, Reto R., *Les Origines et la formation de la littérature courtoise en occident (500–1200)*, 2 vols (Paris: H. Champion, 1944–60).

Bloch, Marc, *Feudal Society*, 2 vols. trans. L. A. Manyon (Chicago: University of Chicago Press, 1961).

Bouchard, Constance B., "The Structure of a Twelfth-Century French Family: The Lords of Seignelay," *Viator*, 10 (1979), pp. 36–59.

Bouchard, Constance B., *Strong of Body, Brave and Noble: Chivalry and Society in Medieval France* (Ithaca, NY: Cornell University Press, 1998).

Bouchard, Constance B., *"Those of my Blood": Constructing Noble Families in Medieval Francia* (Philadelphia: University of Pennsylvania Press, 2001).

Bourdieu, Pierre, *Outline of a Theory of Practice* (Cambridge: Cambridge University Press, 1977).

Bumke, Joachim, *The Concept of Knighthood in the Middle Ages*, trans. W. T. H. and E. Jackson (New York: AMS Press, 1982; original German edn, 1977).

Burgess, Glyn S., "The Term 'Chevalerie' in Twelfth-Century French," in P. Monks and D. D. R. Owen, eds, *Medieval Codicology, Iconography, Literature and Translation: Studies for Keith Val Sinclair* (Leiden: Brill, 1994), pp. 343–58.

Burke, Peter, *The French Historical Revolution: The Annales School, 1929–1989* (Stanford, CA: Stanford University Press, 1990).

Charny, Geoffrey de, *A Knight's own Book of Chivalry*, trans. Elspeth Kennedy (Philadelphia: University of Pennsylvania Press, 2005).

Crouch, David, *William Marshal: Knighthood, War and Chivalry, 1147–1219*, 2nd edn (London: Longman, 2002).

Crouch, David, *Birth of Nobility: Constructing Aristocracy in England and France, 900–1300* (London: Longman, 2005).

Crouch, David, *Tournament* (London: Hambledon and London, 2005).

Daniel of Beccles, *Urbanus magnus*, ed. J. Gilbert Smyly (Dublin: Hodges, Figgis & Co., 1939).

Douglas, David C., "Companions of the Conqueror," *History*, 38 (1943), pp. 129–47.

Duby, Georges, *La Société aux XIe et XIIe siècles dans la région mâconnaise* (1953; rev. edn, Paris: École des Hautes Études en Sciences Sociales, 1988).

Duby, Georges, *The Chivalrous Society*, trans. Cynthia Postan (Berkeley and Los Angeles: University of California Press, 1977).

Duby, Georges, "The Nobility in Medieval France," in Georges Duby, *The Chivalrous Society* (Berkeley and Los Angeles: University of California Press, 1977), pp. 94–111.

Duby, Georges, "Lineage, Nobility and Knighthood: The Mâconnais in the Twelfth Century – a Revision," in Georges Duby, *The Chivalrous Society* (Berkeley and Los Angeles: University of California Press, 1977), pp. 59–80.

Duby, Georges, "Youth in Aristocratic Society: Northwestern France in the Twelfth Century," in Georges Duby, *The Chivalrous Society* (Berkeley and Los Angeles: University of California Press, 1977), pp. 112–22.

Duby, Georges, *William Marshal: The Flower of Chivalry* (New York: Pantheon Books, 1985).

Elias, Norbert, *The Court Society*, trans. Edmund Jephcott (New York: Pantheon Books, 1983).

Elias, Norbert, *The Civilizing Process*, trans. Edmund Jephcott (Oxford: Blackwell, 1994).

Evergates, Theodore, "Nobles and Knights in Twelfth-Century France," in Thomas N. Bisson, ed., *Cultures of Power: Lordship, Status and Process in Twelfth-Century Europe* (Philadelphia: University of Pennsylvania Press, 1995), pp. 11–35.

Flori, Jean, *L'Idéologie du glaive: Préhistoire de la chevalerie* (Geneva: Droz, 1983).

Flori, Jean, *L'Essor de la chevalerie, XIe–XIIe siècles* (Geneva: Droz, 1986).

Fougères, Étienne de, *Le Livre des manières*, ed. R. A. Lodge (Geneva: Droz, 1979).

Froissart, Jean, *Chronicles*, trans. Geoffrey Brereton (Harmondsworth: Penguin, 1969).

Gaimar, Geoffrey, *L'Estorie des Engleis*, ed. T. D. Hardy and C. T. Martin, 2 vols., Rolls Series (London: HMSO, 1888–9).

Gautier, Léon, *Chivalry*, ed. Jacques Levron; trans. D. C. Dunning (London: Dent, 1965; original French edn, Paris, 1884).

Gesta consulum andegavorum, in *Chroniques des comtes d'Anjou et des seigneurs d'Amboise*, ed. Louis Halphen and René Poupardin (Paris: A. Picard, 1913), pp. 25–73.

Gillingham, John, "Conquering the Barbarians: War and Chivalry in Twelfth-Century Britain," *Haskins Society Journal*, 4 (1992), pp. 67–84.

Gillingham, John, "1066 and the Introduction of Chivalry into England," in George Garnett and John Hudson, eds, *Law and Government in Medieval England and Normandy: Essays in Honour of Sir James Holt* (Cambridge: Cambridge University Press, 1994), pp. 31–55.

Gillingham, John, "Civilizing the English? The English Histories of William of Malmesbury and David Hume," *Historical Research*, 74 (2001), pp. 17–43.

Gillingham, John, "From *Civilitas* to Civility: Codes of Manners in Medieval and Early Modern England," *Transactions of the Royal Historical Society*, ser. 6, 12 (2002), pp. 267–89.

Green, Judith, "Networks and Solidarities at the Court of Henry I Beauclerc," in David Bates and Veronica Gazeau, eds, *Personal Links, Networks and Solidarities in France and the British Isles (11th–20th Century)* (Paris: Publications de la Sorbonne, 2006), pp. 113–26.

Guerreau-Jalabert, Anita, "La Désignation des relations et des groupes de parenté en latin médiéval," *Archivum latinitatis Medii Aevi (Bulletin du Cange)*, 46–7 (1988), pp. 65–109.

History of William Marshal, ed. A. J. Holden; trans. S. Gregory with notes by D. Crouch, 3 vols (London: Anglo-Norman Text Society, 2002–6).

Hyams, Paul, "What did Henry III of England Think in Bed (and in French) about Kingship and Anger?" in Barbara H. Rosenwein, ed., *Anger's Past: The Social Uses of an Emotion in the Middle Ages* (Ithaca, NY: Cornell University Press, 1998), pp. 92–124.

Innes, Matthew, "'A Place of Discipline': Carolingian Courts and Aristocratic Youth," in Catherine Cubitt, ed., *Court Culture in the Early Middle Ages* (Turnhout: Brepols, 2003), pp. 59–76.

Jackman, Donald, "Rorgonid Right: Two Scenarios," *Francia*, 26 (1999), pp. 129–53.

Jaeger, C. Stephen, *The Origins of Courtliness: Civilizing Trends and the Formation of Courtly Ideals, 939–1210* (Philadelphia: University of Pennsylvania Press, 1985).

Jaeger, C. Stephen, "Mark and Tristan: The Love of Medieval Kings and their Courts," in Winder McConnell, ed., *In hôhem prîs: A Festschrift in Honor of Ernst S. Dick* (Göppingen: Kümmerle Verlag, 1989), pp. 183–97.

Johannes de Hauvilla, *Architrenius*, ed. W. Wetherbee (Cambridge: Cambridge University Press, 1994).

Kaeuper, Richard W., *Chivalry and Violence in Medieval Europe* (Oxford: Oxford University Press, 1999).

Kaeuper, Richard W., "The Societal Role of Chivalry in Romance: Northwestern Europe," in Roberta Krueger, ed., *The Cambridge Companion to Medieval Romance* (Cambridge: Cambridge University Press, 2000), pp. 97–114.

Keats-Rohan, K. S. B., "Two Studies in North French Prosopography," *Journal of Medieval History*, 20 (1994), pp. 3–37.

Keen, Maurice, *Chivalry* (New Haven: Yale University Press, 1984).
Lachaud, Frédérique, "L'Enseignement des bonnes manières en milieu de cour en Angleterre d'après l'*Urbanus magnus* attribué à Daniel de Beccles," in Werner Paravicini and Jörg Wettlaufer, eds, *Erziehung und Bildung bei Hofe* (Stuttgart: Thorbecke, 2002), pp. 43–53.
Le Jan, Régine, *Famille et pouvoir dans le monde franc (VIIe–Xe siècle)* (Paris: Publications de la Sorbonne, 1995).
Le Jan, Régine, "Continuity and Change in the Tenth-Century Nobility," in Anne J. Duggan, ed., *Nobles and Nobility in Medieval Europe: Concepts, Origins, Transformations* (Woodbridge: Boydell, 2000), pp. 53–68.
Livingstone, Amy, "Diversity and Continuity: Family Structure and Inheritance in the Chartrain, 1000–1200," in *Mondes de l'Ouest et villes du monde* (Rennes: Presses Universitaires de Rennes, 1998), pp. 415–29.
Llull, Ramon, *The Book of the Ordre of chyualry*, trans. William Caxton; ed. A. T. P. Byles (London: Early English Text Society, 1926).
Map, Walter, *De nugis curialium: Courtiers' Trifles*, ed. M. R. James, rev. C. N. L. Brooke and R. A. B. Mynors (Oxford: Clarendon Press, 1983).
Martindale, Jane, "The French Aristocracy in the Early Middle Ages: A Reappraisal," *Past & Present*, 75 (1977), pp. 5–45.
Mathew, Gervase, *The Court of Richard II* (London: John Murray, 1968).
Meddings, John, "Friendship among the Aristocracy in Anglo-Norman England," *Anglo-Norman Studies*, 22 (1999), pp. 187–204.
Morillo, Stephen, "*Milites*, Knights and Samurai: Military Terminology, Comparative History and the Problem of Translation," in Bernard Bachrach and Richard Abels, eds, *The Normans and their Adversaries at War* (Woodbridge: Boydell, 2001), pp. 167–84.
Nelson, Janet L., "Ninth-Century Knighthood: The Evidence of Nithard," in C. Harper-Bill et al., eds, *Studies in Medieval History Presented to R. Allen Brown* (Woodbridge: Boydell, 1989), pp. 255–66.
Nelson, Janet L., "Was Charlemagne's Court a Courtly Society?" in Catherine Cubitt, ed., *Court Culture in the Early Middle Ages* (Turnhout: Brepols, 2003), pp. 39–58.
Orderic Vitalis, *Historia Ecclesiastica: The Ecclesiastical History of Orderic Vitalis*, ed. and trans. with introduction and notes Marjorie Chibnall, 6 vols (Oxford: Clarendon Press, 1969–80).
Painter, Sidney, *French Chivalry* (Baltimore: Johns Hopkins University Press, 1940).
Peter of Blois, *Dialogus inter regem Henricum secundum et abbatem Bonevallis*, in R. B. C. Hugyens, ed., "Un écrit de Pierre de Blois réédité," *Revue bénédictine*, 68 (1958), pp. 87–112.
Pitt-Rivers, Julian, "The Kith and the Kin," in Jack Goody, ed., *The Character of Kinship* (Cambridge: Cambridge University Press, 1973), pp. 89–105.
Pizan, Christine de, *The Book of Deeds of Arms and of Chivalry*, trans. Sumner Willard; ed. Charity Willard (University Park, PA: Pennsylvania State University Press, 1999).
Poly, Jean-Pierre, and Bournazel, Éric, *The Feudal Transformation, 900–1200*, trans. Caroline Higgitt (New York: Holmes and Meier, 1991).
Riley-Smith, Jonathan, *The First Crusade and the Idea of Crusading* (Philadelphia: University of Pennsylvania Press, 1986).
Riley-Smith, Jonathan, *The First Crusaders, 1095–1131* (Cambridge: Cambridge University Press, 1997).
Schmid, Karl, "Zur Problematik von Familie, Sippe und Geschlecht, Haus und Dynastie beim mittelalterlichen Adel," *Zeitschrift für die Geschichte des Oberrheins*, 105 (1957), pp. 1–62.
Schmid, Karl, "The Structure of the Nobility in the Earlier Middle Ages," in Timothy Reuter, ed. and trans., *The Medieval Nobility: Studies on the Ruling Classes of France and Germany*

from the Sixth to the Twelfth Century (Amsterdam: North-Holland, 1978), pp. 37–59; original German: "Über die Struktur des Adels im früheren Mittelalter," *Jahrbuch für frankische Landesforschung*, 19 (1959), pp. 1–23.

Settipani, Christian, "Les Comtes d'Anjou et leurs alliances aux Xe et XIe siècles," in K. S. B. Keats-Rohan, ed., *Family Trees and the Roots of Politics* (Woodbridge: Boydell, 1997), pp. 211–68.

Short, Ian, "Literary Culture at the Court of Henry II," in C. Harper-Bill and N. Vincent, eds, *Henry II: New Interpretations* (Woodbridge: Boydell, 2007), pp. 335–61.

Stafford, Pauline, "La Mutation familiale: A Suitable Case for Caution," in Joyce Hill and Mary Swan, eds, *The Community, the Family and the Saint: Patterns of Power in Early Medieval Europe* (Turnhout: Brepols, 1998), pp. 103–25.

Strickland, Matthew, *War and Chivalry: The Conduct and Perception of War in England and Normandy, 1066–1217* (Cambridge: Cambridge University Press, 1996).

Tyerman, Christopher J., "Were There Any Crusades in the Twelfth Century?," *English Historical Review*, 110 (1995), 553–77.

Vale, Malcolm, *The Princely Court: Medieval Courts and Culture in North-West Europe, 1270–1380* (Oxford: Oxford University Press, 2001).

Vincent, Nicholas, "The Court of Henry II," in Christopher Harper-Bill and Nicholas Vincent, eds, *Henry II: New Interpretations* (Woodbridge: Boydell, 2007), 278–334.

Wace, *The Roman de Rou*, ed. A. J. Holden; trans. Glyn Burgess (Jersey: Société Jersiaise, 2002); translation published apart as *The History of the Norman People: Wace's* Roman de Rou, trans. Glyn Burgess (Woodbridge: Boydell, 2004).

Werner, Karl F., "Bedeutende Adelsfamilien im Reich Karls des Grossen: Ein personengeschichtlicher Beitrag zum Verhältnis von Königtum und Adel im frühen Mittelalter," in Wolfgang Braunfels et al., eds, *Karl der Grosse. Lebenswerk und Nachleben*, 4 vols, vol. 1: *Persönlichkeit und Geschichte* (Düsseldorf: L. Schwann, 1965), pp. 83–142; in English (without appendices) as "Important Noble Families in the Kingdom of Charlemagne: A Prosopographical Study of the Relationship between King and Noble in the Early Middle Ages," in Timothy Reuter, ed. and trans., *The Medieval Nobility: Studies on the Ruling Classes of France and Germany from the Sixth to the Twelfth Century* (Amsterdam: North-Holland, 1978), pp. 137–202.

White, Stephen D., "Feuding and Peace-Making in the Touraine around the Year 1100," *Traditio*, 42 (1986), pp. 195–263.

White, Stephen D., "Inheritances and Legal Arguments in Western France, 1050–1150," *Traditio*, 43 (1987), pp. 55–103.

White, Stephen D., *Custom, Kinship and Gifts to Saints: The* Laudatio parentum *in Western France, 1050–1150* (Chapel Hill, NC: University of North Carolina Press, 1988).

Further Reading

Adams, Jeremy DuQ., "Modern Views of Medieval Chivalry, 1884–1984," in Howell D. Chickering and Thomas Seiler, eds, *The Study of Chivalry: Resources and Approaches* (Kalamazoo: Medieval Institute Publications, 1988), pp. 41–90.

Aurell, Martin, "Stratégies matrimoniales de l'aristocratie (IXe–XIIIe siècle)," in Michel Rouche, ed., *Mariage et sexualité au moyen age: Accord ou crise?* (Paris: Presses de l'université de Paris-Sorbonne, 2000), pp. 185–202.

Aurell, Martin, "La Chevalerie urbaine en occitanie (fin X[e]–début XIIIe siècle)," in *Les Élites urbaines au moyen âge* (Paris: Publications de la Sorbonne; Rome: École française de Rome, 1997), pp. 71–117.

Baldwin, John W., *Aristocratic Life in Medieval France: The Romances of Jean Renart and Gerbert de Montreuil, 1190–1230* (Baltimore: Johns Hopkins University Press, 2000).

Barthélemy, Dominique, "Modern Mythologies of Medieval Chivalry," in P. Linehan and J. L. Nelson, eds, *The Medieval World* (London: Routledge, 2003), pp. 214–28.

Barton, Simon, *The Aristocracy in Twelfth-Century León and Castile* (Cambridge: Cambridge University Press, 1997).

Benson, Larry D., "The Tournament in the Romances of Chrétien de Troyes and *L'Histoire de Guillaume le Maréchal*," in L. Benson and J. Leyerle, eds, *Chivalric Literature: Essays on Relations between Literature and Life in the Later Middle Ages* (Kalamazoo: Medieval Institute Publications, 1980), pp. 1–24.

Benson, Larry D., "Courtly Love and Chivalry in the Later Middle Ages," in Robert F. Yeager, ed., *Fifteenth-Century Studies: Recent Essays* (Hamden, CT, 1984), pp. 237–57.

Bumke, Joachim, *Courtly Culture: Literature and Society in the High Middle Ages*, trans. Thomas Dunlap (Philadelphia: University of Pennsylvania Press, 1991).

Cheyette, Fredric L., *Ermengard of Narbonne and the World of the Troubadours* (Ithaca, NY: Cornell University Press, 2001).

Contamine, Philippe, ed., *La Noblesse au moyen age* (Paris: PUF, 1976).

Ehlers, Joachim, "Entourage du roi – entourage des princes: L'Aube d'une société de cour en Allemagne au XIIe siècle," in Alain Marchandisse and Jean-Louis Kupper, eds, *À l'ombre du pouvoir: Les Entourages princiers au moyen age* (Geneva: Droz, 2003), pp. 97–105.

Fleckenstein, Josef, ed., *Curialitas: Studien zu Grundfragen der höfisch-ritterlichen Kultur* (Göttingen: Vandenhoeck & Ruprecht, 1990).

Flori, Jean, "La Chevalerie: Est-elle une manière de vivre?" in Kaspar Elm and Cosimo Fonseca, eds, *Militia Sancti Sepulcri, idea e istituzioni* (Vatican City: [s.n.], 1998), pp. 59–75.

Flori, Jean, *Chevaliers et chevalerie au moyen âge* (Paris: Hachette littératures, 1998).

Flori, Jean, "Noblesse, chevalerie et idéologie aristocratique en France d'oïl (11ème–13ème siècle)," in José Angel Garcíade Cortázar et al., eds, *Renovacion intelectual del occidente europeo (siglo XII)*. XXIV Semana de estudios medievales (Pamplona: Gobierno de Navarra, Departamento de Educación y Cultura, 1998), pp. 349–82.

Gillingham, John, "Love, Marriage and Politics in the Twelfth Century," *Forum for Modern Language Studies*, 25 (1989), pp. 292–303.

Gillingham, John, "The Cultivation of History, Legend and Courtesy at the Court of Henry II," in Ruth Kennedy and Simon Meecham-Jones, eds, *Writers of the Reign of Henry II* (New York: Palgrave, 2007), pp. 25–52.

Jackson, W. H., "Courtly Culture and Aristocratic Representation in Medieval Germany: Some Recent Work," *German History*, 12 (1994), pp. 80–91.

Jaeger, C. Stephen, "L'Amour des rois: Structure sociale d'une forme de sensibilité aristocratique," *Annales ESC*, 46 (1991), pp. 547–71.

Jaeger, C. Stephen, "Courtly Love and Love at Court: Public Aspects of an Aristocratic Sensibility," *Aestel*, 4 (1996), pp. 1–27.

Keen, Maurice, "Chivalry and Courtly Love," *Peritia*, 2 (1983), pp. 149–69.

Köhler, Erich, "Quelques observations d'ordre historico-sociologique sur les rapports entre la chanson de geste et le roman courtois," in Pierre Le Gentil, ed., *Chanson de geste und höfischer Roman* (Heidelberg: C. Winter, 1963), pp. 21–36.

Lansing, Carol, *The Florentine Magnates: Lineage and Faction in an Italian Commune* (Princeton: Princeton University Press, 1991).

Leyser, Karl, "Early Medieval Canon Law and the Beginning of Knighthood," in L. Fenske, W. Rösener, and T. Zotz, eds, *Institutionen, Kultur und Gesellschaft im Mittelalter: Festschrift für Josef Fleckenstein zu seinem 65. Geburtstag* (Sigmaringen: J. Thorbecke, 1984), pp. 549–566; repr. in Karl Leyser, *Communications and Power in Medieval Europe*, ed. T. Reuter (London: Hambelton Press, 1994), pp. 51–71.

Lachaud, Frédérique, "Littérature de civilité et 'processus de civilisation' à la fin du XIIe siècle," in *Les Échanges culturels au moyen âge: XXXIe Congrès de la SHMES, Université du Littoral Côte d'Opale, juin 2001* (Paris: Publications de la Sorbonne, 2002), pp. 227–39.

Morris, Colin, "*Equestris Ordo*: Chivalry as a Vocation in the Twelfth Century," *Studies in Church History*, 15 (1978), pp. 87–96.

Racine, Pierre, "Noblesse et chevalerie dans les sociétés communales italiennes," in *Les Élites urbaines au moyen âge* (Paris: Publications de la Sorbonne, 1997), pp. 137–51.

Reuter, Timothy, "Nobles and Others: The Social and Cultural Expression of Power Relations in the Middle Ages," in Anne J. Duggan, ed., *Nobles and Nobility in Medieval Europe: Concepts, Origins, Transformations* (Rochester, NY: Boydell Press, 2000), pp. 85–98.

Romagnoli, Daniela, ed., *La Ville et la cour: Des bonnes et des mauvaises manières* (Paris: Fayard, 1995).

Scattergood, V. J., and Sherborne, J. W., eds, *English Court Culture in the Later Middle Ages* (New York: St Martin's Press, 1983).

Werner, Karl F., "Du nouveau sur un vieux theme: Les Origines de la 'noblesse' et de la 'chevalerie,'" *Comptes-rendus de l'Academie des inscriptions et belles lettres* (1985), pp. 186–200.

Werner, Karl F., *Naissance de la noblesse: L'Essor des élites politiques en Europe* (Paris: Fayard, 1998).

Chapter Twenty-five

Philosophy and Humanism

Stephen Gersh

Scholars have grown accustomed to dividing the study of medieval philosophy into two segments on partly chronological and partly conceptual grounds, and to using the second segment as the starting point for the analysis. Thus, "later medieval philosophy" is associated with the beginnings of the universities in the thirteenth century together with the relatively speedy adoption of Aristotelian methods and doctrines by the latter's faculties of arts and theology, "early medieval philosophy" being applied as a vague and generic term to whatever methods and teachings were cultivated during approximately seven hundred years preceding the rise of such institutions. Although one might also postulate a "transitional" phase roughly coextensive with the twelfth century, since this period is marked by the translation into Latin of the numerous ancient philosophical writings, long out of circulation in Western Europe, which eventually formed the textual basis of the Aristotelian-inspired university curriculum, a division of medieval philosophy into two segments along the lines described is perfectly defensible. Nevertheless, something important about the nature of philosophy during the Middle Ages is missed by such an analysis. This concerns the question of hermeneutics, which has become so important in modern philosophical, literary, and cultural criticism. As I hope to demonstrate in the discussion to follow, there is a strong case for dividing medieval philosophy according to the hermeneutical criteria applied at the time – and not without an implicit reference to modern hermeneutics – into two phases that might be termed "humanistic" and "scholastic" respectively. These phases should probably be understood as interweaving rather than consecutive, in that the humanistic approach is dominant until the end of the twelfth century, the scholastic tendency is primary during the thirteenth and fourteenth centuries – although a kind of humanism persists as a secondary tradition within more "Augustinian" circles – and the humanistic approach returns to challenge the scholastic dominance in the early fifteenth century. The interweaving of the phases is reinforced by the fact that leading figures of fifteenth-century humanistic philosophy explicitly look back toward their twelfth-century humanistic forebears, somewhat bypassing the contributions of scholastics during the two hundred years in between.

But a question might be raised about the applicability of the term "humanism" to cultural phenomena in general. Fortunately, the meaning of the term has been fully clarified in recent years by Paul Oskar Kristeller.[1] We must therefore distinguish: (1) the expression "Humanism" (German: *Humanismus*) introduced by the pedagogical theorist F. J. Niethammer in 1808 in order to denote the emphasis placed by secondary education on the reading of ancient classics as opposed to practical or scientific pursuits, this usage also being associated retrospectively with: (2) the term "Humanist" (Italian: *umanista*, Latin: *humanista*), which occurs in Italian university documents from *c.* 1490 onward as referring in a strict sense to the teacher of a definite set of disciplines: namely, grammar, rhetoric, history, poetry, and moral philosophy and sometimes by extension to a scholar who applies ideas derived from the study of those disciplines elsewhere: for example, in natural philosophy or music, this usage also being associated retrospectively with: (3) the expression "humane studies" (Latin: *studia humanitatis*) revived by fourteenth-century writers like Francesco Petrarca and Coluccio Salutati from Cicero, Aulus Gellius, and other classical sources in order to denote the liberal or non-vocational education pursued by members of the Roman ruling class. The further question about the applicability of the term "humanism" to cultural phenomena during the Middle Ages – where the actual term did not occur – can perhaps be answered in two ways. First, an immediate historical connection between the Middle Ages and the Renaissance has been plausibly suggested by recent scholars, who argue that the earliest writers in Italy to whom the title of humanist was assigned were in practice combining two authentically medieval traditions that had previously been separated: a method of the literary study of ancient authors cultivated earlier in northern France and the method of official letter writing known as the *Ars Dictaminis*, long established in Italy itself. Secondly, there is the less immediate historical connection but no less compelling historical analogy assumed by modern scholars between the literary interests and textual methods of. on the one hand, Italian humanists such as Petrarca and Salutati together with earlier "proto-humanist" writers such as Albertino Mussato of Padua and Giovanni del Virgilio of Bologna, and, on the other hand, northern French scholars from as early as the Carolingian period, such as Lupus of Ferrières and Heiric of Auxerre.[2]

But the starting point of the present chapter is a comparison not of the humanism in the Renaissance with the "quasi-humanism" of the Middle Ages in general, but of these two cultural phenomena with special reference to *philosophy*. Among the features that scholars have identified as being characteristic of humanism (in one or more of its stages of development noted above), one should perhaps mention here the general adherence to the Ciceronian ideal of combining "wisdom" (*sapientia*) and "eloquence" (*eloquentia*) on the part of both medieval and Renaissance humanists, the difference being that during the earlier period it is mainly eloquence in the sense of grammar that is combined with philosophy, whereas during the later period it is eloquence in the sense of rhetoric that is more at issue.[3] More specifically, medieval and Renaissance philosophical humanisms can be compared and contrasted in terms of (*a*) the relation between moral and natural philosophy – during the Renaissance it is only the study of moral philosophy that is emphasized, whereas during the medieval period philosophical humanism is concerned with the study of both moral philosophy and natural philosophy and perhaps predominantly with the latter;[4] (*b*) the role of Platonism – during the Renaissance humanism occurs in conjunction with the assertion of both Platonic and Aristotelian philosophical viewpoints, whereas it is the Platonic doctrinal position that is universally maintained by the medieval counterpart of humanism;[5] (*c*) the question of anti-Scholasticism – during the Renaissance humanism is associated with both the endorsement and the rejection of scholastic approaches to philosophy, whereas the medieval antecedent of humanism represents an essentially non-scholastic mode of thinking;[6] and (*d*) the relation between cosmological and theological anthropocentrism – during the Renaissance philosophical humanism emphasizes the pivotal role of humanity in both the theological and the cosmological spheres and perhaps predominantly the latter, whereas during the medieval period it is only the theological sphere that is stressed.[7] It is easy to see from this summary that, as characterizations of Renaissance and medieval philosophical humanisms, criteria *b* and *c* are closely connected, and that, in terms of all the criteria other than *a*, the humanism of the Renaissance is a more complex and variegated phenomenon than is its medieval antecedent.

As in the case of comparable phenomena in the later period, medieval humanism is characterized primarily by its admiration for ancient literature. The letters of Lupus of Ferrières (early ninth century) show a medieval scholar at work in the process of collecting and comparing manuscripts in order to obtain the correct readings of classical texts, while the commentaries of Remigius of Auxerre (later ninth century) illustrate the medieval practice of composing prefaces to important works in order to show precisely how they should be interpreted. With respect to the philosophically inclined humanist of the early Middle Ages, a kind of canonical list of ancient authors and works can certainly be established. This consists of a group of pagan Platonic or putatively Platonic works: Plato's own *Timaeus* in the translation by Calcidius (together with the latter's commentary), book VI of Virgil's *Aeneid*, Cicero's *Academics*,[8] Apuleius' *On Plato and his Doctrine*, the *Asclepius* attributed to "Hermes Trismegistus," and Macrobius' *Commentary on Cicero's Dream of Scipio*; various patristic works reporting Platonism in detail: Augustine's *Against the Academics*, book VII of *Confessions*, and *On the City of God*;[9]certain patristic works whose espousal of Platonism is concealed by pseudonymy: the *On Divine Names*, *On Mystical Theology*, and other writings attributed to "Dionysius the Areopagite;" two Aristotelian works: Aristotle's own *Categories* and *On Interpretation*;[10] certain works expressing Platonic and Aristotelian doctrines from a position either overtly Christian or detached from paganism: Boethius' *On the Trinity*, *On the Consolation of Philosophy*, and *On Arithmetic*;[11] and various works that are not explicitly philosophical but serve to contextualize philosophy within the system of knowledge: Cicero's *On Invention*, Augustine's *On Christian Teaching*, and Martianus Capella's *On the Marriage of Philology and Mercury*.[12]

The manner in which this literary material was put to work in the service of philosophy might be summarized as follows. First, the problem of the relation between the pagan philosophical canon and Scripture had to be resolved. The key work was Augustine's *On Christian Teaching*, which explained how the study of pagan liberal arts such as grammar, rhetoric, dialectic, and arithmetic – together determining part of the domain we call "philosophy" – could be justified on the assumptions that such arts either taught methods of speaking, arguing, and interpreting, which could be applied to or elicited from the sacred text, or else stated truths such as the identification of God with Being, the triune nature of the godhead, or the immortality of the human soul, which were "Christian" truths by the very fact that they were true.[13] To this synchronic account of the relation between philosophy and Scripture a diachronic argument was sometimes added. Here, Augustine's suggestion in *On Christian Teaching* that the parallels between Platonism and Christianity were close enough to prove that Plato learned something about the Hebrew scripture when he was traveling through Egypt in search of philosophical wisdom had an impact on medieval perceptions.[14] Secondly, the question of the relation between the various parts of the pagan philosophical canon had to be clarified. The complicated answer involved dividing knowledge into wisdom and eloquence according to the proposal in Cicero's *On Invention*, dividing wisdom into theoretical and practical parts according to Boethius' *On the Consolation of Philosophy*, dividing eloquence into grammar, rhetoric, and dialectic according to Augustine's *On Christian Teaching*, dividing theoretical wisdom into theology, mathematics, and physics according to Boethius' *On the Trinity*, dividing mathematics into arithmetic, geometry, music, and astronomy according to Boethius' *On Arithmetic*, and then mapping the entire system onto the sevenfold "harmony" of the three verbal arts with the four mathematical arts in Martianus Capella's *On the Marriage of Philology and Mercury*.[15] To this synchronic account of the relation between the parts of philosophy a diachronic argument was also added. Thus, Augustine's argument in *Against the Academics* that Plato had originally stated a doctrine approximating to Christianity, that it had been subsequently concealed, and that it had been revealed anew by Plotinus familiarized medieval readers with a cyclic notion of the history of philosophy.[16]

Admiration for ancient literature is indeed a feature shared by medieval and later humanism. But, because of the relatively limited availability of Latin texts and the virtual absence of Greek texts, the medieval humanist's level of philological expertise was lower than that of his later counterpart – a weakness having a significant impact on questions regarding the authenticity and dating of texts and ultimately on the understanding of philosophy and its history. The enduring controversy surrounding "Dionysius the Areopagite" is undoubtedly the most striking illustration of this. Most medieval readers assumed that the theological treatises of the so-called Dionysius the Areopagite were actually written during the apostolic period, whereas modern scholars universally acknowledge that these works are influenced by pagan Platonism of the fifth century CE, the process of historical clarification having begun with Erasmus and Lorenzo Valla during the Renaissance and been completed only in the nineteenth century. Now, although some of the sharper medieval critics noted the generally Platonic character of the doctrines enunciated without necessarily understanding the specific variety of Platonism involved, this feature was explained by the formulation of various hypotheses. For example, it was suggested that the apostolic "Dionysius" had decisively formulated the teachings dimly adumbrated by Plato himself, and that later pagan Platonists concealed these works in a spirit of professional jealousy, and then attempted to pass off the teachings as their own.[17] Clearly, such historical misunderstandings gave the *pseudo*-Dionysius, with respect to the interpretation of the philosophical canon described earlier, an important and in some respects a pre-eminent position.

In light of the textual practices described above, one might perhaps underline three features of the humanistic tradition within medieval philosophy as a whole.[18] First, medieval philosophical humanism is characterized by a belief in the unitary nature of truth: all the authoritative authors and writings are held to exhibit such doctrinal agreement that one can always gloss one author using material derived from another. Secondly, it is assumed that the canonical authors and texts are doctrinally Platonic and therefore approximating to Christian truth, any tension between these positions being manageable in the case of more pedagogical authors or texts but more troublesome in that of authors or texts more technically philosophical. Thirdly, medieval philosophical humanism is characterized by a belief in the alternating concealment and revelation of truth: such a historical hypothesis is obviously useful in reconciling the belief in the unitary nature of truth with the empirical fact of the periodic disagreements that have arisen among different philosophical schools. All three features of the humanistic tradition in medieval philosophy are actually dependent on the relation between Platonism and Christianity emphasized in the case of the second, given that the unitary nature of truth and its alternating concealment and revelation are themselves assumptions of both a typically Platonic and a typically biblical character.[19]

Medieval Philosophical Humanism: Three Phases

Of the three phases in the development of philosophical humanism during the western Middle Ages that we propose to consider in the remainder of this chapter, the earliest might be characterized as "pseudo-Dionysian" – because of the pivotal role played by this author within the intertextual system – and exemplified by the work of Iohannes Scottus Eriugena (*c.* 815–*c.* 877). Eriugena was perhaps the most outstanding of the many Irish scholars working on the European continent under the patronage of the Carolingian kings and bishops, and was celebrated not only for the writing of works based on the Latin liberal arts and Latin patristic tradition such as his *Annotations on Martianus Capella* and *On Divine Predestination*, but also for his translation of Greek patristic works such as the complete treatises of "Dionysius the Areopagite" and certain writings of Gregory of Nyssa and Maximus the Confessor. But most important of all Eriugena's writings was the treatise in five books entitled *On Natures*, in which he synthesized the teachings of all his authorities while transforming them in a highly original and personal manner.

Perhaps the most immediately striking aspect of Eriugena's philosophy is its emphasis on the logical-semantic doctrine of negativity derived from pseudo-Dionysius. According to the doctrine elaborated in *On Natures*, God can be understood and described by using an alternation of negative terms – that is, saying that he is "not-X" – and of affirmative terms – that is, saying that he is "X" – the negative terms being substitutable with excessive terms – that is, saying that God is "above-X" – in that their negativity implies superiority or plenitude rather than inferiority or deficiency.[20] Because the negative terms do not involve correlative oppositions – as God himself does not involve a correlative opposition – whereas the affirmative terms necessarily involve such oppositions, it is argued that negative terms apply more truly to God and affirmative terms less truly[21] and also that negative terms apply literally to God and affirmative terms only metaphorically.[22] Eriugena bases his theory of "divine names" – which is subsequently shown to be an account of metaphysical realities as well as of semantic properties – on the alternation of the "not-X" and "X" mentioned above.[23] He extracts a list of such names from pseudo-Dionysius' scriptural reading – this comprises goodness, being, life, reason, intellect, wisdom, virtue, blessedness, truth, eternity, greatness, love, peace, unity, and perfection[24] – and also assigns the names to the most appropriate Aristotelian categories: for example, being to substance, intellect to place, virtue to quantity, and love to action.[25]

On Natures as a whole is based on a fourfold structure according to which God or Nature can be described as (1) "creating and not created" – the God who transcends his creature as the source of its being, (2) "creating and created" – the God who is immanent in the individual causes of his creatures, (3) "not creating and created" – the God who is immanent in his individual creatures themselves, and (4) "not creating and not created" – the God who transcends his creature as object of its aspiration.[26] The fourfold structure of double terms also represents a dynamic cyclic process between unity and multiplicity both in the sense of a movement of *realities* from unity to multiplicity called "procession" and from multiplicity to unity called "reversion," and of a movement of *concepts* from unity to multiplicity called "division" and from multiplicity to unity called "analysis."[27] The fourfold structure can be simultaneously real and conceptual because the duality of 1 and 4 represents the unity of God who is alternately *conceived* as beginning and as end of all created things, the duality of 2 and 3 represents the unity of the creature that is *really* composed of participated Forms and participating particulars, and the duality of 1–4 and 2–3 represents the unity of God who is alternately *conceived* under his negative and affirmative divine names.[28] The fourfold structure itself seems to have been derived from two fourfold classifications of a similar logical structure applied to substance in Aristotle's *Categories* and to number in Macrobius' *Commentary on the Dream of Cicero* respectively. The interpretation of the structure in terms of the cyclic movement of realities is clearly influenced by pseudo-Dionysius' *On Divine Names*, while the interpretation of the structure in terms of the cyclic movement of concepts is possibly influenced by Boethius' *On Division*.[29] Nevertheless, the combination of these different logical–metaphysical schemata and the elaboration of the relation between the real and the conceptual can be attributed to Eriugena's own creative genius.

The philosophical system of *On Natures* is also based on an analogy between macrocosm and microcosm. Eriugena here seems to combine the version of this idea in Plato's *Timaeus* – where the analogy is between the world soul and the human soul – and the version in Gregory of Nyssa's *On the Image* and Maximus the Confessor's *Ambigua* ("*Problems*") – where the analogy is between the divine sphere and the human sphere. He therefore argues that it is not only the divine nature in a primary sense but also human nature in a secondary sense that must be approached through the alternation of negative terms and affirmative terms, and not only the divine nature in a primary sense but also human nature in a secondary sense that can be understood as embodying a fourfold structure of (1) creating and not created, (2) creating and created, (3) not creating and created, and (4) not creating and not created, and as embodying a dynamic cyclic process between unity and multiplicity in the sense of a movement of realities and concepts.[30] The analogy between macrocosm and microcosm is not an addition to the doctrine explained earlier but an essential part of it. Thus, the *conceptual* aspect of the duality of 1 and 4 and the *conceptual* aspect of the duality of 1–4 and 2–3 both depend on the cognitive relation between the human microcosm and the divine macrocosm.

The work of certain teachers of grammar in the northern French schools during the early twelfth century may be considered as a second phase in the development of medieval philosophical humanism. Since the work of these grammarians embodies an unusually sophisticated intertextual reading of Plato's *Timaeus*, Calcidius, Macrobius, and other Platonic sources, the second phase might be characterized as "Latin Platonic." We shall here consider the leading ideas of three main figures: William of Conches (d. *c.* 1154), the author of commentaries on Plato's *Timaeus*, Macrobius' *Commentary on the Dream of Scipio*, and Boethius' *On the Consolation of Philosophy*, and of the independent treatises *Philosophy of the World* and *Dragmaticon*, Thierry of Chartres (fl. 1121–48), the author of commentaries on Cicero's *On Invention*, the pseudo-Ciceronian *To Herennius*, and Boethius' theological treatises, and of the independent treatises *On the Works of the Six Days*, and Bernard Silvestris (fl. c. 1130–1160), the author of commentaries on *Virgil's Aeneid Books I–VI,* and Martianus Capella's *On the Marriage of Philology and Mercury*, and of the independent work combining poetry and prose entitled *Cosmography.* Although these three writers make common cause in terms of their commitment to philosophical humanism, there are undeniable differences of interest between them. While William of Conches was more influenced by Graeco-Arabic medical literature and Thierry of Chartres was more influenced by Boethian–Pythagorean numerology, Bernard Silvestris exploited both tendencies in a perfect blend of philosophical commentary and literary imitation.

Bernard Silvestris's *Commentary on Virgil's Aeneid Books I–VI* provides us with insights into the character of twelfth-century philosophical humanism in an important preface. Applying to the Virgilian text an exegetical principle that reads Cicero's injunction concerning the combination of eloquence and wisdom in terms of Martianus Capella's precept regarding the marriage of the *trivium* and *quadrivium*, Bernard here identifies, on the one hand, the "poetical fiction" and, on the other, the "philosophical truth" running through the entire epic. The preface further states that the poetical fiction is the journey of Aeneas, narrated in an artificial manner – that is, contrary to the sequence of real events, with the aim of both utility and amusement, that is, by providing "examples" of morality and stylistics; and that the philosophical truth is the course of human life, narrated in the natural manner – that is, following the sequence of real events, with the aim of utility, that is, by assisting the process of self-knowledge, the relation between the poetical fiction and the philosophical truth being allegorical in nature.[31] However, the main body of Bernard's commentary, which further reveals that the poetical fiction culminates in Aeneas' descent into the underworld and the philosophical truth in the human acquisition of knowledge – the ending of the commentary in *Aeneid* VI being highly significant – produces what is nowadays termed a hermeneutical circle.[32] Given that knowledge turns out to be the curriculum of textual and authorial study, which advances the knowledge of oneself and of God, and that this curriculum of study is based on the combination of eloquence or *trivium* with wisdom or *quadrivium*, then the ideal of knowledge advocated by the Virgilian text includes the study of texts such as that of Virgil himself.[33]

In order to understand more fully what the twelfth-century grammarians thought "philosophical truth" to be, we should turn to texts illustrating some of the ways in which the doctrine of first principles within theoretical philosophy was handled.

William of Conches's *Glosses on Plato* represent the most important commentary on the only text by Plato generally known during the Middle Ages, and proceed on the assumption that the *Timaeus* is a systematic study of four causes: the "efficient cause" corresponding to the divine essence, the "formal cause" corresponding to the divine wisdom, the "final cause" corresponding to the divine goodness, and the "material cause" corresponding to the four elements.[34] The first three causes coincide in God and are eternal and non-generated. They are indicated in Plato's references to the Artificer as source of being, to the Paradigm or Ideas in the divine mind, and to the Artificer as object of aspiration, and in their turn intimate the first person or Father, the second person or Son, and the third person or Spirit in the Christian Trinity. The last cause corresponds to the physical aspect of the creature and is non-eternal and generated. The theory of first principles outlined in several passages of Thierry of Chartres's glosses on Boethius' theological treatises is perhaps more remarkable. According to Thierry's *Lectures on Boethius' On the Trinity*,[35] one and the same universe of all things can be considered in four ways: (1) "in absolute necessity" – in God where the Forms of things exist in a transcendentally enfolded state, (2) "in necessity of complication" – where the Forms are unfolded above individual things, (3) "in determinate possibility" – where the Forms are unfolded within individual things, and (4) "in absolute possibility" – in Matter where the Forms of things exist in an immanently enfolded state.[36] Thierry's theory of first principles is remarkable because it strongly emphasizes that the presence of God and his Ideas in the created world is a real one – recalling the presentation of a Stoic-influenced Platonism under the guise of "Old Academic" doctrine in Cicero's *Academics* – and also that the relation between God or his Ideas and the created world is a conceptual one – recalling the fourfold structure of double terms applied to God or Nature in Eriugena's *On Natures*.[37] William of Conches's *Glosses on Macrobius* represent the most important discussion of the only summary of Plotinus' thought available during the Middle Ages, and pay special attention to the doctrine that there is a descending hierarchy of three principles: "God," the unknowable whose difference from created things can be expressed by the figure of the monad, "Intellect," a non-temporal principle that contains the divine Ideas of all genera, species, and individuals, and "World Soul," a temporal principle whose powers in relation to corporeal world can be expressed figuratively through numbers.[38] Plotinus' triad is treated throughout this argument as an intimation of the Christian Trinity, although it is emphasized that heretical language describing relations between the principles such as the reference to God as "creating" Intellect, and facile assimilations of principles to Persons such as that of the World Soul to the Holy Spirit should be avoided.[39]

In order to understand more fully what the twelfth-century grammarians thought "poetical fiction" to be, we should return to the work of Bernard Silvestris himself. As we have seen from the earlier discussion of Bernard's *Commentary on Virgil's Aeneid Books I–VI*, one of the aims of the poetical fiction that complements the philosophical truth of writers like Virgil is to furnish "examples" of morality and stylistics.[40] Since examples are designed to stimulate imitation in the form of practical action rather than of theoretical contemplation, it was inevitable that Bernard would implement the combination of eloquence and wisdom with the composition of a work emulating the classical models. The result in the form of Bernard's *Cosmography* is arguably the high point of twelfth-century philosophical humanism. On the level of poetical fiction, this work provides a narrative of the actions of quasi-mythical figures in an alternation of prose and verse that recalls Martianus Capella's *On the Marriage of Philology and Mercury* and Boethius' *On the Consolation of Philosophy*. On the level of philosophical truth it articulates a metaphysical analogy between divine "macrocosm" and human "microcosm" along the lines advocated by Plato's *Timaeus*,[41] the hierarchical theory of three principles – here called Tugaton, Noys, and Endelichia[42] – borrowed from Macrobius' *Commentary on the Dream of Scipio*,[43] and a cosmological notion of humanity's privileged role in the universe along the lines suggested by the Hermetic *Asclepius*.[44] This last point suggests a new definition of "humanism" as cosmological anthropocentricity, which will have considerable repercussions in a later generation of thought.

Of the three phases in the development of philosophical humanism during the western Middle Ages that we proposed to consider in this chapter, the last combines aspects of the two earlier phases and might therefore be characterized as both "pseudo-Dionysian *and* Latin Platonic." It is exemplified by Nicholas of Cusa (1401–64). Nicholas had been educated in Padua, where he came under the influence of Italian humanism and mathematical innovation, and in Cologne, where he was introduced by Heimeric de Campo to the Platonic philosophical tradition. During an unusually busy career as a canon lawyer, member of the Council of Basel, papal legate, and cardinal, he managed to compose a number of philosophical texts ranging in subject matter from the political, through the metaphysical, to the mathematical, and composed in the genres of both treatise and dialogue. Nicholas's most widely known work is entitled *On Learned Ignorance*. Although this was completed at the relatively early date of 1440, it presents a full exposition of a philosophical system that does not seem to have undergone substantial revision during the writer's later career. This system is based on the relation between three *maxima*, which are called "absolute," "contracted," and "both absolute and contracted" and are studied in *On Learned Ignorance* books I, II, and III respectively. Although the three maxima are identified at the outset as simply corresponding to God, the universe, and Jesus, they approximate more to God through the universe, the universe through God, and the combination of the two as the problematic deepens.[45]

It is in connection with his study of the absolute maximum in book I that Nicholas appropriates the pseudo-Dionysian legacy. Following the method already formalized by Eriugena, *On Learned Ignorance* argues that God can be understood and described by using an alternation of negative terms and affirmative terms, the negative terms being substitutable with excessive terms.[46] It further argues that negative terms apply more truly to God and affirmative terms less truly,[47] and that negative terms apply literally to God and affirmative terms only metaphorically.[48] Nicholas's reasons for maintaining the superiority of the negative over the affirmative method are different from his predecessor's. Whereas Eriugena had argued that it was the oppositional aspect of the affirmative terms that makes them inapplicable to a God to whom nothing is opposed, Nicholas now suggests that it is the proportional aspect of such terms that makes them inapplicable to a God to whom nothing is proportionate.[49] This shift from a more logical to a more mathematical style of argumentation is linked with a series of further innovations introduced by Nicholas into his theory. These include: the identification of the negative moment with the mathematical notion of infinity,[50] the introduction of the privileged philosophical affirmative name of maximum (defined as "that than which a greater cannot be thought" in the wording of Anselm of Canterbury),[51] the situating of God both above and within the alternation of negative and affirmative moments (reflecting a shift from the *On Divine Names* to the *On Mystical Theology* of pseudo-Dionysius as source),[52] and the introduction of the privileged religious affirmative name of the *Tetragrammaton*.[53] The most striking innovation is, however, the principle of "coincidence of opposites," which reformulates the alternation of negative and affirmative moments in a radical manner. According to this notion, opposites are reconciled at the point of junction between God and creature, these opposites being either on the side of the perceived object like maximum and minimum, or on the side of the perceiving subject like learned and ignorant, and either metaphysical like substance and accident or potency and act, or geometrical like straight and curve or triangle and sphere.[54] The principle of coincidence of opposites, by suspending the law of contradiction within its sphere of operation, represents a profoundly un-Aristotelian mode of thought.

Nicholas appropriates the Latin Platonic legacy in connection with his study of the contracted maximum in book II of *On Learned Ignorance*. He hardly dwells on the theory of the four causes extracted from Plato by William of Conches: that is, where the efficient cause corresponds to the Artificer as source of being, the formal cause to the Paradigm or Ideas in the divine mind, the final cause to the Artificer as object of aspiration – these three causes coinciding in God – and where the material cause corresponds to the four elements. Nevertheless, he cites the theory briefly as that of unnamed "Platonists,"[55] contrasts it with the Peripatetic theory of causality,[56] and corrects any possible hierarchical misunderstanding.[57] Nicholas is more actively engaged with the theory of Thierry of Chartres: a writer whom he admires without knowing his actual name.[58] As an instance of outstanding philosophical thought in the "Platonic" manner, he cites the doctrine that one and the same universe can be considered in the fourfold manner in absolute necessity, in necessity of complication, in determinate possibility, and in absolute possibility.[59] But Nicholas feels obliged to correct this doctrine in two ways: first, by observing that the Forms comprising the necessity of complication cannot exist as a real plurality outside God himself[60] and, secondly, by arguing that absolute possibility must be identified not with matter but with God.[61] On the theory of the three principles extracted from Macrobius by William of Conches – that is, where the unknowable God is expressed through the figure of the monad, the non-temporal principle of Intellect contains the divine Ideas of all genera, species, and individuals, and the temporal World Soul is expressed figuratively through numbers – he again does not dwell. Nevertheless, he cites the theory briefly as that of the unnamed Platonists,[62] aligns it with Avicenna's theory of emanation,[63] and corrects its obvious hierarchical implications.[64]

Conclusion

In this chapter we have been following a number of different threads, and the time has come to ask whether these threads can be pulled together into a bundle. The answer can perhaps be given in the form of a summary.

In the second part of the chapter, we have considered some of the doctrinal issues that were central to medieval philosophical humanism, and we have seen that the doctrine that God can be understood and described by using an alternation of negative and affirmative terms is of primary concern to Eriugena; that an analysis of God's relation to creation in terms of a set of causes called efficient, formal, final, and material, in terms of a real-conceptual structure of the absolute-determinate and the necessary-possible, and in terms of the hierarchy of principles called God, Intellect, and World Soul is the project of William of Conches, Thierry of Chartres, and Bernard Silvestris; and that both the doctrine of negative and affirmative divine names and the various analyses of God's relation to creation are of primary concern to Nicholas of Cusa. In the first part of the chapter we asked the question whether the notion of "humanism" – a term that has been conclusively shown by historical analysis to represent a curriculum of grammar, rhetoric, history, poetry, and moral philosophy during the Renaissance – could be utilized in order to distinguish one tradition from another within medieval philosophy. The answer may be discerned if we are permitted to analyze both the Renaissance program of humanism and the humanistic branch of medieval philosophy in the structural manner[65] in terms of the three conceptual oppositions of practical to theoretical, of grammatical-rhetorical to dialectical, and of Platonic to Aristotelian in which (1) the first term of each opposition prevails over the second and in which (2) the first terms of each opposition and likewise the second terms are interrelated. Now it is fair to say that Renaissance humanism definitely elevates the practical above the theoretical, while the humanistic branch of medieval philosophy occasionally does – something shown clearly in the case of Bernard Silvestris; further, that both Renaissance humanism and the humanistic side of the medieval philosophical tradition elevate the grammatical-rhetorical above the dialectical; and, finally, that Renaissance humanism sometimes elevates the Platonic above the Aristotelian, while the humanistic branch of medieval philosophy invariably does – something shown clearly in the case of Nicholas of Cusa. We can, therefore, posit a structural continuity if not a structural identity between the humanistic branch of medieval philosophy and the Renaissance program, and a family resemblance if not a logical universal underlying the humanistic branch of medieval philosophy and Renaissance humanism: a hypothesis that seems to be well founded as soon as one considers some further aspects of the medieval philosophical tradition. Thus, in the second part of the chapter, we have also considered some of the stylistic features that were typical of medieval philosophical humanism, and we have seen that the doctrine that God can be described and understood by using an alternation of negative and affirmative terms in Eriugena and Nicholas of Cusa, and the analysis of God's creation in terms of a set of causes called efficient, formal, final, and material, in terms of a real-conceptual structure of the absolute-determinate and the necessary-possible, and in terms of the hierarchy of principles called God, Intellect, and World Soul in William of Conches, Thierry of Chartres, Bernard Silvestris, and Nicholas of Cusa consisted entirely of the grammatical-rhetorical manipulation of Platonic philosophical texts. In emphasizing the practical and the grammatical-rhetorical aspects to such an extent, the humanistic branch of medieval philosophy – in contrast with the scholastic branch – comes strikingly close to the modern hermeneutics practiced by Martin Heidegger and certain post-Heideggerians. In emphasizing the negative-dialectical aspects of the Platonism associated with such developments, the humanistic branch of medieval philosophy even exhibits certain affinities with the Jacques Derrida's model of deconstructive reading and writing.

A Note on Petrarch

Especially in connection with the second phase in the development of medieval philosophical humanism, it is perhaps worth inserting a note on Petrarch, who was in relation to the slightly later Italian humanism "the first culmination, if not its beginning."[66] Petrarch's connection with our topic is based particularly on the fact that, in his voluminous composition of Latin poems such as the *Africa*, of orations, of prose treatises including dialogues such as the *Secret* and invectives such as *On his own Ignorance and that of Many Others*, and of letters, he exemplifies the full agenda of humanistic studies described at the beginning of this chapter. From the specific viewpoint of philosophical humanism, we can detect strong doctrinal parallels between Petrarch's work in the fourteenth century and that of the northern French grammarians of the twelfth. This conceptual association seems even more justifiable in light of recent historical research establishing clear empirical connections not only in the form of literary dependence but also in that of manuscript ownership between Italian proto-humanists and their predecessors in the French schools of Chartres and Orléans.

Petrarch's most philosophical work is the invective *On his own Ignorance and that of Many Others*. This treatise is written decidedly from the standpoint of the indirect Platonism that we have seen to prevail during the Middle Ages, Augustine's argument about the close affinity between Platonism and Christianity providing the usual ideological justification. At one point, Petrarch mentions among the names of important writers whom Plato influenced Cicero, Virgil, Apuleius, Plotinus, and Porphyry – a list clearly derived from Augustine's *On the City of God* – while in other passages he makes explicit references to such Platonic works as Calcidius' *Commentary on Plato's Timaeus* and Macrobius' *Commentary on Cicero's Dream of Scipio*. For Petrarch, it is clearly Cicero who is the most important writer within this entire tradition: he teaches a doctrine almost indistinguishable from Christian beliefs in such works as *On the Republic*, *On the Laws*, *On the Nature of the Gods*, and *Tusculan Disputations*, although he occasionally makes regrettable lapses into polytheism. That the present treatise makes tentative approaches to the standpoint of the *direct* Platonism that will emerge during the Renaissance has naturally caught the attention of scholars. Thus, Petrarch raises the question of how many books by Plato are in existence in either Latin or Greek, praises the eloquence of Plato as a writer – a judgment presumably requiring some acquaintance with the Platonic dialogues themselves – and describes the Greek codex of Plato, which he possesses but cannot read.

Notes

1 See Kristeller, "The Humanist Movement," pp. 21–2, "Humanism and Scholasticism," pp. 92, 98–9, and "Humanism," pp. 113–14.

2 There is a good recent discussion of the historical connections and the historical analogies between Renaissance and medieval humanism in Mann, "The Origins of Humanism," pp. 5–8.

3 On the Ciceronian ideal in general among the Renaissance humanism, see Kristeller, "The Humanist Movement," pp. 25–6, 29, and "Humanism," pp. 122–3. The shift from a grammatical to a rhetorical reading of the famous dictum about the combination of

wisdom and eloquence reflects the influence of the *Ars Dictamnis* on Renaissance humanism.

4 See Kristeller, "The Humanist Movement," pp. 23, 28–9, "Humanism and Scholasticism," p. 92, and "Humanism," pp. 113–14, 125. Although humanistic methods were sometimes applied to other areas of philosophy, this must be considered as an extended rather than the basic form of humanism. See Kristeller, "Humanism," pp. 131–2.

5 Examples of humanistically inclined Platonists in the Renaissance are Nicholas of Cusa, Marsilio Ficino, and Giovanni Pico della Mirandola. See Kristeller, "The Humanist Movement," pp. 29–30, and "Humanism," p. 136. For the Aristotelianism that remained prominent, see Kristeller, "Humanism and Scholasticism," pp. 90–1, 99–103, and "Humanism," p. 132.

6 Examples of anti-scholastic humanists are Petrarca, Lorenzo Valla, and Desiderius Erasmus. See Kristeller, "Humanism and Scholasticism," p. 90. For the pro-scholastic side of the equation, see the passages cited in the previous note.

7 This remains the most controversial part of the definition of Renaissance humanism, since the notions of anthropocentricity, individualism, and subjectivity are often conflated in the secondary literature. On the theme of the dignity of man, see Kristeller, "The Humanist Movement," p. 32. Kristeller accepts individualism in the sense of expressing personal feelings in descriptive and biographical literature as one of the leading characteristics of humanism. See Kristeller, "The Humanist Movement," pp, 30, 104, and "Humanism," pp. 126–7, 136–7.

8 The role of Cicero in the medieval Platonic tradition is a particularly complicated and important one, although its significance has not always been appreciated by scholars – one may contrast the situation with that of Petrarch, whose treatment of Cicero as the pivotal writer (and as a Christian *manqué*) has been widely discussed. Within the textual reading strategy of medieval philosophers, Cicero functions (1) as theorist of the relation between eloquence and wisdom (in *On Invention*), (2) as reporter of the Old Academic doctrine – i.e. of Platonism (in *Academics* and *Tusculan Disputations*), (3) as cosmologist (in *On the Republic*) – in conjunction with Macrobius' *Commentary on the Dream of Scipio*, and (4) as theorist of topics (in *On Invention* and *Topics*) – in conjunction with Boethius' *Commentary on Cicero's Topics* and *On Topical Differences.* Cicero was also especially known (via Augustine) as translator of Plato's *Timaeus.* Obviously, the study of this complex reception would go beyond the bounds of the present chapter.

9 There are also scattered briefer testimonies regarding Platonism in other works of Augustine such as *On the Blessed Life, Soliloquies, On the Immortality of the Soul, On the True Religion*, and *On Eighty-Three Different Questions.*

10 The situation regarding Aristotle's *Categories* (at least before the thirteenth century) is somewhat complicated, since, although Boethius' Latin translation had some albeit limited circulation, the work was known indirectly through a work attributed incorrectly to Augustine entitled *On the Ten Categories*, through Augustine's autobiographical report of reading the text in his *Confessions*, and through material obviously derived from it in Augustine's *On the Trinity* and Boethius' *On the Trinity.* However, in the minds of medieval readers, this indirect transmission increased rather than diminished the *Categories'* influence.

11 There are also briefer scattered references to Platonism in other works of Boethius such as *On Music* and *On Division.*

12 For detailed accounts of the works listed and their influence during the Middle Ages, see Gersh, *Middle Platonism and Neoplatonism.*

13 See Augustine, *On Christian Teaching*, II. 1. 1, 33. 29–III. 29. 40, 103. 22, for the theory of exegesis. Cf. Augustine, *Confessions*, VII. 9, 101. 8–VII. 21, 112. 42, for the philosophical doctrines of God as Being and as Trinity. Cf. Augustine, *On the City of God*,

X. 30, 307. 1–X. 31, 309. 38, for the philosophical doctrine of the immortality of the soul.

14 Augustine, *On Christian Teaching*, II. 28. 43, 64. 11–29. Cf. Augustine, *On the City of God*, VIII. 11, 227. 1–228. 52.

15 This scheme is set out most clearly (sometimes using diagrams in the MSS) in twelfth-century works like William of Conches, *Glosses on Boethius' On the Consolation of Philosophy*, and Bernard Silvestris, *Commentary on Virgil's Aeneid* and *Commentary on Martianus Capella's On the Marriage of Philology and Mercury*. However, the scheme occurs in partial form in philosophical works from the ninth century onward.

16 Augustine, *Against the Academics*, II. 13. 29, 33. 17–20, III. 7. 14, 42. 1–7, and III. 17. 37ff., 57. 1ff.

17 This argument occurs in the Greek prologue and scholia to Dionysius by John of Scythopolis, one of the Areopagite's earliest defenders. This explanation is echoed in the Latin West in the preface to Iohannes Scottus Eriugena's Latin translation of the writings of Dionysius. On the debates about the authorship and dating of Dionysius in the West, see Luscombe, "Denis the Pseudo-Areopagite."

18 For the editions of medieval philosophical texts to be cited in the following pages, see the Bibliography below.

19 The three features underlined here are encapsulated in the allegorical figure of Philosophy, who dominates Boethius' *On the Consolation of Philosophy* (one of the canonical texts listed above). See especially *On the Consolation of Philosophy*, I, pr. 1, 1–24, where Philosophy's countenance is of inexhaustible vigor yet seemingly not of our time, her robe of imperishable material yet torn in places. Cf. ibid. I, pr. 3, 14–32, where the philosophers who have appropriated the torn fragments of the robe (i.e. non-Platonists) are listed. When Philosophy speaks to Boethius, she refers to "our Plato."

20 Eriugena, *Periphyseon*, I. 674–884. For an English translation of Eriugena's treatise, see the Bibliography below. For a general introduction to Eriugena's thought, see Moran, *The Philosophy of John Scottus Eriugena.*

21 Eriugena, *Periphyseon*, I. 699–776.

22 Ibid. I. 699–776, I. 800–84.

23 Ibid. II. 3142–282. Since the divine names are closely associated with the second species of nature, Eriugena also calls them "primordial causes."

24 Ibid. III. 124–474.

25 Ibid. I. 887ff.

26 Ibid. I. 19–42, II. 1–131, IV. 1–62.

27 Ibid. II. 36–83.

28 Ibid. II. 84–123.

29 On the probable literary sources of the fourfold structure, see Gersh, "Eriugena's Fourfold Contemplation."

30 Eriugena, *Periphyseon*, IV. 590–726, IV. 898–1247.

31 Bernard Silvestris, *Commentary on Virgil's Aeneid*, 1. 1–3. 22. For an English translation of this text, see the Bibliography below.

32 For a full study of this topic, see Gersh, "(Pseudo-?) Bernard Silvestris."

33 The present writer has always found it difficult not to interpret Bernard Silvestris's reading of the *Aeneid* as a subtle reversal of Augustine's reading of the same text in the *Confessions.* Augustine reads Virgil's text literally as a moment within the process of gaining self-knowledge, while Bernard reads the Virgilian text allegorically as equivalent to the entire process of acquiring self-knowledge. Augustine focuses on book IV (the narrative of Dido and Aeneas with its negative connotations of carnality), while Bernard concentrates on book VI (the narrative of Aeneas' descent to the underworld with its positive connotations of spirituality). There is another contrast between the two readings that cannot be

attributed to deliberate parody on Bernard's part (and that also points to the difference between the earlier humanistic mentality of the twelfth century and the later mentality of a writer like Petrarch) – namely, the association of Virgilian reading with a generalized human biography by Bernard and the association of that reading with a highly personal biography by Augustine.

34 See William of Conches, *Glosses on Plato*, 4. 60, 32. 98–9, for summaries of the four causes. The detailed discussion of the efficient cause begins at ibid. 36. 103, of the formal cause at ibid. 43. 110, of the final cause at ibid. 48. 116, and of the material cause at ibid. 50. 118. The best philosophical study of William's thought is undoubtedly Gregory, *Anima Mundi.*

35 Following a widespread custom of the early twelfth century, the *Lectures on Boethius' On the Trinity* (as also the *Commentary on Boethius' On the Trinity*) circulated anonymously and without specific title. The modern editor Häring has convincingly established the authorship of Thierry and has chosen the two convenient titles *Lectures* and *Commentary.* On the philosophy of Thierry, see Häring, "The Creation and Creator of the World," Gersh, "Platonism, Neoplatonism, Aristotelianism," and Dronke, "Thierry of Chartres."

36 Thierry of Chartres, *Lectures on Boethius' On the Trinity*, 2. 2, 154. 10–2. 34, 166. 5. Cf. the related scheme in Thierry of Chartres, *Commentary on Boethius' On the Trinity*, 4. 8, 97. 81–4. 11, 98. 16.

37 The notion of a fourfold structure in general, if not of the structure's constituent terms, seems to have come to Thierry from Augustine, *On the Literal Interpretation of Genesis*, VI. 10, 182. 18–183. 12. In fact, the question of sources at this point is an intricate one, since Thierry is also combining (1) the distinction of "complication" and "explication" in Boethius' *On the Consolation of Philosophy*, and (2) certain ideas about necessity and possibility from Boethius' *Commentaries on Aristotle's On Interpretation.*

38 See William of Conches, *Glosses on Macrobius*, 3A, 165–9, 3BC, 170–81, 5AB, 204–6, 6A, 207–9, 6B, 210–20, for summaries of the three principles. At ibid. 6B2, 226, William establishes a partial link with the four-cause theory of his *Glosses on Plato.* Here, God seems to correspond to the efficient and final causes, Intellect to the formal cause. Thus, World Soul falls outside the scheme of the four causes, and the material cause outside that of the three principles.

39 For God as creating Intellect, see *Glosses on Macrobius*, 6A, 208. For the assimilation of World Soul and Holy Spirit, see ibid. 3A, 167–9, 6A, 208–9.

40 See above, p. 532.

41 See the analogy between world soul and individual soul in Calcidius, *Translation of Plato's Timaeus* 32. 15ff. (Plato, *Timaeus* 39e ff.).

42 Bernard was no doubt attracted by the *recherché* character of these names. Tugaton corresponds to the Greek *to agathon* (the Good): Plato's own name for the highest principle. *Noys* is the usual Greek term for "Intellect," and *Endelichia* a term sometimes associated with "Soul" in the earlier philosophical literature.

43 Bernard's narrative is admittedly based primarily on the actions of Noys, Natura, and Silva. However, Tugaton appears at Bernard Silvestris, *Cosmography*, II. 5. 3, II. 7. 5, and Endelechia at ibid. I. 2. 13–16, I. 2. 167.

44 See the argument about humanity's proportionality at *Asclepius*, 1. 6, 301. 18–303. 13.

45 Nicholas of Cusa, *On Learned Ignorance*, I. 2, 7. 1–8. 17. For a recent English version of Nicholas' treatise, see the Bibliography below. Watts, *Nicolaus Cusanus*, provides a contextualization of Nicholas's thought in intellectual history. The best introduction to the philosophical problematics involved is perhaps Beierwaltes, *Identität und Differenz.*

46 Nicholas of Cusa, *On Learned Ignorance*, I. 4, 10. 1–11. 22, I. 24, 48. 1–I. 26, 56. 20. II. 5, 76. 1–8. Nicholas's knowledge of Eriugena is shown at *Apology for Learned*

Ignorance, 21. 2, 29.17–30. 1. For a comparison of the two writers' doctrines, see Beierwaltes, "Eriugena und Cusanus."
47 Nicholas of Cusa, *On Learned Ignorance*. I. 26, 56. 5–12.
48 Ibid. I. 2, 8. 9–17, I. 10, 19. 15–I. 12, 25. 14.
49 Ibid. I. 1, 5.1–6. 24, I. 3, 9. 10–20, I. 11, 22. 1–24. 9, II. 2, 67. 7–17.
50 Ibid. I. 3, 8. 18–9. 28, I. 12ff., 24. 10ff., I. 26, 54. 19–55. 12, II. 1, 61. 1–65. 10, II. 5, 77. 7–23.
51 Ibid. I. 2, 7. 4–5, I. 4, 10. 4–6, I. 25, 53. 10–13.
52 Ibid. I. 4, 10. 1–11. 22, I. 16, 30. 24–31. 12.
53 Ibid. I. 24, 48. 17–49, 2.
54 See ibid. I. 2, 7. 1–I. 6, 14. 21, II. 2, 66. 24–6, II. 3, 69. 1–13 (maximum-minimum); I. 1, 5. 1–6. 24 (learning–ignorance); I. 10, 20. 9–10 (substance–accident); I. 13, 27. 18–20, I. 16, 30. 5–18 (potency–act); I. 13, 25. 15–27. 17, I. 15, 29. 5–30. 4, I. 16, 32. 1–10 (straight–curved); I 13, 25. 15–27. 17, I. 15, 29. 5–30. 4 (triangle–circle). Nicholas will later venture some cosmological examples such as sun-moon at ibid. II. 4, 74. 16–21, II. 11, 99. 13–103. 9.
55 Ibid. II. 9, 95. 20–8.
56 Ibid. II. 9, 90. 17–92. 5, II. 9, 93. 19ff.
57 Ibid. II. 9, 94. 11ff. For another application of the theory see ibid. I. 21, 43. 10–17.
58 See Nicholas of Cusa, *Apology of Learned Ignorance*, 24. 6–7, where an anonymous commentator on Boethius' *On the Trinity* (clearly identifiable as Thierry on the basis of doctrine) is singled out for praise. See n. 35. On the relation to Thierry, see also McTighe, "Thierry of Chartres and Nicholas of Cusa's Epistemology."
59 Nicholas of Cusa, *On Learned Ignorance*, II. 7, 81.16–II. 10, 99. 12. At ibid. I. 17, 33. 18–20 and I. 23, 46. 22–47.5 he notes the link between this theory and the teaching of Plato or Parmenides.
60 Ibid. II. 9, 94. 23–8.
61 Ibid. II. 8, 87. 21–88. 8.
62 Ibid II. 9, 90. 5–93. 3.
63 Ibid. II. 4, 74. 28–75. 4.
64 Ibid. II. 4, 72. 23–II. 5, 78. 29. It would be possible to continue establishing parallels between Nicholas of Cusa and the earlier writers (especially Eriugena). For example, Nicholas exploits the cyclic process between unity and multiplicity and between multiplicity and unity, the notion of structure which is simultaneously real and conceptual, and the analogy between macrocosm and microcosm. However, these complicated metaphysical ideas cannot be pursued here.
65 For an example of a "structural" analysis of earlier medieval thought, see Gersh, *Concord in Discourse*.
66 I borrow the phrase from Kristeller, "Humanism," p. 128).

Bibliography

Primary Sources

Augustine, *Contra Academicos*, ed. William M. Green. *Corpus Christianorum Series Latina (CCSL)*, 29 (Turnhout: Brepols, 1970).

Augustine, *De Civitate Dei*, ed. Bernhard Dombart and Alfons Kalb, *CCSL* 47–8 (Turnhout: Brepols, 1955).

Augustine, *Confessiones*, ed. Martin Skutella and Lucas Verheijen, *CCSL* 27 (Turnhout: Brepols, 1981).

Augustine, *De Doctrina Christiana*, ed. Joseph Martin, *CCSL* 32 (Turnhout: Brepols 1962).

Augustine, *De Genesi ad Litteram*, ed. Joseph Zycha, *Corpus Scriptorum Ecclesiasticorum Latinorum*, 28/1 (Vienna: Tempsky, 1894).

Boethius, *De Consolatione Philosophiae*, ed. Claudio Moreschini. *Bibliotheca Teubneriana* (Leipzig: Saur, 2005).

Eriugena, *Periphyseon*, ed. Édouard Jeauneau, *Corpus Christianorum Continuatio Mediaevalis*, 161–5 (Turnhout: Brepols 1996–2003). English translation by I. P. Sheldon-Williams, rev. John J. O'Meara (Montreal: Bellarmin, and Washington: Dumbarton Oaks, 1987) (the text translated here antedates that of Jeauneau's edition).

Nicholas of Cusa, *Apologiae Doctae Ignorantia*, ed. Raymond Klibansky. In *Nicolai de Cusa Opera Omnia iussu et auctoritate Academiae Litterarum Heidelbergensis*... II (Leipzig: Meiner, 1932).

Nicholas of Cusa, *De Docta Ignorantia*, ed. Ernst Hoffmann and Raymond Klibansky. In *Nicolai de Cusa Opera Omnia* I (Leipzig: Meiner, 1932). English translation by Jasper Hopkins (Minneapolis: A. J. Banning Press, 1981).

Silvestris, Bernard, *Cosmographia.*, ed. Peter Dronke (Leiden: Brill, 1978). English translation by Winthrop Wetherbee (New York: Columbia University Press, 1973).

Silvestris, Bernard, *Commentum... super sex libros Eneidos Virgilii*, ed. Julian W. and Elizabeth F. Jones (Lincoln, NE: University of Nebraska Press, 1977). English translation by Earl G. Schreiber and Thomas E. Maresca (Lincoln, NE: University of Nebraska Press, 1979).

Thierry of Chartres, *Lectures on Boethius' "On the Trinity."* See Nikolaus M. Häring, *Commentaries on Boethius by Thierry of Chartres and his School* (Toronto: Pontifical Institute of Medieval Studies, 1971).

William of Conches, *Glosae super Macrobium*. See Helen Rodnite Lemay, "The Doctrine of the Trinity in Guillaume de Conches' Glosses on Macrobius" (Dissertation, Columbia University, 1972).

William of Conches, *Glosae super Platonem*, ed. Édouard Jeauneau (Paris: Vrin, 1965).

Secondary Literature

Beierwaltes, Werner, *Identität und Differenz: Zum Prinzip cusanischen Denkens* (Opladen: Westdeutscher Verlag, 1977).

Beierwaltes, Werner, "Eriugena und Cusanus," in Werner Beierwaltes, ed., *Eriugena redivivus: Zur Wirkungsgeschichte seines Denkens im Mittelalter und im Übergang zur Neuzeit* (Heidelberg: Winter, 1987), pp. 311–43.

Dronke, Peter, "Thierry of Chartres," in Peter Dronke, ed., *A History of Twelfth-Century Western Philosophy* (Cambridge: Cambridge University Press, 1988), pp. 358–85.

Gersh, Stephen, "Platonism, Neoplatonism, Aristotelianism: A Twelfth-Century Metaphysical System and its Sources," in Robert L. Benson and Giles Constable, eds, *Renaissance and Renewal in the Twelfth Century* (Cambridge, MA: Harvard University Press, 1982), pp. 512–34; repr. in Stephen Gersh, *Reading Plato, Tracing Plato.*

Gersh, Stephen, *Middle Platonism and Neoplatonism: The Latin Tradition*, 2 vols (Notre Dame, IN: University of Notre Dame Press, 1986).

Gersh, Stephen, "(Pseudo-?) Bernard Silvestris and the Revival of Neoplatonic Virgilian Exegesis," in *Sophiës Maiëtores. Chercheurs de Sagesse: Hommage à Jean Pépin* (Paris: Institut d'Études Augustiniennes, 1992), pp. 573–93; repr. in Stephen Gersh, *Reading Plato, Tracing Plato.*

Gersh, Stephen, *Concord in Discourse: Harmonics and Semiotics in Late Classical and Early Medieval Platonism* (Berlin: Mouton-De Gruyter, 1996).

Gersh, Stephen, *Reading Plato, Tracing Plato: From Ancient Commentary to Medieval Reception* (Aldershot: Ashgate, 2005).

Gersh, Stephen, "Eriugena's Fourfold Contemplation: Idealism and Arithmetic," in Stephen Gersh and Dermot Moran, eds, *Eriugena, Berkeley, and the Idealist Tradition* (Notre Dame, IN: University of Notre Dame Press, 2006), pp. 151–67.

Gregory, Tullio, *Anima Mundi: La filosofia de Guglielmo di Conches e la scuola di Chartres* (Florence: Sansoni, 1955).

Häring, Nikolaus M., "The Creation and Creator of the World according to Thierry of Chartres and Clarenbaldus of Arras," *Archives d'histoire doctrinale et littéraire du moyen âge*, 22 (1955), pp. 137–216.

Kristeller, Paul O., "Humanism and Scholasticism in the Italian Renaissance," in Paul O. Kristeller, *Renaissance Thought and its Sources*, ed. Michael Mooney (New York: Columbia University Press, 1979), pp. 85–105.

Kristeller, Paul O., "The Humanist Movement," in Paul O. Kristeller, *Renaissance Thought and its Sources*, ed. Michael Mooney (New York: Columbia University Press, 1979), pp. 21–32.

Kristeller, Paul, O., "Humanism," in Charles B. Schmitt and Quentin Skinner, eds, *The Cambridge History of Renaissance Philosophy* (Cambridge: Cambridge University Press, 1988), pp. 113–37.

Luscombe, David, "Denis the Pseudo-Areopagite in the Middle Ages from Hilduin to Lorenzo Valla," in *Fälschungen im Mittelalter* I = *Monumenta Germaniae Historica, Schriften*, 33/1 (Hanover: Hahn, 1988), pp. 133–52.

McTighe, Thomas P., "Thierry of Chartres and Nicholas of Cusa's Epistemology," in *Proceedings of the PMR Conference (Villanova University)*, 5 (1980), pp. 169–76.

Mann, Nicholas, "The Origins of Humanism," in Jill Kraye, ed., *The Cambridge Companion to Renaissance Humanism* (Cambridge: Cambridge University Press, 1996), pp. 1–19.

Moran, Dermot, *The Philosophy of John Scottus Eriugena: A Study of Idealism in the Middle Ages* (Cambridge: Cambridge University Press, 1989).

Watts, Pauline, M. *Nicolaus Cusanus: A Fifteenth-Century Vision of Man* (Leiden: Brill, 1982).

Further Reading

Beierwaltes, Werner, ed., *Platonismus in der Philosophie des Mittelalters* (Darmstadt: Wissenschaftlicher Buchgesellschaft, 1969). A collection of essays on major issues and thinkers in the medieval Platonic tradition.

Beierwaltes, Werner, *Denken des Einen: Studien zur neuplatonischen Philosophie und ihrer Wirkungsgeschichte* (Frankfurt am Main: Klostermann, 1985). An important general work containing several articles specifically on medieval Platonism.

Beierwaltes, Werner, "Einheit und Gleichheit: Eine Fragestellung im Platonismus von Chartres und ihre Rezeption durch Nicolaus Cusanus," in Werner Beierwaltes, *Denken des Einen: Studien zur neuplatonischen Philosophie und ihrer Wirkungsgeschichte* (Frankfurt am Main: Klostermann, 1985), pp. 368–84.

Cappuyns, Maïeul, *Jean Scot Érigène: Sa vie, son œuvre, sa pensée* (repr. Brussels: Culture et Civilisation, 1969). A foundational historical study originally published in 1933 but still unsurpassed.

Carabine, Deirdre, *John Scottus Eriugena* (Oxford: Oxford University Press, 2000). Introductory survey of Eriugena and historical context.

Chadwick, Henry, *Boethius: The Consolations of Music, Logic, Theology and Philosophy* (Oxford: Clarendon Press, 1981).

Courcelle, Pierre, *Late Latin Writers and their Greek Sources*, trans. Harry E. Wedeck (Cambridge, MA: Harvard University Press, 1969).

Cranz, F. Edward, *Nicholas of Cusa and the Renaissance*, ed. Thomas M. Izbicki and Gerald Christianson (Aldershot: Ashgate, 2000). A collection of essays that is among the few reliable volumes on Cusanus in English.

Dronke, Peter, *Fabula: Explorations into the Uses of Myth in Medieval Platonism* (Leiden: Brill, 1974). A miscellaneous but often very insightful treatment.

Duclow, Donald F., *Masters of Learned Ignorance: Eriugena, Eckhart, Cusanus* (Aldershot: Ashgate 2006). Collection of essays with good philosophical analyses of Eriugena and Cusanus.

Faes de Mottoni, Barbara, *Il Platonismo medioevale* (Turin: Loescher, 1979). Good introductory survey with selection of texts.

Gersh, Stephen, "Cratylus Mediaevalis: Ontology and Polysemy in Medieval Platonism (to ca 1200)," in John Marenbon, ed., *Poetry and Philosophy in the Middle Ages: A Festschrift for Peter Dronke* (Leiden: Brill, 2001), pp. 79–98; repr. in Stephen Gersh, *Reading Plato, Tracing Plato: From Ancient Commentary to Medieval Reception* (Aldershot: Ashgate, 2005).

Gersh, Stephen, and Hoenen, Maarten J. F. M., eds, *The Platonic Tradition in the Middle Ages: A Doxographic Approach* (Berlin: De Gruyter, 2002). Collection of articles dealing with medieval philosophers' explicit references to Plato and Platonism.

Gregory, Tullio, *Platonismo Medievale, Studi e Ricerche* (Roma: Istituto storico italiano per il Medio Evo, 1958). Includes detailed studies of the medieval tradition of reading Plato's *Timaeus*.

Jeauneau, Édouard, *Études érigéniennes* (Paris: Études augustiniennes, 1987). A collection of essays by the most important modern editor of Eriugena's texts.

Klibansky, Raymond, *The Continuity of the Platonic Tradition during the Middle Ages: With a New Preface and Four Supplementary Chapters* (Millwood, NY: Kraus International Publications, 1982). Reprint of the classic brief survey of 1939.

O'Meara, John J., *Eriugena* (Oxford: Clarendon Press, 1969). The most useful brief introduction to Eriugena's thought in English.

Parent, Joseph-M., *La Doctrine de la création dans l'école de Chartres: Études et textes* (Paris: Vrin, 1938). Remains one of the few general surveys of the famous twelfth-century school.

Senger, Hans-G., *Die Philosophie des Nikolaus von Kues vor dem Jahre 1440: Untersuchungen zur Entwicklung einer Philosophie in der Frühzeit des Nikolaus (1430–1440)* (Münster: Aschendorff, 1971). The definitive study of Cusanus's early development.

Senger, Hans-G., *Ludus sapientiae: Studien zum Werk und zur Wirkungsgeschichte des Nikolaus von Kues* (Leiden: Brill, 2002).

Sheldon-Williams, Inglis P., "The Greek Christian Platonist Tradition from the Cappadocians to Maximus and Eriugena," in A. Hilary Armstrong, ed., *The Cambridge History of Later Greek and Early Medieval Philosophy* (Cambridge: Cambridge University Press, 1967), pp. 425–533. A good introduction to the Greek theological background to Eriugena.

Stock, Brian, *Myth and Science in the Twelfth Century: A Study of Bernard Silvester* (Princeton: Princeton University Press, 1972).

Vansteenberghe, Edmond, *Le Cardinal Nicolas de Cues: L'Action, La pensée* (Paris: Champion, 1920). The standard biography of Cusanus.

Wetherbee, Winthrop, *Platonism and Poetry in the Twelfth Century: The Literary Influence of the School of Chartres* (Princeton: Princeton University Press, 1972).

Chapter Twenty-six

Philosophy and Theology in the Universities

Philipp W. Rosemann

The intellectual heritage that the medieval faculties of arts and theology bequeathed to the modern age was rich but far from unambiguous. On the one hand, the medieval universities saw the creation of systems of philosophical theology whose comprehensiveness and methodological rigor have remained unrivaled. Yet it was also in the medieval universities that, for the first time in the history of Christian thought, philosophy emancipated itself from theology. This philosophy was no longer the handmaiden of theology, assisting it in its tasks of interpreting Scripture and distilling doctrine from the biblical narrative. For this new philosophy, language was not rooted in the divine Word as it had revealed itself in Scripture and the Incarnation; rather, language was to be analyzed as an autonomous phenomenon, by means of the tools of logic and semantics. Many scholars regard the so-called nominalism that championed this approach as a precursor of modern-day analytic philosophy, which still dominates the philosophy departments in the English-speaking world.[1]

This chapter will argue that these two seemingly so different tendencies in later medieval thought can be traced to a common cause: the advent of a new attitude toward text and authorship, and hence of a new conception of knowledge. This transformation possessed a crucial intercultural dimension, since it occurred in the encounter between an older, ultimately patristic Christian tradition and Greek philosophy as assimilated by Islamic thinkers.

The Legacy of the Twelfth Century

The universities of the thirteenth century were corporations that administered common curricula, as well as academic standards and procedures, for otherwise autonomous schools that were associated with ecclesiastical institutions, such as monasteries and cathedrals. This centralization and professionalization[2] of studies completed a development that had begun in the twelfth century, which witnessed the rise of theology as an academic discipline. In the twelfth century theology was for the first time dissociated from immediate pastoral and spiritual ends: the theologians were no longer monks or bishops, as had typically been the case in the past, but rather "masters" who were either hired by ecclesiastical schools or received permission from them to teach independently. These masters were professional intellectuals, who made reflection on the theory of Christianity the center of the lives, rather than communal worship or the care of souls.

The distancing of the masters from the traditional contexts of religious life was paralleled by a similar transformation of the subject of theology itself. *Sacra pagina*, "sacred page," as theology was called in the twelfth century, was now aimed less at spiritual edification and the resolution of pressing doctrinal disputes. Instead, it acquired increasingly pedagogical and academic qualities, such as systematic organization and ease of consultation. At Laon in the north of France, the school of Master Anselm created the *Glossa ordinaria*, or "standard Gloss" – a compilation of excerpts from the Church Fathers and medieval authorities that were placed in the margins and between the lines of the text of Scripture to serve as commentary. The *Glossa ordinaria* presented a highly efficient tool for the study of the Bible in the light of the entire tradition of reflection upon the sacred text.[3] Toward the middle of the century, several masters attempted a revolutionary project: the creation of a comprehensive account of the whole field of theology, an account embracing all the central doctrines that had evolved since the first Christian centuries, and arranging them in a systematic, logical order. The most successful result of this move toward systematization was Peter Lombard's *Book of Sentences.*

Peter Lombard (1095/1100–60), a master at the cathedral school of Notre Dame in Paris, released the *Book of Sentences* for publication in the academic year 1156/7 and again, with revisions, in 1157/8.[4] Divided into four books, the *Sentences* brought together biblical quotations and doctrinal statements (*sententiae*) from the most respected theologians of the tradition, especially Augustine. It ordered these authoritative sources thematically, starting with God and the Trinity (book one) and then moving on to the created order (book two), Christology (book three), and, finally, the sacraments and eschatology (book four). But the *Book of Sentences* was more than a mere sourcebook, in that it endeavored to reconcile doctrinal differences among its authorities in order to arrive at a synthetic statement of Christian thought.

Each of the four books of the *Sentences* falls into chapters: 210 chapters in the first, 269 in the second, 164 in the third, and 290 in the fourth book. The subject matter of each chapter is summarized in a short heading, which is repeated in the general table of contents that appears at the beginning of the *Sentences.* A table of contents makes it possible to consult a book selectively, the choice of topics to be read being determined by the reader's own interests. This kind of approach was new in the twelfth century, for, prior to the rise of academic theology, the paradigmatic medieval style of reading had been contemplative and ruminative. In the monasteries, books served a religious goal: that of assimilating the reader, through words, to the Word; to lead him or her through Scripture, and the great commentators upon Scripture, to the Author himself. Entire books were therefore read slowly and repeatedly, in community, and aloud. The point was to subject oneself to these holy texts, rather than to use them selectively and with the goal to create original ideas. In Peter Lombard and other twelfth-century masters of theology, we see a more professional attitude to the text.[5]

In keeping with the exigencies of an academic reference work, the *Book of Sentences* possessed a variety of other features to facilitate consultation. Not only the individual chapters, but paragraphs within chapters, too, are frequently introduced by short headings, written in red characters. These so-called rubrics (from the Latin *ruber*, "red") let the headings stand out from the text, making it possible to scan the outline of its argument at a glance. Furthermore, Peter Lombard makes sure to document the sources of his authoritative quotations with the greatest accuracy that was possible in his day: through references by author, title, and book or chapter. Here we have the precursor to the (distinctly modern) footnote, which acknowledges the individual ownership of certain texts, distinguishing borrowed ideas and phrases from "original" contributions.[6]

It is clear, then, that in the twelfth century theology moved beyond biblical commentary and the elucidation of individual doctrinal problems. It took off, as it were, from the biblical text, distanced itself from more immediate concerns of the religious life, and gradually constituted itself as methodically articulated theory. And, yet, the theology masters continued to view themselves ultimately as nothing but writers in the margins of Scripture: the term *sacra pagina*, "sacred page," was used to designate both the text of Scripture itself and the theological reflections that were developed at an increasing distance from it. The transformation of *sacra pagina* into full-fledged theological "science" was completed only in the thirteenth-century universities, under the influence of the rediscovered Aristotle and his Islamic commentators.

The Journey of the *Corpus Aristotelicum* around the Mediterranean

It is a mistake to assume that traditions are handed down through history continuously and without breaks. The reception of Aristotle by Latin Christianity is a perfect example of the vicissitudes that a body of writings and thought can undergo as it is transmitted through the ages. When Aristotle died, in 322 BCE, his works initially remained in the possession of the school that he had founded, the Lyceum.[7] In 288 BCE, Neleus, Aristotle's last surviving disciple, inherited them and transferred them to his home town of Skepsis, close to the old Troy. There they subsequently disappeared, buried in a backyard by Neleus's descendants, who were unable to appreciate their significance. Rediscovered in the first century BCE by Apellicon of Teos, the Aristotelian corpus was then disseminated in an edition that Andronicus of Rhodes put together from the materials available to him. We must not imagine, however, that Andronicus shared our modern sense of authenticity and desire to uphold the purity of original texts: "Andronicus (who may simply be the spokesman for a group) corrected, rearranged, and occasionally rewrote the texts, suppressing some passages and adding explanatory glosses to others."[8] Even today, Aristotle's texts are studied on the basis of Andronicus' edition and in the order that he established.

Another caesura in the transmission of Aristotle's works occurred when the intellectual elite of the Western half of the Roman Empire lost its knowledge of Greek. To preserve the philosophical heritage of ancient Greece for his fellow Romans, Boethius (*c.* 475/80–524) undertook the ambitious project of translating all Aristotle's works (and Plato's as well) into Latin, and elucidating them by means of commentaries. Boethius, however, fell out with King Theodoric, in whose service he worked, and was executed for treason. As for his project to render into Latin all the works of Plato and Aristotle, he only ever completed translations of two of Aristotle's writings: the *Categories* and *On Interpretation*. Because of this tragic accident of history, the bulk of the Aristotelian heritage – including Aristotle's ethics, metaphysics, and theology – was to remain inaccessible to the Latin-speaking world for many centuries.

On the other hand, the Greek philosophical tradition continued to flourish in Byzantium long after the fall of the Roman Empire in the West. At the margins of the philosophical and theological mainstream of Byzantine culture, Christian monks in Syria also continued the tradition of Aristotelian learning.[9] After the Muslim conquest of Syria, the culture of these Syriac-speaking Christians, with their background in Greek learning, found itself marginalized once again in its new Arabic environment. Yet this history of continued marginalization – which ultimately led to the virtual disappearance of Syrian Christianity – secured the Syrian Christians a crucial role as cultural mediators. Already under the first caliphs, the Umayyads (661–749), the original Arab culture had started to undergo profound transformations. The Arabs had little experience in the practical matters of running their ever-expanding empire, and learned eagerly from their subjects, whom they often employed in their service. Moreover, under the rule of the 'Abbāsids, who succeeded the Umayyads, a systematic effort to improve the intellectual level of Arab culture was initiated. In order to obtain important scientific and philosophical literature, the 'Abbāsid caliph "al-Ma'mūn sent emissaries to Byzantium to seek out and purchase for him books of 'ancient learning,' which were then ordered to be translated by a panel of scholars."[10] One of the most eminent and prolific of these scholars, Ḥunain bin Ishāq (809–73), was a Syrian Christian, as were several other members of the original team of translators and commentators.

The efforts made by the Islamic culture to assimilate the Greek heritage bore copious fruit. Between the ninth and the thirteenth centuries, a rich and diverse intellectual culture developed in the Islamic world, drawing upon many sources – including Aristotelian and Neoplatonic philosophy, Greek astronomy, medicine, and other sciences – that were unavailable in the West. From the tenth century, Spain became one of the centers of Islamic thought – indeed, of the Mediterranean intellectual culture in general. Ibn Rushd or, according to the Latinized form of his name, Averroës (1126–98) lived and worked there, as did his contemporary Moses Maimonides, who, despite his Jewish faith, composed his works in Arabic. When Toledo was reconquered in 1085, it soon developed into a hub of Christian intellectual activity. From the middle of the twelfth century onward, it became a center of translation, not unlike Baghdad 300 years earlier.[11] Works by Islamic and Jewish philosophers, as well as Arabic versions of Greek works hitherto unknown to the West, were rendered into Latin by translators such as Dominicus Gundissalinus and Gerard of Cremona (twelfth century), Alfred of Sarashel, Michael Scotus, and Herman the German (thirteenth century). Michael Scotus left Spain sometime before 1220, having been hired to work at the court of Emperor Frederick II in Sicily, another important center of translating activity.[12] The translation of Averroës's meticulous Aristotelian commentaries, which is due in part to Michael, was to constitute one of the dominant influences upon the intellectual development of the Latin West in the thirteenth century. Averroës's so-called "Long Commentaries" were accompanied by full quotations of Aristotle's text, so that the translation of Averroës also rendered Aristotle's own thought accessible. Ibn Sīnā (Avicenna, *c.* 980–1037), too, was translated and proved influential. He defended an Aristotelianism much more colored by Neoplatonic strands of thought and open to traditional religion than that of Averroës.

Thus, the Aristotelian heritage became accessible to the Christian thinkers of Western Europe in two very different waves. First, Boethius's translations made available certain elements of Aristotle's methodology, which quickly became an integral part of early medieval philosophy and theology. Then, several centuries later, when the Aristotelian corpus had completed its long and complex journey around the Mediterranean, Christianity saw itself confronted with a much more serious challenge: Aristotle's ethics, metaphysics, and theology presented a powerfully argued case for a non-Christian world view. This world view, however, did not reach Western Europe unalloyed, but was accompanied by a large body of Muslim and Jewish literature developed in dialogue with the Aristotelian heritage. It is against this background that one must understand the profound changes that Western philosophy and theology underwent in the thirteenth century.

Thirteenth-Century Scholasticism: The New Aristotle

Aristotle's philosophy can be characterized as a naturalism, in the sense that it attempts to account for the structures of the world by invoking natural, rather than supernatural, causes. There is room for god in Aristotle's thought, but this god is not the Christian creator, who is deeply concerned for the well-being of his creatures and periodically intervenes in history. Rather than attributing providence to his god, Aristotle defines him as "self-thinking thought" (*Metaphysics*, bk XII, ch. 9). This means that the Unmoved Mover – another term Aristotle uses – is completely self-enclosed, knowing nothing of the world. This structure of perfect autonomy and self-knowledge serves as the paradigm of all existence: for every being, according to Aristotle, attempts to emulate, in its own way, god's perfect self-reflexivity. In procreation, for example, "human begets human" (as Aristotle frequently declares in the *Metaphysics*), a horse begets a horse, and a mouse a mouse: in other words, the species returns upon itself as the progeny turns out to mirror the progenitor. Through such causal similarity, god's self-thinking thought is the ultimate driving force, the "final cause," of everything that happens in the universe. And, just as god's self-reflexivity describes a never-ending circle, so the changes that are governed by the law of causal similarity will continue for all eternity: the world is neither created, nor will it come to an end. Aristotle requires fifty-four gods, in addition to the first Unmoved Mover, to account for the motion of the heavenly bodies.

Aristotle's metaphysical naturalism is reflected in his ethics, which knows nothing of salvation, an afterlife, or renunciation of worldly pleasures. For Aristotle, the ultimate happiness that humans can strive for consists in *theōria* – the kind of theoretical contemplation that is the goal of philosophy. *Theōria* does not require mortification of the body, as the spiritual masters of Christianity would have taught, but moderation: the right amount of courage, food, sex, wealth, and so forth – not too much but also not too little.

The new Aristotle arrived in Western Europe gradually during the last decades of the twelfth and the first half of the thirteenth century. The first translations, which were often partial, were later superseded by complete ones. The *Nicomachean Ethics* is a case in point: books I, II, and III were known before 1210, but the complete text of the work had to wait until the 1240s before the English theologian and scholar

Robert Grosseteste translated it into Latin. Similarly, the Aristotelian works that were originally translated from the Arabic later became available in more faithful Greco-Latin versions. For example, the Arabico-Latin version of the *Metaphysics* that circulated by around 1225 was rivaled by a growing series of Greco-Latin translations of the same text – namely, the *Metaphysica vetustissima*, *vetus*, and *media*: the "oldest," "old," and "middle" *Metaphysics*. The Flemish Dominican William of Moerbeke, an extremely prolific translator of Aristotle and other Greek texts, produced the first complete Greco-Latin translation of the *Metaphysics* in the 1260s, by revising and completing the "middle" version.[13] Avicenna's works began to be read in the Christian West as early as the 1160s, while Averroës's commentaries made their entry into the Latin world from the 1220s onward.

The new Aristotle, with his strange non-Christian ideas, caused a considerable stir. What is more, the commentaries of Averroës that the Christian thinkers eagerly consulted as soon as they became available only emphasized the naturalism of Aristotle's thought, with few concessions to religious sensibilities (which is why Averroës was extremely controversial in the Islamic world as well). Thus, in his commentary on Aristotle's treatise *On the Soul*, Averroës developed a doctrine ("monopsychism") according to which all humanity shares only one intellect!

The first reaction to these challenges was predictably negative. Aristotle's writings on natural philosophy (which included metaphysics) were condemned several times: in 1210 and 1215 at the University of Paris, and in 1245 at Toulouse, where students had flocked to avoid the Parisian interdict of any public teaching of Aristotle's physical and metaphysical works. In 1228, Pope Gregory IX wrote to the theology faculty in Paris, admonishing the masters to guard against the incursions of philosophical reason onto the field of theology. A few years later, however, the pope's attitude already began to soften. In 1231 he composed a series of letters concerning the study of Aristotle at Paris; in one of these, he envisioned a doctrinal examination of Aristotle's *Physics* by a commission of masters, so that, purged of errors, the work could be made available for general study. In 1255 the University of Paris reversed course completely, prescribing the inclusion of all Aristotle's known works in the curriculum of the arts faculty.[14] Timothy Noone has remarked that we do not know "the precise stages through which the increased acceptance of Aristotle's works was achieved," but he rightly notes: "that the medieval universities made the alien texts of Aristotle the primary texts for their curricula is a remarkable fact and testimony to the desire on the part of intellectuals of the time to assimilate and appropriate whatever was of value in the earlier pagan culture."[15] The assimilation of Aristotelianism into the Christian tradition is usually considered to have culminated in the thought of Thomas Aquinas (1224/5–74).

Thomas Aquinas

On the basis of his reading of Aristotle, Aquinas redefined theology – the old "sacred page" – as scientific knowledge: "Sacred doctrine is a science," he declared audaciously in the opening pages of his *Summa theologiae*.[16] This means that theology no longer viewed itself as a sophisticated kind of biblical commentary or as spiritual reflection; it has completed its mutation into a professional academic discipline, proceeding according to the inherent logic of its subject matter and the demands of pedagogical clarity. The famous prologue to the *Summa* left no doubt about Aquinas's departure from the old ways:

> Since the teacher of Catholic truth must not only instruct those who are [already] advanced, but [since] it is also incumbent upon him to educate beginners – according to this [word] of the Apostle, "As unto little ones in Christ, I gave you milk to drink, not meat" [1 Cor. 3: 1–2] – the main point of our intention in this work is to hand down what pertains to the Christian religion in a way that is appropriate for the education of beginners. We have, in fact, weighed the fact that those who are novices in this [field of] teaching are greatly hindered in those [works] that have been written by various individuals: on the one hand, [this is] because of the multiplication of useless questions, articles, and arguments; on the other, because those [points] that are necessary for them to know are handed down not according to the order of the discipline (*secundum ordinem disciplinae*), but according to what was necessary to the explication of books, or according to what the occasion of disputing allowed; finally, [this is] because the frequent repetition of the same things engenders distaste and confusion in the souls of the listeners. Striving to avoid these and similar [problems], we have attempted, with the confidence of divine assistance, to address what pertains to sacred doctrine briefly and lucidly, as the subject matter permits.[17]

As long as theology is tied to "the explication of books" (in particular, of course, the books of Scripture), it will have to be repetitious, just as the biblical text is – with its four different accounts of Christ's life in the Gospels, for example. Moreover, Scripture is not structured logically, like a science, but rather narratively, according to the order of the stories that it tells about the history of Israel and the life of Christ. By referring to the explication of books, Aquinas may also have had in mind Peter Lombard's *Book of Sentences*, because from the 1220s the *Sentences* was adopted as the standard textbook on which advanced lectures in the theology faculties were based.

The academic practice of public disputations, which originated in the schools of the twelfth century, constitutes an equally unsatisfactory tool – so Aquinas judges – for the presentation of a theological synthesis, since these disputations remain too unsystematic, just like the works of many of his predecessors who failed to distinguish the central elements of theology from useless material. Therefore, theology must be robustly restructured in accordance with its own inherent order and – which is the same thing – with the demands of sound pedagogy.

This is what Aquinas sets out to accomplish in the *Summa*. To be sure, Aquinas does not deny that the first principles of his new science have to be believed. But that, he explains, is not fundamentally different from the situation that obtains in science as Aristotle defines it, for many branches of knowledge are unable to prove their principles. Optics, for instance, relies on the principles of geometry, which it employs without proof, and music assumes the validity of arithmetic in its analysis of musical proportions. Analogously, the "divine science" of theology depends upon principles that only God and the saints in heaven truly understand.[18]

The *Summa theologiae* is an attempt to unfold the entire field of theology from a limited set of credal principles, like an Aristotelian science. This is why, in the *Summa*, quotations from Scripture and the tradition are no longer structuring elements but rather serve to illustrate and buttress conclusions that are arrived at independently, through philosophical reasoning. Nevertheless, the overall composition of the *Summa* still reflects the division of books in Peter Lombard's *Sentences*: in Aquinas, too, we move from a treatment of God's essence and the Trinity to creation (including the human being at its center), Christology, the sacraments, and eschatology. Therefore, in its arrangement the *Summa* betrays its origins as a rethought *Sentences* commentary. However, influenced by Aristotle's naturalism, Aquinas has made some crucial structural changes.

Peter Lombard treated the question of human virtue in a number of different contexts in the *Book of Sentences*, but, as Marcia Colish points out, "his principal analysis of virtue . . . occurs in Book 3, in connection with the moral aptitudes of the human Christ."[19] The Lombard regarded Christology as the most apt context for the treatment of virtue, since, in his view, all virtue is modeled upon the example of Christ. To be virtuous really means nothing else, at bottom, than to follow Christ. In the *Summa theologiae*, by contrast, Thomas moves the treatment of virtue into the so-called "treatise on man," that is to say, Division 1 of Part II of the work. This is because Aquinas, following Aristotle, recognizes the possibility of natural virtue – virtue that comes not from faith in Christ but rather from the inherent powers of human nature. Aquinas will readily admit that this kind of natural virtue remains imperfect by comparison with the fullness of virtue that properly belongs to the Christian life and hence requires grace; but he insists that grace builds upon nature and does not destroy it: *gratia non tollit naturam*. In other words, it would be a mistake to explain supernaturally – by reference to God, Christ, the Holy Spirit, and grace – what can be accounted for naturally. This is also why the *Summa* develops a detailed doctrine of natural law – that is to say, of ethical principles that do not invoke the Ten Commandments or the requirements of charity, but embody standards of behavior based on reason alone.

The *Summa theologiae* is an extremely impressive piece of work. While it does not reduce faith to reason, it pushes the philosophical penetration of theology to its limits. The spirit of the *Summa* is very different from that of Augustine's *Confessions* or even Peter Lombard's *Sentences*. These earlier works of the Christian tradition did not employ the Aristotelian language of deductive science but were permeated by the metaphors of Scripture. Rather than adopting a narrative, biographical framework, as Augustine did, or viewing theology as part of the "sacred page" like Peter Lombard, Aquinas's *Summa* foregrounds methodology and scientific precision. The *Summa* is, therefore, a much more explicitly *constructed* work; the author is clearly in charge of his material, rather than merely functioning as a glossator of Scripture or a mouthpiece of the tradition. Such changed practices of authorship were made possible by the rapid spread, in the thirteenth century, of tools of composition such as concordances and indexes.[20] Aquinas himself created an alphabetic index of the main topics in Aristotle's *Nicomachean Ethics*.[21] This tool allowed him to use ideas from Aristotle in highly creative and original ways by weaving them into other contexts. Without their biblical dictionaries, tables of contents, alphabetical indices, and diagrams summarizing the structure of Peter Lombard's entire theology, the thinkers of the thirteenth century would not have been able to create the synthesis of Aristotelianism and the Christian tradition that is the hallmark of this period.

Recent Thomists have emphasized that the *Summa* has a spiritual side to it; that it would be misread as a dry, scientific manual: "The modern reader of Aquinas . . . is in constant need of the reminder," Peter Candler notes, "that the pedagogical culture in which Thomas studied and taught cannot be abstracted from the 'form of life' which makes such inquiry intelligible. Thomas is, after all, a Dominican religious."[22] Although Aquinas's shift of emphasis from spirituality to pedagogy – from scriptural imagery to scientific precision – is undeniable, Candler's point is well taken. Thomas Aquinas himself, it seems, understood the limits of this approach. For the *Summa theologiae*, which may be the greatest work of philosophical theology that the Western tradition has ever produced, remained unfinished – and not because Aquinas died prematurely but because he decided not to complete it. After a mystical experience, he declared that all he had hitherto written appeared like nothing but "straw" to him. "This surely indicates that its fragmentary character belongs to the total implication of the *Summa theologica*."[23] Aquinas realized that the divine science must stop short of creating the impression that it can offer a comprehensive account of the faith.

The Condemnation of 1277

Nevertheless, there was increasing unease in certain Christian intellectual circles over the central role that Aristotle's philosophy had acquired in the thought of some of their colleagues. Aquinas was by no means the most radical Aristotelian of his time. Teaching in the Parisian theology faculty, he in fact opposed the ideas of some masters in the faculty of arts who had come to believe in an almost complete autonomy of philosophy from theology – a belief that was fostered not only by Aristotle's naturalism but also by the administrative independence of the arts from the theology faculty. In other words, while most students went through the arts in order to acquire the skills necessary for further studies in theology (or law or medicine), the material covered in the arts faculty – grammar, rhetoric, logic, mathematics, natural philosophy, and ethics – could also be regarded as possessing independent value. Thus, arts masters such as Siger of Brabant (*c.* 1240–82) and Boethius of Dacia (precise dates unknown) felt emboldened to develop a much purer Aristotelianism than Thomas Aquinas. Boethius, for instance, authored a treatise *On the Eternity of the World*, in which he argued for the eternity of the world as the only philosophically defensible position. Boethius acknowledged that this position was not compatible with the Christian faith – to which he was ultimately prepared to defer – but he insisted that theology should not interfere with the autonomy of philosophical inquiry. Boethius, then, was left with conflicting spheres of truth that he was unable to reconcile.[24]

These developments did not fail to cause a swift reaction from ecclesiastical authorities. In 1276, Peter of Spain – a renowned philosopher, theologian, and physician whom many scholars identify with the author of the standard medieval textbook on logic, the *Summulae logicales* – became pope under the name of John XXI. In January of 1277, the new pope instructed the bishop of Paris, Étienne Tempier, to conduct an inquiry on the disquieting trends at the university in his diocese. This inquiry quickly led to "the most important doctrinal censure of the medieval period,"[25] the condemnation of March 7, 1277 in which Tempier censured 219 philosophical theses, threatening with excommunication anyone daring to entertain even one of them. The censured propositions cover many different areas; what they have in common is their origin in a radical Aristotelianism. Proposition 3, for example, concerns Aristotle's theory of God's self-thinking thought: "That God does not know anything other than himself." Proposition 9 maintains the eternity of the world and the law of causal similarity that underpins it: "That there was no first human being and that there will not be a last one; rather, the generation of human from human always was and always will be." Aristotle has no doctrine of an afterlife; hence proposition 15: "That after death, the human being loses all goods." Since there is no room for faith in Aristotle, proposition 37 maintains: "That one should not believe anything except what is self-evident or what can be demonstrated from self-evident principles." Again, for Aristotle the highest happiness to which human beings are able to attain consists in philosophical contemplation: "That there is no more excellent condition than to devote oneself to philosophy" (proposition 40). According to Aristotle, there are fifty-five gods rather than one: "That there are several first movers" (proposition 66). Proposition 169 is inspired by Aristotle's ethics of moderation, as opposed to Christian renunciation of the flesh: "That complete abstinence from the carnal act corrupts virtue and the [human] species." Some of the censured theses are not taken directly from Aristotle but reflect the teachings of his Arabic commentators; thus, for example, proposition 121 concerns Averroës's teaching, according to which all human beings share only one intellect: "That the intellect, which is the human being's ultimate perfection, is radically separate."[26]

What has puzzled modern scholars is Bishop Tempier's claim, in the introduction to the condemnation, that the condemned theses were defended by a number of masters in the Parisian arts faculty. This claim is puzzling, because even the purest Aristotelians– the likes of Siger of Brabant and Boethius of Dacia – refrained from drawing the most radical consequences from Aristotle's naturalism; in other words, they never denied the truth of the Christian faith. There is no known master, for example, who claimed "that the statements of the theologian are based on myths" (proposition 152). It is not impossible, of course, that the intellectual climate that the teachings of certain masters generated at the arts faculty gave rise to a kind of Enlightenment ethos, as Kurt Flasch has claimed.[27] Others have conjectured that perhaps, in his condemnation, Bishop Tempier did not have in mind only ideas actually taught at the University of Paris but the entire Greco-Arabic world view that had been filtering into the West since the beginning of the century. Therefore, Tempier "invented" certain theses that no one was (yet) willing to defend.[28]

Be this as it may, one point is clear: the Parisian condemnation of 1277, which was quickly followed by a similar one at Oxford, marked the end of the kind of Aristotelianism that both the radical Aristotelians and Thomas Aquinas had espoused. In our own day, Aquinas's synthesis between the Christian tradition and the new Aristotle has often been hailed as the ultimate accomplishment of medieval Christian thought. Indeed, the papal encyclical *Aeterni Patris* of 1879 not only endorsed but in many ways gave birth to this view.[29] The medievals themselves, however, were far from eager to embrace Thomism after 1277. Instead, they looked for alternative ways of thought.

The Nominalist Alternative

These alternatives came at first from a rereading of Augustine, the trusted Church Father, whose doctrines had been tested by hundreds of years of debate before the introduction of the new Aristotle. But of course the scholastics of the late thirteenth century could not simply return to an older state of affairs in intellectual history, pretending that somehow Aristotle and his Arabic commentators did not have to be reckoned with. In response to this challenge, Henry of Ghent (*c.* 1217–93), a theologian who had served on the committee that Bishop Tempier consulted in drawing up the syllabus of 219 censured theses, developed a system of thought that took inspiration from both Augustine and Avicenna. Avicenna represented a version of Aristotelianism that was tempered by Neoplatonic ideas as well as by Avicenna's commitment to the Islamic faith. (The French medievalist Étienne Gilson coined the untranslatable expression *augustinisme avicennisant* to describe the result of this synthesis: "Avicennizing Augustinianism."[30]) Yet, if Henry's "Augustinianism gone Avicennian" managed to marry traditional elements of Christian thought with more recent trends, it did nothing to stop the movement of Christian theology toward more and more abstract, technical modes of presentation. This is, in fact, the paradox of academic theology after the condemnation of 1277: wishing to defend the core of the Christian intellectual tradition against the presumptions of Aristotelian naturalism, the proposed alternatives only accelerated the professionalization of theology and its detachment from pastoral and spiritual concerns.

From the beginning of the fourteenth century, a distinction took center stage in scholastic philosophy and theology that had not been unknown to earlier generations of thinkers, yet had remained marginal in their discussions. The distinction in question concerned the difference between God's ordained power (*potentia ordinata*) and his absolute power (*potentia absoluta*). If one considers God's omnipotence absolutely, his power is unlimited, so that there is nothing he could not do. For example, as John Duns Scotus (*c.* 1266–1308) explained, God could bestow eternal life on anyone, even a non-Christian who completely lacked faith. Yet, from the point of view of God's ordained power, this is impossible, since we know from God's self-revelation in the Scriptures that eternal life requires faith.[31] In other words, through the covenant into which he has entered with his people, God has committed himself to a certain predictable order of action.

The emphasis on the distinction between *potentia ordinata* and *potentia absoluta* had the purpose of ensuring that God could not be caught in the net of Aristotelian naturalism – that is, in an all-embracing causal system in which he would be reduced to a philosophical principle subject to the same structures of explanation as any other part of the world. God's absolute power remains forever mysterious and unpredictable. In reality, however, or from the point of view of his ordained power, we can trust that God will honor his pact with his people, a pact in which he has spelled out the "rules of the game," as it were. The guarantee for the validity of this pact is not metaphysical, however; rather, it is *personal* and *historical*: as a person endowed with free will, God has historically – in the Scriptures – promised his people to stand by them.[32]

The approach to Christian thought that is based upon the *potentia ordinata/potentia absoluta* distinction undoubtedly does more justice to certain aspects of the Christian faith than Aristotelianism: for, in the Scriptures, God appears as a personal being acting in history, not as the Unmoved Mover or self-thinking thought. The God of the Bible wants human beings to have faith in him, not to build theological systems.

The full implications of the distinction did not take long to unfold. In William of Ockham (*c.* 1285–1347), we witness the rise of "nominalism," various forms of which were to dominate the universities throughout the fourteenth century. The nominalists – *nominales*, as contemporaries called them – maintained that universal, abstract concepts possess no reality outside the human mind. They are mere "names" (*nomina* in Latin). So, for example, when we say "dog," there is nothing that corresponds to this concept in the world of real things; the concept is the result of our mind's abstracting certain common features from individual dogs and bundling them in the name "dog." In antiquity, Plato had defended a position at the extreme opposite of the spectrum, for Plato claimed that individual, real-life dogs are dogs only because they "participate" in dogness – an ideal essence in which all the central features of dogs are brought together and that is even more real than individual dogs. The Platonic assumption generates a metaphysics that is extremely otherworldly, aiming as it does at a grasp of ideal realities that are immaterial and insensible. Nominalism has the opposite consequence: if concepts such as dog, human being, cause, matter, essence, and so forth are nothing but mental constructs and "names," then philosophy must abandon the metaphysical quest for abstract principles that ground the sensible world and focus on the empirical reality of individual things instead. Furthermore, philosophy acquires a strong logical and semantic bent, since its principal task now is to ensure that the language we use about the world functions correctly. If there is no common essence of humanity that philosophical analysis can try to describe, then at least it must make sure that we use the term "human being" in grammatically and semantically sound ways. Thus understood, philosophy functions without any immediate theological concerns.

The late medieval move toward nominalism was intimately connected with the distinction of the two divine powers. God's absolute power is not amenable to rational investigation, and the realities that he created by virtue of his ordained power are radically contingent upon his free will. The deep structure of the world, then, is not to be sought in necessary connections between causes and effects that form a vertical chain ultimately leading back to the Creator. These connections were the subject matter of much of Aristotelian metaphysics. Rather, to do justice to its contingency, reality has to be approached horizontally and on its own terms.

If, for philosophy, the distinction of the two divine powers had the effect of redirecting its efforts toward semantic and logical analysis, theology for its part could now no longer rely on metaphysics. Ockham and the nominalist school consequently rejected the Thomistic conception of theology as a science. For Ockham, science was evident knowledge of necessary truth, truth generated by syllogistic discourse. Since theology derives its certainty from faith, which does not satisfy this rigorous definition of knowledge, it cannot be regarded as scientific. This does not mean that Ockham denied theology its rational structure, insofar as it draws conclusions from principles of faith, from authoritative statements of the tradition, and from Church dogma, weaving them into a logically coherent whole. But he made it clear that this enterprise is very different from philosophy, even if it uses the same tools.

Ironically, these tools were in large measure derived from the methodological works in the Aristotelian corpus: the *Categories* and *On Interpretation*, which contain a philosophy of language, and the *Prior* and *Posterior Analytics*, which are devoted to logic. Thus, nominalism largely implemented its anti-Aristotelian program by means of Aristotelian theories. This is one of the main reasons why the philosophy and theology of the nominalists did not have a more traditional flavor than the ideas of their predecessors, despite the nominalists' express desire to avoid the problems that led to the condemnation of 1277. The philosophy that flourished at the faculty of arts generated collections of *sophismata* and *insolubilia* – logical riddles that could be resolved only through endless distinctions of mind-boggling subtlety. Commentaries on Peter Lombard's *Book of Sentences* – itself already a fairly dry textbook – were the main literary genre in which university theology conducted its discussions. Even these theological discussions, however, were no longer devoted to deep metaphysical speculation but to the minutiae of rules of reasoning and the meaning of words. Indeed, important parts of theology that could not readily be approached in this manner were simply omitted. Furthermore, *Sentences* commentaries were not designed any more to come to a deeper understanding of the theology adumbrated in the Scriptures and rendered explicit by the Church Fathers and later authorities. They were now filled with detailed refutations of the views of contemporaries on obscure logical issues. To possess knowledge, therefore, meant to master the small points of these debates among various shades of nominalism. A late medieval *Sentences* commentary, although technically devoted to theology, was the antipode of a text that could form the object of spiritual contemplation.

Reactions to Nominalism

The nominalists themselves quickly came to understand the limitations of their approach, which engendered distaste among contemporaries who were hungry for the spiritual edification that more traditional theology had provided. Already in the fourteenth century, leading nominalists such as Gregory of Rimini (*c.* 1300–58) had therefore tried to temper the *via moderna* (the "modern way," as nominalism was called to distinguish it from the "old way," the *via antiqua*, of the thirteenth century) by means of extensive recourse to Augustine. Toward the end of the medieval period, at the dawn of the Reformation, Gabriel Biel (*c.* 1425–95) wrote a *Sentences* commentary in which he attempted to be faithful to Ockham and the nominalist current of thought while also incorporating significant aspects of Thomism. This kind of syncretism became popular in later medieval theology. One of the greatest synthetic efforts of late medieval theology was due to a thinker who worked outside the university context: Denys the Carthusian (1402/3–71), a monk who spent most of his life at the Charterhouse of Roermond in the Low Countries. Even by medieval standards, Denys's *Sentences* commentary was monumental: it fills seven folio volumes in its modern edition. In this work, Denys set out to provide a synthesis of the theology of the entire medieval tradition – with the exception, however, of nominalism. His attachment to the mysticism of Pseudo-Dionysius the Areopagite, a mysterious fifth-century Syrian monk whose writings were formative for medieval theology, gave his *Sentences* commentary a welcome spiritual bent that was sorely missed in more academic contexts. Denys dedicated several of his writings to Nicholas of Cusa (*c.* 1401–64), who, like Denys, was a mystical thinker strongly influenced by Pseudo-Dionysius and the tradition of Christian Neoplatonism. Nicholas of Cusa, too, wrote outside the traditional university milieu, developing an audacious system of thought that incorporated mathematical and nominalist elements into its world view.

No straight line leads from later medieval thought to the philosophy of modernity and the theology of the Reformation. Modern philosophy would not have become possible, however, without the Aristotelian revolution of the thirteenth century, with the Christian rediscovery of the possibility of a philosophy that develops autonomously, outside the framework of theology and faith. It is precisely this kind of philosophy – inspired by the "stinking Aristotle," as Luther liked to say – that the Reformers rejected, especially insofar as they saw it as encroaching upon authentic Christian reflection. The Reformation hoped to return to a purer, more primitive stage of the Christian tradition, in which Scripture still stood at the center of theology, rather than *summae* attempting to build theological "science." But it is never possible to return to an earlier stage in intellectual history, to recover it in its original identity. This is perhaps the paradox of the Reformation: aspiring to return to a past not affected by the vicissitudes of scholasticism, it marked the beginning of modern Christianity.

Notes

1 The Canadian philosopher Claude Panaccio has recently made an attempt to introduce medieval nominalist theories into current debates in analytic philosophy; see his book *Les Mots, les concepts et les choses.*

2 See Colish, "From the Sentence Collection to the *Sentence* Commentary and the *Summa*," and Chenu, "The Masters of the Theological 'Science.'"

3 For the state of research on the *Glossa ordinaria*, see the excellent summary in Lenherr, "Die *Glossa Ordinaria* zur Bibel als Quelle von Gratians Dekret," esp. pp. 97–101.

4 On Peter Lombard and his *Sentences*, see Rosemann, *Peter Lombard.*

5 On medieval reading techniques, see Illich, *In the Vineyard of the Text.*

6 The modern notion of authorship is brilliantly analyzed and questioned by Michel Foucault in his essay "What Is an Author?"

7 The following sketch is based upon Hellmut Flashar, ed., *Die Philosophie der Antike*, vol. 3: *Ältere Akademie, Aristoteles – Periparos*, pp. 191–3.

8 Brunschwig,. Lloyd, and Pellegrin, eds, *Greek Thought*, p. 558.

9 See Brock, *Syriac Perspectives on Late Antiquity*, *Studies in Syriac Christianity*, and *Syriac Studies: A Classified Bibliography.*

10 Fakhry, *History of Islamic Philosophy*, p. 12. Also see Gutas, *Greek Thought, Arabic Culture.*

11 For an overview of the translation movement, see Van Steenberghen, *La Philosophie au XIIIe siècle*, pp. 67–81, 101–7.

12 See Manselli, "La corte di Frederico II e Michele Scoto."

13 The Greco-Latin translations of the works of Aristotle are being edited in the series *Aristoteles latinus*, coordinated by the Philosophy Institute of the Catholic University of Louvain, Belgium (the *Metaphysics* appears in the three parts of volume 25). On the current state of the project, see Brams, "L'*Aristoteles latinus*" (includes a list of published and projected volumes), and "The Latin Aristotle and the Medieval Latin Commentaries."

14 The various condemnations and papal interventions, as well as the statute of 1255, are analyzed in Van Steenberghen, *La Philosophie au XIIIe siècle*, pp. 81–101, 321–3.

15 Noone, "Scholasticism," p. 60.

16 Thomas Aquinas, *Summa theologiae*, pt I, qu. 1, art. 2, in *Opera omnia*, vol. 4, p. 9.

17 Ibid., General Prologue (p. 5; my translation).

18 See ibid., pt I, qu. 1, art. 2 (p. 9).

19 Colish, *Peter Lombard*, p. 472.
20 On the rise of concordances and indexes in the late twelfth and thirteenth centuries, see Rouse and Rouse, *Authentic Witnesses*, esp. ch. 6 ("*Statim invenire*: Schools, Preachers, and New Attitudes to the Page") and ch. 7 ("The Development of Research Tools in the Thirteenth Century").
21 See Aquinas, *Tabula libri Ethicorum*, in *Opera omnia*, vol. 48.
22 Candler, *Theology, Rhetoric, Manuduction*, p. 140.
23 Pieper, *The Silence of St Thomas*, p. 89.
24 For further details, see Bazán, "Boethius of Dacia."
25 Wippel, "David Piché on the Condemnation of 1277," p. 597.
26 The quotations are from the new edition of the condemnation by David Piché in *La Condamnation parisienne de 1277*, and follow his numbering. The translations are mine.
27 See Flasch, *Aufklärung im Mittelalter*.
28 Such is de Libera's claim in *Penser au moyen âge*, pp. 123, 194.
29 On the encyclical, see Kerr, *After Aquinas*, pp. 17–21.
30 See Gilson, "Les Sources gréco-arabes de l'augustinianisme avicennisant."
31 See Ioannis Duns Scoti *Opera omnia*, vol. 5: *Ordinatio*, bk I, Prologue, Pars 1, qu. unica, no. 55.
32 See Oberman, "Fourteenth-Century Religious Thought," esp. pp. 5–8.

Bibliography

Aquinas, Thomas, *Opera omnia iussu impensaque Leonis XIII P. M. edita* (Rome: Typographia Polyglotta [and other imprints], 1882–).

Bazán, Carlos, "Boethius of Dacia," in Jorge J. E. Gracia and Timothy B. Noone, eds, *A Companion to Philosophy in the Middle Ages* (Malden, MA: Blackwell, 2003), pp. 227–32.

Brams, Jozef, "L'*Aristoteles latinus*: Bilan d'une édition internationale," in Jacques Follon and James McEvoy, eds, *Actualité de la pensée médiévale* (Louvain-la-Neuve: Éditions de l'Institut supérieur de philosophie; Louvain/Paris: Peeters, 1994), pp. 57–68.

Brams, Jozef, "The Latin Aristotle and the Medieval Latin Commentaries," *Bulletin de philosophie médiévale*, 39 (1997), pp. 9–22.

Brock, Sebastian P., *Syriac Perspectives on Late Antiquity* (Aldershot and Brookfield, VT: Variorum, 1984).

Brock, Sebastian P., *Studies in Syriac Christianity: History, Literature and Theology* (Aldershot and Brookfield, VT: Variorum, 1992).

Brock, Sebastian P., *Syriac Studies: A Classified Bibliography (1960–1990)* (Kaslik, Lebanon: Parole de l'Orient, 1996).

Brunschwig, Jacques, Lloyd, Geoffrey E. R., and Pellegrin, Pierre, eds, *Greek Thought: A Guide to Classical Knowledge*, trans. Catherine Porter (Cambridge, MA: Belknap Press, 2000).

Candler, Peter M., Jr, *Theology, Rhetoric, Manuduction, or Reading Scripture Together on the Path to God* (Grand Rapids, MI: Eerdmans, 2006).

Chenu, Marie-Dominique, OP, "The Masters of the Theological 'Science,'" in Marie-Dominique Chenu, *Nature, Man, and Society in the Twelfth Century: Essays on New Theological Perspectives in the Latin West*, trans. Jerome Taylor and Lester K. Little (Chicago and London: University of Chicago Press, 1968), pp. 270–309.

Colish, Marcia L., "From the Sentence Collection to the *Sentence* Commentary and the *Summa*: Parisian Scholastic Theology, 1130–1215," in Jacqueline Hamesse, ed., *Manuels, programmes de cours et techniques d'enseignement dans les universités médiévales* (Louvain-la-Neuve: Institut d'études médiévales, 1994), pp. 9–29.

Colish, Marcia L., *Peter Lombard*, 2 vols (Leiden: Brill, 1994).

de Libera, Alain, *Penser au moyen âge* (Paris: Seuil, 1991).

Fakhry, Majid, *A History of Islamic Philosophy*, 2nd edn (New York: Columbia University Press; New York: Longman, 1983).

Flasch, Kurt, *Aufklärung im Mittelalter? Die Verurteilung von 1277* (Mainz: Dieterich'sche Verlagsbuchhandlung, 1989).

Flashar, Hellmut, ed., *Die Philosophie der Antike*, vol. 3: *Ältere Akademie, Aristoteles – Periparos*, Grundriss der Geschichte der Philosophie, begründet von Friedrich Ueberweg, völlig neubearbeitete Ausgabe (Basle/Stuttgart: Schwabe, 1983).

Foucault, Michel, "What Is an Author?" (trans. Josué V. Harari), in *Essential Works of Foucault*, ed. Paul Rabinow, vol. 2: *Aesthetics, Method, and Epistemology* (New York: New Press, 1998), pp. 205–22.

Gilson, Étienne, "Les Sources gréco-arabes de l'augustinianisme avicennisant," *Archives d'histoire doctrinale et littéraire du moyen âge*, 4 (1929–30), pp. 5–107; repr. Paris: Vrin, 1981.

Gutas, Dimitri, *Greek Thought, Arabic Culture: The Graeco-Arabic Translation Movement in Baghdad and Early ʿAbbāsid Society (2nd–4th/8th–10th Centuries)* (London and New York: Routledge, 1998).

Illich, Ivan, *In the Vineyard of the Text: A Commentary to Hugh's "Didascalicon"* (Chicago and London: University of Chicago Press, 1993).

Ioannis Duns Scoti, *Opera omnia*, ed. Charles Balić, vol. 5: *Ordinatio, Liber primus, a distinctione undecima ad vigesimam quintam* (Vatican City: Vatican Polyglott Press, 1959).

Kerr, Fergus, *After Aquinas: Versions of Thomism* (Malden, MA: Blackwell, 2002).

Lenherr, Titus, "Die *Glossa Ordinaria* zur Bibel als Quelle von Gratians Dekret," *Bulletin of Medieval Canon Law*, 24 (2000), pp. 97–121.

Manselli, Raoul, "La corte di Frederico II e Michele Scoto," in *L'averroismo in Italia* (Rome: Accademia Nazionale dei Lincei, 1979), pp. 63–80.

Noone, Timothy B., "Scholasticism," in Jorge J. E. Gracia and Timothy B. Noone, eds, *A Companion to Philosophy in the Middle Ages* (Malden, MA: Blackwell, 2003), pp. 55–64.

Oberman, Heiko A., "Fourteenth-Century Religious Thought: A Premature Profile," in Heiko A. Oberman, *The Dawn of the Reformation: Essays in Late Medieval and Early Reformation Thought* (Grand Rapids, MI: Eerdmans, 1986), pp. 1–17.

Panaccio, Claude, *Les Mots, les concepts et les choses: La Sémantique de Guillaume d'Ockham et le nominalisme d'aujourd'hui* (Montreal: Bellarmin; Paris: Vrin, 1992).

Piché, David, *La Condamnation parisienne de 1277* (Paris: Vrin, 1999).

Pieper, Josef, *The Silence of St Thomas: Three Essays*, trans. John Murray, SJ, and Daniel O'Connor (South Bend, IN: St Augustine's Press, 1999).

Rosemann, Philipp W., *Peter Lombard* (Oxford: Oxford University Press, 2004).

Rouse, Mary A., and Rouse, Richard H., *Authentic Witnesses: Approaches to Medieval Texts and Manuscripts* (Notre Dame, IN: University of Notre Dame Press, 1991).

Van Steenberghen, Fernand, *La Philosophie au XIIIe siècle*, 2nd edn (Louvain-la-Neuve: Éditions de l'Institut supérieur de philosophie; Louvain/Paris: Peeters, 1991).

Wippel, John F., "David Piché on the Condemnation of 1277: A Critical Study," *American Catholic Philosophical Quarterly*, 75 (2001), pp. 597–624.

Further Reading

Courtenay, William J., *Schools & Scholars in Fourteenth-Century England* (Princeton: Princeton University Press, 1987). Excellent introduction to the intellectual world of the fourteenth century.

Ghellinck, Joseph de, SJ, *Le Mouvement théologique du XIIe siècle*, 2nd edn (Bruges: "De Tempel"; Brussels: L'Édition universelle; Paris: Desclée-De Brouwer, 1948). Classic study, by one of the great historians of early scholasticism, of the main forces at work in the reshaping of theology in the twelfth century. Dated in places, but not superseded by a better general account.

Messer-Davidow, Ellen, and Shumway, David R., "Disciplinarity: An Introduction," *Poetics Today*, 12 (1991), pp. 201–25. Brief introduction to the history of the division of knowledge into academic disciplines.

Minnis, A. J., *Medieval Theory of Authorship: Scholastic Literary Attitudes in the Later Middle Ages*, 2nd edn (Aldershot, England: Wildwood House, 1988). Study of the new conception of authorship and textuality that emerged in medieval scholasticism.

Oakley, Francis, *Omnipotence and Promise: The Legacy of the Scholastic Distinction of Powers* (Toronto: Pontifical Institute of Mediaeval Studies, 2002). This booklet explains how a momentous transformation in the way the distinction of God's two powers was understood contributed to the crisis of late-medieval nominalism. Interesting reflections on the role of the distinction in early modern thought.

Oberman, Heiko A., *The Harvest of Medieval Theology: Gabriel Biel and Late Medieval Nominalism* (Cambridge, MA: Harvard University Press, 1963). Classic work that paved the way for a new understanding of nominalism through the distinction of God's two powers.

Rosemann, Philipp W., "*Sacra pagina* or *scientia divina*? Peter Lombard, Thomas Aquinas, and the Nature of the Theological Project," *Philotheos: International Journal for Philosophy and Theology*, 4 (2004), pp. 284–300. Analysis of the differences in method and substance between theology conceived as "sacred page" and as science.

Rosemann, Philipp W., *The Story of a Great Medieval Book: Peter Lombard's "Sentences"* (Peterborough, Ontario: Broadview Press, 2007). Short history of the commentaries on the *Book of Sentences* from the twelfth century to the fifteenth, with an attempt to understand the intellectual history of the period through the analysis of this central literary genre.

Weijers, Olga, *Le Maniement du savoir: Pratiques intellectuelles à l'époque des premières universités (XIIIe–XIVe siècles)* (Turnhout: Brepols, 1996). Important study of the "intellectual practices" (the lectures, examinations, literary forms, etc.) that structured the academic culture of the first universities.

Part VII

The European Middle Ages

Chapter Twenty-seven

Medieval Europe in World History

R. I. Moore

The Master Narrative of Academic History

The history of medieval history in the nineteenth and twentieth centuries might be written as that of a series of attempts to secure for it a place in the Master Narrative (as it will be called in this chapter) whose canonization was the founding achievement of academic history in the second half of the nineteenth century. The undisputed basis of that history at least until the 1960s, the Master Narrative told how human achievement had reached its peak in the liberal democracies of the industrial age. Both democracy and capitalist industrialism (which were taken to be inseparable in the authorized version, though not in its Marxist variant) were attributable to the special qualities of European, or Western, or Christian Civilization, and in particular to its synthesis of the rational and democratic traditions of the classical civilization of the ancient Mediterranean with the spiritual power and insights of the Judeo-Christian legacy. This synthesis had been perfected by the Renaissance and Enlightenment, after a millennium of maturation following the decline of the ancient world. Articulated in the Age of (benign) Revolution and diffused in that of Empire, or Improvement, the resultant values imparted to the nations of Europe and the New World both the dynamism that generated world-dominating and world-transforming power and the checks and balances that restrained its exercise, contrasting markedly in both respects with the stagnant and decaying but still absolutist tyrannies of the Middle East and Asia.

During the century or so of its pomp, the Master Narrative structured, with relatively minor national and regional variations, the curriculum for the teaching of history almost everywhere in the developed and much of the developing world. And not only of history, but in varying degrees of all the disciplines that conceived themselves as having developed in a historical fashion, or their subject matter as having been to any degree influenced by its historical contexts and circumstances, including those of the modern languages and literatures, even to an extent of philosophy and ethics. The social sciences too, trapped in the Master Narrative precisely because they self-consciously repudiated historical foundations and historical method, in the main accepted without serious question, even if sometimes under protest, that the ultimate achievement of human progress was the breakthrough to capitalist industrialism, which was the reward of the peculiar virtues that characterized European as opposed to other cultures – freedom, effort, thrift, enterprise, the rule of law, and so on.

The non-European world was, and could be, present in the Master Narrative only as the object of European achievement, and as an invisible but indispensable other, a warning of where different paths might lead; similarly, medieval Europe often appeared as the featureless swamp from which modern man had laboriously extricated himself. To look back at even the better textbooks on Asian societies that were available up to the 1980s is to enter a lost world – even, in some hands, a kind of Eden; in others a Victorian schoolroom in which civilizations were graded with generous acknowledgment of their achievements in the distant past, and a regretful but unsparing enumeration of their more recent short fallings. India had once been top at inventing religions, but became fatally addicted to them, sinking into a long slumber from which occasionally more vigorous outsiders had tried in vain to shake it into wakefulness, only to be frustrated by the unyielding immobility of traditional village society. China had been the brightest star of the infant class, extraordinarily precocious at metal work, canal building, and bureaucracy – in which last it became so entangled that it choked itself almost to death, or smothered in the heap of sand to which it had been perceptively compared by one of its less successful twentieth-century leaders. Islam in its Golden Age had dazzled only to deceive, and decline into a long slumber of superstition and corruption. Japan was the reformed delinquent, which had indulged in adolescent feudalism longer and more recklessly than anybody else, only to emerge at the last moment, right on the eve of graduation, as the one that could modernize and Westernize almost as thoroughly, and even faster, than the West itself. It was the exception that, in the popular, witless, sense, could be dragged in to "prove" almost any rule. But the rule itself was quite clear: all the Rest had had a start in the race to modernity that the West had won, and all had faltered. Faculty opinion was divided as to whether they failed because they were tripped and traumatized by the bullies from the wrong side of the steppes, or because as they grew older their youthful vigor and enterprise were sapped by their own moral and spiritual shortcomings, but failed they undoubtedly had.

In the first formulation of the Master Narrative, current (though not, of course, universally ascendant) from the age of Petrarch (1304–74) to that of Gibbon (1737–96), the European Middle Ages had fulfilled much the same role as the non-European world had done in the nineteenth and twentieth centuries. Consigning a thousand years to "barbarism and religion" performed the essential function of enabling the men (as they were) of the Renaissance and Enlightenment to assume with the maximum of continuity the role that they had claimed for themselves as heirs of the ancients. In the revised version, as the nineteenth-century idea of progress that was finally articulated in contrasting forms by Karl Marx and Max Weber, the millennium of assumed stagnation served to underline the dynamic quality of "modernity," and provided an "other" against which it could be defined, reinforcing the Enlightenment caricature of the "feudal" and "superstitious" Middle Ages. How to respond to the exclusion of their field from the Master Narrative has been a constant dilemma for scholars of the Middle Ages ever since. Romantic medievalism, an eighteenth-century invention, self-consciously repudiated the Master Narrative by valorizing an alternative, non-classical, and even anti-classical character of its own, which reached a peak of acceptance in the Gothic revival and its aftermath. It continued, and continues, to be fuelled by a variety of anti-modernist cultural and political movements. Around the beginning of the twentieth century, in reaction, those who championed history as a scientific discipline in its own right began, rather than challenging the Master Narrative, to claim a place in it for the Middle Ages by pushing the search for the origins of "modernity" back beyond the sixteenth century. In the account that had won widespread acceptance by the 1950s, the twelfth and thirteenth centuries occupied a crucial position as the period when the distinctive institutions of Church and State took shape, and when the recovered learning of classical antiquity was united with the grand synthesis of Catholic theology and piety to lay the foundations of the European civilization that in the nineteenth and for most of twentieth centuries reigned unchallenged as the pinnacle of human achievement.

When spelled out in such elementary terms as they have been above, reduced to the point of caricature, each of the propositions of the Master Narrative now sounds irredeemably tendentious, at best simplistic and at worst self-serving. But the extent to which they have pervaded the entire basis of modern academic thought and structures, irrespective of discipline, means that nobody who grew up in the second half of the twentieth century will seriously disagree that that narrative describes the assumptions that formed the world view not only of history and historians, but, at least in the West, of virtually all thinking (and, *a fortiori*, unthinking) people. Certainly, that was not because it reigned unchallenged. Attacks on the Master Narrative as buttressing the status quo, underwriting privilege, and marginalizing subaltern groups and high cultures or "civilizations" other than that of Western, or Latin, or Protestant, Europe, or of "the West," are almost as old as the narrative itself. Its academic form, indeed, was still in its infancy when the most influential alternative, that of Karl Marx, was formulated in the second half of the nineteenth century – an alternative hardly less Eurocentric, whatever its other merits or demerits, than the Master Narrative itself. But, irrespective of their intellectual caliber, in many cases considerable, both the anti-capitalist and the anti-imperialist historiographies that were elaborated throughout the twentieth century served in the West mainly to reaffirm the loyalties and convictions both of those who accepted them and of those who did not – and hence to reinforce the dominance of the Master Narrative. That was not least, of course, because the social and political systems that the alternatives appeared to propound seemed for compelling reasons to have very much less to commend them than did the liberal democracy in which the Master Narrative reached the triumphant conclusion that was briefly hailed, in the early 1990s, as "The End of History."[1]

The first challenge to the hegemony of the Master Narrative that really disturbed its habitual acceptance in the West was presented by Edward Said's *Orientalism*, published in 1978.[2] Said's arguments did not merely reinforce and reinvigorate those who already agreed with him, but precipitated a gradual and often uncomfortably searching reconsideration, both within and beyond the academy, among those who did not. This impact was not so much a consequence either of Said's qualities as an historian, which were considerable, or of the shortcomings that he also possessed, as because he posed, with a force and vividness that even (or especially) those who disliked his thesis most could not ignore, three propositions that challenged the

Master Narrative at its core: (i) that the narrative itself was founded not on objectively established and incontrovertible fact, but on data selected and shaped to suit the interests of the shapers; (ii) that in doing so they had set aside a multitude of histories other than that of the Master Narrators themselves – explicitly, those of the non-Western civilizations in general and the Islamic world in particular, but also, by implication, the histories of other, perhaps even of all, subordinated communities; and (iii) that these processes were neither incidental nor accidental (which is not to say that they amounted to or relied on calculated falsification), but were elementary, in both senses, to the West's understanding of its own values, and to the manner in which those values were translated into, and deployed as, cultural influence and political power.

None of these propositions was original, of course, but in the history of ideas influence owes less to originality than to timing. Said's book was published after a decade in which the material and political foundations of the postwar consensus in the West had been shaken by a series of crises, including the Vietnam and Six Day wars, to which the responses had included more radical, passionate, and widely based challenges to publicly proclaimed core values than at any time at least since the 1930s. Those responses themselves both drew on and stimulated at the theoretical level the similarly fundamental and perhaps more durable skepticism about the positivist and pragmatist traditions that had been axiomatic in every discipline since religion had ceased to dominate public discourse – let us say, around the end of the nineteenth century.

We need not consider here either the theoretical foundations of these developments – in, for example, the work of Barthes, Foucault, or White in the 1950s, 1960s, and early 1970s – or their consequences and implications in the extraordinary array of new histories. Together with their attendant epistemological and methodological debates, they have transformed the field, for better and worse, since the 1980s, and have been sufficiently scrutinized, both intellectually and ideologically, by capable critics of all persuasions.[3] Our question here is where the history of medieval Europe now stands in the wake of the exposure of European history itself, traditionally conceived, as part of a discourse of domination, and the consequent reduction of its status from that of the central protagonist in the Master Narrative to merely one of the older and more durable characters in a large and miscellaneous cast clamoring for attention on the stage of History. Immense strides have been made since the 1980s in the particular histories of other parts of the world and other "world civilizations," and still more in their integration into a still hesitant and fragmentary but increasingly assured community of discussion in world history. An immediate consequence with particular implications for the ways in which we think about the history of Europe, and of the "neo-Europes," is the utter destruction of the image of "traditional" Asian societies as stagnant and unchanging – an image as much Marx's as Weber's, and still widely taken for granted only a generation or so ago, but now unimaginably remote.

The Master Narrative might have accommodated without undue difficulty merely chronological adjustments consequent upon these advances, as it did, by and large, the very widespread acceptance of Max Weber's view, or variants of it, that the changes that produced a society capable of industrialization in the nineteenth century could be traced from the sixteenth, and directly associated with the events thereof.

But increasingly sophisticated historiography, and especially the broader social ("total") history pioneered by the *Annales* school since the 1930s, had also brought into play an ever wider range of elements, such as skill levels, work disciplines, availability of materials and markets, family structures, conditions of land tenure, political conditions that sustained both freedom and order, economic rationality, religious and ethical underpinnings of all of the above. This opened up new opportunities for comparison between developments in Europe, or the relevant parts of Europe, and in other parts of the world. The cumulative impact of such comparisons, together with advancing knowledge of the non-European world and its cultures,[4] has been fatally to undermine even sophisticated accounts of European distinctiveness.

Thus, for example, Jan de Vries showed how the impetus to use family labor more efficiently by purchasing goods and services transformed the early modern economy.[5] The cobbler and his family saved time for making more and better shoes by buying their beer instead of brewing it – which also enabled them to enjoy better beer; increased profits in turn allowed them to buy a wider range of goods and services, which they had previously provided from their own time and labor, and so to increase still further the number, quality, and variety of their shoes – and so on, and on, setting up the beneficent cycle of advances in the division of labor that gladdened the heart of Adam Smith. In the context of northern Europe and North America in which De Vries first identified his "industrious revolution," it looks like a textbook example of the Protestant Ethic in action, but C. A. Bayly, in his account of *The Birth of the Modern World*, shows that the same complex of cause and effect operated in the eighteenth and early nineteenth centuries in China and Japan, and contributed to the growth of commerce, and the prosperity of Chinese, Arab, and African merchants as well as European ones.[6] That is one of many examples that permit Bayly to describe in the opening section of his book an "Old Regime" that is not simply a European one: similar structures and patterns of life and activity are to be found across most of Europe, Asia, and the Americas, and in parts of Africa too.

The seeds of the changes that would give birth to Bayly's Modern World were scattered equally widely. This is recognizably the same "World of Surprising Resemblances" that Kenneth Pomeranz described, before it was riven by *The Great Divergence* of which he provided a masterly account – the divergence, that is, between those parts of the world that benefited directly from the fruits of European commercial and imperial domination, and of industrialization, in the nineteenth century, and those that did not. Pomeranz methodically disposes of the conventional broad-brush "differences" between Europe and the rest. Comparison at a more precise level, however, suggests to him that by 1800 all the most developed regions of Eurasia, centred on England and the Netherlands, the Yangzi delta and the core regions of Japan (but excepting North India, which still had large reserves of forest), had reached an ecological limit at which they could offset the exhaustion of their land and resources only by continuously adopting increasingly labor-intensive technologies. This would not necessarily have led to the Malthusian collapse widely anticipated in the early nineteenth century, but neither would it have permitted a breakthrough to industrial society. Europe's decisive advantage, which did permit that breakthrough, was that the New World provided not only vast ecological resources otherwise unavailable, but markets for manufactured products that expanded at a comparable rate because of the nature of slavery and the trade that it generated.[7]

The work of Pomeranz and Bayly together summarizes the conclusions and implications of a generation of research that has, in effect, dethroned Europe from the position of moral and cultural superiority that the Master Narrative had celebrated. That is not because they have excluded the possibility of arguing that the developed parts of Europe possessed in one way or another marginal advantages whose cumulative effect was larger than their apparent sum: such cases will continue to be made, and will often, doubtless, have merit. Nor, more importantly, is it because they reveal or describe an early modern (or late early modern) world of uniformly bustling and increasingly entrepreneurial creativity. On the contrary, variety and differentiation are at the heart of the new world history. What has been excluded, once and for all, is the level of generality, the lack both of thematic and regional differentiation, implicit in the caricatured "civilizations" that have hitherto served as the unit of debate. Chris Wickham, in *Framing the Early Middle Ages*, has recently demonstrated both the possibility and the power of applying precisely such differentiated regional comparison to medieval Europe. Whatever Europe was, and whatever part it has played in the making of the modern world, it has to be assessed in the light of the differences between the many histories of Europe's variously defined sets of inhabitants, and equally of the similarities that so many of them turn out to have possessed to counterparts in other parts of the world. The sketch that follows here attempts to show not only how medieval Europe can be included in the new world history, but that it must be regarded as essential to it. The manifest inadequacies and incompleteness of this outline may serve to underline the variety and wealth of the opportunities offered to medievalists by the work of improving it.

Getting away from Gibbon

A preoccupation with the end of the ancient world, and with the preservation and transmission of its legacies, implicit in the Master Narrative, is itself one of the universal legacies of the centuries that we call medieval, and one of the most misleading. In Europe, since long before Gibbon, it has forced the history of those centuries into a procrustean frame of precipitous decline and precarious recovery, until a point – once held to be the fifteenth century, now perhaps the twelfth – when it appeared that a level of "civilization" comparable with that achieved by the ancients was once more attainable. This chapter derives its structure and argument from a different premise, and one that, without claiming a chimerical objectivity, may make it a little easier to stand aside from that long cultural conditioning. It takes as its starting point the simple, not to say banal, observation that both history and historiography necessarily begin with the emergence of cities: "when they first appeared, bringing with them the written word," as Braudel put it, "they opened the door to what we now call *history*."[8]

The dissemination and support of city life, or their reverse, are the prime condition and conditioner of change in history. The simplest definition of the city, as a community that cannot feed itself, echoes the most elementary division of labor, between the producer of food and the consumer of his surplus. By their nature cities must assure their subsistence by transforming the world around them. To do so they are compelled to develop highly specialized skills of coercion and persuasion, planning and accounting, and all the technologies, pre-eminently including literacy, necessary to support them; some hold that agriculture itself is a product rather than, as has usually been supposed, a precondition of city life.[9] Cities are therefore inexorably committed to specialization, and hence to social differentiation, both within themselves and between themselves and their neighbors, and their culture is, from the outset, indispensable to envisaging, representing, underpinning, and justifying a hierarchical social and political order.

It will be noted that this definition embraces communities that we do not ordinarily think of as urban, including, for example, temple complexes, monasteries, and castles – concentrations respectively of religious and of military specialists – whose role in the great expansions of the first millennium CE was everywhere of crucial importance. On the other hand, cities are not found alone: they create markets and subordinate settlements, seek out trading partners and rivals, to form the precisely ranked hierarchies of smaller cities, towns, and villages, dominated by the chief (sometimes referred to as the primate) city.[10] These networks constitute the building blocks of history, far more enduring than the empires and kingdoms that competed to control them. It is to them that the word "civilization" refers in this chapter, meaning, without value judgment, the complex of societies arising from the appearance and expansion of a particular city or group of cities, and united in many though not necessarily all respects by a common adherence or subjection to its literate culture.

Even with these qualifications, of course, we have described for the sake of discussion an ideal type rather than untidy reality, which does not always draw so absolute a distinction even between what is and what is not self-supporting, at either an individual or a collective level. For the present purpose, nevertheless, "the Middle Ages" will be defined by the vicissitudes of city life, which as it happens correspond more or less to the periodization that has long been conventional for Latin Europe and is perhaps becoming so for other regions of Eurasia.[11] About 1,700 years ago city life faltered and in varying degrees receded in most of the relatively restricted areas of dense population and imperial pretensions to which it had spread during the previous three millennia or so, from its earliest sites in the valleys of the Yellow River, and of the Indus, Nile, Tigris, and Euphrates. By about 1,000 years ago it was expanding vigorously, not only in the regions that it had reached by the beginning of the first millennium CE but in many new ones – in fact, in more or less all those in which it has subsequently flourished. By around 1250 what turned out to be lasting citied civilization had been extended to many regions where it had previously been precarious or nonexistent, including northern and Western Europe, Russia, the entire Yangzi basin and Szechuan, Japan, peninsular India, both mainland and island Southeast Asia, central Asia, the African coast of the Indian Ocean, and the valley of the Niger. In the thirteenth and fourteenth centuries CE these civilizations were beset on all sides by invasion from without and famine, insurrection, and disease within – in short, by calamities similar to those that had heralded the end of the ancient world. But almost everywhere they survived, to inaugurate another era of expansion and innovation that issued in the modern world.

These familiar facts raise two simple questions. First, how did regions that had previously been incapable of sustaining city life over very long periods – including northwestern Europe, where most of the cities founded by the Romans failed to outlast them – become capable of doing so? And, secondly, to what did these new civilizations owe the resilience that enabled them, in spite of the catastrophes of the thirteenth and fourteenth centuries, to retain the citied character that was an indispensable condition of all the changes that we associate with modernity – a resilience that it is far from clear, in the second decade of the twenty-first century, that modern society itself will prove able to emulate. Those questions will not be answered directly here, but they will shape this discussion, and in doing so will suggest one possible way – one of many – in which the history of the European Middle Ages can be included in that of a wider world, and better understood as part of it.

The lives of city-dwellers – all city-dwellers – may be seen, from their own point of view, as framed by three sets of relationships. First, the very existence of the city was directly bound up with the hinterland and its inhabitants, which supplied the necessities of life that the city could not produce for itself. Secondly, the security of the hinterland, in most cases, as well as the supply of essential primary products, depended on the city's (or the city region's) relations with the dangerous and primitive world beyond, which represented both in fact and in myth the antithesis of all that the city stood for. In many cases, of course, responsibility for this protection was assumed by the larger political structure, empire, kingdom, or state, of which the city was for the time being a part; indeed, the capacity to provide such protection was an essential condition of the state's existence and an essential rationale for its authority. Thirdly, to both hinterland and wilderness the city appeared, and habitually presented itself, directly or through representation by the state, as an entity firmly, not to say aggressively, united under its gods and rulers. Its ability to do so depended like almost everything else in its life and thought on the relationships between the city-dwellers themselves, and on the nature of the ties that bound them, with varying degrees of volition, to one another. These relationships, between city and hinterland, between "civilization" and "wilderness" or "barbarism," and between the various sections of the urban population, therefore provide an apposite frame in which to sketch the outline of a common history of the citied regions of Eurasia between the fifth and thirteenth centuries – that is, the period when most parts of the world we know established their capacity to sustain city life.

Since that common history has yet to be written, this preliminary sketch must be couched in terms of questions that it will need to address, and of working hypotheses rather than even provisional answers. The procedure, common in "world" or "global" histories, of focusing on the irregular though sometimes spectacular contacts (military, cultural, commercial) between the traditionally conceived macro-regions and their peoples is eschewed: it too easily reifies them into "civilizations," heading for almost inevitable collision. Rather, the focus will be on the particular but nevertheless common experiences of their inhabitants in constructing their lives and working out their destinies.[12] Systematic comparison of the kind that this suggests is beyond the scope of a short essay, of this writer's knowledge, and often of the present state of research, for there are still many parts of the world whose history has been uncovered much less completely than that of Europe. Nevertheless, enough has been achieved, especially since the 1970s, to make this a realistic and practicable approach.[13]

The Expansion of Civilization

The steady expansion of cultivation in the first millennium of the Common Era provides for each of the great civilizations one of the most familiar – though often in detail obscure – foundations of its history. Invasion, political instability and the collapse of the urban economy seem to have precipitated large-scale migration from the north Chinese plains toward the still scarcely settled south in the fourth century, and from the seventh colonization was rapid in the valleys of the Yangzi and its southern tributaries. By 1250 the population had at least doubled, but three-quarters of it was now in the south: while that of most provinces to the north of the Yangzi had remained stable or fallen since 750, those to the south showed increases of anything between 100 percent and 1,000 percent, the most dramatic growth being in the coastal regions.[14]

In north India, too, urban centres and the commercial activity and limited political centralization that they had supported seem to have declined from the fourth century. The extension of field agriculture that followed and the dissemination of agrarian-based social organization from the valleys of the Ganges and the Indus into peninsular India cannot be described with topographical or statistical precision, but it is analogous in scale and consequences to the clearing of the forests and the opening-up of the valleys and plains of northwestern Europe from the eighth century onward. The central Islamic lands, on the other hand, extensively deforested and severely aridified in the previous millennium, were heavily dependent on a fragile ecological balance, and therefore on very particular and complex technologies, including not only sophisticated irrigation systems but the development of new crops and varieties suitable for cultivation at different seasons and in different conditions, and even the creation and maintenance of specialized micro-climates to suit them.[15] Even so, the general pattern of the first millennium described above is often apparent: excavation in Khorezm, between the Aral and Caspian seas, for example, has uncovered evidence that the Sassanian irrigation systems deteriorated markedly in the fourth and fifth centuries, but from the seventh were rebuilt, extended, and technically improved, to be capable of supporting a much greater density of population than their ancient counterpart.[16]

For the most part, of course, expansion did not proceed into virgin or unoccupied territory. How new peoples – new, that is, to the cultivators from whose perspective we inescapably view these events – were brought within the sphere of "civilization," both in the technical sense of this chapter and in the moral one invariably claimed by the conquerors, and how the position that they subsequently occupied in it was defined and determined, must be the central threads in any narrative. Violence, on every scale from heroically celebrated campaigns of conquest and colonization to universal and incessant petty infringements, usurpations, and dispossessions, goes without saying, and in the former case at least is sufficiently recorded. It was the least interesting instrument of conversion to one of the literacy-based religions, which everywhere brought with them not just better devices for irrigation or cultivation, hardier and more fruitful seeds, but social transformation. Wherever a temple or a monastery was established, the people who lived around it were drawn into close and mutually productive relations with it by the lure of status and prestige, differentiated by caste or conversion from their coarser, perhaps still semi-pastoral rivals. So, for a historian of Europe, to read Burton Stein's or David Ludden's accounts of the opening up of the southern part of the Indian subcontinent in the second half of the millennium is to be reminded quite sharply that, for all the great and obvious differences between the Deccan or the Madras plain and Northumbria or Saxony, this is the age of Bede and Boniface.[17] The status that conversion by high-caste brahmins from the north conferred differentiated the people of the plains from those of the mountains, drawing them into the circles of prayer and patronage through which the temples disseminated new crops and techniques, stimulating local exchanges and refining the division of labor. This created the infrastructure for the prosperity of kingdoms of the Pandyas and the Cholas from the tenth to the thirteenth centuries, and the great age of temple building that coincided with them.

Such advantages and inducements proved everywhere irresistible, even where the pagans were not obviously "backward." The Lithuanians, whose Grand Duchy in the middle of the fourteenth century bestrode the routes between the Baltic and the Black Sea, worshipped a panoply of gods and goddesses led by Perkunas of sky and war, whose priests and priestesses read auguries and sacrificed humans and animals when required, though with what level of organization is unclear. But they had Christian subjects, who may have outnumbered them, and had to advertise for more as the development of their territories, and especially their cities, demanded skilled immigrants, and they had Christian neighbors to whom they dispatched their princesses in marriage to build the ever-more tangled web of alliances that security required. By 1386 their entry to Christendom had become unavoidable.[18] In other words, the process of conversion was inherently dynamic. As each new kingdom or territory experienced the increasing wealth, stability, and standing that it gained from the know-how and contacts of the bearers of literate culture, whether they were Christian or Buddhist missionaries, Brahmans from North India or Confucian officials from Chang'an or Loyang, it began to prepare the ground for the next advance. As its wealth increased, its trade became more varied and far flung, its need for skills and services greater, its law and culture more complex, it offered both a more tempting spectacle to the predatory and a more impressive one to the impressionable, drawing them either way into closer relations and eventually, though often not at the first attempt, into conversion.

The Great Transformation

China excepted – and even there we should anticipate that the material reality revealed by archaeology will modify the idealized vision of social organization reflected in official documents – economic development in medieval Eurasia can be seen, very generally, to fall into two rather clearly distinct phases, which we may follow Conrad Totman (writing on Japan[19]) in calling the ages respectively of dispersed agriculturalists and of intensive agriculture. As the difference in the nouns implies, the first is characterized by small and rather loosely connected, even semi-nomadic settlements of relatively independent groups of cultivators; the second by much greater concentrations of population, organized with varying degrees of coercion into a much more closely integrated social and economic system. The terms, of course, are always relative, but the differences they suggest are real and fundamental. Totman's "age of intensive agriculture" in Japan saw a great increase in agricultural production and, more importantly, productivity from the later part of the thirteenth century CE. It was made possible by a number of mutually reinforcing factors including the diffusion of technical advances and better agronomic practice, and the mutation of the diseases, especially smallpox, which for many centuries had caused periodic collapses of population, into illnesses of childhood. When a family could support itself on as little as a hectare of land, people could cluster, or be clustered, in much larger villages, of which "of those that have existed in more recent centuries most seem to date from the 1300s or later,"[20] stimulating increasing artisanal and commercial activity. The diffusion of these changes across Japan and their continuing interaction with one another saw a population estimated at about seven million in 1200 increase to about thirteen million by 1600. It was accompanied by far more than proportionate increases in productivity, and a surplus correspondingly more capable of sustaining military and cultural elites.

The transformation (often identified with "the medieval period") seems to have gathered pace somewhat later in Japan than in most of the core regions of Eurasia, where an accelerating rate of agrarian intensification is often evident by the beginning of the eleventh century, and its dramatic demographic, social, and cultural consequences fully visible by the end of the twelfth.[21] The settling of the working population of much of Western Europe into the pattern of villages that lasted until the Industrial Revolution, for example, is now seen as a development particularly of the tenth century. It was associated with a more aggressive and purposeful lordship over land, exercised both by religious institutions and lay proprietors, and designed to secure a greater surplus especially from the more widespread and systematic cultivation of cereals.[22] That the eleventh century was one of the great ages of temple building, in central and south India as well as in the Ganges valley and Orissa, is one clear sign that what has been called "India's third urbanization"[23] was well under way: it was a result, among other things, of intense competition both between and within the regional kingdoms for which the extension of field agriculture and the revenues and increasingly malleable populations associated with it had laid foundations during the preceding centuries. The increasing scale, variety, and range of exchange that might be expected to accompany these developments are attested from the ninth century by a growing body of inscriptions proclaiming the activity, and especially the philanthropy, of merchant guilds whose members provided trade links among the agrarian communities, notably of South India, Sri Lanka, and Southeast Asia.

It is commonly held that China attained its most remarkable levels of development under the Northern Song dynasty (960–1126). Its annual production of pig iron at that time, for example, was not matched by Great Britain until the 1820s, and the streets of some of its cities were lit by natural gas. However, what used to be regarded as a period of political decline and social stagnation following the overrunning of the north – the ancient heartland of Chinese civilization as well as the economic powerhouse of its extraordinary medieval industrial achievement – by Jurchen invaders is now viewed also as a time of continuing economic growth and social consolidation, particularly in the south. Agrarian development was intensive as well as extensive: great advances in techniques of irrigation, and especially of wet-rice cultivation, underpinned the colonization of the Yangzi basin and a rapid increase of population. Great improvements in communications, including the extension, augmentation, and linking-up of river and canal routes to create in effect a flexible, efficient, and inexpensive nationwide transportation network permitted the expansion and specialization of markets on an immense scale, and a spectacular proliferation of all the trades, activities, and amenities associated with urbanization. Granting all the uncertainties that must attend any such calculation, it seems likely that the great cities that Marco Polo, in the mid-thirteenth century, described with justified astonishment contained a higher proportion of the Chinese population than their counterparts in 1900.

The Middle East and West Asia do not obviously conform to this pattern. The wealth that supported the astonishing florescence of creativity in every sphere of Islam's Golden Age was engendered by commerce. The Arab conquests of the seventh century reunified the Hellenistic and Mediterranean worlds, throwing off the deadweight of the moribund empires of antiquity to create "a garden protected by our spears," a vast market renewed and extended by the foundation of Baghdad in the reign of al-Mansur (754–75) to tap, directly and indirectly, the resources and talents of almost the entire known world. Yet, when that world launched itself, around the millennium, into rapid and productive growth, the Golden Age had already begun to tarnish, the great Caliphate to be eaten away from within as regional potentates from Spain and North Africa to Khorasan shrugged off its tutelage and asserted their effective independence.

The significance of the appearance and early expansion of Islam as a turning point in world history is undeniable, and its consequences and ramifications will certainly occupy a prominent place in any successful attempt to account for the chronology of the great transformations, not least because it was the only world civilization that neighbored all the others. But that is not the whole story. It is not only that merchants and sufis had to eat, that peasants constituted the vast majority of the population of the Islamic world as of every other, that (as we have already noted) here too marked advances in agriculture and agricultural productivity were indispensable, and sustained throughout our period. It is also that the lands between the Hindu Kush and the Pyrenees in the tenth and eleventh centuries illustrate again one of the late twentieth century's major historical insights. To close our eyes as we gaze at one of the crumbling empires that had for so long mesmerized our predecessors is to see on reopening them a new world of emerging regional powers, based upon more effective exploitation of local resources by increasingly specialized and effectively exploited regional communities. Enhanced capacity to create and extract new wealth (though also to plunder it) engendered intense competition for power and prestige, which was expressed, among other ways, in the adornment of great cities and the patronage of artists, craftsmen, and scholars, which sustained the brilliance of the Golden Age up to, and in many places beyond, the disasters of the mid-thirteenth to mid-fourteenth centuries. Under the Seljuqs in Persia and Iraq, the Fatimids, the Ayyubids, the Mamluks in Egyypt and Syria, and throughout the Islamic lands, the eleventh, twelfth, and thirteenth centuries constituted an age of magnificent building and supreme craftsmanship in every art. As in the contemporaneous India of the Chandellas, the Pallavas and the Cholas, or the Europe of the Capetians, the Angevins and the Hohenstaufen, patronage ultimately reflected not only the strength but the weakness of the rulers, not only their grandiose claims but the rivalry of their ambitious subjects, in the military and civic as well as the religious dividends of closer networks of increasingly productive and more efficiently exploited village communities. The splendor of courts and cities necessarily depended on and reflected the specialization of skill and function in every aspect and at every level of social life, and the correspondingly more rigorous and self-conscious differentiation of rank and status that accompanied it. These centuries saw the establishment of what would come to be regarded as the traditional social order of the pre-modern or pre-industrial world, familiar in Europe as the *ancien régime*, and with it of the pattern of civilizations discerned by the enlightened gaze of the great historians of that epoch. It is a pattern that has turned out to be one of the most seductive and enduring parts of their legacy.

The First Great Divergence

Up to around 1000 CE the great expansions of Eurasia's agro-literate societies had proceeded in rather similar ways, and produced many similar social and cultural forms, though at different levels of wealth and attainment. The differences between them were greatly increased in consequence of developments that took place during the eleventh and twelfth centuries. For example, to mention only one, it was at that time that the Latin, or Catholic, clergy became celibate in principle and, at any rate at higher levels, in practice, and that the parish system became universal in Western Europe, the people more or less firmly under the discipline of their priests, the priests of the bishops, and the bishops of the pope. It was also a period during which, as part of the same developments, the Latin Church defined its enemies – most obviously, heretics and Jews within, Greeks and Muslims without – very much more clearly than it had done before, and adopted a much more belligerent posture toward them. Those changes, irrespective of what took place anywhere else, greatly magnified the differences between Catholic Christianity and both Orthodox Christianity and Islam, though they had very little directly to do with the formal doctrines of either, and even less with the direct contacts between them, either commercial or military, which also increased greatly at this time. Rather they were among the results of the much wider upheaval of European society at this period, which some regard as constituting the birth of Europe itself, the appearance of urban civilization for the first time north of the Alps – a civilization that was new and autonomous, not a renewal or a revival, or even a direct successor, of the Mediterranean-based civilization of classical antiquity.[24]

This was, however, only one, though perhaps the most thoroughgoing, of several such upheavals. Indeed, it appears that the eleventh and twelfth centuries saw a crisis of the clerical elites of many of the Eurasian civilizations.[25] In each case it arose from the difficulty experienced by these elites in sustaining their economic and cultural hegemony amid the increasing social complexity caused by intensive economic growth; in each case, but in very different ways, the elites reorganized their economic base and relations with both lay society and central government; and in each they reasserted their cultural predominance by redefining the high culture, the means of recruitment to it and its relations with society at large. The dominant belief systems of the classical world – Confucianism, "Hinduism", Zoroastrianism, Roman paganism – had experienced substantial changes in the early centuries CE, with, at least superficially, striking common elements, including increasing definition of and emphasis on a canonical body of texts, and increasing concentration of cults on fewer objects of veneration. In the eleventh and twelfth centuries the clerical elites, and with them the high cultures, were reconstituted and renewed, to varying degrees and in varying ways. The claim to custodianship of authoritative texts, both sacred and profane, provided sanction for both cultural and governmental authority, and (in varying degrees) controllable mechanisms of recruitment. The recovery and transmission of classical texts, the construction or reconstruction of educational systems, laid the foundations for new systems of thought (masquerading as restored versions of old ones), which have been accepted as defining the respective civilizations.

In China the main instrument of change was the completion of the famous examination system for positions in the imperial bureaucracy, and its installation as (in principle) the sole avenue of recruitment, and the guardian and institutionalizer of the system of thought and ethics later described as "neo-Confucianism." The result was an imposing central authority whose elaborate and sophisticated procedures concealed the essential fact that real power remained even more firmly where it had always been, in the localities, with the gentry families that controlled the land. The families that established their positions at this time were able to sustain them for the remainder of the *ancien régime* (that is, until early in the twentieth century), provided that they could, in practice as well as in precept, supply a successful candidate for the imperial service once in every three generations.[26] In south India the twelfth and thirteenth centuries saw the emergence of assemblies through which the local elites consolidated their authority over more closely integrated and more mature agrarian regions, while formalizing further their social distance from the peasantry.[27] In the very different conditions of the Islamic world an analysis in terms of social stratification is out of the question, on account not only of the recalcitrance of the source materials, but of the extraordinarily various character of the *ulema*, defined, if they were defined at all, not by wealth, inheritance, or institutionally authorized learning, but by *ad hominem* and usually local recognition as such.[28] To the limited extent that pertinent material is available for comparison from region to region, it may be seen that the fragmenting pressure of invasion and warlord regimes produced a sharper division between the civilian elites, which discharged the administrative functions and the religious leadership that, without formal designation or licencing, retained a closer relationship with the mass of the population than its counterparts elsewhere, and with it corresponding and highly volatile social power.[29] In Latin Europe the fragmentation of political authority encouraged by rapid intensive growth concealed an essential unity of political, governmental, and social structures, derived from the common education, culture, and circumstances of the new class of functionaries, the *milites* and *clerici* who staffed the court of every great lord, lay or ecclesiastical. They created an effective counterweight to the power of the noble families from which they sprang, which were compelled, as the price of their survival, to defend the integrity of their patrimonies by forcing younger sons in every generation out of the family's protection, and into that of a royal or episcopal patron whose interests in the longer term might be directly opposed to it.

The most general of the changes that together constituted the great transformations was the drawing and redrawing of boundaries, both literally and metaphorically, in every aspect of activity, and at all social levels. It included, in Europe, North Africa, and the Middle East and the Far East, the definition of frontiers that in many cases foreshadow the modern state system. No less importantly, "the emergence of borderlines out of borderlands"[30] reified the distinctions between civilization and barbarism, or between true religion and paganism, upon which the elites of the advanced agrarian societies founded their claims to cultural hegemony, carrying with it a set of conceptual innovations relating to ethnicity, to loyalty and its objects, and to the construction of political identities. The construction and reconstruction of mental landscapes, of the categories that defined family structures, gender and occupational roles, for example, as well as such distinctions as those between town and country, literate and illiterate, the faithful and the infidel, and so on, were still more important. The extent to which they registered change or simply put on record what had long been the case is always a critical question, and usually a controversial one. Many of these boundaries came to be more vigilantly and aggressively policed, again both literally and metaphorically, in the high Middle Ages than they had been previously.[31] In this way entire societies and cultures, as well as their constituent communities, articulated both their aspirations and their anxieties, and in defining themselves fashioned enduring identities and shaped historical memory.

Eurasia, then, experienced a Great Divergence in the twelfth century, as well as in the nineteenth. The obvious difference is that the first was a divergence of societies and cultures founded on economies in their essentials similar, while in the second rapidly increasing divergence of the economies, with all its consequences, has eroded the differences of culture, to replace them by widening global disparities of wealth and power. Together, however, the two divergences mark an epoch in world history, which both made and was made by the complex and changing identities of the citied societies of Eurasia, and whose successes, failures, and idiosyncrasies have shaped our own world, and formed the talents and tensions with which we confront its anxieties.

Notes

1 Fukuyama, *End of History and the Last Man.*

2 Said, *Orientalism.*

3 Foucault, *Archaeology of Knowledge*; White, *Metahistory*; Burke, *New Perspectives.*

4 Goody, *The East in the West.*

5 De Vries and van der Woude, *First Modern Economy.*

6 Bayly, *Birth of the Modern World*, pp. 51–5.

7 Pomeranz, *Great Divergence*, pp. 31–107.

8 Braudel, *Structures of Everyday Life*, p. 479.

9 Jacobs, *Economy of Cities*, pp. 11–31. Cf. "Whereas cities generally live off an already established agricultural prosperity, Angkor was originally designed to create its own prosperous agriculture" (Rawson, *Arts of Southeast Asia*, p. 44).

10 Cf. Chaudhuri, *Asia before Europe*, pp. 341–66.

11 On the varying implications of the word "medieval" in different traditions, and the consequent chronological confusions, see Reuter, "Medieval: Another Tyrannous Construct?" in Reuter, *Medieval Polities*, pp. 19–37.

12 Cf. "By comparative history he [Marc Bloch] does not mean a feature-by-feature comparison of two or more periods or locales. Rather his goal is to establish a common set of questions about agrarian life – questions which can be applied to Poland and Sicily as well as Normandy and Provence – so that our knowledge of highly disparate places can be brought within a unified framework" (Humphreys, *Islamic History*, p. 285).

13 See, with the author's apology for an apparatus rendered, after it had left his hands, inconsistent sometimes to the point of unintelligibility, Moore, "World History."

14 Elvin, *Pattern of the Chinese Past*, pp. 113–99.

15 Watson, *Agricultural Innovation.*

16 Christian, *History of Russia, Central Asia*, p. 306.
17 Stein, *Peasant State*, pp. 63–89; Ludden, *Peasant History*, pp. 15–41. Cf. also Gernet, *Buddhism in Chinese Society*, e.g. at pp. 94–141.
18 Fletcher, *Conversion of Europe*, pp. 503–7.
19 Totman, *History of Japan*, pp. 33–160.
20 Ibid., p. 148.
21 Superficially the conventional identification of the "medieval" period in Japan with the foundation of the Kamakura *bakufu* in 1185 and the establishment of warrior rule might appear to fit this broader pattern, but Totman's account suggests that this development was, at least chronologically, much less closely related to radical social change than its European counterpart or than the contemporaneous crises (to be discussed later in this chapter) of the Chinese and Islamic elites: a similar chronology is suggested by Adolfson, "Social Change". This is an issue that might reward closer comparative examination, and certainly illustrates the methodological point, elementary but still sometimes misunderstood, that the object of comparison is to identify difference, not likeness.
22 Moore, *First European Revolution*, pp. 30–55.
23 Stein, *History of India*, p. 124.
24 As argued by Moore, *First European Revolution*. Note the analogy with discussion as to whether Song China should be regarded as a continuation of Tang (Standen, *Unbounded Loyalty*, pp. 3–6).
25 Moore, "Eleventh Century in Eurasian History."
26 For a particularly helpful and succinct account, see Fairbank, *New History of China*, pp. 96–107.
27 Stein, *Peasant State*, pp. 216–53.
28 Humphreys, *Islamic History*, pp. 186–206.
29 e.g. Chamberlain, *Knowledge and Social Practice*, pp. 152–75; Lapidus, *Muslim Cities*, pp. 105–13, 130–41.
30 Standen, *Unbounded Loyalty*, p. 1.
31 Moore, *Formation*, especially at pp. 144–71, 183–9.

Bibliography

Abu-Lughod, Janet L., *Before European Hegemony: The World System, AD 1250–1350* (New York: Oxford University Press, 1989).

Adolphson, Mikael S., "Social Change and Contained Transformations: Warriors and Merchants in Japan, 1000–1300," in Johann P. Arnason and Björn Wittrock, eds, *Eurasian Transformations: Tenth to Thirteenth Centuries* (Leiden: Brill, 2004), pp. 309–38.

Arnason, Johann P., and Wittrock, Björn, eds, *Eurasian Transformations: Tenth to Thirteenth Centuries* (Leiden: Brill, 2004).

Barfield, Thomas J., *The Perilous Frontier: Nomadic Empires and China* (Oxford: Blackwell, 1989).

Barraclough, Geoffrey, *Main Trends in History*, expanded and updated by Michael Burns (New York: Holmes and Meier, 1991).

Bayly, C. A., *The Birth of the Modern World, 1780–1914* (Oxford: Blackwell, 2004).

Bourguière, André, et al., eds, *A History of the Family*, 2 vols (Cambridge: Polity Press, 1996).

Braudel, Fernand, *Civilization and Capitalism: 1, The Structures of Everyday Life* (London: Collins, 1981).

Burke, Peter, ed., *New Perspectives on Historical Writing* (Cambridge: Polity Press, 1991).

Chamberlain, Michael. *Knowledge and Social Practice in Medieval Damascus, 1190–1350* (Cambridge: Cambridge University Press, 1994).

Chaudhuri, K. N., *Asia before Europe* (Cambridge: Cambridge University Press, 1990).

Christian, David, *A History of Russia, Central Asia and Mongolia*, I (Oxford: Blackwell, 1998).
Curtin, Philip D., *Cross-Cultural Trade in World History* (Cambridge: Cambridge University Press, 1984).
De Vries, Jan, and van der Woude, Adriaan, *The First Modern Economy* (Cambridge: Cambridge University Press, 1997).
Di Cosmo, Nicola, *Ancient China and its Enemies The Rise of Nomadic Power in East Asian History* (Cambridge: Cambridge University Press, 2002).
Elvin, Mark, *The Pattern of the Chinese Past* (London: Methuen, 1973).
Fairbank, John K., *A New History of China* (Cambridge, MA: Harvard University Press, 1992).
Fletcher, Richard, *The Conversion of Europe* (London: Harper Collins, 1997).
Foucault, Michel, *The Archaeology of Knowledge*, trans. A. M. Sheridan-Smith (London: Tavistock Press, 1972).
Fukuyama, Francis, *The End of History and the Last Man* (New York: Free Press, 1992).
Geary, Patrick, *The Myth of Nations: The Medieval Origins of Europe* (Princeton: Princeton University Press, 2002).
Gernet, Jean, *Buddhism in Chinese Society*, trans. F. Verellen (New York: Columbia University Press, 1995).
Goffart, Walter, *Historical Atlases: The First Three Hundred Years* (Chicago: University of Chicago Press, 2003).
Goody, Jack, *The East in the West* (Cambridge: Cambridge University Press, 1996).
Goody, Jack, *The Theft of History* (Cambridge: Cambridge University Press, 2006).
Heitzman, James, *Gifts of Power. Lordship in an Early Indian State* (New Delhi: OUP India, 1997).
Humphreys, R. Stephen, *Islamic History. A Framework for Inquiry*, rev. edn (Princeton: Princeton University Press, 1991).
Iggers, George G., *Historiography in the Twentieth Century* (Hanover: Wesleyan University Press, 1997).
Jacobs, Jane, *The Economy of Cities* (New York: Random House, 1969; Vintage Books edn, 1970).
Jones, E. L., *The European Miracle* (Cambridge: Cambridge University Press, 1981).
Jones, E. L., *Growth Recurring* (Oxford: Oxford University Press, 1988).
Lapidus, Ira M., *Muslim Cities in the Later Middle Ages* (Cambridge: Cambridge University Press, 1984).
Ludden, David, *Peasant History in South India* (Princeton: Princeton University Press, 1985; Delhi: Oxford University Press, 1989).
Ludden, David, *An Agrarian History of South India* (Cambridge: Cambridge University Press, 1999).
Moore, R. I., "World History," in Michael Bentley, ed., *Companion to Historiography* (London: Routledge, 1997), 941–59.
Moore, R. I., *The First European Revolution* (Oxford: Blackwell, 2000).
Moore, R. I., "The Eleventh Century in Eurasian History", *Journal of Medieval and Early Modern Studies*, 33/1 (2003), 3–21.
Moore, R. I., "The Transformation of Europe as a Eurasian Phenomenon," in Arnason and Wittrock, pp. 77–98.
Moore, R. I., *The Formation of a Persecuting Sociey, Authority and Deviance in Western Europe 950–1250* (Second edition, Oxford: Blackwell, 2007).
Pomeranz, Kenneth, *The Great Divergence: China Europe and the Making of the Modern World Economy* (Princeton: Princeton University Press, 2000).
Rawson, Phillip, *The Arts of Southeast Asia* (London: Thames and Hudson, 1967).
Reuter, Timothy, *Medieval Polities and Modern Mentalities* (Cambridge: Cambridge University Press, 2006).
Said, Edward W., *Orientalism* (New York: Vintage Books, 1994).

Smith, Thomas C., *The Agrarian Origins of Modern Japan* (Stanford: Stanford University Press, 1959).
Standen, Naomi. *Unbounded Loyalty: Frontier Crossings in Liao China* (Honolulu: University of Hawaii Press, 2007).
Stein, Burton, *Peasant State and Society in Medieval South India* (Delhi: Oxford University Press, 1980).
Stein, Burton, *A History of India* (Oxford: Blackwell, 1998).
Totman, Conrad, *A History of Japan*, 2nd edn (Oxford: Blackwell, 2005).
Watson, Andrew M., *Agricultural Innovation in the Early Islamic World* (Cambridge: Cambridge University Press, 1983).
White, Hayden, *Metahistory: The Historical Imagination in Nineteenth-Century Europe* (Baltimore: Johns Hopkins University Press, 1973).
Wickham, Chris, *Framing the Early Middle Ages* (Oxford: Oxford University Press, 2005).
Wolfram, Hervig, *The Roman Empire and its Germanic Peoples* (Berkeley and Los Angeles: University of California Press, 1997).

Further Reading

The issues discussed in this chapter lend themselves readily to further exploration, but not to summary. The modern development of historical studies is well introduced by George G. Iggers, *Historiography in the Twentieth Century* (Hanover: Wesleyan University Press, 1997); Geoffrey Barraclough, *Main Trends in History*, expanded and updated by Michael Burns (New York: Holmes and Meier, 1991); and Peter Burke, ed., *New Perspectives on Historical Writing* (Cambridge: Polity Press, 1991).

There is no satisfactory general account of developing conceptions of the Middle Ages, but Walter Goffart, *Historical Atlases: The First Three Hundred Years* (Chicago: University of Chicago Press, 2003), and Patrick Geary, *The Myth of Nations: The Medieval Origins of Europe* (Princeton: Princeton University Press, 2002), are invaluable. On the Eurocentrism of the Master Narrative see Jack Goody, *The East in the West* (Cambridge: Cambridge University Press, 1996). The broadening of horizons in the 1980s is nicely illustrated by the advance of E. L. Jones from *The European Miracle* (Cambridge: Cambridge University Press, 1981), to *Growth Recurring* (Oxford: Oxford University Press, 1988). The period between the tenth and thirteenth centuries CE as one of transformation in world history is explored from the perspective of several disciplines and most world regions by the contributors to Johann P. Arnason and Björn Wittrock, eds, *Eurasian Transformations: Tenth to Thirteenth Centuries* (Leiden: Brill, 2004). There is almost no aspect of the history of medieval Europe that is not capable of contributing to, and being enriched by, cross-cultural comparison, as all the monographs listed above illustrate, several of them explicitly. Important topics omitted from this account, but that must be approached comparatively, include commerce (see Philip D. Curtin, *Cross-Cultural Trade in World History* (Cambridge: Cambridge University Press, 1984), pp. 90–135; Janet L. Abu-Lughod, *Before European Hegemony: The World System, AD 1250–1350* (New York: Oxford University Press, 1989), the family (André Bourguière et al., eds, *A History of the Family*, 2 vols (Cambridge: Polity Press, 1996)), and the relations between the agrarian societies focused on here and the pastoralists of the steppe (David Christian, *A History of Russia, Central Asia and Mongolia*, I (Oxford: Blackwell, 1998); Hervig Wolfram, *The Roman Empire and its Germanic Peoples* (Berkeley and Los Angeles: University of California Press, 1997); Thomas J. Barfield, *The Perilous Frontier: Nomadic Empires and China* (Oxford: Blackwell, 1989); and Naomi Standen, *Unbounded Loyalty: Frontier Crossings in Liao China* (Honolul: University of Hawaii Press, 2007)). K. N. Chaudhuri, *Asia before Europe* (Cambridge: Cambridge University Press, 1990), though marred by idiosyncrasies of presentation, offers rich comparative discussion of many topics.

Index